Law and Administration

As the branch of law dealing with the exercise of governmental power, and so directly concerned with politics, policy issues and good governance values, administrative law can challenge even the advanced student. In response, this classic text looks at both the law and the factors informing it, elaborating the foundations of the subject. This contextualised approach allows the reader to develop a broad understanding of the subject. The authors consider the distinctive theoretical frameworks which inform study of this challenging subject. Case law and legislation are set out and discussed and the authors have built in a range of case studies, to give a clear practical dimension to the study. This new and updated edition will cement the title's prominent status.

Carol Harlow FBA, QC (Hon), is Emerita Professor of Law at the London School of Economics and Political Science
Richard Rawlings is Professor of Public Law at University College London

The Law in Context Series

Editors: William Twining (University College London), Christopher McCrudden (Lincoln College, Oxford) and Bronwen Morgan (University of Bristol).

Since 1970 the Law in Context series has been in the forefront of the movement to broaden the study of law. It has been a vehicle for the publication of innovative scholarly books that treat law and legal phenomena critically in their social, political and economic contexts from a variety of perspectives. The series particularly aims to publish scholarly legal writing that brings fresh perspectives to bear on new and existing areas of law taught in universities. A contextual approach involves treating legal subjects broadly, using materials from other social sciences, and from any other discipline that helps to explain the operation in practice of the subject under discussion. It is hoped that this orientation is at once more stimulating and more realistic than the bare exposition of legal rules. The series includes original books that have a different emphasis from traditional legal textbooks, while maintaining the same high standards of scholarship. They are written primarily for undergraduate and graduate students of law and of other disciplines, but most also appeal to a wider readership. In the past, most books in the series have focused on English law, but recent publications include books on European law, globalisation, transnational legal processes, and comparative law.

Books in the Series

Anderson, Schum and Twining: *Analysis of Evidence*
Ashworth: *Sentencing and Criminal Justice*
Barton and Douglas: *Law and Parenthood*
Beecher-Monas: *Evaluating Scientific Evidence: An interdisciplinary framework for intellectual due process*
Bell: *French Legal Cultures*
Bercusson: *European Labour Law*
Birkinshaw: *European Public Law*
Birkinshaw: *Freedom of Information: The law, the practice and the ideal*
Cane: *Atiyah's Accidents, Compensation and the Law*
Clarke and Kohler: *Property Law: Commentary and materials*
Collins: *The Law of Contract*
Cranston: *Legal Foundations of the Welfare State*
Davies: *Perspectives on Labour Law*
Dembour: *Who Believes in Human Rights?: The European Convention in question*
de Sousa Santos: *Toward a New Legal Common Sense*
Diduck: *Law's Families*
Elworthy and Holder: *Environmental Protection: Text and materials*
Fortin: *Children's Rights and the Developing Law*
Glover-Thomas: *Reconstructing Mental Health Law and Policy*
Goldman: *Globalisation and the Western Legal Tradition: Recurring patterns of law and authority*

Gobert and Punch: *Rethinking Corporate Crime*
Harlow and Rawlings: *Law and Administration*
Harris: *An Introduction to Law*
Harris, Campbell and Halson: *Remedies in Contract and Tort*
Harvey: *Seeking Asylum in the UK: Problems and prospects*
Hervey and McHale: *Health Law and the European Union*
Holder and Lee: *Environmental Protection, Law and Policy*
Kostakopoulou: *The Future Governance of Citizenship*
Lacey, Wells and Quick: *Reconstructing Criminal Law*
Lewis: *Choice and the Legal Order: Rising above politics*
Likosky: *Transnational Legal Processes*
Likosky: *Law, Infrastructure and Human Rights*
Maughan and Webb: *Lawyering Skills and the Legal Process*
McGlynn: *Families and the European Union: Law, politics and pluralism*
Moffat: *Trusts Law: Text and materials*
Monti: *EC Competition Law*
Morgan and Yeung: *An Introduction to Law and Regulation: Text and materials*
Norrie: *Crime, Reason and History*
O'Dair: *Legal Ethics*
Oliver: *Common Values and the Public–Private Divide*
Oliver and Drewry: *The Law and Parliament*
Picciotto: *International Business Taxation*
Reed: *Internet Law: Text and materials*
Richardson: *Law, Process and Custody*
Roberts and Palmer: *Dispute Processes: ADR and the primary forms of decision-making*
Scott and Black: *Cranston's Consumers and the Law*
Seneviratne: *Ombudsmen: Public services and administrative justice*
Stapleton: *Product Liability*
Tamanaha: *The Struggle for Law as a Means to an End*
Turpin and Tomkins: *British Government and the Constitution: Text and materials*
Twining: *General Jurisprudence: Understanding Law from a Global Perspective*
Twining: *Globalisation and Legal Theory*
Twining: *Rethinking Evidence*
Twining and Miers: *How to Do Things with Rules*
Ward: *A Critical Introduction to European Law*
Ward: *Law, Text, Terror*
Ward: *Shakespeare and Legal Imagination*
Zander: *Cases and Materials on the English Legal System*
Zander: *The Law-Making Process*

Law and Administration

Third Edition

CAROL HARLOW
FBA, QC (Hon), Emerita Professor of Law at the London School of Economics and Political Science

RICHARD RAWLINGS
Professor of Public Law at University College London

CAMBRIDGE
UNIVERSITY PRESS

CAMBRIDGE UNIVERSITY PRESS
Cambridge, New York, Melbourne, Madrid, Cape Town, Singapore, São Paulo,
Delhi, Dubai, Tokyo, Mexico City

Cambridge University Press
The Edinburgh Building, Cambridge CB2 8RU, UK

Published in the United States of America by Cambridge University Press, New York

www.cambridge.org
Information on this title: www.cambridge.org/9780521701792

First published 2009
Reprinted 2010

Printed in the United Kingdom at the University Press, Cambridge

A catalogue record for this publication is available from the British Library

ISBN 978-0-521-70179-2 Paperback

M. Barthélemy, the Dean of the Faculty of Law in the University of Paris, relates that thirty years ago he was spending a week-end with the late Professor Dicey. In the course of conversation M. Barthélemy asked a question about administrative law in this country. 'In England', replied Dicey, 'we know nothing of administrative law; and we wish to know nothing.'

W. A. Robson, 'The Report of the Committee on Ministers' Powers' (1932) 3 *Political Quarterly* 346.

Contents

Preface: Three decades of law and administration

Law and Administration has never been simply a textbook of administrative law. As its title signifies, our primary objective in writing it was to further the study of law in the context of public administration and politics: the 'law in context' approach. We need to remind the contemporary reader that the first edition reflected an era of legal formalism when the study of case law, largely divorced from its social context, was seen as the be-all-and-end-all of legal studies. The formalist approach was reflected both in the dominant casebook method of teaching and the leading administrative law textbooks: de Smith's *Judicial Review of Administrative Action* – a title that speaks for itself – and Wade's *Administrative Law*, a slimmer version of the current well respected text.[1] We saw formalism or legal positivism as largely obscuring both the plural character and the wide parameters of administrative law. Our preoccupations, spelled out clearly in the preface to the first edition, were 'process', 'legitimacy' 'competency' and a functionalist concern with effectiveness and efficiency. We made our points through lengthy case studies of administrative process, focusing especially on social security, immigration and planning law.

Our aim was to further a pluralist approach to the study of administrative law. Throughout our book we emphasised that public bodies possessed their own distinctive ethos, so too did the legal profession. Actors were also presented as individuals, holding different opinions and with differing styles; legal academics were likely to be similarly opinionated. We set out to convey this to our readers by allowing them so far as possible to speak in their own voices. This pluralist approach characterises every edition.

In respect of judicial review, we tried, by the inclusion of case studies, to free the case law from the formalist method that had smothered its political connotations and to re-establish the connections between judicial review and its political context. Judges, Sir William Wade acknowledged, were 'up to their necks in policy, as they had been all through history, and nothing could illustrate this more vividly in our own time than the vicissitudes of administrative

[1] Now H. W. R. Wade and C. Forsyth, *Administrative Law*, 10th edn (Oxford University Press, 2009). The main exception, Griffith and Street's *Principles of Administrative Law*, 5th edn (Pitman Paperbacks, 1973) was out of print and virtually unobtainable.

law.' Judicial review is inevitably controversial, fought out in numerous tiny battles between (as Sir Cecil Carr once put it) 'those who want to step on the accelerator [and] those who want to apply the brake'. Only by recognising this, we argued, could the legitimacy of the judicial transformation of judicial review (see Chapter 3) and its proper place in the unwritten constitution be evaluated. Public law, as Martin Loughlin has since expressed it, is a form of political discourse. This too is a theme of all three editions.

At the date of our first edition, judicial review had recently emerged from a 'period of backsliding' seen by Professor Wade as 'its lowest ebb for perhaps a century'. The step between Lord Reid's famous observation that we did not have 'a developed system of administrative law. . . because until fairly recently we did not need it' (*Ridge v Baldwin*, 1963) and Lord Diplock's assurance that 'this reproach to English law had been removed' (*O'Reilly v Mackman*, 1983) is a huge one, marking judicial review's rapid progression. This edition tracks further major change. The Human Rights Act 1998 has shown itself to be an added bedrock for a new and necessarily more inventive form of judicial review, constructed under the supervision of the Court of Human Rights at Strasbourg. The case law of the Court of Justice of the European Communities has also been increasingly important. Both can be seen today as embedded in the national legal order, forcing the domestic law of judicial review to move beyond its traditional common law framework. As we shall see in Chapter 15, procedural change to the domestic system has ushered in a 'multi-streamed' system of judicial review whose jurisprudential architecture is sometimes well, and sometimes ill, suited to the increasingly complex range of problems our courts are asked to resolve. All this has grounded new arguments, explored in Chapter 3, concerning the legitimacy and competency of judicial process, today expressed in the vocabulary of 'deference' and 'constitutionalism'.

We have never denied the place for judicial review in our constitution. We have on the other hand argued that adjudication is 'an expensive form of decision-taking whose competency ought not lightly to be assumed'. Our early exploration of alternative machinery for redress of grievance such as tribunals and ombudsmen has expanded over time to four chapter-long studies of alternative mechanisms of dispute resolution: from tribunals, inquiries, and ombudsmen to internal complaints-handling machinery more appropriate and proportionate than expensive courts (Chapters 10–13). Nor have we been against accountability and control. Our position is as it always has been that control of the executive and administration can and should be exercised in ways complementary to judicial review that may be more effective. Common to every edition therefore have been extended studies of lawmaking and bureaucratic rule-making, forms of control pioneered both by British 'green light theorists' and by the American writer Kenneth Culp Davies as an alternative to courts. In this edition such an emphasis is, we feel, amply justified by the growing phenomenon of 'juridification' or governance by rules that links the bureaucratic world (Chapter 5) with that of the regulator (Chapters 6 and 7). The worlds of politics and Parliament have so far been affected to a lesser extent: there is as yet no requirement that the legislator should be rational! Chapter 4 nonetheless documents some of the changes undergone in recent years by the legislative process, partly under the influence of self-scrutinising parliamentary committees. Techniques developed in the administrative process or by regulators are today paralleled in Parliament where we find experiments with impact assessment, pre- and post-legislative scrutiny, public consultation, monitoring and evaluation.

Largely by happenstance, each of our three editions has gone to press on the cusp of a new political era. Looking back at the preface to the first edition, published in 1984, it seems unlikely that we had at that stage fully recognised the significance for administrative law of the 1979 election that had brought Margaret Thatcher's reforming Conservative government to power. It is indeed hard to recall the political background against which we were writing; the end of an era in which the state had happily combined steering and rowing, retaining the central position in a planned economy that it had come to occupy in the course of two world wars. Swathes of nationalised industry and state-run public services remained as yet to be privatised and liberalised. Not surprisingly perhaps, we largely overlooked the soon-to-be-expanded discipline of regulation. By then threatening to occupy the whole terrain of administrative law, this had to await the second, 1997, edition, where it occupied a central position. The second edition also focused on the replacement of traditional modes of 'club' or 'trust' government by 'the objective, Weberian model of standardisation and rules'. Under the label of 'a blue rinse', we tracked the reception into the public services of the methodology of 'New Public Management' and mentality of audit, noting the growing challenge posed to the values of administrative law.

There was some surprise that the election of Tony Blair's New Labour government did not bring paradigm change. 'Contracting out' of public services was not, for example, reversed, though its effects were softened. Public/private partnerships and public finance initiatives greatly increased, bringing pressure for control that the courts largely failed to meet, hence for new methods of accountability (see Chapters 8 and 9). There were further challenges for administrative law from the New Labour programme of constitutional reform: the process of devolution, for example, greatly complicated the structure of the lawmaking process, making it harder to know what is and what is not 'the law' (Chapter 4). Nor can we yet foresee what problems may flow from the process of continual administrative change instituted by New Labour under the rubric of modernisation. It has to be said that the picture which emerges in these pages is not one of competence or efficiency; administrative law has had to respond to failing administrative agencies, government departments declared unfit for purpose, whole-scale losses of government information and other serious failures. How far the constant restructuring of central government departments and blocking up of agencies into hyper-agencies has contributed to these administrative catastrophes is hard to tell. Equally, how the overhaul of the piecemeal tribunal system in England and Wales by the Tribunals, Courts and Enforcement Act 2007, the recasting of the public inquiry system by the Inquiries Act 2005 and the restructuring of the courts system in the Constitutional Reform Act 2005 will work out in practice is, at the time of writing, far from clear.

Modernisation has been moving us fast into uncharted administrative territory of 'e-governance' empowered by ICT, bringing promise of greater administrative competence but also new threats to civil liberties and human rights. We ourselves see the pervasive New Labour slogans of 'inclusivity', 'responsive governance' and 'community empowerment' and recourse to the 'soft' terminology of openness, accountability, and participation, as deceptive. Equally, it is insufficient to leave everything to courts, a message driven home through the workings of the political process in the context of the so-called 'war against terror'. This is a lesson we need to remember.

At the same time as we have entered the world of 'public-plus-private', of 'governance through contract' and of 'decentred regulation' described in Chapters 6 to 9, we are moving into a larger world of globalized administration and governance. Here states must compete with governance through transnational agencies and networks of assorted public and private actors. Government, as Martin Shapiro defines it, where administration exists 'as a bounded reality' and administrative law 'prescribes behaviour within administrative organizations' and delineates relationships between 'those inside an administration and those outside it', has arguably broken down. No clear boundary exists (if one has ever existed) between the public and the private. New machinery of control and accountability is clearly necessary if the gains of greater political participation and greater transparency of decision-making associated by Alfred Aman with the administrative law of the 1960s and 1970s are not to be lost. To exemplify, the campaign for freedom of information that came to a head in the 1980s has to a certain extent been won; we now have to take on board and resolve the growing concerns over the emergent 'surveillance society' with its impact on privacy and data protection. Once again we seem to be standing on the cusp of a paradigm change, characterised this time by a rapid re-entry of the state into central areas of economic and financial affairs marked out by economic liberals in the last decade of the twentieth century as sacrosanct areas for private enterprise. We can only speculate on the changes that will be required from administrative law and the contribution administrative law will be able to make.

We cannot end without thanking the many people who have helped to bring this edition to press, starting with our families, who have had to suffer much inattention and, from time to time, some grumpiness. Susan Hunt helped with this, as with every, edition. Sylvia Lough played an equally valuable role. We also had much help and encouragement from Mark Aronson, Julia Black, Peter

Cane, Genevra Richardson and Richard Thomas who read and commented on some of the chapters and gave us the benefit of their expertise. We also thank our publishers, and particularly our copy-editor Jeremy Langworthy, for showing patience and understanding.

Carol Harlow,
Richard Rawlings,
March 2009.

Table of Cases

Table of Statutes

Table of Statutory Instruments

Table of European Union Legislation

1

Red and green light theories

Contents

1. Law and state

Behind every theory of administrative law there lies a theory of the state. As Harold Laski once said, constitutional law is unintelligible except as the expression of an economic system of which it was designed to serve as a rampart.[1] By this he meant that the machinery of government was an expression of the society in which it operated; one could not be understood except in the context of the other. In 1941, Sir Cecil Carr made a similar point in a series of lectures on administrative law given at Harvard University, in the course of which he said:

> We nod approvingly today when someone tells us that, whereas the State used to be merely policeman, judge and protector, it has now become schoolmaster, doctor, house-builder, road-maker, town-planner, public utility supplier and all the rest of it. The contrast is no recent discovery. De Tocqueville observed in 1866 that the State 'everywhere interferes

[1] H. Laski, *A Grammar of Politics* (Allen and Unwin, 1925), p. 578.

> more than it did; it regulates more undertakings, and undertakings of a lesser kind; and it gains a firmer footing every day, about, around and above all private persons, to assist, to advise, and to coerce them' (*Oeuvres*, III, 501). Nassau William Senior, a Benthamite ten years older than Chadwick, a colleague of his on the original Poor Law Commission, had justified this tendency. A government, he thinks, must do whatever conduces to the welfare of the governed (the utilitarian theory); it will make mistakes, but non-interference may be an error too; one can be passively wrong as well as actively wrong. One might go back much earlier still to Aristotle, who said that the city-state or partnership-community comes into existence to protect life and remains in existence to protect a proper way of living. What is the proper standard? That is an age-long issue which is still a burning question of political controversy. The problems of administrative law are approached in the light of that fire. Those who dislike the statutory delegation of legislative power or the statutory creation of a non-judicial tribunal will often be those who dislike the policy behind the statute and seek to fight it at every stage. On the one side are those who want to step on the accelerator, on the other those who want to apply the brake.[2]

In this passage, Carr placed the demise of the minimal state, or state as 'policeman, judge and protector', and the birth of state interventionism, in the early nineteenth century, attributing the change to the work of the economist Nassau Senior and Edwin Chadwick, social and administrative reformer. Barker set two momentous decades of state growth slightly later, in the 1880s, when the number of state employees increased significantly, and the 1890s, when state expenditure as a percentage of national expenditure began to rise. By the end of the nineteenth century all the major political parties had for practical purposes abandoned the ideal of limited government, and accepted the necessity for intervention. The old conception of government as minimal and static was being swept away by a new conception, which was:

> if not dynamic, then at least ambulatory. The old conception had viewed government as administering laws, keeping the peace and defending the frontiers. But it was not a part of government's function to act upon society, nor was it expected that legislation would do much more than sustain clear and established customs. In contrast the new conception was of government as the instigator of movement. This conception of movement was not restricted to the parties of progress or reform; the Conservative and Unionist Party at the beginning of the twentieth century was increasingly characterized, despite opposition, by a commitment to tariff reform, a programme of discriminatory trade duties designed to . . . provide funds for new military and social expenditure at home. Government was not merely to regulate society, it was to improve it.[3]

This was, in short, the beginning of the age of 'collectivism', as Dicey termed socialist theories that favoured 'the intervention of the State, even at some

[2] C. Carr, *Concerning English Administrative Law* (Oxford University Press, 1941), pp. 10–11.
[3] R. Barker, *Political Ideas in Modern Britain*, 2nd edn (Methuen, 1997), pp. 14, 18.

sacrifice of individual freedom, for the purpose of conferring benefit upon the mass of the people.'[4] Dicey acknowledged collectivism grudgingly, although presciently he foresaw its influence as likely to increase in force and volume.

What Carr was saying was hardly novel and, to his American audience, would probably have seemed unexceptional; the link between realist jurisprudence and the 'administrative state' was well established in the USA at the time Carr spoke.[5] English lawyers, on the other hand, might have found the idea unpalatable. The nineteenth-century legal scholars who had laid the foundation stones of English administrative law were certainly alive to the relationship between constitutional law and political theory and were themselves well grounded in both.[6] But this was an era when positivism dominated legal theory and case law was predominantly formalist in its focus on legal principles and concepts. English lawyers understood law as properly isolated from its social context, 'endowed with its own discrete, integral history, its own "science", and its own values, which are all treated as a single block sealed off from general social history, from politics, and from morality'.[7] Barker confirms that a similar outlook obtained amongst political scientists. While the political consequences of 'particular laws and particular legal judgments' met with occasional recognition, the character of the judicial system and the general assumptions of law and lawyers were 'little considered in debates about the political character and goals of the nation', and legal ideas were in general 'invisible'.[8] To question this – as Laski, by describing the judiciary as a branch of government had done and Griffith in *The Politics of the Judiciary*[9] was to do – seemed heretical.

The dominance of positivism in thinking about public law is largely due to the influence of two great men: in the nineteenth century, Albert Venn Dicey (1835–1922), to whom must go the credit of the first sophisticated attempt 'to apply the juridical method to English public law';[10] in the twentieth century, H. L. A. Hart (1907–92), whose *Concept of Law*[11] is a masterpiece of legal positivism. Like Jeremy Bentham (1748–1832) and John Austin (1790–1859), legal philosophers who saw themselves as rationalists and were concerned to excise mysticism and the doctrines of natural law from legal philosophy, Dicey believed that law was capable of reduction to rational, scientific principles. Hart set out 'to understand the legal order in terms of governance through

[4] A. V. Dicey, *Lectures on the Relation between Law and Public Opinion in England during the Nineteenth Century*, 2nd edn (Macmillan, 1914), pp. 64–5.

[5] See R. Gordon, 'Willis's American counterparts: The legal realists' defence of administration' (2005) 55 *UTLJ* 405.

[6] F. Maitland, 'A historical sketch of liberty and equality' in *Collected Papers*, vol. 1 (Cambridge University Press, 1911). p. 1; F. Pollock, *Essays in the Law* (Macmillan, 1922), Nos. 2 and 3.

[7] J. Shklar, *Legalism* (Harvard University Press, 1964), pp. 2–3.

[8] Barker, *Political Ideas in Modern Britain*.

[9] J. Griffith, *The Politics of the Judiciary* (Fontana, 1977).

[10] W. I. Jennings, 'In praise of Dicey (1885-1935)' (1935) 13 *Pub. Admin.*123, 133.

[11] H. L. A. Hart, *The Concept of Law*, 2nd revised edn (Clarendon Press, 1997).

rules', working with the tools of analytic and linguistic philosophy. His work set in place an established legal hierarchy of primary and secondary rules. It is important not to underestimate these achievements. Formalism and conceptual reasoning are essential building blocks of a legal system, which structure judicial decision-making and help to maintain consistency.[12] This in turn helps to underpin the rule of law.[13]

This is not the place to debate the many degrees of positivism. It is, however, helpful to refer to Coyle's recent division of contemporary English jurisprudence into main groupings: (i) a moderate legal positivism, which maintains that 'law can be elucidated without reference to morality, and that it is the duty of judges to determine the content of and apply the law without recourse to moral judgments'; and (ii) liberal idealism, where law is viewed as an open-textured set of principles, rooted in rights derived from 'shared assumptions and beliefs which prescribe for law a particular moral content'.[14] In the evolution of liberal idealism, the 'interpretivist' work of the American theorist Ronald Dworkin[15] has been influential. The two approaches should not, however, be seen as monopolising the field of administrative law. Even if they infuse case law studied in later chapters more radical positions frequently emerge.

2. The Diceyan legacy

(a) Dicey and the rule-of-law state

Dicey's *Introduction to the Law of the Constitution,* published in 1885, acts almost as a substitute for a written constitution. His ideas lock up together to form the ideal-type of a 'balanced' constitution, in which the executive, envisaged as capable of arbitrary encroachment on the rights of individual citizens, will be subject, on the one side, to political control by Parliament and, on the other, to legal control through the common law by the courts. As expressed by Dicey in terms of the twin doctrines of the rule of law and parliamentary sovereignty, the balance necessarily tips in favour of representative government.[16]

The ancient philosophical ideal of the rule of law can be traced to Aristotle's government of 'laws not men' and has been explored by generations of political philosophers. It provides the basis for the idea of 'limited government' and 'constitutionalism' (government limited by law and by a constitution or

[12] N. MacCormick, *Legal Reasoning and Legal Theory* (Clarendon Press, 1994).

[13] See C. Forsyth, 'Showing the fly the way out of the flybottle: The value of formalism and conceptual reasoning in administrative law' (2007) 66 *CLJ* 325.

[14] S. Coyle, 'Positivism, idealism and the rule of law' (2006) 26 *OJLS* 257, 259 citing T. Campbell, *The Legal Theory of Ethical Positivism* (Dartmouth, 1996), p. 1.

[15] R. Dworkin, *Taking Rights Seriously* (Duckworth, 1967) and *Law's Empire* (Fontana, 1986).

[16] M. Vile, *Constitutionalism and Separation of Powers* (Clarendon Press, 1967), pp. 230–3; J. Griffith, 'The common law and the political constitution' (2001) 117 *LQR* 42. See generally on Dicey's legacy, M. Loughlin, *Public Law and Political Theory* (Clarendon Press, 1992), pp. 140–62.

constitutional principles). Below, Martin Shapiro, an American political scientist, nicely encapsulates the conception of 'bounded and billeted' government, central to Anglo-American public law:

> Administrative law as it has historically been understood presupposes that there is something called administration. The administrator and/or the administrative agency or organization exist as a bounded reality. Administrative law prescribes behaviour within administrative organizations; more importantly, it delineates the relationships between those inside an administration and those outside it. Outside an administration lie both the statutemaker whose laws and regulations administrators owe a legal duty to faithfully implement and the citizens to whom administrators owe legally correct procedural and substantive action.
>
> More generally, the political and organization theory that inform our administrative law have traditionally viewed public administration as a set of bounded organizations within which decisions are made collectively. On this view, these 'organs of public administration' are coordinated with one another, subordinated to political authority, and obligated to respect the outside individuals and interests whom they regulate and serve.[17]

In the work of Friedrich Hayek, economist and political theorist, there was a close link between the rule of law and his own strong belief in the limited, minimal or 'night-watchman' state mentioned by Carr. In a passage that looks forward to contemporary faith in the market, Hayek in his early classic, *The Road to Serfdom*, drew a 'general distinction between the rule of law and arbitrary government':

> Under the first, government confines itself to fixing rules determining the conditions under which the available resources may be used, leaving to the individuals the decision for what ends they are to be used. Under the second, the government directs the use of the means of production to particular ends. The first type of rules can be made in advance, in the shape of *formal rules* which do not aim at the wants and needs of particular people . . . Economic planning of the collectivist kind necessarily involves the very opposite of this. The planning authority cannot confine itself to providing opportunities for unknown people to make whatever use of them they like. It cannot tie itself down in advance to general and formal rules which prevent arbitrariness. It must provide for the actual needs of people as they arise and then choose deliberately between them.[18]

Hayek here assumes that, in a rule-of-law state, there must be as much individual freedom as is compatible with the freedom of others, reflecting the ideal of a liberal democratic society, which expects '*freedom from* the state,

[17] M. Shapiro, 'Administrative law unbounded' (2001) 8 *Indiana Journal of Global Legal Studies* 369.

[18] F. Hayek, *The Road to Serfdom* (Routledge, 1944), p. 10. See also F. Hayek, *The Constitution of Liberty* (Routledge and Kegan Paul, 1960) and *Law, Legislation and Liberty* (Routledge and Kegan Paul, 1973-79).

demanding that some individual freedoms, or rights, should be protected from the state and from majority decisions.'[19] This 'thin' rule of law excludes by definition a planned economy or welfare state and is the context for what we have called 'red light theories' of administrative law, where the emphasis is on citizens' rights and on law as a brake on state action. This is a highly contestable proposition which has become the centre of much political controversy.

The emphasis on formal, predictable rules makes the rule-of-law idea attractive to lawyers. Lawyers have willingly adopted the rule-of-law paradigm as a constitutional justification for the judicial power to 'review' governmental and administrative acts and to declare them lawful or unlawful and in excess of power. Dicey's late nineteenth-century restatement of the rule-of-law doctrine comprised three elements – (i) that the state possesses no 'exceptional' powers and (ii) that *individual* public servants are responsible to (iii) the ordinary courts of the land for their use of statutory powers:

> When we say that the supremacy of the rule of law is a characteristic of the English constitution we generally include under one expression at least three distinct though kindred conceptions.
>
> [First] that no man is punishable or can be lawfully made to suffer in body or goods except for a distinct breach of law established in the ordinary legal manner before the ordinary courts of the land. In this sense the rule of law is contrasted with every system of government based on the exercise by persons in authority of wide, arbitrary or discretionary powers of constraint . . .
>
> [Secondly], not only that with us no man is above the law, but (what is a different thing) that here every man, whatever be his rank or condition, is subject to the ordinary law of the realm and amenable to the jurisdiction of the ordinary tribunals.
>
> In England the idea of legal equality, or of the universal subjection of all classes to one law administered by the ordinary courts, has been pushed to its utmost limit. With us every official, from the Prime Minister down to a constable or a collector of taxes, is under the same responsibility for every act done without legal justification as any other citizen . . .
>
> [Thirdly] that the general principles of the constitution (as for example the right to personal liberty, or the right of public meeting) are with us the result of judicial decisions determining the rights of private persons in particular cases brought before the courts; whereas under many foreign constitutions the security (such as it is) given to the rights of individuals results, or appears to result, from the general principles of the constitution.[20]

Dicey's articulation of the rule-of-law principle is so quintessentially English that its opponents readily dismiss it as chauvinistic. Yet Allan thinks Dicey:

[19] P. Dunleavy and B. O'Leary, *Theories of the State: The politics of liberal democracy* (Macmillan, 1987), p. 5.

[20] A. V. Dicey, *Introduction to the Study of the Law of the Constitution*, E. C. S. Wade (ed.),10th edn (Macmillan, 1959) (hereafter *Introduction*), pp. 187–196.

> wise to seek an interpretation of the rule of law which reflected the traditions and peculiarities of English common law. Whatever its faults, Dicey's work recognised the importance of expounding a constitutional philosophy, which could serve as a basis for the systematic exposition and consistent development of legal principle. More recent efforts to give analytical precision to the concept of the rule of law have not always been wholly successful – at least in Britain – and constitutional law has perhaps been weakened in consequence, because its foundations have come to seem uncertain and insecure . . .
>
> At the heart of the problem lies the difficulty of articulating a coherent doctrine which resists a purely formal conception of legality – according to which even brutal decrees of a dictator, if formally 'valid', meet the requirements of the rule of law – without instead propounding a complete political and social philosophy. The formal conception, which serves only to distinguish the commands of the government in power (whatever their content) from those of anyone else, offers little of value to the constitutionalist theorist. And the richer seams of political theory – ideal versions of justice in the liberal, constitutional state – are inevitably too ambitious (because too controversial) to provide a secure basis for practical analysis . . . It seems very doubtful whether it is possible to formulate a theory of the rule of law of universal validity . . . But it does not follow that we cannot seek to elaborate the meaning and content of the rule of law within the context of the British polity – exploring the legal foundations of constitutionalism in the setting of contingent political institutions. That was, of course, Dicey's purpose in *The Law of the Constitution*.[21]

In an exploration of the rule-of-law principle popular with lawyers, Lord Bingham breaks the idea down into eight sub-rules:[22]

1. The law must be accessible and so far as possible intelligible.
2. Questions of legal right and liability should ordinarily be resolved by application of the law and not the exercise of discretion.
3. The laws of the land should apply equally to all, save to the extent that objective differences justify differentiation.
4. The law must afford adequate protection of human rights.
5. Means must be provided for resolving disputes, without prohibitive cost or inordinate delay.
6. Ministers and public officers at all levels must exercise the powers conferred on them reasonably, in good faith, for the purposes for which the powers were conferred and without exceeding the limits of such powers.
7. Adjudicative procedures provided by the state should be fair.
8. The state must comply with its obligations in international law.

Dicey's procedural prerequisites, slightly modernised, all make an appearance but with three significant additions: Principle 6, which purports to include most of the modern principles of judicial review which, given their fluidity and

[21] T. Allan, *Law, Liberty and Justice: The legal foundations of British constitutionalism* (Clarendon Press, 1993), pp. 20–1.

[22] T. Bingham, 'The rule of law' (2007) 66 *CLJ* 67 (slightly paraphrased).

rapidly changing nature, might be thought over-ambitious; and Principles 4 and 8, which pull international and human rights law into the compass of the rule of law. The last two are highly controversial. They cross – or invite us to cross – the boundary between procedural and substantive versions of the rule of law.[23]

The case made for this 'thick' rule of law by those of a liberal persuasion is that law cannot 'serve a bad master'; a rule of law without values is not a true rule of law. A slightly different road to the same end is to incorporate the 'thick' rule of law as a constituent element of democracy.[24] This leads to a still more bounded view of government according to which majoritarian institutions are debarred from overriding normative values of the rule of law (see Chapter 3). As Raz has cogently argued, the danger here is that in seeking to encapsulate a complete social and political philosophy within a single principle, liberals have deprived the rule of law of any useful role independent of their dominant philosophy.[25] Dicey's prioritisation of parliamentary sovereignty has been reversed, tipping the balance in favour of the rule of law (and law courts). As Dicey insisted and Raz is affirming, the core of the rule of law is procedural: it is 'a necessary, but not sufficient condition of other vital, civic virtues – freedom, tolerance and justice itself'.[26]

(b) 'The English have no administrative law'

At the heart of Dicey's exposition of the rule of law lay the concept of formal or procedural equality: the submission of ruler and subject alike to the jurisdiction of the *same* courts of law. Dicey set his face against the French system, where separate and autonomous tribunals attached to the administration handle cases involving the state. Dicey gave a specific and peculiar meaning to the term *droit administratif*, which he maintained had no proper English equivalent:

> Anyone who considers with care the nature of the *droit administratif* of France, or the topics to which it applies, will soon discover that it rests, and always has rested, at bottom on two leading ideas alien to the conceptions of modern Englishmen.
>
> The first of these ideas is that the government, and every servant of the government, possesses as representative of the nation, a whole body of special rights, privileges, or prerogatives as against private citizens, and that the extent of these rights, privileges, or prerogatives is to be determined on principles different from the considerations which fix the legal rights and duties of one citizen towards another. An individual in his dealings with

23 See P. Craig, 'Formal and substantive conceptions of the rule of law: An analytical framework' [1997] *PL* 467; R. Cotterell, *Law's Comunity. Legal theory in sociological perspective* (Clarendon Press, 1995), pp. 160–77, discussing variant continental conceptions of the rule of law.

24 J. Jowell, 'Beyond the rule of law: Towards constitutional judicial review' [2000] *PL* 671.

25 J. Raz, 'The rule of law and its virtue' (1977) 93 *LQR* 195.

26 J. Laws, 'The rule of law - form or substance?' [2007] 4 *Justice Journal* 24.

> the State does not, according to French ideas, stand on anything like the same footing as that on which he stands in dealings with his neighbour.
>
> The second of these general ideas is the necessity of maintaining the so-called 'separation of powers' (*séparation des pouvoirs*), or, in other words, of preventing the government, the legislature, and the courts from encroaching upon one another's province. The expression, however, separation of powers, as applied by Frenchmen to the relations of the executive and the courts, with which alone we are here concerned, may easily mislead. It means, in the mouth of a French statesman or lawyer, something different from what we mean in England by the 'independence of the judges', or the like expressions. As interpreted by French history, by French legislation, and by the decisions of French tribunals, it means neither more nor less than the maintenance of the principle that while the ordinary judges ought to be irremovable and thus independent of the executive, the government and its officials ought (whilst acting officially) to be independent of and to a great extent free from the jurisdiction of the ordinary courts.[27]

It was only towards the end of his long career that Dicey admitted the capacity of the separate French system of administrative courts to control abuse of power. Later still he conceded 'a considerable step towards the introduction among us of something like the *droit administratif* of France', though maintaining that the jurisdiction of 'ordinary law courts' in cases of breach of the law by public officials 'is fatal to the existence to true *droit administratif*'.[28] Dicey's preference was for a unitary court structure, in which administrative cases are handled by 'ordinary' courts and judges and public officials stand at least theoretically on an equal footing with private persons. Underlying this arrangement is the principle strongly favoured by Dicey that relationships of citizens with public officials are not – and should not be – radically different from relations between citizens and private bodies.

(c) State and Crown

But a gaping hole was left in Dicey's theory of equality by the existence of substantial areas of monarchical prerogative power. When Dicey wrote, the Crown was immune from civil proceedings in the 'ordinary courts', a fact that somewhat undercut his argument. The Crown had to be pursued by the special procedure of 'petition of right', a form of *droit administratif* that lasted until the Crown Proceedings Act 1947. The state does not need to possess special powers 'in its own name' if those powers are held by government ministers acting in the name of the Crown.

[27] Dicey, *Introduction*, pp. 336–8. For further exposition, see J. Allison, *A Continental Distinction in the Common Law: A historical and comparative perspective on English public law*, revised edn (Clarendon Press, 2000).

[28] A. V. Dicey, '*Droit administratif* in modern French law' (1901) 18 *LQR* 302 and 'The development of administrative law in England' (1915) 31 *LQR* 148; and see F. Lawson, 'Dicey revisited' (1959) 7 *Political Studies* 109, 207.

Dicey himself defined prerogative power widely, maintaining that 'every act which the executive government can lawfully do without the authority of an Act of Parliament is done in virtue of this prerogative'.[29] This unnecessarily broad definition conflates the Crown's prerogative and common law powers. As we shall see in Chapter 8, this has had serious effects on the law of government contracting. Nevertheless, it is important to understand that the prerogative powers are not merely powers confined to emergency or national security; in the British constitution, the Crown fills the place filled in other constitutions by the notion of executive power.[30] Even on Blackstone's view of prerogative power as 'exceptional',[31] which brings much Crown activity within the ambit of public law and renders it justiciable, this is a matter of some importance.

Until relatively recently, it was accepted that a court faced with a claim of prerogative power could merely pronounce on its validity; the way in which it was exercised could not be reviewed. Not until the seminal ruling of the House of Lords in the *GCHQ* case[32] was it finally established that government is accountable to the courts for its use of prerogative power. In his striking and often-quoted speech, Lord Diplock not only asserted that the prerogative powers form part of the common law but broke new ground in saying that he could 'see no reason why simply because a decision-making power is derived from a common law and not a statutory source, it should *for that reason only* be immune from judicial review'. Accepting his view that no qualitative distinction could be made between statutory and prerogative powers, the House advised that both were subject in the same way to judicial review in respect of their use. In itself, the decision was no more than a warning shot, since the House of Lords endorsed the right of the Prime Minister in her capacity as minister responsible for the Civil Service to withdraw the privilege of joining a trade union from workers at the operational headquarters of the security services. The case, discussed on other grounds in Chapter 3, is a landmark in establishing the justiciability of prerogative power. In recent cases, the courts have tended to intensify the war against prerogative power. *M v Home Office*[33] involved the remnants of Crown

[29] Dicey, *Introduction*, p. 425.

[30] M. Sunkin and S. Payne (eds), *The Nature of the Crown: A legal and political analysis* (Oxford University Press, 1999); T. Daintith and A. Page, *The Executive in the Constitution: Structure, autonomy and internal control* (Oxford University Press, 1999); P. Craig and A. Tomkins (eds), *The Executive and Public Law* (Oxford University Press, 2006).

[31] For a strong rebuttal of Dicey's over-generous definition, see H. W. R. Wade, *Constitutional Fundamentals* (Stevens, 1980), pp. 46–9; and see B. Harris, 'The "third source" of authority for government action' (1992) 108 *LQR* 626; 'The "third source" of authority for government action revisited' (2007) 123 *LQ R* 225.

[32] *Council of Civil Service Unions v Minister for the Civil Service* [1985] AC 374, see p. 107 below.

[33] *M v Home Office* [1994] AC 377, noted in Harlow, 'Accidental death of an asylum seeker' (1994) 57 *MLR* 620. A similar point arose in respect of Scotland after devolution and was settled pragmatically in the same way: see *Davidson v Scottish Ministers* [2005] UKHL 74; *Beggs v Scottish Ministers* [2007] UKHL 3.

immunity, enshrined in s. 21 of the Crown Proceedings Act. This provides that injunctions shall not be granted against the Crown in civil proceedings, an immunity thought previously to cover all mandatory legal remedies, including findings of contempt of court.

M, an asylum seeker, had made several consecutive applications for judicial review at the last of which counsel for the Home Office guaranteed that his removal from the UK would be postponed. Due to a mix-up, M was put on a plane to Zaïre, where he subsequently disappeared. When M's lawyers instituted proceedings, the Court of Appeal held the Home Secretary in contempt of court, circumventing the difficult issue of Crown immunity by holding that he had been acting in his personal capacity. On appeal to the House of Lords, the decision was upheld on the different ground that coercive orders, including findings of contempt, were available against the Crown. Moving decisively on to the constitutional high ground, Lord Woolf invoked the full force of Dicey's statement of the rule-of-law principle, citing it at length. To conceal the innovative nature of the opinion, he then used formalistic reasoning cleverly, distinguishing injunctions as awarded in 'civil proceedings' from the administrative law remedies first introduced by RSC Ord. 53 and later given statutory authority by s. 31 of the Supreme Court Act 1981 (see Chapter 16). In the name of the rule of law, a gaping hole had been blown in the remnants of Crown immunity, even if Lord Woolf took care to warn that the new jurisdiction to issue mandatory orders against the Crown should be used with great care:

> The Crown's relationship with the courts does not depend on coercion and in the exceptional situation when a government department's conduct justifies this, a finding of contempt should suffice. In that exceptional situation, the ability of the court to make a finding of contempt is of great importance. It would demonstrate that a government department has interfered with the administration of justice. It will then be for Parliament to determine what should be the consequences of that finding.

If it is hard to reconcile Crown prerogative power with Dicey's rule-of-law principle, it is harder still to reconcile it with the concept of representative government or doctrine of parliamentary sovereignty. Not surprisingly then, courts have, since the start of the twentieth century, asserted the primacy of parliamentary legislation over the prerogative powers. It is settled law that where statute governs a field of activity, the prerogative powers fall into in abeyance and cannot be used to fill gaps left by Parliament.[34] Whether the principle was truly in issue in the *Fire Brigades* case[35] is a moot point. To understand this famous case, it is necessary to know that the criminal injuries compensation scheme, set up to provide state compensation to victims of violent crime,

[34] *A-G v De Keyser's Royal Hotel* [1920] AC 508.

[35] *R v Home Secretary, ex p. Fire Brigades Union* [1995] 2 AC 513.

had been operated by successive governments under the prerogative power to make *ex gratia* payments, though the courts had, soon after its establishment, assumed jurisdiction to review.[36] There was some feeling that so large a scheme needed to be placed on a statutory footing and in 1988 amendments were introduced in the House of Lords to a criminal justice bill to effect this, in the face of government opposition. The Criminal Justice Act 1988 was stated to come into force 'on such day as the Secretary of State may appoint'. Instead, the Home Secretary introduced legislation to replace the 1988 statutory scheme, which failed to pass the House of Lords. Hoping to delay implementation indefinitely, he replaced the existing prerogative criminal injuries compensation scheme with a new, less generous, scheme, effectively by-passing the 1988 Act. Trade unions representing workers likely to be affected by the cuts in compensation challenged the legality of this action.

There are two different approaches to what had occurred. On the majority view in both the Court of Appeal and the House of Lords, the minister had used the prerogative scheme to stultify the express intention of the legislature; to have recourse to the prerogative power in such circumstances was an abuse of power. As Lord Lloyd put it:

> Ministers must be taken at their word. If they say they will not implement the statutory scheme, they are repudiating the power conferred on them by Parliament in the clearest possible terms. It is one thing to delay bringing the relevant provisions into force. It is quite another to abdicate or relinquish the power altogether. Nor is that all. The Government's intentions may be judged by their deeds as well as their words. The introduction of the tariff scheme, which is to be put on a statutory basis as soon as it has had time to settle down, is plainly inconsistent with a continuing power under section 171 to bring the statutory scheme into force . . .

On another view, the prerogative powers were not really in point. The minister had been exercising a discretionary power granted to him by Parliament, though the exercise of the power was seen by several of the judges as surprising to the point of being unreasonable; the minister had gone so far as to debar himself from exercising his power to make the requisite commencement order, which no reasonable minister would have done. On a third view, held by Lords Keith and Mustill dissenting, the decision was quite simply not justiciable; it was 'of a political and administrative character quite unsuitable to be the subject of review by a court of law':

> It is a feature of the peculiarly British conception of the separation of powers that Parliament, the executive and the courts have each their distinct and largely exclusive domain. Parliament has a legally unchallengeable right to make whatever laws it thinks

[36] *R v Criminal Injuries Compensation Board, ex p. Lain* [1967] 2 QB 864. The operation of the scheme is dealt with in Ch. 17 below.

> right. The executive carries on the administration of the country in accordance with the powers conferred on it by law. The courts interpret the laws, and see that they are obeyed. This requires the court on occasion to step into the territory which belongs to the executive, not only to verify that the powers asserted accord with the substantive law created by Parliament, but also, that the manner in which they are exercised conforms with the standards of fairness which Parliament must have intended. Concurrently with this judicial function Parliament has its own special means of ensuring that the executive, in the exercise of its delegated functions, performs in a way which Parliament finds appropriate. Ideally, it is these latter methods which should be used to check executive errors and excesses; for it is the task of Parliament and the executive in tandem, not of the courts, to govern the country. In recent years, however, the employment in practice of these specifically Parliamentary measures has fallen short, and sometimes well short, of what was needed to bring the executive into line with the law . . .
>
> To avoid a vacuum in which the citizen would be left without protection against a misuse of executive powers the courts have had no option but to occupy the dead ground in a manner, and in areas of public life, which could not have been foreseen 30 years ago. For myself, I am quite satisfied that this unprecedented judicial role has been greatly to the public benefit. Nevertheless, it has its risks, of which the courts are well aware . . .
>
> [S]ome of the arguments addressed [in the Court of Appeal] would have the court push to the very boundaries of the distinction between court and Parliament established in, and recognised ever since, the Bill of Rights 1688 . . . 300 years have passed since then, and the political and social landscape has changed beyond recognition. But the boundaries remain; they are of crucial significance to our private and public life; and the courts should, I believe, make sure that they are not overstepped.[37]

We shall find this division of opinion resurfacing in Chapter 4.

Some years later, the Government of the day attempted a similar manoeuvre in an epic case involving the expulsion of the islanders from their homes in the Chagos Islands in the interests of establishing an American air base. This time the ancient and little-used prerogative power to legislate by Order in Council in colonial territories was in issue. After expulsion orders that had been made against the islanders in 1971 were quashed by the High Court in 2000, the Foreign Secretary (Robin Cook) indicated that the islanders would be allowed to return home. Instead, the Government passed the British Indian Ocean Territory (Constitution) Order and British Indian Ocean Territory (Immigration) Order, which made unauthorised presence on the islands a criminal offence. These Orders were quashed by the High Court on the ground that they were irrational; the Government had failed to take the interests of the islanders into account. This decision was endorsed by the Court of Appeal on slightly different grounds but reversed by the House of Lords. At all three levels, however, there was agreement that the use of the prerogative powers,

[37] [1995] 2 AC 513 (Lord Mustill).

whether for administrative or legislative purposes, was subject to review by the courts.[38]

Now judges are fond of asserting that they 'will be very slow to review the exercise of prerogative powers in relation to the conduct of foreign affairs and the deployment of the armed services, and very slow to adjudicate upon rights arising out of transactions entered into between sovereign states on the plane of international law'.[39] But one by one the 'no-go areas' have become occupied territory. In the *Belmarsh* cases discussed in Chapter 3,[40] the courts made deep inroads into powers of detention without trial claimed by government in the name of defence and security of the state. In *Corner House*,[41] the discretionary powers of the Director of the Serious Fraud Office to conduct an investigation and of the Attorney-General to issue instructions that a prosecution be dropped came under scrutiny. An investigation into allegations of corrupt dealings with officials in Saudi Arabia was dropped when the Director concluded that serious damage to the public interest in relation to security and counter-terrorism was likely if the investigation were to continue. The legal challenge, which sought to prioritise the upholding of the rule of law, reached the House of Lords before collapsing. In the *Prague Airport* case discussed in Chapter 5,[42] the conduct of British officials working overseas came under review by the courts and domestic legislation was held to operate extraterritorially. In *Al-Skeini*,[43] the courts were asked whether acts of torture and atrocities allegedly committed by British soldiers in Iraq came under the jurisdiction of the British courts and, if so, whether they were covered by the Human Rights Act (HRA) and ECHR. By a majority, the House of Lords ruled that the HRA would be applicable when a public authority – in this case the army in Iraq – acted outside British territory but within Parliament's 'legislative grasp'. In the light of this ruling, the Defence Secretary accepted liability for violation of human rights resulting in the death of one of the appellants with a settlement of £3 million.

With the help of the European Convention, the area of immunity from the rule of the law courts is thus shrinking. The invocation of international law before British courts has also expanded very rapidly; domestic courts, as

[38] *R (Bancoult) v Foreign Secretary* [2001] 1 QB 1067 (*Bancoult (No. 1); R (Bancoult) v Foreign Secretary* (*Bancoult (No. 2)* [2006] EWHC Admin. 1038; [2007] EWCA Civ 498 (CA); [2008] UKHL 61 (HL). And see S. Farran, 'Prerogative rights, human rights, and island people: The Pitcairn and Chagos Island cases' [2007] *PL* 414.

[39] *R v Jones (Margaret)* [2006] 2 WLR 772, 783 (Lord Bingham); and see *R (Gentle and Clarke) v Prime Minister and Others* [2008] UKHL 20. The classic case is *Chandler v DPP* [1964] AC 763.

[40] *A and Others v Home Secretary* [2005] 2 AC 68; *A and Others v Home Secretary* [2006] 2 AC 221.

[41] *R (Corner House Research v Director of the SFO* [2008] UKHL 60, overruling the radical judgment of Moses J at [2008] EWHC Admin 714 [56].

[42] *R (European Roma Rights Centre) v Immigration Office at Prague Airport* [2005] 2 AC 1.

[43] *Al-Skeini and Others v Defence Secretary* [2007] UKHL 26. See also *R (Quark Fishing Ltd) v Foreign Secretary* [2006] 1 AC 529.

Lord Rodger recently remarked are finding themselves 'deep inside the realm of international law – indeed inside the very chamber of the United Nations Security Council itself'.[44] The common law is no longer insulated.[45]

Even if Dicey's rule-of-law requirements are now largely satisfied, confidence in our system of government as democratic and 'accountable' is not. The very concept of prerogative power undercuts the fundamental assumption of our parliamentary democracy that power is bestowed by Parliament and government is responsible to Parliament for its use of power. Without the need for parliamentary agreement, governments can sign treaties of great import, such as the Treaty of Accession to the European Communities; only after ratification of the UK Accession Treaty was legislation necessary to deal with incorporation of the Treaty into UK law (see Chapter 4).[46] In similar fashion, the Government can ratify international conventions, such as the ECHR, ratified in 1955 but with provisions not formally incorporated into domestic law until the Human Rights Act was passed in 1998.[47] War can be declared and troops sent into battle in the name of the Crown, though in practice Parliament is normally consulted, as was done in the cases of both the Falklands and Iraq wars. Parliamentary approval is typically necessary only at the point when financial levies or changes to the domestic legal system are required.[48]

In an age of popular democracy, when accountability is a prerequisite of government, this is coming to be seen as unacceptable.[49] The House of Commons Select Committee on Public Administration (PASC), which since the election of the New Labour Government in 1997 has taken upon itself the task of keeping the governance of Britain under regular review, has recently demanded action on ministerial prerogative powers.[50] It called for them to be listed and a parliamentary committee set up to frame appropriate legislation. To stimulate action, PASC listed three of the most important areas to be dealt with – decisions on armed conflict, treaties and passports – appending its own draft bill. One of Gordon Brown's first acts as Prime Minister in 2007 was to issue a Green Paper on the governance of Britain, with a view to making 'the executive, and Parliament, more accountable to the people and to reinvigorate

[44] *R (Al-Jedda) v Defence Secretary* [2007] UKHL58; and see *A and Others v HM Treasury* [2008] EWHC 869.

[45] See further, P. Sales and J. Clement, 'International Law in Domestic Courts: the Developing Framework' (2008) 124 LQR 388

[46] However the European Parliamentary Elections Act 2002 requires statutory approval for the ratification of a treaty increasing the powers of the European Parliament. See further, *R(Wheeler) v Prime Minister* [2008] EWHC 1409.

[47] J. Beatson *et al.*, *Human Rights: Judicial protection in the United Kingdom* (Sweet & Maxwell, 2008).

[48] See for a full survey, HL Constitutional Committee (hereafter CC), *Waging War: Parliament's role and responsibility*, HL 236 (2006) and *Follow up Report*, HL 51 (2007).

[49] A. Tomkins, *Public Law* (Clarendon Press, 2003), pp. 81– 90 and *Our Republican Constitution* (Hart Publishing, 2005).

[50] PASC, *Taming the Prerogative: Strengthening ministerial accountability to Parliament*, HC 422 (2004/05).

our democracy'.[51] This committed the Government to surrendering or limiting powers 'which it considers should not, in a modern democracy, be exercised exclusively by the executive (subject to consultation with interested parties and, where necessary, legislation).' Included in the proposals was a range of important prerogative powers: permitting deployment of troops abroad; requesting a dissolution or recall of Parliament; allowing ratification of international treaties without decision by Parliament; determination of rules governing entitlement to passports and granting of pardons; restriction of parliamentary oversight of the intelligence services; choosing bishops and appointment of judges; direction of prosecutors in individual criminal cases; and establishing the rules governing the Civil Service.

A few of these commitments have already found their way into a draft Constitutional Renewal Bill, the subject of consideration by a Joint Committee of both Houses. This provides that treaties will in future have to be laid before Parliament for approval. They may, in exceptional circumstances, however, still be signed without that consent. So are we about to draw a line under a long history? The Joint Committee did not think so. As Lord Morgan, one of the members remarked: 'Does this not perhaps seem like an area where the Royal Prerogative, instead of being given a decent Christian or un-Christian burial, is in fact alive and well?'[52]

(d) The state and statutory authority

A far stronger criticism of Dicey is that he left English administrative law with a great mistrust of executive or administrative action but without any theoretical basis for its control. By refusing to accept the reality of state power and acknowledge 'the state' as a legal entity possessing inherent powers of government, his theory disguised the inevitable inequality between the state, monarch or government, and citizens. Dicey stultified the growth of a 'special' public law formulated for this basic inequality:

> The fallacy of Dicey's assumptions lies in his contention that the rule of law demands full equality in every respect between government and subjects or citizens. But it is inherent in the very notion of government that it cannot in all respects be equal to the governed, because it has to govern. In a multitude of ways, government must be left to interfere, without legal sanctions, in the lives and interests of citizens, where private persons could not be allowed to do so . . . The refusal of the courts to make planning or policy decisions of government the subject of legal action, also shows that the inequality of government and governed in certain respects is an indispensable fact of organized political life. Where the borderline between governmental freedom and legal responsibility has to be drawn,

[51] *The Governance of Britain*, Cm. 7170 (2007) [43–4]; *The Governance of Britain: Constitutional renewal*, Cm. 7342 (2008).

[52] Joint Committee on the Draft Constitutional Renewal Bill, HC 552 (2007/8), Q 737.

> is, indeed, a very difficult problem. It may be described as the key problem of administrative law. But we can only begin to understand it after having accepted, unlike Dicey, that inequalities between government and citizens are inherent in the very nature of political society.[53]

Dicey argued for the superiority of his individuated model on the moral ground that individuals, even when acting in an official capacity, ought not to be able to shuffle off responsibility for their own misdeeds. His theory of administrative and constitutional law sprang from his belief in liberal individualism and dislike of the collectivism that he saw beginning to flourish around him. Dicey refused to recognise that, in his dealings with the state, the individual does *not* stand on 'anything like the same footing as that on which he stands in dealings with his neighbour'.

> What Dicey suggests by equality is that an official is subject to the same rules as an ordinary citizen. But even this is not true. An official known as a collector of taxes has rights which an ordinary person does not possess . . . All public officials, and especially public authorities, have powers and therefore rights which are not possessed by other persons. Similarly, they may have special duties . . . Dicey was not referring to that part of the law which gives powers to and imposes duties upon public authorities. What he was considering . . . was that, if a public officer commits a tort, he will be liable for it in the ordinary civil courts.[54]

Dicey's polemical account skated lightly over the extent of statutory power, partly, but only partly, because the web of statute and regulation that today confines and structures government was still fragmentary when he wrote. As legislative activity increased and government obtained control of the legislative machinery, so Dicey's theory became less adequate. Dicey, for example, was able to conceptualise police powers, with which he was much concerned, as largely judge-made common law powers, incorporated in 'open textured' precedent. Today, these powers are mainly statutory, embodied for the most part in the Police and Criminal Evidence Act 1984, which empowers a further network of regulations, directives and administrative guidance. The notion of police powers as based on common law citizen arrest is today as unrealistic as the idea that members of the anti-terrorist squad are simply 'citizens in uniform'. This is not the way in which the present-day police force is organised or understood. The same is true of the state.

Like Hayek after him, Dicey condemned wide administrative powers because of their collectivist connotations. Because he viewed the constitution as 'an instrument for protecting the fundamental rights of the citizen, and not an instrument for enabling the community to provide services for the benefit of its citizens', he came to confuse 'discretionary' with 'arbitrary' powers. For Dicey,

[53] W. Friedmann, *Law in a Changing Society*, 2nd edn (Penguin Books, 1964), pp. 276–7.

[54] W. I. Jennings, *The Law and the Constitution* (Athlone Press, 1959), p. 312.

'the constitution excludes wide discretionary authority; therefore it forbids large administrative powers'.[55] The wide administrative powers feared by Dicey were to be restricted in two ways: on one side stood Parliament which, 'because it was still dominated by Whig ideas', would not tolerate administrative interference with individual rights; on the other stood the courts dominated by a similar ideology. Dicey's mistrust of discretionary power was to become, as we shall see in later chapters, a theme dominating administrative law in the second half of the twentieth century. It started administrative law on a collision course with governments that wish to use administrative law 'instrumentally' for socialist or welfare-oriented purposes (below).[56]

(e) Public and private law

Dicey, by setting his face against a 'special' administrative court, helped to set in place the so-called 'private law' model of public law, in which executive and administration are subject to the common law as administered by the ordinary courts. The model underpins Dicey's ideal of *equality*: a vision of government as:

> under the law, and not just any law, but the same law as applies to everyone else. In that way, government is denied the special exemptions and privileges that could lead to tyranny. Moreover, the application of the law to government is placed in the hands of the ordinary courts, who are independent of government, and who can be relied upon to award an appropriate remedy to the citizen who has been injured by illegal government action.[57]

Closely tied to this was Dicey's image of officials as 'citizens in uniform', responsible for their actions to the 'ordinary' courts through the civil law of tort and contract.

A counter-argument advanced forcefully by John Mitchell during the 1960s is that, absent a separate system of administrative law courts, principles appropriate for the control of state power could not evolve.[58] Mitchell coupled the case for a separate administrative jurisdiction with a case for special rules, contrasting the English system with that of France, where a public/private jurisdictional divide was intrinsic to the post-Revolutionary legal order. A separate administrative jurisdiction, staffed by jurists with a specialised training,

[55] Jennings, 'In praise of Dicey (1885–1935)', 132. For Dicey's views, see *Law and Public Opinion*.

[56] The extreme example is Lord Hewart's classic, *The New Despotism* (Ernest Benn, 1929). See further, M. Loughlin, 'Why the history of English administrative law is not written' in Dyzenhaus, Hunt and Huscroft (eds.), *A Simple Common Lawyer* (Hart Publishing, 2008).

[57] P. Hogg, *Liability of the Crown*, 2nd edn (Carswell, 1989), pp. 1–2. See also C. Harlow, '"Public" and "private" law: Definition without distinction' 43 *MLR* 241; J. Allison, *A Continental Distinction in the Common Law: A historical and comparative perspective on English public law*, revised edn (Clarendon Press, 2000).

[58] J. Mitchell, 'The causes and effects of the absence of a system of public law in the United Kingdom' [1965] *PL* 95.

knowledgeable about public administration and specialists in administrative law, had evolved since the nineteenth century. This in Mitchell's view had enabled sophisticated principles of administrative law to be developed appropriate for the control of state power.[59]

We got instead a typical English adjustment: 'droit public – English style'.[60] In a break with the common law tradition, the judges invoked the public/private distinction during the 1970s and 1980s to provide support for a stronger and more extensive system of judicial review, building on a new judicial review procedure introduced in 1978 to assume 'exclusive jurisdiction' in 'public law cases'.[61] In time, this troublesome distinction would largely fade away (see Chapter 15). The Administrative Court of England and Wales, which today handles judicial review applications, is effectively a glorified division of the High Court, from which appeal lies to the civil division of the Court of Appeal and House of Lords.[62] The Administrative Court operates inside the framework of the unitary legal system to which it remains firmly attached; it is, in short, a specialised ordinary court. Tribunals have followed a similar process of 'judicialisation from within and without'. There is no special administrative appeal tribunal like the Australian Appeals Tribunal or as called for by Robson (below). The umbilical cord between tribunals and the 'ordinary courts' is carefully maintained in recent reforms, as discussed further in Chapter 11.

The case for separate principles of public law is not only jurisdictional but also normative. It originates in a view of the state as 'different' and 'exceptional' – endowed with the qualities of Hobbes's 'Leviathan'.[63] The state exercises sovereign power, different in kind from the great powers in practice wielded by private corporations or multinational enterprises (MNEs). The state is seen to possess the monopoly of force; the use of force is illegitimate without state authorisation. The state has financial and economic prerogatives; it controls the currency and collects taxes; its regulatory powers can be used in such a way as to unbalance contractual relations.[64] The state possesses the ultimate power of legislation (see Chapter 4). It acts as representative of the common good in the collective public interest (below). Speaking of the Crown, a metaphor used

[59] See similarly, C. J. Hamson, *Executive Discretion and Judicial Control: An aspect of the French Conseil d'Etat* (Stevens, 1954).

[60] Lord Woolf, 'Droit public – English style' [1995] *PL* 57.

[61] *O'Reilly v Mackman* [1983] 2 AC 237 (Lord Diplock). See also H. Woolf, 'Public law – private law: Why the divide? A personal view' [1986] *PL* 220 and *Protection of the Public: A new challenge* (Stevens, 1990). Contrast D. Oliver, 'Public law procedure and remedies – do we need them?' (2002] *PL* 91.

[62] As provided for by the Constitutional Reform Act 2005, the UK Supreme Court is about to take the place of the House of Lords..

[63] C. B. Macpherson (ed.), *Thomas Hobbes' Leviathan* (1651) (Penguin Books, 1968). And see C. B. Macpherson, *The Political Theory of Possessive Individualism: Hobbes to Locke* (Oxford University Press, 1962).

[64] T. Daintith, 'Regulation by contract: The new prerogative' [1979] *CLP* 41, explained in Ch. 8.

to symbolise the state in many of the common law jurisdictions, the Canadian Supreme Court once said:

> The Crown cannot be equated with an individual. The Crown represents the State . . . It must represent the interests of all members of Canadian society in court claims brought against the Crown in Right of Canada. The interests and obligations of the Crown are vastly different from those of private litigants making claims against the federal government.[65]

Thus the state is not the mere collection of private persons dressed up in official uniforms presented by Dicey; to equate the state with its 'subjects' is therefore profoundly misleading and arguably shows a wilful disregard for power imbalance.[66] Because it does not admit the imbalance, no private law system can provide appropriate answers for public law problems. The special character of the state needs to be matched by a special and distinctive public law.[67]

One reason why the waves of liberalisation, privatisation and managerialism that swept through the English-speaking world during the 1980s created concern amongst public lawyers was anxiety for the *normative* values of their discipline. It was feared that the underlying tendency for public law 'to be swamped and dissolved by the waters of English private law-based common law and statute law' would be accentuated. If the distinction between public law and private law were to be dismantled, it would be 'public law rather than private law which risks being swept away'.[68] Thus Cane describes the public/private division as embodying for its supporters, 'an attractive *normative* theory of the way power ought to be distributed and its exercise controlled'.[69]

One response to problems of inequality is offered by the concept of human rights. Pre-eminently, it may be thought, human rights are a public law concept, since they can be claimed only against the state. In line with this reasoning, the HRA does not have 'horizontal effect'; it is applicable only to public authorities and bodies carrying out public functions.[70] Procedurally the Act is ambivalent, however; it allows the acts of public authorities to be challenged – consonant with the common law tradition – in every type of proceeding. Increasingly too, arguments over human rights are raising normative questions, as the public/

[65] *Rudolph Wolff & Co Ltd and Noranda Inc. v The Crown* [1990] 1 SCR 695, 69 DLR (4th) 392.

[66] See J. Allison, 'Theoretical and institutional underpinnings of a separate administrative law' in Taggart (ed.), *The Province of Administrative Law* (Hart Publishing, 1999), p. 75.

[67] See M. Loughlin, *The Idea of Public Law* (Oxford University Press, 2004) and the review by Allison (2005) 68 *MLR* 344.

[68] M. Freedland, 'The evolving approach to the public/private distinction in English law' in Freedland and Auby (eds.), *The Public Law/Private Law Divide: Une entente assez cordiale?* (Hart Publishing, 2006), p. 107.

[69] P. Cane, 'Accountability and the public/private distinction' in Bamforth and Leyland (eds.), *Public Law in a Multi-Layered Constitution* (Hart Publishing, 2003), p. 276. And see M. Taggart, 'The peculiarities of the English': Resisting the public/private law distinction' in P. Craig and R. Rawlings (eds.), *Law and Administration in Europe* (Oxford University Press, 2003), p. 119.

[70] M. Hunt, 'The 'horizontal effect of the Human Rights Act' [1998] *PL* 423.

private division works in practice to produce outcomes that some think unjust. Why, it is asked, should it be wrong for a state-run nursing home to close its doors or turn away a patient, when a private home can do so with impunity?[71] Surely human dignity is a universal right? Questions like this put the public/private divide in issue.[72]

An alternative response, and one preferred by the authors, is to search for values common to public and private law, capable, if properly handled, of bridging the divide (p. 46 below). Common law principles and concepts are sufficiently flexible to provide appropriate answers to problems involving the state and public authorities.[73] We do not deny that the state has special functions. The legislative process is undoubtedly special, a fact acknowledged in the distinction drawn between lawmaking and administrative rule-making in Chapters 4 and 5. That the common law is holistic does not mean that identical rules should be applied automatically across the board. Specific situations call for thoughtful specific answers and not mechanical application of the totemic word 'public'.

Power has never been the monopoly of the state or its institutions. Today, as Cane wryly observes, 'It is not just that relations between the public and private spheres have become more complex and multi-faceted . . . Rather, the two spheres have become inextricably interwoven in a process better analogised to the scrambling of an egg than to the weaving of a two-stranded rope'.[74] Shapiro's sense of a 'bounded and billeted' administration is rapidly disappearing. Outside the boundaries of the nation state, fragmentation is still more pronounced: states, agencies, international institutions and multinational corporations mingle and exercise ambiguous forms of authority. Separate public and private law principles are hard to apply in the post-modern world of fragmented governmental structures; the outcome is the sterile jurisdictional disputes in which lawyers specialise.

Teubner has argued that 'neither public law, as the law of the political process, nor private law, the law of economic processes, has the capacity to develop adequate legal structures in relation to the many institutional contextures of civil society'.[75] He calls for 'polycontexturality', a frame of mind in which 'the simple distinction of state/society which translates into law as public law *v* private law needs to be substituted by a multiplicity of social perspectives which are similarly reflected in the law.' On just this note, Karen Yeung notes how competition law is:[76]

[71] See *YL v Birmingham City Council* [2007] UKHL 27 discussed at p. 380 below.

[72] See A. Clapham, *Human Rights in the Private Sphere* (Oxford University Press, 1993).

[73] D. Oliver, 'The underlying values of public and private law', and M. Taggart, 'The province of administrative law determined?' in Taggart (ed.), *The Province of Administrative Law*; and see D. Oliver, *Common Values and the Public-Private Divide* (Butterworths, 1999).

[74] Cane, 'Accountability and the public/private distinction', p. 248.

[75] G. Teubner, 'The many autonomies of private law' (1998) 51 *CLP* 393, 396.

[76] K. Yeung, 'Competition law and the public/private divide', in Freedland and Auby (eds), *The Public-Private Divide : Une entente assez cordiale?* (Hart Publishing, 2006), p. 163.

moving beyond its original focus on private economic power to encompass public power, at least in so far as it may impact on the competitiveness of markets. Thus, in its modern guise competition law provides an important means by which economic power, primarily private economic power but increasingly also public economic power, is controlled and restrained.

Her conclusion is that 'the elusive and uncertain public/private divide is unlikely to provide any real assistance'; for relevant principles and values, we must turn to economic theory. Much the same is true in respect of corporations, which should not be free to operate as predators on behalf of their owners or shareholders.[77] Increasingly, they are subject to a range of new regulatory disciplines, seen as the most effective way to tame anti-competitive and predatory behaviour (see Chapter 6).[78] Again, 'good governance' values obtaining in the public sector are gaining ground nationally as principles of 'corporate governance' while on the international scene 'an ethical floor of responsibilities that MNEs should observe is coming into being'.[79]

Used descriptively, the public/private distinction has to be accepted: it is simply a fact, for example, that the HRA is a public law measure applicable only to public authorities and many further examples of rules based on a public/private distinction will be found throughout this book. A procedural distinction, though *not* an exclusive public law jurisdiction, is convenient and sometimes necessary.[80] The model of public law that we owe to Dicey is, like much in English law, incomplete, incoherent and inconsistent. But even when particular outcomes are – as they often are – disappointing, Dicey's equality principle 'conforms to a widely-held political ideal and preserves us from many practical problems'.[81] Quite simply, it is the most practical 'take off point'.[82]

3. Dicey and 'red light theory'

Dicey spoke disparagingly of the French theory of *séparation des pouvoirs* but Vile reminds us that the idea of the balanced constitution, in which executive

[77] As in *NEAT Domestic Trading Pty Ltd v AWB Ltd* (2003) 216 CLR 277.

[78] J. Braithwaite and P. Drahos, *Global Business Regulation* (Cambridge: Cambridge University Press, 2000), p. 531; J. Braithwaite, 'The limits of economism in controlling harmful corporate conduct' (1982) 16 *Law and Society Review* 481; 'Corporate control: Markets and rules' (1990) 53 *MLR* 170.

[79] P. Muchlinski, 'International business regulation: An ethical discourse in the making?' in Campbell and Miller (eds.), *Human Rights and the Moral Responsibilities of Corporate and Public Sector Organisations* (Kluwer Academic, 2004), p. 99.

[80] C. Harlow, 'Why public law is private law: An invitation to Lord Woolf', in Cranston and Zuckerman (eds.), *The Woolf Report Reviewed* (Clarendon Press, 1995).

[81] Hogg, *Liability of the Crown*.

[82] See J. Allison, 'Variations of view on English legal distinctions between public and private' (2007) 66 *CLP* 698, 711.

power is constantly subject to checks and balances from both Parliament and the law courts, is itself a variant on the theme of separation of powers. Noting its peculiar attraction for lawyers, Vile called this 'the theory of law'.

> The 'executive' must act according to the law, the 'government' must exercise leadership in the development of policy; but if the government was subject to the control of parliament, and the executive to the control of the courts, then a harmony could be established between the two roles of the ministers of the Crown. Ministerial responsibility, legal and political, was thus the crux of the English system of government. Whilst it remained a reality the whole edifice of constitutionalism could be maintained; should it cease to be a workable concept the process of disintegration between the legal basis and the operation of the government would begin.[83]

The 'balanced constitution' was an ideal-type. It never really existed and, given the present state of fusion between executive and Parliament, the idea of a constitution held in balance by a *triadic* division of functions is quite simply untenable. It has been tipped hopelessly out of kilter by the rise of political parties and popular democracy.[84] The significance of the balanced constitution lies in its influence on public law.

As administrators gained powers to make regulations and to adjudicate upon matters affecting the state's subjects, lawyers and administrators pulled in opposite directions. Lawyers, trained in the Diceyan mode of thought, regarded these developments as threatening both Parliament and the courts. In consequence, the breakdown – or perceived breakdown – of the doctrine of ministerial responsibility, which formed the political arm of Dicey's balance, brought cries of 'elective dictatorship'.[85] It is not surprising, therefore, to find many authors believing that the primary function of administrative law should be to *control* excesses of state power and, more precisely, subject it to the rule of the law courts. Light-heartedly, we have called this conception of administrative law 'red light theory' because of its emphasis on control. Professor Wade's approach is unequivocal. In the first edition of his leading textbook, he used the metaphor of 'constant warfare between government and governed' to justify a narrow focus on 'the *manner* of the exercise of power'.[86] He expressed overt suspicion of the 'vast empires of executive power' coupled with the expectation that government would 'run amok'. His later definition

[83] Vile, *Constitutionalism and Separation of Powers*, pp. 230, 231.

[84] See the debate between S. Sedley, 'The sound of silence: Constitutional law without a constitution' (1994) 110 *LQR* 270 and Griffith, 'The common law and the political constitution'.

[85] Lord Hailsham, *The Dilemma of Democracy: Diagnosis and prescription* (Collins, 1978), especially Ch. XVI. See also R. Brazier, *Constitutional Reform: Re-shaping the British political system* (Clarendon Press, 1991).

[86] H. W. R Wade, *Administrative Law* (Clarendon Press, 1961), p. 3. This short and incisive text is the basis for H. W. R. Wade and C. Forsyth, *Administrative Law*, 9th edn (Oxford University Press, 2004) (hereafter Wade and Forsyth).

of administrative law as 'the law relating to *the control* of governmental power' hardly comes as a surprise:

> A first approximation to a definition of administrative law is to say that it is the law relating to the control of governmental power. This, at any rate, is the heart of the subject, as viewed by most lawyers. The governmental power in question is not that of Parliament: Parliament as the legislature is sovereign and, subject to one exception [European Community law] is beyond legal control. The powers of all other public authorities are subordinated to the law, just as much in the case of the Crown and ministers as in the case of local authorities and other public bodies. All such subordinate powers have two inherent characteristics. First, they are all subject to legal limitations; there is no such thing as absolute or unfettered administrative power. Secondly, and consequentially, it is always possible for any power to be abused. Even where Parliament enacts that a minister may make such order as he thinks fit for a certain purpose, the court may still invalidate the order if it infringes one of the many judge-made rules. And the court will invalidate it, *a fortiori,* if it infringes the limits which Parliament itself has ordained.
>
> The primary purpose of administrative law, therefore, is to keep the powers of government within their legal bounds, so as to protect the citizen against their abuse. The powerful engines of authority must be prevented from running amok. 'Abuse', it should be made clear, carries no necessary innuendo of malice or bad faith. Government departments may misunderstand their legal position as easily as may other people, and the law which they have to administer is frequently complex and uncertain. Abuse is therefore inevitable, and it is all the more necessary that the law should provide means to check it . . .
>
> As well as power there is duty. It is also the concern of administrative law to see that public authorities can be compelled to perform their duties if they make default . . . The law provides compulsory remedies for such situations, thus dealing with the negative as well as the positive side of maladministration.
>
> *Function distinguished from structure*
>
> As a second approximation to a definition, administrative law may be said to be the body of general principles which govern the exercise of powers and duties by public authorities. This is only one part of the mass of law to which public authorities are subject. All the detailed law about their composition and structure, though clearly related to administrative law, lies beyond the proper scope of the subject as here presented.
>
> What has to be isolated is the law about the manner in which public authorities must exercise their functions, distinguishing function from structure and looking always for general principles.[87]

Wade, perhaps Dicey's greatest and certainly his most influential heir, once described the spirit of Dicey's work as 'enduring' and so, as this chapter demonstrates, it has proved to be. We have chosen to focus on it as an encapsulation

[87] Wade and Forsyth, pp. 4–5 (emphasis ours).

of the red light tradition in English administrative law. The liberal-democratic view of administrative law's objectives, which strongly emphasises freedom *from* the state, derives directly from Dicey, whose account of the British constitution was never, as he seems to have believed, simply a description. It was an *interpretation,* inspired by his own values as well as those of the society in which he lived and worked. The ideology that formed the 'background theory' of his great works included an ardent belief in individualism, in laissez-faire economic policy and in the value of the common law. He showed no apparent interest in other functions for administrative law, such as regulation of relationships between public authorities that today it is increasingly asked to do. Dicey, along with many of his successors, felt that the 'harmony' of the British constitution was under threat from a shift of power away from Parliament and by greatly increased governmental powers (see Chapter 2).[88] Insofar as he recognised and feared the trend to collectivism but suggested no alternative structures by which it might be countered, Dicey must bear some responsibility for the individualistic, citizen-versus-state approach in English administrative law.

4. Ouster clauses and the rule of law

Central to red light theory, as we have taken care to emphasise, is the idea of the rule of law. Closely linked is the view that law courts are the primary weapon for protection of the citizen and control of the executive. Reflecting these sentiments, a leading textbook asserts:

> In matters of public law, the role of the ordinary courts is of high constitutional importance. It is a function of the judiciary to determine the lawfulness of the acts and decisions and orders of the Executive, tribunals and other officials exercising public functions, and to afford protection of the rights of the citizen. Legislation which deprives them of these powers is inimical to the principle of the rule of law.[89]

Whether the Government, acting through the legislature, should be able to exempt governmental activities from judicial oversight or drastically curtail the ambit of judicial review is therefore a crunch constitutional question, crucial to maintenance of the rule of law.

Under the doctrine of parliamentary sovereignty, it is open to Parliament to restrict or entirely exclude judicial review. There are various ways to do this.

[88] See M. Loughlin, *Public Law and Political Theory* (Clarendon Press, 1992), pp. 153–9, where the author calls Dicey's philosophy 'conservative normativism'. And see the debate between E. Barendt, *An Introduction to Constitutional Law* (Clarendon Press, 1998) and A. Tomkins, 'Review article: Of constitutional spectres. Review of Eric Barendt: An Introduction to Constitutional Law' [1999] *PL* 525.

[89] de Smith, Lord Woolf and J. Jowell , *Judicial Review of Administrative Action*, 6th edn (Sweet & Maxwell, 2007) [5-016].

The most extreme is a total 'ouster', 'privative' or 'preclusive' clause, designed to deprive the courts of jurisdiction. Ousters that render decisions wholly unchallengeable in the courts impinge on the constitutional allocation of functions, raising the question whether access to the courts is, as courts are fond of asserting, truly a 'constitutional right'.[90] Less drastic, though still suspect, is retrospective legislation, which has the effect of nullifying a court decision. This may operate either to deprive a litigant of the fruits of a successful lawsuit – a form of retaliation censured by Wade in the context of the *Burmah Oil* case as an 'unusual measure of retaliation'.[91] Slightly less opprobrious is legislation designed to confine the benefits of a successful case to those who fought it, common in social security litigation.[92] Such measures are hotly resented and often provoke judicial retaliation as attacks on the rule of law. Limitation clauses such as the six-week period for challenge frequently found in planning and compulsory purchase statutes are more acceptable.

Judges have developed various strategies to emphasise their opposition to ouster. Ouster clauses are restrictively interpreted. A common law presumption has evolved whereby access to the courts is not to be denied save by clear statutory words;[93] equally, it may be proclaimed a 'constitutional' or 'fundamental' right. The culmination of these approaches came in the celebrated *Anisminic* decision,[94] where Lord Reid showed how an ouster clause can skilfully be 'read down', laying the foundation stone of modern judicial review.

Before we read his speech, it is necessary to understand how limited at that date were the grounds for judicial review. In the case of tribunals such as the Foreign Compensation Commission (FCC), review lay in respect of 'jurisdictional errors' or errors of law concerning the competence of the tribunal to accept jurisdiction in a given case. (This very technical area of law is further discussed in Chapter 11). The effect of judicial invalidation of a decision was an elusive question. Thus Lord Reid in *Anisminic* describes a decision struck down for jurisdictional error as 'a nullity' and 'void', which amounts to saying that it is of no effect whatsoever. In other cases, decisions have been held 'voidable', meaning broadly that they are valid until set aside by a court.[95] The distinction may have important consequences. A void decision has no legal effects, invalidates further decisions dependent upon it, and may create rights to compensation. The rights of third parties will, on the other hand, be frozen out if the decision is merely voidable.

[90] *R v Lord Chancellor, ex p. Witham* [1997] 2 All ER 779 is discussed with further cases at pp. 114, 118 below.

[91] Wade & Forsyth, p 803, discussing *Burmah Oil v Lord Advocate* [1965] AC 75 and the War Damage Act 1965.

[92] T. Prosser, *Test Cases for the Poor* (Child Poverty Action Group, 1983); and see below, Ch. 16.

[93] *Pyx Granite Co Ltd v Minister of Housing and Local Government* [1960] AC 260. And see de Smith, Woolf and Jowell, *Judicial Review of Administrative Action* [4.014–020].

[94] *Anisminic Ltd v Foreign Compensation Commission* [1969] 2 AC 147.

[95] H. W. R. Wade, 'Unlawful administrative action: Void or voidable?' (1967) 83 *LQR* 499 and (1968) 84 *LQR* 95.

The decision in issue in *Anisminic* came from the FCC, a statutory body set up under the Foreign Compensation Act 1950, which from time to time is asked to allocate funds received from foreign governments in respect of losses suffered by British nationals in overseas territories, in this case, after the Suez crisis. Anisminic, a British company claiming compensation, had been nationalised by the Egyptian government and sold to an Egyptian concern, raising the question whether it was a 'British national', for whom the funds were reserved. The FCC made a 'determination' ruling out Anisminic's claim. On appeal, the House of Lords ruled by a majority that an error of law had been made. There was however an obstacle in the form of an ouster clause reading: 'The determination by the Commission of any application made to them under this Act shall not be called in question in any court of law.' By a majority (Lord Morris dissenting), the House went on to decide that the FCC had committed a jurisdictional error against which the ouster offered no protection; the determination was a 'purported determination':

Lord Reid: If the draftsman or Parliament had intended to . . . prevent any inquiry even as to whether the document relied on was a forgery, I would have expected to find something much more specific than the bald statement that a determination shall not be called in question in any court of law. Undoubtedly such a provision protects every determination which is not a nullity. But I do not think that it is necessary or even reasonable to construe the word 'determination' as including everything which purports to be a determination but which is in fact no determination at all. And there are no degrees of nullity. There are a number of reasons why the law will hold a purported decision to be a nullity. I do not see how it could be said that such a provision protects some kinds of nullity but not others; if that were intended it would be easy to say so . . . There are many cases where, although the tribunal had jurisdiction to enter on the inquiry, it has done or failed to do something in the course of the inquiry which is of such a nature that its decision is a nullity. It may have given its decision in bad faith. It may have made a decision which it had no power to make. It may have failed in the course of the inquiry to comply with the requirements of natural justice. It may in perfect good faith have misconstrued the provisions giving it power to act so that it failed to deal with the question remitted to it. It may have refused to take into account something which it was required to take into account. Or it may have based its decision on some matter which, under the provisions setting it up, it had no right to take into account. I do not intend this list to be exhaustive. But . . . if it is entitled to enter on the inquiry and does not do any of those things which I have mentioned in the course of the proceedings, then its decision is equally valid whether it is right or wrong subject only to the power of the court in certain circumstances to correct an error of law . . . [If] they reach a wrong conclusion as to the width of their powers, the court must be able to correct that – not because the tribunal has made an error of law, but because as a result of making an error of law they have dealt with and based their decision on a matter with which, on a true construction of their powers, they had no right to deal. If they base their decision on some matter which is not prescribed for their adjudication, they are doing something which they have no right to do and their decision is a nullity.

The Government reacted swiftly. It tacked onto a bill, coincidentally before the House of Commons, an amendment designed to nullify the decision prospectively. But faced by angry letters to *The Times* from eminent lawyers and a hostile amendment, supported by the Law Lords and carried in the Lords, the Government backtracked. Section 3 of the Foreign Compensation Act 1969 provides for direct appeal to the Court of Appeal on a question of law concerning the construction of an Order in Council made under the Act. No further appeal lies to the House of Lords. Otherwise, save in cases of breaches of natural justice, a determination (including a purported determination) is not to be called in question in any court of law.

The *Anisminic* issue resurfaced suddenly and unexpectedly more than thirty years later in the contentious context of asylum and immigration. As we shall see in later chapters, there had been a continual flow of appeals to tribunals and courts in immigration cases, many of which the Home Office had lost. It was not therefore especially surprising that the bill set out to reform the appeals system; it was surprising to find in it a draconian ouster clause, designed to replace the High Court's jurisdiction with final appeal to a newly constituted Asylum and Immigration Appeals Tribunal (AIT).[96] The motivation was said by the Home Office sponsors to be the need to relieve pressure on the courts from repetitive and unmeritorious appeals – an explanation undercut when the Home Secretary, David Blunkett, announced himself to be 'personally fed up with having to deal with a situation where parliament debates issues and the judges then overturn them'. It was 'time for judges to learn their place'; they did not 'have the right to override the will of the House, our democracy or the role of Members of Parliament in deciding the rules'.[97] A gauntlet had been thrown down to the judges.

The first point that we wish to make about this unfortunate episode concerns drafting. English statutory drafting is said to be both precise and specific and the ouster in Clause 11 of the bill is an especially skilful example. It first dealt directly with the jurisdiction of the courts by providing that 'No court shall have any supervisory or other jurisdiction (whether statutory or inherent) in relation to the [AIT].' It went on to double-bank the ouster:

> No court may entertain proceedings for questioning (whether by way of appeal or otherwise) –
>
> (a) any determination, decision or other action of the Tribunal (including a decision about jurisdiction). . .
>
> (c) any decision in respect of which a person has or had a right of appeal to the Tribunal. . .

In case any loopholes were left, the draftsman added that these provisions were to:

[96] See for a full account, R. Rawlings, 'Review, revenge and retreat' (2005) *MLR* 378.
[97] Quoted by A. Bradley, 'Judicial independence under attack' [2003] *PL* 397.

> (a) prevent a court, in particular, from entertaining proceedings to determine whether a purported determination, decision, or action of the Tribunal was a nullity by reason of -
>
> (b)
>
> (i) lack of jurisdiction,
> (ii) irregularity,
> (iii) error of law,
> (iv) breach of natural justice, or
> (v) any other matter . . .

Only decisions made in bad faith were excepted. Finally, the draftsman anticipated the gateway afforded by the ECHR, providing that the power to challenge a public authority (including the tribunal) for acting incompatibly with the Convention under s. 7(1) of the HRA would be 'subject to subsections (1) to (3) above'.

Publication of the bill created uproar amongst lawyers. A speech from Lord MacKay, a previous Lord Chancellor, in the House of Lords debate shows how the bill's opponents presented it as an attack on the rule of law:

> Those who are familiar with that branch of the law will recognise those words as coming from a speech of the late Lord Reid in the case of *Anisminic*. Those were the grounds on which he held that the decision of the Foreign Compensation Commission in that case was not protected by the statutory ouster, which was elaborate, because the statutory ouster purported to protect determinations of the commission. However broad that protection is, if there is no true determination of the commission, there is nothing to protect. Alert to that problem, those who have put the Bill together sought to avoid it.
>
> In my submission, that is a serious affront to the rule of law. Let me take a breach of natural justice. What the House of Commons has been asked to affirm by the Government – and has affirmed – is that the High Court should be prevented from intervening, even where there is a clear breach of natural justice on the part of the tribunal. . . In my submission, that strikes right at the very heart of the rule of law. Anyone who read the Bill should have appreciated that. . .
>
> [T]he Government were apparently willing to subvert the rule of law in relation to people who might well be at risk of their lives from persecution in a foreign land.[98]

As with *Anisminic*, the Government drew back to a compromise position, providing that parties to an appeal in the AIT may 'apply to the appropriate court, on the grounds that the Tribunal made an error of law, for an order requiring the Tribunal to reconsider its decision on the appeal'.[99] Appeal is, however, strictly limited. An order can be made only if the court 'thinks that the Tribunal may have made an error of law', and only once in relation to each appeal. We shall pick this point up in Chapter 11.

[98] HL Deb., vol. 659, col. 67.

[99] S. 26(1) and (2) of the Asylum and Immigration (Treatment of Claimants, etc.) Act 2004.

The second lesson of this story is that the unwritten constitution is held together by understandings. As the Lord Chancellor, Lord Falconer, appearing before the House of Lords Constitutional Committee, explained:

> I think the rule of law also goes beyond issues such as specific black letter law. I think there are certain constitutional principles which if Parliament sought to offend would be contrary to the rule of law as well. To take an extreme example simply to demonstrate the point, if Parliament sought to abolish all elections that would be so contrary to our constitutional principles that that would seem to me to be contrary to the rule of law. The rule of law goes beyond specific black letter law; it includes international law and it includes, in my view, settled constitutional principles. I think there might be a debate as to precisely what are settled constitutional principles but it goes beyond, as it were, black letter law.[100]

Before we move on from the subject of ouster, we want to highlight a further constitutional development. *Anisminic* was decided long before the HRA 'domesticated' the European Convention in 1998, though after the UK ratified it. ECHR Art. 6(1) contains the important provision that:

> In the determination of his civil rights and obligations . . . everyone is entitled to a fair and public hearing within a reasonable time by an independent and impartial tribunal established by law.

This provision renders total ouster clauses highly suspect. It also requires government to look very carefully at administrative systems both to ensure that adjudicative machinery is in place where this is appropriate and also that the machinery is 'Strasbourg compliant'. We shall follow this important development in Chapter 14.

Again, *Anisminic* was decided before the UK acceded to the European Communities (see Chapter 4). In the years that followed, it was shown that EC law might have something to say on preclusive clauses. The point arose in *Johnston v Chief Constable of the Royal Ulster Constabulary*,[101] a case involving equal opportunities. An Order in force during the Northern Ireland emergency excluded the use of firearms by female members of the Royal Ulster Constabulary (RUC). Ms Johnston sued in an industrial tribunal, arguing that the policy was incompatible with the EC Treaty and Equal Treatment Directive. The RUC relied on a ministerial certificate certifying that the conditions for derogation from the principle of equal treatment had been met which, if accepted, would have ousted the tribunal's jurisdiction. The tribunal made a preliminary reference to the ECJ for an advisory opinion as to the compatibility of the Order with EC law. The ECJ replied:

[100] CC, *Relations between the Executive, Judiciary, and Parliament*, HL 151 (2007) [25].

[101] Case 222/84 *Johnston v Chief Constable of the Royal Ulster Constabulary* [1986] ECR 1651, [1986] 3 WLR 1038. The European Commission was an intervenor in the ECJ in support of Ms Johnston. In issue were s. 53(2) of the Sex Discrimination (Northern Ireland) Order 1976; TEC Art. 141 (ex 119) and Art. 6 of the Equal Treatment Directive (EC 76/207).

The right to an effective judicial remedy

16. The Commission takes the view that to treat the certificate of a minister as having an effect such as that provided for in article 53(2) . . . is tantamount to refusing all judicial control or review and is therefore contrary to a fundamental principle of Community law and to article 6 of the directive. . .
18. The requirement of judicial control stipulated by that article reflects a general principle of law which underlies the constitutional traditions common to the member states. That principle is also laid down in articles 6 and 13 of the European Convention of Human Rights . . .
20. A provision which, like article 53(2) . . . requires a certificate such as the one in question in the present case to be treated as conclusive evidence that the conditions for derogating from the principle of equal treatment are fulfilled allows the competent authority to deprive an individual of the possibility of asserting by judicial process the rights conferred by the directive. Such a provision is therefore contrary to the principle of effective judicial control laid down in article 6 of the directive.

We have highlighted ouster clauses because of their great constitutional importance, not only to red light theorists. In national law, ouster clauses demonstrate the respective constitutional weightings of the rule of law and parliamentary sovereignty. The rule of law is, however, an ideal that transcends the national legal order. Our example therefore serves as a reminder that the UK is no longer an island. As we shall see in subsequent chapters, multi-level systems of law and governance are coming into being into which we are increasingly integrated.

5. 'Green light theory'

The red light view of English administrative law as an instrument for the *control* of power and protection of individual liberty, the emphasis being on courts rather than on government, did not go unchallenged. In the period between the two world wars an alternative tradition grew up, which we have called 'green light theory'. In using this metaphor, we do not wish to suggest that green light theorists favour unrestricted or arbitrary action by the state; what one person sees as control of arbitrary power may – as Carr suggested – be experienced by another as a brake on progress. But while red light theory looks to the model of the balanced constitution and favours strong judicial control of executive power, green light theory sees in administrative law a vehicle for political progress and welcomes the 'administrative state'. In saying this, we must remember that both red and green light theories originated in earlier eras and try to understand their historical context. Both were, as Taggart reminds us:

> forged on the anvil of the emerging welfare state. Green light theorists looked to the truly representative legislature to advance the causes of workers, women, minorities and the disadvantaged. For them, the role of law was to facilitate the provision of statutorily

> established programmes of public services. Parliament was trusted to deliver socially desirable results, and so giving effect to Parliament's intention comported with those theorists' ideological leanings . . . A corollary to this approach was a deep suspicion of judges, who as a class were seen as hostile to collectivism and the welfare state. Employing Victorian canons of statutory interpretation to read down and in some instances scuttle entirely, social welfare legislation, the judiciary were viewed often as the enemy.[102]

During Dicey's lifetime, the state grew exponentially. To some, including Dicey, this was frightening; it meant inroads into private property rights and individual freedoms and called for the protection of the law. To others it was unequivocally good. State action was necessary if the lot of the underprivileged in society was to be improved: pensions and unemployment benefit had to be funded; slum clearance required planning and compulsory purchase; and so on. Law was an essential tool in this crusade. As a green light was given to the interventionist state, law had to become proactive.

Writing at the London School of Economics in the interwar period, and conscious of the close relationship between law, politics and social policy, Laski, Robson and Jennings were able to draw inspiration from abroad. In the United States, where realist and sociological jurisprudence were influential, the gaps between law, politics and administration were narrower. Before the New Deal, the Supreme Court had on several occasions restricted federal government power to regulate economic activity, through the medium of the commerce clause of the US Constitution and their freedom of contract doctrine.[103] After the election of President Roosevelt in 1933, the Court showed every sign of reviving this case law.[104] Under the shadow of the President's happily unfulfilled threat to pack the Supreme Court, the Court gradually retreated, ceding economic power to the executive. The Supreme Court not only recognised the legitimacy of federal government intervention in the economy but also – and perhaps more importantly – 'all but abandoned the idea that it had some special role in enforcing a line between constitutional law and politics'.

> The modern economy's complexity and the wide range of public goals the national government could pursue . . . limited the contributions the Court could make. And, conversely, the political structure of Congress, in which states had substantial representation, made Congress better than the Court in determining whether any particular proposal crossed the line dividing national power from state power.[105]

[102] M. Taggart, 'Reinvented government, traffic lights and the convergence of public and private law. Review of Harlow and Rawlings: *Law and Administration*' [1999] *PL* 124, 125.

[103] *Lochner v New York* 198 US 45 (1905).

[104] *Schechter Poultry Corp v United States* 295 US 528 (1935).

[105] C. Sunstein, 'Constitutionalism after the New Deal' (1987) 101 *Harv. LR* 421 likens the change to a 'constitutional amendment'; G. Lawson, 'The rise and rise of the administrative state' (1994) 107 *Harv. LR* 1231 calls it 'unconstitutional'.

Roosevelt's New Deal had set in place a new 'administrative state', with which lawyers had eventually to come to terms; it had, in short, necessitated the new attitude to state interventionism for which radical scholars in England were working.

The new school of English administrative law writing was less insular and less hostile to collectivism than Dicey. Highlighting the international character of the movement, Gordon describes the voice of Canadian John Willis as 'instantly recognisable':

> He is clearly one of the gang – the legal realists who were concerned to expand the authority of administrative agencies to govern new areas of economic life; to promote their virtues as policy makers and adjudicators over those of their chief rivals, the courts; to defend them against charges of arbitrariness and absolutism; and to limit the scope of judicial review of their decisions. The voice is familiar in style as well as substance – the slashing sharp-pointed satirical barbs aimed to puncture the inflated claims of judicial 'formalism' and the blunt no-nonsense plain style used to highlight the virtues of civil servants' 'functionalism' . . . Willis and the American realists are evidently steeped in a common set of argumentative modes and rhetorics as well as common aims.[106]

Gordon goes on to underscore the significant fact that all the principal intellectual defenders of the administrative state in the US had at some time held important posts in the New Deal administration. Jaffé, another member of 'the gang', wrote in his memorial to Landis, who had launched the first comprehensive defence of the administrative state,[107] that 'our generation – that of Landis and myself – judged the administrative process in terms of its stunning performance under the New Deal'.[108] In Canada, Willis wrote that he wished 'to talk administrative law with a civil servant and political science accent,' to be a 'government man' and a 'what actually happens man'.[109]

A further influence in providing a new model in which green light theories of administrative law could flourish was the work of the French jurist, Léon Duguit (1859–1928). Duguit's theory was premised on a socialistic state in which strong government was a necessity[110] and whose activities stretched far

[106] R. Gordon, 'Willis's American counterparts: The legal realists' defence of administration' (2005) 55 *UTLJ* 405, 405-6.

[107] J. Landis, *The Administrative Process* (Yale University Press, 1938).

[108] L. Jaffé, 'James Landis and the administrative process' (1954) 78 *Harv. LR* 319, 322–3.

[109] J. Willis, 'The McRuer Report: Lawyer's values and civil servant's values' (1968) 17 *UTLJ* 351. And see L. Sossin, 'From neutrality to compassion: The place of civil service values and legal norms in the exercise of administrative discretion' (2005) 55 *UTLJ* 427. For an Australian parallel, see P. Bayne, 'Mr Justice Evatt's theory of administrative law: Adjusting state regulation to the liberal theory of the individual and the state' (1991) 9 *Law in Context* 1.

[110] Duguit's main works in this field were *Traité du droit constitutionnel*, 5 vols. (1911) and *Les transformations du droit public* (1913), tr. H. and F. Laski, *Law in the Modern State* (Allen and Unwin, 1921). Duguit developed his theory of public law under the influence of Emile Durkheim (1858–1917), whose great work on the *Division of Labour* (1893) started life as a dissertation on 'the relationship of individualism and socialism'.

beyond the traditional areas of law, order, justice and defence. He believed in a collectivist state whose function was to secure the provision of public services. These he defined as including 'any activity that has to be governmentally regulated and controlled because it is indispensable to the realisation and development of social solidarity . . . so long as it is of such a nature that it cannot be assured save by governmental intervention'.[111] The definition is broad enough to encompass all the main preoccupations of contemporary administrative law.

Duguit's theory laid the basis not only for a welfare state but also for a corporatist state in which planning and the control of private economic activity in the interests of the collectivity were legitimate state activities; he predicted indeed that transport, mining and electricity would ultimately become public services. Yet he rejected the idea of the state as a corporate entity with a legal life and legal powers of its own. The state was merely a collection of individuals 'interdependent upon one another even for their daily and elementary needs'. The state had 'duties' rather than 'rights' or 'powers'; sovereignty itself was a misconception.[112] In Duguit's 'modern theory of the state', 'the one governmental rule is the governmental obligation to organize and control public services in such a fashion as to avoid all dislocation. The basis of public law is therefore no longer command but organization . . . government has . . . a social function to fulfil.'[113]

Like the green light theorists who built on his work, Duguit did not believe in absolute power and was strongly anti-authoritarian.[114] Power was subject to inherent limitations, and the rulers, defined as those who possessed the power of implementing decisions, had only a limited mandate to act in the public interest or in the interests of social solidarity:

> In whatever manner the business of the state is managed, its fundamental idea is clear: government must perform certain definite functions. As a consequence a public service is an institution of a rigorously objective order controlled by principles equally imposed on the government and its subjects.[115]

In Duguit's ideal state, the function of public law was first and foremost to provide the framework inside which the efficient operation of the public services could at all times be assured. Administrative law limited state action in two distinct ways: (a) through the notion that the state can act only in the public interest and for the public good; and (b) through the principle that the state must observe the law. Regulation and rules, which set out the principles of

[111] Duguit, *Law in the Modern State*, p. 48.

[112] *Ibid.* See, similarly, H. Laski, *A Grammar of Politics* (Allen and Unwin, 1925), pp. 44–88.

[113] Duguit, *Law in the Modern State*, p. 49.

[114] H. Laski, 'M. Duguit's conception of the state' in Goodhart *et al.*, *Modern Theories of Law* (Oxford University Press, 1933), p. 56.

[115] Duguit, *Law in the Modern State*, pp. 51–4.

operation, at once seemed more important than the adjudication of disputes. Duguit's theory does, of course, find a place for adjudication. In case of doubt, administrative courts pronounce on the legality of administrative action. They have a third function. Duguit believed that the state was fully responsible for its acts and that every citizen was entitled to equality of treatment. Where a citizen suffered abnormal loss in the interest of the collectivity, compensation was due; loss caused by a state enterprise must be repaired by the state. Disputes between citizen and state were to be referred to administrative courts. These two ideas formed a complete new theory of administrative liability.

New accounts of administrative law showing the influence of these various ideas began to appear in England. Essentially these were administration-centred and collectivist in character. As Ivor Jennings saw the task of the lawyer, it was not to declare that:

> modern interventionism is pernicious, but, seeing that all modern states have adopted the policy, to advise as to the technical devices which are necessary to make the policy efficient and to provide justice for individuals . . . The problem to be discussed is the division of powers between administrators and judges and, given that judges must exercise some functions, the kind of courts and the judicial procedure necessary to make the exercise of the functions most efficient.[116]

For Jennings, administrative law was all the law relating to administration:

> It determines the organisation, powers and duties of administrative authorities. Where the political organisation of the country is highly developed, as it is in England, administrative law is a large and important branch of the law. It includes the law relating to public utility companies, and the legal powers which these authorities exercise. Or, looking at the subject from the functional instead of the institutional point of view, we may say that it includes the law relating to public health, the law of highways, the law of social insurance, the law of education, and the law relating to the provision of gas, water, and electricity. These are examples only, for a list of the powers of the administrative authorities would occupy a long catalogue.[117]

One senses here the functionalist concern with how things actually work. Jennings saw a new, descriptive role for academic administrative law, with a growing emphasis on statutory and regulatory regimes rather than the general principles of case law; he himself published a sectoral study of housing law.[118] In extended studies of new and developing areas of administrative activity, vertical rather than horizontal studies were made. Typically interdisciplinary in nature, such studies drew on the ideas of non-lawyers to explain and provide

[116] W. I. Jennings, 'Courts and administrative law' (1936) 49 *Harv. LR* 426, 430.

[117] Jennings, *The Law and the Constitution*, p. 194.

[118] Jennings, 'Courts and administrative law'.

context for legal rules. They were to promote a 'hiving off' of administrative law into its component parts – welfare, planning, housing, immigration, etc. – which tends to disguise its true structure. It is easier to confine the definition of administrative law to the general principles governing control of the use of power if the component parts of public administration have been hived off and treated separately. It is important to remember, however, that 'the organisation of this complexity is itself a form of public law, and executive self-regulation is a source of rules as worthy of analysis by the public lawyer as are those made by courts and legislatures'.[119]

Citing Jennings's definition with approval in the first English textbook devoted to administrative law,[120] Griffith and Street explained that their book would focus primarily on three questions:

- First, what sort of powers does the Administration exercise?
- Secondly, what are the limits of those powers?
- Thirdly, what are the ways in which the Administration is kept within those limits?

This certainly does not suggest a permissive attitude to power – an unlikely stance for Griffith, who believed that 'societies are by nature authoritarian. Governments even more so.'[121]

If for red light theorists the answer lay in courts and the rule of law, green light theorists saw judges and lawyers differently. Openly advocating reform of the antiquated legal system, they viewed the legal profession as too old-fashioned to reform itself. Green light theory focused on *alternatives to courts.* Thus Robson described the Donoughmore Committee, set up in 1931:

> to consider the powers exercised by or under the direction of (or by persons or bodies appointed specially by) Ministers of the Crown by way of (a) delegated legislation and (b) judicial or quasi-judicial decision, and to report what safeguards are desirable or necessary to secure the constitutional principles of the sovereignty of Parliament and the supremacy of the law . . .[122]

as paralysed by 'the dead hand of Dicey'.[123] Attacking at the same time legal reasoning and the profession, he damned the Report for rejecting the opportunity of a 'boldly-conceived system of administrative courts' headed by an administrative appeals tribunal, in favour of accepting 'the patchwork quilt of ill-constructed tribunals which at present exists, and endeavour[ing] to remedy some of their more obvious defects'.

Robson was not complaining that lawyers are *wrong* in seeking to protect

[119] T. Daintith, 'Book review' [2006] *PL* 644, 646.
[120] J. Griffith and H. Street, *Principles of Administrative Law*, 5th edn (Pitman, 1973), p. 4.
[121] J. Griffith, 'The political constitution' (1979) 42 *MLR* 1, 2.
[122] *Report of the Committee on Ministers' Powers*, Cmnd 4050 (1932), p. 1.
[123] W. Robson, 'The Report of the Committee on Ministers' Powers' (1932) 3 *Pol. Q.* 346, 359.

individual rights – though green light theorists did undoubtedly query their narrow focus on the right of property. His complaint was that their conceptual tools were inadequate for the task. He alleged that a profession which was incapable of reforming the legal system ought not to be let loose on the administrative process:

> The disappointing feature of the Report is its failure to make any significant contribution to the structure of the system. Instead of endeavouring to increase the sense of responsibility and independence of the administrative tribunals, the Report relies on a hostile judiciary to provide 'checks and balances'. It recommends, accordingly, that the supervisory jurisdiction of the High Court to compel ministers and administrative tribunals to keep within their powers and to hear and determine according to law be maintained; and further, that anyone aggrieved by a decision should have an absolute right of appeal to the High Court on any question of law.[124]

Robson was not arguing for a robotic administrative law or a public administration devoid of values – very much the reverse. What he worked for was justice for the many – what Street would later call 'justice in the welfare state'.[125] What Robson would have thought of the contemporary restructuring of the system of administrative tribunals by the Tribunals, Courts and Enforcement Act 2007 is an interesting question (see Chapter 11).

6. 'Green light theory' and control

Because they look in at administration from outside, lawyers traditionally emphasise external control through adjudication. To the lawyer, law is the policeman; it operates as an external control, often retrospectively. But a main concern of many green light writers was, as already suggested, to *minimise* the influence of courts: courts, with their legalistic values, were seen as obstacles to progress, and the control that they exercise as unrepresentative and undemocratic. 'The lawyers', said Robson, 'still regard themselves as champions of the popular cause; but there can be little doubt that the great departments of state . . . are not only essential to the well-being of the great mass of the people, but also the most significant expressions of democracy in our time.'[126]

In the same mode, we find Hutchinson seeking to re-politicise the notion of 'control':

> [Courts] take an overly historical approach to deciding disputes; they rely on an adversarial process; they limit the amount of relevant information on which decisions can be made; they are ignorant of bureaucratic concerns and workings; they allow access to only a limited

[124] *Ibid.*, pp. 360–1.

[125] H. Street, *Justice in the Welfare State*, 2nd edn (Stevens, 1975).

[126] W. Robson, *Justice and Administrative Law*, 3rd edn (Stevens, 1951), p. 421.

> number of individuals; they fail to monitor the impact of their decisions; they ignore the claims of collective interest; they adopt a negative cast of mind; and they are imbued with an individualistic philosophy. In short, the work of the courts is qualitatively incoherent and quantitatively ineffective. They engage in an inescapably political enterprise and function in a way that is incompatible with their self-imposed democratic responsibilities . . . [I]t will be necessary to give up on the courts entirely in the campaign to develop a better organisational ethic and democratic practice.
>
> In seeking to repoliticise the vast administrative regions of contemporary society and to oblige the ship of state to sail under democratic colours, it is necessary to throw liberalism overboard and cast off the moorings of the public/private distinction. On a democratic voyage of discovery there is no chart to follow and no grand manual of statecraft to consult. On the oceans of possibility, empowered citizens must be allowed to dream their own destinations and steer their own courses.[127]

Red light theory prioritises courts; green light theory prefers democratic or political forms of accountability. Thus Laski advocated citizen participation in the form of parliamentary advisory committees – a precursor of the modern, departmental Select Committees – to oversee the work of government departments. He also advised attaching to each department a 'users' committee of citizens affected by its operations plus a small, 'clearly impartial' investigatory committee to deal with serious charges against departments – a proposal with considerable resonance in the age of 'citizen participation' and 'focus groups'.[128] Committees were seen as an extension of the long tradition of lay participation in governance.[129] Griffith set out his personal creed in 'The Political Constitution',[130] where he caustically dismissed the idea of a justiciable and enforceable Bill of Rights, arguing for a collectivist view of 'rights' as group interests or 'claims' to be evaluated through the political process. On the other hand, Griffith stressed the need for access to information, open government, a free and powerful press, decentralisation through local government and a strengthened Parliament.

But if the red light 'model of law' is to be abandoned, many feel that something other than the traditional 'model of government' must take its place. Few would wish to set sail in a barque as frail as that of ministerial responsibility. And because it revealed the inadequacies of ministerial responsibility, Crichel Down is often described as the beginning of modern English administrative law. Briefly to revisit that forgotten controversy, Crichel Down had been acquired as a bombing range by the Air Ministry before World War II.

[127] A. Hutchinson, 'Mice under a chair: Democracy, courts and the administrative state' (1990) 40 *UTLJ* 374, 375–6, 403.

[128] W. Gwyn, 'The Labour Party and the threat of bureaucracy' (1971) 19 *Political Studies* 383, 389.

[129] K. Wheare, *Government by Committee* (Oxford University Press, 1955).

[130] Griffith, 'The political constitution'. See now G. Gee, 'The political constitutionalism of JAG Griffith' (2008) *Legal Studies* 20.

Subsequently, when no longer required for these purposes, it was transferred to the Ministry of Agriculture. A dispute arose when the Ministry, wishing to dispose of the land, tried to let it to a new tenant instead of allowing its original owners to buy it back. Fierce objections from the latter forced a public inquiry, which established the responsibility of civil servants both for the policy and also for its execution.[131] Controversially, the minister, Sir Thomas Dugdale, accepted responsibility and resigned.

To most commentators, Crichel Down exposed a world of administrative policy and decision-making apparently immune from political and parliamentary controls. To Griffith 'the fundamental defect revealed was not a failure in the constitutional relations of those involved nor the policy decisions nor even the length of the struggle [the complainant] had to wage. It was in the method and therefore in the mental processes of the officials'.[132] Content to rely on 'that personal integrity which is so much more than an absence of corruption', Griffith concluded that the civil service must be left to put its own house in order. For those who were less trusting, yet did not wish to tip the balance too far in the direction of judicial control, the challenge was to provide alternatives.

Discussing red light theories, we talked of 'control' through courts. We did not stop to unpack the word. Control can be symbolic or real; it can mean to check, restrain or govern. Griffith and Street clearly sensed latent ambiguities, remarking that 'A great deal turns on the meaning which is attached to the word "controls". Banks control a river; a driver controls his car. The influence of a parent over a child may be greater than the power of a prison guard over a convict.'[133] Here the 'controls' are direct and internal rather than indirect and external. To extend our metaphors, however, a river bank may be inspected by an officer of the water board – today more probably the official of a privatised water authority or regulatory agency – to see that it is in good repair; a policeman may stop the driver and caution him for speeding; a health visitor may advise the child's parents to exert a different kind of influence; and the prison guard may be questioned by the board of visitors. These are all external controls, but they are not judicial. Dicey's controls were also external, as the concept of 'checks and balances' implies.

The first control on administrative activity is (as Shapiro indicated) legislative. The second is internal, hierarchical and supervisory.[134] Consider the doctrine of individual ministerial responsibility, central to the argument over Crichel Down. One function of the doctrine is to require the minister, as head of his department, to supervise the activities of his subordinates by establishing

[131] *Report of the Inquiry into Crichel Down*, Cmnd 9176 (1954) and HC Deb., vol. 530, cols. 1182–302.

[132] J. Griffith, 'The Crichel Down Affair' (1955) 18 *MLR* 557, 569.

[133] Griffth and Street, *Principles of Adminstrative Law*, p. 24.

[134] See further T. Daintith and A. Page, *The Executive in the Constitution: Structure, autonomy and internal control* (Oxford University Press, 1999).

policies and checking the way in which they are implemented. The doctrine also provides for external control through responsibility to Parliament, but this is envisaged as a last resort. So Griffith hints at the superiority of internal control when he prescribes as a remedy for Crichel Down 'more red tape not less'.

A different distinction is between prospective and retrospective control. Legislation is prospective in that it controls administrative activity by prescribing its bounds. Judicial review of administrative action is primarily retrospective, although it also possesses a prospective dimension. Lawyers assume and administration tacitly accepts that judicial rulings set boundaries for future conduct.[135]

Lawyers like to assume that administrators approach law in the same way as lawyers, ranking it hierarchically and respecting its binding and boundary-setting nature. Dimock – a lawyer by training – suggests that law 'controls' the administrator in three different ways: (i) it tells him what the legislature expects him to accomplish; (ii) it fixes limits to his authority; and (iii) it sets out the substantive and procedural rights of the individual and group.[136] The order may be significant: administrators are necessarily policy-orientated or, to put this differently, interested in outcomes. Positively, administrators see law as a set of pegs on which to hang policies; negatively, as a series of hurdles to be jumped before policy can be implemented, in which sense law acts as a brake. If law conflicts with policy, the official tries to change the law and, if this proves impossible, may sometimes set it aside or ignore it. There is much evidence too that officials do not always respect the hierarchy of legal norms. Junior officials may follow policy directives from above in preference to legislation and they do not always know of the existence of case law or realise its significance. In short, the values and objectives of the two professions differ and they may be unsympathetic to each other's viewpoints. As public administrators, Rosenbloom and O'Leary complain that 'administrative law texts aimed at law students and legal practitioners lack a realistic grasp of what most public administrators actually do, the organisational settings in which they work, and the values that inform their activities. They [lawyers] focus on overhead and control functions, not on implementation and service delivery.'[137]

7. Allocation of functions

Discussing the allocation of functions in the English governmental and administrative system, Ganz criticised the way in which theories of the balanced constitution seek to distinguish 'legislative', 'judicial' and 'administrative' functions.[138] For Ganz, decision-taking is a spectrum, ranging from 'fixed rules at one end to a purely discretionary act at the other. No clear lines can be

[135] P. Atiyah, *Pragmatism and Theory in English Law* (Stevens, 1987).

[136] M. Dimock, *Law and Dynamic Administration* (Praeger, 1980), p. 31.

[137] D. Rosenbloom and R. O'Leary, *Public Administration and Law*, 2nd edn (Marcel Dekker, 1996), pp. vi, vii.

[138] G. Ganz, 'Allocation of decision-making functions' [1972] *PL* 215, 216.

drawn where the one activity stops and the other begins as they shade off into one another imperceptibly.' Lawmaking is, for example, a continuous process, starting normally in a government department, where policy is formulated and drafts made before they are submitted to Parliament, which technically 'makes' the law.[139] The process ends again with the executive, responsible for seeing the law brought into force. In terms of separation-of-powers theory, the action passes from one organ of government to another but the stages are not discrete. Every stage of the process involves value judgements and everything turns on the choice of the decision-maker:

> Rules are themselves value judgements whereas discretion is the power to make a value judgement. In practice the difference may not be very great . . . where the rule contains words such as 'reasonable' which amount to a delegation of discretion to make value judgements . . .
>
> When the problem arises of who should make decisions in a particular field the controversy should centre not on whether these involve the application of rules or discretion but on who should make the necessary value judgements. Looking at this from the point of view of the legislature there is a wide area of choice.
>
> Parliament may make the value judgements itself and embody them in reasonably precise rules in statutes. This narrows the area of discretion to be exercised by whoever is charged with the application of the rules but does not eliminate it. The choice has to be made between the courts, administrative tribunals and sometimes even ministers or independent statutory bodies as interpreters of the rules laid down.
>
> In many areas it is not, however, possible or even desirable to formulate value judgements in the shape of detailed rules. Especially in a new field it may be necessary to make value judgements on a case-to-case basis. This can be done by laying down rules embodying very broad standards or conferring wide discretionary powers. These powers may also be given to courts, administrative tribunals, Ministers or a specially created statutory body.[140]

Here Ganz makes two points which have proved central to the development of modern administrative law. The first concerns administrative discretion, a topic to which we return in Chapter 5; the second concerns the primacy of the democratically elected legislature. In common with other green light theorists, Ganz believed that judges should not interfere with the allocation of functions as established by statute; by so doing, they substituted the court for the rightful decision-maker chosen by Parliament. And she forcefully links the procedural question of allocation of functions with the question of *values*. Where courts cross jurisdictional boundaries to impose 'judicial' procedures on the administration, they are in fact substituting their own values for those of the administration. The argument advanced is two-pronged: on the one

139 M. Zander, *The Law-Making Process*, 6th edn (Cambridge University Press, 2005).

140 Ganz, 'Allocation of decision-making functions'.

hand, administrative procedures are more accessible and 'user-friendly' than courts; equally important, the new institutions are less imbued with old ideas and ideologies.

Ganz's position typifies green light theory. It is also a mirror image of a statement from a very different source. In the celebrated *Wednesbury* case,[141] the Sunday Entertainments Act 1932 empowered local authorities to license cinemas for Sunday performances, subject to such conditions 'as the authority think fit to impose'. The defendants banned entry to children under 15 and the cinema sought a declaration that the condition was ultra vires:

> *Lord Greene MR:* When an executive discretion is entrusted by Parliament to a body such as the local authority in this case, what appears to be an exercise of that discretion can only be challenged in the courts in a strictly limited class of case . . . it must always be remembered that the court is not a court of appeal. When discretion of this kind is granted the law recognizes certain principles upon which that discretion must be exercised, but within the four corners of those principles the discretion, in my opinion, is an absolute one and cannot be questioned in any court of law. What then are those principles . . .?
>
> The exercise of such a discretion must be a real exercise of the discretion. If, in the statute conferring the discretion, there are to be found expressly or by implication matters which the authority exercising the discretion ought to have regard to, then in exercising the discretion it must have regard to those matters. Conversely, if the nature of the subject-matter and the general interpretation of the Act make it clear that certain matters would not be germane to the matter in question, the authority must disregard those irrelevant collateral matters . . .
>
> I am not sure myself whether the permissible grounds of attack cannot be defined under a single head. It has been perhaps a little bit confusing to find a series of grounds set out. Bad faith, dishonesty – those of course, stand by themselves – unreasonableness, attention given to extraneous circumstances, disregard of public policy and things like that have all been referred to, according to the facts of individual cases, as being matters which are relevant to the question. If they cannot all be confined under one head, they at any rate, I think, overlap to a very great extent. For instance, we have heard in this case a great deal about the meaning of the word 'unreasonable' . . . [a word which] has frequently been used and is frequently used as a general description of the things that must not be done. For instance, a person entrusted with a discretion must, so to speak, direct himself properly in law. He must call his own attention to the matters which he is bound to consider. He must exclude from his consideration matters which are irrelevant to what he has to consider. If he does not obey those rules, he may truly be said, and often is said, to be acting 'unreasonably'. Similarly, there may be something so absurd that no sensible person could ever dream that it lay within the powers of the authority. Warrington LJ in *Short v Poole Corporation* [1926] Ch 66 gave the example of the red-haired teacher, dismissed because she had red hair. That

[141] *Associated Provincial Picture Houses Ltd v Wednesbury Corporation* [1948] 1 KB 223. And see M. Taggart, 'Reinventing administrative law' in Bamforth and Leyland (eds.), *Public Law in a Multi-Layered Constitution.*

> is unreasonable in one sense. In another sense it is taking into consideration extraneous matters. It is so unreasonable that it might almost be described as being done in bad faith; and, in fact, all these things run into one another . . .
>
> It is true to say that, if a decision on a competent matter is so unreasonable that no reasonable authority could ever have come to it, then the courts can interfere. That, I think, is quite right; but to prove a case of that kind would require something overwhelming, and, in this case, the facts do not come anywhere near anything of that kind. [The] proposition that the decision of the local authority can be upset if it is proved to be unreasonable, really [means] that it must be proved to be unreasonable in the sense that the court considers it to be a decision that no reasonable body could have come to. It is not what the court considers unreasonable, a different thing altogether. If it is what the court considers unreasonable, the court may very well have different views to that of a local authority on matters of high public policy of this kind. Some courts might think that no children ought to be admitted on Sundays at all, some courts might think the reverse, and all over the country I have no doubt on a thing of that sort honest and sincere people hold different views. The effect of the legislation is not to set up the court as an arbiter of the correctness of one view over another. It is the local authority that are set in that position and, provided they act, as they have acted, within the four corners of their jurisdiction, this court, in my opinion, cannot interfere.

Controversy surrounds the meaning of this famous passage. Are there two tests contained within it?

1. that the authority must act only after consideration of relevant factors (the ultra vires test)
2. that the authority must not act 'unreasonably'.

Or did Lord Greene intend a single test? If the first interpretation is correct, then, after all procedural factors have been exhausted, the court is left with an overriding discretion to intervene whenever it sees extreme unreasonableness: 'if a decision on a competent matter is so unreasonable that no reasonable authority could ever have come to it, then the courts can interfere'. If the second interpretation is correct, the court can oversee the range of factors which the decision-maker must take into consideration or must not consider – for example, he should not take into account wholly irrelevant questions, such as a school-teacher's red hair – but must stop short either of dictating the weight to be given to the various factors or of evaluating the final decision. In later chapters, we shall see how the courts have grappled with these issues.

We might compare the operation of the classical *Wednesbury* test to a plot of land, whose boundaries it is the court's duty to patrol. Provided the decision-maker does not put a toe outside the plot he is protected from judicial review. In the classical English formula, the decision-maker must not exceed 'the four corners of his discretion'; in the terminology of the ECtHR, this is the decision-maker's 'margin of appreciation'. The judge, who cannot review the merits of a decision, retains less discretion than if he possessed an independent power of evaluation. Yet this distinction is not really as clear as it seems. As the court sets the boundaries, it can in practice adjust them virtually at will by adding or subtracting factors which the decision-maker should have considered or not considered.

Shortly before Lord Irvine (New Labour's first Lord Chancellor) introduced the Human Rights Bill into Parliament, he found it expedient to affirm the true sense of the *Wednesbury* test. Irvine called it 'shorthand for that constitutional school of thought which advocates self-restraint in public law matters. Moreover, it is shorthand which the vast majority of lawyers would still acknowledge to be the guiding principle of our system of judicial review'. He wrote that Lord Greene had:

> outlined substantive principles of judicial review which truly reflect the constitutional basis which he ascribed to them. First that a decision-maker has a broad discretion as to the factors which are to be taken into account before a decision is made, a discretion which is only restricted if the governing statute clearly requires that a particular factor *must* be considered, or *must not* be considered. Second, the celebrated principle of *Wednesbury* unreasonableness, that once the decision-maker has properly determined the range of relevant considerations, the weight to be given to each consideration is a matter within its discretion and a decision will only be struck down as unreasonable where it is so unreasonable that no reasonable decision-maker could have made it.[142]

We shall return to this debate in Chapter 3.

8. Towards consensus?

Our objective in the first edition of this book was to reinstate the link between public law and politics, restoring an essential dimension of administrative law which had temporarily been mislaid. Identifying two sharply contrasted positions, we labelled them red and green light theory, distinguishing their opposing attitudes to the functions of state, government and judiciary:

> Red light theorists believed that law was autonomous to and superior over politics; that the administrative state was dangerous and should be kept in check by law; that the preferred way of doing this was through adjudication; and that the goal should be to enhance liberty, conceived in terms of the absence of external constraints. Green light theorists . . . believed that law was not autonomous from politics; that the administrative state was not a necessary evil, but a positive attribute to be welcomed; that administrative law should seek not merely to stop bad administrative practice, and that there might be better ways to achieve this than adjudication; and that the goal was to enhance individual and collective liberty conceived in positive and not just negative terms.[143]

142 Lord Irvine, 'Judges and decision-makers: The theory and practice of *Wednesbury* review' [1996] *PL* 59, 63.

143 The convenient summary comes from A. Tomkins 'In defence of the political constitution' (2002) 22 *OJLS* 157.

At one level, these differences reflect an accepted theoretical division in Anglo-American legal theory;[144] at another, a political divide. It is no coincidence that so many green light theorists were supporters of Roosevelt's New Deal or, like Laski and Griffith, avowed supporters of the British Labour Party. It is this which made their views controversial.

Times change and politics change with them. Attitudes to the state and the way the state is organised changed very sharply in the last decades. The New Deal policies in which green light theory was rooted came to be superseded in their country of origin by a liberal economic revolution worthy of being termed a 'new constitutional order'.[145] Today, this new order is itself under threat of demolition by an emergent 'New, New Deal'. In the UK, a Conservative 'blue rinse' caused concern, as indicated earlier, for the values of public law; New Labour substituted new values and embarked, as we shall see in the next chapter, on a quiet constitutional revolution and mission to modernise. The 'law/government' divide recorded in this chapter has given ground before the notion of 'governance' – a 'new process of governing; or a changed condition of ordered rule; or the new method by which society is governed'.[146] This idea is further unpacked in Chapter 2. We shall find Teubner's theme of hybridisation or 'polycontexturality' echoed in a shift away from 'state-centred' to 'decentred' regulation (see Chapter 6). What changes will be necessary in light of the financial disasters of 2008 it is too soon to say.

Perhaps red and green light theory has had its day? We do not think so. Even if the battle has migrated, the old opponents are still squaring up. The law-versus-democracy battle rages in the context of the HRA, as courts, empowered by the Act, have moved centre stage (see Chapter 4). Red and green light theories are both well represented in the European Union, where the search for 'bounded and billeted' government continues.[147] The idea captures an inevitable tension between administrative law's two main functions. The problem of balance finds expression in an administrative lawyer's simple definition as 'the control of power, and the maintenance of a fair balance between the competing interests of the administration (central government, local government or specialised agencies) and the citizen'.[148] It was also articulated by Richard Crossman, an avowed socialist who, as a Cabinet minister in Harold Wilson's

[144] See further P. Atiyah and R. Summers *Form and Substance in Anglo-American Law: A comparative study of legal reasoning, legal theory and legal institutions* (Clarendon Press, 1987); M. Horwitz, *The Transformation of American Law, 1780-1860* (Harvard University Press, 2006) and *The Transformation of American Law 1870-1960: The crisis of legal orthodoxy* (Oxford University Press, 1992); N. Duxbury, *Patterns of American Jurisprudence* (Clarendon Press, 1995).

[145] M. Tushnet, *The New Constitutional Order* (Princeton University Press, 2003), p. 36.

[146] R. Rhodes, *Understanding Governance* (Open University Press, 1997), p. 6.

[147] C. Harlow, 'European administrative law and the global challenge', in Craig and de Burca (eds.), *The European Union in Perspective* (Oxford University Press, 1999).

[148] D. Yardley, *Principles of Administrative Law* (Butterworths, 1981), p. viii.

1964 Labour Government, was responsible for introducing a parliamentary ombudsman (see Chapter 13):

> The growth of a vast, centralised State bureaucracy constitutes a grave potential threat to social democracy. The idea that we are being disloyal to our Socialist principles if we attack its excesses or defend the individual against its incipient despotism is a fallacy . . . For the Socialist, as much as for the Liberal, the State Leviathan is a necessary evil; and the fact that part of the Civil Service now administers a Welfare State does not remove the threat to freedom which the twentieth-century concentration of power has produced . . .
>
> In Britain we are faced with the following dilemma. Since the abuses of oligopoly cannot be checked by free competition, the only way to enlarge freedom and achieve a full democracy is to subject the economy to public control. Yet the State bureaucracy itself is one of those concentrations of power which threaten our freedom. If we increase its authority still further, shall we not be endangering the liberties we are trying to defend?[149]

We have used the lens of red and green light theory to highlight a number of attitudes to this dilemma. Jennings admits that 'judges must exercise some functions'. Griffith acknowledges that the development of judicial review 'during this century, and especially over the last thirty-five years, has brought great benefits and has been a restraint on overweening princes'.[150] Are we to call Wade a green light theorist when he says that the detailed law about the composition and structure of administrative bodies is 'clearly related to administrative law'?

It would be wrong to leave the subject, however, without any mention of a growing consensus over administrative law values. This has crystallised around a trilogy of values – transparency, participation and accountability – that reflect the 'good governance' programmes of international institutions.[151] Taggart, for example, lists openness, fairness, participation, impartiality, accountability, honesty and rationality as core values of constitutional and administrative law.[152] The leading Australian textbook on judicial review calls for 'a legal system which addresses the ideals of good government according to law', including: openness, fairness, participation, accountability, consistency, rationality, accessibility of judicial and non-judicial grievance procedures, legality and impartiality.[153]

Harden gives accountability – in the sense of giving an account of one's conduct so that it may be evaluated and, in appropriate cases, sanctioned[154]

149 R. Crossman, *Socialism and the New Despotism* (Fabian Tract No. 298, 1956).

150 J. Griffith, *The Politics of the Judiciary*, p. xvii.

151 C. Harlow, 'Global administrative law: The quest for principles and values' (2006) 17 *European J. of International Law* 187.

152 M. Taggart, 'The province of administrative law determined' in Taggart (ed.), *The Province of Administrative Law*, p. 4.

153 M. Aronson, B. Dyer and M. Groves, *Judicial Review of Administrative Action*, 4th edn, (Lawbook Co. of Australia, 2009), p. 1.

154 See M. Bovens, 'Analysing and assessing accountability: A conceptual framework' (2007) 13 *ELJ* 447; D. Oliver, *Government in the United Kingdom: The search for accountability, effectiveness and citizenship* (Open University Press, 1991).

– the central place on any list of good governance values because there is no real possibility of 'exit' from public goods or from the 'obligations which public authorities are entitled to impose on individuals'.[155] With many red light theorists, Mulgan sees legal accountability as:

> in some respects the most powerful form of external review of executive action. Judicial hearings increasingly require the government to disclose publicly what it has done and why; they allow members of the public the right to contest such government actions, and they can force the government into remedial action. Indeed, an effective, independent judicial system is a fundamental prerequisite for effective executive accountability.[156]

Later chapters of this book, however, describe very varied forms of accountability machinery, ranging from formal parliamentary proceedings through public inquiries and ombudsman investigations to judicial review and, in Chapter 17, the sanction of liability.

As Mulgan suggests and Austin has argued more explicitly, 'government would only become truly democratic and accountable and its citizens would only have a meaningful right of participation in the making of decisions which affect them, if there was full access to governmental information.' [157] In this way, freedom of information crept onto the administrative law agenda during the 1970s, when 'government in the sunshine' became a fashionable catchphrase.[158] Government in the sunshine, however, cuts across the dominant British tradition of 'government behind lace curtains'. It was not until the Freedom of Information Act 2000 came into force in 2005, after much pressure and endless official prevarication, that we could begin to talk of a transparent government system in Britain. Even then, when we look at the Act's provisions in greater detail in Chapter 10, we shall find no ringing declaration or positive right of access to official information; instead, we shall find twenty-three specific exemptions from disclosure.

The parallel shift inside administrative law from individuated to participatory due process is normally associated with Stewart's powerful plea for the reformation of American administrative law.[159] Classical English administrative law was, on the other hand, very sparing in its protection of *collective* interests, as green light theorists were quick to point out. Prosser suggests, however, that citizen participation is the goal towards which public law should be working. 'However deficient participation may be in practice, it aspires to, and allows us

[155] I. Harden, 'Citizenship and information' (2001) 7 *EPL* 165, 167.

[156] R. Mulgan, *Holding Power to Account: Accountability in modern democracies* (Macmillan, 2003), pp. 75–6.

[157] R. Austin, 'The Freedom of Information Act 2000: A sheep in wolf's clothing?' in *Changing Constitution*, 6th edn (2007).

[158] I. Harden and N. Lewis, *The Noble Lie: The British constitution and the rule of law* (Hutchinson, 1986); R. Austin, 'Freedom of information: The constitutional impact' in *Changing Constitution*, 2nd edn (1989).

[159] R. Stewart, 'The reformation of American administrative law' (1975) 88 *Harv. LR* 1667.

to work towards, the development of institutions for the expression of the ideal of discussion free from domination, with equal power to affect decisions given to all those affected'.[160] This view anticipates by many years the commitment of New Labour politicians to participatory, consultative and responsive governance (see Chapter 2), documented in a report from PASC.[161] The independent 'Power Inquiry' was more ambitious than PASC, whose report is notably short on ideas for citizen input. The Inquiry optimistically concluded that citizens were *not* apathetic; there was strong participation in areas from voluntary work to pressure politics. It needed to be downloaded, an ideal that has found expression in New Labour's plans for the restructuring of local government (see p. 86 below).[162]

Our own approach to problems of public administration and values is pragmatic. We 'do not demand consistency with some overarching theory of the administrative state'; we are 'prepared to accept new ways of addressing problems, even though they make a theoretical jumble of the legal culture'.[163] We have simply set out to show that there is no single finite question or set of questions for administrative law to answer, revolving around a single attitude to the state's relationships with its subjects. Similarly, there can be no finite list of values. Lawyers, we have argued, suffer from a professional deformation; they are too easily inclined to assume a judicial answer to every problem. Equally, they show a predisposition to leave the judicial branch of government unexamined.

160 T. Prosser, 'Towards a critical public law' (1982) 9 *JLS* 1, 11.

161 PASC, *Public Participation: Issues and innovations*, HC 373 (2001/2).

162 *Power to the People: An independent inquiry into Britain's democratic system* (London: Rowntree Trust) 2006

163 S. Shapiro, 'Pragmatic administrative law' in *Issues in Legal Scholarship: The reformation of American administrative law* (Berkeley Electronic Press, 2005).

2

The changing state

Contents

1. The Trojan horse

In Chapter 1 we focused on the political dimension of administrative law, an unfashionable approach in 1983, when the first edition of this book appeared. At that time we felt the need to assert at the outset our view of administrative law as neither neutral nor objective but as reflecting the expectations that society has of 'the state'. We did not, on the other hand, feel the need to include in our book a structural account of British government. We were writing for readers who were relatively informed about British history and politics, many of whom had undergone a course in public law or British government. This could, we felt, be relied upon as a satisfactory foundation for the study of administrative law. Moreover, British government seemed to us at the time relatively simple. We thought of the state as unitary and highly centralised. Central government was made up of the great departments of state, some like the Home and Foreign Offices with eighteenth-century roots, others modern statutory additions. A few major public services were operated directly by central government, notably the National Health Service (NHS), but more usually, as with housing or social services, they were the responsibility of local government, the only democratically elected competitor to Parliament. Some nationalised industries were, like British Rail, still on the scene but most were on their way out. Few concessions were made to regionalism, regional government was not on our radar screen and although the European Communities Act was on the statute book, to have looked outside the territorial boundaries of our nation state would not have crossed our minds! Declining to define the term 'state', not then in general use amongst lawyers, all that we felt it necessary to say was that 'most people would associate the state with central government, many would include local authorities, some would go on to provide a catalogue of nationalized industries and public enterprises like water authorities, public services like the NHS, boards committees, commissions and inspectorates, the police, all the multifarious public authorities which make up the "public sector" of our complicated society'.

This pragmatic treatment of British government was, we suggested, an historical legacy, reflecting a characteristic British dislike of theory. As Prosser once remarked, Britain has an extended and powerful state apparatus yet lacks a theory of the state: 'There is no systematically developed legal concept of the state as a sort of moral unifier standing above the struggles of civil society.'[1] The apparatus of the modern state has simply grown up around us, starting with a raft of important nineteenth-century reform measures, Lord Shaftesbury's Factory Act 1833, Edwin Chadwick's Poor Law Act 1834 and some very salutary public health legislation in which Chadwick (the father of modern public administration) also played a significant part.[2] The effect of the reforms was both regulatory and centralising, setting a pattern from which we have never since departed:

> The first stage was the discovery of some 'intolerable' evil, such as the exploitation of child labour. Legislation was passed to prevent this. In the second stage, however, it was

[1] T. Prosser, 'The state, constitutions and implementing economic policy: Privatization and regulation in the UK, France and the USA' (1995) 4 *Social & Legal Studies* 507, 510. See also K. Dyson, *The State Tradition in Western Europe* (Martin Robertson, 1980).

[2] O. MacDonagh, *Early Victorian Government 1830-1870* (Weidenfeld and Nicolson, 1977), Ch. 6. Many of the institutions of government are, as indicated, older.

discovered that the legislation was ineffective. New legislation was passed with stronger provisions and inspectors were employed to ensure enforcement. Third, many of the new groups of professionals recruited to enforce legislation themselves became lobbyists for increases in the powers of their agencies. Fourth, this growing corps of professional experts made legislators aware 'that the problems could not be swept away by some magnificent all embracing gesture but would require continuous slow regulation and re-regulation'. Finally, therefore, a quite elaborate framework of law was developed with a complex bureaucratic machine to enforce it. The professionals helped to transform the administrative system into a major organization with extensive powers, almost without Parliament realizing it.[3]

This is a political process with which we are still familiar.

Hill reminds us that the reforming zeal of the nineteenth century was not directed solely at substantive social evils; this was a time of substantial administrative reform when the apparatus of the regulatory state, which we have come to take for granted, was being established. The modern British civil service was set in place and its character determined by the 1853 Northcote-Trevelyan Report, whose lines endured for more than a century.[4] There was substantial local-government reform, starting with the Municipal Reform Act 1835, which set in place a structure that has largely survived later efforts at radical reform.[5] And the state was extending its coercive powers. Chadwick's Poor Law Act 1834 acted as Trojan horse for a raft of public-health measures that made, according to Hill, a potent contribution to the state's regulatory coercive powers. Peel's Metropolitan Police Act 1829, introduced to deal with threatened public disorder, was followed by county, borough and metropolitan police Acts in 1856, which firmly established the principle of professional policing.[6] There were waves of legal reform throughout the century. Common law procedure was reformed in 1854 and Dicey's beloved unitary jurisdiction established with the Judicature Act 1870.[7] It is surprising how much of the machinery by which these nineteenth-century reforms were implemented – boards, committees, commissions, and inspectorates – remains in place today (though naturally remodelled). Boards of Visitors, now the Independent Monitoring Board, still act as 'watchdog' to the prison system; Her Majesty's Inspectorate of Constabulary (HMIC) exercises a supervisory role over police forces; everywhere committees proliferate.[8] Providing familiar landmarks in the institutional landscape, these structures give a comforting sense of stability

[3] M. Hill, *The State, Administration and the Individual* (Fontana, 1976), pp. 23–4.

[4] The Northcote-Trevelyan *Report on the Organisation of the Permanent Civil Service* (C 1713, 1853) is reprinted with the *Fulton Report on the Civil Service*, Cmnd 3638 (1968).

[5] By the Local Government Act 1972, following the *Redcliffe-Maud Report: Reform of Local Government in England*, Cmnd 4276 (1970).

[6] H. Parris, 'The Home Office and the provincial police in England and Wales, 1856-1870' [1961] *PL* 230.

[7] W. Cornish and G. Clark, *Law and Society in England, 1750 -1950* (Sweet and Maxwell, 1989).

[8] K. Wheare, *Government by Committee* (Clarendon Press, 1955).

and continuity, which helps to disguise the fact that the structure of British government, like the countryside, follows no particular pattern or principle; it is changing and contingent and evolves in an ad hoc fashion. The haphazard structure is also comforting in the very different sense that the 'bits and pieces' of which it is made up help to disguise the increasingly regulatory and coercive character of the modern state.

2. Bureaucracy and central government

In Hill's account the onward march of bureaucracy, which underpins the complex public services that are the hallmark of a modern state, is briefly noted. Without a substantial bureaucracy, the modern regulatory welfare state would be impossible; its services would simply fall apart. For analysis of this modern phenomenon we still turn to the German sociologist Max Weber (1864–1920). Bureaucracy – identified by Weber as a phenomenon typical of mass industrial societies, occurring in both public and private sectors – entailed objectivity: business was discharged 'according to calculable rules' and 'without regard for persons'.[9] Both elements of the Weberian equation retain their resonance today and are indeed essential for the operation of our mass administrative welfare and social service systems. Administration 'without regard for persons' implies the principles of equal treatment and non-discrimination that underlie today's egalitarian democracy, culminating in the passage of the Equality Act 2006 and establishment by the New Labour Government of the Equality and Human Rights Commission in 2007 with a mandate to help eliminate discrimination, reduce inequality, protect human rights. And mass administration according to objective principles is best carried out through 'calculable rules': rules favour consistency and equal treatment; discretion involves choice, selection and discrimination. These central principles of public administration are discussed at length in Chapter 5.

The link made by Weber between bureaucracy and rules helps to explain why bureaucracy has become a significant factor in 'juridification' – an 'ugly word' coined by Teubner to describe the tendency of modern and post-modern societies to formalise and encapsulate all social relations in terms of law. Teubner regards juridification as the logical conclusion of bureaucracy, hence a universal feature of modern administration.[10] Much of the administrative law we shall study in later chapters concerns 'cycles of juridification', in which rules are set in place; courts are invoked to interpret and resolve disputes over verbal ambiguities invariably contained in rules; further rule-making,

[9] M. Rheinstein (ed.), *Max Weber on Law in Economy and Society* (Harvard University Press, 1954). See also D. Beetham, *Bureaucracy*, 2nd edn (Open University Press, 1996).

[10] G. Teubner, 'Juridification: Concepts, aspects, limits, solutions' in Teubner (ed.), *Juridification of Social Spheres* (de Gruyter, 1988). See also C. Hood and C. Scott, 'Bureaucratic regulation and new public management in the United Kingdom: Mirror-image developments?' (1996) 23 *JLS* 321.

directed at specific problems thrown up by judicial interpretation is stimulated; and further requests for judicial clarification are made. Juridification, Teubner predicted, would in time prove dysfunctional, leading to consequential 'depoliticization of the social environment' and (we would add) a shrinking private or deregulated sphere. Juridification and with it the shrinking area of pure discretion available to administrators are key issues for administrative law (see Chapter 5). The increasingly regulated and juridified societies that have emerged in the last half-century profess transparency but, we shall suggest, are far from transparent; profess to be participatory, though public participation is marginal; and demand accountability, though accountability is illusory. These problems resurface throughout this book.

The British civil service set in place by Northcote-Trevelyan was Weberian to a limited extent. At the apex was a small Whitehall elite (the Whitehall mandarins).[11] This made it very much a 'trust society', in which much responsibility was delegated and relationships were unwritten, based on trust and a shared work culture – a behavioural pattern that has, somewhat surprisingly, survived juridification and is still the norm.[12] The civil service saw itself as neutral and impartial: a servant to any master. The key principles on which it was based were integrity, political impartiality, objectivity, selection and promotion on merit, and responsibility through ministers to Parliament.[13] These understandings were a crucial part of the professional practices, ethical standards and ideology that evolved in the senior civil service. On one side of the political line, a sense of loyalty to the Government of the day went with an obligation to inform and advise; on the other stood the convention of ministerial responsibility, according to which a minister was (at least nominally) responsible to Parliament for what went on in his department.[14] A culture of secrecy obtained throughout the central civil service, only starting to break down with the introduction of freedom of information legislation that became operative in 2005 (see Chapter 10).

Serious modification of the traditional pattern started with the government of Margaret Thatcher, based on managerial ideas borrowed from the private sector. Changing career patterns in the higher echelons of the civil service, the introduction of short-term contracts and 'performance-related pay', led to a breakdown of traditional hierarchical arrangements, to some extent undercutting the 'trust' model of government. The process of erosion continued under Tony Blair with the growing practice of appointing political advisers, by definition not objective, to senior civil service posts. These new arrangements were

[11] F. Parris, *Constitutional Bureaucracy* (Allen & Unwin, 1951); P. Hennessey, *Whitehall* (Fontana, 1989).

[12] E. Page and B. Jenkins, *Policy Bureaucracy: Government with a cast of thousands* (Oxford University Press, 2005).

[13] Confirmed in *The Civil Service: Continuity and Change* Cm. 2627 (1994), pp. 8–9; Treasury and Civil Service Committee, *The Role of the Civil Service* HC 27 (1993/4).

[14] D. Woodhouse, *Ministers and Parliament: Accountability in theory and practice* (Clarendon Press, 1994); A. Tomkins, *The Constitution after Scott* (Clarendon Press, 1998), pp. 38–41.

perceived inside and outside the civil service as a threat to the unwritten ethos, shoring up demands for a formal, 'juridified' structure.

The terms of the Nolan Committee, set up in the wake of a 'sleaze' scandal involving MPs, was 'to examine current concerns about standards of conduct of all holders of public office'. Simply but magisterially, the Committee enunciated seven principles of public life – selflessness, integrity, objectivity, accountability, openness, honesty and leadership – and described them as applicable 'to all aspects of public life'. Set out by the Committee 'for the benefit of all who serve the public in any way', the Nolan principles form a set of 'good governance values', which today cover the civil service, local government, and other public bodies, including agencies and universities.[15] Nolan again urged replacement of the tacit understandings of British government by something more precise.

Written but non-justiciable codes of practice, available to the public on the Cabinet Office site and applicable to ministers as well as civil servants, now govern standards and questions of ethics and propriety in public life. These exhort civil servants to carry out their tasks 'with dedication and a commitment to the Civil Service and its core values: integrity, honesty, objectivity and impartiality':

- 'Integrity' is putting the obligations of public service above your own personal interests.
- 'Honesty' is being truthful and open.
- 'Objectivity' is basing your advice and decisions on rigorous analysis of the evidence.
- 'Impartiality' is acting solely according to the merits of the case and serving equally well governments of different political persuasions.

These core values are said to 'support good government and ensure the achievement of the highest possible standards in all that the Civil Service does, helping the Civil Service to gain and retain the respect of Ministers, Parliament, the public and its customers'. The standards are monitored by the Cabinet Secretary and Committee on Standards in Public Life, a permanent body responsible to Parliament, which now regulates standards. There is also a Commissioner for Standards. The Parliamentary Commissioner for Administration (PCA) has also published principles of good administration (see Chapter 12).

Despite these reforms, pressure mounted for legislation to acknowledge and protect the autonomy of the civil service. The House of Commons Select Committee on Public Administration (PASC), which has given itself the task of keeping administration and public services regularly under review, warned against taking the public service ethos for granted; it required 'nourishment and cultivation'.[16] PASC asked for a 'Public Service Code' approved by

[15] Lord Nolan, *First Report of the Committee on Standards in Public Life*, Cm. 2850 (1995), p. 14.

[16] PASC, *The Public Service Ethos*, HC 263 (2001/2).; Ninth Report of the Committee on Standards in Public Life, *Defining the Boundaries within the Executive: Ministers, special advisers and the permanent civil service*, Cm. 5775 (2003) with the *Government Response*, Cm. 5964 (2003).

Parliament to be adopted by all bodies providing public services, and a new Civil Service Act with a statutory public service code to govern standards of ethical behaviour, service delivery, administrative competence and democratic accountability.[17] The code would require civil servants to carry out their duties (a) efficiently; (b) with integrity and honesty; (c) with objectivity and impartiality; (d) reasonably; (e) without maladministration and (f) according to law. A further candidate for statutory protection was the independent Civil Service Commission, responsible for appointments to the civil service, in principle by merit and open competition.

PASC was also concerned with co-ordination: to see the 'extensive network of bodies concerned with the regulation of standards of conduct in public life' re-organised and structured. PASC warned that political trust could never be a matter merely of rules but, although a rule-based system should not be a substitute for 'a culture of high standards', it ought to be recognised that the protection of standards was an important objective in its own right. The machinery of ethical regulation 'is an integral and permanent part of the constitutional landscape. This makes it necessary to ensure that it is sensibly organised and securely based'.

PASC recommended a new Public Standards Commission, established by statute to work with the constitutional watchdogs, and provide a framework in which there could be coherent development of the regulatory system. The best option was a statutory commission, which would encourage co-operation between the 'ethical auditors', and provide 'robust forms of both independence and accountability'. The report had been produced in the expectation that it would:

> generate constructive reactions from Parliament, Government, the watchdogs themselves, those who are subject to their scrutiny, and the public itself. The reform of ethical regulation in British public life should be undertaken openly, consensually, and on the basis of principle. There must be an end to ad hocery. It is time to recognise that machinery for the regulation of conduct in public life is a permanent part of our constitutional arrangements, and needs now to be put on a proper statutory footing.[18]

A draft Constitutional Renewal Bill[19] was promoted by the Government in 2008 to do some of these things. It would provide a statutory basis for the Civil Service Commission which handles public service appointments, though it notably stops short of assuring the Commission's financial independence. It requires it to publish guidelines. It would provide the minister for the civil service with powers to 'manage' the civil service and requires

[17] Cabinet Office, *A Draft Civil Service Bill*, Cm. 637 (2004); *Draft Civil Service Bill: A consultation document*, Cm. 6373 (2004); PASC, *A Draft Civil Service Bill: Completing the reform*, HC 128 (2003/4).

[18] PASC, *Ethics and Standards* [112–13].

[19] *The Governance of Britain – Draft Constitutional Renewal Bill*, Cm. 7342-ii (2008) noted in A. Le Sueur, 'Gordon Brown's new constitutional settlement' [2008] *PL* 21. And see PASC, *Constitutional Renewal: Draft Bill and White Paper*, HC 499 (2007/8).

him to publish a Code of Conduct for the national civil service, with separate codes for Wales and Scotland. As a minimum this must require civil servants – but not special advisers, who are to be covered by a separate code – to act with integrity, honesty, objectivity and impartiality. These terms are not defined. A complaints system must be provided. The three codes, for the civil service, diplomatic service and special advisers, would have to be laid before Parliament, though they would not require parliamentary approval.

The bill, which was hardly the new start that PASC had wanted, was scrutinised by two select committees, neither of which was entirely satisfied. The Joint Committee responsible for scrutiny was concerned at failure to define the term 'civil servant' and clarify who and which services would be covered by the bill. PASC, though favouring new civil service legislation that was 'focussed and limited to a few clauses', thought that 'a few clauses more [were] required to give adequate protection to the core values of the civil service'.[20] Claiming time was necessary to deal with the committees' suggestions, the Government held the bill back for 2009.[21]

We have looked at these changes in some detail as an illustration of the steady trend to 'juridification' in public life. In principle the change to statute was meant to reduce reliance on trust and unstructured discretion and, according to the White Paper, to ensure that the civil service was 'not left vulnerable to change at the whim of the Government of the day without proper parliamentary debate and scrutiny'. But as PASC was concerned to emphasise at every stage in the discussion, 'a rule based system should never substitute for a culture of high standards, rooted in the traditions of public life and shared by all those who participate in it.'[22] In response, the Government expressed its commitment to high standards in public life, as reinforced in the *Ministerial Code* of 2007 and the *Civil Service Code* of 2006. It endorsed the view that 'a rule based system should never substitute for a culture of high standards, rooted in the traditions of public life'. Hard law, as PASC concluded, is not always superior to soft law.

3. The blue rinse

The keywords of Margaret Thatcher's programme for public administration were management, regulation, contract and audit. The market creed extended deep into public administration as the collectivist welfare state was

[20] Joint Committee on Constitutional Renewal Bill, HC 166 (2007/8), Ch. 6; PASC, Constitutional Renewal: Draft Bill and White Paper, HC 499 (2007/8), Recommendation 4 and [15].

[21] HC Deb., col. 800, WA, (Mr V. Coaker) (29 January 2009).

[22] PASC, *Ethics and Standards: The Regulation of Conduct in Public Life*, HC 121 (2006/7); *Government Response*, HC 88 (2007/08) and *Further Report*, HC 43 (2008/9). For ministerial conduct, see PASC *The Ministerial Code: a case for independent investigation* , HC 1457 (2005/6); *Government Response*, HC 1088 (2007/8).

remodelled as a market in democratic goods and the notion of choice became a fetish.[23]

Hood has classified the wave of 'New Right' administrative reforms that swept through the public services (and subsequently through the English-speaking world during the 1980s) in terms of four mega-trends:[24]

1. attempts to *slow down or reverse government growth* in terms of overt public spending and staffing
2. a shift towards *privatisation and quasi-privatisation* and away from core government institutions, with renewed emphasis on 'subsidiarity' in service provision
3. the development of *automation,* particularly in information technology, in the production and distribution of public services
4. the development of a more *international* agenda, increasingly focused on general issues of public management, policy design, decision styles and intergovernmental co-operation, on top of the older tradition of individual country specialisms in public administration.

(a) Privatisation and the contract culture

The phrase 'contract culture' marks a cultural shift to an administrative model based on private-sector management, where contract operates to structure and confine discretion through the simulation of markets rather than through the panoply of regulation associated with administrative law. To successive Conservative governments market accountability became so important that a highly artificial form of 'market-mimicking' became the practice within publicly funded enterprises. The NHS, for example, was suddenly required to operate as a modified market in which fund-holding general practices were freed to purchase services from hospital trusts and other operators. Cleaning services, rubbish collection and even prisons were contracted out to private providers. Compulsory competitive tendering (CCT) compelled local authorities to outsource their services. These developments are explained in Chapter 8.

Contract was a means of enforcing standards in downloaded public services but it added layers of bureaucracy and legalism. Even in simple service contracts the quest for 'quality assurance' can prove an exacting task, demanding lengthy documentation. The same is true of EU public procurement procedures, applicable to public contracting throughout the European Community (see Chapter 9). In complex transactions, such as occurred during the privatisation of British Rail, the paperwork was extensive, while the network of contracts necessitated

[23] N. Lewis, *Choice and the Legal Order: Rising above politics* (Butterworths, 1996).

[24] C. Hood, 'A public management for all seasons' (1991) 69 *Pub. Admin.* 3; G. Drewry, 'The new public management' in Jowell and Oliver (eds.), *The Changing Constitution*, 4th edn (Clarendon Press, 2000).

by the multi-billion public/private partnerships is still more challenging as we can see from the case study of the London Underground in Chapter 9.

The 'contract culture' is not necessarily restricted to contract in the full legal sense of an agreement enforceable in the courts; it includes bargains and agreements 'intended to be binding' but lacking the full force of law. 'Pseudo-contracts' are introduced to underline the obligations of individuals, as with the Jobseeker's Allowance, or to specify service providers' obligations to the consumer. That these are not true contracts is immaterial, as we shall see in Chapter 8.

The Citizen's Charter, introduced by John Major as the start of a 'ten-year programme of radical reform', aimed at a steady improvement in standards. The White Paper mentioned a medley of interlocking 'themes, principles mechanisms and implementation vehicles', focusing on four: quality, choice, standards and value:

> **Quality** referred to a sustained new program for improving the quality of public services. **Choice** meant that wherever possible competing providers would be the best spur to improved quality. Choice also meant that, even where competition was not possible, the users of services would be consulted about the level and nature of those services. **Standards** evoked the notion that citizens must be told what the service standards are and be able to act where service is unacceptable. And last but not least, **value** referred to taxpayers' rights to receive public services on a value-for-money basis within a tax bill the nation can afford.[25]

The shift to contract was largely a deception. The charters, left unenforceable, were not true contracts and, as public lawyers noted, classical public law protections and direct citizen participation in the making of policies and rules might be seriously curtailed. On the credit side, however, both PASC and the New Labour Government have recognised the Citizen's Charter as having 'a lasting impact on how public services are viewed in this country. The initiative's underlying principles retain their validity nearly two decades on—not least the importance of putting the interests of public service users at the heart of public service provision.'[26]

(b) Managerialism and new public management

American public administration had traditionally been managerial, prizing efficiency, economy and effectiveness, the British Civil Service much less so. Civil service 'mandarins' were generalists, bringing the values of probity and consistency to the conduct of public policy. In the 1980s, Margaret Thatcher's 'New Right' government wanted something more entrepreneurial, driven by the

[25] *The Citizen's Charter: Raising the standard*, Cm. 1599 (1991), p. 2. See Barron and Scott, 'The Citizen's Charter Programme' (1992) 55 *MLR* 526.

[26] PASC, *Citizen's Charter to Public Service Guarantees: Entitlement to public services*, HC 411 (2007/8) [17] and *Government Response*, HC 112 (2007/8).

whip of 'customer satisfaction'. The thread running through her administrative reforms was a transformation of public law notions of citizenship and accountability through concepts of market and consumerism.[27] Public-choice theory demanded changes in the role of the state, a narrowing of its functions to maximise space for private interests; in Osborne and Gaebler's celebrated metaphor, 'The state steers, it does not row'.[28] This meant restructuring government:

> so as to strip away, through privatisation and contracting-out, functions that private profit or non-profit organisations can perform better, and to reorganise the functions that remain in the interest of greater effectiveness and efficiency ('new public management'). Privatisation and contracting-out not only reduce the scope of executive action, but promote its further diversification and fragmentation, by reason of the need to design specialised systems for the continuing regulation of privatised activity that offer better guarantees of expertise, fairness, predictability and independence than do traditional structures of administration.[29]

Breaking up the homogeneity of the state was one objective; rendering what remained more efficient the second. The term applied in Britain to this decisive change in administrative style was 'new public management' (NPM).

Essentially, NPM is a managerial technique of administration, characterised by rules, accountability and quantitative audit. Two aspects of the package are especially relevant to the development of administrative law. The first is a shift in dominant *values* associated with a more limited conception of government. The second is the shift from courts to auditors as external control machinery and the NPM methodology of standard-setting, measurement and control, evolving into 'value for money' (VFM) audit.[30]

(c) The audit society

Public audit has a long history, represented by the independent office of Comptroller and Auditor-General. The C&A-G is an officer of the House of Commons, responsible to the powerful Public Accounts Committee (PAC) for the audit of central government.[31] Central to the Thatcher reforms was the transformation of public audit into a proactive system entrusted with the duty of

[27] M. Freedland and S. Sciarra (eds.), *Public Services and Citizenship in European Law: Public and labour law perspectives* (Clarendon Press, 1998), pp. 9–10.

[28] Thatcher's administrative reform programme was strongly influenced by D. Osborne and T. Gaebler, *Reinventing Government* (Addison Wesley, 1992).

[29] T. Daintith, 'Book review' [2006] *PL* 645.

[30] Further explained in M. Mulreany, 'Economy, efficiency and effectiveness in the public sector: Key issues' in Hardiman and Mulreany, *Efficiency and Effectiveness in the Public Domain* (Irish Institute of Public Administration, 1991). And see P. Hoggett, 'New modes of control in the public service' (1996) 74 *Pub. Admin.* 9.

[31] See *The Role of the Comptroller and Auditor General*, Cmnd 8323 (1981); J. McEldowney, 'The control of public expenditure' in *Changing Constitution*, 6th edn (2007). The official title of the PAC is now Public Accounts Commission.

'auditing for change'. The audit process was to assume a position of central importance in public service delivery and throughout British public administration. A new institutional focus was provided by the National Audit Act 1983, which set in place a National Audit Office (NAO) to work under the Comptroller.[32] The Act empowered the NAO to examine and report on the economy, efficiency and effectiveness of public spending. This new professionalism greatly strengthened the arm of the PAC, already the most prestigious and powerful of the Select Committees, traditionally chaired by an Opposition backbencher.

At local level, the district auditor had long had powers to question expenditure, surcharge councillors and appeal where appropriate to the courts.[33] The Local Government Finance Act 1982 replaced the district audit service with a centralised Audit Commission, intended as 'a driving force in the improvement of public services', promoting good practice and helping those responsible for public services 'to achieve better outcomes for citizens, with a focus on those people who need public services most'.[34] Currently responsible to the Minister for Communities and Local Government, who appoints Commissioners and may give directions to the Commission, the Commission employs members (who are not necessarily accountants) and commissions audits from private sector firms. The Commission's main functions are: the appointment of auditors to local authorities, most local NHS bodies and foundation trusts, police and probation authorities; inspection of public housing authorities and associations; performance assessments of local authorities and fire and rescue authorities.[35] Crucially, the Commission also has powers to 'undertake national studies of economy, efficiency and effectiveness in local public services and housing associations' and, in the NHS, make studies of financial management, enabling value-for-money or VFM comparisons to be made. It oversees the development of performance indicators for local government to serve as the basis for league tables of performance with which we are all familiar in the education field. Initially greeted with suspicion as a tool to increase the central government grip on local government, the Audit Commission, like the NAO, has emerged as strikingly independent.

The key to audit's successful expansion was VFM. Unlike financial audit, which is merely a protection against corruption, obvious waste and illegality, VFM audit 'is intended both to evaluate and to shape the performance of the auditee in three dimensions: economy, efficiency and effectiveness'. The NAO's chosen definitions of these financial virtues show how audit has fanned out to cover policy issues:

[32] See also the Government Resources and Accounts Act 2000. There have been separate audit arrangements for Northern Ireland since 1921. The Scotland Act 1998 established the Scottish Commission for Audit (Audit Scotland) responsible to the Scottish Assembly and the Public Audit (Wales) Act 2004 established the Wales Audit Office.

[33] In its modern form the system dates back to the Local Government Act 1972.

[34] Audit Commission, *Annual Report and Accounts*, HC 808 (2007).

[35] Audit Commission Act 1998 as amended by the Local Government Act 2000, noted in Radford, 'Auditing for change: Local government and the Audit Commission' (1991) 54 *MLR* 912.

- Economy: minimising the cost of resources used or required – **spending less**
- Efficiency: the relationship between the output from goods or services and the resources to produce them – **spending well**
- Effectiveness: the relationship between the intended and actual results of public spending – **spending wisely.**

Audit machinery gained ground during the 1990s through promising *control*. Power argued, however, that the promise was illusory. What in fact resulted from the primacy of 'The Three Es' was an 'audit explosion', characterised by a 'certain set of attitudes or cultural commitments to problem solving' and dominated by a cluster of technical values – independent validation, efficiency, rationality, visibility. And because audit was 'an idea as much as . . . a concrete technical practice and there is no communal investment in the practice without a commitment to this idea and the social norms and hopes which it embodies', Britain was rapidly transformed into 'an audit society'.[36] Take the 'league tables' authorised by the Education (Schools) Act 1992 with a view to allowing parents to exercise their power of choice in education. These arguably had the effect of substituting easily calculable examination results for community knowledge and first-hand experience of a school's environment – one reason why reliance on VFM and performance indicators as governing principles of public administration has proved controversial.

On the credit side, statistical comparison, like rules, favours transparency, consistency and equal treatment. It may act as 'a wake up call' or trigger an inquiry into a potential problem. (Compare here the managerial use of complaints to improve unsatisfactory areas of administration discussed in Chapter 10.) Many would see the overriding of local autonomy, knowledge and community as a small price to pay when measured against greater efficiency and the norm of equal treatment that dominates politics in the twenty-first century. Yet quantification has limitations as a tool for evaluation. Crude performance indicators may be misinterpreted – a high surgical death rate may indicate a hospital that handles difficult cases rather than institutional negligence – or fear of the consequences of publicity may deter the quest for improvement and become 'a new form of image management rather than a basis for substantive analysis'.[37] Audit may also bring perverse consequences, as when a target to meet all police calls within fifteen minutes brings a rise in traffic accidents; in order to free-up hospital beds patients are discharged into conditions of inadequate care, resulting in further illness or even death; or train timetables are manipulated to ensure that the target maximum of trains arriving on time can be reached. Power's conclusion was that audit shapes activities in significant ways, bleaching out alternative value systems:

[36] M. Power, *The Audit Society: Rituals of verification* (Oxford: Oxford University Press, 1997), p. 4.

[37] M. Power, *The Audit Explosion*, (London: Demos, 1994), p. 48.

> The most influential dimension of the audit explosion is the process by which environments are made auditable, structured to conform to the need to be monitored ex post . . . The standards of performance themselves are shaped by the need to be auditable . . . At the same time, organisations may be encumbered with structures of auditability embodying performance measures which increasingly do not correspond to the first order reality of practitioners' work . . . The general point is that the system of auditing knowledge is increasingly self-referential. It models organisations for its own purposes and impacts to varying degrees upon their first-order operations . . . Concepts of performance and quality are in danger of being defined largely in terms of conformity to auditable process.[38]

Audit, with its central government standard-setting obligations, inspectorates and centrally appointed auditors, also exacerbates tension between the desire for centralisation and for local community, an equation that Power felt needs re-balancing by 'a new respect for local specificity'.[39] Another effect of audit is to impoverish the discipline of public administration, substituting a single form for multiple forms of accountability. Audit impinges too on the primacy of public law as the principal mechanism for control of public administration, imposing itself even on judicial process (see Chapter 3). Like the public/private distinction discussed in Chapter 1, this is not merely a procedural but a normative question of values.

(d) Agencification 1: downloading

The 1980s saw a series of efficiency studies of central government, with some delegation of financial responsibility to 'accountable units'. The Ibbs or 'Next Steps' Report recommended 'a quite different way of conducting the business of government':

> The central Civil Service should consist of a relatively small core engaged in the function of servicing Ministers and managing departments, who will be the 'sponsors' of particular government policies and services. Responding to these departments will be a range of agencies employing their own staff, who may or may not have the status of Crown servants, and concentrating on the delivery of their particular service, with clearly defined responsibilities between the Secretary of State and the Permanent Secretary on the one hand, and the Chairmen or Chief Executives of the agencies on the other.[40]

The core of the Ibbs Report is recognition of 'two (or perhaps many more) Civil Services. Essentially, on the one hand, there are top people we all think

[38] *Ibid.*, p. 8.

[39] *Ibid.*, p. 43. There has been a response to this fear in the White Paper, *Citizens in Control*, Cm. 7427 (2008). And see p. 86 below.

[40] Efficiency Unit, *Improving Management in Government: The next steps. Report to the Prime Minister* (HMSO, 1988) (hereafter *The Ibbs Report*) [44]; G. Drewry, 'Forward from FMI: The next steps' (1988) *PL* 505 and 'Next steps: The pace falters' (1990) *PL* 322.

we know about, now about 3,500, to be entitled the Senior Civil Service, plus their supporters; on the other hand, about 500,000 invisible people, who do the work.'[41] Ibbs recommended hiving off the invisible people to Next Steps Agencies (NSAs), a new type of administrative agency that was emphatically *not* autonomous: indeed, it lacked legal personality to contract. An NSA was, however, closely tied into its parent department by a Framework Document, defining its functions and goals, plus a network of 'contracts' and 'performance indicators', in which departmental policy was embedded. Performance indicators were to act as:

> instruments of hands-off managerial control and democratic accountability: central departments, particularly the Treasury, need PIs to exercise control without breathing down the necks of the new chief executive. Parliament and the public need PIs to ensure that agencies are delivering the desired services efficiently and effectively.[42]

The underlying assumption that two types of executive function, policy-making and implementation, could easily be identified proved incorrect. Research shows that, at every level of the Civil Service, policy and execution are inextricably linked; even junior officials make policy decisions in the implementation of statutory schemes and are often responsible for ministerial policy choices.[43] Clean severance is equally impossible with NSAs. Cracks and gaps appear and serious accountability issues flow from the division of functions between agency chief executives appointed by ministers and the minister, notionally responsible to Parliament.[44] There is moreover no very clear view of what ministerial responsibility entails. The Crichel Down inquiry had established that a civil servant was 'wholly and directly responsible to his minister';[45] later governments, however, sought to distinguish 'responsibility' (where a minister is responsible for ministerial acts and omissions that contribute to a policy or operational failure) from 'accountability' (where a minister, though not directly culpable, has a duty to explain to Parliament what went wrong). Not surprisingly, the distinction does not recommend itself to House of Commons committees.[46]

Using the Home Office (HO) as our example, let us look a little more closely at the problems, feeding in changes and events that have occurred during the twelve-year period of New Labour Government. The HO had been allowed to

[41] P. Kemp, 'The mandarins emerge unscathed' (1994) 2 *Parliamentary Brief* 49.

[42] N. Carter, 'Learning to measure performance: The use of indicators in organisations' (1991) 69 *Pub. Admin.* 85, 87.

[43] Page and Jenkins, *Policy Bureacracy*.

[44] R. Baldwin, 'The next steps: Ministerial responsibility and government by agency' (1988) 51 *MLR* 622; G. Drewry, 'The executive: Towards accountable government and effective governance?' in *Changing Constitution*, 5th edn (2004); D. Oliver and G. Drewry, *Public Service Reforms: Issues of accountability and public law* (Pinter, 1996).

[45] HC Deb., vol. 530, col. 285 (Sir David Maxwell-Fyfe).

[46] See especially Public Service Committee, *Ministerial Accountability and Responsibility*, HC 313 (1995/6); PASC, *Politics and Administration: Ministers and civil servants*, HC 122 (2007).

grow into a 'hyper-ministry', where the Home Secretary, with the help of three ministerial secretaries of state and three parliamentary secretaries, ruled over an empire of 70,000 staff working in six directorates. It had acquired a set of sometimes incompatible functions centred on criminal justice, immigration and prison administration. Four executive agencies and thirteen further NDPBs had been added, including inspectorates of prisons, probation and police. Until the reforms of 2007 (see Chapter 11) the HO was responsible for eight sets of tribunals. There was no particular rationale for these arrangements; they had simply evolved as part of the haphazard progression of British government.

Of the major HO responsibilities, immigration and nationality remained for the time being an in-house directorate (IND), though shortly afterwards it was superseded by the UK Borders Agency. As we shall see in later chapters, the performance of IND with its pendant tribunals provided much of the staple fare of judicial review. Policing has remained a largely local function, for which the HO has supervisory responsibility. Forty-three police forces remain in England and Wales, each under the control of a tripartite police authority, composed of magistrates, local councillors and independent members. The police authority shares responsibility for policing with the chief constable of the force. The Home Secretary's substantial supervisory powers, however, include responsibility for efficiency, and the central government inspectorate (HMIC) is situated in the HO. Appointment of a chief constable requires approval of the Home Secretary and the Police Act 1996 allows the Home Secretary to dismiss a chief constable in the interests of efficiency. The HO sets standards and performance targets and issues guidance on the interpretation of the law. These powers are underpinned by the fact that most of the policing budget comes from central government rather than from local government funds; in addition, substantial special grants can be made for specific purposes, reflecting central-government policies and priorities.

There are two main justifications for retaining local control of police forces: the first stresses the need for community consent to policing policy and co-operation with police; the second is constitutional, viewing localism as a safeguard against the evils of the police state. But as 'law and order' has crept higher up the political agenda to figure prominently in party manifestos and bring powerful ministers down, the motives for centralisation have strengthened. In practice every major post-war reform has been a move towards centralisation. The Police Act 1996 was preceded by a fierce argument over centralisation, which was resisted. A decade later, centralisation was once more on the agenda after an HMIC report concluded that the current structure was 'no longer fit for purpose'; a majority of forces 'do not provide adequate levels of protective service, such as counter terrorism activity and dealing with serious organised crime'.[47] Strongly supported by John Reid, then Home Secretary, proposals

[47] HMIC, *Closing the Gap: Review of the "fitness for purpose" of the current structure of policing in England and Wales* (August, 2007)

for amalgamation to around seventeen forces met strong resistance from the police; amalgamations could not be agreed; the proposals had to be abandoned and were referred back for further consultation. Suggesting a turnaround, recent proposals emphasise the value of local and community policing and talk of 'empowerment' and the need to give the public a stronger say in holding the police to account locally.[48]

Prison management had been partly hived-off under the previous Conservative governments to the Prisons Agency (PA) and partly privatised. In two separate episodes involving maladministration, the cracks in the accountability system became obvious. In the first, a series of high-profile escapes from high-security prisons led to a very public dispute between Michael Howard, then Home Secretary, and Derek Lewis, chief executive of the PA. Refusing to resign, Howard blamed the agency for 'operational' maladministration, distinguishing this from his responsibility for 'policy issues'. Lewis also rejected responsibility, arguing that financial decisions taken by the HO had closed off his policy options. Ironically it was Lewis, who possessed no public law accountability function, who had to resign.[49] This split responsibility led the Treasury and Civil Service Committee to recommend that agency chief executives should be personally answerable to a parliamentary committee.[50] A recent think-tank report wants to dig more deeply. It blames the 'anachronistic and inadequate accountability arrangements' for a civil service that is 'still too often amateur and insular, poor at strategic thinking, leadership and performance management' – a severe judgement lent some credence by the chronicle of breakdowns and malfunctions documented in this book.[51]

The second set of problems involved the HO more directly. It erupted under New Labour, when discovery of a serious backlog of asylum claims was followed by disclosure of a number of escapes from open prisons and further media revelations that over 1,000 foreign nationals, who should on their release from prison have been considered for deportation, were at large in Britain, their whereabouts unknown to the police. The response was in terms of classical ministerial responsibility: Charles Clarke was axed and replaced by John Reid. Before his own resignation could be demanded, Dr Reid quickly announced reforms and, a few weeks later, laid his action plan in the House of Commons library.[52] The HO would be split in order better to focus on its core

[48] Sir R. Flanagan, *The Review of policing: Final report* (Home Office, 2008); Home Office, *From the Neighbourhood to the National: Policing our communities together*, Cm. 7448 (2008). And see Policing and Crime Bill 2008–9.

[49] See *Review of Prison Service Security in England and Wales and the Escape from Parkhurst Prison on Tuesday 3rd January 1995*, Cm. 3020 (1995); A. Barker 'Political responsibility for UK prison security: Ministers escape again' (1998) 76 *Pub. Admin* 1.

[50] *The Ibbs Report* [46]; *The Role of the Civil Service*, HC 27 (1993–4) [171].

[51] G. Lodge and B. Rogers, *Whitehall's Black Box: Accountability and performance in the senior civil service* (IPPR, 2006).

[52] *From Improvement to Transformation: An action plan to reform the Home Office so it meets public expectations and delivers its core purpose of protecting the public* (Home Office, 2006).

purpose of protecting the public. It would be radically reshaped, with responsibility for prisons passing to the DCA (now the Ministry of Justice). The IND would be hived-off as an executive agency, with a second new executive agency, the National Policing Improvement Agency, assuming responsibility for police modernisation and improvement. Inside the Home Office, there would be a new top team with a reshaped Home Office Board and fifteen immediate changes at director level. A new 'contract' would be developed between ministers and officials, 'clarifying respective roles and expectations in relation to policy, operational delivery and management'.

Two points are relevant here. First, a hyper-ministry had been broken up in response to claims of inefficiency and lack of co-ordination; this has implications for 'joined up government', a policy priority for New Labour. Secondly, the venerable Home Office had, by virtue of Crown prerogative, been transmuted by ministerial fiat into a 'department of homeland security' focusing on terrorism, security and policing (for which it still has only supervisory responsibility). Only in response to an Opposition 'urgent question' did the Home Secretary make a short statement to the House of Commons, provoking a fiery and largely unsympathetic debate.[53] To complaints about the way in which the reforms had been handled and announced, Dr Reid replied only that 'it was not and has never been the normal practice of Administrations to make oral statements on the machinery of government. It certainly was not the practice of the last Conservative Government. Indeed, proposals were often announced by way of press release from Downing Street.'

(e) Agencification 2

The usual justification for quangos (an acronym for quasi-autonomous non-governmental organisations) is the need for protection from direct government control and ministerial intervention. Gordon Brown's first act as Chancellor of the Exchequer was to promote the Bank of England Act 1998, freeing the Bank of England from government control (though we do not usually think of the Bank as an agency). The significance of this change became evident during the 'credit crunch' of 2008. The British Broadcasting Corporation (BBC) was granted a Royal Charter in 1927 as an independent corporation with a Board of Directors and Director-General to act as the monopoly purveyor of broadcasting inside the country. The design was adopted specifically to denote independence from interference by government and day-to-day scrutiny by Parliament. The structure has been largely successful. After the Hutton Inquiry (see Chapter 12), however, changes were made. Following the resignation of the Director-General, nominal changes saw the BBC Board restructured as a 'Trust'.

As government took on more functions, quangos proliferated. When Margaret Thatcher came to power, around 2,400 'official bodies' existed and more than

[53] See HC Deb., cols. 1639–52 (29 March 2007).

30,000 'quangurus' were appointed by ministers.[54] Elected with a mandate for 'quangocide', Mrs Thatcher set up the Pliatzky Committee to advise[55] and a handful of quangos bit the dust. Yet her own management programme gave birth to new types of agency: NSAs, which became the standard way to download service-delivery functions; and a new type of regulatory agency, the 'Ofdogs'.

At a time when almost all of state industry has been transferred from the public to the private sector, it is hard to remember that management of industry and commerce were once recognised state functions. But as Friedmann observed, the distinction between the control of government over nationalised industry and the indirect control of regulation might be largely nominal:

> The mixed economies which today characterize the political and economic systems of many States . . . have a combination of managerial and regulatory administrative functions. Certain industries and public utilities are operated by the State itself – either through government departments or with increasing frequency through semi-autonomous public corporations, responsible to government but equipped with more or less far-reaching managerial autonomy . . . At the same time, the bulk of industry and business, which remains in private ownership, is subject to varying degrees of public supervision and regulation, while another set of public authorities administers the various social services.[56]

As swathes of state-run nationalised industry were returned to the private sector, a crop of regulators, the 'Ofdogs', sprang up. These semi-autonomous public bodies, hybrid entities poised uneasily between public and private law, were initially set up to represent the public interest in privatised public services with substantial powers to regulate prices and protect competition.[57] The first Ofdogs were highly individual with a single regulator at the helm. This left room for much individual discretion and also led to complaints that relationships with ministers by whom the regulator was appointed were too cosy and lacked transparency. Partly for such reasons, the model has today been changed. Single regulators have been replaced by Boards composed of 'stakeholders', on which consumers typically have representation (see Chapter 6).

The regulatory state showed itself an aggressive coloniser and regulators were soon functioning throughout the public sector, replacing not only publicly owned industry and government departments but also traditional inspectorates. Ofsted, the Office for Standards in Education, for example, replaced a departmental inspectorate with an independent agency. The 'new Ofsted' or Office for Standards in Education, Children's Services and Skills, which came into being on 1 April 2007, is a 'super-regulator' combining the work of four separate inspectorates. Its mandate, to carry out 'a comprehensive system of

[54] P. Holland, *The Governance of Quangos* (Adam Smith Institute, 1981), p. 7; C. Hood, 'the politics of quangocide' (1980) 8 *Policy and Politics* 247.

[55] *Report on Non-Departmental Public Bodies*, Cmnd 7797 (1980).

[56] W. Friedmann, *Law in a Changing Society* 2nd edn (Penguin Books, 1964), pp. 273–4.

[57] M. Moran, *The British Regulatory State: High modernism and hyper-innovation* (Oxford University Press, 2003), p. 2.

inspection and regulation covering childcare, schools, colleges, children's services, teacher training and youth work', crosses the public/private border, extending to the inspection and registration of childminders and some independent schools.[58] Its powers should not be underrated: Ofsted can directly close down a failing school and indirectly determine the shape of local education when its reports spark ministerial intervention. Its view of the national syllabus, or the way that reading should be taught, may mean that history *must* stop at World War II or that reading *can only* be taught through phonics. Ofsted justifies these powers with the claim that it is a 'non-ministerial government department' accountable to Parliament. It stresses its 'impartiality and integrity', promising to 'report impartially, without fear or favour'. These are questionable claims, which seek to divert attention from its awkward 'quasi-autonomous' status; the link between agencies and their sponsoring departments is still close, bringing complaints of ministerial interference. Yet only ministers and through them the departments for which they take responsibility, are accountable in a real sense to Parliament.[59]

As with NSAs, the relationship between Parliament and non-departmental public bodies (NDPBs) is problematic. Officially, an NDPB is 'a body which has a role in the processes of national government, but is not a government department or part of one and which accordingly operates to a greater or lesser extent at arm's length from ministers.' [60] This definition begs most of the questions about accountability. NDPBs spend large sums of public money (which is of course audited) yet are widely perceived as unaccountable. There is no 'firm or clear theoretical framework that dictates which functions should rest directly under the control of elected politicians or quasi-autonomous bodies.'[61] There is a contrast here with devolved government. The Public Appointments and Public Bodies etc. (Scotland) Act 2003 regulates appointment procedure[62] and in Wales, where corruption in non-accountable quangos was a very sore point before devolution, those that have not been abolished are brought directly under the control of the Welsh Assembly.[63]

In the post-war period, the growing numbers of 'quanguru' appointments greatly increased the scope for political patronage, creating complaints of 'sleaze' and corruption. Minimum standards have now been set by the Committee on Public Standards:[64]

[58] S. 162A of the Education Act 2002; the Education and Inspections Act 2006; Ofsted Strategic Plan 2007–2010, *Raising standards, improving lives.*

[59] PASC, *Quangos*, HC 209 (1998/9); and see S. Weir and D. Beetham, *Political Power and Democratic Control in Britain* (Routledge, 1999).

[60] *Public Bodies: A Guide for Departments* (2008) [2.1], available on the civil service website.

[61] PASC, *Government by Appointment: Opening up the patronage state*, HC 165 (2003/4).

[62] Scottish Executive, *Public Bodies: Proposals for change* (2001).

[63] R. Rawlings, *Delineating Wales: Constitutional, legal and administrative aspects of Welsh devolution* (University of Wales Press, 2003), pp. 355–61.

[64] Second Report of the Committee on Standards, *Local Public Spending Bodies: Vol. 1*, Cm. 3270 (1996).

- Appointment should be open and nominations encouraged from a wide range of people.
- Management should be transparent.
- A code of conduct should be published for guidance of quangos' members.
- There should be clear statements on complaints and on 'whistleblowing'.

The Office of the Commissioner for Public Appointments (OCPA, a new, one-person quango) was set up in 1995 to oversee appointments, to be joined after devolution by regional OCPAs. The OCPAs monitor ministerial appointments to ensure they are made on merit. Codes of practice were put in place. There are around 11,000 appointments annually to quangos, ranging from BBC trustees to tribunal members and members of expert agencies, such as NICE, the National Institute for Clinical Excellence (see below). The majority remain in the hands of ministers, leaving significant opportunities for government patronage and raising concerns over accountability and expertise. Gordon Brown has undertaken to 'explore the scope for improving appointments processes in line with the best practice of the Commissioner for Public Appointments', promising a wider role for Parliament in public appointments.[65] In line with this promise, a list of sixty suitable appointments has been agreed with the Liaison Committee and a pilot of pre-appointment hearings for key public appointments is being trialled.[66]

The Blair government tried to pass responsibility for scrutiny to select committees of the Westminster Parliament but, as their chairmen have objected, select committees were not created for this purpose and are unequal to the task.[67] As Flinders cynically observes:

> the whole constitutional framework of the British state was designed to ensure that Parliament adopted a passive rather than an active role in relation to the administration. The role of Parliament was, and remains today, to hold ministers responsible for the way in which they steer the ship of state – venturing into the scrutiny of detailed administration only in response to serious policy failures where the link between policy and operations is unclear.[68]

[65] *The Governance of Britain*, Cm. 7170 (2007) [72–81]. See also PASC, *Public appointments: Confirmation hearings*, HC 731-i (2006/7), evidence given by Ms Gaymer, the Commissioner for Public Appointments (19 June 2007); Sixth Report of the Committee on Public Standards, *Reinforcing Standards,* Cm. 4557 (2000); PASC, *Quangos*, HC 219 (1998/9) and 1st Special Report, HC 317 (1999/2000).

[66] Liaison Committee, *Pre-appointment Hearings by Select Committees: Government response to the Committee's first report of session 2007-08*, HC 594 (2007/8).

[67] Liaison Committee, *Shifting the Balance? Select Committees and the Executive*, HC 300 (1999/2000).

[68] M. Flinders, 'MPs and icebergs: Parliament and delegated governance' (2004) 57 *Parliamentary Affairs* 767, 778; and see M. Flinders, 'Distributed public governance in Britain' (2004) 82 *Pub. Admin.* 883.

NDPBs may have decreased numerically since Tony Blair vowed to 'sweep away the quango state'[69] but culling has largely been achieved through amalgamation, as with the inspectorates taken into Ofsted, or the Commission for Equality and Human Rights (CEHR). In the name of 'joined-up government', this new 'super-agency' brings together the existing Commission for Racial Equality, Disability Rights and Equal Opportunities Commission, with new human-rights responsibilities tacked on. Whether super-agencies will prove any more effective in handling their varied tasks than 'hyper-ministries' such as the Home Office, is very doubtful. In time, like hyper-ministries, they may have to be broken up. Agencies are, however, unlikely to disappear; they have too many advantages for government. Agencification allows the inexorable growth of public power to be screened behind a fictional 'rolling back' of the state. By combining powers of regulation with a 'hands-off' look, they also allow government to be more interventionist, permitting an unparalleled extension of social engineering, such as we have seen with the 'new Ofsted' – and, indeed, the new Department for Children, Schools and Families. Finally, in an era of globalisation, agencies play a crucial part in the 'policy networks' through which states co-ordinate their policies and co-operate, making up in global space for the absence of a permanent administration, as they are beginning to do in the European Union.[70] In the present globalised state of world affairs, with global trade and finance, energy, security and environmental problems now at the apex of political agendas, the progression towards agencification can only accelerate.

4. The risk and security society

(a) The 'third way'

Mrs Thatcher's reforms marked a paradigm shift (a notion used by Kühn to describe a radical transformation of an existing order). When in 1997 New Labour replaced the long period of Conservative government, the expectation was that the transformation would be reversed. Giddens summarised the positions:[71] 'the neo-liberals want to shrink the state; the social democrats, historically, have been keen to expand it. The third way argues that what is necessary is to reconstruct it – to go beyond those on the right "who say government is the enemy", and those on the left "who say government is the answer".' No new paradigm shift occurred. The floor of Thatcher's reforms remained in place, to be reconstructed but not demolished – new themes modified without jettisoning the Thatcher blueprint for public service delivery. To the chagrin of

[69] Cabinet Office, *Opening up Quangos* (1997); *Quangos: Opening the* doors (1998). In 2008, there were 790 NDPBs, of which 198 were executive agencies and 410 advisory NDPBs: Cabinet Office, *Public Bodies* (2008). And see Cabinet Office, *Executive Agencies: A guide to departments* (2008), both available on the Cabinet Office website.

[70] See D. Geradin *et al.*, *Regulation Through Agencies in the EU: A new paradigm for European governance* (Edward Elgar, 2005).

[71] T. Giddens, *The Third Way* (Polity Press, 1998), pp. 47–8.

many, privatisation was not reversed; as we shall see, public utilities are still in private ownership, competitive but subject to regulation. Private sponsorship was welcomed in 'city academies' (specialised schools established with participation from the private sector) and in the private finance initiative (PFI), which provides – or until recently provided – investment capital for capital-intensive projects such as airports or hospitals (see Chapter 9). The 'contract culture' continues to flourish: consumer choice remains a fetish[72] and 'pseudo-contracts' thrive, notably in the field of education and youth opportunity (see Chapter 8). Audit and other NPM techniques, in place throughout the public services, have widened and deepened – indeed, the New Labour Government has added to the toolkit available for the measurement and control of public services. Agreements between the Treasury and departments or public bodies set minimum standards against which the body is measured annually. The agreements act as a useful 'tin-opener', enhancing the capacity of the Treasury to delve inside departments and engage in direct policy-making and agenda control.[73] The Treasury has emerged with the Cabinet, Cabinet Office, Prime Minister and his staff as the 'core executive', which stands at the heart of the government machine and through which modern government is conducted.[74]

The visible sense of continuity did not mean that New Labour lacked ideas for the reform of government institutions: very much the reverse. To New Labour, 'reform of the state and government should be a basic orienting principle of third way politics – a process of the widening and deepening of democracy'.[75] Where Thatcher's keywords had been choice, management, regulation, contract and audit, Tony Blair's were modernisation, reform, responsiveness, accessibility and voice, inclusion and equality. The challenge would be to achieve these objectives in the context of an economic revolution comprising skills, technology and work practices; the social revolution comprised in amplifying women's life chances; and a political revolution caused by the demand for a 'new relationship' between citizens and government. The slogan of 'third-way politics' implied consensus, co-operation and inclusiveness: 'bringing everyone into the tent'. The state envisioned by New Labour was a 'strategic and enabling' state able, in an age of globalisation to 'avoid the pitfalls of the big or small state argument and reinvent the effective state', its overt purpose being to redistribute power to the people.

Ten years later, *Building on Progress*, a Cabinet Office policy document published just before Gordon Brown took office as Prime Minister, described the 'core idea of the strategic and enabling state':

72 PASC, *Choice, Voice and Public Services* HC 49 (2004/5).

73 D. Judge, *Political Institutions in the UK* (Oxford University Press, 2005), p. 159; PASC, *On Target*, HC 62-2 (2002/3), p. x. See also C. Thain, 'Economic policy', in Dunleavy *et al.*, *Developments in British Politics 6* (Macmillan, 2000).

74 R. Rhodes and P. Dunleavy, *Prime Minister, Cabinet and Core Executive* (Palgrave, 1995); M. Birch and I. Holliday, 'The Blair government and the core executive' (2004) 39 *Government and Opposition* 1.

75 Giddens, *Third Way*, p. 69; T. Blair, 'Introduction', *Modernising Government*, p. 4.

> Enabling citizens to take power is both right in itself and also indispensable to meeting the objectives of government that cannot be met in any other way.
>
> The modern state needs to work in a new way – less about command and control and more about collaboration and partnership. This reflects the kind of citizen we have today: inquiring, less deferential, demanding, informed.
>
> The core idea of the strategic and enabling state is that power is placed in the hands of the people. It is a vision of the state in which we increase the range of opportunities for engagement; we empower citizens to hold public institutions to account; and we ensure that citizens take joint responsibility with the state for their own well-being.

The state had five main functions, as:[76]

- direct provider of services
- commissioner of services, where the state specifies the required outcome but pays a supplier to provide the service
- regulator, ensuring that standards are complied with
- provider of information so that citizens can make informed choices
- legislator to set down clear rules of behaviour.

(b) 'Modernising government'

Thus New Labour aimed to graft onto the managerial values of efficiency, effectiveness and customer satisfaction prioritised by previous Conservative governments the softer, more responsive and participatory values of public service, with a view to building an inclusive and egalitarian society. The goal was a system that was both responsive and accessible: a 'people's democracy' or 'stakeholder society'.[77] A White Paper published shortly after Blair came to power affirmed commitment to public service but stressed that 'public servants must be the agents of the changes citizens and businesses want'. Linking choice to improved service standards and delivery, it insisted on 'forward looking, inclusive and fair' policies. There were five key commitments:[78]

- to be forward looking in developing policies to deliver outcomes that matter, not simply reacting to short-term pressures
- to deliver public services to meet the needs of citizens, not the convenience of service providers
- to deliver efficient, high-quality public services and not tolerate mediocrity
- to use new technology to meet the needs of citizens and business, and not trail behind technological developments
- to value public service, not denigrate it.

[76] Cabinet Office Policy Review *Building on Progress: The role of the state* (May 2007) [1.10–15] (excerpts). Compare Giddens, *The Third Way*, pp. 46–7.

[77] Giddens, *The Third Way*, p. 1, quoting Blair, 1998.

[78] *Modernising Government*, Cm 4310 (1999).

The inevitable clash of values plays out in a PASC study of the effects of audit culture on public administration.[79] Five main justifications for the audit culture were identified by PASC: (i) targets provide a clear statement of what government is trying to achieve; (ii) they provide a clear sense of direction; (iii) they focus on results; (iv) they provide a basis for monitoring; (v) they provide better public accountability. PASC concluded that a clash of 'two cultures at work in the Government's approach to public service reform' was inhibiting progress. There was a lack of proper integration between 'the performance culture', where the focus was on 'the organic ingredients of durable change and improvement' and 'the measurement culture', which aimed to track quantitative achievement in the public services. The 'measurement culture' was typified by targets, its time frame shorter, its techniques more mechanistic. Both had their place, but it was important that 'the former is not crowded out by the latter'. Urging the Government to give consumers and stakeholders greater 'voice' – a consistent theme of New Labour administration – PASC asked that targets be as few as possible, focusing on key outcomes and reforming the way in which they were set, with a widened consultation process to involve professionals, service users, Parliament and select committees.

This new 'stakeholder style', first tried out in local government[80] emerged as a key feature of policy for public service delivery under Gordon Brown. The emphasis changed. Talk of efficient service provision gave way before a rhetoric of concern for the needs of users and user satisfaction. Information, consultation and involvement became the watchwords of a government that professed to see 'active citizenship, as well as being a good in itself . . . as a route to improving local public services and strengthening local accountability'. Under the rubric of 'transformational government', the greater emphasis on responsiveness to people was attributed to 'a logical extension of the public service reforms that have gone before'.[81]

(c) The risk society

The 'cradle-to-grave' welfare state had nourished a risk-averse society, increasingly preoccupied with protection against risk.[82] Citizens born in state hospitals and educated in state schools had come to believe that the state could and should wrap every citizen in a personal security blanket. 'Security' took on the extended meaning of 'being protected from or not exposed to danger. This involves protection against unwanted and damaging change – loss of income,

[79] PASC, *On Target? Government by measurement*, HC 62 (2002/3), *Government Response*, HC 1264. And see C. Hood *et al.*, *Regulation Inside Government* (Oxford University Press, 1999).

[80] Department for Communities and Local Government, *Unlocking the Talent of Our Communities*, n. 145 below.

[81] See PASC, *User Involvement in Public Services*, HC 410 (2007/8) and *Government Response*, HC 998 (2007/8).

[82] U. Beck, *Risk Society: Towards a new modernity*, tr. Ritter (Sage Publications, 1992). And see Organisation and Risk in Late Modernity, (2009) 30 *Organization Studies* (Special Issue).

livelihood or home, for instance'.[83] The state had come to be perceived as the main insurance against personal disaster, with consequences for administrative law. Any failure of risk regulation invariably brings public pressure for a public inquiry (see Chapter 13). There are invariably demands for compensation, exemplified in the ombudsman investigation into occupational pensions, a case study that forms the focal point of Chapter 12. Perhaps more significantly, government has drawn on the desire for security to legitimate an authoritarian and interventionist style of government (below).

New Labour's interest in risk regulation was signalled early on. Pragmatically, *Modernising Government* explained:

> Much government activity is concerned with managing risks, in the workplace, in what we eat and in protecting the environment. We need consistently to follow good practice in policy making as we assess, manage and communicate risks. Government needs to develop its capacity to handle risk by:
>
> - Ensuring decisions take account of risks;
> - Firmly establishing risk management techniques;
> - Organising to manage risk;
> - Developing skills; and
> - Ensuring quality.[84]

A decade later, risk has become 'the new buzzword of administrative governance', a 'risk commonwealth' has evolved, where 'the task of public decision-makers is increasingly being characterised in terms of the identification, assessment, and management of risk and the legitimacy of public decision-making is also being evaluated on such a basis'.[85] Every activity of government, from economic development to national security strategy, is defined in terms of risk.[86] Risk analysis is the core of managerial and regulatory practices;[87] risk and impact assessments are a mandatory element in all forms of management and rule-making (see Chapters 4 and 5). Risk triggers regulation, which becomes increasingly bound up with the control, identification and classification of degrees of risk (see Chapter 6).[88] The technical nature of the enterprise

[83] D. Oliver, 'The underlying values of public and private law' in Taggart (ed.), *The Province of Administrative Law* (Hart Publishing, 1997), p. 226.

[84] Cm. 4310 (1999). See also Cabinet Office, *Risk: Improving government's capability to handle risk and uncertainty* (HMSO, 2002), p. 4.

[85] E. Fisher, 'The rise of the risk commonwealth and the challenge for administrative law' [2003] *PL* 455. See also M. Power, *Organising a World of Risk Management* (Oxford University Press, 2007).

[86] See Sir David Omand, *The National Security Strategy: Implications for the UK intelligence community* (IPPR, 2008).

[87] J. Black, 'The emergence of risk-based regulation and the new public risk management in the United Kingdom' [2005] *PL* 512.

[88] C. Hood *et al.*, *The Government of Risk: Understanding risk regulation regimes* (Oxford University Press, 2001).

necessitates delegation of policy and standard-setting to expert bodies, often to 'networks' of rule-making committees and agencies established within the EU to which the UK is merely one contributor.

Power describes the 'risk management of everything' as the 'motif for one of the major public policy challenges of the early twenty-first century . . . Risk management is now at the centre stage of public service delivery and is a model of organisation in its own right.' Like the audit 'rituals' to which it is intimately connected:

> risk management is much more than a technical analytical practice; it also embodies significant values and ideals, not least of accountability and responsibility. Historically, a public politics of risk management, particularly in the field of health, has been concerned with the transparency and accountability of scientific expertise in decisions about risk acceptance. Since the mid-1990s, risk management and private corporative governance agendas have become intertwined, if not identical . . . [B]eing a 'good' organisation has become synonymous with having a broad and formal risk management programme. Risk analysis, the traditional home territory of risk management, has been subsumed within a larger accountability and control framework.[89]

Risk is an 'over-arching concept', a benchmark of 'good governance', straddling the border between public administration and corporate governance.

We should not assume, however, that as administration becomes more rule-bound, transparency and accountability increase. Rules become more technical and complex, diminishing transparency as 'all purpose' legislators, generalist judges and the public at large find themselves defeated by obscure technical language; accountability is diminished by the struggle to evaluate difficult scientific material. As public lawyers, we cannot admit the right of science and technology to stay outside democratic processes. 'Experts cannot be relied upon automatically to know what is good for us, nor can they always provide us with unambiguous truths; they should be called upon to justify their conclusions and policies in the face of public scrutiny.'[90]

(d) E-governance and the IT revolution

Drawing on Foucault's concept of 'governmentality', Morison sees e-governance as a weapon for deconstructing the classical model of 'bounded government' based on the concept of sovereignty, with power shared between the executive and legislature.[91] In tune with New Labour rhetoric, Morison argues for an open,

[89] M. Power, *The Risk Management of Everything* (London: Demos, 2004), pp. 10, 11.

[90] Giddens, *The Third Way*, p. 59. And see M. Shapiro, 'The problems of independent agencies in the United States and European Union' (1997) 4 *Journal of European Public Policy* 276.

[91] J. Morison, 'Modernising government and the e-government revolution' in Bamforth and Leyland (eds.), *Public Law in a Multi-Layered Constitution* (Hart Publishing, 2003). The term is borrowed from M. Foucault, 'Governmentality' and 'The subject and power', in Faubion (ed.), *Michel Foucault, Power: The essential works*, vol. 3 (Penguin Books, 2000).

pluralist and 'bottom up' governance system in which power and sovereignty are 'diffused through a diverse number of sites'. New Labour experiments with 'transformational government' (described earlier) may have similar roots.

This opens the possibility of a democratic control system premised on true participation. In the post-modern context of globalised governance, these ideas are important. Faced with a diverse population of many linguistic groups distributed in twenty-seven nations, the European Commission has, for example, put its faith in e-governance, constructing its plans for participatory democracy around a user-friendly website.[92]

(e) ICT and participation

At home, PASC, taking evidence for a report on public participation, was enthusiastic about the potential of e-governance: it saw 'the advent of e-government and the Internet [as] important opportunities for extending public participation. Some wholly new forms of participation could open up by offering the possibility of responding to questions at the click of a mouse.'[93] Not everyone was so keen; it was suggested that the beneficiaries would be well-organised pressure groups, 'poised and eager to step into the vacuum left by the decline in traditional political activity. [ICT] could therefore actually intensify the exclusion of groups which do not have physical or psychological access to it.' A further effect might be 'to make government seem joined up, when behind the scenes the reality was that the structures were disconnected'.[94] Cautiously, an international academic conference concluded that e-governance could foster and enhance accountability and legitimacy of public service by promoting interactive, participatory, open and good administration. It could 'dramatically transform' public-sector organizations and processes and impact on traditional Weberian bureaucratic organisations:

> E-governance serves as a strong catalyst for organizational change, namely networking and collaboration. It is also instrumental in facilitating re-engineering processes and integrated services for citizens . . . Bureaucracy may become more customer-friendly enterprise managed in a more businesslike manner . . . The government's operation of and management of e-governance depends on the performance of administrative changes [sic]. Otherwise, the government runs the risk of estranging itself from its citizens.[95]

[92] European Commission, *White Paper on European Governance*, COM (2001) 428 final [2001] OJ C287, p.1; and see C. Joerges, 'Deliberative supranationalism: Two defences' (2002) 8 *European Law Journal* 135.

[93] PASC, *Public Participation: Issues and innovations*, HC 373 (2001/2). See also R. Silcock, 'What is e-government?' (2001) *Parliamentary Affairs* 88; I. Snellen, 'Electronic governance; Implications for citizens, politicians and public servants' (2002) 68 *International Review of Administrative Sciences* 183.

[94] Evidence to PASC, HC 373-i.

[95] Pan Suk Kim, 'Introduction: Challenges and opportunities for democracy, administration and law' (2005) 71 *International Review of Administrative Sciences* 101-2. See also J. Morison, 'Online government and e-constitutionalism' [2003] *PL* 14.

(f) ICT and agency failure

At the practical level, British government's experiments with ICT have so far proved an abject failure. The vast sums lavished on it have not to date paid off; indeed, ICT now makes up a substantial proportion of the workload of complaint-handling services. The list of abandoned computer projects is said to total £2 billion, including a new benefits card sponsored by the Department of Work and Pensions based on outdated technology.[96] Expenditure on the National Programme for IT in the NHS launched in 2002 and designed to reform the way the NHS uses information, has so far totalled £3,550 million. Two reports from the NAO suggest that the programme is four years behind time and shows only modest returns.[97]

When the Inland Revenue (IR) made overpayments of over £2.2 billion in the tax-credit scheme, letters to more than 1.9 million families to claw back the overpayment were automatically generated. Because these could take no account of personal circumstances, great hardship was caused. Blaming the complexity of the system, the PAC warned that 'schemes that are intrinsically complex carry the risk of being too difficult for the intended beneficiaries to understand and for departments to handle'; this was not something that ICT could rectify.[98] The same point was made by the PCA:

> The cases I have investigated are striking in the sheer range and extent of processing errors affecting tax credit claims during the first two years, leading to overpayments for which customers were not responsible, but which they had to repay. A heavier burden was placed on customers than was reasonable to spot the wide variety of mistakes and omissions which occurred as a result of processing faults. . . . [This highlights] the importance, when designing new systems, of starting from the customer perspective and maintaining customer focus throughout the development of the programme. It also highlights the dangers of introducing a 'one size fits all' system. Such systems, whilst superficially providing a fair and consistent and efficient service for all customers can, by failing to pay sufficient regard to the different circumstances and needs of specific client groups, have entirely unintended harsh and unfair consequences for more vulnerable groups.[99]

The Child Support Agency (CSA) was a new NSA established in 1991[100] to take over responsibility for the collection of child maintenance from absent parents. From the start, its performance fell far below what was acceptable. Amongst its

[96] NAO, *Government on the Internet: Progress in delivering information and services online*, HC 529 (2006/7).

[97] NAO, *The National Programme for IT in the NHS*, HC 1173 (2005/6); *The National Programme for IT in the NHS: Progress since 2006*, HC 484 (2007/8).

[98] PAC, *Tax Credits and deleted tax cases*, HC 412 (2005/6); IR standard report: *New Tax Credits*, HC 782 (2005/6); *Tax Credits: Getting it wrong?*, HC 1010 (2006/7).

[99] PCA, *Tax Credits: Putting things right*, HC 124 (2005/6).

[100] By the Child Support Act 1991; and see *Children Come First*, Cmnd 1263 (1990). For the full story of the problems, see G. Davis, N. Wikeley and R. Young, *Child Support in Action* (Hart Publishing, 1998).

many problems were serious IT failures. For the next fifteen years it became a 'repeat player' in every one of administrative law's main accountability forums and the subject of many adverse reports. Three years after it became operative, a Special Report from the Parliamentary Accounts Committee (PAC) revealed that the CSA's operating costs (some £224.52 million) routinely exceeded the maintenance collected (£206.78 million, of which £96.46 million went to the DSS and £110.31 million to parents with care). Uncollected debt from parents stood at over £1,127 million, less than 5 per cent of which was thought to be collectable.[101] The scale of the problems is demonstrated by the caseload of the CSA's Independent Case Examiner (ICE) who, on appointment in 1998, received 28,000 complaints.[102] Consequential problems for the complaints-handling machinery are dealt with in Chapter 10.

IT was not of course the only cause of the CSA's breakdown. Some of the problems flowed from badly thought-through policies and badly drafted legislation (see Chapter 4). Mundane maladministration was noted by the various watchdogs, such as widespread delays, poor communication and inaccurate information to clients, badly trained staff, and failures of communication with other agencies. Time and again, these are shown in reports from the 'watchdogs' to be problems endemic to British public administration. There was a general failure, noted by two PCAs, to learn from previous mistakes. Sir William Reid criticised the hurried way in which the scheme had been implemented:

> Maladministration leading to injustice is likely to arise when a new administrative task is not tested first by a pilot project; when new staff, perhaps inadequately trained, form a substantial fraction of the workforce; where procedures and technology supporting them are untried; and where quality of service is subordinated to sheer throughput.[103]

But driven to review the matter separately, the Select Committee on Work and Pensions, (CWP) concluded that unsatisfactory IT provision in the CSA was the root of the problem.[104] In evidence, the CSA's chief executive said (before resigning):

> it is not possible to operate a large, complex business in today's world without having a sophisticated level of computer support, both for the processing activity, the client contact activity, and the management information needed to run the business. So if you wanted a summary of how I feel, it is that I am seriously disappointed over the last 18 months.[105]

[101] PAC, *Child Support Agency: Client funds account 1996-9*, HC 313 (1997/8).

[102] CSA Independent Case Examiner, First Report (1998). Of these, 1,078 were investigated. Complaints reduced in 2004–05, 2,973 complaints were received, of which 1,257 were accepted for investigation.

[103] PCA, *Investigation of Complaints against the Child Support Agency*, HC 135 (1994/5), p. iii.

[104] CWP, *DWP's Management of Information Technology Projects: Making IT deliver for DWP customers*, HC 311 (2004/5); *Government Response to the Committee's Third Report into the DWP's Management of Information Technology Projects*, HC 1125, (2004/5).

[105] CWP, *The Performance of the CSA*, HC 44-i (2004/5) [19].

The PCA reported a return to an older technology:

> The computer failings have meant that the CSA have had to deal with an increasing number of cases manually. We recognise the need to do so in order to ensure that individual claims are processed as quickly as possible. However, operating both electronic and manual systems alongside one another have given rise to concerns about the impact on standards of data recording. We are concerned that processing claims manually may generate problems of its own.[106]

A £486 million upgrade sanctioned by the New Labour Government in the hope of ending the sorry saga collapsed, forcing a £1 billion claims write-off. A new review was commissioned. The Government announced a redesign of the child support system; the CSA would be wound up and a new start made with a Child Support and Enforcement Commission.[107]

(g) Data protection issues

Collection and storage of private information raises issues other than efficiency; it has serious implications for data protection and privacy. Data may be collected from individuals in many ways: in immigration procedures at borders, in police fingerprint and DNA banks or in new identity cards. It may be stored for long periods of time,[108] accessed by many individuals and exchanged with other public bodies. The reported loss of computer 'smartcards' used to give access to the NHS database, for example, raised concerns over access to confidential patient records and identity fraud. Errors on the police DNA database are capable of causing wrongful convictions and of following innocent citizens from childhood into later life. Late in 2007, a junior official at Revenue and Customs (HMRC) lost two disks containing personal details of 25 million child-benefit claimants, an error compounded by the automated sending of 7.25 million personalised letters of apology containing the claimant's name, address, National Insurance and child-benefit numbers. There was public outrage; the head of department resigned; the Chancellor announced an immediate departmental review.[109] A subsequent trawl through government departments for information about data protection did nothing to lessen concern: an NHS agency had accidentally published on its website full details of the C.V.s of junior doctors applying for NHS positions; a private

[106] Parliamentary Commissioner for Administration, *Annual Report for 2004/5*.

[107] DWP, *A New System of Child Maintenance*, Cm. 6979 (2006). The change was effected by the Child Maintenance and Other Payments Act 2008, which established the Child Maintenance and Enforcement Commission, to which child maintenance functions are gradually being transferred.

[108] But see *S and Marper v United Kingdom*, App. No. 30562/04 [2008] ECHR 1581 (4 Dec. 2008), where the UK arrangements were held to violate ECHR Art. 8.

[109] HC Deb., 28, col. 308, November 2007 (Alistair Darling). This led on to a Cabinet Office report, *Data Handling Procedures in Government*, HC 984-I (2007/8).

contractor to the Driving Standards Agency had lost a hard disk from its secure facility based in Iowa containing just over 3 million records including names and postal addresses – a stark warning of the international dimension of e-governance. The incidents cast doubt both on a projected 'child register' or database containing details of every child or young person in the country under the age of eighteen and on the controversial £5 billion scheme for a National Identity Register.[110] Immediate changes to the law were announced to allow the Information Commissioner to carry out spot-checks on government departments and a 'wide ranging review of data sharing and data protection' by the Information Commissioner authorised (see Chapter 10). No concessions were made on identity cards.

5. The security state

A report made for the Information Commissioner sounded a note of alarm. IT warned that we were sleepwalking into 'a surveillance society', where surveillance encounters were now 'just part of the fabric of daily life. Unremarkable'.[111] It was possible to view this situation as progress towards efficient administration; an alternative viewpoint, however, was that it undermined key democratic values of transparency, accountability, choice, power and empowerment, leaving individuals at a serious disadvantage in controlling the effects of surveillance. Because surveillance varied in intensity geographically and in relation to social class, ethnicity and gender, it also raised issues of discrimination and social exclusion. The debate was too often seen as purely technological in character; these wider issues needed to be brought out into the open and openly debated. In a later response to a government proposal for a 'super-database' to monitor phone lines and internet usage, the Information Commissioner demanded 'the fullest public debate about the justification for, and implications of, a specially created database – potentially accessible to a wide range of law enforcement authorities – holding details of everyone's telephone and internet communications. Do we really want the police, security services and other organs of the state to have access to more and more aspects of our private lives?'[112]

These sombre warnings were taken up in a fuller report from the House of Lords Constitution Committee, which contains around forty precise recommendations. The report stressed the importance of personal privacy and the paramount need for:

[110] ICO, 'The Identity Cards Bill: The Information Commissioner's concerns', October 2005. The Bill became law in the Identity Cards Act 2006.

[111] *Report on the Surveillance Society made for the Information Commissioner by the Surveillance Studies Network* (September, 2006). See also House of Lords Science and Technology Committee, *Personal Internet Security* HL 165 (2006-07); Home Affairs Committee, *Inquiry into 'A Surveillance Society'*, HC 58 (2006/7).

[112] Address introducing the Annual Report for 2008 (15 July 2008), available on website.

> executive and legislative restraint to the use of surveillance and data collection powers as necessary conditions for the exercise of individual freedom and liberty. Privacy and executive and legislative restraint should be taken into account at all times by the executive, government agencies, and public bodies.
>
> Before introducing any new surveillance measure, the Government should endeavour to establish its likely effect on public trust and the consequences for public compliance.[113]

Essentially, the Committee was recommending extension of the administrative law protections dealt with in later chapters of this book: expansion of the remit of the Information Commissioner, whose functions are dealt with in Chapter 10; impact assessments and consultation with the Information Commissioner and with groups representative of the public at an early stage in policy formation (see Chapter 4); statutory regimes and codes of practice for the use of CCTV systems; judicial oversight of surveillance systems and so forth. The operation of the police DNA bank should be more tightly regulated and there should also be greater oversight of the powers of surveillance granted by the Regulation of Investigatory Powers Act 2000 and greater publicity of the tribunal set up under the Act. Compensation should be made to people subject to unlawful surveillance. An immediate response from the Home Secretary rejected claims of a surveillance society, claimed that surveillance was necessary to counter terrorism and called for 'common sense' guidelines on CCTV and DNA.

The *Report on the Surveillance Society* had also noted that cradle-to-grave health and welfare, 'once the proud promise of social democratic governments', had, with the help of data-retrieval systems, been 'whittled down to risk management'. Risk regulation provides a ready justification for an ever more intrusive and regulatory state (a point made earlier). A benevolent gloss is given to state regulatory power by the word 'welfare' but welfare has always had a darker side. Chadwick's nineteenth-century poor-law reforms aimed to make relief sufficiently unpleasant to minimise claims, and complaints were regularly heard of subsequent social assistance schemes that they were designed for the purpose of 'regulating the poor'.[114] The Conservative 'welfare-to-work' ideology, taken up and expanded by New Labour, was designed to force benefit-seekers into work.[115] The 'pseudo-contracts' signed by jobseekers on which benefits are conditional (see Chapter 8) are a form of social control that push benefit recipients back to work. But benefits may be forfeited not only by the work-shy but by those who have 'transgressed against legislative codes regulating human behaviour, whether in the form of non-fulfilment of the terms of an anti-social behaviour order (ASBO), failure to make child maintenance

[113] Constitution Committee, *Surveillance: Citizens and the State*, HL 18 (2008/9) [452].

[114] F. Piven and R. Cloward, *Regulating the Poor: The functions of public welfare* (Tavistock Publications, 1971), p. xvii.

[115] DWP, *Reducing Dependency, Increasing Opportunity: Options for the future of welfare to work* (2007).

payments as an absent parent, or being deemed an "anti-social neighbour", even though their behaviour may have no direct links with the social security system'.[116] Again, affirmative concepts of human rights, which cast positive duties on the state, have the effect of authorising state intervention into areas of private life such as parental discipline.[117] It sounds beneficent to say that 'in order to address inequality adequately, child rearing must be repositioned as a public rather than a private concern and the state must take responsibility for inculcating the practice of good parenting'. To announce 'intensive care sin bins' for 'reckless and disruptive families' or 'pre-birth intervention' to identify 'the kids and families that are going to be difficult in the future' is less benign. The implication in the term 'Respect Tsar' is of an 'increasingly coercive and authoritarian approach to family policy, which has seen ever greater use of compulsion, fines and imprisonment'.[118]

A heavy-handed use of criminal law for purposes of social engineering characterised Tony Blair's government, which in its nine-year tenure added 3,023 offences to the statute book – one for almost every day in power. Many were designed to force changes in conduct not widely considered criminal or even immoral, such as smacking children, failing to send them to school, not wearing seat belts, using mobile telephones while driving, smoking or dropping litter in a public place. More questionable was the use of civil law penalties such as ASBOs, a practice that intentionally undermines the rule of law procedural protections of criminal process. Breach of an ASBO is a criminal offence punishable with imprisonment.[119]

In the name of security, public-order powers became more stringent, controlling the way people behaved in public and vesting extensive discretionary powers in the police. The Crime and Disorder Act 1999 provided for 'dispersal areas' in which groups may be dispersed and for the removal of young people to their place of residence in areas where 'anti-social behaviour is a significant and persistent problem'. A challenge mounted to these provisions, on the ground that they give a near arbitrary power for police to remove to their place of residence any young person 'not in the control of a parent or

[116] P. Larkin, 'The "Criminalization" of Social Security Law: Towards a punitive welfare state?' (2007) 34 *JLS* 295, 299.

[117] See, e.g., *Williamson v Education Secretary and Others* [2002] EWCA 1926, which explores the right of parents to authorise corporal punishment in the light of s. 131 of the School Standards and Framework Act 1998, which extends the prohibition on corporal punishment to private schools.

[118] Citations from DfES, *Every Parent Matters* (2007); V. Gillies, 'Perspectives on Parenting responsibility: Contextualizing values and practices' (2008) 35 *JLS* 95, 98–9. See also C. Henricson, 'Governing parenting: Is there a case for a policy review and statement of parenting rights and responsibilities?' (2008) 35 *JLS* 150.

[119] See P. Ramsay, 'The responsible subject as citizen: Criminal law, democracy and the welfare state' (2006) 69 *MLR* 29. ASBOs were introduced by the Anti-Social Behaviour Act 2003. In 2007, plans were announced to extend this system with ASBO-type attendance orders for those who fail to turn up to school or training courses after the school leaving age is raised to eighteen; violators will face fines of up to £200.

responsible person aged 18 or over', failed.[120] Demonstrations within the vicinity of Parliament required notice to the police; authorisation and breach of the conditions was a criminal offence. The provisions have been used to inhibit an individual from camping outside Parliament in protest against the Iraq war; a woman has also been charged simply for reading out a list of the dead near the Cenotaph in Whitehall.[121]

Under s. 44 of the Terrorism Act 2000 the police may stop, search and detain any individual in an area designated as being at high risk of terrorism even if not suspected of a crime; challenge in the courts has failed.[122] Every piece of legislation in this area adds new criminal offences to the list. Gordon Brown as a new Prime Minister promised a new beginning, reminding his audience that 'liberty belongs to the people not governments'.[123] Less than a month later, he asked Parliament to extend police powers of detention without charge to 42 days. Such measures have not only exacerbated judicial relationships with the executive (see Chapter 3) but have made serious inroads on the concept of civil liberties as conceived in a supposedly liberal-democratic state.

6. 'Hollowing out of the state'

So far in this chapter we have been discussing the role and functions of the state. The implication is that the state is one and indivisible: a centralised and homogeneous single unit. Even in the post-war era of 'big government' this has never been the case. Rhodes coined the famous metaphor of 'hollowing out of the state'[124] to highlight the way that the functions of central government had apparently been depleted during the 1990s. They had been transferred sideways to agencies or the private sector or upwards from national governments to the EU, leaving a hollow centre. New Labour's devolution programme took the process further, adding potential rivals to central government.

(a) Local government

Before devolution, the only institution capable of rivalling the democratic credentials of Parliament was local government. Democratically elected and to an extent free from central-government intervention, local government constituted a 'quasi-autonomous source of political power in the British

[120] *R (W and PW) v Metropolitan Police Commissioner and Richmond LBC* [2006] EWCA Civ 458.

[121] Ss. 132–8 of the Serious Organised Crime and Police Act 2005; *R(Haw) v Home Secretary* [2006] 3 WLR 40. These sections are to be repealed by the forthcoming Constitutional Renewal Bill.

[122] *R(Gillan) v MPC* [2006] UKHL 12; *Austin v MPC* [2009] UKHL 5.

[123] Speech at the University of Westminster, 25 October 2007.

[124] R. Rhodes, 'The hollowing out of the state: The changing nature of the public service in Britain' (1994) 65 *Pol. Q.* 138.

system'.[125] This was a source of tension when different political parties controlled the different power levels. But as government became more centralised, local government slowly lost the essential attributes of self-government.[126] Lacking the legal protections of a written constitution,[127] local government is at the mercy of any government that can obtain a parliamentary majority for abolition – as Margaret Thatcher, angered by consistent opposition to her policies, did with metropolitan counties and the Greater London Council in the Local Government Act 1985. The devolution settlements discussed in the next section radically changed central–local relationships, with responsibility transferred to the three devolved governments.

There are two ways to analyse central–local relations in Britain. The first is as an *agency model*, in which local government has strictly limited powers and disposes of little autonomous discretion. In this model, power emanates from the centre and 'trickles down' to other public bodies, reflecting the traditional view of sovereignty as attaching to Crown and Parliament. 'Inferior parts of government' need specific sanction for any form of activity in which they wish to engage[128] and local government possesses only 'earned' autonomy, conditional on doing what central government wants, and – perhaps more important – doing it in ways approved by central government.[129] Not surprisingly, this 'ultra vires' perspective on local government finds favour with courts wedded to the doctrine of legal sovereignty. The judiciary has consistently downplayed local government's democratic credentials, ruling that it has no inherent powers over and above those contained in or necessarily ancillary to statute.[130]

A more positive way to look at central–local relationships is as a *partnership* in which high-policy decisions are taken centrally but the local partner has political input and some independent discretion. Which of the two models is operative largely depends on the attitude for the time being of the senior partner. In the immediate post-war period, the partnership model prevailed, with much of the service delivery in education, housing, social services and land-use planning entrusted to local authorities. For King, this was 'something

[125] A. King, *Does the United Kingdom Still Have a Constitution?* (Sweet & Maxwell, 2001), p. 27.

[126] M. Loughlin, 'The demise of local government' in V. Bogdanor (ed.), *The British Constitution in the Twentieth Century* (Oxford University Press, 2003).

[127] In 1998, the UK ratified the European Charter of Local Self-Government, 1985 but took no implementing steps.

[128] See M. Taggart, 'Globalization and administrative law' in Huscroft and Taggart (eds.), *Inside and Outside Canadian Administrative Law* (University of Toronto Press, 2006), p. 261.

[129] G. Jones and M. Stewart, 'Central–Local Relations since the Layfield Report' (2002) 28 *Local Government Studies* 7; S. Leach and M. Stewart, *Local Government: Its role and functions* (Joseph Rowntree Foundation, 1992).

[130] *Bromley London Borough Council v Greater London Council* (p. 103 below); *Wheeler v Leicester City Council* (local authority unable to develop and enforce an independent 'local' policy on race relations, see p. 114 below); *R v Lewisham LBC, ex p. Shell United Kingdom Ltd* (contract compliance, see p. 363 below); *R v Somerset County Council, ex p. Fewings* [1995] 1 WLR 1037 (local council bound to use land in the interests of all inhabitants unable to impose an anti-hunting ban). See V. Mehde, 'Steering, suporting, enabling: The role of law in local government reforms (2006) 28 *Law & Policy* 164

of a golden age for local authorities'; in terms both of independence from Whitehall and the scope of their activities, they operated virtually as 'local statelets'.[131] The 'golden age' ended abruptly with the election of Margaret Thatcher who, faced with the need to scale-down local government spending and borrowing, introduced restrictive financial controls. Central government reasserted its pre-eminence and, stripping local government of many of its powers and much of its capacity for independent action, accentuated its dependent position.[132] A cycle of juridification set in as relations between the two tiers of government worsened and courts were called in to adjudicate disputes and interpret the complex provisions of new legislation.[133] Under New Labour, the partnership model has been partially reinstated with the Central Local Partnership established for discussion of topics of mutual interest (including finance) and modification of the strict ultra vires rule in the Local Government Act 2000.[134]

The position of local government has always been undermined by inability to set its own taxes; indeed, the history of local government in the late twentieth century revolves around arguments over finance. Local taxes raise no more than 20 per cent of income and are subject to a cap by central government; the main source of local authority income is central government grants, some distributed according to a formula, others more specific – an invitation to control. No government has so far dared to redress the balance by introducing a locally administered council tax.[135] New Labour's Local Government Act 1999, applicable to England and Wales, to some extent loosened the financial corset, though much central government regulation of local authority finance remained in place. Loan applications by local authorities require ministerial permission; councils that have, in the view of central government, 'overspent' can have their vital central government grants reduced; and so on.[136] And although compulsory competitive tendering was replaced by 'best-value tendering', conditions remained onerous (see Chapter 8). Subjection to VFM quality audit by the independent Audit Commission further restrained policy choices. There were several thousand performance indicators, with reserve powers to intervene for failure to achieve 'best value'.

In *Modernising Government*,[137] the incoming government committed itself to 'making life easier for the public by providing public services in integrated,

[131] King, *Does the United Kingdom Still Have a Constitution*, p. 27.

[132] M. Loughlin, 'Central–local relations' in *Changing Constitution*, 4th edn (2000), p. 138 and 'The demise of local government' in Bogdanor (ed.), *The British Constitution in the Twentieth Century*.

[133] *Ibid.*, pp. 149–60.

[134] I. Leigh, 'The new local government' in *Changing Constitution*, 6th edn (2007).

[135] See *Report of the Committee of Inquiry into Local Government Finance*, Cmnd 6453 (1976) (the Layfield Report) and *Place-shaping: A shared ambition for the future of local government* (HMSO, 2007) (the Lyons report).

[136] P. Vincent-Jones, 'Central–local Relations under the Local Government Act 1999: A new consensus?' (2000) 63 *MLR* 84. And see ss. 136–40 of LGPIHA 2007.

[137] *Modernising Government*, Cm 4310 (1999).

imaginative and more convenient forms like single gateways' (one-stop shops). The essence of 'joined-up government' was to:

> re-engineer governance processes so as genuinely to reunify or re-orientate them to meet the needs of the client groups being served. Ideally, joining-up should make the governance process as simple and transparent as possible instead of citizens or organisations having to deal on connected issues with a maze of different agencies.[138]

Concerned for 'the less articulate and more vulnerable', whose dependence on public services was greater, PASC in its report on audit stressed the need for *standardisation*, demanding common reporting standards and regular monitoring by the NAO.[139] Yet in the same year, the Education and Skills Committee in a report on English secondary education concluded that the policy of centrally set targets had 'now served its purpose'; each school should be left to set its own targets, subject to review by local authorities and OFSTED.[140] This minor divergence highlights the constant tension between the drive to centralise (equality, efficiency, and economy of scale) and the call for localism and community.

In his major review of local government,[141] Sir Michael Lyons, stressed the latter need, calling for 'greater local choice'. Dismissing concerns about 'post-code lotteries' and public calls for 'the same services and levels of service, to be delivered in all areas', he insisted that government targets should be fewer and better focused. *Strong and Prosperous Communities*,[142] a 'more streamlined and proportionate performance regime' was promised with 'more freedom and powers to bring about the changes they want to see'. The promise is implemented in Part 7 of the Local Government and Public Involvement in Health Act 2007(LGPIHA), which not only restricts the number of authorities affected by 'best value' requirements but abolishes the need for performance indicators in England; in respect of Wales, where the Welsh Assembly has made different policy choices, the Act bestows measure-making powers.[143]

More generally, New Labour presents local government through the lens of community empowerment and as a focal point for community renewal and 'voice'.[144] *Strong and Prosperous Communities*[145] promised to strengthen

[138] PASC, *Making Government Work: The emerging issues*, HC 94 (2001/2) [6].

[139] PASC, *On Target: Government by measurement*, HC 62 (2002/3); *Choice, Voice and Public Services*, HC 19 (2004/5).

[140] Select Committee on Education and Skills, *Secondary Education: Pupil Achievement*, HC 513 (2002/3).

[141] Sir Michael Lyons, *National Prosperity, Local choice and Civic Engagement* (May, 2006).

[142] Department for Communities and Local Government, *Strong and Prosperous Communities*, Cm. 6939 (2006) [2].

[143] See further, Welsh Assembly Government, *Making the Connections: Delivering better services for Wales* (2004); *Beyond Boundaries: Citizen-centred local services for Wales* (the Beecham Review) (2006).

[144] DTLR, *Modern Local Government In Touch with the People* (1998).

[145] DCLG, *Strong and Prosperous Communities*, Cm. 6939 (2006). And see Local Democracy, Economic Development and Construction Bill (2009).

the ability of councillors to act as champions for their community via a new 'Community Call for Action'; to increase community management and ownership of community assets to serve local communities better; and to download management and administration (for example, by setting up tenant management schemes and local parish councils). The LGPIHA provides for 'community governance petitions' to trigger policy reviews by a local authority and frees councils from the need for central-government approval of local bylaws. *Communities in control: Real people, real power* takes the process further, announcing (somewhat ironically, in view of its record) that the Government:

> want to shift power, influence and responsibility away from existing centres of power into the hands of communities and individual citizens. This is because we believe that they can take difficult decisions and solve complex problems for themselves. The state's role should be to set national priorities and minimum standards, while providing support and a fair distribution of resources.[146]

In line with this commitment, the Government is to introduce a statutory 'duty to promote democracy' and extend the existing 'duty to involve' local people in key decisions, which covers police authorities and key arts, sporting, cultural and environmental organizations. An Empowerment Fund of at least £7.5 million will go to the DWP to support voluntary organisations and volunteers, especially young people, the disabled and socially excluded. Alongside, government is working on proposals for a two-tier system of local government formed of counties and blocked-up districts and based on regional structures.

(b) Devolution

The centralising trends of the Thatcher government stimulated regional resentment. In Wales, administration was largely in the hands of the Welsh Office, which controlled the lion's share of public spending. Many functions had been transferred to agencies, notably the Welsh Development Agency, whose affairs had provoked much concern.[147] In Scotland, where nationalism was traditionally stronger, the fires were stoked by Thatcher's introduction of the hated 'poll tax'. Following advisory referendums in the two nations, legal force was given to Labour's longstanding promises of devolution by the Scotland and Government of Wales Acts 1998. The devolution settlements, like the Human Rights Act 1998, were crafted to take account of the ruling doctrine of parliamentary sovereignty: it is theoretically always open therefore to the Westminster Parliament to legislate for the devolved areas.

As introduced, the arrangements for devolution were 'asymmetric', based

[146] Executive summary, *Communities in control: Real people, real power* (July 2008).
[147] Rawlings, *Delineating Wales*, pp. 29–31.

on very different models and statutory provisions.[148] Limitations on the Welsh Assembly, restricted to passing secondary legislation, were lessened by the Government of Wales Act 2006, following the report of the Richard Commission.[149] But Acts of Parliament cover England and Wales except where otherwise indicated and the legal system remains technically that of England and Wales.[150] In Northern Ireland, where government had first been devolved in 1921, direct rule was restored in 1973 in response to escalating violence. In 1998, the New Labour Government succeeded in negotiating the Belfast or 'Good Friday' agreement between the major political parties, which set in place a new and complex 'consociational' model of devolved government;[151] devolution had once more to be shelved, however, and had in practice to await the Northern Ireland (St Andrews Agreement) Acts of 2006 and 2007. There have since been substantial moves to normal governance in the province.[152]

The fact that regional executives responsible to regional legislatures are now competent in internal matters (with important exceptions for human rights and EU affairs, where the UK government retains responsibility) has changed the remit of many central government departments, notably the Home Office and Departments of Health and Education. New complaints machinery, including changes to the existing ombudsman systems, was also necessary (see Chapter 10). Devolved government has opened the way to policy divergence of a kind not previously possible in the highly centralised British system, where government had at its disposal in the last resort the weapon of statute law.

According to Oliver, one effect of devolution has been to introduce 'more highly juridified political and administrative processes than operate at UK level'. This raises questions as to 'how rules governing political behaviour can be enforced, as to the implications of involving the courts in disputes abut breaches of norms, and the relative advantages and disadvantages of non-judicial mechanisms for resolving disputes where rules governing inter-institutional relationships have been breached'.[153] Some highly technical

[148] C. Turpin and A. Tomkins, *British Government and the Constitution*, 6th edn, (Cambridge University Press, 2007), Ch. 4; and see N. Burrows, *Devolution* (Sweet & Maxwell, 2000); A. Trench, *Devolution and Power in the United Kingdom* (Manchester University Press, 2007).

[149] *Report of the Commission on the Powers and Electoral Arrangements of the National Assembly for Wales* (2004). And see R. Rawlings, 'Law making in a virtual Parliament: The Welsh experience' in Hazell and Rawlings (eds.), *Devolution, Law Making and the Constitution* (Imprint Academic, 2005).

[150] Rawlings, *Delineating Wales*, pp. 317–21.

[151] *Agreement Reached in the Multi-Party Negotiations*, Cm. 3883 (1998). And see C. McCrudden, 'Northern Ireland' in *Changing Constitution*, 5th edn (2004); and 'Northern Ireland and the British Constitution since the Belfast Agreement' in *Changing Constitution*, 6th edn (2007).

[152] G. Anthony, 'The St Andrews Agreement and the Northern Ireland Assembly' (2008) 14 *EPL* 151.

[153] D. Oliver, *Constitutional Reform in the UK* (Oxford University Press, 2003), p. 241. And see B. Winetrobe, 'Scottish devolution: Developing practice in multi-layer governance' in *Changing Constitution*, 6th edn (2007).

points have fallen to be decided by the House of Lords and Privy Council.[154] As for the formal mechanism for resolution of 'devolution issues',[155] the various actors have so far shown restraint and a willingness to make the system work. The general tendency, contrary to Oliver's prediction, has been not to resort to litigation and formal law change but to rely on understandings and 'soft law'.[156] No doubt this has been helped by the existence of national, political parties and the common formation, style and code of ethics of the public servants presently operating the system. In time this may change.[157] Or change might come about through a rise in nationalism, signalled by the election in 2007 of the first Scottish nationalist government committed to full independence or at least reform of the devolution settlement with greater control of the Scottish budget.[158] On the English side of the border, where some commentators feel that a 'gaping hole' exists in the constitutional arrangements for the largest country in the Union, a renewed interest in regional assemblies, for which the English have so far shown little appetite,[159] is possible. More likely, though undesirable, are attempts to change Parliament's lawmaking procedures to curtail the rights of Scottish representatives to vote on purely English measures.[160]

(c) The European Union

Regionalisation shares out the powers of the nation-state without necessarily diminishing the total. Transfer of state power to a supranational entity such as the European Union (EU) is a different type of 'hollowing out'. Although this may not at first be realised, powers are subtracted from the sum available to national governments and transferred to a 'higher' level, a process with direct impact on national sovereignty. Giddens catches the inherent tension between 'uploading' and 'downloading' in the globalised world of post-modern politics and governance:

154 Notably *Somerville and Others v Scottish Ministers* [2007] UKHL 44, which concerns the very important relationship of the Scotland Act to the UK Human Rights Act 1998; and see G. Gee, 'Devolution and the courts' in Hazell and Rawlings (eds.), *Devolution, Law Making and the Constitution.*

155 Competence is transferred to the new Supreme Court by s. 40 and Sch. 9 of the Constitutional Reform Act 2005.

156 R. Rawlings, 'Concordats of the constitution' (2000) 116 *LQR* 257.

157 See R. Rhodes (ed.), *Decentralizing the Civil Service: From unitary state to differentiated polity in the United Kingdom* (Open University Press, 2003).

158 The Scottish Government, *Choosing Scotland's Future: A national conversation: Independence and responsibility in the modern world* (August 2007).

159 A local referendum on an assembly for the north-east was defeated by nearly 80%: see R. Laming, 'The future of English regional government', Federal Union website.

160 R. Hazell (ed.), *The English Question* (Manchester University Press, 2006) reviewed by Bogdanor [2007] *PL* 169; B. Hadfield, 'Devolution and the changing constitution: Evolution in Wales and the unanswered English question', in *Changing Constitution*, 6th edn (2007).

> Globalisation 'pulls away' from the nation-state in the sense that some powers nations used to possess, including those that underlay Keynesian economic management, have been weakened. However, globalisation also 'pushes down' – it creates new demands and also new possibilities for regenerating local identities . . . Globalisation also squeezes sideways, creating new economic and cultural regions that sometimes cross-cut the boundaries of nation-states.[161]

Since its inauguration as a common market, the EU has rapidly accumulated power. There has a steady upwards 'delegation' of national state functions, with a consequential impact on national sovereignty. Significant steps on the road have been the Single European Act 1986, which delegated wide powers to the European Commission in the interests of completing the single market; the Treaty of European Union (TEU), which formalised the co-operation beginning to take place in the areas of policing, immigration and justice and introduced the idea of co-operation in the field of foreign policy. The EU is a regime very prone to 'mission creep', often working through agencies, such as Europol, established to co-ordinate the transnational activities of national police forces, or Eurojust, which helps to co-ordinate the criminal and civil justice systems of member states. Few lawyers know, for example, about the programme for harmonisation of our civil law or that the Commission has programmes in the area of legal aid. This raises serious questions over accountability.[162]

More relevant to the subject matter of this book is the EU's growing regulatory power. We shall find in Chapter 6 that many of our national regulatory systems, in fields like competition, telecommunications and many others, should bear the label 'manufactured in Brussels'. Partly due to the technicality of much of the subject matter, people are only beginning to be aware of the role played by the EU in regulating food safety or horticultural and veterinary chemicals and agricultural production generally. And the less than transparent operation of EU rule-making processes means that probably only the 'Euro-elite', visiting Brussels regularly, and officials who meet constantly in the committees and corridors of the Commission, are fully conscious of the EU's upward pull. This again creates problems for political accountability.[163]

Many years ago, Lord Denning famously compared the Treaty of Rome to an 'incoming tide flowing into the estuaries and up the rivers'. The simile, with its notion of invasion, took hold. Since those early days, it has been customary to think of EU law as an outsider and to measure its impact on British law, or 'spill-over effect'.[164] Principles of judicial review, such

[161] T. Giddens, *The Third Way*, p. 31.

[162] D. Curtin, 'Delegation to EU non-majoritarian agencies and emerging practices of public accountability' in Geradin *et al.*, *Regulation Through Agencies in the EU*.

[163] C. Harlow, *Accountability in the European Union* (Oxford University Press, 2002).

[164] G. Anthony, 'Community law and the development of UK administrative law: Delimiting the "spill-over" effect' (1998) 4 *EPL* 253 and *UK Public Law and European Law: The dynamics of legal integration* (Hart Publishing, 2002). See also Turpin and Tomkins, *British Government and the Constitution*, Ch. 5.

as proportionality or legitimate expectation, have been imported from Europe. Structural change has been imposed on administrative systems, as with the EU public procurement directives that strictly regulate government contracting (see Chapter 8). The impact of EU law may sometimes be unexpected, unintentional and even unwelcome, as in *Watts*, where an NHS patient, upset by her long wait for a hip replacement, went to France for the operation and subsequently claimed reimbursement from the NHS. Ruling this to be permissible, ECJ took the opportunity to criticise NHS procedure, saying in the course of its judgment that a 'rationing system' was only legitimate if:

> based on objective, non-discriminatory criteria which are known in advance, in such a way as to circumscribe the exercise of the national authorities' discretion, so that it is not used arbitrarily. Such a system must furthermore be based on a procedural system which is easily accessible and capable of ensuring that a request for authorisation will be dealt with objectively and impartially within a reasonable time and refusals to grant authorisation must also be capable of being challenged in judicial or quasi-judicial proceedings.[165]

As the 'spill-over effect' became more widely recognised, the approach to EU law changed. New books are appearing, which look on EU law as part of domestic public law to be drawn on when necessary. How British courts treat EU law is itself a subject of study.[166] Bamforth talks of the arrival of a 'multi-layered constitution' in which a 'multi-level jurisdiction' operates.[167] This idea is explored in Chapter 15. Sir Konrad Schiemann writes:

> The light in which a lawyer views a set of facts and the way he formulates the legal problem is very much conditioned by the legal system which he is applying. In this country the courts are now more often in a position where they can apply one or more of four legal systems which are interacting - public international law, the law of the European Union, the law of the ECHR and the common law as modified by Equity and statute.[168]

If the EU is a force for 'hollowing out' state power, it is equally a force for centralisation. The EU deals with its member states, responsible in EU law for implementing its policies (TEC Art. 10). This is reflected at national level by the reservation of legislative and policy-making powers in EU matters for the Westminster government. At the same time, the EU has committed itself to the doctrine of subsidiarity, whereby decisions should be taken as close as possible

165 Case C-372/04 *R (Yvonne Watts) v Bedford Primary Care Trust and Health Secretary* [2006] ECR I-4325 [115-6]. In consequence of this judgment, the European Commission is preparing proposals to facilitate patient travel abroad in search of treatment.

166 R. Gordon, *EC Law in Judicial Review* (Oxford University Press, 2007).

167 N. Bamforth, 'Courts in a multi-layered constitution' in Bamforth and Leyland (eds.), *Public Law in a Multi-Layered Constitution*.

168 K. Schiemann, 'Introduction' in Gordon, *EC Law in Judicial Review*, p. ix.

to the people.[169] In fact, the machinery is not in place for enforcement of the doctrine. Only recently have national parliaments begun to receive proper recognition in the EU's constitutional arrangements;[170] regional governments and sub-national parliaments have still more limited representation in EU law and policy-making processes.[171] The EU has nonetheless been a force for disaggregation, providing an alternative to national power structures that makes regional 'opt out' look feasible. It has helped to dismantle Shapiro's picture of 'bounded' government, responsible to a national legislature and billeted firmly in the national constitution (p. 5 above).

For better or worse, the UK has become a player in a multi-level system of governance,[172] in which the policy-making process is not only creeping steadily upwards but being dispersed amongst 'policy-making networks' of public and private players. National public servants work alongside EU officials, agencies, private corporations and the voluntary sector. Transparency has declined through the opacity of the EU treaty-making, lawmaking and policy-making processes. A worrying 'democratic deficit' has come into being, reducing opportunities for citizen participation.[173] A forceful transnational court (the ECJ) has impinged on national legal orders, changing the balance of power between courts and government.[174] This is a challenging context for public lawyers and one that threatens 'some of the most benign developments of modern administrative law'.[175]

7. A state of change

The contours of public administration have changed very rapidly in recent years. Constitutional change has come suddenly and sporadically. It has been disconnected and too little thought has been given to the possible consequences of some of the reform. Prosser's view of English public law as a 'journey without maps'[176] is vindicated in this chapter, which records a

[169] TEC Art. 5; and see A. Estella, *The EU Principle of Subsidiarity and its Critiques* (Oxford University Press, 2002); N. Barber, 'The limited modesty of subsidiarity' (2005) 11 *ELJ* 308; I. Cooper, 'The watchdog of subsidiarity' (2006) 44 *J CMS* 281.

[170] European Scrutiny Committee, *Democracy and Accountability in the European Union and the Role of National Parliaments*, HC 152 (2001/2); T. Raunio, 'Always one step behind? National legislatures and the European Union' (1999) 34 *Government and Opposition* 180.

[171] E. Bomberg and J. Petersen, 'EU decision-making: The role of sub-national authorities' (1998) 46 *Pol. Studies* 219.

[172] See K-H Ladeur (ed.), *Public Governance in the Age of Globalization* (Ashgate, 2004).

[173] S. Andersen and T. Burns, 'The European Union and the erosion of parliamentary democracy: A study of post-parliamentary governance', in Andersen and Eliassen (eds.), *The European Union: How democratic is it?* (Sage, 1996); R. Bellamy, 'Still in deficit: Rights, regulation and democracy in the EU' (2006) 12 *ELJ* 725.

[174] D. Wincott, 'Does the European Union pervert democracy? Questions of democracy in new constitutionalist thought on the future of Europe' (1998) 4 *ELJ* 411.

[175] A. Aman Jr, 'Administrative law for a new century', in Taggart (ed.), *The Province of Administrative Law*, pp. 75, 95.

[176] T. Prosser 'Journey without maps?' [1993] *PL* 346.

number of divergent attitudes to the state and its functions. Some of the differences have political origins: 'big state' socialism contrasted strongly with Margaret Thatcher's approach. Others are temporal in character, in the sense that they have to be accommodated. Thatcher's privatisation programmes and reforms to public administration were, for example, a revolution which subsequent governments have had to digest.

Later chapters consider the new administrative law that emerged and is still emerging from these changes. We shall find that regulation and regulatory theory have come to occupy the centre of our discipline (see Chapters 6 and 7); that contract has emerged from the shadows to become a powerful tool for service delivery and for 'steering' (see Chapters 8 and 9); and that a steady process of juridification is a marked feature of modern bureaucratic systems (see Chapter 5). This is partly due to the process of institutional fragmentation and 'hollowing out of the state' recorded in this chapter. Primarily, however, juridification is an aspect of computerisation. ICT has brought us to the edge of an age of 'e-governance' which we do not as yet know how to handle.

National politics are increasingly concerned with transnational or global issues. Policy-development is moving upwards. National economic policy is bound up with world trade, while the equality principle that has so rapidly gained ground at national level is beginning to encompass global poverty and development.[177] Nowhere is this more evident than in the environmental field. The Stern Review, commissioned by HM Treasury, reflects the new international dimension to environmentalism:

> The Review takes an international perspective. Climate change is global in its causes and consequences, and international collective action will be critical in driving an effective, efficient and equitable response on the scale required. This response will require deeper international co-operation in many areas – most notably in creating price signals and markets for carbon, spurring technology research, development and deployment, and promoting adaptation, particularly for developing countries.[178]

A government statement that sustainable development should become a cross-cutting basis for policy across government blends economic advance with environmentalism.[179] In response, we have seen a rapid 'greening of administrative law', with new regulatory machinery (see Chapter 7) and new cutting-edge principles.

We spoke of Margaret Thatcher's reforms as marking a paradigm shift, ushering in an era of economic liberalism. Globalisation, the progression of

[177] D. Trubek and A. Santos (eds.), *The New Law and Economic Development: A critical appraisal* (Cambridge University Press, 2006).

[178] HM Treasury, *Stern Review on the Economics of Climate Change* (Cambridge University Press, 2006).

[179] UK Cabinet Office, *Securing the Future: Delivering UK sustainable development strategy* (March 2005).

e-governance and, latterly, a new environmentalism, all pose serious challenges for our discipline. As optimist Alfred Aman Jr sees it, 'A major role for law in the global era is to help create the institutional architecture necessary for democracy to work, not only within the institutions of government but also beyond them in the sphere where the private sector governs'.[180] Taggart, recalling that 'old pictures of a political and legal scene remain current long after it has been dramatically altered', once criticised public lawyers for slowness in coming to grips with the challenges of 'the blue rinse'.[181] In time, however, they did respond and the chapters that follow deal with their responses.

Today, we stand on the edge of a new paradigm shift. Triggered by the 'credit crunch' in 2008, and the subsequent economic recession, nationalisation and quasi-nationalisation are at least on the agenda. There are cries for new regulators and new forms of regulation and talk at the political level of a 'New, New Deal'. For administrative law, this is undoubtedly a challenge but it is also an opportunity.

180 A. Aman Jr, *The Democracy Deficit* (New York University Press, 2004), p. 136.

181 M. Taggart (ed.), 'The Province of Administrative Law Determined' in M. Taggart (ed.), *The Province of Administrative Law* (Hart Publishing, 1997) p. 2. Taggart is citing Justice Felix Frankfurter, writing in the context of Roosevelt's New Deal. See now R. Stewart, 'US administrative law: A model for Global Administrative Law?' (2005) 68 *Law and Contemporary Problems* 63, a Special Issue on the problems of global administrative law.

3

Transforming judicial review

Contents

1. Beginnings

Kenneth Culp Davis, a leading American academic visiting England in the 1960s, described English judicial review as restricted by an old-fashioned, positivist corset 'astonishing to one with a background in the American legal system'. English judges strove to avoid consideration of the policy aspects of the issues they decided and the typical lawyer:

> responds with consternation to an inquiry into the soundness of the policies embodied in a judicial decision, and, if he persists, the inquirer is gently reminded that judges do not consider policy questions and that only Parliament can change the law; the task of the judge is wholly analytical – to discover the previously existing law, and to apply it logically to the case before the court.[1]

Not only were judges precluded from considering 'policy questions' but the lawmaking powers of the judiciary were scarcely recognised.[2] The judicial

[1] K. C. Davis, 'The future of judge-made public law in England: A problem of practical jurisprudence' (1961) 61 *Col. Law Rev.* 201, 202.

[2] P. Atiyah and R. Summers, *Form and Substance in Anglo-American Law: A comparative study of legal reasoning, legal theory and legal institutions* (Clarendon Press, 1987).

function was seen as limited to 'discovering' previously existing law and applying it logically to the case before the court. A strict interpretation of the doctrine of precedent inhibited rapid changes of direction and it was accepted that only Parliament could change the law. As Lord Reid (perhaps too modestly) put it, if doctrine had developed in such a way as to cause injustice, appellate judges should, if they could, 'get the thing back on the rails', but 'if it has gone too far we must pin our hopes on Parliament'.[3] Jaffé attributed the different behaviour of English and American judges to constitutional factors; it had always been anticipated that the federal American judge would 'assume a role in the polity far greater than that played by his *confrère* in Britain'.[4]

English political scientists confirmed this view of courts. For King, the judiciary was not at this time 'an autonomous source of political power' in the British system of government:

> The courts were important, of course, as they are in every properly functioning constitutional system. British judges' independence of both the government and Parliament, and their insistence that the state as well as its citizens should be subject to the rule of law, were and are essential bulwarks of good government. Compared, however, with the role of the courts in many other countries, the role of the courts in the United Kingdom was severely circumscribed. Judges might occasionally be said to have 'made policy' as a result of their individual decisions or series of decisions, but they could not declare Acts of Parliament unconstitutional, because there was no capital-C constitution in Britain, and they could not determine that Acts of Parliament or acts of government were in breach of the bill of rights because there was no bill of rights.[5]

World War II had marked a period of exceptionally strong executive government, acceptable only in periods of national emergency. It marked too a period of judicial deference, when judges joined with Parliament to endorse executive authority and power. Their obsequious attitude was encapsulated by the majority speeches in *Liversidge v Anderson*.[6] The draconian Defence of the Realm Act 1914 and the regulations made thereunder had empowered the Home Secretary to intern an alien without trial if 'he had reasonable cause to believe' that the internee was of hostile origin or associations. The

3 Lord Reid,'The judge as law-maker' (1972) XII *Journal of the Society of Public Teachers of Law* 22.

4 L. Jaffé, *English and American Judges as Lawmakers* (Clarendon Press, 1969), p. 83, a view traceable to the classic work of Alexis de Tocqueville, *Democracy in America* (1835). By the late 1990s, Jaffé's remark might have seemed controversial to Americans: see A. Scalia, *A Matter of Interpretation: Federal courts and the law* (Princeton University Press, 1997); M. Tushnet, *The New Constitutional Order* (Princeton University Press, 2003).

5 A. King, *Does the United Kingdom Still Have a Constitution?* (Sweet & Maxwell, 2001), p. 25. See also Barker, p. 3 above.

6 *Liversidge v Anderson* [1942] AC 206. See also *McEldowney v Forde* [1971] AC 632 (Lord Diplock dissenting).

question for the House of Lords was whether this formula conveyed an *objective* or *subjective* discretion: in other words, did the Home Secretary have to spell his reasons out to a court? By a majority of four to one, the House held that he did not: the discretion was subjective. One lonely member of the House of Lords (Lord Atkin) maintained that the formula permitted, nay demanded, review for reasonableness.[7] Seven years later, Sir Alfred Denning was prepared to defend the decision. The wartime powers of detention represented 'the high-water mark of power of the executive of this country' but the power was not abused; 'it was administered by men who could be trusted not to allow any man's liberty to be taken away without good cause'. There was parliamentary accountability in the shape of 'a conscientious and careful Home Secretary who was answerable to a Parliament which was ever vigilant in defence of liberty'.[8] But the lecture series stressed also the historical role of the common law in keeping the balance 'between individual freedom and social duty'. While not denying the necessity of strong executive powers for social purposes, Sir Alfred pointed to their increasing extent: 'they touch the life of every one of us at innumerable points: and they are an inseparable part of modern society'.[9] Over the substance of the powers, the courts could have little control; these were matters for government and Parliament; the courts' 'most important task' was to see that the powers are not exceeded or abused.

Schwarz and Wade blamed the 'lingering effect of the wartime spirit of abnegation and sacrifice' for an administrative law 'at its lowest ebb for perhaps a century. The leading cases made a dreary catalogue of abdication and error.'[10] But the authors thought a turn-around still possible if it were realized that 'Britain had in the past developed much more administrative law than the legal profession understood';[11] they looked, in other words, for a renaissance. According to Wade, it was the judges who 'executed a series of U-turns which put the law back on course and responded to the public mood'. In response to a 'public reaction against administrative injustice' too strong to be ignored, a new judicial policy was adopted 'to build up a code of rules of administrative fair play which [judges] take for granted as intended by Parliament to apply to all statutory powers, and perhaps even to prerogative powers, and to insist on preserving their jurisdiction even in the face of legislation purporting to exclude it'.[12] The move was justifiable to Wade because 'the judges appreciate,

[7] R. Heuston, '*Liversidge v Anderson* in Retrospect' (1970) 86 *LQR* 33.

[8] A. Denning, *Freedom under the Law* (Stevens, 1949), p. 16. History does not support his view: see A. Simpson, *In the Highest Degree Odious: Detention without trial in wartime Britain* (Clarendon Press, 1992).

[9] Denning, *Freedom under the Law*, p. 100.

[10] B. Schwarz and H. Wade, *Legal Control of Government: Administrative law in Britain and the United States* (Clarendon Press, 1972), pp. 320–1.

[11] *Ibid.* See similarly Sir Leslie Scarman, *English Law: The new dimension* (Stevens, 1974).

[12] H. W. R. Wade, *Constitutional Fundamentals* (Stevens, 1980), p. 62.

much more than does Parliament, that to exempt any public authority from judicial control is to give it dictatorial power, and that this is so fundamentally objectionable that Parliament cannot really have intended it.'[13] In these classical red-light pictures of the evolution of 'administrative law', our present happy state is owed to the judiciary. And Lord Diplock (only too willing to take credit) regarded 'the progress towards a comprehensive system of administrative law . . . as having been the greatest achievement of the English courts in my judicial lifetime.'[14]

A quantum leap had been taken by the millennium, when King called the judiciary a 'living presence in the constitution in a way that it was not before'. How had this significant turn-around been achieved? As we shall see, judicial review expanded exponentially during the 1970s and 1980s, as the judiciary regained confidence lost during two wartime regimes. The common law, which Lord Scarman saw as incapable of rejuvenation, confounded his pessimistic predictions and, with some assistance from continental Europe, showed a remarkable capacity for renaissance. Accession to the European Communities brought structural change, as national courts were incorporated into the 'new legal order' of Community law (see *Factortame*, p. 180 below). The indirect effect was to re-balance the relationship between judiciary, executive and legislature, very much to the profit of the judges. (Discussion of these momentous developments is reserved for Chapter 4.) Alongside, human rights law was flowing in through the European Convention. Finally, the HRA gave the judiciary a new power base, underpinning its authority. Today, as Lord Diplock forecast in the *GCHQ* case (p. 107 below), the jurisprudence of the ECJ and ECtHR form important components of the 'multi-streamed jurisdiction' that has come into being – a new context where judges are learning to grapple with and domesticate European and international law. In the rest of this chapter, we shall examine the 'onward march of judicial review' under the following heads:

- *Rebuilding judicial review* in the post-war period, when old principles were affirmed and new principles set in place
- *Rapid expansion* of judicial review during the 1970s and 1980s, with executive discretion as its target
- *Rationality* as the key concept of judicial review
- *Rights-based review*
- *The shadow of the Convention*
- *Rights, unreasonableness and proportionality*
- *The Human Rights Act and after*

[13] *Ibid.*, p. 65.

[14] *R v IRC, ex p. National Federation of Self-Employed* [1982] AC 617, 641. Speaking extrajudicially, Lord Diplock had claimed that the English system was 'nearly as comprehensive in its scope as *droit administratif* in France': see [1974] *CLJ* 233, 244.

2. Rebuilding judicial review

A formalist agenda for administrative law accompanied judicial formalism.[15] Cotterell, situating judicial review within constitutional theory, described it as a 'modest underworker', by which he meant that the judicial role was no more and no less than to police the rule of law through interpretation (compare Lord Reid's earlier account above).[16] Less restrained was Hutchinson's metaphor of 'mice under the executive chair' (though we should note that the author thought mice better suited than lions to a popular democracy).[17] Judges were concerned to avoid accusations of meddling in policy. They perceived themselves to be debarred from substituting their decision as to the merits of a case for that of the primary decision-maker, a view expressed by Lord Greene in his classical *Wednesbury* judgment (p. 42 above). A passage from a judgment of Lord Donaldson makes the point nicely. The Court of Appeal was faced with an application from Michael Foot, then Leader of the Opposition, to review the findings of the Boundary Commission, an independent statutory body set up by and answerable to the Home Secretary which exists to review the boundaries of parliamentary electoral constituencies. Faced with the argument that the matter was not justiciable, Lord Donaldson was careful to explain why this was not so:

> Since a very large number of people are interested in this appeal and since it is most unlikely that our decision, whether for or against the applicants, will meet with universal approval, it is important that it should at least be understood. In particular it is important that everyone should understand what is the function and duty of the courts.
>
> Parliament entrusted the duty of recommending changes in English constituency boundaries to the commission. It could, if it had wished, have further provided that anyone who was dissatisfied with those recommendations could appeal to the courts. Had it done so, the duty of the court would, to a considerable extent, have been to repeat the operations of the commission and see whether it arrived at the same answer. If it did, the appeal would have been dismissed. If it did not, it would have substituted its own recommendations. Parliament, for reasons which we can well understand, did no such thing. It made no mention of the courts and gave no right of appeal to the courts.
>
> There are some who will think that in that situation the courts have no part to play, but they would be wrong. There are many Acts of Parliament which give ministers and local authorities extensive powers to take action which affects the citizenry of this country, but give no right of appeal to the courts. In such cases, the courts are not concerned or involved as long as ministers and local authorities do not exceed the powers given to them

[15] M. Taggart, 'Reinventing administrative law' in Bamforth and Leyland (eds.), *Public Law in a Multi-Layered Constitution* (Hart Publishing, 2003).

[16] R. Cotterell, 'Judicial review and legal theory' in Richardson and Genn, *Administrative Law and Government Action* (Clarendon Press, 1994). See also R. Cranston, 'Reviewing judicial review', *ibid.*

[17] A. Hutchinson 'Mice under a chair: Democracy, courts and the administrative state' (1990) 40 *UTLJ* 374.

> by Parliament. Those powers may give them a wide range of choice on what action to take or to refrain from taking and so long as they confine themselves to making choices within that range, the courts will have no wish or power to intervene. But if ministers or local authorities exceed their powers – if they choose to do something or to refrain from doing something in circumstances in which this is not one of the options given to them by Parliament – the courts can and will intervene in defence of the ordinary citizen. It is of the essence of parliamentary democracy that those to whom powers are given by Parliament shall be free to exercise those powers, subject to constitutional protest and criticism and parliamentary or other democratic control. But any attempt by ministers or local authorities to usurp powers which they have not got or to exercise their powers in a way which is unauthorised by Parliament is quite a different matter. As Sir Winston Churchill was wont to say, 'that is something up with which we will not put'. If asked to do so, it is then the role of the courts to prevent this happening.[18]

Rigorously applying the *Wednesbury* test, the Court of Appeal ruled that the applicant had failed to show that the Commission had reached conclusions that no reasonable Commission could have reached.

We can relate this statement to Lord Wilberforce's description of the role of judges in judicial review made in the celebrated *Bromley* case (p. 103 below). According to Lord Wilberforce, two possibilities were open to the judge:

- to construe statute to determine the extent of administrative powers (the principle of 'narrow' ultra vires) or
- in addition to apply general principles of administrative law, such as the reasonableness doctrine ('wide' ultra vires).

In reality, the formulation is ambiguous. When, for example, Lord Donaldson tells us that the courts 'can and will intervene' if public authorities do or refrain from doing something when 'this is not one of the options given to them by Parliament', is he describing 'narrow' or 'wide' ultra vires? The difference, as this chapter will reveal, could be significant. A similar ambiguity is evident when Allan says that judicial review 'exists to safeguard legality. The rule of law requires that public authorities act only within the limits of their powers, *properly understood*.'[19] There is scope for a good deal of judicial activism in the two emphasised words. He himself admits that 'administrative and political choice may become closely intertwined with legal principle'.

In a trilogy of famous cases decided at the end of the 1960s, the House of Lords intervened decisively to give judicial review a new lease of life. The 1969 case of *Anisminic* (see p. 27 above) used the idea of a body of general administrative law principles to render null and void virtually any decision taken in defiance of these principles. Also in 1963, *Ridge v Baldwin* (see p. 622 below)

[18] *R v Boundary Commission for England, ex p. Foot* [1983] QB 600.

[19] T. Allan, *Law, Liberty and Justice: The legal foundations of British constitutionalism* (Clarendon Press, 1993), pp. 183–4.

reinstated into decision-taking rules of procedural fairness that had fallen into abeyance, using them as an aid to statutory interpretation. In *Padfield*,[20] the third case in the trilogy, the House of Lords moved to control ministerial discretionary power, boldly walking down the path they had refused to take in *Liversidge v Anderson*.

The Agricultural Marketing Act 1958 set up a milk-marketing scheme that forced producers to sell their product to the Milk Marketing Board, which periodically fixed prices on a regional basis. Section 19 provided that, in case of dispute, complaints could be referred to a committee of investigation 'if the Minister in any case so directs'. On receipt of the committee's report, the minister could revoke or amend the scheme, 'if he thinks fit so to do after considering the report'. Producers in the south-east region complained that the fixed price did not adequately reflect increased costs in transporting milk from other regions but the Board declined to fix new prices on the grounds that an increase to the complainants would be at the expense of other areas. The minister refused to refer the matter to the committee of investigation, stating in a letter that, if the complaint were upheld, the minister would be expected to give effect to the committee's recommendations by laying a statutory order before Parliament, which he was unwilling to do. Padfield sought mandamus to compel a reference. By a majority, Lord Morris dissenting, the House of Lords issued the order:

> *Lord Reid:* The Minister is, I think, correct in saying that the board is an instrument for the self-government of the industry. So long as it does not act contrary to the public interest the Minister cannot interfere. But if it does act contrary to what both the committee of investigation and the Minister hold to be the public interest the Minister has a duty to act. And if a complaint relevantly alleges that the board has so acted, as this complaint does, then it appears to me that the Act does impose a duty on the Minister to have it investigated. If he does not do that he is rendering nugatory a safeguard provided by the Act and depriving complainers of a remedy which I am satisfied that Parliament intended them to have . . .
>
> It was argued that the Minister is not bound to give any reasons for refusing to refer a complaint to the committee, that if he gives no reasons his decision cannot be questioned, and that it would be very unfortunate if giving reasons were to put him in a worse position. But I do not agree that a decision cannot be questioned if no reasons are given. If it is the Minister's duty not to act so as to frustrate the policy and objects of the Act, and if it were to appear from all the circumstances of the case that that has been the effect of the Minister's refusal, then it appears to me that the court must be entitled to act.
>
> *Lord Morris:* The language here is, in my view, purely permissive. The Minister is endowed with discretionary powers. If he did decide to refer a complaint he is endowed with further discretionary powers after receiving a report . . . If the respondent proceeded properly to exercise his judgment then, in my view, it is no part of the duty of any court to act as a Court of Appeal from his decision or to express any opinion as to whether

[20] *Padfield v Minister of Agriculture, Fisheries and Food* [1968] AC 997.

> it was wise or unwise . . . A court could make an order if it were shown (a) that the Minister failed or refused to apply his mind to or to consider the question whether to refer a complaint or (b) that he misinterpreted the law or proceeded on an erroneous view of the law or (c) that he based his decision on some wholly extraneous consideration or (d) that he failed to have regard to matters which he should have taken into account.

The minister duly referred the dispute to the committee, which recommended change. In turn, the minister reported to the House of Commons that 'it would not be in the public interest for me to direct the Board to implement the change'.[21]

Austin accused the House in *Padfield* of ignoring an important distinction between 'objective' and 'subjective' discretion: objective discretion was derived from statute and imposed 'defined or ascertainable predetermined criteria' by which, and solely by which, the decision-maker had to make his choice: in other words, it was always confined and structured. Formulae such as 'if in his opinion', 'if he thinks fit', 'if he deems', 'if he considers', etc., ought to be interpreted as conferring subjective discretion because they contain no benchmarks against which the decision-maker's choices can be measured. The implication of *Padfield* must be that:

> if the source of the power does not impose any objective criteria, the courts will imply such criteria; the disturbing element in this development is that the courts may simply be replacing their own subjective views for those of a person such as a Minister who is better qualified and equipped to exercise the power. In short, they may supply their own criteria rather than implying them from the terms of the empowering legislation.[22]

There are two accusations here: first that, in substituting their subjective views for those of the appointed decision-maker, the judges had strayed outside the traditional boundaries of their constitutional function; secondly, that the principles on which they operated were just as discretionary and unstructured as the discretions they purported to discipline. Judicial review did not, in other words, measure up to the standards of rational decision-making imposed by the judges on the executive and administrators. Rationality was to become the focal point of judicial review.

3. Rapid expansion

Padfield, with its emphasis on control of discretionary power, was to set the tone of judicial review for the next two decades. As Jowell observes:

[21] HC Deb., vol. 781, cols. 46–7 (Mr Cledwyn Hughes).

[22] R. Austin, 'Judicial review of subjective discretion: At the Rubicon: whither now?' (1975) 28 *CLP* 150, 154.

> In the space of just five years the attitude of the courts to the administration turned dramatically. Power conferred broadly was no longer read as necessarily conferring unfettered discretion. In *Padfield* it was even said that unfettered discretion is not recognised in law. There were of course cases the other way. Where national security was involved, the courts would tend to defer to the executive, but the position had been reached where virtually no state power was unreviewable. And the courts were increasingly ready to extend their categories of review.[23]

Two closely linked aspects of Lord Reid's trend-setting reasoning in *Padfield*, based on flexible purposive principles of statutory interpretation, foreshadowed this rapid expansion. First, he had asserted, quite contrary to the ruling in *Liversidge v Anderson*, that ministerial failure to give reasons was not without consequences – the court was entitled to draw its own inferences from an absence of evidence to support the decision-maker's conclusions; secondly, that the court could make its own evaluation of the weight of evidence before the decision-maker to a degree ostensibly precluded by the *Wednesbury* principle. These are points of great significance. In contrast to EU law, which imposes a positive duty for all its institutions to give reasoned decisions,[24] English law imposes no *overall* duty to give reasons[25] and, although in later chapters we shall see our courts inch towards a requirement of reasons, they have never yet gone so far as to impose a general duty.[26] Yet Shapiro talks of reasons, which permit courts properly to assess the administrative reasoning process, as the basis of all rational judicial review. It is also, Shapiro argues, a tool for expansion: 'hard look' scrutiny of reasons enables courts 'to run through, replay or reconstruct the decision-making process'[27] while remaining ostensibly on the legitimate judicial terrain of procedure. This mirrors Lord Diplock's approach in the notorious *Bromley* case.[28]

The Labour majority on the GLC had promised before election to reduce

[23] J. Jowell, 'Administrative law' in V. Bogdanor (ed.), *The British Constitution in the Twentieth Century* (Oxford University Press, 2004), p. 387.

[24] TEC Art. 253 establishing a duty for all EC institutions to give reasons for their acts and decisions: see P. Craig, *EU Administrative Law* (Oxford University Press, 2006), pp. 360–72.

[25] A start was made with the Tribunals and Inquiries Act 1958, which provided that, if a request is made at or before the time of judgment, the tribunal must give reasons for its decision. The provision is consolidated by s. 10 of the Tribunals and Inquiries Act 1992: and see n. 26 below).

[26] S. A. de Smith Lord Woolf and J. Jowell, *Judicial Review of Administrative Action*, 6th edn (Sweet & Maxwell, 2007), 7-087–108; and see G. Richardson, 'The duty to give reasons: Potential and practice' [1986] *PL* 437; P. Craig, 'The common law, reasons and administrative justice' (1994) 53 *CLJ* 282; P. Neill, 'The duty to give reasons: The openness of decision-making' in Forsyth and Hare (eds.), *The Golden Metwand and the Crooked Cord* (Oxford University Press, 1998).

[27] M. Shapiro, 'The giving reasons requirement' (1992) *University of Chicago Legal Forum* 179, 183, 206. American courts are, however, as inconsistent as their British counterparts: see J. Beermann, 'Common law and statute law in US federal administrative law', in Pearson, Harlow and Taggart (eds.), *Law in a Changing State* (Hart Publishing, 2008).

[28] *Bromley London Borough Council v Greater London Council* [1983] 1 AC 768.

bus and tube fares by 25 per cent. This was done by a grant to the London Transport Executive enabling it to budget for a deficit. The funds were provided a 'precept' or levy on the London boroughs, falling on the ratepayers (those who paid local taxes) of all boroughs. Bromley, a borough controlled by Conservatives, challenged the legality of the scheme. Dividing those affected by the policy of fares subsidy into passengers, residents, ratepayers and electors, Lord Diplock drew on the equitable principle of 'fiduciary duty' to prioritise the interests of ratepayers:

> *Lord Diplock:* My Lords, the conflicting interests which the GLC had to balance in deciding whether or not to go ahead with the 25 per cent reduction in fares, notwithstanding the loss of grant from central government funds that this would entail, were those of passengers and the ratepayers. It is well established that a local authority owes a fiduciary duty to the ratepayers from whom it obtains moneys needed to carry out its statutory functions, and that this includes a duty not to expend those moneys thriftlessly but to deploy the full financial resources available to it to the best advantage; the financial resources of the GLC that are relevant to the present appeals being the rate fund obtained by issuing precepts and the grants from central government respectively. The existence of this duty throws light upon the true construction of the much-debated phrase in section 1(1) [of the Transport (London) Act 1969] 'integrated, efficient and economic transport facilities and services'. 'Economic' in this context must I think mean in the economic interests of passengers and the ratepayers looked at together, i.e. keeping to a minimum the total financial burden that the persons in these two categories have to share between them for the provision by the LTE in conjunction with the railways board and the bus company of an integrated and efficient public transport system for Greater London . . . I think that the GLC had a discretion as to the proportions in which that total financial burden should be allocated between passengers and the ratepayers. What are the limits of that discretion . . . does not, in my view, arise, because the GLC's decision was not simply about allocating a total financial burden between passengers and the ratepayers, it was also a decision to increase that total burden so as nearly to double it and to place the whole of the increase on the ratepayers. For, as the GLC well knew when it took the decision to reduce the fares, it would entail a loss of rate grant from central government funds amounting to some 50 million, which would have to be made good by the ratepayers as a result of the GLC's decision. So the total financial burden to be shared by passengers and the ratepayers for the provision of an integrated and efficient public passenger transport system was to be increased by an improvement in the efficiency of the system, and the whole of the extra 50 million was to be recovered from the ratepayers. That would, in my view, clearly be a thriftless use of moneys obtained by the GLC from ratepayers and a deliberate failure to deploy to the best advantage the full financial resources available to it by avoiding any action that would involve forfeiting grants from central government funds. It was thus a breach of the fiduciary duty owed by the GLC to the ratepayers. I accordingly agree with your Lordships that the precept issued pursuant to the decision was ultra vires and therefore void.

Here Lord Diplock uses the 'wide' ultra vires principle in two distinct ways. First, he re-formulates Lord Greene's doctrine of *Wednesbury* unreasonableness in a way that anticipates his speech in the *GCHQ* case (p. 107 below), using it to structure administrative discretion as a model of reasoned decision-making. Secondly, a supposed general principle of administrative law (fiduciary duty)[29] is introduced as a 'relevant consideration' in the light of which the statutory duty *must* be interpreted. Invoking the first limb of the *Wednesbury* principle, Lord Diplock had actually turned it on its head. This striking example of judicial creativity caused public uproar, provoking accusations from politicians that the judges were 'arrogating to themselves political decisions', and academic criticism of the 'insular and pedantic reasoning' on which the decision was based. The more pragmatic response of the GLC was to double fares. Later they introduced new proposals (the 'Balanced Plan') in an effort to conform to the judgment while maintaining their policy of fares subsidy. A second challenge to the legality of the Balanced Plan was rejected by the High Court.[30]

4. Rationality

Herbert Simon based his model of 'bounded rationality', in which information-gathering is a prerequisite of rational decision-making, on the maxim 'No conclusions without premises.' If they are not to act arbitrarily and capriciously in taking decisions, decision-makers need to narrow down their choices: to find a way, as Simon put it, of 'avoiding distraction (or at least too much distraction) and focusing on the things that need attention at a given time'.[31] Rational choice is the process of 'selecting alternatives which are conducive to the achievement of previously selected goals' or 'the selection of the alternative which will maximise the decision-maker's values, the selection being made following a comprehensive analysis of alternatives and their consequences'. Rationality does not dictate goals but acts as a pathway to a goal: 'all reason can do is help us reach agreed-on goals more efficiently'. Inside public administration, we have seen that rationality underlies the audit methodology of NPM described in Chapter 2; it is also the rationale of both regulatory theory and risk regulation described in Chapter 6. To one experienced judge, administrative and judicial rationality are linked: 'The model of bounded rationality has in common with administrative law a focus on process and procedure; there is, at least on the

[29] The idea of fiduciary duty can be traced to *Roberts v Hopwood* [1925] AC 578, where the House of Lords supported a district auditor's surcharge on councillors for paying to men and women a standard minimum wage above the national average. Lord Atkinson described the council as standing 'somewhat in the position of trustees or managers of the property of others'.

[30] HC Deb., vol. 12, col. 418 (Mr Lyon). See J. Griffith, 'The Law Lords and the GLC', *Marxism Today* (Feb 1982) 29. See also D. Pannick, 'The Law Lords and the needs of contemporary society' (1982) 53 *Pol. Q* 318. And see *R v London Transport Executive, ex p. Greater London Council* [1983] 2 WLR 702.

[31] H. Simon, *Reason in Human Affairs* (Blackwell, 1983), pp. 2, 5, 77, 106.

surface, a good fit with the terminology of rational decision-making.'[32] Thus the first limb of the *Wednesbury* test directs the decision-maker to accumulate his evidence, taking into account all relevant and excluding all irrelevant material but – at least as applied by Lord Greene – does not question the decision-maker's objectives. *Padfield* adds a secondary dimension: reasons render the decision-maker's reasoning transparent, opening it up to external scrutiny.

But as judicial review increasingly impinged on discretionary decision-making, the contrast between the standards required of administrators and those of judicial decision-making, which remained inherently discretionary, began to stand out. To be rational, judicial review too should be reasoned: it 'makes sense only if the judge is in a position to enunciate or explain the rule on which his decision is based'.[33] And there was a further reason why judicial review needed to be presented as rational. The malleable nature of its general principles opened the judges to the complaints of 'playing politics' made after the *Bromley* case. Green light theorist John Griffith was not afraid to label the judiciary's decisions 'political':

> In our system for two principal reasons, the judiciary have a wide scope for the making of political decisions. First, statute law does not seek with any precision to indicate where, between Ministers and judges, final decision making should lie. Secondly, judges themselves, in the common law tradition of judicial creativity, frequently invent or re-discover rules of law which enable them to intervene and to exercise political judgment in areas that hitherto had been understood to be outside their province. In the event, for these two reasons, legislators and Ministers and public authorities are continuously being surprised to discover that, in the view of the judges, they do not have the powers they thought they had.[34]

By encouraging a more logical and coherent approach, proponents of judicial review felt this type of argument could be refuted. Decision-making seems more objective if presented as rational and scientific. (Consider, for example, the use made by Lord Diplock of the fiduciary principle to neutralise the hotly political *Bromley* decision.) Jowell and Lester attacked the loose texture of *Wednesbury* unreasonableness for conferring subjective or 'strong' discretion on the judiciary, arguing that 'intellectual honesty requires a further and better explanation as to why the act is unreasonable'.[35] A change in terminology from

[32] See J. Laws, 'Wednesbury' in Forsyth and Hare (eds.), *The Golden Metwand and the Crooked Cord*.

[33] J. Kahn, 'Discretionary power and the administrative judge' (1980) 29 *ICLQ* 521, 525. See now D. Dyzenhas and M. Taggart, 'Reasoned decisions and legal theory' in Edlin (ed.), *Common Law Theory* (Cambridge University Press, 2007).

[34] J. Griffith, 'Constitutional and administrative law', in Archer and Martin (eds.), *More Law Reform Now!* (Barry Rose, 1983), p. 55; and see J. Griffith, *The Politics of the Judiciary* (Fontana, 1977).

[35] J. Jowell and A. Lester, 'Beyond *Wednesbury*: Substantive principles of administrative law' [1987] *PL* 368, 371.

'reasonableness' to 'rationality' seemed to point in the desired direction. In the highly charged *GCHQ* case[36] where the change was made, it was especially important for judicial review to appear scientific, objective and apolitical. The case was fought by the civil-service unions, which had members working in the general communications headquarters of the security services (GCHQ) when the Foreign Secretary suddenly announced to the House of Commons that GCHQ employees would no longer be allowed to join a trade union. The unions argued that they had not been consulted. The minister stood on the prerogative powers, arguing that they were non-justiciable. The House of Lords ruled (i) that the prerogative powers were in general justiciable (see p. 10 above); and (ii) that the unions had a 'legitimate expectation' of being consulted before the change was made. However, the House found for the Government on the ground (iii) that security and the defence of the realm were involved.

Usually cited as the basis of the modern doctrine of judicial review, Lord Diplock's three principles still conform largely to the classical grounds as they had evolved over the centuries, though he left room for the development of new principles. But scrutinise Lord Diplock's account of the *Wednesbury* principle carefully. Has he conflated two separate principles: rationality and a subsidiary category of '*Wednesbury* unreasonableness'? Boundaries are also set by Lord Diplock's reference to 'decisions of a kind that generally involve the application of government policy'. Here, he suggests, judicial process is not adapted to provide the right answer, because the decisions involve 'competing policy considerations which, if the executive discretion is to be wisely exercised, need to be weighed against one another: a balancing exercise which judges by their upbringing and experience are ill-qualified to perform'. Later in the chapter we shall see this limitation evolve into the 'deference' principle increasingly used in human rights cases:

> *Lord Diplock:* Judicial review has I think developed to a stage today when . . . one can conveniently classify under three heads the grounds upon which administrative action is subject to control by judicial review. The first ground I would call 'illegality', the second 'irrationality' and the third 'procedural impropriety'. That is not to say that further development on a case by case basis may not in course of time add further grounds. I have in mind particularly the possible adoption in the future of the principle of 'proportionality' which is recognised in the administrative law of several of our fellow members of the European Economic Community . . .
>
> By 'illegality' as a ground for judicial review I mean that the decision maker must understand correctly the law that regulates his decision-making power and must give effect to it. Whether he has or not is *par excellence* a justiciable question to be decided, in the event of dispute, by those persons, the judges, by whom the judicial power of the state is exercisable.

[36] *Council of Civil Service Unions v Minister for the Civil Service* [1985] AC 374.

> By 'irrationality' I mean what can by now be succinctly referred to as '*Wednesbury* unreasonableness'. It applies to a decision which is so outrageous in its defiance of logic or of accepted moral standards that no sensible person who had applied his mind to the question to be decided could have arrived at it. Whether a decision falls within this category is a question that judges by their training and experience should be well equipped to answer, or else there would be something badly wrong with our judicial system . . .
>
> I have described the third head as 'procedural impropriety' rather than failure to observe basic rules of natural justice or failure to act with procedural fairness towards the person who will be affected by the decision. This is because susceptibility to judicial review under this head covers also failure by an administrative tribunal to observe procedural rules that are expressly laid down in the legislative instrument by which its jurisdiction is conferred, even where such failure does not involve any denial of natural justice . . .
>
> While I see no a priori reason to rule out 'irrationality' as a ground for judicial review of a ministerial decision taken in the exercise of 'prerogative' powers, I find it difficult to envisage in any of the various fields in which the prerogative remains the only source of the relevant decision-making power a decision of a kind that would be open to attack through the judicial process upon this ground. Such decisions will generally involve the application of government policy. The reasons for the decision-maker taking one course rather than another do not normally involve questions to which, if disputed, the judicial process is adapted to provide the right answer, by which I mean that the kind of evidence that is admissible under judicial procedures and the way in which it has to be adduced tend to exclude from the attention of the court competing policy considerations which, if the executive discretion is to be wisely exercised, need to be weighed against one another: a balancing exercise which judges by their upbringing and experience are ill-qualified to perform. So I leave this as an open question to be dealt with on a case to case basis . . .

Paul Craig, who describes himself as a 'liberal interpretivist' sympathetic to the concept of a principled and orderly legal universe infused by liberal values,[37] sees the new judicial review as a spectrum, with the classical, limited *Wednesbury* test of reasonableness lying at one end and 'judicial substitution of judgment, whereby the court imposes what it believes to be the correct meaning of the term or issue in question' at the other. 'The theme that runs throughout this area is therefore the desire to fashion a criterion that will allow judicial control, without thereby leading to substitution of judgment or too great an intrusion on the merits'.[38] With this in mind, an enthusiastic and critical academic literature with great faith in rationality has stimulated the evolution of new principles which are perceived or can be presented as evaluative in character – including the proportionality principle mentioned by Lord Diplock and imposed by the ECtHR in human rights cases (below). Both the rationality and proportionality tests act as constraints on the decision-maker but also

[37] P. Craig, 'Theory and values in public law: A response' in Craig and Rawlings (eds.), *Law and Administration in Europe* (Oxford University Press, 2003) and 'Theory, "pure theory" and values in public law' [2005] *PL* 429.

[38] P. Craig, *Administrative Law*, 6th edn (Sweet and Maxwell, 2008), p. 615.

on the adjudicator, prompting them to articulate the reasoning on which their decisions are based. This point is illustrated in the *Miss Behavin'* case, below.

5. Rights-based review

According to Dworkin's 'principle of political integrity', law must be *morally* principled and both adjudicators and lawmakers are duty bound 'to make the total set of laws *morally* coherent'.[39] Dworkin famously distinguished 'principle' from 'policy', severing the legal universe of rules and principles from the world of policy and politics. 'Policy' relates to the general or public interest; is characteristically concerned with economic or social priorities; and is not required, according to Dworkin, to be consistent. 'Principles' are concerned with justice and fairness and are governed by values of integrity and consistency. MacCormick exposes the fallacy:

> Even if it be the case . . . that moral values and principles have some objective truth and universal validity, it remains also the case that people inveterately disagree about them . . . Political principles are . . . also subjects of inveterate disagreement. Legal systems result from a patchwork of historical assertions of contentious and changing political principles, political compromises and mere political muddles. That from which laws emerge is controversial, even if some or all of the controversies concern moral issues on which there may in principle be a single right answer.[40]

Dworkin's work, with its hint of a 'single right answer',[41] has profoundly influenced the debate over law and values. It has helped, as Allan explains, to set the scene for a 'principled' judicial review based on the concept of rights:

> Dworkin's account of the distinction between principle and policy makes a helpful contribution to the task of defining the nature and limits of public law. Questions of principle are those which concern the scope and content of individual rights, as opposed to the general welfare or the public interest. Matters of public interest or public policy should be determined by the political branches of the government – executive or legislature. Questions of right, by contrast, are peculiarly the province of the courts. As counter-majoritarian entitlements or 'trumps' over general utility or the public interest, the relative insulation of the judges from the ordinary political process ought to be specially conducive to their protection and enforcement . . . [A]dministrative law may be helpfully interpreted as a system of public law rights and the legitimate boundaries of judicial review may be found in the process of defining and enforcing those rights.[42]

[39] R. Dworkin, *Law's Empire* (Fontana, 1986), Ch. 6.

[40] N. MacCormick, *HLA Hart* (Stanford University Press, 1981), p. 30. See also J. Waldron, *Law and Disagreement* (Harvard University Press, 1999).

[41] R. Dworkin, 'No right answer?' in Hacker and Raz (eds.), *Law, Morality and Society* (Oxford University Press, 1977) but see M. Weaver, 'Herbert, Hercules and the plural society: A "knot" in the social bond' (1978) 41 *MLR* 660.

[42] Allan, *Law, Liberty and Justice: The legal foundations of British constitutionalism*, p. 7.

This highly artificial distinction is naturally hard to apply, if only because so many of the disputes on which courts are called to adjudicate concern a conflict between individual and collective interests. Arguably, rights-based theories of law create an automatic bias towards individualism. This is accentuated by the classical view of English administrative law as concerned in essence with 'individual versus state' disputes.[43] As we saw in Chapter 2, however, the natural bias came to seem justifiable in light of the increased powers and interventionist character of the regulatory state.

Allan leaves open the question whether 'rights' have a moral content, though elsewhere he suggests that the common law embodies 'albeit imperfectly, a set of constitutional values transcending the ordinarily more transient, and particular, rules enacted by the legislature'.[44] Sir John Laws, who also sees values as 'immanent in the common law', more openly expresses his view that 'constitutional rights' are 'higher-order law':

> The democratic credentials of an elected government cannot justify its enjoyment of a right to abolish fundamental freedoms. If its power in the state is in the last resort absolute, such fundamental rights as free expression are only privileges; no less so if the absolute power rests in an elected body. The byword of every tyrant is 'My word is law'; a democratic assembly having sovereign power beyond the reach of curtailment or review may make just such an assertion, and its elective base cannot immunise it from playing the tyrant's role . . .
>
> A people's aspiration to democracy and the imperative of individual freedoms go hand in hand. Without democracy the government is by definition autocratic; though it may set just laws in place, and even elaborate a constitution providing for fundamental rights, there is no sanction for their preservation save revolution . . . the need for higher-order law is dictated by the logic of the very notion of government under law.[45]

We have now reached the point of concluding that a democratic constitution must be preserved against incursions on its core values, even if this entails some limitations on the powers of government and Parliament. But the view that the 'good constitution' must recognise and entrench 'a bedrock of rights' as 'higher-order law' to which 'even Parliament is subject' challenges our accepted constitutional order; Griffith has indeed called the position 'unbalanced' and 'tenable only on a misreading of constitutional history'.[46]

[43] P. McAuslan, 'Administrative law, collective consumption and judicial policy' (1983) 46 *MLR* 1.

[44] T. Allan, 'Fairness, equality, rationality: Constitutional theory and constitutionalism' in Forsyth and Hare, *The Golden Metwand*, p. 17.

[45] J. Laws, 'Is the High Court the guardian of fundamental constitutional rights?' [1993] *PL* 59, 61; 'Law and democracy' [1995] *PL* 72, 84 and 'The constitution: Morals and rights' [1996] *PL* 622.

[46] J. Griffith, 'Judges and the constitution' in Rawlings (ed.), *Law, Society and Economy* (Oxford University Press, 1997) and 'The brave new world of Sir John Laws' (2000) 63 *MLR* 159. Support for this view comes from J. Goldsworthy, *The Sovereignty of Parliament: History and philosophy* (Oxford University Press, 1999). P. Craig, 'Constitutional foundations, the rule of law and supremacy' [2003] *PL* 92 seeks to align the rival positions, arguing that parliamentary sovereignty was never as absolute as modern interpretations of Dicey pretend.

An unwritten constitution without a bill of rights in which parliamentary sovereignty is the dominant constitutional norm sits uncomfortably with the concept of a 'higher-order law' logically prior to the democratic system with the judiciary as custodian. Poole calls the proposition 'nothing less than the reconfiguration of public law as a species of constitutional politics centred on the common law court. The court, acting as primary guardian of a society's fundamental values and rights, assumes, on this account, a pivotal role within the polity.'[47] An added problem with the idea is that judges are unelected and, we might add, that Britain has no 'Big-C' Constitutional Court.[48]

'Higher-order law' must logically precede the democratic system as it operates for the time being. It cannot therefore depend, as the *ultra vires* principle supposedly does, on the 'will' or 'intent' of Parliament; its general principles must be embedded in the common law and form the context in which statute is interpreted.[49] To underpin this point a giant stride was necessary: 'to dismiss rival conceptions – in particular those that take legislative sovereignty as their starting point or otherwise underestimate the normative potential of the common law – as being anomalous within British constitutional history.'[50] We are moving close to the doctrine of 'common law constitutionalism' by which parliamentary sovereignty was to be reconfigured. Lord Woolf in a public lecture treated the rule of law as a *grundnorm* or primary rule that neither Parliament nor the courts could repudiate:

> If Parliament did the unthinkable, then . . . the courts would also be required to act in a manner which would be without precedent. Some judges might choose to do so by saying that it was an irrebuttable presumption that Parliament could never intend such a result. I myself would consider there were advantages in making it clear that ultimately there are even limits on the supremacy of Parliament.[51]

Lord Woolf chose not to expand on what the unthinkable might be. Would it, for example, cover David Blunkett's planned ouster clause that we met in Chapter 1?

It was left to Lord Steyn in *Jackson* to hypothesise circumstances in which the courts might take action. The issue was whether the Hunting Act 2004, passed without the consent of the House of Lords in terms of the Parliament

[47] T. Poole, 'Back to the future? Unearthing the theory of common law constitutionalism' (2003) 23 *OJLS* 435, 449 and 'Questioning common law constitutionalism' (2005) 25 *Legal Studies* 142. See similarly D. Feldman, 'Public law values in the House of Lords' (1990) 106 *LQR* 246.

[48] See on the constitutional relationship between the three branches of government subsequent to the Constitutional Reform Act 2005, House of Lords Constitution Committee, *Relationships between the executive, the judiciary and Parliament*, HL 151 (2006/7). And see R. Bellamy, *Political Constitutionalism* (Cambridge University Press, 2007).

[49] D. Oliver, 'Is ultra vires the basis of judicial review?' [1987] *PL* 543; P. Craig, 'Competing models of judicial review' [1999] *PL* 428; C. Forsyth and M. Elliott, 'The legitimacy of judicial review' [2003] *PL* 286.

[50] Poole, 'Back to the Future', pp. 439–40.

[51] H. Woolf, 'Droit public - English style' [1995] *PL* 57, 68–9.

Acts 1911 and 1949, was valid. In the course of argument, the Attorney-General had asserted that no exceptions other than that contained in the 1911 Act of legislation to extend the life of Parliament are placed on the use of the Parliament Acts. Clearly uncomfortable with an interpretation that would extend to constitutional change as fundamental as abolition of the House of Lords or monarchy without further safeguards, the Court of Appeal had proposed reading in a limitation to except 'fundamental constitutional change' from the purview of the Acts. Some of the Law Lords also hinted at possible constitutional limitations; Lord Steyn was the most forthright. The Acts could theoretically be used to introduce 'oppressive and wholly undemocratic legislation' or:

> to abolish judicial review of flagrant abuse of power by a government or even the role of the ordinary courts in standing between the executive and citizens. This is where we may have to come back to the point about the supremacy of Parliament. We do not in the United Kingdom have an uncontrolled constitution as the Attorney General implausibly asserts . . . The classic account given by Dicey of the doctrine of the supremacy of Parliament, pure and absolute as it was, can now be seen to be out of place in the modern United Kingdom. Nevertheless, the supremacy of Parliament is still the *general* principle of our constitution. It is a construct of the common law. The judges created this principle. If that is so, it is not unthinkable that circumstances could arise where the courts may have to qualify a principle established on a different hypothesis of constitutionalism. In exceptional circumstances involving an attempt to abolish judicial review or the ordinary role of the courts, the Appellate Committee of the House of Lords or a new Supreme Court may have to consider whether this is a constitutional fundamental which even a sovereign Parliament acting at the behest of a complaisant House of Commons cannot abolish.[52]

Any such power (on which the Law Lords reserved their position) could only be a 'nuclear deterrent'; otherwise it would be a wholly undemocratic remedy for an undemocratic malady.

More moderately, Goldsworthy argues that it is not for the judges *alone* to revoke (implicitly or otherwise) the doctrine of parliamentary sovereignty. The doctrine is not, as it is sometimes said to be, judge-made and judges have no authority unilaterally to change or reject it. The unwritten constitution depends on a measure of consensus, implicit in the way Dicey hives off legal from political sovereignty. Change, which has to start somewhere, can be initiated either by Parliament or by the courts; but it has to be ratified by an 'official consensus'.[53] Governments recognise this when they seek approval of constitutional change in a referendum, as was done before

[52] *Jackson v Attorney General* [2005] EWCA Civ 126; [2005] QB 579 (CA); [2005] UKHL 56, [2005] 3 WLR 733 (HL) [102]. The other Law Lord to express similar views was Lord Hope [103] and, more tentatively, Baroness Hale [159] and Lord Carswell [194].

[53] Goldsworthy, *The Sovereignty of Parliament*, pp. 244–5.

devolution. Judges recognise it by drawing back from cases that involve 'political questions', as they did when asked to derail ratification of the Maastricht Treaty.[54]

To read an exception for 'fundamental constitutional change' into the Parliament Acts, as the Court of Appeal did in *Jackson*, would not shake the constitution. Courts can, as Goldsworthy said, legitimately institute change, affording an opportunity of parliamentary reconsideration and public debate. But notice the language used by the judges: 'fundamental constitutional change'; 'in exceptional circumstances' (Lord Steyn); 'if Parliament did the unthinkable' (Lord Woolf). The Parliament Acts might require re-thinking in the light of the Attorney-General's claims. There might – or might not – be support for the position that they should not be used for purposes of 'fundamental constitutional change'. But to have ruled that the Parliament Acts should not be used to pass the Hunting Bill would almost certainly have been unwise. Hotly contested though it was, the Bill was not generally regarded as involving fundamental constitutional change. This was indeed later confirmed by the Law Lords, when the Hunting Act survived the test of proportionality, used by the House to measure compatibility with the European Convention.[55] There was wide popular support from around 50 per cent of the population for anti-hunting measures, promised and put to the people in the Labour Party's election manifesto. Thus the unelected House of Lords could be seen as overstepping its powers; as Baroness Hale put the position, 'The party with the permanent majority in the unelected House of Lords could forever thwart the will of the elected House of Commons no matter how clearly that will had been endorsed by the electorate.'[56] To invalidate the Act might therefore have provoked the 'unthinkable'.

6. The shadow of the Convention

In Chapter 1 we quoted Lord Bingham to the effect that the rule of law demands (i) adequate protection of human rights plus (ii) compliance with the state's international law obligations. This 'thickened' conception of the rule of law justifies judges, as self-styled guardians of the rule of law, in turning to human rights law and precepts of international law as a source of values and principles. Before 1998, successive governments had left the judiciary in an awkward dilemma. They had ratified the European Convention (1951) and agreed the right of individual petition (1966). Yet they had several times expressly declined to incorporate the ECHR into English law. In *ex p. Brind*,[57]

[54] *R v Foreign Secretary, ex p. Rees-Mogg* [1994] 1 All ER 457. And see R. Rawlings, 'Legal politics: The United Kingdom and ratification of the treaty on European Union (Part two)' [1994] *PL* 367, 369–75.

[55] *R (Countryside Alliance) v Attorney-General* [2007] UKHL 52.

[56] *Jackson v Attorney General* [156–7].

[57] *R v Home Secretary, ex p. Brind* [1991] 1 AC 696.

the House of Lords confirmed our 'dualist' legal tradition, which does not automatically incorporate international conventions into domestic law. They held indirect 'judicial incorporation' impossible; only the legislature could take such a radical step. In construing any ambiguous provision in domestic legislation, the courts would presume that Parliament intended to legislate in conformity with the ECHR; but it did not form part of UK law and was not directly enforceable in a British court.

Although *Brind* closed the door to judicial incorporation, it could not close the door on the ECHR; it only fuelled the argument for legislative incorporation. By the 1990s, the UK was a constant defendant in the Court of Human Rights at Strasbourg (ECtHR). Rights-conscious litigants and determined pressure groups versed in the techniques of the international human rights movement were pushing hard for the Convention to be applied at domestic level. Extrajudicially, leading members of the judiciary called for incorporation.[58] In their judicial capacity, judges often treated the ECHR as 'persuasive', reading it 'as a series of propositions, [which] largely represent legal norms or values which are either already inherent in our law, or, so far as they are not, may be integrated into it by the judges'.[59] A new rights-base for judicial review seemed to be under construction. In a highly significant test case brought on behalf of immigrants, the Court of Appeal demanded legislative authorisation for a government policy introduced by regulation that amounted in their view to 'inhumane treatment'.[60] A right of access to the court began to be seen as constitutional in character.[61] In *Wheeler v Leicester Corporation*,[62] Browne-Wilkinson LJ drew on the traditional common law freedom to 'do anything not expressly proscribed by law' to protect freedom of speech and conscience. The movement, in which Laws J participated, can clearly be linked to his interest in 'higher-order law'.

The position fell to be tested in *ex p. Smith*, a case brought by Stonewall, a campaigning group, on behalf of five claimants administratively discharged from the armed forces for homosexual tendencies in accordance with an MOD policy document issued in 1994. All had exemplary service records. They sought judicial review on the basis: (i) of a breach of the ECHR and (ii) that on any test of reasonableness the policy was irrational. Sir Thomas Bingham MR explained:

[58] T. Bingham, 'The European Convention on Human Rights: Time to incorporate' (1993) 109 *LQR* 390; N. Browne-Wilkinson, 'The infiltration of a Bill of Rights' [1992] *PL* 397.

[59] T. Poole, 'Legitimacy, rights and judicial review ' (2005) 25 *OJLS* 697.

[60] *R v Social Security Secretary, ex p. JC WI* [1996] 4 All ER 385 (p. XXX below).

[61] *R v Lord Chancellor, ex p. Witham* [1997] 2 All ER 779; and see *Simms* and *Daly* (p. 118 below).

[62] *Wheeler v Leicester Corporation* [1985] 2 All ER 151 (CA); [1985] AC 1054 (HL) noted in A. Hutchinson and M. Jones, 'Wheeler-dealing: An essay on law, politics and speech' (1988) 15 *JLS* 263. See similarly Lord Steyn in *Simms* (see p. 118 below); *Anderson v UK* (1997) 25 EHRR 172; and compare Mason CJ in *Nationwide News Pty Ltd v Wills* (1992) 177 CLR 1; *Australian Capital Television Pty Ltd v Commonwealth* (1992) 177 CLR 106.

> [T]he court may not interfere with the exercise of an administrative discretion on substantive grounds save where the court is satisfied that the decision is unreasonable in the sense that it is beyond the range of responses open to a reasonable decision-maker. But in judging whether the decision-maker has exceeded this margin of appreciation the human rights context is important. The more substantial the interference with human rights, the more the court will require by way of justification before it is satisfied that the decision is reasonable in the sense outlined above . . .
>
> It was argued for the ministry . . . that a test more exacting than *Wednesbury* was appropriate in this case . . . The Divisional Court rejected this argument and so do I. The greater the policy content of a decision, and the more remote the subject matter of a decision from ordinary judicial experience, the more hesitant the court must necessarily be in holding a decision to be irrational. That is good law and, like most good law, common sense. Where decisions of a policy-laden, esoteric or security-based nature are in issue, even greater caution than normal must be shown in applying the test, but the test itself is sufficiently flexible to cover all situations.
>
> The present cases do not cover the lives or liberty of those involved . . . [but] the appellants' rights as human beings are very much in issue. It is now accepted that this issue is justiciable. This does not of course mean that the court is thrust into the position of primary decision-maker. It is not the constitutional role of the court to regulate the conditions of service in the armed forces of the Crown, nor has it the expertise to do so. But it has the constitutional role and duty of ensuring that the rights of citizens are not abused by the unlawful exercise of executive power. While the court must properly defer to the expertise of responsible decision-makers, it must not shrink from its fundamental duty 'to do right to all manner of people'.[63]

A wide range of options was open to the Court of Appeal in *Smith*. It might have ruled:

(i) that the issue fell within the area of prerogative defence powers and was non-justiciable (see Lord Diplock in the *GCHQ* case)

(ii) applying the rules of natural justice, that no one should be dismissed without a fair hearing (*Ridge v Baldwin*, see Chapter 14)

(iii) that the policy was valid if it was not 'so unreasonable that no reasonable defence minister would adopt such a policy' (standard *Wednesbury* review)

(iv) that the policy was so unreasonable that Parliament must be invited to endorse it in statute (the *JCWI case*, see p. 114 above) – this option was complicated by the fact that a parliamentary committee had recently confirmed the impugned policy[64]

[63] *R v Ministry of Defence, ex p. Smith and Grady* [1996] 1 All ER 257. A third claim that the EU equality directives had been breached is not dealt with here.

[64] In *Nottinghamshire County Council v Environment Secretary* [1986] AC 240 and *R v Environment Secretary, ex p. Hammersmith and Fulham London Borough Council* [1991] 1 AC 521 the Law Lords had hesitated to scrutinise policy decisions in matters recently considered by Parliament.

(v) that in cases involving apparent violations of an ECHR right, the proportionality test should be applied (but see *Brind*).

What the Court of Appeal did was to refine option (iii) by recognising three broad categories of *Wednesbury* unreasonableness, applicable to different types of case:

(a) 'extreme deference', as in security cases, the so-called 'super-*Wednesbury* test'
(b) standard *Wednesbury* unreasonableness, generally applicable[65]
(c) 'anxious scrutiny', available where an important interest is at stake and particularly in human rights cases, a position already adopted by the House of Lords in *Bugdacay*.[66]

This simple analysis is intended to demonstrate how broad the discretion of the judiciary actually is. Several forms of 'judgment discretion' are illustrated: first, the choice involved in classification – into which of categories (i) to (v) to fit the case; secondly, the discretion latent in the standard of review is revealed in (a) to (c) and (v) as flexible and shifting; thirdly, the flexibility of the general principles, demonstrated earlier in respect of the *Wednesbury* principle. The three-tier structure of (a) to (c) brings additional flexibility, allowing judges an escape route from the already flexible standard of *Wednesbury* review. Each choice on the scale is a step to greater intensity.

Believing that the previous case law rendered success unlikely and that domestic remedies would be viewed by the ECtHR as effectively exhausted, the applicants took the road to Strasbourg. In *Lustig-Prean and Beckett*, the ECtHR unanimously found a violation of Art. 8, which protects private and family life, home and correspondence; in *Smith and Grady*, delivered on the same day, the Court found a violation of Art. 8 together with a violation of ECHR Art. 13 (right to an effective remedy):

Article 8: The Court considered the investigations, and in particular the interviews of the applicants, to have been exceptionally intrusive, it noted that the administrative discharges had a profound effect on the applicants' careers and prospects and considered the absolute and general character of the policy, which admitted of no exception, to be striking. It therefore considered that the investigations conducted into the applicants' sexual orientation together with their discharge from the armed forces constituted especially grave interferences with their private lives.

As to whether the Government had demonstrated 'particularly convincing and weighty reasons' to justify those interferences, the Court noted that the Government's core

[65] See A. Le Sueur, 'The rise and ruin of unreasonableness?' (2005) 10 *Judicial Review* 32; T. Hickman, 'The reasonableness principle: Reassessing its place in the public sphere' (2004) 63 *CLJ* 166.

[66] *Bugdacay v Home Secretary* [1987] AC 514. See also *R (Thangarasa and Yogathas) v Home Secretary* [2002] UKHL 36. And see N. Blake, 'Judicial review of expulsion decisions' in Dyzenhaus (ed), *The Unity of Public Law* (Hart Publishing, 2004), p. 242.

argument was that the presence of homosexuals in the armed forces would have a substantial and negative effect on morale and, consequently, on the fighting power and operational effectiveness of the armed forces. The Government relied, in this respect, on the Report of the Homosexual Policy Assessment Team (HPAT) published in February 1996. The Court found that, insofar as the views of armed forces' personnel outlined in the HPAT Report could be considered representative, those views were founded solely upon the negative attitudes of heterosexual personnel towards those of homosexual orientation. It was noted that the Ministry of Defence policy was not based on a particular moral standpoint and the physical capability, courage, dependability and skills of homosexual personnel were not in question. Insofar as those negative views represented a predisposed bias on the part of heterosexuals, the Court considered that those negative attitudes could not, of themselves, justify the interferences in question any more than similar negative attitudes towards those of a different race, origin or colour.

Article 13:

The sole issue before the domestic courts in the context of the judicial review proceedings was whether the policy was irrational and that the test of irrationality was that expounded by Sir Thomas Bingham MR in the Court of Appeal. According to that test, a court was not entitled to interfere with the exercise of an administrative discretion on substantive grounds save where that court was satisfied that the decision was unreasonable, in the sense that it was beyond the range of responses open to a reasonable decision-maker. In judging whether the decision-maker had exceeded this margin of appreciation, the human rights context was important, so that the more substantial the interference with human rights, the more the court would require by way of justification before it was satisfied that the decision was reasonable.

The Court also noted that Sir Thomas Bingham MR emphasised that the threshold beyond which a decision would be considered irrational was a high one and it considered that this was confirmed by the judgments of the High Court and of the Court of Appeal. Both of those courts had commented very favourably on the applicants' submissions challenging the Government's justification of the policy and both courts considered that there was an argument to be made that the policy was in breach of the United Kingdom's Convention obligations. The Court observed that, nevertheless, those domestic courts were bound to conclude, given the test of irrationality applicable, that the Ministry of Defence policy could not be said to be irrational.

The Court therefore found that the threshold at which the domestic courts could find the policy of the Ministry of Defence irrational had been placed so high that it effectively excluded any consideration by the domestic courts of the question of whether the interference with the applicants' private lives had answered a pressing social need or was proportionate to the national security and public order aims pursued by the Government, principles which lie at the heart of the Court's analysis under Article 8.

The Court concluded, accordingly, that the applicants did not have an effective domestic remedy in relation to the violation of their right to respect for their private lives.[67]

[67] *Lustig-Prean and Beckett v UK* (1999) 29 EHRR 493; *Smith and Grady v UK* (1999) 29 EHRR 548.

Smith and Grady was one of a number of judgments in which the ECtHR hinted that judicial review was an inadequate vehicle for the protection of human rights. This jurisprudence embarrassed the British judiciary, making them:

> more sensitive to the fault-line in the British legal system that had resulted in repeated failures to give sufficient legal protection to individual rights. It caused our senior judges to take European Convention law more seriously than had been the case in the 1970s and 1980s; and, eventually, to support moves to make Convention rights directly enforceable in British courts.[68]

Reluctance of successive governments to 'bring the Convention home', coupled with the unwillingness of the judges to do the work of the legislature, had left the national judges in a very exposed position.

Two transitional cases, decided on facts occurring before the HRA came into force, confirmed the new judicial power base in human rights. In *Simms*,[69] the prison authorities sought to bar interviews with journalists seeking to investigate the possibility of wrongful conviction by banning them from making professional use of material obtained during prison visits. The restriction was contained in rule 37 of the Prison Rules, subordinate legislation made under authority of s. 47(1) of the Prison Act 1952. Lord Steyn affirmed the status of freedom of expression as the 'primary democratic right, without which the rule of law is impossible' and the House, confirming that it could be defeated by 'only a pressing social need', refused to allow 'the safety valve of effective investigative journalism' to be outlawed.

In *Daly*, where the practice of reading prisoners' correspondence with legal advisers during cell searches was challenged successfully, the House moved towards a convergence of common law and Convention rights, in readiness for the implementation of the HRA 1998, about to come into force. Concluding that the prison security manual was ultra vires, Lord Bingham added significantly:

> I have reached the conclusions so far expressed on an orthodox application of common law principles derived from the authorities and an orthodox domestic approach to judicial review. But the same result is achieved by reliance on the European Convention. Article 8.1 gives Mr Daly a right to respect for his correspondence. While interference with that right by a public authority may be permitted if in accordance with the law and necessary in a democratic society in the interests of national security, public safety, the prevention of disorder or crime or for protection of the rights and freedoms of others, the policy interferes with Mr Daly's exercise of his right under article 8.1 to an extent much greater than

[68] A. Lester, 'Human rights and the British Constitution', in Jowell and Oliver (eds.), *The Changing Constitution*, 5th edn (Clarendon Press, 2005), p. 69.
[69] *R v Home Secretary, ex p. Simms* [2000] 2 AC 115.

> necessity requires. In this instance, therefore, the common law and the convention yield the same result. But this need not always be so. In *Smith and Grady* [see p. 116 above], the European Court held that the orthodox domestic approach of the English courts had not given the applicants an effective remedy for the breach of their rights under article 8 of the convention because the threshold of review had been set too high. Now, following the incorporation of the Convention by the Human Rights Act 1998 and the bringing of that Act fully into force, domestic courts must themselves form a judgment whether a Convention right has been breached (conducting such inquiry as is necessary to form that judgment) and, so far as permissible under the Act, grant an effective remedy.[70]

A widely quoted passage from Lord Hoffmann in *Simms* confirmed that the HRA would not unravel the traditional relationship between Parliament and the courts. It would, however, strengthen and intensify the courts' interpretative powers:

> Parliamentary sovereignty means that Parliament can, if it chooses, legislate contrary to fundamental principles of human rights. The Human Rights Act 1998 will not detract from this power. The constraints upon its exercise by Parliament are ultimately political, not legal. But the principle of legality means that Parliament must squarely confront what it is doing and accept the political cost. Fundamental rights cannot be overridden by general or ambiguous words. This is because there is too great a risk that the full implications of their unqualified meaning may have passed unnoticed in the democratic process. In the absence of express language or necessary implication to the contrary, the courts therefore presume that even the most general words were intended to be subject to the basic rights of the individual. In this way the courts of the United Kingdom, though acknowledging the sovereignty of Parliament, apply principles of constitutionality little different from those which exist in countries where the power of the legislature is expressly limited by a constitutional document.
>
> The Human Rights Act 1998 will make three changes to this scheme of things. First, the principles of fundamental human rights which exist at common law will be supplemented by a specific text, namely the European Convention. But much of the Convention reflects the common law . . . [s]o the adoption of the text as part of domestic law is unlikely to involve radical change in our notions of fundamental human rights. Secondly, the principle of legality will be expressly enacted as a rule of construction in section 3 and will gain further support from the obligation of the Minister in charge of a Bill to make a statement of compatibility under section 19. Thirdly, in those unusual cases in which the legislative infringement of fundamental human rights is so clearly expressed as not to yield to the principle of legality, the courts will be able to draw this to the attention of Parliament by making a declaration of incompatibility. It will then be for the sovereign Parliament to decide whether or not to remove the incompatibility.[71]

70 *R (Daly) v Home Secretary* [2001] UKHL 26 [23] quoting the ECtHR cases of *Golder v UK* (1975) 1 EHRR 524; *Silver v UK* (1983) 5 EHRR 347; *Campbell and Fell v UK* (1984) 7 EHRR 137.

71 See for further exposition of the principle of legality *R v Shayler* [2002] UKHL 11 [56] (Lord Hope).

7. Rights, unreasonableness and proportionality

For Lord Steyn in *Daly*, the time had come to acknowledge that neither the standard *Wednesbury* test nor the stiffer test of 'anxious scrutiny' was 'necessarily appropriate to the protection of human rights'. Citing the three-stage *de Freitas* test of proportionality, he observed that it was 'more precise and more sophisticated than the traditional grounds of review'. Review for proportionality was not merits review and most cases would be decided in the same way whichever approach was adopted but the *intensity* of review was somewhat greater under the proportionality approach. There were two main differences:[72]

(i) Proportionality may require the reviewing court to assess the balance which the decision maker has struck, not merely whether it is within the range of rational or reasonable decisions.
(ii) The proportionality test may go further than the traditional grounds of review inasmuch as it may require attention to be directed to the relative weight accorded to interests and considerations.

Lord Cooke went rather further, labelling *Wednesbury*:

> an unfortunately retrogressive decision in English administrative law, insofar as it suggested that there are degrees of unreasonableness and that only a very extreme degree can bring an administrative decision within the legitimate scope of judicial invalidation. The depth of judicial review and the deference due to administrative discretion vary with the subject matter. It may well be, however, that the law can never be satisfied in any administrative field merely by a finding that the decision under review is not capricious or absurd.[73]

Let us look at this more closely. The *Wednesbury* test (p. 42 above) starts from the premise that the administration possesses a virtually unfettered power of policy- and decision-making, provided only:

- that the official can point to the source of his powers
- that the official has taken into account only relevant considerations and
- that the action taken does not seem to a judge to be wholly unreasonable.[74]

A proportionality test, on the other hand, forces the official to take as his starting-point the interests of the individual, limiting the *scope* of the decision as well as the way in which it is taken. In its current judicial formulation,[75] the *de Freitas* test requires the administrator to ask:

72 [2001] UKHL 26 [27]
73 [2001] UKHL 26 [32].
74 See Taggart, 'Reinventing administrative law'. And see A. Le Sueur, 'The rise and ruin of unreasonableness?' [2005] *Judicial Review* 32; D. Thomas, 'How irrational does irrational have to be?: *Wednesbury* in public interest, non-human rights cases' [2008] *Judicial Review* 258.
75 *De Freitas v Permanent Secretary of Ministry of Agriculture, Fisheries, Lands and Housing* [1999] 1 AC 69, 80; *Huang and Kashmiri v Home Secretary* [2007] UKHL 11 [19] (Lord Bingham). The formulae used in EU and ECHR law vary quite considerably: see E. Ellis (ed.), *The Principle of Proportionality in the Laws of Europe* (Hart Publishing, 1999).

- whether the legislative objective is sufficiently important to justify limiting a fundamental right
- whether the measures designed to meet the legislative objective are rationally connected to it
- whether the means used to impair the right or freedom are no more than is necessary to accomplish the objective.

This three-limbed test is, however, subject to a rider added in *Huang* by Lord Bingham of an 'overriding requirement of fair balance': i.e., that the interests of society must be weighed against those of groups and individuals.

In the *Denbigh High School* case, a school dress code was contested as a violation of the religious freedom of a strict Muslim student (ECHR Art. 9(1)). In the Court of Appeal, Brooke LJ used the proportionality principle to impose a rigorous evaluative process on the governors, listing six crucial questions that the governors should have asked:

1. Has the claimant established that she has a relevant Convention right which qualifies for protection under Art. 9(1)?
2. Subject to any justification that is established under Art. 9(2), has that Convention right been violated?
3. Was the interference with her Convention right prescribed by law in the Convention sense of that expression?
4. Did the interference have a legitimate aim?
5. What are the considerations that need to be balanced against each other when determining whether the interference was necessary in a democratic society for the purpose of achieving that aim?
6. Was the interference justified under Art. 9(2)?[76]

The governors had approached the issues from an 'entirely wrong direction'. Their starting point – compatible with *Wednesbury* – had been that the school uniform policy 'was there to be obeyed: if the claimant did not like it, she could go to a different school'. They should have started from the premise that 'the claimant had a right which is recognised by English law, and that the onus lay on the School to justify its interference with that right'.

In the House of Lords, it was the Court of Appeal's turn to be derided for setting the governors an 'examination paper' that the Court of Appeal would have failed. According to Lord Hoffmann:

> The fact that the decision-maker is allowed an area of judgment in imposing requirements which may have the effect of restricting the right does not entitle a court to say that a justifiable and proportionate restriction should be struck down because the decision-maker did not approach the question in the structured way in which a judge might have done. Head teachers and governors cannot be expected to make such decisions with textbooks on human rights law at their elbows. The most that can be said is that the way in which the

[76] *R(SB) v Headteacher and Governors of Denbigh High School* [2005] EWCA Civ 199 [75].

> school approached the problem may help to persuade a judge that its answer fell within the area of judgment accorded to it by the law.[77]

Here the decision-making function is squarely allocated to the administrative authority, which is free to go about its business in its own way provided that the outcome is justifiable and proportionate. *Judges* apply the proportionality questions to decide whether this is so.

But is there a missing dimension here? Whatever the language used, the governors were surely required to address 'the gist' of questions 1 and 2 above: namely, whether the uniform policy impinged disproportionately on the schoolgirl's personal religious beliefs? The proportionality test is designed to ensure on the one hand that they do so and on the other that the judges can see that they have done so. This second point emerges more clearly from the *Miss Behavin'* case involving a licence to open a sex shop in Belfast. The City Council applied their minds to the statutory criteria, taking into account 'the character of [the] locality, including the type of retail premises located therein, the proximity of public buildings such as the Belfast Public Library, the presence of a number of shops which would be of particular attraction to families and children and the proximity of a number of places of worship'. They refused a licence. Sharply critical of the judicial tendency to focus on procedural failings rather than outcome, Lord Hoffmann asked:

> What was the Council supposed to have said? 'We have thought very seriously about your Convention rights but we think that the appropriate number of sex shops in the locality is nil.' Or: 'Taking into account article 10 and article 1 of the First Protocol and doing the best we can, we think that the appropriate number is nil.' Would it have been sufficient to say that they had taken Convention rights into account, or would they have had to specify the right ones? A construction of the Human Rights Act which requires ordinary citizens in local government to produce such formulaic incantations would make it ridiculous. Either the refusal infringed the respondent's Convention rights or it did not. If it did, no display of human rights learning by the Belfast City Council would have made the decision lawful. If it did not, it would not matter if the councillors had never heard of article 10 or the First Protocol.[78]

But if the City Council failed entirely (as it apparently did) to *consider* the issue of free speech and opinion, was it perhaps acting, in *Wednesbury* terms, both irrationally and unreasonably? Lord Hoffmann leaves the judges in the

[77] *Begum v Headteacher and Governors of Denbigh High School* [2006] UKHL 15 [68]. And see R. Gordon, 'Structures or mantras? Some new puzzles in HRA decision-making' [2006] *Judicial Review* 136; T. Poole, 'Of headscarves and heresies: The *Denbigh High School* case and public authority decision-making under the Human Rights Act' [2005] *PL* 685; N. Gibson, 'Faith in the courts: Religious dress and human rights' (2007) 66 *CLJ* 657.

[78] *Belfast City Council v Miss Behavin' Ltd* [2007] UKHL 19, Lord Hoffmann at [13], Baroness Hale at [37]. And see C. Knight, 'Proportionality, the decision-maker and the House of Lords' [2007] *Judicial Review* 221.

unfortunate position of effectively making a discretionary decision on the merits without any guidance from the true decision-makers. Baroness Hale's approach was more nuanced. Acknowledging that the local authority was 'much better placed than the court to decide whether the right of sex shop owners to sell pornographic literature and images should be restricted', she thought its views were:

> bound to carry less weight where the local authority has made no attempt to address that question. Had the Belfast City Council expressly set itself the task of balancing the rights of individuals to sell and buy pornographic literature and images against the interests of the wider community, a court would find it hard to upset the balance which the local authority had struck. But where there is no indication that this has been done, the court has no alternative but to strike the balance for itself, giving due weight to the judgments made by those who are in much closer touch with the people and the places involved than the court could ever be.

In the difficult *Herceptin* case,[79] rationality and not proportionality was in issue. The Swindon primary healthcare trust (PCT) was responsible for treatment and funding, subject to mandatory *directions* from the Minister of Health and ministerial *guidance* to which trusts must 'have regard'. The only ministerial statement was a press release, apparently intended for circulation through the NHS, in which the minister expressed her wish to see Herceptin used more widely but saw it as 'an issue for individual clinicians'. She added, 'I want to make it clear that PCTs should not refuse to fund Herceptin solely on the grounds of its cost.'

In establishing policy, the PCT looked to two further sources of guidance: NICE, the NHS agency which has overall responsibility for approving drugs for use in the NHS, which had not yet reported on Herceptin; and a 'stakeholders' advisory forum'. In 2005, the PCT set out its policy on 'off-licence drugs' in 'Clinical Priorities Policy for Commissioning Selected Services'. This weighty document was rather more complex than Brooke LJ's six questions; it committed the PCT to: take into account and weigh all the relevant evidence; give proper consideration to the views of the patient or group of patients involved, and accord proper weight to their needs against other groups competing for scarce resources; take into account only material factors; act in the utmost good faith; and make a decision that is in every sense reasonable. In addition, an 'ethical framework' had been developed to enable the PCT 'to make fair and consistent decisions that treat patients equally'. In principle the PCT did not commission drugs unlicensed for use in the UK but there was a policy and procedure for considering 'exceptional' cases on their merits where the PCT did not have a policy in place. Not every PCT took this line; a 'post-code lottery' was happening.

[79] *R (Rogers) v Swindon NHS Primary Care Trust* [2006] EWCA Civ 392 reversing Bean J [2006] EWHC 171 Admin.

R, who was in the early stages of breast cancer, asked to be treated with Herceptin, which was refused. After an exhaustive consideration of the situation, Swindon refused to make any exception to its general policy; it was not licensed or approved by NICE and it would be wrong to 'introduce a dangerous precedent of disregarding the contribution made by the licensing and appraisal process'. Funding was not a factor; R's was not an exceptional case.

In an application for judicial review, Bean J exhaustively reviewed the decision-making process, finding that the PCT policy was neither irrational nor did it breach the applicant's right to life. The Court of Appeal overruled his finding. Although Sir Anthony Clarke MR conceded that the court could not hold the policy arbitrary solely because it referred to unidentified exceptional circumstances, he invoked a 'general principle of consistency' to hold that it was irrational, without clinical evidence of exceptional circumstances, to treat one patient but not another:

> The essential question is whether the policy was rational; and, in deciding whether it is rational or not, the court must consider whether there are any relevant exceptional circumstances which could justify the PCT refusing treatment to one woman within the eligible group but granting it to another. And to anticipate, the difficulty that the PCT encounters in the present case is that while the policy is stated to be one of exceptionality, no persuasive grounds can be identified, at least in clinical terms, for treating one patient who fulfils the clinical requirements for Herceptin treatment differently from others in that cohort.
>
> The PCT has not put any clinical or medical evidence before the court to suggest any such clinical distinction could be made. In these circumstances there is no rational basis for distinguishing between patients within the eligible group on the basis of exceptional clinical circumstances any more than on the basis of personal, let alone social, circumstances . . . Here the evidence does not establish the possibility of there being relevant clinical circumstances relating to one patient and not another and, in the case of personal characteristics, there is no rational basis for preferring one patient to another.[80]

Crawling over the decision-making process, the Court of Appeal had taken every opportunity (in Shapiro's words) 'to run through and reconstruct' it and, by obliging the PCT to 'replay' it, they had made an answer favourable to the appellant virtually inevitable. Some months after *Rogers*, NICE ruled that the NHS must fund Herceptin, though it warned that long-term risks and even benefits of the drug were still unknown. Was this decision influenced by the fear of further litigation? Decision-making is not necessarily more rational for taking place in the shadow of litigation.

We have set out the decision-making processes in the *Herceptin* case in some detail because they are illustrative of the way administrative decisions are actually arrived at. Decision-making can be seen as a chain made up of links contributed by a 'network' of different actors. The minister supplies (or

[80] [2006] EWCA Civ 392 [63] [82].

ought to supply) general 'guidance', which is not to be read as binding. NICE is responsible for ensuring the safety of drugs and giving guidance on their appropriate uses, which may, in the state of scientific evidence, be contestable. The primary decision-maker is the PCT, which has used a consultation process to feed in the views of patients. What, in this process, is the role of courts?

One approach to this question would look to Ganz's view of the allocation of functions (p. 40 above). Parliament has allocated decisions in this area to the PCT, which is composed of experts. Courts are peripheral to the main decision-making process and should confine themselves to a restricted reading of the *Wednesbury* test. This means that a court should intervene only where there is a clear failure to examine relevant evidence, obvious resort to irrelevant factors or a clear breach of human rights. This is in essence the view of decision-making expressed by Lord Hoffmann in *Denbigh High School* and *Miss Behavin'*. A second way to approach the problem is through the concept of 'polycentric' decisions as expounded by the jurist Lon Fuller. A polycentric decision is one that affects third parties not before the court or, as we should probably say today, a decision with 'spin off'. Fuller argued in a famous and judicious essay that polycentric decisions were unsuited to the adjudicative process and ought not to be justiciable.[81] Thus whether or not the PCT explicitly took resources into account in their policy, in the background the issue was unavoidable. Indeed, even Sir Anthony Clarke suggested that the *Herceptin* case might have gone very differently:

> if the PCT had decided that as a matter of policy it would adopt the Secretary of State's guidance that applications should not be refused solely on the grounds of cost but that, as a hard-pressed authority with many competing demands on its budget, it could not disregard its financial restraints and that it would have regard both to those restraints and to the particular circumstances of the individual patient in deciding whether or not to fund Herceptin treatment in a particular case. In such a case it would be very difficult, if not impossible, to say that such a policy was arbitrary or irrational.

Here Sir Anthony seems to be admitting that the decision not to fund Herceptin was within the PCT's powers. So surely it was precisely the type of decision where judges should show 'deference' to professionals, subject only to the 'last resort limb' of the *Wednesbury* test that the outcome of the decision-making process is not wholly unreasonable? Resources for health are finite and have to be rationed; many patients suffer from the lack of facilities that are simply not available. According to the *Annals of Oncology*,[82] increasing the availability of Herceptin would put great pressure on the NHS budget and lead to cuts in services for less high-profile diseases and conditions. £109 million

[81] L. Fuller, 'The forms and limits of adjudication' (1978) 92 *Harv. LR* 353; J. Allison, 'Fuller's analysis of polycentric disputes and the limits of adjudication' (1994) 53 *CLJ* 367.

[82] M. Neyer *et al.*, 'An economic evaluation of Herceptin' (2006) 17 *Annals of Oncology* 381.

would be needed to give Herceptin to the 5,000 women diagnosed each year with early-stage breast cancer. No extra funding was available. One NHS trust needed £1.9 million annually to pay for Herceptin for seventy-five patients; it could find this only if it did not treat 355 patients with other cancers, sixteen of whom might otherwise be cured. In the past, courts have wisely fought shy of decisions involving resource allocation, knowing they lack adequate experience and expertise (see Chapter 15). Nor did they have access to relevant statistical evidence and, if they had, would not necessarily have known how it should be interpreted.

Much time has, in the authors' view, been wasted in disputing the when and where of proportionality and the pros and cons of proportionality and reasonableness. Applying the tests to the cases we have cited will show that in most cases – as Lord Steyn made clear in *Daly* – the outcome will be the same whichever test is applied. Proportionality rules out outcomes unnecessary or disproportionate to the ends to be achieved; so too the rationality limb of the *Wednesbury* test can be used (as Lord Diplock used it in *Bromley*) to rule out disproportionate outcomes. But although the proportionality test is perceived as more intensive, irrational outcomes are not always disproportionate, as the *Herceptin* case suggests. Both tests are in reality flexible and plastic; both can act as 'tin-openers' for intensive forms of judicial review. Whenever they wish to, the judges are well able to move the goal posts. What is really in issue is *intensity*.[83] A prime virtue of proportionality from the standpoint of the judges, and the nub of Lord Hoffmann's objection in *Miss Behavin'*, is that the principle allows them to disguise just how close they have moved to review on the merits.

8. The Human Rights Act and after

According to the New Labour Government which fashioned it, the purpose of the HRA was not to create new rights. Its primary purpose was 'to bring rights home' and, by so doing, to spare litigants the long and expensive 'trek to Strasbourg'.[84] The HRA is not a 'Bill of Rights'; all that it does is to annex Convention Articles, making it unlawful for a public authority to act in such a way as to contravene them. Nor does it confer on British courts a power of 'constitutional review' in the full sense of that term. The HRA was intentionally designed to be compatible with the doctrine of parliamentary sovereignty and also to resolve issues of judicial and executive boundaries. Statute law is not to be overridden, annulled or otherwise invalidated; it is not, as under EU

[83] See M. Elliott, 'The Human Rights Act 1998 and the standard of substantive review on rationality and proportionality (2001) 60 *CLJ* 301; R. Clayton and K. Ghaly, 'Shifting standards of review' [2007] *Judicial Review* 210.

[84] See *Rights Brought Home: The Human Rights Bill*, Cm. 3782 (1997). And see J. Jowell, J. Cooper and A. Owers (eds.), *Understanding Human Rights Principles* (Hart Publications, 2001); J. Jowell and J. Cooper (eds.), *Delivering Rights: How the Human Rights Act is working* (Hart Publishing, 2003).

law, to be set aside or 'disapplied'. Section 4 of the HRA allows a superior court to issue a 'declaration of incompatibility' stating that an Act of Parliament is incompatible with the ECHR; secondary legislation may be struck down, unless the terms of the parent statute make this impossible. Before this drastic step can be taken, however, the court must 'so far as it is possible to do so' make every effort to read and give effect to primary and subordinate legislation 'in a way which is compatible with the Convention rights' (s. 3).[85] Thus the Act places a duty on courts not to be lavish with the new 'declarations of incompatibility' authorised by s. 4; they must turn first to s. 3. Exactly how courts should balance these two provisions is a matter of some controversy. While some feel that declarations of incompatibility should be treated as 'routine and unproblematic',[86] the courts have in practice taken a 'prudential' approach, interpreting the s. 3 interpretative duty quite broadly. In eight years, since the Act came into force in 2000, twenty-five declarations of incompatibility were made, of which eight were overturned on appeal.

That no direct clash with Parliament or the executive has occurred so far is largely due to the prudence of the judges, who have not by and large used their new powers to push their tanks far onto governmental turf. They have, for example, been noticeably unwilling to create economic and social rights to housing, social security etc., preferring to leave questions of resource allocation to government. In *Spink*, for example, where ECHR Art. 8 was invoked to persuade a court to interpret a statutory duty so as to impose financial obligations towards children on local authorities, the attempt foundered, just as a pre-Act case had done.[87] In *N v Home Secretary*,[88] the sad case of a claimant raped by armed forces in Uganda who had contracted AIDS, N contested deportation on the ground that her treatment would be terminated. Lord Nicholls explained why hers was not an 'exceptional case' and why the prospect of serious or fatal relapse on expulsion could not make expulsion into inhuman treatment for the purposes of ECHR Art. 3: 'It would be strange if the humane treatment of a would-be immigrant while his immigration application is being considered were to place him in a better position for the purposes of Article 3 than a person who never reached this country at all.' Courts, which can afford to be more generous when the affirmation of rights costs the taxpayer little or nothing, are wise to recognise that judgments occasioning substantial redistribution of resources will raise cries of 'government by judges'.[89]

85 On 'reading down' under s. 3 and principles of interpretation generally, see A. Lester and D. Pannick (eds.), *Human Rights Law and Practice*, 2nd edn (Butterworths, 2004).

86 T. Campbell, 'Incorporation through interpretation' in Campbell *et al.* (eds.), *Sceptical Essays in Human Rights* (Oxford University Press, 2001); D. Nicol, 'Law and politics after the Human Rights Act' [2006] *PL* 722. And see T. Hickman, 'The courts and politics after the Human Rights Act: A comment' [2008] *PL* 84.

87 *R (Spink) v Wandsworth LBC* [2005] EWCA Civ 302, citing the ECtHR case of *KA v Finland*, [2003] 1 FLR 201; *R (G) v Barnet LBC* [2003] 3 WLR 1194. Compare *ex p. Tandy* (p. 720).

88 *N v Home Secretary* [2005] 2 AC 296.

89 See T. Macklem, 'Entrenching Bills of Rights' (2006) 26 *OJLS* 107.

9. Rhetoric meets reality

An era that had commenced with the wartime detention case of *Liversidge v Anderson* ended with the terrorist attack of 9/11 and a subsequent 'war on terror' that made order and security the overriding priority. This was a testing context for the courts, shown in earlier chapters to be given to bold words and cautious action in reviewing executive action taken in defence of the realm. Yet Austin calls this 'the litmus test of the new constitutional order. Only if the courts are willing to protect the basic values of the rule of law, democracy and fundamental human rights in the face of emergency measures, will the new constitutionalism be seen as having real substance.'[90]

The Terrorism Act 2000 consolidated and expanded temporary legislation, originally enacted in 1974 in response to the IRA terrorist campaign, which included wide stop-and-search powers in designated areas. Detention without trial, first reinstated during the Northern Ireland conflict, resurfaced in the Anti-Terrorism, Crime and Security Act 2001 in respect of non-UK nationals. The Act also expanded the period of detention of terrorist suspects, strengthening the special procedures before the Special Immigrations Appeals Commission (SIAC). The Prevention of Terrorism Act 2005, passed in response to the decision in *A (No. 1)* (below), introduced control orders. The Terrorism Act 2006 extended pre-trial detention in terrorist cases to twenty-eight days, hotly contested in Parliament as too high. Almost immediately the Government proposed raising the limit to forty-two days with a new Counter-Terrorism Bill, meeting sufficient outcry to withdraw the proposal.[91] The Counter-Terrorism Act 2008 substituted post-charge questioning of terrorist suspects with judicial authorisation for renewable periods of 48 hours. The increasingly authoritarian style of a government apparently unconcerned about serious inroads on civil liberties was undoubtedly putting pressure on a judiciary charged with protecting human rights. Ought the judicial tanks to be more strongly deployed on the executive lawn?

In the justly famous case of *A (No. 1)*[92] the appellants had been certified and detained under ss. 21 and 23 of the 2001 Act, which provided for detention without trial of foreign nationals suspected of terrorist activity, the only right of appeal being to SIAC, where neither the allegations nor the evidence on which they were based were fully available to detainees. Detainees were also debarred from choosing their own counsel, instead having allocated to them SIAC-appointed, security-cleared 'special advocates' – a procedure subsequently challenged as a breach of ECHR Article 6(1). Before introducing the 2001 Act, the Government had invoked ECHR Art. 15, which

[90] R. Austin, 'The New Constitutionalism, Terrorism and Torture' (2007) 60 *CLP* 79, 97.

[91] See JCHR, *Counter-Terrorism Policy and Human Rights (Eleventh Report): 42 Days and Public Emergencies*, HC 635 (2007/8); House of Lords Constitution Committee, *Counter-Terrorism Bill: The Role of Ministers, Parliament and the Judiciary*, HL 167 (2007/8).

[92] *A and Others v Home Secretary* [2005] 2 AC 68.

permits derogation in emergency situations, to derogate from ECHR Art. 5, concerned with unlawful arrest and detention. The case of *A* and others now challenged the Act as incompatible with ECHR Art. 5 and as discriminatory in terms of ECHR Art. 14.

By a majority of eight to one (Lord Walker dissenting), the House issued a declaration of incompatibility on the grounds of violations of Arts. 5 and 14; the provisions interfered disproportionately with the applicants' right of personal freedom and were also discriminatory in their application to foreign nationals alone. A greater intensity of review was said by Lord Bingham to be required in determining questions of proportionality, while the duty of the courts to protect Convention rights would be emasculated if either the SIAC judgment were held 'conclusively to preclude any further review' or, in a field involving indefinite detention without charge or trial, there were excessive deference to ministerial decision. But no such hard look was applied to the question of derogation, which the House ruled (Lord Hoffmann vigorously dissenting) fell outside the competence of the domestic courts.[93] Here Lord Bingham, considering the issue of derogation, looks back to the classical Anglo-American doctrine of 'political question', ruling that the Home Secretary could not be challenged:

> *Lord Bingham*: I would accept that great weight should be given to the judgment of the Home Secretary, his colleagues and Parliament on this question, because they were called on to exercise a pre-eminently political judgment. It involved making a factual prediction of what various people around the world might or might not do, and when (if at all) they might do it, and what the consequences might be if they did . . . It would have been irresponsible not to err, if at all, on the side of safety. As will become apparent, I do not accept the full breadth of the Attorney General's argument on what is generally called the deference owed by the courts to the political authorities. It is perhaps preferable to approach this question as one of demarcation of functions or . . . 'relative institutional competence'. The more purely political (in a broad or narrow sense) a question is, the more appropriate it will be for political resolution and the less likely it is to be an appropriate matter for judicial decision. The smaller, therefore, will be the potential role of the court. It is the function of political and not judicial bodies to resolve political questions. Conversely, the greater the legal content of any issue, the greater the potential role of the court, because under our constitution and subject to the sovereign power of Parliament it is the function of the courts and not of political bodies to resolve legal questions. The present question seems to me to be very much at the political end of the spectrum . . . The appellants recognised this by acknowledging that the Home Secretary's decision on the present question was less readily open to challenge than his decision (as they argued) on some other questions. This

[93] The House of Lords brushed aside warnings from the UN Human Rights Committee, Newton Committee of Privy Councillors and Joint Committee on Human Rights (JCHR) that the derogation was questionable: see JCHR, *Review of Counter-Terrorism Powers*, HC 173 (2003/4). The majority position was later confirmed by the ECtHR in *A and Others v UK*, Application No. 34455/05 (19 February 2009).

> reflects the unintrusive approach of the European Court to such a question. I conclude that the appellants have shown no ground strong enough to warrant displacing the Secretary of State's decision on this important threshold question.

Lord Hoffmann's approach was very different. Holding that the situation had been insufficient to permit derogation from the ECHR, Lord Hoffmann saw the government's duty to protect the lives and property of its citizens as a duty that is 'owed all the time and which it must discharge without destroying our constitutional freedoms'. Nothing could be more antithetical to the instincts and traditions of the people of the United Kingdom than a power to detain people indefinitely without charge or trial:

> I would not like anyone to think that we are concerned with some special doctrine of European law. Freedom from arbitrary arrest and detention is a quintessentially British liberty, enjoyed by the inhabitants of this country when most of the population of Europe could be thrown into prison at the whim of their rulers. It was incorporated into the European Convention in order to entrench the same liberty in countries which had recently been under Nazi occupation. The United Kingdom subscribed to the Convention because it set out the rights which British subjects enjoyed under the common law.
>
> The exceptional power to derogate from those rights also reflected British constitutional history. There have been times of great national emergency in which habeas corpus has been suspended and powers to detain on suspicion conferred on the government. It happened during the Napoleonic Wars and during both World Wars in the twentieth century. These powers were conferred with great misgiving and, in the sober light of retrospect after the emergency had passed, were often found to have been cruelly and unnecessarily exercised. But the necessity of draconian powers in moments of national crisis is recognised in our constitutional history. Article 15 of the Convention, when it speaks of 'war or other public emergency threatening the life of the nation', accurately states the conditions in which such legislation has previously been thought necessary . . .
>
> What is meant by 'threatening the life of the nation'? . . . I think that it was reasonable to say that terrorism in Northern Ireland threatened the life of that part of the nation and the territorial integrity of the United Kingdom as a whole. In a community riven by sectarian passions, such a campaign of violence threatened the fabric of organised society. The question is whether the threat of terrorism from Muslim extremists similarly threatens the life of the British nation . . . Terrorist violence, serious as it is, does not threaten our institutions of government or our existence as a civil community. For these reasons I think that the Special Immigration Appeals Commission made an error of law and that the appeal ought to be allowed.

The divergent approaches surfaced again in *A (No. 2)*,[94] where the issue was the admissibility in SIAC hearings of evidence possibly obtained by torture

[94] *A and Others v Home Secretary* [2006] 2 AC 221, overruling the shameful Court of Appeal decision to hold the evidence admissible: see [2005] 1 WLR 414 (Laws and Pill LJJ, Neuberger LJ dissenting). See on burden of proof *Saadi v Italy* [2008] ECHR 179 [129–133].

overseas. The House of Lords ruled such evidence inadmissible if it could be established on a balance of probabilities that torture had been involved. A minority (Lords Nicholls, Bingham and Hoffmann) refused to place the onerous burden of proof on the applicant: it was for SIAC 'to initiate or direct such inquiry as is necessary to enable it to form a fair judgment whether the evidence has, or whether there is a real risk that it may have been, obtained by torture or not'. The Court of Appeal followed this lead in the later case of *Othman*, where the issue was the possible use by courts in Jordan of evidence obtained by torture, ruling that, where the applicant raised a plausible reason for thinking that a statement might have been procured by torture, it was for SIAC proactively to institute enquiries. The decision to return the applicant to Jordan was annulled but overturned on appeal. The House of Lords ruled that SIAC procedures did not violate ECHR Art. 6(1). SIAC was entitled to make decisions based on 'closed evidence', reviewable only on questions of law. The House also legitimated the government practice of taking 'assurances' from foreign governments that deportees would not be subjected to torture and would receive a trial compatible with the requirements of Art.6. [95]

In *A* (*No. 2*), Lord Bingham's scholarly opinion had ranged exhaustively over international law, the UN Convention on Torture and the ECHR, by which he thought SIAC should 'throughout be guided'; Lord Hoffmann saw the issue as falling firmly within the parameters of the common law; the rejection of torture had a constitutional resonance for the English people which could not be overestimated. This attempt to re-root the international law of human rights in the traditional constitutional ground of civil liberties does not merit Dyzenhaus's charge of 'Anglo-Saxon parochialism'.[96] Rather, the strategy anticipates arguments that the measure of legislation is 'Convention-compliance', thus avoiding the 'ceiling' and the 'mirror image' fallacies discussed later in the chapter. It stands as a useful reminder too that human rights did not spring fully fledged from twentieth-century international law texts but grew painfully within communities and national legal orders so that all who live in the society, and not only judges and other national political actors, retain responsibility for the propriety of the rules and practice. This is what is meant – or ought to be meant – by 'rights-consciousness' or 'a culture of human rights awareness'.

The tanks were not yet far enough onto the lawn for the government to resent the intrusion; there were no acid ministerial statements. On the other hand, the government was not minded to concede its rightful policy-making function. The declaration of incompatibility made in *A* (*No. 1*) had placed it in a predicament; the jurisprudence of the ECtHR meant that suspects could

[95] *Othman (Jordan) v Home Secretary* [2008] EWCA Civ 290 appealed in *RB (Algeria) and OO (Jordan) v Home Secretary* [2009] UKHL 10.

[96] D. Dyzenhaus, 'An unfortunate outburst of Anglo-Saxon parochialism' (2005) 68 *MLR* 673, 674. See also T. Poole, 'Harnessing the power of the past? Lord Hoffmann and the *Belmarsh Detainees* case' (2005) 32 *JLS* 534.

not be deported to places where there was a real risk of ill treatment;[97] now it was questionable how they could be lawfully detained. Legislation was clearly needed. But the position was complicated by the absence of all-party agreement, doubt whether the proposed bill would pass the Lords and the imminence of an election. A compromise was reached with the Prevention of Terrorism Act 2005, which, in line with the House of Lords ruling on discrimination in *A (No. 1)*, applied also to British nationals. The Act introduced 'control orders' of two types: 'non-derogating control orders' made by the Home Secretary but subject to review by a High Court judge; and 'derogating control orders', which required a derogation from the ECHR made by ministerial order followed by application for a judicial order, allowing the merits of the proposed order to be scrutinised. This hairline distinction did not recommend itself to the Joint Committee on Human Rights (JCHR), which described the control orders as 'falling not very far short of house arrest' and thought the regime likely to infringe several ECHR articles, in addition to being incompatible with 'the most basic principles of a fair hearing and due process long recognised as fundamental by English common law'.[98]

The matter was soon to be tested. The 'Belmarsh detainees', still in custody and about to be made subject to non-derogating control orders, went back to court. In a two-part judgment, Sullivan J ruled that the attenuated procedures used in review, including the refusal to release evidence to the accused or his counsel and the deplorably low standard of proof in a case akin to criminal proceedings, violated the requirement of a fair trial before an independent and impartial tribunal. Maintaining the control order in force, he granted a declaration of incompatibility with ECHR Art. 6(1). On appeal, a specially constituted court found it possible, taking a purposive, common-law approach, to 'read down' the relevant statutory provisions so as to hold the procedures compatible with Art. 6(1). The case was remitted for reconsideration on the new criteria set out by the Court of Appeal, including a finding that proceedings concluding in a control order were not, for Convention purposes, 'criminal' in character.[99] With further decisions from the lower courts that more restrictive control orders, amounting effectively to house arrest for 18 hours each day, fell outside the scope of a non-derogating control order, this finding reached the House of Lords, where the disparate rulings revealed a serious divergence of opinion.

The House of Lords divided first on whether control orders amounted to

[97] *Chahal v United Kingdom* (1996) 23 EHRR 413. *Chahal* was later upheld in *Saadi v Italy* (ECtHR, Grand Chamber, Application no. 37201/06, 28 Feb. 2008), a test case in which the UK intervened unsuccessfully to argue that the protection of national security could be weighed against the risk of inhuman treatment.

[98] See *Counter-Terrorism Policy and Human Rights: Draft Prevention of Terrorism Act 2005 (Continuance in force of sections 1 to 9) Order 2006*, HC 915 (2005/6) with special reference to Arts. 6(1)–(3) and 5(4); J. Hiebert 'Parliamentary review of terrorism measures' (2005) 68 *MLR* 676.

[99] *Re MB* [2006] EWHC Admin 1000; *SSHD v MB, E and JJ* [2006] EWCA Civ 1141.

a deprivation of liberty under ECHR Art. 5, which Lord Bingham and Lady Hale saw as a question of fact and circumstance, while Lords Hoffmann and Carswell thought that Art. 5 covered only 'literal physical restraint'.[100] Again, the House was ambiguous over the time for which curfews could be imposed: there was unanimity that a twelve-hour period was lawful but also a suggested maximum of sixteen hours from Lord Brown.[101] Finally, only Lord Hoffmann squarely endorsed the 'special advocate' procedure before SIAC as Convention-compliant. Lord Bingham thought the use of 'closed material' would always be non-compliant while the majority, hedging their bets, felt that it could be made to work fairly and compatibly in many cases but a result might be produced on occasion that would not be compatible with Convention rights.[102] Some very mixed messages were being sent. So opaque was the reasoning of the House of Lords on these various issues that the rulings proved almost impossible to apply. After grappling conscientiously and at some length with possible interpretations, the Court of Appeal sent the issue back to the House for resolution.[103]

A (No. 1), first of the *Belmarsh Detainees* cases, has been called 'one of the most constitutionally significant ever decided by the House of Lords' yet in terms of immediate outcome the significance was largely symbolic.[104] In other areas the HRA had produced some tangible results, as, for example, in *Al-Skeini*, where the House of Lords asserted the rule of human rights law overseas in time of war in respect of a prisoner who had died of his injuries while in the custody of British troops[105] and the JCHR followed on swiftly with searching questions over assurances it had received concerning the use of illegal interrogation techniques by the British army in Iraq.[106] The case of terrorism was very different. Four years after *A (No. 1)*, with the detention and deportation sagas not finally ended and many of the detainees still

[100] *Home Secretary v JJ* [2007] UKHL 45.

[101] *Home Secretary v JJ*, *Home Secretary v E* [2007] UKHL 47; *Home Secretary v MB and Others* [2007] UKHL 46.

[102] *Home Secretary v MB and Others* [2007] UKHL 46. But see now the judgement of the Grand Chamber in *A and Others v United Kingdom*, Application No. 3455/05 (19 February 2009).

[103] *SSHD v AF, AM and AN* [2008] EWCA Civ 1148 (Sir Anthony Clarke MR and Waller LJ, Sedley LJ dissenting).

[104] By February 2009, of 38 individuals subject to control order, 23 had been released, of whom 6 had been deported. 1 order was revoked and 2 not renewed: see Third and Fourth Reports of the Independent Reviewer pursuant to s. 14(3) of the Prevention of Terrorism Act 2005 (18 February 2008, 3 February 2009).

[105] *Al-Skeini v Defence Secretary* [2007] UKHL 26. One claimant, Baha Mousa, succeeded. Five who lost on the ground that they were not in the control of the British army have applied to the ECtHR for redress. The Ministry of Defence immediately responded with an admission that human rights had been violated and a settlement of £2.83 million.

[106] See JCHR, *UN Convention Against Torture: Discrepancies in evidence given to the Committee About the Use of Prohibited Interrogation Techniques in Iraq*, HC 527 (2007/8). The allegation was that evidence given to the JCHR for its report *The UN Convention Against Torture (UNCAT)*, HC 701 (2005/6) that the judgment in *Ireland v UK* [1978] 2 EHRR 25, dealing with interrogation techniques used in Northern Ireland, had been properly implemented in Iraq, was false.

under control orders, the House of Lords, though free with rhetoric, had not on close examination moved far from its repressive pre-HRA decision in *Rehman*.[107] There it had declined to review a deportation order made by the Home Secretary on the ground that he was 'undoubtedly in the best position to judge what national security requires even if his decision is open to review'. Ewing and Tham feel driven to conclude that, after the excitement that followed the landmark case of *A (No. 1)*, 'normal service appears to have been resumed, in terms of the approach of the courts'. Even parliamentary committees appear unhappy with the depth of the deference shown by the courts towards the legislature and their respect for parliamentary sovereignty.[108]

It was not, as it happens, the *Belmarsh Detainees* cases but a ruling from Sullivan J, involving Afghan asylum seekers who had hijacked an aeroplane in Afghanistan and landed at Stansted, which provoked the political storm.[109] The procedure adopted by the Home Office was undoubtedly questionable, since the minister had delayed a decision on the Afghans' application for asylum until such time as internal guidance on humanitarian protection could be amended and the policy applied retrospectively to their case. Nonetheless, the Prime Minister, Tony Blair, publicly labelled the judge's ruling 'an abuse of common sense'. He called on his Home Secretary to change the law 'to ensure the law-abiding majority can live without fear' and asked for a 'profound re-balancing' of the debate on civil liberties, adding for good measure that amendments to the HRA might be necessary to require judges to balance the rights of the individual with public safety, which they 'do not always do'. Ex-Home Secretary David Blunkett fuelled the fire by branding the HRA 'the worst mistake of Labour's first term', while David Cameron for the Opposition poured oil on the promising flames by calling for a 'British Bill of Rights' to enshrine and protect fundamental British liberties (such as jury trial, equality under the law and civil rights) and to protect ECHR rights 'in clearer and more precise terms'. The Home Office and DCA responded that the HRA had *not* seriously impeded the Government's objectives on crime, terrorism and immigration; rather, it had been used in a number of high-profile cases as 'a convenient scapegoat for unrelated administrative failings within Government.'[110] A measured intervention from the JCHR blamed the Government for failing to tackle 'far-fetched stories' about the HRA and to put the case for the important rights it enshrined. The Act had:

107 *SSHD v Rehman* [2001] UKHL 47.

108 K. Ewing and J.-C. Tham, 'The Continuing Futility of the Human Rights Act' [2008] *PL* 668. And see E. Bates, 'Anti-terrorism control orders: liberty and security still in the balance' (2009) 29 *Legal Studies* 99.

109 *R (S,M, S and Others) v SSHD* [2006] EWHC 1111 (Admin). Sullivan J quashed the ministerial order refusing exceptional leave to remain.

110 DCA, *Review of the Implementation of the Human Rights Act* (25 July 2006); JCHR, *The Human Rights Act: The DCA and Home Office reviews*, HC 1716 (2005/6) [40].

> created no new rights. In fact, it enabled rights the UK had signed up to in the European Convention on Human Rights (ECHR) in 1950 (which UK lawyers had played a major part in drafting and which in large part they based on the common law) to be enforced in the UK courts. None of the rights in the Convention – such as the right to life or the right to a fair trial – are, in themselves, remotely controversial. Their application in specific cases may involve striking a difficult balance between competing rights, or accepting the implications of absolute rights, such as the right to life or the right not to be tortured. The universality of human rights – their application to everyone in the UK, including criminals and foreign nationals – can also prove challenging for some.
>
> The universality of human rights can, and should, be a major force for good, especially in the way public services are delivered – including to many vulnerable groups in our society. Human rights are the basic set of rights that we all enjoy by virtue of being human. The Human Rights Act obliges public authorities, including Government departments, to act in accordance with that basic set of rights. They must act proactively to enhance the human rights of the people with whom they deal. The Human Rights Act could and should act as a lever to improve the way in which services are delivered to the public, underpinning good practice with an enforceable legal obligation.[111]

Gratefully accepting this escape route, the Government confirmed commitment to its Human Rights Act.[112] But warning shots had been fired.

10. Lions, mice or bulldogs?

In this chapter we have tried to show how, from the baseline of 'abdication and error' deplored by Schwarz and Wade, the role of the judges in judicial review has been steadily enlarged. During the 1980s, judicial review was rebuilt and greatly strengthened by what would become in time the Administrative Court. We moved from a position where King (p. 96 above) saw the judiciary as 'inclined to defer to the executive' to something in the nature of a separation-of-powers constitution. The new model was concreted in by the Constitutional Reform Act 2005, which created a newly autonomous Supreme Court. Emphasising continuity, the Act confirms 'the existing constitutional principle of the rule of law' and requires the Lord Chancellor to 'uphold the continued independence of the judiciary'.[113]

Meanwhile, judicial review has assumed a central position in the rule-based, evaluative processes that characterise present-day public administration and has itself been reconstructed in the image of a more principled, more rational,

[111] JCHR, *The Work of the Committee in 2007 and the State of Human Rights in the UK*, HC 270 (2007/8) [5–6].

[112] Ministry of Justice, *Rights and Responsibilities: Developing our Constitutional Framework*, Cm 7577 (2009).

[113] There is no space here to deal in detail with the Constitutional Reform Act 2005 but see the Special Issue devoted to the topic at (2004) 24 *Legal Studies* 1–293. And see House of Lords Constitution Committee, *Relations between the executive, the judiciary and Parliament: Follow-up Report*, HC 177 (2007/8).

system. The common law, according to a senior Lord Justice of Appeal, 'is growing incrementally as human rights principles, regarded as commonplace overseas, have been invading the nooks and crevices'.[114] Conscious that the eyes of the outside world would be on them, he concludes, the judges have taken their role as guardian of human rights very seriously. But they have shown no immediate inclination to indulge in extrajudicial sharpshooting or test the boundaries of their new powers and, despite occasional judicial overreaching, have not yet gone so far as to imperil their legitimacy.

To a limited extent, the national courts are offered an escape route by the Court of Human Rights at Strasbourg. The relationship between national courts and Strasbourg under the HRA is very different to that with the Court of Justice at Luxembourg. In arriving at its conclusion, a court or tribunal determining a question that has arisen in connection with a Convention right must 'take into account' any judgment, decision, declaration or advisory opinion of the ECtHR (s. 2(1)); it is not *bound* by that Court's jurisprudence. Space is left by the HRA for British courts to exercise their 'margin of appreciation' by departing from the ECtHR's jurisprudence, even if, for reasons of comity and expedience, they prefer 'in the absence of special circumstances' to follow 'clear and constant' leads from Strasbourg.[115]

Lord Bingham has suggested, however, that the human rights function of a British judge is to act as a 'mirror', positioned to reflect the jurisprudence of the Strasbourg Court. Our courts are reduced 'to keep[ing] pace with the Strasbourg jurisprudence as it evolves over time: no more, but certainly no less'.[116] If so, the readiness of the 'modest underworkers' of classical administrative law to transfer their services to a new master in Strasbourg would be worrying. If national courts were to *lower* the platform of rights protected by Strasbourg, the UK would be placed in breach of its international commitments; if the domestic court were to feel inhibited from moving the platform *up*, the position would be less satisfactory still. In *Re P*, however, Lord Hoffman expressly departed from the 'mirror principle', saying:

> I . . . do not think that your Lordships should be inhibited . . . by the thought that you might be going further than the Strasbourg court. But what if you were? Say the Strasbourg court were to . . . say that these are delicate questions, capable of arousing religious sensibilities in many Member States, and should therefore be left to the national 'margin of appreciation'?
>
> My Lords, in my view this should make no difference . . . 'Convention rights' within the

[114] H. Brooke, 'Human rights beyond the hostile headlines: New developments in practice' (2007) 4 *Justice Journal* 8.

[115] R. Masterman, 'Taking Strasbourg jurisprudence into account; Developing a 'municipal law of human rights' under the Human Rights Act' (2005) 54 *ICLQ* 907; M. Amos, 'The impact of the Human Rights Act on the United Kingdom's performance before the European Court of Human Rights' [2007] *PL* 655.

[116] *R (Ullah) v Special Adjudicator* [2004] UKHL 26 [20].

> meaning of the 1998 Act are domestic and not international rights. They are applicable in the domestic law of the United Kingdom and it is the duty of the courts to interpret them like any other statute . . . In the interpretation of these domestic rights, the courts must 'take into account' the decisions of the Strasbourg court. This language makes it clear that the United Kingdom courts are not bound by such decisions; their first duty is to give effect to the domestic statute according to what they consider to be its proper meaning, even if its provisions are in the same language as the international instrument which is interpreted in Strasbourg.[117]

This certainly accords with Parliament's intention. The HRA contains no 'ceiling' on human rights and does not act as 'mirror' for the Strasbourg jurisprudence; as the Lord Chancellor said during debate on the bill, 'our courts must be free to try to give a lead to Europe as well as to be led'.[118] It was not the intention of Parliament to reduce our judges to 'mice under the Strasbourg throne'.

There is a certain irony in the fact that a judiciary empowered to check the executive in an unprecedented fashion seems *largely* content (we emphasise the word 'largely') to operate inside a classical framework of procedural judicial review, modelling the clay of new principles closely to the shape of the old moulds. It has been said, for example, that the approach of British courts to proportionality 'is orientated towards the limiting of other state organs and already builds itself into a theory of legitimacy: "rights" are for courts, "policy" is for legislatures and executives . . . Questions of "sufficiently important public objective" and "essential core" are for the judiciary.'[119] Are these not the very questions discussed by Dworkin so many years ago?

Although the rhetoric of constitutionalism has not gone away, the tone of the debate has moderated. The vigorous language of 'higher-order law', 'the imperative of individual freedoms' and 'quintessentially British liberty' is gently dissolving into a language of 'deference'. Questions of 'deference' arise according to Lord Hope when, in the context and circumstances of a case, it seems appropriate for the courts to recognise an area of judgment 'within which the judiciary will defer, on democratic grounds, to the considered opinion of the elected body or person whose act or decision is said to be incompatible with the Convention'.[120] What these areas might be is a matter of precedent and judicial discretion. For Lord Steyn, deference is a question of 'institutional competence' in the sense both of legitimacy and expertise. There are no longer any 'no-go areas' but a court may, after scrutiny, 'recognise that in a particular case and in respect of a particular dispute, Parliament or the

[117] [2008] UKHL 38 [29–30] [33–34].

[118] HL Deb., vol. 583, col. 514; and see J. Lewis, 'The European ceiling on human rights' [2007] *PL* 720.

[119] J. Rivers, 'Proportionality and variable intensity of review' (2006) 65 *CLJ* 174, 180.

[120] *R v DPP, ex p. Kebilene* [2000] AC 326, 381 (Lord Hope).

executive may be better placed to decide certain questions'.[121] Laws LJ has tried to construct a spectrum, ranging from the nearly absolute case of state security (a paradigm of special executive responsibility) to the case of criminal justice, a paradigm of judicial responsibility, where it might 'barely exist at all'.[122] So, is this new language a reintroduction, albeit 'in pastel colours',[123] of the supposedly discredited notion of justiciability? Does the 'spectrum theory of deference' differ greatly from the three-stepped *Wednesbury* reasonableness test (p. 42 above)?

The HRA did not, as we have been at pains to emphasise, create a power of constitutional review. It called for 'structured dialogue' between judges and lawmakers about the nature and extent of human rights. The HRA empowered not only the judiciary but also Parliament. Government took on board the principle of 'mainstreaming' or consistently measuring the impact of policy development on human rights. This new practice has, in Gearty's view, contributed more than any other measure to 'the infiltration of human rights considerations deep into Whitehall'.[124] Parliament has responded to its role with new committees, such as the JCHR which, as we shall see in the next chapter, has begun to provide a distinctive and independent voice. This understated 'dialogue model', which 'requires us to talk, to persuade, to argue, to fight the political fight, and not to rely on judicial guardians to protect us from the crowd' is properly, in Gearty's words, 'the human rights mask that the United Kingdom has chosen to wear'.[125] The JCHR, which believes a 'Bill of Rights and Freedoms' to be desirable 'in order to provide necessary protection to all, and to marginalised and vulnerable people in particular', takes a similar view of the appropriate balance of power:

> Adopting a Bill of Rights provides a moment when society can define itself. We recommend that a Bill of Rights and Freedoms should set out a shared vision of a desirable future society: it should be aspirational in nature as well as protecting those human rights which already exist. We suggest that a Bill of Rights and Freedoms should give lasting effect to values shared by the people of the United Kingdom: we include liberty, democracy, fairness, civic duty, and the rule of law.
>
> Adopting a Bill of Rights and Freedoms is a constitutional landmark, and could have a far-reaching impact on the relationship between Parliament, the executive and the courts. We recommend that the Bill of Rights and Freedoms should build on our tradition

[121] J. Steyn, 'Deference: A tangled story' [2005] *PL* 346, 351; J. Jowell, 'Judicial Deference and human rights: A question of competence' in Craig and Rawlings (eds), *Law and Administration in Europe*; R. Clayton, 'Principles for judicial deference' [2006] *Judicial Review* 109.

[122] *International Transport Roth GmbH v Home Secretary* [2003] QB 728. It should be noted that the 'spectrum theory' has not found favour with the judiciary generally.

[123] T. Allan, 'Human rights and judicial review: A critique of "due deference"' (2006) 65 *CLJ* 671, 682.

[124] C. Gearty, *Principles of Human Rights Adjudication* (Oxford University Press, 2004), p. 211.

[125] C. Gearty, *Can Human Rights Survive?* (Cambridge University Press, 2006), p. 97.

of parliamentary democracy, and we do not believe that courts should have the power to strike down legislation. A UK Bill of Rights and Freedoms should, as with the Human Rights Act, apply to legislation whenever enacted, unless Parliament decides to pass incompatible legislation, and makes clear its intention to do so.[126]

[126] JCHR, *A Bill of Rights for the United Kingdom*, HC 150-I (2007/8); *Government Response*, HC 145 (2008/9). And see Justice, *A Bill of Rights for Britain?* (2007); F. Klug, 'A Bill of Rights: Do we need one or do we already have one?' [2007] *PL* 701; Ministry of Justice, *Rights and Responsibilities*.

4

Making the law

Contents

1. Legislation and constitutional change

Since at least the nineteenth century, a first objective for lawyers has been to arrange legal norms logically and in a hierarchical fashion. This is the essence of both Dicey's nineteenth-century doctrine of parliamentary sovereignty and Hart's celebrated theory of primary and secondary rules (see Chapter 1), each of which seeks to establish when and why rules are binding and to be obeyed. The fact that the constitution is unwritten sets statute law at the apex of the hierarchy of legal norms; the prerogative powers, historical rival of parliamentary legislation, are nowadays subordinate to statute and those remnants of the prerogative legislative powers that remain in respect of colonial territories are controversial and subject to review by the courts.[1] At the other end of the spectrum, the borders between law and non-law are not always easily discernible. It may often be hard to differentiate the confusing 'ragbag of rules, regulations, orders, schemes, byelaws, licences, directives, warrants, instruments of approval or minutes' that bear the label delegated legislation,[2] from the confusing ragbag of directives, circulars, guidance, guidelines and codes of practice that clutter the desks – and computer screens – of bureaucrats. Discussion of this mass of 'soft law', generated by the use of rule-making as a standard technique of modern bureaucracy and e-governance, is reserved for Chapter 5.

A sharp line is commonly drawn between statute law, which falls into the field of constitutional law, and secondary legislation which, merely by virtue of being made by the executive or other authorised public bodies, falls within the purview of administrative law. We have never been entirely comfortable with this distinction and shall not attempt to maintain it here. In a separation-of-powers analysis, the role of the executive in lawmaking may pass virtually unnoticed, while the traditional vision of 'Parliament the lawmaker' disguises the fact that parliamentary input into legislation is in practice rather modest – sometimes little more than its input into the making of delegated legislation. The parliamentary stage of lawmaking occupies fractional space on a continuum from policy-making to implementation in which the action passes from one institution to another in an effort to get a law on to the statute book and in force. Ministers and civil servants, politicians and lawyers participate at both policy-making and legislative stages of the process. We shall see too that with greatly improved procedures for parliamentary scrutiny of delegated legislation and EU law these forms of lawmaking are no longer so clearly differentiated from statute.

The package of constitutional reform introduced after the 1997 election again makes the boundary difficult to maintain. The devolution legislation and the HRA were all designed expressly to be compatible with the doctrine of parliamentary sovereignty, as was the earlier European Communities Act 1972 (ECA), passed after the UK acceded to the European Communities. Yet each in its different ways disturbed and significantly modified the traditional hierarchy of rules. As noted in the last chapter, the HRA altered the balance of power between legislature and judiciary, provoking hot debate over the true nature of parliamentary sovereignty. In this chapter, we follow the theme of 'dialogue', assessing the contribution of the Westminster Parliament to 'mainstreaming' human rights. The HRA and ECA both contain swingeing executive powers to legislate by delegated legislation, commonly known as 'Henry VIII clauses'. In the case of the European Union (EU), where the

[1] *R (Bancoult) v Foreign Secretary (No. 2)* [2008] UKHL 61. And see Ch. 1, p. 13.

[2] J. Griffith and H. Street, *Principles of Administrative Law*, 3rd edn (Pitman, 1973), p. 32.

'primacy' doctrine of EC law developed by the ECJ poses a direct challenge to parliamentary sovereignty, the fiction of 'delegation' on which Anglo-American administrative law is premised seems to us unhelpful in resolving the delicate issue of whether EU legal instruments are or are not 'delegated' legislation.[3]

Although it may be technically correct to classify 'devolved legislative competence' as lawmaking under delegated powers, the output is not 'delegated legislation' in the same sense as statutory instruments subject to scrutiny by the Westminster Parliament. If anything more complex, lawmaking procedures in Northern Ireland are, as we write, only just being tested.[4] In addition, the three representative bodies have adopted their own procedures, which differ – and may in the future differ more – from those used at Westminster.[5]

The Scotland, Northern Ireland and Government of Wales (GWA) Acts 1998 created devolved institutions with substantial, though variant, lawmaking and rulemaking powers. The Scottish Parliament can pass primary legislation, known as 'Acts of the Scottish Parliament' (ASP). Bills are subject to possible legal challenge by the Law Officers for a four-week period if they are thought to be outside the lawmaking powers of the Scottish Parliament and any provision of an ASP outside its legislative competence is 'not law'. This covers provisions incompatible with the ECHR and EU law (both areas for which the UK retains responsibility).[6] At least for a limited period, ASPs can amend or repeal Westminster Acts in respect of Scotland; vice versa, Westminster Acts can modify the law of Scotland in both reserved and devolved areas, if necessary by amendment or repeal of ASPs. Under the so-called 'Sewel convention' the consent of the Scottish Parliament is normally required, an issue on which the Scottish Parliament is not unnaturally highly sensitive.[7] Powers are also available under the Scotland Act for UK ministers to amend Scottish law in devolved areas by subordinate legislation.

In Wales, where the Assembly does not possess plenary legislative powers, the Westminster Parliament makes statute law. The amending GWA 2006 allows the Welsh Assembly to make laws known as 'measures', which will have similar effect to an Act of Parliament in areas where the Assembly has legislative competence; these are listed in the Act and can be amended either by a new Westminster Act or a 'Legislative Competence Order', which will transfer

[3] See P. Lindseth, 'Democratic legitimacy and the administrative character of supranationalism: The example of the European community' (1999) 99 *Col. Law Rev.* 628.

[4] But see G. Anthony and J. Morison, 'Here, there, and (maybe) here again: The story of law making for post-1998 Northern Ireland' in Hazell and Rawlings (eds.), *Devolution, Law Making and the Constitution* (Imprint Academic, 2005).

[5] See N. Jamieson, 'The Scots statutory style and substance' (2007) 28 *Stat. Law Rev.* 182.

[6] Ss. 29 and 33 of the Scotland Act 1998; G. Gee, 'Devolution and the courts' in Hazell and Rawlings (eds.), *Devolution, Law Making and the Constitution.*

[7] CC, *Devolution: Its effect on the practice of legislation at Westminster*, HL 192 [6]; A. Page and A. Batey, '*Scotland's Other Parliament*' [2002] *PL* 501. The Sewel convention was originally developed in Northern Ireland to cover relations between Westminster and the Stormont Parliament between 1922–1972.

specific powers from Westminster to the Assembly and is subject to approval by both the Assembly and UK Parliament. A two-stage process, involving pre-legislative scrutiny of a proposed LCO by committee and approval by the Assembly and Parliament of a draft LCO, is necessary; a complex process demanding careful co-ordination. The GWA also provides that, if in the future authorised by popular referendum, the Assembly may make Welsh statutes.[8] Under s. 33, the Secretary of State for Wales must consult the Assembly after the beginning of each Westminster parliamentary session on the Government's legislative programme and thereafter on Bills agreed for introduction.[9]

These are only a few of the complexities noted by the House of Lords Constitution Committee (CC) as raising 'barriers for the ordinary reader' to 'full access to and understanding of the law of the land'.[10] For legislation on devolved subjects it is, for example, necessary to look to ASPs, Acts of the Westminster Parliament, and now to Welsh Assembly Measures. As for secondary legislation, the network of regulation has become so tangled that the Scottish Parliament wants a programme of consolidation, especially where rules originally made by UK ministers have been successively amended by the Scottish ministers.[11] Adding to concern that devolution has brought increased reliance on delegated legislation is the problem that some measures may be subject to scrutiny by two Parliaments, which may not always see eye to eye. The effect on lawmaking procedures at Westminster, not fully appreciated at the time of devolution, is also considerable – so complicated as to persuade the Lords Constitution Committee that it may defy attempts at resolution within the structures of 'asymmetrical devolution'. The complexities 'derive from the nature of the devolution settlement, and it would be difficult to mitigate them without seeking to re-model the structure of that settlement'.[12] In practice, conventions and inter-institutional agreements have had to be evolved to flesh out relationships between the partners, so far with success. [13]

2. Parliament and courts

We should be careful not to underrate the symbolism of a formal parliamentary contribution to lawmaking. Parliament provides the ultimate seal of democratic legitimacy, marking the giving of assent on behalf of citizens to measures that are to have binding force. In the 'small c' constitution (see p. 96)

[8] A. Trench, 'The Government of Wales Act 2006: The next steps to devolution in Wales' [2006] *PL* 687.

[9] S. 33 re-enacts s. 31 of the 1998 Act, on which see R. Rawlings, 'Quasi-legislative devolution: Powers and principles' (2001) 52 *NILQ* 54 and 'Law making in a virtual Parliament: The Welsh experience' in Hazell and Rawlings (eds.), *Devolution, Law Making and the Constitution.*

[10] CC, *Devolution: Inter-institutional relations in the United Kingdom*, HL 28 (2002/03).

[11] Scottish Parliament Subordinate Legislation Committee, (21 September 1999) col. 31.

[12] HL 192 (2003/04) [17].

[13] See, e.g., R. Rawlings, 'Concordats of the constitution' (2000) 116 *LQR* 257.

there is a sentiment strong enough to amount to a convention that constitutional matters and other matters of great import ought to be reserved for full debate in Parliament, even if there are differences over what these matters are and where the lines are to be drawn. This explains why in the *JCWI* case (p. 114 above) the Court of Appeal asked for *parliamentary* ratification of a regulatory power to strip asylum seekers of their right to welfare benefits leaving them destitute. And fear of what may be done to an unwritten constitution when parliamentary sovereignty is the highest constitutional norm lies behind the warning shots fired by Lord Steyn in *Jackson v Attorney-General* (p. 111 above). In *Jackson*, the appellants were contending that the Hunting Act 2004 was not a 'true' statute, despite the fact that the procedure adopted was in full accordance with that laid down in the Parliament Act 1949. This involved the second contention that the 1949 Act was not a 'true' statute; it was a form of secondary legislation made in terms of the 1911 Act. Lords Bingham and Nicholls made short work of the argument. Lord Bingham thought the meaning of the term 'Act of Parliament' was not 'doubtful, ambiguous or obscure. It is as clear and well understood as any expression in the lexicon of the law. It is used, and used only, to denote primary legislation.' Nor was an Act of Parliament required to 'state on its face' that it was made by the authority of the 1911 Act. Hence legislation made under the 1911 Act was not 'delegated or subordinate or derivative in the sense that its validity is open to investigation in the courts, which would not be permissible in the case of primary legislation'.[14] Lord Steyn did not dissent, though he addressed the issue somewhat differently:

> The word Parliament involves both static and dynamic concepts. The static concept refers to the constituent elements which make up Parliament: the House of Commons, the House of Lords, and the Monarch. The dynamic concept involves the constituent elements functioning together as a law making body. The inquiry is: has Parliament spoken? The law and custom of Parliament regulates what the constituent elements must do to legislate: all three must signify consent to the measure. But, apart from the traditional method of law making, Parliament acting as ordinarily constituted may functionally redistribute legislative power in different ways. For example, Parliament could for specific purposes provide for a two-thirds majority in the House of Commons and the House of Lords. This would involve a redefinition of Parliament for a specific purpose. Such redefinition could not be disregarded.[15]

What occurred when the Countryside Alliance came back to court seeking judicial review of the Hunting Act makes the distinction between primary and secondary legislation amply clear. In terms of classical English judicial review the case was obviously untenable; quite simply statute law is not reviewable. To ground their action, the Alliance had to turn to the European streams of the

[14] *Jackson v Attorney-General* [2005] UKHL 56 [24], noted in Plaxton, 'The concept of legislation: *Jackson v HM Attorney General*' (2006) 69 *MLR* 249.

[15] *Jackson* [81]. The argument is a variant on the so called 'new theory of sovereignty' addressed by R. V. F. Heuston, *Essays in Constitutional Law* (Stevens, 1961).

'multi-streamed jurisdiction', arguing (i) that the Hunting Act contravened their right of property under ECHR Art. 1, Protocol 1 and (ii) that the Act violated their freedom under the EC Treaty to offer services and trade. Both arguments were categorically rejected.[16]

Partly for historical reasons, the courts treat the democratic credentials of Parliament with great respect, as we saw in *ex p. Smith* (p. 114 above), where the court refrained from questioning policy that Parliament had recently considered. *Jackson* is, however, one of a number of recent cases that has seen judicial review creep ever closer to Parliament. A turning point was the *Fire Brigades* case,[17] in which both sides of the constitutional argument were represented. Section 171(1) of the Criminal Justice Act 1988 had been introduced by the House of Lords and passed by Parliament in the face of government opposition to place the *ex gratia* criminal injuries scheme on a statutory footing (see Chapter 17). The Act was stated to come into force 'on such day as the Secretary of State may appoint'. Instead, the Home Secretary introduced legislation to replace the statutory scheme, which failed to pass the Lords. Hoping to delay implementation indefinitely, he replaced the existing scheme with a new, less generous 'tariff-based' *ex gratia* scheme, effectively by-passing the 1988 Act. Trade unions representing workers likely to be affected by cuts in compensation challenged the legality of this action.

Two very different viewpoints inform the arguments in this case which triggered considerable disagreement in both Court of Appeal and House of Lords, though both finally agreed by narrow majorities that the procedure adopted had been improper. Lord Mustill represents the traditional view that legislation is ineffective until it comes into force, reasoning that gave the whip hand to government and legitimated the use of the prerogative in the teeth of Parliament's expressed wishes. For the majority, Lord Lloyd thought it was an abuse of power to stultify the express intention of the legislature by recourse to the prerogative:

> *Lord Mustill* (dissenting): Parliament has its own special means of ensuring that the executive, in the exercise of its delegated functions, performs in a way which Parliament finds appropriate. Ideally, it is these latter methods which should be used to check executive errors and excesses; for it is the task of Parliament and the executive in tandem, not of the courts, to govern the country. In recent years, however, the employment in practice of these specifically Parliamentary measures has fallen short, and sometimes well short, of what was needed to bring the executive into line with the law . . .
>
> To avoid a vacuum in which the citizen would be left without protection against a misuse of executive powers the courts have had no option but to occupy the dead ground in a manner, and in areas of public life, which could not have been foreseen 30 years ago. For myself, I am quite satisfied that this unprecedented judicial role has been greatly to the public benefit. Nevertheless, it has its risks, of which the courts are well aware . . . Some

[16] *R (Countryside Alliance) v Attorney-General* [2007] UKHL 52.
[17] *R v Home Secretary, ex p. Fire Brigades Union* [1995] 2 AC 513.

> of the arguments addressed [in the Court of Appeal] would have the court push to the very boundaries of the distinction between court and Parliament established in, and recognised ever since, the Bill of Rights 1688 . . . 300 years have passed since then, and the political and social landscape has changed beyond recognition. But the boundaries remain; they are of crucial significance to our private and public life; and the courts should, I believe, make sure that they are not overstepped.
>
> *Lord Lloyd:* If one assumes that the postponement for five years was a valid exercise of the power conferred by Parliament, then of course the Home Secretary would be free to continue the existing non-statutory scheme in the meantime, as he has in the past, or substitute another scheme, whether more or less favourable to the victims of violent crime. But the assumption begs the question. It is the decision of the Home Secretary to renounce the statutory scheme, and to surrender his power to implement it, which constitutes the abuse of power in the present case . . .
>
> Ministers must be taken at their word. If they say they will not implement the statutory scheme, they are repudiating the power conferred on them by Parliament in the clearest possible terms. It is one thing to delay bringing the relevant provisions into force. It is quite another to abdicate or relinquish the power altogether. Nor is that all. The Government's intentions may be judged by their deeds as well as their words. The introduction of the tariff scheme, which is to be put on a statutory basis as soon as it has had time to settle down, is plainly inconsistent with a continuing power under section 171 to bring the statutory scheme into force . . . In granting . . . relief, the court is not acting in opposition to the legislature, or treading on Parliamentary toes. On the contrary: it is ensuring that 'powers conferred by Parliament are exercised within the limits, and for the purposes, which Parliament intended'.

Courts are also reluctant to trespass on parliamentary territory or tempt retaliation by scrutinising the internal proceedings of Parliament.[18] Thus when Lord Bingham in *Jackson* examined the history of the Parliament Acts in very great detail, he expressed his feelings that this was a somewhat strange exercise. This has meant that the courts did not until recently turn to parliamentary debates etc. to aid interpretation. *Pepper v Hart*[19] was the first occasion when this was done. It was held that, when statute is obscure or ambiguous, reference can be made to *Hansard* debates and other parliamentary or official material as an aid to statutory construction. Following *Pepper v Hart*, however, doubts were expressed whether the practice would play into the hands of government, which was in a position to manipulate statements made to Parliament and so obtain an advantage inside the judicial process.[20] More recently, the new style

[18] *Pickin v British Railways Board* [1974] AC 765; and see H. W. R. Wade, 'The basis of legal sovereignty' [1955] *CLJ* 172.

[19] *Pepper (Inspector of Taxes) v Hart* [1993] AC 593.

[20] *Jackson* [65]. See for discussion S. Styles, 'The rule of Parliament: Statutory interpretation after *Pepper v Hart* (1994) 14 *OJLS* 151; Lord Steyn '*Pepper v Hart*: A Re-examination' (2001) 21 *OJLS* 59; S. Vogenauer, 'A Retreat from *Pepper v Hart*? A Reply to Lord Steyn' (2006) 26 *OJLS* 629; P. Sales, '*Pepper v Hart*: A footnote to Professor Vogenauer's reply to Lord Steyn' (2006) 26 *OJLS* 585

of explanatory notes to draft bills published on the internet has raised similar doubts; both have been described as likely to lead to a 'politicisation of judicial interpretation'.[21] This fear has led the Speaker to protest that courts were starting to delve too deeply into parliamentary affairs in an effort to seek out and identify the underlying reasons for legislation; there are no circumstances, he has argued, where it is appropriate for a court to refer to the record of parliamentary debates in order to decide whether an enactment is compatible with the European Convention. The House of Lords did not entirely accept this view. Especially in human rights cases, Lord Nicholls said in *Wilson*:

> the court may need additional background information tending to show, for instance, the likely practical impact of the statutory measure and why the course adopted by the legislature is or is not appropriate. Moreover, as when interpreting a statute, so when identifying the policy objective of a statutory provision or assessing the 'proportionality' of a statutory provision, the court may need enlightenment on the nature and extent of the social problem (the 'mischief') at which the legislation is aimed. This may throw light on the rationale underlying the legislation.[22]

In *Huang and Kashmiri*[23] Lord Bingham took a bolder line. Faced with the classic argument that Immigration Rules and supplementary instructions, made by the minister and laid before Parliament, should be assumed to have 'the imprimatur of democratic approval and should be taken to strike the right balance between the interests of the individual and those of the community', Lord Bingham distinguished the Immigration Rules from housing policy which, he said, had:

> been a continuing subject of discussion and debate in Parliament over very many years, with the competing interests of landlords and tenants fully represented, as also the public interest in securing accommodation for the indigent, averting homelessness and making the best use of finite public resources. The outcome, changed from time to time, may truly be said to represent a considered democratic compromise. This cannot be said in the same way of the Immigration Rules and supplementary instructions, which are not the product of active debate in Parliament, where non-nationals seeking leave to enter or remain are not in any event represented.

To proceed down this road would indeed amount to 'major shift in the British constitution' and one fraught with danger and difficulty, as the Speaker's decision to intervene in the *Wilson* case suggests.

[21] R. Munday, 'In the wake of "good governance": Impact assessment and the politicisation of judicial interpretation' (2008) 71 *MLR* 385.

[22] The Speaker was intervening in *Wilson v First County Trust* [2003] UKHL 40 [63]. See also *R v Environment Secretary, ex p. Spath Holme* [2001] 2 AC 349.

[23] *Huang and Kashmiri v Home Secretary* [2007] UKHL 11 [17]. In *Kay v Lambeth LBC* [2006] 2 AC 465 the House of Lords had adopted a more passive approach in respect of housing law.

Less intrusive and more legitimate would be recourse to a statement made under s. 19 of the HRA. This obliges a Minister to make and publish a written statement on introducing legislation either that the provisions of the bill are in his view compatible with the Convention or that, although he is unable to make a statement of compatibility, the Government nevertheless wishes the House to proceed with the bill. For a statement of compatibility to be made, 'the balance of arguments' must favour the view that a bill will survive judicial scrutiny. The section is an important 'firewatching' innovation, operating to concentrate the minds of ministers, all those who have to advise ministers, and Parliament itself on the risk of inadvertently violating human rights law. In *Animal Defenders International*,[24] the question was whether s. 321(2) of the Communications Act 2003, which regulates political advertising, was compatible with ECHR Art. 10. The Law Lords looked to the Commons proceedings, where the minister had stated her inability to make a s. 19 statement because of uncertainty over the meaning of an ECtHR case. The JCHR, which thought the prohibition on political advertising might well be incompatible, had advised the Government to examine ways in which 'more limited but workable and Convention-compliant restrictions could be included in the Bill'; this advice had been endorsed by the Joint Committee on the Draft Communications Bill.[25] The Government on legal advice 'judged that no fair and workable compromise solution could be found'. This was accepted by the JCHR after re-consideration[26] and then by Parliament as a whole.

This substantial consideration of the bill when before Parliament helped to guide the House of Lords to the conclusion that a total ban on broadcast political advertising could be justified in a democratic society, and hence has Convention-compatible. That a policy or law has been carefully considered and sealed with the authority of the representative legislature lends substance to the case that it is 'necessary in a democratic society.' As Baroness Hale said:

> Government and Parliament have recently examined with some care whether a more limited ban could be made to work and have concluded that it could not. The solution chosen has all-party support. Parliamentarians of all political persuasions take the view that the ban is necessary in this democratic society. Any court would be slow indeed to take a different view on a question such as this.[27]

Lord Bingham thought that:

[24] *R (Animal Defenders International) v Culture, Media and Sport Secretary*) [2008] UKHL 15. For the view of the ECtHR, see *VgT Verein gegen Tierfabriken v Switzerland* (2001) 34 EHRR 159.

[25] JCHR, HC 1102 (2001/2) [62–4]; Joint Committee on the Draft Communications Bill, HC 876-1 (2001/2).

[26] JCHR, HC 191 (2002/3), HC 397 (2002/3).

[27] *Animal Defenders International*, respectively [52] [33].

> The weight to be accorded to the judgment of Parliament depends on the circumstances and the subject matter. In the present context it should in my opinion be given great weight, for three main reasons. First, it is reasonable to expect that our democratically-elected politicians will be peculiarly sensitive to the measures necessary to safeguard the integrity of our democracy. It cannot be supposed that others, including judges, will be more so. Secondly, Parliament has resolved, uniquely since the 1998 Act came into force in October 2000, that the prohibition of political advertising on television and radio may possibly, although improbably, infringe article 10 but has nonetheless resolved to proceed under section 19(1)(b) of the Act. It has done so, while properly recognising the interpretative supremacy of the European Court, because of the importance which it attaches to maintenance of this prohibition. The judgment of Parliament on such an issue should not be lightly overridden.

3. Parliament the watchdog

(a) The scrutiny function

Parliament's second and more practical scrutiny function is as important as its representative role. Parliament does not 'make' law in the functional sense of drafting bills; this is government's role, with Parliament's drafting role generally confined to amendment.[28] The two Houses do, however, debate, critique, assent to or dissent from, government proposals and do their best to scrutinise the text. For the Lords Constitution Committee, the scrutiny of legislative texts is fundamental to the work of Parliament and more especially the Lords:

> Parliament has to assent to bills if they are to become the law of the land. Acts of Parliament impinge upon citizens in all dimensions of their daily life. They prescribe what citizens are required to do and what they are prohibited from doing. They stipulate penalties, which may be severe, for failure to comply. They can have a significant impact not only on behaviour but also on popular attitudes. Subjecting those measures to rigorous scrutiny is an essential responsibility of both Houses of Parliament if bad law is to be avoided and the technical quality of all legislation improved. Parliament has a vital role in assuring itself that a bill is, in principle, desirable and that its provisions are fit for purpose. If Parliament gets it wrong, the impact on citizens can on occasion be disastrous; and history has shown examples of legislation that has proved clearly unfit for purpose . . .
>
> Our starting point is that the process by which Parliament considers bills should be structured, rigorous and informed, and sufficient to ensure that Members have adequate opportunity to weigh the merits of the bill and consider the detail. We believe that legislation is most likely to emerge fit for purpose if Parliament has the opportunity to be involved at all stages of the legislative process and has mechanisms to digest informed opinion and comment from concerned citizens and interested organisations. Parliament does not operate in a vacuum. It is important that those affected by, or with knowledge of or having

[28] M. Zander, *The Law-Making Process* (Cambridge University Press, 2004); D. Miers and A. Page, *Legislation*, 2nd edn (Butterworths, 1990).

> an interest in proposed legislation should have an opportunity to make their voices heard while the legislation is being considered rather than after it has taken effect . . .[29]

The Committee, suggesting – not for the first time – that the paradigm had not been achieved, endorsed a 1947 description of Parliament 'as an overworked legislation factory'.[30]

Statistics kept by the Commons confirm this description.[31] Overall, the number of pages of legislation is substantially higher than forty years ago, although the number of statutes 'has if anything been declining'. Starting in 1951 with sixty-four Acts, the statutory load peaked in 1964 with ninety-eight Acts, levelling out in 2006 with fifty-five. Statutes were getting longer: from just under 4,000 pages of statute law in 1951 to 6,000 in 1964, though the figure dropped to 2,712 in 2005, reflecting a sharp rise in delegated legislation (p. 163 below). Contemplating the statistics, the Modernisation Committee made the redundant point that, 'given a smaller volume of legislation each year, Parliament could devote more time to scrutinising it'. But the Committee saw no way out: 'the volume of legislation is largely a function of the programme of the Government of the day rather than a matter of procedural changes in the House'.[32] And governments, we suggested, are becoming steadily more intrusive while, in parallel, there has been a consistent trend to rule-based governance. We have become a highly regulated society.

Lord Renton, who chaired an important Commons report on the quality of legislation, disliked the tendency to push everything into primary legislation. Discussing the Water Act 1989 (418 pages long with 194 sections and 27 schedules) he observed that it contained 'a good deal of law which consists of mere instruction to government departments . . . This is not a suitable device for legislation . . . Internal matters of this kind are best dealt with by the ordinary machinery of government . . . and departmental circulars can play an important part.'[33] This preferred division of functions, in which Parliament 'outlines' policy, leaving it to the administration to finalise detail, dates back to the nineteenth century. In practice, the division is often disregarded. Secondary legislation may be hotly political; instead of simply implementing the 'nuts and bolts' of government policy', it may be used to change policy, 'sometimes in ways that were not envisaged when the primary enabling legislation was passed', and its relative obscurity, which seldom attracts the attention of the media or

[29] CC, *Parliament and the Legislative Process*, HL 173-I (2003/4). And see M. Russell, *Reforming the House of Lords: Lessons from overseas* (Constitution Unit, 2000).

[30] L. Amery, *Thoughts on the Constitution*, 2nd edn (Oxford University Press, 1964), p. 41.

[31] HC Library, *Acts & Statutory Instruments: Volume of United Kingdom Legislation 1950 to 2007*, SN/SG/2911 (Jan. 2008).

[32] Modernisation Committee, *The Legislative Process*, HC 1097 (2005/6) [7] [9].

[33] *Report of the Committee on the Preparation of Legislation*, Cmnd 6053 (1975). See also Lord Renton, 'Current drafting practices and problems in the United Kingdom' (1990) 11 *Stat. Law Rev.* 11, 14.

even of MPs, makes it an ideal way to hide 'bad news'.[34] This makes the style of much modern legislation highly specific and complex. The long Bills today presented to Parliament have codifying tendencies, though codification is usually incomplete. There is an unhappy common law practice of 'legislation by reference', which leaves the searcher to trawl through partially repealed statutes and regulations to discover the true state of the law (though there is now an online data base of revised legislation making it easier to find accurate texts of legislation in force). The Pensions Act 2007, which we meet again in Chapter 12, consists of seventy-eight pages of thirty-seven detailed and highly technical sections, containing a dense list of repeals and revocations with the dates they come into force; nine powers to make regulations or orders vested in the minister or agencies; and eight complex schedules, which take up more space than the sections. Since schedules are unlikely to be debated, they are a good place to hide controversial provisions – though efforts have been made to phase-out some of the 'dirty tricks' available to governments for this purpose[35] through 'programming', whereby a timetable is agreed for each stage of a bill with time allocated in advance to the more controversial clauses; and 'carry-over', which allows consideration of bills to be spread over a parliamentary year.[36]

The Constitution Committee emphasises that:

> for Parliament to examine bills effectively, it needs to understand them. That encompasses the purpose of the bill and the provisions designed to achieve that purpose. For many years, the way in which bills were brought before Parliament was not conducive to aiding understanding. Bills were often drafted in fairly obscure language with no accompanying material to explain the provisions and no clear explanation of the effect of provisions that substituted words for those in earlier Acts. Members were dependent on the Minister's speech on Second Reading and explanations offered in response to probing amendments.[37]

Draftsmen are currently instructed to use accessible language and the explanatory notes that since 1998–9 accompany bills are fuller, clearer and available online. General (previously Standing) Committees, used for detailed scrutiny of bills, can now if they wish operate more like a Select Committee, taking evidence, which widens public access and engages the attention of interested professional bodies and their advisers at a pre-legislative stage. The Constitution Committee thinks this procedure, so far little used, should become standard practice.

[34] E. Page, *Governing by Numbers: Delegated legislation and everyday policy-making* (Hart Publishing, 2001), p. 3, citing the Scrutiny Committee (p. 164 below).

[35] See Modernisation Committee, *Committee Stage of Public Bills: Consultation on alternative options*, HC 810 (2005/6), pp. 3–5.

[36] Modernisation Committee, *Programming of Bills*, HC 1222 (2002/3) contains statistics of use of programming and guillotine. See also Procedure Committee, *Programming of Legislation*, HC 235 (2004/5) and *Government Response*, HC 1169 (2004/5).

[37] *Parliament and the Legislative Process*, HL 173 (2003/4) [76].

(b) Impact assessment

Amongst the mounting piles of documents available to today's legislator are Impact Assessments (IAs). Originating as the chief analytical device for 'better regulation', IAs were, by 2005, administratively required for all forms of UK regulation, from codes of practice to formal legislation, where policy changes could affect the public sector, charities, the voluntary sector or small businesses. The types of impact considered had moved from business matters to include health, gender, race, sustainability, rural issues, human rights and older people.[38]

A basic template made available by the National Audit Office (NAO)[39] tells officials what to cover in a full regulatory impact assessment:

- *Purpose and intended effect* – identifies the objectives of the regulatory proposal
- *Risks* – assesses the risks that the proposed regulations are addressing
- *Benefits* – identifies the benefits of each option including the 'do nothing' option
- *Costs* – looks at all costs including indirect costs
- *Securing compliance* – identifies options for action
- *Impact on small business* – using advice from the [DTI] Small Business Service
- *Public consultation* – takes the views of those affected, and is clear about assumptions and options for discussion
- *Monitoring and evaluation* – establishes criteria for monitoring and evaluation
- *Recommendation* – summarises and makes recommendations to ministers, having regard to the views expressed in public consultation.

According to Cabinet Office guidance,[40] the IA process is continuous. An *initial IA* should inform and ideally accompany a submission to ministers seeking agreement to a proposal and include best estimates of the possible risks, benefits and costs. A *partial RIA* accompanies the near-mandatory public consultation with relevant questions and enquiries. The *full/final RIA* updates and builds upon the analysis in the light of consultation, further information and analysis. 'You can then submit the full RIA to ministers with clear recommendations. It becomes a final RIA when it is signed by the responsible minister and placed in the libraries of the Houses of Parliament.' (You will see this progression illustrated in the *Greenpeace* case at p. 177 below).

The NAO has been keen to emphasise the contribution of IAs 'to the Government's aim of modernising policy making':

[38] See BRTF, *Regulatory Impact Assessment Guidance* (2005 version).

[39] NAO, *Better Regulation: Making good use of regulatory impact assessments*, HC 329 (2001/2), p. 16.

[40] Cabinet Office, *Regulatory Impact Assessment overview* (2005 version).

> Identifying the options for achieving the desired policy outcome and the costs and benefits associated with each option should help assess how policies are likely to work in practice and to develop policies that secure the desired results while avoiding unnecessary burdens. By making RIAs publicly available, members of the community should be able to understand what a proposed regulation is seeking to achieve and what it means for them, and to challenge assumptions with which they disagree. This should contribute to making policies inclusive and decision making transparent. By facilitating Ministerial and parliamentary scrutiny of regulation and subsequent evaluation of whether regulation has achieved what was intended, RIAs should help establish accountability for the regulatory process.[41]

But sampling the quality of the 150–200 final IAs produced each year, the NAO expressed disappointment. Often IAs were not used in the right way. There was a lack of clarity in analysis and persistent weaknesses in the assessments; they were too discursive; and there was a general lack of consistency in the analysis undertaken and presentation of results. Consequently, IAs were only occasionally used to challenge the need for regulation and influence policy decisions; they 'have not yet been a tool which has dramatically altered the regulatory landscape or the way Government thinks about regulation'.[42]

The methodology has today become an inherent part of new public management theory and discourse, intended to suggest that management, administration and now lawmaking are scientific disciplines: from 'rational' administration to 'evidence-based legislation'. 'Better' legislation is no longer merely well-drafted, clear and accessible – as the Hansard Society in a major report on the legislative process insisted that it should be.[43] Better legislation in this new regulatory context is part of a scientific – or pseudo-scientific – pursuit of rational policy development, aimed at 'smart' regulation: in other words, a regulatory strategy that 'offers the best mixtures of regulatory instruments and institutions'.[44] Echoing Power's criticisms of the flattening effects of audit (p. 61 above), Baldwin reminds us that not everything is capable of being measured:

> Smart regulation involves too many variables, estimates and judgments to lend itself to the RIA process. To evaluate it by using RIA processes involves something approaching a category mistake . . . It is difficult to see how ongoing regulatory co-ordination, with all its flexibilities, can be tested in advance by a RIA process as if it is a static single-shot system.[45]

41 NAO, *Better Regulation*, pp. 3–4. The acronym RIA stands for regulatory impact assessment, later generalised as IA.

42 NAO, *Evaluation of Regulatory Impact Assessments 2005-06*, HC 1305 (2005/6), pp. 3–4, 12; NAO, *Regulatory Impact Assessments and Sustainable Development* (2006), p. 2. And see T. Ambler *et al.*, *Regulators: Box tickers or burdens busters?* (British Chambers of Commerce, 2006).

43 Hansard Society, *Making the Law: Report of the Hansard Society Commission on the legislative process* (1992).

44 R. Baldwin, *Rules and Government* (Clarendon Press, 1995), p. 485; J. Black, '"Which arrow?": Rule type and regulatory policy' [1995] *PL* 94. And see below, Ch. 6.

45 Baldwin, *Rules and Government*, pp. 503, 506–7.

This warning should be borne in mind when we move to considering post-legislative scrutiny.

(c) 'Mainstreaming': the Joint Committee on Human Rights

Feldman, former academic adviser to the JCHR, feels that a 'human rights culture' is beginning to emerge in Parliament. This has brought substantial improvements in every area of parliamentary scrutiny, including delegated legislation, where there exists 'the added incentive that, unlike primary legislation, subordinate legislation is normally invalid and ineffective to the extent of any incompatibility with a Convention right, which concentrates the mind wonderfully'.[46] This is an important point. Section 10 of the HRA authorises a minister, where either the domestic courts or ECtHR have found legislation to be incompatible with the Convention, to 'make such amendments to the legislation as he considers necessary to remove the incompatibility'. This 'fast track' procedure allows any minister who sees 'compelling reasons' to do so, to amend statute law by means of delegated legislation, a so-called 'Henry VIII clause' that Parliament normally resents. In this case, the assumption is that government's motives for using 'fast-track procedure' will always be the benign wish to bring the law into compliance with human rights standards. This assumption, we have begun to see, is not always correct. Evidence that the JCHR takes its scrutiny powers seriously is therefore welcome.

The JCHR, set up and charged with 'considering human rights issues in the UK' has emerged as central to the effectiveness of Parliament in maintaining human rights standards:

> In many other jurisdictions with constitutional bills of rights, or other legal protections of human rights, court judgments are the single most important source of interpretation of the rights protected. In the UK's institutional arrangements for protecting human rights, however, Parliament, as well as the judiciary, has a central role to play in deciding how best to protect the rights which are considered to be fundamental. This means that in our system, when courts give judgments in which they find that a law, policy or practice is in breach of human rights, there is still an important role for Parliament to play in scrutinising the adequacy of the Government's response to such judgments and, in some cases, deciding for itself whether a change in the law is necessary to protect human rights and, if so, what that change should be.[47]

Taking as its starting point the s. 19 statement, the JCHR effectively 'shadows the minister', scrutinising all government and private bills in accordance with a sifting system and reporting to the House on those with implications

[46] D. Feldman, 'The impact of human rights on the UK legislative process' (2004) 25 *Stat. Law Rev.* 91,102.

[47] JCHR, *Monitoring the Government's Response to Court Judgments Finding Breaches of Human Rights*, HC 728 (2006/7) [1].

for human rights. Its approach, set out in every scrutiny report, has been to interpret its brief widely; to these ends it is prepared to take account of conventions other than the ECHR to which the UK is a signatory, such as the UN Refugee Convention, Convention against Torture and Convention on the Rights of the Child.[48] Where the explanatory notes or human rights memoranda accompanying a bill are inadequate, the minister is likely to face questioning from the JCHR, which pays special attention to any 'clear pattern of incompatibility, i.e. if reports from us and our predecessors have repeatedly raised the same incompatibility issues and the Government does not appear to have addressed them'.[49] The Committee may then make repeated reports (p. 157 below).

After eight years' experience, the JCHR published a lengthy review of its working practices, explaining how such a small Committee could manage its demanding mandate:

> The Committee intends to maintain its predecessors' undertaking to scrutinise all Government and private bills introduced into Parliament for their human rights implications. It will seek however to focus its scrutiny on the most significant human rights issues raised by bills in order to enhance its ability to alert both Houses to them in a timely way. To this end it will implement a new sifting procedure, to be carried out by its Legal Adviser under the Chairman's delegated authority according to certain criteria to establish the significance of human rights issues raised by a bill . . . The Committee's Reports on bills will be shorter and more focused, and the Committee intends more regularly to reach a view on issues of proportionality which may arise . . . The Committee also re-emphasises the importance of a substantial improvement in the quality and consistency of the information which the Government provides to Parliament on the human rights implications of bills at the time of their introduction.[50]

The reduction in overall work brought about by the sifting process would be used to expand pre-legislative scrutiny, 'in order to draw the attention of Parliament and the Government to any potential pitfalls in relation to a proposed policy course'; post-legislative scrutiny would also be undertaken 'to assess whether the implementation of legislation has produced unwelcome human rights implications'. Thematic inquiries, such as that into deaths in custody,[51] would continue, and inquiry work would start into 'major unexpected developments and significant human rights issues of national concern' where the Committee felt it could make an 'important and useful contribution' to parliamentary and public debate. There are also 'regular evidence sessions' with the human rights

[48] JCHR, *The UN Convention Against Torture (UNCAT)*, HC 701 (2005/6); *The UN Convention on the Rights of the Child*, HC 81 (2002/3).

[49] JCHR, *Monitoring the Government's Response to Court Judgments*, HC 728 (2006/7)

[50] See JCHR, *The Committee's Future Working Practices*, HC 1575 (2005/6) [40-2]. The JCHR has 12 members and has had two Labour Chairs: Jean Corston MP and Andrew Dismore MP.

[51] See JCHR, *Deaths in Custody*, HC 137 (2004/5); *Government Response*, HC 416 (2004/5).

minister, and work with the newly established Commission for Equality and Human Rights is projected. The regular discussions with government, process of hearing and sifting evidence, issuing reports, and receiving and responding to government responses are all, of course, relatively formal but they certainly fall within the description of 'dialogue'.[52]

The JCHR takes into consideration the broad political or public impact of prospective legislation, including the extent to which it has attracted public and media attention and 'reputable NGOs or other interested parties have made representations'; it is becoming something of a focal point for human rights lobby groups. In publishing special reports, it tries to pick up missed opportunities to promote and protect human rights and significant topical issues, using a broad proportionality test to weigh the importance of an affected right, the number of people likely to be affected, their vulnerability, the strength of justification for the interference and the extent to which the UK's 'most significant positive obligations are engaged'. Amongst subjects chosen are the cases for a Human Rights Commission and Children's Commissioner for England and latterly the 'British Bill of Rights'.[53] Noting the popular preference for social and economic rights, the JCHR has included these in its analysis, asserting that they are more than merely political aspirations and merit the same degree of consideration as civil and political rights.

> The popular misconception which we noted in our Report on *The Case for a Human Rights Commission*, that human rights are a 'criminal's charter', cannot be as easily applied to economic, social and cultural rights. Rights to adequate healthcare and education, to equal treatment in the workplace, and to protection against the worst extremes of poverty, deal in the substance of people's everyday lives. In a society which is setting out to build a 'culture of rights' this public identification with core economic and social rights is not insignificant.[54]

We should not infer from this that the JCHR refrains from reporting on controversial civil-liberties issues; very much the reverse. Exchanges with government over terrorism are best described as a ping-pong match. A stream of reports on counter-terrorism and asylum bills has flowed from the Committee, giving it considerable expertise strengthened by contacts with experts (such as Lord Carlile, the Government's independent adviser on terrorism) from whom it takes evidence. This has allowed the JCHR to develop and fiercely promote its own policies. In its report on the 2008 Counter-Terrorism Bill, for example,

[52] E.g., JCHR, *Life Like Any Other? Human rights of adults with learning disabilities*, HC 73 (2007/8), *Government Response*, Cm. 7378 (2008); JCHR, *The Human Rights of Older People in Healthcare*, HC 378 (2006/7) *Government Response*, HC 72 (2007/8).

[53] *The Case for a Human Rights Commission*, HC 489-I (2002/3); *The Case for a Children's Commissioner for England*, HC 666 (2002/3); *A British Bill of Rights*, HC 150-iii (2007/8); and see n. 52 above.

[54] JCHR, *The International Convention on Economic, Social and Cultural Rights*, HC 1188 (2003/4) [29].

it set out its choice of the 'five most significant human rights issues which are in need of thoroughgoing parliamentary scrutiny and debate': pre-charge detention; post-charge questioning; control orders and special advocates; the threshold test for charging and the admissibility of intercept. It went on to consider these issues in considerable detail, with a view to 'framing the debate on the Bill'.[55]

The JCHR was not particularly impressed by the judgments in terrorism cases discussed in Chapter 3. In its own '28 days report', the JCHR 'reached the firm conclusion that the system of special advocates, as currently conducted, fails to afford individuals a fair hearing, or even a substantial measure of procedural justice'. It recommended that:

- the Secretary of State be placed under a statutory obligation always to provide a statement of the gist of the closed material
- the prohibition on any communication between the special advocate and the individual (or their legal representative) after the special advocate has seen the closed material be relaxed
- the low standard of proof in SIAC proceedings be raised.[56]

When the Government rejected all its recommendations, the JCHR urged it to re-visit the matter, expressing regret that the Government had not seen fit to discuss the House of Lords judgment in *MB* with the special advocates themselves. Widening the 'dialogue' and inviting the judges to join it, the JCHR accused the Law Lords of timidity and obscurity, remarking that the High Court had found considerable difficulty in deciding exactly what was required to give effect to the confusing judgments:

> We welcome the decision of the House of Lords in *MB* that it would be a breach of an individual's right to a fair hearing if a control order could be made where the essence of the case against him is entirely undisclosed to him. We have frequently made the same observation in our reports on the control order legislation. However, we are surprised at the Lords' interpretation of the scope of their power under section 3 of the Human Rights Act to read words into a statute to avoid an incompatibility with a Convention right. In 2005, in the Prevention of Terrorism Act, Parliament grappled with how to strike the right balance between the right to a fair hearing and keeping sensitive information secret. It decided (against our advice) to strike that balance by placing a duty on courts in control

[55] *Counter-Terrorism Policy and Human Rights (Eighth Report): Counter-Terrorism Bill*, HC 199 (2007/8); JCHR, *Counter-Terrorism Policy and Human Rights (Twelfth Report): Annual renewal of 28 Days 2008 Counter-Terrorism Policy and Human Rights (Twelfth Report): Annual renewal of 28 Days 2008*, HC 825 (2007/8); *Counter-Terrorism Policy and Human Rights: Government responses to the Committee's Twentieth and Twenty-first Reports and other correspondence*, HC 756 (2007/8); *Counter-Terrorism Policy and Human Rights (Fourteenth Report): Annual Renewal of Control Orders Legislation*, HC 37 (2008/9).

[56] See *Government Reply to the Nineteenth Report from the Joint Committee on Human Rights Session 2006-07: Counter-Terrorism policy and human rights: 28 days, intercept and post-charge questioning*, Cm. 7215 (2007).

> order proceedings to receive and act on material even the gist of which is not disclosed to the controlled person. It used mandatory language to make that intention clear. To weaken Parliament's clear mandatory language by 'reading in' the words 'except where to do so would be incompatible with the right of the controlled person to a fair trial' does, as Lord Bingham observed, 'very clearly fly in the face of Parliament's intention'.
>
> The scheme of the Human Rights Act deliberately gives Parliament a central role in deciding how best to protect the rights protected in the ECHR. Striking the right balance between sections 3 and 4 of the Human Rights Act is crucial to that scheme of democratic human rights protection. In our view it would have been more consistent with the scheme of the Human Rights Act for the House of Lords to have given a declaration of incompatibility, requiring Parliament to think again about the balance it struck in the control order legislation between the various competing interests. In any event, we think it is now incumbent on Parliament to consider again, in detail, exactly what a 'fair hearing' requires in this particular context, in light of the House of Lords judgment, and to amend the control order legislation accordingly.[57]

The Committee went on to make detailed proposals as to steps the Government should take immediately in the forthcoming counter-terrorism legislation, arguing that 'counter-terrorism measures which breach human rights are ultimately counter-productive and therefore worse than ineffective in countering terrorism: they risk exacerbating the problem'.

In a later report on renewal of control orders,[58] the Government was sharply reminded that no response had been made to the many earlier reports on extension of pre-trial detention, which were therefore reiterated. The Committee complained also that it could not report on two measures raising significant human rights issues because these had been introduced too late in the proceedings. This was not the first complaint of failure to deal fairly with the Committee by laying reports etc. in time; indeed, consistent failures in this respect prompted the JCHR in its latest report on counter-terrorism to recommend that the independent adviser on terrorism should, like the PCA, report directly to Parliament, effectively transforming him into a parliamentary officer.

It is not the first time that the JCHR has taken issue with the courts. After *Leeds v Price*,[59] where the House of Lords had refused to set aside the domestic rules of precedent in order to allow a lower court to take into consideration a subsequent decision of the ECtHR that was clearly inconsistent, the JCHR tartly remarked:

[57] HC 199 [46–7] referring to *Home Secretary v MB and Others* [2007] UKHL 46 and *Home Secretary v E* [2007] EWHC 233 (Admin) (Beatson J).

[58] *Counter-Terrorism Policy and Human Rights (Ninth Report): Annual renewal of control orders legislation*, HC 356 (2007/8) [33], citing *Third Report of the Independent Reviewer pursuant to section 14(3) of the Prevention of Terrorism Act 2005* (18 Feb. 2008). See to the same effect the HL Merits of Statutory Instruments Committee, *Draft Prevention of Terrorism Act 2005 (Continuance in force of sections 1 to 9) Order 2008*, HL 51 (2007/08).

[59] *Leeds Corporation v Price* decided with *Kay v Lambeth Corporation* [2006] UKHL 10. The case concerned the right of local authorities to evict unauthorised occupiers from their land. The GJCHR was supporting the Government, which intervened to argue for a relaxation of the doctrine of precedent in the circumstances of the *Leeds* appeal.

> It is likely that the decision in *Leeds v Price* effectively excludes the judicial branch from having any significant role in the implementation of Strasbourg judgments against the UK. We are concerned that, without Parliament becoming involved, responsibility for the effective implementation of the judgments of the ECtHR will remain principally with the Government. If judgments are not given effect domestically and individuals are required to go to Strasbourg in order to gain just satisfaction, this will also contribute to the significant burden faced by the ECtHR as a result of repetitive cases. The effect of the House of Lords decision in *Leeds v Price* is to make it all the more important that there is effective parliamentary scrutiny of the Government's response to ECtHR judgments finding the UK in breach of the Convention and places an extra onus on Parliament to ensure that the law is changed as swiftly as possible following a finding of violation.[60]

The JCHR takes its monitoring of government responses to declarations of incompatibility and implementation of Strasbourg judgments seriously; its reports are, indeed, the best hope of finding out what is going on.[61] 'Dialogue' with ministers is detailed and specific. Following the ECtHR judgment in *Hirst v UK*[62] concerning the voting rights of convicted prisoners, for example, the JCHR commented unfavourably on Lord Falconer's timetable for implementation. In reply, the difficulty of this contentious matter was pleaded; it was under consultation. Six months later, when the timetable had slipped again, the chairman wrote asking for an updated timetable. The Committee had to register its disappointment in its 2008 report that no concrete timetable had as yet been set, raising serious questions regarding the government's sincerity.

Nicol has argued that the intention in the HRA was to give 'politicians a stake in the rights-game' and Parliament 'a voice of its own'.[63] One consequence of this pluralist model of rights-formation is that parliamentarians may develop conceptions of rights that diverge from those of government and judiciary. If the JCHR is the voice of Parliament for these purposes, then it is a surprisingly radical and independent voice. Its input into the human rights 'dialogue' is uncompromising and its influence in its continuous dialogue with ministers considerable. It is not afraid to voice views that differ starkly from those of the courts. It is a source of information not only for the two Houses but also for the general public. As indicated earlier, the JCHR has emerged as a focal point for human rights campaigners, who regularly give evidence for its reports. On occasion, it could indeed be seen to be acting more like a human rights commission or lobby group than a committee of MPs.

[60] *Monitoring the Government's Response to Court Judgments*, HC 728 (2006/7) [13].

[61] See JCHR, *Implementation of Strasbourg Judgments: First progress report*, HC 954 (2005/6); *Monitoring the Government's Response to Court Judgments Finding Breaches of Human Rights*, HC 728 (2006/7) and HC 1078 (2007/8) [47]–[63].

[62] *Hirst v UK*, App. No. 74025/01 (6 Oct. 2005).

[63] D. Nicol, 'The Human Rights Act and the politicians' (2004) 24 *Legal Studies* 451, 452 and 'Law and Politics after the Human Rights Act' [2006] *PL* 722.

(d) Pre-legislative scrutiny

The practice of making bills available in draft for public consultation and pre-legislative scrutiny followed a recommendation from the Modernisation Committee in 1997.[64] By 2007, forty-five bills had been subject to this procedure – fewer than the Committee had hoped.[65] Pre-legislative scrutiny is concerned not so much with drafting style – though perhaps it ought to be – as with human rights issues, spending implications, regulatory impact assessment and delegation of powers. In some ways therefore the new scrutinising work duplicates that of other parliamentary committees, though it has the advantage that the 'fire-watching' comes at a stage when change is still possible. Time remains a serious problem; some complex bills are published in stages; essential draft regulations are often unavailable and a terse recommendation that all draft bills 'be accompanied by a comprehensive set of draft secondary legislation' has not always prevailed.[66]

There is near-universal agreement that pre-legislative scrutiny is 'a good thing': parliamentary officials indicate that it saves time at later stages; the Constitution Committee welcomes it, pointing specifically to the advantages for regional elected assemblies; the Law Society and other professional bodies see it as playing a significant part in improving the quality of bills. For the Hansard Society, it is 'an extremely positive development' because the public can be involved. The House of Lords Constitution Committee, hoping to see pre-legislative scrutiny extended, has recommended technical improvements, such as checklists, for a more consistent approach; greater access to information; evidence-taking facilities and so on.[67] A Scrutiny Unit has also been set up to deal with the problem that scrutinising committees are increasingly asked to survey a mass of documentary and statistical material, dealing with technical subjects such as resource budgeting, which are beyond their expertise. The Unit, set up in 2002, comprises seventeen staff, including lawyers, economists and an accountant; it advises on the reading of documentation and statistical material used in pre-legislative scrutiny, including regulatory impact assessments.

The Modernisation Committee sees pre-legislative scrutiny as aiding consensus and helping Parliament to 'connect with the public':

> Pre-legislative scrutiny of draft bills, one of the most successful Parliamentary innovations of the last ten years, should become more widespread, giving outside bodies and individuals a chance to have their say before a bill is introduced and improving the quality of the bills that are presented to Parliament. Members who have served on pre-legislative committees should

[64] Modernisation Committee, *The Legislative Process*, HC 190 (1997/8).

[65] House of Commons Library, *Pre-Legislative Scrutiny*, SN/PC/2822 (November 2007), p. 7.

[66] A. Kennon, 'Pre-legislative scrutiny of draft bills' [2004] PL 478, 488.

[67] HC 1097 (2005/6) [20]; Hansard Society, 'Pre-Legislative Scrutiny' (2004) 5 CC, *Issues in Law Making*; HL173-I (2003/4). And see CC, *Pre-legislative Scrutiny in the 2006-7 Session*, HL 129 (2007/8) and *Follow-up*, HL 43 (2007/8).

> be invited to return for the standing committee stage, drawing on their experience with the draft bill to contribute to the detailed consideration of the bill itself . . . there is evidence that, by informing Members more thoroughly about the issues surrounding a bill, pre-legislative scrutiny can make the Parliamentary stages of a bill more challenging for Ministers.
>
> As a matter of routine, Government bills should be referred to committees which have the power to take evidence as well as to debate and amend a bill, and these committees should be named public bill committees. This is not intended to be a substitute for pre-legislative scrutiny; it is to enable the Members who will be going through the bill in detail to inform themselves about its contents and to give the Minister a chance to respond to questions from the Committee, a process which is likely to be more fruitful than a series of debates on 'probing' amendments.
>
> The standing committee stage itself could be improved by increasing the notice period for amendments – giving Members more time to prepare for debates – and Members should have the opportunity to table brief explanations of their amendments. The House should take the first steps towards computerising standing committee papers and providing onscreen access to papers in committee rooms. In the longer term, this could have far-reaching implications for the way that Members use standing committee papers, for example, by providing hypertext links between different documents and showing how the bill would look if particular amendments were made . . .
>
> A more flexible approach to the timing of bills could bring some benefits. In particular, a move away from the 'standard' one-day debate on second reading could allow for longer second reading debates on some bills, and shorter debates on others.
>
> Parliament should improve the quality of the information it provides both for its own Members and for the public. A new series of 'legislation gateways' on the internet will provide a single source of information for each bill and the House of Commons Library will produce a Research Paper covering the committee stage of most bills, supplementing the Reports that are currently produced before second reading.[68]

The implications of these recommendations are considerable, bringing a very real risk of overload. The plethora of committees – general committees, departmental select committees, the JCHR, the constitutional committees of the two Houses, and so on – which all now take a hand in scrutinising legislation brings the further danger of overlapping and contradictory recommendations, reducing any impact they might have.

(e) Post-legislative scrutiny

Parliament is also starting to take an interest in the output end of the legislative sequence, toying with the idea of post-legislative scrutiny. As Jean Corston, when Chair of the JCHR, explained in a letter to the Constitution Committee:

> As legislators, we need to pay as much attention to what happens after we have finished our specialised task of making the law as we do to the processes by which we achieve

[68] Modernisation Committee, *The Legislative Process*, HC 1097 (2005/6) [11].

> the law. The professional deformation against which we perhaps have to be most wary is supposing that legislating is the most effective way to achieve our ambitions, and that lawmaking is a precise science which can result in a perfect product. Our responsibility does not begin with a Bill's introduction to Parliament or end with the royal assent. Improving the efficiency with which we process legislation is only a small part of improving our effectiveness.[69]

The Constitution Committee favoured post-legislative scrutiny on the ground that it would allow implementation to be regularly monitored.[70] It did not, however, expand on how precisely this was to be done, limiting its advice to the recommendation that all legislation should be reviewed within three years either of commencement or passage of the legislation. The matter was then referred to the Law Commission which, after lengthy consultation, published essentially cautious recommendations,[71] fearing that post-legislative scrutiny would simply serve to reopen contentious political debates, while the huge resource implications would fall largely on already over-burdened departments. Warily, it concluded that the approach should be evolutionary and should build on what was already in place.

In its belated response, the Government chose to draw attention to its record of reforms,[72] including:

- more frequent publication of bills in draft, allowing pre-legislative scrutiny both inside and outside Parliament
- publication of a draft legislative programme[73]
- introduction of published Explanatory Notes on Bills and Acts
- measured use of 'carry-over' of bills from one session to the next so as to help make better use of parliamentary time
- renaming of Commons standing committees on bills as 'public bill committees' and fuller explanatory material, to promote greater public understanding
- oral evidence-taking as a standard part of public bill committee work on programmed government bills starting in the Commons
- written evidence taking procedures in public bill committees.

On post-legislative scrutiny, the Government agreed with the Law Commission's cautious approach. There were lessons to be earned from selective post-legislative scrutiny not only where problems were identified but also where things had gone well, but any more formal structure must be proportionate. It must:

[69] *Parliament and the Legislative Process*, HL 173-ii, pp. 164–7.

[70] *Parliament and the Legislative Process*, HL 173-i (2004/5), Ch. 5.

[71] Law Commission, *Post-Legislative Scrutiny*, CP No 178 (2006) and *Post-Legislative Scrutiny*, Cm. 6945 (2006).

[72] Office of the Leader of the House of Commons, *Post-Legislative Scrutiny: The government's approach*, Cm. 7320 (2008).

[73] Published in July, anticipating the traditional Queen's Speech in November; see House of Commons Library, *Draft Queen's Speech*, SN/PC/4398.

- concentrate on appropriate Acts and not waste resources attempting detailed reviews of *every* Act
- avoid re-running what are basically policy debates already conducted during passage of the Act
- reflect the specific circumstances of each Act (for example, associated secondary legislation or surrounding policy environment)
- be complementary to the scrutiny which can already take place, in particular through existing Commons select committee activity.

The initiative should therefore be left to Commons committees. All Acts would receive a measure of post-legislative scrutiny within government and a memorandum would be prepared as a basis for scrutiny by the appropriate departmental select committee; some Acts, on a considered and targeted basis, would go on to receive more in-depth scrutiny.

There are, in fact, strong arguments against post-legislative scrutiny, which have not been properly investigated. The first, mentioned by the Law Commission, concerns resources; post-legislative review as envisaged would add substantially to the burdensome paperwork generated by regular pre-legislative impact assessment. The second is that it is not clearly within the legislator's remit and its close links with impact assessment mean that, if it is to work properly, there must be co-operation with administration, alone capable of monitoring the administrative process. This raises questions as to how Parliament could react. The legislative process is not within Parliament's grasp: space for amending legislation needs to be found in the crowded government bill programme. So Parliament would need to authorise 'fast track' procedures, which it does not like, as it has done in the case of deregulation (see p. 168 below). For government, the main concern is to avoid replaying policy arguments. The hope that this can be averted by a 'cooling-off period' of three to five years is simply naïve. Has the Countryside Alliance, for example, abandoned opposition to the Hunting Act four years (and two House of Lords challenges) after the Act came into force? Have anti-abortionists given up hope of seeing the Abortion Act repealed? The prospect of post-legislative scrutiny would breathe new life into buried political disputes.

4. Delegated legislation

Ideally, legislation and the regulations needed to implement it should form part of a single scheme and be drafted by the same team;[74] in practice this counsel of perfection is seldom met. The fact that the style of drafting secondary legislation 'is on the whole worse than that for primary legislation' can partly be explained by the fact that it is not drafted by specialist parliamentary draftsmen but by departmental lawyers who 'despite best efforts and training perhaps do

[74] Australian ARC, *Rule Making by Commonwealth Agencies* (Australian Government Publishing Service, Report No. 35, 1992), Ch. 4.

not have the opportunity to build up the necessary skill and expertise.'[75] The instructions on which the text is based often come from junior civil servants, who may themselves occasionally draft statutory instruments without the advice of parliamentary draftsmen or even the help of departmental lawyers.[76] These drafting problems, creating a greater need for scrutiny, should not be overlooked.

After World War II, when delegated powers had proliferated, the Statutory Instruments Act 1946 (SIA) was passed. It provided that statutory instruments as defined in the Act must be laid before Parliament for approval. In 'affirmative procedure', regulations need confirmation by the House, although this may in practice occur before the scrutiny committee has reported on them or the vote may be purely formal after a debate in a general committee. In 'negative procedure', a statutory instrument enters into force unless a motion to annul is successfully moved. The first scrutiny committee was the Committee on Statutory Instruments established in 1944. A survey of the markedly inadequate arrangements in 1971 led to a measure of rationalisation, when the Committee merged with the Special Orders Committee of the Lords to form the Joint Committee on Statutory Instruments (JCSI), which scrutinises all statutory instruments or drafts requiring affirmative resolution.[77]

The JCSI publishes around thirty scrutinising reports annually plus an annual report.[78] Its remit is to scrutinise the text of regulations for drafting faults and ensure that they conform to certain overriding principles: a statutory instrument should not impose a tax; its parent legislation must not oust the jurisdiction of the courts; it should not have retrospective effect without the express authority of the parent legislation. It can also be referred on the ground that there is doubt whether it is *intra vires*; that it makes an unusual or unexpected use of its powers; or on 'any other ground which does not impinge upon the merits of the instrument or the policy behind it'. The JCSI also monitors departmental progress in updating the regulatory stock but, in contrast to the Committee on the Merits of Statutory Instruments set up by the Lords in 2003, is not empowered to look at policy.

The Merits Committee can draw to the attention of the House of Lords any instrument considered to be 'politically or legally important or that gives rise to issues of public policy likely to be of interest to the House',

75 Hansard Society, *Making the Law*, 285 (Law Society representations).

76 Page, *Governing by Numbers*, Ch. 6. And see E. Page and B. Jenkins, *Policy Bureaucracy: Government with a cast of thousands* (Oxford University Press, 2005), pp. 48–9, 61–2.

77 HC Standing Order 151, HL 74. Commons Members sit separately as the Select Committee on Delegated Legislation to deal with those instruments which need to be laid only before the House of Commons.

78 The Annual Report not only contains statistics but list 'laggards' and 'leaders' in rectification: see, e.g., JCSI, *Scrutinising Statutory Instruments: Departmental Returns, 2006*, HC 917 (2006/7). And see J. Hayhurst and D. Wallington, 'The Parliamentary scrutiny of delegated legislation' [1988] *PL* 255.

which 'imperfectly achiev[es] its policy objectives', inappropriately delegates legislative power or incorrectly transposes EU law. Reviewing the area, the Merits Committee has stressed that, because statutory instruments cannot be amended during parliamentary scrutiny, it is essential that they be well formulated and well explained when presented. It has criticised lack of clarity in explanatory memoranda, inappropriate implementation of EU directives and insufficient progress in the consolidation of successive instruments, and censured 'failures to engage in "grass roots" consultation where regulations are being made which will affect the lives of ordinary citizens'.[79] The Committee blames in-house departmental procedures: the absence in some departments of a strategic approach to the making of statutory instruments, especially long-term planning and programme management measured against milestones. This suggests that departments do not take secondary legislation seriously. The Law Commission is in agreement, seeing the onus for improvement as lying on government: it should 'give more thought to consolidation of secondary legislation with the aim of improving accessibility'. More specifically, the related provisions of primary and secondary legislation 'should be capable of being accessed in a coherent fashion by a straightforward and freely available electronic search.'[80]

It could be retorted that Parliament does not take scrutiny sufficiently seriously. Indeed, the Clerk to the House of Lords Delegated Powers and Deregulation Committee notes 'widespread agreement that Parliament's consideration of secondary legislation is second rate'.[81] The main cause is the rise in number and length of statutory instruments (not all of which are laid before Parliament). In 1951, there were 2,144 but the numbers registered have doubled since the 1980s, from around 2,000 to over the 4,000 mark. The devolved administrations have naturally provided a major boost. Again, the volume rose from 2,970 pages in 1951 to 4,370 in 1964; by 2005, the figure had jumped dramatically, to almost 12,000 pages annually. The numbers of those subject to only negative procedure had also risen exponentially at Westminster. In fact, very few statutory instruments are discussed on the floor of the House of Commons: in the three sessions beginning 2004–05, for example, just 37:

> Does this matter? I think that most people involved in the parliamentary process would say that it does. The volume of secondary legislation has increased, is increasing and is unlikely to diminish. Statistics which the Government has recently provided show that this increase is particularly true for negative instruments which Parliament at present almost always nods through without comment. At the same time, the importance of much of the content of secondary legislation is increasing. It covers increasingly complex issues, perhaps especially

[79] Merits Committee, *The Management of Secondary Legislation*, HL 149 (2005/6) [122].

[80] Law Commission, *Post-Legislative Scrutiny* [4.14–15]. The Commission favoured an additional parliamentary joint committee.

[81] P. Tudor, 'Secondary legislation: Second class or crucial?' (2000) 21 *Stat. Law Rev.* 149, 150.

> in relation to information technology, where the goalposts are constantly changing and which is therefore a prime candidate for secondary legislation. And it covers issues which are increasingly sensitive, for example, relating to immigration and asylum issues.[82]

It is not that Westminster's Scrutiny Committees are not useful but their scope is limited and their procedures a little old-fashioned; they do not avail themselves, for example, of scrutiny techniques used elsewhere in government.[83] By no means all secondary legislation comes within the parameters of the SIA; not all statutory instruments are subject to affirmative procedure; very few of those subject to negative procedure are actually considered by Parliament. The Scrutiny Committees are unable to make amendments but are reliant on negotiation with departments. They can recommend debate either in committee or on the floor of the House but only a tiny handful of measures reported to the House is actually debated.[84]

The Procedure Committee blames Parliament for 'too great a readiness . . . to delegate wide legislative powers to Ministers, and no lack of enthusiasm on their part to take such powers. The result is an excessive volume of delegated legislation'.[85] Parliamentary procedure is 'palpably unsatisfactory, and offers the House scarcely any opportunity for constructive and purposeful discussion', while negative procedure allows instruments to slip through 'unregarded, undebated and often unnoticed by Members'. The Committee thinks the forty-day scrutiny period too short; it should be extended to the sixty days allowed to the Deregulation Committee (see p. 167 below) and a new Standing Order made forbidding a final decision in advance of the recommendations of the JCSI. A new and significant proposal to experiment with a new, 'super-affirmative' procedure, applicable to both affirmative and negative instruments, would require departments to signal particularly complex or significant affirmative orders to the House for channelling to the most appropriate committee of its choice.[86] Forcefully pointing out that almost all its proposed reforms had 'been pioneered . . . and shown to be eminently workable' elsewhere, including the scrutiny of primary legislation, the Procedure Committee concluded that this cast the failures of the system into even starker relief and rendered 'the task of modernising scrutiny of delegated legislation even more pressing'.[87] But in 2002, it had yet again to record stalemate; its two previous reports had received no government response nor had changes in Standing Orders or amendment been made to the SIA. Once again the Procedure

[82] *Ibid.*

[83] D. Oliver, 'Improving the scrutiny of bills: The case for standards and checklists' [2006] *PL* 219; HL 173-I (2003/4), from [88].

[84] On the need to manage the laying process, see HL 149 (2005/6) [71–4]. See also T. St. John Bates, 'The future of parliamentary scrutiny of delegated legislation: Some judicial perspectives' (1998) 19 *Stat. Law Rev.* 155.

[85] Procedure Committee, *Delegated Legislation*, HC 152 (1995/6).

[86] *Delegated Legislation*, HC 152 [57].

[87] Procedure Committee, *Delegated Legislation*, HC 48 (1999/2000) [51].

Committee stressed the need for a sifting process; this time the Government rejected the proposal out-of-hand.[88]

(a) Deregulation and 'Henry VIII clauses': A case study

If delegated legislation is a necessary evil, executive powers to amend or repeal primary legislation retrospectively are regarded less complacently. Because it allows the executive to override the express wishes of Parliament and permits primary legislation to be overridden by secondary legislation, the so-called 'Henry VIII clause' is widely seen as an unconstitutional threat to parliamentary sovereignty and meets a hostile reception.[89] Yet we have already met several sweeping Henry VIII clauses, notably s. 10 of the HRA, which empowers a minister to act by order to 'make such amendments to the legislation as he considers necessary' to remove the incompatibility to one of the Convention Rights set out in Schedule 1 of the Act. Section 2 of the European Communities Act 1972 (ECA), discussed in greater detail below, not only contains powers to transpose EC law into the domestic legal order by Order in Council but also makes EC regulation directly applicable inside the UK. There is some sense that the use of Henry VIII clauses is increasing and that its legitimacy is less contested.

The Lords set up its committee on the Scrutiny of Delegated Powers in 1992 in response to the sweeping powers proposed in the Deregulation and Contracting Out Bill, described by Lord Rippon as 'a Henry VIII clause squared'.[90] The purpose of this bill was to allow the Conservative government to move quickly to lessen burdens falling on industry due to over-regulation. Expecting trouble, the Government had referred its bill to the Procedure Committee, which set out to ensure that 'no Act of Parliament is repealed or amended under this new power without examination at least as thorough as if the change had been made by a Bill passing through the House'.[91] But complaining that the outcome was inevitable because its deliberations were proceeding in parallel with debates on the bill, Opposition members ultimately boycotted the Committee. In the Lords, a government concession was secured to extend the normal scrutiny period of forty days for delegated legislation to sixty days, the start of 'super-affirmative' procedure (above). With these supposed precautions, the 'fast track procedure' went into operation. It was not much used: by the end of 1996, the Deregulation Unit of the Cabinet Office charged with deregulation had introduced only forty-four measures, of which

[88] Procedure Committee, *Delegated Legislation: Proposals for a Sifting Committee*, HC 501 (2002/3), *Government Response*, HC 684 (2002/3).

[89] See e.g., V. Korah, 'Counter-inflation legislation: Whither parliamentary sovereignty?' (1976) 92 *LQR* 42.

[90] Lord Rippon, 'Henry VIII clauses' (1989) *10 Stat. Law Rev*. 205, 206 and 'Constitutional anarchy' (1990) 11 *Stat. Law Rev*. 184. See also C. Himsworth, 'The Delegated Powers Scrutiny Committee' [1995] *PL* 34.

[91] *Delegated Legislation* , HC 152 [16].

three had attracted the notice of Parliament; by 2000, the total was only forty-eight. The Unit blamed the restrictive terms of the enabling legislation.

The New Labour Government now in power therefore proposed reinforcing the earlier legislation. It would extend the procedures to the public sector, allowing statutory instruments to be used to relieve *government agencies* of burdens, provided they were not the 'sole beneficiaries' of a deregulation measure. Even more controversially, the bill contained a 'mega-Henry VIII clause', allowing repeal by statutory instrument laid and approved by a resolution of each House of Parliament of any Act (whether or not in force) passed at least two years before the day on which an Order, including an Order made under the 1994 Act, was made.[92]

Government was moving on to dangerous ground. But it gave the usual undertakings not to use the legislation for 'highly controversial' measures and Parliament perhaps felt that it could rely on the vigilance of its Scrutiny Committees using 'super-affirmative' procedure: a two-stage consideration of Orders in each House obliging a minister wishing to make an Order to lay before Parliament after the first sixty-day scrutiny period a statement of any 'representations' received. As passed by Parliament, the Regulatory Reform Act 2001 had the acquiescence of its Select Committees.[93] Again it was not much used: only twenty-seven Orders had been made by the end of 2005. Reviewing the Act, the Cabinet Office concluded that it was not 'fit for purpose'; its ability to deliver regulatory measures was 'not as wide-ranging as hoped' so that the number of reforms delivered was 'significantly lower than expected'.[94]

In view of the fact that publication had been preceded by a review, by a consultation paper and by wide consultation, the uproar that greeted an amending bill in 2005 was perhaps unexpected. As introduced in January 2006, the bill would have allowed a minister to make provision by Order for reform or repeal of any public general or local Act plus a wide range of subordinate legislation and also to implement Law Commission recommendations with or without changes. There was power for ministers to act by negative procedure and, even though Parliament could request 'super-affirmative procedure', it would be for the minister to decide whether to apply it. The bill contained restrictive preconditions, based on fairness and proportionality.

Reports poured in from Select Committees criticising the bill 'in robust terms'. The Regulatory Reform Committee called it 'potentially the most constitutionally significant bill that has been brought before Parliament for some years'[95] and highlighted the perils of proposals that 'would change the way that

[92] House of Commons Library, *The Legislative and Regulatory Reform Bill: Bill 111 of 2005/6*, Research Paper 06/06 (2006), pp. 13–14.

[93] D. Miers, 'Regulatory reform orders: A new weapon in the armoury of law reform' (2001) 21 *Public Money and Management* 29.

[94] Cabinet Office, *Review of the Regulatory Reform Bill* (July, 2005); *A Bill for Better Regulation: Consultation document* (July, 2005).

[95] Select Committee on Regulatory Reform, *Legislative and Regulatory Reform Bill*, HC 878 (2005/6).

primary legislation was amended'. The minister faced aggressive questioning.[96] PASC, leaping with a slim excuse into the fray, pointed out that the bill itself provided a striking example of the advantages of legislative procedure as it currently existed. The bill gave government powers 'entirely disproportionate to its stated aims' and the Government, which had undertaken to amend it, must 'ensure that by the time it leaves this House it provides adequate safeguards against the misuse of the order making powers it contains'.[97] The media gleefully reported a government climb-down; amendments would be introduced so that the bill could 'no longer be misconstrued as an attempt by government to take a wider constitutional power' and a statutory veto on the 'fast track' procedure would be given to the two Regulatory Reform Committees.

As finally passed by Parliament, the Legislative and Regulatory Reform Act 2006 contains stringent limitations. The Act first provides that regulatory activities shall be targeted only at cases in which action is needed. It authorises ministers to make by Order in Council any provision 'aimed at removing or reducing any burden, or the overall burdens, resulting directly or indirectly for any person from any legislation' but strictly defines the term 'burden' and also limits the persons to whom the powers can be transferred or delegated. Relevant in the present context, it provides that Orders can be made only by statutory instrument that is subject to 'super-affirmative procedure' and have to be laid before and approved by a resolution of each House of Parliament.

What light does the affair shed on the effectiveness of the 'modernised' parliamentary legislative procedures? At first sight, they were not very effective; of nine suggestions from various select committees, only three were accepted. On the other hand, a proposal seen:

> by those interested in constitutional protection, as alarming, ended as an Act within the scope of accepted precedent. It also seems that the reports of the various select committees had some influence in persuading the government to table amendments that were able largely to satisfy those most concerned. On that basis it is misconceived to think that because all accepted amendments to the Bill were government amendments, the same result would have been achieved had those parliamentary stages not been required. All the amendments were preceded by pressure that might have resulted in amendments imposed against the wishes of government, or even House of Lords defeat and loss of the Bill, had the government continued to disregard issues perceived to be of constitutional importance.[98]

[96] Select Committee on Regulatory Reform, *Operation of the Regulatory Reform Act 2001*, HC 774 (2005/6).

[97] PASC, *Legislative and Regulatory Reform Bill*, HC 1033 (2005/6) [13]. See also CC, *Legislative and Regulatory Reform Bill*, HL 194 (2005/6).

[98] P. Davis, 'The significance of parliamentary procedures in control of the executive: A case study: The passage of Part 1 of the Legislative and Regulatory Reform Act 2006' [2007] *PL* 677, 693–4. And see A. Brazier, S. Kalitowski and G. Rosenblatt, *Law in the Making: Influence and change in the legislative process* (Hansard Society, 2008).

5. Access and participation

(a) Pre-legislative consultation

When the first scrutiny committees were being set up in 1952, an MP remarked: 'It has been perhaps rather noticeable that all through this afternoon we have been discussing this merely from the point of view of Parliament and MPs. We have not let the public creep into the discussion at all.' Indeed, a proposal to allow members of the public to complain of, or ask for changes in, regulations was dismissed on the ground that 'aggrieved persons have their grievances brought to the attention of the House by Members.'[99] The general public has in fact never been totally excluded from the lawmaking process but consultation was – and still is – largely voluntary. Griffith and Street's foundational textbook[100] contains a lengthy account of informal government consultation procedures, emphasising their importance. Consultation, according to the authors, had a threefold purpose: (i) to put the administration 'in full possession of the facts and viewpoints which bear on the particular matter'; (ii) 'to enable those affected, from powerful groups to ordinary individuals, to state their case against the proposed action and to urge that it be modified or dropped'; (iii) for public explanation. Amongst appropriate techniques, the authors mention advisory committees, direct consultation and public inquiries, developing around that time as an important vehicle for consultation in the area of land use planning (see Chapter 13).

Wade and Forsyth call pre-legislative consultation with interests and organisations likely to be affected 'one of the firmest and most carefully observed conventions':

> It is not a matter of legal right, any more than it is with Parliament's own legislation. But it is so well settled a practice that it is most unusual to hear complaint. It may be that consultation which is not subject to statutory procedure is more effective than formal hearing which may produce legalism and artificiality. The duty to consult is recognised in every sense except the legal one.[101]

In some ways, this passage marks a transition, coinciding with a perceived decline in consultation and in publication of preliminary Green and White Papers under Margaret Thatcher, which provoked demands for a British equivalent of the American Administrative Procedure Act.

The AAPA applies in the absence of alternative statutory provision to all federal administrative authorities and agencies, obliging them to give notice of proposed rule-making and (as understood in Britain) affords to 'interested persons the opportunity to participate in the rule-making through submission of written data, views or arguments with or without opportunity to

[99] HC 310 (1952/3), p. 141.

[100] J. Griffith and H. Street, *Principles of Administrative Law*, 5th edn (Pitman, 1973), pp. 118–36.

[101] Wade and Forsyth, *Administrative Law*, 9th edn (Oxford University Press, 2004), p. 896.

present the same orally in any manner'. In practice, the American experience has been very mixed; it has been said to impede agency action and lead to serious 'dilution of the regulatory process'[102] – one reason perhaps why a general right of consultation has not so far been conceded in Britain. In 1992, however, the Hansard Society noted 'deep dissatisfaction with the extent, nature, timing and conduct of consultation'. There was a lack of coherent policy; civil service guidelines did not appear to be followed; there were inconsistencies of approach between and even within government departments, agencies and other statutory bodies. The result was 'a mixture of good and bad consultation practice, and, more fundamentally . . . a distortion of the whole consultation process.' The Hansard Society called for a leisurely and prolonged two-stage consultation process at 'rough draft' and 'final draft' stage; this would give an opportunity for experts and those likely to be affected to make their views known. It also favoured published guidelines 'drawing on best practice' and influenced by the 'advice and experience of those most directly involved'.[103]

In his study of delegated legislation, Page identifies three separate types of consultation: *indirect consultation* of committees, advisory and other bodies known to be interested; a *staged consultation exercise*, based on an explanatory or exploratory paper, often published on the Internet; and *at large consultation* by politicians and civil servants testing their ideas informally at the development stage.[104] All may involve the general public, though in practice it is mainly interest groups or those who give evidence to parliamentary committees who make a meaningful response. Civil servants take consultation seriously; they 'generally make serious efforts to consult relevant groups' and will 'consult anyone interested in the consultations'.[105] But government retains discretion; representations can be ignored, though it is unwise to do so, as interest groups help to ensure that regulations will not prove so unpopular as to prove unenforceable. In this perspective, consultation is designed for 'stakeholders', rather than the public at large; it is, in other words, a 'Three Es' method of ensuring the interests of the main players. It also serves the purposes of 'joined-up government', acting as an 'NPM' technique for rectifying fragmented public administration, especially the impact of devolution; the Legislative and Regulatory Reform Act 2006, for example, lists the Welsh

[102] R. Hamilton, 'Procedures for the adoption of rules of general applicability: The need for procedural innovation in administrative rulemaking' (1972) 60 *Calif. LR* 1276, 1312–3, writing just as the UK and US models were compared by B. Schwarz and H. W. R. Wade, *Legal Control of Government: Administrative law in Britain and the United States* (Oxford University Press, 1972), p. 97. See J. Rossi, 'Participation run amok: The costs of mass participation for deliberative agency decisionmaking' (1997) 92 *Northwestern Univ. L. Rev.* 173.

[103] Hansard Society, *Making the Law*, pp. 17–18, 226 and Recommendations 150, 162.

[104] Page, *Governing by Numbers*, p. 129. Page examined 46 statutory instruments of which 11 involved no consultation, 6 indirect consultation, 12 at-large consultation, and 17 staged consultation.

[105] *Ibid.*, p. 142.

Assembly as potential consultee, requiring a second round of consultation if the whole or any part of the proposals undergoes change. This is like a staged consultation exercise confined to elite stakeholders.

The theme recurs in the context of statutory consultation rights, common in the fields of planning, social security and local governance. The Social Security Act 1992, for example, set up a Social Security Advisory Committee (SSAC), which must be consulted on new legislation and changes to regulation, and also advises on Green and White Papers; whether its advice will be followed is quite another matter. The SSAC has its own consultative network and also posts consultation exercises on the Internet[106] (Page's indirect consultation). Similarly, the Deregulation and Contracting Out Act 1994 allowed 'those with expert knowledge of the subject, and those who will be affected by the legislation, [to] have access to the process'.[107] Before making an Order under s. 1 of the Act, the minister has to consult (a) such organisations as appear to him to be representative of interests substantially affected by his proposals; and (b) such other persons as he considers appropriate (Page's 'at large' consultation). This is despite the fact that the Act was designed to introduce the possibility of 'dialogue between Parliament and people – largely absent from the consideration of much primary legislation'.

The UK Cabinet Office has issued a code of practice, available on the Cabinet Office website, on running a consultation and identifying and engaging with stakeholders. This sets out six consultation criteria which must be followed in all consultation documents:

- Consult widely throughout the process, allowing a minimum of twelve weeks for written consultation at least once during the development of the policy.
- Be clear about what your proposals are, who may be affected, what questions are being asked and the timescale for responses.
- Ensure that your consultation is clear, concise and widely accessible.
- Give feedback regarding the responses received and how the consultation process influenced the policy.
- Monitor your department's effectiveness at consultation, including through the use of a designated consultation co-ordinator.
- Ensure your consultation follows better regulation best practice, including carrying out a regulatory impact assessment if appropriate.

(b) Citizen participation

Before considering contemporary policies for citizen participation, it is helpful to look at Arnstein's 'ladder of citizen participation', devised just as 'citizen

[106] A. Ogus, 'SSAC as an independent advisory body: Its role and influence on policymaking' (1998) 5 *J. of Social Security Law* 156.

[107] *Delegated Legislation*, HC 152-ii, p. 73 (Mr Barry Field).

Citizen control	8
Delegated powers	7
Partnership	6
Placation	5
Consultation	4
Informing	3
Therapy	2
Manipulation	1

Fig. 4.1 Arnstein's ladder of citizen participation

participation' became fashionable with planners at the end of the 1960s (see Fig. 4.1 above). Arnstein conceived the idea in the course of her work in US federal social programmes, where contacts with 'rubberstamp advisory committees' and 'manipulative neighbourhood councils' persuaded her that citizen participation was largely a sham; it 'juxtapose[d] powerless citizens with the powerful in order to highlight the fundamental divisions between them'.[108] Arnstein believed that there was 'a critical difference between going through the empty ritual of participation and having the real power needed to affect the outcome of the process'. It is useful to bear Arnstein's theory in mind when thinking about participation and consultation in British government and public administration.

Experiments with citizen participation started in the UK during the 1960s and '70s, when planners came to see it as the only way to stave off the vigorous protests and demonstrations that increasingly accompanied large-scale planning projects.[109] The Skeffington Committee, set up to advise on 'the best methods, including publicity, of securing the participation of the public at the formative stage in the making of development plans for their area',[110] talked ambitiously of a continuous dialogue between the people and the planners, allowing the people 'to take an active part throughout the plan-making process', and even of 'citizen control'. Never realised, the ideology of Skeffington still remains a potent influence in environmental matters, where public participation is today the subject of international conventions ratified by the UK. The governing Aarhus Convention, which requires public participation,[111] has

[108] S. Arnstein, 'A ladder of citizen participation' (1969) 35 *J. of the American Institute of Planners* 216.

[109] See R. Damer and C. Hague, 'Public participation in planning: A review' (1971) 42 *Town Planning Review* 217.

[110] Report of the Skeffington Committee, *People and Planning* (1969). See now J. Cullingworth (ed.), *Fifty Years of Urban and Regional Policy* (Continuum Publishers, 2001); Y. Rydin and M Pennington, 'Public participation and local environmental planning: The collective action problem and the potential of social capital' (2000) 5 *Local Environment* 153.

[111] The Aarhus Convention on Access to Information, Public Participation in Decision-making and Access to Justice in Environmental Matters. And see M. Lee and C. Abbot, 'The usual suspects? Public participation under the Aarhus Convention' (2003) 66 *MLR* 80; R. Macrory and S. Turner, 'Participatory rights, transboundary environmental governance and EC law' (2002) 39 *CML Rev.* 489.

been implemented by the European Commission and applies generally across the EU. In its *White Paper on European Governance* (strongly influenced by academic theories of deliberative democracy), the European Commission has recognised participation as a 'good governance' standard and committed itself generally to greater access for citizens to the policy-making process,[112] an ambition attainable, in view of the geographical area and cultural differences, largely through ICT. Whether this diluted form of participatory democracy or 'e-governance' adds up to anything more than therapy or placation (rungs 2 and 5) is a very moot point.

As we noticed in Chapter 2, however, consultation is currently an obsession in British government. Committed to being 'responsive', New Labour has seized the opportunity of technical advance, which has opened the way to consultation with the public and 'e-governance' (p. 75 above). Consultation is said both to inform the public about government policies and let them have their say (rungs 3 and 5). Page, however, has doubts about motives for consultation in the civil service, suggesting it is largely a way of 'making sure that interested parties know that there is likely to be a change in the law and checking that there are no mistakes or ill-conceived portions of the proposed legislation' (rung 3).[113] The decision is often finalised *before* consultation, though the consultees may not be aware of this, in which case it is purely placatory, buying time for the public to adapt to unpopular change (rungs 5 or 1).

The fashion has also penetrated the Commons, which has authorised tentative experiments in taking evidence by standing committees (rungs 4 and 3). The idea was endorsed in 2003 by the Constitution Committee:

> The legislative process is not an insulated one. It is important that Parliament is aware of the views of others. Parliamentarians may not themselves be expert or especially well informed about the subject matter of a bill. It is essential that Parliament has the means to hear from experts and informed opinion in order to test whether a bill is fit for purpose. However, input should not be confined to such opinion. Citizens may have strong views on the subject. Parliamentarians should be in a position to know whether a measure is objectionable to citizens on ethical or other grounds. A measure may be technically feasible – and enjoy the assent of those affected by it – but it may not necessarily be desirable in the view of citizens. Parliamentarians do not have to go along with the views expressed to them by individuals, but it is important that citizens have an opportunity to express their views on measures before Parliament. It is then up to MPs and peers to assess the strength of feeling and the extent to which it is persuasive or informed.

[112] European Commission, *White Paper on European Governance* COM (2001) 428 (Brussels, 25.7.2001). And see A. Follesdal, 'The political theory of the White Paper on Governance: Hidden and fascinating' (2003) 9 *EPL* 73; O. Gerstenberg and C. Sabel, 'Directly-deliberative polyarchy: An institutional ideal for Europe?' in Joerges and Dehousse (eds.), *Good Governance in Europe's Integrated Market* (Oxford University Press, 2002).

[113] Page, *Governing by Numbers*, p. 148.

> The opportunity to be heard should apply to citizens operating individually and collectively. Groups have a right to make their opinions heard, but so too do citizens who are not organised in groups. Our intuitive view is that groups often have the knowledge and the means to make their voices heard: individual citizens often do not. We are concerned therefore to explore to what extent the means do and should exist in order to ensure that citizens have the opportunity to express their opinions on legislation being considered by Parliament.[114]

Ironically, a strong alternative motivation for consultation comes from concern over public disillusion with representative democracy and its institutions, setting in train a search for 'more innovative methods' to encourage citizen participation and encourage 'civic voluntarism' (rung 8).[115] The unofficial 'Power Inquiry', which hoped to counter widespread indifference to politics by 'rebalancing the system towards the people', set out to stimulate a culture of political engagement in which it would be normal for 'policy and decision-making to occur with direct input from citizens' (rung 6).[116] Amongst its concrete recommendations we read:

- All public bodies should be required to meet a duty of public involvement in their decision and policy-making processes.
- Citizens should be given the right to initiate legislative processes, public inquiries and hearings into public bodies and their senior management.

A White Paper, *Communities in Control*, aims overtly at rung 8 (though rungs 5 and 1 are also possibilities). The document purports to examine 'who has power, on whose behalf is it exercised, how is it held to account, and how it can be accessed by everyone in local communities', the stated objective being:

> to pass power into the hands of local communities. We want to generate vibrant local democracy in every part of the country, and to give real control over local decisions and services to a wider pool of active citizens.
>
> We want to shift power, influence and responsibility away from existing centres of power into the hands of communities and individual citizens. This is because we believe that they can take difficult decisions and solve complex problems for themselves.[117]

(c) Consultation and judicial review

The emergence of participation as a 'good governance value' plus the routine concession of consultation rights by public bodies suggests that courts might

[114] *Parliament and the Legislative Process*, HL 173-I (2003/4) [13] [14].

[115] PASC, *Public Participation: Issues and innovations*, HC 373 (2000/1).

[116] Rowntree Trust, *Power to the People: The report of Power: An independent inquiry into Britain's democracy* (March 2006), Recommendations 23, 24; and see House of Commons Library, *Power to the People: The report of Power: An independent inquiry into Britain's democracy*, Standard Note: SN/PC/3948 (2006).

[117] DCLG, *Communities in Control: Real people, real power*, Cm. 7427 (2008), p. 11.

be called on to protect them.[118] But although statutory consultation rights provide an opening for judicial review, English courts have been slow to accept it.[119] They have occasionally intervened to insist that consultation must permit 'a real and not an illusory opportunity to make representations', as when an Education Secretary, acting under legislation which made consultation mandatory, left four days for parental consultation on a new system of comprehensive schools.[120] In less flagrant cases, judges have tended to interpret statutory consultation requirements as 'directory' rather than 'mandatory', a leniency that contrasts oddly with the firm position taken by the House of Lords in *Padfield* (p. 101 above). And if protection of statutory consultation rights has been weak then protection of non-statutory consultation has been weaker still. Without a statutory basis, protection was virtually limited to situations where assurances had been given until the *GCHQ* case (p. 107 above), in which a trade union was held to have a 'legitimate expectation' of being consulted before policy change, laid a stronger foundation.[121]

An appeal brought by Bapio Action on behalf of newly qualified doctors, who had trained in the UK in the expectation of being permitted to work here but later found their limited leave to remain suddenly withdrawn, not only contains a classic statement of the position in English law but also tells us much about the hazards of informal rule-making. The Immigration Rules, which contained the policy change, have to be laid before Parliament but are technically not statutory instruments; they have been allocated a hybrid status between a statutory code and non-statutory guidance by the courts. Responsibility for the rules rests with the Home Office, which refused on this occasion to amend them. Undeterred, the Department of Health pressed on with guidance, of which Lord Bingham said in the House of Lords:

> To speak of the guidance being 'issued' is to suggest a degree of official formality which was notably lacking. It appears that the guidance was published on the NHS Employers' website in terms approved by the Department, but no official draft, record or statement of the guidance has been placed before the House, which has instead been referred to an e-mail beginning 'Dear All' sent by an official of the Immigration and Nationality Directorate of the Home Office in response to confusion caused by some earlier communication. It is for others to judge whether this is a satisfactory way of publishing important governmental decisions with a direct effect on people's lives.[122]

[118] See R. Stewart, 'The Reformation of American administrative law' (1975) 88 *Harv. LR* 1667; F. Bignami, *Three Generations of Participation Rights in European Administrative Proceedings* (JMWP 11/03, 2003).

[119] S. A. de Smith, Lord Woolf and J. Jowell, *Judicial Review of Administrative Action*, 6th edn (Sweet & Maxwell, 2007) [7-052–6].

[120] *Lee v Education Secretary* (1967) 66 LGR 211; *Bradbury v Enfield London Borough Council* [1967] 1 WLR 1311.

[121] *Re Liverpool Taxis Association* [1972] 2 All ER 589. For legitimate expectation see Ch. 5.

[122] *R (Bapio Action) v Home Secretary* [2008] UKHL 27 [10] (Lord Bingham); [2007] EWCA Civ 1139 [50] [43–5] (Sedley LJ).

Both appellate courts found these procedures wholly inadequate: the guidance directly and intentionally affected immigration law and practice by imposing on the possibility of employment in the public sector a restriction beyond those contained in the rules. Faced with the argument in the Court of Appeal that government has a duty 'at least as a prima facie rule', to consult prior to rule-change, Sedley LJ thought that implying a duty to consult from a 'practice of consultation' in a case where there were no statutory consultation provisions was a step too far:

> Many people might consider it very desirable – but thinking about it makes it rapidly plain that if it is to be introduced it should be by Parliament and not by the courts. Parliament has the option, which the courts do not have, of extending and configuring an obligation to consult function by function. It can also abandon or modify obligations to consult which experience show to be unnecessary or unworkable and extend those which seem to work well. The courts, which act on larger principles, can do none of these things.

In *R (Greenpeace) v Trade and Industry Secretary*, an application to quash a government decision to reverse a longstanding policy on nuclear energy by supporting 'nuclear new build', Sullivan J took a bolder line, ruling that a consultation exercise was 'very seriously flawed'. This time, however, the judge was working from a statutory basis:

> The purpose of the 2006 Consultation Document as part of the process of 'the fullest public consultation' was unclear. It gave every appearance of being an issues paper, which was to be followed by a consultation paper containing proposals on which the public would be able to make informed comment. As an issues paper it was perfectly adequate. As *the* consultation paper on an issue of such importance and complexity it was manifestly inadequate. It contained no proposals as such, and even if it had, the information given to consultees was wholly insufficient to enable them to make 'an intelligent response'. The 2006 Consultation Document contained no information of any substance on the two issues which had been identified in the 2003 White Paper as being of critical importance: the economics of new nuclear build and the disposal of nuclear waste. When dealing with the issue of waste, the information given in the 2006 Consultation Document was not merely wholly inadequate, it was also seriously misleading . . . There could be no proper consultation, let alone 'the fullest public consultation' as promised in the 2003 White Paper, if the substance of these two issues was not consulted upon before a decision was made. There was therefore procedural unfairness, and a breach of the claimant's legitimate expectation that there would be 'the fullest public consultation' before a decision was taken to support new nuclear build.[123]

This judgment takes consultation seriously, seeing it as making a real contribution to rational risk assessment and decision-making (Arnstein, rung 4 or 3). The case was a strong one because it was based on an assurance in a White Paper. *Our Energy Future: Creating a low carbon economy* had promised in

[123] *R(Greenpeace) v Industry Secretary* [2007] EWHC 311 [116–20] (Sullivan J).

bold type that 'before any decision to proceed with the building of new nuclear power stations, there would need to be the fullest public consultation and the publication of a White Paper setting out the Government's proposals'. Consultation duly followed, with a programme of seminars and round table meetings, based on a full technical questionnaire for experts and a 'summary document' for the general public. Because the decision was ruled unlawful, all these procedures would have to be replayed. This clearly provides an incentive for public authorities to draw back, for fear of litigation, from the more generous consultation practices recently introduced to all but mandatory statutory consultation.

What followed the judgment illustrates the limited possibilities of consultation and, indeed, of judicial review (see Chapter 16). The minister (Alistair Darling) immediately issued a statement confirming the Government's faith in both the consultation process and the case for new nuclear power stations from which they clearly were not going to resile. Two White Papers followed from the Department for Business, Enterprise and Regulatory Reform. The first promised further consultations; the second endorsed the consultation exercise:

> In May 2007 we launched a consultation to examine whether nuclear power could also play a role in meeting these long-term challenges, alongside other low-carbon forms of electricity generation. We set out our preliminary view that it is in the public interest to give energy companies the option of investing in new nuclear power stations. The purpose of the consultation was to subject this preliminary view, and the evidence and arguments for it set out in our consultation document, to a thorough and searching public scrutiny . . .
>
> Following the consultation we have concluded that, in summary, nuclear power is:
>
> - Low-carbon – helping to minimise damaging climate change
> - Affordable – nuclear is currently one of the cheapest low-carbon electricity generation technologies, so could help us deliver our goals cost effectively
> - Dependable – a proven technology with modern reactors capable of producing electricity reliably
> - Safe – backed up by a highly effective regulatory framework
> - Capable of increasing diversity and reducing our dependence on any one technology or country for our energy or fuel supplies.
>
> Having reviewed the evidence, and taking account of these points, the Government believes nuclear power should be able to play a part in the UK's future low-carbon economy. We have also carefully re-examined the impact of excluding nuclear power from our future energy mix. Our conclusion remains that not having nuclear as an option would increase the costs of delivering these goals and increase the risks of failing to meet our targets for reducing carbon dioxide emissions and enhancing energy security.[124]

[124] *Meeting the Energy Challenge: A White Paper on energy*, Cm. 7124 (2007); *Meeting the Energy Challenge: A White Paper on nuclear power*, Cm. 7296 (2008).

This summary from John Hutton's introduction formed the basis for an Energy Bill, now the Energy Act 2008. A parallel Planning Bill (now the Planning Act 2008) was introduced, ostensibly to co-ordinate and replace the disparate systems governing planning approval for major infrastructure proposals, with the objective of streamlining decisions and avoiding long public inquiries.[125] The Act sets in place a new and 'independent' Infrastructure Planning Commission, which will make its decisions in the light of 'national policy statements' issued by the Government. Before any such statement can be issued, the minister must either 'carry out such consultation, and arrange for such publicity, as [he] thinks appropriate in relation to the proposal' or 'consult such persons, and such descriptions of persons, as may be prescribed'; he must also 'have regard to the responses to the consultation and publicity in deciding whether to proceed with the proposal'.

6. Climbing the ladder: EC law

(a) EC law and sovereignty

Nothing in the EC Treaties, ratified by the UK in 1972 and 'brought home' by the European Communities Act 1972 (ECA), suggested change in the constitutional doctrine of parliamentary sovereignty; indeed, not even the contentious Treaty of Lisbon, signed by the Government in 2007, dares openly to mention the 'primacy' of EU law.[126] Primacy, like parliamentary sovereignty, is a doctrine articulated by judges, read into the EC Treaties by the ECJ in the seminal case of *Van Gend en Loos*.[127] At the time of UK accession, it is probable that neither MPs nor a largely apathetic public were aware of the Court's radical case law[128] or appreciated the effect of the arcane formula in s. 3(1) ECA, which provides:

> For the purposes of all legal proceedings any question as to the meaning or effect of any of the Treaties, or as to the validity, meaning or effect of any Community instrument, shall be treated as a question of law (and, if not referred to the European Court, be for

[125] The bill derived from the *The Eddington Transport Study* and *Review of Land Use Planning* (HMSO, December 2006) and *Planning for a Sustainable Future*, Cm. 7120 (2007) on which 12 weeks was allowed for consultation. And see below.

[126] 'EC law', which we use throughout for continuity, refers to law made under the EC Treaties (TEC); 'EU law' covers all forms of law made by the EU under the Maastricht Treaty of European Union (TEU) and TEC.

[127] Case 26/62 *Van Gend en Loos v Nederlandse Administratie Belastingen* [1963] ECR 1. For discussion see M. Shapiro, 'The European Court of Justice' in Craig and de Burca (eds.), *The Evolution of EU Law* (Oxford University Press, 1999).

[128] The White Paper, *The United Kingdom and the European Communities*, Cmnd 4715 (1971) [29] had said: 'There is no question of any erosion of essential national sovereignty; what is proposed is a sharing and an enlargement of individual sovereignties in the general interest.' For the full story, see D. Nicol, *EC Membership and the Judicialization of British Politics*, (Oxford University Press, 2001).

> determination as such in accordance with the principles laid down by and any relevant decision of the European Court).

To paraphrase, the ECA – in sharp contrast to the HRA – incorporates the jurisprudence of the ECJ into the domestic legal hierarchy and renders it *binding* on the national courts. The two judicial hierarchies are linked through TEC Art. 234, which sets in place a 'preliminary reference procedure' whereby national courts ask for advisory opinions from the ECJ on questions of EC law that arise in the course of domestic judicial proceedings. Subordinate courts or tribunals 'may' take the decision to refer; final appellate courts 'must' do so. Since 2003, a Member State whose courts wrongly fail to refer or otherwise make a 'manifest error' of EC law may be liable to compensate injured parties.[129]

The EC Treaty made provision for two different types of EC legislative act: a *regulation,* 'binding in its entirety and directly applicable in all Member States' and a *directive,* binding only 'as to the result to be achieved', which left to the Member States 'the choice of form and method' to be employed in implementation (TEC Art. ex 189).[130] ECA s. 2(1) provides:

> All such rights, powers, liabilities, obligations and restrictions from time to time created or arising by or under the Treaties, and all such remedies and procedures from time to time provided for by or under the Treaties, as in accordance with the Treaties are without further enactment to be given legal effect or used in the United Kingdom shall be recognised and available in law, and be enforced, allowed and followed accordingly . . .

Section 2(2) empowers ministers to carry out UK obligations where EU law is not directly applicable or effective by ministerial regulation or Order in Council.[131] These are 'prospective Henry VIII clauses' that, in the first case, allow an external lawmaker to make laws directly applicable within the United Kingdom.[132]

The message of *van Gend en Loos* reached the British public with the momentous *Factortame* case, where the House of Lords for the first time in history set aside (in technical parlance, 'disapplied') an Act of the UK Parliament in response to an ECJ ruling.[133] Perhaps curiously, since EC law

[129] Case C-224/01 *Köbler v Republic of Austria* [2003] ELR I-10239.

[130] The ECJ later blurred the distinction with its doctrine of 'direct effect', making directives enforceable in litigation by individual litigants in national courts, provided their provisions are sufficiently clear, precise and unconditional: Case 41/74 *Van Duyn v Home Office* [1974] ECR 1337; Case 43/75 *Defrenne v Sabena* [1976] ECR 455; and see T. Hartley, *The Foundations of European Community Law*, 6th edn (Oxford University Press, 2007), Ch. 7.

[131] See s. 2(2) and (4) of the ECA. The procedure is subject to reservations requiring statutes listed in Sch. 4. Around 50% of implementation of EU directives is effected under s. 2(2).

[132] N. Barber and A. Young, 'The rise of prospective Henry VIII clauses and their implications for sovereignty' [2003] *PL* 112.

[133] Case C-213/89 *R v Transport Secretary, ex p. Factortame (No. 2)* [1990] ECR I-2433.

was not obviously relevant to domestic legal procedure, s. 21 of the Crown Proceedings Act 1947 was in issue. Factortame had applied for an interim injunction pending a hearing in the ECJ of a question concerning compatibility of the Merchant Shipping Act 1988 with EC law. The House of Lords ruled that English law did not permit injunctions against the Crown but made a reference under TEC Art. 234 to ask whether an injunction should be ordered under EC law. The enigmatic reply was received that 'a national court which, in a case before it concerning Community law, considers that the sole obstacle which precludes it from granting interim relief is a rule of national law must set aside that rule'. Interpreting this to mean that interim relief should be available, the House of Lords awarded an interim injunction.

Mindful that the step taken by the House of Lords might be misunderstood, Lord Bridge took care to stress *Parliament's* responsibility for this momentous step:

> Some public comments on the decision of the Court of Justice . . . have suggested that this was a novel and dangerous invasion by a Community institution of the sovereignty of the UK Parliament. But such comments are based on a misconception. If the supremacy within the European Community of Community law over the national law of member states was not always inherent in the EEC Treaty it was certainly well established in the jurisprudence of the Court of Justice long before the United Kingdom joined the Community. Thus whatever limitation of its sovereignty Parliament accepted when it enacted the European Communities Act 1972 was entirely voluntary. Under the terms of the Act of 1972 it has always been clear that it was the duty of a United Kingdom court, when delivering final judgment, to override any rule of law found to be in conflict with any directly enforceable rule of Community law. Similarly, when decisions of the European Court of Justice have exposed areas of United Kingdom statute law which failed to implement Council directives, Parliament has always loyally accepted the obligation to make amends. Thus there is nothing in any way novel in according supremacy to rules of Community law in those areas to which they apply and to insist that, in the protection of rights under Community law, national courts must not be inhibited by rules of national law from granting interim relief in appropriate cases is no more than a logical recognition of that supremacy.[134]

The precise legal effects and constitutional implications of the *Factortame* case fall outside the scope of this book.[135] What is important here is that the case exposed the reality of EU membership: the national legal order was no longer wholly autonomous; it was subject not only to the influence of external legal orders but, in respect of EU law, to their directions.

Whether the courts would go further and 'disapply' a statute that *explicitly*

[134] *R v Transport Secretary, ex p. Factortame (No. 1)* [1989] 2 WLR 997, 1011.

[135] See H. W. R. Wade, 'Sovereignty: Revolution or evolution?' (1996) 112 *LQR* 568; P. Craig, 'Sovereignty of the United Kingdom Parliament after *Factortame*' (1999) *Yearbook of European Law* 221.

overrides EC law is still not decided. The issue was indirectly addressed in 'The Metric Martyrs' case'. The 'martyrs' were convicted of trading with imperial instead of metric weights and measures contrary to regulations made in terms of s. 2(2) of the ECA (above). The tortuous argument was advanced that these regulations were invalid, because the power to make them had been removed by s. 1(1) of the Weights and Measures Act 1985, which had impliedly repealed s. 2(2) of the ECA. (Under the doctrine of implied repeal, an earlier Act of Parliament is taken to be repealed by a subsequent Act with which it is inconsistent). Faced with a more extreme argument from counsel that Parliament could not *explicitly* repeal the ECA, Laws LJ gave an extreme response:

> Whatever may be the position elsewhere, the law of England disallows any such assumption. Parliament cannot bind its successors by stipulating against repeal, wholly or partly, of the ECA. It cannot stipulate as to the manner and form of any subsequent legislation. It cannot stipulate against implied repeal any more than it can stipulate against express repeal. Thus there is nothing in the ECA which allows the Court of Justice, or any other institutions of the EU, to touch or qualify the conditions of Parliament's legislative supremacy in the United Kingdom.[136]

What followed has been widely cited, but is decidedly controversial:

> In my opinion a constitutional statute is one which (a) conditions the legal relationship between citizen and State in some general, overarching manner, or (b) enlarges or diminishes the scope of what we would now regard as fundamental constitutional rights. (a) and (b) are of necessity closely related: it is difficult to think of an instance of (a) that is not also an instance of (b). The special status of constitutional statutes follows the special status of constitutional rights. Examples are the Magna Carta, the Bill of Rights 1689, the Act of Union, the Reform Acts which distributed and enlarged the franchise, the HRA, the Scotland Act 1998 and the Government of Wales Act 1998. The ECA clearly belongs in this family. It incorporated the whole corpus of substantive Community rights and obligations, and gave overriding domestic effect to the judicial and administrative machinery of Community law. It may be there has never been a statute having such profound effects on so many dimensions of our daily lives. The ECA is, by force of the common law, a constitutional statute. Ordinary statutes may be impliedly repealed. Constitutional statutes may not . . . A constitutional statute can only be repealed, or amended in a way which significantly affects its provisions touching fundamental rights or otherwise the relation between citizen and State, by unambiguous words on the face of the later statute.

This proposition – never tested in the House of Lords – throws doubt on the classical hierarchy of legal norms. Like Lord Steyn's dissent in *Jackson*, it

[136] *Thoburn v Sunderland City Council* [2002] 3 WLR 247 [59] and [62–4] (emphasis ours). And see T. Allan, 'Parliamentary Sovereignty, Law, Politics and Revolution' (1997) 113 *LQR* 443.

forms part of the debate over common law constitutionalism in which Sir John Laws played a conspicuous part (p. 110 above). It remains to add as a footnote that the European Commission announced in September 2007 that it was withdrawing its 2009 time limit for metrication, that 'supplementary indications' (namely, imperial measures) had always been permissible and would be allowed indefinitely. The regulations are, however, still in force, a typical example of 'gold-plating'.

(b) Textual quality

Since 1999, it has been possible, with Council agreement, for EU legislation to be adopted immediately after first reading in the European Parliament (EP). This so-called 'fast track' route now accounts for over half of legislation made by 'co-decision procedure' (the standard EU lawmaking method in which Council and Parliament supposedly have equal rights). Up to 10,000 EU regulations and directives are currently in force. There is constant complaint (especially from business) about over-regulation and about the poor textual quality of EU legislation, which is published in over twenty languages and passes through many stages of negotiated policy-making and drafting. The EP has called the output 'opaque and confused' and simplification is a Commission priority; its Transparency Initiative and Better Regulation Agenda aim to simplify and codify the existing stock of legislation under a rolling programme.[137]

Policy and regulatory proposals are now assessed to ensure quality, and systemic impact assessments are overseen by an independent Impact Assessment Board and published. Difficulties of transposition are supposedly being tackled: 'in partnership with Member States, a more effective approach is being developed to handle difficulties in implementing and ensuring conformity with Community law.'[138] But much of the subject matter is highly technical, dealing, for example, with permitted levels of chemicals in animal feed, foodstuffs or pesticides, general health and safety issues or mesh dimensions of drift nets, and legislation may take the form of 'implementing regulations', resembling, though not identical to, delegated legislation in national law, where the European Parliament has limited scrutiny powers.[139] Typically, the UK has a single representative, civil servant or scientific expert on the EU scientific

[137] See *Final Report of the Mandelken Group on Better Regulation* (Brussels, 2005); European Commission, *Implementing the Community Lisbon Programme: A strategy for the simplification of the regulatory environment*, COM(2005) 535 final; European Commission, *A Strategic Review of Better Regulation in the EU*, COM(2005) 689 final, p. 9. And see Ch. 6.

[138] *European Transparency Initiative* SEC(2005) 1300; *Green Paper*, COM(2006) 194 final; Commission Communication, *Second Strategic Review of Better Regulation in the European Union*, COM(2008) 32, 33, 35 final. 164 measures are covered for 2005–2009; 91 had been proposed or adopted, 44 in 2008.

[139] See for explanation of Comitology, M. Andenas and A. Turk, *Delegated Legislation and the Role of Committees in the EC* (Kluwer Law International, 2000) and for a critique, F. Bignami, 'The democratic deficit in European Community rulemaking: A call for notice and comment in comitology' (1999) 40 *Harv. Int'l LJ* 451.

'Comitology' that advises and supervises the Council and Commission in lawmaking.

National pride in British drafting at first led British draftsmen to 'translate' EU texts, using common law concepts and drafting style, rather than using the practice of 'copy out' whereby the EU text passes unaltered into domestic law. Not only does this leave room for error but provides government with opportunities to incorporate new policy, raising fears of 'unnecessary over-implementation'. The output has been castigated by the Commons as 'stuffed with jargon, badly translated, or victims of the sort of muddled thinking that even the most limpid translation cannot cure'.[140] The House of Lords Merits Committee, in a report warning that scrutiny is generally weak and needs strengthening', has also criticised the habit of 'legislation by reference', especially where criminal penalties are introduced:

> We consider that those affected by regulations (particularly those required to obey or enforce them) should be able to understand their obligations from the face of the instrument itself . . . look for evidence in the EM of what guidance the department or others is providing to stakeholders to explain the new obligation to ensure that it is fulfilled. The Committee's test of clarity and guidance is higher for an instrument which creates penalties and sanctions for non-compliance by individuals.[141]

Concerned over incoherence, the Cabinet Office commissioned the Davidson Review, which advised departments to review existing UK legislation before transposition with a view to creating a single coherent regulatory scheme. Drafters should avoid 'copy out'; 'gold-plating' (extending the scope of European legislation); 'double-banking' (failing to eliminate overlap); and 'regulatory creep' (over-zealous enforcement).[142] This counsel of perfection is likely to meet deaf ears.

(c) Parliamentary scrutiny

We have been careful to emphasise elsewhere in this book not only the growing influence of EC law but also the growing dominance of the EU in policy-making. In many areas, policy, especially regulatory policy, is more often than not 'made in Europe' and framed in EC regulations, which form part of UK law, and directives, which have to be implemented (see Chapter 6). All that the UK Parliament can do in this situation is see that the EU

[140] ESC, *The Role of National Parliaments in the European Union*, HC 51, HC 51-xxviii, Cm 3446 (1996) [112]. A. Cygan, 'Democracy and accountability in the European Union: The view from the House of Commons' (2003) 66 *MLR* 384; and see L. Ramsay, 'The copy out technique: More of a "cop out" than a solution?' (1996) 17 *Stat. L. Rev.* 218.

[141] ESC, *Special Report: The work of the Committee in Session 2005-06*, HC 275 (2005/6) [15].

[142] Cabinet Office, *Review of the Implementation of EU Legislation* (Dec. 2006); and see NAO and PAC, *Lost in Translation: Responding to the challenge of European Law*, HC 26 and 590 (2005/6).

instructions are carried out faithfully: Parliament is, in other words, an agent or delegate of the EU institutions.[143] It follows that the UK Parliament, if it is to maintain (and even improve) its place in lawmaking, must endeavour to scrutinise and control the flood of EU legislation. Yet for many years the Commons slumbered, slow to appreciate the effects of EU membership and unwilling to co-operate with the European Parliament. It was left to the Lords, encouraged by its judicial members, to make the running. In 1972, the Lords set up what is now its European Union Committee (EUC), with a broad and simple remit 'to consider EU documents and other matters relating to the EU'. It soon established a Europe-wide reputation through the strength of its reports. The EUC, divided into specialist areas, focuses on policy, though it does sometimes undertake scrutiny: in 2007, for example, its specialist subcommittees conducted parallel inquiries into the impact of the Lisbon Treaty on the UK with a view to informing Parliament's debates on ratification.[144] As similar reports were issued by the Lords Constitution Committee and Commons European Scrutiny Committee (ESC), MPs on this occasion had little excuse for being ill-informed when they came to debate ratification.

The EUC emphasises the importance of getting in early:

> Once European regulations, directives and decisions have been through the law-making processes enshrined in the Treaties (which to varying degrees involve the Commission, the European Parliament and national government ministers operating in the Council), it is in practice too late for national parliaments to seek to reverse them, even if the EU instrument in question has to be given effect in the United Kingdom by means of domestic primary or secondary legislation.[145]

Both Houses regularly report on the Commission's Annual Work Programme, now discussed directly with the Commission and its officials in Brussels and Westminster.

The basis for Commons scrutiny was the Foster Committee, appointed in 1972 'to consider procedures for scrutiny of proposals for European Community Secondary Legislation'.[146] A Select Committee set up in 1973 was strengthened in 1980, when the Commons managed to win from government

[143] As argued by J. Steiner, 'From direct effects to *Francovich*: shifting means of enforcement of Community law' (1993) 18 *EL Rev* 3.

[144] EUC, *The Treaty of Lisbon: An impact assessment*, HL 62 (2007/8) and *Government Response*, Cm. 7389 (2008); HLCC, *European Union (Amendment) Bill and the Lisbon Treaty: Implications for the UK constitution*, HL 84 (2007/8); ESC, *EU Intergovernmental Conference*, HC 1014 (2006/7); *The Conclusions of the European Council and Council of Ministers*, HC 86 (2007/8), HC 16-iii (2006/7).

[145] EUC, *Review of Scrutiny of European Legislation* HL 15 (2002/3) [12]. See also EUC, *Enhanced Scrutiny of EU Legislation with a United Kingdom Opt-in*, HL 25 (2008/9).

[146] For an account of scrutiny, see Department of the Clerk to the House, *European Scrutiny in the House of Commons* (2005); HC Research Paper 05/85, *The United Kingdom Parliament and European Business* (2005).

the power of 'scrutiny reserve'.[147] This prohibits ministers from giving agreement in the Council or in European Council to any proposal on which the European Scrutiny Committee (ESC) has not completed its scrutiny or which awaits consideration by the House. This resolution gives the House essential purchase over the Government's activities in EU affairs. Its exceptions for urgency are, however, used very frequently; in up to seventy cases annually, the reserve is bypassed, often in respect of highly controversial pieces of legislation, such as that providing for the European arrest warrant and the setting up of a new European defence procurement agency.

Early Commons attempts at scrutiny were unsystematic and there were problems not only with bulk but also access and timing. An important report from the Procedure Committee, largely accepted by the Conservative government in 1988, moved to revise procedures in the hope that MPs would take more interest, the debates would be better attended and the House better informed.[148] There are now three European Standing Committees, which handle texts referred to them by the ESC and provide liaison with departmental Select Committees, in particular the Foreign Affairs Committee, which also handle European affairs. The ESC handles around 1,200 documents annually and has had to be strengthened with seven subcommittees. Under Standing Order No. 143, the ESC considers:

(i) any proposal under the Community Treaties for legislation by the Council or the Council acting jointly with the European Parliament
(ii) any document which is published for submission to the European Council, the Council or the European Central Bank
(iii) any proposal for a common strategy, a joint action or a common position under Title V of the Treaty on European Union which is prepared for submission to the Council or to the European Council (second pillar)
(iv) any proposal for a common position, framework decision, decision or a convention under Title VI of the Treaty on European Union which is prepared for submission to the Council (third pillar)
(v) any other document relating to European Union matters deposited in the House by a Minister of the Crown.

Its coverage is wide, taking in not just draft Regulations, Directives and Decisions but other documents such as EU Green and White Papers and

[147] Resolution of the House of 3 Oct. 1980, HC Deb., vol. 991, col. 843, now Resolution of the House of 17 Nov. 1998.

[148] Procedure Committee, *European Community Legislation*, HC 622 (1989/90) and *Government Response*, Cm. 1081 (1990). See also Modernisation Committee, *The Scrutiny of European Business*, HC 791 (1997/8); *Scrutiny of European Business*, HC 465 (2004/5); A. Cygan, 'European Union Legislation Before the House of Commons: The work of the European Scrutiny Committee' in Andenas and Türk (eds.), *Delegated Legislation and the Role of Committees in the EC*; T. Raunio and S. Hix, 'Backbenchers learn to fight back: European integration and parliamentary government' (2000) 23 *W. European Politics* 142.

Commission reports. 'We frequently question the likely effectiveness, cost, consistency or result of a measure, or ask the Government to justify its policy towards it, and we certainly regard it as an important part of our work to ensure that the Government has considered any potential problems and has done what it can to remedy them.'[149] The Committee has the power (rarely used) to refer documents formally to departmental Select Committees and (very rarely) to recommend a debate on the floor of the Commons. It also keeps under review the Commission's programme for regulatory simplification and scrutinises important EU texts with a view:

> to ensur[ing] that members are informed of EU proposals likely to affect the United Kingdom, to provide a source of information and analysis for the public, and to ensure that the House and the European Scrutiny Committee, and through them other organisations and individuals, have opportunities to make Ministers aware of their views on EU proposals, seek to influence Ministers and hold Ministers to account.'[150]

The EUC and ESC co-operate, with some procedural differences: the EUC operates a 'sift' based on an explanatory memorandum from the Government, to select the most significant documents; the ESC considers *all* documents and there is no formal sift, since the purpose is not to examine the merits of documents but to report to the House whether they are legally or politically important and so worthy of a debate. In practice, however, the ESC calls its whole procedure a sift, since it is faced weekly with a pile of thirty to forty documents and relies heavily on briefing from its advisers.[151] A complaint running through every review is difficulty of access: the Commission regularly fails to make essential documents available; they are incomplete, badly translated, late (sometimes 'long after the legal deadline') or 'in bits and pieces and without a clear explanation of their status, and sometimes under misleading headings'. Council agendas are unpredictable and obscurely drafted; legislative proposals come forward 'shortly before the Council decided on them, and long before an official text reached national Parliaments, let alone the citizens who would be directly affected' and the Council was even prepared to discuss legislation on the basis of unofficial texts that were not available to the public at all.[152] All of this puts pressure on the parliamentary process.

The House of Lords EUC now sees scrutiny as comparing favourably with other national parliaments and the ESC has concluded that the new provisions of the Lisbon Treaty, designed to increase participation from national parliaments, will not make much difference to its work.[153] Open Europe, an

[149] ESC, 30th Report HC 63 (2002/3) [11].

[150] ESC, 30th Report HC 63 (2002/3) [25].

[151] HC 465-i (evidence of ESC Chairman, Jimmy Hood MP).

[152] ESC, *European Scrutiny in the Commons*, HC 361 (2007/8). See also European Parliament, Committee on Constitutional Affairs, Frassoni Report, PE400 629v02-00.

[153] ESC, *Subsidiarity, National Parliaments and the Lisbon Treaty*, HC 563 (2007/8); and see *Government Response*, HC 1967 (2008/9).

independent business think-tank devoted to reform of European institutions, has, however, compared the UK Parliament unfavourably with those of Denmark and other member states. Open Europe wants to see the Commons Standing Committees, which it calls a 'black hole', abolished. It would like the ESC, in consultation with specialist committees, to take its own decisions and it wants a mandate from the ESC to be necessary before government signs up to any EU legislation or political agreements. Alternatively, the ESC should have a 'kind of "red card" role' to mandate rejection of proposals that seem to breach the subsidiarity principle. Open Europe's five-point minimalist programme[154] asks for:

1. a *statutory* scrutiny reserve
2. substitute ESC members to ensure full participation (having substitutes for each member to ensure full attendance – rather than an average 40 per cent non-attendance – would improve the quality of debate)
3. a weekly 'question time' with the UK's Permanent Representative in Brussels on the issues which are expected to come up at CoReper that week
4. meetings of the Scrutiny Committee whenever the EU institutions are in session
5. joint rights of attendance and participation for MEPs, Peers, MEPs, MSPs etc., to attend and speak in committee.

In principle, Open Europe's programme is right, though whether scrutiny reserve would be a practical proposition for twenty-seven national parliaments is doubtful, as is the question whether scrutiny by national parliaments could ever be meaningful in a polity with twenty-plus languages and legal orders.[155]

7. Restoring the balance

In Chapter 3, we expressed our support for a modified 'dialogue' model of human rights protection in which the responsibility was shared between the institutions of government, demanding a measure of co-operation between executive, legislator, administration and courts. We focused there on the work of courts. In this chapter, we have tried to redress the balance, turning our attention to the work of legislators, in particular committees of the Lords and Commons. Looking at the role of the JCHR in 'mainstreaming' human rights, for example, we found it impressively vocal, with some success in getting its voice heard.

We followed this theme further, looking at efforts of the two Houses, with co-operation from New Labour Governments, to enhance their role in the law-making process. We looked at Parliament's efforts to stand up for its legislative

[154] Open Europe, *Getting A Grip: Reforming EU scrutiny at Westminster* (2006). Contrast HL 15 (2002/3) [60–70].

[155] T. Raunio, 'Always one step behind? National legislatures and the European Union' (1999) 34 *Government and Opposition* 180.

prerogatives, fighting a battle of attrition against the 'Henry VIII clause' and the Regulatory Reform Act. Slowly, Parliament has been bringing itself into the modern age through techniques like pre- and post-legislative scrutiny and impact assessment, giving itself a measure of control over the textual quality of law and secondary legislation. We have tried to evaluate the contribution of the two Houses of Parliament and their various Scrutiny Committees to making law accessible and comprehensible. Recognising the cardinal importance of our membership of the EU, we have asked whether Parliament gives sufficient recognition to the fact that so much UK legislation is for practical purposes 'made in Europe', according it sufficient scrutiny. Policy legitimacy and textual coherence of lawmaking in the EU are matters of consequence and concern, to which only the House of Lords European Union Committee gives enough time. All this adds up to a considerable burden on Parliament.

Lawmaking, as we have observed it in this chapter, remains largely the prerogative of an elite. We rely on Cabinet ministers, civil servants, departmental lawyers, parliamentary counsel and the law officers together with parliamentarians not only to reinforce awareness of constitutional principles inside and outside government but more importantly to carry out scrutinising functions forcefully and with integrity. Often downplayed, the impact of MPs and peers, whether individual or collective, may be greater than is commonly recognised.[156] The role of the general public is more diffuse. The official line is that 'the people' can and do participate in government. The reality is, we have suggested, that participation is largely notional, seldom moving above rungs 4 and 5 of Arnstein's ladder.[157] The public acts, and has to act, through civil society organisations, through political parties[158] and through the media. This in turn acts on government and Parliament as well as on the public. Together these various interests form what Davis has called a network of 'individual small binders' that act as watchdogs and 'protectors of the constitution'.[159] Their contribution is as important as, though not more important than, that of the courts.

[156] Brazier, Kalitowski and Rosenblatt, *Law in the Making: Influence and change in the legislative process*.

[157] A. King, *Does the United Kingdom Still Have a Constitution*? (Sweet and Maxwell, 2001), Ch. 2.

[158] D. Nicol, 'Professor Tomkins' house of mavericks' [2006] *PL* 467.

[159] P. Davis, 'The significance of parliamentary procedures in control of the executive' [2007] *PL* 677, 700.

5

Rules and discretion

Contents

1. Law and 'soft law'

Towards the end of World War II, Robert Megarry, a young English barrister specialising in property law, came across Inland Revenue (IR) guidance on concessions to the taxpayer. Megarry was intrigued by these 'administrative notifications'. Were they enforceable? Were they or were they not 'law'? In his view the arrangements:

> operating in favour of the individuals concerned at the expense of taxpayers as a whole, are technically not law, but although no Court would enforce them, no official body would fail to honour them, and as they are not merely concessions in individual cases but are intended to apply generally to all who fall within their scope, the description of 'quasi-legislation' is perhaps not inept. Announcements operating against the individuals concerned, on the other hand, will normally be open to challenge in the Courts and so can be said to have the practical effect of legislation only to the extent that the expense, delays and uncertainties of litigation in general, and of opposing the unlimited resources of the Administration in particular, make those affected prefer to be submissive rather than stiff-necked.[1]

[1] R. Megarry, 'Administrative quasi-legislation' (1944) 60 *LQR* 125.

Subsequent case law showed courts at first looking on the IR concessions with disfavour. In *Cook*,[2] for example, the IR had agreed, as a concession, to accept excise duty in instalments rather than by a single, immediate payment. The Lord Chief Justice remarked: 'One approaches this case on the basis, and I confess for my part an alarming basis, that the word of the Minister is outweighing the law of the land.' Yet the court did not actually halt the 'illegal' practice. In the celebrated *Federation* case (p. 696 below) where third parties tried to challenge a discretionary IR concession, the House of Lords treated it as reasonable and sensible. Parliament too has condoned similar practices: for example, the Select Committee on the PCA has encouraged the IR to make concessions without express statutory authority while, perhaps more importantly, the Public Accounts Committee long ago accepted the need for extra-statutory concessions.[3]

The world in which Megarry operated (or more precisely, in which he thought he was operating) was the world of law and regulation described in the previous chapter. This body of law was arranged hierarchically and classified, as we saw in *Jackson*, by the way it was made: statutes made by Parliament, statutory instruments approved by Parliament and so on through a 'ragbag' of rules, regulations, orders, etc., which does not need parliamentary approval but was identified by Griffith and Street as delegated legislation. This ragbag was also classified by source; to constitute law a text must be traceable to and authorised by a superior rule of law; otherwise it could be declared ultra vires and invalidated by a court. Unlike the term 'statutory instrument', however, 'quasi-legislation' was not, as Ganz observed, a term of art. It covered:

> a wide spectrum of rules whose only common factor is that they are not directly enforceable through criminal or civil proceedings. This is where the line between law and quasi-legislation becomes blurred because there are degrees of legal force and many of the rules to be discussed do have some legal effect. It is also not possible to draw a clear distinction between law and quasi-legislation on purely formal lines i.e. the mechanism by which it is made. A legally binding provision may be contained in a circular whilst a code of practice may be embodied in a statutory instrument. We draw the line at rules which have a limited legal effect at one end of the spectrum and purely voluntary rules at the other end.[4]

Megarry's concern as a practising lawyer was with issues very like those that prompted the Statutory Instruments Act 1946. The SIA regularised provision

[2] *R v Customs and Excise Commissioners, ex p. Cook* [1970] 1 WLR 450. (The applicants were held not to have standing); *IRC v National Federation of Self-Employed and Small Businesses* [1981] 2 All ER 93.

[3] PAC, HC 300 (1970/1), pp. 408–10.

[4] G. Ganz, *Quasi-Legislation: recent developments in secondary legislation* (Sweet & Maxwell, 1987), p. 1. The Australian government prefers the term 'Grey-letter law': see Commonwealth Interdepartmental Committee on Quasi-regulation, *Grey-letter Law*, (Canberra, 1997); R. Creyke and J. McMillan, 'Soft law in Australian administrative law' in Pearson, Taggart and Harlow (eds), *Law in a Changing State* (Hart Publishing, 2008).

for parliamentary scrutiny of statutory instruments and provided for publication. In contrast, neither oversight nor publication was stipulated in respect of the mass of 'announcements by administrative and official bodies' that lay largely out of sight on the fringes of the law. Neither the rules nor the policies they incorporated were, in today's terminology, 'transparent'. Megarry called for 'some uniform official method of publication'. In this he was unsuccessful. There is still no equivalent of the American Administrative Procedure Act to regulate administrative rule-making. There is no European-style Official Journal in existence, and no register of documents such as the EU institutions now maintain is held or promulgated by government institutions. 'E-governance' and ICT have, however, made an important contribution in this respect. Many of the rules and policies discussed in this chapter, including the IR concessions, are directly available online to the public, and accessed easily through *Directgov* and departmental or local government websites.

We should not assume, however, that further unpublished rules are not in circulation behind the scenes. The 'ragbag' of delegated legislation is paralleled in a litter of 'rules, manuals, directives, codes, guidelines, memoranda, correspondence, circulars, protocols, bulletins, employee handbooks and training materials'[5] that clutter the desks (and computer files) of bureaucrats. Rules of this type are not really, as Megarry saw them, 'quasi-legislation'. All have some claim to the term 'rule' but not all can claim to be 'law' nor would they find a place within the legal hierarchy of rules. 'Soft law', as it has come to be called, is a term that covers 'any written or unwritten rule which has the purpose or effect of influencing bureaucratic decision-making in a non-trivial fashion'[6] or, to put this differently, 'rules of conduct that, in principle, have no legally binding force but which nevertheless may have practical effects'.[7] Rule-making is a natural and autonomous administrative function which, in tandem with regulation, has become one of the four 'output functions' of modern government, the others being rule application and rule interpretation.[8] Rule-making is 'the most important way in which bureaucracy creates policy' and in some respects 'rivals even the legislative process in its significance as a form of governmental output'.[9] As we shall see, the rules are usually tempered by discretion.

Soft law may be used in preference to hard law because it is simply not worth setting the lawmaking process in operation; this is particularly true of the EU, where the lawmaking procedures are exceptionally complex. On other occasions, resort to rules may be deliberate, to evade the openness of the law-

[5] From L. Sossin and C. Smith, 'Hard choices and soft law: Ethical codes, policy guidelines and the role of the courts in regulating government' (2003) 40 *Alberta Law Rev.* 871.

[6] *Ibid.*

[7] F. Snyder, 'Soft law and institutional practice in the European Community' in S. Martin (ed.), *The Construction of Europe: Essays in honour of Emile Noël* (Kluwer International, 1994), p. 197.

[8] D. Easton, 'An approach to the analysis of political systems' (1957) 9 *World Politics* 383.

[9] W. West, 'Administrative rule-making: An old and emerging literature' (2005) 65 *Pub. Admin. Review* 655.

making process. Inside government departments, where much rule-making happens, decisions to make rules are not always taken on rational grounds. Rules are 'bargained over and they are built'; choice is constrained by the political, legal and regulatory context.[10] Legislation based on a broad consensus may, for example, seem right for a change in the law affecting civil liberties but if government senses parliamentary opposition or parliamentary time is in short supply, it may give way to the temptation to avoid the parliamentary process. It may turn first to ministerial regulation (less parliamentary scrutiny) or, where even this seems difficult, use internal, departmental policy-making to supplement or subvert the law; cases such as *Anufrijeva* (p. 210 below) suggest, for example, that practices like this are common within the Home Office immigration service. Again, soft law may form part of an official legal hierarchy in which secondary or delegated legislation is used by the executive to flesh out Acts of Parliament or make procedural rules, which need to be amplified, interpreted or expanded by soft law in the form of guidance or circulars.

For centuries, to use a simple example, police procedures were governed by the common law, which governed matters such as arrest or detention. The law was expressed as broad general concepts, using terms such as 'reasonable suspicion', 'excessive force' or 'within a reasonable time'. From time to time, case law established boundaries: at what point someone must be told the grounds for his arrest, for example.[11] This left much scope or 'strong discretion' for individual officers to decide how to proceed. During the nineteenth century, as professional police forces were gradually set in place, the common law was amplified by specific local statutes and bylaws governing police practices in different parts of the country. Occasional general statutes, such as the Criminal Law Act 1967, which dealt with arrest in serious cases, applied countrywide. In 1978, the decision was taken to tidy up the mess and codify police procedures and a Royal Commission was appointed with a view to standardisation and greater transparency.[12] The subsequent Police and Criminal Evidence Act 1984 (PACE) codified the common law principles, replacing them by a hierarchy of rules. PACE is more specific than the common law, setting out in detail the procedures governing search, seizure, detention and arrest. PACE also authorises the Home Secretary to issue Codes of Practice, which are statutory instruments and must be laid in draft before Parliament for approval. The Home Office (HO) Codes of Practice are published and available on-line. Together, they 'provide the core framework of police powers and safeguards around stop and search, arrest, detention, investigation, identification and interviewing detainees'.

But the HO also issues 'guidance' on important police practices such as arrest, stop-and-search or caution. These are addressed primarily to those who

[10] J. Black, '"Which arrow?": Rule type and regulatory policy' [1995] *PL* 94, 95.

[11] *Christie v Leachinsky* [1947] AC 573.

[12] *Report of the Royal Commission on Criminal Procedure*, Cmnd 8092 (1981).

have to operate the codes or have an interest in knowing how they are operated ('stakeholders'). The Prosecution Team Manual of Guidance (available online) was, for example:

> prepared for use by members of the prosecution team, police officers and Crown Prosecutors concerned with the preparation, processing and submission of prosecution files. It contains advice and guidance about how to complete each of the constituent manual of guidance forms, along with a description of each type of prosecution file and its application in practice on matters such as arrest, questioning and cautioning suspects.

The code is transparent in the sense of being available on the HO website and accessible by the general public, who are not, be it noted, consulted on its content (Arnstein, rung 3). HO circulars also regularly provide guidance to chief constables on changes in the law or important judicial decisions. Further guidance to officials may be contained in unpublished departmental memorandums or even letters to junior officials answering specific inquiries on departmental policy. Whether or not a lawyer would characterise these informal documents as 'rules' is questionable but they are certainly intended by their authors to have some practical effect.

Not every code of practice has a statutory basis like the PACE codes. The model procedural code sponsored by the Council on Tribunals in 1991 was advisory only; as we shall see in Chapter 11, however, legislation has recently introduced a formal rule-making power. The PCA's 'Principles of Good Administration' (see Chapter 12) and the more detailed codes of good administrative practice negotiated with local authorities by the local government ombudsmen (see Chapter 10) are other important examples of this type of soft law. Self-regulatory bodies such as the Advertising Standards Authority or Press Council issue similar codes of practice to formulate their policies and explain and communicate them to stakeholders and the public (see Chapter 7). Look at the website of the Health and Safety Executive (HSE) and you will find many different examples of soft law. There is, for example, interpretative guidance on the Adventure Activities Licensing Regulations and the set of highly technical rules of good practice dealing with hazardous substances, aimed at and comprehensible only to experts. It is often hard for the public to know whether guidance of this type is *prescriptive*, as it may be where the agency possesses statutory rule-making powers, or a voluntary code, indicative of good practice but not binding. The HSE also publishes on its website its internal operational instructions and guidance used 'to carry out its core operational work of inspecting, investigating, permissioning and enforcing', said to be presented 'essentially in the same way as it is made available to HSE staff but with some additional explanation for an external audience'. There are further references to operational circulars, minutes and inspection packs, available online. These could be rules addressed to the regulators (in this case HSE inspectors) or notifications of rules addressed to the regulated (stakeholders) to instruct them on compliance with the law. They could also be aimed at the general public to provide information on the work of the agency or even to give guidance on third-party rights. The legal status of this type of rule may then cause difficulty. If, for example, the HSE specifies operational procedures for inspections, what is the position if an inspectorate departs from the established procedures in making an inspection? Are the rules binding? Can they be challenged? Does the guidance give rise to third-party rights? We shall see later how the courts have tried to deal with problems of this kind.

The Highway Code deals specifically with this point. Breach of the Highway Code is not in itself an offence because it does not have statutory or regulatory force. Its provisions, which have no formal legal basis, are 'good practice' standards, issued for purposes of guidance, though they may nonetheless be taken into account in judging criminal and civil liability. Breach of some of the provisions, contained in Road Traffic Acts or regulations made under the Acts, is an offence however. The function of the Highway Code in this case is to inform the public on the law. The website of the Department for Transport, responsible for the Highway Code, clarifies the position:

> Many of the rules in the Code are legal requirements, and if you disobey these rules you are committing a criminal offence. You may be fined, given penalty points on your licence or be disqualified from driving. In the most serious cases you may be sent to prison. Such rules are identified by the use of the words **'MUST/MUST NOT'**. In addition, the rule includes an abbreviated reference to the legislation which creates the offence. An explanation of the abbreviations can be found in 'The road user and the law'.
>
> Although failure to comply with the other rules of the Code will not, in itself, cause a person to be prosecuted, The Highway Code may be used in evidence in any court proceedings under the Traffic Acts (see 'The road user and the law') to establish liability. This includes rules which use advisory wording such as 'should/should not' or 'do/do not'.

The informal nature of the Code and the fact that its text may change is reinforced by the warning that 'In any proceedings, whether civil or criminal, only the Department for Transport's current printed version of the Code should be relied upon.'

2. Some reasons for rules

One reason for the juridification that Teubner sees as characteristic of post-modern society is that rules are really the only efficient way to organise complex societies and carry out the diverse functions that in previous chapters we associated with the state. Just as regulation and risk regulation depend on rule-making so too do the complex mass systems of service delivery in welfare and social services or of tax collection and immigration control. Administration becomes a cycle of juridification in which policies expressed as rules move up to the lawmaker and down to rule interpretation and rule application by the administration. Rules are used to manage rule application by junior officials (the 'line' or 'street level' bureaucrats) who 'individuate' rules by using their discretion to apply them to specific cases. Rule application leads up in case of dispute to rule interpretation by hierarchical superiors, then outwards to tribunals and courts. The cycle recurs if an adjudication calls for further interpretative rules, or provokes the bureaucrat to produce more, and more specific, rules. This may be done by formal rule-change or interpretative circulars and guidance.

In this account of juridification, rule-making is portrayed as a bureaucratic phenomenon, springing up inside and motivated by bureaucracy and its needs. We here assume a Weberian interpretation of bureaucracy as inherently hierarchical: senior managers formulate policies or record policy and practice as rules for the 'line bureaucracy' to apply. Similarly, the doctrine of ministerial responsibility assumes that ministers and 'mandarins' make policy decisions while rule application, implementation and routine decision-making are delegated to subordinates: the 'Carltona model' of public administration.[13] This widely-accepted stereotype has made a powerful contribution to the way in which rules are perceived but recent research suggests that it may be misleading. We should not so readily assume that:

> 'policy' – the broad strategic direction of government – is set by the top, whether politicians or civil servants, and the detailed elaboration of this policy is, to use a phrase coined in a different context, 'embellishment and detail'. The top deals with the broad issues, and the narrow gauge work is done lower down . . .
>
> [T]here is prima facie evidence to challenge the assumption that a hierarchy in the importance of decisions coincides with organisational hierarchy. Many important strategic policy issues involve settling detail, many strategic policy decisions emerge from the work of those developing detail, and those working at this level have substantial discretion and influence in shaping policy in this sense.[14]

Policy, in other words, is not necessarily imposed from the top; it may evolve at ground level and permeate upwards. Similarly the choice of rule-type is not always made by ministers, experienced senior civil servants, parliamentary draftsmen or legal advisers. It may be a matter of happenstance, involving no more than rubber-stamping of the decision of a junior civil servant, who decides not only what the minister 'needs to see and what he does not need to see' but also what can be done informally by rule-making and what requires the stamp of ministerial and legislative approval. Rule-making is not a wholly rational process though it ought to exhibit some elements of rationality.

The introduction of ICT and evolution of e-governance (see Chapter 2) have

[13] *Carltona v Commissioner of Works* [1943] 2 All ER 560 (CA).

[14] E. Page, 'The civil servant as legislator: Lawmaking in British administration' (2003) 81 *Pub. Admin.* 651; E. Page and B. Jenkins, *Policy Bureaucracy: Government with a cast of thousands* (Oxford University Press, 2005), pp. 2 and 72–108.

brought about fundamental changes in the way large-scale service-delivery agencies operate. In the world of K. C. Davis, whose influential work on rule-making is discussed below, police officers and public service workers were *individuals* who interacted directly with individual citizens. They possessed and, unlike computers, were capable of using, substantial discretion in allocating or withholding benefits and services, in problem-solving and sometimes in imposing sanctions. Contrast the modern office, where:

> window clerks are being replaced by Web sites, and advanced information and expert systems are taking over the role of case managers and adjudicating officers. Instead of noisy, disorganized decision-making factories populated by fickle officials, many of these executive agencies are fast becoming quiet information refineries, in which nearly all decisions are pre-programmed by algorithms and digital decision trees. Today, a more true-to-life vision of the term "bureaucracy" would be a room filled with softly humming servers, dotted here and there with a system manager behind a screen.[15]

The decision-making process has been 'routinised' and has evolved into a two-way process in which a computer screen (or mobile telephone) always connects implementing officials to the organisation. Insofar as they are directly in contact with citizens, this is always through or in the presence of these contacts. A step further and the organisation is translated into a 'system-level bureaucracy', where:

> routine cases are handled without human interference. Expert systems have replaced professional workers. Apart from the occasional public information officer and the help desk staff, there are no other street-level bureaucrats . . . The process of issuing decisions is carried out – virtually from beginning to end – by computer systems.[16]

Whether or not ICT is wiping out the discretion of street-level bureaucrats, as Bovens and Zouridis maintain, is contestable; their functions have, however, certainly changed, very much to the profit of supervisors.[17] Rules, as we saw in Chapter 2, play a central part in NPM methodology, which is highly dependent on rules. Not only do rules allow street-level bureaucrats to be guided and directed, they also allow them to be tested and controlled; with the help of rules, their work can be audited, measured and evaluated in the ways described by Power. So long as NPM remains the predominant mode of public administration therefore, rules are likely to remain an indispensable tool.[18]

[15] M. Bovens and S. Zouridis, 'From street-level to system-level bureaucracies: How information and communication technology is transforming administrative discretion and constitutional control' (2002) 62 *Pub. Admin. Rev.* 174, 175.

[16] *Ibid.*, p. 180. The term 'street-level bureaucracy' was introduced by M. Lipsky, *Street-level Bureaucracy: Dilemmas of the individual in public services* (Russell Sage Foundation, 1980) in an era of face-to-face encounters between individuals.

[17] F. Jorna and P. Wagenaar, 'The "iron cage" strengthened? Discretion and digital discipline' (2007) 85 *Pub. Admin.* 214.

[18] C. Hood and C. Scott, 'Bureaucratic regulation and new public management in the United Kingdom: Mirror-image developments?' (1996) 23 *JLS* 321.

Computers are not designed for the exercise of discretion, so that automation, which facilitates standardisation, also demands it. Computers, in other words, speak the language of rules. This 'fourth generation legislation', however, takes the form of the algorithms, decision-trees and checklists that make up computer programs, an innovation that has radically changed the balance of power between ministers and mandarins and the computer programmers and expert technicians responsible for the implementation of policy.[19] The former may now have to take responsibility for systems that they can neither operate nor understand – a deficiency enough in itself to explain the many public procurement failures and technological breakdowns met with in the Child Support Agency and NHS. Nor are our democratic representatives well equipped to deal with the technological revolution; as we saw in Chapter 4, they are experiencing difficulty in catching up. Bovens and Zouridis argue that democratic control over the executive can only be restored by opening up to public scrutiny 'the electronic forms, decision trees, and checklists used by the organisation to make decisions'.[20] This will allow independent experts to act as monitors, a view of e-governance that relates surprisingly closely to Foucault's concept of 'governmentality' (p. 75 below).

Recent changes in the organisational structure of government have also hastened the trend to administration through rules. The downloading of administration to executive agencies is conducted, as we saw, through 'pseudo-contracts', whose terms are simply a privatised form of rule. As functions have been hived-off to agencies and devolved to regional government, the quest for equality has meant that locally administered services are supervised by and subjected to the policy guidance of central government or inspected, monitored and regulated by a regulator. Equally, the 'joined up government' initiatives and creation of 'hyper-ministries' and 'super-agencies' (see Chapter 7) depend on the ability of diverse organisations to communicate with each other. They communicate with rules: the circulars, guidance and memorandums met already but also through concordats and other agreements between the public servants who work in central and devolved government and help to hold the British state together.

One process in which authorities at several levels have to collaborate is land-use planning. Central and regional government, district, county and metropolitan district councils all exercise planning functions as well as national parks authorities. Several central government departments are also involved. The principal responsibility rests with the Department of Communities and Local Government (DCLG) but the Department of Environment (now DEFRA) has some responsibilities and many 'stakeholder' interests and the Department for Transport deals with major projects for roads, railways and, highly controversial, airports. In recent years too, responsibility for environmental policy

[19] R. de Mulder, 'The digital revolution: From trias to tetras politica' in Snellen and van de Donk (eds.), *Public Administration in an Information Age: A handbook* (IOS Press, 1998).

[20] Bovens and Zouridis, 'From street-level to system-level bureaucracies', p. 183.

has increasingly been transferred to the EU, adding a further link to the communication chain.[21] For many years, the complex administrative structure was knit together by a set of interpretative circulars issued to planning authorities by central government, published as *The Encyclopedia of Planning Law*. This loose-leaf publication, updated regularly and available to the general public through public libraries, is supplemented in the era of e-governance by the publication of all regulations, codes, circulars and official letters on the DCLG website. Elements of this body of soft law may be questioned and fall to be judicially interpreted, as in the *Newbury* case,[22] where the minister relied heavily on a departmental circular in deciding a planning appeal. Newbury argued that the circular glossed the law and was inaccurate. Lord Fraser called the circular 'erroneous in law' and the House agreed in thinking that the minister's decision, if based on it, would have been unlawful.

The EU, with few service-delivery functions or duties of direct administration, which are largely exercised by national or regional administrations, is a regime devoted to regulation and held together by rules; one view of its chief executive body, the European Commission, is as a super-regulator, whose main function is rule-making, standardisation and the harmonisation of rules.[23] The network of administrations and European agencies of which the Commission is the focal point is held together by committees and rules. The setting-up of EU agencies, with important liaison functions with national administrations, third states and agencies, has added to the need for rules which, as EU agencies possess neither legislative nor executive functions, are advisory and interpretative.[24] In recent years too, governance in the EU has come increasingly to rely on a 'soft governance' format, the 'Open Method of Co-ordination', in which guidelines, codes of practice and other informal instruments agreed between the Commission and representatives of national governments are substituted for formal EU legislation made by 'the Community method'.[25] A tissue of non-binding or not fully binding inter-institutional agreements, codes of conduct, frameworks, resolutions, declarations, guidance notes, circulars, codes of practice, communications and no doubt other forms of 'soft law' has come into being.[26] Although technically not binding, these texts, though usually

[21] C. Demke and M. Unfried, *European Environmental Policy: The administrative challenge for the Member States* (European Institute of Public Administration, 2001).

[22] *Newbury District Council v Environment Secretary* [1980] 2 WLR 379.

[23] G. Majone, 'The rise of the regulatory state in Europe' (1994) 17 *W. European Politics* 77.

[24] G. Majone, 'Managing Europeanization: The European agencies' in Peterson and Shackleton, *The Institutions of the European Union*, 2nd edn (Oxford University Press, 2006).

[25] J. Scott and D. Trubek, 'Mind the gap: Law and new approaches to governance in the European Union' (2002) 8 *ELJ* 1; D. Trubek and L. Trubek, 'Hard and soft law in the construction of social Europe: The role of the open method of coordination' (2005) 11 *ELJ* 343.

[26] K. Wellens and G. Borchardt, 'Soft law in European Community law' (1989) 14 *EL Rev.* 267; M. Cini, From Soft Law to Hard Law? Discretion and Rule-making in the Commission's State Aid Regime, EUI, RSC 2000/35 (2000); L. Barani, 'Hard and soft law in the European Union: The case of social policy and the open method of coordination' W*ebpapers on Constitutionalism and Governance beyond the State* 2 (2006), available online.

published, are enforceable largely through peer-group pressure; from time to time they may surface and fall to be interpreted by the ECJ or national courts.[27]

A final explanation for the pervasiveness of rules in contemporary society takes us outside bureaucracy into civil society in an era of human rights. The advent of New Labour to government in 1997 brought greater commitment to an equal and inclusive society, which we find illustrated in the wording of the Equality Act 2006.[28] The overriding general duty laid on the new Commission for Equality and Human Rights is to exercise its functions:

> with a view to encouraging and supporting the development of a society in which:
>
> (a) people's ability to achieve their potential is not limited by prejudice or discrimination
> (b) there is respect for and protection of each individual's human rights
> (c) there is respect for the dignity and worth of each individual
> (d) each individual has an equal opportunity to participate in society
> (e) there is mutual respect between groups based on understanding and valuing of diversity and on shared respect for equality and human rights.

Prioritising values connected with equality has had the incidental effect of greatly enhancing the case for rules. There is a widely held belief that rules support fairness, consistency and equal treatment; contrariwise, administrative discretion contributes to inconsistency and inequality of treatment. Rule-making can also be portrayed as contributing indirectly to equality by extending the possibility of participation in the policy-making process from stakeholders to the public at large. On the other hand, the fact that rules operate 'in all-or-nothing fashion' (as Dworkin has put it) creates serious conflict with the principle of 'individuation' favoured by courts; rules may maintain consistency while giving rise to unfairness. The world of rules is neither consistent nor symmetrical and West, summarising the qualities for which rule-making is valued, concludes that most of its goals 'conflict with most of the others'.[29]

3. Structuring discretion

Red light theorists, we saw in Chapter 1, have always put their trust in courts as the *primary* means of controlling what Lord Hewart once called 'administrative lawlessness';[30] green light theorists prefer legislation and 'firewatching' techniques. American professor Kenneth Culp Davis was emphatically not a

[27] J. Klabbers, 'Informal instruments before the ECJ' (1994) 31 *CML Rev.* 997; O. Treib *et al.*, *Complying with Europe: European Union harmonization and soft law in the Member States* (Cambridge University Press, 2005).

[28] The Act replaced three earlier agencies, the Commission for Racial Equality, the Equal Opportunities Commission, and the Disability Rights Commission, with a new umbrella agency, the CEHR.

[29] West, 'Administrative rule-making', p. 659.

[30] Lord Hewart, *The New Despotism* (Ernest Benn, 1929), Ch. 4.

red light theorist; indeed, his celebrated book, *Discretionary Justice*, opened by dissociating its author from Dicey's 'extravagant version of the rule of law'.[31] Davis saw that the control courts purported to exercise was inadequate; it was largely retrospective; it was external; it operated on the surface, 'pushing bricks on the nice part of the house'. He was concerned to bring inside the parameters of administrative law the 'dark and windowless' areas of administration, such as policing, pre-trial, parole and immigration procedures. It troubled Davis that administrative lawyers were focusing narrowly on areas of administrative activity – judicial review, tribunals and inquiries – that were already relatively open and controlled. He wanted to open windows on the arbitrariness that, he believed, thrives in darkness:

> If we stay within the comfortable areas where jurisprudence scholars work and concern ourselves mostly with statutory and judge-made law, we can at best accomplish no more than to refine what is already tolerably good. To do more than that we have to open our eyes to the reality that justice to individual parties is administered more outside courts than in them, and we have to penetrate the unpleasant areas of discretionary determinations by police and prosecutors and other administrators, where huge concentrations of injustice invite drastic reforms.[32]

Davis focused on the widely dispersed administrative discretion in the hands of the 'street-level bureaucracy' whose decisions he thought were, all too often, unlawful. He saw rule-making as the most effective technique for controlling the arbitrary decisions of the police and immigration officers whose practices he had studied. Rule-making would open up the administrative process and procure fairer, more consistent decisions. Rules, because they were written down and could be published, assisted transparency; they were more easily accessible than unpublished policies formulated in terms of wide administrative discretion. Because rules were general, rule-making encouraged comprehensive solutions to problems that 'go beyond the facts of individual cases'. It permitted broader participation by stakeholders and provided opportunities for public participation; indeed, Davis described bureaucratic rule-making hopefully as 'a miniature democratic process'. (We have to remember that Davis was thinking in terms of the American Administrative Procedure Act (AAPA), which prescribes a more open and participatory rule-making procedure than that found at the time in Britain).

These ideas gained ground rapidly with administrative lawyers, who saw Davis's approach as advantageous in terms both of individual and collective fairness and effective policy development.[33] Rules were 'rational' and sat more

[31] K. Culp Davis, *Discretionary Justice* (Greenwood Press, 1969).

[32] *Ibid.*, p. 215

[33] West, 'Administrative rule-making'.

easily with Herbert Simon's model of rational administration. Rule-making was more efficient than individuated decision-making, enabling agencies to accomplish their statutory objectives more expeditiously than incremental policy development through individuated, adjudicated decisions.[34] Discretion permitted discrimination and was capable of unexpected and capricious change. Rules *structured* discretion and helped to ensure that policies approved by the public were actually implemented and observed; they were therefore a more effective weapon for control of administrative discretion than courts could ever be. The influence of these ideas cannot be overestimated. For a decade or more they became the perceived wisdom, prompting a large literature and inducing the belief that control of discretionary power was administrative law's paramount task.[35] The potential disadvantages of complexity and rigidity were downplayed.

The essential novelty of Davis's thesis lay in his conclusion that 'the degree of administrative discretion should often be more restricted; some of the restricting can be done by *legislators* but most of this task must be performed by *administrators*'.[36] His definition of discretion was simple and pragmatic. 'A public officer has discretion whenever the effective limits of his power leave him free to make a choice among possible courses of action and inaction.'[37] Discretion derived in the first instance from legislation or regulations but it did not stop there: 'The degree of discretion depends not only on grants of authority to administrators but also on what they do to enlarge their power.'[38] Davis saw that street-level bureaucrats possessed relatively high degrees of discretion unfettered by hierarchical, organisational authority. He focused on internal control through the hierarchical structures of the bureaucracy itself, arguing that it should be encouraged to 'structure' its discretion by formulating its policies as rules. The rules would not only be used internally for the guidance of the line- or street-level officials but also by the public, which would be able to access them for purposes of evaluation – very much the function of modern freedom of information legislation. Davis did not, however, argue that discretion could or should be eliminated; it was an essential part of a decision-making process:

> Even when rules can be written, discretion is often better. Rules without discretion cannot fully take into account the need for tailoring results to unique facts and circumstances of particular cases. The justification for discretion is often the need for individualized justice. This is so in the judicial process as well as in the administrative process.

[34] See further, J. Mashaw, *Bureaucratic Justice* (Yale University Press, 1983).

[35] West, 'Administrative rule-making'. And see R. Baldwin and J. Hawkins, 'Discretionary justice: Davis reconsidered' [1984] *PL* 570; D. Galligan, *Discretionary Powers: A legal study of official discretion* (Clarendon Press, 1990); K. Hawkins (ed.), *The Uses of Discretion* (Clarendon Press, 1991).

[36] Culp Davis, *Discretionary Justice*, p. 215 (emphasis ours).

[37] *Ibid.*, p. 4.

[38] *Ibid.*, p. 215.

> Every governmental and legal system in world history has involved both rules and discretion. No government has ever been a government of laws and not of men in the sense of eliminating all discretionary power.[39]

In his celebrated metaphor of discretion as 'the hole in the doughnut', Dworkin expressed the realisation that discretion is always shaped and structured by rules. 'Discretion does not exist except as an area left open by a surrounding belt of restriction. It is therefore a relative concept. It always makes sense to ask, "Discretion under which standards?" or "Discretion as to which authority?"'[40] Davis, on the other hand, thought in linear terms, believing it was possible 'not merely to choose between rules and discretion but to find the optimum point on the rule-to-discretion scale'.[41] This might suggest that rule-making is, as some economists think, a rational or largely rational process.[42] Many attempts have been made, mostly by those who write about regulatory theory, to fit rule-type to function and select the most appropriate rule-type from the toolkit of rules (see Chapter 6). Braithwaite has suggested, for example, that precise rules are better suited to regulating simple matters but that, as the situation or phenomena become more complex, principles deliver more consistency than rules.[43] But even when rule-makers try to be scientific, they often fail: their rules may, for example, be premised on mistaken assumptions as to how people will act, or fail properly to take into consideration the views of stakeholders.[44] This hints at important problems not only for rule-making but also for the supposedly scientific techniques of impact assessment discussed in Chapter 4 and, still more severe as we shall see in Chapter 6, for risk regulation.

4. Rules, principles and discretion

(a) Discretion to rules

At this point we need to think a little more deeply about the nature and quality of rules. We have so far been thinking in terms of Megarry's procedural distinction between 'law' and 'quasi-law' or, as we termed it, 'soft law'. This, however, is not the only way rules can be classified. Legal theorists distinguish 'rules', defined as applicable generally or 'across the board', from 'principles', which are less specific and more flexible, leaving a greater degree of discretion to the decision-maker – one reason why they recommend themselves to judges. Rules operate 'in all-or-nothing fashion'[45] or 'attach a definite detailed

39 *Ibid.*, p. 17.
40 R. Dworkin, *Taking Rights Seriously* (Duckworth, 1978), p. 31.
41 Culp Davies, *Discretionary Justice*, p. 215.
42 C. Diver, 'The optimal precision of administrative rules' (1983) 93 *Yale LJ* 65.
43 J. Braithwaite, 'Rules and principles: A theory of legal certainty' (2002) 27 *Australian Journal of Legal Philosophy* 47.
44 R. Baldwin, *Rules and Government* (Clarendon Press, 1995), pp. 140–1.
45 R. Dworkin, 'The model of rules I' in Dworkin, *Taking Rights Seriously* (Duckworth, 1978), p. 24.

legal consequence to a definite detailed state of fact'.[46] This is certainly a quality of the statutory drafting discussed in Chapter 4.

Rules embody policies which, according to Jowell, are transformed into rules by a 'process of legalisation':

> Policies are broad statements of general objectives, such as 'To provide decent, safe and sanitary housing,' 'To prevent unsafe driving.' The policy is legalised as the various elements of housing and driving are specified, providing, for example, for hot and cold running water, indoor toilets, maximum speed limits and one-way streets. A rule thus is the most precise form of general direction, since it requires for its application nothing more or less than the happening or non-happening of a physical event. For the application of the maximum speed rule, all we need do is determine factually whether or not the driver was exceeding thirty miles per hour . . . [47]

Dworkin famously distinguished 'policy' from 'principle'. A government may (as we saw) accept the 'abstract egalitarian principle' that it must treat its citizens as equals. (This broad general principle, we should note, is open to many different interpretations.) It then uses the principle to shape legislative strategies. 'Decisions in pursuit of these strategies, judged one by one, are matters of policy, not principle; they must be tested by asking whether they advance the overall goal, not whether they give each citizen what he is entitled to have as an individual.'[48] Principles, on the other hand, embody *rights* which act as 'trumps' over these decisions of policy in that government is required to respect them on a case-by-case, decision-by-decision basis.

Principles, according to Jowell, differ from rules in that they 'prescribe highly unspecific actions'. In a distinction reminiscent of Dworkin, Jowell tells us that principles:[49]

> arise mainly in the context of judicial decision-making. They involve normative moral standards by which rules might be evaluated. They are frequently expressed in maxims, such as 'No man shall profit by his own wrong,' 'He who comes to court shall come with clean hands.' They have developed in the judicial context over time, and are less suited to administrative decision making because they do not address themselves to economic, social or political criteria, but to justice and fairness largely in the judicial situation. A principle that may arise in the administrative context would be the maxim: 'Like cases shall receive like treatment.'

Perhaps more relevant to our subject are the principles that citizens should be equally treated by the administration; that policies should be consistent and

[46] J. Raz, 'Legal principles and the limits of law' 81 *Yale LJ* 823 (1972).

[47] J. Jowell, 'The legal control of administrative discretion' [1973] *PL* 178, 201.

[48] R. Dworkin, *Law's Empire* (Fontana, 1986), p. 223.

[49] A well-known definition by Roscoe Pound cited by J. Jowell, 'The legal control of administrative discretion'.

consistently administered; that intervention with citizen's rights should be proportionate to administrative policy-goals, etc.

As Jowell explains, rules are not simply the antithesis of discretion but are points on a continuum:

> Discretion is rarely absolute, and rarely absent. It is a matter of degree, and ranges along a continuum between high and low. Where he has a high degree of discretion, the decision-maker will normally be guided by reference to such vague standards as 'public interest' and 'fair and reasonable'. Where his discretion is low, the decision-maker will be limited by rules that do not allow much scope for interpretation. For example, a police officer's discretion is high when he has the power to regulate traffic at crossroads 'as he thinks fit.' If he were required to allow traffic to pass from East to West for three minutes and then from North to South for two minutes, subject to exceptional circumstances, then his discretion would be greatly reduced. A traffic light possesses no discretion at all.[50]

While some rules, like Jowell's example, are highly specific and not malleable, others are open-textured and flexible, leaving more room for discretion. Rules normally embody discretion because they can seldom be formulated with sufficient precision to eliminate it. Rules may also incorporate principles, just as principles may modify rules and reduce their specificity. Rules are also subject to interpretation, a judicial activity leaving much room for discretion.

Let us test these ideas against the hypothetical case of Anne, an unsighted woman who wishes to go into a café in a public park owned by Parktown local council with her guide dog.[51] A park bylaw provides: 'No dog may enter an establishment where food is served', a highly specific instruction leaving minimal room for interpretation. Would it apply, for example, to tables in front of a stall serving only cold drinks, tea and coffee? A notice on the café door repeats the bylaw. Yolande, a waitress, refuses to let the guide dog in. Anne objects and calls the manageress, Mrs Brown, arguing that the bylaw contravenes s. 22 (3) of the Disability Discrimination Act 1995 (DDA), which provides:

> It is unlawful for a person managing any premises to discriminate against a disabled person occupying those premises—
>
> (a) in the way he permits the disabled person to make use of any benefits or facilities;
> (b) by refusing or deliberately omitting to permit the disabled person to make use of any benefits or facilities.

Mrs Brown thinks that Yolande has not discriminated. She has applied the rule literally: no dogs are admitted under any circumstances. But s. 24(1) of the DDA states that a person does discriminate against a disabled person if:

50 *Ibid.*

51 For further examples and explanation of the way rules operate, see W. Twining and D. Miers, *How to Do Things with Rules*, 4th edn (Butterworths, 1999).

> (a) for a reason which relates to the disabled person's disability, he treats him less favourably than he treats or would treat others to whom that reason does not or would not apply; and
> (b) he cannot show that the treatment in question is justified.

This rather tortuous wording leaves much space for 'judgement discretion'. Technically perhaps, Mrs Brown's interpretation satisfies (a) but it certainly seems to gainsay the legislative intention.

So, can Yolande prove justification? By s. 24(3)(a), treatment is justified when action is taken 'in order not to endanger the health or safety of any person (which may include that of the disabled person)'. This rule embodies discretion, which is very lightly 'structured'; it comes towards the 'strong' end of Jowell's scale. Yolande may refuse to admit the guide dog if she is sure in her own mind that health or safety could be endangered; in the light of *Padfield* (p. 101 above), however, she will have to give reasons for her belief. *Padfield* passes discretion to the adjudicator. What is the applicable standard? Must the risk be low, high or very high? Is it enough that Yolande believes it to be high? Here the *Wednesbury* principle, according to which Yolande's discretion can be reviewed if it is manifestly unreasonable, is applicable.

But s. 24(3)(a) goes on to provide that the defence can only be claimed if 'it is reasonable, in all the circumstances of the case for [the defendant] to hold that opinion'. This formula transfers strong discretion to the adjudicator or judge reviewing the case, who is left to decide what is 'reasonable'. This 'judgement discretion' is structured first by reference to the *Wednesbury* principle that Yolande's conduct must not be so unreasonable that no reasonable waitress would act like that and, secondly, to 'vague standards' as to what conduct actually meets this test. This, John Griffith would argue, is what judges do every day (see p. 105).

A further possibility is opened by the fact that this incident took place in a public park. The DDA 2005 modifies the 1995 Act, inserting a new s. 49A. This specifies the duties of public authorities, amongst which we find a general duty to have due regard in carrying out its functions to:

> the need to take steps to take account of disabled persons' disabilities, even where that involves treating disabled persons more favourably than other persons.

Perhaps Parktown's bylaw offends this provision? If so, Parktown should have issued guidance to employees. But how detailed should that guidance be? Is it enough to set out or draw attention to the provisions of s. 49A? Should the guidance be interpretative, reformulating the section in simple language? Should it deal specifically with guide dogs? If it is too general, those at whom it is aimed (the street-level bureaucracy) may not understand it; if it is too detailed, they may not bother to read it, or may not understand it if they do. Perhaps, the bored and bemused reader might observe, it would be better to rely on the good sense of the manageress; from which we might deduce either that there is no optimum point on the rules/discretion scale or that rules are not the optimal means of administration.[52] To Taggart:

> the line between law and discretion is unstable, and has broken down in important respects in recent years . . . [I]n truth there is no bright line separating law and discretion. The key is to recognise that, both in interpreting particular words in statutes and in divining the limits of broadly conferred discretionary powers, lawyers and judges are engaged in exactly the same interpretative process.[53]

So, we might add, with equal justification, are officials, administrators and other members of the street-level bureaucracy.

(b) Rules to discretion

Our 'No dogs' rule is a classic example of an 'over-inclusive rule' that does not admit of any exceptions. There are several ways to mitigate the harsh effects of over-inclusive rules. The first is to pile rule upon rule. Our bylaw could, for example, be amended to read: 'No dogs other than guide dogs may enter an establishment where food is served.' One reason why modern legislation tends to be too specific is precisely this wish to cover every possible contingency. Specific amendments may, however, store up problems for the future, opening the way (for example) to arguments over the meaning of the words 'establishment' and 'guide dog'. Another solution is a change of rule-type as Braithwaite (above) recommends: to turn from specific rules to principles. A more general notice – 'Dogs can enter this café only with the manager's permission' – would allow staff to admit dogs at their discretion. In exercising discretion, Mrs Brown would then be subject to Jowell's 'normative moral standards by which the rules might be evaluated'. These would include the statutory equality principle, general common law principles and prevalent community values, all of which are sufficiently flexible to allow the admission of guide dogs.

In the real world of the British social security system, where protagonists of rule-based administration were especially vocal during the 1960s, Titmuss emerged as a major advocate for discretion. Titmuss saw that welfare systems needed discretion for two fundamental reasons:

> First, because as far as we can see ahead and on the basis of all we know about human weaknesses and diversities, a society without some element of means-testing and discretion is an unattainable goal. It is stupid and dangerous to pretend that such an element need not exist . . . Secondly, we need this element of individualised justice in order to allow

[52] Baldwin, *Rules and Government*, p. 16; K. Hawkins, 'The use of legal discretion: Perspectives from law and social science' in Hawkins (ed.), *The Uses of Discretion*.

[53] M. Taggart, 'Australian exceptionalism in judicial review' (2008) 36 *Federal Law Review* 1, 13.

> a universal rights scheme, based on principles of equity, to be as precise and inflexible as possible. These characteristics of precision, inflexibility and universality depend for their sustenance and strength on the existence of some element of flexible, individualised justice.[54]

Consistency, in other words, is not always a desirable goal.

The third solution to our guide dog problem, which most people would see as most sensible, is simply to waive the over-inclusive rule. This is the discretionary power of 'selective enforcement', which sociologists see as necessary to deal with over-inclusive rules. We would all condemn a policeman for prosecuting an ambulance driver who breaks the speed limit when rushing to A&E. Again, the Licensing Act 2003 provides that a licence to sell alcohol lapses automatically on death of the licensee unless a transfer is applied for within seven days. When the Neath Council applied this provision to a grieving widow who had failed to apply within the statutory period, the local MP called the decision 'shockingly offensive', castigating the council for applying the law in 'such a rigid and insensitive way'. Quite correctly the council replied that it had no discretion in the matter, but local opinion was so clearly on the side of the bereaved family that it had to find some way out of the impasse. It did not resort to 'selective enforcement'; this might have interfered with the rights of third parties and is, in any event, much harder in these days of transparency, accountability, audit and inspection. Instead, it advised the licensee how to operate within the rules by serving food and beverages but not alcohol until a new licence could be applied for and granted – a solution that the MP thought inadequate.

We need to be careful here. It is one thing to applaud selective enforcement when it is used to mitigate the severity of a rule that has created a 'hard case'. It is important to bear in mind, however, that this is not the only or even the most usual way in which powers of selective enforcement can be used. It was indeed the selective enforcement by police officers of the rules supposed to govern stop-and-search procedures to target unpopular groups such as drug users that prompted Davis's rule-making theory. Quite correctly, Davis suspected that police officers routinely disregard the rules in favour of their own belief that some classes of people are simply undesirable and ought, if the officer wants to do this, to be stopped and searched at the officer's whim. (We shall pick this point up in *Gillan*, see p. 215 below). So civil libertarians are right to be afraid of police discretion because it can be so easily abused; and welfare lawyers are right to be frightened of discretion because of its potency as a weapon for social control. Welfare lawyers in particular have always stressed the need for consistency and equal treatment in decision-taking and pointed to the lack of transparency and opportunities for arbitrariness in discretionary decision-making.[55] (Note how the argument is becoming circular.)

[54] R. Titmuss, 'Welfare "rights", law and discretion' (1971) 42 *Pol. Q.* 113, 131.

[55] M. Partington, 'Rules and discretion in British social security law' in Gamillsheg (ed.), *In Memoriam Sir Otto Kahn Freund* (Stevens, 1980), p. 621.

Was Davis unduly optimistic about the power of rules to counter misuse of discretion? Reiss, a sociologist, thought he had closed his eyes to how people really behave:

> Davis relies on rule making as the principal means for confining discretion, on openness of discretionary processes as the major means for structuring discretion, and on supervision and review as the major means for checking discretion. These are, of course, the classic means and processes operating in modern bureaucracies. What is absent from his treatment, however – a deficiency that may puzzle behavioural scientists – is both a consideration of the relative importance of these factors and a consideration of how bureaucracies can turn these means to ends of justice or can find ways to circumvent them so that decisions go against the interests of individual parties.[56]

Goodin takes this argument to its logical conclusion, arguing that problems of bad faith or deficient institutional culture cannot be overcome merely by replacing discretion with rules.[57] One reason is that rules can never be drafted with sufficient precision, another that some discretion is 'inevitable' in the sense of being 'logically necessary to the operation of a system of rules at all'. Such discretions are inherent to the system: the choice to make rules ('policy discretion') can, for example, be shifted all around the system: 'from lower-level officials to higher ones, or onto judges, or onto Parliament, or whatever'. It cannot, however, ever entirely be eliminated. 'Judgement discretion', used whenever rules are interpreted, is equally hard to eliminate. Judges, as Cohen once remarked, are not slot-machines.[58] Even when the rules a court has to apply are apparently specific, judges have at their disposal principles, including the general principles of administrative and human rights law, to modify the rules. (See Lord Steyn in *Anufrijeva*, p. 210 below).

All the objectionable features of discretion – secrecy, inaccessibility, unfairness, arbitrariness – are possible in a rule-based system. Goodin instances a discretion that is objectionable because reasons do not have to be given for its use, such as a dress code in a bar or restaurant. Reasons are demanded; officials circumvent the rule by providing only 'boiler plate reasons', which re-state the reasons in terms of the rule ('you cannot come in because you are not properly dressed'.) The considerations that dictate abuse of discretion will drive the administrator to use rules in identical fashion. The question of rules and discretion is thus largely immaterial because only changes in administrative culture will bring about real change. 'Rules cannot, at least without substantial costs in other respects, prevent arbitrariness and other vices; for much the

56 A. Reiss, 'Book review of K. C. Davis, *Discretionary Justice*' (1970) 68 *Michigan L. Rev.* 789, 795.

57 R. Goodin, 'Welfare, rights and discretion' (1986) 6 *OJLS* 232.

58 F. Cohen, 'Transcendental nonsense and the functional approach' (1935) 35 *Col. Law Rev.* 809.

same reasons that discretionary decisions display those attributes, rule-based decisions *can,* and *probably will.*'

> 'Bad' clients find that officials stand on the letter of the law or lodge unnecessary appeals designed to postpone payment; 'good' clients may receive the benefit of loopholes and ambiguities. Some seek to 'neutralize administration' by tying it in its own rules; e.g. by lodging unnecessary appeals which use up resources and time and may even be designed to overload the system to provoke concessions. Consultation procedures may be contested at every stage in the hope that a development plan or new regulations can be postponed indefinitely.[59]

In short, badly disposed officials and badly disposed welfare clients understand only too well how to play games with rules. Goodin's conclusions are reinforced by modern studies of accountability, which tend to show that work conditions and professional willingness to conform make it hard to control the behaviour of police and public servants simply by recourse to rules.[60]

In *Anufrijeva*,[61] Miss A was an asylum seeker entitled to income support pending a decision on her application. The rules applicable were laid down in the Income Support (General) Regulations 1987, which provided that a person lost the right to income support on ceasing to be an asylum seeker and ceased to be an asylum seeker on the date when the claim was 'recorded by the Secretary of State as having been determined'. A negative decision was recorded in her file together with the reasons for the officer's decision: 'This woman has cited numerous mishaps throughout the 1990s and puts her woes down to an encounter her father had with a drunken solicitor in 1991. There is no credibility in any of this and no Convention reason anyway.' The decision was notified directly to the Benefits Agency but was not at the time notified to the applicant. Unknowingly, Miss A went to claim benefit and was told that she had been struck off. Following a determination that she was not entitled to asylum, the case was returned to an immigration officer to consider her case for 'exceptional leave to remain'. It was not until she had failed to attend two interviews that Miss A received formal notice of the decision recorded in her file.

The Immigration Rules prescribe that someone refused leave to enter following the refusal of an asylum application shall be provided with a notice informing him of the decision and of the reasons for refusal. The notice of refusal shall also explain any rights of appeal available to the applicant and inform him of the means by which he may exercise those rights. Miss A therefore claimed entitlement to income support on the ground that these provisions were incompatible with the view that a decision that had not been notified was final; until notification, it remained provisional.

59 Goodin, 'Welfare, rights and discretion'.

60 See, e.g., R. Reiner, *The Politics of the Police*, 3rd edn (Oxford University Press, 2000.

61 *R v Home Secretary, ex p. Anufrijeva* [2003] UKHL 36.

Though somewhat cynical of the HO justification of expense and administrative convenience for what had become a routine procedure, Lord Bingham found the wording clear and unambiguous. Parliamentary draftsmen had no difficulty in distinguishing between the *making* of a determination or decision and *giving notice of it* to the party affected. The words did not say and could not be fairly understood to mean 'recorded by the Secretary of State as having been determined . . . on the date on which it is so recorded and notice given to the applicant'. That would be to rewrite the rules. Furthermore, while Lord Bingham was willing to accept that the Home Secretary was 'subject to a public law duty to notify the appellant of his decision on her asylum application and, if it was adverse, his reasons for refusing it', any implied duty would be to give notice within a reasonable time. Failure to give notice within a reasonable time would be a breach of the Home Secretary's public law duty but would not necessarily nullify or invalidate his decision.

In strong contrast, Lord Steyn's speech for the majority described HO practice as a clear breach of a constitutional principle requiring access to the courts and of the rule of law: whatever the 'niceties of statutory language . . . the semantic arguments . . . cannot displace the constitutional principles'. Lord Steyn went on to say:

> In oral argument before the House counsel stated that the Secretary of State did not condone delay in notification of a decision on asylum. These were weasel words. There was no unintended lapse. The practice of not notifying asylum seekers of the fact of withdrawal of income support was consistently and deliberately adopted. There simply is no rational explanation for such a policy. Having abandoned this practice the Secretary of State still seeks to justify it as lawful. It provides a peep into contemporary standards of public administration. Transparency is not its hallmark. It is not an encouraging picture . . .
>
> The arguments for the Home Secretary ignore fundamental principles of our law. Notice of a decision is required before it can have the character of a determination with legal effect because the individual concerned must be in a position to challenge the decision in the courts if he or she wishes to do so. This is not a technical rule. It is simply an application of the right of access to justice. That is a fundamental and constitutional principle of our legal system . . .
>
> This view is reinforced by the constitutional principle requiring the rule of law to be observed. That principle too requires that a constitutional state must accord to individuals the right to know of a decision before their rights can be adversely affected. The antithesis of such a state was described by Kafka: a state where the rights of individuals are overridden by hole in the corner decisions or knocks on doors in the early hours. That is not our system. I accept, of course, that there must be exceptions to this approach, notably in the criminal field, e.g. arrests and search warrants, where notification is not possible. But it is difficult to visualise a rational argument which could even arguably justify putting the present case in the exceptional category.[62]

[62] [2003] UKHL 36 [24] [26] [28].

These contrasting methods of interpretation tell us more about the relationship of 'principles' and 'rules'. Lord Steyn would certainly support the textbook statement that 'the standards applied by the courts in judicial review must ultimately be justified by constitutional principle, which governs the proper exercise of public power in any democracy'.[63] With Dworkin and Jowell, he clearly sees both rules and policies as giving way to principles that embody human rights; principles 'trump' rules, in Dworkin's phrase. Lord Bingham's guiding principle differs. He believes that, under the rule of law:

> Ministers and public officers at all levels must exercise the powers conferred on them reasonably, in good faith, for the purposes for which the powers were conferred and without exceeding the limits of such powers.[64]

This classical principle of English judicial review points towards his more conservative style of judicial interpretation according to which statutory texts, unless clearly ambiguous, must be interpreted literally.

The principle ultimately applied by the House of Lords, that a decision comes into force only when notified, is far-reaching and will need amplification by further rules. It may be sufficient to issue guidance to immigration officials that notice of determinations must be given to persons affected, a policy change easily underpinned by ICT: computers can be programmed to generate letters of notice whenever a final determination is filed. But has the decision wider implications? If so, circulars akin to HO circulars to the police may be necessary, warning officials of the new judicial requirement.

Lord Steyn's picture of a 'consistent and deliberately adopted *practice*' of non-notification suggests much deeper problems. It reminds us of the *Afghan hijackers* case (p. 134 above), where a HO minister and his senior officials deliberately timed their decision-making with a view to defeating an asylum claim. It is not so much systemic incompetence in an immigration service characterized by a previous Home Secretary as 'unfit for purpose' (p. 65 above) as systemic wrongdoing stemming from a HO culture of hostility to asylum seekers. This picture receives confirmation from an external review of the Border and Immigration Agency (now the UK Border Agency) conducted by the Independent Asylum Commission (IAC).[65] The IAC called the immigration service 'shameful for the UK' and a 'shameful blemish on the UK's reputation' – strong words, only slightly mitigated by its overall finding that the service was 'improved and improving'. The service still 'denies sanctu-

[63] S. A. de Smith, Lord Woolf and J. Jowell, *Judicial Review of Administrative Action*, 6th edn (Sweet & Maxwell, 2007), [1-016], part of an introductory chapter in the last edition that seems to align the authors with common law constitutionalism.

[64] T. Bingham, 'The rule of law' (2007) 66 *CLJ* 67.

[65] Interim findings of the IAC, *Fit for Purpose Yet?* (2007). The IAC, set up by the Citizen Organising Foundation with the support of London Citizen, is funded by charitable organisations. See also JCHR, *The Treatment of Asylum Seekers*, HC 60 (2006/7) and *Government Response*, HC 47 (2006/7).

ary to some who genuinely need it and ought to be entitled to it; is not firm enough in returning those whose claims are refused; and is marred by inhumanity in its treatment of the vulnerable'. The IAC was particularly concerned by the quality of initial decisions, largely made (as we saw in *Anufrijeva*) on the subjective impressions of a single caseworker, whose opinion as to the reliability of testimony was often based on prejudice.[66] Coupled with an adversarial stance in the appeals process, this operated to prejudice asylum seekers, who were often unable to do justice to their case because of ignorance and vulnerability. The prevalent 'culture of disbelief' amongst decision-makers, exacerbated by inadequate qualifications and training, led to 'some perverse and unjust decisions'.

This directly supports Goodin's view that the best hope of administrative change lies in changing the street-level culture, reinforcing changes with street-level accountability regimes.[67] This is how the Agency hopes to improve the immigration process: first, it is recruiting higher calibre staff with improved qualifications; and, secondly, it is testing a new asylum model whereby a single asylum case worker 'owns' a case from its initiation until final outcome: not more rules but greater discretion based on trust and responsibility in the 'street-level bureaucracy'. This is a shift away from modern management-controlled, juridified bureaucracy back towards the discretionary administrative processes preferred by Titmuss.

In the *Prague Airport* case,[68] the HO feared a flood of East European Roma asylum seekers at British airports. Immigration officers were therefore stationed at Prague airport to give pre-entry clearance to passengers before boarding. The Race Relations (Amendment) Act 2000, passed to apply the Race Relations Act 1976 to public authorities, contained substantial exceptions for immigration, and the Immigration (Leave to Enter and Remain) Order 2000 was widely drafted so as to give immigration officers 'strong discretion' in the matter. Art. 7(1) stated:

> An immigration officer, whether or not in the United Kingdom, may give or refuse a person leave to enter the United Kingdom at any time before his departure for, or in the course of his journey to, the United Kingdom.

The Minister followed this up with an authorisation, made under the 1976 Act, permitting officials to subject persons to a 'more rigorous examination than other persons in the same circumstances' by reason of that person's ethnic or

[66] See also NAO, *Improving the Speed and Quality of Immigration Decisions* HC 535 (2003/4); R. Thomas, 'Assessing the credibility of asylum claims: EU and UK approaches examined' (2006) 8 *Eur. J. of Migration and Law* 79.

[67] P. Hupe and M. Hill, 'Street-level bureaucracy and public accountability' (2007) 85 *Pub. Admin.* 279, 291–2.

[68] *European Roma Rights Centre v Immigration Officer at Prague Airport* [2004] UKHL 55 noted in R. Singh, 'Equality: The neglected virtue' (2004) *EHRLR* 141.

national origin. The HO expanded this regulatory framework with internal guidance to make the instructions more specific. The guidance, as Lord Steyn read it, was designed to show immigration officers how to carry out their functions at Prague Airport. It stated:

> The fact that a passenger belongs to one of these ethnic or national groups [including Roma] will be sufficient to justify discrimination – without reference to additional statistical or intelligence information – if an immigration officer considers such discrimination is warranted.

Acting for the Roma, the ERRC complained that the procedures were carried out in an unlawfully discriminatory manner, in that would-be travellers of Roma origin were subjected to longer and more intrusive questioning than non-Roma, required to provide proof of matters taken on trust from non-Roma and far more of them were refused leave to enter than were non-Roma. Perhaps surprisingly, the HO chose not to stand on the ministerial authorisation but argued that their procedures did not in any event amount to discrimination: 'individual differences in treatment were explicable, not by ethnic difference, but by more suspicious behaviour'.

By a majority, the House of Lords held that it was discriminatory to single out a particular group of immigrants for harsher treatment on the ground that they were more likely to be asylum seekers. Such conduct is 'the reverse of the rational behaviour we now expect from government and the state . . . If distinctions are to be drawn, particularly upon a group basis, it is an important discipline to look for a rational basis for those distinctions.' As Lady Hale put it:

> The Court of Appeal accepted that the judge was entitled to find that the immigration officers tried to give both Roma and non-Roma a fair and equal opportunity to satisfy them that they were coming to the United Kingdom for a permitted purpose and not to claim asylum once here. But they considered it 'wholly inevitable' that, being aware that Roma have a much greater incentive to claim asylum and that the vast majority, if not all, of those seeking asylum from the Czech Republic are Roma, immigration officers will treat their answers with greater scepticism, will be less easily persuaded that they are coming for a permitted purpose, and that 'generally, therefore, Roma are questioned for longer and more intensively than non-Roma and are more likely to be refused leave to enter than non-Roma' . . . The Roma were being treated more sceptically than the non-Roma. There was a good reason for this. How did the immigration officers know to treat them more sceptically? Because they were Roma. That is acting on racial grounds. If a person acts on racial grounds, the reason why he does so is irrelevant . . . The law reports are full of examples of obviously discriminatory treatment which was in no way motivated by racism or sexism and often brought about by pressures beyond the discriminators' control: the council which sacked a black road sweeper to whom the union objected in order to avoid industrial action, the council which for historical reasons provided fewer selective school places for girls than for

> boys. [69] But it goes further than this. The person may be acting on belief or assumptions about members of the sex or racial group involved which are often true and which if true would provide a good reason for the less favourable treatment in question. But 'what may be true of a group may not be true of a significant number of individuals within that group' [fn omitted]. The object of the legislation is to ensure that each person is treated as an individual and not assumed to be like other members of the group . . .
>
> The combination of the objective of the whole Prague operation and a very recent ministerial Authorisation of discrimination against Roma was, it is suggested, to create such a high risk that the Prague officers would consciously or unconsciously treat Roma less favourably than others that very specific instructions were needed to counteract this. Officers should have been told that the Directorate did not regard the operation as one which was covered by the Authorisation. They should therefore have been given careful instructions in how to treat all would-be passengers in the same way, only subjecting them to more intrusive questioning if there was specific reason to suspect their intentions from the answers they had given to standard questions which were put to everyone.
>
> It is worth remembering that good equal opportunities practice may not come naturally. Many will think it contrary to common sense to approach all applicants with an equally open mind, irrespective of the very good reasons there may be to suspect some of them more than others. But that is what is required by a law which tries to ensure that individuals are not disadvantaged by the general characteristics of the group to which they belong. In 2001, when the operation with which we are concerned began, the race relations legislation had only just been extended to cover the activities of the immigration service. It would scarcely be surprising if officers acting under considerable pressure of time found it difficult to conform in all respects to procedures and expectations which employers have been struggling to get right for more than quarter of a century.[70]

Once again we find emphasis on culture: this time the culture of discrimination. Whether or not the ministerial authorisation was operative at Prague Airport, the thinking that underlay it remained the same so that the rules structured and defined the officials' discretion. The culture would continue to infuse the institutional decision-making; only a change of heart and rigorous training could eliminate it.

Lord Brown, who (as Simon Brown LJ) had contributed to the Court of Appeal decision in *Prague Airport*, advanced the opposite side of this argument in *Gillan*.[71] The allegation was that police had used stop-and-search powers under s. 44 of the Terrorism Act 2000 in a case to which it was not applicable; they had also used the powers in a discriminatory fashion to pick out and search one of the defendants because he was from an ethnic minority. Lord Brown thought the common police practice of 'intuitive

69 See *R v Commission for Racial Equality, ex p. Westminster City Council*) [1985] ICR 827; *R v Birmingham CC, ex p. Equal Opportunities Commission* [1989] AC 1155.

70 [2004] UKHL 55 [81–5].

71 *R (Gillan) v Metropolitan Police Commissioner* [2006] UKHL 12 [77] [84]. The two viewpoints resurfaced in *AL(Serbia) v Home Secretary* [2008] 1 WLR 1434, where the problems of the consistency principle were again addressed.

stop-and-search' well justified. It was not wrong to take ethnic origin into account provided always, as the HO guidance authorised by PACE provided, that the power was used sensitively and the selection made for reasons connected with the perceived terrorist threat and not on grounds of racial discrimination:

> Imagine that following the London Underground bombings last July the police had attempted to stop and search everyone entering an underground station or indeed every tenth (or hundredth) such person. Not only would such a task have been well nigh impossible but it would to my mind thwart the real purpose and value of this power. That, as Lord Bingham puts it . . . is not 'to stop and search people who are obviously not terrorist suspects, which would be futile and time-wasting [but rather] to ensure that a constable is not deterred from stopping and searching a person whom he does suspect as a potential terrorist by the fear that he could not show reasonable grounds for his suspicion.' It is to be hoped, first, that potential terrorists will be deterred (certainly from carrying the tools of their trade) by knowing of the risk they run of being randomly searched, and, secondly, that by the exercise of this power police officers may on occasion (if only very rarely) find such materials and thereby disrupt or avert a proposed terrorist attack. Neither of these aims will be served by police officers searching those who seem to them least likely to present a risk instead of those they have a hunch may be intent on terrorist action.

Lord Brown accused the House of supporting practice that was 'not merely wrong but also silly':

> [I]t is important, indeed imperative, not to imperil good community relations, not to exacerbate a minority's feelings of alienation and victimisation, so that the use of these supposed preventative powers could tend actually to promote rather than counter the present terrorist threat. I repeat . . . that these stop and search powers ought to be used only sparingly. But I cannot accept that, thus used, they can be impugned either as arbitrary or as 'inherently and systematically discriminatory' . . . simply because they are used selectively to target those regarded by the police as most likely to be carrying terrorist connected articles, even if this leads, as usually it will, to the deployment of this power against a higher proportion of people from one ethnic group than another. I conclude rather that not merely is such selective use of the power legitimate; it is its *only* legitimate use. To stop and search those regarded as presenting no conceivable threat whatever (particularly when that leaves officers unable to stop those about whom they feel an instinctive unease) would itself constitute an abuse of the power. Then indeed would the power be being exercised arbitrarily.

Davis may have been over-optimistic in thinking that rules would radically change the behaviour of the New York drugs squad by structuring the discretion. Whether or not it was rule-based, police conduct would display much the same attributes as their discretionary decisions. Rules that undermine bureaucratic efficiency, principles or values that are seen as too costly or cut across the prevailing administrative ethos will be pushed to one side and simply ignored.

Thus doubt is cast both on rule-making as a tool for structuring and confining discretion and on the juridified world of rules and rule-change, where conduct that falls outside the rules is seen as capable of being corrected by a further flurry of rule-making. In the real world, as Goodin recognised, the strongest influences on decision-making are social conditioning, group morality, attitudes of mind and prejudices. Something much more difficult and subtle than blind obedience to rules is required of street-level bureaucrats as well as judges.

5. Rules, individuation and consistency

The due-process principles that prevailed in *Anufrijeva* are designed for the protection of individuals: they grant to the 'individual or groups against whom government decisions operate' the chance to make their views known and participate in the decision-making process.[72] They are part of the adjudicative value of 'individuation', by which we mean that someone entrusted with discretionary power has an obligation to consider the merits of the *specific case* with which he is confronted; he cannot simply apply a rule. In English administrative law, this is expressed in the classical principle that 'a decision-making body exercising public functions which is entrusted with discretion must not, by the adoption of a fixed rule or policy, disable itself from exercising its discretion in individual cases. It may not "fetter" its discretion.'[73] In the *Lavender* case,[74] for example, the Minister of Housing and Local Government adopted a policy whereby he would not exercise his statutory power to grant planning permission for mineral working 'unless the Minister of Agriculture is not opposed to working'. Unless the agricultural objection had been waived, the minister simply refused planning permission. This somewhat extreme application of the 'joined up government' policy was quashed as illegal by the High Court.

The suggestion is then that every rule may have an exception and that discretion involves at least a limited power of free choice that must be personally exercised. (This belief informed our earlier, common-sense qualification of the 'No dogs' rule that guide dogs should be treated as exceptional.) As Galligan puts it:

> There is an idea buried deep in the hearts of various constitutional theorists and judges that 'to discipline administrative discretion by rule and rote is somehow to denature it'. According to this idea, there is something about the nature of discretionary power which requires each decision to be made according to the circumstances of the particular situation,

[72] They are often described as 'dignitary values': see J. Mashaw, 'Dignitary Process: A political psychology of liberal democratic citizenship' (1987) 39 *Univ. of Florida LR* 433. And see below, Ch. 14.

[73] de Smith, Woolf and Jowell, *Judicial Review of Administrative Action* [9-002].

[74] *H. Lavender & Son v Minister of Housing and Local Government* [1970] 1 WLR 1231.

> free from the constraints of preconceived policies as to the ends and goals to be achieved by such power. The circumstances of the situation will indicate the proper decision and policy choices must remain in the background.[75]

As we saw earlier, the 'non-fettering' view of discretionary power encouraged lawyers to look coldly at the practice of 'quasi-legislation' and it was not until the 1970s that courts took the first steps towards getting to grips with the phenomenon of bureaucratic rule-making. In the *British Oxygen* case, the Board of Trade had power to award investment grants in respect of new 'plant'. BOC asked for £4 million in respect of gas cylinders each valued at £20 but was refused because the Board had a rule of practice not to approve grants on items valued individually at less than £25. The House of Lords upheld the practice and Lord Reid made this important statement of the individuation principle:

> It was argued . . . that the Minister is not entitled to make a rule for himself as to how he will in future exercise his discretion . . . The general rule is that anyone who has to exercise a statutory discretion must not 'shut his ears to an application' . . . I do not think there is any great difference between a policy and a rule. There may be cases where an officer or authority ought to listen to a substantial argument reasonably presented arguing a change of policy. What the authority must not do is to refuse to listen at all. But a Ministry or large authority may have had to deal already with a multitude of similar applications and then they will almost certainly have evolved a policy so precise that it could well be called a rule. There can be no objection to that, provided the authority is always willing to listen to anyone with something new to say – of course I do not mean to say that there need be an oral hearing. In the present case the respondent's officers have carefully considered all the appellants have had to say and I have no doubt that they will continue to do so.[76]

Here the House of Lords acknowledged that discretion entails a power in the decision-maker to make policy choices, not just to deal with the individual case, but to develop a coherent and consistent set of guidelines which seek to achieve ends and goals within the scope of powers. In short, 'discretion' must include the discretion to make rules.[77]

With the evolution of mass, ITC-based administrative systems, matched by judicial development of the consistency, or equal treatment, principle, the 'no-fettering' rule has become increasingly hard to apply. In the recent *Ealing* case, it crept into the contemporary world of audit only to be sidelined.[78] The Audit Commission was required by s. 99 of the Local Government Act 2003 to 'produce a report on its findings in relation to the performance of English local

[75] D. Galligan, 'The Nature and function of policies within discretionary power' [1976] *PL* 332.
[76] *British Oxygen Co Ltd v Ministry of Technology* [1970] 3 WLR 488.
[77] Galligan, 'The Nature and function of policies within discretionary power', p. 332.
[78] *Audit Commission v Ealing Borough Council* [2005] EWCA Civ 556. See also *R (Ahmad) v Newham LBC* [2009] UKHL 14.

authorities in exercising their functions'. In 2004 the Audit Commission had, after extensive consultation, published a document entitled *Comprehensive Performance Assessment Framework 2004*, extracts from which read:

10. The CPA framework brings together judgements about:

- Core service performance in education, social services, housing environment, libraries and leisure, benefits, and use of resources; and
- The council's ability measured through a corporate assessment.

. . .

12. Each of the individual service judgements and the use of resources judgement are awarded a score of 1 to 4, with 1 being the lowest score and 4 being the highest. These are then combined into an overall **core service performance score** of 1 to 4.
13. Each of the themes scored within the corporate assessment (ambition, prioritisation, focus, capacity, performance management, achievement of improvement, investment, learning and future plans) are also awarded scores of 1 to 4. These are then combined to reach an overall **council ability score** ranging from 1 to 4.
14. The overall CPA category ('excellent', 'good', 'fair', 'weak' and 'poor') is reached by combining the overall core service performance and council ability scores in the form of a matrix (see below). Where a council has not yet achieved a specified level of performance on education, social care or financial management (or scores a 1 on any other service), rules apply which limit a council's overall category, see paragraphs 29–30.

CORE SERVICE PERFORMANCE

Scores		1	2	3	4
COUNCIL	1	poor	poor	weak	fair
ABILITY	2	poor	weak	fair	good
	3	weak	fair	good	excellent
	4	fair	good	excellent	excellent

. . .

Rules

29. Rules limit a council's overall CPA category where a council's score falls below a specified level on education, social care or financial standing, or scores a 1 on any other service.
30. The rules are as follows:

- [Rule 1] A council must score at least 3 (2 stars) on education, social services star rating, and financial standing to achieve a category of 'excellent' overall;
- [Rule 2] A council must score at least 2 (1 star) on education, social services star rating and financial standing to achieve a category of 'fair' or above; and
- [Rule 3] A council must score at least 2 (1 star) on all other core services to achieve a category of 'excellent' overall.

Ealing achieved scores of 3 on each of core service performance and council ability. Applying the approach set out at paragraph 14 of the CPA Framework it would have been categorised as 'good', if the matter had stopped at that point. However, Ealing had received a zero star rating from the Commission for Social Care Inspection (CSCI) with the result that under Rule 2 Ealing could not be categorised as better overall than 'weak', effectively dropping two categories. Notified that its performance was 'weak', Ealing LBC applied for judicial review.

Following *Lavender*, Walker J held that by simply accepting the verdict of the CSCI, another statutory body, in respect of Ealing's social services performance, the Audit Commission had fettered or unlawfully delegated its discretionary powers. The Court of Appeal disagreed:

> The principle that a body given a statutory power by Parliament must exercise that power itself and not delegate its exercise to another is well-established in administrative law . . . The real issue is whether the Audit Commission's approach as set out in rule 2 offends against the principle. It is conceded by Ealing that the Audit Commission is entitled to adopt the professional judgments of the CSCI, as embodied in the assessments on the vertical and horizontal axes of the annexed matrix, as its own. That is an understandable concession, since the CSCI is the inspectorate specialising in the assessment of local authorities' social care performance. It would be absurd for the Audit Commission to have to re-assess all those findings itself, and that cannot have been Parliament's intention.
>
> Does this mean that the Audit Commission has unlawfully delegated its s. 99 decision to the CSCI? On reflection we have concluded that it does not. The matrix which embodied these weightings or trade-offs was publicly available in the SSI/CSCI Operating Policies document and it must be the case that the Audit Commission was familiar with it and with the weightings attached to the various 'scores' on the two axes. The Audit Commission must be taken to have been content with those weightings and to have adopted them. This is not a case where the CSCI made its own separate judgments from time to time about the star rating of an individual authority. The star ratings follow automatically from the 'scores', to which Ealing takes no objection. It is a mechanical exercise, once one has the scores and the matrix. As the . . . Audit Commission puts it at paragraph 4(c):
>
>> the social services star rating is not based on the subjective judgment of the Chief Inspector, but is arrived at by the application of a set of transparent and objective rules to those judgments. There is no discretion involved in translating those judgments into a star rating.
>
> This is, therefore, a very different case from *Lavender*. There the relevant Minister's policy was to allow his decision to be dictated by what another Minister decided *in any individual case*. Here the Audit Commission has in effect adopted as its own a series of weightings, produced by the CSCI, which result in a star rating in an entirely predictable way. In our view it is entitled to do that. It is not delegating its decision in any individual case to the CSCI, since the CSCI does not make any such individual decision once it has arrived at the 'scores'. It is simply that the Audit Commission has itself decided to adopt certain principles for achieving its categorisation.

Commenting on the fact that Ealing had chosen not to challenge the CSCI decision about its score, the Court of Appeal decided that no real prejudice had been suffered. Does this suggest that the only way to challenge rules is by resort to a second-stage adjudicative process, more discretionary, more individuated and better able to handle exceptions?

That computerised mass service delivery makes insufficient allowance for special circumstances and is thus incompatible with the *individuated* decision-making required by the administrative law watchdogs was the concern of the Australian Administrative Review Council in a report on automated assistance. The AARC thought that automated assistance could offend 'the administrative law values of lawfulness and fairness because it could fetter the decision maker in the exercise of their discretionary power'. Conceding its use 'as a tool to guide officers', the AARC set out firm guidelines: officers trained to 'understand the relevant legislation', able 'to explain a decision to the affected person', and capable of making the decision manually, should always be on hand.[79] In one sense, this undercuts the benefits of ICT. It is just because trained and expert officials are *not* on hand in sufficient numbers that we turn to ICT to deal with mass administrative systems. It is a mistake to think that ICT can be programmed for 'individuation'; it is for equal treatment and consistency that we turn to its data storage and retrieval capacities.

To balance consistency with individual treatment in such situations is an almost impossible task, as shown by a study of the effects of computerisation on administrative decision-making conducted for the then UK Department of Social Security.[80] Not unexpectedly, this revealed that computerisation pushed departmental decision-making towards the 'bureaucratic justice' model of administrative decision-making, in which the goal is the consistent and accurate application of rules and the means of redress are administrative and hierarchical:

> Thus it was likely to lead to an even more bureaucratized system rather than one that was more sensitive to the needs and circumstances of claimants or one that made it easier for them to assert their rights. The main reasons for this were that the DSS adopted a 'top-down' orientation to computerisation that gave priority to the interests of the government rather than a 'bottom-up' orientation that would have given priority to the interests of the claimants or staff; and that the aim of the programme was to make administrative savings rather than to improve quality of service (whatever that might mean).[81]

With automated systems, rules have taken over from discretion and individuation. The emphasis is managerial with heavy reliance on audit and other

[79] AARC, *Automated Assistance in Administrative Decision Making* (Commonwealth of Australia, 2004) [16] [17].

[80] M. Adler and P. Henman, 'Computerisation and e-government in social security: A comparative international study' (2003) 23 *Critical Social Policy* 139.

[81] M. Adler, 'Fairness in context' (2006) 33 *JLS* 615, 626.

performance measures to bring about improvements in service delivery. Once again, we find a clash of values between the 'top-down', managerial or bureaucratic model of accountability through rules and 'the legal and consumerist models of administrative justice that embody "bottom-up" orientations.'[82]

6. Bucking the rules

The previous cases have in common that they involve challenge to the idea of policy-making through rules. But what is to happen in the reverse case, where the administration wishes to depart from rules or policies on which a third party seeks to rely? In the *US Tobacco* case,[83] UST had negotiated permission to market oral snuff, subject to the condition that it would not be marketed to young persons. On the strength of this assurance, UST built a factory in Scotland. Later, the minister, acting on the advice of an expert advisory committee, changed the rules by making regulations to ban oral snuff. Although the regulations were subject to annulment by negative resolution, had been laid before the House of Commons and were not annulled, UST argued that they were ultra vires the parent Consumer Protection Act 1987, which did not cover public-health issues. When this argument failed, UST contended that it had been led to believe that it could market snuff, had acted on this expectation, and the concession could consequently not be withdrawn so long as the original conditions were observed. This is the notion of 'administrative estoppel', according to which a promise or representation is held to bind the promisor where the promisee acts on it to his detriment even though the conditions necessary to constitute a binding contract are not fulfilled.[84] Estoppel effectively fetters the administrative discretion and is capable of creating substantive rights. Rightly, this argument failed also; it was held that the Minister could not fetter his statutory discretion to take action in the public interest unless the action taken was unfair or unreasonable. All that UST achieved was the classical 'halfway house' of natural justice (see Chapter 14). It had not had access to the scientific advice underpinning the ministerial decision hence had no real opportunity to combat it; 'such a draconian step should not be taken unless procedural propriety has been observed and those most concerned have been treated fairly'.

The outcome, similar to the *BOC* case, sets in place a sensible framework within which courts and administration can operate. On the one hand, public authorities must be capable of acting in the public interest, retaining the power to change their policies, as they justifiably did in the *US Tobacco* case. The role of the courts is procedural; it is their duty to ensure that any individual whose

[82] *Ibid.*, p. 634.

[83] *R v Health Secretary, ex p. United States Tobacco International Inc.* [1982] QB 353.

[84] See *R v Liverpool Corpn, ex p. Liverpool Taxi Fleet* Operators' *Association* [1972] 2 WLR 1262; *Lever Finance Ltd v Westminster City Council* [1971] 1 QB 222; *Western Fish Products Ltd v Penrith District Council* [1981] 2 All ER 204.

interests are affected receives a fair hearing. There is a strong case, however, against allowing ultra vires decisions to stand. Public bodies do not always act honourably: consider, for example, the case of a local authority which sets out to bind its successor to a policy that it had contested in local elections; or look forward to the cases in Chapter 8, which show public authorities dealing with public funds in a way that courts thought entirely improper. Thus the classical rule is that not even contract is strong enough to bind an authority to an unlawful decision; courts should be slow, as the Court of Appeal remarked in *Rowland*,[85] 'to fix a public authority permanently with the consequences of a mistake, particularly when it would deprive the public of their rights'. Finding that it had been mistaken in treating a reach of the Thames as private water, the Thames Water Authority removed the 'Private' notices, allowing the public access. The Court of Appeal held this action to be lawful and taken in the public interest, though it recognised that a shark had recently swum into the national waters. In *Stretch v United Kingdom*,[86] S had been granted a building lease with an option to renew, which turned out, when he sought to exercise it, to have been beyond the powers of the local authority. The ECtHR ruled that a 'legitimate expectation' had been created, treating this as a disproportionate deprivation of 'property' under ECHR Protocol 1.

We first met the idea of legitimate expectation in the *GCHQ* case (p. 107 above), where it was held that a trade union must be consulted before any sudden change of policy (removal of the right to belong to a trade union) was taken. In *AG of Hong Kong v Ng Yuen Shiu*,[87] the Hong Kong government had announced changes in its policy of repatriating illegal immigrants. The promise of a personal interview and individual consideration of each case was made, on the strength of which illegal immigrants were asked to give themselves up. When the applicant responded, he was given no opportunity to present a case. The Privy Council ruled that the promise had created procedural expectations which must be observed; no repatriation without interview. The Privy Council did not, however, rule on the substantive issue.

These 'halfway house' cases imply procedural rights to make a case, not substantive entitlements; the decision is returned to the allotted decision-maker, which, in the light of the existing policy, may or may not be a right worth having. As Lord Reid put it somewhat wryly in *British Oxygen*, 'In the present case the respondent's officers have carefully considered all the appellants have had to say and I have no doubt that they will continue to do so.' Only occasionally is there a hint of something better, as in the exceptional *Khan* case,[88] where the Khans had written to the Home Office to inform themselves about current policy on entry for adoption. A reply set out four conditions to be

[85] *Rowland v Environment Agency* [2003] EWCA Civ 1885.

[86] *Stretch v UK* (2004) 38 EHHR 12 noted in Blundell, 'Ultra vires legitimate expectations' [2005] *Judicial Review* 147. In *Rowland*, the CA held the action taken to be proportionate.

[87] *AG of Hong Kong v Ng Yuen Shiu* [1983] 2 AC 629.

[88] *R v Home Secretary, ex p. Asif Khan* [1985] 1 All ER 40.

satisfied. The Khans' application to adopt satisfied all four conditions but was rejected on another ground. The Court of Appeal held that the HO was held to its guidance on policy, unless there had been proper notification of policy change and the Khans had been given an opportunity to make representations, which should be seriously considered, as to the added condition. This is 'procedure plus', carrying the implication that the new decision must be favourable.

The new and stronger doctrine of substantive legitimate expectation derives from *Coughlan* where C, a severely disabled elderly woman, went to live in a nursing home run by a health authority, acting on an assurance that this would be her 'home for life'.[89] Later, the authority decided for financial reasons to close the home. Challenged, it argued that the overriding public interest entitled it to break the 'home for life' assurance. Lord Woolf speaking for the court first disposed of the 'no fettering' argument as one that would 'today have no prospect of success' and then outlined three possible outcomes, the first two uncontentious, the third contestable:

(a) The court may decide that the public authority is only required to bear in mind its previous policy or other representation, giving it the weight it thinks right, but no more, before deciding whether to change course. Here the court is confined to reviewing the decision on *Wednesbury* grounds.
(b) The court could decide that the promise or practice induced a legitimate expectation of, for example, being consulted before a particular decision is taken. Here it is uncontentious that the court itself will require an opportunity for consultation unless there is an overriding reason to resile from it. The court itself will judge the adequacy of the reason advanced for the change of policy, taking into account what fairness requires.
(c) Where the court considers that a lawful promise or practice has induced a legitimate expectation of a *benefit which is substantive,* not simply procedural, authority now establishes that here too the court will in a proper case decide whether to frustrate the expectation is so unfair that to take a new and different course will amount to an abuse of power. Here, once the legitimacy of the expectation is established, the court will have the task of weighing the requirements of fairness against any overriding interest relied upon for the change of policy.

In the instant case, the authority knew of the promise and its seriousness; it referred to its new policies and the reasons for them; it knew that something had to yield, and it made a choice which, whatever else can be said of it, could not easily be challenged as irrational. Could the court go further? Lord Woolf thought that it could:[90]

[89] *R v North and East Devon Health Authority, ex p. Coughlan* [2000] 2 WLR 622 [57] noted in Craig and Schonberg, 'Substantive legitimate expectation after *Coughlan*' [2000] *PL* 684.

[90] [2000] 2 WLR 622 [66] [71], citing *R v IRC, ex p. Unilever plc* [1996] STC 681; R *v IRC, ex p. Preston* [1985] AC 835 and *R v MAFF, ex p. Hamble (Offshore) Fisheries Ltd* [1996] 2 All ER 714.

> In the ordinary case there is no space for intervention on grounds of abuse of power once a rational decision directed to a proper purpose has been reached by lawful process. The present class of case is visibly different. It involves not one but two lawful exercises of power (the promise and the policy change) by the same public authority, with consequences for individuals trapped between the two. The policy decision may well, and often does, make as many exceptions as are proper and feasible to protect individual expectations . . . If it does not . . . the court is there to ensure that the power to make and alter policy has not been abused by unfairly frustrating legitimate individual expectations. In such a situation a bare rationality test would constitute the public authority judge in its own cause, for a decision to prioritise a policy change over legitimate expectations will almost always be rational from where the authority stands, even if objectively it is arbitrary or unfair . . .
>
> Fairness in such a situation, if it is to mean anything, must for the reasons we have considered include fairness of outcome. This in turn is why the doctrine of legitimate expectation has emerged as a distinct application of the concept of abuse of power in relation to substantive as well as procedural benefits, representing a second approach to the same problem. If this is the position in the case of the third category, why is it not also the position in relation to the first category? Legitimate expectation may play different parts in different aspects of public law. The limits to its role have yet to be finally determined by the courts. Its application is still being developed on a case by case basis. Even where it reflects procedural expectations, for example concerning consultation, it may be affected by an overriding public interest. It may operate as an aspect of good administration, qualifying the intrinsic rationality of policy choices. And without injury to the *Wednesbury* doctrine it may furnish a proper basis for the application of the now established concept of abuse of power . . .

Drawing on EC law, where substantive legitimate expectation is a well-recognised principle,[91] the Court of Appeal ruled that to resile from the clear promise of a 'home for life' was unjustified and constituted 'unfairness amounting to an abuse of power'. Admitting with some justification that the courts' role in relation to category (c) was 'still controversial', Lord Woolf felt that they could nonetheless 'avoid jeopardising the important principle that the executive's policy-making powers should not be trammelled by the courts'. How precisely?

That the representations made to C should have figured (as they did) in the local authority assessment is not in dispute; we know that rational decision-making and procedural fairness are standard requirements of administrative law and we have seen too how far a court may take 'hard look review'. The problem comes, as the Court of Appeal explained in the later case of *Bibi*, at the stage when the court has to decide what to do. There the council, acting under a mistake of law, indicated that it would allocate publicly funded housing with

[91] In *Hamble (Offshore) Fisheries Ltd* (above), Sedley LJ had reviewed the EC jurisprudence. See further, J. Schwarze, *European Administrative Law* (Sweet & Maxwell, 1992), pp. 1134–5; P. Craig, 'Substantive legitimate expectations in domestic and community law' [1996] *CLJ* 289.

security of tenure to B; when the mistake came to light, the assurance was withdrawn. Seeking to dispel the fog surrounding the subject, Schiemann LJ specified 'three practical questions' that arose in all legitimate expectation cases:

- First, what has the public authority, whether by practice or by promise, committed itself to? This involves only evaluation of the facts.
- Secondly, has the authority acted or does it propose to act unlawfully in relation to its commitment? At this stage, he explained:

> The law requires that any legitimate expectation be properly taken into account in the decision making process. It has not been in the present case and therefore the Authority has acted unlawfully . . . when the Authority looks at the matter again it must take into account the legitimate expectations. Unless there are reasons recognised by law for not giving effect to those legitimate expectations then effect should be given to them. In circumstances such as the present where the conduct of the Authority has given rise to a legitimate expectation then fairness requires that, if the Authority decides not to give effect to that expectation, the Authority articulate its reasons so that their propriety may be tested by the court if that is what the disappointed person requires.[92]

- Third, what should the court do? Can it come to a substantive decision itself? Must it send the matter back for a new decision? This was the solution the Court of Appeal chose:

> The court, even where it finds that the applicant has a legitimate expectation of some benefit, will not order the authority to honour its promise where to do so would be to assume the powers of the executive. Once the court has established such an abuse it may ask the decision taker to take the legitimate expectation properly into account in the decision making process.

We might call this outcome 'procedural fairness plus'. It does not, as the Court of Appeal emphasised, *tie* the authority to its assurances; it remained free to take the same decision again in the light of 'the current statutory framework, the allocation scheme, the legitimate expectations of other people, its assets both in terms of what housing it has at its disposal and in terms of what assets it has or could have available'. It must, however, throw the assurances it had given into the balance, which had not in the instant case been done. This is the right outcome, because the primary duty of a public body is a *collective* duty to constituents and the public at large.[93] Moreover, a polycentric decision or decision with 'spin off' is involved as indicated in the phrase 'the legitimate expectations *of other people*'.

Coughlan, where the authority had taken its assurance into account in

[92] *R(Bibi and Al-Nashid) v Newham LBC* [2002] 1 WLR 237 [22] [46–8].
[93] See *O'Rourke v Camden LBC* [1997] 3 WLR 86 (Lord Hoffmann).

arriving at the decision to close, effectively gives the court two bites at the same cherry: first the court looks at the procedure by which the decision was taken; then it goes on to review the decision itself, applying a test of fairness and rationality, tying the authority to its assurance as though a contract had been signed. Unanimously, the Court of Appeal concluded:

> The decision to move Miss Coughlan against her will and in breach of the Health Authority's own promise was in the circumstances unfair. It was unfair because it frustrated her legitimate expectation of having a home for life in Mardon House. There was no overriding public interest which justified it. In drawing the balance of conflicting interests the court will not only accept the policy change without demur but will pay the closest attention to the assessment made by the public body itself. Here, however, as we have already indicated, the Health Authority failed to weigh the conflicting interests correctly. Furthermore, we do not know . . . the quality of the alternative accommodation and services which will be offered to Miss Coughlan. We cannot prejudge what would be the result if there was on offer accommodation which could be said to be reasonably equivalent to Mardon House and the Health Authority made a properly considered decision in favour of closure in the light of that offer. However, absent such an offer, here there was unfairness amounting to an abuse of power by the Health Authority.

In terms of outcome, the Court of Appeal said only that the saving in closing the home would be 'in terms of economic and logistical efficiency in the use respectively of Mardon House and the local authority home'. But if the effect were to tie the authority indefinitely to the retention of an uneconomic facility, then this outcome must appear unrealistic and based on unconvincing reasoning that violates principles of economic and efficient public management. For public-service managers who, in contrast to unelected judges, are asked to combine the delivery of high quality, efficient, helpful and user-friendly public services with the requirements of VFM, it invokes the spectre of open-ended financial commitments, where assurances offered in different economic and legal climates have to be redeemed at great cost to the public. Times change and space must be left for policy-makers to change their mind, as Sales and Steyn argue:

> Legal protection for legitimate expectation . . . means that, in effect, the decision-maker is taken to have acted with (to some degree) binding effect at the earlier point in time when it promulgated the policy or assurance, so that the policy or assurance determines how it must act at the later stage when an actual decision in a particular case is called for. And this is so even though at that later stage the decision-maker, on further reflection, would otherwise treat as relevant to (and, it may be, determinative of) its decision factors which are not recognised as such in the statement of policy or the assurance. It is not uncommon for a decision-maker to change its mind when it has more information about the consequences of a decision, or a better understanding of the views and interests of those affected by the decision (who may have had no awareness of or opportunity to comment

on the assurance when it was given). Or it may simply be confronted with unanticipated situations falling within the scope of the policy or assurance. What seemed like a good idea at the time the policy or assurance was promulgated may not seem like a good idea in all the circumstances when the time for action arises.[94]

After *Coughlan*, Craig identified four main situations that might give rise to a legitimate expectation:[95]

1. A general norm or policy choice, which an individual has relied on, has been replaced by a different policy choice.
2. A general norm or policy choice has been departed from in the circumstances of a particular case.
3. There has been an individual representation relied on by a person, which the administration seeks to resile from in the light of a shift in general policy.
4. There has been an individualised representation that has been relied on. The administrative body then changes its mind and makes an individualised decision that is inconsistent with the original representation.

Unpicking this classification, we can see for example that situations 1 and 3 both involve the power to change administrative policy to which, in the public interest, the 'no fettering principle' ought to apply. In *Re Findlay*,[96] for example, the Home Secretary, changing the settled practice whereby the first review of a life sentence came after three years, announced in a speech to the Conservative Party conference that in future reviews would be held back until three years before the expiry of the 'tariff' period, while certain murders would automatically carry minimum sentences of not less than twenty years. It was argued that this policy could not apply retrospectively to prisoners who had acquired a 'legitimate expectation' that their cases would be considered at a certain time, which could not be retracted. A strong case one might think and, dissenting in the Court of Appeal, Browne-Wilkinson LJ certainly thought so. The House of Lords, on the other hand, did not consider that the Home Secretary had acted unlawfully. Lord Scarman envisaged a two-stage process, the first general, the second individuated:

The most that a convicted prisoner can legitimately expect is that his case will be examined individually in the light of whatever policy the Secretary of State sees fit to adopt provided always that the adopted policy is a lawful exercise of the discretion conferred upon him by the statute. Any other view would entail the conclusion that the unfettered

[94] P. Sales and K. Steyn, 'Legitimate expectations in English public law: An analysis' [2004] *PL* 564, 569. But see Y. Dotan, 'Why administrators should be bound by their policies' (1997)17 *OJLS* 23.

[95] P. Craig, *Administrative Law*, 5th edn (Sweet & Maxwell, 2003), p. 641, judicially approved in *R (Rashid) v Home Secretary* [2005] EWCA Civ 744 [44]. And see I. Steele, 'Substantive legitimate expectations: Striking the right balance?' (2005) 121 *LQR* 300; M. Elliott, 'Legitimate expectations and the search for principle' [2006] *Judicial Review* 281.

[96] *Re Findlay* [1985] AC 318. See also *R v Home Secretary, ex p. Hargreaves* [1997] 1 All ER 397.

> discretion conferred by the statute upon the minister can in some cases be restricted so as to hamper, or even to prevent, changes of policy. Bearing in mind the complexity of the issues which the Secretary of State has to consider and the importance of the public interest in the administration of parole I cannot think that Parliament intended the discretion to be restricted in this way.

So the prisoners failed and if the outcome seems harsh, it is because it seems to breach the well-known rule of law principle against retrospectivity; the review date of existing prisoners ought in fairness to have been preserved. In *Walker* too,[97] a case involving policy changes in the application of the criminal injuries compensation scheme to members of the armed forces, Lord Slynn summarised the applicant's legitimate expectations as being: 'to have the policy in force at the time of the incident applied to him and to be given the opportunity to make representations that he was in the scheme and outside the exclusion', both of which he had. It 'would have been better' to give similar publicity to the change as had been given to the original proposal but this did not amount to 'unfairness which would justify the courts interfering'. In practice too, most cases of general policy change will fail on the grounds either, as in *Findlay* and *Walker*, that no one has 'acted to their detriment',[98] or that the representations are insufficiently specific and not aimed at individuals. In *Begbie*,[99] for example, B took advantage of the Conservative government's assisted-places scheme for private education on the strength of statements made by the Opposition as to their intentions if elected. When made, the transitional arrangements were found not to cover her situation but a challenge based on the earlier statements failed.

Craig's situations 3 and 4 both involve some form of individual representation. In both, there is a clear expectation of a chance to argue that a policy change should not apply to one's case. Situation 4 cases are special and bear a strong family resemblance to estoppel, which is narrower and more clear-cut than the concept of substantive legitimate expectation which has replaced it. Substantive legitimate expectation extends to 'enforce the continued enjoyment of the content – the substance – of *an existing practice or policy*, in the face of the decision-maker's ambition to change or abolish it',[100] a wider and notably inchoate category. Perhaps the belief that public law has 'already absorbed whatever is useful from the moral values which underlie the private law concept of estoppel'[101] is incorrect.

In *Naharajah and Abdi*,[102] Laws LJ tried to counter concern over the breadth of judicial discretion by recourse to proportionality. Asserting that public

[97] *R v Ministry of Defence, ex p. Walker* [2000] 1 WLR 806 (Lord Slynn).
[98] See also *R (Bancoult) v Foreign Secretary* [2008] UKHL 61.
[99] *R (Begbie) v Department of Education and Employment* [1999] EWCA Civ 2100.
[100] *R (Bhatt Murphy) v Independent Assessor* [2008] EWCA 755 [32] (emphasis ours).
[101] *R v Sussex CC, ex p. Reprotech (Pebsham) Ltd* [2003] 1 WLR 348 [33–5].
[102] *R (Naharajah and Abdi) v Home Secretary* [2005] EWCA Civ 1363 [68].

bodies ought to deal straightforwardly and consistently with the public (a standard which he compared to a Convention right), he contrasted individual promises (situation 4) with general policy change:

> Thus where the representation relied on amounts to an unambiguous promise; where there is detrimental reliance; where the promise is made to an individual or specific group; these are instances where denial of the expectation is likely to be harder to justify as a proportionate measure . . . On the other hand where the government decision-maker is concerned to raise wide-ranging or 'macro-political' issues of policy, the expectation's enforcement in the courts will encounter a steeper climb. All these considerations, whatever their direction, are pointers not rules. The balance between an individual's fair treatment in particular circumstances, and the vindication of other ends having a proper claim on the public interest (which is the essential dilemma posed by the law of legitimate expectation) is not precisely calculable, its measurement not exact.

Almost immediately, the distinction was blurred in *Rashid*,[103] where the Court of Appeal learned that implementation of a policy not to relocate asylum seekers to the Kurdish autonomous zone of Iraq had been patchy and, despite internal inquiries, the HO had 'never got to the bottom of how some caseworkers knew and some did not'. Asked to reconsider R's case on the ground that he had not had the benefit of the policy, the HO chose to take into consideration changed circumstances which, three years later, had purportedly rendered Iraq a safe destination. Counsel asked the Court of Appeal not be fixated with labels but to take an overall view, which it did, quashing the decision simply as a 'conspicuous unfairness requiring the intervention of the court'. The case was 'not the typical case of legitimate expectation'; it was quite irrelevant that R, who was unaware of the policy, did not rely on it; he was entitled to rely on it and it must be applied.

In *Bhatt Murphy*,[104] the Court of Appeal flatly turned down an attempt to hold ministers to the terms of a compensation scheme subsequently withdrawn and replaced. Unfortunately, this did not deter Laws LJ from another trawl through the unsatisfactory cases:

> A very broad summary of the place of legitimate expectations in public law might be expressed as follows. The power of public authorities to change policy is constrained by the legal duty to be fair (and other constraints which the law imposes). A change of policy which would otherwise be legally unexceptionable may be held unfair by reason of prior action, or inaction, by the authority. If it has distinctly promised to consult those affected or potentially affected, then ordinarily it must consult (the paradigm case of procedural expectation). If it has distinctly promised to preserve existing policy for a specific person or group who would be substantially affected by the change, then ordinarily it must keep its promise

[103] *R (Rashid) v Home Secretary* [2005] EWCA Civ 744.

[104] [2008] EWCA 755 [50].

> (substantive expectation). If, without any promise, it has established a policy distinctly and substantially affecting a specific person or group who in the circumstances was in reason entitled to rely on its continuance and did so, then ordinarily it must consult before effecting any change (the secondary case of procedural expectation). To do otherwise, in any of these instances, would be to act so unfairly as to perpetrate an abuse of power.

In *SSHD v R(S)*,[105] however, a differently constituted Court of Appeal tackled the issue more robustly. A backlog of undecided immigration cases had been postponed to allow administrative targets to be met. Dismissing 'abuse of power' as 'a magic ingredient, able to achieve remedial results which other forms of illegality cannot match', the court focused on *remedy*. Carnwath LJ took a *Padfield* approach, insisting that 'the issue is not so much whether the unfairness is obvious or conspicuous, but whether it amounts to illegality which on reconsideration the Department has the power to correct. If it has such power, and there are no countervailing considerations, it should do so'. The case would be remitted for re-determination, though in the expectation that the outcome would be indefinite leave to remain. Lightman J added:

> I have the gravest difficulty seeing how the fact that the challenged administrative act or decision falls within one category of unlawfulness as distinguished from another, and in particular the fact that it constitutes an abuse of power giving rise to conspicuous unfairness, can extend the remedies available to the court. It may of course be relevant in the choice of the available remedy and the terms of the guidance to the administrative body on any reconsideration of its previous decision or of the appropriate action to be taken.

We shall pick this valuable reminder up in a later chapter.

Legal certainty is to be judged, a legal positivist would insist, by the ability of the judges clearly to articulate and consistently to apply a dependable body of legal principle. This they are manifestly failing to do here. Craig's four situations overlap because they are descriptive rather than prescriptive; they fluctuate in tune with a fluctuating case law based on concepts devoid of hard legal content. The reasoning is replete with what Groves calls 'motherhood statements', designed to lend legitimacy to limp reasoning by tying it into some unassailable notion of 'goodness':

> The phrase 'abuse of power' suggests that there has been a breach of a basic tenet of public law but it is usually used in a conclusionary rather than an explanatory manner. This approach enables abuse of power to be used as a motherhood statement that can be invoked as a wider principle or justification in English public law without any clear explanation of what might constitute an abuse of power or whether a new ground of review can be said to fall within the scope of that term.[106]

[105] *SSHD v R(S)* [2007] EWCA Civ 546 [60] [74].

[106] M. Groves, 'The surrogacy principle and motherhood statements in administrative law' in Pearson, Harlow and Taggart (eds.), *Law in a Changing State* (Hart Publishing, 2008), p. 90.

Less forcefully, Elliott reads *Rashid* as implying 'a possibility of intervention simply where something has gone badly wrong, even if the court cannot quite put its finger on it'. Substantive legitimate expectation operates:

> in the light of exceptional circumstances, to liberalise the application of existing heads of review (thus ensuring the protection of the norms underpinning them) by facilitating intervention in circumstances closely analogous to, but technically outwith, those in which such heads of review would usually operate.[107]

When public bodies fail or unfairly decline, as in *Rashid*, to redress the situation of those trapped by policy change or misleading representations, there is a temptation for judges to step in and redress the grievance; this is, after all, an aspect of their age-old constitutional function. They are well justified in demanding procedural fairness. Within limits (discussed in Chapter 3) review based on the established principles of illegality and irrationality is also justifiable. They can legitimately remit, making it hard to deny the applicant a favourable outcome; we have called this procedural fairness plus. They might even take the extra step of requiring the decision-maker to consider transitional arrangements, something which, taking into account what was said in Chapter 4 about impact assessment, would certainly be good administrative practice. Further they should not go.

The situation of administrators is not helped by principles of judicial review that are contradictory and confusing. Currently, courts are telling administrators to act consistently but never to 'fetter their discretion'. They are to follow the rules and apply them consistently and without discrimination but must not refuse to listen to representations. They must where appropriate consider making exceptions even at the expense of consistency. Rule-making, we learned earlier in this chapter, is supposed to be a procedurally fair, rational, reasoned and consistent process. Rules are designed to help administrators towards the approved values of consistency, fairness and equal treatment. The same must surely be true of judicial rule-making. If the judiciary wishes to introduce a reserve or equitable category of relief for exceptional cases, judges should say so openly. At least that would give the opportunity for a principled and rational debate in which we could all participate.

[107] M. Elliott, 'Legitimate Expectation, Consistency and Abuse of Power' [2005] *Judicial Review* 281, 285.

6

Regulation and governance

Contents

1. Essence

Regulation is of the essence of administrative law, constituting much of the interface between the state and the individual or 'legal persons'. To a greater or lesser extent, and in a myriad of different ways, citizens, small business, large corporate and even multinational enterprise fall into its domain. As prime machinery of governance, regulation has epitomised the contemporary mixing in administrative law of public with private powers: 'steering not rowing'. The recent UK process of regulatory reform itself is an archetypal example of domestic administrative law development in a global context.

Regulation wears a distinctly 'green light' hue as one of the chief instruments for the achievement of policy objectives. Epitomised today in the rise of 'the regulatory state', its day-to-day workings are of the first importance in the functioning economy. As such, regulation is a hot topic of political debate: not least when some 'disaster' occurs as with the current credit crunch. The style and substance of regulation connects in turn with competing – shifting – views of the role of the state. According to a recent, highly influential, report to government:

> The world in which regulators operate continues to change, both with the pressure on business of a more competitive world, and the changing regulations that need to be enforced. As a society, we have increased expectations that regulations can and will protect consumers, businesses, workers and the environment, coupled with an increasing need to keep our businesses efficient and flexible to face new competitive challenges. Our regulatory system has the pivotal role in resolving the regular conflict between prosperity and protection.[1]

Tasked to consider the inspectorial and enforcement activities of public regulatory systems operating at UK level and in England and Wales, the same review highlights the scale of the activity:[2]

> Regulation in the review's scope is delivered through 63 national regulators, and 468 local authorities. Regulators at national level employ about 41,000 individuals, of whom about 12,000 work primarily on inspection and enforcement. There are just under 20,000 people working in local authority regulatory services of whom 5,500 work primarily on inspection and enforcement. National regulators in the review's remit carry out at least 600,000 inspections each year, and local authorities carry out approximately 2 ½ million. National regulators send out 2.6 million forms a year. Statistics are not collated for the number of forms sent out by local authorities . . . Regulatory bodies at national and local level . . . have a combined budget of around £4 billion.

Underpinning its central place in administrative law is regulation's great capacity for reinvention. A wide array of tools and techniques – and many different combinations of them – is on offer. Classic issues of rules and discretion

[1] P. Hampton, *Reducing Administrative Burdens: Effective inspection and enforcement* (HM Treasury, 2005) (hereafter, '*Hampton Review*'), p. 1.

[2] *Ibid.*, pp. 11–12.

or compliance and sanction are given a very contemporary edge in the never-ending quest for properly responsive forms of regulation, as with impact assessment (see p. 152 above) and – with a view to 'structuring', 'confining' and 'checking' (see p. 200 above) – risk-based regulation ('RBR'). Indirect means of harnessing private endeavour in the public interest, for example official validation of self-regulatory systems ('meta-regulation') or the twinning of government and non-government agencies ('co-regulation'), have also been favoured. And whereas in earlier years regulation was the by-product of privatisation, today the tentacles of the regulatory state stretch increasingly far and wide: public power renascent.

All this brings issues of control and accountability sharply into focus: 'who regulates the regulators?' As we see in the next chapter, traditional 'red light' techniques of judicial review may be of little consequence in view of the highly dynamic and technically complex nature of the regulatory process. Since regulation may or may not be recognisably 'public' in character, difficulties also arise over the reach of supervision. In practice, a premium is placed on the use of audit-style techniques. The rise of regulatory agencies operating outside the hierarchical lines of ministerial control and responsibility reflects and reinforces the challenge to classic constitutional techniques in an age of governance; alternative means for directing their efforts are actively explored by ministers, as by codifying principles of regulatory policy and practice. How best to secure legitimacy in view of such competing values as independence and accountability, or due process and efficiency and effectiveness (see p. 285 below)? Meanwhile, complex regulatory networks are notoriously difficult to pin down – 'mind the gap'.

(a) Regulatory reform: Changing fashion

Characterised by 'a constant up-grading of instruments [and] the establishment of an array of regulatory policies, institutions and tools, many of them innovative and unprecedented,'[3] the UK has been a world leader in regulatory reform. While many shared strands naturally exist, not least the overarching EU connection, several main phases can be identified over the course of a generation, revealing different emphases in administrative law aims and methods and legislative and institutional development.

The Conservative 'blue rinse' is an obvious starting place. Together with privatisation, which focused attention on utility regulation, the chief mantra in this first phase was the deregulatory one of 'lifting the burden'.[4] Flanking themes were increased interest by government in techniques of self-regulation and a distinct preference for regulation by agency 'at arm's length'

[3] OECD, *Government Capacity to Assure High Quality Regulation: Regulatory reform in the United Kingdom* (2002), p. 6; and see M. Moran, *The British Regulatory State: High modernism and hyper-innovation* (Oxford University Press, 2004).

[4] DTI, *Lifting the Burden*, Cmnd 9571 (1985).

from ministers. Viewed in historical perspective, this amounted to change in, and challenge to, an old regulatory culture, not least because, in paradoxical fashion, privatisation led to a more legalistic – juridified – relationship between the state and the private sector as more explicit regulatory structures were established (a process of 're-regulation').[5] Contemporary observers noted how older, informal structures of regulation had been breaking down under the pressure of powerful economic, technological, and ideological forces.[6]

In the words of Tony Blair's fresh-faced minister in 1997:

> Some regulation is necessary for public and consumer protection, for example to ensure food safety, and to carry out the functions of Government. 'Deregulation' implies that regulation is not needed. In fact good regulation can benefit us all – it is only bad regulation that is a burden. That is why the Government's new regulatory policy will concentrate on ensuring that regulations are necessary, fair to all parties, properly costed, practical to enforce and straightforward to comply with.[7]

Following the lodestar of 'better regulation' in this next phase thus meant re-balancing the policy debate, which in turn implied a somewhat broader approach to matters of administrative law design and technique, as with regulatory impact assessment (see p. 152 above). A set of principles for regulatory reform,[8] which themselves reflect and reinforce the wider quest for 'good governance', were operationalised and particular interest taken in both harnessing and taming systems of self-regulation. Concern about regulatory agencies' own accountability was much to the fore, resulting in substantial institutional re-working and larger ('joined-up') structures. A regulatory doctrine of proportionality would feature prominently in a drive for greater regulatory 'responsiveness', with emphasis placed on risk-based methodologies (see p. 73 above).

One of the most radical programmes of regulatory reform anywhere in the world, a key element of keeping the economy strong; in this way was a third phase officially advertised: better regulation – 'mark II'.[9] Its hallmark as New Labour engaged in a third term in office was an attempt to re-work the day-to-day routines of regulation in a more 'targeted' fashion: in Gordon Brown's words, 'to deliver better regulatory outcomes while driving down the

[5] C. Veljanovski, *Selling the State* (Weidenfeld & Nicolson, 1987).

[6] J. Kay and J. Vickers, 'Regulatory reform: An appraisal' in Majone (ed.), *Deregulation or Re-regulation? Regulatory reform in Europe and the United States* (Pinter, 1990), p. 223. See further M. Moran and T. Prosser (eds.), *Privatisation and Regulatory Change in Europe* (Open University Press, 1994).

[7] Cabinet Office news release, 3 July 1997 (Chancellor of the Duchy of Lancaster, David Clark).

[8] Better Regulation Task Force (BRTF), *Principles of Good Regulation* (Cabinet Office, 2003).

[9] Department for Business Enterprise and Regulatory Reform (BERR), *Next Steps on Regulatory Reform* (2007).

cost to business of complying with regulation'.[10] A swing back in favour of deregulation would be grounded in another bout of institutional reform and in what rapidly emerged as the full-blooded discipline of 'risk-based regulation' ('RBR').[11] Designed to achieve large-scale reductions in the regulatory load on business, there would be a strong dose of audit technique.[12] A drive to raise compliance, not least by tackling those operators who persistently flout their regulatory responsibilities, has seen a major revamp of the sanctions 'tool-kit'.[13] Associated features include an accretion of ministerial order-making powers for steering the work of 'arm's length' regulators, a general legislative codification of better regulation principles, and a large-scale replacement of Dicey's 'ordinary courts' with regulators and tribunals. Aiming to promote consumer 'voice', ministers have also looked to consolidate.[14] Super-regulators would now be mirrored in a super consumer advocate.

Naturally, the rhetoric of 'better regulation' has not always matched the reality. Estimates have put the cost of regulation to the UK economy at 10–12 per cent of GDP (similar to the annual take in income tax). While much of this will be 'policy costs' directly attributable to the regulatory goal, 'thousands of small, sometimes invisible' administrative costs 'represent a huge cumulative burden':

> Within the £100 billion plus total are laws covering social, economic, political and technical issues such as minimum wage, maternity rights, environmental protection and consumer safety . . . People may rightly vote for cleaner air, longer holidays or safer travel. No one votes for red tape or excessive monitoring, inspection and form filling . . . Red tape costs . . . account . . . for . . . around 30% of total regulatory costs.[15]

In the twin contexts of an enlarged EU and – epitomised by China and India – of heightened global competition, the external pressures for further regulatory reform have appeared unrelenting. According to a 2006 report from the European Commission:

> British business has become more vocal in criticising the UK's regulatory burden. Puzzlingly, the best available evidence suggests that the UK's overall levels of regulation are actually relatively light, if not in some specific areas of regulation. Furthermore, the government pursues regulatory reform energetically. Nonetheless, summary data indicates that other countries, including many of the UK's EU partners, appear in recent years to have been

[10] Chancellor of the Exchequer Gordon Brown, *Budget 2005*. Although the developments are typically more muted, the agenda encompasses the public and third (voluntary) sectors.

[11] *Hampton Review*.

[12] BRTF, *Regulation – Less is More: Reducing burdens, improving outcomes* (2005) [hereafter, '*Arculus Review*'].

[13] R. Macrory, *Regulatory Justice: Making sanctions effective* (Cabinet Office, 2006) [hereafter, '*Macrory Review*'].

[14] DTI, *Consultation on Consumer Representation and Redress* (2006).

[15] Sir David Arculus, foreword to BRTF, *Annual Report 2004–5*.

> deregulating faster than the UK. The primary cause of British business criticism could reflect these signs that, in a globalising world, regulation in the UK is now not significantly lighter than in some other Member States, or in other developed economies. Whereas in earlier years, when the UK's regulatory burden was much lighter than in other countries, British business enjoyed the competitive advantage of lower regulatory compliance costs and, therefore, operating costs than their external competitors. Today, however, as regulatory regimes outside the UK have apparently gained ground on the UK, the competitive advantage may have shrunk. That, in turn, may be a factor behind the UK's recent inability to further close its productivity gap with other advanced countries.[16]

Today, amid the wreckage of a banking system, yet another phase of regulatory reform is signalled. Calls for 'more regulation' are all around; and understandably so, with the state suddenly playing the role of underwriter of last resort on an unprecedented scale. Whether this heralds the end of a neo-liberal era, or (as appears more likely) a series of pragmatic adjustments designed to produce 'a firmer grip on the tiller', remains to be seen of course. One important measure will be the degree of policy slop-over: the extent to which institutional responses in terms of the financial crisis are read across into other regulatory sectors. From the standpoint of the administrative lawyer, it would be strange indeed if the better regulation agenda, and the hitherto fashionable nostrums of risk-based regulation, escape unscathed. As illustrated in later sections, there has been a pervasive sense of complacency.

2. Classification, explanation and formulation

Regulation is a slippery concept. As seen in earlier chapters the term is sometimes used loosely to describe any form of behavioural control – effectively the main output function of government. It is often used in economics to describe all activity of the state, including nationalisation, taxation and subsidy, determining or altering the operation of markets. More manageably, according to Selznick,[17] regulation refers to sustained and focused control exercised by a public agency over activities that are socially valued. This well-known formulation betrays its roots in an age of government. It usefully delineates the central core of activity for administrative lawyers but, given the rise of complex and fragmented processes of regulation involving both state and non-state actors, needs supplementing.

There is far more to regulation than simply passing a law. The stress on 'sustained and focused control' points to the need for detailed knowledge and close and continuing involvement with the regulated activity. 'Full-blown' regulation involves 'a combination of three basic elements: rule formulation;

[16] J. Sheehy, 'Regulation in the UK: Is it getting too heavy?' (2006) 3(7) *ECFIN Country Focus* 1, 5.

[17] P. Selznick, 'Focusing organisational research on regulation' in Noll (ed.), *Regulatory Policy and the Social Sciences* (University of California Press, 1985).

monitoring and inspection; enforcement and sanctions'.[18] The idea of a continuous 'regulatory cycle' serves to highlight the strong sense of dynamics. Again, regulation is not only about preventing unwanted behaviours; much of it has a determinedly facilitative flavour, effectively enabling commerce on the basis of an orderly market framework.

Regulation is commonly associated with *public* control exercised over *private* business. An 'executive' model, in which public regulation is the direct responsibility of central or local government, may be contrasted with an 'agency' model. 'Self'-regulation' by the private sector, classically defined as 'an institutional arrangement whereby an organisation regulates the standards of behaviour of its members',[19] may appear at first sight to fall outside the subject matter of administrative law. Government however may in effect be delegating the regulatory function, or there may be subtle blends, such as self-regulation within a statutory framework, or full-grown hybrids of public and private control, which command our attention. Less familiar as a category is 'bureaucratic regulation' (of government bodies by other government bodies). Incorporating standard administrative law machinery – auditors, inspectors, ombudsmen, regulatory agencies – it finds a home in different chapters of this book.

(a) Competing theories

Regulation is an old battleground of ideas.[20] And if the great twentieth-century debate between state-centred welfare economics and neo-liberalism wore an increasingly dated air, recent regulatory perspectives are only properly understood by reference to it. Writing in the late 1990s, Gunningham and Grabosky made the point explicitly: 'the challenge for regulatory strategy is to transcend this ideological divide by finding ways to overcome the inefficiencies of traditional regulation on the one hand and the pitfalls of deregulation on the other. That is, to move beyond the market–state dichotomy'.[21]

As classically conceived, economic regulation involves 'governmental efforts to control firms' decisions about price, output, product quality, or production process'.[22] Full of meaning for administrative law 'green lighters',[23] this has

[18] C. Hood and C. Scott, 'Bureaucratic Regulation and New Public Management in the United Kingdom Mirror-Image Developments?' (1996) 23 JLS 321, 336.

[19] R. Baggott, 'Regulatory reform in Britain: The changing face of self-regulation' (1989) 67 *Pub. Admin.* 436.

[20] A good introduction is M. Ricketts, 'Economic regulation: Principles, history and methods' in Crew and Parker (eds.), *International Handbook on Economic Regulation* (Edward Elgar, 2006); and see generally, R. Ekelund (ed.), *The Foundations of Regulatory Economics* (Edward Elgar, 1998).

[21] N. Gunningham and P. Grabosky, *Smart Regulation: Designing environmental policy* (Clarendon Press, 1998), p. 10. See generally B. Morgan and K. Yeung, *An Introduction to Law and Regulation* (Cambridge University Press, 2007).

[22] S. Breyer and R. Stewart, *Administrative Law and Regulatory Policy*, 3rd edn (Little Brown, 1992), p. 1.

[23] J. Landis, *The Administrative Process* (Yale University Press, 1938).

been the realm of public-interest theories of regulation predicated on 'market failure' – circumstances in which the interaction of market forces fails to generate allocative efficiency. Typical justifications are externalities, where price does not reflect costs imposed on society (environmental protection); difficulty with expressing consumer preference (food labelling); 'moral hazard', as with avoiding extravagant consumption of free services; and excessive competition and predatory pricing. Market disciplines being at a premium, the case is a compelling one for regulation of monopolies, as also of anti-competitive practices.[24] Even Prime Minister Thatcher took the point, in the case of the 'Ofdogs' (see p. 249 below).

Policies of redistribution, transferring wealth from the advantaged, have not been in vogue. Yet distributional concerns remain on the regulatory agenda, illustrated by universal service obligations imposed on major utilities companies.[25] Regulation is sometimes advocated as producing socially desirable results that are inefficient ('cross-subsidisation'). And there is of course a considerable history of government regulation designed to further social policy, as that big new feature on the administrative law landscape the Commission for Equality and Human Rights (see p. 200 above) reminds us.

Public-interest theory is comfortable theory, indicating the design and operation of regulation in the pursuit of collective goals. It became a subject of increased scepticism as economic and social regulation proliferated in the 1960s and 1970s in Western industrialised countries. The limits to centralised institutional capacity – in Hayek's words,[26] 'the fiction that all the relevant facts are known to some one mind, and that it is possible to construct from this knowledge of the particulars a desirable social order' – could not be wished away. Private-interest theories of regulation gained ground, the basic thesis being that 'interest groups demand more or less regulation according to the self-interest of their members and public officials supply more or less regulation according to what benefits their self-interest'.[27] Producers, benefiting from homogeneity of interest and low organisational costs, might override more general preferences or diffuse interests. According to Stigler,[28] 'regulation is acquired by the industry and is designed and operated primarily for its benefit' – the problem of 'regulatory capture'.

Concerns about the excessive burden of regulation filtered into Britain from

[24] For the resulting legal framework, see R. Whish, *Competition Law* (Butterworths, 6th edn, 2008); also, T. Prosser, *The Limitations of Competition Law: Markets and public services* (Oxford University Press, 2005).

[25] T. Prosser, *Law and the Regulators* (Clarendon Press, 1997); M. Feintuck, *The Public Interest in Regulation* (Oxford University Press, 2004).

[26] F. A. Hayek, *Law, Legislation and Liberty*, vol. 1 (Routledge, 1973,), p. 13.

[27] R. Pearce, S. Shapiro and P. Verkeuil, *Administrative Law and Process*, 2nd edn (Foundation Press, 1992), p. 17. See generally C. Sunstein, *After the Rights Revolution: Reconceiving the regulatory state* (Harvard University Press, 1990), Ch. 3.

[28] G. Stigler, 'The theory of economic regulation' (1971) 2 *Bell Journal of Economics* 1; and see the classic by M. Olson, *The Logic of Collective Action* (Oxford University Press, 1965).

the US, where matters were compounded by rule-bound or legalistic techniques of 'command and control' operated by sprawling federal agencies. The cure, explained Stewart, might be worse than the disease:

> The legal commands adopted by central agencies are necessarily crude, dysfunctional in many applications, and rapidly obsolescent . . . These dysfunctions not only overburden the regulated entities but also cause them to fail at their intended goal. Legal blueprints . . . inevitably fall short of postulated outcomes and produce unintended side effects when officials attempt to apply them to unforeseen or changed conditions . . . Centralisation of information and decision-making . . . is generally far more costly for the government to administer than alternatives that place greater reliance on market incentives. [29]

Ogus, drawing on this country's rich history of administrative law, showed a wider field of choice, classifying individual techniques of public regulation by the degree of state intervention.[30] At one end of his spectrum came information regulation (as audit methodology requires of public services (see Chapter 2)). At the opposite end, firms would be prohibited from undertaking an activity without obtaining 'prior approval' (licensing). In between, there was standard-setting, with compliance more or less closely prescribed and sanctioned across the full range of 'target', 'performance' and 'specification' standards. Other classic instruments in the armoury included competition rules and price caps.

By the 1990s, the search for a regulatory 'third way' was nonetheless accelerating. From the perspective of socio-legal theory, regulatory failure was not simply a problem of too much law. For Teubner, juridification 'signifies a process in which the interventionist social state produces a new type of law, regulatory law, [which] "coercively specifies conduct in order to achieve particular substantive ends"'.[31] It tends to be 'particularistic, purpose oriented and dependent on assistance from the social sciences'. Drawing on autopoiesis, the theory of self-generating and self-referring systems normatively closed but cognitively open, Teubner identified a 'regulatory trilemma':[32] regulatory law tends to be ignored, or to damage the life of the system being regulated, or to impair the integrity – premised on autonomy and generality – of the legal system. This brand of reflexive theory suggested constitutive approaches to self-regulation (designing processes and organisational structures to ensure that other, wider interests are taken into account in decisions).

[29] R. Stewart, 'Madison's nightmare' (1990) 57 *University of Chicago LR* 335, 343, 356. See further S. Breyer, *Regulation and its Reform* (Harvard University Press, 1982).

[30] See A. Ogus, *Regulation: Legal form and economic theory* (Clarendon Press, 1993).

[31] G. Teubner, 'Juridification: Concepts, aspects, limits, solutions' in Teubner (ed.), *Juridification of Social Spheres* (Walter de Gruyter, 1987). See also J. Black, 'Constitutionalising self-regulation' (1996) 59 *MLR* 24.

[32] G. Teubner, *Law as an autopoietic system* (Blackwell, 1993). See also N. Luhmann, *A Sociological Theory of Law* (Routledge, 1985).

(b) Responsive regulation

So influential has the concept been that no administrative law book could be complete today without reference to 'responsive regulation'. As expounded by Ayers and Braithwaite in the early 1990s,[33] it means designing regulatory frameworks which stimulate and respond to the pre-existing regulatory capacities of firms, keeping regulatory intervention to the minimum required to achieve the desired outcomes, while retaining the regulatory capacity to play a more forceful hand. Stress is laid on the need for creative combinations of techniques tailored to particular circumstances and especially on enforcement as involving a progression through different compliance-seeking tools:

> Central to our notion of responsiveness is the idea that escalating forms of government intervention will reinforce and help constitute less intrusive and delegated forms of market regulation . . . By credibly asserting a willingness to regulate more intrusively, responsive regulation can channel market place transactions to less intrusive and less centralised forms of government intervention. Escalating forms of responsive regulation can thereby retain many of the benefits of laissez-faire governance without abdicating government's responsibility to correct market failure . . . Regulatory agencies will be able to speak more softly when they are perceived as carrying big sticks. [34]

The 'responsive regulator' thinks in terms of a hierarchy of regulatory strategies: in model form, the face of a pyramid.

Appropriately defined as 'the bringing to bear' of regulatory requirements on those bodies or persons sought to be influenced or controlled,[35] a broad conception of enforcement is central to this approach. The model illuminates this, beginning with the least intrusive interventions at the base, moving towards the apex

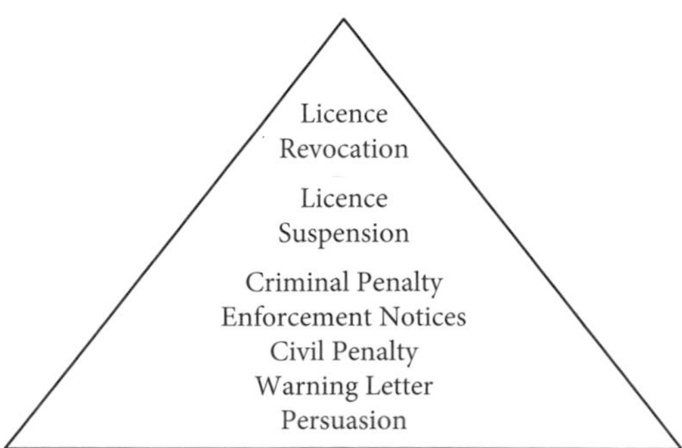

Fig 6.1 Model enforcement pyramid

[33] I. Ayres and J. Braithwaite, *Responsive Regulation: Transcending the deregulation debate* (Oxford University Press, 1992).

[34] *Ibid.*, pp. 4, 6.

[35] R. Baldwin and M. Cave, *Understanding Regulation: Theory, strategy and practice* (Oxford University Press, 1999), p. 98.

through enforcement actions of increasing severity. The very shape of the pyramid highlights the tendency for most enforcement activity to be of a determinedly routine nature. 'Tit-for-tat': the model also suggests how agencies can seek to calibrate their actions, so that increasingly strict measures are applied to the recalcitrant and less interventionist ones adopted in the light of closer compliance.

The approach suggests a strong dose of 'restorative justice',[36] such that the offender is given an opportunity to put things right. An agency may play up proactive 'fire-watching' responses (greater investment by the firm in safety systems). The drastic remedies at the apex are appropriately characterised as a brooding presence, rarely called upon, and a powerful background influence ('regulation in the shadow of the law'. 'To reject punitive regulation is naïve; to be totally committed to it is to lead a Charge of the Light Brigade. The trick of successful regulation is to establish a synergy between punishment and persuasion.'[37]

Long and tall, short and squat – differently shaped pyramids can be used to model different regulatory regimes according to the available techniques and how these are operationalised.[38] Yet as Scott observes, in the world of fragmented interests and networks 'contemporary regulatory law is rarely within the control of a single regulatory unit with capacity to deploy law coherently for instrumental purposes'.[39] The influence of political, social and economic environments on regulatory enforcement styles is also well attested. In a leading study of environmental regulation, Hutter points up a broad range of factors – from close relationships with regulatees to low costs of inspection, and on through a low incidence of serious breaches to lack of media interest – as conducive to informal, collaborative, enforcement work.[40] Carefully 'calibrating' actions is not so simple even within a single agency.

(c) Regulation *à la mode*

Recent regulatory theory has consciously expanded on 'responsive regulation'. Acknowledging that in the real world of agency design and activity the significant and legitimate roles of other stakeholders are themselves critical factors, Gunningham and Grabosky introduced the concept of 'smart regulation':

> The central argument [is] that, in the majority of circumstances, the use of multiple rather than single policy instruments, and a broader range of regulatory actors, will produce better

[36] J. Braithwaite, *Restorative Justice and Responsive Regulation* (Oxford University Press, 2002).
[37] Ayres and Braithwaite, *Responsive Regulation*, p. 25.
[38] B. Hutter, *Compliance: Regulation and environment* (Oxford University Press, 1997). There are close parallels with the idea of the 'complaints pyramid' discussed in Ch. 10.
[39] C. Scott, 'Regulation in the age of governance: The rise of the post-regulatory state', in Jordana and Levi-Faur (eds.), *The Politics of Regulation: Institutions and regulatory reforms for the age of governance* (Elgar, 2004) 158. See also, R. Baldwin and J. Black, 'Really responsive regulation' (2008) 71 *MLR* 59.
[40] B. Hutter, *The Reasonable Arm of the Law?* (Oxford University Press, 1998).

> regulation. Further, that this will allow the implementation of complementary combinations of instruments and participants tailored to meet the imperatives of specific environmental issues. By implication, this means a far more imaginative, flexible and pluralistic approach to environmental regulation than has so far been adopted in most jurisdictions.[41]

Their ideal type of a whole 'pyramid', with public agencies on the first face (government regulation), businesses on the second one (self-regulation), and 'surrogate' or 'quasi'-regulators (whether other businesses or NGOs) on the third face, usefully highlights the complex interactions taking place in the regulatory frameworks of governance. The 'smart regulator' thinks of blends of responses to mixes of problems:

> One might begin with a less intrusive instrument such as . . . education (i.e., using second parties), but then recruit another instrument if the first exhausts its responsive potential (e.g., third party audit or government mandated community right to know), and end up (where all else fails) with highly coercive instruments, such as government enforcement of command and control regulation . . . Ideally, one would use a combination of instruments in sequence to achieve a co-ordinated and gradual escalation up one or more faces of the pyramid from base to peak.[42]

Given the prominent role of NGOs and an especially wide choice of regulatory instruments (e.g. tradeable permits), environmental law and policy appears a natural home for smart regulation. But will the need for consultation requirements properly to empower third party 'surrogates' be assigned a high priority? (Refer back to Arnstein's 'ladder', see p. 173 above). The attractions of smart regulation may themselves be a weakness: 'co-ordinated. . . escalation' sounds like a leap of faith. And administrative lawyers beware: the determinedly fluid, multiparty approach poses major challenges in terms of accountability.

On show in, for example, financial regulation and – increasingly – regulation of the professions (see p. 323 below), the indirect technique of 'meta-regulation'[43] merits special attention. The contemporary blending of public and private powers is exemplified by the attempt of government regulators to exercise control through leverage of internal – commercial – control systems. Linked to principles of corporate governance, this approach calls for much care and ingenuity on the part of the agency as Parker explains:

> Regulators and rule-makers will themselves have to revise and improve their strategies constantly in light of the experience and evaluation of corporate self-regulation. [First], law and regulators must help *to connect the internal capacity for corporate self-regulation*

41 Gunningham and Grabosky, *Smart Regulation*, p. 4.

42 *Ibid.*, p. 400.

43 J. Braithwaite, 'Meta risk management and responsive regulation for tax system integrity' (2003) 25 *Law and Policy* 1; B. Morgan, 'The economisation of politics: Meta-regulation as a form of non-judicial legality' (2003) 12 *Social and Legal Studies* 489.

> *with internal commitment to self-regulate*, by motivating and facilitating moral or socially responsible reasoning within organisations . . . Secondly, law and regulators should hold corporate self-regulation accountable, and facilitate the potential for other institutions of society to hold it accountable, by *connecting the private justice of internal management systems to the public justice of legal accountability, regulatory co-ordination and action, public debate and dialogue* . . . The most important standards for corporate self-regulation processes allow regulators, the public and the law to judge the companies' own evaluations of their performance, and whether they have improved it on the basis of those evaluations – *meta-evaluation*.[44]

As deployed for public regulatory purposes of risk management, the strategy involves, in Power's words,[45] 'turning organisations inside out'. Self-evidently, however, such an approach can be fraught with difficulty, not least because of the problem of 'fit'. Rash is the meta-regulator who assumes that the design of firms' internal control systems echoes its own public interest objectives.

The term 'co-regulation' is increasingly used to describe public/private partnerships with the specific purpose of 'sustained and focused control'.[46] In Britain, as demonstrated by OFCOM (see p. 330 below), it has come to be associated with one particular model, the sub-delegation of powers by a public agency to a self-regulatory organisation (SRO). Typically, the statutory agency retains backstop powers in case the scheme proves not to work but also to assist the self-regulator in dealing with 'rogue' members of the scheme – the proverbial 'big stick in the cupboard'.[47] For its part, responsible for the day-to-day activity, the SRO must work in partnership with, but subject to control over remit and periodic review by, the agency. Bartle and Vass see on offer:

> a new regulatory paradigm . . . involving a form of regulatory 'subsidiarity', whereby the detailed implementation and achievement of regulatory outcomes can be delegated ('downwards') to industry and private sector agreements . . .
>
> Developing regulation within a co-regulatory framework is an example of how the practice of regulation evolves to achieve better cost-effective outcomes, but is dependent, if public confidence is to be secured and maintained, on good regulatory governance . . . Accountability of both the regulators and the regulated, through transparency of process and reporting, is the essential mechanism required. [48]

44 C. Parker, *The Open Corporation: Self-regulation and democracy* (Cambridge University Press, 2002), p. 246. See also, C. Coglianese and D. Lazer, 'Management based regulation: Prescribing private management to achieve public goals' (2003) 37 *Law and Society Review* 691.

45 M. Power, *The Risk Management of Everything: Rethinking the politics of uncertainty* (Demos, 2004).

46 The European Commission is much enamoured with the concept: *Better Lawmaking* COM (2003) 770. See further, F. Cafaggi, 'New modes of regulation in Europe: Critical rethinking of the recent European paths', in Cafaggi (ed.), *Reframing Self-regulation in European Private Law* (Kluwer, 2006).

47 D. Currie (Chairman of OFCOM), speech to the Advertising Association, 19 May 2003.

48 I. Bartle, and P. Vass, *Self-Regulation and the Regulatory State* (CRI, 2005), pp. 4, 40.

A mix of self-regulatory flexibility and responsiveness with government regulation's hard edge has obvious attractions, but equally the high dependency on meta-regulation – by one partner of another – makes it vulnerable. Efficient and effective workings of the 'essential mechanism' of accountability can scarcely be assumed in a split system.

Conceptually speaking, there is clear overlap with the expansive category of 'self-regulation' traditional in the professions. Today, it is increasingly diluted by a rising tide of external involvement, publicly appointed lay members, formal complaints systems (see Chapter 10) and statutory reporting requirements. This has culminated in a new species of agency, the sector-specific 'meso-regulator' targeted on the professions (see p. 327 below). A separate tier of meta-regulation is inserted, with the aim of closer 'steering' of traditionally autonomous bodies, e.g. the relationship of the Legal Services Board and Bar Council.[49] As well as sucking up some of the powers, the meso-regulator thus sits above the professional self-regulation, exercising leverage. Infused, like co-regulation more generally, with ideas of 'smart' regulation, the model offers a form of agency-based 'sustained and focused control' militating against 'capture'. Once again, however, it raises concerns about complexity and duplication, and possible infighting: where does the buck stop?

'Pure' self-regulation is the more notable by its absence:

> Self-regulation has for all intents and purposes become 'embedded' within the regulatory state . . . The traditional view of self-regulation as an activity remote or removed from the interests of the regulatory state is an anachronism . . . Where self-regulation operates, it operates with the sanction, or support or threat of the regulatory state. The modern regulatory state has become all pervading in the ambit of its attentions, and self-regulation has now to be seen in this context – simply as one of the 'instruments' available to the regulatory state.[50]

Harnessing or enrolling non-state actors in complex systems of 'collaborative governance' is another way of characterising the development – state power in a velvet glove. Central government is left with the problem of squaring the desire for authoritative action with its reliance on other bodies to deliver on its policies. The tools used to try to steer decentralised regulation produce, and are produced by, a 'thickening at the centre'.[51]

All this highlights the scale of the challenge to standard conceptions of government and of formal law as discussed in earlier chapters. Aman underscores the theme:

> The cumulative effect of various market approaches to regulation, regulatory structures and procedures is to introduce a new mix of private and public power . . . The overall context

[49] See Part 2 of the Legal Services Act 2007; also DCA, *The Future of Legal Services: Putting consumers first*, Cm. 6679 (2005).

[50] Bartle and Vass, *Self-Regulation and the Regulatory State*, pp. 3–4.

[51] J. Black, 'Tensions in the regulatory state' [2007] *PL* 58, 63.

of globalisation frames these developments. The emphasis on global competition and economic growth coupled with the general weakness of any individual single state in the face of globalisation processes encourages more negotiation on the part of the state as well as regulatory approaches more sympathetic to the cost-conscious demands of multi-national businesses and government as well.[52]

Let us examine the several phases of UK regulatory reform against this backdrop.

3. Blue-rinsed regulation

'There should always be a presumption *against* regulation unless it is strictly necessary . . . The temptation to over-regulate must be restricted.' So said Prime Minister Major in emphasising the high priority given by the Conservatives to lifting the burden on business.[53] A Deregulation Unit was tasked to co-ordinate initiatives across Whitehall and the work gained impetus from the Deregulation and Contracting Out Act 1994 (see p. 172 above). Compliance Cost Assessment (CCA) was introduced,[54] an appraisal technique designed to generate information on the total compliance costs for business sectors and individual firms, and also the effect on national competitiveness. Notably, this attempt at more 'rational' regulation – which prefigures the increasingly broad process of impact assessment under New Labour (see p. 152 above) – was shot through with discretionary judgement. Preparing a CCA would, in the words of the Government manual, 'largely involve making *assumptions* about the consequences of regulation and producing *estimates* as to the extent of the impact on business'.[55] Anticipating the current drive for more flexibility at ground-floor level, there was also talk of 'ensuring compliance rather than over-zealous enforcement'. This was the message of an enforcement code tellingly entitled *Working with Business*. Typical of the time, Citizen's Charter principles – information and advice 'in plain language', 'courteous and efficient service', accessible complaint procedures – featured prominently.[56]

Prevailing ideas of 'good' regulation were spelt out in guidance to officials engaged in the basic administrative law task of rule-formulation.[57] The first theme, proportionality, geared with the developing evaluation process. 'Think

52 A. Aman, 'Administrative law for a new century', in Taggart (ed.), *The Province of Administrative Law* (Hart, 1997), 117.

53 DTI, *Thinking About Regulating: A guide to good regulation*, (1994), foreword. The policy development can be followed through a series of White Papers: *Lifting the Burden* (see n 4 above); *Better Business Not Barriers*, Cmnd 9794 (1986); *Releasing Enterprise* Cm. 512 (1988); also DTI, *Deregulation: Cutting red tape* (1994).

54 Deregulation Initiative, *Checking the Cost of Regulation: A Guide to compliance cost assessment*, (1996).

55 *Ibid.*, p. 8.

56 DTI, *Thinking About Regulating*, pp. 10–12; DTI and Citizen's Charter Unit, *Working With Business: A code for enforcement agencies* (1996).

57 *Ibid.*

small first', the second theme, reflected the concern that 'over-regulation harms small businesses most'. A special 'litmus test' for small business was developed, to test impact. 'Go for goal-based regulations' was the third theme; provisions 'should specify the goal and allow businesses to decide how to achieve this goal'. In the event, a wedge of detailed prescriptive rules in areas such as health and safety and consumer protection was abandoned in favour of broader target standards.[58]

The manual naturally included a checklist.[59]

Good regulation – ten points to think about

1. Identify the issue . . . Keep the regulation in proportion to the problem.
2. Keep it simple . . . Go for goal-based regulation.
3. Provide flexibility for the future . . . Set the objective rather than the detailed way of making sure the regulation is kept to.
4. Keep it short.
5. Try to anticipate the effects on competition or trade . . . Try to find ways of regulating which cause the least market disruption . . .
6. Minimise costs of compliance . . . Think small first.
7. Integrate with previous regulations.
8. Make sure the regulation can be effectively managed and enforced . . . If [it] cannot be enforced fairly at a reasonable cost, think again.
9. Make sure that the regulation will work and that you will know if it does not . . . Consider how you will monitor the results, costs and any side-effects or changes in behaviour . . .
10. Allow enough time . . . for . . . consulting people inside and outside government.

The obvious danger was sub-optimal control. Allied to the presumption against regulation was a stress in evaluation on costs over benefits. Similarly, in the absence of American-style rule-making procedure (see p. 170 above), consultation exercises were concentrated on the regulated industries, rather than groups representing consumers.[60] While other EU states were also pursuing deregulatory policies, the UK under the Conservatives was 'notable for the ideological vigour of its commitment'.[61] All this serves to highlight the political dimension in regulatory strategy and design.

[58] The process is traceable to the Health and Safety at Work Act 1974: see for a comparative study, R. Baldwin and T. Daintith (eds.), *Harmonisation and Hazard* (Graham & Trotman, 1992).

[59] DTI, *Thinking About Regulating*, pp. 20–1.

[60] *Ibid.*, pp. 13–15; Ogus, *Regulation*, Ch. 16.

[61] T. Daintith, 'European Community law and the redistribution of regulatory power in the United Kingdom' (1995) 1 *ELJ* 134, 137. For a retrospective, see C. Scott and M. Lodge, 'Administrative simplification in the United Kingdom', in OECD, *From Red Tape to Smart Tape* (2003).

(a) 'Ofdogs'

The so-called 'Ofdogs', which emerged as a necessary by-product of the Conservatives' large-scale privatisation of the utilities, demonstrate a major shift in UK administrative law in favour of the agency model of public regulation. Bodies such as OFTEL (the Office of Telecommunications, 1984), OFGAS (the Office of Gas Supply, 1986) and OFFER (the Office of Electricity Regulation, 1989) came to litter the regulatory landscape. Predictably, given the scale and complexity of the privatisation process, a steep learning curve for government and agencies alike, diversity in powers and performance was a common trait. There were, however, standard components in what became known for a brief historical moment as regulation 'UK style':[62]

- a *single, independent* regulatory agency, headed by a director-general (D-G), for each industry
- within a general regulatory framework provided by the privatisation statute, practical operations predicated on a system of *licensing*
- control of the dominant firm via a *price-cap formula*, intended to incentivise greater efficiency
- the D-Gs as part of a regulatory *network*, the competition authorities included
- latterly, emphasis on *quality* regulation as part of the economic regulation.

As a compact agency, a non-ministerial government department operating at arm's length from, though subject to the patronage of, the minister, the Ofdog model typified fragmentation of the traditional government framework. There was a strong sense of personalisation associated too with vesting of the powers in the D-G, making these watchdogs peculiarly vulnerable to criticisms of excessive discretion and lack of accountability.[63] Ofdogs possessed substantial licensing powers, control being exercised both on entry to the industries and through modification and enforcement of the terms and conditions. By so structuring and confining the discretion of individual operators, and especially the privatised firms like British Telecom that initially faced little competition, the D-Gs were able to engage in 'structural regulation' (the way in which the market is organised) as well as 'conduct regulation' (behaviour within a market). Expressing the dominant concern with regulatory failure, the D-G of Electricity Supply considered that regulation was 'a means of "holding the fort" until competition arrives'.[64] The D-G of OFTEL spoke of competition as 'a regulatory weapon; by allowing interconnection on favourable terms, 'a regulator does not need to wait, hoping that it will occur, but

[62] C. Veljanovski, 'The regulation game' in Veljanovski (ed.), *Regulators and the Market* (IEA, 1991); also, M. Armstrong, S. Cowan and J. Vickers, *Regulatory Reform: Regulation of economic activity* (MIT Press, 1994).

[63] C. Graham, *Is There A Crisis in Regulatory Accountability?* (CRI, 1995).

[64] S. Littlechild, *Regulation of British Telecommunications Profitability* (HMSO, 1983) [4.11].

can take active steps to encourage it'.[65] Detailed licence provision came to look 'cumbersome and inappropriate' as structural regulation for competition began to bear fruit.[66]

Adopted across a wide range of industries, the licence rule 'Retail Price Index (RPI) – X' for limiting the profits and prices of the dominant firm was described by contemporaries as 'the most distinctive feature of monopoly regulation in Britain'.[67] This meant the now privatised utility company could raise prices for a defined 'basket' of its wares by no more than the rate of retail price inflation minus X per cent, with 'X' representing a regulatory judgement of its cost-efficiency potential – a major ongoing exercise of agency discretion. This incentivising approach duly illustrated the propensity for juridification. Originally trumpeted as a straightforward means of economic regulation,[68] RPI–X was the focus of progressive rule development; the emergence of a hierarchy or subspecies of rules structuring and confining commercial discretion more closely. Otherwise, an operator like BT was free to change individual prices, affecting different classes of consumer, provided the average was met.[69]

Regulation 'UK style' also demonstrates the important role in governance of regulatory 'tiers' and 'webs'. An industry-plus-agency model view of arrangements is too simplistic; the interconnectedness of split regulatory functions between institutions was an essential feature.[70] Ministers retained significant powers, e.g. on market entry and payment of subsidies. Behind the D-Gs stood the competition authorities, in the shape of the Monopolies and Mergers Commission and the Office of Fair Trading (OFT). Their potential involvement constituted both regulation 'in the shadow of regulation' (leverage on the dominant firm in e.g. a licence renegotiation) and a measure of so-called 'network accountability' (the D-G having to justify his policy to other regulatory actors).[71] Reference to the MMC also served as a check on the D-G's exercise of discretion.[72]

There were changing attitudes to 'quality regulation', broadly defined to include customer service issues and standards of supply.[73] In line with the

[65] As in telecommunications: see B. Carsberg, 'Office of Telecommunications: Competition and the Duopoly Review: in Veljanovski (ed.), *Regulators and the Market*, p. 100.

[66] Hansard Society and European Policy Forum, *Regulation of Privatised Utilities* (1996), p. 9.

[67] R. Rees and J. Vickers, 'RPI – X price-cap regulation' in Bishop, Kay and Mayer (eds.), *The Regulatory Challenge* (Oxford University Press, 1995), p. 358. 'CPI-X regulation' (Customer Prices Index – X) is a later formulation.

[68] In contrast to American 'rate of return' regulation: see D. Helm, 'British utility regulation theory, practice and reform' (1994) 10 *Oxford Rev. of Economic Policy* 17.

[69] See further, C. Hall, C. Hood and C. Scott, *Telecommunications Regulation: Culture, chaos and interdependence inside the regulatory process* (Routledge, 2000).

[70] B. Hogwood, 'Developments in regulatory agencies in Britain' (1990) 56 *International Rev. of Administrative Sciences* 595.

[71] C. Scott, 'Accountability in the regulatory state' (2000) 27 *JLS* 28.

[72] S. Lipworth, 'Utility regulation and the Monopolies and Mergers Commission, retrospect and prospect' in Borrie and Beesley (eds.), *Major Issues in Regulation* (IEA, 1993).

[73] J. Bowdery, *Quality Regulation and the Regulated Industries* (CRI, 1994).

strong market ideology prevailing in the early 1980s, no direct provision was made for this in the early privatisation schemes of telecommunications and gas. Yet RPI–X could in such conditions have perverse effects, the incentive for the dominant firm to reduce costs providing a corresponding incentive to reduce quality.[74] The problem was tackled in typically incremental fashion. Individual regulators such as OFTEL took action to shore up standards by negotiation and informal agreement. Later privatisation statutes, on electricity and water, created specific powers to establish performance standards binding on the licence-holders. Eventually, embodying the philosophy of John Major's Citizen's Charter programme, the Competition and Service (Utilities) Act 1992 brought such quality regulation powers up to the level of the strongest. In hindsight, this more consumerist 'feel' heralded the next phase of UK regulatory reform under New Labour. The pendulum was swinging.

4. 'Better regulation'

'The job of government is to get the balance right, providing proper protection and making sure that the impact on those being regulated is proportionate'.[75] In so seeking to re-orient policy away from deregulation, the incoming Labour administration gave 'better regulation' a determinedly consensual flavour. 'Politicians differ about the appropriate level of intervention, but all governments should ensure that regulations are necessary, fair, effective, affordable and enjoy a broad degree of public confidence.'[76] The agenda was a huge one, reaching into most aspects of government activity. A Regulatory Impact Unit was created in the Cabinet Office to help drive it, together with the 'Better Regulation Task Force', an independent advisory body composed largely of business people and charged with 'challenging' departments. The '"thickening" of the centre' soon included a 'better-regulation minister' for each department, a Whitehall network of 'better-regulation units' and, showing the role for bureaucratic regulation, a designated Cabinet committee (the 'Panel for Regulatory Accountability') to vet departmental plans. Replacing the Conservatives' Deregulation and Contracting Out Act 1994, the Regulatory Reform Act 2001 provided the essential legislative framework (see p. 168 above).

First promulgated by the BRTF in 1997, a five-fold set of regulatory principles rapidly became the orthodoxy, being mainstreamed in the policy process through the detailed template of regulatory impact assessment (see p. 152 above). As an archetypal piece of 'soft' law designed to influence the hard legal product, relevant Cabinet Office guidance shows the parallels with legal precept, as well as the twin policy elements of continuity and change:

[74] See National Consumer Council, *In the Absence of Competition* (HMSO, 1989).

[75] BRTF, *Principles of Good Regulation*, 3rd edn (Cabinet Office, 2003), p. 1.

[76] *Ibid.*

Principles of Good Regulation

The principles are a useful toolkit for assessing and improving the quality of regulation. Use them to inform and shape your consultation, particularly in the planning stages:

- Proportionality
  Policy solutions should be appropriate for the perceived problem or risk: you don't need a sledgehammer to crack a nut!
- Accountability
  Regulators/policy officials must be able to justify the decisions they make and should expect to be open to public scrutiny.
- Consistency
  Government rules and standards must be joined up and implemented fairly and consistently.
- Transparency
  Regulations should be open, simple and user friendly. Policy objectives, including the need for regulation, should be clearly defined and effectively communicated to all stakeholders.
- Targeting
  Regulation should be focused on the problem. You should aim to minimise side effects and ensure that no unintended consequences will result from the regulation being implemented.

Once you have drafted your policy proposal and policy options, check that it complies with all of the five principles. If you have planned and carried out your consultation well, it should meet these criteria anyway.[77]

The stress on 'targeting' would smooth the path of risk-based methodologies on the administrative law frontline. 'Enforcers should focus primarily on those whose activities give rise to the most serious risks'. 'Consistency' would be assigned wide currency as an administrative value. 'Regulators should . . . work together in a "joined-up" way . . . new regulations should take account of other existing or proposed regulations . . . regulation should be predictable in order to give stability and certainty . . . enforcement agencies should apply regulations consistently across the country'.[78] Better to combat the over-zealous interpretation of rules and guidance – 'regulatory creep'[79] – an additional premium would be placed on transparency.

A push for hybrid and indirect strategies shows the influence of contemporary regulatory theory:

> The level of risk involved in any activity should determine the level of protection necessary. However. . . no solution will eradicate risk, and we have found no evidence that indicates

[77] Cabinet Office, *Principles of Good Regulation* (1998), p. 1.
[78] *Ibid.*, p. 4–5.
[79] BRTF, *Avoiding Regulatory Creep* (2004).

> that state regulation is necessarily more effective than alternative arrangements at reducing risk. There will always be cases of people breaking laws and failing to meet mandatory requirements. And sometimes, the out-of-touch nature of regulations will encourage a climate of evading the rules. In contrast, rules that have been developed closely with, or indeed by, those whose behaviour is to be controlled might be more readily complied with. The rules should be targeted to ensure that they require the minimum standards necessary to deliver adequate protection. A common feature of all effective systems, however, is the potential for the imposition of real sanctions. [80]

In seeking so to reconcile an expansive role for the regulatory state with 'light-touch' regulation based on securing operator-led solutions, the task force had effectively incorporated self-regulation as part of better regulation. The state should not only let industry and commerce 'row', but also do more 'steering'.

(a) Changing institutional geography

With concerns about regulatory accountability a main driver, substantial changes in the institutional geography were in train. Time was called on the individualised 'Ofdogs', the preference now being for the standard regulatory structure of a commission or board with collective responsibility for decisions. The benchmark is Part 1 of the Utilities Act 2000, which replaced OFGAS and OFFER with GEMA, the Gas and Electricity Markets Authority; similar re-workings soon included the OFT, OFCOM, and the Office of Rail Regulation (ORR).[81] The Act also represented a golden opportunity to demonstrate New Labour's commitment to a more rounded approach to regulation. A primary duty to protect the interest of consumers, ministerial powers to intervene to help disadvantaged groups, and provision for the furtherance of environmental objectives, mark the changed philosophy.[82]

The rise of the 'super-' or 'mega-' regulator reflects and reinforces broader trends in agencification (see Chapter 2). Take the Financial Services Authority (FSA), which became the single regulator for the industry in 2001, finally combining the responsibilities of nine separate bodies. One of the first integrated financial regulators in the world, it thus substituted for an old model of institutional regulation, in which different sets of financial institutions (insurance, securities, etc) had their own regulatory bodies, a 'thematic' or 'functional' model defined holistically in terms of engagement in commercial financial activity. Behind this lay the Financial Services and Markets Act 2000 which, in

[80] BRTF, *Alternatives to State Regulation* (2000), p. 26; also BRTF, *Imaginative Thinking for Better Regulation* (2003).

[81] See respectively, Enterprise Act 2002, Communications Act 2003, and Railways and Transport Safety Act 2003.

[82] Utilities Act 2000, Parts 2–4; P. Leyland, 'UK utility regulation in an age of governance' in Bamforth and Leyland (eds.), *Public Law in a Multi-layered Constitution* (Hart Publishing, 2003).

sweeping away the pre-existing mix of statutory regulation and self-regulation, afforded the FSA major new enforcement powers (see p. 263 below). As the agency's first policy director confirms, concerns about coherence, consistency and targeting featured prominently in the choice of institutional design:

> With the growth in the number of multiple-function firms, the need for communication, coordination, cooperation and consistency across specialist regulatory bodies [has] become increasingly acute and increasingly difficult to manage efficiently . . . A single regulator can take advantage of a single set of central support services . . . introduce a unified statistical reporting system for regulated firms . . . operate a single database for the authorisation of firms . . . avoid unnecessary duplication or underlap across multiple specialised regulators, introduce a consolidated set of rules and guidance . . . offer a single point of contact to both regulated firms and to consumers.
>
> In addition to pure scale economies, a single regulator ought to be more efficient in the allocation of regulatory resources across both regulated firms and types of regulated activities. One crucial element of this is the development of a single system of risk-based supervision under which regulatory resources are devoted to those firms and those areas of business which pose the greatest risk when judged against the objectives of protecting consumers, maintaining market confidence . . . and reducing financial crime . . . A single regulator ought to be best placed to resolve efficiently and effectively the conflicts which inevitably emerge between the different objectives of regulation. This is because a single management structure should be better able to identify, to decide upon and to implement a collectively agreed resolution . . . A single regulator ought to be able to avoid the unjustifiable differences in supervisory approaches and the competitive inequalities imposed on regulated firms through inconsistent rules which have arisen across multiple specialist regulators.[83]

OFCOM, the Office of Communications, is another big beast in the administrative law jungle. Launched in 2003 in place of five regulatory bodies, its origins lie in the dynamics of convergence in the sector. As such, the agency is a leading illustration of regulatory structures and processes being driven by technological change. According to the White Paper:

> The current system for media and communications regulation is a reflection of the way communications developed in the twentieth century, with different content and distribution channels. We need a regulatory body with the vision to see across these converging industries, to understand the complex dynamics of competition in both content and the communications networks which carry services. It should not demand the same regulation for each medium, but must see across the whole sector and help build a coherent system . . . It will be essential for the regulator to have delegated powers to act independently in response to fast-changing circumstances.[84]

[83] C. Briault, *The Rationale for a Single National Financial Services Regulator* (FSA, 1999), pp. 15, 18, 20–2. See further on the practical experience, G. Walker, 'Financial Services Authority' in Walker and Blair (eds.), *Financial Services Law* (Oxford University Press, 2006).

[84] DTI, *A New Future for Communications*, Cm. 5010 (2000), pp. 11, 77. See also NAO, *The Creation of OFCOM: Wider lessons for public sector mergers of regulatory agencies*, HC 1175 (2005/6).

OFCOM may be likened to a giant spider – at the centre of a more or less finely woven regulatory 'web'. Highlighting the place in 'better regulation' for mixes of public and private power, the agency must 'have regard to . . . the desirability of promoting and facilitating the development and use of effective forms of self-regulation'.[85] This has grounded the policy of co-regulation, taken in the White Paper to mean:

> situations in which the regulator would be actively involved in securing that an acceptable and effective solution is achieved. The regulator may for example set objectives which are to be achieved, or provide support for the sanctions available, while still leaving space for self-regulatory initiatives by industry, taking due account of the interests and views of other stakeholders, to meet the objectives in the most efficient way. The regulator will in any case have scope to impose more formal regulation if the response of industry is ineffective or not forthcoming in a sufficiently timely manner.[86]

5. Better regulation – mark II

The most recent period of UK regulatory reform has seen the focus widen beyond government departments to include regulatory agencies, inspectorates and local authorities.[87] Yet more bureaucracy 'to improve the productivity of the UK economy by removing unnecessary regulation . . . or reducing the costs associated with complying':[88] the reader will appreciate the irony. Created in 2007, the Department for Business, Enterprise and Regulatory Reform is 'to help ensure business success in an increasingly competitive world'. Successor to the Regulatory Impact Unit, the Better Regulation Executive has concentrated on fostering risk-based approaches; the BRTF meanwhile has metamorphosed into, first, a beefed-up Better Regulation Commission, and thence, underscoring the broad policy orientation, the Risk and Regulation Advisory Council.[89] Moving on from the Regulatory Reform Act 2001, there are two successive legislative flagships: the Legislative and Regulatory Reform Act (LRRA) 2006, and the Regulatory Enforcement and Sanctions Act (RESA) 2008. Principles have been laid on principles and placed on a statutory footing, and bureaucratic regulation has abounded, in a fresh attempt to embed the 'best practice' of better regulation.

(a) Hampton

Three independent reviews commissioned by ministers, of which the Hampton review, *Reducing Administrative Burdens: Effective inspection and enforcement*,

[85] Communications Act 2003, s. 3(4).
[86] DTI, *A New Future for Communications*, p. 83.
[87] A theme elaborated by BERR, *Next Steps on Regulatory Reform*.
[88] NAO, *Regulatory Reform in the UK* (2008), p. 2.
[89] BRC, *Public Risk: The next frontier for better regulation* (2008).

is the best known, established new policy. Given a typically ad hoc and piecemeal development over many years, the basic finding that 'the system as a whole is uncoordinated and good practice is not uniform' was eminently predictable. Hampton homed in on risk-based regulation:

> Risk assessment - though widely recognised as fundamental to effectiveness - is not implemented as thoroughly and comprehensively as it should be. Risk assessment should be comprehensive, and should be the basis for all regulators' enforcement programmes. Proper analysis of risk directs regulators' efforts at areas where it is much needed, and should enable them to reduce the administrative burden of regulation, while maintaining or even improving regulatory outcomes.[90]

Glossing over the limitations of RBR methodology (see p. 275 below), Hampton was thus concerned both to widen and deepen its already very considerable application, not least at the local level. This would involve a major deregulatory push in the form of adjustment to the means of enforcement and greater stress on the facilitative – pro-enterprise – role of regulators.

Hampton elaborated a series of principles for regulatory enforcement:

- Regulators, and the regulatory system as a whole, should use comprehensive risk assessment to concentrate resources on the areas that need them most.
- Regulators should be accountable for the efficiency and effectiveness of their activities, while remaining independent in the decisions they take.
- All regulations should be written so that they are easily understood, easily implemented, and easily enforced, and all interested parties should be consulted when they are being drafted.
- No inspection should take place without a reason.
- Businesses should not have to give unnecessary information, nor give the same piece of information twice.
- The few businesses that persistently break regulations should be identified quickly, and face proportionate and meaningful sanctions.
- Regulators should provide authoritative, accessible advice easily and cheaply.
- When new policies are being developed, explicit consideration should be given to how they can be enforced using existing systems and data to minimise the administrative burden imposed.
- Regulators should be of the right size and scope, and no new regulator should be created where an existing one can do the work.
- Regulators should recognise that a key element of their activity will be to allow, or even encourage, economic progress and only to intervene when there is a clear case for protection.[91]

[90] *Hampton Review*. And see BRC, *Risk, Responsibility, Regulation: Whose risk is it anyway?* (2006).

[91] *Hampton Review*, p. 43.

Chancellor of the Exchequer Gordon Brown spoke of a new era of trust (which today, in light of the happenings in the financial sector, appears remote!):

> In the old regulatory model – which started in Victorian times – the implicit regulatory principle has been 100% inspection of premises, procedures and practices irrespective of known risks or past results. The theory has been to inspect every one continuously, demand information whole-scale, and require forms to be filled in at all times, the only barrier to the blanket approach being lack of resources. The new model we propose is quite different. In a risk based approach there is no inspection without justification, no form filling without justification, and no information requirements without justification. Not just a light touch but a limited touch. Instead of routine regulation attempting to cover all, we adopt a risk based approach which targets only the necessary few.
>
> A risk based approach helps move us a million miles away from the old assumption – the assumption since the first legislation of Victorian times – that business, unregulated, will invariably act irresponsibly. The better view is that businesses want to act responsibly. Reputation with customers and investors is more important to behaviour than regulation, and transparency – backed up by the light touch – can be more effective than the heavy hand. So a new trust between business and government is possible, founded on the responsible company, the engaged employee, the educated consumer – and government concentrating its energies on dealing not with every trader but with the rogue trader, the bad trader who should not be allowed to undercut the good.[92]

A further round of institutional reform was part of the logic:

> Some of the problems identified . . . are rooted in, or exacerbated by, the complicated structure of regulation in the UK . . . There are many small regulators at national level – of the 63 regulators covered by the review, 31 had fewer than 100 staff, and 12 had fewer than 20. Small regulators, although focused, are less able to join up their work, and are less aware of the cumulative burdens on businesses. It is more difficult and more expensive to have a comprehensive risk assessment system if data is split across several regulators with similar areas of responsibility. In such circumstances, a holistic view of business risk becomes difficult, if not impossible.[93]

We dealt earlier with the Legislative and Regulatory Reform Act as a discreditable attempt by ministers to undermine Parliament's constitutional prerogatives (see p. 168 above). But this should not obscure its important role in promoting compliance with the principles of better regulation. As well as removing or reducing burdens (see further below), Part I permits the minister by order to create or abolish regulatory bodies and transfer functions, amend the constitutions of statutory regulatory bodies and modify the way in which regulatory functions are exercised, under this broad rubric.[94]

[92] HM Treasury, *Chancellor launches Better Regulation Action Plan*, press release 24 May 2005.

[93] *Hampton Review*, p. 6.

[94] LRRA, s. 2.

Hampton had set in train a mass cull of separate agencies, with the landscape of administrative law becoming home to an expanded breed of 'super-regulators'.[95] Take the Health and Safety Executive (HSE). It is now merged with its erstwhile twin, the Health and Safety Commission, so integrating an array of informational, advisory and lobbying functions.[96] To the not inconsiderable remit of the safety of workers and the public in workplaces are added some very particular regulatory responsibilities, e.g. those of the Adventure Activities Licensing Authority. How long – echoing concerns about the new CEHR (see p. 70 above) – before serious complaints are generated of an unwieldy and/or insufficiently specialist agency?

Hampton also triggered substantial rationalisation of the regulatory activities of local government in the important domains of trading standards and environmental protection. At the heart of this is the rapid emergence of the 'Local Better Regulation Office', first as a government-owned company, and now on a statutory footing with powers to issue guidance to local authorities (with a backstop power to direct compliance).[97] Subject in turn to ministerial powers of direction, guidance and review,[98] LBRO is clearly intended to be a significant player in the close regulatory web or network being spun. LBRO's remit is to:

> - get local authorities to adopt risk-based enforcement and reduce the number of business inspections and information requests
> - manage up the quality of local enforcement services
> - give local authorities a smaller and agreed list of priority areas for enforcement,[[99]] instead of the long and unprioritised list they get at present
> - better co-ordinate local enforcers so that (i) business receives consistent advice on compliance and (ii) multi-size business gets a clear home or lead authority, instead of regulation by multiple authorities.[100]

(b) 'Regulatory Procedures Act'

Breaking new ground in our administrative law system, LRRA Part 2 contains important provisions on the exercise of regulatory functions. Earlier 'soft law' statements of better regulation are given a harder edge across the piece:

> Any person exercising a regulatory function . . . must have regard to the [following] principles: (a) regulatory activities should be carried out in a way which is transparent,

95 HM Treasury, *Implementing Hampton: From enforcement to compliance* (2006).

96 See Legislative Reform (Health and Safety Executive) Order 2008, SI No. 960.

97 RESA, ss. 6–7.

98 RESA, ss. 15–17.

99 See the *Rogers Review of National Enforcement Priorities for Local Authority Regulatory Services* (Cabinet Office, 2007).

100 HM Treasury, *Implementing Hampton*, p. 48. Hampton had envisaged a yet more powerful Consumer Trading Standards Agency.

accountable, proportionate and consistent; (b) regulatory activities should be targeted only at cases in which action is needed . . .

In this Act 'regulatory function' means –

(a) a function under any enactment of imposing requirements, restrictions or conditions, or setting standards or giving guidance, in relation to any activity; or
(b) a function which relates to the securing of compliance with, or the enforcement of, requirements, restrictions, conditions, standards or guidance which under or by virtue of any enactment relate to any activity.[101]

Supplementing this is ministerial power to make a statutory code – tertiary legislation – to which, when 'determining any general policy or principles' or 'setting standards or giving guidance generally', a regulator must also have regard.[102] The framework governs most statutory regulators, including many 'super-agencies';[103] so too, a long list of 'executive' regulatory functions exercised by ministers or by local authorities in England and Wales.[104] As an authoritative distillation of 'best practice', the end product may be likened to a miniature 'Regulatory Procedures Act'. Presented as 'a central part of the Government's better regulation agenda', the Regulators' Compliance Code enshrines Hampton's recommendations about enforcement activity:[105]

- *Economic progress* – regulators to consider the impact of their regulatory interventions on economic progress and to keep their activities under review with a view to minimising burdens, especially for small business.
- *Risk assessment* – to precede and inform all aspects of approaches to regulatory activity. Risk methodologies to be regularly reviewed and updated.
- *Advice and guidance* – regulators to provide general information, advice and guidance to make it easier for regulated entities to understand and meet their obligations.
- *Inspections* – to be justified and targeted on the basis of risk assessment.
- *Information requirements* – regulators to balance the need for information with the burdens this entails for operators. Regulatory data to be shared where this is practicable, beneficial and cost effective.
- *Compliance and enforcement action* – regulators to incentivise and reward good levels of compliance, for example by lighter reporting requirements. Sanctions policies to be consistent with 'Macrory penalties principles' (see p. 263 below).

101 LRRA, ss. 21, 32.

102 LRRA, s. 22. So replacing a voluntary code, *Enforcement Concordat: Good practice guide for England and Wales* (1998), which had in turn replaced the Conservatives' one: DTI and Citizen's Charter Unit, *Working with Business*.

103 In some areas of economic regulation, there is a sector-specific version: see e.g. Communications Act 2003, s. 3 (OFCOM).

104 Legislative and Regulatory Reform (Regulatory Functions) Order 2007, SI No. 3544. Devolution allows Scotland, Wales and Northern Ireland to go their own way: LRRA, s. 24.

105 BERR, *Regulators' Compliance Code* (2007).

- *Accountability and process* – regulators to ensure effective consultation and feedback opportunities and to provide effective and timely complaints procedures.

This is a milestone in the ongoing juridification of UK regulatory policy and practice. As so often with tertiary legislation the precise legal effects are hard to pin down however. In principle, judicial review is a possibility (failure to give specific obligations due weight). Any decision to depart from the Code would need to be carefully reasoned and based on material evidence. Then again, the framework operates subject to any other legal requirement affecting the exercise of a regulatory function (including of course EC obligations). While the inspector should operate in accordance with general policy or guidance, the Code does not apply directly to enforcement activity in individual cases.

(c) Arculus

Appearing in tandem with Hampton, the Arculus review *Regulation: Less is more* had as its chief target the administrative costs of regulation to business. It recommended a massive dose of audit-style technique: burdens should be measured[106] and, through a system of departmental simplification plans, reduction targets agreed, across Whitehall.

By 'simplification' Arculus in fact meant a wide range of administrative law actions, which businesses as 'stakeholders' should be actively encouraged to suggest:[107]

- *Deregulation* – removing regulations from the statute book, leading to greater liberalisation of previously regulated regimes
- *Consolidation* – bringing together different regulations into more manageable form and restating the law more clearly
- *Rationalisation* – using 'horizontal' legislation [such as a general duty not to trade unfairly] to replace a variety of sector-specific 'vertical' regulations and resolving overlapping or inconsistent regulations
- *Administrative burden reductions* – making forms simpler or clearer, increasing the intervals between information requests, sharing data etc.

This presented an ongoing challenge to government since with a view to promoting change in the regulatory culture Arculus demanded that departments identify offsetting measures when introducing new administrative burdens. The inherently crude approach of 'one in, one out' was championed as an:

> easily understood description of the way we want people who are involved in putting administrative burdens on others to think and to behave. It is about prioritising, about

[106] According to a rough and ready model of 'standard cost' borrowed from the Netherlands: *Arculus Review*, pp. 12, 19–23.

[107] HM Treasury, *Simplification Plans* (2006), p. 5.

> putting the more important things ahead of the less important, and accepting that, if we try to do everything, we know that either we ourselves or those around us will not be able to cope. Regulatory bodies need to work out which are the most important regulations, which we can do without and which ones can be removed from the regulatory basket. If ministers do want new laws they will need to . . . drop other proposals – thus *stemming the flow*, or repeal existing laws – thus *reducing the stock*.[108]

Arculus spoke of achieving 'an outstanding return on investment for the UK – potentially a greater than 1% increase in GDP'.[109] Rules and regulations being such a major output function of (New Labour) government, one is entitled to be sceptical. A strong start has been made however. The measurement exercise having identified annual administrative costs from regulation of £13.4 billion, departments committed to the challenging target of a 25 per cent net reduction by 2010. By early 2008, some twenty separate simplification plans were up and running, containing hundreds of detailed proposals.[110] And 'audit of audit', the NAO has been specifically tasked with evaluating their delivery.[111] How different is all this from 'good regulation' Conservative style? The pendulum had swung back.

Take the HSE, which 'deals with many areas of the economy where strong regulation and enforcement are key to public confidence'.[112] Illustrating how the different policy strands are interwoven, a 'Sensible Risk Management' initiative, designed as the name suggests to encourage a more proportionate approach to assessing and managing risk in the work-place, is centre-stage in the agency's simplification plan. As well as 'forms projects' designed to reduce agency-inspired paperwork, flanking developments include such determinedly practical measures as a simplified process for checking building contractors' competence, rationalising the guidance on control of hazardous substances to make it more accessible, and re-targeting inspection of heavy industrial equipment. Perhaps hopefully, agency officials believe that 'none of the changes will result in a reduction in worker or public safety';[113] if so, it is a remarkable indictment of previous regulatory practice.

Woe betide the 'arm's length' agency that does not toe the line. Should restructuring under the LRRA seem a little drastic then ministers are empowered under Part 4 of RESA to require regulators to review the burdens they impose, reduce any that are 'unnecessary' (disproportionate), and report

108 *Arculus Review*, p. 6. Revamping an over-loaded impact assessment system was part of the package.

109 *Ibid.*, p. 3.

110 BERR, *Delivering Simplification Plans: A summary* (2008). See further, Regulatory Reform Committee, *Getting Results: The Better Regulation Executive and the impact of the regulatory reform agenda*, HC 474 (2007/8).

111 NAO, *Reducing the Cost of Complying with Regulations*, HC 615 (2006/7).

112 HSE, *Simplification Plan 2006: Executive summary.*

113 *Ibid.*

annually on progress.[114] From a legal standpoint, this is one step on from the generalised taking-account requirements of the Regulators' Compliance Code. The guidance duly warns of judicial review if an agency's review 'is of insufficient detail'.[115]

(d) Macrory

Tasked with ensuring that, as Hampton recommended, sanctions are 'consistent and appropriate for a risk based approach to regulation',[116] the Macrory review, *Regulatory Justice: Making sanctions effective*, focused on classic compliance issues. Ministers quickly embraced the central recommendation of a more flexible and transparent set of regulatory sanctions designed to 'reduce the burden on legitimate business by dealing effectively with the rogues and reducing the need for inspection'.[117]

Macrory confirmed the fact of a highly fragmented set of arrangements heavily reliant on criminal prosecution should operators prove unwilling or unable to follow advice and comply with legal obligations.[118] Largely centred on the magistrates' courts, and, commonly, offences of strict liability [119] punctuated from time to time by high-profile prosecutions (as in the notoriously difficult matter of 'corporate manslaughter'[120]), this constituted a blunt instrument:

> Criminal sanctions currently are often an insufficient deterrent to the 'truly' criminal or rogue operators, since the financial sanctions imposed in some criminal cases are not considered to be a sufficient deterrent or punishment . . . In instances where there has been no intent or wilfulness relating to regulatory non-compliance a criminal prosecution may be a disproportionate response . . . Criminal sanctions are costly and time-consuming for both businesses and regulators. In many instances, although non-compliance has occurred, the cost or expense of bringing criminal proceedings deters regulators from using their limited resources to take action. This creates what has come to be known as a *compliance deficit.*
>
> Criminal convictions for regulatory non-compliance have lost their stigma, as in some industries being prosecuted is regarded as part of the business cycle. This may be because

114 The duties apply automatically to the big economic regulators like OFCOM and OFWAT. See further, Select Committee on Regulators, *UK Economic Regulators* HL 189 (2006/7), Ch. 7.

115 BERR, *Guide to the Regulatory and Enforcement Bill* (2007) 51.

116 *Macrory Review*, p. 4.

117 Cabinet Office press release, 28 November 2006. So following in the footsteps of other common law countries: see C. Abbott, 'The regulatory enforcement of pollution control laws: The Australian experience', (2005) 17 *JEL* 161.

118 K. Hawkins, *Environment and Enforcement: Regulation and the social definition of pollution* (Oxford University Press, 1984); D. Vogel, *National Styles of Regulation: Environmental policy in Great Britain and the United States* (Cornell, 1986).

119 See A. Simester, *Appraising Strict Liability* (Oxford University Press, 2005).

120 But see the Corporate Manslaughter and Corporate Homicide Act 2007. The Act lifts Crown immunity to prosecution.

> both strict liability offences committed by legitimate business and the deliberate flouting of the law by rogues is prosecuted in the same manner with little differentiation between these two types of offender . . .
>
> Since the focus of criminal proceedings is on the offence and the offender, the wider impact of the offence on the victim may not be fully explored. There has been a limited evolution of the rights and needs of victims in the area of regulatory non-compliance.[121]

An expansive sanctions 'tool kit' that includes administrative fines and other non-criminal penalties was identified as the way forward, coupled with careful targeting and general use of variable and fixed monetary administrative penalties (MAPs).[122] As well as greater flexibility in the design of statutory notices, traditionally geared towards criminal sanctions, a role in cases of serious breach for enforceable undertakings was recognised. Voluntary but legally binding agreements of this kind provide a means for taking industry considerations and resources into account and for redress to affected parties.[123] Fitting with emergent EU requirements centred on environmental protection,[124] the use of criminal procedure could then be refined and sharpened.[125] Regulators could be expected to opt for prosecution over civil sanctions in 'top-end' offences such as cartels (the OFT), deliberate or reckless industrial pollution, and corporate killing (the HSE). MAPs would typically occupy the middle ground, with statutory notices clustered round minor or technical breaches.

The concepts of 'responsive' and 'smart' regulation thus gained tangible expression. A capacity to move up and down the hierarchy (or 'enforcement pyramid') of sanctioning options is implicit, underscoring flexibility. Subsequently incorporated in the Regulators' Compliance Code, the 'Macrory penalties principles' deal with structuring sanctions. Paralleling a move in the general criminal law, they are designed to open up such possibilities as restorative justice. Sanctions should:

- aim to change the behaviour of the offender (perhaps involving 'culture change within an organisation or a change in the production or manufacturing process')
- aim to eliminate any financial gain or benefit from non-compliance
- be responsive and consider what is appropriate for the particular offender and the regulatory issue ('the regulator should have the ability to use its

[121] *Macrory Review,* pp. 15–16. See also A. Ogus, 'Better regulation-better enforcement' in Weatherill (ed.), *Better Regulation* (Hart, 2007).

[122] So building on major sector-specific developments, e.g. the Financial Services and Markets Act 2000 which affords the FSA a wide range of administrative, civil and criminal sanctioning powers, including MAPs. The Health and Safety Offences Act 2008 is in similar vein.

[123] C. Parker, 'Restorative justice in business regulation? The Australian Competition and Consumer Commission's use of enforceable undertakings' (2004) 67 *MLR* 209.

[124] See Cases C-176/03 *Commission v Council* [2005] ECR 1-7879 and C-440/05 *Commission v Council* [2007] ECRI–9097; and, latterly, Commission, Directive 2008/99/EC on the Protection of the Environment through Criminal Law.

[125] See further R. Baldwin, 'The new punitive regulation' (2004) 67 *MLR* 351.

discretion and, if appropriate, base its decision on what sort of sanction would help bring the firm into compliance')

- be proportionate to the nature of the offence and the harm caused
- aim to restore the harm caused by regulatory non-compliance (such that 'business offenders take responsibility for their actions and its consequences')
- aim to deter future non-compliance ('firms should never think that non-compliance will be ignored or that they will "get away with it"').[126]

A more flexible sanctioning toolkit demands additional safeguards, most obviously to protect business from heavy-handed implementation. Assuming agency compliance with the Hampton principles of enforcement as a basic requirement, Macrory prescribed a seven-fold operating framework.[127] Regulators should:

- publish an enforcement policy
- measure outcomes ('impact') not just outputs (numbers of agency interventions)
- justify their choice of enforcement actions year on year to stakeholders, ministers and Parliament
- follow up their enforcement actions where appropriate
- enforce in a transparent manner (e.g. disclosing when and against whom action has been taken)
- be transparent in the way in which they apply and determine administrative penalties
- avoid perverse incentives that might influence the choice of sanctioning approach (e.g. internal 'targets' for different types of enforcement action or correlation with salary bonuses).

This too is taken up in the statutory code. Take accountability, where further emphasis is laid on the regulator's responsibility to render itself responsible:

> Regulators should ensure that clear reasons for any formal enforcement action are given to the person or entity against whom any enforcement action is being taken . . . Complaints and relevant appeals procedures for redress should also be explained . . .
>
> Regulators should provide effective and timely complaints procedures . . . that are easily accessible to regulated entities and other interested parties. They should publicise their complaints procedures, with details of the process and likely timescale for resolution. Complaints procedures should include a final stage to an independent, external person.

Creating a specialist regulatory tribunal, whereby MAPs would be made compliant with the institutional-procedural requirements of Art. 6, was the obvious

[126] *Macrory Review*, pp. 30–1. And see K. Yeung, *Securing Compliance* (Hart Publishing, 2004).
[127] *Ibid.*, pp. 32–3.

next step.[128] This fits both with a trend in economic regulation, where new life is breathed into the tribunal technique (see p. 321 below), and, in the form here of a 'General Regulatory Chamber', with the general move to a unified tribunal system able to accommodate new specialisms (see Chapter 11).

(e) New dispensation

Reworking Macrory's ideas, Part 3 of RESA provides for four broad categories of civil sanctions, which will now be available to regulators of all shapes and sizes:[129]

- fixed monetary penalty, with the amount of the relevant penalty prescribed in statutory instrument
- imposition of 'discretionary requirements', which include (a) variable monetary penalty, (b) 'compliance notice', requiring the operator to take specified steps to ensure that the offence does not continue or recur, and (c) 'restoration notice', requiring specified steps to restore the position, so far as possible, to what it would have been had the offence not been committed
- stop notice to prohibit the carrying on of a particular activity until the operator takes specified steps to come back into compliance, coupled with a duty to pay compensation in prescribed cases
- enforcement undertaking.

To levy a fine or impose other discretionary requirements the regulator must be 'satisfied beyond reasonable doubt' that the person has committed the particular regulatory offence; stop orders on the other hand require that the regulator 'reasonably believes that the activity . . . presents a serious risk of causing serious harm', and enforcement undertakings 'reasonable grounds to suspect' that the offence has been committed. Official estimates suggest that 30,000–40,000 prosecutions each year could metamorphose into civil sanctions. With rights of appeal both on liability and sanction, the General Regulatory Chamber may expect to be busy.

By choosing not to prosecute, regulators would be 'effectively ousting the jurisdiction of the ordinary courts'.[130] Invoking Dicey, the Lords' Constitutional Committee thus bewailed the looming 'transfer, on an unprecedented scale, of responsibilities for deciding guilt and imposing financial sanctions . . . away from independent and impartial judges to officials'. However, much like the famous Donoughmore Committee (see p. 36 above), this very contemporary articulation of 'red light' concerns was ill fated. Able to deploy in the politi-

[128] *Macrory Review*, pp. 53–6.

[129] RESA ss. 39–50 and Schs. 5–7. Echoing the compliance code, a regulator must publish detailed guidance on its enforcement and sanctions policies and be prepared to 'name and shame': RESA ss. 63–5.

[130] CC, *Regulatory Enforcement and Sanctions Bill*, HL 16 (2007/8), p. 3.

cal arena the twin facts of tribunal appeal and judicial review, ministers were well placed to see off this fundamentalist challenge to the onrush of regulatory power.

Ministerial tentacles are everywhere in what may be likened to a licensing system. Regulators are not automatically awarded the new powers. Rather, it is a matter of discretion to make rules by statutory instrument.[131] In order to be eligible, the minister must be satisfied that a regulator is in compliance with – of course – the five general principles of better regulation. This is the realm of 'Hampton implementation reviews' involving the NAO. The minister may also give directions suspending and revoking suspensions of regulators' powers to apply the sanctions in relation to particular offences (e.g. when the minister is satisfied that the agency has regularly failed to abide by Hampton principles of enforcement in that context).[132] Looking forwards, a patchwork of rules and regulations could result, a re-fragmented framework in which civil sanctions are available from time to time. 'The arrangements . . . risk being too complex and inaccessible to conform to one of the most basic facets of the rule of law, namely that the laws ought to be reasonably certain and accessible', warned the Constitution Committee.[133]

Whereas Macrory was concerned to increase public confidence, not least by establishing a more transparent system, much was heard in the legislative debates of the dangers of an adversarial 'ticket-writing culture' and of the regulatory focus shifting from 'catching the rogues' onto legitimate business.[134] Significant concessions were extracted under the banners of procedural fairness and protection from abuse of power. Thus procedures for levying fixed as well as variable monetary penalties must include a 'notice of intent' stage, so allowing the person to make written representations before the final decision is made; a monetary penalty cannot exceed the maximum fine for a summary offence. Importantly however, the Government resisted calls[135] for caps on variable monetary penalties for the more serious offences. The policy of being able to capture the benefit gained from non-compliance – a 'big stick in the cupboard' – would otherwise have been compromised.

(f) Consumer voice: Super-advocate

Regulatory arrangements designed for an age of international capital inevitably raise the question: who, amid the cacophony of voices, is actually heard? Echoing the general move in administrative law beyond individual protection to issues of collective access (see Chapter 4), the 2006 DTI *Consultation*

[131] Via affirmative resolution procedure: RESA ss. 36, 62. 'Ministers' for these purposes includes Welsh ministers.
[132] RESA ss. 66–8.
[133] CC, *Regulatory Enforcement and Sanctions Bill*, p. 2.
[134] See e.g. HL Deb., vol. 701, cols. 8–40 (third reading).
[135] CC, *Regulatory Enforcement and Sanctions Bill*, p. 4.

on Consumer Representation and Redress carefully emphasised the range of modalities:

> There are different forms of representation that consumers require. They value contact that can provide helpful information and advice. They may have complaints that need resolution or redress. And they need their interests to be promoted in the formulation and implementation of the policy framework within which everything happens. [136]

Conservative privatisation cast a long shadow. As explained further in Chapter 7, disparate consumer bodies had been created following the sector-specific model of the Ofdogs to whom they were largely subservient. Despite best efforts in policy development and advocacy, the National Consumer Council, set up as a company in 1975 and largely funded by the Government, was never able to make good the deficiency.[137] As part of the quest for a more rounded approach to economic regulation, fresh-faced New Labour had in turn focused on separating consumer representation from the regulatory offices so as to 'encourage more open debate on regulatory decisions and raise the profile of consumers within the regulatory process'.[138] As DTI made clear, the resulting hotchpotch of independent consumer councils, each with its own dedicated staff and resources, defined functions and rights to information, was no longer considered fit for purpose:

> The fragmented nature of consumer representation in the UK means that there is not a single, coherent, voice for the consumer which can reflect priorities across the different markets, or which can speak with expertise and authority for all consumers in discussion with companies, with Government, or in Europe. Consolidation. . . into a single, coherent, body would bring a number of specific benefits, including the critical mass to engage effectively. . . and the benefit of being able to draw on experience and expertise from a number of sectors. The new structure should also allow a reduction in the overall cost of consumer representation. [139]

This dovetailed with Hampton's view of an institutional geography of super-regulators. In this way 'manipulation' and 'therapy' or relegation to the bottom rungs of Arnstein's 'ladder of participation' (see p. 173 above) would be avoided, or so the argument went:

> The new 'Consumer Voice' would bring together specific duties and powers held by the existing sectoral consumer bodies with the National Consumer Council's remit as a

[136] DTI *Consultation on Consumer Representation and Redress* (2006) [2.4]. And see M. Harker, L. Mathieu and C. Price, 'Regulation and Consumer Representation' in Crew and Parker (eds.), *International Handbook on Economic Regulation.*

[137] See NCC, *In the Absence of Competition* (HMSO, 1989).

[138] DTI, *A Fair Deal for Consumers: Modernising the Framework for Utility Regulation*, Cm. 3898 (1998), p. 16.

[139] DTI, *Consultation on Consumer Representation and Redress* [2.19].

> wide-ranging single, independent, consumer champion, creating a powerful body, able to target resources appropriately to tackle consumer detriment wherever and whenever it emerges.
>
> The main functions of Consumer Voice would be to represent consumers in all markets, and provide information and advice on the consumer perspective to business, to Government, and to sectoral regulators. Consumer Voice would undertake cross-sectoral research proactively to identify key consumer issues, and play a key role in formulation of public policy both in the UK and in Europe . . . Sectoral duties that Consumer Voice would need to take on would include input into price reviews or other proposals that would have a major impact on consumers. The arrangements to establish Consumer Voice would take account of the need to retain sectoral expertise.[140]

The legal base is Part 1 of CEARA, the Consumers, Estate Agents and Redress Act 2007. In providing for three core elements, (a) representative function, (b) information function, and (c) research function, the Act speaks generously of the 'consumer' and of 'consumer matters', so ensuring a broad and flexible jurisdiction.[141] Subsequently given the title 'Consumer Focus', the new body has a regional presence in the different parts of the UK.[142] In determining priorities, it is required to proceed in transparent and consultative fashion through forward work programmes.[143] Illustrating the need for different actors to work constructively together, 'co-operation arrangements' must be entered into, including with the Office of Fair Trading, which continues to take the lead on consumer protection. The watchdog has powers to demand information from regulators and from operators but these are hedged round by ministerial restriction and cumbrous procedures.[144]

Some sectoral arrangements such as the gas and electricity and postal sectors fit better together than others; other bodies such as OFCOM's 'consumer panel', essentially concerned with policy advice, have been left intact.[145] But given the basic prescription of cohesion, empowerment and simplification, the new super-advocate can be expected to grow; there are many little-known consumer bodies that could easily be incorporated in a 'one-stop shop'.[146] Whether the consolidation comes at the expense of loss of focus – too many diverse topics for the 'super-advocate' properly to handle – remains to be seen.

[140] *Ibid.* [2.10] [2.12].

[141] 'Consumer' means 'a person who purchases, uses or receives . . . goods or services which are supplied in the course of a business': CEARA, s. 2.

[142] CEARA, s. 1 and Sch. 1. See further, Consumer Focus, Work Programme to March 2010 (2008).

[143] CEARA, s.10. Back-up powers include the power to investigate 'any matter which appears to the Council to be, or to be related to, a problem which affects or may affect consumers generally or consumers of a particular description'.

[144] CEARA, ss. 19, 23–8.

[145] See for details, DTI, *Summary of Responses and Government Response to Consultation on Consumer Representation and Redress* (2006).

[146] Examples are the Air Transport Users' Council and the Rail Passengers' Council.

Better complaints and redress systems are part of the package. Effectively standardising 'best practice', CEARA further empowers regulators to prescribe complaints-handling standards and the minister to insist that operators join an industry scheme such as an ombudsman.[147] 'Consumer Direct', a government-created telephone and on-line advice service, has been extended to cover enquiries and simple complaints in those sectors covered by the new super-advocate.[148] From the perspective of administrative law, this all illustrates the holistic idea of individual and collective 'voice', and more particularly the 'improvement' role of grievances, an aspect on which we focus in Chapter 10. 'Complaints data flowing back to Consumer [Focus] from Consumer Direct and the ombudsman [systems] will be a key input to the advocacy work.'[149]

6. Risk-based regulation

In earlier chapters we have emphasised the place of RBR as the dominant regulatory policy in recent years. It is then important to examine the way in which RBR operates in practice, with a view to assessing its place in administrative law. An appropriate angle of approach is in terms of rules and discretion, with RBR as a method of supposedly rational reasoning which structures and confines the agency's exercise of power. The determinedly mathematical style further attests the broad influence of audit technique.

Encapsulating the better regulation principle of 'targeting', RBR means (i) setting regulatory standards on the basis of assessment of risks of a given sector or activity; and (ii) assessing the risks that individual operators pose to an agency's goals and ordering regulatory activities accordingly. The methodology covers a wide spectrum of approaches: from an entire risk-based perspective or framework of regulatory governance to, at a minimum, the piecemeal use of technical risk-based tools commonly grounded in cost–benefit analysis.[150] Further illustrating how IT transforms the structures and use of public power, as with 'screen-level' and even 'system-level' bureaucracy (see p. 197 above), it is characterised by 'a move away from informal qualitatively based standard setting towards a more calculative and formalised approach'.[151] Imagine trying to construct and apply the targeting technologies described below using an old-fashioned card index!

The Environment Agency is a leader in the field, the more so in the light

[147] CEARA, ss. 42, 46–50. Otelo, the first established ombudsman for electronic communications, provided a model.

[148] See DTI *Consultation on Consumer Representation and Redress*, Ch. 5.

[149] *Ibid.* [2.16].

[150] C. Hood, H. Rothstein and R. Baldwin, *The Government of Risk: Understanding risk regulation regimes* (Oxford University Press, 2004); E. Fisher, *Risk Regulation and Administrative Constitutionalism* (Hart, 2007).

[151] B. Hutter, *The Attractions of Risk-based Regulation* (Centre for Risk and Regulation, 2005), p. 3.

of burgeoning EU requirements.[152] The risk-based format is part of a self-consciously 'modern approach' to regulation.[153] At the heart of this is 'Operator and Pollution Risk Appraisal' (OPRA), a screening methodology for profiling businesses which graphically illustrates the multiple factors and enumerations associated with the basic formula: *risk = impact* x *probability*. Take the hazards of industrial pollution:

> First, we look at the environmental risk of the specific processes. This includes the following:
>
> - what hazardous substances are stored?
> - what hazardous substances could be emitted?
> - how frequent is the process and how complicated is it?
> - how is the hazard controlled at source?
> - how are environmental emissions reduced?
> - how sensitive is the local environment to pollution?
> - are emissions likely to cause annoyance, such as a smell?
>
> We give each of these attributes a score from 1 (low hazard) to 5 (high hazard). We then add these together to give a total Pollution Hazard Appraisal (PHA) score. [A] map shows these scores for each process divided into bands – Band A for lowest pollution hazards and Band E for highest pollution hazards.
>
> Then, we look at the operator and their ability to manage the environmental risks of the processes they are engaged in. We look at the following attributes:
>
> - recording and use of information
> - knowledge and implementation of authorisation requirement
> - plant maintenance
> - management and training
> - process operation
> - incidents, complaints and non-compliance events
> - recognised environmental management systems.
>
> We give all of these attributes a score from 1 (low performance) to 5 (high performance) which we then add together to get the Operator Performance Appraisal (OPA). The datasets show Band A for the best operator, down to Band E for the worst operator.[154]

The methodology has increasingly informed the day-to-day enforcement work. The EA regularly founds requests for new plans and adaptations on poor scores for specific items, while sharply limiting the use of inspection post-Hampton.[155] There is however 'a certain level of imprecision . . . We try to be objective but

[152] The ECJ has itself elaborated a broad ranging 'precautionary principle': Case T-70/99 *Alpharma v Council* [2002] ELR II-3475; Case T-13/99 *Pfizer* [2002] ECR II-3305.

[153] EA, *Delivering for the Environment* (2005).

[154] EA, *Pollution hazards* (*IPC OPRA*) (2007), p. 1.

[155] HM Treasury, *Implementing Hampton*, pp. 18–19.

our officers do have to use judgement to apply scores.'[156] The agency has had to introduce a system of regional checks, with a view to ensuring that scores are applied accurately and consistently. Goodin, urging the inevitability of some discretions (see p. 209 above), could have predicted this.

The HSE has long experience of risk-based decision-making. For a national regulator comprising a staff of several thousand, and charged with ensuring compliance in literally hundreds of thousands of workplaces, it could scarcely be otherwise. HSE pioneered a more systematic approach, so detailing the scientific basis and criteria by which it would decide upon the degree and form of regulatory control across myriad sectors.[157] Here as elsewhere, however, public perceptions of risks and what is desirable to contain them are not always reconcilable with the technical 'expert'-driven modelling used in RBR.[158] HSE is well aware that the methodology is contestable:

> It may be [not] be possible to derive a quantifiable physical reality that most people will agree represents the 'true' risk from a hazard . . . The concept of risk is strongly shaped by human minds and cultures. Though it may include the prospect of physical harm, it may include other factors as well, such as ethical and social considerations, and even a degree of trust in the ability of those creating the risk (or in the regulator) in ensuring that adequate prevention and protective measures are in place for controlling the risks . . . Human judgment and values . . . determine which factors should be defined in terms of risk and action made subject to analysis . . .
>
> Even using all available data and best science and technology, many risk assessments cannot be undertaken without making a number of assumptions such as the relative values of risks and benefits or even the scope of the study. Parties who do not share the judgmental values implicit in those assumptions may well see the outcome of the exercise as invalid, illegitimate or even not pertinent to the problem. [159]

(a) 'ARROW'

As a targeting technology ARROW – the elaborate 'Advanced Risk Response Operating Framework' of the Financial Services Authority – has taken RBR to new heights. In modelling the system, the designers naturally began with the statutory objectives assigned the new agency: market confidence, public understanding, consumer protection and reduction of financial crime.[160] However in light of such a broad mandate, considered difficult to operationalise,[161] they focused on how, why and in what circumstances these might *not* be achieved.

[156] EA, *More about OPRA Scores* (2007), p. 1.

[157] HSE, *Reducing Risk, Protecting People* (2001).

[158] As notoriously with food technologies: M. Lee, *EU Regulation of GMOs* (Edward Elgar, 2008).

[159] HSC, *A Strategy for Work Place Health and Safety in Great Britain to 2020 and Beyond* (2004), p. 11.

[160] Financial Services and Markets Act 2000, s. 2.

[161] C. Sergeant, 'Risk-based regulation in the Financial Services Authority' (2002) 10 *J. of Financial Regulation and Compliance* 329.

'Risks to objectives' (RTOs), e.g. financial failure or market abuse, were duly classified as arising from three main sources: external environment, consumer and industry wide developments and the individual institutions themselves. As well as 'watch lists' of particular firms, senior agency officials now felt sufficiently confident to embark on 'risk maps':

> We started out with an impact analysis, and that involved trying to identify measures to show what would be the size of the impact on the FSA's ability to deliver its objectives if a particular risk materialised. We then drew on supervisors' judgements and their existing knowledge of particular sectors and institutions . . . We allocated institutions to four impact bands – high, medium one, medium two and low . . . In cases like banks and building societies, we were looking at total assets and liabilities . . . In other cases, like credit unions, we looked at the number of members as perhaps the best measure . . . Of the 9,000 firms we currently supervise . . . roughly 80% by number of institutions are low impact, roughly 15% are medium two, roughly 4% are medium one and less than 1% is high impact. [Conversely] on market share, the high impact [firms] account for roughly 65% of the total market share, medium one roughly 24%, medium two 8%, and low impact . . . just over 3% . . .
>
> The next stage was to assess the likelihood or probability . . . Particular kinds of risk – credit risk, market risk, operational systems and control risk – involved building up a risk profile of each institution . . . Some of those aspects are quite easy to quantify, questions like financial strength; others of course are much more qualitative and require informed judgement by the regulator – judgement of the quality of management for example. We have also . . . tried to take account of the effect of external environmental factors . . . Problems from one institution in a particular country or a region can quickly spill over into other institutions in that region that have a UK presence . . .
>
> Assessments for high and medium impact firms show that it is only 0.5% of these firms [that are] rated both high impact and high probability – that is probably just as well from a regulator's point of view . . . [162]

It was assumed that the thoroughness of the probability assessment would be driven by the firm's impact rating. Whereas those designated 'low' impact might have little individual supervision, 'high' and 'middling' impact firms should expect visits of varying frequency to review operating and control systems ('meta-regulation'). FSA supervisors should in turn be generating tailored sets of 'risk-mitigation programmes' for firms to adopt: a determinedly contemporary form of 'fire-watching' underwritten by reporting requirements and ultimately enforcement action. Best practice requires the process to be highly dynamic however, such that material changes of circumstance are closely monitored and individual risk assessments adapted accordingly. In particular, 'vertical' (firm-based) supervision needs to be supplemented by

[162] M. Foot, 'Our new approach to risk-based regulation' (FSA, 2000), pp. 2–3. See also, FSA, *A New Regulator for the New Millennium* (2000).

thematic or 'horizontal' analysis of market developments, as under the broad rubric of 'external environment'.[163]

In structuring the exercise of regulatory power, ARROW confines it. Because only the risks to the FSA's own objectives are factored, those relating e.g. to shareholder value typically fall under the radar. 'It is not our role to restrict appropriate risk taking by authorised firms.'[164] A self-assessment lays bare the regulatory philosophy that has prevailed hitherto:

> Given the many possible events that could have a negative effect on the financial markets and our limited resources, our risk-based approach is based on a clear statement of the realistic aims and limits of regulation. In other words, we accept that we can never entirely eliminate risks to the statutory objectives we have been set by Parliament – our 'non-zero failure' approach. And although the idea that regulation should seek to eliminate all failures may look superficially appealing, in practice this would impose prohibitive costs on the industry and consumers . . . We regularly review the amount of risk we are prepared to accept and focus our resources on the risks that matter most. By doing so, we believe we can make the greatest overall difference in the UK financial services market, without stifling competitiveness.[165]

'Regulatory competition' (especially with the American securities markets) has been a main driver. 'Delivering a lighter regulatory touch for those firms that pose less risk to our statutory objectives, [ARROW] has been one of our principal methods of delivering regulation in an efficient and economic way'.[166] As such, it is intimately bound up with FSA experiments in 'principles-based' regulation: the replacement of detailed rules with short, high-level, requirements – e.g. 'a firm must conduct its business with integrity' – and accompanying guidance.'[167] An approach, that is, which assumes a high degree of trust.

Following a lengthy review, the FSA concluded that ARROW needed fine-tuning. Launched in 2006, 'ARROW II' aimed at:

> - Better communication with firms concerning our assessment of them;
> - Greater efficiency and effectiveness on our management of risk, and sharing and making better use of the knowledge we have;
> - Greater proportionality and consistency in response to risks, applying our resources where they will make the most difference;
> - Improved skills and supervisory knowledge of our staff;
> - A major overhaul to our risk model, allowing better comparison of risks in different areas so we can more reliably devote our resources to the areas of greatest risk.[168]

163 FSA, *The Firm Risk Assessment Framework* (2006) Chs. 3–4 ('ARROW II').
164 Foot, 'Our new approach to risk-based regulation', p. 1.
165 'ARROW II', p. 7.
166 'ARROW II', p. 5.
167 FSA, *Principles-based Regulation: Focusing on the outcomes that matter* (2007); C. Ford, 'New governance, compliance, and principles-based securities regulation' (2008) 45 *American Business Law Review* 1.
168 'ARROW II', p. 6.

(b) Balance sheet

RBR has a range of attractions, not least for the super-regulator. The more mathematical bent gives such agencies a common language, allows for comparison across different parts ('to which sectors should we direct resources?'), and constitutes a means for hierarchical control of junior officers' discretion. As such, this rapidly developing methodology not only echoes the administrative law themes of 'structuring' and 'confining' discretion with rules introduced by Davis (see Chapter 5), but has increasingly operated on a scale and with an intensity he could never have envisaged.

RBR links with other indirect strategies, so helping to frame the mixing of public with private powers typical of 'governance'. Chiefly, it unlocks the potentials of 'meta-regulation'. As the basis on which much in the 'risk maps' is constructed, and monitoring functions performed, gaining leverage through firms' own systems of governance is an article of faith. Agency resources are conserved and the primary responsibility for ensuring appropriate standards is vested where it is thought to belong. In the form of 'responsive regulation', RBR admits of carrots as well as sticks, with suitably conscientious operators earning more autonomy – less supervision – over time.[169] The methodology also allows opportunities for 'co-regulation' with trade associations and professional bodies in the context of a more principles-based approach.[170]

Agencies may also favour RBR as a useful source of legitimacy. The FSA for example has made much of the apparent objectivity and transparency of ARROW: 'From the point of view of those we regulate, our interventions in the marketplace can be justified in terms of the level of risk to our statutory objectives and consequent harm that would otherwise be present.'[171] This however begs the question: 'who decides which "failures" are acceptable and which are not?' Contentious decisions are 'masked in the technical structure of the risk-based framework'. For proper accountability, the regulators themselves 'need to be "turned inside out"'.[172]

Much depends on the regulator's own appetite for risk. While commonly presented as 'light-touch', RBR can prove burdensome for operators by reason of a voracious appetite for data. The calculations themselves may be daunting, not least because of the difficulty of comparing incommensurables in such (contested) fields as health and safety. There is, too, an inherent problem of equity. Things that look rational to the regulator may seem different from the standpoint of individuals who suffer in consequence, as when it turns out

169 See e.g. 'ARROW II', p. 27. This approach is also prevalent in the public sector, as in the case of 'foundation hospitals': see, M. Goddard and R. Mannion, 'Decentralising the NHS: Rhetoric, reality and paradox' (2006) *J. of Health Organisation and Management* 67.

170 See e.g. FSA, *Confirmation of Industry Guidance* (2006).

171 'ARROW II', p. 7.

172 J. Black, 'The Emergence of risk-based regulation and the new public risk management in the United Kingdom' (2005) *PL* 512, 547–8.

that small operator 'low impact' firms commonly serve poorer sections of the community. Viewed from the perspective of judicial review, the principles of equality and consistency or non-discrimination cast a shadow.

The risk is that risk-based tools 'will be too literally and slavishly believed in'.[173] Not only is the technical complexity of 'risk maps' apt to obscure the underlying process of reducing structures and activities to numbers. Such apparently rational systems can also gloss over systemic risk or the big picture. The enterprise in fact has a paradoxical flavour. By dealing with uncertainty on the basis that the exercise of public power can be effectively ordered and managed by means of algorithm, RBR runs the risk of hobbling the responsiveness of the agency. 'If the safest thing to do is to follow the framework, the safest thing to do is not to respond to any circumstances or events which are not anticipated by that framework.'[174] In the case of the FSA, such elements have now been brutally exposed by a seizing-up of the financial markets and a sudden economic recession. Future historians will surely remark on how an era of transnational financial speculation – all too easily off the official radar screen – helped constitute the conditions of mass regulatory failure at domestic level.

(c) Disaster

2007 witnessed a harbinger of bad economic climes: the first major run on a British bank since the mid-nineteenth century. An aggressive player in the mortgage-lending market, Northern Rock had fallen victim to the worldwide credit crunch, so being driven – in very public fashion – to seek emergency funding from the Bank of England. Faced with thousands of depositors queuing to withdraw their savings, ministers eventually passed the Banking (Special Provisions) Act 2008, which allowed for nationalisation. While the bank's executives obviously bore primary responsibility for a reckless business strategy (borrowing 'short' and lending 'long'), the City of London's much-vaunted regulatory structure had hardly distinguished itself. According to the Treasury Select Committee, the establishment of a 'tripartite framework', with the Treasury, the Bank of England, and the FSA each having discrete responsibilities for the maintenance of the financial system, had resulted in a lack of leadership and coherent view. And while ARROW sounded well, the FSA had 'systematically failed in its duty as a regulator to ensure Northern Rock would not pose such a systemic risk'.[175] The FSA's own audit confirmed a catalogue of error: no detailed financial analysis; lengthened periods between risk assessments; no risk mitigation programmes failure to re-assess as market conditions worsened and so on. The affair had effectively highlighted the fact that RBR methodology is only as good as the personnel:

[173] Hutter, *The Attractions of Risk-based Regulation*, p. 13.

[174] Black, 'The emergence of risk-based regulation', p. 543.

[175] Treasury Select Committee, *The Run on the Rock*, HC 56 (2006/7), p. 34, and *Financial Stability and Transparency*, HC 371 (2007/8). A permanent statutory regime for dealing with failing banks is now provided by the Banking Act 2009.

> More management time should be spent on assessing and engaging with internal supervisory judgements and decisions, as well as on assessing and challenging firms in particular areas . . . One of the themes emerging . . . has been the apparent ease with which individual members of staff have been able not to comply with established processes (for example recording key meetings, document filing, updating the FSA's database).[176]

Some fine-tuning was suggested, in the form of a supervisory enhancement programme aimed at securing more rigorous use of the existing framework. ARROW, despite the bad miss, remains in place. Yet fuelling the demand for heightened supervision, the problems appear deep-rooted. In light of the subsequent turmoil across the financial markets, a more thoroughgoing agency response has been called for as part of a package of (international) institutional and market reforms. More intrusive and more systemic, the talk now is of 'a major shift' in the FSA's supervisory approach with:

- increased resources devoted to high impact firms and especially large complex banks
- focus on business models, strategies, risks and outcomes, rather than primarily on systems and processes
- development of capabilities in macro-prudential analysis
- focus on technical skills as well as probity of approved persons
- increased analysis of sectors and comparative analysis of firm performance
- investment in specialist prudential skills
- more intensive information requirements on key risks (e.g. liquidity)
- major intensification of bank balance sheet analysis and oversight of accounting judgements
- focus on remuneration policies.[177]

Time will tell.

7. The EU (and global) connection

The scale of regulatory policy-making at Community level is today enormous, ranging from environmental protection to competition law, and consumer product safety to the regulation of banking and financial services. Reasons are not difficult to find. As highlighted in the drive to the Single Market in the 1980s,[178] the profusion of national regulatory regimes has long been recognised as a barrier to Member State trade. Also, Community regulation is a relatively inexpensive instrument of governance for the institutions, which enhances their power and status.[179]

[176] FSA, *Supervision of Northern Rock* (2008), p. 8. And see FSA, *Financial Stability and Depositor Protection* (2008), p. 8

[177] FSA, *The Turner Review: A regulatory response to the global banking crisis* (March, 2009), p. 8.

[178] Commission, *White Paper on Completing the Internal Market*, COM (85), p. 310.

[179] G. Majone, *Regulating Europe* (Routledge, 1996).

The early preference for harmonisation or integrated regulation proved cumbersome, and discouraging of innovation by producers. The so-called 'new approach' was to restrict harmonisation to minimum essential requirements and leave the task of either filling in the details or fixing standards above minimum requirements to the Member States or the Comitology.[180] Post-enlargement, the emphasis has shifted to the principle of subsidiarity, whereby regulation within the EU should be pursued at the lowest level consistent with effectiveness, and 'soft law' techniques of governance such as OMC (see Chapter 5).[181] The Commission has also in the last few years embraced the idea of 'better regulation'.[182] Today, much is heard in Brussels of 'impact assessment' and 'regulatory simplification'.[183]

All this has a profound impact on regulation in the domestic administrative law system. Whether at UK or regional level, government departments, local government and independent agencies have a positive role to play, by virtue of the many shared and indirect elements in the administration of Community law. At the same time, the capacity of domestic regulators and legislators to dictate a regulatory strategy may be closely affected; it has to be remembered that the Commission may take action against Member State infringements of Community law (TEC Arts. 226, 228). The emphasis has been on erosion of national regulatory jurisdictions but there are other more subtle implications for domestic regulatory practice. As the Davidson review showed (see p. 184 above), 'over-implementation' is all too easy. The obligation on the UK government to demonstrate effective compliance with, and enforcement of, Community norms leads inevitably to juridification,[184] centralisation and oversight of local regulatory power – in the context of devolution a potential source of friction.[185] A key UK policy aim in recent years has been the export of 'better regulation' to Brussels.[186] Given the scale of inter-penetration of regulatory law and practice, what otherwise would be the point of a radical national reform agenda?

(a) Rule of networks

Featuring diverse and fluid forms of collaboration and co-ordination across the multi-level system, as also a broad range of actors (ministers and officials,

[180] Premised on the principle of 'mutual recognition', established in the famous *Cassis de Dijon* case: Case 120/78 *Rewe-Zentrale AG v Bundesmonopolverwaltung für Branntwein* [1979] ECR 649.

[181] Commission, *White Paper on European Governance*, COM (2001) 428.

[182] Commission, *Better Regulation for Growth and Jobs in the European Union*, COM (2005) 97, and *A strategic review of Better Regulation in the European Union*, COM (2006), 689.

[183] Commission, *Action Plan for Reducing Administrative Burdens in the European Union*, COM (2007), 23. See further, Weatherill (ed.), *Better Regulation*.

[184] T. Daintith, 'European Community law and the redistribution of regulatory power in the United Kingdom' (1995) 1 *ELJ* 134.

[185] As evidenced by the collaborative provisions of the *Concordat on Co-ordination of European Union Policy Issues*, Cm. 5240 (2001).

[186] See e.g. the joint statement by the Irish, Dutch, Luxembourg, UK, Austrian and Finnish Presidencies, *Advancing regulatory reform in Europe* (2004). For the EU policy development from a UK perspective, see EUC, *Regulation in the EU*, HL 33 (2005/6).

committees and agencies, and public and private bodies and groupings), European regulatory development exemplifies the growth of network governance.[187] This too has important ramifications for national administrative law. Reducing the decision-making burden by co-operating on supervisory approaches and standards with specialist foreign counterparts has obvious attractions, especially with risk-oriented regulatory regimes.

The OFT is part of the 'European Competition Network', a decentralised and multi-level system in which enforcement of EC competition law is a shared responsibility of the Commission and national agencies. Provision for the exchange of confidential information and re-allocation of cases with a cross-border dimension is at the heart of this.[188] Relevant 'soft law' developments promoting consistency include detailed Commission guidelines, a pan-European system of liaison officers and a plethora of working groups for establishing best practice.[189] The OFT thus wears two hats, being part of the domestic administrative law system while becoming increasingly integrated in the EU administration.[190]

We have also seen the rise of 'the European agency'[191] to which national sectoral counterparts will be 'networked' in. We can see this especially with the Food Standards Agency, set up like its European counterpart – the European Food Standards Agency – in the wake of the BSE crisis ('mad cow disease').[192] The national agency's website is replete with contributions to, and opinions emanating from, the scientific advisory work of EFSA. The pace of development is well illustrated by the Civil Aviation Authority's 2006 annual review:

> Aviation regulation in Europe has been changing at almost every level and there is little that the CAA does that is not affected in some way. A few examples make the point: our consumer responsibilities bring us into contact with European rules on denied boarding, cancellations and delays; our airspace responsibilities immerse us in the Single European Sky (SES); our economic work is involving us in Europe-wide discussions on topics such as slot allocation and airspace charging; and our safety responsibilities bring us into close contact with the European Aviation Safety Agency (EASA). EASA is the body which started operations

[187] H. Hofman and A. Turk (eds.), *EU Administrative Governance* (Edward Elgar, 2006); D. Curtin and M. Egeberg (eds), *Towards a New Executive Order in Europe?* (West European Politics special issue, 2008).

[188] Regulation 1/2003 on the implementation of the rules on competition laid down in Arts. 81–2 of the Treaty.

[189] I. Maher, *The Rule of Law and Agency: The case of competition policy* (Chatham House, 2006).

[190] See further, E. O'Neill and E. Scaife, *UK Competition Procedure: The modernised regime* (Oxford University Press, 2007).

[191] D. Gerardin, R. Munoz and N. Petit (eds.), *Regulation through Agencies in the EU: A new paradigm of European governance* (Edward Elgar, 2006). Confusingly however, these bodies are not 'regulatory agencies' as that term is commonly understood in the Anglo-American tradition, being more or less strictly confined to making individualised decisions, to advisory functions and exercising influence, and to information and co-ordination. See further, P. Craig, *EU Administrative Law* (Oxford University Press, 2006), Ch. 5.

[192] Food Standards Act 1999.

in September 2003 and which is now responsible for aircraft certification and maintenance regulation across Europe. There are plans to add operations and licensing to those responsibilities shortly. [[193]] All EU Member States and their National Aviation Authorities (NAAs) are committed to the EASA system. For safety regulation this is undeniably the way of the future and promises significant benefits, provided EASA's supporting systems and regulatory framework are fully fit for purpose to realise those benefits, and sound working relationships are fostered between EASA and NAAs throughout Europe. For the CAA, it is crucial that EASA develops the ability to assist us and the British aviation industry in delivery of the Government's key safety policy objective, which is to maintain the UK's present high safety standards, identify possible threats and seek appropriate improvements.[194]

European regulatory harmonisation is facilitated through a bewildering array of formal and informal 'horizontal' networks of national bodies. Some are situated at the heart of the functioning economy, e.g. 'European Regulators Groups' for electricity and gas and for telecommunications, and the 'Committee of European Securities Regulators' (CESR). These influence policy agendas and cannot be lightly dismissed as talking shops.[195] From the standpoint of national administrative law, a growing trend (whereby domestic routines of enforcement become more Europeanised) is very significant. This is illustrated by the creation in 2005 of the Community Fisheries Control Agency, a response to the problem of dwindling stocks and of unscrupulous local practice that Commission infringement action has been unable to halt.[196] While the domestic authorities (for English and Welsh waters, the Marine and Fisheries Agency) remain responsible for securing compliance, CFCA is given powers to coordinate control and inspection activities and the deployment of Member State resources against illegal fishing.

(b) Going global

With the increased exercise of regulatory authority by international or transnational institutions across many fields,[197] national authorities must also master the art of standard-setting on the global stage, not least with a view to enabling national regulatory policies and practices. Examples are all around. Though today much of its policy-making effort is driven by European initiatives, the Financial Services Authority engages with a range of international

[193] Regulation 216/2008 on common rules in the field of civil aviation and establishing a European Aviation Safety Authority.

[194] CAA, *Annual Review 2006*, pp. 3–4.

[195] D. Coen and M. Thatcher, *After Delegation: The evolution of European networks of regulatory agencies* (CEPR, 2006).

[196] Regulation 768/2005 establishing a Community Fisheries Control Agency. And see e.g. Case C-304/02 *Commission v France* [2005] I-6263.

[197] J. Braithwaite and P. Drahos, *Global Business Regulation* (Cambridge University Press, 2000); A-M Slaughter, *A New World Order* (Princeton, 2004).

bodies.[198] Looking forwards, international co-operation and co-ordination in this regulatory sphere will no doubt increase in the wake of the world-wide credit crunch.[199] Or take the CAA, which has 'playing a full part in international aviation organisations in support of the UK's needs' in its mission statement. For a self-styled world leader in the sector, how could it be otherwise? Top of the list is the International Civil Aviation Organisation;[200] national regulation is moulded in its image.

Demonstrating a very wide range of lobbying, negotiating and general networking activity, the case of the Food Standards Agency suffices to underscore the theme:

> With the diverse range of foods from around the globe available to people in the UK and with free trade and markets within the European Union, the Agency aims to ensure that imported foods meet the required UK standards, in order to protect the safety and interests of the consumer. As a result the Agency is playing an increasingly important role internationally, representing the UK Government on joint international bodies and making food safety information available to other countries and organisations. Developing relations with international organisations plays an equally important role, and the Agency has an interest in the work of several international organisations . . . The most significant fora in which other countries participate and the FSA has a varied interest are:
>
> - Codex Alimentarius Commission
> - World Health Organisation (WHO)
> - Food and Agriculture Organisation of the United Nations (FAO)
> - World Trade Organisation (WTO)
> - World Organisation for Animal Health (OIE)
>
> In particular, the FSA negotiates on behalf of the UK Government in the joint FAO/WHO body, Codex Alimentarius Commission, which was created to develop food standards, guidelines and related texts such as codes of practice. By active involvement in meetings and contributing to the EU's input to Codex, the Agency aims to influence the standards set for food traded globally and for better consumer involvement in the development of standards.[201]

8. Conclusion

British regulatory practice has come a long way in a short time, taking on much greater prominence. This reflects in part the transformation in state forms, and in part changes in regulatory style and culture (the processes of formalisation and juridification described in earlier chapters). Illuminating the political dimension of administrative law – so often downplayed – the path

[198] Especially the Basel Committee on Banking Supervision.
[199] See now the communiqué from the G20 Summit in London in 2009.
[200] (Chicago) Convention on International Civil Aviation (9th edn, 2006).
[201] Food Standards Agency, *How we work: International ordering* (2008).

of UK regulatory reform is characterised by mood-swings. The fashion for 'deregulation' inevitably raised concerns about sub-optimal control; attempts at 're-balancing' under the more generous rubric of better regulation have recently led to a conscious effort at 'de-burdening'. European and global forces of marketisation have created a strong lobbying role for domestic agencies in supranational regulatory networks.

State actors have also been experimenting with an array of regulatory tools and techniques. A classic administrative law device like licensing is given fresh twists; anti-trust powers are more widely disseminated among agencies; the new empire of risk-based regulation colonises more and more areas of economic and social life; the future belongs, or so it seems, to 'regulatory justice'. The endless official statements of regulatory principle sound well but there is a real risk of 'over-juridification': regulators being hamstrung by too many rules and too much codification. The process of regulation is itself increasingly regulated. In the name of 'better regulation' bureaucratic regulation is piled on bureaucratic regulation and central control is reasserted through a plethora of directions and guidance.

The most recent phase of UK regulatory reform shows the administrative law landscape changing dramatically. An elite group of super-regulators has emerged as a great power in the land. Officially justified in terms of efficiency and effectiveness, let us hope they do not come to resemble lumbering elephants. Reflecting and reinforcing ideas of 'responsive regulation' and 'collaborative governance', creative blends of government and self-regulation are also much to the fore. Modish techniques of meta-, meso-, and co-regulation show major vulnerabilities however. As with RBR, regulators may be blinded.

Complex mixes of public with private power have been engendered. First came the strong move away from the explicitly 'public' – privatisation coupled with private law. With an eye to good governance values, concerns were raised about the ability of administrative law to reach out and encompass the new modalities (see p. 94 above). Increased 'harnessing' of private power has followed, with self-regulatory systems themselves being hollowed out in the service of the regulatory state. All this presents us with another set of challenges in terms of institutional design and accountability. Today, far from a general retreat of public power, regulatory governance casts a lengthening shadow.

7

Regulatory design and accountability

Contents

As major repositories of public power, the institutional design and accountability of regulatory agencies are important matters. The more so, it may be said, in this era of 'super-agencies'. A host of questions arises for the student of law and administration. Will the statutory framework provide sufficient guidance? Is the agency given the appropriate tools for the job? Are good governance values such as transparency properly reflected in the design? Individually and collectively are the external lines of accountability up to the task? Or are they apt to confuse (or be confused)? We see immediately that, embedded though they now are as generally accepted statements of regulatory best practice, the better regulation principles do not exhaust the field.

'Public + private' as well as 'public vs private',[1] contemporary developments happening under the broad rubric of 'governance' give all this an additional twist. In what ways are self-regulatory organisations (SROs) appropriately harnessed in the public interest? How is the delegation and re-delegation of powers in a co-regulatory system properly organised? Alternatively, a problem exacerbated in the EU context,[2] how in this challenging landscape of overlapping functions and fluid networks can the consumer interest be properly vindicated and effective lines of accountability secured? We will see serious efforts being made to match the advance in agency powers with more open and protective procedures, but this should not be allowed to obscure the underlying potential with systems of governance for 'passing the buck'.

1. The agency model

(a) Risen tide

The rise of agencies in general, and regulatory agencies in particular, is a recurring theme in this book. Consider the position some forty years ago, when, in a comparative study, Schwartz and Wade[3] commented on the sharp distinction with administrative law in the US. The American federal system had long been agency-oriented, partly by reason of the New Deal (see p. 33 above). Instruments of government regulation such as the Interstate Commerce Commission (1887) and the Federal Power Commission (1930) were a chief battleground for law as an instrument of administrative policy and in defence of private rights, and, latterly, for law as a resource for wider, collective interests (interest representation).[4] In contrast, Schwartz and Wade observed, 'this kind of regulatory agency scarcely exists in Britain' and is 'difficult to compare with British institutions'. Perhaps this was an exaggeration, given the role of such bodies as the Monopolies Commission (1948) and the Independent Television Authority (1954), as well as a crop of agencies then on the horizon, including the Civil Aviation Authority (1972) and the Health and Safety Commission (1974).[5] Nonetheless, it conveyed an essential truth, that Britain did not have a strong tradition of using the agency model of government regulation.

[1] L. Salamon in Salamon (ed.), *The Tools of Government: A guide to the new governance* (Oxford University Press, 2002).

[2] J. Scott and D. Trubek, 'Mind the gap: Law and new approaches to governance in the European Union' (2002) 8 *ELJ* 1.

[3] B. Schwartz and H. Wade, *Legal Control of Government* (Clarendon Press, 1972).

[4] See for an excellent overview, G. Lawson, *Federal Administrative Law*, 3rd edn (West, 2004).

[5] T. Prosser, *Law and the Regulators* (Clarendon Press, 1997), Ch. 2; M. Moran, *The British Regulatory State* (Oxford University Press, 2003), Ch. 3.

One explanation lay in the dominant Westminster style of government. Premised on ministerial responsibility, and so on a simple principal-agent model or chain of delegation[6] from legislature to executive and hence civil servants, the centralist practices of parliamentarianism did not readily permit the development of independent regulatory agencies (IRAs).[7] In addition, agencies that combine powers treated as distinct in Dicey's 'balanced constitution' were considered constitutionally awkward or even monstrous.[8] Another explanation is of course the post-war preference for public ownership as distinct from the private sector-plus-regulator model. Schwartz and Wade believed that 'it would never be thought right' in Britain to devolve the control of major industries such as rail or power 'where decisions of the utmost political and economic importance have to be taken and for which responsibility to Parliament is indispensable'.[9]

Conversely, the explanations for the rise of the regulatory agency go beyond political fashions. Independence from, or an arm's-length relationship with, government is said to facilitate the continuity of, and flexibility or responsiveness in, policy formulation and implementation, and also a disinterested expertise. In addition, that is, to helping to deflect criticism or political responsibility and reducing government overload.[10] The specialist, multi-functional agency fits well the model of government regulation as sustained and focused control. Expressive of the demand for 'joined-up' regulatory activity, as well as for economies of scale, the new breed of super-agency reflects and reinforces these general elements, not least in complex and contested matters of risk regulation. And the push in this direction from Europe is ongoing.

Two parliamentary reports show just how far the UK administrative law system has travelled. In a wide-ranging study of regulatory accountability published in 2004, the Constitution Committee (CC) aimed to reconcile the values of independence and control. Post-privatisation there was however no rolling back the agencies. 'Traditional mechanisms of accountability may therefore have to be reinforced, or reviewed and adapted, where necessary, to the new arrangements.'[11] A 2007 review of economic regulators by the ad hoc Select Committee on Regulators (RC) assigned 'quasi-constitutional status' to what

[6] D. Kiewiet and M. McCubbins, *The Logic of Delegation* (University of Chicago Press, 1991); K. Strom, W. Muller and T. Bergman (eds.), *Delegation and Accountability in Parliamentary Democracies* (Oxford University Press, 2003).

[7] The use of boards and commissions had declined in the nineteenth century as government expanded and Parliament demanded more direct ministerial control of state activity; see Ch. 2 above.

[8] R. Baldwin and C. McCrudden, *Regulation and Public Law* (Weidenfeld & Nicolson, 1987), Ch 1.

[9] Schwartz and Wade, *Legal Control of Government*, p. 41. C. Walker, 'Governance of the critical national infrastructure' [2008] *PL* 323, gives another perspective.

[10] See on the broad historical development, M. Everson, 'Independent agencies: Hierarchy beaters' (1995) 1 *ELJ* 180; and M. Thatcher, 'Regulation after delegation: Independent regulatory agencies in Europe' (2002) 9 *JEPP* 954.

[11] CC, *The Regulatory State: Ensuring its accountability,* HL 68 (2003/4), p. 6.

was now tellingly described as 'the regulatory estate'.[12] 'It was taken as read by the regulators, the regulated and the Government that the regulators are to be fully independent and that no undue influence should be put on them at any point.'[13]

While the independence of regulatory agencies from elected authority is commonly regarded as their chief virtue, not least in the markets, the agency model of regulatory governance itself implies sophisticated wiring systems. For reasons of coherence and control, those 'steering' must themselves be 'steered'. In the typically understated language of Whitehall: 'it is helpful for regulators to be given guidance by government on issues that are matters of public policy'.[14] Encompassing such matters as 'standards in public life' (see p. 54 above), but centred in particular on VFM audit (below), flanking techniques of bureaucratic regulation are much in evidence. There is independence, and there is independence.[15]

(b) Design kit

But if powerful regulatory agencies were here to stay, how should they be designed (and evaluated)? Spurred by the evident defects of the Ofdog model (see p. 249 above), the search for 'legitimacy' – as expressed in terms of the core values which agencies need to satisfy in order to merit and receive public approval[16] – became a leitmotif of UK administrative law in the 1990s. An important link was being made with regulatory effectiveness: 'many regulators operate without sufficient legitimacy to do their job with full confidence, weakening the regulatory environment and prompting agencies to operate defensively'.[17]

Baldwin has identified five main sources of agency legitimacy[18] (there is naturally considerable overlap with the various principles of 'good' and 'better' regulation propounded by successive governments[19]):

- *Legislative mandate*: agency action deserves support when authorised explicitly by the people's representatives in Parliament. The greater the agency discretion however, the less a statutory mandate can be used to justify actions and policies.

12 See HL Deb., vol. 700, cols. 1224–50.

13 RC, *UK Economic Regulators*, HL 189 (2006/7), p. 71.

14 BERR, *Government Response to the Select Committee on Regulators* (2008), p. 4.

15 See further, M. Thatcher, 'The third force? Independent agencies and elected politicians in Europe' (2005) 18 *Governance* 347.

16 R. Baldwin, *Rules and Government* (Clarendon, 1995). Note also the pioneering study by J. Freedman, *Crisis and Legitimacy: The administrative process and American government* (Cambridge University Press, 1978).

17 Constitutional Reform Centre, 'Regulatory agencies in the United Kingdom' (1991) 44 *Parl. Affairs* 504, 507.

18 Baldwin, *Rules and Government*.

19 As also with a well-known set of models of administrative justice devised by Mashaw: see p. 447 below.

- *Expertise*: traditional rationale for agency model and redolent of 'trust'; sits comfortably with wide agency discretion.[20] Much to the fore, and frequently contested, in the vital arena of risk regulation,[21] it finds tangible expression in judicial 'deference' to highly technical regulatory decisions (see p. 314 below).
- *Efficiency*: range of measures, including productive efficiency (agency costs), contribution to allocative efficiency (for example, by regulating for competition), and contribution to dynamic efficiency (for example, by encouraging product innovation). It is a standard 'better regulation' component in the choice of regulatory instruments by policy-makers and agency officials.
- *Due process*: expressive of the search in public law for a better quality of administrative justice. It places a premium on agencies adopting fair administrative procedures, maximising consistency and equality of treatment, transparency and participation of outside interests. (One might wish to add good governance values and respect for human rights.)
- *Accountability*: view of agency decisions being rendered more acceptable by effective means of scrutiny or 'answerability', which itself is 'a key discipline on regulators'.[22] It is given a very contemporary edge by the new regime of regulatory sanctions (see p. 265 above).

For the architects and controlling minds of agencies there are several key messages.[23] One is of an irreducible core of both legal and administrative elements. 'Strong claims across the board point to regulation that deserves support, generally weak claims indicate a low capacity to justify'. Performance under different headings may also be linked. A regulatory process perceived as unfair could well suffer low levels of co-operation, so impeding fulfilment of the mandate. While trade-offs are inevitable, appropriate weightings being 'the meat and drink' of regulatory debates, institutional designs scoring very poorly in a particular category are best avoided. 'What matters is the collective justificatory power'. Here *theta* values of due process and *sigma* values of efficiency and effectiveness (see p. 61 above) may come into conflict. Formal participation requirements are a rightful democratic attribute and necessary instrument for institutional learning; on the other hand they can be a recipe for delay and indecision (a factor which clearly influenced the Ofdog model).

The practical relevance is illustrated in the evidence to Parliament. Take the model of legislative mandate. This is the standard stuff of administrative law: to step outside the statutory terms of reference is illegitimate or, in the language

[20] See for the classic 'green light' defence of the expert agency, J. Landis, *The Administrative Process* (Yale University Press, 1938).

[21] E. Fisher, *Risk Regulation and Administrative Constitutionalism* (Hart Publishing, 2007), Ch. 2.

[22] CC, *The Regulatory State*, p. 7.

[23] As elaborated in R. Baldwin and M. Cave, *Understanding Regulation* (Oxford University Press, 1999), Ch. 6.

of judicial review, ultra vires. A broad formulation is typical however, with objectives couched in general terms, pregnant perhaps with conflict. With a view to flexibility and responsiveness, rarely is an agency 'a mere transmission belt for implementing legislative directives in particular cases'.[24] So what constitutes an effective statutory remit?

> The regulators were unanimous in their belief that clarity was the most important quality . . . Clarity enabled regulators to readily understand their purpose, to focus their mind quickly on the work in hand . . . Clarity . . . brought other major benefits: increased legitimacy for the regulator; greater consistency in regulators' decision making; a greater likelihood of an internally well-organised, well-run regulator; greater opportunities to monitor regulatory performance successfully; increased ability for regulated industries and consumers to judge the legitimacy and appropriateness of regulatory policies and actions.[25]

Agencies, the Select Committee on Regulators concluded, are 'most likely to be effective when they are working towards limited and relatively narrowly defined duties and objectives'.[26] But we note the tensions. This is not the logic of New Labour's re-balancing of regulatory policy, with more emphasis on social and latterly environmental factors (see p. 236 above); similarly, the rise of the super-regulator is administrative law code for wide-ranging discretion. We see, too, why ministerial guidance is at such a premium. Varying the constitutional theme of hierarchy of legislative instruments, there also is a significant role for graded systems of primary legislative obligation in structuring agency discretion. DTI explained to the Constitution Committee that regulators operate 'under a hierarchy of statutory duties to achieve a range of public policy objectives . . . Some of these duties express matters which are to be achieved through the exercise of the regulators' functions, others identify issues or concerns which the regulator must take into account when exercising its functions . . . In some cases, though not all, one or more duties is identified as having primacy or precedence over other duties.'[27]

Ambiguities in the legislative mandate make it difficult to determine the effectiveness of an agency in realising its objectives. There are other general problems in measuring performance. Tasked for many years with a three-fold social project[28] (to work towards the elimination of racial discrimination, to promote equal opportunity, and to encourage good relations between people of different ethnic and racial backgrounds) the Commission for Racial Equality, a forerunner of CEHR, is a classic example. What would have happened in the absence of the regulator's efforts? How is the agency's performance to be separated from that of the regulated? And how does it relate to parallel statutory obligations lat-

[24] R. Stewart, 'The reformation of American administrative law' (1975) 88 *Harv. LR* 1667, 1675.

[25] RC, *UK Economic Regulators* , p. 23.

[26] *Ibid.*, p. 24.

[27] Evidence to CC, *The Regulatory State*, p. 373.

[28] Under the auspices of the Race Relations Act 1976, s. 43.

terly imposed on most public authorities?[29] Market regulation presents similar difficulties, as when an agency is tasked with promoting sectoral efficiency.

We touch here on a long-standing dispute in law and economics over efficient action or results as a value independent of distributional considerations. Evidencing the more purist market ideology of the time, it was an article of faith that Ofdogs limit themselves as far as possible to the maximisation of economic efficiency.[30] The approach was also designed to shore up agency legitimacy: to help structure and confine discretion, and to ground decisions in technical expertise. Practical workings confirmed however that discretion and dispute were endemic: for example, an agency policy of consumer protection could be at variance with promotion of competition; a price control designed to curb the profitability of the dominant firm might reduce market entry. And should economic criteria enjoy such a dominant position? In view of the Utilities Act 2000 (see p. 253 above), and indeed of the HRA, the retort by Prosser was prescient. Public lawyers 'are concerned . . . to develop theories of non-arbitrary decision-making, which are not necessarily economic based but which involve other conceptions of legitimacy and rights . . . for example, through employment of Dworkin's concept of a right to equal respect and concern . . . The same values [of individual autonomy] used to justify market provision may also justify rights of access to the necessities of life through non-market mechanisms.'[31] Then again, after a period of New Labour, could it be that the Regulators' Committee heralds a swing back?

> It is . . . important that regulators' remits are not continuously expanded . . . When the original privatisation statutes were put in place, the regulators' duties were more focussed than they are now on their economic roles of regulating monopolies, promoting competition and setting prices. Determining which policy issues were for government and which for regulators was therefore relatively clear-cut. However, the later increase in the importance within the regulators' roles of other duties (particularly social and environmental duties) means that there is now a less clear distinction . . . Government should be careful not to offload political policy issues onto unelected regulators.[32]

The Committee's report itself serves to illustrate the slippery nature of 'efficiency'. Take agency costs – never popular. At one with the general picture painted by Hampton (see p. 234 above), those of the chief economic regulators have increased substantially in recent years, totalling almost £700m in 2006–7. The common explanation is more staff. Although minded to warn against 'regulatory creep', the Committee (advised by the NAO) could see no obvious

[29] Race Relations (Amendment) Act 2000 and now the Equality Act 2006. See for relevant 'baseline' research: CRE, *Towards Racial Equality* (2003).

[30] C. Foster, *Privatisation, Public Ownership and the Regulation of Natural Monopoly* (Blackwell, 1992).

[31] T. Prosser, 'Privatisation, regulation and public services' (1994) 1 *Juridical Review* 3, 17: drawing in turn on older legal principles associated with 'common callings' (see p. 344 below).

[32] RC, *UK Economic Regulators*, pp. 24–5.

scope for operational cost savings; the trend was largely attributable to the 'significant extensions in their remits'.[33]

The wider regulatory reform agenda has cast its spell. We saw the quest for economic efficiency exemplified in impact assessment and by the drive for 'simplification' in the wake of Arculus. With agencies having to adhere to better regulation principles their choice of particular instruments and methodologies has also been influenced. 'Regulators should commit to evaluating the impact of their work and monitoring the extent to which they are providing value for money . . . The principles of proportionality and targeting . . . both . . . address aspects of efficiency . . . We would encourage other regulators to consider risk-based regulation more explicitly, particularly as a means of using regulatory resources more efficiently'.[34]

Another piece in the jigsaw, rule design, is a particular concern of administrative law (see Chapter 5). Giving it a highly contemporary edge is the question whether a principles-based approach of the kind pioneered by FSA (see p. 274 above) should be adopted in market regulation more generally. Efficiency gains could be anticipated both in terms of agency resources and administrative burdens on operators; preventing 'loopholes' is also attractive. Looking at it through the lens of small and medium enterprise however, the Regulators' Committee was understandably cautious. Agencies should be sensitive to differential impacts; some operators may benefit from a more directive approach. 'The principles basis may make regulation less predictable and so increase regulatory uncertainty with the possible consequence of increasing the cost of capital . . . This concern applies with increasing force as one moves towards smaller regulated businesses which will not have the same lines of contact with the regulator as will the larger ones.'[35] Furthermore, the collapse of trust associated with the current global financial crisis clearly puts in issue the viability of this form of 'regulatory bargain'.

The design-kit is valuable; it does not do however to be overly mechanical. Not only will Baldwin's varying logics of regulatory legitimation play differently in different contexts; ultimately, there is no way of avoiding the contested nature of the trade-offs between them. Different views of the state are reflected in, and reinforced by, this selection of values (see Chapters 1–2). Attention is here directed to a major advance on the Ofdog model, which sees due process and agency accountability taken much more seriously.

(c) A new model

An exercise of broad agency discretion fuels calls for transparency, allowing all information to be brought forward and the basis of regulatory policy to be clear.

[33] *Ibid.*, p. 35.
[34] *Ibid.*, pp. 36–8.
[35] *Ibid.*, p. 39.

There is further a powerful demand for inclusive or participative procedures to ensure that all affected interests are allowed a 'voice', so underwriting the legitimacy of the agency's decisions. The concern of the Constitution Committee with scrutiny in the regulatory state itself speaks volumes. 'Accountability is a control mechanism which is an integral part of a regulatory framework . . . Effective regulation therefore requires effective accountability.'[36]

When setting up the Ofdogs, the Conservatives paid scant attention. Trotting out the traditional control of Parliament and courts, ministers rejected the American-style model of interest representation (see p. 170 above), seeing it as excessively rigid and adversarial.[37] Pointing up the absence of an Administrative Procedure Act, public law critics bewailed the 'startling difference' between the two national systems; the British understanding of due process was 'highly impoverished'.[38] As against pluralist values or ideas of deliberative democracy, the formal institutional framework reflected an old domestic style, so facilitating a closed, bipolar dialogue between regulators and regulated, devoid of hearings.

Individual D-Gs in fact built up some innovative procedures of their own, better to allow for inputs from competitors and user groups. As against the danger of fuzzy compromise between competing special interests, the advantages both in terms of administrative rationality and institutional legitimacy were evidently not lost on the regulators. OFTEL was the market leader in this exercise of agency procedural discretion inside a skeletal statutory framework (of course licensees still enjoyed a privileged position in the broader discussion):

> In principle, OFTEL will consult on all issues that have significant impact on consumers and operators. The only issues on which OFTEL would not consult are those which are of too little consequence to merit the expense . . . or of such a high level of commercial confidentiality that consultation would be damaging . . . The Director General's policy is to develop the maximum transparency in the consultation process – hence to include as full an exposition of his reasons as practicable.[39]
>
> The transparency of the regulatory process . . . is particularly important in telecoms where there is increasing competition in different segments of the market and where regulatory decisions can have different effects on different players. OFTEL needs to have a clear picture . . . It is vital therefore that proposals for change are fully aired and discussed with all the stakeholders in the industry.[40]

[36] CC, *The Regulatory State*, p. 7.

[37] J. Steltzer, 'Regulatory methods: A case for hands across the Atlantic?' in Veljanovski (ed.), *Regulators and the Market* (IEA, 1991).

[38] C. Graham and T. Prosser, *Privatising Public Enterprises* (Oxford University Press, 1991), pp. 239, 256. For a slightly different perspective, see A. McHarg, 'Separation of functions and regulatory agencies: Dispute resolution in the privatised utilities', in Harris and Partington (eds), *Administrative Justice in the 21st Century* (Hart Publishing, 1999).

[39] OFTEL, *Annual Report 1993* [1.12].

[40] NAO, *The Work of the Directors General*, HC 645 (1995/6), p. 64.

It was left to the incoming Blair government to declare a step-change in legislative practice, duly inaugurated in the Utilities Act 2000. 'We believe that the framework needs strengthening to improve accountability and achieve a right balance of interests between consumers and shareholders.'[41] The national trend has latterly been in favour of stronger process requirements, linking better regulation Hampton-style to broader constitutional developments in judicial review and freedom of information. Globalising forces in the market economy have also been influential, as evidenced by a highly developed rule-making schema for the FSA:

> When the Financial Services Authority proposes to make any rules, it must first publish a draft accompanied by a cost-benefit analysis and an explanation of the purpose of the proposed rules and must invite representations on them. When the rules are published the Authority must also publish a general account of the representations received and its response to them; differences must be justified by cost benefit analysis . . . In addition, the Authority is obliged to maintain effective arrangements for consulting practitioners and consumers on the extent to which its general policies and practices are consistent with its general duties, and to establish, and to consider representations by, a Practitioner Panel, and a Consumer Panel, to represent those interests.[42]

Concerns in the early years of privatisation about rough-and-ready agency procedures have dissipated (with the focus shifting to problems of network accountability: p. 306 below). It is today the accepted norm that public consultation precedes (and reasons-giving follows) a major regulatory decision. Of course the adequacy in a particular case may be open to dispute. The recent findings of the Regulators' Committee are eminently predictable:

> We have heard no evidence to suggest that regulators' consultation exercises are lacking in depth; indeed, quite the opposite . . . As well as being thorough, regulators' procedures were praised for being open . . . Witnesses from the regulated industries also praised the regulators' commitment to continual improvement of these processes. There is a recognition that communication between regulator and regulated has improved considerably in recent years . . . There is certainly a positive story to tell . . .
>
> But it would be wrong to overlook the more critical comments we have received . . . Some raised doubts over the extent to which regulators took seriously the responses . . . some were critical of time-scales imposed on consultations . . . some complained that the burden consultation exercises put on them was too great . . . some felt that, on occasion, certain regulators side-stepped the consultation process altogether when formulating policy . . .
>
> Industry needs reassurance that the time it invests in responding to consultation is time well spent and is meaningful in the decision-making process.[43]

[41] DTI, *A Fair Deal for Consumers: Modernising the framework for utility regulation*, Cm. 3898 (1998), p. 3. And see BRTF, *Economic Regulators* (2001).

[42] T. Prosser, 'The powers and accountability of agencies and regulators', in Feldman (ed.), *English Public Law* (Oxford University Press, 2004), p. 321.

[43] RC, *UK Economic Regulators*, p. 51–2.

Let us take stock. Conveying the sense of advances in agency powers being matched with more open and inclusive procedures, Prosser in 2004 spoke approvingly of a 'new regulatory model' emerging in the utilities.[44] Displaying by now familiar features, the template contrasts strongly with the original Ofdog model (see p. 249 above):

- regulatory commission
- clarification of key duties, with priority given to consumers and competition, and injection of social and environmental objectives
- enhanced enforcement powers ('wider' and 'deeper')
- heightened process requirements, including transparency
- strengthened consumer voice

We see how recent developments – better regulation 'mark II' – accentuates this. The institutional architecture of regulatory commissions is a *sine qua non* of the move, Hampton-style, to super-agencies. And the process requirements framed by LRRA (a miniature 'regulatory procedures act'), the super-consumer advocate established by CEARA, and the administrative penalties regime of RESA, must be factored in.

Looking at IRAs more generally, the model needs supplementing:

- Infusion of risk-oriented methodologies

For reasons discussed further in s. 3, the authors also would insist on another – quintessentially administrative law – bullet point:

- Expanded *ex post facto* forms of accountability ('answerability').

2. Regulatory development: A case study

How does the general regulatory development play out in individual agencies? The water regulator OFWAT makes a suitable case study. Leading two lives, first as an Ofdog, and latterly as a regulatory commission, the agency neatly illustrates the changed institutional template. Increasingly inclusive and transparent procedures also show the different phases of UK regulatory reform, with initial 'soft law' contributions from the D-G and then harder-edged requirements of 'better regulation'. Practical workings further serve to point up continuing pressures for change – the sense of regulatory development as a process, not an event. Enforcement had not been the agency's forte; officials, however, are acquiring a taste for Macrory-type administrative penalties. Even the lack of market competition, which has cast the water industry apart in the evolution of the utilities since privatisation, is being addressed.

OFWAT does water regulation; water regulation is not OFWAT. Usefully illustrating the complexities of regulatory governance and the multi-level context, the agency itself comprises part of a network featuring government

[44] Prosser, 'The powers and accountability of agencies and regulators', p. 318.

departments, other IRAs, and – increasingly prominent – EC actors. Division and interconnectedness of regulatory functions is a defining feature. As discussed in s. 3 of this chapter, administrative lawyers need to focus on the resulting problems of diffuse accountabilities.

The contemporary element of 'greening' in administrative law deserves special attention. Typically, we see this economic regulator starting out narrowly focused on price control, and then, expressive of New Labour's less concentrated form of market ideology, taking on a broader legislative mandate. Water management is today at the cutting edge of public policy; the agency must think 'sustainable development', but also deal with the fact of conflicting interests which casts a lengthening shadow over the exercise of regulatory choice:

> Water resources in England and Wales (especially in south east England) are threatened by below average rainfall in the short-term and climate change in the longer-term. The use of these resources is also facing increasingly tight regulation in order to meet ever-higher ecological requirements. Simultaneously, demand for water is increasing because of population growth, a decreasing average household size and growing use of water-intensive appliances.[45]

(a) Ofdog

When privatising the industry in the Water Act 1989, the Thatcher government recycled the model of vertical integration in the pre-existing 'professional bureaucratic complex'.[46] Ten regional water authorities, each covering a main river catchment area in England and Wales,[47] metamorphosed into ten regional companies, with the integrated utility functions of providing clean water, sewerage and sewage treatment. Some thirty surviving local companies, providing a quarter of the total water supply, were also brought inside the framework. While control of pollution and management of rivers became the responsibility of a National Rivers Authority (later gobbled up in the Environment Agency), the legislation dealt with economic regulation in standard Ofdog fashion through a sectoral framework with long-term licensing and price control operated by the DG for Water Services (OFWAT).

The DG's primary duties were to exercise powers 'in the manner that he considers is best calculated' to ensure (a) that the water and sewerage companies carried out their functions properly and (b) that the companies could finance this by securing a reasonable rate of return on their capital. The secondary

[45] Lords Science and Technology Committee, *Water Management*, HL 191 (2005/6), p. 3. And see M. de Villiers, *Water: The fate of our most precious resource* (Mariner, 2001).

[46] W. Maloney, 'Regulation in an episodic policy-making environment: The water industry in England and Wales' (2001) 79 *Pub. Admin.* 625. And see W. Maloney and J. Richardson, *Managing Policy Change in Britain: The politics of water* (Edinburgh University Press, 1995).

[47] Scottish legislation is distinct, culminating in the Water Services etc (Scotland) Act 2005.

duties included promoting economy and efficiency; facilitating competition; and safeguarding the interests of customers, especially vulnerable groups (for example, there should be 'no undue preference' in fixing charges). Other (tertiary) duties included having regard to particular environmental issues, such as conservation of flora and fauna.[48] Self-evidently, much depended on the D-G's regulatory philosophy. Under former Treasury official Sir Ian Byatt, D-G throughout the 1990s, a light-touch approach became the orthodoxy.[49] 'We regulate at arm's length wherever possible. We provide incentives to companies to operate efficiently. It is for the companies to decide how they manage their activities and meet their obligations.'[50] To operationalise matters, the D-G had four indispensable sources of in-house expertise: water engineers, economists, accountants (for complex calculations of cost of capital and asset base, etc), and regulatory lawyers (for drafting of licences and dealing with, for example, competition law disputes).

Faced with the classic monopoly conditions of a network industry, such as high transport costs of water, OFWAT had to make do with 'yardstick competition',[51] so using comparative efficiency measurement to inform an industry-wide system of price control that could scarcely be abandoned. Practical workings confirm the methodological difficulties both in terms of hydrological and demographic variation between regions [52] and the classic problem of asymmetry of information between regulator and regulated (below). The 'big business' element must be factored into the equation. With a supply area of 5,000 square miles, Thames Water has some 8 million water customers.[53]

The regulatory rule 'RPI+K' was adopted for the purpose of determining an annual average price cap, with a 'K factor' set for each company in the light of overall industry potential, and differential potential between operators, for efficiency gains. This has combined the need for continuing high levels of investment, especially given strengthening EU requirements (see p. 299 below), with the typical Ofdog incentivising element (see p. 250 above). 'We do not control profits or dividends. If companies exceed our efficiency assumptions they will be more profitable. Customers will benefit from these efficiencies at future price reviews. It is for the companies to decide whether to share these benefits with customers by charging less than their price limits allow between price

48 See ss. 2–3 of the (consolidating) Water Industry Act 1991.

49 Sir Ian Byatt, 'The water regulation regime in England and Wales' in Henry, Matheu and Jeunemaître (eds.), *Regulation of Network Utilities: The European experience* (Oxford University Press, 2005).

50 OFWAT *Annual Report 2005-6*, p. 5.

51 R. Baldwin and M. Cave, *Understanding Regulation: Theory, strategy and practice* (Oxford University Press, 1999), Ch. 18.

52 D. Bailey, 'The emerging co-existence of regulation and competition in the water industry' (2002) 25 *World Competition* 127.

53 OFWAT has generally opposed mergers in the industry precisely because of the need for benchmarking: see Competition Commission, *Water Merger References Guidelines* (2004).

reviews.'[54] The periodic reviews were set at five-yearly intervals, so affording the companies sufficient scope to improve efficiency and generate additional profits.[55] The initial determination in 1994 was very favourable to the industry: evidently, there was greater slack than the agency calculated. With water prices rising significantly, large-scale profit-taking was no source of popular legitimacy for OFWAT.[56] Further highlighting the importance of agency discretion, the 1999 periodic review wrought substantial change, with the demand for environmentally friendly investment programmes making inroads.[57]

'Learning by doing' is an apt description of OFWAT in the early years. Here, as elsewhere in the utility sector, the new breed of regulators had to experiment with complex modalities of econometrics and financial modelling in largely uncharted territory. 'Nobody knew what the cost of capital was . . . because nobody had borrowed for utilities in these markets.'[58] The closed, elite and informal practices familiarly associated with state corporatism lingered on. 'Detailed discussions were held with each company prior to publication of OFWAT's decisions: in almost every case the draft K factors distributed to the companies in 1994 were revised upwards.'[59] Departmental wrangling with the Treasury behind the scenes compounded matters: the ministerial guidance commonly conveyed mixed messages.[60] As Sir Ian conceded, a 'disinterested expertise' could only take the agency so far in the real world of regulatory politics:

> How do you do trade-offs? The customer of course wants water at a reasonable price, the customer wants clean drinking water and the customer wants a good environment, particularly on the beaches . . . At the [1999] review we thought that out of a bill of something like £230 the bill could have come down by as much as £60 for efficiency but £30 was ploughed back into higher quality. We thought that was broadly a reflection of the responses which we got from the various actors, trying to put them together in a judgmental rather than a systematic way.[61]

Increasingly however, the Ofdog took 'substantial steps with a view to improving . . . openness, consultation and clarity'.[62] Further illustrating the positive

[54] OFWAT, *Regulating the Companies: The role of the regulator* (2006), p. 2. And see J. Cubbin, 'Efficiency in the water industry' (2005) 13 *Utilities Policy* 289.

[55] The licensing system also allows for interim determinations if costs or revenues change materially. A cautious approach is implicit since this would otherwise blunt the incentive effect of the price-cap model.

[56] Commons Environmental Audit Committee, *Water: Periodic review 2004 and the environmental programme*, HC 416 (2003/4) puts this in historical perspective.

[57] See Commons Environmental Audit Committee, *Water Prices and the Environment*, HC 597(1999/2000).

[58] Sir Ian Byatt, Evidence to CC, HL 68 (2003/4), Q12

[59] Maloney, 'Regulation in an episodic policy-making environment', p. 639.

[60] See on this aspect, Commons Environmental Audit Committee, *Water: Periodic review* 2004.

[61] Evidence to CC, HL 68 (2003/4), Q 5.

[62] Hansard Society and European Policy Forum, *Report of the Commission on the Regulation of Privatised Utilities* (1996), p. 56.

exercise of procedural discretion in a permissive statutory framework, the D-G was especially keen to shore up regulatory legitimacy in the markets:

> It is essential that we approach our tasks in a transparent way, designed to minimise unnecessary regulatory uncertainty . . . We hold workshops to describe and discuss our policy approaches and meet the companies and others to discuss issues . . . We try to ensure that the basis of regulation is fully understood by the companies themselves and their own investors, bondholders and other lenders. This helps to hold down the cost to them of raising finance and thereby, through the system of incentive-based price cap regulation, the cost of customers' bills. As examples, we now publish our forecasts of companies' regulatory capital values and the financial model we use to set price limits.[63]

With no serious prospect of 'exit', and with only basic statutory provision in the form of regional 'customer service committees' (CSCs) appointed by the D-G to investigate complaints and make representations to the companies,[64] the exercise of consumer voice became a pressing issue. Individual complaints could be dealt with in standard pyramidal fashion – internal review by the companies, possible further review by a CSC, and evaluation by OFWAT of those few cases raising significant regulatory issues – but what of collective interest representation by a dedicated consumers' champion? An agency-sponsored development was typically incremental. Regular rounds of meetings with CSCs led on to an 'OFWAT National Customers Council' composed of CSC chairmen which, in order 'to achieve a higher public profile' and 'clearer separation from OFWAT', was later armed with a memorandum of understanding and re-launched as 'WaterVoice'. Yet by definition such soft law arrangements could only go so far. 'The DG . . . appoints the staff . . . Watervoice is funded by the DG who is responsible as Accounting Officer for its expenditure . . . OFWAT provides WaterVoice with advice, information and briefing.'[65] The case for a statutory body was further underlined when WaterVoice indicated some blemishes on OFWAT's generally 'satisfactory' record:

> The technical content, complexity and length of OFWAT consultation documents are not conducive to effective public consultation and participation in the debate, thereby limiting input to those with special knowledge . . . OFWAT does publish its conclusions following public consultation but we believe that as a matter of good practice OFWAT should always include sufficient analysis and explanation of decisions so that respondents can see to what extent their individual views have been influential.[66]

Showing the increased importance in the national administrative law system of 'anti-trust', the Competition Act 1998 introduced a whole new dimension

[63] OFWAT, *Memorandum of Evidence* to CC, HL 68 (2003/4), p. 3.

[64] Water Industry Act 1991, ss 28–9.

[65] WaterVoice, *Memorandum of Evidence* to CC, HL 68 (2003/4), pp. 1–2.

[66] *Ibid.*, pp. 3–4.

to the regulation. This was all the more significant for OFWAT because of the fact of regional monopolies. As a utility regulator, the agency now had concurrent competition law powers with OFT in the sector.[67] The whole process of considering allegations of market abuse by a dominant firm, imposing interim measures, carrying out investigations, and imposing financial penalties, itself means substantial agency discretion:

> When we receive a [competition] complaint we consider carefully, amongst other things: the consumer harm involved; the complainant's views; the benefits of setting a precedent for the market; the size of the market; and our resource constraints. We cannot investigate a complaint under the CA98 unless we have reasonable grounds for suspecting an infringement . . . We are unlikely to consider complaints unless they are supported by substantive evidence and information, although we do take account of the resources available to the complainant . . . OFWAT has discretion to decide on the most appropriate powers to use . . . It may not always be appropriate to investigate a complaint under the CA98. For example, we may be developing policy that will address the issues raised by the complainant.[68]

Matched with a right of appeal to the Competition Appeal Tribunal (see p. 321 below), this major accretion of powers has proved a mixed blessing. Big business repeat players, typically deploying City commercial and public-law specialists, make the most formidable adversaries. As the agency laments: 'we have spent a lot of time and resources defending appeals to CAT'.[69]

(b) Benchmark

Set in 2004, the current price control covers the period 2005–10. The exhaustive periodic review process preceding it shows quite how far the Ofdog model had evolved. Placing more emphasis on sustainable development and on the affordability of water for low-income families,[70] the ministerial guidance was itself the subject of a public/private deliberative cycle: initial statement, draft business plans from the companies, summary report by OFWAT and advices from other agencies in the network, principal statement.[71] OFWAT's own two-year timetable comprised: (a) consultation on and elaboration of agency methodology, (b) agency consideration of draft and final business plans, (c) setting of and consultation on draft determinations, and (d) setting of final determinations. An independent review group set up by OFWAT judged it 'about right'. In contrast to the Department (which was considered 'more

[67] Competition Act 1998 s. 54 and Sch. 10; and see Enterprise Act 2002.

[68] OFWAT, *Report on Competition Complaints* (2006), pp. 3–4; and see DTI and Treasury, *Concurrent Competition Powers in Sectoral Regulation* (2006).

[69] OFWAT, *Annual Report 2005–6*, p. 23.

[70] See also Water Industry Act 1999 (prohibiting disconnection of domestic users for non-payment).

[71] DEFRA, *Principal Guidance to the DG of Water Services* (2004).

opaque'),[72] there was 'a high level of satisfaction' with the agency's conduct of the process, with 'even the most critical parties' considering it a further 'major improvement':

> [The process] was seen as more transparent, with OFWAT being prepared to listen to representations in, for the most part, an open-minded way; to explain how it had modified its approach in responses to consultation papers; and provide feedback on . . . submissions made by individual companies. The overall process was thought to have been well planned and managed, with . . . delay in the issue of Ministerial Guidance as the only blip in the timetable . . . Virtually all respondents respected the role of the Director-General personally in the price setting process, and commended his independence and integrity.[73]

Of course substance may colour views of procedure:

> Consumer orientated organisations believed OFWAT should have given more weight to customer interests, and the WaterVoice committees felt that communications with them deteriorated sharply after the Draft Determinations. The Environment Agency and other environmental groups felt that OFWAT treated environmental improvements as optional investments – rather than integral parts of company investment programmes – and made them subject to disproportionate scrutiny while, at the same time, exaggerating the contribution of the environmental programme to bill increases. They were also concerned over what they see as the tendency of companies to bid up costs for environmental schemes through gaming. For their part, the water companies considered that whilst OFWAT was generally open and transparent in relation to the methodologies it deployed, this was not the case at the end in relation to the way OFWAT dealt with issues of efficiency and capital maintenance . . .
>
> Despite these differences, we found no one advocating radical change to the processes adopted by OFWAT . . . or in OFWAT's approach or behaviour. The process is seen as being now essentially on the right lines.[74]

The detail of the resulting price control shows the huge importance of this regulatory regime. Whereas for 2000–5 the K factor had been assigned a negative average value (-1.5 per cent), OFWAT now determined an average annual increase in the price cap before inflation of 4.3 per cent.[75] As well as reflecting increased operating costs, this was to enable a £17 billion capital investment programme, including £8.5 billion for repairs to an ageing infrastructure and – largely to comply with EU requirements – £ 5.5 billion on quality and environmental improvements. The increased price limit was both substantially lower

[72] Water UK, *Future Regulation of the Water Industry: Simpler, smarter, better* (2006), p. 13.

[73] OFWAT, Independent Steering Group, *Report into the Conduct of the 2004 Periodic Review* (2005), p. 4.

[74] *Ibid.*, p. 6.

[75] OFWAT, *Future Water and Sewerage Charges 2005-2010: Final determinations* (2004). With expected average annual household bills in 2009-10 of £297 (excluding inflation).

than that originally requested by the companies (6.2 per cent), and, following representations from the 'green' lobby, significantly higher than those suggested in the agency's draft determination (3.1 per cent). As for the incentivising element, what OFWAT termed 'demanding but achievable' challenges, such as operating cost efficiencies of some 1.3 per cent each year, assumed that 'all the companies, especially the less efficient, will improve further and faster than the economy as a whole'. Major variation in tariffs between companies by reason of different revenue requirements and revenue base was an inevitable outcome.[76]

The aftermath points up issues of 'grievance' and channels of redress (see Chapter 10). As agency officials are grimly aware, there never will be universal satisfaction, least of all among individual consumers. 'The level of the price limits meant that we saw a significant increase in the numbers and complexity of complaints about bills.'[77] The extent to which this individual expression of 'voice' was futile was not explained. The companies were seemingly content, or at least chose not to unsettle the markets. None requested a re-determination by the Competition Commission, as under the Ofdog template they were entitled to do.

(c) New model agency

'The Ofdog is dead: long live OFWAT!' The acronym is retained but the D-G's powers are no more, having been transferred to a regulatory commission through a typical piece of New Labour amending legislation, the Water Act 2003.[78] To support the increased range of work, the 'Water Services Regulation Authority' boasts sub-directorates of regulatory finance and competition, network regulation, and consumer protection, as well as operations, corporate affairs and legal services.

The revamped legislative mandate[79] includes as a primary duty: 'to protect the interests of consumers, wherever appropriate by promoting effective competition between persons engaged in, or in commercial activities connected with, the provision of water and sewerage services'. Both objective and means clearly fit Prosser's 'new regulatory model'. A key message is that OFWAT should think long-term:[80] 'consumers' is defined to mean all users of water, current and future. This is underwritten by a secondary duty 'to contribute to the achievement of sustainable development'. There is a further link to the wide-ranging requirements of the EC Water Framework Directive,[81] which speaks of 'common principles . . . to promote sustainable water use'.

[76] With expected average increases in household bills ranging from 7% (Anglian) to 25% (South West, Southern, and Wessex).

[77] OFWAT, *Annual Report 2005-06*, p. 3.

[78] Implementation sensibly took place after completion of the 2004 periodic review

[79] Water Act 2003, s. 39.

[80] See for the policy development, DEFRA, *Directing the Flow: Priorities for future water policy* (2002).

[81] Directive 2000/60/EC; now supplemented by the Groundwater Directive 2006/118/EC.

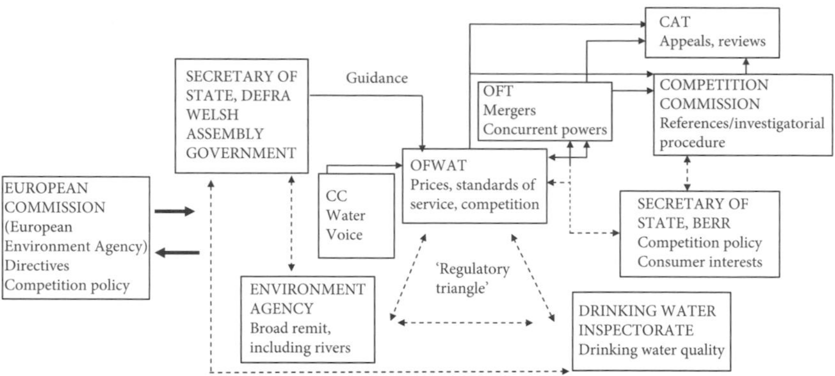

Fig 7.1 Water, water everywhere: Simplified map of a regulatory network

Figure 7.1 illustrates the broader networking context. Better to hold the system together, the Act demonstrates a particular technique of regulatory governance: legal duties to co-operate, underpinned by inter-organisational requirements to make pseudo-contractual MoUs.[82]

Take standards for (a) drinking water and (b) discharge of used water back into the environment. As set out in regulations, these are the responsibility of ministers, with advice from the Drinking Water Inspectorate (DWI), an arm's-length body established at the time of privatisation, and the EA, respectively. The European connection features strongly: drinking water for example must be 'wholesome' at the time of supply, this being defined by quality standards largely derived from a 1998 Directive.[83] DWI and EA do separate monitoring and enforcement under the European Commission's more or less watchful eye.[84] OFWAT must be in the loop precisely because 'environmental and quality regulation is incorporated as a constraint into economic regulation'.[85] Or, as the ministerial guidance patiently explains,[86] since the companies must maintain such standards, the agency when setting the price cap has to allow them the financial wherewithal. No wonder then that working relations with the Secretary of State and the Welsh Assembly government[87] as relevant political authorities, and with DWI and EA in an expert triangular network, are officially described as 'close'.[88] Conversely, we see how accountability is blurred. Informed of increased prices, the irate

[82] Water Act 2003, ss. 35, 52. See further, P. Leyland, 'UK utility regulation in an age of governance' in Bamforth and Leyland (eds), *Public Law in a Multi-Layered Constitution* (Hart Publishing, 2003).

[83] Drinking Water Directive, 98/83/EC.

[84] See for the potential of infringement proceedings, Case C-278/01 *Commission v Spain* [2003] ECR I-14141.

[85] CC, HL 68 (2003/4), p. 17.

[86] DEFRA, *Social and Environmental Guidance to OFWAT* (2008).

[87] The Government of Wales Act 2006 carefully ties Wales into an integrated England and Wales water-resources system: ss. 101, 114, 152.

[88] OFWAT, *Regulating the Companies*, p. 5.

customer asks: 'Who is responsible?' The answer, conveniently, is 'everybody' and 'nobody'.

A Guaranteed Standards Scheme (originally part of the Citizen's Charter programme, p. 247 above) shows ministers acting in concert with OFWAT. Commonly sanctioned by an automatic compensation payment, these minimum service requirements on, for example, water pressure, maintenance of supply and both making and keeping appointments, have recently been extended. OFWAT's contribution is to monitor compliance ('league tables'), determine unresolved disputes, and recommend changes to the rules as determined by the minister in statutory instrument.[89]

We note too the important place for interest representation. The 2003 Act substituted for customer service committees and WaterVoice a separate statutory body, the Consumer Council for Water. A national body with a regional presence, CCW has broad-ranging powers to make representations, as well as handle complaints, and also a power to mount its own investigations.[90] More particularly, it can acquire and review information about consumer matters and the views of consumers (regular tracking surveys), provide advice and information to consumers and public authorities, and publish statistical information about complaints (company comparisons). While given broad rein as a consumer advocate, the watchdog is not unleashed however; powers to obtain and publish information from the industry are tightly restricted.[91] Note too the sectoral dimension. CCW is a prime candidate for takeover by the new super-consumer advocate.[92]

The Act is a repository of better regulation. Not only must OFWAT have regard to the 'big five' principles of transparency, accountability, proportionality, consistency and targeting[93] but the agency also has enhanced enforcement powers: Macrory-style administrative fines.[94] These are applicable in a wide range of circumstances – contravention of statutory requirement, breach of licence condition, failure to meet minimum performance standard. Any such penalty must be of an amount 'reasonable in all the circumstances of the case', up to a maximum of 10 per cent of annual turnover.

(d) Continuing dynamics

With the price control established, monitoring activity centres on four main topics: levels of service; security of supply and efficient usage; financial performance and expenditure; and unit costs and relative efficiency. Buttressed

[89] Water Supply and Sewerage Services (Customer Service Standards) Regulations 2008, SI No. 594.

[90] Water Act 2003, ss. 43, 46–7. And see CCW, *Forward Work Programme 2008–09 to 2010–11*.

[91] Water Act 2003, ss. 43–4.

[92] CEARA, s. 31 makes express provision.

[93] Water Act 2003, s. 39.

[94] Subject of course to a right of appeal: Water Act 2003, ss. 48–9.

by reports from other agencies in the network, OFWAT's main source of data is each company's annual regulatory return. As well as extolling the virtues of effective corporate governance (internal controls), the agency has tried hard to mitigate the problem of asymmetry of information. A variant on meta-regulation, independent expert 'reporters' are placed inside the companies, tasked with examining, and then advising OFWAT on, the accuracy and completeness of regulatory information.[95] An informal European network of agencies allows yardstick competition based on international comparisons.[96]

A recent burst of enforcement action is significant. The first example concerns water leakage – an emotive topic. The 2004 periodic review factored in a £3 billion investment by the companies designed to achieve levels of loss a third lower than the recorded peak in the mid-1990s; annual leakage targets for each company were duly incorporated in the determination.[97] Substantial and repeated failure by Thames Water to comply put the company in breach of its statutory duty to ensure a secure and efficient water supply,[98] triggering the exercise of formal enforcement powers. To enhance credibility, OFWAT is seen moving sharply up the 'enforcement pyramid': from increasingly frequent reporting requirements and detailed investigation of company performance to a voluntary binding undertaking extracted in lieu of an enforcement order.[99] A major precedent for UK regulatory practice post-RESA, this is very much in the mould of the 'Macrory penalty principles'. The maximum administrative fine possible was £66 million: instead the company agreed an extra £150 million investment from its own resources and tougher medium-term targets[100] – 'restorative justice'.

The second example bears directly on the functioning – and limitations – of the regulation. Several companies have recently been fined by OFWAT for misreporting. The largest penalty – £36 million – was against Severn Trent for providing false information about its customer-service performance and using the figures to justify increases in household bills.[101] Using criminal law as back-up, OFWAT had meanwhile referred to the Serious Fraud Office further allegations against the company of faked data on water leakage; Severn Trent eventually pleaded guilty to two charges of fraud and was fined £2 million. The fact that the affair only came to light through the exertions of a company 'whistleblower' speaks volumes about the continuing regulatory difficulty of asymmetry of information.

95 OFWAT, *Reporters' Protocol* (2003).

96 OFWAT, *International Comparison of Water and Sewerage Service* (2008); and see International Water Association, *Competition and Economic Regulation in Water: The future of the European water industry* (2006).

97 See OFWAT, *Security of Supply, Leakage and Water Efficiency 2005–06 report.*

98 Water Industry Act 1991, s. 37.

99 Water Industry Act 1993, ss. 18–19.

100 OFWAT, *Security of Supply*, App. 5.

101 OFWAT, *Final Determination*, 2 July 2008. The company also apologised to its customers and reduced bills.

The structure of the industry is again in issue. Following the well-trodden path, OFWAT has begun to take market competition seriously.[102] While naturally pointing up the achievements since privatisation – £70 billion of capital investment by 2010, better standards of service, increased environmental and drinking water compliance, greater efficiency[103] – the agency concedes comparatively low levels of innovation in the sector. Together with ministers, it is currently looking at ways to disaggregate contestable markets such as retail services from natural monopoly activities. The pre-existing methodology serves for 2010–15,[104] but a single price cap for each company thereafter looks unlikely:

> Our strategy is to take some key steps to open markets . . . and to enable competition to prove itself. New steps can be taken as our knowledge increases. As markets are opened, we will look for opportunities to withdraw regulation where competitive pressures provide sufficient protection for consumers. But until this happens, or where competition cannot provide this protection, we will continue to regulate in a manner that robustly challenges monopoly service providers.[105]

Reviewing the regulatory system in 2005, the Lords Science and Technology Committee was highly critical: 'OFWAT currently focuses too narrowly on keeping water prices down and insufficiently on security of supply in terms of long-term planning, network renewal and the promotion of efficiency.' The Committee highlighted the particular difficulty of achieving the kind of integrated policy approaches required for sustainable development, urging joint initiatives: 'we have seen insufficient evidence to convince us that the potential consequences of climate change are being adequately factored'.[106]

The 'greening' of the regulation has suddenly gathered pace. Designed to frame the agency's policy-making in the 2009 periodic review and thereafter, recent ministerial guidance is notably firm. OFWAT is 'expected to consider . . . environmental outcomes in their broadest sense' and 'to draw on its unique perspective, skill and experience to maximise its contribution to sustainable development'.[107] This signals a raft of regulatory initiatives on, for example, water conservation, sustainable abstraction levels, and the industry's carbon footprint. Happily, the agency sees 'no conflict' between sustainable

[102] OFWAT, *Review of Competition in the Water and Sewage Industries* (2008). There has been much prodding, especially by CAT (below) and also the Select Committee on Regulators.

[103] OFWAT, *International Comparison*. See also I. Byatt, T. Balance and S. Reid, 'Regulation of water and sewerage services' in Crew and Parker (eds.), *International Handbook on Economic Regulation* (Edward Elgar, 2006).

[104] See OFWAT, *Setting Price Limits for 2010–15: Framework and approach* (2008).

[105] OFWAT, *Review of Competition*, p. 4. And see DEFRA, *Future Water: The government's water strategy for England* (2008).

[106] Lords Science and Technology Committee, *Water Management*, pp. 39, 109.

[107] DEFRA, *Social and Environmental Guidance* [2.4]; drawing on the major policy document, DEFRA, *Future Water*.

development and its other legal duties: 'sustainable development should inform our work and "permeate" through it'.[108]

But there will be hard choices, not least in view of economic recession (and the difficulty of borrowing in the markets). Risk methodologies already feature prominently:

> The industry has already developed accepted approaches to assessing risk in some areas. For example, water resource plans include technical assessments of required allowances for 'headroom' and 'outage' in handling risk to the supply/demand balance . . . Reducing risk often also carries costs, and these tend to increase exponentially as risk diminishes. For example, it would be prohibitively expensive to attempt to remove all risk of hosepipe bans during dry years . . . In assessing the approach to handling risk, we support a realistic approach that builds on empirical understanding of likelihood, consequences, and the costs associated with interventions to address risk. We do not support removing the risk altogether, as costs will outweigh the likely benefits.[109]

OFWAT's vision is of good corporate governance: 'a sector made up of sustainable organisations, taking account of their economic, social and environmental impacts, acting to address the key sustainable development challenges ahead, and delivering high quality, good value and safe services to customers'.[110] Let us see.

3. Accountability matters

(a) Multiple accountabilities

How, in its *ex post facto* sense (see p. 46 above), might regulatory accountability be analysed? In addressing the three basic questions of 'who is accountable, to whom and for what', the Constitution Committee[111] adopted a '360° view'. The model (see Fig 7.2) ranges across state, business and civil society as befits an age of governance.

The model serves in classic 'law in context' fashion to remind administrative lawyers that traditional accountability mechanisms are part, but only part, of a bigger picture of multiple accountabilities. The Committee went on to highlight the importance and diversity of the various channels:

> Regulators carrying out public functions wield considerable powers and must accept that these powers carry responsibilities, including the duty to explain to all interested parties, whether they are parliamentary select committees, Ministers, regulated companies,

[108] OFWAT, *Contributing to Sustainable Development* (2006), p. 6. See also OFWAT, *Sustainable Development Action Plan* (2007) *Preparing for the Future: OFWAT's climate change policy statement* (2008) *and Water Today, Water Tomorrow: OFWAT and sustainability* (2009).

[109] *Ibid.*, p. 12. And see *OFWAT's Strategy: Taking a forward look* (2008).

[110] OFWAT, *Setting Price Limits for 2010–15*, p. 2.

[111] CC, *The Regulatory State*, p. 20.

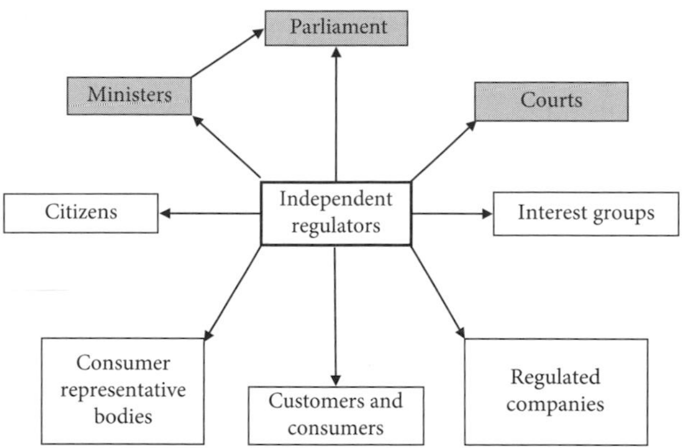

Fig 7.2 360° view of multiple accountabilities

> consumers or citizens. We recognise that this duty is likely to be exercised in different ways, and to different extents, for the different interested parties. It will depend on statutory and formal requirements, good practice, and an understanding of the information needs of each party . . . Equally, the rights of the various interested parties to expose the regulator to scrutiny will vary. Parliamentary select committees have a right to summon regulators to appear before them; this is a right not normally available to the individual citizen.[112]

A spatial form of classification is illustrated. As well as 'upward' accountability to constitutionally superior state institutions, there is the role of 'downward' accountability to consumers and citizens and of course to operators (note how, following Hampton, this is buttressed by the 'hard law' principle that regulators themselves take accountability seriously: p. 258 above):

> We draw a distinction between regulators exercising a duty to explain – extending to all the bodies identified in [the model] – and being required to respond to demands made by those who gave them their powers. Citizens, consumer bodies and regulated bodies lack the power to summon regulators to justify their actions. We have reflected this distinction in [the model]. The shaded boxes comprise the bodies that exercise power directly in relation to the regulators. These are the bodies that are responsible for scrutiny and formal review . . . Parliament is at the apex in that it passes the law creating the regulatory bodies and is the body responsible for calling Government to account.[113]

The potentially corrosive effect on regulatory effectiveness of competing pulls and/or excessive burdens of justification is indicated. Accountable to a plethora of different forums, all of which apply a different set of criteria, the regulator is faced with *the problem of many eyes.*[114] Even so, the model is deceptively

[112] *Ibid.*, p. 19.

[113] CC, *The Regulatory State*, p. 20.

[114] M. Bovens, 'Analysing and assessing accountability: A conceptual framework' (2007) 13 *ELJ* 447, 172; and see J. Black, 'Constructing and contesting legitimacy and accountability in polycentric regulatory regimes' (2008) 2 *Regulation and Governance* 137.

simple. 'Horizontal' accountability to other public bodies, as with bureaucratic regulation and pre-eminently audit, is a glaring omission. Perhaps too, this parliamentary committee needs reminding of the European Union. Where is the Commission?

The true challenge for accountability presented by interconnected and overlapping functions of regulatory networks is glossed over. As our own simplified model of water regulation illustrates, regulatory 'spaces' are far more cluttered than the 360° view implies, centred as it is on the accountability of individual regulators. That there is no thoroughgoing solution for this *problem of many hands*[115] is shown by the best attempt at providing one. Convinced of the potential for harnessing 'dense networks of accountability within which public power is exercised . . . for the purpose of achieving effective accountability or control', Scott suggests two alternative models. In his 'interdependence' model, actors who are 'dependent on each other in their actions because of the dispersal of key resources of authority (formal and informal), information, expertise, and capacity to bestow legitimacy' form a mutual accountability network. As shown above with OFWAT, 'each of the principal actors has constantly to account for at least some of its actions within the [regulatory] space, as a precondition to action.'[116] This autonomous self-responsibility may be a substitute for the formal accountability to public law institutions eroded by network governance or (as Scott suggests) may be supplemented by formal accountability to public law institutions. In his second 'redundancy' model, 'overlapping (and ostensibly superfluous) accountability mechanisms reduce the centrality of any one of them'.[117] Scott describes this as a 'belt-and-braces' model of accountability, in which two or more independent mechanisms, each capable of working on its own, are deployed to ensure the system does not fail. Exploiting 'redundancy' – ratcheting up the pressure to explain and justify by invoking multiple accountability machineries – is what clever campaigners do.

Scott's strategy of reinforcing network checks and balances shows some useful potentials.[118] As discussed in the next section, it is of the essence of 'steering' that the presence of state agents in a regulatory network can operate as a control device to limit opportunistic behaviour by private parties and ensure respect for the public interest. And in policy domains with a strong EU dimension, the supervisory powers vested in the Commission may help to shore up and fill gaps created by network governance or left by decreased accountability at national level. A set of multi-level governance arrangements as sophisticated as the European Competition Network (see p. 278 above)

[115] D. Thompson, 'Moral responsibility of public officials: The problem of many hands' (1980) 74 *Am. Pol. Sci. Rev.* 905.

[116] C. Scott, 'Accountability in the regulatory state' (2000) 27 *JLS* 38.

[117] *Ibid.*, p. 52

[118] See also S. Wilks and B. Doern, 'Accountability and multi-level governance in UK regulation' in Vass (ed.), *Regulatory Review 2006–07* (CRI, 2007).

shows how mutual accountability can be given tangible expression in never-ending rounds of meetings and formal and informal reviews; the design militates against (national) agency 'capture'. The joint accountability of the Network is harder to secure.[119] Leaving aside the chance of 'simultaneous failure' of accountability systems (for example, for lack of information),[120] the redundancy model is problematic. Gaps may be left. 'Redundancy' itself implies a significant element of inefficiency. 'Mutual accountability networks' tend to be more concerned with policy input and long-term relationships than retrospective evaluation, rendering accountability difficult. With participants rendered complicit in decisions, there is a risk of degeneration into a complacent 'old boy network' – the accountability function blunted by mutual interest – and there are obvious problems of transparency. The lines of responsibility and accountability are apt to be blurred, presenting fresh opportunities for passing the buck. It is therefore questionable whether a mutual accountability network can be shored up so as to add the requisite element of legitimacy to the accountability process.[121]

As we said of ministerial responsibility, few would wish to venture a vessel as flimsy as internal network checks and balances. The rise of regulatory governance itself suggests strengthening the capacities of classical, external, techniques of political and legal accountability. One notable feature is the increased blending of audit technique with parliamentary scrutiny in a form of hard-edged and free-flowing techno-political accountability.[122] Efforts are also made to thicken regulatory accountability through core administrative law methods, as part of 'the transforming of judicial review' (see Chapter 3), and especially by an application of high-class tribunal technique in key economic sectors. Let us look at this more closely.

(b) Audit and political accountability

Audit is much to the fore with regulatory governance.[123] Grounded in budgets and resource allocation, but capable of application across the full range of agency practices of rule formulation and implementation and enforcement, the broad and flexible rubric of VFM gives this historic forum of accountability a very contemporary appeal. Control via ministers being a hollow hope, MPs can seek to reclaim lost ground by piggybacking on the technical investigations

[119] See further, C. Harlow and R. Rawlings, 'Promoting accountability in multi-level governance: A network approach' (2007) 13 *ELJ* 542.

[120] Scott, 'Accountability in the regulatory state', p. 60.

[121] As regulation moves increasingly outside the state, these accountability problems become more serious. See C. Harlow, *Accountability in the European Union* (Oxford University Press, 2002).

[122] In Ch. 13 we will see the Parliamentary Ombudsman also playing an increasingly prominent role in regulatory accountability.

[123] See for a self-assessment, E. Humpherson, 'The National Audit Office's audit programme in perspective' in Vass (ed.), *Regulatory Review 2006–07* (CRI, 2007).

and evidence of the NAO, which now has extended jurisdiction over NDPBs. This allows for NAO reports to be followed up in hearings by the PAC (see p. 59 above).[124]

Matters are complicated however because the NAO wears two hats. As the better-regulation agenda expanded so this arch-bureaucratic regulator began to play an increasingly active role as policy guardian and advocate. This is the stuff of reports on the conduct of impact assessment (see p. 152 above); on progress with reduction of administrative burdens (see p. 261 above); and of 'Hampton implementation reviews' (see p. 266 above). Recent events point up the twin dangers of overstretch and complacent acceptance of the network 'view'. Tasked by the Treasury with a major review of the FSA,[125] the NAO produced a highly laudatory report: the ARROW system of RBR was 'rigorous' in application; 'rich in process', the agency could now think about 'streamlining'.[126] Little hard evidence was produced to substantiate these claims. As the failure of Northern Rock and the FSA's own highly critical review (see p. 276 above) soon confirmed, it was a flabby piece of work.

The NAO could usefully concentrate on expanding the support given to a select group of select committees. A summary of Parliament's capacities by the Hansard Society[127] shows why this particular instrument of political accountability is at a premium:

Specific powers:

- vote appropriations to pay for the industry regulatory bodies
- overturn relevant ministerial decisions in the form of Orders (for example, RROS).

General scrutiny powers:

- oral and written answers and statements on regulatory bodies' activities
- formal submission of regulatory bodies' annual reports
- debates in Westminster Hall on regulatory bodies' work (generally poor attendance)
- answerability of regulatory bodies to the PAC via the NAO
- select committee work: formal evidence from regulatory bodies (and stakeholders) in the course of investigations; private briefings by regulators; frequent appearances by agency chief executives.

Starting from a low base, select committees' contribution thickened with New Labour in office. As well as numerous ad hoc inquiries into regulatory matters occasioning public concern, particular committees have shown themselves

124 Government Resources and Accounts Act 2000 (Rights of Access by Comptroller and Auditor General) Order, SI No. 1325; Government Resources and Accounts Act 2000 (Audit of Public Bodies) Order 2003, SI No. 1326.

125 Under s. 12 of the Financial Services and Markets Act 2000.

126 NAO, *The Financial Services Authority*, HC 500 (2006/7), p. 4.

127 Hansard Society, *Parliament at the Apex: Parliamentary scrutiny and regulatory bodies* (2003).

important repeat players, most obviously the Commons Trade and Industry (now Business and Enterprise) Committee.[128] Adding to the mix are the Commons' Regulatory Reform Committee, the Lords' Delegated Powers and Regulatory Reform Committee and Merits of Statutory Instruments Committee (see Chapter 4). The very fact of inquiries into regulatory accountability, and into the role of the economic regulators, by Lords committees (see p. 284 above) is significant. Nor should the added value of scrutiny by the devolved parliaments and assemblies in the more intimate conditions of small-country governance be overlooked.[129] Economic regulation is commonly constructed UK-wide, but bold is the agency which, operating locally, steadfastly ignores the views or moral suasion of, for example, the Scottish Parliament. All this represents a valuable counter-weight to the rise of non-majoritarian regulatory institutions epitomised in the 'super-agency' and underscores the importance of not being subsumed in some intricate 'mutual accountability network'. The particular value in fields dominated by experts of an unruly element of political accountability should not be underestimated. Uncomfortable lines of questioning cannot always be brushed aside; later, for example, we see MPs prick a cosy consensus on co-regulation.

Nevertheless, overall contribution is necessarily modest. Problems reflect, or are epitomised in, the experience of the many regulatory contexts of EU multi-level governance. The subjects are so technical that reports are prone to gather dust, far from the public view. Committee resources and expertise are, on the other hand, limited. Better to match the 'rule of networks' (see p. 277 above) – and so maximise the accountability potential inside the national system – there is a pressing need at Westminster to expand links with other Member States' parliaments, as well as with the European Parliament.[130]

Undue fragmentation of the scrutiny arrangements is a recipe, as the Constitution Committee has pointed out,[131] for decidedly mixed results. Where, in the form of a dedicated committee able to absorb, probe and disseminate the lessons of experience across the piece, is the machinery to ensure that regulators collectively are accountable to Parliament? The Constitution Committee outlined its preferred model:

> The functions . . . should include the right to be consulted over any proposal to confer statutory powers on a new regulator, or to add to those of an existing regulator, in good time for its comments to be taken into account during pre-legislative scrutiny. Other functions should include:

[128] See e.g. Commons Trade and Industry Committee, *Fuel Prices*, HC 279 (2004/5), and *Security of Gas Supply*, HC 632 (2005/6).

[129] R. Rawlings, *Delineating Wales: Constitutional, Legal and Administrative Aspects of National Devolution* (University of Wales Press, 2004), Ch. 11.

[130] See K. Auel and A. Benz (eds), *The Europeanisation of Parliamentary Democracy* (*J. of Legislative Studies* special issue, 2005).

[131] CC, *The Regulatory State*, Ch. 10. And see P. Norton, 'Select Committees and the accountability of the regulatory state' in Vass (ed.), *Regulatory Review 2006–07* (CRI, 2007).

- Having regard to such issues as potential duplication or overlap of regulatory activities, and the clarity of hierarchies of objectives
- Identifying and promoting good practice in its role as the parliamentary counterpart of the lead Government department and the Regulatory Impact Unit of the Cabinet Office
- Examining whether regulation is guided by . . . the BRTF principles
- Satisfying itself that appointment processes for regulators conform to Nolan principles
- Monitoring the regularity and scope of RIAs produced by Government and by IRAs
- Focusing on annual reports of regulatory bodies with a view to maintaining the consistency and co-ordination of parliamentary scrutiny.[132]

To which the authors would add:

- Examining the complex entanglements of the regulatory state or opaque networks.

This is unfinished business. 'The question of who regulates the regulators has not been answered and will not go away. There is a need for a wider, and continuing, review.'[133] Recently the Commons has taken the lead. Exploiting a broadly worded mandate, the Regulatory Reform Committee has moved on from scrutinising draft orders to conduct a general inquiry into the design and impact of the regulatory reform agenda. Attesting the role for creative forms of techno-political accountability, we find the NAO helping to work up the Committee's work programme.[134] Engagement with stakeholders, from business and trade union representatives to the National Consumer Council, and with an array of government and academic experts, further illustrates the special value of select committees' inquisitorial technique. The end result is a promising beginning:

> We have recommended regular parliamentary scrutiny of the BRE through annual reporting to Parliament. We believe that the BRE should . . . focus more on setting clearly defined and prioritised targets and then measuring against them – both for itself and for Departments and (where relevant) Agencies. The BRE should itself scrutinise the robustness of reporting in programmes such as the Administrative Burdens Reduction Programme. We have also suggested that Government Departments provide information on progress in burdens reduction in their Annual Reports. That information would then be available for scrutiny by the relevant Departmental Select Committee.[135]

(c) Judicial supervision (I): Standards

Regulation raises some classic issues of legal accountability. How far can the 'ordinary courts' reasonably go in scrutinising the decisions of expert

[132] *Ibid.* [201].

[133] RC, *UK Economic Regulators* [1.29]. This ad hoc committee was only a temporary expedient.

[134] NAO, *Regulatory Reform in the UK* (2008), p. 2.

[135] Regulatory Reform Committee, *Getting Results: The better regulation executive and the impact of the regulatory reform agenda*, HC 474 (2007/8), p. 3.

repeat-players in the many complex areas of market regulation? What is the role of procedural review in promoting transparency, etc., in powerful non-majoritarian bodies? How in the shaping of jurisdiction should the courts respond to the 'public + private' equation of governance?

In addressing the key question of intensity of review, we start from the idea that judicial review of expert regulatory bodies is traditionally in de Smith's famous phrase 'sporadic and peripheral'. With exceptions,[136] a deferential attitude to regulatory autonomy, with agencies granted considerable latitude in matters of judgement, long characterised the case law.[137] The general trend of juridification in the regulatory process, as exemplified by the Regulators' Compliance Code, together with the broader transformation of judicial review (see Chapter 3), suggests a less permissive view.[138] Recent procedural-fairness cases illustrate this. A circumspect approach to substantive review still prevails however; an experienced practitioner notes, 'advancing irrationality challenges in a regulatory context is notoriously tough'.[139] As Ogus reminds us, considerations of relative institutional competence loom large here:

> Regulatory rule-making often [involves] the 'polycentric problem': issues cannot be resolved independently and sequentially; they are, rather, interdependent and a choice from one set of alternatives has implications for preferences within other sets of alternatives. The decision-maker must take into account the whole network before she can reach a single decision. The adversarial setting of the judicial process does not lend itself to grappling with this problem, not the least because judicial intervention is generally sought after the rules have been promulgated.[140]

In breeding the Ofdogs, the Thatcher government showed little appetite for judicial review. The determinedly subjective and permissive language of the privatisation statutes locked up together with a continued use of informal techniques of regulatory bargaining and the technical complexity of much of the subject matter to reduce its potency. A decade of operations saw only a handful of cases. In the event,[141], far from the so-called 'hard look' doctrine of judicial examination of the basis of regulatory decisions once fashionable in America,[142] the judges stressed the breadth of the statutory discretion, declining to become involved in detailed questions of fact.

[136] As in *Laker Airways v Department of Trade* [1977] QB 643 and, with a chilling effect on formal investigations for social regulatory purposes, *Hillingdon LBC v Commission for Racial Equality* [1982] AC 779.

[137] See generally J. Black, P. Muchlinski and P. Walker (eds.), *Commercial Regulation and Judicial Review* (Hart Publishing, 1998).

[138] See e.g. R. Macrory, 'Environmental public law and judicial review' (2008) 13 *Judicial Review* 115.

[139] T. de la Mare, 'Regulatory judicial review: The impact of competition Law' (ALBA lecture, 2007), p. 4.

[140] A. Ogus, *Regulation: Legal form and economic theory* (Clarendon Press, 1994), p. 117.

[141] As in *R v Director-General of Gas Supply, ex p. Smith* (31 July 1989, unreported); *R v Director-General of Telecommunications, ex p. Let's Talk (UK) Ltd* (6 April 1992, unreported).

[142] *Vermont Yankee Nuclear Power Corpn v NRDC* 435 US 519 (1978); but see n. 146 below.

A City regulation case from the same period, *Ex p. Panton*,[143] is a striking example of light-touch review. At issue were disciplinary decisions of the Securities and Futures Authority, one of the statutorily empowered SROs later replaced by the FSA.

> *Sir Thomas Bingham MR:* The clear intention is that bodies established under the Act should be the regulatory bodies and it is not the function of the court in anything other than a clear case to second-guess their decisions or, as it were, to look over their shoulder . . . These bodies are amenable to judicial review but are in anything, other than in very clear circumstances, to be left to get on with it. It is for them to decide on facts whether it is or it is not appropriate to proceed against a member as not being a fit and proper person. It is essentially a matter for their judgment as to the extent to which a complaint is investigated.

It is noteworthy also that the Monopolies and Mergers Commission did not lose a single judicial review case during the long years of Conservative rule despite regular challenges.[144] The closest squeak came in the *South Yorkshire Transport* case.[145] The issue was whether, as the MMC had determined, a particular merger came within the meaning of the statutory phrase 'a substantial part of the United Kingdom', so empowering an investigation. In a benchmark ruling echoing the later American approach,[146] the House of Lords made clear that while as a 'jurisdictional fact' the matter was susceptible to review, it did not entail a 'hard-edged' question yielding one correct answer:

> *Lord Mustill:* This clear-cut approach cannot be applied to every case, for the criterion itself may be so imprecise that different decision-makers, each acting rationally, might reach different conclusions when applying it to the facts of a given case. In such a case the court is entitled to substitute its own opinion for that of the person to whom the decision has been entrusted only if the decision is so aberrant that it cannot be classed as rational: the present is such a case. Even after eliminating inappropriate senses of 'substantial' one is still left with a meaning broad enough to call for the exercise of judgement rather than exact quantitative measurement. Approaching the matter in this light I am quite satisfied that there is no ground for interference by the court, since the conclusion at which the Commission arrived was well within the permissible field of judgement.

A greater use of litigation already appeared likely as New Labour came to power in 1997. For Scott, seeking to explain a small stream of utility cases:

143 *R v Securities and Futures Authority, ex p. Panton* (20 June 1994, unreported). The earlier *Datafin* case (see p. 316 below) had effectively established that the SFA was subject to judicial review.

144 See *R v Monopolies and Mergers Commission, ex p. Argyll Group plc* [1986] 1WLR 763; also, *R v Monopolies and Mergers Commission, ex p. Stagecoach Holdings plc*, The Times 23 July 1996. And see J. Swift, *Judicial Control of Competition Decisions in the UK and EU* (Competition Commission, 2004).

145 *South Yorkshire Transport v Monopolies and Mergers Commission* [1993] 1 WLR 23.

146 The famous '*Chevron* doctrine', whereby the statute is construed in accordance with the specific intention of Congress where evident, and, where not, the agencies are allowed reasonably to exercise judgement discretion: *Chevron USA Inc v NRDC* 467 US 837 (1984).

> Liberalisation has had the effect of multiplying the number of players participating in each sector (both regulatory and commercial) and tended to threaten the consensual, bureaucratic models of provision and regulation which carried over from the era of public ownership. Increasingly these more numerous players are seeking to test their rights and obligations against the legal frameworks of each sector . . .
>
> The key instances of litigation have occurred under circumstances where restrictions that had hitherto applied have been lifted or have been in the process of being lifted. Thus we have seen dominant incumbent firms seeking to improve the regulatory conditions as they face competition . . . a dominant incumbent challenging the UK implementation of EC liberalisation measures . . . new entrants seeking to improve the conditions of entry . . . and a pressure group challenging the relaxation of minimum service levels.[147]

In *Scottish Power*,[148] the refusal of the Director-General of Electricity Supply to reopen a consensual modification of the company's licence in light of the MMC's recommendation of more favourable terms for another company was quashed for *Wednesbury* unreasonableness. Since the D-G had put forward no 'preventing reason', he could scarcely complain at this use of judicial review as an agent for rationality in the regulatory process.

Judicial insistence on transparency and dialogue in regulation sits comfortably with the all-pervasive principles of better regulation. This kind of procedural review came to prominence in *Interbrew*,[149] a first defeat for the Competition Commission (the more powerful successor to the MMC). The company contested the minister's decision to accept the Commission's recommendation[150] that it be required to divest itself of a recently acquired UK brewing business. The Commission's failure to raise with Interbrew the remedy it was considering was held to amount to procedural unfairness:

> *Moses J:* There can be no doubt but that the Commission owed a duty of fairness in conducting its investigation as to the merger. The content of the duty will vary from case to case but generally it will require the decision maker to identify in advance areas which are causing him concern in reaching the decision in question . . . I accept that the Commission was under no obligation to undertake a two-stage procedure revealing firstly its provisional views as to the consequences of a duopoly and, at the second stage, inviting comments upon a proposed remedy. I also accept that the Commission was under time restraints . . . But that, in my judgment, would not have prevented the issue being raised in a way which would have given Interbrew a fair opportunity to deal with it.

147 C. Scott, 'The juridification of relations in the UK utilities sector' in Black, Muchlinski and Walker, *Commercial Regulation and Judicial Review*, pp. 20, 56.

148 *R v Director-General of Electricity Supply, ex p. Scottish Power plc* (3 February 1997, unreported). For other contemporary examples see *Mercury Communications Ltd v Director-General of Telecommunications* [1996] 1 WLR 48 and *Save Our Railways* (see p. 405 below).

149 *Interbrew SA v Competition Commission* [2001] EWHC Admin 367.

150 Today it is the agency and not the minister that has the prime decision-making responsibility in monopolies and mergers: Enterprise Act 2002.

Legal accountability works to promote, and is itself promoted by, the increased amount of information and explanation available from the regulators. The courts, in other words, play a composite role, constituting machinery for accountability but contributing also to public accountability by, for example, buttressing reasoned decision-making (see Chapter 14). Indicative perhaps of future developments, the *Eisai* case[151] shows the outlines of what Shapiro has called 'synoptic dialogue':[152] the regulator is being asked to supply evidence to show that the decision-making process, and ultimately the decision, is fair and rational. The dispute centred on the economic model used by NICE (see p. 123 above) to appraise the clinical benefits and cost-effectiveness of new medicines for NHS purposes. Wishing to have the whole matter re-opened, a pharmaceuticals company aggrieved by restrictive guidance on the availability of its products complained that the full workings of the methodology had not been disclosed in the public consultation. Protestations by the agency that this was a recipe for more technical wrangling and delay failed to move the court.

> *Richards LJ:* Procedural fairness does require release of the fully executable version of the model. It is true that there is already a remarkable degree of disclosure and of transparency in the consultation process; but that cuts both ways, because it also serves to underline the nature and importance of the exercise being carried out. The refusal to release the [workings] stands out as the one exception to the principle of openness and transparency that NICE has acknowledged as appropriate in this context. It does place consultees (or at least a sub-set of them, since it is mainly the pharmaceutical companies which are likely to be affected by this in practice) at a significant disadvantage in challenging the reliability of the model. In that respect it limits their ability to make an intelligent response on something that is central to the appraisal process.

The judicial resolve to avoid substantive matters of economic regulation has nonetheless held firm despite regular testing. The *GNER* case[153] centred on the rail regulator's policy of differential charging, whereby franchise holders, but not their competitors, had to pay substantial fixed track charges on the basis of greater operational costs. Dismissing a complaint of unlawful discrimination, Sullivan J held fast to the principle of no second-guessing:

> Ascertaining the cost that is directly incurred as a result of operating any particular train service is a complex and difficult task, and the answer to the question: 'what is that cost?' will be very much a matter of expert judgment. In a nutshell, the Office of the Rail Regulator considers that the variable track access charge, although imperfect, is the best answer that can be provided

151 *R (Eisai Ltd) v National Institute for Health and Clinical Excellence* [2008] EWCA Civ 438.

152 M. Shapiro, 'The giving reasons requirement' (1992) *University of Chicago Legal Forum* 179, 183; and see p. 103 above.

153 *R (Great North Eastern Railway Ltd) v Rail Regulator* [2006] EWHC 1942. Other cogent examples are *R (London and Continental Stations & Property Ltd.) v Rail Regulator* [2003] EWHC 2607 and *R (Centro) v Transport Secretary* [2007] EWHC 2729.

on the information presently available . . . Given the ORR's expertise in this highly technical field the Court would be very slow indeed to impugn the ORR's view . . . It is in any event no part of the Court's function to substitute its own view on matters of economic judgment: the question is not whether the ORR's approach to this issue makes good sense in terms of transport economics, but whether it is compliant with the [relevant] Regulations . . .

Where the statutory framework confers such a large measure of discretion upon the Regulator it would not be appropriate to focus solely upon the wording of the Act and to ignore the very detailed policies which are applied by the ORR . . . When these policies and practices are considered it is clear that the market conditions under which franchised operators and open access operators are able to seek access to the railway infrastructure are, in practice, very different indeed.

Regulatory lawyers have naturally been interested to explore Convention rights. Since economic regulation necessarily impinges on 'civil rights and obligations' the procedural requirements of Art. 6 feature prominently and have driven an expansion of statutory appeal rights as part of the 'new regulatory model'. The right to peaceful enjoyment of possessions in Art. 1 of the First Protocol is also in play: deprivation of possessions must be 'in the public interest' and 'subject to conditions provided by law'. We see how the substantive and procedural constraints on the Macrory-style use of financial penalties are neatly tailored to promote compliance, especially via the proportionality principle, so exploiting the very extensive margin of appreciation for acting in the public interest customarily allowed under this Article.[154]

In *Marcic v Thames Water Utilities Ltd*,[155] the Court of Appeal and House of Lords clashed over the judicial role. M's property had suffered repeated flooding from sewerage systems operated by TW, which made his house virtually unsaleable; only major drainage works could resolve the problem. The Court of Appeal awarded damages under the HRA for a breach of Art. 1 of Protocol 1 and Art. 8, as well as in the tort of nuisance. TW had failed to demonstrate that its scheme of priorities struck a fair balance between the competing interests of M and other customers. But how did this square with a regulatory system predicated on OFWAT's power to make an enforcement order?[156] Implicit in 'sustained and focused control' is that public regulation of statutory undertakings constrains free-ranging private law rights of action; the graded responses of the 'enforcement pyramid' must have room to operate. Insisting that the regulation must be considered in the round, the House of Lords refused to allow M to side-step OFWAT (to which he had in fact never complained).

Lord Nicholls: The claim based on the Human Rights Act 1998 raises a broader issue: is the statutory scheme as a whole, of which this enforcement procedure is part,

[154] *Lithgow v UK* (1986) 8 EHRR 329; *R (SRM Global Master Fund) v HM Treasury* [2009] EWHC 227.

[155] [2002] EWCA Civ 64; [2003] UKHL 66.

[156] The case pre-dates the agency's power to impose financial penalties. An enforcement order would have generated individual rights to damages.

> Convention-compliant? In the present case the interests Parliament had to balance included, on the one hand, the interests of customers of a company whose properties are prone to sewer flooding and, on the other hand, all the other customers of the company whose properties are drained through the company's sewers. The interests of the first group conflict with the interests of the company's customers as a whole in that only a minority of customers suffer sewer flooding but the company's customers as a whole meet the cost of building more sewers. As already noted, the balance struck by the statutory scheme is to impose a general drainage obligation on a sewerage undertaker but to entrust enforcement of this obligation to an independent regulator who has regard to all the different interests involved. Decisions of the Director are of course subject to an appropriately penetrating degree of judicial review by the courts. In principle this scheme seems to me to strike a reasonable balance. Parliament acted well within its bounds as policy maker . . . The malfunctioning of the statutory scheme on this occasion does not cast doubt on its overall fairness as a scheme.

Lord Hoffman explained that in complex matters of economic regulation the courts should proceed cautiously, including in human rights cases. (Linked themes are the circumspect approach in resources cases (see Chapter 16) and an evident concern to keep the lid on HRA damages claims (see Chapter 17)):

> When one is dealing with the capital expenditure of a statutory undertaking providing public utilities on a large scale . . . the matter is no longer confined to the parties to the action. If one customer is given a certain level of services, everyone in the same circumstances should receive the same level of services. So the effect of a decision about what it would be reasonable to expect a sewerage undertaker to do for the plaintiff is extrapolated across the country. This in turn raises questions of public interest. Capital expenditure on new sewers has to be financed; interest must be paid on borrowings and privatised undertakers must earn a reasonable return. This expenditure can be met only by charges paid by consumers. Is it in the public interest that they should have to pay more? And does expenditure on the particular improvements with which the plaintiff is concerned represent the best order of priorities? These are decisions which courts are not equipped to make in ordinary litigation. It is therefore not surprising that for more than a century the question of whether more or better sewers should be constructed has been entrusted by Parliament to administrators rather than judges.

(d) Judicial supervision (II): Reach

The proliferation of indirect forms of governance raised the question of amenability to judicial review. In the 1980s 'the Datafin project'[157] entailed the assertion of jurisdiction in cases stated to involve 'public power'. But how far could this sensibly go? With one eye on the caseload, how should the courts

[157] So dubbed by M. Aronson, 'A public lawyer's responses to privatisation and outsourcing' in Taggart (ed.) *The Province of Administrative Law* (Hart Publishing, 1997).

deal with a mass of self-regulatory organisations (SROs) more or less, or not at all, connected with the state (see p. 326 below)? Simply to abstain might offend against the historical role of judicial review, protection of individuals from abuse of power; this was an argument raised by a range of applicants scrambling to gain entry into judicial review procedure.[158] Alternatively, was there not a need to adjust judicial review jurisdiction to meet the twin realities of SROs being 'steered' by, and exercising powers on behalf of, government? It is important to keep in mind however that judicial review is only one form of judicial supervision. Not before time, the courts have begun to mix and match 'public' and 'private' law doctrines better to reflect the subtle mixes of 'public' and 'private' power.

The *GCHQ* case had expanded the reach of common law principles of judicial review (see p. 107 above): but what then? Three broad positions were possible:[159]

1. Judicial review should operate to keep statutory and prerogative bodies under supervision, it being geared towards, and confined to, the exercise of explicitly governmental and legal powers.
2. Judicial review should apply to any exercise of regulatory power actually delegated by the state. This fits with the move to indirect forms of administration, and encompasses some, but importantly not all, forms of self-regulation.
3. Judicial review should extend to the exercise of monopoly power over an important sector of national life. This conveys a different sense of publicness to (2), being premised not on a connection with the state but on the amount of power exercisable.

The leading case of *R v Panel of Take-overs and Mergers, ex p. Datafin plc*[160] shows the judges moving beyond (1) to (2), and even flirting with (3). A non-statutory SRO, the Panel devised and operated the relevant City Code. It had no direct statutory, prerogative or common law powers, nor was it in contractual relationship with the financial market or with individual dealers, but it clearly was a major actor in the regulatory network. Supported by statutory powers which presupposed its existence, and boasting a City-wide membership which included nominees of the Bank of England, its decisions could result in the imposition of sanctions. When the Panel rejected Datafin's complaint of breach of the Code by a rival bidder, the Court of Appeal held it susceptible to judicial review:

158 For diverse reasons: no other cause of action; special relevance of tests of legality, fairness and irrationality; and superior public law remedies (quashing orders). Employment cases were much to the fore, see e.g. *R v East Berkshire Health Authority, ex p. Walsh* [1985] QB 152.

159 A fourth position, that judicial review should regulate all forms of power, public or private, exercised by the state or otherwise, was never seriously on the agenda.

160 [1987] QB 815. See D. Pannick, 'Who is subject to judicial review and in respect of what?' [1992] *PL* 1

> *Lord Donaldson MR:* In all the reports it is possible to find enumerations of factors giving rise to the jurisdiction, but it is a fatal error to regard the presence of all those factors as essential or as being exclusive of other factors. Possibly, the only essential elements are what can be described as a public element, which can take many different forms, and the exclusion from the jurisdiction of bodies whose sole source of power is a consensual submission to its jurisdiction . . . The Panel . . . is without doubt performing a public duty and an important one . . . In this context I should be very disappointed if the courts could not recognise the realities of executive power and allowed their vision to be clouded by the subtlety and sometimes complexity of the way in which it can be exerted.

Since a public element could be found in most walks of life, the reasoning was potentially explosive. Whereas previously, in establishing the limits of the supervisory jurisdiction, the courts had looked at the *source* of a body's power, the judges had now encompassed in the test the *nature* of the power being exercised.

But matters were not so simple. From the viewpoint of the regulator, 'the decisive interest' of the case lay in 'the guidelines . . . indicating that the jurisdiction would be sparingly exercised'.[161] Not only had Lord Donaldson spoken of the 'considerable latitude' owed to a SRO interpreting its own rules; he had further asserted the court's discretionary power to limit public law remedies (see Chapter 16). Intervention should be by declaration and should be 'historic rather than contemporaneous' in order to sustain orderly markets. The reasoning in *Datafin* was a poor solution: discouraging to litigants, it conjured the shadow but denied the substance of judicial review.

In asserting jurisdiction, the court had failed to provide appropriate guidance, sparking a predictable welter of litigation, and complex and contradictory case law. Subsequent cases focused on the need to find 'not merely a public but potentially a governmental interest'[162] in the regulation (an approach akin to position (2)). Requiring of the judges 'a greater perspicacity and insight into governmental intentions than most politicians and civil servants would claim',[163] a court might ask whether 'the Government would have assumed the powers being exercised "but for" self-regulation?' Alternatively, it might ask whether the body had been 'integrated' in a system of regulation approved or defined by government, such as co-regulation.[164] This both fitted the facts of *Datafin* and marked a substantial limitation on the scope of the project but, as would later be candidly admitted, it was as often as not 'a matter of feel'.[165] The Bar Council, the Advertising Standards Authority, the Press Complaints Commssion (see p. 462 below), and a not-for-profit company regulating

[161] Lord Alexander, ' Judicial review and City regulators' (1989) 52 *MLR* 640, 644.

[162] *R v Chief Rabbi of the United Hebrew Congregations, ex p. Wachmann* [1992] 1 WLR 1036 (Simon Brown J).

[163] R. Cranston, 'Reviewing judicial review' in Richardson and Genn (eds.), *Administrative Law and Government Action* (Clarendon Press, 1994), p. 48.

[164] *R v Chief Rabbi of the United Hebrew Congregations, ex p. Wachmann.*

[165] *R (Tucker) v Director General of the National Crime Squad* [2003] ICR 599 (Scott Baker LJ).

farmers' markets have all been held amenable to the jurisdiction; the contrary list is a bewildering array of bodies ranging from the Football Association to Lloyds of London, the Labour Party and the Chief Rabbi.[166] As Aronson explained,[167] the root of the difficulty lay in the project's binary logic. The public/private dichotomy it assumed did not match the social reality – made ever more apparent as regulatory reform progressed – of mixed power with both public and private elements.

Datafin left an unresolved tension between recognition of institutional power as a reason for subjecting a body to review and exemption of bodies with a contractual source of power. It had previously been held in *Law v National Greyhound Racing Club Ltd*[168] that the NGRC was not the kind of body covered by judicial review, its licensing powers being derived from contract. In effect, the club had been treated as a 'domestic tribunal'. Post-*Datafin*, the key question was whether the contract 'exception' should be disapplied in a type (3) monopoly situation. Matters came to a head in *R v Jockey Club Disciplinary Committee, ex p. Aga Khan*.[169] The Jockey Club never had been drawn into a co-regulatory partnership with government; its great powers of organisation and control of all aspects of horse racing were exercised through its rulebook, which constituted a contract for those in the industry. One of his horses having failed a dope test and been disqualified, the applicant sought judicial review. This attempt further to extend the frontiers of the jurisdiction signally failed however.

> *Sir Thomas Bingham MR*: Those who agree to be bound by the Rules of Racing have no effective alternative to doing so if they want to take part in racing in this country . . . But this does not . . . alter the fact . . . that the powers which the Jockey Club exercises over those who (like the applicant) agree to be bound by the Rules of Racing derive from the agreement of the parties and give rise to private rights . . . It would in my opinion be contrary to sound and long-standing principle to extend the remedy of judicial review to such a case.[170]

Not all public lawyers were dismayed. Aronson urged the need to broaden horizons: 'the way in which the state has restructured itself . . . will even raise questions as to whether the best way of handling an issue might not be an adaptation of private law doctrines'.[171] Some tools lay close to hand. Lord Denning

[166] See Lord Woolf, J. Jowell and A. Le Sueur, *de Smith's Judicial Review*, 6th edn (Sweet & Maxwell, 2007), Ch. 3.

[167] Aronson, 'A public lawyer's responses to privatisation and outsourcing'; and see J. Black, 'Constitutionalising self-regulation' (1996) 59 *MLR* 24.

[168] [1983] 1 WLR 1302.

[169] [1993] 1 WLR 909.

[170] The decision would later be reaffirmed for the purpose of the current procedural rules, introduced in 2000: *R (Mullins) v Jockey Club* [2005] EWHC 2197. And see below, Ch. 15.

[171] Aronson, 'A public lawyer's responses to privatisation and outsourcing', p. 70. See also, D. Oliver, 'Common values in public and private law and the public/private divide' [1997] *PL* 467.

had conjured a supervisory jurisdiction that was neither contractual nor grounded in judicial review in the context of restraint of trade. Such was *Nagle v Fielden*,[172] in which the Jockey Club's refusal to license a female racehorse trainer was held challengeable as contrary to public policy. Previously overshadowed by *Datafin*, this parallel common law control was ripe for reinvigoration. Alternatively, where the court could find – or construct – a contractual nexus in the self-regulation, implied terms could be used to impose good governance values.[173] The *Bradley* case[174] in 2004 shows the potentials. A five-year ban imposed by the Appeal Board of the Jockey Club struck at B's livelihood; the Club could be said to have promised that it would give effect to a *lawful* decision of the Board. Effectively bridging the public/private 'divide', Stephen Richards J held that both features generated a supervisory function, 'very similar to that of a court on judicial review':

> Given the difficulties that sometimes arise in drawing the precise boundary . . . I would consider it surprising and unsatisfactory if a private law claim in relation to the decision of a domestic body required the court to adopt a materially different approach from a judicial review claim in relation to the decision of a public body. In each case the essential concern should be with the lawfulness of the decision taken: whether the procedure was fair, whether there was any error of law, whether any exercise of judgment or discretion fell within the limits open to the decision maker, and so forth . . . The supervisory role of the court should not involve any higher or more intensive standard of review when dealing with a non-contractual than a contractual claim.

The court should still show deference; it was the secondary decision-maker in the sense familiar from *Huang*. As Lord Phillips observed on appeal, 'professional and trade regulatory and disciplinary bodies are usually better placed than is the court to evaluate the significance of breaches of the rules or standards of behaviour governing the professions or trades to which they relate'. The ban was upheld, so serious were the findings of corrupt practice.

The HRA gives all this an extra twist. Specifying a modified 'public functions' test, s. 6 of the Act reflects the broad impetus – and limitations – of the *Datafin* project. As we see in the next chapter, a line of cases, some involving SROs, but mostly concerning the contractualisation of public services,[175] take a cautious approach to amenability to Convention rights.

172 [1966] 2QB 663.

173 As sign-posted by a string of trade union disciplinary cases, e.g. *Lee v Showmen's Guild* [1952] QB 329 and *Edwards v SOGAT* [1971] Ch 354; and see Ch. 8 below.

174 *Bradley v Jockey Club* [2004] EWHC 2164; [2005] EWCA Civ 1056. See also *Mullins v McFarlane* [2006] EWHC 986. An independent Horseracing Regulatory Authority is now in place.

175 The leading authority being *YL (by her litigation friend the Official Solicitor) v Birmingham City Council and Others* [2007] UKHL 27. For cases involving SROs, see *R (Beer) v Hampshire Farmers Markets Ltd* [2004] 1 WLR 233 and *R (Mullins) v Jockey Club* [2005] EWHC 2197.

(e) Thickening legal accountability: High-class tribunals

The trend in economic regulation today is a closer form of legal 'answerability' with statutory appeals and reviews by high-powered tribunals substituted for judicial review. Reflecting and reinforcing the increased role for competition law in market regulation, the Competition Appeal Tribunal (CAT) is the prime example.[176] Adjudicating on decisions of the Competition Commission, the OFT, and sectoral agencies like OFCOM, CAT fits neatly into Prosser's 'new regulatory model'. The logic of CAT – effectively a specialist regulatory court – is creative tension or less 'deference'. A leading practitioner notes the crude equation: 'review of experts by generalists – wide margin of appreciation; review of experts by other experts (potentially even 'more expert experts') – narrow margin'.[177] Possible non-compliance with Art. 6 ECHR, stemming from the limitations of judicial review (see further Chapter 14), is also avoided.

CAT's great strength is its cross-disciplinary nature: a panel of legal chairmen and a panel of members with backgrounds in business and accountancy, regulation and economics. Specially tailored rules of procedure render it better equipped for 'hard look' review than the Administrative Court; complex factual issues and technical evaluations are well catered for:

> The Tribunal will pay close attention to the probative value of documentary evidence. Where there are essential evidential issues that cannot be satisfactorily resolved without cross-examination, the Tribunal may permit the oral examination of witnesses. As regards expert evidence, the Tribunal will expect the parties to make every effort to narrow the points at issue, and to reach agreement where possible.[178]

In fact CAT has a split jurisdiction.[179] First it deals with appeals on the merits, the strong version of legal 'answerability'. Although the Court of Appeal may step in occasionally to clip its claws,[180] CAT can thus range much more freely than does the ordinary judicial watchdog. Indicative of the 'hard look' approach, the Tribunal has elaborated its own checklist. The regulator's decision is tested to see whether it 'is incorrect or, at the least, insufficient, from the point of view of (i) the reasons given; (ii) the facts and analysis relied on; (iii) the law applied; (iv) the investigation undertaken; or (v) the procedure followed'.[181] Point (ii) speaks volumes.

[176] Closely followed by the Financial Services and Markets Tribunal, which deals with disciplinary decisions and proceedings taken for market abuse.

[177] de la Mare, 'Regulatory judicial review', p. 6.

[178] CAT, *Guide to Proceedings* (2007), p. 13.

[179] Competition Act 1998; Enterprise Act 2002.

[180] As when CAT, claiming a supervisory role, sought to impose on the regulator a timetable for re-investigation: *OFCOM v Floe Telecom Ltd* [2006] EWCA Civ 768.

[181] *Freeserve v Director General of Telecommunications* [2003] CAT 5.

In *Albion*,[182] a CAT case concerning (the lack of) competition in the water industry, the first market entrant since privatisation struck a deal to supply a large industrial user. The incumbent supplier responded in classic monopolistic style by imposing hefty charges for use of its pipes. OFWAT rejected Albion's complaint of abuse of dominant position. Strongly rebuking the regulator, CAT pressed the need for more 'regulating for competition':

> The effect of [OFWAT's] decision is to render uneconomic Albion's proposal to supply Shotton Paper . . . The consequent removal of choice for the customer and the potential elimination of the [market entrant] are matters which the Tribunal views with serious concern . . . Irrespective of the justification in principle for a policy designed to enable incumbents to recover their sunk and common costs and fund investment . . . the particular application . . . maintains a retail price which is not shown to be cost-based and which the evidence strongly suggests to be excessive.

Second, in certain cases concerning mergers and market investigations a different balance has been struck, with CAT statutorily enjoined 'to apply the same principles as would be applied by a court on an application for judicial review'. Predictably since legal principles are generally malleable (see Chapter 5), and judicial review principles particularly so (see Chapter 3), this requirement has been a recipe for conflict between CAT and both regulators and judges. Question: where (as effectively with *GNER*) the Administrative Court would choose 'super-*Wednesbury*' (see p. 314 above), is it open to CAT to use 'ordinary *Wednesbury*' or even 'anxious scrutiny' as the standard of review?

A 2004 merger case, *IBA Health Ltd*,[183] shows the jostling for position. In upholding a complaint against the OFT, CAT ventured to suggest that because it was an expert body there was no direct read-over of the restrictive case law on judicial review. The Court of Appeal was naturally more conservative. 'If and in so far as CAT did not apply the ordinary principles of judicial review as would be applied by a court . . . then they failed to observe the mandatory requirements'. Even so, the judges allowed that some stretching was permitted. 'CAT was right to observe that its approach should reflect the "specific context" in which it had been created as a specialist tribunal.' Giving substance to the idea of a 'synoptic dialogue', CAT duly exploited the opportunity in *UniChem*.[184] 'The Tribunal has jurisdiction, acting in a supervisory rather than appellate capacity, to determine whether the OFT's conclusions are adequately supported by evidence, that the facts have been properly found, that all material factual considerations have been taken into account, and that material

182 *Albion Water Ltd v Water Services Regulation Authority* [2006] CAT 23. See further *Dwr Cymru v Albion Water Ltd* [2008] EWCA Civ 536.

183 *Office of Fair Trading v IBA Health Ltd* [2004] 4 All ER 1103.

184 *UniChem v Office of Fair Trading* [2005] CompAR 907, where CAT also drew on the leading ECJ authority of Case C-12/03P *Commission v Tetra Laval* [2005] ECR I-987. See also *Tesco plc v Competition Commission* [2009] CAT 6.

facts have not been omitted.' The message is clear: for securing effective legal accountability, cutting-edge market regulation demands technically superior forms of adjudication. Given New Labour's predilection for handing decisions of major economic significance to super-regulators, this type of close scrutiny has added value. 'If the CAT does not control, it may be argued that these agencies are in a real sense uncontrollable.'[185]

4. Breaking the mould

Public power exercised through indirect means is still public power and public lawyers in an age of governance must engage with the forms, functions and activities of hybridised systems ranged across a continuum from self-regulation to highly developed species of meta-, meso-, and co-regulation.[186] We started with the metaphor of government steering not rowing: a light hand on the tiller. Now we see that under New Labour the steering has increased in many sectors.

(a) Self-regulation in issue

Britain was once described as 'something of a haven for self-regulation'.[187] Prevalent in major parts of industry, in the City of London and in the professions, this reflected and reinforced the attributes of co-operation, informality and discretion, the high degree of trust associated with an elite or 'club' style of government. The second half of the twentieth century saw a decline; the more so, once a distinctive regulatory reform agenda took hold in the 1980s. While self-regulatory organisations (SROs) continued to play a vital role across broad swathes of the functioning economy, such arrangements came increasingly to be, in Moran's words, 'institutionalised, codified and juridified'.[188] The regulatory culture was being transformed on the back of efforts to redefine self-regulation 'to encompass the public interest, the interests of users as well as practitioners'.[189]

The Financial Services Act 1986, the classic example from the Thatcher years, constitutes the 'halfway house' between a pre-existing network of self-governing bodies expressing 'group' values, and the current structures of super-agency and RBR. At the heart of the scheme lay a blend of statutory and self-regulation: a more elaborate and hierarchical system of rules and procedures than hitherto.[190] The state was becoming 'a more pervasive presence

[185] B. Kennelly, 'Judicial review and the Competition Appeal Tribunal' (2006) 11 *Judicial Review* 160, 163.

[186] J. Freeman, 'Private parties, public function and the real democracy problem in the new administrative law' in Dyzenhaus (ed.), *Recrafting the Rule of Law* (Hart Publishing, 1999).

[187] R. Baggott, ' Regulatory reform in Britain: The changing face of self-regulation' (1989) 67 *Pub. Admin.* 436, 438.

[188] M. Moran, *The British Regulatory State: High modernism and hyper-innovation* (Oxford University Press, 2003), p. 69.

[189] A. Page, `Self-regulation: The constitutional dimension' (1986) 49 *MLR* 141, 164.

[190] L. Gower, '"Big bang" and City regulation' (1988) 51 *MLR* 1.

than ever in financial markets'[191] but the Act was nonetheless a compromise and one which New Labour was ultimately unwilling to tolerate. Catching the public mood, the National Consumer Council[192] was also busy with a shopping list of reforms – public appointments, procedures for consultation and rule-making and complaint mechanisms. The theme was one of 'regulated autonomy',[193] with the delegation of state authority implied by self-regulation needing to be matched by an injection of good governance values. The BRTF later took up the baton under New Labour, reading across into self-regulation its five-fold principles of better regulation.[194]

Countervailing trends can be seen at work. On the one hand – the spread of state tentacles – there is more taming of self-regulation. On the other hand, embedding self-regulation in the regulatory state points up additional possibilities for SROs alongside, or as an alternative to, government agencies. Given the problems of overload associated with direct forms of state intervention, as also the ideological attraction of more private autonomy, policy-makers may prefer to hazard the route of making self-interested, collective action contribute to the achievement of public-policy objectives.[195] The danger with self-regulation is that regulatory capture is there from the outset[196]; the lack of legitimacy cannot be wished away.

Collective self-regulatory systems come in all shapes and sizes.[197] The degree of monopoly power and the relevance of the regulation for third parties are key variables. Does the SRO regulate all the suppliers in a market, including non-members? If so, it is a prime candidate for harnessing. Legal status and degree of formality are important design choices. The body may or may not have been specially created for the purpose. It may or may not have statutory powers. It may be merely an unincorporated association, be constituted under a (private) Act of Parliament, or, as is more commonly the case, be a company limited by guarantee (so having a basic constitutional structure in the form of the company memorandum and articles). And is there in effect a 'mini legal system': a well-established and generally recognised set of practice rules as with doctors and lawyers? The rules themselves may have binding force, sanctioned perhaps by a disciplinary tribunal,[198] or they may be more or less voluntary ('soft law'). Different approaches to access and consumer voice are again of interest. Are

[191] M. Moran, 'Thatcherism and financial regulation' (1988) 59 *Pol. Q.* 20, 26.

[192] National Consumer Council, *Self-Regulation* (1986) and *Models of self-regulation* (2000).

[193] P. Birkinshaw, N. Lewis and I. Harden, *Government by Moonlight: The hybrid parts of the state* (Routledge, 1990); C. Graham, 'Self-regulation' in Richardson and Genn (eds.), *Administrative Law and Government Action*.

[194] BRTF, *Self Regulation* (1999).

[195] See the pioneering work of W. Streeck and P. Schmitter (eds.), *Private Interest Government* (Sage, 1985).

[196] J. Kay, 'The forms of regulation' in Goodhart and Seldon (eds.), *Financial Regulation – Or Over-Regulation* (IEA, 1988), p. 34.

[197] A. Ogus, 'Rethinking self-regulation' (1995) 15 *OJLS* 97; I. Bartle and P. Vass, *Self-Regulation and the Regulatory State* (CRI, 2005).

[198] B. Harris, *Disciplinary and Regulatory Proceedings*, 4th edn (Jordan, 2006) is the leading text.

there formal processes of consultation with designated 'stakeholders' such as consumer groups? Is there a more flexible mix of formal and informal discussions with interested parties amounting to a regulatory negotiation?[199] And what, ultimately, is the input from government across the broad regulatory cycle of rule formulation, monitoring and inspection, enforcement and sanctions, for example under the banner of 'better regulation'?

Picking up on ideas of 'decentred regulation' or 'regulation in many rooms', BRTF's analysis highlights themes of flexibility and responsiveness, and of cost-effectiveness and expertise:[200]

- Self-regulatory rules are by definition developed by those directly involved in the industry or profession and so can be said to best reflect the issues and needs of the particular sector.
- It can be quicker to achieve self-regulation than statutory regulation.
- Self-regulation can generate a sense of ownership within the profession or industry and so is more likely to secure a high level of compliance.
- It can harness common interest in maintaining the reputation of those involved in the activity.
- It can be easily adapted or updated to reflect changing circumstances or industry developments.
- In some areas, especially the professions, it may be disproportionately expensive or difficult for government to acquire the specialist knowledge necessary to regulate effectively.
- Self-regulation can provide a quicker and cheaper means of redress.
- It can harness the close relationship between the industry/profession and its clients.

To which we might add:

- Self-regulation is cheap, because the regulated bear the burden of the costs of regulation.

The dangers are conveniently summarised by BRTF in terms of coverage and – as envisaged by private interest theories of regulation in terms of 'rent-seeking' – of conflicts of interest:[201]

- All those who trade in the profession or sector will not necessarily operate within the self-regulatory rules.
- It may be difficult to ensure that consumers appreciate the implications of trading with those who operate outside the rules.
- Consumers may not be aware of who or what is covered.
- There is a danger of self interest being put ahead of the public interest and

[199] As discussed in the agency context in the US: see J. Freeman and L. Langbein, 'Regulatory negotiation and the legitimacy benefit' (2000) 9 *New York University Environmental Law J.* 60.

[200] BRTF, *Self Regulation*, p. 4.

[201] *Ibid.*, p. 5.

self-regulation may lead to anti-competitive behaviour, especially in terms of restricting market entry beyond the restrictions required to protect consumers.

- The organisations involved in enforcement may not be open and transparent about their processes and outcomes.
- There may be a general lack of public confidence in the ability of or the incentives for a self-regulatory body to provide effective consumer protection, and to impose appropriate sanctions when rules are broken.

To which we would add:

- There is the problem of accountability and control through the acquisition of power by bodies not answerable in the conventional way through the political process and the diffusion of government responsibility.

(b) Harnessing: Policy options

The scope for creative blends of self-regulation and government regulation – forms of 'responsive regulation' whereby different combinations of techniques are identified and applied in a myriad of contexts – is demonstrated. We see how the concept of self-regulation is both sufficiently flexible to accommodate a considerable degree of official involvement and shades naturally into ideas of 'partnership' and 'co-regulation'. The broad policy options can be viewed as a continuum:

(i) pure self-regulation
(ii) tacitly supported self-regulation
(iii) coerced self-regulation
(iv) sanctioned self-regulation/formally identifiable elements of meta-regulation
(v) mandated self-regulation/ substantial elements of meso-regulation
(vi) fully-fledged co-regulation.

As an ideal type, category (i) conveys the classical idea of voluntary arrangements, of bottom-up control in the functioning economy where the collective group, industry or profession desires self-regulation and takes the initiative. Whereas, at a minimum, the regulatory state exhibits 'a passive interest' liable to be engaged should some major 'shock' afflict the legitimacy of a self-regulatory system.[202] Government relying on the body's regulatory functions, as reflected in a decision for the time being not to take legal powers: such is (ii), self-regulation with the tacit support of state actors. As illustrated by the Press Complaints Commission (below, p. 462), category (iii) denotes the not unfamiliar scenario of the SRO formulating and applying a system of controls in response to threats – real or perceived – that otherwise government regula-

[202] Bartle and Vass, *Self-Regulation and the Regulatory State*, p. 3.

tion will be forthcoming. Subsequently of course the SRO may gain acceptance, such that reliance for effective workings on 'the shadow of the state' diminishes.

In (iv), state actors are seen playing a more active role, such that ideas of meta-regulation come to the fore. Formulated by the SRO, requirements are subjected to official approval: private ordering bears the stamp of public interest. The design and workings of trade association codes of practice are a prime example of this; statutory regulators would simply be overwhelmed otherwise.[203] Category (v), in which the SRO is required to establish and apply norms within a prescribed framework, is often termed statutory self-regulation. Very familiar in the professions, this harnessing or enrolment of non-state actors in what increasingly looks like 'collaborative governance' is epitomised today by sector-specific meso-regulation. The paradigm being that of 'partnership working', category (vi) shows the mixing of public with private power taken to new heights in formally established twin regulatory arrangements. This may be coupled as in (v) with strong elements of meta-regulation.

Better to convey the flavour, we have chosen some examples for closer inspection. First comes fundamental reform of professional self-regulation in health and social care. Currently being implemented in the name of patient protection, it exemplifies the continuing advance of the regulatory state. Meso-regulation is centre-stage. OFCOM-inspired co-regulation is the second illustration, or rather two versions of it. Critically related to the effectiveness of meta-regulation in underpinning the joint arrangements, the good and the ugly of this fashionable technique are on offer. In addition, in Chapter 10 on complaint systems we examine the Press Complaints Commission. Highly self-regulatory in terms of content, its workings show both the many advantages of voluntary systems and an ongoing struggle for legitimacy.

(c) Meso-regulation: Health- and social-care professionals

The 2007 White Paper *Trust, Assurance and Safety: The regulation of health professionals in the 21st century*[204] effectively challenged a bastion of self-regulation. The prompt was the long-running public inquiry into events involving mass murderer Harold Shipman, highlighting concerns that in matters of regulation the culture of the medical profession was too focused on doctors' interests.[205] Itself part of a larger package of reforms, which includes a new super-regulator (the Care Quality Commission) to oversee health and social-care provision in England generally,[206] the resulting statutory provision

[203] See e.g. FSA, *Confirmation of Industry Guidance* (2006).

[204] Cm. 7013 (2007).

[205] Dame Janet Smith, *Fifth Report of the Shipman Inquiry: Safeguarding patients* (2001); DoH *Learning from Tragedy: Keeping patients safe*, Cm. 7014 (2007).

[206] See Health and Social Care Act 2008, Part I.

takes the modern trend of increased legislative intervention in the regulatory affairs of the professions to new heights.

The case for reform was grounded in the present-day realities of clinical practice. Here as elsewhere, public trust is at a premium in view of less deference and greater technical complexity:

> There is emerging and growing public pressure for the relationship between the health professional and the patient to be an open, honest and active partnership, and a declining public willingness to accept passively and unquestioningly the clinical judgements that are made for them. The system that regulates health professionals, in its governance and its ability to provide objective assurance, needs to respond to these pressures, which will increase as the global economy and the open information society gather pace.
>
> As the technical ability to intervene effectively continues to accelerate, patient and public expectations of health professionals are rising proportionately and the work of health professionals is becoming more complex and specialised. Accordingly, the scope for human error increases, putting growing pressures on health professionals who strive to fulfil their fundamental ambitions and instincts to deliver clinical excellence. Our system of regulation needs to adapt and respond to those pressures.[207]

The policy development further illustrates the influence of better regulation principles across the piece, as with targeting and proportionality. Ministers also recognised the role of due process and accountability as vital sources of regulatory legitimacy. Testifying to the high standards of most health professionals, the White Paper said:

> We need a system . . . that is better able to identify people early on who are struggling . . . so that they have a fair chance to improve . . . and a system that is better able to detect and act against those very rare malicious individuals who risk undermining public and professional confidence.
>
> Sustaining confidence also means patients need to be assured that, when there are problems with health professionals, their concerns will be listened to and acted upon and that they will receive timely explanations . . . Professional regulation is about fairness to both sides of the partnership between patients and professionals. To command the confidence of both, it must also be *seen to be fair*, both to patients and to health professionals.[208]

Although nostrums of RBR infused the policy development, the Government's chief medical officer had to concede that 'there are real challenges in constructing a rigorous, comprehensive and robust assessment that can put accurate costings on the risks and benefits that need to be weighed carefully in an ideal analysis of professional regulation'. This was something of an understatement:

[207] *Trust, Assurance and Safety*, Cm. 7013 (2007), p. 16
[208] *Ibid.*, p. 2.

> Empirical information on the prevalence of death, injury, disability and mental distress caused by inadequate professional competence or malicious, discourteous or abusive conduct is not available. Even if it were, it would be difficult to cost. What price do we put on the benefits of patients' peace of mind and public confidence? How do we cost lives scarred by grief in families who have lost those they love? Can we measure the frustration and anxiety of health professionals enmeshed unnecessarily in national professional regulatory procedures? How do we measure the costs of a sense of having been unjustly treated? We are more dependent than we would wish to be on using judgement.[209]

The detailed provision in Part II of the Health and Social Care Act 2008 shows how the tentacles of the regulatory state spread in different ways. Take the demand for 'fire-watching' at the ground-floor level, where the role of private providers outside the NHS must be factored into the equation. The Act empowers a system of 'responsible officers' to help identify and handle cases of poor professional performance in organisations employing or contracting with doctors.[210] Putting in issue the very concept of professionally led regulation, the policy of 'assuring independence' sees – as a minimum requirement – parity of lay members with professional representatives on the relevant SROs, which include the General Medical Council, the Nursing and Midwifery Council, and the General Social Care Council. As for 'fire-fighting' in the form of fitness-to-practise cases, investigation and prosecution of doctors is separated from adjudication, better to allay concerns about the dominance of private practitioner interest. The hitherto imperious GMC retains basic functions such as registration but has otherwise lost out to a new corporate body, publicly appointed: the Office of the Health Professions Adjudicator.[211] The rules on enforcement are also stiffened: the civil, rather than criminal, standard of proof now applies across the sector.

A beefed-up system of meso-regulation fits the New Labour penchant for rationalisation. The drive was on for greater coherence and consistency in the face of diverse legal frameworks that, profession by profession, had been built up and amended over many years.[212] Officially described as a 'statutory overarching body', the Council for the Regulation of Health Care Professionals had been established in 2003 to promote best practice and the interests of patients and the public in the activities of the SROs.[213] Tasked with monitoring and reporting on their performance, investigating complaints against them, and providing government with advice, CRHB enjoyed a form of legal privileged access, given standing to refer fitness-to-practise decisions to the High Court on grounds such as undue lenience. The 2007 White Paper looked to add a more strategic approach centred on common protocols for local investigations

209 *Ibid.*, pp. 19–20
210 HSCA, ss. 119–20.
211 HSCA, ss. 98–110.
212 *Trust, Assurance and Safety*, p. 23.
213 NHS Reform and Health Care Professions Act 2002.

by the SROs.[214] Formally re-launched as the Council for Healthcare Regulatory Excellence (CHRE), the agency must regularly state how far, in its opinion, each SRO 'has complied with any duty imposed on it to promote the health, safety and well-being of patients and members of the public'. It must also learn lessons from complaints by 'investigating particular cases with a view to making general reports on the performance by the regulatory body of its functions or making general recommendations to the regulatory body affecting future cases'.[215]

Given the size and diversity of the sector, let alone the challenge involved in altering professional mindsets, these arrangements will provide a sharp test of meso-regulation. Will CHRE have sufficient resources to exercise real leverage or will it find itself squeezed? Or will the agency veer towards the hands-on, with the clear potential for duplication and infighting? Or will it pursue a more 'sweethearting' relationship, leaving itself vulnerable to criticisms of capture? Coupled with specific duties to inform and consult the public, the answers will in part be dictated by the use of new ministerial powers of direction 'as to the manner in which the Council exercises its functions' and 'to require the Council to investigate and report on a particular matter'. The outline of one of Scott's 'accountability networks' is visible, with the various actors or tiers of regulation put in continuing dialogue – interdependency. The statutory agency could however easily find itself piggy-in-the middle.

(d) Co-regulatory empire: OFCOM

For the designers of OFCOM, co-regulation was an alluring prospect. OFCOM would be able to stand back from regulation or reduce regulatory burdens where it could see effective self-regulation, allowing the super-agency to concentrate its resources in those areas where co- or self-regulation was not a practical proposition.[216] Flexible self-regulatory norms fitted the highly dynamic nature of the sector: 'we are moving away from a traditional model where the regulator opines intermittently on the importance of particular things, and the industry reacts, to one where we are actually working with the industry in an iterative process'.[217]

In benign conditions these potentials may be realised. Take broadcast advertising, the lifeblood of most commercially financed television and radio. Here OFCOM could enrol two organisations experienced in operating and adjudicating industry codes and well versed in upholding the basic principles of 'legal, decent, honest and truthful' advertising: CAP, the Committee of

214 *Trust, Assurance and Safety*, p. 9.

215 HSCA, s. 115.

216 OFCOM, *The Future Regulation of Broadcast Advertising* (2003), p. 8.

217 EUC, *Television Without Frontiers*, HL 27 (2006/7), Q. 125; and see M. Feintuck and M. Varney, *Media Regulation: Public interest and the law*, 2nd edn (Edinburgh University Press, 2006).

Advertising Practice, and ASA, the Advertising Standards Authority. This had the advantage of creating a 'one-stop shop' for advertising-content standards at a time of much convergence in the sector, while avoiding accusations of regulatory creep.

OFCOM's code-making and complaints-handling functions were delegated by statutory order[218] to two new limited companies sharing in the mixed industry and lay membership of CAP and ASA: the Broadcast Committee of Advertising Practice and the Advertising Standards Authority (Broadcast). There was the necessary caveat of the agency retaining its power to carry out any statutory function or duty ('no fettering'). To detail the respective roles, responsibilities and functions of the co-regulatory parties, 'soft law' in the form of a 'pseudo-contractual' MOU was used.[219] Agency officials had also to devise criteria for delegation. Ranging beyond better regulation principles, these provide a useful template for testing co-regulatory systems:[220]

- beneficial to consumers
- clear division of responsibilities between co-regulatory body and OFCOM
- accessible to members of the public
- independence from interference by interested parties
- adequate funding and staff
- achieve and maintain near-universal participation
- have effective and credible sanctions available
- auditing and review by OFCOM
- public accountability
- consistency with similar regulation
- independent appeals mechanism.

ASA and CAP were naturally keen to emphasise the notion of 'regulatory subsidiarity' in the form of partnership working:

> Co-regulation can only be truly effective where each partner . . . has full confidence in the role to be performed by the other . . . OFCOM's . . . role in such a partnership [should be] as an enabler and evaluator for co-regulation and not [to] second guess the decisions of the contractor . . . OFCOM should therefore have, as a default, a 'hands-off' posture towards the day-today operation of its co-regulatory partners. Indeed, these partners will only be useful if their independence is respected and any right for OFCOM routinely to interfere with the functions and procedures of its partners would be likely to undermine their authority. There would also be double jeopardy for those whose actions were to be regulated. This could mean, for example, leaving an adjudicatory body largely to determine – within the context

[218] Contracting Out (Functions Relating to Broadcast Advertising) and Specification of Relevant Functions Order 2004, SI. No 1975.

[219] *Memorandum of Understanding between OFCOM, ASA (B), BCAP and BASBOF (MoU)* (2004). BASBOF (the Broadcast Advertising Standards Board of Finance) would deal with the industry levy.

[220] OFCOM, *Consultation on Criteria for Transferring Functions to Co-regulatory Bodies* (2003).

> of OFCOM's statutory obligations – the standards appropriate for its sector, and to judge upon these free from pressure by OFCOM. This is not, however, to suggest that OFCOM have no input in the setting of acceptable standards. With OFCOM retaining statutory responsibility – and therefore Parliamentary accountability – for those contracted out functions, it should routinely maintain constructive communications with its partners on all areas of mutual concern. Equally, should public policy develop on issues dealt with by a particular co-regulatory relationship, these might legitimately and formally be raised by OFCOM with the body to whom it had contracted out any of its functions.[221]

The MoU explains the complex relationship further:

> OFCOM retains all its legal powers stemming from the Act, and is therefore ultimately able to make Code changes. It will however not normally seek to do so, as OFCOM recognises that BCAP is the 'self' in self-regulation and in the spirit of the desire by all parties to ensure that the new system is a success, undertakes to use this power only in exceptional circumstances. This allows for the fact that there may be occasions when . . . OFCOM has to insist that a rule(s) should be amended or introduced and BCAP is unwilling to do so . . . This may include the introduction of a prohibition on certain categories of product/service.[222]

It being made a condition of their licences that operators ensure compliance both with the BCAP codes and with ASA (B) directions, enforcement was the crux of the matter:

> ASA(B) will communicate its decisions clearly and promptly to all parties in response to a complaint/challenge . . . Decisions in relation to upheld complaints/challenges may instruct the advertiser and broadcaster to change the advertisement prior to further broadcast, instruct the broadcaster to restrict transmission as directed, or instruct the broadcaster to cease broadcasting the advertisement altogether . . .
>
> If, in the opinion of the Director General of ASA(B), a broadcaster fails to comply fully and promptly with a decision of ASA(B) . . .demonstrates a repeated disregard for decisions of ASA(B) or . . . commits one or more code breaches of sufficient seriousness to warrant in ASA(B)'s opinion a statutory sanction, the DG shall . . . refer the matter to OFCOM for OFCOM to consider further action. OFCOM undertakes to consider any such referrals promptly and to impose any such proportionate sanctions as it deems appropriate in the circumstances in support of ASA(B), taking into account any representations from the broadcaster(s) concerned. Such sanctions may include a formal reprimand, a fine, a warning about possible revocation of the broadcaster's licence or, ultimately, the actual termination of the licence.[223]

Considerable effort is needed to work the machinery effectively. The MoU details multiple liaison arrangements; it also specifies 'no surprises' – the two

[221] ASA and CAP, *Joint response to OFCOM Consultation on Criteria for Transferring Functions to Co-regulatory Bodies* (2004), pp. 3–4.

[222] *MoU*, pp. 6–8.

[223] *Ibid.*, pp. 13–14.

watchdogs should bark in unison. A strong dose of meta-regulation of the SROs – reporting to and monitoring by OFCOM across a range of performance indicators – is part of the prescription.

The design epitomises contemporary trends in regulatory governance. A determinedly mixed system of state and non-state supervision sets OFCOM at the centre of a regulatory web: sustained and focused control is premised on close collaboration. The model has so far functioned tolerably well. The standards of ASA (B) adjudication are underpinned by the work of an independent reviewer; another specialist body, the Broadcast Advertising Clearance Centre, performs the important 'fire-watching' role of pre-transmission examination and clearance of advertisements. Consumer representation on a BCAP advisory committee allows for external involvement in the code-making.[224] OFCOM meanwhile has been freer to focus on major issues of public concern.[225] With 'levels of mutual confidence and trust between practitioners, the self-regulatory authority and the statutory regulator that are arguably unparalleled elsewhere in Europe',[226] the agency has agreed the system to at least 2014.[227]

(e) Co-regulatory failure

Elsewhere in OFCOM's co-regulatory empire, trouble had been brewing. Regulation of one of the fastest growing areas, telecom premium rate services (PRS) and specifically 'participation TV', saw the agency authorised to approve the self-regulatory code of an 'enforcement authority', while again retaining powers to impose licence conditions and levy sanctions.[228] In practice, this meant ICSTIS (the Independent Committee for the Supervision of Standards of Telephone Information Services), a part-time industry body already dealing with the matter. The MoU duly provided: 'ICSTIS will have the role of administering and enforcing the Code, subject to the need to refer cases to OFCOM when network operators have failed to comply with an ICSTIS Direction.'[229] With few detailed reporting requirements, meta-regulation of the SRO was noticeably thin however. Much was being taken on trust.

Enter investigative journalists, who uncovered instances of callers to TV quizzes and competitions being tricked. This prompted ICSTIS, clearly not the most proactive of regulators, to introduce such basic measures as 'publication of complete, accurate, and easily understood rules' for interactive TV.[230] But

224 See for details, ASA, *Annual Reports*.

225 See e.g. OFCOM, *Final Statement on the Television Advertising of Food and Drink Products to Children* (February 2007).

226 OFCOM chief executive Ed Richards, speech to ISBA, March 2007.

227 A policy that sits comfortably with developing EU requirements: see M. Burri-Nenova, 'The new Audiovisual Media Services Directive' (2007) 44 CML Rev. 1689.

228 Communications Act 2003, ss. 120–4.

229 *Memorandum of Understanding between OFCOM and ICSTIS* (2005), p. 1.

230 ICSTIS, press release 8 March 2007; and see *Statement of Expectations for Call TV Quiz Services* (2006).

where was OFCOM, the agency with statutory responsibility for consumer protection? Actively engaged in the co-regulatory process, or so the Select Committee was told:

> Since the advent of such services, OFCOM and ICSTIS have worked closely together to ensure that they minimize confusion when telling consumers who to complain to, as well as maximizing their enforcement efforts and certainty for broadcasters and premium rate service providers about regulatory requirements and compliance. OFCOM and ICSTIS produced detailed new rules and guidance in 2006 as a result of viewer concern, the regulators' own monitoring and the rise in the number of Call TV quiz shows on television platforms. These new rules and guidance were aimed at ensuring best practice in the industry and providing appropriate consumer protection. As a result of OFCOM guidance and ICSTIS' rules, there were significant changes in the way Call TV quiz shows operated and the way they broadcast – with increased transparency for the viewer . . . Nevertheless, neither regulator is complacent. Both OFCOM and ICSTIS are keeping this area under review and are planning separate consultations.[231]

Understandably, the MPs were not convinced:

> Confusion has arisen from the involvement of both OFCOM and ICSTIS in regulation, a split which is confusing for the public and which complicates the procedure for dealing with complaints. A single regulator, in our view OFCOM, should take the lead and give direction; and that single body should take responsibility for registering all complaints and forwarding them as necessary.[232]

The Select Committee's report served as a valuable 'tin-opener', calling into question the production standards used in participation TV, involving some of the country's most popular shows. The super-agency had to fall back on classical techniques of government regulation, launching a whole series of formal investigations, which 'raised serious concerns for OFCOM about the scale of compliance failure in this area, and the impact on trust between broadcasters and viewers.' The resulting industry-wide review revealed a can of worms. At the heart of the problem lay 'the absence of systems designed to require, ensure and audit compliance. In the absence of such systems individual mistakes, whether the result of technical failure, misjudgement, negligence or deliberate deceit, too often went unnoticed or unreported and sometimes ignored.'[233]

Much of the difficulty lay in the complex contractual relationships between broadcasters, production companies and service providers, leading 'to lack of clarity about who was responsible to whom and for what, and to lack of due

[231] Commons Culture, Media and Sport Committee, *Call TV quiz shows*, HC 72, (2006/7), Evidence, p. 49.

[232] *Ibid.*, p. 3.

[233] OFCOM, *Report of the Ayres Inquiry into Television Broadcasters' Use of Premium Rate Telephone Services in Programmes* (2007), pp. 1–2.

diligence'[234] in the industry. But this was compounded on the regulatory side, which was quintessentially soft-touch. Co-regulation itself operated to blunt the effective exercise of public power:

> Failures of compliance could have continued on such a scale, and gone largely undetected, only if successive regulatory regimes had been less than fully effective . . . While ICSTIS is able to bar a service provider for periods . . . it has never done so in the case of a broadcast use of PRS. ICSTIS can impose fines of up to £250k for each offence, but the usual figure has been a fraction of that sum. [OFCOM's] Broadcasting Code requires broadcasters to observe the ICSTIS Code, so a breach of one is technically a breach of the other. But the risk of double jeopardy, or of OFCOM judging a broadcaster while, on the same facts, ICSTIS judges its service provider, has meant that most cases of alleged non-compliance associated with PRS in broadcasting have in the past been handled by ICSTIS alone . . . Many of the stakeholders I spoke to called for more clarity between ICSTIS and OFCOM . . . Memorably, one major service provider said he thought ICSTIS were convinced that the industry would resist tougher regulation: 'we wouldn't,' he said, 'we would welcome it but just want them to get on with it'.[235]

The aftermath points up the role – and limitations – of financial penalties as a regulatory sanction. As well as reputational damage, the formal investigations eventually resulted in millions of pounds' worth of fines including against all four main terrestrial broadcasters. The largest, a £6 million penalty levied on ITV for 'institutionalised failure', was reduced in view of an £8 million compensation fund set up by the company. PRS had however delivered very large profits and, with OFCOM restricted to fining 5 per cent of turnover, the Macrory penalty principle of eliminating 'any financial gain or benefit from non-compliance' was hardly respected.

Restoring credibility meant re-visiting the regulatory design. The imposition of a prior-approval system was a major dent in OFCOM's light-touch philosophy. Re-launched as 'PhonepayPlus' with a viewers' online advice and complaints service, the SRO announced that it would not hesitate to revoke a permission for breach of the conditions of a level playing field. A new 'compliance code panel', functionally separate and with equal numbers of lawyers and lay members, further illustrates the theme of regulated autonomy.[236] Revamping the broadcasters' licences to pinpoint their own ultimate responsibility for the programmes was another very necessary regulatory step in light of the fog engendered by complex contractual chains.[237]

New governance arrangements were made by formal framework agreement. As against the co-regulatory paradigm of partnership working, regulatory responsibility has been taken back and agency accountability sharpened. The SRO is reduced to little more than a satellite:[238]

[234] *Ibid.*, p. 4.

[235] *Ibid.*, pp. 4–5.

[236] PhonepayPlus, *The PhonepayPlus Sanctions Guide* (2008).

[237] OFCOM, *Participation TV: Protecting viewers and consumers* (2008).

[238] OFCOM/ PhonepayPlus, *Framework Agreement* (2008), pp. 1–2.

- OFCOM recognises PhonepayPlus as its agency, designated to deliver the day-to-day regulation of the market, by approving the PhonepayPlus Code of Practice. Regulatory strategy, scope and policy are developed in dialogue with PhonepayPlus, but final decisions will rest with OFCOM.
- OFCOM and PhonepayPlus will agree medium term and annual objectives, strategies and related funding arrangements. Final decisions on these matters rest with OFCOM but will be informed by recommendations from the PhonepayPlus Board based on their knowledge of the sector and relevant trends.
- OFCOM will provide one member on the appointment or re-appointment panels of members of the PhonepayPlus Board and the Chief Executive. All appointments and re-appointments shall be subject to approval by OFCOM.
- PhonepayPlus will propose and agree with OFCOM performance measures and efficiency targets for [its] activities. These should at minimum cover complaint handling, the processing of serious cases that require adjudication, the operation of the Contact Centre and supporting web and Interactive Voice Response (IVR) services, the compliance support activity, and operation of the prior permission (licensing) arrangements.

The affair serves as a warning. There is a pervasive sense at the beginning of agency officials believing their own co-regulatory propaganda; key items in the organisational template were not read across. With cutting-edge enterprise offering substantial commercial rewards and ample scope for nefarious practice, and co-regulatory design weighted towards the self-regulatory aspect, conditions were ripe for regulatory failure – ineffectiveness – at the expense of consumers. Distancing the Government regulator from the coalface raises question marks over the credibility of sanctions, not least when the SRO appears insufficiently attuned to different business models and/or lacks the resources to keep pace. The chain of delegated authority was unnaturally extended and diffuse. The affair highlights the frailty of regulator-on-regulator checks in the 'mutual accountability network', suggesting weaknesses in Scott's model. A real injection of political accountability was required to right matters.

5. Conclusion

Going back some twenty years, the institutional design of 'blue-rinsed' regulation exhibited serious deficiencies. Calculations of economic efficiency were emphasised by the Ofdogs, but the twin facts of agency discretion and competing interests could not be discounted. Failures of due process, transparency and accountability put in issue the legitimacy of agency action. Prosser's 'new regulatory model' bears testimony to a raft of changes in the intervening period centred on, but not confined to, the chief economic regulators. There is a pervasive sense of agency empowerment: wider ends (extensive legislative mandates), greater means (elaborate tools and techniques of enforcement), larger capacities (commission and expert staff). Credit where credit is due: much has also been done in recent years to clean up agency practice. Closed, bilateral approaches have largely given way to open, multilateral processes and consultation, even collective consumer 'voice'. At first internally driven as in the case of OFWAT, this development found proper recognition in statute and today is buttressed through the codification of 'good governance' obligations. British independent regulators have come of age.

External lines of accountability have also strengthened, if from a very low base. Experience confirms the strong role for audit techniques in 'regulating the regulators' – the more so when managerial and political accountability are combined through the select committee system. While reasserting the independence of regulators, the committees themselves have effectively framed the case for transparency and answerability; how better to rebut assertions of agency capture? The contributions of legal accountability are typically varied. Recent cases show the utility of regulatory judicial review on the procedural side; inflexible legal modes of classification are avoided in the aftermath of 'the Datafin project'; codification of better regulation principles inevitably means more opportunities for formal legal challenge. Yet questions of institutional competence loom large in this frequently technical and highly complex field. Courts, though still nominally in control, could see themselves sidelined by high-powered tribunals, an important feature of the fast-changing administrative law landscape. In substantive matters, CAT is not so easily bamboozled!

The problems of network accountability are more intractable. Taking water management as an example, we saw how complex webs of regulatory governance blur institutional responsibilities. Matters are naturally compounded in the EU context; opaque networks of public and private actors stretch across the different layers of governance. Another major factor is central government seeking to enhance its steering capacity, whereby agencies are not only empowered but also subjected to a glut of legislative rules and bureaucratic regulation (see Chapter 6). Building internal network checks and balances is a necessary but insufficient response. Democratic oversight – a dose of externality – is at a premium in these conditions.

Self-regulation poses in acute form the difficulty of securing the public interest. Equally, it is an integral part of light-touch thinking. It therefore presents government with both a challenge and an opportunity. Ideas of meta- and co-regulation are made more explicit in this age of governance (hybridisation). If carefully designed and operated, these types of indirect administration have considerable appeal. This however is a big 'if'. We sense that more bracing climes are starting to expose the shallowness of some of these regulatory fashions.

8

Contractual revolution

Contents

Forty years ago, contract was a low-lying feature in the administrative law landscape. This mirrored state forms, at the time the classic welfarist model of direct service provision by integrated, hierarchical, public bodies. It also reflected the non-development of a distinctive 'public law' body of legislation and jurisprudence.[1] On the one hand, Dicey dominant, the basic premise was that government contracts should be subject to the ordinary private law;[2] on the other, a history of Crown immunities and privileges reinforced the sense of an internal, executive-owned activity devoid of formal legal regulation.[3] Public procurement in its traditional format of buying in goods and services was both big business and largely hidden from view. Behind the scenes, a well-established 'law of the contract' was in operation, a reservoir of standard terms and conditions on which officials could draw when specifying performance and to anticipate disputes.[4]

Today in contrast, contract and regulation are twin pillars of the new architecture of governance.[5] Underpinning the development is the capacity of this great instrument of economic exchange for multi-tasking. In the guise of 'pseudo-contract' (see p. 198 above) it is *a way of modelling institutional relations* (all those MoUs). Under the broad rubric of 'contracting out' it is *the vehicle for the delivery of many public services.* And as a repository for rules, principles and standards it functions as *an alternative source of regulation.*

Illustrating the sheer scale of the development, as also the particular elements of continuity and change (government using contracts since time immemorial but doing so in recent times in a variety of novel ways), Davies has identified:

> at least six (albeit somewhat fluid) categories of contracting activity in which the government engages: procurement; providing services by contracting with private bodies ('contracting out'); the private finance initiative (PFI) and other public/private partnerships (PPPs); 'agreements' between the government and self-regulatory organisations; various types of agreement internal to government such as NHS contracts or Next Steps agency framework documents; and contracts of employment with staff.[6]

Reflecting 'a contract culture' (see p. 57 above), some effects are immediately apparent. Policies of outsourcing stretch across, and so blur, the public/private 'divide'. Private-sector notions of contract infuse public administration: the discipline of markets or market mimicking, the individualist ethos of freedom

[1] H. Street, *Governmental Liability* (Cambridge University Press, 1953) Ch. 3; J. Mitchell, *The Contracts of Public Authorities* (Bell, 1954).

[2] For accounts from elsewhere in the common law world, see P. Hogg and P. Monahan, *The Liability of the Crown*, 3rd edn (Carswell, 2000) and N. Seddon, *Government Contracts*, 3rd edn (Federation Press, 2005).

[3] T. Daintith, 'Regulation by contract: The new prerogative' (1979) 32 *CLP* 41.

[4] C. Turpin, *Government Procurement and Contracts* (Longman, 1989).

[5] R. De Hoog and L. Salamon, 'Purchase-of-service contracting' in Salamon (ed.) *The Tools of Government: A guide to the new governance* (Oxford University Press, 2002); P. Vincent-Jones, *The New Public Contracting* (Oxford University Press, 2006).

[6] A. Davies, *Accountability: A public law analysis of government by contract* (Oxford University Press, 2001), p. 1. 'Contracts' with individuals directed e.g. to behaviour management are a major omission (see below).

of choice. Contractual ideas of mutual obligation permeate government policies concerning the rights and responsibilities of the citizen. Contract as an organisational tool shows destructive, as well as constructive, properties. Through the contractual model the bureaucratic hierarchies and organisational forms previously associated with 'government' have been challenged or subverted.

The many parallels to UK regulatory reform will not be lost on the reader. Instigated by the Conservatives as part of 'the blue rinse', this general process of 'contractualisation' has been taken to new heights by New Labour. Precepts of VFM, or of a role for contract in delivering 'the three Es'; injections of business acumen and creativity; creative mixes of public with private power – once again, it all fits. The literature shows the UK development as part of a broader convergence associated with approaches to public management[7] and growing internationalisation of public procurement practice and procedure.[8] This country can, however, plausibly claim to be *the* world leader in contractual forms of governance, encompassing at one extreme massively complicated financial deals for public services (see Chapter 9) yet extending in a different direction into the realms of individual behaviour management and social control of an underclass (see p. 351 below).

The tension between ministers' wishes for authoritative action and promotion of a system of 'distributed public governance' (see p. 246 above) pervades the administrative framework. There is further 'thickening at the centre', this time in the service of the so-called 'contracting state'.[9] To enhance its steering capacity over multiple public purchasers, the Treasury typically deploys a mixed bag of sticks and carrots. We find more soft law (pre-contractual administrative 'guidance'); more standard terms (contract colonising new areas); and – yes – more bureaucratic regulation (audit technique). Matters are compounded by the fact that much in contractual governance is impregnated with controversy, not only in the broad ideological sense (the role of the state), but also in particular projects (as when the authority would prefer to use alternative methods). As contract has emerged centre stage in administrative law, so political tensions have heightened and contract's hidden political dimension has surfaced.

Sparking further questions about the suitability of the framework, statutory regulation has also spread. In the drive to open up publicly funded activities to the market, local government typically bore the brunt; this was successively the realm of the Conservatives' compulsory competitive tendering (CCT) and New Labour's best-value regime (see Chapter 2). An important product

7 J-B Auby, 'Comparative approaches to the rise of contract in the public sphere' (2007) *PL* 40; and see J. Freeman and M. Minow (eds.), *Outsourcing the US* (Harvard University Press, 2006).

8 S. Arrowsmith, *The Law of Public and Utilities Procurement*, 2nd edn (Sweet and Maxwell, 2005).

9 I. Harden, *The Contracting State* (Open University Press, 1992).

of the Single Market has been the deep penetration of national rules on the making of particular government contracts by EU law, such that the former is commonly the expression of the latter. The regime of public procurement has itself required major reform, once more illustrating the limits and limitations of rules and the irrepressible character of discretion (see Chapter 5). We see too the regulatory pendulum swinging on 'contract compliance' or the controversial use by government of the private legal form to promote broader policy objectives.[10] The expansive uses of contract have exposed tension and uncertainty in the case law over both executive freedom of action and the public/private 'border'. This has been marked by a series of flashpoints culminating, as we shall see, in fierce controversy over the amenability of contracted-out public services to the HRA.

Contractual governance is no panacea. There are some sharp lessons to be learned about the functional limitations of the private legal form. The contractual allocation of risk to the private sector has obvious attractions, but with vital public services it is easier said than done. Alternatively, the role for regulation by contract points up classic 'red light' concerns about possible abuse of state power; the more so, when the individuals concerned have little with which to bargain. Executive use of the private legal form strengthens rather than weakens the case for protective arrangements.[11] Contract has the potential to enhance managerial and administrative forms of accountability through specification, but equally discretions can go unchecked in a jungle of terms and conditions and technical detail.[12] And the propensity of contract to squeeze out political accountability should never be forgotten. All the more reason for administrative lawyers to proclaim good governance values![13]

1. Old and new

(a) Shadow of the Crown

Any discussion of government contract is complicated by the legal fiction of 'the Crown' (see p. 9 above). Since 'the Crown' is said to have all the powers of a natural person, including the power to enter into contracts, the activity is afforded a broad and flexible framework. However this operates to limit democratic accountability. The focus naturally being on the general estimates of expenditure, the idea of Parliament refusing funds to fulfil a contract has gone

[10] C. McCrudden, *Buying Social Justice: Equality, government procurement, and legal change* (Oxford University Press, 2007).

[11] M. Aronson, 'A public lawyer's responses to privatisation and outsourcing' in Taggart (ed.), *The Province of Administrative Law* (Hart, 1997).

[12] A. Davies, *Accountability: A public law analysis of government by contract* (Oxford University Press, 2001).

[13] M. Taggart, 'The impact of corporatisation and privatisation on administrative law' (1992) 51 *Australian J. of Public Administration* 368; A. Aman, *Politics, Policy and Outsourcing in the United States: The role of administrative law in a changing state* (Hart Publishing, 2008).

untested.[14] Conversely, HM Treasury as the lead player has the maximum possibility to drive forward new and perhaps controversial policies of contractual governance using internal, soft-law techniques.

In addition, the Crown enjoys certain immunities. Section 21 of the Crown Proceedings Act 1947[15] provides that no injunction or order for specific performance lies against the Crown in 'civil proceedings',[16] although in lieu a declaration can be made. Again, the payment of money by way of damages or otherwise cannot be enforced against the Crown by the normal processes of execution or attachment (s. 25). A special defence of 'executive necessity' to an action for breach of contract against the Crown has been derived from the old case of *The Amphitrite*.[17] An undertaking not to requisition a foreign ship in wartime was held unenforceable. In so denying compensation, the judge carefully distinguished the situation of commercial contracts and spoke generally of the need to preserve executive freedom of action in matters concerning 'the welfare of the state'.

All this raises questions about the meaning of the term 'Crown'[18] and the legal position of ministers and agencies.[19] As Crown agents, ministers have general authority to make contracts on behalf of the Crown. But do they in addition have an independent capacity to make contracts in their own name? *Town Investments* is one well-known authority denying this.[20] Similar questions arise in the context of devolution. In Wales as in Scotland[21] ministers are now 'Ministers of the Crown'.[22] Agencification further complicates matters. Where statute is used, the realm of Crown proceedings is apt to be diminished. In *British Medical Association v Greater Glasgow Health Board*[23] the board was set up to perform functions on behalf of the Crown but nonetheless was denied the protection of s. 21. Then again, 'the Crown' represents fertile territory for pseudo-contract in its internal administrative form. As NSAs (see p. 63 above) vividly illustrate, it takes two to contract. In Freedland's words, there is 'a sort

[14] The best-known common law authority is *New South Wales v Bardolph* [1934] 52 CLR 455.

[15] Prior to the CPA there was no legal right to sue the Crown. In contract, as distinct from tort, petition of right procedure could be used to mount a claim for damages (as in *The Amphitrite*, below).

[16] The restriction that Lord Woolf circumnavigated for the purpose of judicial review in *M v Home Office* (see p. 10 above).

[17] [1921] 3 KB 500.

[18] See especially here, J. McLean, 'The Crown in contract and administrative law' (2004) 24 *OJLS* 129.

[19] As also, historically, of civil servants. Moving on from arcane understandings of the prerogative, it was eventually accepted in *R v Lord Chancellor's Department, ex p. Nangle* [1992] 1 All ER 897 that civil service employment was based on formal contract.

[20] *Town Investments v Department of the Environment* [1978] AC 359. See C. Harlow, 'The Crown: Wrong once again?' (1977) 40 *MLR* 728.

[21] See A. Tomkins, 'The Crown in Scots law' in A. McHarg and T. Mullen (eds), *Public Law in Scotland* (Avizandum, 2006).

[22] Government of Wales Act 2006, ss. 48, 89.

[23] [1989] AC 1211.

of double legal fiction, whereby a non-corporation is deemed to enter into non-contracts'.[24]

Contracting out prompts the question: 'what is sacrosanct?' An answer was given in s. 71 of the Deregulation and Contracting Out Act 1994, in light of the general provision of order-making power to authorise the exercise of ministerial functions by private bodies.[25] Judicial activity; functions interfering with individual liberty; power of entry, search or seizure into or of any property; power or duty to make subordinate legislation: we here find an important set of excepted or non-delegable core public functions. A sharp reminder of the innate flexibility of the domestic administrative law system in the absence of a written constitution, the list is also notably minimalist.

(b) Ordinary law: Contract technology

Governing, as it does, such matters as capacity and formation, implied terms and performance, and termination and remedies, the general common law of contract still provides much of the formal legal framework of government contracting. Indeed, many of the technical challenges associated with contractual governance will be familiar to the private commercial lawyer. Similarly many tools and techniques are read across from the business to the public sphere, where certain key issues are accentuated in the light of collective interest. From time to time, there clearly is a need for adjustment. If, for example, the government contractor defaults, the continuity of essential public services may be jeopardised. Statutory step-in powers may be required. Or take the twin doctrines of 'consideration' and 'privity of contract', central to the English private legal concept. Questions about the 'rights' of 'third parties' are brought sharply into focus with contracting-out of public services. English law has moved cautiously in freeing-up the classical bipolar model of contract by the Contracts (Rights of Third Parties) Act 1999.[26] Provided that the public purchaser can bargain successfully with the contractor to include terms that protect the consumer interest, as also that 'on a proper construction' the contract does not exclude enforcement by the beneficiary, it may be possible for the citizen/service-user to obtain redress for poor performance.

Some fifty years ago Mitchell was pleading for a distinctive body of law that would be more sensitive to the distinctive characteristics of government contract.[27] A principle of governmental effectiveness should be established, such that no contract would be enforced in any case where some essential governmental activity would be thereby rendered impossible or seriously impeded. On the other hand, a principle of compensation should be developed

[24] M. Freedland, 'Government by contract and public law' [1994] *PL* 86.

[25] By analogy with the famous *Carltona* principle: p. 196 above.

[26] See R. Stevens, 'The Contracts (Rights of Third Parties) Act 1999' (2004) 120 *LQR* 292.

[27] Mitchell, *The Contracts of Public Authorities*.

in situations where the administration reneged on its own contractual obligations. Remember the criticism that Dicey, by refusing to accept the reality of state power and so disguising the inequality between the state and its citizens, had disabled effective legal control of the state machine (see Chapter 1). For Mitchell, the collective interest and the private-sector interest needed re-balancing with compensation as 'a check', the existence of which would provide a safeguard for individual rights.

Extrapolated from the French system of administrative law, the project failed of course, run aground in the shoals of Diceyan 'background theory'. However we hear continuing echoes of the argument. For Davies, reflecting on the contractual revolution in public services:

> Government contracts pose some problems, not encountered in contracts between private actors, which can only be addressed through a more developed *public law* regime. Government contracting is thus an area in which the public/private divide ought to be drawn more sharply. This would not necessarily entail a 'public law of contract' entirely separate from the private law of contract. Instead it would involve the development of a 'law of public contracts': a set of public law doctrines which would supplement or modify the ordinary law of contract where the government was one of the contracting parties.[28]

The fact is that 'English law does not cope well with the wider public interests which might be at stake in government contracting.' As well as the difficulty of ensuring democratic accountability, which then places a special premium on audit technique (see Chapter 9), the representation of service recipients in the contractual decision-making is in no way guaranteed. But as Davies also concludes, a separate law of public contracts is impractical: it would have to meet the 'significant objection' of 'the difficulty of determining its scope of application'.[29]

The way forward lies in a continuing set of pragmatic adjustments, framed on the one hand by Dicey's equality principle, whereby 'the take off point' (see p. 22 above) is that government liability closely parallels private liability, and, on the other, by the Single Market and EU public procurement regime. While there still is no 'Government Contracts Act', there are, to reiterate, special rules for many government contracts. Nor is judicial review the courts' only way of improving legal accountability. We would expect attempts to transcend the artificiality of the public/private distinction to intensify, as by a stress on underlying common-law values.[30]

[28] A. Davies, 'English law's treatment of government contracts: The problem of wider public interests' in Freedland and Auby (eds), *The Public-Private Divide – Une Entente Assez Cordiale?* (Hart Publishing, 2006), p. 113.

[29] *Ibid.*, pp. 128–9.

[30] See further, with reference to revivifying old common law obligations for essential public services, M. Taggart, 'The province of administrative law determined?' in Taggart (ed.), *The Province of Administrative Law* (Hart Publishing, 1997) and 'Common law price control, state-owned enterprises and the level playing field' in Harlow, Pearson and Taggart (eds.), *Administrative Law in a Changing State* (Hart Publishing, 2008).

With the Treasury naturally preferring to keep the courts at arm's length, formal legal principles have in any case played a limited role. Long-standing techniques of internal or bureaucratic law (administrative directions, codes of practice, established procedures) occupy the space. The secretive lore of central government procurement is one classic example; the torrent of Treasury communications promoting PFI is another (see p. 417 below). Again, the 'law of the contract' offers much by way of a flexible 'contract technology' able, in Mitchell's terms, to be more sensitive to the special demands of government contract. As Turpin explained in a famous study, model or standard terms and conditions also constitute a vehicle of internal hierarchical control:

> The 'law' created by the agreement of the parties is 'subordinate' law, in that the conditions for its creation are regulated by the general law of the land; and it is 'particular' law, applicable only to the parties who have by their contract brought it into existence. It is in operation as law only during the continuance of the contract. In government contracting, however, there are many basic terms that are not freshly devised for each contract, but are supplied from sets of standard conditions adopted by government departments for regular use. In this case, the 'rules' applicable to each contract have a continuing existence in the Government's standard conditions. It is only by their incorporation in each individual contract that they take effect as law for the parties, but the standard conditions have a quasi-obligatory character with respect to all relevant contracts in so far as government contracts staff are directed to incorporate them.[31]

A seemingly draconian authority, the survival[32] of *The Amphitrite* points up how this contract technology helps to suppress the role of the general law in relation to liability and dispute resolution. Government contracts commonly contain variation clauses which make provision for compensation, as also so-called break clauses, permitting the authority to terminate the contract at any time. Exactly the kind of public interest considerations and remedies associated with the French *contrat administratif*[33] are thereby factored in.

(c) 'New prerogative': 'New contractual governance'

Herbert Hart once referred to making a contract 'as the exercise of limited legislative powers by individuals'.[34] For 'individuals' read 'executive' or 'agency' and the huge potential of government contracting as a vehicle for rules becomes apparent. In a classic paper published in 1979, Daintith identified 'regulation by contract' as 'the new prerogative':

[31] Turpin, *Government Procurement and Contracts*, pp. 105–6.

[32] There is limited case law. See in particular *Robertson v Minister of Pensions* [1948] 1 KB 227 and *Crown Lands Comrs v Page* [1960] 2 QB 274.

[33] See for a modern account, L. Richer, *Droit des contrats administratifs*, 4th edn (LGDJ, 2004).

[34] H. L. A. Hart, *The Concept of Law*, 2nd edn (Clarendon, 1994), p. 96.

> Government contracting . . . incorporates, into standard terms and allocation procedures, clauses and public requirements which by their breadth and importance pass far beyond the mutual objectives of the contracting parties and which, therefore, might normally be promoted by statutory regulation . . . Government has discovered a means of using its increasing economic strength vis-à-vis private industry so as to promote certain policies in a style, and with results, which for a long time we have assumed must be the hallmark of Parliamentary legislation: [i.e.], officially promulgated rules backed by effective general compulsion. This means the power to rule without parliamentary consent, which is the hallmark of prerogative.[35]

It has to be remembered that this was the era of the corporate state, the immediate context being the then Labour Government's non-statutory tactic of blacklisting government contractors who refused to abide by its general incomes policy. Legally speaking too, such swingeing economic policies of 'contract compliance' appear a thing of the past, given EC public procurement policy and indeed *GCHQ* (see p. 107 above). But more subtle exercises of 'regulation by contract' are of the very essence of today's 'contracting state': another variation on the theme of 'steering not rowing'. Public service franchising, whereby, via the machinery of auction, market rules are laid out as contractual conditions and then made the subject of monitoring and supervision, is one technique providing many examples (see Chapter 9).[36] Raising concerns about control and accountability, Daintith had also unknowingly signalled the future.

As a technique of government, regulation by contract is commonly grounded in the *dominium* power of the state – the deployment of wealth in aid of policy objectives.[37] This being fuelled by the great public power of taxation, we see immediately the strength of the Treasury's position at the heart of a network of public purchasers. We note too the attractions for policy-makers in terms of contemporary regulatory theory. As against *imperium* or the command of law (see Chapter 4), regulation by contract suggests greater flexibility and shared ownership, as well as less formal accountability.

A recent survey by Vincent-Jones[38] suggests a three-fold, functional classification:

- Administrative contracts: these are contractual arrangements intended (or having the potential) to increase the transparency and effectiveness of the operation of the machinery of government. They are associated with the attempt to separate the political and managerial aspects of government,

[35] T. Daintith, 'Regulation by contract: The new prerogative' (1979) 32 *CLP* 41, 41–2.

[36] For alternative, sector-specific, potentials, see e.g. E. Orts and K. Deketelaere, *Environmental Contracts: Comparative approaches to regulatory innovation in the United States and Europe* (Kluwer, 2002).

[37] T. Daintith, 'The techniques of government' in Jowell and Oliver (eds.), *The Changing Constitution* (Clarendon, 1994).

[38] P. Vincent-Jones, *The New Public Contracting* (Oxford University Press, 2006).

and to clarify bureaucratic roles through performance-based management systems (see Chapter 2).

- Economic contracts: these are contractual arrangements directed at improving public services through competition and/or the devolution of management powers to public purchasing or commissioning agencies in a variety of hybrid forms beyond simple market or bureaucratic organisation. Policy initiatives are about the better use and co-ordination of resources (see Chapter 9).
- Social control contracts: these are adaptations of the contractual mechanism used in the regulation of relationships between individual citizens and state authority. They entail entitlements contingent upon reciprocal responsibilities and their arrangements perform a more or less overt disciplinary function (see below).

The contractual revolution is seen here spreading rapidly beyond the sphere of economics into public administration and social policy as a distinctive mode of governance, characterised by the delegation of contractual powers and responsibilities to public bodies in regulatory frameworks preserving central controls and powers of intervention. The development is highly instrumental in character, with contract norms being harnessed in each situation – within government, in the economic organisation of public services, and in state–citizen relationships – for the attainment of determinate public policy purposes. For yesterday's 'new prerogative', read today's 'new public contracting'.

Reflecting a paradigm shift in law and administration (see Chapter 2), the close interplay of contractual with regulatory forms of governance takes many forms.[39] Just as consensual elements are evident in the practices of traditional regulation so the success of regulation by contract will typically depend on the culture of regulation and compliance in which it is set.[40] The term 'regulation by contract' is also used today to denote the burgeoning use of contract-type arrangements as the instrument of intra- and inter-governmental co-ordination. Earlier we mentioned 'framework documents' defining the goals and functions of NSAs and 'concordats' dealing with relationships between Whitehall and the devolved administrations. To these may be added devices such as the 'public service agreement' and the seemingly ubiquitous memorandum of understanding.

We note the different conceptual understandings in play: contract in the strict, formal, sense of 'thing'; and contract(ualism), as contemporary developments in governance lead us to insist, more generously defined in terms

[39] C. Donnelly, *Delegation of Governmental Power to Private Parties: A comparative perspective* (Oxford University Press, 2007).

[40] See M. Considine, 'Contract regimes and reflexive governance: Comparing employment service reforms in the United Kingdom, the Netherlands, New Zealand and Australia' (2000) 78 *Pub. Admin.* 613.

of 'core notions of reciprocity, mutuality of obligations, and rights balanced by responsibilities'.[41] In Chapter 2 we saw for example that the language of contract can be used in an expansive way, encompassing (and so modelling) a variety of arrangements which are not themselves directly legally enforceable in the courts ('pseudo-contract'). Sanction, after all, can take many forms. Woe betide the Government unit that consistently fails to deliver on PSA commitments!

Contractualism begets contractualism, so increasingly ordering the state and its modes of delivery. Freedland and King speak of a 'pyramid' of contract.[42] Premised on a high degree of central co-ordination through detailed output specification and the setting of standards, contractual governance at UK level is thus seen as determinedly systemic in character, comprising both macro- and micro-levels of operation. An alternative description is 'cascades of contracts',[43] as when there are agreements of various kinds between the Treasury and the Department, the Department and the NSA, the NSA and local units, the local units and private suppliers of services, and the private suppliers of services and subcontractors.

(d) Functional limitations

Paradoxical it may seem, but contract theorists have done much in recent times to enrich our understanding of the limitations of the private legal form.[44] At the root of this is insistence on the need to understand the social matrix of norms, understandings and expectations in which a contract is embedded.[45] As Wightman notes pithily, 'the behaviour of the parties cannot be read off from the terms of any agreement'.[46] The long-term interests of both parties may bind them together regardless of any potential legal sanction, a feature highlighted by public bodies commonly being repeat players in the field of contract. It would be strange indeed if, in the case of essential public services, the relationship was never given priority over the

[41] Vincent-Jones, *The New Public Contracting*, p. 13; drawing on I. Macneil, *The New Social Contract* (Yale University Press, 1980); and see R. Brownsword, *Contract Law: Themes for the 21st century*, 2nd edn (Oxford University Press, 2006).

[42] M. Freedland and D. King, 'Contractual governance and illiberal contracts: Some problems of contractualism as an instrument of behaviour management by agencies of government' (2003) 27 *Cambridge Journal of Economics* 465.

[43] J. Boston, 'The use of contracting in the public sector: Recent New Zealand experience' (1996) 55 *Australian Journal of Public Administration* 105.

[44] See generally R. Hillman, *The Richness of Contract Law: An analysis and critique of contemporary theories of contract law* (Kluwer, 1997); S. Smith, *Contract Theory* (Clarendon, 2004).

[45] P. S. Atiyah, *The Rise and Fall of Freedom of Contract* (Clarendon, 1990); and see D. Campbell, H. Collins and J Wightman (eds.), *Implicit Dimensions of Contract: Discrete, relational and network contracts* (Hart Publishing, 2003).

[46] J. Wightman, 'Book review' (2003) 15 *Journal of Environmental Law* 99, 101; and *Contract: A critical commentary* (Pluto Press, 1996).

deal.[47] Of course the argument should not be pressed too far. As Collins reminds us:

> The contractual framework does not disappear when the injured party prefers to ignore the breach of contract and to emphasise instead the norms derived from the business relation or economic interest. The contractual framework may be invoked at any time. It will be resuscitated if the parties perceive that the long-term relationship is about to terminate or the considerations of economic self-interest now point in the direction of strict contractual enforcement. In the absence of these conditions, however, which will normally represent the situation in successful trading relations, we should expect the contractual framework to be temporarily occluded.[48]

In analysing contract as a social institution, contract theorists stress the concept of 'presentiation'.[49] Nowhere is the self-conscious attempt, through planning, 'to bring the future into the present' better illustrated than in the case of the private finance initiative. Some of these arrangements for the supply of public services and infrastructures are very long-term – a shaping of the future landscape that distinguishes the UK experiment in contractual governance. Public law values of flexibility and (democratic) responsiveness are threatened; there is even a sense of the classic 'no-fettering' rule (see Chapter 5) being flattened. Amid all the (Treasury) talk of risk allocation, there is however a pervasive sense of contractual 'incompleteness'.[50] 'Presentiating' some thirty years of modernisation of the London Tube (see p. 425 below) is not so easy.

Macneil's famous analysis of 'discrete' and 'relational' contracts[51] is very relevant to public procurement and its legal regulation. Signalled by the demand for repeated bouts of competitive bidding, we will see how EU policies have pressed national practice firmly in the direction of the discrete or individuated model. How else could entrenched local preferences associated with relational factors of stability and co-operation be overpowered? But this fuels complaints of high transaction costs; today, there is an element of re-balancing, with more space for contractual dialogue and mutual learning. 'Public purchasing is a skill which requires the judicious exercise of knowledge, expertise and, yes, discretion.'[52]

47 As in business contracts: see S. Macaulay, 'Non-contractual relations in business: A preliminary study (1963) 28 *American Sociological Review* 55 and H. Beale and T. Dugdale, 'Contracts between businessmen: Planning and the use of contractual remedies' (1975) *BJLS* 45.

48 H. Collins, *Regulating Contracts* (Oxford University Press, 1999), pp. 137–8. The implications for judicial reasoning are disputed: G. Gava and J. Greene, 'Do we need a hybrid law of contract?' (2004) 63 *CLJ* 605.

49 I. Macneil, *The New Social Contract* (Yale University Press, 1980), p. 60

50 O. Hart, *Firms, Contracts and Financial Structure* (Oxford University Press, 1995).

51 I. Macneil, 'The many futures of contracts', (1974) 47 *Southern California Law Review* 691 and 'Relational contract theory: Challenges and queries' ((2000) 94 *Northwestern Univ. L. Rev.* 877. But see D. Campbell, 'Ian Macneil and the relational theory of contract' in Campbell (ed.), *Selected Papers of Ian Macneil* (Sweet and Maxwell, 2001).

52 P. Trepte, 'Book review' [2007] *PL* 608.

The modern focus in contract theory on 'relationality' as a quality of social exchange highlights the importance to smooth and effective workings of core elements of voluntarism and reciprocity, fairness and trust. This suggests a difficulty with the use by government of contract in a highly instrumental – one is tempted to say, 'green light' – fashion. Instancing the regulation of individuals by pseudo-contract, Vincent-Jones lays stress on 'the negative effects of policy-driven regulation on the relational elements of trust and cooperation that are essential to realising the capacity of contract to benefit both the parties and society more generally.'[53]

2. Pseudo-contract: Regulation and responsibilisation

Pseudo-contract has increasingly been used to model relations between the state and the individual. In Chapter 2, we saw how in neo-liberal fashion Thatcherism presented the citizen as both the dominant partner and consumer, with John Major's Citizen's Charter then making the core idea of services in return for taxes explicit (while avoiding justiciable service-delivery rights). The alternative dimension of contractual governance *of* the individual was already emerging however in the shape of regulation by pseudo-contract; ultimately, 'contract' as a technique of social control, contrary to its classic liberal meaning (the virtues of consent and freedom of choice). This type of approach has taken off under New Labour in a further reconceptualising of state/citizen relationships. We see a systematic and highly instrumental use of pseudo-contract across key strands of public policy: from attempts at 'diversion' from criminal law process, to tackling deviance, and on through the integrative potential of education to 'work not dole'. Reflecting particular policy aims, the degree – and balance – of promise and threat in such arrangements varies. Rooted however in ideas of 'responsibilisation',[54] of 'growing' individuals as self-determining and self-willing agents, a common theme is contractualisation as an explicit means of 'regulated self-regulation'.[55]

Administrative lawyers generally have been slow to engage with this phenomenon, in part, no doubt, because of a lack of judicial review cases associated with use of the contractual form. Yet there are many relevant aspects. Executive power may be dressed in private garb, but we see the creeping

[53] Vincent-Jones, *The New Public Contracting*, p. 30; drawing on D. Campbell and D. Harris, 'Flexibility in long-term contracts: The role of co-operation' (1993) 20 *JLS* 166.

[54] A. Deacon and K. Mann, 'Agency, modernity and social policy' (1999) *Journal of Social Policy* 413; N. Rose, 'Government and control' in Garland and Sparks (eds.), *Criminology and Social Theory* (Clarendon, 2000).

[55] See on this element, A.Yeatman, 'Interpreting contemporary contractualism' in Dean and Hindess (eds.), *Governing Australia: Studies in contemporary rationalities of government* (Cambridge University Press, 1998) and H. Collins, 'Regulating contract law' in Parker, Scott, Lacey and Braithwaite (eds.), *Regulating Law* (Oxford University Press, 2004).

tentacles of state regulation. As a vehicle for pre-emptive intervention in citizen's lives, pseudo-contract colonises more areas: less liberty. We are back with K. C. Davis and the 'dark and windowless' areas of administrative law. Administrative lawyers are – or rather should be – concerned to ensure proper procedural protection. What are the guarantees of 'fair dealing' for the disadvantaged citizen in these highly personalised forms of 'negotiated' regulation? The technique also falls to be evaluated as one of a range and mix of state interventions. How and in what conditions is it effective? Questions arise about the use and proportionality of sanctions. While these agreements are not enforceable in the conventional contractual manner, 'breach' by the regulated individual may trigger other, sharper, enforcement methods such as preventative civil orders and even penal sanctions, or denial of benefits and privileges.

(a) Control contracts

Pseudo-contract as a tool of social work became widespread in the 1980s. There were checklists of tasks for 'clients' such as alcoholics or drug addicts, behaviour modification schemes incorporating rewards and sanctions tailored to 'progress', and conditions or requirements for the use of care facilities. For policy-makers concerned to inculcate a greater sense of individual responsibility among particular target groups 'contract' offered an enticing mix of specification, tailored process, and symbolic value (fitting with NPM, it also provided a measure of 'productivity' of social work, serving both to define and limit, and to deflect from central government, public-service responsibilities):[56]

> A Social Work contract was taken to have particular advantages for the *relationship* between the social worker and client. The first of these was that it treated clients with *respect* and helped them become more *responsible* for their choices . . . A further benefit was that contracts were thought to supply a definite spur to *motivation* and *achievement.* Because contracts provided a clear specification of the goals of social work intervention they made it possible (sometimes all too possible) to see what progress had been achieved. Clients would be motivated by their involvement in drawing up the contract, by their consent to what it contained, by the incentive of the reciprocal promises of the Social Work Department and, where applicable, by fear of sanctions if it broke down . . . A final set of functions related to control by the social worker and her *accountability.* Contracts were capable of helping both social workers and clients gain more control of their interaction so as to better achieve their aims.[57]

56 See Freedland and King, 'Contractual governance and illiberal contracts'.

57 D. Nelken, 'The use of "contracts" as a social work technique' (1987) 40 *CLP* 207, 215–16. In a policy context of 'care in the community', the technique could also facilitate multi-agency engagement.

Mixing 'carrot and stick', the resort to 'contract' as part of an expanding pattern of state interventions under New Labour has been fuelled by concerns about antisocial behaviour. 'Where families and parents are failing to meet their responsibilities to their communities, we will work with them until they do.'[58] Within a few years, the regulation had taken on the character of a complex set of written rules including 'parental contracts', 'acceptable behaviour contracts' (below), 'youth offender contracts',[59] and generalised 'home-school agreements'.[60] The centre provides copious administrative guidance and standard forms.

In a situation of unequal power how real is agreement? A contractual rhetoric of 'voluntariness' cannot disguise the fact of many of these 'state-based control contracts' being 'imposed upon the individual to a greater degree than similar-looking private contractual arrangements'.[61] Criminologists point up the particular normative force of this kind of individualised contractual governance:

> Given the language of choice, autonomy and voluntariness, in which contracting is couched, the failure of a given party to adhere to their self-imposed and agreed part of the bargain means that they have failed themselves – by breaking their own promise – as well as their obligations to others. This failure appears as more serious than the failure to fulfil a command ordered of them. Hence, failure to honour an agreement serves to legitimate more fundamental interventions into people's lives. In certain circumstances, this may justify a more punitive response.[62]

Parenting contracts show the widening sphere. The Anti-Social Behaviour Act 2003 empowered youth-offending teams to 'contract' with the parents where there is reason to believe that the child or young person 'has engaged, or is likely to engage', in criminal conduct or antisocial behaviour.[63] Such powers have subsequently been given to a range of bodies, including local authorities and housing associations.[64] The 2003 Act likewise made parenting contracts another instrument in the 'tool-box' of interventions in cases of truancy or

[58] White Paper, *Respect and Responsibility: Taking a stand against anti-social behaviour*, Cm. 5778 (2003), p. 12; and see A. Von Hirsch and A. Simester (eds.), *Incivilities: Regulating offensive behaviour* (Oxford University Press, 2006).

[59] Inaugurated by the Youth Justice and Criminal Evidence Act 1999 (as consolidated in the Powers of Criminal Courts (Sentencing) Act 2000). The relevant White Paper is *No More Excuses: A new approach to tackling youth crime in England and Wales*, Cm. 3809 (1997).

[60] Rolled out across the state-sector under the auspices of the School Standards and Framework Act 1998, HSAs demonstrate a much greater sense of reciprocity: A. Blair, 'Home-School Agreements: A legislative framework for soft control of parents' (2001) *Education Law Journal* 79.

[61] S. Mackenzie, 'Second-chance punitivism and the contractual governance of crime and incivility: New Labour, old Hobbes' (2008) 35 *JLS* 214, 222.

[62] A. Crawford, 'Contractual governance of deviant behaviour' (2003) 30 *JLS* 479, 503–4.

[63] Anti-Social Behaviour Act 2003, s. 25.

[64] Police and Justice Act 2006, ss. 23–5.

exclusion from school.[65] This now extends to situations where the school or LEA has reason to believe that the child's conduct 'has caused, or is likely to cause' significant disruption.[66]

Mixing discipline with support, the 'contract' typically consists of two main elements. The first is a parenting programme: the vehicle for various therapies, founded in turn on agency assessments or risk-evaluations. The second is 'restrictive covenants': ways in which the parent is tasked with controlling their child, for example by ensuring regular school attendance. Modelled in terms of a regulatory 'enforcement pyramid' (see p. 242 above), relevant sanctions underwrite the place of such 'contracts' in the hinterland of formal law. Up from this level of intervention lies the 'parenting order',[67] whereby, on pain of penal sanction, parents can be required to take steps to address their child's misbehaviour.[68] Administrative guidance explains:

> As contracts are voluntary there is no penalty for refusing to enter into or failing to comply with one. However, previous failure to co-operate with support offered through a contract is a relevant consideration for a court when deciding whether to make a parenting order. Therefore contracts provide YOTs with additional authority when attempting to secure voluntary co-operation from parents.[69]

Commonly paired with parenting contracts, 'acceptable behaviour contracts' for children and young persons have been much in vogue. Pioneered in London at the beginning of the decade, by 2006 some 18,000 'ABCs' had been made by local enforcement agencies in England and Wales[70] despite the fact that there was no explicit statutory framework[71] – a new 'new prerogative' indeed! The ABC is officially considered a 'second-tier approach' to anti-social behaviour, on from the cheap, if not so cheerful, warning letter, and ahead of the more costly and judicially determined Anti-Social Behaviour Order (ASBO). The innate flexibility of pseudo-contract means however that ABCs themselves can be used incrementally:

> The contract specifies a list of anti-social acts in which the person can be shown to have been involved, and which they agree not to continue. The contract can also include positives, i.e. activities that will help prevent recurrence, such as attending school. The main

[65] Anti-Social Behaviour Act 2003, s. 19: see DCSF, *Guidance on Education-Related Parenting Contracts, Parenting Orders and Penalty Notices* (2007).

[66] Education and Inspections Act 2006, s. 97.

[67] Originally introduced in the Crime and Disorder Act 1998, ss. 8–10. See for an unsuccessful HRA challenge, *R (M) v Inner London Crown Court* [2003] EWHC 301.

[68] Anti-Social Behaviour Act 2003, ss. 20–2, 26–8, as amended.

[69] Home Office, *Parenting Contracts and Orders Guidance* (2004) [2.13].

[70] House of Commons Debates, vol. 456, col. 358W (31 January 2007). And see K. Bullock and B. Jones, *Acceptable Behaviour Contracts: Addressing anti-social behaviour in the London Borough of Islington* (Home Office, 2004).

[71] See Home Office, *Acceptable Behaviour Contracts and Agreements* (2007).

> aim is to lead perpetrators towards recognition both of the impact of their behaviour and of the need to take responsibility for their actions. For this reason it is important that the individual should be involved in drawing up the contract.
>
> Where behaviour is more problematic – either because it is persistent or because it is serious – then support to address the underlying causes of the behaviour should be offered in parallel to the contract. This may include diversionary activities (such as attendance at a youth project), counselling or support for the family . . . Legal action (such as an application for an ASBO or a possession order, if the perpetrator is in social housing) should be stated on the contract where this is the potential consequence of breaking the agreement.[72]

The use made of ABCs at local level has been variable.[73] The guidance itself exhibits concerns: for children still at primary school a parental intervention 'may be preferable'; perhaps hopefully, 'practitioners will be aware of the need to guard against racial stereotyping'.[74] The guidance speaks of multiple 'triggers' for ABCs: complaints to housing officers; police intelligence; discussions with residents, etc.[75] The obvious administrative benefit of ABCs – no need to establish a formal evidence chain – is another piece in the jigsaw of risk-oriented state interventions eroding civil liberties. What, one might ask, of the rule of law?

We are back too with the functional limitations of contract, the chief relational elements of trust and co-operation being under threat in this highly disciplinary context. The methodology may also be criticised for glossing over underlying causes of social problems; is it just a matter of responsibilisation? The NAO gives a suitably cautious assessment:

> 65 per cent of the people in our sample who received an Acceptable Behaviour Contract did not re-engage in anti-social behaviour. However Contracts were less effective with people aged under 18 where just over 60 per cent of our cases displayed further anti-social behaviour. This outcome could be due to a failure to engage the young person sufficiently in forming a contract and to support them, for example in disengaging from the society of certain of their peers . . . In practice, it is possible that other factors unrelated to the intervention, such as changes in family circumstances, may have contributed partly or wholly to changes in behaviour.[76]

(b) Contractualising welfare, etc.

One of the more controversial Conservative reforms to the Welfare State was the Job Seeker's Allowance, which replaced unemployment benefit and income

72 *Ibid.*, pp. 1–2, 9.
73 See NAO, *Tackling Anti-Social Behaviour*, HC 99 (2006/7).
74 Home Office, *Acceptable Behaviour Contracts*, pp. 3, 11.
75 *Ibid.*, pp. 4–5.
76 NAO, *Tackling Anti-Social Behaviour*, pp. 6, 19.

support for the unemployed. The scheme was designed to focus the efforts of claimants on looking for work, as well as securing better VFM.[77] To this end the 'Job Seeker's Agreement' was created as a condition precedent of receiving benefit, its requirements typically including targets for job applications.[78] Highlighting the element of compulsion, as also of one-sidedness, the employment officer would only 'contract' if satisfied that compliance would secure the general statutory requirements of availability for work and actively seeking employment. The claimant could hardly shop elsewhere.[79]

New Labour ministers built enthusiastically on the JSA, reinforcing the view of unemployment largely in terms of an individual's capacities and capabilities. A 1998 Green Paper set the tone. 'At the heart of the modern welfare state will be a new contract between the citizen and the Government based on responsibilities and rights.' The talk was of 'opportunity instead of dependence':[80] splendidly envisioned in terms of 'the Third Way', active engagement of the citizen with the state (see p. 71 above). Promoted as a 'New Deal', this meant determinedly conditional income-maintenance programmes of 'workfare' with requirements to undertake training or join work schemes to enhance employability.[81] Over time, different sets of 'contractual' conditions have evolved for lone parents, people with disabilities, etc. The reconfiguration of the state–citizen relationship is made abundantly clear:

> In a contributory system, establishing the right to protection is the end result of a process during which the claimant via his/her contributions 'demonstrates' his/her responsible behaviour. Conditions are mainly attached before the claim is made . . . Conversely, in the new arrangements, the claim for support marks the beginning of a different process whereby conditions are attached after the claim is made. What is strengthened here is the 'right' of the state to 'steer' and monitor the claimant's behaviour after the claim is made.[82]

In the face of stubbornly high rates of detachment from the labour market[83] the contract culture is underpinned by the Welfare Reform Act 2007.[84] A

[77] White Paper, *Job Seeker's Allowance*, Cm. 2687 (1994).

[78] Jobseekers' Act 1995, ss. 1, 9.

[79] See J. Fulbrook, 'The Job Seekers' Act 1995: Consolidation with a sting of contractual compliance' (1995) 24 *Industrial Law J.* 395.

[80] Green Paper, *A New Contract for Welfare: New ambitions for our country*, Cm. 3805 (1998), pp. 1–2; and see S. White, 'Social rights and the social contract: Political theory and the new welfare politics' (2000) 30 *B. J. Pol. Sci.* 507.

[81] See especially, DWP, *Building on New Deal: Local solutions meeting individual needs* (2004). There is a strong comparative element: see J. Handler, 'Social citizenship and workfare in the US and Western Europe: From status to contract' (2003) 13 *Journal of European Social Policy* 229.

[82] E. Carmel and T. Papadopoulos, 'The new governance of social security in Britain' in Millar (ed.), *Understanding Social Security: Issues for social policy and practice* (Policy Press, 2003), p. 5.

[83] See for criticism of the regulatory 'effectiveness', F. Field and P. White, *Welfare Isn't Working* (Reform, 2007).

[84] See Green Paper, *A New Deal for Welfare: Empowering people to work*, Cm. 6730 (2006).

major revamp extending conditionality, the legislation replaces incapacity benefit with the tellingly titled 'employment and support allowance'. A subsequent Green Paper speaks of strengthening the 'benefit contract' between the state and the individual: government will provide personalised support in exchange for an obligation to work for all those capable. Framed by 'powers to require those who need it to undertake training', and by 'tougher sanctions' for those failing to take relevant steps, this is the world of tailored 'back-to-work action plans'.[85] Showing how the different strands of contractual governance intertwine, the Green Paper also speaks of 'modernising and strengthening the welfare to work market', a new 'right to bid' for public, private and voluntary providers. 'Individual responsibility is at the heart of these reforms. For people to exercise responsibility, we need to increase choice'.[86]

The general dynamic shows no sign of slackening – quite the reverse. 'Contractual relations' between state and citizen feature prominently in a Cabinet Office strategy review. 'Could we move from an implicit one-way contract based on outputs to one based on explicit mutually agreed outcomes? . . . How might this work in key areas like healthcare, schooling, policing and family support?':[87]

> Our actions are an important determinant of whether we will live productive and healthy lives, in clean and sustainable environments, in communities free from fear or isolation. Unfortunately all too often we fail – collectively and individually – to behave in the way required to achieve these outcomes. There is an increasing recognition that cultural factors are important determinants of our behaviour . . . Where there are gaps in both underlying attitudes, values, aspirations and self-efficacy as well as in actual behaviour . . . this suggests an approach based on combining addressing the cultural factors along with smoothing this into behaviour through enabling, incentivising, and encouraging measures . . . 'Encouraging' measures include contracts and codifications to build a consistent behavioural path of achievement . . . explicit or implicit contracts whereby the citizen is incentivised to engage in co-productive behaviour . . . clear agreements between whole groups . . . reinforced by . . . rewards or greater responsibility.[88]

The Orwellian overtones are all too apparent: contract from cradle to grave?

[85] DWP, *No One Written Off: Reforming the welfare state to reward responsibilities* (2008), pp. 12–13. And see in turn DWP, *Raising Expectations and Increasing Support: Reforming welfare for the future*, Cm. 7506 (2008). The relevant legislation – the Welfare Reform Bill – is currently before Parliament.

[86] *Ibid.*, pp. 118, 120.

[87] PM's Strategy Unit, *Strategic Priorities for the UK* (2006), p. 26.

[88] PM's Strategy Unit, *Achieving Culture Change: A policy framework* (2007), pp. 10–11, 115.

3. Outsourcing: Policy and structures

(a) Central . . .

The public sector currently spends £160 billion a year on purchasing goods and services. The amounts have mushroomed in recent years, with the popularity of outsourcing and historically high levels of government investment. The Treasury recognises that 'all of us, as taxpayers who use and fund public services, have the right to expect government to meet the highest professional standards when it procures on their behalf'.[89]

Twenty-five years ago the Conservatives were trying to achieve this. The Central Unit on Procurement was established to advise departments on their increasingly important – and varied – procurement strategies.[90] Coming on top of the substantial body of principles and procedures that had evolved over many years, its administrative guidance, with titles like 'model forms of contract', 'specification writing', 'quality assurance' and 'disputes resolution', quickly multiplied. Greater emphasis than hitherto was placed on VFM; and elaborate processes of market testing, whereby in-house teams had to compete against external bidders, were developed.[91] Underlining the close linkage with NPM, a 1995 White Paper spoke of integrated processes 'covering the whole cycle of acquisition and use from start to finish, to ensure quality and economy'.[92] Continuous information flows, shared understandings, and migration of personnel between purchasing departments and their major suppliers, were typical of a 'procurement community',[93] strongly corporatist in ethos. But fitting with the drive to the Single Market, the official orthodoxy was now liberalisation and genuine competition.

'Pragmatic not dogmatic' was the predictable catchphrase of the incoming Blair government's administrative guidance on market testing and contracting out. In delivering on ministers' commitment to a modern, responsive and customer-focused range of services, senior Whitehall managers should bear in mind that competition was only one option, and that, as against lowest price, VFM meant 'better quality services at optimal cost'.[94] Market-type disciplines would however remain a central element in the programme of public-sector reform at UK level.[95]

The aim, of course, was 'better' procurement. The Gershon review[96] in 1999 highlighted a lack of consistency and common process among Whitehall

[89] HM Treasury, *Transforming Government Procurement* (2007), p. 1.

[90] Cabinet Office, *Government Purchasing* (HMSO, 1984).

[91] Office of Public Service and Science, *The Government's Guide to Market Testing* (HMSO, 1993).

[92] *Setting New Standards: A Strategy for government procurement*, Cm. 2840 (1995), p. 6.

[93] Turpin, *Government Procurement and Contracts*.

[94] Cabinet Office, *Better Quality Services Handbook* (HMSO, 1998), p. 1.

[95] See NAO, *Benchmarking and Market Testing the Ongoing Services Component of PFI Projects*, HC 453 (2006/7).

[96] HM Treasury, *Review of Civil Procurement in Central Government* (1999).

departments, as well as 'a very wide spectrum' between best and worst practice. Agencification itself was a reason for greater centralisation of procurement practice and procedure:

> The fragmentation and lack of co-ordination of these activities results in the Centre lacking the 'clout' necessary to lead Government procurement into the 21st Century . . . There is a widespread recognition of the need for, and benefit of, a central body which ensures consistency of policy, avoids re-invention of wheels, catalyses appropriate aggregation and promotes best practice.[97]

So was born the Office of Government Commerce, a separate entity inside the Treasury with its own chief executive, responsible for improving VFM by driving up standards and capability in procurement. OGC quickly elaborated a whole range of strategies, from promoting effective competition for government business to securing improvements in the management of large, complex and novel projects, and on through to support for the wider public sector in procurement matters.[98] So-called 'conventional procurement' – departments buying in the goods and services they need using in-house units – should be treated as only one option, alongside PPPs and PFI (which themselves take many forms, see Chapter 9).[99] Soft law was laid on soft law as OGC took over, reworked, and extended, the administrative guidance.

OGC has had ownership of 'the Gateway Process', treated as mandatory in central government for complex procurement, IT-enabled and construction programmes, whereby projects are independently reviewed at critical stages in their life cycle to determine whether they should proceed further and if so whether changes are necessary. While somewhat cumbersome in nature, the reviews are rightly prized for providing 'an external challenge to the robustness of plans and processes'.[100] A trading arm, OGC buying.solutions, able to assess and access a vast array of products and services on behalf of public sector bodies, was an obvious next step. How better to promote 'best practice' than through a set of pre-tendered contracts?[101] OGC also leads for the UK on EU and, as regards the WTO, OECD and UNCITRAL,[102] international procurement policy issues. Reflecting the highly porous nature of the national and transnational regulatory frameworks, this is important work. Echoing developments among the super-agencies (see Chapter 6), the aim is to ensure a two-way traffic, whereby international legal development 'both

97 *Ibid.*, p. 4.

98 OGC, *Procurement Policy Guidelines* (2001). Procurement being an aspect of devolved government, OGC's remit is correspondingly limited however.

99 OGC, *Procurement Strategies* (2007).

100 OGC, *Gateway Review for Programmes and Projects* (2007), 1. But see NAO, *Delays in Administering the 2005 Single Payments Scheme in England*, HC 1631 (2005/6).

101 There is also a well-established, UK-wide, professional network centred on the Chartered Institute of Purchasing and Supply.

102 United Nations Commission on International Trade Law.

influences and is influenced by the developing UK domestic procurement policy agenda'.[103]

Evidently, however, things have not gone well. The search is on for major efficiency gains as this huge collective purchasing power is harnessed to equip the UK with world-class public services in the face of growing challenges of global competition, changing demographics and increasing pressures on natural resources. A Treasury-led revamp of policies and processes inaugurated in 2007 promises to transform government procurement:

> Government needs to harness the benefits that businesses can offer . . . through a procurement function . . . that is increasingly adaptable, flexible and knowledgeable about the commercial world . . . The positive influence of procurement can go far beyond simply securing the goods and services it requires – it can also transform the market to the benefit of others . . . Effective procurement . . . has the capacity to drive the efficiency of suppliers and their supply chains, demonstrating the added importance of conducting procurement to the highest professional standards.[104]

Policy-makers have also come to elaborate not one but two overarching principles of procurement policy and practice:

> The challenge is to meet the public's demands for increasingly high quality public services at good value for money and in a sustainable way . . . The Government is determined to be at the forefront of sustainable procurement, making the government estate carbon neutral by 2012. The OGC will help delivery, encouraging departments to develop the expertise to value whole life costs and benefits.[105]

The 'greening' of administrative law thus augments demands for more centralisation and hierarchy, greater professionalism, and heightened modalities of internal regulation:[106]

- Recognising its importance to public service delivery, departments will strengthen their procurement capability with greater direction and support from the top.
- Departments will collaborate more in the purchase of goods and services common across more than one department, to get better value for money.
- A new Major Projects Review Group will ensure that the most important and complex projects are subject to effective scrutiny at the key stages.
- OGC will have strong powers to set out the procurement standards

103 OGC, *Policy and Standards* (2007), p. 1.

104 HM Treasury, *Transforming government procurement*, p. 3; and see CBI, *Innovation and Public Procurement* (2007).

105 HM Treasury, *Transforming government procurement*; and see Sustainable Development Task Force, *Procuring the Future* (2006).

106 HM Treasury, *Transforming government procurement.*

departments need to meet, monitor departments' performance against them, and ensure remedial action is taken where necessary.
- Overseeing the changes needed across government, the OGC will be a smaller, higher-calibre organisation and work closely with departments and suppliers to improve capacity and effectiveness.

Some basic nostrums of 'good' procurement have been recycled (in the next chapter, we see some of them honoured in the breach). A procuring authority should:

- be clear on the objectives of the procurement from the outset
- be aware of external factors that will impact on the procurement such as the policy environment or planning issues
- communicate those objectives to potential suppliers at an early stage, to gauge the market's ability to deliver and explore a range of possible solutions
- consider using an output or outcome based specification, to give suppliers – who naturally know more about business than potential buyers – more scope to provide innovative solutions
- follow a competitive, efficient, fair and transparent procurement process, and communicate to potential suppliers at the outset what that process will be
- be clear about affordability – the resources available to spend on the particular good or service. . .The procurer has to select on the basis of whole-life value for money, but in setting budgets for individual projects departments also needs to make decisions about relative policy priorities and needs
- establish effective contractual management processes and resources in good time to drive excellent supplier performance throughout the contract. [107]

(b) . . . and local

Local government procurement presents its own challenges. Margaret Thatcher aimed primarily at forcing the market on councils: 'subjecting in-house provision of services to competition would expose the true cost of carrying out the work and lead to greater efficiency in the use of resources and, hence, to better value for money for local authorities and for the tax-payers.'[108] Consistent with the Conservatives' general programme, compulsory competitive tendering was also a way of reducing the size of the public sector and the power of trade unions. Since local government had traditionally been very reliant on in-house provision, the policy had huge potential.

In central government, policies of outsourcing and market testing could be implemented through soft law; in local government,[109] where councils

[107] *Ibid.*, pp. 4–5: drawing on NAO, *Improving Procurement*, HC 361 (2003/4).

[108] Department of the Environment, *Competing for Quality: Competition in the provision of local services* (1991) [1.4].

[109] Local Government Planning and Land Act 1980, Part III; Local Government Act 1988; Local Government Act 1992.

were independent legal entities, statutory intervention was necessary. As well as complying with EU procurement rules on the tender process (below), an authority would have to solicit bids both from its own service unit and from private-sector providers and act in making the award so as not to restrict, distort or prevent competition. The regulatory design became ever more elaborate as CCT was progressively applied across local government services. Whitehall became increasingly 'involved in policing the "rules of the game" and plugging loopholes'.[110] Legal paper proliferated in a rising spiral of command and recalcitrance.[111] Despite the fierce element of compulsion, CCT had not delivered a thriving market in local services by the time the Conservatives left office;[112] in-house teams continued to win the great majority of 'contracts'.[113] The greater long-term impact stemmed from the requirement to operate on a trading basis and the resultant spread of commercialism – that is to say, a cultural shift in local government, from a public service base to a business organisation base.[114]

The replacement of CCT with the regime of 'best value' in local services was a flagship policy of the incoming Blair government. Competitive tendering would now be a strictly voluntary activity, so drawing the sting of complaints of excessive legalism or domination by Whitehall and neglect of service quality.[115] Typically however, the Conservative blueprint for public-service delivery was being modified, not jettisoned (see Chapter 2); there would be no rolling back of local contractual governance. Amid the plethora of performance standards and indicators, market testing and contracting out were ways of showing compliance with a best value authority's duty of making arrangements 'to secure continuous improvement' in service functions.[116] Then again:

> The introduction of Best Value, and with it the very active promotion of strategic service delivery partnerships by Central Government, marked a subtle, though significant, change

[110] A. Cochrane, 'Local Government' in Maidment and Thompson (eds.), *Managing the United Kingdom* (Sage, 1993), 224. And see *R v Environment Secretary, ex p. Haringey LBC* (1994) 92 LGR 538.

[111] We dealt with this more fully in C. Harlow and R. Rawlings, *Law and Administration* (Butterworths, 2nd edn 1997), Ch. 9.

[112] Competitive pressures were partly blunted by employee protection under the Acquired Rights Directive [1977] OJ C61/26. See M. Radford and A. Kerr, 'Acquiring Rights – Losing Power' (1997) 60 *MLR* 23.

[113] Although competition levels and in-house success rates varied considerably between services: see K. Walsh and H. Davis, *Competition and Service: The Impact of the Local Government Act 1988* (HMSO, 1993). Since the authority could not contract with itself, the in-house transaction would be pseudo-contract.

[114] J. Greenwood and D. Wilson, 'Towards the contract state: CCT in local government' (1994) 47 *Parl. Affairs* 405.

[115] DETR, *Modernising Local Government: Improving local services through best value* (1998) [1–2]; and see M. Geddes and S. Martin, 'The policy and politics of best value' (2000) 28 *Policy and Politics* 379.

[116] Local Government Act 1999, s. 3. But see ODPM, *Best Value and Performance Improvement* (2003).

> in public sector procurement strategy. Best Value brought public sector procurement into step with private sector thinking which had long maintained that key supplier relationships should be organised on an enduring partnership rather than short-term contract basis.[117]

More recently, a national procurement strategy for England has been pursued, replete with rolling targets. The talk is of 'smart' procurement, emphasis on specifying outcomes not functions and on payment by results. Institutional developments – local buying consortia and regional centres of excellence – reflect the demands for greater co-operation and co-ordination in the sector. This builds on the important missionary work of the '4ps', a general source of procurement advice and assistance to local government first established under the Conservatives (see p. 418 below). The forces of change are unrelenting:

> The Strategy . . . has laid the foundations for the next phase: the transformation of local public services. [The Department] and our partners will work with local authorities to underpin a radical value for money programme to deliver the ambition set out in the 2007 Budget of at least 3% annual cashable efficiencies . . . whether delivered through smarter procurement, re-engineering services or any other innovative approaches . . . While priority has been accorded to the delivery of efficiency gains, the role of procurement in the promotion of the economic, social and environmental well being of communities [is] a central feature.[118]

(c) Buying social justice

Use of the great commercial power of government contracting to achieve political and social objectives has a long and chequered history.[119] Such strategies of contract compliance touch on basic ideological questions: social engineering, however beneficial, versus a purist conception of VFM and business autonomy. From a 'green light' standpoint, the technique may be a viable alternative to criminal sanctions or individual complaint and adjudication as a way of regulating operator behaviour, or else a useful supplement. The proactive, or fire-watching, qualities are valuable, as is also the scope for flexibility or negotiated compliance. Familiar in the US as a distinctive technique of administrative action, especially in relation to race and sex discrimination,[120]

[117] DCLG, *The Long-term Evaluation of the Best Value Regime* (2006), p. 93.

[118] Department for Communities and Local Government, *The National Procurement Strategy for Local Government: Final report* (2008), p. 45; and see Audit Commission, *Healthy Competition* (2007).

[119] Reaching back to 'the Fair Wages Resolution', first promulgated by the House of Commons in 1891. See O. Kahn-Freund, 'Legislation through adjudication: The legal aspects of fair wages clauses and recognised conditions' (1948) 11 *MLR* 274. (This is now the realm of the statutory minimum wage.)

[120] For a valuable comparative study see R. Dhami, J. Squires and T. Modood, *Developing Positive Action Policies: Learning from the experiences of Europe and North America* (DWP, 2006).

contract compliance eventually came to be sanctioned by statute for Northern Ireland.[121]

In the 1980s many councils, led by the Greater London Council, resorted to contract compliance to enforce equal opportunities. Special units developed to monitor and advise contractors, with the ultimate sanction of termination of contract or disbarment from tendering.[122] Some authorities went further, refusing to contract with firms that had business dealings in (apartheid) South Africa or connections with the nuclear industry. Matters came to a head in *R v Lewisham LBC, ex p. Shell UK Ltd*,[123] when this practice was challenged by the UK subsidiary of a powerful multinational with other subsidiaries operating in South Africa. There are close similarities with the *Wheeler* case (see p. 114 above). Whereas the council sought to justify the boycott on the basis of its statutory duty to promote good race relations within the borough, the court focused on the pressure put on the company to end trading links and found improper purpose: 'It is to be remembered that Shell UK was not acting in any way unlawfully.'

Prime Minister Thatcher had seen enough. A striking example of 'imperium' to curb 'dominium', s. 7 of the Local Government Act 1988 required local authorities to disregard 'matters which are non-commercial matters for the purposes of this section'. The list included contractors' terms and conditions of employment; conduct in industrial disputes; involvement with defence or foreign policy or location in any country; and any political, industrial or sectarian affiliation.[124] The Act effectively corralled the use of contract compliance by local authorities,[125] which was in any case already being stunted by developments in Community law (see p. 383 below).

With New Labour in power, the core idea of *buying social justice* began again to creep up the agenda. After all, the further the 'contractual revolution' progressed, the greater the potential scope for this type of policy lever (today some 30 per cent of British companies are contracted by the public sector). McCrudden, the leading commentator, has produced a basic template for determining 'how best to introduce social policies, and *which* such policies should be integrated into the process of public procurement' (as with the modelling of regulatory legitimacy (see Chapter 7), major value judgements cannot be avoided however):

[121] Fair Employment (Northern Ireland) Act 1989: see C. McCrudden, R. Ford and A. Heath, 'Legal regulation of affirmative action in Northern Ireland: An empirical assessment', (2004) 24 *OJLS* 363.

[122] Institute of Personnel Management, *Contract Compliance: The United Kingdom experience* (1987).

[123] [1988] 1 All ER 938.

[124] The prohibition covered all types of procurement contract regardless of their financial value (with a tightly drawn exception for race relations (s. 18)).

[125] The message was driven home via judicial review: *R v Islington LBC, ex p. Building Employers' Confederation* [1989] IRLR 382.

> First, linkages should be chosen that are effective in achieving the aim of the procurement and delivering the social policy. This is likely to mean concentrating procurement resources on delivering only the most important policy goals so as not to overload the system. This is a crucial point. Not every public policy can, or should, be taken into account in procurement. Second, potential suppliers should understand clearly from the outset what categories of information and service standards may be expected . . . Third, choosing which government policies should be integrated into procurement will need to be carefully considered and justified, with the criteria clearly specified . . . Integration does not mean that all such polices should be integrated, or in the same way, or to the same depth. Fourth, linkages should be chosen that are as consistent as possible with the other aspects and values of the procurement process. Fifth, linkages should be chosen that are justifiable. Departments are accountable for their expenditure and, therefore, will need to determine whether any extra costs that may result . . . are justified.[126]

The curb on councils was loosened through the Local Government Act 1999 as part of the move to 'best value'.[127] Contracting authorities could now factor workplace issues and in particular take account of the equal-opportunities practices of potential providers where this was relevant to service delivery. While pragmatic concerns about the burden on business typically hold sway, more recent developments show the policy-makers becoming more ambitious in promoting such linkages within the broad framework of VFM.[128] Showing the potential of blending social with economic considerations, central government has moved, for example, to specify skill levels and training for those providing contracted services. 'It is important for Government to lead by example . . . There will be benefits for those who use public services, the individual employee, and the employer.'[129] Contract compliance can be an especially useful tool for crossing the public/private 'divide' in the context of positive duties. We note how the new generation of legislative duties on public bodies to promote equality[130] encompasses the dominium power and hence government contracting: for example, questioning bidders about the make-up of their work force. As part of a proposed package of reforms centred on the idea of a single equality duty, ministers recently signalled further changes to procurement policy so as to require suppliers, as well as public bodies, to detail

[126] McCrudden, *Buying Social Justice*, p. 578.

[127] Local Government Best Value (Exclusion of Non-commercial Considerations) 2001, SI No. 909; DETR, *Best Value and Procurement: Handling of workplace matters in contracting* (2001).

[128] As also of course EC law: see generally, OGC, *Buy and Make a Difference: How to address social issues in public procurement* (2008).

[129] Cabinet Office, *Access to Skills, Trade Unions and Advice in Government Contracting* (2008), p. 1. Government contractors are further 'encouraged' actively to publicise trade union representation and rights at work.

[130] Race Relations (Amendment) Act 2000; Disability Discrimination Act 2005; Equality Act 2006; and see above Ch. 5.

pay gaps.[131] Contract compliance is here seen as a way to 'drive transparency' into a large wedge of the private sector, so contributing to delivery of the Government's targets.[132]

Contract compliance can also help in promoting human rights protection for service users. The lack of direct 'horizontal' effect of the HRA (see p. 20 above), and more especially a restrictive case law denying the statutory Convention rights in contexts of 'contracting out', has given this a very contemporary edge. Indeed, majority speeches in the leading case of *YL*[133] (see p. 380 below) make the link expressly: 'The contractual terms which a local authority is often able to impose on a proprietor of a care home with whom it makes arrangements may well ensure that a person's rights against the proprietor are pretty similar in practice to those which would be enjoyed against the local authority.'[134]

Ministers have issued multi-sectoral guidance:

> The most fruitful way for public authorities to proceed when attempting to contract to secure the protection of human rights for service users is via the specification of services . . . The public authority should detail . . . the activities which it considers will be required to be performed by the supplier, including output specifications relating to processes where these help to define the performance characteristics of the service . . .
>
> There are several advantages . . . It provides all potential suppliers with a very high degree of certainty as to what will be required from them . . . It enables the public authority to ensure that there is a mutual understanding as between itself and the supplier that the services will be delivered in a particular, HRA compliant way . . . It enables the public authority to fully reflect the needs of relevant stakeholders in the service delivered. Where appropriate, users of the service could be invited to feed into the process of drawing up the specification, thus [meeting] end user expectation that human rights issues have been satisfactorily addressed . . . It provides transparency as to the way in which the public authority has sought to secure the discharge of the HRA obligations it has. Flowing from this, it assists the public authority in monitoring and enforcement of those obligations (and auditing bodies similarly) . . . It may be possible to adopt greater commonality . . . A public authority consensus view as to the way in which certain issues should be dealt with could be fed into all relevant contracts. In this way, the culture of respect for human rights can be fostered.[135]

How realistic is this? From a human rights perspective, the risks of inconsistency, associated on the one hand with a diverse range of public contracting

[131] Government Equalities Office, *Framework for a Fairer Future: The Equality Bill*, Cm. 7431 (2008).

[132] *The Equality Bill: Government response to consultation*, Cm. 7454 (2008). Imposing pay audits across the private sector was evidently considered a step too far.

[133] *YL (by her litigation friend the Official Solicitor) v Birmingham City Council and Others* [2007] UKHL 27.

[134] Lord Neuberger [149]; echoing Lord Woolf in the *Leonard Cheshire* case (see p. 379 below).

[135] ODPM, *Guidance on Contracting for Services in the Light of the Human Rights Act* (2005).

bodies and, on the other, with highly variegated local markets, loom large. While there clearly are potentials for public deliberation – a more 'responsive' form of contractual governance – the practical difficulties of promoting genuinely participative modes of rule-making with the private legal form cannot be gainsaid. There is also the problem of enforceability by service-users with the Contract (Rights of Third Parties) Act 1999 providing only a partial solution. As shown in *YL*, sophisticated contractual 'webs' applying human rights standards can be developed to smooth the way through, for example, tripartite contracts between the public purchaser, operator and end-user. But will they be?

The limitations of contractual technique are shown. Take the commercial difficulties of negotiating contractual terms with uncertain implications; the guidance did not recommend generic compliance clauses (see p. 380 below) on grounds of higher bid costs and likely market resistance. 'Suppliers might feel unable to price risk.'[136] Yet as the British Institute of Human Rights observes, a specification-based approach to 'presentiation' sits uncomfortably with the idea of an all-embracing 'living law':

> The successful implementation of contract specifications requires the public authority to identify whether the delivery of the particular service engages human rights issues and the steps that need to be taken to ensure the relevant rights are respected. Whether this is even possible is debatable, since human rights questions arise in a multitude of different potential situations some of which cannot be predicted. It is not possible in our view to take such a prescriptive approach to human rights protection. In any event, to have the chance of protecting human rights in this way, even partially successfully, the public authority would need to have a very good understanding of human rights issues . . . In the vast majority of public bodies, human rights have remained in the domain of legal services or human resources. In light of this, it seems difficult to understand how an approach based on contract specification could be effective in protecting the human rights of service users.[137]

But while it lacks the glamour of human rights adjudication, public lawyers should not lose sight of the valuable spaces for dialogue inherent in the contractual process, as also the sense of shared 'ownership' familiarly associated with the private legal form. Contract compliance remains a useful part of the equipment for the hard slog of mainstreaming human rights values where it really matters – beyond the courtroom. Irrespective of the statutory coverage, we could expect to see the gradual elaboration of model clauses, no doubt with inputs from the Commission for Equality and Human Rights.

[136] *Ibid.*, p. 2.

[137] JCHR, *The Meaning of Public Authority under the Human Rights Act*, HC 410 (2006-07), p. 21(BIHR evidence); and see BIHR, *The Human Rights Act: Changing lives* (2007).

4. Flashpoints

The interaction of the conceptual framework of ordinary private law with, on the one side, the needs of public policy and administration and, on the other, demands for individual protection, infuses the case law. Perhaps confusingly, the courts are found in certain situations holding fast to, or dismantling, old exceptions or privileges in favour of a private law model, and in others edging towards a public law one. Fuelled by the ever-increasing economic and social significance of the 'contractual revolution' – public procurement as big business (disappointed tenderers), outsourced public-service delivery (afflicted users) – alternative ways of developing legal accountability are naturally the subject of exploration. Judicial review has been weak however in the very area where administrative development has been strong. The prevailing common law ethos of government contracts as subject to general private law doctrines facilitates the use of informal administrative or negotiated rules. A public law system would supervise and monitor such arrangements; here the result has been judicial reluctance to apply to the contract function common law doctrines of judicial review that apply to other government activities; as also, in the context of contracted out public services, Convention rights. At one with a strong dose of neo-liberalism, the inhibition is connected with the consensual basis of contract and freedom of contract.[138] Let us look more closely.

(a) From incapacity to restitution

Unlike the Crown, statutory bodies such as local authorities have no general capacity to contract. The ultra vires principle applies to contract as to other activities and the scope of the power will be dependent upon the construction of the relevant legislation. Historically, cases have been few and far between, a reflection both of broad and flexible legal frameworks,[139] and of light-touch judicial scrutiny (a power to contract easily implied[140]). Providing that 'a local authority shall have power to do anything . . . which is calculated to facilitate, or is conducive or incidental to, the discharge of any of its functions', s. 111 of the Local Government Act 1972 embodied this approach.[141]

Contrariwise, the undermining of traditional relationships by the assertion of a strong central will became a familiar theme during the long years of

[138] See P. Cane, *An Introduction to Administrative Law*, 4th edn (Clarendon, 2004), pp. 294–301. But see E. McKendrick, 'Judicial control of contractual discretion' in Auby and Freedland (eds.), *The Public-Private Divide.*

[139] J. Griffith, *Central Departments and Local Authorities* (Allen and Unwin, 1966); M. Loughlin, *Local Government in the Modern State* (Sweet and Maxwell, 1986).

[140] *Attorney-General v Great Eastern Railway* (1880) 5 App Cas 473 is the standard authority.

[141] See likewise s. 2 of the Local Government Act 2000 and s. 60 of the Government of Wales Act 2006 (general power to promote or improve the economic, social or environmental 'well-being' of the area/country).

Conservative government.[142] Operationalised by audit in terms of 'regularity' (see p. 60 above), more structured and restrictive legislation brought the ultra vires principle to the fore. Local authorities meanwhile sought to protect expenditure programmes through creative accounting and innovative financing techniques. The scene was set for a flood of litigation on the power to contract, involving some very special kinds of arrangement: multi-million pound 'interest swaps'.

Led by Hammersmith, various councils had resorted to the futures market, exchanging debt with different banks with a view to benefiting from movements in interest rates. For several years a matter of doubt, the question whether these swap transactions were within the powers of the authorities became pressing as the market turned against them. In *Hazell v Hammersmith and Fulham LBC*[143] the local auditor sought a declaration of ultra vires, such that the contracts would be void and unenforceable against the public body. The main issue was whether, in the absence of express powers, the transactions could be brought within the general wording of s. 111. This in turn involved the question of the relationship with a very detailed set of provisions on borrowing set out in Schedule 13 to the same Act. The House of Lords roundly rejected the characterisation of the contracts as an appropriate means of debt management on the part of local government:

> *Lord Templeman:* A power is not incidental merely because it is convenient or desirable or profitable. A swap transaction undertaken by a local authority involves speculation in future interest trends with the object of making a profit in order to increase the available resources of the local authorities . . . Individual trading corporations and others may speculate as much as they please or consider prudent. But a local authority is not a trading or currency or commercial operator with no limit on the method or extent of its borrowing or with powers to speculate. A local authority is a public authority dealing with public monies . . . Schedule 13 establishes a comprehensive code which defines and limits the powers of a local authority with regard to its borrowing. This schedule is . . . inconsistent with any incidental powers to enter into swap transactions.[144]

Faced with huge loss of profits, the banks naturally called foul. There was much talk of the adverse impact of the case on the financial markets, both in terms of the cost of future credit to local government and damage to the City of London's international reputation. The Bank of England was sufficiently concerned to press the case, unsuccessfully, for what the Governor was pleased to call 'retro-corrective' legislation to restore 'the principle of the sanctity of

142 M. Loughlin, *Legality and Locality: The role of law in central-local government relations* (Clarendon, 1996); I. Leigh, *Law, Politics and Local Democracy* (Oxford University Press, 2000).

143 [1992] 2 AC 1.

144 For criticism see M. Loughlin, 'Innovative financing in local government: The limits of legal instrumentalism' [1990] *PL* 372; [1991] *PL* 568.

conduct'. *Hazell* however is one of those public law cases involving many diverse and competing interests. Take the local taxpayers. Why should they bear the risk? For Lord Templeman, protection of the public is uppermost. Again, the risk of ultra vires was no more hidden from the banks than from the local authorities; indeed, dispensing with specialist legal advice, some banks had turned a blind eye to the issue.[145] And what, it may be asked, of 'government under law', or of the role of ultra vires in buttressing the system of representative democracy? Note that, presented with the auditor's claim and hence the task of statutory interpretation, the court in *Hazell* had only a binary choice.

Might a distinction be drawn between cases of 'simple' ultra vires, as in *Hazell*, and of abuse of power? Even due diligence and search on behalf of the private contractor may not reveal the transaction that is capable of being lawful but is unlawful by reason of the purpose for which it was made. The issue came to the fore in *Crédit Suisse v Allerdale BC*,[146] where the bank tried to enforce a contract of guarantee relating to a failed development scheme. The case further illustrates the 'defensive use' of ultra vires, with the council pleading both the insufficiency of s. 111 and – the arrangement being made in order to avoid the strict borrowing limits set by central government – improper purpose. For the bank, much was made of the potential prejudice in government contracts to the private party, especially in terms of expectation losses (the classic contract calculus). It was argued that ultra vires contracts made by public bodies should not be treated as void automatically; the court should be able to uphold a contract where the other party acted in good faith. An analogy was drawn with the discretionary character of remedies in judicial review procedure, the argument being that since the enforceability of the guarantee turned on issues of public law, the same principles should apply in considering the consequences of a breach of public law in civil proceedings. The bank lost on all the main issues however. The Court of Appeal conceded little by way of flexibility in the interpretation and application of local authority powers.[147] And the doctrine of ultra vires was applied to maximum effect – no distinct categories, no public law discretion:

> *Neill LJ:* I know of no authority for the proposition that the ultra vires decisions of local authorities can be classified into categories of invalidity . . . Where a public authority acts outside its jurisdiction in any of the ways indicated by Lord Reid in *Anisminic* [p. 27 above] the decision is void. In the case of a decision to enter into a contract of guarantee, the consequences in private law are those which flow where one of the parties to a contract lacks capacity.

145 See E. McKendrick, 'Local authorities and swaps: Undermining the market?' in Goode and Cranston (eds.), *Making Commercial Law* (Oxford University Press, 1997).

146 [1996] 4 All ER 129.

147 See further the conjoined appeal, *Crédit Suisse v Waltham Forest London Borough Council* [1996] 4 All ER 176.

This is hardly satisfactory. Observe how the counterparty suffers the worst of the public/private law dichotomy: deprived of private law rights by public law yet unable in a commercial forum to take advantage of public law discretions. *Crédit Suisse* also cut against government policy, raising doubts over the guarantees and indemnities offered by statutory authorities in PPPs and under PFI. The predictable outcome was a dose of legislative pragmatism to mitigate the rigour of the common law. The Local Government (Contracts) Act 1997 is designed to provide contracting parties with a safe harbour while preserving the public protection of ultra vires. In consequence:

- Every statutory provision conferring or imposing a local government function confers power to contract for the provision of assets or services for the purposes of discharging that function.
- Local authorities can certify that they have power to enter into particular medium- or long-term contracts (as associated with PFI), so blocking arguments in private law proceedings of unenforceability.
- Conversely, rights of challenge of the auditor and – via judicial review – of local taxpayers are preserved.
- The court is further empowered however to permit the (otherwise 'void') contract to continue, so avoiding a possible disruption to services, and (if the parties have not otherwise stipulated) to award the private contractor compensation.

This is a neat little code which, by drawing the sting of *Crédit Suisse*, calms nerves. Administrative procedure is prioritised, elements of party autonomy factored, and the judges assigned a reserve power or back-up function. While some fine-tuning is in order, for example allowing for a contract to continue only on a transitional basis,[148] the model could usefully be applied to other agency-oriented fields of contractual governance.

It is one thing to declare the contract of a public body ultra vires, another to sort out the consequences. Take the situation following *Hazell*. Unable to claim damages for breach, the banks looked to the principle of unjust enrichment. Restitution had emerged in the early 1990s as a major growth area in domestic law.[149] Key doctrinal issues remained to be resolved however, a feature duly highlighted by the fluid and interactive character of the interest swap market.[150] To blow the whistle and seek to restore the players to their original position would prove a somewhat arbitrary exercise given the mixing of public and

[148] See A. Davies, 'Ultra vires problems in government contracts' (2006) 122 *LQR* 98. The radical alternative would be to afford statutory bodies like local authorities a general power of competence (for the problems, see R. Carnwath, 'The reasonable limits of local authority powers' [1996] *PL* 244).

[149] The essential 'breakthrough' case was *Lipkin Gorman v Karpnale Ltd* [1991] 2 AC 548.

[150] See further, P. Birks and F. Rose (eds.), *Lessons of the Swaps Litigation* (Mansfield Press, 2000).

private bodies, and redistribution of the risk through separate parallel deals, in the market.[151] Bear in mind polycentricity and the limitations of adjudication (which tends to isolate and focus on particular transactions).

Matters came to a head again in *Kleinwort Benson Ltd v Lincoln City Council*.[152] Could the bank recover payments made in the mistaken belief that they were pursuant to a binding contract or did an old (but much criticised) common law rule of no recovery for mistake of law prevent this? Recognition of the claim would allow for greater legal flexibility through the principle of unjust enrichment in cases of contractual incapacity. Showing scant sympathy for the financially hard-pressed local authority, the House of Lords did so,[153] subject to general defences such as change of position. The ruling is one of a number that establishes restitution in the judicial 'tool-kit' of remedies against public bodies, including in non-contractual contexts, a dimension to which we return in Chapter 17.

(b) To fetter or not to fetter

The common law principle that a public authority must retain the freedom to exercise its discretionary power in the public interest is well established (see Chapter 5). But how far – *The Amphitrite* aside – should this 'no fettering' principle be pressed in the case of contract? With competing values in play of security of contract and party autonomy, and of government effectiveness and political responsiveness, the question admits of no simple answer. Two different approaches are found in the early authorities. One involves a very strict test whereby the contract is void if it overlaps the subject matter of a statutory power.[154] The other, ultimately favoured by the House of Lords,[155] entails the more benign test of incompatibility between the purpose of the statutory power and the contractual purpose. That this allows the use of contract as a tool of statutory purpose is of great contemporary significance; as when, so facilitated, long-term PFI-type arrangements cut at the public law values expressed by 'no fettering' (see Chapter 9).

The test of incompatibility operates to defeat blatant attempts to rewrite statutory obligations. A classic example is *Stringer v Minister of Housing and Local Government*,[156] where the local authority made a formal agreement with Manchester University to discourage development in the vicinity of the Jodrell

[151] As with back-to-back contracts where the local authority's transaction would be ultra vires and the counter-party's 'balancing' transaction with another bank perfectly valid.

[152] [1999] 2 AC 349. See further, for the sea of uncertainty, *Westdeutsche Landesbank Girozentrale v Islington London Borough Council* [1996] AC 669.

[153] Building on *Woolwich Equitable Building Society v Commissioners of Inland Revenue* [1993] AC 70.

[154] *Ayr Harbour Trustees v Oswald* (1883) 8 App Cas 623.

[155] *British Transport Commission v Westmoreland County Council* [1958] AC 126, drawing on *Birkdale District Electric Supply Co Ltd v Southport Corpn* [1926] AC 355.

[156] [1970] 1 WLR 1281.

Bank telescope. The contract was held ultra vires since it bound the council to contravene the planning laws by a failure to consider all specified matters. Again in *R (Kilby) v Basildon DC*,[157] the Housing Act 1985 stipulated several ways to vary a council tenancy 'and not otherwise'. A clause in K's agreement purporting to give the tenants' committee a power of veto thus amounted to unlawful contractual fettering of the authority's management powers. Void *ab initio*, it could not found a legitimate expectation that the procedure would be followed.

Difficulties arise when – typical of a multi-functional body like a local authority – two potentially discordant statutory powers are involved. Take *R v Hammersmith and Fulham London Borough Council, ex p. Beddowes*.[158] Acting under a statutory power to dispose of land held for housing purposes, the ruling Conservative group resolved to sell off part of an estate to property developers and to enter into covenants over the remainder precluding the council from exercising a statutory power to provide housing via new tenancies. The contract, bitterly opposed by the Labour opposition, was signed a few hours before control of the council changed hands following local elections. A resident sought judicial review on the basis that the covenants were an unlawful fetter on the council's powers as a housing authority. By a majority, the Court of Appeal dismissed the challenge:

> *Fox LJ:* What we are concerned with in the present case are overlapping or conflicting powers. There is a power to create covenants restrictive of the use of retained land; and there are powers in relation to the user of the retained land for housing purposes. In these circumstances, it is necessary to ascertain for what purpose the retained land is held. All other powers are subordinate to the main power to carry out the primary purpose . . . Now the purpose for which the . . . estate is held by the council must be the provision of housing accommodation in the district. The council's policy in relation to the estate . . . seems to be consistent with that purpose. The estate is in bad repair and the policy is aimed at providing accommodation in the borough of higher quality than at present by means of a scheme of maintenance and refurbishment . . . If the purpose for which the power to create restrictive covenants is being exercised can reasonably be regarded as the furtherance of the statutory object, then the creation of the covenants is not an unlawful fetter. All the powers are exercisable for the achieving of the statutory objects in relation to the land, and the honest and reasonable exercise of a power for that purpose cannot properly be regarded as a fetter upon another power given for the same purpose.

Surely this formulation is too broad? The wide definition of 'primary purpose' basically deprives the no-fettering principle of legal effect. Covenants not in furtherance of a statutory power would anyway be unlawful. There is much to be said for the dissenting judgment in terms of representative democracy and electoral choice:

[157] [2006] EWHC 1892 (Admin).

[158] [1987] 2 WLR 263. See also *Dowty Boulton Paul Ltd v Wolverhampton Corporation* [1971] 1 WLR 204.

> *Kerr LJ:* The court must consider with the greatest care whether the decisions of the . . . council were actuated by policy reasons based upon the proper discharge of the authority's powers and functions as a housing authority, or by extraneous motives . . . The decision to contract . . . for the development, subject to these covenants, was an unreasonable and impermissible exercise of the powers and functions of a housing authority in the *Wednesbury* sense. Its predominant motivation was to fetter the political aspects of the future housing policy and not the implementation of the then . . . housing policy for reasons which were reasonably necessary at the time.

(c) Tendering and after: Judicial review

The sheer size of the government contracts market makes the case for legal protection of the public interest compelling. First, there is the ideal of fair access to the commercial benefits as expressed in principles of equal treatment and open competition. Secondly, the reality of informal networks fuels the argument for firm rules against bad faith and improper influence. According to Bailey:

> Hesitancy over the application of general public law standards concerning considerations, rationality and fairness . . . is misplaced. Each of these standards is sufficiently flexible to protect the legitimate interests of public authorities . . . Proper attention would then be placed, as appropriate, to the dimension of the public interest in the decision-making process in question . . . The rule of law requires public bodies to be held legally accountable in respect of abuses of power and unfairness . . . Public law principles properly applied need not distort the normal processes of commercial negotiations between parties simply because one party happens to be a public body; a remedy will only be available where the public interest is engaged.[159]

This is not however a convincing case for judicial review simply because of the public status of a body: an institutional test.[160] It is not immediately obvious either that, in ordinary commercial contracts like leases, corporate interests dealing with public bodies should have greater protection than any other contracting parties, or that, when operating in competition with private enterprise, public bodies should be subject to additional constraints. It is important to bear in mind also the practical problems of expense, delay and potential hardship to a successful bidder associated with legal action.

A suitable alternative would be the ombudsman system (see Chapter 13). However 'action taken in matters relating to contractual or other commercial transactions' is specifically excluded from investigation by the PCA.[161] The justification traditionally given is that ombudsmen are concerned with the relations between government and governed, and should be excluded from

[159] S. Bailey, 'Judicial review of contracting decisions' (2007) *PL* 444, 463.

[160] 'Core' public authorities are of course subject to Convention rights for all their activities (HRA, s. 6): p. 377 below.

[161] Parliamentary Commissioner Act 1967, Sch. 3 [9].

activities like outsourcing in which public bodies are not acting in a distinctively governmental fashion.[162] Today this will not wash. Wearing her other 'hat' of Health Services Commissioner, the PCA reviews the actions and decisions of contractors in the realm of publicly funded health and social care services.[163] In constructing ombudsman 'one-stop shops' for their territories, the devolved administrations have also taken the opportunity to align the jurisdiction with the essential fact of contractual governance.[164] The general barrier on local government ombudsmen investigating contractual and commercial transactions was recently lifted,[165] so opening up a whole new front of external administrative accountability in England. Why, it may be asked, the double standard?

The old assumption[166] that decisions relating to procurement are not reviewable on the basis of common law principles has come under pressure. In tandem with the *Lewisham case* in the 1980s was *ex p. Unwin*,[167] in which decisions to remove a firm from the council's list of contractors and to prevent it from tendering for renewal of an existing contract were held to be subject to the requirements of procedural fairness. In neither case did the court stop to consider whether there was a 'public element' to the contractual decisions, the functional test commonly associated with limitations on, or reluctance to exercise, the supervisory jurisdiction.[168] Another more liberal case is *ex p. Donn*,[169] in which the decision-making procedure of a Legal Aid Committee in awarding a contract to represent claimants was held amenable to judicial review. According to Ognall J, the 'public dimensions' of the matter took it outside the realm of a commercial function. In *Molinaro*,[170] Elias J came to the same conclusion in a case involving the licensing of premises and change of user: 'Manifestly, the Council was not simply acting as a private body when it sought to give effect to its planning policy through the contract.'

'Exceptions that prove the rule' is one way of describing this short list of judicial interventions. The Divisional Court's decision in *R v Lord Chancellor's Department, ex p. Hibbit and Saunders*[171] has stood foursquare against treating

162 See *Observations by the Government on the Select Committee Review of Access and Jurisdiction*, Cmnd 7449 (1979).

163 Health Service Commissioners Act 1993, s. 7(2)(a). See M. Seneviratne, *Ombudsmen: Public services and administrative justice* (London: Butterworths, 2002), pp. 162–7.

164 See e.g. Public Services Ombudsman (Wales) Act 2005, Sch. 2.

165 Local Government and Public Involvement in Health Act 2007, s.173.

166 See S. Arrowsmith, 'Judicial review and the contractual powers of public authorities' (1990) 106 *LQR* 277.

167 *R v London Borough of Enfield, ex p. T F Unwin (Roydon) Ltd* [1989] COD 466. See also *R v Hereford Corpn, ex p. Harrower* [1970] 1 WLR 1424.

168 As with 'the *Datafin* project' (Ch. 7). Not that the 'public law' element found has always been obvious: see e.g., *R v Barnsley Metropolitan Borough Council, ex p. Hook* [1976] 1 WLR 1052.

169 *R v Legal Aid Board, ex p. Donn & Co* [1996] 3 All ER 1.

170 *R (Molinaro) v Kensington LBC* [2001] EWHC Admin 896.

171 [1993] COD 326; drawing on the judgment of Woolf LJ in *R v Derbyshire County Council, ex p. Noble* [1990] ICR 808. See also *Mass Energy Ltd v Birmingham CC* [1994] Env LR 298.

contractual powers in the same way as other governmental powers for the purpose of judicial review. The dispute involved the proper ambit of post-tender negotiations, a major issue in the design of procurement procedures pitting administrative pressures for flexibility and VFM against concerns of a level playing field and equal treatment. One of the unsuccessful bidders for a contract to supply court reporting services managed to persuade the court of a breach of legitimate expectation that was 'unfair' and caused 'prejudice'. But the challenge was dismissed for lack of jurisdiction.

> *Rose LJ:* It is not appropriate to equate tendering conditions attendant on a common law right to contract with a statement of policy or practice or policy decisions in the spheres of Inland Revenue, immigration and the like, control of which is the especial province of the State and where, in consequence, a sufficient public law element is apparent.
>
> *Waller J:* In considering whether a decision can be judicially reviewed, it is critical to identify the decision and the nature of the attack on it. Unless there is a public law element in the decision, and unless the allegation involves suggested breaches of duties and obligations owed as a matter of public law, the decision will not be reviewable.

Hibbit is one of many cases, some already discussed, others to come (see Chapter 15), in which the court has attempted to set the boundaries of judicial review, at a time and in a context where the boundary lines of public and private organisation are fast being overridden. The conceptual difficulty when a 'public law' oriented jurisdiction is faced by a governmental system increasingly premised on private law techniques is manifest. Administrative lawyers must again think in terms of transcending the 'divide' or of blending public and private law methodologies. The potential of implied contract is shown by *Blackpool and Fylde Aero Club Ltd v Blackpool Borough Council*,[172] a case involving bids for a local authority concession. It was held to be breach of a right to have a bid considered when the plaintiff's tender was mistakenly treated as late and excluded from the competition. The fact that the purchaser was a public body was treated as a relevant factor in finding the contract.

The pressures for a reworking of the conceptual limitation on judicial review are unrelenting. The role of the common law principles is naturally bound up with the juridification of procurement stemming especially from EC policies. Heightened litigiousness, as well as the increased resort to contractual techniques in public services, fuels the jurisprudential argument whenever gaps appear in the relevant statutory codes. A pair of Welsh cases shows the courts holding strictly to *Hibbit*. In *Menai Connect*[173] complaints of relevant considerations being ignored and of mistake of fact failed to trigger the supervisory jurisdiction: 'It is not every wandering from the precise paths of best practice that lends fuel to a claim for judicial review.' In the second case, *Gamesa*

[172] [1990] 3 All ER 25.

[173] *R (Menai Connect Ltd) v Department for Constitutional Affairs* [2006] EWHC 727 (Admin). See also *R (Cookson and Clegg) v Ministry of Defence* [2005] Eu LR 517.

Energy,[174] the judge accepted that the tendering process was clouded with irrationality but nonetheless dismissed the challenge for going to 'the nuts and bolts parts of the exercise.' The approach taken is that exercise of the supervisory jurisdiction is appropriate only for claims of illegality, bad faith or serious misconduct (typically fraud) amounting to abuse of process. As with the light-touch approach in regulation, there is an understandable judicial nervousness about becoming embroiled in such dynamic and multi-polar forms of commercial decision-making.

The 2006 Court of Appeal case of *Supportways*[175] raised the question of amenability to judicial review at the later stages of contract management. A service review by the council had left the incumbent firm facing the loss of its franchise to supply housing-related support services to vulnerable people. Complaining of a flawed assessment of cost-effectiveness, but with no contractual entitlement to a fresh review and not much interested in damages as a remedy, the company sought to have the assessment quashed and re-done properly. The court was firm. There was no sufficient nexus between the conduct of the service review and the public law powers of the council to ground the supervisory jurisdiction. The fact that the contractual obligations in question were framed by reference to the council's statutory duties did not make them public law duties:

> *Neuberger LJ:* It cannot be right that a claimant suing a public body for breach of contract, who is dissatisfied with the remedy afforded him by private law, should be able to invoke public law simply because of his dissatisfaction, understandable though it may be. If he could do so, it would place a party who contracts with a public body in an unjustifiably more privileged position than a party who contracts with anyone else, and a public body in an unjustifiably less favourable position than any other contracting party . . . It is one thing to say that, because a contracting party is a public body, its actions are, in principle, susceptible to judicial review. It is quite another to say that, because a contracting party is a public body, the types of relief which may be available against it under a contract should include public law remedies, even where the basis of the claim is purely contractual in nature.

The Diceyan equality principle is not to be lightly discarded.

(d) Service provision: Convention rights

Ministers when promoting the HRA clearly had in mind the changing basis of public service delivery; the classical international law rubric of 'vertical' effect, protection of citizens' rights against encroachment by the state, would

[174] *R (Gamesa Energy UK Ltd) v National Assembly for Wales* [2006] EWHC 2167 (Admin).

[175] *Hampshire CC v Supportways Community Services Ltd* [2006] EWCA Civ 1035. See also *Mercury Energy Ltd v Electricity Corporation of New Zealand* [1994] 1 WLR 521.

be adapted in light of the more complex, less hierarchical, arrangements of contractual and regulatory governance.[176] Brought into sharp focus by the expanded role of the private and voluntary sectors in areas like social housing and residential care, the issue for the courts has been the *scale* of the adaptation: generous, very generous, or not so generous, in terms of the reach of protection.

Cane has said that 'the only way of deciding whether a function is public or private is to apply normative criteria about the desirable reach of human rights norms. Functions are "public" or "private" only because we make them so for particular and varied purposes'.[177] Unfortunately, the Human Rights Act did not take this route. The relevant provision is s. 6, which provides that 'it is unlawful for a public authority to act in a way which is incompatible with a Convention right'. It then gives some basic guidance about amenability to jurisdiction:[178]

> (3) In this section 'public authority' includes –
>
> (a) a court or tribunal, and
> (b) any person certain of whose functions are functions of a public nature . . .
>
> (5) In relation to a particular act, a person is not a public authority by virtue only of subsection (3)(b) if the nature of the act is private . . .
>
> (6) "An act" includes a failure to act.

This leaves the courts to navigate inside a threefold conceptual framework:

- *'Core' or 'standard' public authorities*: these are left undefined but Lord Nicholls reads in an 'instinctive classification' of 'bodies whose nature is governmental' that draws on such factors as special powers, democratic accountability, public funding, an obligation to act only in the public interest, and a statutory constitution.[179] Ranging through central government departments and the devolved administrations to the police and local authorities, 'core' public authorities are thus akin to an elephant: difficult to describe but easily recognised. They are also termed 'pure' public authorities since – irrespective of the seemingly 'private' nature of particular activities – they must act compatibly with Convention rights in all they do. Contractual activity is no exception.
- *'Hybrid', 'mixed function' or 'functional' public authorities*: these are bodies required to comply with Convention rights when exercising a function of a

[176] See especially *Rights Brought Home: The Human Rights Bill*, Cm. 3782 (1997) [2]; also, HC Deb. col. 773 (16 February 1998) (Home Secretary Jack Straw).

[177] P. Cane, 'Church, State and human rights: Are parish councils public authorities?' (2004) 120 *LQR* 41, 45.

[178] Consistent with the general policy of the statute, s. 6 also contains special exceptions for parliamentary activities.

[179] *Aston Cantlow and Wilcote with Billesley Parochial Church Council v Wallbank* [2003] 3 WLR 283 [7].

public nature (s. 6(3)(b)), but not when doing something where the nature of the act is private (s. 6(5)). The categorisation follows *Datafin* (see p. 317 above) in looking to the nature of the power, but in making no reference to the source of the power or to 'institutional' factors (relationship with government) appears to go further. Where contracted-out service delivery stands is questionable.

- *'Courts and tribunals'*: The inclusion of courts and tribunals in the section lays on those bodies a continuing duty to develop the common law in the light of ECHR requirements in cases between individuals.[180] But the proposition that s. 6(3)(a) imports, but is limited to, 'indirect horizontal effect' is now generally accepted, and properly so in view of the design of the statute.[181] It is this lack of full horizontal effect – no direct obligation on private parties to comply with Convention rights – that places a premium on the meanings otherwise ascribed under s. 6 to 'a public authority'.

Adopting a classical liberal position on the importance of private space in which actors can pursue their own conception of the good, Oliver[182] warns against using s. 6 to 'roll back the frontiers of civil society' thus undermining values of pluralism and individual autonomy. To avoid the unpredictability otherwise associated with 'functions of a public nature', she thinks that only those activities involving the exercise by private bodies of specifically legally authorised coercion,[183] or authority over others which would normally be unlawful for a body to exercise, should be caught under s. 6(3)(b). A strong dose of pragmatism is also advisable given the many pressures on non-governmental service providers and the enormous range of decisions that the statutory formula might otherwise be read to encompass:

> A generous interpretation could encourage litigation between private parties which would generate legal uncertainty and have negative effects for the many bodies, often charitable or not-for-profit, providing services for disadvantaged people . . . Litigation or the risk of it could inhibit, and divert resources from, what most of us would regard as desirable activity in civil society . . . [It] could [be made] difficult or impossible for these bodies to take important managerial decisions about closure or modernisation of facilities . . . without being exposed to. . . the risk of having to obtain clearance . . . if services are being provided under contract, or . . . of being sued and thus being second-guessed by the courts . . . It would be discriminatory . . . if the nature (as 'public' or 'private') of a function that is performed by a

[180] The best known examples are in the realm of breach of confidence and privacy law; see further below, Ch. 17.

[181] For the doomed attempt to import the value of universality into s. 6, see Sir W. Wade, 'Horizons of horizontality' (2000) 116 *LQR* 217; and see, M. Hunt, 'The "horizontal effect" of the Human Rights Act' [1998] *PL* 423.

[182] D. Oliver, 'The frontiers of the state: Public authorities and public functions under the Human Rights Act' [2000] *PL* 476 and 'Functions of a public nature under the Human Rights Act' [2004] *PL* 329.

[183] As with the detention in hospital of mental health patients: *R(A) v Partnerships in Care Ltd* [2002] 1 WLR 2610.

> private organisation . . . depended on whether it was being provided under a contract with the recipient of the services, or a contract with a public authority . . . or under no contract and voluntarily.[184]

This argument can however be turned on its head. Short of full horizontal effect, some form of 'discrimination' is inevitable. Parliament's JCHR has naturally championed a broad interpretation of 'functions of a public nature', so warning against 'a serious gap' in human rights protection for the many vulnerable people dependent on contracted out public services.[185] 'A function is a public one when government has taken responsibility [for it] in the public interest . . . A State programme or policy . . . may delegate its powers or duties through contractual arrangements without changing the public nature of those powers or duties . . . It is the doing of [the] work as part of a government programme which denotes public function.'[186]

Faced with the open-ended language of s. 6, the courts have struggled from the outset. In *Leonard Cheshire*,[187] long-stay residents of a care home run by a large charitable organisation, whose places were funded by the local authority under a contractual arrangement, wished to challenge the decision to close the home and disperse them. Partly on the basis of promises of a 'home for life', Art. 8 was invoked, as it had been in *Coughlan* (see p. 224 above).This put the reach of the HRA in issue and hence, in a very practical way, the legally recognised contours of the state. Clearly concerned about the burdens otherwise imposed on small- to medium-size service providers, Lord Woolf dismissed the argument of a 'hybrid' case under s. 6(3)(b) on the ground that the charity was not 'enmeshed' in the council's activities. Other factors mentioned were that the charity was not exercising statutory powers and the absence of material distinction between the services provided by the care home to publicly and privately funded residents. Other than requiring the residents to look to the ('core') local authority for Convention rights, Lord Woolf had, by jumbling institutional and functional factors, provided little by way of practical guidance.

A recurrent issue in the cases is the appropriate degree of alignment between the reach of judicial review in the guise of (a) Convention rights and (b) common law principles: for example, should the limitations on 'the *Datafin* project', previously established in contract-type cases,[188] be read

[184] Oliver, 'Functions of a Public Nature', p. 342.

[185] JCHR, *The Meaning of Public Authority under the Human Rights Act*, HC 382 HL 39 (2003/4), p. 26. See also P. Craig, 'Contracting Out, the Human Rights Act and the Scope of Judicial Review' (2002) 118 *LQR* 551.

[186] JCHR, *The Meaning of Public Authority under the Human Rights Act*, HC 382 HL 39 (2003/4), pp. 46–7; and see *The Meaning of Public Authority under the Human Rights Act*, HC 410 (2006/7).

[187] *R (Heather) v Leonard Cheshire Foundation* (2002) 2 All ER 936. It is interesting to compare Lord Woolf's reasoning in distinguishing *Poplar Housing and Regeneration Community Association Ltd v Donoghue* [2002] QB 48 with his *Coughlan* judgment.

[188] As discussed in Ch. 7; and see *R v Servite Houses and Wandsworth LBC, ex p. Goldsmith and Chatting* (2000) 2 LGLR 997.

across? Pragmatic concerns to do with the manageability of 'a multi-streamed jurisdiction' (see Chapter 15), as where common law and Convention rights claims arise in a single case, point to the necessity for rough equivalence.[189] Clearly concerned to preserve some flexibility, Lord Hope in *Aston Cantlow* spoke of the common law authorities being helpful but not determinative.[190]

Aston Cantlow involved a somewhat arcane dispute: whether the historic liability of a private landowner to pay for local church repairs was overridden by Art. 1 of the ECHR First Protocol (peaceful enjoyment of possessions). The Court of Appeal thought it 'inescapable' that s. 6 bit, the parochial church council being part of 'the church by law established'. The speeches in the House of Lords were indicative, in Lord Nicholls' words, of a 'generously wide' interpretation of 'functions of a public nature',[191] yet the House took a relatively narrow approach to the particular case, reversing the Court of Appeal. Section 6 (3)(b) was circumnavigated with the help of the private law analogy of a restrictive covenant[192] and property law trumped human rights. But the speeches left unanswered the authority of *Leonard Cheshire*, which had not been mentioned. The law relating to Convention rights in the context of contractual governance was now hopelessly confused.

The scene was set for the difficult case of *YL*.[193] An elderly lady suffering from Alzheimer's disease lived in a home owned and operated by Southern Cross Healthcare Ltd, a market leader in residential accommodation and nursing services as regulated under the Care Standards Act 2000. Tasked with the classic welfare-state duty to 'make arrangements for providing' accommodation and care for such vulnerable persons, the council was funding most of the cost. As well as numerous provisions about service standards, both the tripartite contract (between council, company and claimant) and the company's master contract (with the council) contained a generic compliance clause to 'at all times act in a way which is compatible with the Convention rights'. Southern Cross retained the contractual right to terminate the placement 'for good reason', a right which it sought to exercise following a breakdown in relations with YL's family. This right the Official Solicitor's lawyers aimed to trump with a direct application of the Art. 8 right to respect for a person's home, raising the question whether Southern Cross was netted by s. 6. Government lawyers intervened to support a broad interpretation but, by a three to two majority, the House of Lords chose to tread more carefully.

[189] *R (Hammer Trout Farm) v Hampshire Farmers Markets Ltd* [2003] EWCA Civ 1056; *R (Mullins) v Jockey Club* [2005] EWHC 2197. See also (post *YL*), *R (Weaver) v London & Quadrant Housing Trust* [2008] EWHC 1377.

[190] [2003] 3 WLR 283 [52].

[191] [2003] 3 WLR 283 [11].

[192] And on the basis that a public authority could not be a 'victim' for ECHR purposes. See further M. Sunkin, 'Pushing forward the frontiers of human rights protection: The meaning of public authority under the Human Rights Act' (2004) *PL* 643.

[193] *YL (by her litigation friend the Official Solicitor) v Birmingham City Council and Others* [2007] UKHL 27; noted by Palmer (2007) 66 *CLJ* 559.

The minority (Lord Bingham and Lady Hale) looked at matters through the lens of the welfare lawyer. Echoing the JCHR, their starting point was the modern state's acceptance of responsibility for social welfare. In Lord Bingham's words, 'the intention of Parliament is that residential care should be provided, but the means of doing so is treated as, in itself, unimportant'. A contextual and purposive approach was called for, centred on protection of the individual:

> Those who qualify for residential care . . . are, beyond argument, a very vulnerable section of the community . . . Despite the intensive regulation to which care homes are subject, it is not unknown that senile and helpless residents of such homes are subjected to treatment which may threaten their survival, may amount to inhumane treatment, may deprive them unjustifiably of their liberty and may seriously and unnecessarily infringe their personal autonomy and family relationships. These risks would have been well understood by Parliament when it passed the 1998 Act.[194]

In seeking so to infuse the 'mixed economy of care' with legal accountability through Convention rights, Lady Hale mentioned a series of factors, predictably more functional than institutional in character, indicative of amenability to jurisdiction:

> One important factor is whether the state has assumed responsibility for seeing that this task is performed. In this case, there can be no doubt . . . Another important factor is the public interest in having that task undertaken. In a state which cares about the welfare of the most vulnerable members of the community, there is a strong public interest in having people who are unable to look after themselves . . . looked after properly . . . Another important factor is public funding. Not everything for which the state pays is a public function. The supply of goods and ancillary services such as laundry to a care home may well not be a public function. But providing a service to individual members of the public at public expense is different . . . Another factor is whether the function involves or may involve the use of statutory coercive powers . . . Finally there is the close connection between this service and the core values underlying the Convention rights and the undoubted risk that rights will be violated unless adequate steps are taken to protect them.[195]

Viewing the case through a commercial law lens, the majority saw things very differently. Lord Scott was robust: the 'contractual revolution' could not be reduced to a matter of means; in repressing direct service provision, it had wrought substantive – capitalist – ends. 'Private' enterprise was exactly that:

> Southern Cross is a company carrying on a socially useful business for profit. It is neither a charity nor a philanthropist. It enters into private law contracts with the residents in its care homes and with the local authorities with whom it does business. It receives no

[194] *YL* [16] [19]. See further, JCHR, *The Human Rights of Older People in Healthcare*, HC 378 (2006/7).

[195] *Ibid.* [66–71]

> public funding, enjoys no special statutory powers, and is at liberty to accept or reject residents as it chooses (subject, of course, to anti-discrimination legislation which affects everyone who offers a service to the public) and to charge whatever fees in its commercial judgment it thinks suitable. It is operating in a commercial market with commercial competitors.
>
> For these reasons I am unable to conclude that Southern Cross, in managing its care homes, is carrying on a function of a 'public nature' . . . As to the act of Southern Cross that gave rise to this litigation, namely, the service of a notice terminating the agreement . . . it affected no one but the parties to the agreement. I do not see how its nature could be thought to be anything other than private.[196]

The swing votes of Lords Mance and Neuberger highlighted the difficulty of differentiating between privately and publicly funded residents, as well as the positive role for contract as a vehicle of human rights protection.[197] Engaging in a nicely 'structured dialogue' with the lawmaker (see p. 138 above) over the nature and extent of human rights protection, Lord Neuberger concluded by saying:

> It may well be thought to be desirable that residents in privately owned care homes should be given Convention rights against the proprietors. That is a subject on which there are no doubt opposing views, and I am in no position to express an opinion. However, if the legislature considers such a course appropriate, then it would be right to spell it out in terms, and, in the process, to make it clear whether the rights should be enjoyed by all residents of such care homes, or only certain classes (e.g. those whose care and accommodation is wholly or partly funded by a local authority).[198]

In honouring a commitment to reverse *YL*, however, ministers have taken a strictly limited approach. According to s. 145 of the Health and Social Care Act 2008:

> A person ('P') who provides accommodation, together with nursing or personal care, in a care home for an individual under arrangements made with P under the relevant statutory provisions is to be taken . . . to be exercising a function of a public nature in doing so.

This leaves *YL*, in the absence of general valedictory legislation,[199] as good authority across a broad swathe of contracted public service provision. In the case of care homes it leaves self-funded individuals excluded from the protec-

[196] *Ibid.* [26] [33–4].

[197] *Ibid.* [117] [149] [151]. The decisions on amenability to jurisdiction at common law were also considered of 'real assistance' at [156]. See conversely, *R (Weaver) v London & Quadrant Housing Trust* [2008] EWHC 1377.

[198] *Ibid.* [171].

[199] The government has been consulting on the matter: see JCHR, *A Bill of Rights for Britain?* HC 150 1 (2007/8) [281–5].

tion of Convention rights now afforded to publicly funded residents – a wholly unattractive form of public/private 'dichotomy'. But this is not necessarily, as Lords Mance and Neuberger hinted, the end of the story. We must not forget that *YL* was tried on the preliminary issue of whether Southern Cross, in providing accommodation and care for the appellant, was exercising public functions for the purpose of s. 6 of the 1998 Act. No other outcome was necessary, as Southern Cross had withdrawn the request to remove the appellant from the home before the House of Lords hearing. Had it been otherwise, the House might well have explored other ways round the problem, turning first to techniques of contract compliance (see p. 362 above). Had it been shown that ECHR standards were infringed, the contractual obligation to 'at all times act in a way which is compatible with the Convention rights' might have come into play. Or it might have been argued that the contractual right to terminate 'for good reason' could not cover a breach of human rights protection. More boldly, implied terms could be read into care contracts that treatment will not be degrading.

5. Contract-making: Europeanisation

Nowhere is the contemporary blending of domestic administrative law with EU law better illustrated than in the special 'administrative procedures act' on public procurement effectively comprised by the Public Contracts Regulations 2006 and the Utilities Contracts Regulations 2006.[200] The regulations are part of a convoluted legal development involving repeated use of the ECA 1972 to make delegated legislation drawing down into administrative practice and procedure the overarching legal requirements of the Single Market.[201] Typically however, the EU requirements not only drive, but are also driven by, national developments in law and administration. Reflecting classic debates about rules and discretion (see Chapter 5), the evolving regime raises general questions about the efficacy and scale of the regulation of public contract making. It is also notable for innovations in the realm of remedies.

(a) Development

The European Commission has over the years been very active in the field, targeting a mass exercise in dominium power estimated to account for over 15 per cent of Member States' total GDP. A legal framework centred on public contracts being awarded in an open, fair and transparent manner has, as policy rationales, the elimination of discrimination on national grounds, economic

[200] Respectively, SI Nos. 5 and 6 of 2006.

[201] S. Arrowsmith, 'Legal techniques for implementing directives: A case study of public procurement' in Craig and Harlow (eds.), *Law Making in the European Union* (Kluwer, 1998) and 'Implementation of the new EC Procurement Directives' (2006) 15 *PPLR* 86.

efficiency and European competitiveness in the global market,[202] VFM for awarding authorities, and anti-corruption. The paradox is immediately apparent: burgeoning regulation in the cause of market liberalisation.[203]

A major programme of legislative reform initiated by the Commission in the mid-1980s was designed to break the stranglehold of domestic preference in public purchasing.[204] As against the various 'pull factors' ranging from the consciously national ('Buy British') to the collateral or social, and on through administrative convenience or, as the contract theorist might insist, the virtues of trust and co-operation associated with 'repeat' contracting, earlier efforts had achieved conspicuously little.[205] Application of basic Treaty articles by the ECJ remained sporadic and peripheral,[206] relevant directives lacked an effective enforcement mechanism and in practice were largely ignored.[207] The reform programme involved widening control by bringing in the utilities[208] and deepening it by strengthening procedural requirements and establishing a new regime of sanctions. Different activities – works, supplies, services – were each made the subject of a specific directive, which received general underpinning from the Remedies or Compliance Directive.[209] 'Contracting authorities' were broadly defined to include central government, local government and public agencies; thresholds were used to exempt minor contracts.

The use of 'a pathway model', whereby public purchasers are prescribed a whole series of steps to follow, is significant in terms of administrative law technique. Involving stress on the transparency of decision-making and the use of objective criteria specified in advance, the design reflected the familiar assumption that whenever there is broad administrative discretion arbitrariness or discrimination follows automatically. Perhaps however 'pathways model' is the better description. In recognition of demands for competition and manageability in routine transactions, and for greater flexibility in complex (large-scale) contracts, public purchasers were given the choice of one of three award procedures:

- *open procedure* – all interested firms being allowed to tender
- *restricted procedure* – tenders being invited from a list of firms drawn up by the authority

202 International legal ordering in the shape of the WTO's Government Procurement Agreement (GPA) underscores this aspect.

203 M. Chiti, 'Regulation and market in the public procurement sector' (1995) 7 *European Review of Public Law* 373; S. Arrowsmith, 'The past and future evolution of EC procurement law: from framework to common code?' (2006) 35 *Public Contract Law J.* 337.

204 Commission White Paper, *Completing the Internal Market,* COM (85) 310.

205 Evidenced by very low rates of import penetration: W. S. Atkins Management Consultants, *The Cost of Non-Europe in Public Procurement* (1988).

206 For an exception that proves the rule, see Case 45/87 *Commission v Ireland* [1988] ECR 4035.

207 See Directive 71/305 (Works), Directive 77/62 (Supplies); and generally F. Weiss, *Public Procurement in European Community Law* (Athlone Press, 1992).

208 Which were given their own, rather more flexible regime: Directives 93/38 (Utilities), 92/13 (Utilities Remedies).

209 Directives 93/37 (Works), 93/96 (Supplies), 92/50 (Services), 89/665 (Compliance).

- *negotiated procedure* – the contractual terms being negotiated with chosen contractors, the use of which has however been strictly confined precisely because of the informality.[210]

As well as formal implementation by statutory instrument,[211] this regime in turn became the subject of mass soft-law guidance inside the domestic system.[212] We touch here on a defining feature of EU procurement law in recent years: a fast-moving jurisprudence that sees the ECJ filling gaps in the directives, elaborating relevant factors, and utilising general principles in the cause of market integration pre- and post-Enlargement.[213] Take the principle of transparency. In support of equal treatment, the ECJ has in this context afforded it an expansive meaning, to the extent of requiring elements of rule-based decision-making.[214] Again, take the vexed issue of contract compliance to achieve social objectives. Whereas the Commission typically urged market purity, the Court in a well-known line of cases mitigated this. Provided there were no discriminatory effects, it could be lawful to incorporate local policy objectives like combating unemployment in the contractual conditions for performance; likewise, as an award criterion, provided that, for example, the relevant environmental factors related to the subject matter of the contract.[215] The case law has thus accommodated New Labour's cautiously rounded approach to use of the dominium power.

Reviewing the scheme in the late 1990s, the Commission initially suggested little change. The economic impact being relatively limited, with public purchasing continuing to operate overwhelmingly along national lines, the existing framework should be given more time to bite.[216] As the consultation made clear, however, this meant skating over a series of difficulties with formal legal ordering demonstrated by the rules.[217] Take the problem of over-rigidity. Considerable compliance costs were being imposed and hard to justify. Rather than improving the efficiency of purchasing, such

[210] Case C-71/92 *Commission v Spain* [1993] ECR I-5923.

[211] See e.g. Public Works Contracts Regulations 1991, SI No. 2680.

[212] So paralleling the Commission's use of the interpretative communication: notably, *Public Procurement and Protection of the Environment* COM (2001) 274 and *Public Procurement and Social Policy* COM (2001) 566.

[213] C. Bovis, 'Developing public procurement regulation: Jurisprudence and its influence on law making' 43 *CML Rev.* (2006) 461.

[214] See especially Cases C-496/99 *Commission v CAS Succhi di Frutta SpA* [2004] ECR-I 3801, C-340/02 *Commission v France* [2004] ECR I-9845 and C–532/06 *Lianakis* [2008] ECRI–251. In Case C-324/98 *Telaustria* [2000] ECR I-10745 the Court produced the idea of positive obligations of transparency arising outside the ambit of the directives.

[215] Case 31/87 *Gebroeders Beentjes BV v Netherlands* [1989] ECR 4365); Case C-225/98 *Commission v France ('Calais Nord')* [2000] ECR I-7455; Case C-513/99 *Concordia Bus Finland v Helsinki* [2002] ECR I-7213.

[216] Commission Green Paper, *Public Procurement in the European Union: Exploring the way forward* (1996) COM (96) 583, pp. 5–6.

[217] Commission, *Communication on Public Procurement and the European Union* (1998) COM, 143.

a framework might so easily inhibit efficient practices with the rise of more formal and compartmentalised arrangements operating to undermine the important relational values of co-operation and co-ordination. Transparency, meanwhile, was scarcely a given. Whereas the Commission had spoken of 'a few rules based on common sense',[218] complaints about the un-readability of a fragmented and often highly technical legal framework were legion. And there was ample scope for 'games with rules' and for 'boiler plate' reasons (see p. 729 below).

Directives conceived at the start of the 1990s increasingly smacked of a lost world. There was now the little fact of an IT revolution to contend with which would soon be opening up whole new vistas in the shape of an electronic, pan-European, public purchasing market place.[219] Changing contractual modalities had also to be factored into the equation, ranging through PPP and PFI, and from electronic auctions to streamlining 'framework agreements' (establishing general terms for future contracts with participating suppliers). This all struck a strong chord in the UK, which proved a voluble critic.[220]

A major revamp eventually resulted (with implementation in the UK in the 2006 regulations). The talk now was of simplification, modernisation and flexibility.[221] The core directives were reduced to three in number: a consolidated public-sector directive,[222] a revised directive on utilities,[223] and the compliance directive. Many technical distinctions were ironed out; incorporation of court rulings into the legislation added clarity. 'Simplification', however, should not be confused with 'simplicity'. The re-design in fact sends out mixed messages. Better to accommodate more collaborative forms of government contracting, the regulatory framework is loosened in certain respects. Aimed at curbing discretion, there are also elements of deepening and widening.[224]

The most prominent feature is a fourth pathway:

- *competitive dialogue procedure* – providing space for discussions with suppliers to develop suitable solutions, on which chosen bidders are then invited to tender.

[218] Commission, *Public Procurement in Europe: The Directives* (1994), p. 3.

[219] See Commission Communication, *Action Plan for the Implementation of the Legal Framework for Electronic Public Procurement* (2004); and, on the internal market website, the 'SIMAP' and 'TED' (Tenders Electronic Daily) resources.

[220] HM Treasury, *Investigating UK Business Experiences of Competing for Public Contracts in Other EU Countries* (2004) ('the Wood Review').

[221] Commission, *Communication on Public Procurement*, p. 3; and see, for an upbeat assessment of the growing regulatory 'impact', Commission, *Report on the Functioning of Public Procurement Markets in the EU* (2004).

[222] Directive 2004/18/EC on the co-ordination of procedures for the award of public works contracts, public supply contracts and public service contracts.

[223] Directive 2004/17/EC co-ordinating the procurement procedures of entities operating in the water, energy, transport and postal services sectors. The directive reflects the view that purchasers in liberalised sectors (e.g. telecoms) should not be covered.

[224] Through e.g. detailed provisions on framework agreements and e-auctions. See C. Bovis, 'The new public procurement regime of the European Union' 30 (2005) *EL Rev.* 607.

Designed to facilitate the complex, longer-term, contracting commonly associated with PFI (see Chapter 9), while avoiding the opacity inherent in the negotiated procedure, it is very much a compromise; CDP offers up its own challenges. Sitting comfortably with the contract theorist's desiderata of co-operation and mutual learning, it can also be slow, expensive and resource intensive. Early planning and preparation are called for; the public purchaser must be nimble:

> Under the competitive dialogue procedure all substantial aspects of the bid need to be agreed before conclusion of the dialogue. The dialogue process should be used to identify the best means of satisfying the Authority's needs. The dialogue should continue until the Authority has identified and defined its requirements with sufficient precision to enable final bids (which meet those requirements) to be made. At that time the Authority should be able to identify one or more solutions to its requirements (since, as a result of the separate dialogues, different solutions may have been developed). A call for final bids should then be made and the winning bidder selected. After final bids have been submitted, it is only permissible to clarify, specify and fine tune. This does not necessarily mean that the Contract has to be complete in every detail at this stage, but it does mean that, after this time, no changes may be made to the basic features of the bid which are likely to distort competition or have a discriminatory effect.[225]

(b) On the straight and narrow

Let us follow the reworked pathway model (as with a public-works contract). The application of the directive/national regulations having been ascertained,[226] there are requirements to advertise (today electronically) in the EC Official Journal and on the use of European technical specifications (or a properly designated substitute). Such specifications may be defined 'in terms of performance or functional requirements' but any such requirements must be 'sufficiently precise to allow an economic operator to determine the subject of the contract and a contracting authority to award the contract'.[227] Next come selection of a contract award procedure, with the regulations making clear that from the choice of four pathways the open and restricted procedures are the standard options,[228] and selection of (an) appropriate (number of) bidders. An authority, in determining whether to exclude firms from tendering on the basis

225 HM Treasury, *Standardisation of PFI Contracts*, 4th edn (2007) [32.1.2 –3]. See further, HM Treasury and OGC, *Guidance on Competitive Dialogue* (2008).

226 For the thresholds see Public Contracts Regulations 2006, Art. 8 (as amended). Defence procurement, hitherto the chief subject-matter exclusion, is currently the subject of another legislative package; see Commission, Proposal for a Directive on the coordination of procedures for the award of certain public works contracts, public supply contracts and public service contracts in the fields of defence and security, COM (2007) 766.

227 Public Contracts Regulations 2006, Art. 9(7).

228 *Ibid.*, Art. 12. Sub-sub-pathways such as electronic auctions are made the subject of separate Articles.

of standing and competence, 'shall' do so in the light of fraud or corruption and 'may' do so for other relevant offences (environmental crime perhaps).[229] This brings national officials to the actual award process and post-decisional procedures (steps 6 and 7). The pathway model, we learn, is both determinedly logical and complex. The length of the regulations – some 80 pages – speaks volumes. Perhaps fortunately, the OGC supplies public purchasers with a flow chart.[230]

The crucial award stage embodies Davis-type techniques for control of discretion (see p. 200 above). In the provisions set out below,[231] rules are thus deployed in order to minimise the scope for abuse and so that procurement decisions can be more easily monitored. Take paragraph 2, a nice example of *structuring* discretion with a checklist of relevant factors. This puts flesh on the bones of the 'most economically advantageous' test (which (translating as VFM) it is UK government policy to use). The drafting dictates a commercial outlook and, reflecting the jurisprudence, gives some additional leeway.[232] Paragraphs 3 and 4 show the attempt at *confining* discretion. Underpinned by developments in IT, and linking with audit technique, public purchasing is shaped in terms of mathematical formulae. The Commission championed these novel provisions, saying that the previous stipulation[233] had undermined the pathway model by allowing too much discretion.[234] (How much the rewording will achieve other than increased administrative cost remains to be seen.) The *checking* of additional discretions is shown in the special anti-dumping provisions of paragraph 6.

Criteria for the award of a public contract

1. 30 (1) Subject to regulation 18(27) [specifying 'the most economically advantageous' test in competitive dialogue procedure] and to paragraph 6 . . . of this regulation, a contracting authority shall award a public contract on the basis of the offer which –

    (a) is the most economically advantageous from the point of view of the contracting authority; or

    (b) offers the lowest price.

(2) A contracting authority shall use criteria linked to the subject matter of the contract to determine that an offer is the most economically advantageous including quality, price, technical merit, aesthetic and functional characteristics, environmental characteristics, running costs, cost effectiveness, after sales service, technical assistance, delivery date and delivery period and period of completion.

[229] *Ibid.*, Art. 23.

[230] See OGC, *EU Procurement Guidance* (2008).

[231] Public Contracts Regulations 2006, Art. 30.

[232] Social and environmental considerations as contractual conditions of performance are also provided for: Art. 39.

[233] Use 'where possible' of the 'descending order of importance' approach (now mandated as the second string in [5]).

[234] Commission, *Explanatory Memorandum to Proposal for a Directive on the Co-ordination of Public Sector Award Procedures*, COM (2000) 275, p. 12.

> (3) Where a contracting authority intends to award a public contract on the basis of the offer which is the most economically advantageous it shall state the weighting which it gives to each of the criteria chosen in the contract notice or in the contract documents . . .
> (4) When stating the weightings referred to in paragraph (3), a contracting authority may give the weightings a range and specify a minimum and maximum weighting where it considers it appropriate in view of the subject matter of the contract.
> (5) Where, in the opinion of the contracting authority, it is not possible to provide weightings for the criteria referred to in paragraph (3) on objective grounds, the contracting authority shall indicate the criteria in descending order of importance in the contract notice or contract documents . . .
> (6) If an offer for a public contract is abnormally low the contracting authority may reject that offer but only if it has – (a) requested in writing an explanation . . . (b) taken account of the evidence provided in response . . . and (c) subsequently verified the offer . . . being abnormally low with the economic operator . . .

The pathway model needs fencing. As well as public notice of the contract award, the national regulations faithfully specify strengthened reasons-giving requirements, extending at the request of a rival bidder to 'the characteristics and relative advantages of the successful tender'.[235] Linkage with provisions on remedies is immediately apparent. A raft of information and record-keeping requirements buttresses the monitoring role of the Commission. Reflecting and reinforcing the judicial contribution, there are now clear legislative statements of general principle. Article 4(3) of the Regulations provides: 'A contracting authority shall (in accordance with Article 2 of the Public Sector Directive) – (a) treat economic operators equally and in a non-discriminatory way; and (b) act in a transparent way.'

Showing EU law as a source of judicial review, the first important case arising under the new regulations, *R (Law Society) v Legal Services Commission*,[236] is directly in point. The dispute was over the new unified contract between the Commission and solicitors wishing to undertake publicly funded work, following on the Government White Paper *Legal Aid Reform: The way ahead*.[237] Prioritising flexibility to the extent of allowing for major policy change, the Commission had included in this 'take it or leave it' arrangement wide-ranging powers of unilateral amendment. But was this sufficiently 'transparent' in light of the ECJ jurisprudence? The Court of Appeal thought not:

> *Lord Phillips CJ:* What is . . . plain is that among the most important factors for compliance with the principle of transparency are the definition of the subject matter of the contract and need for certainty of terms. That is why . . . Regulation 4(3) requires the contracting authority 'to act in a transparent way' and why Regulation 9(7) requires technical

[235] Public Contracts Regulations 2006, Art. 32.

[236] [2007] EWCA Civ 1264. See also *Letting International Ltd v Newham LBC* [2008] EWHC 1583.

[237] Cm. 6993 (2006).

specifications in terms of performance or functional requirements to be 'sufficiently precise to allow an economic operator to determine the subject matter of the contract. . .'

It is true that the LSC could not make arbitrary or improper amendments. That would follow not only from general principles of public law, but also from the Regulations and no doubt also from an implied term to that effect in the Unified Contract or from the express term . . . that the LSC will act as a 'responsible public body'. But that would not achieve the transparency of the contractual terms . . . Nor is it achieved by the point that the parameters of the possible amendments had been published in *Legal Aid Reform: The way ahead.* The right reserved to amend the contract . . . 'to facilitate a Reform of the Legal Aid Scheme' is on its face not limited to amendments to give effect to proposals in the White Paper. The power to make amendments is better to comply with the LSC's statutory duties or fulfil its statutory functions . . . The power also includes changes consequent on 'new approaches to procurement and contracting'.

It cannot therefore be said that there are any effective limitations, still less that the parameters of change will be known to the profession. The power of amendment is so wide in this case that it amounts to a power to rewrite the Contract.

How far can this reasonably go?[238] Together with the competing values of security of contract and government responsiveness, the issue is raised of the limitations to contract in terms of presentiation. Judges need to understand that bleeding out contractual discretion in the name of transparency can defeat the object.

(c) Enforcement and remedy

This regime places great reliance on private legal action to police it (the Commission can only do so much by way of infringement proceedings). Designed to promote quick and effective means of redress, the 1989 Compliance Directive introduced special provisions on remedies, which function alongside the ordinary remedies of English law.[239] Just like the famous cases of *Factortame* and *Francovich* (see Chapter 4), they operate to erode the procedural autonomy of national law in order to establish the means for the vindication of EC rights.[240]

The pre-contractual remedies are wide-ranging. The national court thus has powers to make an interim order halting progress, to set aside a decision or amend any document, and to award damages to firms for breach of duty. Once a contract is made, however, damages have hitherto been the only available remedy. Aggrieved suppliers in fact have little incentive to seek damages in this situation. The courts are not well equipped to assess relevant matters, as with

238 The successful challenge itself prompted a more collaborative approach to legal aid reform: see joint statement by the Legal Services Commission, Law Society and Ministry of Justice, 2 April 2008.

239 See on judicial review, *R (Cookson) v Ministry of Defence* [2005] EWCA Civ 811.

240 Whereas the original design was typically skeletal, the ECJ has done much to fill out the rules using the general EC principle of effectiveness. See e.g. Case C-81/98 *Alcatel* [1999] ECR I-7671.

the relative economic advantage of competing bids. Essentially a contribution to company costs, the remedy has no real corrective effect.[241] Commission research confirms that the action for damages is rarely used; recourse to the pre-contractual remedies is more common, but varies considerably among the Member States.[242] The UK was found to have the lowest rate of litigation (remedies actions in just 0.02 per cent of tendering processes). One explanation would be high rates of compliance. The Commission, however, singles out the high litigation costs associated with the domestic choice of review body – in England and Wales, the High Court.[243]

Another bout of reform is currently being implemented: more prescription through codification. Bearing ample testimony to the difficulties of formal regulation, a new Compliance Directive[244] addresses two main aspects. First, pre-contractual remedies sound well, but they may be defeated by a 'race to signature' by awarding authorities. The ECJ had previously held that where, as in the UK, a national system of remedies did not allow a supplier to overturn a concluded contract, and failed to guarantee the possibility of challenging an award decision pre-contractually, it was non-compliant.[245] A good example of national administrative law being driven from Luxembourg, a mandatory standstill period between award decision and contract award was thus included in the 2006 regulations.[246] Similar requirements in the new directive underwrite this.[247]

The second aspect calls for the fashioning of a novel remedy in domestic administrative law. The Commission's research had further highlighted the limited coverage of 'the pathway model'.[248] Thresholds and exemptions aside, attention focused on what the ECJ has termed 'the most serious breach of Community law in the field of public procurement on the part of a contracting authority',[249] namely the direct award of a contract which should have been subject to a transparent and competitive award procedure. The directive accordingly provides for the remedy of 'ineffectiveness' (which will also operate to sanction breaches of the standstill period). The national authorities can choose whether this entails retrospective cancellation (of all contractual

[241] A familiar complaint among practitioners: see e.g. A. Brown, 'Effectiveness of remedies at national level in the field of public procurement' (1998) 7 *PPLR* 89.

[242] Commission, *Impact Assessment Report: Remedies in the field of public procurement* SEC (2006) 557.

[243] *Ibid.*, p. 18.

[244] Directive 2007/66/EC amending Council Directives 89/665/EEC and 92/13/EEC with regard to improving the effectiveness of review procedures concerning the award of public contracts. Member States have two years in which to implement.

[245] In Case C-81/98 *Alcatel* [1999] ECR I-7671.

[246] Of 10 days: Public Contracts Regulations 2006, SI No 5 [32(3)].

[247] See OGC, *Consultation on the Approach to Implementation of the EU Remedies Directive* (2008).

[248] With an estimated 16% of total public procurement in the Member States advertised in the EU Official Journal: Commission, *Impact Assessment Report*, p. 9.

[249] Case C-26/03 *Stadt Halle* [2005] I-1 [37]. See also Joined Cases C-20/01 and 28/01*Commission v Germany* [2003] ECR I-03609.

obligations), or, coupled with powers to impose fines and shorten the contract period, prospective cancellation (of those obligations yet to be performed).[250] Echoing recent developments in the national system (see p. 370 above), a boost for restitutionary remedies is implicit.

The practical significance remains to be seen. Intended to increase operator confidence in the fairness of the procedures across the EU, the new dispensation certainly offers more opportunities and incentives to litigate. Underlying difficulties with the enforcement model of private legal action cannot be wished away however. It is unrealistic to expect many tenderers to engage in formal legal conflict with prospective major customers. Not before time, a pan-European approach to ADR is beginning to emerge in this sector.[251] Determinedly more collaborative, and operated through official channels (giving operator anonymity), the method has much untapped potential.

6. Conclusion

The contractual revolution is thoroughgoing. Instigated by the Conservatives, and vigorously pursued under New Labour, it sees the private legal model operating to define and reconstitute the role of government and relations with the private sector, and with the citizen, and to formalise (and fragment) intra- and inter-governmental relationships. The label of 'the contracting state' is today both an accurate description and a misnomer. Grounded in the idea of contract as an alternative source of rules, the state is here seen taking on a new set of co-ordinating and activating roles; the Treasury is typically at the apex. This echoes contemporary developments in regulation; a recurring theme of these chapters is the read-across between regulatory and contractual techniques of governance.

All this presents administrative lawyers with an immense challenge. Far from a 'solution', juridification in the shape of detailed contractual provision is part of the problem. While the courts have typically played a limited role in this sphere, the statutory regulation is marked by a profusion of rules presenting its own difficulties. A closer engagement with the expanded forms of contractual governance is required for good governance values to be properly vindicated; case studies in the next chapter will highlight the importance of embedding requirements of due process and accountability in contractual schemes from the outset. In a world of mixed administrations, of heavy reliance on the creative interaction of public and private power in service provision, mixtures of law are called for, transcending the public/private 'divide'. Administrative lawyers must not be intimidated.

250 Directive 2007/66/EC, Art. 2d. National meaning must also be given to various exemptions, etc. See further, J. Golding and P. Henty, 'The new remedies directive of the EC: Standstill and ineffectiveness' [2008] Public Procurement Law Rev. 146.

251 European Public Procurement Network, *Complain in Good Time!* (2005).

9

Contract, contract, contract

Contents

The aim of this chapter is to look more closely at contracting as a state activity. In light of the pursuit of new forms of governance what better to examine than the functional development of contract in the economic sphere as a way of delivering public services and infrastructures? We have selected two types of regime of great importance in the changing landscape of law and administration. Exhibiting a wide variety of designs, the first one, public franchising, highlights the overlap of contractual with regulatory techniques of governance. As well as contract as a source of administrative rules, there is a significant history here of deficiencies in, and attempts to improve, the procedure and accountability of agencies. Our second selection, public/private partnerships and 'the private finance initiative' (PPP/PFI), wears a distinct political hue, this being the favoured child of New Labour. There is a pervasive sense of experimentation – sometimes, it must be said, at the expense of the taxpayer – coupled with levels of contractual detail that can appear almost wilfully complex. The question of the extent to which risks in public enterprise can in fact be passed to the private sector is sharply posed.

1. The franchising technique

Franchising as a tool of governance is operative today across a diverse range of activities, from London buses to legal aid, and from cable television to the National Lottery.[1] Harnessing private enterprise in the delivery of services, this fresh lease of life for an old technique epitomises the influence of NPM and the rise in administrative law of contract-type arrangements. The Conservatives' legacy is manifest.

Franchising entails the allocation of exclusive or protected rights to carry on an activity for a certain period of time, typically using the mechanism of an auction to determine entry to the market. The basic premise is that competition *for* the market effectively substitutes for competition *within* it: to enjoy special rights, the private firm first has to engage in competition to secure those rights.[2] Public or governmental franchising may be viewed either as one form of regulation, or as a complement to, even a substitute for, traditional regulatory instruments. As with contracting out, with which it overlaps, the technique is appropriately considered as a *process*, involving both the design and operation of award procedures, and monitoring, negotiation, and sanction under the rubric of franchise management. There is ample scope for agency discretion.

Flexibility of application – the scope for tailoring the technique to different market types and conditions – is a particular virtue. From the Treasury viewpoint, a franchising arrangement may have the considerable benefit of shifting the revenue risk to the service provider. Franchising allows competition for loss-making activities because negative tender prices can take the form of subsidy. The franchise as a source of rules can be used explicitly in defence of 'the public interest' as through specifications for quality. Then again, there is room for explanation in terms of public choice – franchising as the product of rent-seeking behaviour by private-interest groups.

The development has been fuelled by loss of faith in the alternatives.

[1] While such activity is distinguished by its 'public' purpose, commercial franchising provides many instructive parallels. See for a useful overview, J. Adams, J. Hickey and K. Prichard Jones, *Franchising*, 5th edn (Tottel, 2006).

[2] See, generally, R. Blair and F. Lafontaine, *The Economics of Franchising* (Cambridge University Press, 2005).

According to an influential theory of public franchising derived from regulatory economics, the market disciplines unleashed by a properly designed system of allocation undermine the case for traditional modes of regulation: contract terms and conditions constitute the appropriate legal instrument of public control:

> Franchising can be viewed essentially as a mechanism for increasing market contestability. It does so by allowing firms to bid for the rights to supply before they have committed resources to the enterprise, i.e. by reducing the level of sunk costs associated with entry. Of equal importance is the fact that franchising is a mechanism for providing the regulator with information about the competitiveness of potential suppliers. Such information generation is entirely absent under traditional regulation and nationalisation and is a major advantage of the franchising method. Another advantage of franchising over traditional forms of regulation is that it provides a sanction on poor performance, namely the threat of franchise termination, which may in some circumstances be a more credible sanction than the threat of take-over faced by a regulated enterprise. [3]

Franchising as a policy choice fits with the search for 'a third way' in regulation (see p. 241 above). The state retains an element of control, ultimately expressed through the power (not) to renew the franchise; on the other hand, commercial responsiveness and inventiveness can be facilitated in light-touch fashion through respect for managerial freedoms. Of course the benefits of a competition for the market cannot always be realised, as where too few potential franchisees can be found for competitive bidding, where performance cannot easily be benchmarked, or where substitution of poor performers is impractical.[4] In practice, franchising is commonly combined with conventional regulatory tools.

While franchising has the potential to enhance accountability through specification, the issue arises of the legitimacy of franchisor action. The technique likewise highlights the challenge for administrative law presented by government by contract. Reconciling desiderata of VFM and of process-values like fairness, consistency and transparency with precepts traditionally associated with private autonomy, such as commercial confidentiality, is not easy.[5]

(a) Allocation: Fairness

In 'public-interest franchising' the system is geared to selecting the bid which will best serve public-interest goals. Echoing themes in regulatory design (see

[3] S. Domberger, 'Economic regulation through franchise contracts' in Mayer and Thompson (eds.), *Privatization and Regulation: The UK experience* (Clarendon Press, 1986), pp. 275–6.

[4] R. Baldwin and M. Cave, *Franchising as a Tool of Government* (CRI, 1996), p. 49.

[5] But see D. Oliver, 'Common values in public and private law and the public/private divide' [1997] *PL* 467.

Chapter 7), this maximises agency discretion. Subjective judgement is involved in the choice and weighing of different factors; the legislative mandate is less of a guide as dimensions to the 'public interest' multiply. Alternatively, there is 'price-bidding franchising': the highest bid in the auction being successful, or else the bid that accepts to charge service users the lowest price. Combinations of these two basic models abound;[6] given monopoly, it is hard to ignore pricing, while price competition alone creates incentives to reduce quality, etc.

Changing priorities over time are illustrated by the development of franchising in commercial analogue television. Unkindly characterised as 'the apotheosis of the great-and-the-good paternalistic mode of British public administration',[7] the model that originally took root in the 1950s was heavily reliant on 'public interest'. The franchisor, successively the Independent Television Authority and the Independent Broadcasting Authority (IBA), was given virtually untrammelled discretion in the allocation of regional franchises; detailed standards of impartiality, decency, quality, etc. were stipulated in the contracts awarded to the successful bidders.[8] This chief example of public franchising in Britain became increasingly criticised however. Noting 'an atmosphere of prevailing mystery', Lewis stressed the need for rational decision-making and structuring and confining of discretion.[9] With hindsight, the call for American-style procedures (notice and comment, open hearings, reasons) anticipated the debates in administrative law over the Ofdogs (see Chapter 6).

Eventually, commercial pressures coupled with technological advance saw the whole basis of public control challenged. The digital age was dawning. The Broadcasting Act 1990, which provided for both 'Channel 5' and the 'Channel 3' regional franchises, involved a shift in favour of price bidding. Consistent with a policy of deregulation, s. 17 provided that what was now the Independent Television Commission (ITC) 'shall, after considering all the cash bids submitted . . . award the licence to the applicant who submitted the highest bid'. But Parliament would not wear a pure price bidding system.[10] Franchises could be awarded otherwise if it appeared to the Commission that there were 'exceptional circumstances': cases where the quality of the service proposed by the preferred bidder was 'exceptionally high', or where it was 'substantially higher' than that proposed by the highest bidder. Threshold

[6] P. Klemperer, 'What really matters in auction design' (2002) 16 *J. of Economic Perspectives* 169.

[7] M. Elliott, 'Chasing the receding bus: The Broadcasting Act 1980' (1981) 44 *MLR* 683, 692. See further, A. Briggs and J. Spicer, *The Franchise Affair: Creating fortunes and failures in independent television* (Century, 1986).

[8] See Television Act 1954, ss. 3, 6. The discretion of the agency was largely confirmed in the Independent Broadcasting Authority Act 1973, and the Broadcasting Acts 1980 and 1981.

[9] N. Lewis, 'IBA programme contract awards' [1975] *PL* 317.

[10] M. Cave and P. Williamson, 'The reregulation of British broadcasting' in Bishop, Kay and Mayer, *The Regulatory Challenge* (Oxford University Press, 1995).

requirements relating to the sustainability of a service were imposed. Today, of course, the industry is different again. Plagued by diminishing market share, Channel 3 and Channel 5 are but one part of OFCOM's regulatory empire constituted under the Communications Act 2003. In 2004 the surviving companies' analogue licences were duly replaced by digital ones, with the agency setting the financial terms based on its own assessment of what each broadcaster would bid in a competitive tender.[11] Amid the plethora of TV channels domestic and foreign, the original ITA and IBA system appears nothing less than quaint.

Given both a valuable monopoly and a lack of automaticity in the auction process, it would be strange indeed if franchise allocations were not the subject of legal challenge. The courts have again taken a light-touch approach in the commercial context however. Take the allocation of Channel 3 licences under the Broadcasting Act 1990. Suggesting rather more exercise of discretion than Parliament had envisaged, only eight of the sixteen franchises went to the highest bidder, the rest being excluded at the threshold stage.[12] In *TSW Broadcasting Ltd*,[13] one of the unsuccessful companies complained of procedural unfairness, the argument being that staff advice to the Commissioners had presented an unfair and inaccurate assessment of its bid. Appreciative of the need for regulatory flexibility, and positively discouraging of future challenges, the House of Lords proved deferential. In Lord Templeman's words, 'judicial review should not be allowed to run riot. The practice of delving through documents and conversations and extracting a few sentences which enable a skilled advocate to produce doubt and confusion where none exists should not be repeated.' Another round of litigation followed the allocation of the Channel 5 franchise in 1995. In *Virgin Television*,[14] the company argued that the eventual winner, C5B, had unfairly been allowed to increase its shareholders' funding commitment in response to agency inquiries about sustainability at the threshold stage. Rejecting the complaint of no level playing field, the Court of Appeal held that the invitation to tender, while ruling out changes to a cash bid or to programme proposals, did allow the franchisor this measure of dialogue. Fairness should not mean treating the agency like a post box. Predictably, the parallel complaint that Virgin's own disqualification on quality grounds was *Wednesbury* unreasonable also failed:

> *Henry LJ:* Matters of judgment were entrusted to an expert body by Parliament. That body was also made responsible for finding the facts on which such judgment would be based, in circumstances where the level of quality threshold was to be set by the Commission

[11] OFCOM, *Conclusion of the Review of Channel 3 and Channel 5 Financial Terms* (2005).

[12] Cave and Williamson, 'The reregulation of British broadcasting'.

[13] *R v Independent Television Commission, ex p. TSW Broadcasting Ltd* [1996] EMLR 291.

[14] *R v Independent Television Commission, ex p. Virgin Television Ltd* [1996] EMLR 318.

> and no-one else. Of its nature such an exercise is . . . judgmental in character and, therefore, one upon which opinions may readily differ. Especially is this so within this area of decision-making where the exercise is not simply a quantitative exercise . . . but involves a qualitative analysis and judgment . . . It has to follow that a very heavy burden falls on the party seeking to upset a qualitative judgment of the nature described and arrived at by the qualified and experienced body which is the Commission.

First established under the Conservatives, the National Lottery is a classic example of monopoly public franchising. Reflecting different public interests in the regulation of gambling, the agency was given a substantial mix of responsibilities: secure all due propriety, protect the interests of participants, and maximise the amount of money available to good causes.[15] Today a full-blown regulatory commission (the National Lottery Commission (NLC)),[16] it was originally an Ofdog (the Office of the National Lottery (OFLOT)). Following the award in 1994 of the first franchise to Camelot (a powerful consortium of companies), the lottery rapidly became one of the largest in the world in terms of sales, some £5 billion annually.

How then in 1999 would the newly established NLC conduct the second franchise allocation (for 2001–8)? The founding statute typically gave maximum procedural discretion, allowing the agency to decide whether or not to hold a competition. NLC decided to do so, with a view to promoting innovation and achieving the best return for good causes. From this process a serious challenger to the incumbent emerged: 'The People's Lottery', a 'not-for-profit' organisation headed by business celebrity Richard Branson. Having reserved the power so to do in the Invitation to Apply (ITA), the Commission later aborted the process, saying that neither bidder met the necessary criteria. For TPL it was a problem of finance; in Camelot's case the integrity of a key supplier (GTECH) was in issue, although the Commission had previously appeared to accept the company's explanations. With time pressing and on the assumption that Camelot would not meet its concerns, NLC launched a new process of negotiations solely with TPL. The resulting case, *R v National Lottery Commission ex p. Camelot*,[17] stands for greater judicial supervision. Having embarked on a competitive process, NLC now found itself fixed with requirements of fairness accompanying that process, to the extent of a finding (as in recent legitimate-expectation cases – Chapter 5) of abuse of power.

> *Richards J:* I find it remarkable that . . . the Commission chose to allow TPL the opportunity to allay its concerns but to deny a similar opportunity to Camelot. Such a marked lack of even-handedness between the rival bidders calls for the most compelling justification,

[15] National Lottery Act 1993, s. 4; and see D. Miers, 'Regulation and the public interest: Commercial gambling and the National Lottery' (1996) 59 *MLR* 489.

[16] National Lottery Acts 1998 and 2006.

[17] [2001] EMLR 43.

> which I cannot find in the reasons advanced by the Commission . . . Fairness required that each bidder should have the *opportunity* to allay the Commission's concerns . . . The fact that the Commission had been completely silent about its continuing concern contributes to the unfairness of counting Camelot out . . . on the ground that it could not meet that concern within a month . . .
>
> One of the individual strands to Camelot's case is that it had a legitimate expectation of consultation before the Commission reached its decision on the way forward following the termination of the ITA procedure. In my view the conditions for a legitimate expectation . . . were not made out . . . There was no clear and unambiguous representation . . . On the other hand . . . the absence of consultation is an additional factor to be taken into account in assessing the overall position. Where the actual procedure decided on is very unfair to Camelot, as it is, the fact that it was decided on without giving Camelot any opportunity to make representations about it serves to increase the degree of unfairness overall.
>
> The Commission's decision to negotiate exclusively with TPL was, in all the circumstances, so unfair as to amount to an abuse of power . . . The Commission, while intending to be fair, has decided on a procedure that results in conspicuous unfairness to Camelot – such unfairness as to render the decision unlawful. That broad point is perhaps more important than the precise legal analysis . . . The ultimate question is whether something has gone wrong of a nature and degree which requires the intervention of the court. In my judgment it has.

The case ultimately led to a different regulatory outcome: following reconsideration by NLC, Camelot retained the franchise. Procedural lessons have been learned. For award of the current franchise (2009–18), NLC engaged in a lengthy rule-making process replete with consultation.[18] A set of 'hurdles' or required threshold standards, ranging from financial soundness to technology operation, was closely geared to its statutory responsibilities. The agency added a modification phase to the evaluation process, an express opportunity for dialogue aimed at securing the strongest bids possible. Specifically on the basis of greatest forecast returns to good causes, it was then a matter of choosing, and finalising arrangements with, the preferred bidder – in the event, Camelot.

(b) Going on: Franchise management

The prominence afforded the auction should not detract from important issues in the continuing franchise relationship. The legitimacy of sales procedure is undermined if subsequently there is insufficient emphasis on compliance. Take attempts by the franchisee to renegotiate terms. The spectre is raised of opportunistic behaviour and over-bidders aiming to recoup monopoly profits. Why should the state 'insure' against 'the winner's curse'? The issue is

[18] NLC, *A Lottery for the Future* (2005) and *Statement of Main Principles* (2005).

vividly illustrated by a gigantic auction: the sale in 2000 of licences for the next generation of mobile telephones.[19] Some 150 rounds of bidding later, the five licences collectively reached £22.5 billion: roughly 4,000 per cent higher than the minimum or 'reserve' price. Commercial euphoria having evaporated, the Treasury understandably showed little sympathy. These were proceeds on the 1980s privatisation scale.

There must be scope however for adaptation in the light of changed circumstances. Managing the franchise in part means managing the tensions associated with service specification: the need to elaborate and maintain a sufficiently precise description of the successful bidder's obligations, while allowing for flexibility and responsiveness to both public and private demands. This stage of the franchising process further highlights the interface with regulation. Such are the complexities of public services that the franchise, as a source of rules, will be incomplete; the franchisor has a degree of flexibility in the enforcement function. The agency, by monitoring and negotiation, is commonly involved in mandating aspects of the operation – precisely the kind of task familiarly associated with regulatory agencies (see Chapter 7).

The NLC exemplifies this aspect. Its Compliance Directorate is based inside Camelot's headquarters affording quick and easy access to systems and records. Ensuring the security of the operator's IT programme is a chief priority. A Licensing Directorate has the ultimate fire-watching role of vetting individuals and entities to ensure they are 'fit and proper'. It conducts evaluative studies, such as testing new games in light of the Commission's social regulation responsibilities (prevention of underage or excessive play). Flanking elements include approval of codes of practice, for example on advertising, and inspection of retail premises to check provision of information. Building on the financial and technical detail that Camelot must supply under its licence, a Performance Team seeks to mitigate the problem of no direct comparators through various information sources: players' complaints, opinion research, and market data. Legitimacy demands that the franchisor have a series of sanctions: 'the enforcement pyramid'. Breaches of licence are publicised via the Commission's annual reports and website. The 'sticks' include powers to give directions and extract financial penalties.[20] 'Franchising in the shadow of the law', NLC may apply to the High Court for an order requiring Camelot to remedy a licence breach. As well as the threat of non-renewal of franchise, NLC may, *in extremis*, have the licence revoked.[21] This watchdog has chosen to nibble, imposing fines, for example, for reporting and internal control-systems failures.[22]

[19] K. Binmore and P. Klemperer, 'The biggest auction ever: The sale of the British 3G Telecom licenses' 112 *Economic Journal* (2002) 74.

[20] National Lottery Act 1998, s. 2.

[21] National Lottery Act 1993, ss. 9–10.

[22] NLC, *Annual Report 2005–6*, p. 8

The franchisor may however be weakly placed to ensure compliance. Danger of loss of continuity of service can make the threat of 'the big stick' appear hollow. Much turns on substitutability: today in TV the 'blank screens' problem scarcely features; the same could not be said of the National Lottery. Refranchising is another major concern, since the advantages of incumbency are liable to undermine the competition.[23] Notwithstanding the agency's best efforts at a level playing field, is it so surprising to learn that Camelot had only one competitor for the current franchise and won on the basis that it would probably generate higher sales?[24] The further question is raised of the optimum length of the franchise term. While a short term is good for discipline, minimising incumbent advantage and emphasising instead competition and agency leverage, a long franchise minimises transaction costs and is apt to stimulate investment.

The style of franchise management is naturally informed by the general philosophy of the franchise system. In a one-to-one relationship with Camelot, and with a direct interest in its financial viability, NLC is determinedly collaborative. 'We will work with the operator to encourage it to continue to grow sales across every channel to ensure continued growth in returns to good causes.'[25] Showing the space for changed regulatory dynamics, a recent internal review sees 'better regulation' principles being read across. Hampton has cast its spell, prompting NLC to make good a surprising omission: the lack, hitherto, of a formally defined risk-assessment structure.

> Government established the remit of the regulator, who was free to determine the approach to and model of regulation. This needed to reflect the particular circumstances... when the National Lottery was launched . . . a newly established operator, inexperienced players and an inexperienced regulator . . . The key to . . . success . . . would be that it inspired confidence among players, and that its reputation would be unquestioned. The regulatory model was therefore designed to reflect the degree of risk that these circumstances posed. It was characterised by a detailed and prescriptive framework which was underpinned by the need for the operator to obtain consent or approval in advance of taking action . . .
>
> The Commission has sought to develop and evolve its approach to regulation by focusing on the objectives and outcomes of its decisions . . . In some commercial areas it has attempted to move away from the detailed control of inputs . . . For example, it has moved away from the licensing of individual games and now grants class licences. These allow the operator to launch certain types of games, within prescribed guidelines, without prior consent from the Commission . . .
>
> The Commission wishes to continue to move towards the regulation of outputs, and away from the detailed regulation of inputs, [adopting] controls which are proportionate

[23] O. Williamson, 'Franchise bidding for natural monopolies: In general and with respect to CATV' (1976) 7 *Bell J. of Economics* 73.

[24] NLC, *Statement of Reasons: Licence to run the National Lottery* (August 2007).

[25] NLC, *Annual Report 2005–6*, p. 8.

> to the outcomes it is seeking. It proposes to begin by identifying areas in which such an approach could be developed with the minimum of risk to the National Lottery and to players . . . It would expect to provide the operator with greater commercial freedom, but would seek to balance this with the application of firmer sanctions for non-compliance.[26]

Enough has been said to highlight the danger of 'franchisor capture'. NLC is notably keen to stress the various forms of oversight of agency activity, beginning with the NAO.[27] As Baldwin and Cave note, 'resort to a competitive allocative process should not be seen as a substitute for accountability and openness concerning the nature of the service to be offered or the steps taken to ensure delivery'.[28]

2. Overground

Britain's railways have in recent times been a chief test bed of the franchising technique. The development epitomises the close connection of contractual and regulatory forms of governance and the fact of mood swings in matters of institutional design and accountability. On show is a succession of elaborate 'contracting regimes' – contract as a major source of rules flanked or supported by individual regulatory mechanisms.[29] The twin themes of juridification and fragmentation in public service provision (see Chapter 2) are powerfully illustrated; there has been much vicissitude.

(a) Context and architecture

Nationalised by the Attlee government in 1948[30] but commonly starved of investment, from the 1960s to the 1990s Britain's railways experienced a slow decline. As a subsidy-ridden, highly unionised, natural monopoly, the industry was not an early candidate for Conservative policies of privatisation. Indeed, the fully integrated network that was British Rail (formerly British Railways) fell victim not to Margaret Thatcher but to John Major, under the Railways Act 1993. In familiar fashion, the White Paper claimed that by re-introducing competition and levering in private investment there would be greater efficiency and innovation, a higher quality of service and better VFM. After an initial boost, the level of subsidy would gradually reduce and ultimately be replaced

[26] NLC, *Review of Approach to Regulation* (2006), pp. 3, 7 –8.

[27] NLC, Memorandum to CC, *The Regulatory State: Ensuring its accountability*, HL 68-III (2003/4).

[28] Baldwin and Cave, *Franchising as a Tool of Government*, p. 283.

[29] M. Considine, 'Contract regimes and reflexive governance: Comparing employment service reforms in the United Kingdom, the Netherlands, New Zealand and Australia' (2000) 78 *Pub. Admin.* 613.

[30] In the then standard fashion of a state-owned corporation: see Transport Act 1947.

by net payments to the Treasury as franchised services turned to profit.[31] This was remarkably sanguine. BR had for some years been making substantial efficiency gains, such that the productivity of its workforce was among the highest of any European railway.[32] The scope for service improvement – or for cutting costs without jeopardising the public interest in both a safe network and a network that comprises an important part of the transport infrastructure – was correspondingly reduced.

Public ownership relies on an internal command structure for co-ordination and organisation; in contrast, in the words of a contemporary, 'the rail network has been privatised by lawyers, and it will be run on a regime dictated by legal documents'. The new service would be governed by 'possibly the most complicated contractual matrix ever drawn up'.[33] Characterised by a high degree of functional separation, both vertical and horizontal, as well as interdependency, rail privatisation thus involved a fundamental restructuring of the industry.[34] It was said that separate ownership of the infrastructure would encourage private-sector involvement in operations and ensure fair treatment between train operators wanting track access.[35]

Under the original scheme, the central player was Railtrack, a publicly listed company that owned and managed most of the operational infrastructure, including the track and signalling equipment. It granted access to passenger-train-operating companies (TOCs), the individual winners of twenty-five regional franchises. Railtrack was responsible for the timetable and the franchisees for running the trains and for day-to-day station operations. Other important players included rolling stock companies (ROSCOs), owners and lessors of trains to the operators; infrastructure service companies (ISCOs), responsible for maintenance; and freight companies. With various support companies and subcontractors, the system was divided into over a hundred separate legal entities.

Flanking the Department, which retained powers of direction and guidance, two new agencies were cast in the Conservative mould of small, personalised units: the Office of the Rail Regulator (ORR) and the Office of Passenger Rail Franchising (OPRAF).[36] As well as licensing the operators, overseeing the general operation of the railways, and enforcing competition law, ORR was tasked with periodic reviews of the level of access charges paid to Railtrack by the train operators.[37] OPRAF was made responsible for the entire franchise

[31] DfT, *New Opportunities for the Railways,* Cm. 2012 (1992) [1] [19–21].

[32] *Ibid.* [3]. See generally, T. Gourvish, *British Rail 1974 to 1997: From integration to privatisation* (Oxford University Press, 2002).

[33] J. Edwards, 'Big ticket' (1996) 6 *Legal Business* 22.

[34] R. Freeman and J. Shaw (eds), *All Change: British Rail privatisation* (Mcgraw-Hill, 2000); also, J. Shaw, *Competition, Regulation and the Privatisation of British Rail* (Ashgate, 2000).

[35] DfT, *New Opportunities for the Railways* [12].

[36] Railways Act 1993, s. 1.

[37] Railways Act 1993, ss. 4, 8: see J. Stittle, 'Regulatory control of the track access charges of Railtrack PLC' (2002) *Public Money and Management* 49.

process: tender, negotiation and award, monitoring and enforcement.[38] Its Franchising Director would commonly be disbursing significant amounts of taxpayers' money to the TOCs in the form of subsidy. Meanwhile, a third set of arrangements covered safety; while the mega HSE provided general supervision, Railtrack – notably wearing two hats – would take the lead role.[39] Could all this possibly add up to the efficient and effective service that the public required?

(b) 'Everything must go'

Expressive of the Conservatives' philosophy, and on the basis of a genuine commercial opportunity ripe for exploitation, the initial approach to rail-passenger franchising was modelled as a series of business disposals for a fixed term (typically seven years). Subject to a 'safety net' – obligations not to let services fall below specified base levels – managerial freedoms would be maximised. Ministers having accepted that most franchises would require some subsidy, the bid requesting least from the public purse was generally to be successful. Using a narrow financial conception of VFM, space on the network would thus be allocated to those showing the greatest appetite for business risk.[40]

Not that this appeared on the face of the statute, the provisions of which were typically skeletal. Take the core concept of a franchise agreement with the franchising director 'under which another party undertakes . . . to provide . . . throughout the franchise term those services for the carriage of passengers by railway to which the agreement relates'. There was broad discretion to determine content, both in relation to major specified items (operator payments/subsidies, 'the fares to be charged for travel') and otherwise ('subject to any [statutory] requirements a franchise agreement may contain any such provisions as the Franchising Director thinks fit').[41] Ministers could again steer through instructions and guidance.[42] Common themes in the 'blue rinsed' approach to state power were forthcoming – a light touch:

> In general the Franchising Director should ensure, within the resources available to him, that the franchise system provides good value for money, encourages competition in the railway industry and protects the interests of passengers . . . He should also leave maximum scope for the initiative of franchisees under franchise agreements imposing requirements no more burdensome than are required in his opinion to achieve his objectives . . . He should act so far as possible to enable franchisees to plan the future of their businesses with a reasonable degree of assurance.[43]

[38] Railways Act 1993, ss. 5, 23–31, 57–8.

[39] S. Hall, *Hidden Dangers: Railway safety in the era of privatisation* (Allan, 1999).

[40] NAO, *The Award of the First Three Passenger Rail Franchises*, HC 701 (1995/6).

[41] Railways Act 1993, ss. 23, 28–9.

[42] Railways Act 1993, s. 5.

[43] OPRAF, *Passenger Rail Industry Overview* (1996), p. 53.

Standard terms in the franchise agreement included incentive payments linked to quality of service; prices, for certain designated classes of ticket; and obligations on the franchisee to participate in inter-operator arrangements. OPRAF, however, was keen to prescribe only the basic parameters:

> It is the Franchising Director's policy that operators should retain a substantial degree of freedom in managing their businesses, protecting the availability, quality and safety standards of rail services. A vital part of the franchising strategy is that operators have opportunities to introduce extra services for which there is public demand. It is also part of the policy that high quality operation is more likely to result if there are fair rewards for the operators.[44]

Procedure was a subject of strong agency discretion. OPRAF was proactive, taking steps to generate competition and, following pre-qualification centred on finance and managerial competence,[45] to advise, clarify and negotiate bids. But there was disdain for process-values in the form of publicly articulated criteria and reasoned decisions.[46] The pre-qualification document was emphatic:

> You are invited to lodge an application to pre-qualify in respect of any one or more of the Passenger Services summarised in . . . this document . . . The Franchising Director will treat as confidential any information so designated by an applicant. [He] reserves the right to refuse pre-qualification and shall not be obliged to give any reason for such refusal . . . If you pre-qualify, you will be asked to sign a confidentiality agreement as a precondition to receiving an [invitation to tender]. The Franchising Director will evaluate tenders in accordance with criteria to be set out in the [Invitation to Tender] and associated information. [He] reserves the right not to accept a tender on the grounds of price or otherwise and without giving any reason for his decision.

A procedure in which not even the invitation to tender was published lacked legitimacy; whither taxpayers' money? Attention is drawn to the speed and scale of rail franchising – the political imperative to complete the task ahead of the 1997 general election. OPRAF's methods were notably rough and ready.

OPRAF did not go unchallenged in the courts. *Save Our Railways*[47] was a major piece of campaigning litigation sponsored by the unions. At issue were the minimum-required service levels in the first seven franchises offered by the Director. With the minister's approval, the agency had set most of these safety nets substantially below existing service levels, reasoning – in determinedly

[44] OPRAF, *Bulletin* (August 1995), p. 1.

[45] Railways Act 1993, s. 26(3).

[46] See OPRAF, *Annual Report 1995–1996*, pp. 8–13.

[47] *R v Director of Passenger Rail Franchising, ex p. Save Our Railways* (1995) Times, 18 December.

economic fashion – that either services would be sustained by demand or unwarranted subsidies for loss-making services avoided. But what, it was asked, of the hierarchy of rules (see Chapter 4)? Laid before Parliament, the relevant instruction stated: 'for the initial letting of franchises, your specification of minimum service levels . . . is to be based on that being provided by BR immediately prior to franchising':

> *Sir Thomas Bingham MR:* 'Based on' is not a term of art, and it is not an exact term. It permits some latitude. It is obvious that every train timetabled by BR need not continue to run. There may be changes, and within limits it is for the Franchising Director to rule on the extent of the changes. His is the primary judgment. But there is a limit to the changes which may be made without ceasing to comply with the instruction . . . The changes must in our view be marginal, not significant or substantial . . . The Franchising Director's approach . . . is an intelligible and no way irrational approach. But it is not in our view an approach which gives effect to the instruction.

The procedural values of lawyers had clashed with the policy judgements of government.[48] The pressure group hoped that specifications would be amended to meet the instructions; the minister, however, preferred 'to clarify' the rules 'to ensure that they reflect beyond doubt the policy that we have always followed'.[49] Save Our Railways won the case but lost the campaign.

In arranging for franchise management, the architects had to confront the weakness of a purely contractual approach (damages 'inefficacious because the principal losses are incurred by consumers, not the franchisor'[50]). Showing the flexibility of statute-based franchising technique, the way round lay in a specially designed public contract grounding additional remedies. A franchise agreement would include such terms as customer compensation, a performance bond and termination for serious default. The Franchising Director was under a duty to act to prevent or rectify any breach of the agreement, if necessary by means of statutory order and financial penalty.[51] OPRAF's own approach to implementation was naturally informed by the general philosophy of the franchise system. Geared to negotiated compliance, not strict enforcement, the preference for a light-touch, even quiescent, role was clearly signalled:[52]

> The Franchising Director intends to develop a constructive and collaborative relationship with each franchise operator. [He] intends to found this relationship on the following general principles:

48 This is reminiscent of *Laker Airways v Department of Trade* [1977] QB 643.
49 HC Deb. vol. 268, col. 1238.
50 A. Ogus, *Regulation: Legal form and economic theory* (Clarendon Press, 1993), p. 332.
51 Railways Act 1993, ss. 57–8.
52 OPRAF, *Passenger Rail Industry Overview* (1996), p. 101.

- to manage the achievement of his objectives, not the activities of the operator;
- to require the operator to provide information only if this is required in relation to one of [his] objectives; and
- to minimise the burden placed on the operator.

(c) A few years later

OPRAF scarcely had time to engage in franchise management before being abolished by the incoming New Labour government. The reform was part of a determinedly 'third way' approach to the railways beyond, in Tony Blair's words, 'the sterile debate between wholesale privatisation and old-style state control'.[53] The Transport Act 2000 established a major new arm's-length agency, the Strategic Rail Authority (SRA). It was meant to cure the hole in the heart of contractual governance on the railways: the lack of industry leadership and thus of a clear, coherent, programme of future development.[54] Far from the contract theorist's ideal of a collaborative and dynamic approach to problem solving premised on mutual interest, ministers were having to respond to the day-to-day realities of 'conflicting priorities and . . . relationships at the front-line [which] have too often been adversarial'.[55] The relational qualities of trust and co-operation, we are reminded, cannot be created by fiat.[56]

But was this papering over cracks in the original construction? Paradoxically, part of the difficulty arose from an increasingly overcrowded network: the industry had now entered on a period of sustained traffic growth.[57] As well as subsuming OPRAF's functions, SRA was tasked, subject to ministerial powers of direction and guidance, with keeping network capacity under review, identifying investment needs, and promoting integration with other modes of transport.[58] Relations with the government rapidly soured; the SRA chairman complained that 'almost every breath we draw has to be cleared by Ministers'.[59] Replicating the sense of a cluttered regulatory space, the new agency was also working alongside ORR, now re-launched as a regulatory commission (the 'Office of Rail Regulation').[60] Soon the wider picture was of a rail industry in crisis. Highlighting poor

53 Quoted in R. Jupe, 'Public (interest) or private (gain)? The curious case of Network Rail's status' (2007) 34 *JLS* 244, 252.

54 DETR, *A New Deal for Transport: Better for everyone*, Cm. 3950 (1998); *Transport 2010: The 10 year plan* (July 2000).

55 *The Future of Rail: White Paper*, Cm. 6233 (2004), p. 16.

56 A theme elaborated here by T. Prosser, 'The privatisation of British Railways: Regulatory failure or legal failure?' (2004) 57 *CLP* (2004) 213.

57 Producing over one billion passenger journeys each year: see Transport Committee, *Passenger Rail Franchising: Government response*, HC 265 (2006/7).

58 Transport Act 2000, ss. 201–22.

59 Transport, Local Government and the Regions Committee, *Passenger Rail Franchising and the Future of Railway Infrastructure*, HC239 (2001/2) [30].

60 Railways and Transport Safety Act 2003, ss. 15–16.

maintenance of the track and signalling systems, a series of fatal accidents[61] led to speed restrictions across the network, a period of major disruption. Unable to meet the huge costs of new investment, Railtrack was forced into administration by ministers[62] and subsequently replaced with Network Rail, a 'not-for-dividend' company initially supported through, and made accountable to, the SRA.[63]

Defects in the franchising model became increasingly apparent in this difficult business environment. Indicative of a lack of realism in the original price-bidding system, many TOCs demanded additional subsidy in the face of escalating costs.[64] Absent strong provisions on quality standards, as also a lack of incentive for those TOCs on short-term franchises, service performance and the overall reliability of passenger trains worsened; nor, since the contracts were based on historic levels of performance, was there much scope for regulating for improvement.[65] A major complicating factor was interdependency or the blurring of responsibility. While TOCs routinely blamed track and signalling problems for service deficiencies, the network provider pointed to breakdowns of trains and shortages of drivers. Another element in the huge contractual matrix, and originally designed to encourage efficiency, an internal industry system of compensation provisions was now a vehicle for the circulation of millions of pounds.

The touchstone is agency enforcement, or rather the lack of it. Early efforts exposed the functional limitations of fines: large penalties on monopoly service providers struggling with costs were seen as counter-productive. Subtle techniques of restorative justice – new contractual commitments perhaps in recompense for misdemeanors – did not always fit the message of passenger representations.[66] SRA soon faced the classic problem of the failing franchise. Should public money be poured in, so making a mockery of the original auction process, or should the arrangement be terminated, with possible disruption for the travelling public? Doing both saw the agency castigated by the Treasury Committee:

> In our view, the essence of private sector involvement is that the private sectors pays if it gets its sums wrong. It is outrageous that such astonishingly large sums of taxpayers' money have been used to prop up palpably failing businesses such as £58 million in the case of Connex. While we accept that failures in the initial franchise process may have been

[61] See especially, Lord Cullen, *The Ladbroke Grove Rail Enquiry Report* (2001).

[62] Marked by an unsuccessful tort action by shareholders: *Weir v Transport Secretary* [2005] EWHC 2192 (Ch).

[63] L. Whitehouse, '"Railtrack is dead – long live Network Rail?" Nationalisation under the Third Way' (2003) 30 *JLS* 217

[64] SRA, *Franchising Policy Statement* (2002), pp. 5–6.

[65] R. Gladding, 'Rail regulation in the UK: The role of quality in the passenger rail franchises' (2004) 14 *Utilities Law Rev.* 151.

[66] OPRAF, *News Releases*, 14 March 1997.

> to blame originally, we cannot understand why action was not taken earlier by the SRA. As a result of this failure to monitor Connex properly the SRA bailed out a company using taxpayers' money only to strip it of its franchise a short time later. The SRA's management of this franchise has been woefully poor.[67]

With the first round of franchises drawing to a close, the SRA in 2002 signalled a new form of partnership, with the TOCs focused on delivering reliable performance, meeting passenger needs and containing short- and long-term costs. In a division of labour reminiscent of NSAs (see p. 63 above), agency discretion would thus expand at the expense of managerial autonomy. The talk now was of an expanded role for contract as a source of rules and of a more robust approach premised on a 'smart' regulatory mix of sticks and carrots:

> The SRA is firmly of the view that it should specify service levels and quality standards and the private sector should be charged with delivery. This is the essence of a successful relationship between the public and private sectors . . .
>
> The SRA sees the new Franchise Agreement as a contract with a more precise specification of the franchise proposition in terms of the service to be run, the performance standards to be met, and the rewards for achievement. The agreement will clearly identify the criteria and rewards for a successful franchise. However, it will also effectively penalise poor performance with a set of known financial and other consequences, including the real possibility of terminating an underperforming franchise.[68]

(d) A few years more

The SRA scarcely had time to make a difference before it too was abolished in a development that crystallises concerns about the broad trends of agencification and fragmentation. Reporting in 2004, the Transport Committee drew attention to 'a serious mismatch between the SRA's objectives, powers and responsibilities'.[69] How could the agency be 'strategic' when it had 'no control over the infrastructure which largely determines overall rail performance'? 'Back to government' – ministers duly performed a U-turn:

> When the SRA was conceived and legislation first introduced into Parliament, the scale of the industry's problems was not yet apparent, and a leadership model based on influence and persuasion seemed appropriate. In the light of changing circumstances . . . this has proved not to be the case . . . Without more direct powers the SRA has found itself in an increasingly difficult position. It cannot act as an industry leader, because it is positioned outside the industry in the public sector . . .

[67] Transport Committee, *The Future of the Railway*, HC 145 (2003/4) [122].
[68] SRA, *Franchising Policy Statement*, p. 9.
[69] Transport Committee, *The Future of the Railway*, p. 7.

> It must be for Ministers, accountable to Parliament and the electorate, to set the national strategy for the railways, but in the current industry structure this is not the case. Under the new arrangements, the Government will set the level of public expenditure, and take the strategic decisions on what this should buy.[70]

Flanking developments underwrite the themes of consolidation and rationalisation in a major illustration of re-regulation. ORR is today the sole industry regulator, combining arm's-length calculations of the revenue needed by Network Rail to meet the Government's objectives[71] with additional responsibilities for consumer protection and railway safety. Network Rail is directly responsible for ensuring that the network delivers a reliable service: a government statement of 'reasonable requirements', which ORR is under a duty to enforce, is incorporated in the company's licence.[72] In-house maintenance is the preferred model: less formal contract, more British Rail-type understanding of the infrastructure; and the Department has direct control of the TOCs' franchising process.[73]

The 'new, new' approach to franchise allocation currently on offer emphasises reliability and is noticeably more risk-averse. The Department wants to pre-qualify at the threshold stage:

> those who can be expected to submit attractive, competitive and realistic bids, and who will then be capable of delivering a high-quality service at the price which they have offered. To achieve this, the accreditation questionnaire invites applicants to provide evidence of their competence and experience, which the Department will assess. For assessing the responses the Department uses pre-determined scoring systems, as follows:
>
> - approximately 50-70% of the total score available is awarded for demonstrating a proven track record of service delivery and financial management in relevant areas of activity (which may not necessarily be within the UK) . . .
> - 30-50% of the score is awarded for demonstrating appropriate resources for bidding, the ability to manage mobilisation issues and the quality of outline plans for the development and management of the Franchise . . .
>
> In its scoring, the Department will assess and weight any past failure to deliver on contractual commitments on price and quality in a UK rail franchise, whether it arises from over-optimistic bidding or from poor management.[74]

70 *The Future of Rail : White paper*, pp. 6, 33; Railways Act 2005; and see P. Leyland, 'Back to government? Re-regulating British Railways' (2005) 12 *Indiana J. of Global Legal Studies* 435.

71 The High Level Output Specification (HLOS) for the improvements in safety, reliability and capacity that ministers intend to buy is contained in the White Paper, *Delivering a Sustainable Railway*, Cm. 7176 (2007).

72 *The Future of Rail: White paper*, pp. 45–7.

73 Allowing for closer alignment with Network Rail's regional structure, the number of franchises is also reduced.

74 DfT, *Guide to the Railway Franchise Procurement Process* (2008), p.2.

The system is clearly weighted in favour of repeat players, while imposing a discipline of continuous assessment. The obvious danger is failure to realise the benefits of a competition.[75] Again:

> The Department will undertake a risk-assessment of the bidder's delivery plans. This will ask three key questions. What is the risk of failure? Are the potential adverse impacts of failure limited to the financial position of the bidder, or could they impact on the taxpayer and the travelling public? Would the failure be one that would emerge progressively, giving the bidder and the Department time to take corrective action, or could it emerge very abruptly?
>
> In the light of this assessment, the Department will have to exercise its judgement in deciding whether the risks associated with accepting a bid which superficially offers the best proposition on price and reliability are so great that it justifies preferring another bid.[76]

How far we have since travelled from the laissez-faire days of OPRAF! The Department speaks of wielding 'the big stick':

> OPRAF and the SRA have in the past rescued failing franchises, rather than putting in an *operator of last resort* (OOLR) and then re-letting the franchise. The Department will not follow that precedent. Such rescues may have been justified in a relatively immature market where there was only limited experience of commercial passenger-service operation for bidders to draw on, and only limited evidence on which they could base revenue and cost forecasts. Given a more mature market, franchisees must build resilience into both their operational and financial plans to deal with the changes in the economic environment to which a passenger rail operation may be subject. Revenue-risk sharing mechanisms have been built into new franchise contracts, which cushion franchisees against a major downturn in revenue due to circumstances beyond their control (in return for a share for the Department of the potential upside), together with *force majeure* provisions.[77]

There is greater openness. As well as sponsoring lengthy 'stakeholder' consultations on franchise specification,[78] the Department has established a public register of franchise agreements, with information on each operator's contractual commitments. 'Both passengers and taxpayers', it is solemnly declared, 'are entitled to know what has been purchased on their behalf'. Nevertheless, much in this system of contractual governance remains shrouded in mystery:

[75] Especially in view of major concentration of ownership in the sector: Transport Committee, *Passenger Rail Franchising*, HC 1354 (2005/6), pp. 26–7.

[76] DfT, *Guide to the Railway Franchise Procurement Process*, p. 4. See further, NAO, *Letting Rail Franchises 2005-2007*, HC 1047 (2007/8).

[77] *Ibid.*, pp. 5–6; and see for practical illustration, the demise of the GNER franchise: DfT press release, 15 December 2006.

[78] If not always to the satisfaction of consumer groups: Transport Committee, *Passenger Rail Franchising*, pp. 12–17.

> The Department also regards commercial confidentiality as essential. It cannot secure the best deal for passengers and taxpayers unless it can operate a commercially confidential procurement procedure. The Department will not, therefore, release any information on unsuccessful bids, because doing so could result in lower VFM in subsequent franchising rounds. Nor will the Department release information which allows a comparison to be made between the winning bid and the second-placed and other bids as this could have market consequences for the winning bidder. Access to bid information is very tightly restricted within the Department. Likewise, the Department insists that bidders do not discuss with anyone the details of their bid or their discussions with the Department.[79]

Nor should it be assumed that 'back to government' means direct ministerial responsibility on the classical Westminster model:

> Ministers do not wish or need to be involved in the procurement commercial decisions, including the pre-qualification of bidders, the award of contracts, or the management and termination of contracts. These will be handled on their behalf by officials. Within the Department a designated committee of senior officials, the Contract Award Committee (CAC), take the decisions on selecting those suppliers who are invited to tender, and subsequently, the winning bid. During this process the names of bidders are anonymised, i.e. the members of the CAC do not know the identities of the bidders whose scores and risk-assessments are presented . . . Contract-signature occurs the day before the award is announced to the financial markets and to Parliament. It is only at the contract signature stage that the identity of the winning bidder is disclosed to Ministers and senior officials.[80]

How convenient!

(e) A new golden age?

A report on franchising from the Transport Committee in 2006 shows MPs far from convinced that government policy was finally on the right track:

> Our inquiry exposed fundamental tensions at the very heart of the Government's model. The Government has embraced the notion that private enterprise is best at delivering high-quality, innovative services such as the passenger railways, and yet it does not trust companies to deliver these services without highly detailed and specific contractual requirements which reduce the scope for innovation . . . It wants risk to be transferred from the public to the private sector, and yet risk cannot be transferred in anything other than name because, as everyone knows, no Government could afford to let the railways go bust. The Government hails the growth in passenger patronage, and yet it does not provide the long-term strategy and investment to increase capacity on the network. It wants coordination and yet continues to operate a system of fragmentation. Finally, the Government wants

[79] DfT, *Guide to the Railway Franchise Procurement Process*, p. 7.
[80] *Ibid.*, pp. 6–7.

> the private sector to invest, take risks and innovate, and yet it prioritises price above all of these. There is scant evidence that the current model balances and optimises the benefits from conflicting priorities. It looks more like a muddle that provides little more than a complex, costly and mediocre means of maintaining the status quo.[81]

Not before time the Department was developing a long-term strategy, revealed in the 2007 White Paper *Delivering a Sustainable Railway*. The industry, it was said, had 'turned a corner'.[82] Huge new tranches of public investment in the network were signalled, together with a raft of quality improvements by the TOCs, financed by additional customer revenues. As against managing decline, with which this story of the railway began, ministers now reckoned on a utility that:[83]

- could handle double today's level of freight and passenger traffic
- would be even safer, more reliable and more efficient
- would deliver a substantially reduced carbon footprint
- could cater for a more diverse, affluent and demanding population.

In light of the current economic downturn, this golden age of rail may be some way off!

3. Loads of money: PPP and PFI

A key component of Treasury strategy for the delivery of modern, high-quality public services, and for advancing UK competitiveness, public–private partnerships[84] epitomise the idea of contractual governance. While PPPs cover a broad range of business structures and partnership arrangements,[85] from outsourcing to joint ventures and the sale of equity shares in state-owned business, the principal vehicle is PFI, the Private Finance Initiative. As a way of delivering major capital investment, PFI represents both an alternative to and, since the public sector is not generally the owner and operator of the assets, a transformation beyond the traditional paradigm of government contract. PFI differs from other forms of PPP in that the private contractor not only carries out the project but also arranges finance.

PFI has spawned various sub-species. The common type is 'DBFO', where the private sector designs, builds, finances and operates facilities such that services are 'sold' to the public authority via a unitary charge. Basing the level of payment on the performance of the firm against agreed standards of service or 'output' specifications provides an incentivising element. Then there is

[81] Transport Committee, *Passenger Rail Franchising*, p. 7.

[82] *Delivering a Sustainable Railway*, Cm. 7176 (2007), p. 15.

[83] *Ibid.*, p. 7. See also, Transport Committee, *Delivering a Sustainable Railway: A 30-year strategy for the railways?* HC 219 (2007/8).

[84] HM Treasury, *Public Private Partnerships: The government's approach* (2000).

[85] C. Donnelly, *Delegation of Governmental Power to Private Parties: A comparative perspective* (Oxford University Press, 2007).

'DBF', where the public sector does not own the asset, such as a hospital or school, but rather 'rents' it over the term of the contract. Different again, and with old antecedents in toll roads, are financially free-standing projects, where the private-sector supplier recovers costs through direct charges on individual users. Public-sector involvement is limited to assistance with planning, licensing and other enabling procedures. Alternatively, what are often called 'concession contracts' may involve an element of public subsidy; a contribution perhaps to asset development designed to ensure the viability of the project.

New Labour ministers have not been afraid to experiment. An initial policy document in 1997 spoke of new models emerging 'as the Government looks to encourage PPPs, accelerate the flow of good projects and encourage investment'.[86] A major policy review of PFI in 2003 confirmed that ministers would 'investigate potential new areas . . . such as . . . prisons estate, urban regeneration, waste management . . . and social housing'.[87] In another review in 2006 the Government highlighted its commitment 'to developing procurement vehicles . . . through PFI in alternative ways'.[88] A further review in 2008 signposted a chief role for 'innovative procurement approaches . . . in addressing the complex infrastructure investment challenges ahead'.[89] This extends to the so-called 'integrator model', which sees the public body appointing a private partner to manage a PFI process. The general policy has in fact been pursued with an almost religious fervour: to the extent in early 2009 of committing several billion pounds in government loans to shore up PFI projects amid the credit crunch.[90]

(a) Rationale

The standard rationale is VFM; achieved through private-sector innovation and management skills delivering significant performance improvement and efficiency savings.[91] To this end, the Treasury aims to specify the appropriate conditions for PFI (as against a public sector scheme or traditional procurement process):

- there is a major capital investment programme, requiring effective management of risks associated with construction and delivery
- the private sector has the expertise to deliver
- the structure of the service is appropriate, allowing the public sector to define its needs as service outputs that can be adequately contracted for in a way that ensures effective,

[86] HM Treasury, *Partnerships for Prosperity: Private finance initiative* (1997), p. 2.

[87] HM Treasury, *PFI: Meeting the investment challenge* (2003), p. 11.

[88] HM Treasury, *PFI: Strengthening long-term partnerships* (2006), p. 27.

[89] HM Treasury, *Infrastructure Procurement: Delivering long-term value* (2008), p. 11. As for the attraction of foreign capital (via a role for the state in creating markets for private investment), see *ibid.*, Ch. 3

[90] HC Deb. vol. 488, col. 47 WS.

[91] As for the attraction of foreign capital (via a role for the state in creating markets for private investment), see *ibid.*, Ch. 3.

equitable and accountable delivery of public services in the long term, and where risk allocation between public and private sectors can be clearly made and enforced

- the nature of the assets and services identified as part of the PFI scheme are capable of being costed on a whole-life, long-term basis
- the value of the project is sufficiently large to ensure that procurement costs are not disproportionate
- the technology and other aspects of the sector are stable, and not susceptible to fast-paced change
- planning horizons are long-term, with assets intended to be used over long periods into the future
- robust incentives on the private sector to perform can be set up.[92]

PFI and complex IT, for example, is not a clever mix; a bitter experience of burgeoning cost and interminable delay[93] underscores the need of public authorities for more short-term flexibility due to fast changing service requirements. The Treasury considers that for 'small' investment – projects of less than £20 million in capital value – the VFM benefits are unlikely to outweigh the very considerable start-up costs in PFI of bidding and borrowing. The third condition clearly indicates not only the policy sensitivities but also the limitations of contractual technique in front-line service delivery (see Chapter 8).

Appropriate sharing of risk is the key to ensuring that the VFM benefits are realised. Indeed the Treasury speaks of successful PFI arrangements achieving 'an optimal apportionment' of risk between the public and private sectors.[94] The basic contours of the deal are thrown into sharp relief:

The benefits of PFI flow from ensuring that the many different types of risks inherent in a major investment programme are borne by the party best placed to manage those risks . . . The Government does not seek to transfer risks to the private sector in a PFI project as an end in itself. Where risks are transferred, it is to create the correct disciplines and incentives on the private sector, which then drive value for money through more effective risk management. In general, the Government underwrites the continuity of public services, and the availability of the assets essential to their delivery, but the private sector contractor is responsible for its ability to meet the service requirements it has signed up to. Where it proves unable to do so, there are a number of safeguards in place for the public sector to ensure the smooth delivery of public services, but the contractor is at risk to the full value of the debt and equity in the project. The full value of that debt incurred by the project, and the equity provided by contractors and third parties, is the cap on the risk assumed by the private sector.[95]

Transferred risks will typically include meeting required standards of delivery, cost-overrun risk during construction, timely completion of the facility (no

92 HM Treasury, *PFI: Strengthening long-term partnerships*, p. 32.

93 See e.g. PAC, *Department of Health: The national programme for IT in the NHS*, HC 390 (2006/7).

94 HM Treasury, *Meeting the investment challenge*, p. 35.

95 HM Treasury, *PFI: Strengthening long-term partnerships*, p. 38.

payments until available), latent defects, and industrial action. Certain market risks associated with the scheme may also be included; for example, in some road schemes, those associated with volume and type of traffic. Conversely, as well as general inflation, the Treasury anticipates the retention of risks directly associated with public law values of flexibility and responsiveness. 'Whether the service specified in the contract is required and adequate to meet the public demand and expectations' may admit of no easy assessment; likewise, 'the possibility of a change in public sector requirements in the future' is hardly remote in elongated PFI-type arrangements.[96] Contract technology such as variation machinery designed to mitigate these risks is at a premium.

This is only half the story. With most PFIs, the risks transferred to the private sector will be reallocated, using a central consortium company and subcontracts; highly intricate forms of debt financing and re-financing are commonly involved.[97] From the standpoint of the administrative lawyer there are significant issues here of openness and accountability. The public authority which engaging in PFI does not look to the robustness of the private framework is foolish.

For a Labour Chancellor concerned, on the one hand, to make good years of underinvestment in public-service infrastructure and, on the other hand, to (be seen to) maintain a tough fiscal stance, PFI-type arrangements have also proved highly convenient in terms of government accounting. A form of 'off balance sheet' financing, the capital expenditure or resultant debt may not score as public expenditure. Since today's large-scale investment programme becomes tomorrow's current spending, associated tax increases can be postponed. Meanwhile, other capital projects not suitable for PFI can be prioritised, using the Government's own resources or power of dominium. Like all mortgages this comes at a cost: to be borne by future taxpayers and service users. It should also be recalled that direct government borrowing, backed by tax revenues, and so virtually risk-free, is a cheap way of raising funds. So PFI-type arrangements do not provide public authorities with a cheaper source of finance, but rather with another potential source of funding, generally at a higher capital cost than traditional procurement. No wonder the Treasury has been concerned to stress the VFM benefits derived from risk transfers.

(b) Scale

The figures provide graphic illustration. Following a slow start under the Conservatives, between 1997 and 2007 at least fifty PFI deals have been signed each year. By the end of 2008, the total capital value of PFI contracts was some £66 billion. Estimated to 2031–2, future revenue payments arising under them

[96] *Ibid.*, pp. 39–40.

[97] D. Asenova and M. Beck, 'The UK financial sector and risk management in PFI projects' 23 *Public Money and Management* (2003) 195; and see PAC, *Update on PFI Debt Refinancing and the PFI Equity Market*, HC 158 (2006/7).

Table 9.1 Largest UK PPP/PFI contracts 1987–2006

Project	Government Department	Year Signed	£m*
London Underground	Transport	2002	16,179
Channel Tunnel Rail Link	Transport	1996	4,178
Aldershot Garrison (rebuild)	Defence	2006	1,800
Barts & London NHS (hospital redevelopment)	Health	2006	1,100
National Air Traffic Control	Transport	2001	800
Skynet 5 (satellite communications)	Defence	2003	750
Future C Vehicles (construction/mechanical equipment)	Defence	2005	600
Birmingham NHS (hospital)	Health	2006	560
Colchester Garrison	Defence	2006	539
Highways Agency (integrated digital services)	Transport	2005	490
M6 toll road	Transport	2000	485

*Capital value of signed deals

amounted to £180 billion. Meanwhile, projects valued at £13 billion were in the pipeline. Overall, PFI-type arrangements have accounted for 10–15 per cent of public-sector capital investment in the UK under New Labour.[98] Although other countries, especially in Europe, have been turning to PPP, there is little on the scale of British practice.[99] Some of the projects are gargantuan.

(c) Behind the scenes

The policy implementation demonstrates the great importance of the inherent – discretionary – powers of government.[100] PFI has been pressed forwards using a combination of Treasury 'sticks and carrots', policy guidance and information, and standardised 'contract technology', and through dedicated networks.

Crystallised in the so-called 'Ryrie rules',[101] a cautious attitude to private-finance contracting prevailed in the early years of the Thatcher government.

[98] *Public Private Finance Yearbook* (Centaur Media, 2008).

[99] See D. McKenzie, *PFI in the UK and PP in Europe* (International Financial Services, 2009).

[100] Public procurement being a devolved responsibility, PFI also illustrates how Treasury discretion is today more confined to England. The Welsh Assembly government for example has been noticeably reticent: Welsh Labour/Plaid Cymru, *One Wales* (2007), Ch. 3.

[101] See Treasury Committee, *The Private Finance Initiative*, HC 146 (1995/6).

According to this piece of Treasury orthodoxy, investors should not be offered significantly more security than that available on private-sector projects; efficiency gains should be clearly commensurate with the commercial cost of raising risk capital. Such investment should be additional to, and not substitute for, the investment otherwise made through government borrowing to discharge core responsibilities. But as enthusiasm for private-sector involvement took hold, the Ryrie rules were progressively relaxed until by 1993 this classic piece of soft law was officially 'retired'. As new Treasury guidance put it ever so delicately, 'the Government has now made clear that it wants deals, not rules'.[102]

New Labour's step-change involved an immediate revamp of administrative practice and procedure.[103] Much effort went into streamlining; for example, Treasury certification of commercial viability could now be provided ahead of the detailed negotiations at the procurement stage. Internal incentives were developed; PFI investments, the Treasury explained, might now be treated as an addition to departmental budgets rather than being counted against them. To deal with the problem of many local PFI projects not being viable without additional revenue support, machinery for applications by local authorities for 'PFI credits' was elaborated.[104] In what Freedland termed 'the transition from regulatory control to positive-policy-driven regulation',[105] contractual governance thus took on, in paradoxical fashion, a determinedly green light hue.[106]

Techniques of contractual governance themselves generate new administrative structures. A burgeoning support and approvals infrastructure exists for PFI, again orchestrated by the Treasury. The OGC provides general supervision and modelling of VFM. Networking with individual procuring authorities, Private Finance Units are responsible for implementation at departmental level. Testing the deliverability of projects prior to the formal procurement process is the task of an interdepartmental Project Review Group. Reflecting the changed focus as capital assets come on stream, a PFI Operational Taskforce was recently established to tackle key relational issues such as managing variations, 'contractor distress' and refinancing.[107]

PFI is a land fit for advisers and consultants. The Public Private Partnership Programme ('4ps') is a key player. Established in 1996 by the local government associations, the company is self-described as a delivery specialist. As

[102] HM Treasury, *The Private Finance Initiative: Breaking new ground* (1993), p. 7. See also, HM Treasury Private Finance Panel, *Private Opportunity, Public Benefit: Progressing the public finance initiative* (1995).

[103] HM Treasury, *Partnerships for Prosperity*.

[104] DETR, *Local Government and the Private Finance Initiative* (1998).

[105] M. Freedland, 'Public law and private finance: Placing the private finance initiative in a public law frame' [1998] *PL* 288, 302–3.

[106] Not least in the health service, where corporatisation has gone hand in hand with acute local political sensitivity: see NHS Executive, *Public Private Partnerships in the National Health Service: The private finance initiative* (2007).

[107] HM Treasury, *PFI: Strengthening long-term partnerships*, p. 79.

well as training and skills development, it offers hands-on project support to local authorities in priority sectors like school building. Epitomised at central-government level by Partnerships UK, which is itself a PPP, there are strong elements of latter-day corporatism. Described as having 'a unique public-sector mission', PUK brings together senior officials and lieutenants of industry, operating as a PFI developer in partnership with procuring authorities.

The lawyers have contributed standard terms and conditions. Stated aims are to foster a common understanding of the main risks, to engender consistency of approach across a range of similar projects, and to reduce the time and cost of negotiation.[108] But the role of such 'virtual' legal material in underpinning Treasury control and audit should not be underrated. Several hundred pages long, and repeatedly modified, the model form and guidance also demonstrates the great complexity of PFI-type arrangements. Fitting the familiar paradigm of large-scale commercial contracting, there are sheaves of detail on issues such as commencement and duration, service availability and maintenance, delay and dispute resolution. Some much worked-over provisions on management and monitoring of payments, on price variation and early termination, and on final ownership of the capital asset, illustrate the particular concern in PFI with risk sharing.

Take a familiar flashpoint: the question of 'fettering' (see p. 217 above):

> It is important that, in entering into any Contract, a local authority is not fettering itself in the performance of its normal public duties . . . Equally however, the Contractor will want to know that if the Authority expressly agrees to do something in the Contract and fails to do it, then (without seeking to fetter the local authority . . .) the Contractor should enjoy his contractual rights and remedies. . . The obligations of the Authority in any Contract should be limited (normally being confined to payment and perhaps some access and co-operation provisions) and clearly stated in any event. If there is any doubt around the relationship of any of these provisions with any statutory duty, the position should be clarified in the Contract. On any local authority project the Authority should always ensure that it does not undertake any obligations in the Contract which could conflict with its statutory duties and powers . . .[109]

The 'required drafting' on 'authority step-in', where the public body takes over some or all of the contractor's obligations for a period, mimics much in regulation:

> If the Authority reasonably believes that it needs to take action in connection with the Service:
>
> (i) because a serious risk exists to the health or safety of persons or property or to the environment; and/or

[108] HM Treasury, *Standardisation of PFI Contracts*, 4th edn (2007) [1.2.1].
[109] *Ibid.* [1.4.5].

> (ii) to discharge a statutory duty,
> then the Authority shall be entitled to take action . . .
>
> Following service of . . . notice, the Authority shall take such action . . . as it reasonably believes is necessary . . . and the Contractor shall give all reasonable assistance to the Authority . . . Where the Authority steps-in upon Contractor breach, the Authority should continue to pay the Contractor as where there is no breach . . . The Authority should, however, be entitled to set off any costs it incurs.[110]

Taking the example of improvements to social housing, a priority area of PFI activity, Figure 9.1 sketches the many stages in a project process. It highlights the close interplay of central and local government through the machinery of planning and approval of PFI credits. Looking forwards, the Treasury sees the need for public bodies to do more 'front-end' work in PFI, engaging and informing the market and developing 'robust project governance'.[111] 'A sound outline business case', explains 4ps, 'will document a systematic approach to analysing the current service, setting out the evaluation criteria, examining the different project and procurement options, identifying the best value solution, and considering key implementation issues'.[112] Paper must again be piled on paper.

(d) Major concerns: Fine-tuning

That PFI has proved controversial is an understatement. As well as 'disguised form of privatisation',[113] the litany of complaint includes:[114]

- Government becomes overly vulnerable to the vagaries of the market; some PFI contracts produce 'mega-profits' at the taxpayers' expense.
- Many PFI contracts fail to provide 'real' risk transfer from the public to the private sectors; whatever the contract may say, with essential services the public sector remains the guarantor of last resort.
- Limited pool of willing and able PFI contractors undermines competitive discipline.
- Elongated, multifaceted and large-scale PFI arrangements are peculiarly susceptible to contractor failure, a source both of service disruption and further public expense.

[110] *Ibid.* [29.2] [29.4].

[111] Better to achieve compliance with EU requirements: *ibid.* [32.1.2].

[112] 4ps, *A Map of the PFI Process Using Competitive Dialogue* (2006), p. 6. See on competitive dialogue procedure, p. 386 above.

[113] Raising the spectre of 'two-tier' employment terms and conditions; see for the various commitments on workforce protection, HM Treasury, *PFI: Strengthening long-term partnerships*, pp. 36–8.

[114] P. Gosling, *PFI: Against the public interest* (UNISON, 2005); A. Pollock, D. Price and S. Player, *The Private Finance Initiative: A policy built on sand* (UCL, 2005).

Preparation and selection of schemes	Formal PFI procurement process	Post-contract award
Bidding round Investment programme based on PFI credits activated by Department	*Tendering process launched* If project accepted, notice in OJEC (see p. 378 above)	*Manage contract* (perhaps for thirty years) Performance measurement (against output specification) – payment of performance-based unitary charge – potential variation and early termination issues
Expressions of interest Local authorities invited to submit outline proposals	*Pre-qualification and short-listing of bidders*	
Preliminary review Filtering by Department, based on appropriateness and deliverability of individual schemes	*Evaluation, clarification and dialogue on detailed bids*	*Evaluate project*
Outline business case Approved outline proposal worked up with output specification	*Evaluation, clarification and selection of preferred bidder* Fine-tuning, final due diligence etc	
Endorsement and credit approval Reviews by Department and Partnership UK Assessment and determination by Policy Review Group	*Award contract*	

Fig 9.1 Illustrative PFI project process[114]

- Increasingly huge revenue commitments limit the spending options of future administrations.
- There is a lack of transparency: blurred lines of accountability.

This must be put in perspective. Traditional public-procurement process is littered with examples of delay and cost overrun at great expense to the public purse: big projects are big projects. The pathology of PFI – all those headlines when things go wrong – is precisely that. Official research paints a different picture. In a Treasury sample of sixty-one completed projects, 88 per cent came in on time or early, with no cost overruns on construction borne by the public sector.[116] PUK, in a study of the operational phase of 500 projects,

[115] Adapted from DCLG, *Advice for Local Authorities Who Are New to Housing PFI* (2006).
[116] HM Treasury, *PFI: Meeting the investment challenge*, p. 43.

judged overall performance 'at least satisfactory' in 96 per cent; services were provided 'in line with the contract or better' in 89 per cent. With increased standardisation and experience of project management, use of the legal technology had also improved; 83 per cent of contracts were described 'as always or almost always accurately specifying' the services currently required.[117] A full assessment is obviously impossible until current ministers are long gone. But recent imbroglios over cash-flow problems in heavily PFI-engaged hospital trusts[118] are indicative of future wrangles in different economic climes.

The Treasury 'seeks to ensure that PFI is as open and transparent as possible. As well as improving accountability, this approach leads to better management of programmes and projects, and helps the private sector plan its investments in PFI.'[119] Warm words, but the policy development has been tepid. Scrolls of online information about capital values and estimated future payments should not disguise the great respect paid commercial confidence and interests.[120] Only recently has the Treasury insisted that departments publish the original VFM assessments; NHS 'best practice' of publishing executive summaries of projects[121] has been likewise slow to spread.[122]

In this context the contribution of audit technique takes on added value. The NAO has published over sixty reports of investigations into PPP/PFI deals: nearly 1,000 recommendations have resulted from subsequent hearings by the PAC.[123] Demonstrating the flexible fire-watching role, a series of methodological and systemic reviews has covered such topics as comparative assessment of VFM and improvements to tendering process.[124] While basking in the glow of positive findings in many cases, fine-tuning is for the Treasury part of the job. 'The NAO's critical review function has been demonstrably beneficial in highlighting areas of PFI procurement policy that required attention.'[125] An early-warning system based on real evidence of PFI in practice, and ongoing assessment of projects to ensure VFM is maintained during procurement, illustrate this. There is however an underlying tension. VFM is classically viewed as an instrument of regulatory control, not least in the internal processes of government accounting, but it is seen dominating the normative discourse in favour of PFI.[126] The Treasury wears two hats.

Seeing 'a myopic method of modernisation', political scientist Matthew Flinders makes the broader point:

[117] HM Treasury, *PFI: Strengthening long-term partnerships*, p. 45; and see D. Chevin (ed.), *Public Sector Procurement and the Public Interest* (Smith Institute, 2005).

[118] See e.g. Audit Commission, *Learning the Lessons from Financial Failure in the NHS* (2006).

[119] HM Treasury, *PFI: Strengthening long-term partnerships*, p. 24.

[120] As provided for in ss. 41 and 43 of FOIA. See further Ch. 10.

[121] See DoH, *Code of Practice on Openness in the NHS* (2003).

[122] HM Treasury, *Standardisation of PFI Contracts* [26], hammers home the message.

[123] Available with a text search facility on the NAO website.

[124] And see NAO, *A Framework for evaluating the implementation of Private Finance Initiative projects*, 2 vols. (2006).

[125] HM Treasury, *PFI: Meeting the investment challenge*, p. 4.

[126] Freedland, 'Public law and private finance'.

> PPPs represent a Faustian bargain in that forms of PPP may deliver efficiency gains and service improvements in some policy areas but these benefits may involve substantial political and democratic costs. The short term benefits of PPPs may therefore be outweighed by a number of long-term problems . . . regarding increased fragmentation, complexity and opaque accountability channels.[127]

(e) Practical issues

Day-to-day operational experience has revealed a variety of practical problems. A major bugbear is the high cost of developing detailed bids for PFI projects; the tendering period also tends to be long drawn-out.[128] Perhaps then it is not surprising to hear of 'the private sector becoming . . . more selective';[129] weak competitive discipline does not suggest full VFM however. Reshaping the process by doing more 'front-end' work sounds well, but in an often hard-pressed public sector how realistic is this? A City insider draws attention to some basic facts of life:

> The process of risk allocation is, in the standard mantra, about the allocation of risks to those best able to manage and control them. In practice, there are a number of instances of risks being allocated to those least able to resist them. For example, during the competitive tendering and negotiation process bidders may accept risks simply in order to stay in the game, without adequate consideration on either side as to the sustainability of the position; in other situations political commitments and timetables have apparently left procuring authorities with no choice but to assume risks which the private sector could . . . more suitably bear.[130]

The Treasury describes flexibility under PFI contracts in the following terms:

> One of the key benefits of PFI is the requirement for the public sector to define accurately its requirement through an output-based specification and to consider and provide for mechanisms to change its requirements over time. This is a discipline that does not generally exist within conventional procurement . . . Evidence suggests public sector managers appreciate the long-term certainty over maintenance and service provision created by PFI, but want greater flexibility to make minor variations and greater alignment of incentives to agree and complete variations.[131]

Most PFI contracts are changed within a few years of being let. That this commonly involves minor modifications to operational assets highlights

[127] M. Flinders, 'The politics of public-private partnerships' (2005) 7 *Brit. J. of Politics and International Relations* 215–16, 234.

[128] In one study, 2 years average for PFI schools, 3 years for PFI hospitals, and 4 years for other PFI projects: NAO, *Improving the PFI Tendering Process*, HC 149 (2006/7).

[129] *Ibid.*, p. 5.

[130] T. Stone, *PFI : Is there a better way?* (KPMG, 2006), p. 6.

[131] HM Treasury, *PFI: Strengthening long-term partnerships*, p. 6.

the extraordinarily detailed specification in many of these public/private transactions.

Where major increases in capacity are involved, the quest for VFM can be acutely challenging. The NAO warns of 'complex interface issues with the ongoing risks and obligations borne by the incumbent private sector contractor' making competitive tendering less attractive at this stage.[132]

In the Treasury's words, 'relations between the public and private parties to a PFI contract represent a key factor in influencing operational performance'.[133] Emphasis is put on the importance of 'partnership working' (itself a not insignificant administrative cost):

> PFI projects involve long term relationships between authorities and contractors who, at first sight, appear to have inherently different objectives. A successful outcome for both parties can only be achieved if they are prepared to approach projects in a spirit of partnership. This requires an understanding of each other's business and a common vision of how best they can work together . . . A good partnership relationship is one where both sides are open, share information fully and work together to solve problems. It is not easy to secure this form of relationship . . . Authorities must develop a staffing and training plan to ensure that they have staff with the right skills and experience to manage the contract . . . Authorities should regularly re-assess . . . to identify ways in which relationships can be improved.[134]

The Treasury declares that relations at managerial level are generally 'good' and often 'very good'. Notably however, with many more PFI projects in the operational phase, there is growing recognition of the 'balance to be struck between partnering and contract management and enforcement'.[135] While not anticipating much use of the formal process of arbitration made available under the model form, the Treasury has distanced itself from those authorities 'reluctant to levy deductions' for poor performance 'for fear of spoiling the relationship with the private sector'.[136]

The National Physical Laboratory affair, where the company's faulty designs caused massive delays in the construction, sheds light on the problems of enforcement. Rather than act unilaterally, the department eventually agreed a termination, the first one in a major PFI contract to involve serious non-performance. In an age of governance, we learn, it is not only judicial review or tort law which induce official caution:

> The [company's] approach to the project became more adversarial as its problems mounted. The Department strove to avoid compromising its contractual position. It was prepared to

[132] NAO, *Making Changes in Operational PFI contracts*, (HC 205 (2007/8), p. 13.

[133] HM Treasury, *PFI: Strengthening long-term partnerships*, p. 63.

[134] NAO, *Managing the Relationship to Secure a Successful Partnership in PFI Projects*, HC 375 (2001/2), pp. 3, 5.

[135] HM Treasury, *PFI: Strengthening long-term partnerships*, pp. 63, 65–6.

[136] *Ibid.*, p. 65; and see HM Treasury, *Standardisation of PFI Contracts*, Ch. 28.

> accept lower performance requirements providing that the relaxations did not compromise scientific research. Prudently in the circumstances, the Department refrained from requesting changes to the specification, and so avoided obscuring [the company's] design responsibilities. Despite being of the view that some construction phases had been wrongly certified as complete, the Department paid the required unitary charge in full, adhering to legal advice that it was under an obligation to do so . . .
>
> At least three times from 2001 onwards, the Department considered terminating the contract on the basis of default by [the company]. However, each time, the Department was advised that there was a risk that to do so would expose it to a claim for damages. The Department was also concerned that it might not be able to find another contractor to take on the project.[137]

The NAO concluded:

> The Authority should be prepared to set limits on its partnering role when the Contractor's continued poor performance seriously jeopardises the successful delivery of the project, and, where necessary, re-establish any rights that may have been eroded . . . and avoid actions that will inadvertently transfer risk back to the Authority . . . Under normal circumstances, issuing variations in good time is sensible . . . But this project demonstrates that refraining from issuing variations, which would have changed the nature of the works, helped the Department successfully avoid counter claims that it shared responsibility for the poor performance of the new facilities . . .
>
> As part of its risk planning, the Authority should prepare fallbacks/contingency arrangements so that it is not forced to compromise its contractual position in order to maintain services . . . Terminating a contract for reasons of an alleged default by the Contractor is unlikely to be straightforward. Reliance on the threat of termination alone is therefore not an adequate substitute for effective arrangements that confirm, before the contract is signed, that the Contractor can meet its obligations.[138]

4. Underground

Unique in scale and complexity, and mired in political controversy, the PPP arrangements for the London Tube – a £17 billion modernisation programme lasting thirty years – demand special attention. Contract technique has been pushed to extraordinary lengths, both in terms of the allocation of (financial) risk and flexibility for the future (all those 'known and unknown unknowns'). The resulting governance machinery has taken the contemporary juggling of public interest and private autonomy in the contractual sphere to new heights, but has proved inadequate; the arrangements show a substantial accountability deficit. We find the contract theorist's desiderata of trust and planning, and co-operation and mutual interest, tested to destruction.

[137] NAO, *The Termination of the PFI Contract for the National Physical Laboratory*, HC 1044 (2005/6), p. 4.

[138] *Ibid*., pp. 6–7.

(a) Set-up

The earlier model of the Tube[139] under local government control was famously on show in *Bromley* (see p. 103 above). The subsequent abolition by the Conservatives of the Greater London Council saw the establishment of London Underground Ltd ('LUL') as a wholly owned subsidiary of London Regional Transport ('LRT'), a statutory agency firmly under the thumb of central government.[140] There followed years of fluctuating Treasury subsidy, inevitably resulting in disruption to long-term maintenance and renewal programmes, coupled in the 1990s with worst-case examples of conventional procurement (cost overruns on the Central Line upgrade and the Jubilee Line extension project of over 30 per cent). Against this backdrop, and on the basis of a satisfactory train operating performance, the incoming Labour Government opted for a partial privatisation along the lines of the horizontal business structure previously devised for the national railway.[141] While LUL would still be running (and ticketing) the trains, responsibility for maintenance, replacement and upgrade of the network (including the trains) would pass to three private-sector infrastructure companies. These 'Infracos' were to bring in project management expertise and innovation, while being suitably rewarded PFI-style through the infrastructure service charge ('ISC') payable by LUL under their contracts. Greasing the wheels, the Treasury agreed a regime of stable funding, whereby, subject to monitoring and review, the Department would make annual grants to cover the ISC.[142]

The arrangements must be read in the light of New Labour's commitment to restore London-wide local democracy in the form of an Assembly and 'a powerful directly elected Mayor with hands-on responsibility for transport, economic development, strategic planning and the environment'.[143] The legislative framework for the PPP was made part of the subsequent devolution statute, the Greater London Authority Act 1999. Implementation would see LUL become part of Transport for London (TfL), a functional body of the GLA, the primary role of which is to implement the Mayor's transport strategy and to manage transport services across the capital. Whereas Whitehall expected the PPP deals to be done and dusted prior to the Mayor taking office, the process became bogged down in all the technical detail. To ministerial dismay, enter former leader of the GLC Ken Livingstone, implacably opposed to the PPP and elected Mayor of London in 2000.

139 The system has a long and chequered history. Mostly built by separate, for-profit, companies, the lines were brought under the auspices of a public corporation, the London Passenger Transport Board, in 1933. At nationalisation in 1948 the system was combined with the rest of the nation's railways. Control of the Tube passed to the Greater London Council in 1969.

140 London Regional Transport Act 1984.

141 HC Deb. vol. 308, cols. 1539–42 (Deputy Prime Minister John Prescott); and see S. Glaister, 'UK transport policy 1997-2001' (2002) *18 Oxford Rev. of Economic Policy* 154.

142 NAO, *London Underground: Are the Public Private Partnerships likely to work successfully?* HC 644 (2003/4) and *London Underground PPP: Were they good deals?* HC 645 (2003/4).

143 *A Mayor and Assembly for London*, Cm. 3897 (1998), Foreword.

So could the PPP be stopped? The attempt was made in the High Court[144] on the basis of the transport strategy listed in the Act as one of the Mayor's responsibilities. Produced in record time, the policy was one of unified management control of the Tube system by TfL 'in order for it to ensure a safe, efficient and reliable system'. Counsel's argument was that LRT and LUL had no power to enter into the proposed arrangements because to do so would place TfL in the 'impossible position' of inheriting the contracts while also being under a statutory duty to facilitate implementation of the Mayoral strategy. Understandably the court was not about to unpick the legislation. Devolution notwithstanding, the 1999 Act had given ministers, through LRT, the last word:

> *Sullivan J:* Presented by Parliament with such a detailed statutory framework, it is simply not open to the Court to draw the implication that Parliament must have intended that a further restriction should be imposed upon the exercise of powers expressly conferred by the 1999 Act. Parliament has said what it wishes LRT to do during the transitional period. It is to facilitate the carrying into effect of PPP agreements whilst at the same time having regard to the Mayor's Transport Strategy. If, having regard to the Strategy, LRT nevertheless concludes that it would be appropriate to enter into the proposed PPP agreements, the 1999 Act enables it to do so . . .
>
> Entering into [these] agreements may be wise, as asserted by the Government, LUL and LRT, or it may be foolish, as claimed by the Mayor and . . . TfL. The electorate will, in due course, have an opportunity to express its views in the ballot box about that issue. That may be small comfort for those who oppose the Government's proposals, but it is as it should be, because judgments about the merits, as opposed to the legality of entering into the proposed PPP agreements, must be made by elected politicians and not by judges.

The roles and relations of the different players at the start of the PPP are illustrated in Fig. 9.2. Ownership of LUL was finally transferred to that reluctant contractual partner, TfL, in 2003. In the meantime, two of the three contracts had been placed with the same consortium, Metronet. With a total equity of £350 million, this featured subsidiaries of leading civil engineering firms such as WS Atkins and Balfour Beatty. Tube Lines, a smaller consortium, bid successfully for the 'JNP Infraco'.

Informed by the burgeoning experience of PFI, the transfer (or otherwise) of risk was much bargained about. So-called political risk featured prominently. To deal with the banks' concerns, especially over the continued disagreement between TfL and the government about the PPPs, lenders of £3.8 billion ('the senior debt') were given 95 per cent protection in the event of termination. Again:

[144] *R (Transport for London) v London Regional Transport* (30 July 2001, unreported). A second judicial review challenge by the Mayor collapsed at the permission stage.

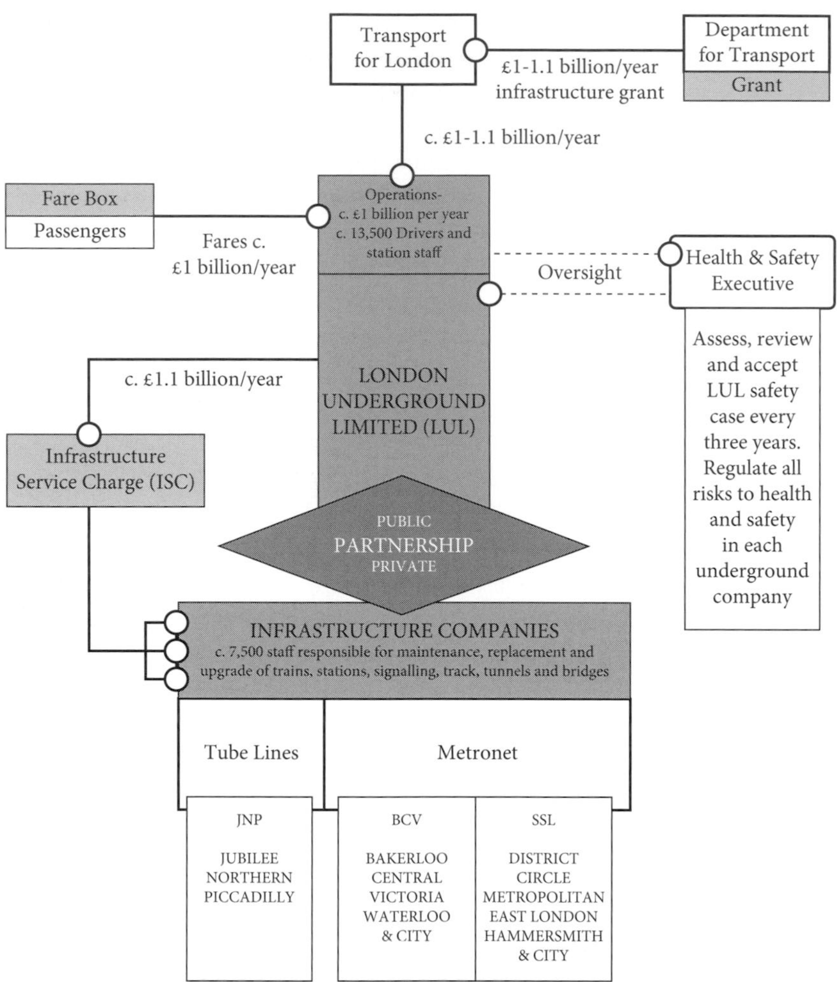

Fig 9.2 Responsibilities and funding flows under the London Tube PPPs[145]

> There are caps, caveats and exclusions to project risks borne by the Infracos. The risk of cost overruns in repairing assets of unknown condition, such as tunnel walls, is excluded because knowledge of their residual life and associated costs is incomplete. In the case of assets whose condition has been fully identified against specific engineering standards, the cost overruns that the Infracos have to bear are capped, so long as the Infracos can demonstrate that they are acting economically and efficiently. In the case of Metronet the limit in each 7½ years period [see below] is £50 million . . . Exclusions to the risks borne by the Infracos include passenger demand, lower income with fewer users and capacity constraints in the face of increased use. These are borne by London Underground.[146]

145 Source: NAO, *London Underground PPP*. See further European Commission, *London Underground Public Private Partnership* (2002) (decision on compatibility with state aid control).

146 PAC, *London Underground PPP*, HC446 (2003/4), pp. 3, 11.

The complexity of the legal arrangements is mind-boggling. The original contractual documentation ran to 28,000 pages – over two million words.[147] Determining the precise amounts of money paid to the Infracos on a monthly basis, a chief feature has been the use of hundreds of intricate mathematical formulae to calculate both bonuses and penalties or abatements. Take the following – transparent to whom?

> Service Consistency for a Line Grouping (Y^*) shall be calculated in the relevant Capability Model by the following formula:
>
> Y^* = (vis x wis) + (vmn x wmn) + (vdb x wdb) + (vtm x wtm) + (vcd x wcd) + (vms x wms) + (vfyr x wfyr) + (vfyt x wfyt) + (vfa x wfa) + (vfb x wfb) + (vfta x wfta) + (vftb x wftb).
> *Whereas:*
> wis, wmn, wdb, wtm, wcd, wms, wfyr, wfyt, wfa, wfb, wfta, and wftb are Fixed Parameters defined in the relevant Capability Model Data;
> *and*
> vis, vmn, vdb, vtm, vcd, vms, vfyr, vfyt, vfa, vfb, vfta, & vftb are Infraco Measures set out in the relevant Capability Model Data and the relevant Capability Model where applicable.[148]

The transaction costs of the deals were some £500 million, or 3 per cent of the net present value. With legal fees for advice to LUL amounting to £30 million, City solicitors were big gainers.[149]

And yet, notwithstanding all the detail, the London Tube PPPs are the chief example in UK procurement law and practice of what contract theorists term 'incompleteness by design'.[150] The need for flexibility, or the exercise of discretion on a rolling basis, was a central element of the bargain. While they enabled a vast and intensive programme of work, the agreements very deliberately did not specify the work to be undertaken. Instead, deliverables were set in terms of the service provided to passengers, using three main measures (into which the individual mathematical formulae would feed):[151]

- *availability*: a measure of day-to-day reliability based on whether assets are available for service
- *capability*: a measure of what the assets are capable of delivering in terms of capacity and reduced journey time
- *ambience*: a measure of the quality of the travelling environment.

Fixed prices for the whole thirty years was not thought to represent good VFM: LUL could not confidently predict its service requirements for the distant

147 See generally C. Wolmar, *Down the Tube: The battle for London's underground* (Aurum Press, 2002).

148 London Underground PPP Contracts, Sch. 1 [1] to the Performance Measurement Code.

149 Transport Committee, *The London Underground and the Public-Private Partnership Agreement*, HC 45 (2007/8), p. 15; NAO, *London Underground PPP*, p. 14.

150 H Collins, *Regulating Contracts* (Oxford University Press, 1999), p. 161.

151 See Mayor of London, *London Underground and the PPP* (*Annual Report, 2006*), Ch. 3.

future.[152] So, while establishing a long-term relationship between LUL and each Infraco, the agreements provided for LUL to restate its requirements at periodic reviews every seven and a half years and for the ISC to be reset to reflect changes in costs. Provision was also made for 'extraordinary reviews', so allowing charges to be modified within a review period should Infracos experience cost shocks beyond their control.[153]

How then, from a governance perspective, might all this indeterminacy be managed? Given the flammable mix of public and private interests, trusting to a co-operative ethos represented a leap of faith (for investors). An important role in the PPPs for dispute procedures like arbitration familiar from commercial contract might be anticipated. Equally however, being more reactive or 'fire-fighting' in nature, such machinery can only do so much in the crafting of future responsibilities. A special – and specialised – statutory personage was born: 'the Public-Private Partnership Agreement Arbiter'.[154]

(b) Juggling

The statute assigned the Arbiter two main functions: to give directions on matters specified in the PPP agreements, when referred to him by one of the parties; and to give guidance on any matter relating to a PPP agreement, when so requested by either or both of the parties.[155] While armed with information-gathering powers, the Arbiter has had no unilateral power to change provisions in the PPP agreements; a direction made on a disputed matter within his remit might also be set aside by agreement of the parties. In giving directions or guidance, the Arbiter is required to take account of any factors notified by the parties or duly specified in the contract; he must also 'act in the way he considers best calculated to achieve' four different objectives:[156]

- to ensure that LUL has the opportunity to revise its requirements under the PPP Agreements if the proper price exceeds the resources available
- to promote efficiency and economy in the provision, construction, renewal, or improvement and maintenance of the infrastructure
- to ensure that if a rate of return is incorporated in a PPP Agreement, a company which is efficient and economic in its performance of the requirements in that PPP Agreement would earn that return
- to enable the Infracos to plan the future performance of the PPP Agreements with reasonable certainty.

Duly functioning as a source of administrative rules, the agreements detailed the kinds of financial and technical issues the Arbiter might be asked to

[152] See for analysis by a regulatory economist, S. Glaister, 'The London Underground Arbiter: Effective public utility regulation?' in P. Vass (ed.) *Regulatory Review 2002–03* (CRI, 2003).

[153] *London Underground PPP Contracts*, Sch. 1 [9], Pts 2 and 3.

[154] As constituted under the Greater London Authority Act 1999, ss. 225–7.

[155] Greater London Authority Act 1999, ss. 229–30.

[156] *Ibid.*, s. 231.

address. Chief among these is a task naturally touching on many different interests: the determination – via directions – of the key financial terms of the PPP agreements at the periodic (and extraordinary) reviews.[157]

How might all this be conceptualised? As the name suggests, the Arbiter is more than an arbitrator, less than a regulator.[158] On the one hand, ranging beyond the standard institutional limitations of adjudication/arbitration, the Arbiter was clearly conceived as an authoritative and constructive repeat player, so exercising a close and continuing – and on occasion, at the heart of the financial deal, decisive – influence. On the other hand, the remit is restricted (notably excluding enforcement); the role is reactive (in the sense of being party-driven); and the periodic review function is potentially limited (by narrow terms of reference). The Arbiter, in other words, cannot provide the sustained and focused control familiarly associated with a regulatory agency. We shall find him successively main actor and bit-part player in the drama.

Organisationally speaking, the Arbiter is a throwback to the days of small-scale, highly personalised, arm's-length agencies, with notable strengths in law, accountancy and economics.[159] With a view to the legitimacy of agency action in such a contested and technically difficult policy domain, 'better regulation' principles have again been read across:

> The [Arbiter's] aim . . . is to give sound and timely guidance and directions on relevant aspects of the PPP Agreements when . . . requested, and to work constructively with the Parties in support of their key objective of providing . . . a modern and reliable metro service in a safe, efficient and economic manner. We seek to achieve this by:
>
> - working within a clear, transparent and consistent framework
> - giving reasoned guidance and directions which are based on well developed analysis shared with the Parties and procedures which achieve predictability in process and outcome
> - establishing effective dialogue with the PPP Parties and other stakeholders to facilitate timely response to requests for guidance or direction, while maintaining our independence
> - operating to high standards of accountability in all our actions.[160]

At the heart however of this challenging essay in administrative law is a decidedly contestable analytical concept, that of the 'Notional Infraco':

> In the PPP Agreements, adjustments to costs are made by reference to those that would be incurred by a 'Notional Infraco'. [This] is defined as being 'an assumed entity . . . that carries out its activities in an overall efficient and economic manner and in accordance with

[157] See on the process, PPP Arbiter, *Procedural Framework for Use in the Giving of Directions and Guidance* (2007) and *Procedural Approach to Periodic Review* (2009).

[158] C. Bolt, *Regulating London Underground* (City University, 2003) and *Regulating by Contract and Licence: The relationship between regulatory form and its effectiveness* (CRI, 2007).

[159] See PPP Arbiter, *Role, Approach and Procedures* (2003). The first office-holder, economist Christopher Bolt, has combined the job with the chairmanship of ORR.

[160] PPP Arbiter, *Draft Directions on Reference from Metronet BCV Ltd*, 16 July 2007, p. 1.

> Good Industry Practice, that has specified characteristics including the same contractual commitments as Infraco and also has Infraco's responsibilities for future performance of the Contract.' Good Industry Practice is in turn defined as meaning 'the exercise of the degree of skill, diligence, prudence and foresight and practice which could reasonably and ordinarily be expected from a skilled and experienced person'.
>
> The guidance from the Parties to the Arbiter expands on these definitions . . . It says that 'what should be expected of an Infraco working to Good Industry Practice [includes]:
>
> - establishing and maintaining whole life asset planning and maintenance regimes;
> - ensuring the right competence is available, including appropriate external advice when needed;
> - recognising that systems and assets must be useable in practice and taking appropriate steps to ensure this, looking at comparable industries where relevant and taking account of practical constraints;
> - recognising the time and resources needed for systems integration and taking appropriate steps to make it possible'
>
> The guidance also emphasises the distinction between good and 'best' practice. It indicates for example that the Arbiter should not base his determination on 'an assumption that all the Infracos could reasonably be expected to achieve the financial performance previously demonstrated by the best Infraco, unless there is a clear reason for this assumption'.[161]

This doppelganger-type reasoning has echoes of the *Wednesbury* test. However, far from a deferential approach, the methodology has seen the Arbiter and his team of experts playing a strong creative role. 'The Agreements recognise that it is impossible to provide a cookbook recipe that will produce *the* right answer if followed properly, not least given that the assessment is dynamic and needs to be relative to changes in the market.'[162]

(c) Implosion

The Infracos made some bold plans:

- three hundred and thirty-six new trains by 2014 and an additional forty-two trains by 2019
- all rolling stock currently more than ten years old replaced by 2019
- all lines to have modern signal and control systems by 2016, providing automatic train operation and automatic train protection
- a total of 80 per cent of the Underground's 400-plus kilometres of track replaced over the life of the contract
- capacity increased within ten years by 22 per cent on the Jubilee line; 14 per cent on the Victoria line; and by 18 per cent on the Northern line, with increases on other lines over the period of the agreements

[161] C. Bolt, *Regulating London Underground*, pp. 15–16.
[162] *Ibid.*, p. 21.

- ten of London's busiest stations modernised or refurbished within ten years
- a programme of modernisation and refurbishment at other stations, including a network of 'step-free' stations, with ongoing refurbishments every seven and a half years
- all infrastructure fully maintained and renewed to achieve a network-wide state of good repair by the end of the third review period.

The service requirements generated a front-loaded expenditure profile, whereby the Infracos would experience negative cash flow in the first period. In PFI-type fashion, this meant the Infracos raising project finance to cover the shortfall, and the public paying more, later. The very long length of the contracts is explained by the need to have sufficient time, not only completely to revamp the network, but also, through fares, etc., to remunerate the private-sector financial input. Conversely, the profile reveals the particular vulnerability of this form of public contracting in the early years.

Performance soon confirmed both the potentials and pitfalls of the PPP arrangements.[163] On the one hand, Tube Lines was commonly delivering plans to time and to budget while generating substantial dividends for its shareholders, much as ministers intended. Attention is drawn to the nature of the consortium's supply chain. Major supply contracts had been awarded by open tender, so engendering a healthy competitive discipline inside the private sector part of the PPP. Metronet, on the other hand, became a byword for inefficiency and service disruption. This was not entirely surprising since the consortium had a tied supply chain, the big subcontracts being parcelled out among the sponsors in cosy corporatist fashion.[164] By early 2007, TfL was estimating delays totalling twenty-seven years in Metronet's station upgrades programme; cost overruns were perhaps as much as £1.2 billion.[165] The Arbiter in a monitoring report remarked on the consortium delivering 'significantly less than was expected in its bid'.[166]

The arrangements created ample space for blame shifting not only between, but also across, the public and private sectors. While conceding deficiencies, it was Metronet management's contention that much of the difficulty arose from additional works required by LUL or changes to standard. 'Events', most obviously the terrorist bombings of the London Tube in July 2005, should not be discounted. Conversely, with Metronet already in receipt of £3 billion in contractual payments, TfL's very public line was not a penny extra. Vindication of Mayor Livingstone's determined struggle against the PPP was the not so subliminal message.

[163] London Assembly Transport Committee, *A Tale of Two Infracos* (2007).

[164] PPP Arbiter, *Annual Metronet Report 2006*, Ch. 3.

[165] TfL, *London Underground and the PPP: The fourth year* (2007). And see *London Underground Ltd v Metronet Rail BCV Ltd and Metronet Rail SSL Ltd* [2008] EWHC 502 (TCC).

[166] PPP Arbiter, *Annual Metronet Report*, p. 8.

By June 2007 Metronet was on its knees. Confronted with weekly cash flow deficits of £10–15m and by forecast losses for the coming year in excess of £1 billion,[167] the banks and the shareholders not unnaturally called time on further credit. Metronet executives were thus driven to seek an 'extraordinary review' of the BCV Infraco agreement, so triggering the independent assessment of efficiency and economy. Such was Metronet's plight that, as part of the reference for a direction increasing the ISC, it requested an interim award of some £550 million. The Arbiter issued his draft interim directions[168] within a matter of weeks. Applying the methodology of the 'Notional Infraco', it was not at all however what Metronet wanted to hear. Efficient costs for the year, assessed at £243 million above the existing baseline, were discounted to £121 million in extra ISC for the company's failure to match good industry practice. Evidently concerned that this might be throwing good money after bad, the Arbiter also provisionally determined no payments for six months, conditions that Metronet executives regularly certify the Infraco as a going concern and funding for any shortfalls, and the appointment of an independent monitoring trustee. A striking example of administrative law powers in an age of public–private partnership, this was nothing less than a death sentence. Enter the Administrators, the product of an immediate High Court application by the Mayor 'in order to maintain the efficient running of the London Tube'.[169] Aiming to transfer each Infraco as a going concern, so fulfilling the statutory purpose of the PPPs,[170] was all very well, but how could this be achieved? With the private sector now proving shy, the Administrators had to deal solely with TfL.[171]

Although the big company shareholders in the consortium had lost their original equity stake of £350 million, they were now not only free of accrued liabilities but also in profit from the valuable subcontracts. Nor did they appear to suffer much reputational damage. As regards the impact on the travelling public, Parliamentary investigation further highlighted the extent of Metronet's service-delivery failure: only 40 per cent of station upgrades and 65 per cent of track renewal completed as scheduled.[172] As for the public purse, ministers were soon paying out an additional £2 billion, mostly by reason of

[167] *Metronet - Statement of Administrators' Proposals*, 27 November 2007.

[168] PPP Arbiter, *Reference from Metronet BCV Ltd: Interim level of ISC pending a direction on ISC at Extraordinary Review: Draft directions* (16 July 2007).

[169] *In the matter of Metronet Rail BCV Ltd and in the matter of Metronet Rail SSL Ltd* (18 July 2007).

[170] *Metronet - Statement of Administrators' Proposals*. For the special provisions on PPP administration orders and transfer, see Greater London Authority Act 1999, ss. 220–4 and Schs. 14–15.

[171] TfL made withdrawing the earlier request for 'extraordinary review' a condition of offer. In *Directions on Form and Structure of Extraordinary Review and Net Adverse Effects: Initial thoughts* (September 2007) the Arbiter had indicated a less unfavourable approach to Metronet.

[172] Transport Committee, *The London Underground and the Public-Private Partnership Agreement*, p. 31.

the 95 per cent guarantee to lenders.[173] In the face of continuing heavy losses, TfL also had to make available some £900 million in emergency-loan funding to the Administrators in order to underpin the works programme. The costs of administration were estimated at a further £600 million. Re-engaged to sort out the legal and financial mess, beneficiaries included City firms that advised on the design of the PPPs.

Metronet's business was later transferred to two TfL nominee companies,[174] to be managed on a stand-alone basis until a long-term structure was agreed with the Treasury. Possible options included bringing the maintenance element of the contracts back into the public sector and letting individual contracts for upgrades and major investment work. Whatever arrangements finally emerged however,[175] the rebuff to Treasury policy on public contracting had been very real. According to the Transport Committee, 'the failure of Metronet fatally damages the Government's assumption that the involvement of the private sector will always result in efficient and innovative approaches to contracts'.[176]

(d) Lessons

Examination of the London Tube PPPs reveals major design faults. Take the tied supply chain (a common feature of PFI-type projects). As the intended beneficiaries, Metronet's shareholders could not be relied upon to address the inefficiencies. Competitive bidding for the Infracos was no substitute for healthy market disciplines through the whole lifecycle of the modernisation programme. Government, in other words, was insufficiently alive to the dangers for the public interest of this blurring of supplier and shareholder functions. There was also insufficient transfer of risk properly to grease the wheels of corporate governance. With few assets of its own, Metronet was little more than a buffer between the consortium and the contractual obligations under the PPP. Rather than be pressured to improve performance, the parent companies could down tools with very limited liability. Likewise, with the risk to lenders being so heavily offset, the financial institutions had less incentive to hold Metronet to account for escalating costs. Meanwhile, the sharp £50 million cap on the cost overruns absorbed by the Metronet Infracos did little to encourage innovation. Looking forward, the Transport Committee emphasises the need for 'detailed assessment . . . of the suitability of the proposed structure of delivery organisations, of bidders' specific expertise and of the strength of

173 HC Deb. Vol. 471, cols. WS 74–6.

174 *In the matter of Metronet Rail BCV Ltd and in the matter of Metronet Rail SSL Ltd* (23 May 2008).

175 In a changed political climate following election of a new Mayor of London (the Conservative, Boris Johnson).

176 Transport Committee, *The London Underground and the Public-Private Partnership Agreement*, p. 12.

the incentives to efficiency'.[177] So much it may be said for the costly endeavours of the government's City advisers.

Too contractual, insufficiently regulatory, the independent supervisory mechanism has been under-powered. While respect for commercial judgement was an essential ingredient of the relationship, the PPP Arbiter should have been able to self-start the reporting function under the banner of affordability and VFM. In the event, his intervention via the extraordinary review was both resolute and too late. The lack of an early-warning system, whereby the fact of rapidly spiralling costs could have been authoritatively established, was a serious omission. The affair vividly illustrates how public and private discretions alike may otherwise go untracked amid a mass of complex legal documentation. Both sides were all too eager to 'pass the buck'.

The high degree of uncertainty concerning the investment the Infracos had to make should have been a warning. Important transaction costs were bound up in the central design feature of less presentiation, more incompleteness. The sheer scale of the enterprise maximised the scope for disagreement. More and more detailed contractual provision formed part of the problem. The contract theorist might ask, 'trusting and co-operative relationship – what trusting and co-operative relationship?' Imposing the PPP on a powerful and recalcitrant elected authority was itself redolent of failure. Protecting lenders against political risk was one thing, ensuring the parties would constructively address contractual stresses and strains to their mutual benefit quite another. We are reminded of the difficulty of transferring risk in public services and infrastructures. To keep the Tube trains running means the taxpayer is inevitably forced to play the role of safety net. In conclusion, there are important lessons to be learned here about the functional limitations of contractual ordering and the importance of vindicating public law values like transparency and accountability.

177 *Ibid.*

10

Into the jungle: Complaints, grievances and disputes

Contents

1. Informal justice

(a) Origins

Much of the energy of modern administrative law has been spent on alternative dispute resolution (ADR). Alternative to what? In the course of the next chapters, we shall see that this question can have several answers. We could be talking of inquisitorial alternatives to adversarial procedure; of documentary procedure as alternative to oral hearings; of internal review as alternative to tribunals; of inquiries as alternative to ministerial appeals (such as we find in the education and planning systems); of arbitration and mediation instead of litigation. There is a natural tendency, however, for administrative lawyers to think in terms of tribunals as alternatives to courts. This is, as we shall see, how the debate has evolved.[1]

A famous nineteenth-century aphorism described justice 'like the Ritz hotel', as open to rich and poor, marking a growing concern over what would we should today call the 'access to justice' problem. The simile was a telling one. Litigation, even in essential areas, was quite simply beyond the means of the majority of the population. Legal services for the poor were exceptional. In criminal law there were 'poor person's defences' but even this provision was not formalised until the twentieth century.[2] In civil cases, unpaid legal assistance was virtually restricted to charitable provision and the 'pro bono' activities of the legal profession. Despite patchy efforts at reform, this situation did not change materially until the introduction of the Legal Aid and Advice Act 1949.[3] A period of relative generosity in the provision of legal aid ensued only to be followed by a serious turndown since 1990.[4]

Not only were courts inaccessible but they had also gained a reputation for conservatism. Judiciary and Bar Council alike were notable for opposition to law-reform measures. The courts' performance in deciding statutory appeals against, for example, railway and canal companies was poor; worse still was the experience of arbitration under the Workmen's Compensation Acts of 1897 and 1906, largely carried out by county court judges. Intended as 'inexpensive' machinery for dispute resolution, the procedure led to a flood of conflicting decisions emanating from pro- and anti-employer judges, swamping the Court of Appeal. The experience induced government to experiment with alternatives. The Old Age Pensions Act 1908 set up local committees to arbitrate disputes, with appeal to the Local Government Board. Benefit disputes under the National Insurance Act 1911 were settled by local 'courts of referees' with appeal to an Insurance Commissioner, bypassing the 'ordinary' courts. Thus the foundation of a modern system of welfare tribunals 'providing a free service to their users and in front of [which] legal representation was unnecessary' was being laid at the turn of the century.[5]

These were, however, by no means the *first* administrative tribunals. Stebbings sets their origin in the nineteenth-century period of reform

1 H. Genn, 'Tribunals and informal justice' (1993) 56 *MLR* 393, 394. And see C. Glasser and C. Harlow, 'Legal services and the alternatives: The LSE tradition' in Rawlings (ed.), *Law, Society and Economy* (Clarendon Press, 1996).

2 By the Poor Persons Defence Act 1930. See further B. Abel-Smith and R. Stevens, *Lawyers and the Courts* (Heinemann, 1967).

3 *Ibid.*, Ch. VI. And see *Report of the Committee on Legal Aid and Legal Advice in England and Wales*, Cmnd 6641 (1945) (the Rushcliffe Committee).

4 Legal Action Group, *A Strategy for Justice* (LAG, 1992). And see the Courts and Legal Services Act 1999 and the Legal Services Act 2007.

5 Abel-Smith and Stevens, *Lawyers and the Courts*, p. 117. And see R. Wraith and P. Hutchesson *Administrative Tribunals* (Allen and Unwin, 1973), p. 28.

when Factories Acts were passed, the poor-law system was reformed, the first public-health regulation set in place and a miscellany of Boards, Commissions and inspectorates installed, charged with implementation (see Chapter 2):

> It was clear and foreseeable that this controversial increase in government interference with the private, professional and property affairs of individuals would give rise to disputes between individuals and between individuals and the state. The provision of a system of dispute resolution was necessary and urgent if the smooth implementation of the legislation was to be ensured, because the opportunity of raising grievances and having them properly addressed was central to pacifying hostile public opinion.
>
> Because the requirements in each case were very specific, the choice of dispute-resolution body was not a straightforward one. First, the personnel had to possess specialist knowledge because the rules to be implemented were not those of the common law, but novel and technical administrative regulations. The restructuring of land rights, for example, would demand a knowledge of agricultural practice and management, while ensuring an efficient and safe railway system would require a knowledge of railway management and engineering skills. Secondly, disputes had to be resolved quickly so as not to hinder the implementation of government policy and to meet public demand, and to do so the procedures had to be simple and informal. The process had to be accessible to be acceptable to the public, and that meant that it had to be affordable. This could only be ensured by making legal representation unnecessary and by keeping the proceedings local. Furthermore, most disputes would be minor ones of fact rather than principle or law, and might be very numerous.
>
> With these very specific requirements, the established organs of dispute resolution were seen to be inadequate. Though the regular courts of law had the advantages of familiarity, authority, independence, tested procedures and respected judges, they were too slow and the requirement for legal representation also made them prohibitively expensive. And while the judges were experts in law and the handling of evidence, they did not possess the new and necessary technical knowledge. The courts were not suited to handling large numbers of small disputes quickly, and the judges themselves were reluctant to adjudicate what they saw as not law but administrative regulation . . . As the limitations of the established institutions of the regular legal system were appreciated, the dispute-resolution function was given to the implementing bodies themselves. It was at this point, when the administrative body acquired adjudicative functions, that the modern statutory tribunal was recognisable.
>
> Each Act laid down its tribunal's composition, its jurisdiction and to some extent its procedures. When the procedures were not found in the parent Act, each tribunal constructed its own. It is clear from the evidence that the tribunals drew on the courts of law, other orthodox legal processes and institutions, as well as general legal values for their composition and procedures. Nevertheless each was self-contained, an ad hoc body individually conceived to suit the subject matter of the legislation it sought to implement and undertaking a mixture of legislative, administrative and policy functions with strictly circumscribed

> and subordinate adjudicatory powers. Subject-specificity was all-important because it determined the detail of a tribunal's composition, procedures and, most importantly, its jurisdiction. Each was sui generis and developed in almost total theoretical and practical isolation.[6]

At this early date, Stebbings argues, the pattern was already set of heterogeneous 'bespoke tribunals', designed specifically for a single purpose without any overall design or guiding principles. This is the pattern that we live with today and have to try to rationalise. It is in the same sense that we ourselves talk of the administrative justice landscape as a 'jungle': a dense and obscure region on the borders of administrative law, in which subsists a tangled mass of gripes and grumbles, grievances and complaints.[7]

(b) Donoughmore to Franks

In the search for court-substitutes, green light theory came into its own. Many green light theorists were actively involved in the early years of the twentieth century in working for reform of legal services.[8] Laski campaigned for legal aid. Robson, who criticised courts for doing 'absolutely nothing to modernize, to cheapen or to bring into accord with modern needs a fantastic procedure which has been obsolete for at least a century',[9] never ceased to argue for a systematised administrative justice 'in the main independent of the courts of law'. He believed that to submit tribunals to judicial control was to reintroduce 'the legalism and unfreedom of the formal judicature, the avoidance of which is one of the main objects sought to be obtained by the machinery of administrative justice'.[10] *Justice and Administrative Law*, Robson's wide-ranging study of 'Trial by Whitehall',[11] compared and contrasted judicial and administrative decision-making. It looked not only at areas such as vehicle licensing and planning where rights of appeal were vested directly in ministers but also contributed studies of little-known tribunals such as railway courts, transport and war damage tribunals, and tribunals for children's homes. The study extended to the 'domestic tribunals' of 'voluntary organisations', as Robson called the various self-regulatory professional bodies, such as trade associations and trade unions, universities

[6] C. Stebbings, 'Comment: A Victorian legal legacy – the bespoke tribunal' (Council on Tribunals, *Adjust*, April 2007). And see C. Stebbings, *Legal Foundations of Tribunals in Nineteenth Century England* (Cambridge University Press, 2006); H. Arthurs, *Without the Law: Administrative justice and legal pluralism in nineteenth-century England* (University of Toronto Press, 1985); Wraith and Hutchesson, *Administrative Tribunals*.

[7] R. Rawlings, 'In the jungle' (1987) 50 *MLR* 110.

[8] C. Glasser, 'Radicals and refugees: The foundation of the *Modern Law Review* and English legal scholarship' (1987) 50 *MLR* 688.

[9] W. A. Robson, 'The Report of the Committee on Ministers' Powers' (1932) *3 Political Quarterly* 346.

[10] *Ibid.*

[11] W. A. Robson, *Justice and Administrative Law*, 3rd edn (Stevens, 1951).

and the legal and medical professions, charged with the task of hearing complaints against their members.

Amongst Robson's objectives and the objectives of his followers was the development of user-friendly machinery for the resolution of 'small claims'. But not even the keenest advocates of informal justice were at this stage prepared to move far from the legal paradigm. Thus much of Robson's classic study was devoted to identifying judicial qualities and the characteristics of adjudication. He saw the need to bring 'some measure of consistency and system' into their activities, arguing for the laying down of 'certain overriding principles to be applied by all administrative tribunals in the manner best suited to their individual functions'.[12] He also favoured the establishment of an administrative appeals tribunal for better oversight and control. Robson focused on ministerial and administrative decision-making and the way administrators took decisions. His was, in other words, a 'top-down' rather than a 'bottom-up' approach.

Street, on the other hand, looked at the clientele for administrative justice, highlighting its special needs:

> Here is a class of litigant often unfamiliar with the legal process and lacking the financial means to pay to be represented at hearings. Nervous, inarticulate, over-awed, mistrustful of bureaucracy, impatient of legal forms – he is indeed a special case . . . He must be around the table with people, some of whom he sees as like himself, people to whom he can speak freely, who will be tolerant of his fumbling, discursive, often irrelevant, disorderly presentation of his case. Accessibility to justice in the land of welfare benefits is not merely helping the claimant; it is ensuring beforehand that there is a tribunal, an atmosphere, a procedure welcomely receptive and comforting to him.[13]

Although this passage hints at a new, 'bottom-up' perspective on administrative justice focused on complainants and their needs, Street did not move far on to the terrain of ADR. He dismissed conciliation as a technique for resolving welfare disputes 'as an excuse for the adjudicator not discharging his hard appointed task of finding out what the facts in dispute are and applying the relevant law to them'.[14] There is no suggestion either that a mediator, arbitrator or ombudsman might be more 'welcomely comforting' to welfare claimants than oral, court-type proceedings. Street relied on tribunals as the primary means for dispensing 'justice in the welfare state'.[15] For all his mention of tribunal users, his remained largely a 'top-down' perspective, in which tribunals are court substitutes. Tribunals existed, or so Wade argued, to dispose of dis-

[12] *Ibid.*, Ch. 8.

[13] H. Street, 'Access to the legal system and the modern welfare state: A European report from the standpoint of an administrative lawyer' in Cappelletti (ed.), *Access to Justice and the Welfare State,* (European University Institute, 1981) 310.

[14] *Ibid.*

[15] See H. Street, *Justice in the Welfare State*, 2nd edn (Stevens, 1975).

putes 'smoothly, quickly and cheaply'; the object was not the best article at any price but the best article consistent with efficient administration.[16] A model of administrative justice was emerging in which courts and tribunals formed the top two tiers of a pyramid of dispute resolution of which the bottom two were internal review and administrative adjudication. Administrative lawyers were slow to take note of any but the top two tiers. Equally, they were slow to characterise tribunals and inquiries as forms of ADR, even though, at least by the 1980s, the movement for alternatives to civil justice, emanating from the US, was growing fast.[17]

The Franks Committee on Tribunals and Inquiries,[18] which followed Crichel Down in 1955 and is discussed in Chapter 11, was a landmark for administrative justice. If, as Robson had asserted, Donoughmore suffered from the 'dead hand of Dicey',[19] then Franks, with its attempt to sever 'administrative' from 'judicial' functions, suffered from the dead hand of Donoughmore. Franks characterised tribunals as 'machinery for adjudication', a definition with permanent effects. It not only recommended extending the supervisory jurisdiction of the High Court and Lord Chancellor's Department (in strong contrast to Robson's preference for an administrative appeals tribunal) but also the introduction of legal representation, legal advice and legal aid. With Franks, the judicialisation that Robson feared was well under way and the link with ADR had to all intents and purposes been broken. As Wade put it contemporaneously, 'a new system for the dispensation of justice [had] grown up side by side with the old one'.[20]

For twenty years or more, tribunals were to be pushed towards a court-substitute function until finally it came to be accepted that they were 'a third tier in the administration of civil justice',[21] a characterisation that reached its zenith with the Tribunals, Courts and Enforcement Act 2007. Franks also laid the foundation for the four-level structure mentioned earlier, in which level 1 (primary adjudication) and level 2 (internal review) were characterised as *administrative*. *Adjudication* kicked in only with two further levels of appeal, to a tribunal (level 3) and finally, appeal on a point of law to the courts (level 4). The division, justified in terms of cost and numbers, had several unfortunate consequences. On the one hand, the influence of adversarial trial-type procedure was boosted, discouraging experiment and

16 H. W. R. Wade, *Administrative Law* (Clarendon Press, 1961), p. 196.

17 See R. Abel, *The Politics of Informal Justice* (Academic Press, 1982); J. Auerbach, *Justice Without Law?* (Oxford University Press, 1983); Cappelletti (ed.), *Access to Justice and the Welfare State*; and C. Glasser and S. Roberts (eds), 'Special Issue, Dispute Resolution: Civil justice and its alternatives' (1993) 56 *MLR* 277- 470.

18 *Report of the Committee on Administrative Tribunals and Enquiries*, Cmnd 218 (1957). For the Donoughmore Committee, see above, p. 36.

19 Robson, 'The Report of the Committee on Ministers' Powers' .

20 Wade, *Administrative Law*, pp. 196-7.

21 Abel-Smith and Stevens, *Lawyers and the Courts*, p. 264. See also, JUSTICE–All Souls Review, *Administrative Justice: Some necessary reforms* (Clarendon Press, 1988).

innovation; on the other, appeals might be founded on shoddily prepared and reasoned cases conducted by junior administrative officials without much understanding of due process or judicial review. As Ison was cynically to remark:

> Even when statute law prescribes an alternative, such as an inquisitorial model, there is still pressure for a tribunal to gravitate to the adversary system. It is promoted in several ways; the heavy concentration on adversarial processes in legal education, judicial review, legal history, and the general inclination of the legal profession to see court proceedings as a model to be emulated. Excess capacity in the legal profession also seems to be stimulating an aversion to procedural models in which lawyers might seem to be superfluous.[22]

It could be argued too that Franks gave to the notion of adjudication an individualistic flavour, advantageous to individuals and corporate bodies flying under the 'individual' flag of convenience. Collective interests, which might receive a more sympathetic hearing in administrative and democratic decision-making, often take second place in adversarial proceedings.[23] Reinforcing this paradigm is the expanding influence of ECHR Art. 6(1) (the 'human rights for lawyers' clause), limiting the extent to which 'alternatives' to trial-type procedure can be a final method of determining civil rights and obligations (below, Chapter 14).

In its consideration of inquiries, the reasoning of Franks was similarly shaped by the Donoughmore analysis. Franks did not, as it might properly have done, focus on inquiries as a paradigm of inquisitorial procedure but saw its task as being to find 'a reasonable balance' between 'judicial' and 'administrative' functions. The general conclusion was that neither terminology was appropriate; inquiries were a 'halfway house' between the administrative and judicial.[24] But while Franks carefully stressed the hybrid function of inquiries and the ever-present policy element, the effect of bracketing tribunals and inquiries encouraged an assumption that 'what is right for a tribunal is also right for an inquiry'. The tendency to convergence was accentuated by the focus on planning inquiries, already more procedurally standardised and judicial than ad hoc inquiries (below). When Franks demanded a statutory code of procedure for planning inquiries, the inevitable result was to increase procedural formality. Thereafter the debate would crystallise around 'how much "judicialisation" the inquiry procedure can stand'.[25]

[22] T. Ison, '"Administrative justice": Is it such a good idea?' in Harris and Partington (eds), *Administrative Justice in the 21st Century* (Hart Publishing, 1999), p. 26. See also L. Mulcahy, 'Sliding scales of justice at the end of the century: A cause for complaints', *ibid.*

[23] Ison, '"Administrative justice"', 27. And see A. Chayes, 'The role of the judge in public law litigation' (1976) 89 *Harv. LR* 1281.

[24] Cmnd 218 [272–4] quoted below, p. 575.

[25] B. Schwartz and H. Wade, *Legal Control of Government: Administrative law in Britain and the United States* (Oxford University Press, 1972), p. 163.

To sum up, administrative lawyers had by the 1960s accustomed themselves to two main alternatives to court proceedings. Tribunals, accepted as 'machinery for adjudication', were seen essentially as small claims courts, dealing with matters such as entitlement to welfare benefits, insufficiently important for courts. We follow the post-Franks moves to judicialisation in Chapter 11. Inquiries, on the other hand, were accepted as a specifically English, 'advanced and sophisticated' contribution to administrative law and practice.[26] But although their hybrid and inquisitorial character was admitted in theory, in practice they too came under pressure to conform to trial-type procedure as witnesses to inquiries began, for example, to see themselves as parties and demand individual representation. We trace this development in Chapter 13. Our main aim in this chapter is to trace the movement for ADR in the sense of alternatives to civil justice into a wider search for 'proportionate dispute resolution' (PDR). Against a background of a rising tide of complaints to public bodies government has not unnaturally shown much interest in ways of damming the flood. We shall focus on internal complaints-handling machinery, designed to prevent complaints from escalating into disputes; on private complaints-handling systems and on the ombudsman system, based on investigative and negotiatory techniques.

2. Digging down

If courts form the top tier of the administrative-justice pyramid and tribunals the second, then ombudsmen represent a further downwards step. Working alongside and not in competition with courts, ombudsman schemes were introduced for 'the little man': as a means of 'giving protection to the citizen against injustice caused by faulty administration'.[27] The ombudsman widened the net to trawl for 'grievances' or 'complaints' as well as full-blown 'disputes' that courts supposedly could settle but, as Rawlings noted, this extension to 'small claims' did not demand a great change in the traditional top-down perspective.[28] Both tribunals and ombudsmen were an informal alternative to courts: a form of 'relief road' to deal with cost, overload and delay. Mitchell saw ombudsmen as filling a gap better filled by an administrative court,[29] while Schwartz and Wade, who thought the 'most surprising feature' of the Office of the Parliamentary Commissioner for Administration (PCA) was the absence of legal staff, were unwilling to allocate the new arrival more than a place 'on the outskirts of' administrative law. He should be welcomed 'as an important ally in the campaign for administrative justice, who will work alongside an independent judiciary and legal profession and supplement the rule of law

[26] JUSTICE–All Souls Review, *Administrative Justice* [10.3].

[27] JUSTICE–All Souls Review, *Administrative Justice* [5.5]; *The Citizen and the Administration* (London: JUSTICE) 1961.

[28] Rawlings, 'In the jungle'.

[29] J. Mitchell, 'The ombudsman fallacy' [1962] *PL* 24.

with the rule of administrative good sense and even of generosity' but he 'stands outside the field of administrative law'. They did, however, note that the PCA dealt with 'large numbers of substantial cases with great thoroughness and fairness'; it was unjust to see the ombudsman as dealing 'only with trivialities'.[30]

From a 'bottom-up' perspective, this landscape would be read very differently. Ombudsmen not only offer an informal, cost-free alternative to courts but also possess other advantages. Ombudsmen do not deal in rights; they are free to arbitrate and negotiate, qualities not generally recognised as features of adjudication.[31] And although ombudsmen are independent, they do not stand as impartial arbiters between equal adversaries but see it as part of their role to redress the balance of power between individuals and large institutions. We shall look more closely at this in Chapter 12. Other techniques of administrative justice can be re-situated on the landscape of ADR. Ministerial appeals, for example, acquire a certain logic if classified – as Robson saw them – as the concluding stage in an administrative decision-making process. The inquisitorial role of those who chair public inquiries is more acceptable if inquiries are something different from adjudication. This is indeed, the nub of the argument over inquiry procedure, as we shall see in Chapter 13.

The point we are making is that the core commitment of ADR is to extra-judicial forums for dispute-handling. These forums are not to be described as court substitutes but as *appropriate* and *proportionate* techniques for the handling of complaints: 'horses for courses', as one might say. Take the example of complaints to MPs, who handle as many as 3 million constituency letters annually. Their effectiveness is tacitly recognised by government departments, which have in place special arrangements for handling both MPs' and ombudsman inquiries. How should we categorise these complaints? A 'top-down' perspective focuses on the notorious 'MP filter' at which many incumbents of the office chafe, which provides that all complaints to the PCA must be submitted through an MP. This filtering function we might see as either a way of maintaining the workload of the PCA (the real dispute-resolution machinery) within manageable proportions, or as an obstacle to access to justice. A 'bottom-up' perspective would evaluate the MP's service as a complaints-handling system in its own right. It might then appear as an effective, cheap and accessible complaints system, providing quick, cost-free solutions for very ordinary people and taking the load from more formal dispute-resolution machinery. This, however, calls for empirical research. And complaints to MPs serve another crucial function; they keep the representatives of the people in touch with their constituents, helping to show them where the regulatory

[30] Schwartz and Wade, *Legal Control of Government*, pp. 64–6, 71.

[31] R. Gregory, 'The Ombudsman in perspective' in R. Gregory *et al., Practice and Prospects of the Ombudsmen in the United Kingdom* (Edwin Mellon Press, 1995), p. 11.

shoe pinches.[32] We shall find this theme appearing in managerial theories of complaints-handling.

We might in much the same way consider the provisions for conciliation and informal resolution in the police complaints system, which call for police complaints to be informally resolved at the police station, subject to the important proviso that (a) the complainant consents to this and (b) the conduct in question would not justify criminal proceedings or a disciplinary charge (s. 85 of PACE). Again, this provision is not merely a filter for trivial complaints; it operates also as an exercise in public relations, bringing police and people together. But is this how complainants see it? We simply do not know whether the provision discourages complainants; once again we need empirical research.[33] We might find that in practice the requirement undercuts effective dispute resolution and casts doubt on the legitimacy of the police complaints system. If so, should the system be reformed? Conciliation of this type is a function that a tribunal could not perform, though an ombudsman or mediator could. A tribunal might, on the other hand, seem more legitimate, at least if sufficiently independent.

A bottom-up approach to administrative justice, the present PCA has recently argued, starts with the citizen's first experience of the administration and extends to:

> the parts of the administrative justice system that tend to get overlooked, either because they seem remote from where the real judicial action is or because they appear as only a tenuous blip on the administrative radar screen. I might, of course, well say that Ombudsmen schemes figure high on the list, and I will return to the Ombudsman question shortly. I want, however, to start at a more basic level, not with courts, or tribunals or Ombudsmen or even with the users of the administrative justice system itself, but with those countless citizens who have no option but to be more or less regular recipients of the administrative decisions of the state, whether as claimants for welfare benefits, as users of the health and social care systems, as householders or tax payers or in countless other ways. And I want to start there because it is with the citizen as user of public services and decision-making that the administrative justice system must ultimately come to terms.[34]

(a) Bureaucratic justice

Like the 'access to justice movement', the 'bottom-up' approach to administrative justice first emerged as a subject of socio-legal scholarship in the United States. Mashaw's 'bottom-up' study of bureaucratic justice in welfare administration

32 R. Rawlings, 'The MP's Complaints Service' (1990) 53 *MLR* 22.

33 See M. Harris, 'The place of informal and informal review in the administrative justice system' in Harris and Partington (eds), *Administrative Justice in the 21st Century*.

34 PCA, Speech at the launch of the AJTC (20 November 2007), available online.

was a seminal influence.[35] Defining 'administrative justice' in terms of 'the myriad of first-instance decisions rather than the much smaller number of an appeal or complaint', Mashaw was searching for:

> an 'internal law of administration' that guides the conduct of those who make routine decisions more effectively than the external controls so beloved of administrative lawyers, who look to courts and – to a lesser extent – to tribunals and other forms of accountability, such as ombudsmen, for judgments that will secure the achievement of administrative justice.[36]

Mashaw famously identified three separate models of administrative justice: *bureaucratic rationality*, a managerial model in which the primary goal is effective programme implementation and the legitimating values are accuracy and efficiency; the *professional treatment* model, which is interpersonal and based on service, and aims at client satisfaction; and the model of *moral judgement*, a legal model of fairness and due process, characterised by externality and independence. This was later redefined by Adler as a model of legality and the assertion of rights.[37] Mashaw argued that any dispute-resolution system is dominated by one of these models according to the culture of those who operate it. Others may of course be present as, for example, where a private ombudsman observes standards of natural justice. Although the models are competitive, there can be 'trade-offs' between them.

An equally influential study by Felstiner, Abel and Sarat of the way in which disputes originate focused on the transformation of grievances into disputes:[38]

- stage 1, **perception** (naming)
- stage 2, **grievance** (blaming)
- stage 3, **dispute** (claiming).

Perception, the first stage, is realisation of injury. To interpolate a modern British example, litigation by victims of the Iraq war started to reach the British courts when soldiers, accustomed to a regime of military discipline, first began to perceive that their status was not exceptional: they had 'rights' commensurate with those of the civilian population. A grievance emerges at the second stage of 'blaming', when the victim looks around for someone on whom to pin responsibility for his injury. Grievances are to be distinguished from grumbles

[35] J. Mashaw, *Bureaucratic Justice: Managing social security claims* (Yale University Press, 1983).

[36] M. Adler, 'Fairness in context' (2006) 33 *JLS* 615, 619.

[37] M. Adler, 'A socio-legal approach to administrative justice' (2003) 25 *Law and Social Policy* 324, where Adler's modified five-model structure was launched.

[38] W. Felstiner, R. Abel and A. Sarat, 'The emergence and transformation of disputes: Naming, blaming and claiming' 15 *Law and Society Review* 631 (1980-1).

('a complaint against no one in particular') by the fact that 'the injured person must feel wronged and believe that something might be done in response to the injury'. The third transformation occurs when someone with a grievance voices it to the person or entity believed to be responsible and claims redress. A claim is then transformed into a dispute when it is 'rejected in whole or in part. Rejection need not be expressed in words. Delay that the claimant construes as resistance is just as much a rejection as is a compromise or partial rejection or an outright refusal.'[39]

The authors are making three important and novel points:

- First, legal sociologists should pay more attention to the early stages of disputes and to factors that determine when and whether a claim will evolve into a grievance and emerge as a dispute.
- Secondly, the forum to which the grievance is assigned affects the way in which the dispute unfolds and may 'transform' it; courts in particular 'individuate' the idea of grievance (a point made earlier by us).
- Finally, the authors questioned the idea common in 'top-down' studies of dispute-resolution that the level of complaints was too high; 'a healthy social order is one that minimises barriers inhibiting the emergence of grievances and disputes and preventing their translation into claims for redress.'[40]

These were both 'bottom-up' studies but with different objectives. Mashaw's main concern was to avoid disputes altogether by procedures designed to get the primary decision right. The approach of the second study was to channel grievances into appropriate and proportionate means of resolution, in much the same way as K. C. Davis hoped to structure administrative discretion by a sophisticated structure of rules. This opens the way to a search for 'proportionate' dispute-handling mechanisms.

These new lines of inquiry were soon replicated in British socio-legal studies. Contributing a seminal study of government complaints-handling, Birkinshaw inverted the traditional 'top-down' approach. He set out to:

> establish what [departments] did in relation to grievances from the public affected by their administration, and to study what connections there were between these informal practices and the more formal procedures for complaint resolution or dispute settlement culminating with Ombudsmen and Courts of Law.[41]

Rawlings too set out to redress the balance, taking note of the finding that, 'even within the parameters of institutionalised complaining most people

[39] *Ibid.*, pp. 635–6.
[40] *Ibid.*
[41] P. Birkinshaw, *Grievances, Remedies and the State*, 2nd edn (Sweet and Maxwell, 1994), p. xi.

seek informal redress'.[42] He blamed the top-down focus for ignorance of the 'unstructured, fluid and poorly publicised internal procedures which handle the great bulk of grievances ventilated by citizens against public bodies'. His own focus was on 'bottom-up studies of how people usually behave when seeking redress'; on non-judicial means of dispute resolution between citizens and administration; and on informal procedure for the redress of grievance. Similarly, Mulcahy and Tritter describe complaint systems as 'low level grievance procedure', which a modern state should know how to address:

> Complaints systems are important and should be recognised as needing as much attention as other systems for dispute resolution. The systems represent the mass end of a disputes market; systems which users may choose to access rather than the courts. In addition, we have an overloaded court system. Access to the courts and tribunals is severely limited by financial and procedural factors as well as those based on knowledge. As the expanding state produces more opportunities for injustice low level procedures represent a cheap, accessible and often more appropriate way to resolve disputes.[43]

This is an argument which needs to be considered carefully. Dispute resolution is the lawyer's trade; it is central to his function. It is natural for lawyers to see law in terms of their clients' interests and through the spectacles of dispute resolution; for the practitioner indeed, everything else could be said to be tangential. If this were the whole story, much of the content of earlier chapters – structuring through rule-making, regulation, etc. – would be peripheral to administrative law because it is not concerned with disputes and dispute resolution. As an explanation of lawyers' attitudes to ADR the statement is, however, helpful. Unless they work inside the administration, the lawyers' concern is essentially with the pathological. In red light theories of administrative law, the right of access to a court, common law adversarial procedures and the due-process rights that characterise them are the ultimate protections bestowed by the rule of law. This is why lawyers are so often guilty of 'squaring the circle' by reinstating them and why 'unmet need', the core concept of the access-to-justice movement, is conceived in terms of the extension of legal or quasi-legal services to new clients and new types of dispute. Administrative tribunals and the more visible and sophisticated forms of administrative justice can be fitted within a top-down, access-to-justice model, though the participation of lawyers will usually push them towards judicialisation. Internal machinery for complaints-handling is a way of protecting adjudicative machinery from

[42] R. Rawlings, *Grievance Procedure and Administrative Justice: A review of socio-legal research* (Economic and Social Research Council, 1987). And see L Mulcahy *et al.*, *Small Voices, Big Issues: An annotated bibliography of the literature on public sector complaints* (University of North London Press, 1996).

[43] L. Mulcahy and J. Tritter, 'Rhetoric or redress? The place of the citizen's charter in the civil justice system' in Willetts (ed.), *Public Sector Reform and the Citizen's Charter* (Blackstone, 1996), p. 109.

a flood of complaints conceived as 'trivial'. The assumption here (which every lawyer knows to be mistaken) must be that every important dispute will reach a court and that every dispute that does reach a court is important. On this view, complaints are trivial; they constitute an administrative problem demanding administrative measures.

A bottom-up approach treats complaints very differently. A research study conducted for the Nuffield Foundation, for example, selected people who had experienced a 'non-trivial justiciable problem' and asked how they had dealt with these.[44] The conclusion was that individuals took action (i.e., moved from grumbling to grievance and dispute) if:

- the grievance was serious either because of its impact or because a vulnerable person (a child, the aged, or a person suffering from a disability) was involved
- there was an expectation of positive outcome
- the victim had knowledge of how to proceed and
- could access the right procedure
- had adequate personal and financial resources
- had previous experience of favourable outcomes.

This tells us how and to a limited extent why complainants fall off the complaints ladder. It does not, however, resolve the question where dispute-resolution mechanisms should kick in.

3. Complaints: Is anybody there?

(a) The Citizen's Charter

In Chapter 2, we saw that complaining formed an essential component of John Major's Citizen's Charter. The Charter was a manager's and public customers' charter, closely linked to market ideology. It aimed not only to raise the standards of public service delivery but also to empower the citizen when service delivery was substandard. It gave market citizens 'voice'.[45] The Charter adopted a 'stakeholder' approach to complaining and suggested a new function for complaints: the so called 'gift' function of informing managers of defects in the service.[46] The Charter advocated proper redress when things went wrong; 'at the very least the citizen is entitled to a good explanation, or an apology'. It called for better machinery for redress of grievances and adequate remedies,

[44] M. Adler *et al.*, *Administrative Grievances: A developmental study* (National Centre for Social Research, 2006). See also D. Leadbetter and L. Mulcahy *Putting It Right For Consumers: Complaints and redress procedures in the public services* (National Consumer Council, 1996).

[45] See A. Hirschman, *Exit, Voice And Loyalty: Responses to decline in firms, organizations and states* (Harvard University Press, 1970). And see M. Conolly, P. Mckeown and G. Miligan-Byrne, 'Making the public sector more user friendly? A critical examination of the Citizen's Charter' (1994) *Parl. Affairs* 1.

[46] See J. Barlow and C. Moller, *A Complaint is a Gift* (Berrett-Koehler, 1998).

including compensation where appropriate.[47] Significantly, however, the Charter steered clear of creating legal rights.

Shortly after the Charter was unveiled, a Citizen's Charter Task Force was set up to advise on complaints procedure. Its priorities were made clear in a series of discussion papers, culminating in a checklist for 'putting things right'.[48] The Unit recommended all public services to 'define a complaint. This definition needs to be understood by all staff and users of the service.' It underscored the principle of easy access, insisting that all public services should 'have in place formal written guidance on how to recognise and handle all complaints, whether they concern operational or policy matters'. Staff should be familiar with these and be trained to 'fulfil their role and responsibilities within them'. An effective complaints system should be:

- easily *accessible* and well-publicised
- *simple* to understand and use
- *speedy*, with established time limits for action, and keeping people informed of progress
- *fair*, with a full and impartial investigation
- *effective*, addressing all the points at issue, and providing appropriate redress
- *informative*, providing information to management so that services can be improved.

Appropriate redress, including financial compensation, should be offered and the Unit 'should take the lead in producing guidance on redress in public services'. Equating fairness with equality, the Task Force urged:

> All public services must be seen to be delivering their services on the basis of fair and equitable treatment of all their users. The same principle applies to the handling of complaints. All parties involved in a complaint – the users of services, those complained about, and others – must be assured that the complaint will be dealt with *even-handedly*. Users need to feel that they will be treated on an impartial view of the facts, and not on the basis of any irrelevant personal differences, discrimination or inherent resentment against them from having 'caused trouble'. Staff, and other parties involved, need to be assured that any complaint will be fairly investigated to establish whether there are grounds for complaint, and then responded to in an open and straightforward way. Demonstrably fair systems encourage people to complain and staff to respond positively, within the framework of policy.[49]

[47] G. Drewry, 'Citizen's Charters: Service quality chameleons', (2005) 7 *Public Management Review* 321. And see A. Page, 'The Citizens Charter and administrative justice' in Harris and Partington (eds), *Administrative Justice in the 21st Century*.

[48] *Effective Complaints Systems: Principles and Checklist* (Cabinet Office, 1993); *If Things Go Wrong. . .*, Discussion Papers 1–5 (Cabinet Office, 1994); *Putting Things Right* (Cabinet Office, 1995); *Good Practice Guide* (HMSO, 1995). And see C. Adamson, 'Complaints handling: Benefits and best practice' (1991) 1 *Consumer Policy Rev.* 196.

[49] *Putting Things Right.*

In contrast to lawyers, who stress independence, and ombudsmen, who highlight investigation, the managerial approach emphasises high-quality in-house complaints systems. The Task Force favoured conciliation and mediation by 'trained and independent' mediators but warned against closing off the possibility of further review. This would involve access to someone *outside line management* who should (i) be clearly independent of the public service concerned and (ii) be free from interference by the organisation about how they carry out any investigation, once the remit and powers are set.[50] This guide to good practice today forms the framework for complaints-handling throughout the public service.

Local authorities were at first slow to introduce complaints procedures. By 1992, however, the local ombudsman or CLA was reporting that the practice was on the increase as part of customer-care and quality-assurance programmes; some authorities were going further and appointing an internal ombudsman.[51] Like the Charter Unit, the CLA has always recommended a relaxed and non-adversarial attitude to complaints. In its first code of practice issued jointly with local-authority associations it advised that complaints should not be too narrowly defined:

> The definition should certainly cover the small minority of matters which are clearly complaints and may end as allegations of injustice caused by maladministration and be referred to a [local ombudsman]. It should also, however, cover those other approaches to authorities, whether for advice, information, or to raise an issue which, if not handled properly, could lead to a complaint.[52]

Because the emphasis is on improving services, the current version of the advice suggests that *any* 'expression of dissatisfaction' should be treated as a complaint. A council needs to demonstrate commitment to a good complaints system and the need for the system should be appreciated at all levels:

> A good complaints system is an opportunity for a council to show that it wants to be open and honest; that it cares about providing a good service; and that it genuinely values feedback on whether there are any problems which need attention. So staff who handle complaints need to be positive, understanding, open-minded and helpful; and they should let it be seen that the council takes complaints seriously and deals with them sympathetically.[53]

50 *Good Practice Guide*, p. 29. There are seven more criteria concerning resources, access, publicity and expertise.

51 CLA, *Annual Report for 1990/91* [5]. And see J. Greenwood, 'Facing up to the Local Ombudsmen: Are internal complaints procedures adequate?' (1989) 15 *Local Government Studies* 1.

52 *Complaints Procedures: A code of practice for local government and water authorities for dealing with queries and complaints* (Local Authorities Association, 1978).

53 CLA, *Guidance on Good Practice*, available on line. See also British and Irish Ombudsman Association, 'Principles of good complaint handling' (April 2007).

As the Public Administration Select Committee (PASC) has recently emphasised, the Citizen's Charter had a lasting impact on how public services are viewed in this country:

> The initiative's underlying principles retain their validity nearly two decades on – not least the importance of putting the interests of public service users at the heart of public service provision. We believe this cardinal principle should continue to influence public service reform, and encourage the Government to maintain the aims of the Citizen's Charter programme given their continuing relevance to public service delivery today.[54]

(b) New Labour: Towards PDR

The conception of complaints as a 'gift' to management was introduced with new public management (NPM). It sits very comfortably, however, with New Labour's nostrum of 'responsive government'. Equally, the 'bottom-up' view of complaining sits well with the New Labour commitment to 'inclusive government' and its deliberately egalitarian style. Complaints are taken seriously as a way to make contact with people and to encourage public participation. Every department and all local authorities should carry on their websites information about their complaints systems and, after the Freedom of Information Act 2000 (FOIA) came into force in 2005, on arrangements for access and complaints to the Information Commissioner. *Directgov*, the official government website, publishes practical information on how to make complaints about government, public bodies and the media, as does the OFT at consumerdirect.uk, a government-funded advice service with specially trained advisers, which gives practical advice on how to complain and resolve disputes. *Consumerdirect* stresses the advantages of ADR:

- It can lead to compensation (Other satisfactory outcomes may include a formal apology, a change in procedures, etc.).
- It may cost you less than a court procedure.
- It is confidential.
- It is less formal than going to court.

However, it also warns that resort to a mediator or arbitrator may end by depriving the consumer of his or her legal rights.

The government has consistently pushed departments to review and modernise elderly complaints systems, where possible simplifying systems and bringing them together. The Department of Health has, for example, undertaken major reviews of the complex complaints machinery for which it is responsible, resulting in a new mediated redress system for cases of clinical negligence[55] and

[54] PASC, *From Citizen's Charter to Public Service Guarantees: Entitlements to Public Services*, HC 411 (2007/8) Recommendation 1 and [17].

[55] See DH, *Making Amends* (2003); NHS Redress Act 2006.

currently a public consultation on a wider survey of social service complaints.[56] These bottom-tier arrangements were not enough, however, to satisfy the National Audit Office (NAO). Its survey of central-government redress systems was highly critical of complaint-handling mechanisms within departments, concluding that complainants often needed time, persistence and stamina to pursue their complaints to a satisfactory conclusion through the jungle of processes often difficult to access, understand and use.[57]

The NAO's motivation for wanting improvement was largely financial. Comparing the overall public expenditure costs of handling complaints and appeals, it estimated that each new complaints case cost on average £155; appeals cost £455, while an ombudsman investigation might cost as much as £1,500 to £2,000, a figure queried by the NAO on VFM grounds. The total cost to government of handling around 1.4 million cases annually was nearly £510 million without counting in further costs of at least £198 million incurred through legal aid in immigration, asylum and social security appeals – nearly 2 per cent of overall administrative costs. When, on the other hand, a complaint was settled by 'street level' personnel the cost was as low as £10 per case – a powerful motive for early settlement! The general conclusion of the report was that departments and agencies should ensure citizens had easy access to information about where to seek redress and that departments and agencies should actively manage their redress processes to provide accurate, timely and cost effective responses to those citizens. There were two main obstacles to achieving this goal: first, the complexity of segmented complaints systems organised and run by individual departments; secondly, the adversarial nature of appeals:

> Current redress systems are arranged in a 'ladder' or 'pyramid' format, which copies the arrangements of law courts, with a hierarchy of procedures. Basic cases are solved locally and informally, and higher tier procedures become progressively more formal and more expensive, as well as involving fewer cases. In a legal context this pattern reflects a fundamental assumption that two parties to an action will naturally behave in an adversarial manner. It is not clear that such a foundational assumption is appropriate in many areas of citizen redress . . . The aim now is to be able to assure citizens and senior managers and ministers alike that as much as possible administrative operations and decisions are 'right first time'. The most recent White Paper in this area . . . spells out this fundamental shift in government and public expectations of citizen-focused and actively managed redress procedures even more clearly.[58]

[56] DH, *Listening to People: A consultation on improving social services complaints procedures* (2000); DH, *Learning from Complaint: Social services complaints procedures for adults* (2008); *Making Experiences Count: The proposed new arrangements for handling health and social care complaints* (2008), available online.

[57] NAO, *Citizen Redress: What citizens can do if things go wrong with public services*, HC 21 (2004/5).

[58] *Ibid.* [4] [6]. For the White Paper, see below.

This passage epitomises the managerial, bottom-up approach to complaints-handling which focuses (like Mashaw and Adler) on procedures apt for getting the initial decision right.

In the New Labour context of responsive government, however, handling complaints effectively is not just about getting value for money. In an echo of the academic literature, PASC recently reminded us in a report that formed part of a wider inquiry into *Public Services: Putting people first* that 'crucially, it is about establishing a responsive relationship between the apparatus of the state and the people who use this apparatus'.[59] PASC chose to focus on:

- how citizens know what they can complain about and who they can complain to
- arrangements for handling complaints within departments
- how complaints are used by public services to address problems and inform service design and delivery
- whether there is a role for a central government body to issue guidance and hold departments to account for how they handle complaints.

PASC recommended a 'caseworker approach' to complaint handling so that complainants have an identifiable person to deal with. This would entail defining 'complaint' widely and setting in place complaints systems easy for people to identify, understand and use.

A recent White Paper underlines the present government's holistic approach to administrative justice:

> A good service delivery organization must be designed with [the legitimate needs of the user] in mind. To make this a reality the system has to have the following features:
>
> - the decision-making system must be designed to minimise errors and uncertainty;
> - the individual must be able to detect when something has gone wrong;
> - the process for putting things right or removing uncertainty must be proportionate – that is, there should be no disproportionate barriers to users in terms of cost, speed or complexity, but misconceived or trivial complaints should be identified and rooted out quickly;
> - those with the power to correct a decision get things right; and
> - changes feed back into the decision making system so that there is less error and uncertainty in the future.[60]

This leads on to PDR as the ambitious idea lying at the heart of an overall strategy for administrative justice:

[59] PASC, *When Citizens Complain*, HC 409 (2007/8). The first in the series was *Choice, voice and public services*, HC 49 (2004/5).

[60] DCA, *Transforming Public Service: Complaints, redress and tribunals*, Cm. 6243 (2004) [1.7].

> Our strategy turns on its head the Department's traditional emphasis first on courts, judges and court procedure, and secondly on legal aid to pay mainly for litigation lawyers. It starts instead with the real world problems people face. The aim is to develop a range of policies and services that, so far as possible, will help people to avoid problems and legal disputes in the first place; and where they cannot, provides tailored solutions to resolve the dispute as quickly and cost effectively as possible. It can be summed up as **'Proportionate Dispute Resolution'**.
>
> We want to:
>
> - minimise the risk of people facing legal problems by ensuring that the framework of law defining people's rights and responsibilities is as fair, simple and clear as possible, and that State agencies, administering systems like tax and benefits, make better decisions and give clearer explanations;
> - improve people's understanding of their rights and responsibilities, and the information available to them about what they can do and where they can go for help when problems do arise. This will help people to decide how to deal with the problem themselves if they can, and ensure they get the advice and other services they need if they cannot;
> - ensure that people have ready access to early and appropriate advice and assistance when they need it, so that problems can be solved and potential disputes nipped in the bud long before they escalate into formal legal proceedings;
> - promote the development of a range of tailored dispute resolution services, so that different types of dispute can be resolved fairly, quickly, efficiently and effectively, without recourse to the expense and formality of courts and tribunals where this is not necessary;
> - but also deliver cost-effective court and tribunal services, that are better targeted on those cases where a hearing is the best option for resolving the dispute or enforcing the outcome.

4. Review, revision and reappraisal

(a) Internal review

A common way to ration judicial review is to require applicants to exhaust alternative remedies before coming to court. In Chapter 16, we shall see how this rule, originally applicable to tribunal hearings, has been extended to mediation and ADR. In similar fashion, complainants may be required – or permitted – before they move to the higher tiers of the complaints model to have recourse to internal review. Sometimes there is statutory provision for a reappraisal: ss. 9 and 10 of the Social Security Act 1998, for example, provide that decisions may be both 'revised' and 'superseded'. More commonly, reconsideration is a 'naturally occurring administrative procedure' which, without precluding rights of appeal, may do away with the need for adjudication: it is, in other words, a normal step in a complaints-handling procedure.

Top-down assessment of internal review might regard it, like the MP filter in the PCA system, merely as a device for filtering out trivial complaints. Or Wade's test of simpler, speedier, cheaper and more accessible justice than in ordinary courts might be applied. Sainsbury, in an early study of internal review in the social security system,[61] used criteria applied to the tribunals of speed, independence and impartiality, participation, costs and quality of decision-making. His conclusions were that internal review scored heavily on cost and speed but had the incidental effect of discouraging appeals to the upper tiers (tribunals and courts) of the complaints pyramid. He thought that internal review scored low on participation. 'What participants primarily want is to be able to participate in the process, to be treated with respect and dignity, to have an impartial decision-maker look at their case, and to receive a fair hearing.'[62]

Internal reviews are inherently quicker than tribunal hearings because neither the parties nor the tribunal need the comprehensive paperwork on which adversarial procedure depends. The system should also be more flexible and more responsive to sudden increases in demand or backlogs; staff can be moved temporarily or relatively junior temporary staff employed. We now know, however, that this is an optimistic assessment. If an administrative system goes badly wrong, as occurred with the infamous child support agency[63] and when tax credit payments were introduced (below), departments may be flooded with requests for reconsideration, bringing the system to a standstill. As we shall see in Chapter 12, ombudsmen can deal with this problem by setting up a group complaint. Appeals to tribunals, on the other hand, may have the unfortunate effect in practice of filtering out complaints from all but the most determined.

Internal review necessarily lacks independence, since the system is set up and managed by a government department or in the case of housing, local authorities; indeed a successful challenge of the Housing Benefit and Council Tax Benefit Review Board was mounted to the ECtHR on this very ground.[64] An empirical study of housing-benefit review suggests, however, that complainants may be less concerned with independence than lawyers like to think; only in the last resort are they greatly affected by the absence of independence, the lawyer's primary concern. Benefit applicants approach internal review in the light of a 'last-chance saloon' with a mixture of confidence in and scepticism of the system. The driving force to both review and appeal is necessity and desperation rather than conscious ideological preference, though a second strong motivation, to call bureaucracy to account, does suggest a need for externality and independence.[65]

[61] R. Sainsbury, 'Internal reviews and the weakening of social security claimants' rights of appeal' in Richardson and Genn (eds.), *Administrative Law and Government Action* (Clarendon Press, 1994), p. 288–9.

[62] Sainsbury, *ibid.*, p. 306.

[63] See G. Davis, N. Wikeley and R. Young, *Child Support in Action* (Hart Publishing, 1998).

[64] *Tsfayo v UK* [2006] ECHR 981.

[65] D. Cowan and S. Halliday, *The Appeal of Internal Review* (Hart Publishing, 2003), pp. 118, 152, 170–4.

This introduces questions of principle for administrative lawyers, of which we have perhaps lost sight in the previous discussion of PDR. A PDR approach to internal review of decision-making would probably ask whether it plays an effective part in the overall system of bureaucratic rationality. Is it a useful and normal part of the administrative justice landscape? Lawyers are asking a rather different question. Do these types of complaint system measure up to the legal template of due process? Are their procedures fair and sufficiently independent?

Complaints systems come in all shapes and sizes; their structure, remit and procedures are very variable. We have selected three review systems for a closer look. The first is the internal review system set up by the Inland Revenue to investigate complaints about tax and valuation; this raises questions about independence and efficiency and merits comparison with the ombudsman and social fund inspectorate discussed in Chapter 11. Our second study is of the Press Complaints Commission, a self-regulatory system based, like private ombudsmen, on consent. We then turn to freedom of information, which allows us to contrast the very new statutory system set in place by the FOIA with the previous 'soft law' system policed by the PCA. A final section looks at the major ombudsmen systems in the United Kingdom, their functions and relations with the courts.

(b) Internal review: The Adjudicator's Office

The Adjudicator's Office (AO)[66] was devised as an independent 'middle tier' between internal procedure and the PCA, who regularly deals with large numbers of complaints over tax matters. It was introduced by the IR in 1993 specifically to encourage adherence to Citizen's Charter standards of service and complaints handling. No legislation was required; the office is contractual. The service is free to complainants.

The Adjudicator (RA) calls herself 'a fair and unbiased referee', works independently of the units she investigates and has an independent budget. The complainant must be fairly persistent; fortunately, however, the first RA (Elizabeth Filkin) devised a guide through the complex internal complaints machinery![67] Starting with a phone call to the person or office dealing with the case, the complainant moves up to the local complaints manager, then up again to review by a senior officer not involved in the case, before the RA is involved. Alongside, a complainant could turn to his or her MP or to the PCA, who will normally expect internal review to have been exhausted. Appeal also lies to a tribunal and judicial review may be a possibility, though here again internal remedies must normally be exhausted.

[66] The original title was Revenue Adjudicator, changed to Adjudicator when HM Revenue amalgamated with Customs as HMRC and the AO gained jurisdiction over the Valuation Office Agency (VOA). For convenience, we use RA and RI throughout.

[67] HMRC, *Complaints and Putting Things Right* (April 2007 version).

Essentially, the remit of the AO is maladministration. Like an ombudsman, she handles complaints about mistakes, unreasonable delays, poor or misleading advice, inappropriate staff behaviour and the use of discretion, comparing what has occurred against the IR's published standards and codes of practice. The AO cannot look at matters of government or departmental policy or 'matters which can be considered on appeal by independent tribunals', including disputes about matters of law or the amount of tax, etc., due from the complainant or the amount of tax credit awarded. The AO cannot deal with a complaint that has been or is being investigated by the PCA. Complaints involving requests for information and complaints under the FOIA or Data Protection Act go directly to the Information Commissioner (IC) (see p. 473 below). The AO's role is:

> to consider whether or not HMRC or the VAO have handled the complaint appropriately and given a reasonable decision. Where we think they have fallen short, we will recommend what they need to do to put matters right under the terms of their guidance on complaints. This may include making suggestions for service improvements where we think this could be of benefit to the wider public.
> We cannot require HMRC or the VAO to do anything outside the terms of their guidance on complaints . . . Nor can we ask them to act outside their current procedural guidance.[68]

Much has depended on the personality of the appointees. Elizabeth Filkin had a background in citizens' advice and was strongly committed to securing the independence of the scheme, actual and perceived. Describing herself as a 'mediator . . . striving to engineer and conciliate settlement', she sought to resolve claims through mediation.[69] Her methods were designed to be 'user-friendly', i.e. informal and reliant on telephone calls and personal interview. Again like an ombudsman, the RA has no powers of compulsion, though her recommendations have to date apparently been complied with. There is a high rate of adverse findings: of 1,615 and 2,581 complaints in the first two years (1993–5), 64 per cent and 51 per cent respectively were upheld. In 2004, 1,419 investigations were conducted (against 926 in the previous year), of which 46 per cent were successful. This temporary rise was explained by complaints over tax credits, where 56 per cent were successful; in 2007–8, however, when tax credits were still an issue, 2,017 cases were received, a rise of 1,419 over the previous year, suggesting a general rise in complaints. Seven hundred and fifty-seven (44 per cent) of complaints were upheld and 1,720 settled. In her last Annual Report Elizabeth Filkin recorded that, in her five years in office, she had 'seen a dramatic change' in the way the organisation dealt with the public. She named 1997 as a watershed year, when there was 'significant improvement' in how the IR dealt with complaints (in its partner,

[68] *Annual Report for 2006*, available online.

[69] E. Filkin, 'Mediation not confrontation', *Taxation Practitioner* (April 1994). Of 503 complaints completed and 233 upheld in 2002/3, 160 were handled by mediation.

the Contributions Agency, by way of contrast, a 'staggering' 80 per cent of complaints had been upheld).

In an early evaluation of the office, Morris, an academic observer, gave the AO high marks for openness, fairness and effectiveness. 'Taxpayers have been provided with a speedy, high level and effective complaints service under the direction of an individual who is obviously strongly committed to stimulating higher standards of administration throughout the Revenue'.[70] As we shall see, this has not been entirely borne out. The second AO, Dame Barbara Mills QC, was highly critical of the time taken by her predecessor to resolve complaints; 'the average age of open cases – at more than six and a half months – was simply unacceptable'.[71] By 2008, the AO had made inroads on its backlog; 98.43 per cent of complaints were settled in forty-four weeks and the average turn-around time was just over twenty-three weeks. This typifies the broadly managerial approach of the present RA, who previously headed her own department. She tells us that she wants 'to maximise opportunities to work constructively with the organisations in learning from complaints, to use 'our experiences with the few to make changes for the benefit of the many'.[72] And in a passage redolent of the 'complaints as gifts' attitude to complaints-handling, she has said:

> A key aspect of our work is helping the organisations to improve their service to the public. To ensure that mistakes are not repeated and that lessons are learned, we aim to monitor our results, identifying trends and particular areas of concern. We feed this information back to the organisations, prompting them to make improvements to their service.[73]

But is this the primary function of office, expressly established as a 'small claims' system?

The tone of the RA's remarks in dealing with mismanagement of the tax credit scheme nicely illustrates her approach. Early on she expressed her 'strong concerns' at an area said to make up 'the bulk' of complaints to the AO but chose to see things as 'going in the right direction'. Her reports consistently highlight progress made in bringing the problem under control.[74] In 2007–8, for example, when 80 per cent of her docket consisted of tax credit complaints and 48 per cent were upheld, she welcomed a softening of the rules on recouping overpayments from beneficiaries (COP 26), though she added:

> Despite the progress made over the last few years, there are still features of the tax credits system which cause a minority of claimants real difficulties; especially for those whose circumstances change frequently. There are also still a significant number of claimants

[70] P. Morris, 'The Revenue Adjudicator: The first two years' [1996] *PL* 309, 312, 315.

[71] *Annual Report for 1999.*

[72] *Annual Report for 2003.*

[73] *Annual Report for 2008.*

[74] *Annual Report for 2006* and *Annual Report for 2007.*

> with problems, the origins of which can be traced back to difficulties with the system they encountered in 2003/04. It is important all these claimants are treated properly and fairly; and having in place a fit for purpose COP 26 lies at the forefront of achieving this. For these reasons, it is also important [the IR] continue to improve their complaints handling for tax credits claimants . . . Securing such improvements will be a challenge.[75]

This 'softly, softly' approach to administrative practices that for *five long years* have caused great hardship before concessions were finally worked out can be contrasted with the more forthright findings of the PCA. After working with the PCA on complaints-handling, the IR introduced a caseworker system for tax credit complaints whereby each complaint was allocated to a dedicated caseworker whose name and contact details were given to the customer. The PCA's Special Report on tax credits contained twelve hard-hitting recommendations, two very broad in character:

- Consideration should be given to writing off all excess and overpayments caused by official error which occurred during 2003-04 and 2004-05.
- Consideration should be given to the adoption of a statutory test for recovery of excess payments and overpayments of tax credits, consistent with the test that is currently applied to social security benefits, with a right of appeal to an independent tribunal.[76]

It would seem that these recommendations had not been followed. Perhaps this is one reason why the PCA's Revenue caseload remains so high. In 2007–8, the IR occupied second place on the list of most-complained-about departments, with 1,791 complaints, of which 82 involved tax credits and 60 per cent were upheld. It is a matter for concern also that 512 of the total complaints were against the AO, of which 68 were accepted for investigation and 15 per cent fully upheld,[77] perhaps because the IR is the first-tier appeal.

The first three-year term of office brought criticism of a 'substantial and worrying independence deficit'. Despite the fact that the IR's contract with the RA can only be terminated for gross inefficiency or serious misconduct, this is sufficient to exclude the office from the Association of Ombudsmen. Morris, evaluating the early years, paid tribute to the reputation of the first AO as 'an independent and impartial complaints-handler' but nonetheless saw the AO scheme as 'clearly flawed in terms of perceived independence and accountability'. Complainants themselves seem less concerned with independence than with outcome: the percentage of those 'very satisfied' with the service has fallen from 41% in 2003–4 to 36% and 29% in the last two years, though those not

[75] *Annual Report for 2007/8.*

[76] The PCA reports, *Tax credits: Putting things right*, HC 124 (2004/5); *Tax credits: Getting it wrong?* HC 1010 (2006/7) are discussed below at p. 541. The citation is from HC 124 [5.61] [5.65]. The Annual Report for 2006/7 showed that tax credits remained a major source of complaint: in all there were 1,142 PCA complaints, 828 in all areas except tax credits, where 120 new complaints came in, of which 15 were summarily closed.

[77] PCA, *Annual Report for 2007/8*, HC 1040 (2007/8).

satisfied remained at 33%.[78] Yet 84% of 249 surveyed in 2004 thought it important that the office existed while 65% saw it as 'fairer than the office complained about'. They were, however, not asked the direct question whether they would prefer an *independent* adjudicator. And perhaps they had already voted with their feet, turning to the more obviously independent PCA.

(c) Self-regulation: press complaints

The present system of press self-regulation dates from the early 1990s and rests on the twin pillars of the *Editors' Code of Practice* and the Press Complaints Commission (PCC) as grievance machinery.[79] The self-regulatory system has often come under attack and been recommended for abolition and replacement by a statutory tribunal with powers to restrain publication and fine newspapers.[80] Despite considerable pressure, successive governments have so far managed to avoid this outcome in favour of perseverance and strengthening of the system.[81]

The rationale for self-regulation is a powerful one: 'to maintain the freedom of the press – vital in an open and democratic society – the industry has to regulate itself; otherwise the door is open to Government influence, censorship, even control'.[82] And we must not forget the background against which the struggle for autonomy rages; there is a long history of censorship of all forms of self-expression, including books, theatre and cinema in Britain. The present self-regulatory system operates on a most sensitive interface between openness and secrecy and, in human rights terms, between the right to respect for private and family life (ECHR Art. 8) and the right to freedom of expression and 'to receive and impart information' (ECHR Art. 10).[83] Thus, as the preamble to the Code puts it:

> It is essential that an agreed code be honoured not only to the letter but in the full spirit. It should not be interpreted so narrowly as to compromise its commitment to respect the rights of the individual, nor so broadly that it constitutes an unnecessary interference with freedom of expression or prevents publication in the public interest.

[78] P. Morris, 'The Revenue Adjudicator', 321. Contrast D. Oliver, 'The Revenue Adjudicator: A new breed of ombudsperson?' [1993] *PL* 407, who believes accountability to be secured by the possibility of complaint to the PCA and PASC.

[79] The first Press Council, established on a trial basis in the face of widespread calls to rein in 'media excesses', was set up in 1953: see R. Shannon, *A Press Free and Responsible: Self-regulation and the Press Complaints Commission 1991-2001* (John Murray, 2001), p. 11.

[80] See the recommendations of the two Calcutt Committees: *Report on Privacy and Related Matters*, Cmnd 1102 (1990); *Review of Press Self-Regulation*, Cmnd 2135 (1993).

[81] *Privacy and Media Intrusion*, Cmnd 2918 (1995).

[82] Culture, Media and Sport Committee (CMSC), *Privacy and Media Intrusion*, HC 458 (2002/3), p. 24; *Government response*, Cm. 5985 (2002/3); and *CMSC reply*, HC 213 (2003/4).

[83] See *von Hannover v Germany* (2005) 40 EHRR 1. And see H. Fenwick and G. Phillipson, *Media Freedom under the Human Rights Act* (Oxford University Press, 2006).

The Code must naturally be read in the context both of market forces and of media law more generally. We should note the strong contrast too with the more modern media: broadcasting, film and television have always been subject both to censorship and licensing and are today regulated by a statutory regulator, Ofcom, which has a remit to see that people who watch television and listen to the radio are protected from harmful or offensive material, from being treated unfairly in television and radio programmes and from having their privacy invaded. (Ofcom publishes a code of practice, has investigatory powers and a complaints-handling service available online). We need to bear in mind also that responsibility is shared with the formal legal system. 'The press', as the PCC keenly reminds us, 'is subject to plenty of different pieces of legislation as well . . . A complex mesh of criminal and civil law . . . restrains newspapers' investigation, newsgathering and publication, in print or online'.[84] Historically, English courts have been very slow to recognise privacy as an interest worthy of protection[85] and only in the last few years are embryonic forms of liability beginning to emerge. A recent case brought by Max Mosley strikes a warning note however; in an action based on breach of confidence and human rights, a judge awarded damages of £60,000 for publication of material concerning the plaintiff's sexual habits.[86]

The Code itself remains firmly in the ownership of the industry. While subject to ratification – 'sanctioning' – by the PCC, it is framed and revised by a committee made up of independent editors of national, regional and local newspapers and magazines. It can thus plausibly be presented as 'the cornerstone of the system of self-regulation to which the industry has made a binding commitment'. More particularly, 'it is the responsibility of editors and publishers to implement the Code and they should take care to ensure it is observed rigorously by all editorial staff and external contributors'. There is also a role for contract; the Code is now routinely incorporated in editors' and journalists' contracts of employment, so opening the way to internal disciplinary proceedings. This form of 'tertiary rule' has a status of its own under the Human Rights Act (HRA). Section 12(4) provides that, in proceedings relating to 'journalistic, literary or artistic' material, the court 'must have particular regard' to 'any relevant privacy code' (statutory or otherwise).[87] Like the self-regulatory system, the exception was the product of heavy industry lobbying.

The Code contains three types of provision. There are cross-cutting requirements of accuracy in reporting and respect for privacy; there is a range of highly specific clauses; and last but not least there are public interest

[84] PCC, Evidence to CMSC, *Self-regulation of the Press*, HC 375 (2006/7). And see generally, G. Robertson and A. Nicol, *Media Law*, 5th edn (Sweet and Maxwell, 2007).

[85] *Malone v Metropolitan Police Commissioner* [1979] Ch 344. And see Lord Bingham, 'Tort and human rights' in P. Cane and J. Stapleton (eds), *The Law of Obligations: Essays in celebration of John Fleming* (Clarendon Press, 1998).

[86] *Mosley v News Group Newspapers Ltd* [2008] EWHC 1777. And see *Campbell v MGN* [2004] UKHL 22; *OBG Ltd v Allan, Douglas v Hello* [2007] UKHL 21.

[87] *Sugar v BBC* [2009] UKHL 9.

qualifications – 'the right to know'. The Code leaves much space for 'judgement discretion'.

1. **Accuracy**

(i) The press must take care not to publish inaccurate, misleading or distorted information, including pictures
(ii) A significant inaccuracy, misleading statement or distortion once recognised must be corrected, promptly and with due prominence, and – where appropriate – an apology published . . .

. . .

3. **Privacy**

(i) Everyone is entitled to respect for his or her private and family life, home, health and correspondence, including digital communications. Editors will be expected to justify intrusions into any individual's private life without consent.
(ii) It is unacceptable to photograph individuals in a private place without their consent.

'Private places' are defined as 'public or private property where there is a reasonable expectation of privacy'. The Code provides for exceptions to the privacy restrictions where they can be demonstrated to be in the public interest and this term is defined:

1. The public interest includes, but is not confined to:

(i) Detecting or exposing crime or serious impropriety
(ii) Protecting public health and safety
(iii) Preventing the public from being misled by an action or statement of an individual or organisation.

2. There is a public interest in freedom of expression itself.

Illustrating the inherent flexibility of self-regulation, the Code is very much 'a living document'. It 'cannot stand still. It must keep pace with changing society. That is one of its strengths.'[88] It has in fact been amended some thirty times, usually with a view to deepening or widening the regulation. A major shock to the system, the death of Diana, Princess of Wales, generated a raft of amendments such as a ban on material obtained by 'persistent pursuit' and an extension of children's protection. Again, the HRA prompted some careful redrafting, illustrated in the privacy clause cited above. Better to reflect the lessons of PCC adjudications, the Code is now subject to annual review and a readily updated 'Editor's Codebook' has recently been produced, fleshing out the regulation with details of relevant rulings and interpretations.

[88] PCC, *Annual Review 2005*, p. 17.

Tasked with dealing with complaints, the PCC is neatly characterised by current chairman Sir Christopher Meyer as being in a state of 'permanent evolution'[89] in response partly to the ongoing injection of good governance values into self-regulatory systems (see Chapter 7), especially in the form of institutional 'checks and balances'; partly to pressure from a series of parliamentary inquiries, such as a Culture, Media and Sport Committee (CMSC) report emphasising the importance of better-regulation-type measures in commanding the confidence of government, Parliament, and, crucially, the public.[90] Funded in the usual way at arm's-length from the industry, the PCC today has both a permanent staff and a clear majority of Board members who are not journalists. 'This amounts to a degree of structural independence that is unsurpassed in any press self-regulatory body throughout the world.'[91] Flanking developments include an independent 'charter commissioner', whereby the PCC's handling of a complaint can be challenged on judicial-review-type grounds; and an independent 'charter compliance panel', empowered retrospectively to examine complaints files and to report generally on quality of service. In practice, most PCC casework concerns the accuracy of articles, with a further substantial wedge related to issues of privacy (see below). Happily, the panel finds 'much to praise, not least in the care and patience the complaints officers show in dealing with individual complaints, and in negotiating the satisfactory resolution of complaints'.[92] As we shall see, not everyone agrees!

'Free, fast and fair' is the PCC mantra. From the complainant's standpoint, a key advantage of the self-regulatory system is that 'it costs nothing . . . you do not need a solicitor or anyone else to represent you'.[93] Notably, of the several thousand complaints the PCC handles each year, over 90 per cent are classified as being from ordinary members of the public. The PCC also prides itself that, 'excluding complaints where no breach of the Code is established, or no further action is required, nine out of ten complaints are resolved; and it only takes us, on average, just 25 working days to do so'.[94] Approximately 50 per cent of complaints (about 3,600 annually) fall outside the scope of the Code, in which case a letter is sent to the complainant and the case is merely recorded; of the rest, an apparent breach is found in about 65 per cent. The PCC then contacts the editor who may offer to resolve the complaint by mediation through the PCC. Remedies secured through conciliation may include a published or a private apology, undertakings about future conduct, confirmation of internal disciplinary action, *ex gratia* payments or donations to charity.

It seems that between 20–25 per cent of all complaints received are not resolved through conciliation. Unless the PCC deems that a major principle

[89] PCC, *Annual Review 2003*, p. 7.
[90] CMSC, HC 458, p. 3.
[91] PCC, Evidence, HC 458-ii.
[92] Charter Compliance Panel, *Annual Report 2006*, p. 2.
[93] PCC, *Key Benefits of the System of Self-Regulation* (2006), p. 1.
[94] PCC, *Annual Review 2005*, p. 4.

is at stake, it lets them go; otherwise, it moves on to a formal adjudication. Questions are raised by the fact that formal adjudications have slackened off in recent years, a phenomenon explained away by the PCC as the consequence of a maturing system with less need for 'precedents.'[95] It could equally be explicable in terms of lack of public confidence in the system, fuelled by the presence on the PCC of a minority of members drawn from the industry, creating an institutional or structural bias, though this is not entirely confirmed by Annual Reports. The number of complaints is rising. So is the number resolved satisfactorily and, surveyed regularly by the PCC, complainants seem to be satisfied: 82% of those surveyed in 2007 thought the investigations thorough, 76% expressed overall satisfaction and 81% thought the review sufficiently fast (compare the Information Commissioner, below, p. 477).[96] But noting that around 70–80% or more of complaints never reach adjudication (as in 2001, when only 41 out of 3,003 complaints were adjudicated and only 19 upheld) the Campaign for Press and Broadcasting Freedom in evidence to the CSMC took a rather different view. This appalling 'wastage of complaints' was entirely in line with the record of the Press Council and PCC, which had 'never had the power to make their judgments stick'. Both had acted as 'little more than lightning conductors, taking the strain when press behaviour has provoked the public and politicians to despair'.[97]

The effectiveness of its non-adversarial conciliation techniques lies at the heart of the PCC's defence of self-regulation:

> The overwhelming majority of breaches of the Code are either the result of an oversight or mistake, or a professional decision made in good faith that falls on the wrong side of the line. It is very rare in the Commission's experience for journalists or editors deliberately to flout the rules . . . The question for the Commission is not how to achieve perfection but how to raise standards and how to deal with the breaches of the Code that will inevitably arise. Over the years, [the Commission] has developed a wide range of remedies. In the context of privacy intrusion, these include the removal of offending material from websites . . . the publication of apologies [and] undertakings about future conduct . . . In addition, following negotiation the Commission also sometimes secures *ex gratia* payments [or] donations to charity . . . Conciliated settlements such as these are popular because, in addition to them being meaningful, they are quicker to achieve either than formal rulings or certainly action through the courts . . . They are discreet and do not involve public argument . . . There is limited risk – there is not a 'winner takes all' outcome where the complainant may end up with nothing . . . The process is designed to be harmonious and to take the heat out of a situation.[98]

95 *Ibid.*, p. 9. For the full statistics, see the Table at HC 458 [12].

96 PCC, *Annual Review for 2007*, available online. There were 4,340 complaints (a 70% increase) in 2007, with 1,229 rulings, 822 investigations and 245 privacy rulings.

97 Campaign For Press and Broadcasting Freedom, Submission to the Culture Media and Sport Committee of the House of Commons in relation to their inquiry on 'Privacy and Media Intrusion' (7 February 2003).

98 PCC, Evidence, HC 375, pp. 16–20.

There will be times when conciliation is not appropriate. The publication may refuse to make an offer; the complaint may in the PCC's judgement involve 'an important matter of principle that requires amplification and publicity throughout the industry'. Should the complaint then be upheld on the basis of a formal adjudication, the PCC's power of sanction is triggered: the publication must print its criticisms, according to the Code, 'in full and with due prominence'. But what is the value of the word 'must' in a system without sanctions? And what amounts to 'due prominence' is a running sore in the system, despite a more generous attitude by editors since 2007. The litany of complaints also includes the 'opaque procedures' associated with conciliation and the absence of any substantive right of appeal or further review by (e.g.) an ombudsman.[99] This contrasts unfavourably with the FOI system discussed below.

The PCC has come to recognise the need to be more proactive or 'regulatory'; better to draw together the system's two functions in a sustained and focused control. While it has no powers of prior restraint, urging self-restraint on editors behind the scenes is now considered a vital aspect of the work, as is advice and assistance to those at the centre of high-profile stories. Time is also spent on self-promotion ('visibility'); training and education for the industry; and – of course –networking on the international plane; the PCC is a leading player in the Alliance of Independent Press Councils of Europe. Even so, this essentially complaints-based system remains vulnerable to the criticism of being structurally too limited. Where are the audit functions that a regulator would surely exercise?

Equally, the PCC is weak on accountability, partly because the courts, on the rare occasions when judicial review has been sought against the PCC, have proved reluctant to become involved. The *Anna Ford* case concerned a challenge by the well-known TV presenter after her complaint over publication of photographs of her and her partner on a public beach had been rejected (Code 3(ii), see p. 464 above). Assuming that the matter came within his jurisdiction, Silber J emphasised that the PCC should enjoy broad discretion when interpreting the words 'a reasonable expectation of privacy' in the Code. This standard judicial policy of light-touch review in the regulatory field is duly couched in the language of 'deference' – though it may of course owe something to the general weakness of the law relating to privacy:

> The type of balancing operation conducted by a specialist body, such as the Commission is still regarded as a field of activity to which the courts should and will defer. The Commission is a body whose membership and expertise makes it much better equipped than the courts to resolve the difficult exercise of balancing the conflicting rights of Ms. Ford . . . to privacy and of the newspapers to publish . . . So the threshold for interference by the courts is not low as it must be satisfied that it is not merely desirable but clearly desirable to do so.[100]

[99] J. Coad, 'The Press Complaints Commission: Are we safe in its hands?' (2005) 16 *Entertainment Law Review* 167.

[100] *R (Ford) v Press Complaints Commission* [2001] EWHC 683 Admin [28].

For its part, the PCC as chief agent of the self-regulatory system must not only pay heed to the many calls for a statutory privacy law but also carefully navigate the gap between a gently expansionary Strasbourg jurisprudence, a reluctant legislature and a judiciary unwilling to fill legislative gaps. Perhaps then it is not surprising to learn that, moving on from the Anna Ford imbroglio, the PCC is keener than ever to stress its role as 'protector of privacy'.[101]

Given its origins, the system may, in one sense, be accounted a huge success: effectively staving off statutory regulation for some two decades. Thus, reviewing the work of the PCC in 2003, the CMSC once more felt able to conclude that 'overall, standards of press behaviour, the Code, and the performance of the PCC have improved over the past decade'.[102] Elsewhere, however, the PCC has had a poor press, especially amongst lawyers. Robertson and Nicol feel that 'the PCC has failed to demonstrate many virtues in self-regulation. It has designed an ethical code which it declines to monitor, and its decisions are accorded a degree of cynicism, bordering on contempt, by editors.'[103] And the Campaign for Press and Broadcasting Freedom sees self-regulation as 'manifestly devised to protect the proprietors from independent regulation of standards':

> The most important problems with the PC and the PCC have related to their lack of independence. These bodies have relied almost exclusively since the early 1980s on monies from the newspaper proprietors. They have therefore never acted in a manner which is truly independent of the interests of those proprietors . . . [T]his lack of independence has been exhaustively documented. So too has the fundamental weakness of self regulation, that is the PCC's unwillingness to develop a system of penalties that will make its judgments meaningful. The Press Complaints Commission has survived because of the political power that the press wields and not because it is impossible to devise a workable alternative.[104]

Perhaps lawyers should look to the performance of their own profession, as Sir Stephen Sedley did recently in a highly critical review of the courts' performance in the areas both of privacy and defamation. He too thought statutory regulation essential. Appointing a regulator would have the effect of 'getting the inflationary and punitive elements out of the courts' which, he implied, having made a mess of actions for libel were 'now going to be trying actions, under whatever name, for invasion of privacy'. If it were empowered to impose penalties, a regulatory body would need to 'observe appropriate standards of due process' but this could be done without 'mimicking trial procedures':

[101] PCC, *Annual Review 2005*, p. 5.
[102] CMSC, HC 458, p. 3.
[103] Robertson and Nicol, *Media Law*, p. 676.
[104] CMSC, HC 458-ii, Annex 55.

> All one can safely say is that there is no serious case for preserving anything of the Press Complaints Commission, the industry's voluntary self-regulator, except its Code of Practice, which – as often happens – sets out admirable principles which the more aggressive of its subscribers seem to have very little difficulty in circumventing.[105]

Giving the watchdog more 'bite', such as a power to fine publications for breaches of the Code, would encourage a firmer line in the face of an industry driven by commercial considerations and be consistent with the recommendations of the Macrory review on regulatory sanctions generally (see p. 262 above). But this apparently modest reform goes to the very nature of the present system. Echoing recent controversy over the powers of ombudsmen, the PCC expressed its resolute opposition:

> Introducing the power to fine would in fact be significantly counter-productive . . . It would seriously undermine the Commission's main work as a dispute resolution service . . . At the moment, there are many borderline cases that are resolved to the complainant's satisfaction thanks to the goodwill of the editor because of the conciliatory nature of the system . . . Such cases would fall by the wayside . . . The worst features of a compensation culture would inevitably be imported, with lawyers coming between the complainant and the newspaper to prevent a speedy and common-sense resolution to a complaint in search of more money . . . The Commission's authority would be seriously undermined if a publication refused to pay a fine. Without legal powers to demand payment, the Commission would be powerless to act in such circumstances. With legal powers, the system would no longer be self-regulatory. The current structure would have to be dismantled.[106]

A recent CMSC report followed three scandals that cast grave doubt on the credentials of the press for self-regulation: the persistent harassment by photographers of Kate Middleton amidst speculation that an engagement to Prince William was about to be announced; the conviction and sentencing of Clive Goodman, a *News of the World* reporter, for conspiracy to intercept communications without lawful authority; and the release by the Information Commissioner of a list of publications employing journalists who had had dealings with a particular private investigator known to have obtained personal data by illegal means.[107] Not surprisingly in these circumstances, the report was highly critical of the press. Why then did it once again recommend retention of the present scheme?

> To draft a law defining a right to privacy which is both specific in its guidance but also flexible enough to apply fairly to each case which would be tested against it could be almost impossible. Many people would not want to seek redress through the law, for reasons of

[105] S. Sedley, 'Sex, libels and Video-surveillance', the Blackstone Lecture 2006, available online.
[106] PCC, Evidence, HC 458-ii.
[107] IC, *What Price Privacy?* HC 1056 (2005/6); *What Price Privacy Now?* HC 36 (2006/7).

> cost and risk. In any case, we are not persuaded that there is significant public support for a privacy law.
>
> We do not believe that there is a case for a statutory regulator for the press, which would represent a very dangerous interference with the freedom of the press. We continue to believe that statutory regulation of the press is a hallmark of authoritarianism and risks undermining democracy. We recommend that self-regulation should be retained for the press, while recognising that it must be seen to be effective if calls for statutory intervention are to be resisted.[108]

No doubt with relief, the PCC welcomed the 'numerous constructive comments and suggestions' contained within the report. No doubt gratefully, the Government agreed the report's conclusion that self-regulation of the press should be maintained. There was no case for statutory regulation. A free press is a 'hallmark of our democracy'.[109] So that's all right!

(d) Freedom of information: 'The full Monty'

Before the Act

Discussing transparency in Chapter 2, we described official secrecy as deeply embedded in our political culture. For nearly a century, government had been regulated by official secrets legislation, which put government firmly in control of what official information was released into the public arena.[110] Some concessions had been wrung from reluctant governments and a generally unwilling civil service over the years: some specific legislation gave rights of access, for example, to personal files, health and safety information and local government documents.[111] But the first real inroad on the culture of secrecy came through 'soft law' in the shape of the 1977 'Croham Directive', an internal civil-service instruction authorising publication of limited, factual materials, which significantly restricted policy matters and advice to ministers.[112]

John Major took a further step in the direction of openness to which he was personally committed but, for reasons of expense and because he had to compromise with Cabinet and civil service, chose to act through 'soft law'.[113] A White Paper published in 1993 proposed an informal Code of Practice on government information.[114] Asserting that 'Open Government is part of

[108] CMSC, *Self-regulation of the Press*, HC 375 (2006/7) [53–4].

[109] CMSC, *Self-regulation of the Press: Replies to the Committee's Seventh Report of Session 2006-07*, HC 1041 (2007/8).

[110] The Official Secrets Act 1911 and later Acts were revised by the Official Secrets Act 1989.

[111] See generally, P. Birkinshaw, *Freedom of Information*, 3rd edn (Cambridge University Press, 2001).

[112] See R. Austin, 'Freedom of information: The constitutional impact' in Jowell and Oliver (eds.), *The Changing Constitution*, 3rd edn (Clarendon Press, 1994).

[113] B. Worthy, 'John Major's information revolution? The Code of Access ten years on', Online Journal Of Open Government vol. 3, no. 1 (2007).

[114] *Open Government*, Cmnd 2290 (1993) [1.7].

an effective democracy', the White Paper tried to restrict access only where there were 'very good reasons for doing so'. It aimed at 'a more disciplined framework for publishing factual and analytical information about new policies, and reasons for administrative decisions'. The new Code[115] applied to all departments, agencies and authorities falling within the jurisdiction of the PCA. The Code was non-justiciable, though non-disclosure could be the subject of complaint to the PCA, causing Hazell to comment that the PCA was 'ill equipped to carry out a judicial function'.[116] One might equally argue that the PCA's investigatory procedure, his investigators' familiarity with civil service methods and attitudes and assured access to documents and files in practice made his office the most appropriate method of dispute resolution.

The scheme was dismissed by Birkinshaw as 'part of a wider conspiracy to protect secrecy', though he did admit elsewhere both that the arrangements had procedural advantages and that the PCA had set about this work in a 'spirited fashion'.[117] But although rejected as 'a last-ditch attempt' to forestall Freedom of Information legislation,[118] the soft law scheme was a sure sign that the climate of secrecy was, albeit slowly, thawing. It brought into the public domain much previously secret information. On the other hand, it contained a warning sign in the shape of a long list of protected areas.

A minor change was made to the PCA's normal competence: in freedom-of-information cases, to show that maladministration had caused injustice was unnecessary, it would be enough that information had not been given out in accordance with the Code.[119] Even so, the number of complaints was small: over the years 1994–2005, 208 complaints were investigated, of which 152 were at least partially upheld.[120] The PCA expressed disappointment at the public's minimal use of the new facility and surprise at the small use made by the press of the arrangements. The Select Committee blamed absence of publicity and delay on the PCA's part in investigating complaints;[121] the PCA blamed departments, which were 'sometimes unwilling to allow him to see the disputed information in the first place or to accept his verdict if he recommended that this information should be released: sometimes it was a case of both.'[122] The Office of Public Service, speaking for departments, retorted that most requests received a favourable response: of 2,600 requests received by

[115] *Open Government: Code of practice on access to government information*, 2nd edn (Cabinet Office, 1997).

[116] R. Hazell, 'Freedom of information: The implications for the Ombudsman' (1995) 73 *Pub. Admin.* 263.

[117] P. Birkinshaw, 'I only ask for information' [1993] *PL* 557, 563.

[118] R. Austin, 'The Freedom of Information Act 2000: A sheep in wolf's clothing?' in Jowell and Oliver (eds.), *The Changing Constitution*, 6th edn (2007), p. 404.

[119] Cmnd 2290 [4.19].

[120] PCA, *Access to Official Information: Monitoring of the non-statutory codes of practice 1994–2005*, HC 59 (2005/6), Annex 4.

[121] Select Committee on the PCA, *Open Government*, HC 84 (1995/6).

[122] PASC, *Your Right to Know: The government's proposals for a Freedom of Information Act*, Cm. 3818 (1997).

central government departments, only 89 had been rejected in whole and 21 in part.

By the year 2000, things had begun to change. Journalists had realised the Code's potential and MPs and campaigners had begun to use it. Conflicts arose. Things came to a head when the PCA (Sir Michael Buckley) clashed with the Home Office and Cabinet Office over their protracted refusals to provide information in two highly political cases. He had to issue a draft report saying that 'lack of co-operation from the two departments had effectively made it impossible for him to carry out his work properly' before the documentation was produced.[123] An inquiry by the Select Committee led to a truce, with the Cabinet Office signing a memorandum of understanding. This, according to the PCA, 'helped in general to produce a more consistent level of response from departments, [but] continued to fail to have much impact in those cases involving the politically sensitive areas of Ministerial interests and the Ministerial Code of Conduct'.[124]

The truce was short-lived. Ann Abraham, the new PCA, was soon mired in fresh conflict in a case involving the ministerial code of conduct and gifts to ministers. The Cabinet Office had delayed for nearly sixteen months to advise departments how to handle requests, finally advising them to refuse disclosure claiming exemption 12 of the Code (personal privacy).[125] Although the PCA disagreed, the Cabinet Office did not concede, making this the second case of refusal to release information in accordance with a PCA recommendation. Two further cases involving *The Guardian* newspaper followed, cover ministers' financial interests and the Attorney-General's advice on the legality of the Iraq war. On both occasions it was claimed that 'disclosure of that document or information, or of documents or information of that class, would be prejudicial to the safety of the state or otherwise contrary to the public interest' (s. 11(3) of the Parliamentary Commissioner Act 1967), resulting in the investigation being dropped (though on the first occasion the Government backed down, quashing the certificate in the face of a threatened judicial review).[126]

Surveying ten years' experience of FOI complaints, Ann Abraham concluded:

> During the decade or so of its existence the Code, and the Ombudsman's policing of it, resulted in a significant enlargement in the kind of information that was routinely released into the public domain . . . But it was not a smooth process and, although the Ombudsman frequently dragged departments to water, departments often showed a marked reluctance

[123] PCA, *Access to Official Information: Declarations made under the Ministerial Code of Conduct*, HC 353 (2001/2); PCA, *Investigations Completed February-April 2002*, HC 844 (2001/2).

[124] HC 59 (2005/6) [26]. And see PASC, *Ombudsman Issues: Third Report*, HC 448 (2002/3); Government Response, Cm. 5890 (2003).

[125] PCA, *Investigations Completed November 2002-June 2003*, HC 951 (2003/4), Case A/703.

[126] HC 59 (2005/6) [27].

> (or outright refusal) to drink. This manifested itself most noticeably through delays in responding to the Ombudsman; very often this was in response to statements of complaint and draft reports but sometimes showed itself in a refusal to even provide the Ombudsman with relevant papers.[127]

She warned of the implications for the statutory regime, now imminent. We were about to test a second, statutory model.

After the FOIA

Two modern statutes are relevant to access to information: the FOIA 2000 (below) and the Data Protection Act (DPA) 1998. The DPA governs the use and retention of personal information. It provides that information is processed 'fairly and lawfully' for specified purposes and not further processed or retained 'in any way that is incompatible with the original purpose'. The DPA is more extensive than the FOIA as it extends into the private sector, while the FOIA covers only public authorities as defined in the Act. Environmental information is covered by a different regime. The Aarhus Convention, to which the EU is a signatory, was implemented by an EU Directive and transposed into British law by the Environmental Information Regulations 2004.[128] The difference is significant. Exemptions from disclosure under Aarhus are narrower than those in the domestic FOIA. In Scotland too, where freedom of information is a devolved responsibility, the legislation passed by the Scottish Parliament in 2002 is in some ways more open than the FOIA.[129]

The role of Data Protection Commissioner under the 1998 Act is now combined with that of Information Commissioner (IC), who has the twin functions of promoting access to official information and protecting individuals. This dual role of promoting openness while at the same time ensuring privacy has been called 'a major contradiction at the heart of the [scheme].'[130] The IC believes, however, that the twin functions are compatible. Moreover, their combination is essential to a proper balancing of the two opposing values, more especially in the information age, which augments the risks and challenges.[131]

[127] *Ibid.* [34].

[128] Directive 2003/4/EC on public access to environmental information implemented by the Environmental Information Regulations, SI 2004/3391. And see the Aarhus Convention on Access to Information, Public Participation in Decision-Making and Access to Justice in Environmental Matters (25 June 1998) noted in P. Coppel, 'Environmental information: The new regime' [2005] *PL* 12.

[129] See Freedom of Information (Scotland) Act Environmental Information (Scotland) Regulations, SI 2004/520.

[130] HL Deb, col. 431 (25 October 2000) (Earl of Northesk).

[131] IC, *Annual Report for 2005/6*, p. 2. And see P. Kleve and R. de Mulder, 'Privacy protection and the right to information: In search of a new symbiosis in the information age', *Information Abstracting Privacy Law Journal* (2 June, 2008), available online.

Section 1 of the FOIA entitles any person making a request for information to a public authority:[132]

- to be informed in writing by the public authority whether it holds information of the description specified in the request, and
- if that is the case, to have that information communicated to him.

Applications must be made in writing or electronically (s. 8(1)) and an effort must be made to identify the information requested; 'fishing expeditions' are discouraged.

The FOIA imposes three different types of exemption from disclosure:

- absolute or 'class-based exemptions', such as the exception for security matters in s. 23
- public interest exemptions based on prejudice to the public interest, such as that in s. 36 for information likely to prejudice 'the effective conduct of public affairs'
- qualified exemptions subject to the *double* public interest test set out in s. 2(2)(b) that in all the circumstances of the case, the public interest in maintaining the exemption outweighs the public interest in disclosing the information.[133]

One constant user of access to information machinery, David Hencke of *The Guardian* newspaper, has called the Act 'a useful tool enabling our journalists to put into the public domain material which should indeed be there'.[134] In fact, the twenty or so exemptions from disclosure spelled out in the FOIA make this one of the world's more restrictive pieces of information legislation.[135]

The restrictive character of the scheme, the numerous exemptions, the prevailing civil-service 'culture of secrecy and partial disclosure' and the complex and occasionally obscure text of the Act all mean that decisions under the FOIA are highly likely to be contested. It has indeed been argued that disputes will escalate as the players learn how to manoeuvre within the rules.[136] And, as we shall see, the PCA's experience with ministerial certification has been repeated; a ministerial certificate can bar access and stands as 'conclusive

[132] For the purposes of the Act, a 'public authority' is an authority listed in Sch. 1 or designated by ministerial order made under s. 5 as exercising functions of a public nature or under contract; the term extends to publicly owned companies.

[133] See IC, *Awareness Guidance No. 3: The public interest test* (April, 2006).

[134] Quoted by the Constitution Committee, *Freedom of information: One year on*, HC 991 (2005/6) [9–10]. See also A. MacDonald, 'What hope for freedom of information legislation in the UK?' in Hood and Heald (eds.), *Transparency: The key to better governance?* (Oxford University Press, 2006), p. 143.

[135] Austin, 'The Freedom of Information Act 2000: A sheep in wolf's clothing?', p. 409. And see Constitution Unit, *Balancing the Public Interest: Applying the public interest test to exemptions in the UK Freedom of Information Act 2000* revised May, 2006, available online

[136] A. Roberts, 'Dashed expectations: Governmental adaptation to transparency rules' in Hood and Heald (eds.), *Transparency.*

evidence' of the fact that non-disclosure is 'required for the purpose of safeguarding national security'.[137] This provision in particular is unlikely to go unchallenged.

The IC is an independent Officer of the Crown directly answerable to Parliament. The second incumbent is Richard Thomas, a lawyer who has worked for the National Consumer Council and Office of Fair Trading. His office, funded by the Department for Constitutional Affairs, is best described as a multi-tasked regulatory public body; its work is 'more like an ombudsman on our Freedom of Information work and more like a regulator on the data protection work'. The IC takes his data-protection functions seriously, regularly commenting on plans for identity cards, plans to fingerprint all passengers using Heathrow airport and – all too frequently – on loss of data held by government departments. He has warned too of the dangers of 'sleepwalking into a surveillance society' as large and very vulnerable data banks are set up by national governments and made available to transnational bodies.[138] (The IC is our representative on the EU group of data supervisors).

The IC possesses rule-making functions, which take the shape of Codes of Practice for public authorities, on which he must be consulted by the Lord Chancellor (ss. 45 and 46 FOIA). Guidance may also be issued to public authorities and to data protection individuals and commercial concerns. To these rule-making powers are added investigatory functions with powers of entry and inspection and enforcement functions with powers of sanction. Enforcement powers to improve compliance with the Act include:

- power to issue decision notices
- 'good practice recommendations' where an authority's practices do not conform to the codes of practice
- 'information notices' requesting information to assist complaint investigations and (a sharp contrast here to the PCA)
- enforcement notices directing an authority to amend its practices.

If an authority fails to comply with a decision notice, it is enforceable as a contempt of court. After the episode when 35 million IR records went missing (see p. 79 above) the Government moved swiftly to enhance the IC's investigatory powers, empowering him 'to carry out inspections of organisations which collect and use personal information and to put in place new sanctions for the most serious breaches of data protection principles'. We need to question whether these roles are compatible with the IC's adjudicatory functions.

[137] Technically, under s. 53 FOIA, the certificate must come from a department's 'accountable person' but s. 8 ensures that this will be a Law Officer, Minister of the Crown or Welsh Assembly First Secretary.

[138] See ICO, Surveillance Studies Network, *A Report on the Surveillance Society: Full Report* (September 2006). And see now, Constitution Committee, *Surveillance: Citizens and the State*, HL 18 (2008/9).

(e) Handling complaints

The FOIA replaces complaint to the PCA (who retains competence in complaints about management of the Commissioner's office) by a new four-level complaints-handling system, a structure carefully chosen because 'systems supervised by a Commissioner can be operated with a greater degree of informality and more cheaply than can a system under which courts adjudicate':[139]

- Level 1 is a request to a department for internal review. This step, which is compulsory, has itself generated complaints of delays. Expressing itself as troubled and dissatisfied, the Commons Constitution Committee has welcomed the IC's commitment to put pressure on public authorities to complete internal reviews more quickly.[140]
- Level 2 is appeal to the IC, who may issue a decision notice stating that an authority has made a wrongful decision, or an enforcement notice, which is served on authorities that fail or decline to make a decision or refuse to comply with the IC's decisions. The notice must be reasoned and mention the right of appeal to the Information Tribunal (Level 3).
- Level 3 is the Information Tribunal (IT). The IT consists of a legally qualified chair with two lay members with expertise in the subject, representing the interests of applicants and public authorities. A separate National Security Appeals Panel hears appeals against 'ministerial override certificates'. The IT can conduct its proceedings on paper or, if requested, with a hearing. It may in the course of the hearing review the IC's findings of fact. This places the IC in an unusual and ambivalent position; he is at one and the same time the subject of the appeal and respondent in the proceedings. The IT may substitute a new decision notice for one that it finds to be unlawful, taking into consideration the public interest (s. 58 FOIA). As we shall see, it issues mandatory orders. Disobedience is a contempt of court.
- Level 4 is the High Court, which deals with appeals from the IT.

As the IT is *not* a complaints system, it cannot handle complaints about the IC's performance, of which there have been many.

A managerial (NPM) approach to evaluation of this system would be statistical: delays, throughput, compliance with targets and consumer satisfaction can all be measured and evaluated. Here the system would not score well. The FOIA came into force with a serious backlog of (data-protection) complaints for which the office was clearly unready; it was indeed thought that more than eight years might be needed to clear the backlog. After one year, witnesses were telling the Constitution Committee that some had 'waited months' for the IC to start investigating their complaints and felt too that the quality of

[139] J. Wadham and J. Griffiths, *Blackstone's Guide to the FOIA 2000*, 2nd edn (Oxford University Press, 2005), p. 129.

[140] HC 991 [20-4]. And see H. Brooke, 'The UK's openness watchdog lacks teeth and transparency', *Open Government, the Online Information Journal*, vol. 3, issue 1 (2005).

investigation and information provided in the decision notice were inadequate. Only 135 decision notices had been issued by an apparently reluctant IC (Elizabeth Filkin). The office of the IC was not itself open.

The IC apologised and introduced a new policy: only complaints where 'a useful purpose would be served' by a decision notice would in future be investigated, unless there were reasonable grounds to suspect deliberate wrongdoing or conduct requiring censure, the case involved principle, or 'it would be manifestly unreasonable in the particular circumstances not to proceed with the case'.[141] Note how a complaints-handling system can be flexible; a tribunal would find it hard to abandon trivial complaints in this way.

One year on again and things were perhaps improving. The annual workload remained high: almost 6,000 FOI complaints were received in 2006–7. Review now averaged eighteen days with 53% of FOI cases resolved within one month. Three hundred and thirty-nine decision notices (13% of cases) had been served and published. Perhaps more important, the Annual Report confirmed that the authority took remedial action in 78% of successful cases. But customer satisfaction was low, with only 42% of individuals recording satisfaction and there were ninety-two appeals to the IT. We should not read too much into these bare statistics, though they do lend tentative support to the view that the IC is in danger of being overwhelmed by complaints.

Two high-profile cases show how determined campaigners can use the new institutions to drag information into the public sphere. The first concerns attempts to view the Attorney-General's advice to the Government concerning the legality of the Iraq war.[142] We saw how a request for information and complaint to the PCA made under the Code of Practice was blocked by recourse to the security exemption in the Parliamentary Commissioner Act 1967. Once the FOIA was in force, campaigners could try again. They took their unsuccessful request for disclosure to the IC, who issued an enforcement notice to the Law Officers.[143] Once again, the Cabinet Office refused to disclose the Opinion and the case returned to the IC for a determination of 'the public interest'.

The IC summarised the Cabinet Office claim to exemption as a 'class claim'. It was based first on the need to be free to consider important and sensitive policy issues without inhibition and also on the importance of maintaining the convention of Cabinet collective responsibility. In a careful and thorough balancing exercise, the IC weighed the pros and cons of non-disclosure against his own chosen public-interest criteria in favour of publication and openness, which were:

- participation in public debate on issues of the day
- gravity and controversial nature of the subject matter
- accountability for government decisions

[141] IC, 'A robust approach to FOI complaint cases' (May 2006), available on IC website.
[142] See P. Sands, *Lawless World* (Allen Lane, 2005), p. 196 on legality.
[143] Enforcement Notice to Legal Secretariat of Law Officers (25 May 2006).

- transparency of decision making
- public government decisions

The IC ruled in favour of disclosure though he did add a caveat that disclosure would not necessarily set a precedent in respect of other Cabinet minutes. Perhaps controversially he added:

> The Commissioner considers that a decision on whether to take military action against another country is so important, that accountability for such decision making is paramount. Though not strictly relevant, acceptance by the current Prime Minister that decisions to go to war should ultimately be referred to Parliament reinforce arguments flowing from the gravity of subject matter.[144]

Amongst factors that the IC took into consideration were promoting accountability for their actions by public authorities and furthering understanding of and participation in 'issues of the day'. But were these factors truly present? The decision to make war had been discussed in every imaginable public forum, including the Hutton and Butler Inquiries (see p. 601 below) on which opponents of the war had pinned their hopes. What followed was a rudimentary proportionality test. It is at least arguable that the public interest in disclosure should not in the instant case have outweighed a public interest in Cabinet solidarity and free discussion; or, under the rubric of legal privilege, in fearless and frank legal advice from the Law Officers of the Crown.[145]

The second case is set against the background of allegations of abuse of MPs' allowances. We know from Chapter 2 that written, though non-justiciable, codes of practice now govern the behaviour of ministers, that the Committee on Standards in Public Life is now a standing committee, that there is a code of conduct for MPs and that a Parliamentary Commissioner for Standards (PCS) has been appointed. In the case of Derek Conway MP, the Committee on Standards and Privileges found a 'serious breach of the rules' in respect of payment of allowances to his son for work that had not been carried out. It recommended a ten-day suspension and demanding an apology to the House. It asked the PCS to investigate and published a wider report recommending to the House a new scheme for the employment of family members supported by a new register.[146]

The IC was now asked to investigate a set of cases where a request for details, including invoices, of expenditure by Tony Blair and other Members had been refused by the House of Commons.[147] The Speaker claimed that the

144 IC, Decision Notice of 19 February 2008, Ref FS50165372.

145 The Justice Secretary promptly issued a ministerial certificate vetoing publication: HC Deb., col. 153 (24 Feb. 2008). The Foreign Secretary subsequently confirmed an inquiry into the Iraq War: HC Deb., col. 312 (25 Mar. 2009).

146 CSP, *Conduct of Mr Derek Conway*, HC 280 (2007/8); CSP, *Employment of Family Members through the Staffing Allowance*, HC 436 (2007/8).

147 IC, Decision Notice, FS50083202 and FS50134623 (16 January 2008).

information was personal data protected by the DPA, that disclosure would be unfair and, because it involved publication of addresses, presented a security risk. The IC issued an Information Notice requiring the House to make the requested information available for his examination. Confirming that much of the information was covered by the DPA and acknowledging a right to some privacy, the IC's decision was that the House had 'failed to communicate to the complainant such of the information specified in his request as did not fall within any of the absolute exemptions from the right of access nor within any of the qualified exemptions under which the consideration of the public interest in accordance with s. 2 would authorise the House to refuse access'. He therefore required the House to disclose aggregate monthly sums including the number of staff members 'but excluding any reference to named staff members'. Instantly, the House of Commons appealed to the tribunal.

The IT held an oral hearing at which evidence was given on oath. Drawing on its own earlier precedents, it substituted a decision that 'all the information held by the House which falls within each complainant's request or requests must be disclosed to that complainant' subject to exceptions for sensitive personal data, which could be edited out. In the course of the judgment, the IT said:

> It is not our function to say what system ought to be operated by the House. But we cannot avoid making some assessment of the existing system, since we cannot decide the issues which are before us without arriving at a view on the effectiveness of the existing controls. The laxity of and lack of clarity in the rules for [Additional Claims Allowance] is redolent of a culture very different from that which exists in the commercial sphere or in most other public sector organisations today . . . Moreover the [published] information . . . does not match the system as actually administered, and hence as actually experienced by MPs. In our judgment these features, coupled with the very limited nature of the checks, constitute a recipe for confusion, inconsistency and the risk of misuse. Seen in relation to the public interest that public money should be, and be seen to be, properly spent, the ACA system is deeply unsatisfactory, and the shortfall both in transparency and in accountability is acute.[148]

A further appeal followed.[149] Scrutinising the tribunal judgment with approval, the High Court concluded that it could not interfere with its decision 'on the basis of what the appropriate outcome might be if the Tribunal were not addressing the deeply flawed system which the Tribunal believed had "so convincingly established" the necessity of full disclosure'. Not before time, and in the face of the High Court, the Speaker conceded. Nonetheless, the affair casts

[148] IT Appeals Nos. EA/2007/0060, 0061, 0062, 0063, 0122, 0123, 0131, *Corporate Officer of the House of Commons v Information Commissioner and Dan Leapman et al.*, on appeal from IC FS50070469, FS50051451, FS50079619, FS50124671, 26 February 2008, available online.

[149] *Corporate Officer of the House of Commons v Information Commissionerand Others* [2008] EWHC 1084 Admin.

light on the question we asked earlier concerning the combination posts of IC and DPC.

We would not of course wish to imply that the FOIA and its supporting machinery can be evaluated by its performance in a couple of high-profile cases. Some important questions are, however, raised. First and foremost we would put the extent of the IC's discretion. In the House of Lords debates on the FOIA, a speaker asked whether the IC would be 'bound by strict rules'.[150] There are no such rules, though guidance has, as we saw, been issued by the IC himself. Secondly, we asked if the dual role of IC and DPC creates a fundamental clash of interests. Typically, the cases show the IC having to balance conflicting interests in privacy and openness both of which he is supposed to represent. This must cast doubt on his objectivity; indeed, his own preferences are often obvious. Finally, we remarked on the IC's ambiguous status, describing the office as a regulatory agency with a complaints-handling capacity and adjudicative capacity. His adjudicative decisions are subject to a series of appeals. Otherwise, in common with many regulators, the IC is barely accountable; he is not like the PCA, a parliamentary officer, accountable to a select committee. This suggests structural defects with the multi-faceted model, which have not really been resolved.

5. Ombudsmania

The work of our first ombudsman, the PCA, is surveyed in Chapter 12. In this chapter, we want to look at the rapid spread of the ombudsman technique as a method of complaints-handling. The technique has established itself as a central component of administrative justice and ombudsmen have spread widely in the private sector.[151] Their inquisitorial and largely documentary procedure (though ombudsmen occasionally hold hearings) can help to resolve disputes informally in a quick and effective fashion. For the complainant, the ombudsman service is relatively trouble-free; all he has to do is complain. No expensive lawyers are necessary, no evidence has to be amassed, no case has to be proved; the ombudsman takes over control of the investigation. Ombudsmen normally have power to trawl through (government) documents and offices and question officials informally and the possible disadvantage that recommendations – never judgments – of public ombudsmen are not usually enforceable is offset by the fact that they are usually obeyed; some may even be indirectly enforceable on application to a court.[152] Private ombudsmen

150 HL Deb, col. 224 (14 November 2000) (Viscount Colville).

151 M. Seneviratne, *Ombudsmen Public Services and Administrative Justice* (Butterworths, 2002); M. Harris, 'The Ombudsman and administrative justice' in Harris and Partington (eds), *Administrative Justice in the 21st Century.*

152 As, e.g., with the Northern Ireland Commissioner for Complaints: see The Commissioner for Complaints (Northern Ireland) Order 1996, SI No. 1297/1996 (NI 7); The Public Services Ombudsman (Wales) Act 2005. The Widdecombe Report, *The Conduct of Local Authority Business*, Cmnd 9800 (1986) recommended similar powers for the CLA in England and Wales.

operate in a framework of self-regulation and, like the PCC, are responsible to the industries which set them up and fund them. The schemes are usually contractual with the terms contained in a Code of Practice and operate as an 'alternative' to courts. The fact that a complainant could go to court is therefore not a bar to an ombudsman investigation as it is with most public ombudsmen. Again, public-sector ombudsmen investigate maladministration, while some private-sector schemes allow their ombudsman to look at the merits of a decision as well as the way in which it was taken. The decisions of private ombudsmen may, for contractual reasons, be binding on the body against which the complaint has been made.

The reader will not be surprised to learn that there is little rhyme or reason in the existing system; it just 'growed up'. A Health Services Commissioner (HSC) was appointed in 1973, an office today held by the PCA;[153] in 1974, a local ombudsman service, the CLA, was appointed on a three-member regional basis.[154] The ombudsman idea was taking off. Today there are ombudsmen for Scotland and Wales, where the systems were rationalised on devolution,[155] and Northern Ireland has several ombudsmen. There are ombudsmen for prisons and probation. Statutory ombudsmen have been created for financial and legal services, replacing previous self-regulatory systems.[156] A Pensions Ombudsman was installed by the Social Security Act 1990. Ombudsmen have also spread widely in the private sector, with ombudsmen for building societies, estate agents and many more, achieving wide acceptance and popularity as an all-purpose complaints-handling technique.[157] To help complainants through the maze, the British and Irish Ombudsmen Association (BIOA) lists hundreds of ombudsmen and other complaint-handling bodies who may be able to help with complaints. Nonetheless, citizens find it hard to navigate.

There are other strong reasons for rationalisation, as recommended by the Colcutt report in 2000.[158] The split competences leave cracks into which complaints may fall. In the notorious Balchin case, for example, Mr and Mrs Balchin complained of maladministration by the DoT in confirming road orders in respect of a bypass without seeking an assurance from Norfolk

[153] National Health Service (Reorganisation) Act 1973. The Health Service Commissioners Act 1993 consolidates the legislation governing the three separate health service ombudsmen for England, Scotland and Wales.

[154] Local Government Act 1974 now updated and replaced by the Local Government and Public Involvement in Health Act 2007.

[155] Scottish Public Services Ombudsman Act 2002; Public Services Ombudsman (Wales) Act 2005; M. Seviratne, 'A new Ombudsman system for Wales' [2006] *PL* 6.

[156] The Financial Ombudsman Service, set up by the Financial Services and Markets Act 2000, combines ombudsman services for banking, insurance, personal pensions and private finance. For legal services, see ss. 21-6 of the Courts and Legal Services Act 1990; R. James and M. Seneviratne, 'The Legal Services Ombudsman: Form versus function?' (1995) 58 *MLR* 187.

[157] R. James, *Private Ombudsmen and Public Law* (Ashgate Publishing, 1997).

[158] *Review of the Public Sector Ombudsmen in England: A Report by the Cabinet Office* (HMSO, 2000). And see M Elliott, 'Asymmetric devolution and ombudsman reform in England' [2006] *PL* 84.

County Council that they would be given adequate compensation for the impact of the bypass on their home. They approached the CLA but the CLA declined competence. Three successive PCA reports followed, each of which was successfully reviewed by the High Court.[159] Finally, investigations run in parallel by the two ombudsmen services produced an apology and compensation for events that went back nearly twenty years. The unhappy saga led the PCA to comment in her fourth report on the problems caused by cases that crossed more than one Ombudsman jurisdiction:

> Whilst the Local Government Ombudsman and I have collaborated closely throughout our respective investigations, the restrictions on our ability to work together have nevertheless meant that we have not been able to provide the sort of fully-joined up and coherent service for Mr and Mrs Balchin that we should be able to provide to all citizens who have such complaints.[160]

The new legislation advised by Colcutt has never been forthcoming, though the problem has been to a limited extent alleviated by a Regulatory Reform Order.[161]

One would perhaps assume that ombudsman systems were not amenable to judicial review. They are, after all, an alternative mode of dispute resolution based on inquisitorial procedure and accountable to democratically elected bodies. But there has in fact been a creeping spread of judicial review, with courts showing themselves increasingly willing to review procedures and lay down conditions for exercise of the discretionary powers to investigate.[162] Typically, the challenges ask for compliance with the rules of natural justice established by the courts in judicial review – a further illustration of the strength of the common law, adversarial template. In *Seifert and Lynch*, for example, a finding of maladministration by the Pensions Ombudsman was attacked on the grounds that a relevant letter had not been disclosed to the applicants who had therefore had no opportunity to comment on it. It was held that the PO must follow not only the statutory procedure but also the rules of natural justice. In justification, Lightman J explained:

> A determination by the ombudsman can damage or destroy reputations, as well as impose financial penalties . . . It is not open to the ombudsman to make a determination save in

159 *R (Balchin and Others) v Parliamentary Commissioner for Administration* [1996] EWHC Admin 152; [1999] EWHC Admin 484.

160 PCA, *Redress in the Round: Remedying maladministration in central and local government*, Case No. C.57/94 (2005).

161 Regulatory Reform (Collaboration etc. between Ombudsmen) Order 2007 (SI 2007/1889). Around 10 joint inquiries have since been started.

162 E.g., *R v Local Commissioner for Administration, ex p. Bradford MCC* [1979] QB 287; *R v Local Commissioner for Administration, ex p. Eastleigh Borough Council* [1988] QB 855; *R v Local Commissioner for Administration ex p. Croydon London Borough Council* [1989] 1 All ER 1033.

> respect of the allegations in the complaint . . . of which he has given notice to the appellants. It is highly desirable that the ombudsman, rather than simply transmitting copies of his correspondence with the complainant, (save in simple and obvious cases) expresses in his own words in plain and simple language what he perceives to be the substance of the allegation . . . The respondents must know at least the gist of what he has learnt, so as to enable them to have a fair crack of the whip and a fair opportunity to provide any answer they may have. Whilst the procedure before the ombudsman is intended to be quick, inexpensive and informal, these are the minimum requirements for fairness and accordingly for a decision that can be allowed to stand.[163]

We return to ombudsmen in Chapter 12.

6. Administrative justice?

The traditional top-down view of courts as the standard machinery for dispute-resolution within the state, and tribunals as court substitutes, had certain advantages. It helped to control numbers: litigation is costly and slow and requires persistence – a paradigm rationing device though a cause of concern to the access to justice movement. Perhaps more important, clashes of values were largely avoided. It was surely reasonable, if tribunals were court substitutes, to submit them to trial-type procedures and require due process principles to be observed.

The new bottom-up approach of administrative lawyers has spawned a new discipline, which acknowledges no strict distinction between administration and adjudication but embraces within its frontiers 'all official decision-taking procedures which directly affect the individual citizen'.[164] This already broad remit is complicated by the view of administrative justice as a set of values, which far exceed the simple Franks formula of openness, fairness and impartiality. There is a set of public-service standards culled from the Citizen's Charter: information and openness, choice and consultation, courtesy and helpfulness, putting things right and value for money. There are modern good-governance values such as confidentiality, transparency, secrecy, fairness, efficiency, accountability, consistency, participation rationality, equity and equal treatment. There is the ever-extending catalogue of human rights. These often conflicting values set an impossibly wide agenda.

The 'complaints-are-gifts' ideology of contemporary public administration has brought into view a plethora of new material for administrative lawyers to work on. This has arguably resulted in blurring an important line between *disputes* – the traditional stuff of administrative law – and the *grievances*, complaints, gripes, grumbles, moans, comments and observations which belong on the other side of the line. This in turn blurs a second distinction between

163 *Seifert and Lynch v Pensions Ombudsman* [1997] 1 All ER 214.

164 M. Partington, 'Restructuring administrative justice? The redress of citizens' grievances' (1999) 52 *Current Legal Problems* 173, from which the list of values in the text is taken.

the 'redress mechanisms' that come into play when someone unhappy with the outcome of a decision seeks to challenge it, and the view that administrative justice starts at the bottom with primary decision-making. On this view, fairness could be premised (as both Mashaw and Adler argue) on one of several models. Staff training, standard-setting, audit – all the machinery of NPM – would be more important than due-process values.The most appropriate form of dispute-resolution would likely be internal review and/or an ombudsman, rather than a tribunal or court. This divergence of goals is summed up in the idea of proportionate dispute resolution.

PDR is, according to the present government, a flexible vision of administrative justice, which aims at better ground floor decision-making and early and appropriate advice to minimise the risk of legal problems. The Government aims to:

- promote the development of a range of tailored dispute resolution services, so that different types of dispute can be resolved fairly, quickly, efficiently and effectively without recourse to the expense and formality of courts and tribunals where this is not necessary
- but also deliver cost-effective court and tribunal services, that are better targeted on those cases where a hearing is the best option for resolving the dispute or enforcing the outcome.[165]

The institutions, processes and procedures that we have studied in this chapter do not suggest that this is happening. Choice and allocation of machinery is random, encouraging the growth of a complaints industry and culture that, the NAO suggests, absorbs an inordinate amount of public expenditure – perhaps as much as £830 million annually.[166] There are issues as to coherence. Either the systems are too fragmented or, if joined up, as with the Information and Data Protection Commissioners, overloaded. Could the outcome be more rational? Yes, but only if disputes were more restrictively defined.

Towards the end of her speech made at the launch of the AJTC, Ann Abraham described administrative justice as lying at the heart of the compact between citizens and their administration:

> It is after all in the daily encounters between citizen and state that most people experience the Executive at first hand. It is in those encounters that most people get a sense of the sort of administration they are dealing with. It is in the quality of those encounters that most people either detect, or more often fail to detect, signs that they are viewed by the state as persons not cogs, citizens not ciphers.[167]

[165] *Transforming Public Services: Complaints, redress and tribunals*, Cm. 6243 (2004), p. 6.

[166] LSE Public Policy Group, Evidence to PASC: PASC, *From Citizen's Charter to Public Service Guarantees*.

[167] PCA, Speech at the launch of the AJTC (20 November 2007).

Like the PCA, the Administrative Justice and Tribunals Council, whose work we describe in the next chapter, sees improvements in the area of administrative justice as crucial to good governance.[168] They 'serve to strengthen the compact between the citizen and the state by helping to entrench principles of fairness and transparency in relationships between decision makers and those whose interests they serve'. The Administrative Justice and Tribunals Council welcomes the idea of a 'right' to administrative justice. PASC too has welcomed the news that the Ministry of Justice is considering administrative justice as a 'candidate for inclusion in a British Bill of Rights':

> The right to fair and just administrative action is arguably one of the common law's greatest achievements, and in other countries which have recently adopted a Bill of Rights it has been accorded constitutional status . . . **We agree that this right is a strong candidate for inclusion in a UK Bill of Rights as a nationally distinctive right.**[169]

[168] AJTC, *Annual Report for 2007/8*, available online.

[169] PASC, *A Bill of Rights for the UK?* HC 165 (2007/8) [128]. Ministry of Justice, *Rights and Responsibilities: Developing our constitutional framework* (Cm 7577, 2009) [3.39–3.46].

11

Tribunals in transition

Contents

In Chapter 10, we introduced the topic of administrative justice, adopting a bottom-up approach. We considered ways of resolving disputes without resort to the formal machinery of tribunals and courts. The commonly held view of tribunals as court substitutes was recorded but never unpacked. It is now time to consider this view more carefully and look more closely at the evolution of tribunals. They have moved a long way from humble beginnings to the place they occupy today as the standard machinery for alternative dispute resolution in administrative law. Situated near the top of the pyramid, they now possess their own integrated tribunals service and, at appellate level, stand in near proximity to the courts. We shall see that procedures have also converged, with courts becoming more flexible after Lord Woolf's review of civil procedure and tribunals becoming more formal. The Tribunals, Courts and Enforcement Act 2007 (TCEA) sees a partial assimilation of the two adjudicative systems,

Table 11.1 Cases disposed of annually by selected Tribunal Service tribunals[1]

	2005–6	2006–7	2007–8
Social Security and Child Support Appeals (SSCSA)	262,857	254344	256,565
Mental Health Review	10,420	18,851	19,500
Commissioners Office (TCO) (income tax)	5,523	5,689	5,807
Asylum and Immigration Tribunal (AIT)	114,692	166,191	161,538
All Tribunal Service tribunals	497,485	566,461	548,592

representing, we shall argue, a final acknowledgment of the position of tribunals as court substitutes.

Without tribunals, the court system would quite simply break down and machinery for alternative dispute resolution would need to be heavily augmented. As Table 11.1 shows, some tribunals handle very large case loads. The combined total of enquiries addressed to the Parliamentary Commissioner for Administration (PCA) and Health Services Commissioner (see Chapter 12) averages 12,000 annually, of which around 1,000 are accepted for investigation. The load of the Commission for Local Administration is larger, averaging 18,000 complaints annually, of which in the region of 90 per cent are determined. County courts, perhaps the nearest comparator, registered over 2 million cases in 2007 and proceeded to 18,400 trials with 53,200 small-claims hearings. Employment tribunals (which are not strictly speaking 'administrative' tribunals) disposed of over 107,000 cases in 2006–7 alone. Over seventy separate sets of tribunals were then in operation, hearing around six times as many cases as courts.

In this chapter, we shall trace the evolution of administrative tribunals, using social security and immigration tribunals as illustrative of our main themes. We do not pretend that the two sets of tribunals are 'typical' or, indeed, that 'one size fits all' in the tribunal context. There is a wide diversity and range of tribunals, making them hard to classify or sort. We try nonetheless to answer some of the questions about the utility of tribunals for dispute resolution and the appropriateness of the traditional, adversarial model in the contemporary setting. In recent years, we shall see that oral hearings and lay members (like the traditional jury system) have come under threat from a more managerial model of dispute resolution – Mashaw's model of bureaucratic justice. This 'new public management' angle on dispute resolution is increasingly prevalent within government departments preoccupied with cost and efficiency and underlies the current interest in proportionate dispute resolution (PDR). In certain areas, a move away from judicialisation has been triggered. Thus we find the Council

[1] Table adapted from *Tribunals Service Annual Reports, 2006–7, 2007–8.*

on Tribunals, the tribunals watchdog, repackaged as the Administrative Justice and Tribunals Council (AJTC), marking its wider mandate to review the whole field of administrative justice with special emphasis on PDR. Alongside, tribunals are being bypassed by new innovative systems. Later in the chapter we look briefly at the Social Fund Inspectorate, a prototype of modern 'inspectorial justice' but harking back to the time when the dispute-resolution function was a stage in the decision-making process given, as Stebbings tells us, 'to the implementing bodies themselves' (see p. 439 above).

1. Franks and after: Establishing values

Many of the characteristics of the contemporary tribunal system can be traced to Franks. Its first and most significant legacy was the finding that 'tribunals should properly be regarded as machinery provided by Parliament for adjudication rather than as part of the machinery of administration'.[2] This conclusion, a marked chang e from the previous view of tribunals as a stage in the administrative process,[3] was by no means inevitable. As Richardson and Genn have recently noted, 'Tribunals do not have to lie within the judicial arm of government with all the necessity for independence that that involves. In Australia, they are seen as part of the executive. But in the United Kingdom the judicial model is firmly entrenched.'[4] As we shall see, the 'entrenchment' is very recent and still incomplete. Not until the Leggatt review of the tribunal system in 2001[5] was a unitary tribunals system seriously contemplated, let alone one that took the administration of tribunals away from their sponsoring central government departments, many of which (and notably the Home Office) hotly opposed change.

In practice, tribunals still occupy very different positions in decision-making chains. Some, like the Information Commissioner discussed in the previous chapter, or the Civil Aviation Authority (CAA), which has the duty of granting operating, route and air transport licences as well as air operator's certificates, possess a combination of regulatory and adjudicative functions. The CAA's licensing functions may or may not be classified as adjudicative. The procedures, set out in regulations, permit the CAA to hold hearings and provide for representation from interested parties, which points to an adjudicative function; that appeal lies to a government minister[6] points in the contrary direction. In contrast, the Independent Appeals Service (AS) (now incorporated into the Tribunal Service) is, in Ison's terms (see p. 443 above), a third-level

[2] *Report of the Committee on Tribunals and Inquiries*, Cmnd 218 (1957) (hereafter 'Franks') [40].

[3] See the discussion of Robson's *Justice and Administrative Law* at p. 440 above.

[4] G. Richardson and H. Genn, 'Tribunals in transition: Resolution or adjudication?' [2007] *PL* 116. The difference has constitutional origins and it should not be assumed that the Australian Administrative Appeals Tribunal lacks independence.

[5] Sir Andrew Leggatt, *Tribunals for Users: One system, one service* (HMSO, 2001) (hereafter Leggatt). Many years earlier, the move had been recommended in a study by J. Farmer, *Tribunals and Government* (Weidenfeld and Nicolson, 1974).

[6] See the Licensing of Air Carriers Regulations 1992, SI 2292/1992 made under the authority of the Civil Aviation Act 1982.

complaints-handling body responsible for appeals on decisions on social-security matters, including disability, child support and vaccine damage, after a second-level internal review. It stresses its *independent* status while at the same time describing itself as an 'executive agency of the Ministry of Justice'.

The primary legacy of Franks was its chosen mantra of 'openness, impartiality and fairness',[7] keywords that have dominated every subsequent major reconsideration of administrative justice. They have also helped to set in place a model of adjudication in which independence and impartiality are intertwined. Impartiality is not the same thing as independence, though the two are often in practice confused. Baroness Hale sees independence as *institutional* and related to the structural framework of the adjudicative machinery; impartiality, on the other hand, is *functional* and refers to the adjudicator's approach to his task.[8] Impartiality can (as we shall see is the case with the Social Fund Inspectorate) be achieved without institutional independence, though the latter helps 'to maintain a distance between the decision-maker and both the subject-matter of the dispute and the personalities involved, and in that sense can be seen as instrumental to achieving impartiality and hence good outcomes'.[9] The tendency to conflate the two values was already visible in Franks, which said:

> In the field of tribunals openness appears to us to require the publicity of proceedings and knowledge of the essential reasoning underlying the decision; fairness to require the adoption of a clear procedure which enables parties to know their rights, to present their case fully and to know the case which they have to meet; and impartiality to require the freedom of tribunals from the influence, real or apparent of departments concerned with the subject-matter of their decisions.[10]

In this way, Franks helped to initiate debate on structural independence for tribunals, a demand reinforced after the introduction of the Human Rights Act (HRA) by the growing impact of ECHR Art. 6(1) (see Chapter 14). The debate culminated in the Leggatt review and TCEA, which formally links tribunals for the first time to the court service. Franks failed, however, to establish any principled reason for deciding *when* a specific administrative or ministerial decision required reference to a tribunal or court or indeed whether the reference should be to a court or tribunal, commenting only that, in the absence of 'special considerations', courts, not tribunals, should adjudicate. It left the critical question wide open, focusing on the existing system. It also recommended a new 'tribunals watchdog', the Council on Tribunals, with powers to tackle questions of allocation. In fact, successive governments prevented the Council from fulfilling this

[7] Franks [41].

[8] *Gillies v Work and Pensions Secretary* [2006] UKHL 2 [38]. The question is further discussed in the context of procedural justice below.

[9] *Gillies* [121].

[10] Franks [42].

role.[11] But the Council did provide an ongoing stimulus for reform, even though never empowered to operate in the regulatory manner envisaged by Franks.

By an application of the procedural values of openness, impartiality and fairness, Franks aimed to push tribunals closer towards the common law adjudicative ideal-type. Some of the modifications it recommended (such as the duty to give reasons on request) were incorporated in the Tribunals and Inquiries Act 1958, while others (such as the opening-up of hearings to the public) required no more than secondary legislation or administrative action. Although not every recommendation was accepted, a measure of judicialisation was achieved and as tribunals were slowly remade in the image of the ordinary courts, it became more possible to view them merely as 'court substitutes' – a utility court model selected because they provided 'simpler, speedier, cheaper and more accessible justice'.[12] Only recently has this model come under fire.

Franks opened the way for a judicialisation of tribunal procedure, based on the trial-type model: in other words, the oral and adversarial procedures of the 'ordinary courts'. It envisaged legally qualified chairmen; 'orderly' procedures; public hearings; full reasons to be given for decisions; developed systems of precedent; and more. A right to legal representation and extension of the provision of legal aid was also recommended. This, however, has never been fully implemented. Legal aid remains exceptional in tribunals and an ongoing battle surrounds it.[13] There is much research to show that appellants find it hard to represent themselves, tend to take any opportunity (such as legal aid or community legal services) to secure representation, and do very much better when represented. This is especially true of immigration tribunals, whose users may speak little English and be unfamiliar not only with asylum law but also with the legal and administrative system generally. An important survey by Genn and Genn[14] found that most immigrants obtained information about their right of appeal direct from the immigration service, while a second study showed 'considerable problems with information about rights and procedures as well as difficulties with language and literacy. It is likely that some of these barriers apply equally to other types of immigration appeal.'[15] There is correspondingly little evidence to support Leggatt's view that 'the vast majority

[11] Franks [30]. See for discussion the JUSTICE–All Souls Review, *Administrative Justice: Some necessary reforms* (Clarendon Press, 1988) (hereafter JUSTICE–All Souls), Ch. 9.

[12] H.W.R. Wade and C. Forsyth, *Administrative Law* (Oxford University Press) 2004, p. 884. And see H. Genn and G. Richardson (eds.), *Administrative Law and Government Action: The courts and alternative mechanisms of review* (Clarendon Press, 1994).

[13] See JUSTICE–All Souls [9.29–38]; Legal Action Group, *Justice: Redressing the balance* (LAG, 1997) 70–4; Council on Tribunals, *Review of Tribunals: The Council's response* (September, 2000) [28–32]. Legal representation is not available in all tribunals and its extent varies considerably: see Table I in M. Adler and J. Gulland, *Tribunal Users' Experiences, Perceptions and Expectations: A literature review* (November 2003); P. Draycott and S. Hynes, *Extending Legal Aid To Tribunals*, Legal Action Special Feature (June 2007).

[14] H. Genn and Y. Genn, *The Effectiveness of Representation at Tribunals* (HMSO, 1989).

[15] Adler and Gulland, *Tribunal Users' Experiences, Perceptions and Expectations*, citing Gelsthorpe *et al.*, *Family Visitor Appeals: An evaluation of the decision to appeal and disparities in success rates by appeal type*, (Home Office Online Report 26/03, 2003).

of appellants' could be enabled by its proposed reforms (below) 'to put their cases properly themselves'. In the present era of retrenchment, however, no substantial new entitlements to legal aid are likely to be conceded.[16]

Judicialisation from within was accompanied by judicialisation from without; tribunals were for supervisory purposes to come under the rule of the 'ordinary courts'. Franks recommended one full appeal from all tribunal decisions and a statutory right of appeal on a point of law from most tribunals. Ouster clauses were to be cut back, a recommendation generally respected, and judicial review should always be available. By requiring reasoned decisions, Franks believed it would be giving the courts a record on which effective judicial review could be based. Today, these measures are generally taken for granted and judicial control of tribunals is, as we shall see, routinely asserted. To Lord Woolf indeed, tribunals were 'a third tier' in the administration of civil justice,[17] a level that has since been outstripped.

We should not be too ready, however, to accept the stereotype of tribunals as court substitutes. Some, notably employment tribunals, are genuinely so, in the sense that they offer a state-funded service for the resolution of disputes between citizens: in the case of employment tribunals, employers and employees. If we ask why these bodies remain within the tribunal system and are not simply relabelled 'Employment Courts', the answer would come back from users and their representatives that tribunals, with their lay members, are more accessible and less frightening than courts. They are, in other words, prized for qualities that *differentiate* a tribunal from a court hearing. The qualities of cheapness, speed, accessibility and informality with which we have seen tribunals credited are not, in short, simply managerial virtues; they make a positive contribution to proportionate dispute resolution.[18] Speed and cheapness are qualities in principle achievable by any good adjudication or complaints-handling system, including (in Lord Woolf's authoritative opinion) courts.[19] Tribunals have other features that help to make them user-friendly. Professor Bell, for example, emphasised the *participatory* nature of tribunal hearings. This she thought helped to 'foster civic competence, personal responsibility and active involvement rather than over-dependency on professionals and a belief that people are not able to cope'.[20] If this is so, it is partly due to the *oral* character of proceedings; equally important, however, is the presence of *lay members* on tribunals, normally 'representative' of the two parties to the

[16] The White Paper, *Transforming Public Services*, Cm. 6243 (2004) stated that the 'blanket availability of legal aid is unnecessary' [10.3] [10.14] and that current provision through the Community Legal Service 'is about right' [10.15].

[17] Lord Woolf, *Access to Justice* (Lord Chancellor's Department, 1996).

[18] M. Partington, 'Restructuring administrative justice? The redress of citizens' grievances' (1999) 52 *Current Legal Problems* 173. And see R Creyke, 'The special place of tribunals in the system of justice: How can tribunals make a difference?' (2004) 15 *Public Law Review* 220.

[19] Lord Woolf, *Access to Justice*.

[20] K. Bell, 'Social security tribunals: A general perspective' (1982) 33 *NILQ* 132, 147. And see J. Mashaw, 'Administrative Due Process: The Quest for a Dignitary Theory' (1981) 61 *Boston University Law Rev.* 885.

dispute. On the other hand, as the process of juridification noted in Chapters 4 and 5 makes the body of law with which tribunals have to deal steadily more complex, so professional help and advice become more necessary, at one and the same time strengthening the case for legal aid in tribunals and undercutting the case for lay members.

2. Tribunals for users

Leggatt fastened on *participation* as one of three linked principles that should govern the allocation of decisions to tribunals, the other two being *accessibility* to users and the need for special *expertise*. Accepting the popular belief (which has never been properly tested) that tribunals are more accessible than courts, Leggatt thought that 'a tribunal route, rather than redress in the courts, should be the normal option in the interests of accessibility'.[21] There must be 'strong specific arguments' if no appeal was to be provided and recourse left only to judicial review, a route that was 'expensive and difficult for the unassisted'. But Leggatt gave accessibility an unusual meaning, defining it in terms of informality and linking the three qualities of participation, accessibility and expertise:

Participation

First, the widest common theme in current tribunals is the aim that users should be able to prepare and present their own cases effectively, if helped by good-quality, imaginatively presented information, and by expert procedural help from tribunal staff and substantive assistance from advice services. We think the element of direct participation is particularly important in the field of disputes between the citizen and the state. We have found, however, that in almost all areas the decision-making processes, and the administrative support which underlies them, do not meet the peculiar challenges the overall aim imposes. We propose a programme of reform which should enable users to play their part better. The use of tribunals to decide disputes should be considered when the factual and legal issues raised by the majority of cases to be brought under proposed legislation are unlikely to be so complex as to prevent users from preparing their own cases and presenting them to the tribunal themselves, if properly helped.[22]

With the post-Leggatt emphasis on 'tribunals for users', came a greater interest in the special qualities that help to make tribunals user-friendly. Thanks to the 'bottom-up' theories of complaints-handling discussed in the previous chapter, we are beginning to have at our disposal a body of empirical research that helps to bring users into the picture.[23] Research suggests that lay members may play a

[21] Leggatt [1.13].

[22] Leggatt [1.11].

[23] The most significant recent studies are collected in a literature review by M. Partington *et al.*, *Empirical Research on Tribunals: An annotated review of research published between 1992 and 2007* (AJTC, 2007) available online. See also Adler and Gulland, *Tribunal Users' Experiences, Perceptions and Expectations.*

special role in the case of ethnic minorities and that increasing the ethnic diversity of tribunal panels (not necessarily a simple thing to do) might have a positive effect on their perceptions of fairness.[24] This is a point to bear in mind when considering the rapid legalisation of immigration tribunals (see p. 514 below).

We know that tribunal-users are concerned with speed, accessibility, anticipated cost and complexity. Their main concern is, however, with fairness. Users, about half of whom are unrepresented, really do appreciate an opportunity to participate by putting their case. They expect to be listened to, have their views considered and have a real opportunity to influence the outcome. But users are apparently more concerned with impartiality than structural independence, believing that the decision-maker should have an open mind, deal with their case in a neutral, even-handed way and treat them courteously and with respect.[25] These are, as we saw in the last chapter, qualities beginning to be expected of everyone who handles complaints or who makes individuated decisions, whether they work as administrators or adjudicators.

(a) Members and 'expertise'

Leggatt, which consulted specifically on the issue, heard from users that 'the presence of people without an obviously expert qualification helped some users cope with the stressful experience of appearing before a tribunal' and made it easier 'for at least some users to present their cases'. Leggatt concluded that tribunals permitted decisions to be reached 'by a panel of people with a range of qualifications and expertise'; tribunal members who were themselves disabled were thought, for example, to make a major contribution to disability appeals tribunals.[26] This, however, is to confuse personal experience with expertise, giving that term a perverse meaning. Admittedly personal experience is something for which tribunals may be valued, especially perhaps in social security tribunals; it is decidedly not the sort of professional expertise that one would wish for in a tribunal dealing with, for example, aviation safety. Nor is it what Wade was thinking of when he said:

> Specialised tribunals can deal both more expertly and more rapidly with special classes of cases, whereas in the High Court counsel may take a day or more to explain to the judge how some statutory scheme is designed to operate . . . Where there is a continuous flow of claims for a particular class, there is every advantage in a specialised jurisdiction.[27]

This sounds more like the Lands Tribunal, composed equally of lawyers and surveyors, which sits to hear disputes over land valuation. These 'tend to be

[24] H. Genn *et al.*, *Tribunals for Diverse Users*, DCA research series (HMSO, 2006).

[25] *Ibid.*, Ch. 6.

[26] Leggatt [1.12] [7.19].

[27] Wade and Forsyth, *Administrative Law*, pp. 906–7. See also R. Sainsbury and H. Genn, 'Lessons from tribunals' in Cranston and Zuckerman (eds.), *The Woolf Report Reviewed* (Clarendon Press, 1995), p. 426.

legally and factually complex' and legal representation is the norm. The Lands Tribunal has actually received criticism because its 'comparatively formal and adversarial' proceedings have failed to take on board the Woolf changes to civil procedure.[28] Again, in Mental Health Review Tribunals, responsible for hearing applications for release from people detained under the Mental Health Act 1983, a medically qualified practitioner, in practice a psychiatrist, must be appointed in addition to one legally qualified and one lay member for each hearing. The psychiatrist makes a preliminary examination of the applicant.[29]

In the consultation paper on the new tribunal structure,[30] 'expertise' and 'experience' were again conflated. The proposal was 'to create a unified approach to tribunal composition, and better use the experience and expertise non-legal members (NLMs) bring to the tribunal, whether they be accountants, surveyors, service or disability members'. NLMs 'should be used on particular hearings where they bring to the table skills, experience or knowledge that tribunal judges cannot provide'. Some concern was expressed in the consultation that the new structural arrangements (which group tribunals and their members into 'chambers') would lead to 'dilution of skills and expertise' on the part of chairmen and diminution of the role of non-legal members. The Government tried to provide reassurance that this would not be the case: 'the aim is to make the best possible use of the experience and expertise NLMs bring to the tribunal, whilst at the same time avoid placing unnecessary burdens on those who give their time to tribunals to perform this role'. To underline that 'expertise and experience can be equally as important as qualifications in many tribunal hearings', the proposal to call all specialists and experts 'members' was adopted. This, however, can only be read as a move away from the original role of 'lay members' as articulated by Bell and Leggatt.

3. Welfare adjudication: Discretion to rules

(a) From NATs to SBATs

For much of its long history, the question whether social security adjudication was administrative or adjudicative in character was immaterial. Early welfare

[28] Following the Woolf Review, *Access to Justice*; Leggatt [155]. The current Lands Tribunal Rules 1996 (SI 1996/1022 as amended) are to be read with the Lands Tribunals Practice Direction, which states [2.1] that the Civil Procedure Rules have no application but that the Tribunal follows the same overriding objective of 'dealing with a case justly' as the CPR. Following the TCEA 2007, whose provisions are explained below, the Lands Tribunal will become part of a specialised chamber for land, property and housing.

[29] This position is not without its critics: see G. Richardson and D. Machin, 'Doctors on tribunals: A confusion of roles' (2000) 176 *British J. of Psychiatry* 110 and, for a response, H. Prins, 'Complex medical roles in mental health review tribunals' (2000) 177 *British J. of Psychiatry* 182. And see E. Perkins, *Decision Making in Mental Health Review Tribunals* (Policy Studies Institute, 2003). In November 2008, MHRTs became First-tier Tribunals in the Social Entitlement chamber in the reorganised tribunal system (below).

[30] See Ministry of Justice, *Government Response to Transforming Tribunals* (19 May 2008), available online.

tribunals were locally based and 'hearings', if they can be dignified with that name, resembled the Public Assistance Committees which preceded them. Typically, they were informal and held in private, respecting the intimate nature of the requests for assistance with which they had to deal.[31] The Franks Committee accepted the departmental view of National Assistance Tribunals (NATs) (as they had become) as 'an assessment or case committee, taking a further look at the facts and in some cases arriving at a fresh decision on the extent of need.'[32] They were thought to operate satisfactorily (perhaps this only meant that Franks received no grave complaints). The report described NATs as 'special' and exempted them from the general requirement of openness; 'if any or all of these appeals were to be held in public many applicants might be deterred from appealing or even from applying for assistance and the purpose of the legislation might thus be frustrated'.[33]

There were other signs that Franks did not regard NATs as 'machinery for adjudication'. It did not create an appeal to the High Court on a point of law and it made no recommendations about legally qualified chairmen. The only real concession was the admission that 'legal representation should be permitted to the applicant who can satisfy the chairman of the tribunal that he cannot satisfactorily present his case unless he is allowed to employ a lawyer'. It can be seen how these features might help to disguise dissatisfaction with tribunals. Claimants were not legally represented and were hardly likely to know of the prerogative-order procedure (the precursor of modern judicial review procedure) by which decisions could theoretically be challenged. Neither lawyers nor journalists were present to articulate dissatisfaction. It is tempting to see Franks as condoning amateurishness because small sums were at stake or because the concept of welfare as a 'charitable handout' still prevailed.

The Ministry of Social Security Act 1966 did not alter the tribunals system though once again they were renamed: Supplementary Benefit Appeal Tribunals, commonly known as SBATs. The Act made one important change. It introduced the idea of *entitlement* to benefit, albeit in limited areas, perhaps unintentionally setting the scene for adjudicative change. The climate, however, was not yet ready. Mashaw's 'case-committee' model, which, with the tacit approval of Franks, SBATs were supposedly operating, was slow to change. Thus in 1971, we find the Chairman of the Supplementary Benefits Commission (SBC), responsible after 1966 for administering the tribunals system, writing of his gratitude to 'all who act, in whatever capacity, as friendly counsellors to claimants' adding that 'the concept of co-operation, in the

[31] The UATs set up under the Unemployment Assistance Act 1934 became NATs after the National Assistance Act 1948: see T. Lynes, 'Unemployment Assistance Tribunals in the 1930s' in Adler and Bradley (eds.), *Justice, Discretion and Poverty* (Professional Books, 1975). M. Herman, *Administrative Justice and Supplementary Benefits* (London School of Economics, 1972) pp. 13–14 still classified SBATs (below) as administrative.

[32] Franks [180] [182–3]. And see A. Bradley, 'National Assistance Appeal Tribunals and the Franks Report', in Adler and Bradley (eds.), *Justice, Discretion and Poverty.*

[33] Franks [79].

Commission's view, goes to the heart of a successful operation of the scheme'.[34] Bradley, in sharp contrast, was describing the functions of SBATs in standard dispute-resolution terminology. They were instituted, he said:

> to decide *disputes* which the administration of social security has thrown up, disputes which break the surface because a citizen is sufficiently aggrieved by the official decision to appeal against it. It is an important function of tribunals to be able to settle such disputes in an impartial and fair manner. If their decisions are to be accepted, they must observe certain minimum standards both of procedural and of substantive justice.[35]

If Franks had favoured informality, it had also warned that informality without rules of procedure might produce 'an unordered character which makes it difficult, if not impossible, for the tribunal properly to sift the facts and weigh the evidence'.[36] This was an apt description of SBATs, where members received no training, administrative staff received minimal training and legally qualified chairmen were exceptional. Tribunals were inclined to give free rein to prejudice, and ignorance of the simplest legal tenets, such as who ought to prove what or how things should be proved, was common. In an influential study, Lewis contrasted the performance of National Insurance Local Tribunals (NILTs), which dealt with industrial injury claims, with that of SBATs; NILTs were 'usually a model of balancing informal expertise with order and legality'. Praising the 'traditions of English lawyering which can, at its best, rise to lending order to administrative processes without ever meddling', Lewis concluded that:

> criticism of supplementary benefit tribunals is not based upon comparisons with courts of law but is made within a framework of acceptance of the valuable job performed by administrative tribunals at large. Nor is the objection to underdeveloped legal technique an attempt to promote the claims of the legal profession to intellectual leadership of the 'welfare rights movement'. It is simply that the system of appeals from the SBC is vastly important, that it is not operating upon the basis of anything resembling objective standards, that such a state of affairs works to the ultimate detriment of claimants and that some of the fault is a lack of legal expertise.[37]

Researchers who, like Lewis, attended SBATs in the early 1970s, found tribunals that were heavily dependent on the clerk, a departmental employee, and the departmental presenting officer, who in many tribunals sat opposite to the clerk, emphasising his official status and suggesting a spurious objectivity. Regular appearance in tribunals and access to departmental policy gave these departmental officials a misleading appearance of expertise and the fact that many members

[34] Lord Collison, 'Introduction', *SBC Handbook for Claimants* (c.1966).

[35] A. Bradley, 'Reform of Supplementary Benefit Tribunals: The key issues' (1976) 27 *NILQ* 96, 101.

[36] Franks [64].

[37] N. Lewis, 'Supplementary Benefits Appeal Tribunals' [1973] *PL* 257, 258–9.

and chairmen were also magistrates may have reinforced their tendency to turn for advice to the clerk. But unlike the clerk in a magistrate's court, neither clerks nor presenting officers were legally qualified or trained. Their advice on the meaning of statute and regulations and their knowledge of High Court decisions were imperfect and the presenting officer, who had normally worked in a social security office actually deciding claims, was likely to feel a sense of loyalty to the department, share its ethos and accept its understanding of 'the rules'.

Since 1958, chairmen had been appointed by the minister from a panel approved by the Lord Chancellor but they did not need legal qualifications. Of the two members, one was selected by the minister from a panel nominated by trade unions and other representative organisations, the other was appointed by the minister from a list of people 'with knowledge or local experience of people living on low incomes'. In practice, members were often drawn from local citizens' advice bureaux or chambers of commerce in an effort to make them representative of the community. They were strikingly unrepresentative of the population at large, with women, ethnic minorities and young people seriously under-represented, and even less representative of claimants, whose difficulties they often failed to recognise or accept. Lack of training reinforced latent prejudice and bias.[38]

This was a system riddled at every level with unstructured discretion. The first-instance decision-making was left to junior benefit officers, though their discretion was in practice structured by departmental guidance. SBATs were meant to examine the discretionary decisions of benefit officers on their merits and, according to s 15(1)(c) of the 1976 Act, could 'substitute for any decision appealed against any determination which a benefit officer could have made'. Departmental policy was not supposed to bind the 'independent' tribunals but unqualified tribunal members and chairmen did not always understand the status of this 'soft law' nor did they appreciate that SBC directives and codes of practice could not 'bind' either the benefit officer or the tribunal. They tended either to accept SBC policy unquestioningly or to give free rein to personal prejudices. The 'strong' discretion of the three-person tribunal panel was, in other words, not properly 'structured'. Observers were concerned by the way the power of choice was exercised and by the indeterminate nature of the 'rules'.

(b) The Bell Report and after: Orderliness

A mounting tide of pressure from welfare lawyers, academics and action groups led the overseeing department (then the DHSS) to commission a survey of SBATs in which Professor Bell pointed to some of the disadvantages of adversarial procedure in tribunals.[39] Bell concluded that presenting officers did

[38] R. Lister, *Justice for the Claimant: A study of Supplementary Benefit Appeal Tribunals* (Child Poverty Action Group, 1974).

[39] K. Bell, *Research Study on Supplementary Benefit Appeal Tribunals: Review of main findings: Conclusions: Recommendations* (HMSO, 1975).

not understand their role; some could more aptly be described as prosecuting officers. They needed to be of high calibre and properly trained if they were to balance their conflicting duties of 'adviser' and 'presenter'. Without legal qualifications clerks could not be relied on to redress the balance. Clerks, unlike presenting officers, remained with the tribunal while it was deliberating and after the appellant and his representative had left. Some clerks intervened of their own accord in proceedings where they felt the tribunal was going wrong.

The Bell Report was an important stage in the move to orderliness and ultimately to judicialisation of tribunals. It recommended a three-stage programme:

- Stage 1: strengthen existing tribunals, e.g. by appointing legal practitioners as 'Senior Chairmen' to supervise tribunals and institute training schemes.
- Stage 2: improve on existing tribunals by a planned programme of judicialisation. Bell recommended legally qualified chairmen, better provision for representation and a higher calibre of member with strong commitment to the work.
- Stage 3: integrate SBATs with NILTs (not achieved in practice until 1983).

Bell had complained that no right of appeal existed from SBATs to a second-tier appeal body and of the deliberate decision to exclude them from the right to appeal on a point of law to the High Court.[40] As a halfway measure, the appeals system would be restructured to allow a second appeal on a point of law to National Insurance Commissioners, who would be given jurisdiction in both sets of tribunals and rechristened 'Social Security Commissioners'. This was an important step forward.

The majority of Bell's proposals could be implemented administratively. There were immediate moves to introduce training schemes and appoint more legally trained chairmen. Five senior chairmen (legally qualified) were appointed on a regional basis to monitor tribunals and to supervise training who, by 1982, had assumed a 'watchdog' function. The new appeals structure was provided by legislation.[41] Fulfilling an important criterion for tribunals, the Commissioners were specialists, well versed in welfare law, who understood the operation of the welfare system. A substantial volume of precedent was thus built up, which helped to regularise procedure as well as to rule on the interpretation of the complex statutes and regulations.[42] To underpin the new appeals structure, the rules provided for the tribunal to record its reasons and findings of material questions of fact, together with any dissenting opinions.[43]

[40] Under s. 13 of the Tribunals and Inquiries Act 1971.

[41] Ss. 14 and 15 of the Social Security Act 1980.

[42] See T. Buck, 'Precedent in tribunals and the development of principles' (2006) 25 *CJQ* 458.

[43] Supplementary Benefit and Family Income Supplements (Appeals) Rules, SI 1980/1605. The duty is reinforced by s. 10 of the Tribunals and Inquiries Act 1992, which provides statutory authority for a statement of reasons to form part of the record: see J. Tinnion, 'Principles in practice: The statement of reasons' (1995) 2 *Tribunals* 9.

Only a handful of cases reached the Court of Appeal, with a further trickle of applications for judicial review, the normal remedy of last resort.

After Bell, the claimant entering a SBAT would see facing her across a table a lawyer chairman seated between two members. The clerk sat on one side. The claimant and her representative sat opposite with the departmental presenting officer beside her, emphasising their equal status and removing any impression that he was an officer of the tribunal. Every member had the procedural guide. A copy of all relevant statutes, regulations and guidance should be in the room, together with the collected summaries of relevant High Court precedents and Commissioners' decisions to which the presenting officer might want to make reference. The first procedural guide was issued in 1977; revised by the senior chairmen, it was reissued regularly (and is now available online). This, and the extension of training, did much to standardise procedures.

The guide laid particular emphasis on the importance of reasoned decisions, warning against 'boiler-plate reasons'. The tribunal, having considered all the evidence was to decide which facts were established and, where there was a conflict of evidence, indicate clearly which version it accepted:

> It is not sufficient merely to record: 'The facts put forward by the Adjudication Officer (or the claimant) were agreed' or 'Facts as stated'. The space labelled 'Tribunal's unanimous/majority decision' is not simply for a 'rubber stamp decision' . . . The Tribunal's decision should be fully, intelligibly and accurately set out in it. To use expressions such as 'Decision revised' or 'Appeal dismissed' or 'Case adjourned' is not sufficient. The dissenting member's reasons should also be recorded. The wording should be such that neither the claimant nor the AO is left in any doubt as to what the Tribunal has decided. A proper recording of decisions by the chairman is essential; it is his duty to see that this is done.[44]

(c) A presidential system

A further move towards a court model came with the Health and Social Services and Social Security Adjudications Act 1983 (HASSASSA), which provided for benefit decisions to be taken by an adjudication officer with appeal to a SSAT and further appeal to the Social Security Commissioners and Court of Appeal.[45] More important, HASSASSA empowered the Lord Chancellor to appoint a president with regional and full-time chairmen for the tribunals and for these appointments to be held by barristers or solicitors of not less than ten, seven and five years' standing respectively. Appointments of tribunal members would be made by the president and the greater independence of the tribunals was recognised by the fact that staffing, including the post of clerk, was also to be the

[44] *Social Security Appeal Tribunals: A guide to procedure* (HMSO, 1985) [73]. And see Commissioner's Decision (R(SB) 8/84).

[45] See N. Harris, 'The reform of the Supplementary Benefits Appeals System' (1983) *J. of Social Welfare Law* 212. HASSASSA also provided for NILTs and SBATs to be amalgamated.

responsibility of the president.[46] The presidential system and the personality of Judge Byrt, the first president, provided the motor for reform. Judge Byrt used to the full his powers to appoint and train chairmen, making tribunals conform more closely to Mashaw's 'due process' model. Training was steadily upgraded and increased. There was proper access to the regulations and precedent from the Social Security Commissioners. Much was done in addition to make the panels more 'representative', at least in regard to age and gender.

Were these changes solely an instance of 'capture' by a powerful Lord Chancellor and the legal profession? Perhaps they were necessitated by a steady process of juridification. Benefits were no longer a charitable handout to the 'deserving poor'. The welfare system had been transformed, with a sharp move from discretion to rules visible in the governing legislation. It had become a mass service, dealing annually with millions of payments and with a budget of many millions. A complex network of statute and regulations, notable for their textual density, now governed entitlements. The new regime had, in the words of one commentator, 'swept away many of the old (and potentially broad) discretionary powers and replaced them with a much firmer and narrower basis of legal entitlement'.[47] This was a fundamental change of style that demanded to be matched by a corresponding transformation of tribunals. Tribunal work now called for greater technical ability in dealing with arguments based on entitlement under the regulations and a considerable degree of legal expertise was now necessary to interpret them. Hearings had become more formal; proceedings had to be adequately recorded; the papers, decision and record had become more legalistic. Legally qualified chairmen were pushed into a dominant position, often forming a view on the papers submitted without much further exploration of facts. Some observers felt that the changes had gone too far; lay members, whose remit was to play an active and enabling role in proceedings by showing sympathetic understanding of the problem, listening, asking relevant questions, drawing claimants out and generally helping to sort out the case, were being sidelined. The known preference of appellants for informality, for participatory proceedings and for non-legal representation, usually by social workers, whose preference for the 'case-worker model' allowed appellants to participate in presenting their own case, was being undercut.[48]

A study had shown a high correlation between success rates, attendance and representation; only about 7 per cent of appellants who neither attended nor were represented succeeded in their appeal. The authors thought the apparent informality of tribunal proceedings positively misleading; legally relevant factual information and evidence of those facts was necessary for claimants to

[46] HASSASSA, Sch. 4 [8]. Ministerial and Treasury consent was required.

[47] J. Baldwin, N. Wikeley and R. Young, *Judging Social Security: The adjudication of claims* (Clarendon Press, 1992), p. 155.

[48] C. Mesher, 'The 1980 social security legislation: The great welfare state chainsaw massacre?' (1981) 8 *JLS* 119.

make their case and the framework was increasingly that of common law, trial-type procedure.[49] The obvious answer of more representation had, however, never really been on the agenda. The pragmatic solution of an investigatory role for the tribunal was suggested by the Social Security Commissioners: 'its investigatory function has as its object the ascertainment of the facts and the determination of the truth'.[50] Judge Byrt also recognised that chairmen would have to modify their traditional stance of adjudicators in an adversarial system, who should not actively intervene to assist one of the parties to proceedings:

> If the appellant is unrepresented, it makes a mockery of the tribunal system to leave him totally to his own devices to argue his appeal as best he may. The law is so complex that the majority of appellants would not know where to begin, and justice would seldom be done. Keeping its independent judicial role in mind, the tribunal must seek clarification and if necessary the elaboration of all relevant facts . . . the tribunal must create the atmosphere in which such an inquiry might effectively take place. It must do what it can to offset the appellant's feeling of bewilderment and intimidation at attending a court of law . . . The underlying principle is that the tribunal should in all things conduct itself so as to enable the appellant to maximise his performance and himself to feel that he has done so.[51]

This was the 'enabling' role, to be taken up later by Leggatt, which also emphasised chairmen's 'considerable responsibility to ensure that . . . the parties to be heard have the appropriate chance to say what they have to say, to ask the questions that they wish to ask, and to make the submissions that relate to their case'.[52] But chairmen trained in an adversarial system were in practice uneasy in abandoning their traditional impartial and listening role. An alternative way forward was to transform the role of the presenting officer from departmental advocate to a 'friend of the court' function. But this is a difficult balancing act even for a skilled advocate and the presenting officer remained a departmental official. Something nearer to true inquisitorial procedure might be necessary.

To summarise the position as it stood in the late 1980s, judicialisation had, on the surface, won the day. There was a cadre of full- and part-time professional social-security adjudicators and the list of lay members, if not entirely representative, had been pruned. Behind the scenes, however, a very different managerial mentality prevailed. The system was being streamlined. Paper decisions were substituted for oral hearings, which became the exception, and short cuts in the recording of decisions and reasons were authorised. To Lynes, a 'simple and informal' procedure was being deliberately bureaucratised.[53]

[49] Genn and Genn, *The Effectiveness of Representation at Tribunal*. See similarly A. Frost and C. Howard, *Representation and Administrative Tribunals* (Routledge, 1977).

[50] Decision 4 R(S)1/87 (Commissioner Hallett).

[51] In evidence to the Social Services Select Committee, *Social Security: Changes Implemented in April 1988*, HC 437-ii (1988/9) [36–7].

[52] M. Partington, 'Principles in practice: Adjudication' (1994) 1 *Tribunals* 12, 13.

[53] T. Lynes, 'Social security tribunals: New procedures', (June 1997) *Legal Action* 24.

(d) Burying Bell?

By the late 1990s, delay had become a problem: an average time of ten weeks in 1983 had mounted to twenty-six weeks in 1996. With the avowed aim of streamlining the system, the Social Security Act (SSA) 1998 merged all existing appeal tribunals, creating a unified Appeals Tribunal and downloading administration to an executive agency. The tribunal was still under the control of a legally qualified president with members selected from a panel appointed by the Lord Chancellor[54] but a radical change had been made in its actual composition. Section 7 of the SSA provided that a tribunal could be composed of one, two or three members, of whom one should be legally qualified. In cases involving 'a question of fact of special difficulty', the tribunal could call on one or more experts to assist it, 'experts' being narrowly defined in the section as members of the panel with 'knowledge or experience which would be relevant in determining the question of fact of special difficulty'. Regulations provided for revision of decisions and for the allocation of cases by the president. A one-person tribunal had to consist of a lawyer; a two-person tribunal handled incapacity benefit, industrial injury or severe disablement and had to consist of a legally and a medically qualified person; in exacting financial cases, such as those involving child support, the two-person panel consisted of a lawyer and person with financial qualifications; where both medical and financial expertise were necessary, a three-person tribunal could be convened. [55] Almost unnoticed, Adler remarked with some sadness, 'the long tradition of lay involvement' in social security appeals had been brought to an abrupt end in favour of a single, legally qualified person sitting alone; in addition, many of the so called 'hearings' would in fact be paper decisions.[56]

The new managerial arrangements allowed some of the backlog and delays to be cleared: the average waiting time dropped; the clear-up rate improved; costs remained low.[57] There have, however, been other costs. With hindsight, Wikeley sees the move to legally qualified single-person tribunals as completing a transition initiated by the post-Bell reforms of HASSASSA, which 'sig-

[54] Ss. 4–7 of the SSA 1998 noted N. Wikeley, 'Decision making and appeals under the Social Security Act 1998' (1998) 5 *J. of Social SecurityLaw* 104. The amalgamated tribunals were: SSATs, Child Support Appeal Tribunals, Disability, Medical Appeal Tribunals and Vaccine Damage Tribunals. In practice the president is a county court judge. The Appeals Service Agency, an executive agency, has since 2007 been part of the Tribunals Service. From 2009 the tribunals have been amalgamated into the Social Entitlement chamber of the new TCEA structure.

[55] S. 6 of the Social Security and Child Support (Decisions and Appeals) Regulations, SI 1999/91.

[56] M. Adler, 'Lay tribunal members and administrative justice' [1999] *PL* 616, 619.

[57] The average time for an appeal to be heard was 10.4 weeks and the number over 20 weeks old was reduced to 3,421. 262, 816 cases had been cleared (compared with 257,888 in the previous year). Average cost was £260 (well below the NAO's average of £455 and 5% below the agency's target of £273): see Appeals Service, *Annual Report and Accounts 2005/6*, HC 1542 (2006/7).

nalled the beginning of the end for lay members in social security tribunals'. By 1998, managerial professionalism was replacing the due process model of HASSASSA, which had in turn superseded Bell's ideal of participation in social-security adjudication. The TCEA completed the process, winding up appeal tribunals and transferring their jurisdiction to the 'First-tier Tribunal'. Once again we would stress that this move is not unique to social security but 'reflects a wider tendency on the part of governments to seek to increase managerial efficiency in the judicial process, as measured by the throughput of cases'.[58] As indicated earlier, the attitude to 'lay' members has been steadily less positive. Leggatt, for example, recommended that the decision whether or not to ask a lay member to sit should rest with presidents or regional/district chairmen, 'on the basis that they should only do so if they [the members] have a particular function to fulfil'.[59]

(e) Internal review: The Social Fund Inspectorate

As a matter of administrative convenience, social security legislation has long made provision for reviewing and changing decisions without the necessity for appeal or a fresh claim but always on strictly limited grounds. In respect of the 'social fund', which largely replaced with discretionary loans the single, lump-sum payments available under previous legislation,[60] the Social Security Act 1986 went much further. Not only did the Act provide a flexible power for social fund officers (SFOs) to review any decision at any time but it also added two further reviews at the claimant's request: (i) of the officer's initial decision by the same or another SFO; and (ii) a further review by the Social Fund Inspectorate (now known as the Independent Review Service or IRS). The IRS is headed by the Social Fund Commissioner (SFC), appointed by the Secretary of State for Work and Pensions, to whom he is accountable. The SFC appoints the inspectorate, usually, to ensure their familiarity with the system, from within the department (DSS) and is responsible for training. An inspector (SFI) has authority to reopen a decision on the grounds that information was missed or incorrectly recorded or that there is new evidence or that the rules have been wrongly applied. The SFI's decision ends the internal review process.

When the SFI was first mooted in the discretionary area of social fund payments as an alternative to the well-established tradition of tribunal adjudication, the Council on Tribunals objected strongly:

[58] N. Wikeley, 'The judicialisation of Social Security Tribunals' (2000) 63 *MLR* 475, 487, 492. And see N. Wikeley and R. Young, 'The marginalisation of lay members in Social Security Appeal Tribunals' (1992) *JSWFL* 127; S. Vernon, 'Principles in practice: The role of lay members in the tribunal system' (1995) 2 *Tribunals* 5.

[59] Leggatt, Recommendation 147 and [7.25].

[60] The Social Fund introduced a new type of social assistance whereby many benefits took the form of loans: see T. Mullen, 'The Social Fund: Cash-limiting social security' (1989) 52 *MLR* 64.

> The only separate review which a dissatisfied claimant could have would be by another official; apparently he would even be in the same local office as the person who made the original decision. This is not the way to gain the confidence of the public, still less of claimants, in these decisions and reviews.[61]

The Council's concern was lack of independence; it saw the move as 'probably the most substantial abolition of a right of appeal to an independent tribunal since 1958'. What then happened reminds us that we should not be too ready to equate independence and impartiality. The first SFC, a lawyer by training, took a 'top-down view' of internal review. She analysed it as a 'two-stage process' in which the first stage had the characteristics of a review or reassessment, while the second resembled appeal. Correctness of initial decisions was of the first importance and decisions were regularly monitored by the SFC to ensure their quality. Equally important, however, was impartiality:

> When the Inspector reviews, he addresses the same matters as does a court in Judicial Review. At the next stage the Inspector is asking himself whether the decision is the right one in all the circumstances of the case. There is no appeal against the Inspector's decision on the merits of the case. The only further recourse the citizen has, if he is not satisfied, is to apply for judicial review on procedural grounds. The aggrieved citizen has a right to expect that the Inspector will act in a fair and impartial manner, consistent with natural justice, and that the decision will be of a high standard. I place emphasis above all on the quality of the review and the standard of service provided by the IRS . . . By the time a case arrives at the IRS, all the facts of the case should have been established. The original application provides the basis for the first decision. As part of the review process, the applicant has the opportunity to attend an interview at which time further evidence may be provided. When the facts have not been established by the decision maker, or they are not recorded, or disputes of fact remain unresolved Inspectors will, if they are unable to resolve the issues, refer the case back to the [Benefits Agency].[62]

Annual reports, many highly critical of the department, give some idea of the scale of work. In 2007–8, for example, SFIs delivered 19,221 decisions and changed around 50 per cent of the decisions they reviewed. Case readers, who check SFI decisions, found that 89 per cent of a sample met SFI standards; of seventy-five complaints about the SFI service, only thirty-five were upheld. The cost per decision of around £160 compares favourably with the cost of a tribunal hearing.

The Commissioner recognised:

[61] Council on Tribunals, *Social Security: Abolition of independent appeals under the proposed Social Fund*, Cmnd. 9722 (1986) [5] [6] [12].

[62] *Annual Report of the Social Fund Commissioner for 1993/4 on the standards of review by Social Fund Inspectors* (HMSO, 1994).

> the need to complete reviews as quickly as possible, since the people who use our service are generally in urgent need and have already had two decisions on their application at Jobcentre Plus. Nevertheless, the Inspector has a duty to ensure natural justice is served. In order to do this, before he makes a decision, he sends the applicant a copy of the key papers, sets out the facts and issues to be decided, invites the applicant to comment and asks any relevant questions.[63]

Over 90 per cent of straightforward enquiries were completed within twelve working days and within thirty days of receipt for complex enquiries; only in respect of urgent cases did the IRS at 87 per cent fall below its 90 per cent target.

A review by independent researchers shortly after the system became operative[64] concluded that it did have an impact: the quality of initial decision-making had been improved by the flow of substituted and returned decisions from the IRS. Not only had the inspectorate emerged as a scrupulous team of reviewers, laying a sound base for any external appeal, but it was itself 'a centre of excellence' in decision-making. The scrutiny function has been taken very seriously.[65] Closer to the department (now Benefits Agency), the Inspectorate is clearly a better mechanism for feedback and change than reports from a tribunal hearing or the annual report of the president, through which SBATs attempt to instigate change. This function will in any event be lost now social security tribunals have joined the new First-tier chamber.

So should this inspectorial model of adjudication be considered as a way to deliver PDR? The present SFC, Sir Richard Tilt, has said that the SFI model has 'gained much respect in many quarters for its independence, accessibility and high standards'. It is 'a proportionate remedy in the context of the Social Fund, and one which could have application in other jurisdictions'. He hopes that 'the processes at the IRS may have wider applicability'.[66] On the debit side, this is one less opportunity for participation – but perhaps participation, implying a need for attendance at an oral hearing, is not what claimants want.

4. Tribunals watchdog?

The idea of a specialised administrative appeals tribunal, recommended by Robson to the Franks Committee, has never been accepted in Britain (though it did have some influence on the Leggatt proposals for a two-tier tribunal system). Instead, Franks opted for the limited solution of a 'Council on

[63] IRS, Annual Report for 2006/7, p. 28.

[64] G. Dalley and R. Berthoud, *Challenging Discretion: The Social Fund review procedure* (Policy Studies Institute, 1992).

[65] Thus in 2007 the Commissioner gave detailed evidence which influenced the Select Committee on Work and Pensions in its review of the Social Fund: see SCWP, *The Social Fund*, HC 941 (2007/8) [50–7].

[66] SFC, *Annual Report for 2006/7*, available online.

Tribunals' or permanent supervisory body to provide a 'focal point from which knowledgeable advice and guidance could be maintained'. The main function of the Council on Tribunals should be:

> to suggest how the general principles of constitution, organisation and procedure enunciated in the Report should be applied in detail to the various tribunals. In discharging this function they should first decide the application of these principles to all existing tribunals; thereafter they should keep tribunals under review and advise on the constitution, organisation and procedure of any proposed new type of tribunal. We recommend that any proposal to establish a new tribunal should be referred to the Councils for their advice before steps are taken to establish the tribunal. The Councils should have power to take evidence from witnesses both inside and outside the public service, and their reports should be published.[67]

While accepting that the Council's recommendations would be purely advisory, Franks hoped that its influence would be considerable. It envisaged that the Council would have important executive powers, including the appointment of tribunal members (as distinct from chairmen), the formulation of procedural rules and the review of remuneration for tribunal appointees.[68] It would have operated, in short, along the lines of a modern regulatory agency, though without either rule-making or enforcement functions.

These ambitious proposals, not fully implemented, were further undercut by an important structural defect. Unlike a modern regulator, the Council would remain small, with a part-time chairman, not necessarily legally qualified, and no more than ten part-time members, a majority being non-lawyers. While it was to be through the Council that tribunals, after the initial reforms anticipated by Franks, were to be moved towards the adjudicative ideal-type, and future 'tribunals' brought within the ethos, the Council's role was seen as essentially reactive: to report on particular proposals, not to initiate their own proposals. Whether or not a tribunal was to be set up remained a policy matter for departments drafting legislation.

As finally set up, the Council had four major functions: (i) a supervisory role; (ii) a consultative role, laid down by statute, concerning proposed rules for procedure; (iii) an informal consultative role in relation to draft legislation; and (iv) a promotional and propagandist role. It was (as it has remained) a 'shoestring operation', with a staff of six, two part-time chairmen for the Council and its Scottish Committee and part-time lay members, chosen in principle from 'as broad a section of the community as possible' but in practice predominantly

[67] Cmnd 218 [133]. Franks actually wanted two separate councils, one for England and Wales and for Scotland, to keep the constitution and workings of tribunals under continuous review: Cmnd 218 [43]. Instead, s. 1 of the Tribunals and Inquiries Act 1958 created a Council on Tribunals with a Scottish Committee. Ss. 44 and Sch. 7 of the TCEA 2007 replace the Council on Tribunals by the Administrative Justice and Tribunals Council. This too has Scottish and Welsh committees.

[68] Franks [134].

male, white and middle-aged or elderly.[69] A striking omission was any research capacity whatsoever, making the Council dependent on the good nature of legal academics. This is not the way that the Law Commission has to work.

Necessarily, the Council's work was incomplete and its style non-conflictual. Take the statutory power to 'keep under review the constitution and working' of tribunals listed in the Tribunals and Inquiries Acts. This, Professor Street, himself a member, acknowledged, would require 'unannounced and frequent visits', assessment of the quality of the chairman's paperwork and random examination of decision files: all the resources that Judge Byrt had at his disposal to implement HASSASSA or that the Audit Commission possesses. All that the Council could manage was around one hundred visits annually, which were never unannounced. Street was driven to conclude that the Council was 'playing no effective part in ensuring that the personnel are discharging their duties competently . . . Its supervision of tribunals is so slight as to be ineffective.'[70] Equally, its complaints-handling procedure was rudimentary. A promotional leaflet warned the citizen that 'the Council has no power to change a tribunal decision or to provide any other redress', adding vaguely that the PCA (whose services are free) may be able to 'look into allegations of maladministration by the administrative staff of certain tribunals'. The Council itself had no ombudsman function.

The weaknesses of this non-statutory framework were to emerge very clearly during the reorganisation. The Council, which might have expected after forty years of work and experience (including a special report on the organisation and independence of tribunals)[71] to have been at the very least represented *ex officio* on the Leggatt Committee, was reduced to giving evidence to it. Similarly, in 1991, after ten years' work, the Council on Tribunals published an important compilation of model tribunal rules intended for the use of departmental draftsmen.[72] True that, in the absence of rule-making powers, implementation was purely a voluntary matter, reflected in the presentation as 'no more than a store from which Departments and tribunals may select and adopt what they need'. It is nonetheless disappointing to find that the AJTC has only one nominee on the new Tribunals Procedure Committee, which has now taken on the function of drafting model procedural rules.[73] The Committee has a majority of judicial members.

[69] J. Garner, 'The Council on Tribunals' [1965] *PL* 321. For comparison with the more influential Australian Administrative Review Council, see A. Robertson, 'Monitoring developments in administrative law: The role of the Australian Administrative Review Council' in Harris and Partington, (eds.) *Administrative Justice in the 21st Century* (Hart Publishing, 1999).

[70] H. Street, *Justice in the Welfare State*, 2nd edn (Stevens, 1975), p. 63.

[71] Council on Tribunals, *Review of Tribunals: The Council's response* (2000), incorporating Special Report, *Tribunals: Their organisation and independence*, Cm. 3744 (1997).

[72] Council on Tribunals, *Model Rules of Procedure for Tribunals*, Cm. 1434 (1991). The current version is *Guide to Drafting Tribunal Rules* (2003), available on the archived Council website.

[73] See the Tribunal Procedure (Upper Tribunal) Rules 2008, SI 2698/2008. Three sets of procedural rules for First-tier Tribunals were published in 2008: SI 2699/2008, SI 2685/2008, SI 2686/2008. In practice, these were closely based on the Council's model rules.

Barely mentioned by Leggatt, the Council was abolished in the subsequent reorganisation to be replaced by an Administrative Justice and Tribunals Council (AJTC) heralded by the Government as 'a new body and a new remit'.[74] This new remit is very much wider than the old. Not only is the AJTC to keep under review and report on the constitution and working of listed tribunals and statutory inquiries but it must also keep under review *the whole of the administrative justice system*. In its first Annual Report, the AJRC indicated how it understood this gargantuan task:

PURPOSE

Our purpose is to help make administrative justice and tribunals increasingly accessible, fair and effective by:

- playing a pivotal role in the development of coherent principles and good practice;
- promoting understanding, learning and continuous improvement;
- ensuring that the needs of users are central.

VISION

Our vision for administrative justice and tribunals is a system where:

- those taking administrative decisions do so on soundly-based evidence and with regard to the needs of those affected;
- people are helped to understand how they can best challenge decisions or seek redress at least cost and inconvenience to themselves;
- grievances are resolved in a way which is fair, timely, open and proportionate;
- there is a continuous search for improvement at every stage in the process.

VALUES

The values we seek to promote in administrative justice and tribunals are:

- openness and transparency
- fairness and proportionality
- impartiality and independence
- equality of access to justice.[75]

The new Senior President of Tribunals (Sir Robert Carnwath) has spoken of the AJTC as 'a powerful ally in the reform programme, and an independent guardian of the objectives of the service'.[76] These are fine words but built

[74] See *Transforming Public Services*, Cm. 6243 (2004); Sch. 7 of the TCEA 2007; and Ministry of Justice, *Transforming Tribunals, Implementing Part 1 of the Tribunals, Courts and Enforcement Act 2007* CP 30/07 (28 November 2007) [117–28] (hereafter *Transforming Tribunals*).

[75] AJRC, *Annual Report for 2007/8*.

[76] Sir Robert Carnwath, 'Administrative Justice and Tribunals Council: Getting there at last!' (Speech to first conference of the AJTC, 20 Nov 2007) [24], available online.

into the new regime are the old limitations, accentuated by the fact that the tribunals system is itself now more complex and professional; it has gained a professional Tribunals Service and acquired some of the Council's previous functions. Including its Scottish Committee, the AJTC has fourteen members, most of whom have full-time jobs, with a part-time chairman and total budget of just over £1.25 million. Its only realistic strategy is to act as a co-ordinator of networks, fostering co-operation. Without a sizeable research budget, all it can hope to do is to publicise rather than commission research, as it has already started to do. It can 'offer advice and assistance' on policy issues; comment from time to time on Tribunals Service priorities, standards and performance measures; and monitor so far as it is able the progress and performance of tribunals against common standards and performance measures. Once again, it must 'seek to build up influence' over forthcoming legislation and 'raise awareness' of the different approaches within the UK legal systems. There is at long last a co-ordinated tribunals system - but significantly without a tribunals regulatory body.

5. Courts, tribunals and accountability

It seems proper for those tribunals that exercise judicial functions to be accountable to courts. For centuries the prerogative writs of prohibition and certiorari issued from the royal courts to any body carrying out a 'judicial' act, the former to prevent an inferior tribunal from exceeding its jurisdiction, the latter to quash any order made by a tribunal in excess of jurisdiction.[77] In the interwar period, however, when tribunals were still seen as exercising administrative functions, not every tribunal would come within this jurisdiction,[78] and judicial review could be excluded not only by 'ouster' or 'preclusive' clauses but by 'no certiorari' clauses or statutory limitation periods, such as the traditional six-week period for challenging planning decisions.

In the post-war period, the jurisdiction of the courts in respect of tribunals has steadily been extended by statutory rights of appeal.[79] These followed the Franks idea for a two-tier system: appeal on the merits to a specialised tribunal, appeal on a point of law to the High Court and above.[80] In future this structure will be modified by ss 11-13 of the TCEA: there will be appeal from

[77] See for the history, S. A. de Smith, *Judicial Review of Administrative Action*, 4th edn (Stevens, 1980), pp. 25–6 and App. 1. For the modern law, see S. A. de Smith, Lord Woolf and J. Jowell, *Judicial Review of Administrative Action*, 6th edn (Sweet & Maxwell, 2007) Ch. 4.

[78] de Smith, Woolf, and Jowell, *Judicial Review of Administrative Action* [4-053–4]. The position was ameliorated by *R v Electricity Commissioners* [1924] KB 171, where the term 'judicial act' was widely defined by Atkin LJ.

[79] Introduced for the most part by the Tribunals and Inquiries Act 1958; consolidated by the Tribunals and Inquiries Act 1971; and s. 11 of the Tribunals and Inquiries Act 1992. And see Law Commission, *Administrative Law: Judicial review and statutory appeals*, Law Com. No. 226 (HMSO, 1994).

[80] Franks [105–7].

the First-Tier to the Upper (second-tier) Tribunal and, on a point of law with leave, to the Court of Appeal.

The purpose of statutory appeal rights is generally to confer power to reverse the tribunal's decision, something which cannot be achieved by the quashing order (certiorari), which operates merely to quash the decision, remitting it to the tribunal or decision-maker for reconsideration. The TCEA specifically confers the power to remake a decision on both the Upper Tribunal and the Court of Appeal.[81] There are, however, various forms of appeal: some involve a rehearing; others, such as statutory appeal under the Tribunals and Inquiries Act, which is by way of a case stated by the tribunal chairman, or the general appeal on a point of law from an inferior court or tribunal, do not.[82] As we shall see, appeal in immigration cases does not involve rehearing and is a very attenuated form of appeal.

The underlying premise of judicial review has always been that a tribunal (or other administrative body) is entitled to decide wrongly but is not entitled to exceed its statutory jurisdiction or *vires*. From this it followed that judicial review was at first limited to errors in excess of jurisdiction or (later) that were visible 'on the face of the record'.[83] By 1973, however, de Smith was able to report that:

> the English courts have now emphatically repudiated the doctrine that whenever an inferior tribunal has jurisdiction to inquire into a matter for the purpose of giving a decision, its findings thereon, whether they be right or wrong, are conclusive. The proposition that an inferior tribunal has freedom to err within the ambit of its jurisdiction has been eroded rather than repudiated.[84]

The reference was to a complex and subtle case law that had grown up distinguishing jurisdictional from non-jurisdictional errors – and errors of fact, which could usually not be reviewed, from errors of law, which could.[85] Fortunately, this esoteric area of law was rendered largely obsolete by the *Anisminic* case, where Lord Reid used the concept of nullity to extend the courts' supervisory jurisdiction, defining nullity so widely as to cover virtually every imaginable error of law (see p. 21 above). This momentous decision had the effect, according to Lord Diplock, of:

81 Ss. 12 and 14 of the TCEA. On an application for judicial review, a quashed tribunal decision can now be replaced by the court: see RSC, Order 54, see p. 670 below.

82 See for a useful summary, Law Commission, *Administrative Law: Judicial review and statutory appeals*, Law Com No. 226 (HMSO, 1994).

83 *R v Northumberland Compensation Appeal Tribunal, ex p. Shaw* [1952] 1 KB 338.

84 S. A. de Smith, *Judicial Review of Administrative Action*, 3rd edn (Sweet & Maxwell, 1973), p. 105.

85 See on the correspondence of error of law and jurisdictional error, *Pearlman v Keepers and Governors of Harrow School* [1979] QB 56 (Lord Denning MR); *S.E. Asia Fire Bricks v Non-Metallic Mineral Products Manufacturing Employees Union* [1981] AC 363 (PC); *Re Racal Communications Ltd* [1981] AC 374.

> liberat[ing] English public law from the fetters that the courts had theretofore imposed on themselves so far as determinations of inferior courts and statutory tribunals were concerned, by drawing esoteric distinctions between errors of law committed by such tribunals that went to their jurisdiction, and errors of law committed by them within their jurisdiction.[86]

The issues since then have, according to Woolf, Jowell and Le Sueur, changed dramatically so that traditional distinctions and labels, if they cannot yet be declared obsolete, are largely of historical interest.[87] In short, judicial oversight of tribunals has since *Anisminic* followed an expansive path and, as the grounds for review have enlarged and been extended by the HRA, so too has judicial supervision of tribunals.

(a) Review of fact

Anisminic has not, however, disposed of every problem. Once the competence of the courts covered most errors of law and the grounds for review had expanded, it was natural that courts should begin to question the 'no go area' of errors of fact. But as explained by Kirby J in a leading Australian case, judicial review stopped at errors of law:

> The grounds of judicial review ought not be used as a basis for a complete re-evaluation of the findings of fact, a reconsideration of the merits of the case or a re-litigation of the arguments that have been ventilated, and that failed, before the person designated as the repository of the decision-making power.[88]

There are a number of sensible reasons for this restrictive rule, not the least being the need to save time, cost and judicial energy. But leaving these logistical factors aside, review of fact is problematic. An appellate court's ability to detect factual error is much less than its ability to correct errors of law. Unless appeals are to consist of a total re-hearing, it will not see the witnesses nor is it certain that witnesses will give the same evidence or make the same impression on the second court. Assessment of witnesses and credibility is necessarily fairly subjective so that review inevitably means substituting one person or tribunal's subjective view of the facts for that of another. Rule 52.11.1 of the present rules of the Supreme Court for England and Wales does, however, grant a limited discretion to admit new evidence where (i) the fresh evidence

[86] *O'Reilly v Mackman* [1982] 2 AC 237, 278.

[87] de Smith, Woolf and Jowell, *Judicial Review of Administative Action* [4-001–6] The doctrine of jurisdiction and non-jurisdictional errors of law is still of importance in Australia, particularly in immigration cases, where jurisdictional error remains a prerequisite to review: see M. Aronson, B. Dyer and M. Groves, *Judicial Review of Administrative Action*, 4th edn (Lawbook Co, 2008), Ch. 4.

[88] *Re Minister for Immigration and Multicultural Affairs, ex p. Applicant S20/2002* (2003) 198 ALR 59 [114].

could not have been obtained with reasonable diligence for use at the trial; (ii) it probably would have had an important influence on the result; and (iii) it is apparently credible although not necessarily incontrovertible. Moreover, courts have been flirting for some time with the idea that some errors of fact may be reviewable as an error of law.[89] In an appeal from the Lands Tribunal, the Court of Appeal explained how a tribunal could make an error of law in considering facts:

> Judicial review (and therefore an appeal on law) may in appropriate cases be available where the decision is reached 'upon an incorrect basis of fact', due to misunderstanding or ignorance . . . A failure of reasoning may not in itself establish an error of law, but it may 'indicate that the tribunal had never properly considered the matter . . . and that the proper thought processes have not been gone through'.[90]

What has pushed courts towards this changed position is their experience with asylum and immigration cases, which in recent years make up the bulk of the judicial review case-load and feature high on the list of human rights challenges. Home Office handling of appeals has been the subject of constant criticism from courts, adjudicators and immigration tribunals. In one case, Collins J, then President of the Immigration Appeals Tribunal (IAT), said that the Home Office seemed wholly incapable of dealing appropriately with appeals: 'files are not provided, documents are not available, they do not put in evidence that they ought to put in, they fail totally to produce any skeleton arguments, the list goes on and on'.[91] There is widespread criticism too that 'the quality of the reasons given for refusal is often extremely poor' and 'frequently involve legal mistakes, reliance on defective country information taken from the Home Office's own country assessments and inadequate treatment of medical evidence'.[92] Similarly, the IAT has referred to the 'lack of skilled and professional care in reaching the initial decision' as necessarily placing extra burdens on adjudicators.[93] This left tribunals and judiciary in a dilemma.

Leggatt took note that 'complex factual issues are a regular feature of immigration and asylum cases, ranging from the circumstances of an alleged marriage or the obligations within an extended family abroad to the political situation in a country from which asylum is sought'.[94] To the Court of Appeal,

[89] An important step was Lord Slynn's speech in *R v Criminal Injuries Compensation Board, ex p. A* [1999] 2 AC 33. See also *R v Home Secretary, ex p. Launder* [1997] 1 WLR 839; *R v Home Secretary, ex p. Simms* [2000] 2 AC 115. And see Craig, *Administrative Law*, 6th edn (Oxford University Press, 2008) [15.002–4].

[90] *Railtrack Plc v Guinness Ltd* [2003] EWCA Civ 188 on appeal from [2003] RVR 280. The citation is from *R (Alconbury Ltd) v Environment Secretary* [2001] 2 WLR 1389 [53] (Lord Slynn).

[91] *SSHD v Tatar* [2000] 00TH01914 [3] [4], cited in R. Thomas, 'Evaluating tribunal adjudication: Administrative justice and asylum appeals' (2005) 26 *Legal Studies* 462, 481.

[92] JCWI, *Immigration, Nationality and Refugee Law Handbook* (2006), pp. 184, 198, 214.

[93] *Horvath v SSHD* [199] Imm. AR 121.

[94] Leggatt, 152 [23].

'the practice of asylum law is complicated by the fact that it is all about future risk, and on many occasions there are relevant changes of circumstances between the time of the original refusal of asylum and the time of the IAT's decision'.[95] And as the Home Office instructions tell junior staff, 'the case-worker will seldom be able to say with certainty whether or not an applicant will be persecuted if returned to their country'.[96] The position is made more difficult by statutory provisions allowing new facts and changing circumstances to be taken into account by adjudicators at every level of the process (see p. 519 below). Mistakes of fact, poor evidence-handling, opinion and prejudice and Home Office policy are blended in worrying decisions that tempt the courts to expand their supervisory jurisdiction.

In *E v Home Secretary*,[97] the applicant, who had been refused asylum status on the ground that he was not at risk of persecution, sought leave to appeal on the strength of new reports of the real state of affairs in his home country. Permission was refused by the IAT, which viewed the appeal as a disagreement about the factual evidence and therefore said: 'The Tribunal can only determine an appeal on the objective evidence before it at the time of the hearing and those reports were not before the Tribunal.' This left the Court of Appeal to consider whether a decision reached on an incorrect basis of fact could be challenged on an appeal limited to points of law? Their answer was to subsume review of fact under unfairness as a ground of review of law:

> In our view, the time has now come to accept that a mistake of fact giving rise to unfairness is a separate head of challenge in an appeal on a point of law, at least in those statutory contexts where the parties share an interest in co-operating to achieve the correct result. Asylum law is undoubtedly such an area. Without seeking to lay down a precise code, the ordinary requirements for a finding of unfairness are . . . First, there must have been a mistake as to an existing fact, including a mistake as to the availability of evidence on a particular matter. Secondly, the fact or evidence must have been 'established', in the sense that it was uncontentious and objectively verifiable. Thirdly, the appellant (or his advisers) must not been have been responsible for the mistake. Fourthly, the mistake must have played a material (not necessarily decisive) part in the Tribunal's reasoning.[98]

The Court went on to allow the appeal on the ground that the IAT had made an error of law in wrongly failing to consider new evidence in the context of its discretion to direct a rehearing, and remitted the case to the IAT for reconsideration.

Perhaps aware that a can of worms was being opened, later cases seem to have drawn back. In *Subesh*, Laws LJ laid down guidelines for the IAT:

95 *R (Iran) v Home Secretary* [2005] EWCA Civ 982 [41] (Brooke LJ).

96 UK Borders Agency, Asylum Policy Instructions, available on Home Office website.

97 *E v Home Secretary* [2004] QB 1044. The criteria are modified from *R v Criminal Injuries Compensation Board, ex p. A* [1999] 2 AC 33.

98 Ibid [66] (Laws LJ).

> i) It would only very rarely be able to overturn a finding of fact based on oral evidence and the assessment of credibility;
> ii) It could more readily overturn a finding of fact based on documentary evidence specific to the individual case (because the IAT was in just as good a position to assess such evidence), but great caution would be required in those cases where there might be an important relationship between the assessment of the person involved and the assessment of those documents;
> iii) The IAT would be at least as well placed as the adjudicator to assess findings as to the general conditions, or the backdrop, in the country concerned which would be based on the objective country evidence; the more so if the adjudicator had departed without solid justification from a relevant IAT country guidance decision;
> iv) The IAT would be entitled to draw its own inferences as to the application of those general country conditions to the facts of the particular case.[99]

The escalation and intensification of judicial review, the impetus of the HRA and the modern tendency of English courts to invoke what Groves has called vague 'motherhood' concepts such as fairness, legitimate expectation or abuse of power in the interest of combating perceived injustice,[100] have all contributed to greater accountability of tribunals. When coupled with their self-imposed duty of 'anxious scrutiny' in human rights cases, these developments have led the courts to go somewhat further in exercising their supervisory function than they might otherwise have done. The case of immigration tribunals is nevertheless, we would argue, somewhat special. As we shall see in the following section, the intensely difficult task of immigration tribunals has been made more so in recent years by a torrent of asylum appeals and a flood of reforming legislation that has left the tribunals in a constant state of flux.

6. Regularising asylum appeals

Immigration control as we understand it today starts effectively with the Aliens Act 1905. This Act was generous to intending immigrants, severely restricting Home Office powers of exclusion. Under threat of world war, however, these generous provisions were soon replaced by draconian powers to regulate, exclude and deport aliens, with correspondingly minimal powers of review.[101] In the post-war years, immigration continued to be regulated by the Home

[99] *Subesh v SSHD* [2004] EWCA Civ 56. And see *Shaheen v SSHD* [2005] EWCA Civ 1294; *Kaydanyuk v SSHD* [2006] EWCA Civ 368.

[100] M. Groves, 'The Surrogacy Principle and Motherhood Statements in Administrative Law' in Pearson, Harlow and Taggart, *Law in a Changing State* (Hart Publishing, 2008) pp. 88-92.

[101] By the Aliens Restriction Act 1914. On review of wartime powers generally, see *R v Halliday* [1917] AC 260; *Liversidge v Anderson* [1942] AC 206. The executive powers of deportation were unsuccessfully challenged on procedural grounds in *R v Home Secretary, ex p. Hosenball* [1977] 1 WLR 766. The informal advisory procedures (familiarly known as 'Three Wise Monkeys' procedure) were finally outlawed by the ECtHR in *Chahal v UK* (1993) 23 EHRR 413, to which the SIAC procedures discussed in Ch. 3 were a response.

Office and immigration decisions were taken by immigration officers exercising a statutory discretion in accordance with informal Home Office instructions. It was during this period that the UK signed the Refugee Convention, still the governing international legal instrument,[102] and the ECHR, which contains no specific provisions on the subject but provides 'subsidiary protection', especially through Art. 3 (torture and inhumane treatment) (*Chahal*, see p. 132 above).

The genesis of the modern immigration appeals system is the Wilson Committee on Immigration Appeals, which for the first time provided the framework for a statutory appeals system. Although, as we shall see, this has become increasingly complex and convoluted, the framework remains largely in place.[103] Why at a time when the state was considering wider and tougher immigration controls on British subjects was it thought appropriate to introduce appeals to tribunals for intending immigrants refused entry to Britain? On one view, appeals seemed the perfect legal buffer, 'enabling the State to maintain a liberal image while pursuing essentially illiberal policies'.[104] In Wilson itself, however, we find a mix of instrumentalist and non-instrumentalist reasons for procedural protection (see further Chapter 14). It was thought 'fundamentally wrong and inconsistent with the rule of law that power to take decisions affecting a man's whole future should be vested in officers of the executive, from whose findings there is no appeal'. More pragmatically, the system was insufficiently transparent; when the main safeguard was through hierarchical responsibility to the minister and ministerial responsibility to Parliament, it was not clear to potential migrants that what was being done was fair. In a passage that merits comparison with contemporary arguments over 'special advocate procedure' (see p. 129), the Committee pronounced:

> In this situation it is understandable that an immigrant and his relatives or friends should feel themselves from the outset to be under a disadvantage, and so should be less willing than they might otherwise be to accept the eventual decision . . . Complaints quite often express the feeling that the person concerned never had a chance to confront his interrogators on equal terms. Allegations of this kind are hard to counter when the whole process has taken place in private. They reflect unfairly on the officials concerned, and cumulatively they give rise to a general disquiet in the public mind. The evidence we have received strongly suggests that among the communities of Commonwealth immigrants in this country, and among people specially concerned with their welfare, there is a widespread belief that the Immigration Service deals with the claims of Commonwealth citizens seeking

[102] *UN Convention relating to the Status of Refugees of 28 July 1951 and Protocol of 1967* (known as the Refugee or Geneva Convention). In contrast to the ECHR, this Convention has never been 'domesticated'.

[103] *Report of the Committee on Immigration Appeals*, Cmnd 3387 (1967). The very limited appeal rights to the earlier Immigration Boards established under the Aliens Acts 1905 are dealt with in App. II.

[104] L. Bridges, 'Legality and immigration control' (1975) 2 *JLS* 221, 224.

> admission in an arbitrary and prejudiced way. We doubt whether it will be possible to dispel this belief so long as there is no ready way of having decisions in such cases subjected to an impartial review.[105]

Such was the background to the Immigration Appeals Act 1969 and Immigration Act 1971, which institutionalised immigration control and installed the modern system of immigration tribunals.[106] Adopting Wilson's two-tier model, the Act provided that appeals should lie first to adjudicators sitting alone in regional tribunals; secondly, with leave, to the IAT. These were, of course, general *immigration* tribunals and not dedicated tribunals for hearing *asylum* appeals. Provision for asylum appeals was not at that time considered necessary, since Home Office figures show that there were only a couple of hundred applications for asylum each year.[107] This was a system for immigration appeals that incidentally handled asylum cases.

Provision for appeals in asylum cases was grafted onto the tribunal system in 1993[108] when the number of asylum claims threatened to overwhelm the system. Claims, which numbered 3,900 in 1995, peaked in 2002 at around 84,000, when new legislation was introduced to stem the flow. From a structural standpoint, however, the system stayed relatively stable, retaining the two-tier model (adjudicator and IAT) installed by Wilson until 2004. By 2003, there were some 600 adjudicators, sitting individually at twenty-four main hearing centres around the country, many with full-time posts. In that year, they determined some 82,000 cases; the number had almost doubled in just two years. The IAT had also to be expanded and there had been an infusion of lawyers at senior level. No wonder that the Home Office was looking for savings. From modest beginnings as a sub-set of the immigration appeals jurisdiction in the early 1990s, asylum appeals had emerged in the course of a decade as one of the most considerable elements in the UK system of administrative tribunals.

From the early 1990s there was an unremitting flow of immigration legislation, all bringing change. But change remained substantive rather than structural: for example, appeals seen as frivolous and time-wasting could be filtered out of the system by ministerial certification that a claim to asylum was 'manifestly unfounded', in which case the appeal rights stopped at the adjudicator.[109]

[105] Wilson [83–5].

[106] See further, R. Moore and T. Wallace, *Slamming the Door: The administration of immigration control* (Martin Robertson, 1975); M. Travers, *The British Immigration Courts: A study of law and politics* (Policy Press, 1999). The Immigration Appeals Act was re-enacted in Part II of the 1971 Act.

[107] See generally D. Stevens, *UK Asylum Law and Policy: Historical and contemporary perspectives* (Sweet & Maxwell, 2004).

[108] Asylum and Immigration Appeals Act 1993. And see JUSTICE, *Providing Protection : Towards fair and effective asylum procedures* (JUSTICE, 1997).

[109] Sch. 2 of the Asylum and Immigration Appeals Act 1993 as re-enacted in s.1 of the Asylum and Immigration Act 1996 and the Immigration and Asylum and Act 1999. See Thomas, 'Evaluating tribunal adjudication', 466-9 and see *ZT (Kosovo) v Home Secretary* [2009] UKHL 6.

Again, 'fast-tracking' in the form of accelerated appeal procedures meant that, from the outset, the appeals process doubled as a single-tier and two-tier system in asylum. The Asylum and Immigration Act 1996 reduced the appeal rights of asylum-seekers, introducing the bizarre idea of 'non-suspensive appeals' or appeals made by appellants from *outside* the UK, in which – in sharp contrast to the tradition of oral proceedings – the appellant could not physically participate. In the face of continuing criticism of the quality and speed of the adjudication from many quarters, however, attention began to turn to the basic architecture of the system.[110] The fact that around 20 per cent of appeals from adjudicators succeeded was open to two interpretations: on the one hand, it was a not insubstantial proportion – enough to show that the IAT was not a rubber stamp and to demonstrate its credentials in Franks's terms as independent and autonomous 'machinery for adjudication'; on the other, from a managerial standpoint, that *only* 20 per cent of appeals succeeded could be presented as an invitation to do away with 'waste'.[111] Ministers vexed by high numbers of applications for leave to appeal hit at the source of delay by limiting second-tier appeals more closely to a point of law.[112]

Leggatt nonetheless observed how the general trend to judicialisation was being replicated in immigration tribunals.[113] The Nationality, Immigration and Asylum Act 2002 (NIAA), for example, provided for appointments to the IAT to be made by the Lord Chancellor. He also appointed a president, who must hold or have held high judicial office (Sch. 5), a chief adjudicator, and regional adjudicators with administrative responsibilities (Sch. 4). Leggatt also reported that, whatever the IAA's problems in the past:

> great efforts were being made to achieve more consistent decision-making, more effective administration, and much closer working between the Home Office and the Lord Chancellor's Department (LCD). The organisation has taken the opportunity to centralise much of the routine administration . . . allowing the hearing centres to focus on providing a high quality service to users and members.[114]

There was a push for greater consistency through the familiar techniques of 'starred' or binding IAT decisions; authoritative IAT statements on major points of law and principle; and latterly through 'country guideline determinations', or authoritative factual guidance from the IAT on conditions in specific countries.[115] To one of the authors, 'the IAT in its last few years was

[110] Select Committee on the LCD, *Asylum and Immigration Appeals: Written evidence*, HC 777-ii (2002/3).

[111] See R. Thomas, 'Asylum appeals: The challenge of asylum to the British legal system' in Shah (ed.), *The Challenge of Asylum to Legal Systems* (Cavendish, 2005).

[112] S. 101(1) of the Nationality, Immigration and Asylum Act 2002.

[113] Leggatt [149–54].

[114] *Ibid.*, p. 149 [6].

[115] See for practical illustrations, *Hamza v Home Secretary* [2002] UKIAT 05185 and *K (Croatia) v Home Secretary* [2003] UKIAT 00153.

developing a hierarchy and status more appropriate to the importance of its jurisdiction'.[116]

Contemplating incorporation of the IAA into the unified, two-tier structure it was proposing, Leggatt highlighted a 'significant structural anomaly' in the existing two-tier immigration arrangements:

> At present, cases are heard at first instance by legally qualified Adjudicators sitting alone. There is then a general appeal on both fact and law to the Tribunal, comprising a legally qualified chairman and two lay members. This brings in the expert contribution of non-lawyers too late in the process, and creates serious problems for the IAA and for the courts . . . We therefore wish to see the general model applied to immigration and asylum work in the Tribunal System. There should be a first-tier immigration and asylum tribunal, within a separate Division, which should be the sole judge of issues of fact . . . There should be a second-tier tribunal, consisting of a lawyer sitting alone, to hear appeals on a point of law only.[117]

But draconian changes in the provision for welfare and other restrictive policies indicated earlier were gradually bringing asylum claims down from the 2002 peak of 84,130; by 2008, they had fallen to 23,430, the lowest number since 1993. There were also improvements in the rate of primary determinations: by 2007, 40 per cent of new asylum cases were concluded within six months. The backlog of adjudicator decisions was being cleared, with a stable success rate of around 20 per cent.[118] Precisely why a new single-tier appeal system was urgently needed in 2003 was not entirely clear.

The Government's main argument was that judicial review was distorting the work of the specialised immigration tribunals while at the same time overloading the Administrative Court.[119] It is certainly true that both government and judiciary had expressed concern at the level of judicial review applications in immigration. They felt also that 'unmeritorious' claimants could use the multi-tier appeals system (in particular the widespread practice of seeking judicial review of IAT decisions to refuse permission to appeal) to prolong their stay in the country, making it harder to remove them. In response to that specific problem, the NIAA had initiated a streamlined form of statutory review – strict time limits, written submissions and no onward appeal (s. 101(2)).[120] Before this had time to bite, the Government embarked on drastic curtailment of appeal rights, culminating in the dramatic affair of the ouster clause, described in Chapter 1.

[116] R. Rawlings, 'Review, revenge and retreat' (2005) 68 MLR 378, 396.

[117] Leggatt, pp. 152–3 [21] [23].

[118] HO, Asylum Statistics UK for 2003 and 2004, HOSB 13/05, HOSB 11/04.

[119] A. Le Sueur, 'Three strikes and it's out? The UK government's strategy to oust judicial review from immigration and asylum decision-making' [2004] *PL* 225.

[120] The changes may help to explain the diminished use of standard judicial review process in asylum-related cases visible in 2003: see p. 740 below.

As finally passed by Parliament, the Asylum and Immigration (Treatment of Claimants, etc) Act 2004 represented both a capitulation by government and a break with the past. Not only did it introduce for the first time a single-tier system by rolling up the adjudicator system and IAT in a novel Asylum and Immigration Tribunal (AIT) that hears appeals on the merits, but it also attenuated the rights of appeal.[121] Onward appeal is by means of a streamlined, interactive and decidedly limited form of statutory review. Decisions made by single members in the AIT are subject to review by a High Court judge for error of law. Only one application, resulting in an order that the tribunal should 'reconsider' the appeal, can be made in respect of each appeal.[122] The grounds for appeal permit an 'appropriate court' to make a review order 'only if it thinks that the Tribunal may have made an error of law' (ss.103A(2) and (5)). The review is conducted solely on the papers without an oral hearing. Procedural rules further limit reconsideration to cases where there is a 'real possibility' that the appeal would be decided differently on reconsideration.[123] Appeal lies with leave on a point of law to the Court of Appeal and House of Lords. These provisions, making substantial changes in the role and functions of the appellate tribunals, raise concerns about the autonomy, independence and legitimacy of the one-tier tribunal.

This may be why the House of Lords took the opportunity in *Huang and Kashmiri*[124] to give authoritative advice on the function of tribunals in deciding a human rights application in immigration cases. In the human rights claim, the Law Lords saw the tribunal *not* as exercising a secondary, reviewing function but called on it to make its own, independent decision. The first task should be to establish the facts: 'It is important that the facts are explored, and summarised in the decision, with care, since they will always be important and often decisive'. The tribunal should then go on, applying tests of proportionality:

[121] S. 26 of the Act amends s. 81 and repeals ss. 101–3 of the NIAA. It inserts a new s.103 (A–E) before s.104 of the NIAA to cover the new appeals system: see R. Thomas, 'Immigration appeals overhauled again' [2003] *PL* 260.

[122] By Sch. 2 [30], the AIT was empowered for an interim period to review the need for reconsideration of its own decisions. In the event of the review application being unsuccessful, judicial review would usually be blocked out by analogy with *R (G) v Immigration Appeal Tribunal* [2004] 1 WLR 2953. The terms 'error of law' and 'reconsideration' have now been judicially defined: see R. Thomas, 'After the ouster: review and reconsideration in a single-tier tribunal' [2006] *PL* 674, 677–9.

[123] Asylum and Immigration Tribunal (Procedure) Rules 2005, SI 2005/230 as amended by the Asylum and Immigration Tribunal (Procedure)(Amendment) Rules 2008, SI 2008/1088. These authorise the extension of paper reviews and give the senior AIT judges power to remit appeals for further reconsideration by the tribunal. In *DK(Serbia) v Home Secretary* [2006] EWCA 1246, the Court of Appeal gave extensive guidance to the AIT on how these rules should be interpreted.

[124] *Huang and Kashmiri v Home Secretary* [2007] 2 AC 167. The case was decided under the Immigration and Asylum Act 1999 but was stated *obiter* to be applicable to the new, one-tier IAT.

> to consider and weigh all that tells in favour of the refusal of leave which is challenged, with particular reference to justification under [ECHR Art. 8(2), family life]. There will, in almost any case, be certain general considerations to bear in mind: the general administrative desirability of applying known rules if a system of immigration control is to be workable, predictable, consistent and fair as between one applicant and another; the damage to good administration and effective control if a system is perceived by applicants internationally to be unduly porous, unpredictable or perfunctory; the need to discourage non-nationals admitted to the country temporarily from believing that they can commit serious crimes and yet be allowed to remain; the need to discourage fraud, deception and deliberate breaches of the law; and so on . . . The giving of weight to factors such as these is not, in our opinion, aptly described as deference: it is performance of the ordinary judicial task of weighing up the competing considerations on each side and according appropriate weight to the judgment of a person with responsibility for a given subject matter and access to special sources of knowledge and advice.[125]

Once again, the reconstructed system had hardly bedded down when a new consultation paper signalled a sharp change of heart by the Government: it would after all be appropriate for the immigration appeals system to be taken within the two-tier TCEA structure, probably in a separate chamber. More significantly, to relieve the over-burdened judicial review system, the only way to appeal from a decision of the first-tier immigration tribunal would be by application to the Upper Tribunal, which would have exclusive jurisdiction in appeals. Remittal to the First-tier Tribunal would be exceptional, with the Upper Tribunal determining most appeals.[126] Finally, the TCEA would be amended to facilitate transfer of individual judicial review applications into the Upper Tribunal for decision.[127] Insofar as it would bring immigration tribunals inside the new system, the consultation paper is welcome; the suspicion must be, however, that asylum appeals will always be treated as exceptional.

7. Tribunals reformatted

(a) Restructuring[128]

The TCEA established tribunals as 'a vital but distinct part of the independent civil justice system' and their adjudicators as 'full members of the independent judiciary', with full guarantees of independence.[129] It set up a new Tribunals

125 [2007] 2 AC 167 [15–16].

126 UK Border Agency, *Consultation: Immigration Appeals, Fair Decisions; Faster Justice* (August, 2008) [28–36].

127 *Ibid.* [37]. There would be similar provisions for the Scottish Court of Session.

128 For an overview of the Act's main provisions, see House of Commons Library, *The Tribunals, Courts and Enforcement Bill*, Research Paper 07/22 (2007).

129 Sir Robert Carnwath, 'Administrative Justice and Tribunals Council: Getting there at last!' [4]. S. 1 of the TCEA applies s. 3 of the Constitutional Reform Act 2005 to office-holding tribunal members: the senior president, commissioners, adjudicators, panellists.

Service as an executive agency of the Ministry of Justice, which provides common administrative support to the larger tribunals.

The TCEA creates a senior president, appointed by a panel headed by the Lord Chief Justice, with overall responsibility for the new two-tier system of tribunals. Amongst his more important functions are: allocation of tribunals between 'chambers' and judges between tribunals; the provision of training (currently undertaken by the Judicial Studies Board); and chairing the Tribunal Procedure Committee, which takes over the function of preparing procedural rules. Section 2(3) of the TCEA prescribes the senior president's objectives: the need for tribunals to be accessible, fair, quick and efficient and for members to be expert. Significantly, the section adds 'the need to develop innovative methods of resolving disputes that are of a type that may be brought before tribunals' (s. 2(3)(d).

The TCEA creates two new tribunals, each divided into chambers headed by chamber presidents into which it is hoped that most existing jurisdictions will be transferred. The First-tier Tribunal is to comprise six 'generic' chambers to take in the major existing tribunal systems with a combined annual caseload of around 300,000 cases, approximately 190 judges and 3,600 odd members. These will broadly speaking continue to carry out their existing functions.[130] The Upper Tribunal, comprising three chambers, is seen by the Government as 'probably the most significant innovation in the tribunal system' and an opportunity 'to establish a strong and dedicated appellate body at the head of the new system'.[131]

The new structure is seen by Sir Robert Carnwath, its senior president, as an exciting opportunity 'to build a new coherent appellate structure':

> [The Upper Tribunal] will be a superior court of record, presided over by the Senior President. Its powers in relation to tribunal decisions will be as wide as those of the Administrative Court, including judicial review powers under arrangements to be agreed with the Lord Chief Justice. I hope that the Lord Chief Justice will also agree to High Court judges being available to sit on appropriate cases in the Upper Tribunal . . . I see no reason why the Upper Tribunal should not acquire a status and authority in tribunal matters equivalent to that of the Administrative Court in relation to public law generally.[132]

[130] The term 'generic' indicates that the chamber is not specialised (e.g. in tax) but groups together tribunals in the same area. The groupings are not yet finalised. In the first phase, the first-tier chambers seem likely to be: social entitlement; health, education and social care; war pensions and armed forces compensation. In 2009, a tax and duties chamber and general regulatory chamber will join the first tier and, by 2012, an immigration chamber. Employment tribunals will form a separate 'pillar'. Judges and members will be 'ticketed' to sit in particular jurisdictions or 'assigned' to different chambers: see *Transforming Tribunals* [160–4] and Ch. 7 generally.

[131] *Ibid.* [177]. The chambers are: administrative appeals; finance and tax; land. Again, an immigration chamber is contemplated. The first president of the administrative appeals chamber is a High Court judge, Sir Gary Hickinbottom, previously Chief Social Service Commissioner

[132] Carnwath, 'Administrative Justice and Tribunals Council: Getting there at last!'; and Sir Robert Carnwath, 'Tribunal Justice: A new start' [2009] *PL* 48.

The word 'court' is significant. Leggatt's proposals were premised on the model of the Australian Administrative Appeals Tribunal. The TCEA departs radically from the Australian precedent on which it was supposedly modelled.[133]

Tribunals at both levels are given power to 'review' their own decisions for purposes specified in the Tribunal Procedure Rules and may use this power to correct incidental errors, amend reasons or (under s. 9(4)(c)) set the decision aside. Where the First-tier Tribunal does this, it must either re-decide the matter or refer it to the Upper Tribunal (s. 9(5)); the Upper Tribunal's review powers are specified in the Tribunal Procedure Rules (s. 10). Appeal to the Upper Tribunal is on a point of law (s. 11).

Where the Upper Tribunal finds that an error of law infects the decision, it may either remit the decision to the First-tier Tribunal or 're-make the decision' itself (s. 12(2)(b)). Some of the problems mentioned in the immigration context are avoided, however, by giving each tribunal power in exercising its review functions 'to make such findings of fact as it considers appropriate' (ss. 9(8), 10(6), 12(4)(b)). Appeal lies to the Court of Appeal (or an alternative designated court), which is specifically given power to make any decision which the Upper Tribunal or other tribunal or person re-making the decision could make and to 'make such findings of fact as it considers appropriate' (s. 14(4)(a)–(b)). Thus the first English attempt at an administrative appeals tribunal takes the appeal process a little way towards 'merits review' in that tribunals as well as appeal courts are empowered to 're-make' the decision (in other words, substitute their decision for that of the decision-maker). It does not, however, authorise merits review in the full sense of that term, whereby 'the facts, law and policy aspects of the original decision are all reconsidered and a new decision – affirming, varying or setting aside the original decision – is made'.[134] Judicial review of tribunal decisions is intended to become a rarity. In 'highly specialised' areas, such as social security law, which are 'rarely encountered by lawyers', this 'new dedicated judicial institution will bring benefits that the Administrative Court cannot give . . . of supervision by judges who are specialists in the particular law and practice under review'.[135]

How this restructuring will work out in practice is far from clear, since the system is not yet fully operative. Clearly, however, it will, as was intended , push tribunals into the ambit of courts; in future they are likely to be less court substitutes and more quasi-courts. The appointment of tribunal adjudicators by the Judicial Appointments Committee, the 'transfer-in' of High Court judges

[133] See P. Cane, 'Understanding administrative adjudication' in Pearson, Harlow and Taggart (eds.), *Administrative Law in a Changing State* (Hart Publishing, 2008), p. 287, fn. 51.

[134] Australian Administrative Review Council, *Better Decisions: Review of Commonwealth Merits Review Tribunals*, Report No. 39 (1995) [2.2].

[135] Carnwath, 'Tribunal Justice: A new start', p. 57, citing *Cooke v Social Security Secretary* [2001] EWCA Civ 734 (Hale LJ).

to the Upper Tribunal (s. 31(2), training by the judicial studies board , are all factors likely to lead to judicialisation. More significant still is the appointment of a senior Lord Justice of Appeal as first president: this not only enhances the status of the new system but forms an important link, through the regional chief justices, with the 'court judiciary'. The senior president has described the TCEA as both 'a quiet revolution' and an 'evolution'. There can be little doubt as to where he wants the evolution to lead. Cane, however, thinks:

> it is unlikely, in the foreseeable future, that the distinction between courts and tribunals will be abolished in the UK. The more likely result is effective recognition of a branch of government the prime function of which is adjudication . . . consisting of two separate adjudicatory hierarchies. . .running in parallel but converging at the appellate level and sharing the two highest appellate bodies . . . In this dispensation, it will be possible to describe tribunals as a type of court and courts as a type of tribunal; or, more accurately, courts and tribunals as species of adjudicative institution.[136]

(b) Proportionate justice

Leggatt's brief was 'to review the delivery of justice through tribunals other than ordinary courts of law'; he was not asked to consider radical alternatives. Nor was *Transforming Public Services*, the subsequent White Paper[137] particularly innovatory; accepting Leggatt's case for systemic reform as 'convincing', it followed where Leggatt had led. Putting the question whether the changes could happen within the existing institutional structure, the White Paper opined that they could not:

> One option would be to create a new institution of some kind with the job of improving decision-making and resolving disputes informally. But even with such a new institution there would be a need for an authoritative body, with the powers of the court, to have the final word on rights and obligations. We believe the field is too cluttered already with administrative justice institutions. **What we need to do is to create the unified tribunal system recommended by Sir Andrew Leggatt but transform it into a new type of organisation which will not only provide formal hearings and authoritative rulings where these are needed but will have as well a mission to resolve disputes fairly and informally either by itself or in partnership with the decision-making department, other institutions and the advice sector.** [138]

This key passage sets out dual roles for tribunals. From a top-down perspective, tribunals operate as court substitutes, to provide 'authoritative rulings' imbued with the legitimacy of the judicial system. This objective, which suggests the use of trial-type procedures, the new dispensation amply supplies. From a

[136] Cane, 'Understanding administrative adjudication', p. 287.

[137] DCA, *Transforming Public Service: Complaints, redress and tribunals*, Cm. 6243, (July 2004).

[138] *Ibid.* [4. 21].

bottom-up perspective, the tribunal function of informal dispute resolution is endorsed in the last, highlighted sentence, which hints at exploration of novel methods of dispute-resolution. Despite the fact that the White Paper felt that, for the £280 million spent annually on tribunals, a better system could be created, the PDR theme was not developed.[139] It was left to the Council on Tribunals unerringly to pinpoint the omission in a letter accompanying its response to *Transforming Tribunals* and gently reproach the Tribunals Service with them:

> It is understandable that the consultation, like the Act itself, should have a structural focus with an attention to matters of detail. However, the paper sometimes seems to lose sight of the fact that rationalisation and standardisation are not ends in themselves but are part of a wider reform with the needs of users at its heart. There is little about the impact of the proposed changes on users . . . It is disappointing that the Enhanced Advice Project outlined in the 2004 White Paper appears to have been abandoned and that the paper gives no clear indication of how the need for advice will be met . . . The paper has little new to say about the broader administrative justice landscape and proportionate dispute resolution. While there is reference to early dispute resolution projects that have been under way for some time, there is no real sense of strategic direction in taking forward the wider vision of the 2004 White Paper. In the Council's view, this indicates a need for a dedicated policy team within the MoJ but outside the Tribunals Service to look at administrative justice issues in a more holistic way . . . So far as the present consultation is concerned, a subject of special interest to the Council is the proposed mapping of existing non-legal members into the new roles in a way that maximises the opportunity for their flexible use in appeals . . .

In its formal response, the Council expressed its warm support for the development of alternative dispute resolution, though only 'as a means of avoiding tribunals having to decide cases that can be resolved in other ways.'[140] Perhaps ironically, its informal letter had ended:

> The Council was pleased to see the attention paid in the paper to research in the administrative justice field, most of it funded independently of the Ministry of Justice and its predecessors. The Council is looking forward to its new statutory function of making proposals for research into the administrative justice system. An empirical base is essential in order for the Council and government to consider where improvements can be made.

Inside the framework of tribunals, five topics in particular cry out for further examination. The first is the question of merits review. Here we cannot do more than cite the tentative predictions of Sir Robert Carnwath published early in 2009, though once again there are clearly lessons to be learned from

[139] *Ibid.* [5.29] [5.30].

[140] Council on Tribunals, *Review of Tribunals: The Council's Response* (September 2000) [38].

Australia.[141] Carnwath believes that the Upper Tribunal is less likely to embark widely on merits review than to exercise its 'guidance' function constructively to influence appellate tribunals themselves to 'look at the matter in a more flexible way than the traditional approach'. He also predicted that a pragmatic attitude and tests of expediency were likely to develop in the characterisation of issues of fact and law; determinations were likely to depend on whether 'as a matter of policy' the court felt the matter to be one which 'an appellate body with jurisdiction limited to errors of law should be able to review'.[142]

As indicated earlier, review of faulty fact-finding is a source of particular difficulty in immigration appeals and the exceptional difficulties with fact-finding and evaluation of facts was the basis of a special case made by Leggatt for lay (or 'expert') members in immigration tribunals:

> Many cases would not be suitable for hearing by a chairman, even legally qualified, sitting alone and expert members should be used when appropriate at this level. In setting the qualifications for appointment to the tribunal, and to sit in particular cases, we believe that special care should be taken to ensure that those selected bring relevant experience and skills to the decisions to be taken, such as knowledge of conditions in particular countries concerned, or of refugees.[143]

There is no sign that particular attention has been paid to this need in the post-Leggatt reforms; rather the current terminology of 'expert members' marks a rapid slide into professionalism and judicialisation.[144] It follows that the second outstanding issue on the tribunals agenda must, as the AJTC has already suggested, be a proper investigation of the functions of lay members.

The last three questions are clearly linked: the third is the desirability of oral hearings; the fourth is representation; and the fifth inquisitorial procedure. These questions arise whenever the public is consulted, only to disappear from legislation or be shamefully side-lined by government departments.

Whether users really have a preference, as common lawyers like to think, for their 'day in court' is a moot point. Lawyers tend to see adversarial procedure as the best way to produce and test evidence. This is, however, only the case if the applicant and/or a departmental representative attend the hearing, which we have seen is by no means always the case. Sainsbury saw the move to

[141] See Administrative Review Council, *Better Decisions: Review of the Commonwealth Merits Review Tribunals* (Canberra, 1993); P. Cane, 'Merits review and judicial review: The AAT as a Trojan horse' (2000) 28 *Federal Law Review* 213; E. Fisher, 'Administrative law, pluralism, and the legal construction of merits review in Australian environmental courts and tribunals' and L. Pearson, 'Fact-finding in Administrative Tribunals', both in Pearson, Harlow and Taggart (eds)., *Administrative Law in a Changing State* .

[142] Sir Robert Carnwath, 'Tribunal Justice', pp 58–64. The citation is from *Serco v Lawson* [2006] UKHL 3 [34] (Lord Hoffmann). And see similarly *Moyna v Work and Pensions Secretary* [2003] UKHL 44.

[143] Leggatt p. 152

[144] D. Pearl, 'Immigration and asylum appeals and administrative justice', in Harris and Partington (eds.), *Administrative Justice in the 21st Century*.

internal review and investigatory procedure in social-security decision-making as a watering-down of applicants' appeal rights;[145] other users find oral hearings confrontational and oppressive:

> For many appellants an oral hearing may be a daunting thing and it is probably a factor explaining why some appellants fail to appear at their hearings . . . The nature of an oral hearing depends upon where the proceeding is on the spectrum of adversarial – inquisitorial. If the users are responding to questions posed by the tribunal this is very much easier to cope with compared to the preparation and making of representations.[146]

Parking Adjudicators, the only tribunal to move into the age of e-governance by conducting proceedings largely electronically, receive only a minority of requests for oral hearings. This suggests that, at least in the area of 'small claims', oral hearings are only a last resort for the public.[147]

Oral, adversarial proceedings inevitably raise the issue of representation, which we have seen is a matter of controversy. We know that with representation applicants do better and might tentatively deduce that they are probably disadvantaged without it (see p. 490 above). The 'enabling approach' eventually taken by Leggatt put to one side the difficult question of true inquisitorial procedure, in which proceedings become the responsibility of the adjudicator, who accumulates and produces the evidence, calls witnesses and conducts the questioning. Thomas has, however, suggested that inquisitorial procedure, on which he believes the system was originally predicated, might (for obvious reasons) be better suited to immigration cases.[148] Walter Merricks, the Financial Services Ombudsman, has put the case rather more strongly:

> The inquisitorial process is . . . suddenly being discovered as more effective and economical than the traditional adversarial model for arriving at the resolution of disputes. The court model of requiring both parties to assemble all their evidence (the relevant, the marginally relevant and the probably irrelevant) at a hearing for them to be explained orally to a tribunal is being seen as cumbersome, expensive and wildly uneconomic for many disputes.

[145] R. Sainsbury, 'Internal reviews and the weakening of social security claimants' rights of appeal' in Richardson and Genn (eds.), *Administrative Law and Government Action*. But see N. Wikeley, 'Burying Bell: Managing the judicialisation of social security tribunals' (2000) 63 *MLR* 475.

[146] Brian Thompson, evidence to the Leggatt consultation. See also G. Richardson, 'Listening to a range of views' (Spring 2006) *Tribunals* 18–20, an interim account of a Council on Tribunals consultation, *The Use and Value of Oral Hearings in the Administrative Justice System* (2005).

[147] J. Raine, 'Modernising tribunals through ICTS' in Partington (ed), *The Leggatt Review of Tribunals: Academic papers* (Bristol Centre for the Study of Administrative Justice, 2001); C. Sheppard and J. Raine, 'Parking adjudications: The impact of new technology' in Partington and Harris (eds.), *Administrative Justice in the 21st Century*.

[148] Thomas, 'Evaluating tribunal procedure', 477. And see S. Kneebone, 'The Refugee Review Tribunal and the assessment of credibility: An inquisitorial role?' (1998) 5 *Australian Journal of Administrative Law* 78.

> Ombudsmen on the whole don't need hearings. They do not need parties to be represented by lawyers. Their authority entitles them to go straight to the evidence we know to be relevant.[149]

This is a complex topic deserving of more meaningful research to which – as Australian public lawyers have started to do – the AJTC should devote its attention and some of its limited funds.[150]

This chapter ends where the next chapter starts: with inquisitorial procedure as an alternative to tribunals. It also ends where the previous chapter started: with the search for proportionate dispute resolution. Over the course of a century, it has been largely left to tribunals to deliver this. In the era of ICT and e-governance, however, alternative strategies might look better.

[149] In an address to the British and Irish Ombudsman Association, available on the BIOA website.

[150] N. Bedford and R. Creyke, *Inquisitorial Processes in Australian Tribunals* (Australian Institute of Judicial Administration, 2006).

12

The Parliamentary Ombudsman: Firefighter or fire-watcher?

Contents

1. In search of a role

In Chapter 10, we considered complaints-handling by the administration, settling for a 'bottom-up' approach. This led us to focus on proportionate dispute resolution (PDR) and machinery, such as internal review, by which complaints can be settled before they ripen into disputes. In so doing, we diverged from the 'top-down' tradition of administrative law where tribunals are seen as court substitutes. We returned to the classic approach in Chapter 11, looking at the recent reorganisation of the tribunal service and its place in the administrative justice system. We saw how the oral and adversarial tradition of British justice was reflected in tribunal procedure and considered the importance attached to impartiality and independence, values now protected by ECHR Art. 6(1). We, however, argued that recent reshaping of the tribunal system left unanswered key questions about oral and adversarial proceedings and whether they are always the most appropriate vehicle for resolving disputes with the administration. Would we be better served by inquisitorial and investigatory procedure such as is used by the ombudsman? We looked briefly at ombudsman systems within the UK in Chapter 10, noting an unfortunate degree of fragmentation and considering their relationship with courts. Now we want to look more closely at the way in which ombudsmen work, focusing on the Parliamentary Commissioner (PCA), with whose office truly inquisitorial and investigatory procedure first reached our shores in 1967.

An 'ombudsman' is literally a 'complaints man', a title suggesting a general grievance-handling function; alternatively, he may be described as a 'mediator' (the French title) because he aims at negotiated solutions. Ombudsmen have common characteristics, which the International Ombudsman Institute, to which most ombudsman offices belong, has listed in an effort to protect against dilution by the plethora of quasi- or pseudo-ombudsmen that today litter public and private space.[1] For Gregory and Giddings, the essence of the office is:

- an expert, independent and non-partisan instrument of the legislature established by statute or in the constitution;
- clearly visible and readily accessible to members of the public;
- responsible for both acting on its own volition and for receiving and dealing impartially with specific complaints from aggrieved citizens against alleged administrative injustice and maladministration on the part of governmental agencies, officials or employees.[2]

There is a good fit with a British and Irish Ombudsman Association (BIOA) list of criteria for good complaints-handling, namely clarity of purpose; accessibility; flexibility; openness and transparency; proportionality; efficiency and quality outcomes.[3] There is much similarity too with the views of the European Union Ombudsman (EO), expressed in a speech made to the ombudsmen of the twenty-seven Member States.[4] He sees as essential:

- a personal dimension to the office, with a publicly-recognised office-holder
- independence
- free and easy access for the citizen

[1] IOI, *Ombudsman newsletter*, vol. 29, no. 1 (March 2007). See also R. Gregory and P. Giddings, *Righting Wrongs: The ombudsman in six continents* (Amsterdam: IOS Press, 2000).

[2] R. Gregory *et al.*, *Practice and Prospects of the ombudsmen in the United Kingdom* (Edwin Mellon Press, 1995), p. 2. See also G. Caiden *et al.*, 'The institution of ombudsman', in G. Caiden (ed.), *International Handbook of the Ombudsman: Evolution and present function* (Greenwood Press, 1983).

[3] BIOA, *Guide to Principles of Good Complaints Handling: Firm on principles, flexible on process* (April 2007) available online.

[4] N. Diamandouros, Speech to fifth seminar of the national ombudsmen of the EU member states (12 September 2005) available on the EO website.

- primary focus on the handling of complaints, whilst having the power to recommend not only redress for individuals but also broader changes to laws and administrative practices
- use of proactive means, such as own-initiative inquiries and providing officials with guidance on how to improve relations with the public
- effectiveness based on moral authority, cogency of reasoning and ability to persuade public opinion, rather than power to issue binding decisions.

Special stress is rightly laid on the fact that the office is furnished with practically unrestricted access to official papers, empowered to investigate, form judgements, criticise or vindicate, make recommendations as to remedies and corrective measures, and report on but not reverse, administrative action. We might add that in contrast to courts, which normally administer justice publicly, PCA procedure is private, a factor that undoubtedly facilitates full access to documents. Nor do the anonymised reports name individuals.

The procedure of British ombudsmen resembles that of courts in that neither has power to open 'own-initiative' investigations. They must await a complaint (although in practice they may be able to arrange one.) In this respect, the office is not inspectorial nor does it form part of the regulatory machinery of government, though there are certain parallels with the work of auditors, in that government acknowledges a general 'fire-watching' brief for ombudsmen in matters of good administration. But the ombudsman neither possesses the powers of a regulator nor does he act as an 'inspector-general' of state services. As the EO once put it, ombudsmen are concerned not only with redress for individuals but also with 'broader changes to laws and administrative practices'. They are properly fire-watchers as well as firefighters.[5] This is, however, a role that the PCA is trying to build.

2. The PCA's office

Established by the Parliamentary Commissioner Act 1967, the PCA is an officer of the House of Commons, appointed by the Crown on the advice of the Prime Minister. In practice, after some wrangling, appointments are made with the approval of the Leader of the Opposition after consultation with the chairman of the Public Administration Select Committee (PASC). In practice, two terms of five years has been the maximum but this has recently been reduced to a single seven-year term. The desirability of change to a more secure statutory basis has been acknowledged by the government but the change has never been made.[6] Like High Court judges, however, the PCA's tenure is secure: s/he holds office during good behaviour. Appointment through patronage together with the fact that the majority of Commissioners have come from

[5] *Ibid.* And see C. Harlow, 'Ombudsmen in search of a role' (1978) 41 *MLR* 446.

[6] Select Committee on the PCA, *Powers, Work and Jurisdiction of the Ombudsman*, HC 33 (1993/4) [31]. For the government response, see HC 619 (1993/4).

within the public service,[7] have not unnaturally helped to cast doubt on the independence of the office. Thus JUSTICE has campaigned unremittingly for the appointment of a lawyer or someone external to the Civil Service. As argued earlier, however, independence can be distinguished from impartiality. Arguments over independence are moreover often arguments over different values: a lawyer-ombudsman might, for example, be expected to share the values and practices of his profession.

Although different individuals have in fact perceived their role differently, the PCA has invariably seen the office as impartial. PCAs appointed from inside the civil service have not shown particular leniency to their erstwhile colleagues (see the *Channel Tunnel* case, below) while some of the most restrictive interpretations of jurisdiction have been made by lawyer-ombudsmen.[8] Later in this chapter we shall find cases where the PCA has acted more independently and more effectively than a lawyer appointed to hold a ministerial inquiry (*Barlow Clowes*, below); in other cases too PCAs have acted more courageously and more generously than courts.[9] But the view of the office as quasi-judicial has constrained the PCA from acting as 'citizen's advocate' (though it may be felt after reading this chapter that in recent years the position has shifted, perhaps because of the appointment of a Commissioner from NACAB). Civil servants, however, need impartiality; a key administrative benefit of the scheme was that individual civil servants, falsely accused, should be able to clear their name.

The PCA's first office was staffed by ninety or so people and is still not large in civil service terms.[10] At first a handful of lawyers reinforced a staff of career civil servants seconded from central-government departments. From the standpoint of independence this was a controversial practice, though it proved highly effective, providing a built-in understanding of civil service procedure. Today, when recruitment is open and job opportunities, including ombudsman appointments, advertised on the office website, a high proportion of those appointed continue to come from public-service posts.

[7] Sir Edmund Compton, previously Comptroller and Auditor-General, was followed by Sir Alan Marre and Sir Idwal Pugh, both Permanent Secretaries; then came two lawyers, Sir Cecil Clothier and Sir Anthony Barrowclough; Sir William Reid, a Permanent Secretary from the Scottish Home and Health Department; and Sir Michael Buckley, a local government official who had chaired an NHS trust. A break with the past came with the appointment of Ann Abraham in 2002. She had previous ombudsman experience as chair of the BIOA and Legal Services Ombudsman; prior to this, however, she was chief executive of NACAB, the National Association of Citizens Advice Bureaux.

[8] A. Bradley, 'The role of the ombudsman in relation to the protection of citizens' rights' [1980] 39 *CLJ* 304; R. Rawlings, 'The legacy of a lawyer-ombudsman', (June 1985) *Legal Action* 10.

[9] Compare *First Report of the PCA*, HC 20 (2001/2) Case C557/98 (compensation recommended) with *Reeman v DoT and Others* [1997] 2 Lloyds Rep. 648 (no liability in tort for negligent inspection in the same case).

[10] In 2006-7, the offices of PCA and HSC employed around 293 staff, five in senior management. Expenditure on the two offices is currently agreed at £24,026 million, by no means a trivial sum, of which £12,209,000 was spent on handling PCA complaints: see *Resource Accounts 2006/7*, HC 839 (2006/7).

The function of the PCA is to investigate complaints referred by an MP on behalf of individuals or private concerns that have suffered maladministration.[11] In other words, the office is at the disposal of the *general* public; it cannot be used to sort out disputes between public bodies or between public servants and the Government as employer. To succeed, a complainant must satisfy a two-pronged test of 'injustice' caused by 'maladministration' (see p. 534 below). The complainant is required to be someone 'directly affected' by maladministration resident in the UK, or relating to rights and obligations accruing in the UK (s. 6(1)); a complainant cannot act as public advocate to notify the PCA of departmental incompetence. In practice, as we shall see, this rule is mitigated by the office blocking-up frequent complaints into a single investigation or by MPs coming together to refer group complaints. In this type of case, the modern practice is to select around four sample cases, 'parking' the rest and absorbing them into a Special Report laid under s. 10(3).[12] This is something courts cannot easily do.

The 1967 Act offset flexibility with complex limitations. The PCA's jurisdiction covered only central government departments and other public bodies *specifically listed* in Sch. 2 of the Act. Schedule 3 exempted from investigation some key governmental concerns, including all commercial transactions and civil service personnel matters and, originally, all official action taken abroad (this has now been modified to include consular staff). There have since been many changes. Today over 250 bodies are listed, including all central government departments, an odd assortment of quangos, and some privatised bodies.[13] This method of proceeding is hardly transparent and it may help to explain why so many complaints to the PCA fall outside his jurisdiction.

The distinguishing characteristic of the PCA is his close relationship with Parliament. This restricts his remit. The Act provides that only an MP can lay a complaint before the PCA. This 'MP filter' has provoked much criticism, though successive PCAs have in practice learned how to circumvent it.[14] It is true that, in 1967, many MPs agreed with the main Opposition spokesman that the office would be a threat to a system where, it was said, a key feature of our parliamentary democracy was that MPs provided an 'efficient and relatively sophisticated grievance machinery'.[15] JUSTICE on the other hand has always

[11] Health service complaints are made first to the body concerned for resolution; if dissatisfied, the complainant goes directly to the HSC.

[12] Sir Michael Buckley, *Oral Evidence to Select Committee*, HC 62-ii (2001-2) Questions 23, 24.

[13] Sch. 1 of the Parliamentary and Health Service Commissioners Act 1987 expanded the list to more than 100 bodies and allowed for change to be made by a statutory instrument, in practice made almost annually. See also the Health Services Commissioner Act 1993 and the Deregulation and Contracting Out Act 1994.

[14] *Review of Access and Jurisdiction*, HC 615 (1977/8) [10]. The PCA had invented a circuitous way to deal with complaints referred directly by the public by sending them on to the constituency MP to decide whether to refer the complaint back formally. The current website helps complainants to locate their MP but makes no suggestion how to proceed if the MP does not refer, e.g., by contacting another MP.

[15] HC Deb., vol. 734, col. 65. And see G. Drewry and C. Harlow, 'A "cutting edge"? The Parliamentary Commissioner and MPs' (1990) 53 *MLR* 745.

maintained that direct access is essential 'if the Commissioner is properly to fulfil the role of providing redress for citizens with complaints against central administration, and of acting as watchdog against administrative abuse'.[16] This view is beginning to predominate. Over the years, the relationship between MPs and the PCA has changed radically. Hard-worked constituency MPs seem better informed about the office and more willing to use the machinery and there are many high-profile examples of group complaints (below). Defensive attitudes have also changed; a Cabinet Office Review in 2000 found 'almost universal dissatisfaction with the arrangements for access to the PCA via an MP.'[17] Ann Abraham has joined her predecessors in saying that the MP filter acts as a barrier to transparency; removal would help the office in its efforts to become more accessible. PASC has recommended removal.[18] The Government seems to accept the need for change. But legislation is still awaited.

The PCA's remit is maladministration and s. 12(3) of the 1967 Act reads:

> It is hereby declared that nothing in this Act authorises or requires the Commissioner to question the merits of a decision taken without maladministration . . . in the exercise of a discretion vested in [a] department.

At an early stage, however, the Select Committee (SC) encouraged the first PCA, Sir Edmund Compton, to interpret this provision generously so as to encompass 'bad decisions' and 'bad rules', a line followed by subsequent Commissioners.[19] Nonetheless, disputes over discretion and the merits of decisions have arisen on many occasions, especially where decisions complained of are those of a minister, as in the early *Sachsenhausen* and *Court Line* investigations.

Announcing the appointment of a former Comptroller and Auditor-General to an office not yet in being, the minister (Mr Crossman) soothingly explained, 'It is a Parliamentary officer that we want, and Sir Edmund Compton is a most distinguished Parliamentary officer already.'[20] Successive PCAs have set great store by their status as parliamentary officials, a relationship at once an advantage and disadvantage. The PCA is responsible to a Select Committee of the Commons – currently PASC – to which regular reports are made. He lays his reports as parliamentary papers and dispatches individual findings to the referring MP. The Committee follows investigations, summons witnesses and issues its own reports on matters arising. Very occasionally, as in the *Occupational*

[16] JUSTICE, *Our Fettered Ombudsman* (JUSTICE, 1977), pp. 1, 16–19. See also JUSTICE–All Souls Review, *Administrative Justice: Some necessary reforms* (Clarendon Press, 1988), Ch. 5.

[17] R. Kirkham, *The Parliamentary Ombudsman: Withstanding the test of time*, HC 421 (2006/7), p. 11 reports that 66% of MPs surveyed by the office favoured removal. See also the *Colcutt Review of the Public Sector Ombudsmen in England: A report by the Cabinet Office* (HMSO, 2000), p. 20.

[18] See PASC, *4th Report of the Parliamentary Ombudsman for 1998-1999*, HC 106 (1999/2000) [6I] and for the PCA's views, memo to PASC, *ibid.*

[19] *Select Committee on the PCA*, HC 350 (1967/8).

[20] HC Deb., vol. 734, col. 54.

Pensions affair described below, reports are debated on the floor of the House.[21] On the credit side, this lends muscle to the PCA; the powerful Select Committee looming over the PCA's shoulder is usually sufficient to secure compliance. On the debit side, the relationship has sometimes acted as a restraint. The PCA has to be a particular type of person capable of walking a tightrope between government and Parliament. Sir Cecil Clothier, a notably compliant lawyer, once questioned whether he should investigate complaints which Parliament had debated, on the ground that 'Parliament would not tolerate to be corrected by my subsequent investigation if I should arrive at a different conclusion'.[22] Other PCAs have fallen into a cosy relationship with their Select Committee (and vice versa). Thus in one sense the link threatens independence, perhaps the most crucial factor in legitimating complaints machinery; on the other hand, the *Occupational Pensions* case shows how a good relationship to the strongly chaired PASC lent strength to an embattled PCA.

3. From maladministration to good administration

Deliberately, the 1967 Act did not define maladministration, though the Government spokesman, Richard Crossman, described it during debates on the bill as including 'bias, neglect, inattention, delay, incompetence, ineptitude, perversity, turpitude, arbitrariness and so on'.[23] The term has proved elastic. In some cases the two-pronged test of 'maladministration causing injustice' has been glossed by PCAs anxious to extend their competence. Findings not strictly maladministration or maladministration causing injustice have been used to prod departments into action through references to 'errors' or phrases such as 'I was critical of' or 'left with a feeling of unease'. In his Annual Report for 1993, the PCA (William Reid) proposed updating the 'Crossman Catalogue' to give a clearer indication in the language of the 1990s of what was expected of departments. To Crossman's list, Reid added examples with a notably more bureaucratic flavour:

- rudeness (though that is a matter of degree);
- unwillingness to treat the complainant as a person with rights;
- refusal to answer reasonable questions;
- neglecting to inform a complainant on request of his or her rights or entitlement;
- knowingly giving advice which is misleading or inadequate;
- ignoring valid advice or overruling considerations which would produce an uncomfortable result for the overruler;
- offering no redress or manifestly disproportionate redress;
- showing bias whether because of colour, sex, or any other grounds;
- omission to notify those who thereby lose a right of appeal;

[21] See R. Gregory, 'The Select Committee on the Parliamentary Commissioner for Administration 1967–1980' [1982] *PL* 49.

[22] C. Clothier, 'Legal problems of an ombudsman' (1984) 81 *Law Soc. Gaz.* 3108.

[23] HC Deb., vol. 734, col. 51 (Mr Crossman). And see G. Marshall, 'Maladministration' [1973] *PL* 32.

- refusal to inform adequately of the right of appeal;
- faulty procedures;
- failure by management to monitor compliance with adequate procedures;
- cavalier disregard of guidance which is intended to be followed in the interest of equitable treatment of those who use a service;
- partiality; and
- failure to mitigate the effects of rigid adherence to the letter of the law where that produces manifestly unequal treatment.[24]

The advent of 'new public management' (NPM) and the later Citizen's Charter faced the PCA with the question whether departure from standards and performance indicators should constitute maladministration. After discussion, the Committee agreed that the PCA ought to have regard to charter assurances when investigating complaints but should not consider himself bound; 'they leave the Parliamentary Commissioner . . . unfettered in his discretion to determine whether or not maladministration has taken place'. The PCA would help to provide 'independent validation of performance against standards' but departmental standards were not to be the benchmark of maladministration.[25] Ann Abraham's approach is somewhat different. Stressing her fire-watching function, she has spoken of clear agreement right across the public service about a number of key principles with significant constitutional implications. These can be expressed as 'a series of shared understandings:[26]

- a shared understanding of what makes for good public administration: the principles of good administration
- a shared understanding of what needs to be done when things go wrong in public administration or public services: the principles of redress
- a shared understanding of the respective roles of the Ombudsman, Parliament, government and the courts in putting things right when they go wrong, including the key task of making sure lessons are learned by public services.

On all these issues, she was keen to play a positive role.

On the fortieth anniversary of the office, with a view both to transparency and the promotion of good administration, the PCA issued her key *Principles of Good Administration*. Stressing that they were neither a checklist nor 'the final or only means' by which to assess and decide individual cases, she urged public bodies to use their judgement in applying them 'to produce reasonable, fair and proportionate results in the circumstances'. The Principles would be 'broad statements of what we believe public bodies within jurisdiction should be doing to deliver good administration and customer service. If we conclude that a public body has

[24] *Annual Report for 1993*, HC 290 (1993/4) [7].

[25] *The Implications of the Citizen's Charter for the Work of the Parliamentary Commissioner for Administration*, HC 158 (1992/3), evidence at pp. 12–13 (Mr Reid).

[26] PCA, 'The Ombudsman, the constitution and public services: A crisis or an opportunity?' Speech to Constitution Unit Seminar (4 December 2006).

not followed the Principles, we will not automatically find maladministration or service failure. We will apply the Principles fairly and sensitively to individual complaints, which we will, as ever, decide on their merits and in all the circumstances of the case.'[27] The short text is managerial but consumer-oriented:

Principles of Good Administration

Good administration by a public body means:

1 Getting it right
2 Being customer focused
3 Being open and accountable
4 Acting fairly and proportionately
5 Putting things right
6 Seeking continuous improvement

Each of these headings is then broken down and fleshed out in guidance. 'Getting it right' means:

- acting in accordance with the law and with due regard for the rights of those concerned
- acting in accordance with the public body's policy and guidance (published or internal)
- taking proper account of established good practice
- providing effective services, using appropriately trained and competent staff
- taking reasonable decisions, based on all relevant considerations.

The supporting text fleshes out each principle. Thus 'getting it right' reflects a wider context of management and risk assessment:

1. Getting it right

- All public bodies must comply with the law and have due regard for the rights of those concerned. They should act according to their statutory powers and duties and any other rules governing the service they provide. They should follow their own policy and procedural guidance, whether published or internal.
- Public bodies should act in accordance with recognised quality standards, established good practice or both, for example about clinical care.
- In some cases a novel approach will bring a better result or service, and public bodies should be alert to this possibility. When they decide to depart from their own guidance, recognised quality standards or established good practice, they should record why.
- Public bodies should provide effective services with appropriately trained and competent staff. They should plan carefully when introducing new policies and procedures. Where public bodies are subject to statutory duties, published service standards or both, they should plan and prioritise their resources to meet them.

[27] PCA, *Principles of Good Administration* (March, 2007) available online.

- In their decision making, public bodies should have proper regard to the relevant legislation. Proper decision making should give due weight to all relevant considerations, ignore irrelevant ones and balance the evidence appropriately.
- Public bodies necessarily assess risks as part of taking decisions. They should, of course, spend public money with care and propriety. At the same time, when assessing risk, public bodies should ensure that they operate fairly and reasonably.

The text looks to the 'Seven Principles of Public Life' set out by the Nolan Committee, the BIOA Guide (see p. 529 above) and the values and practices of the Civil Service Code.[28] Its general tone is one of fire-watching. The need for personal initiative, responsibility and discretion is stressed.

4. Firefighting or fire-watching?

There has never been full agreement over the PCA's role and functions. The office has an adjudicative and an inspectorial role, in which 'firefighting' and 'fire-watching' are combined. The two functions have seemed on occasion to be pulling it apart.

(a) The small claims court

The perception of ombudsmen as firefighters infused the influential report *The Citizen and the Administration*,[29] which lay behind the legislation. The lawyerly emphasis was not surprising; the report under the direction of Sir John Whyatt, a former judge, was drawn up for JUSTICE, a pressure group of lawyers dedicated, according to its constitution, to the 'preservation of the fundamental liberties of the individual'. Whyatt contended that traditional controls left a gap. Judicial review was too limited, leaving much maladministration (e.g., rudeness or delay) un-redressed and too expensive to challenge save in the exceptional case. Equally, parliamentary procedures were ineffective; adjournment debates and parliamentary questions were uneven contests because only the executive possessed all the relevant information. Ad hoc inquiries were little-used Rolls-Royce machinery unsuited to everyday matters. Into the gap, an ombudsman should be inserted. Directed as it was towards redress of grievances, the Whyatt report did not consider fire-watching functions; the identification of administrative inefficiency with a view to its eradication passed the committee by. Effectively, the role envisaged by the Whyatt report was an administrative small claims court or court substitute, decisively oriented towards small claims. Neither JUSTICE nor the House of Commons

[28] The very different text of the EO, *The European Code of Good Administrative Behaviour* 2005, available online is consonant with the more legalistic definition of maladministration in the EO's Annual Report for 1997 as occurring 'when a public body fails to act in accordance with a rule or principle which is binding upon it'.

[29] JUSTICE, *The Citizen and the Administration* (1961).

analysed the general consequences for administration although, in advocating informal investigatory techniques designed to minimise administrative disruption, JUSTICE did recognise that departments expend resources in investigations. They envisaged the new office as a sort of standing inquiry able to go behind the anonymity of ministerial responsibility. Perhaps it was not surprising that, at a time before departmental select committees became operative, and well before the audit culture had come into being, the PCA was not viewed as an auditor-general or government inspector.

This perception infuses all JUSTICE's later work on the office. Consistent with its initial position, the question of direct access to the PCA has been a constant source of concern to JUSTICE, which has, as already indicated, consistently lobbied for open access, criticised the tendency to appoint career civil servants to the post and campaigned on grounds of independence for the appointment of a lawyer.[30] Its only concession to problems of overload has been that, while elaborate investigations were appropriate for difficult cases, informal methods would produce immediate redress in routine cases. In practice, however, the problem of overload did not arise. It was not until 2000 that a population of over 50 million potential complainants produced 2,000 complaints in a single year. This is surprising. Compare the figures with, say, social security appeals (see p. 487 above); complaints to the Information Commissioner (see p. 477 above); or even to the Revenue Adjudicator (see p. 459 above). Although complaints have risen gradually until they average around 4,000 annually, we must remember that the PCA's jurisdiction has altered substantially, expanding to include new agencies but in other ways retracting as competences have been ceded to regional government and regional ombudsmen. Critics blame the MP filter.

It could be argued from a PDR standpoint that the MP filter helps to get disputes settled at the earliest possible stage. The flaw in this argument lies at the bottom of the pyramid, where the response of MPs to their complaints function and their use of the PCA is unmonitored, unstructured, uncontrolled and sporadic.[31] While some regard themselves as 'statutory pillar boxes', others exercise independent discretion and refuse to pass on complaints. Nor is there any machinery whereby the PCA can rid his office of trivial complaints; he would indeed probably be loath to do this, as trivial complaints occasionally trigger a complex and demanding investigation.

(b) Ombudsmen and courts

Despite the fact that Richard Crossman, the bill's promoter, voiced traditional Labour Party aversion to courts, the Labour Government did not allow the PCA to supplant existing machinery for redress.[32] The statutory solution

[30] See n. 16 above.

[31] See R. Rawlings, 'The MP's Complaints Service' (1990) 53 *MLR* 22, 149; Harlow and Drewry, 'A "cutting edge"? The Parliamentary Commissioner and MPs'.

[32] s. 5(2) of the Parliamentary Commissioner Act 1994.

represents a modest attempt to avoid overlapping remedies. It provides that where a complaint relates to a matter giving rise to a right of appeal to a tribunal or to a court remedy, the PCA shall not investigate unless 'satisfied that in the particular circumstances it is not reasonable to expect [the complainant] to resort or have resorted to it'. But the PCA possesses an overarching discretion, giving him considerable freedom of manoeuvre; s. 5(5) provides that in determining whether to initiate, continue or discontinue an investigation, the PCA shall 'act in accordance with his own discretion'. This discretion has at various times been exercised in very different ways. Sir Idwal Pugh, a former civil servant, used it generously, inaugurating a practice (of doubtful legal validity) of extracting from complainants a promise to refrain from legal action. Sir Cecil Clothier, a lawyer, was also generous, saying:

> Where there appears on the face of things to have been a substantial legal wrong for which, if proved, there is a substantial legal remedy, I expect the citizen to seek it in the courts and I tell him so. But where there is doubt about the availability of a legal remedy or where the process of law seems too cumbersome, slow and expensive for the objective to be gained, I exercise my discretion to investigate the complaint myself.[33]

Less generously, another lawyer, Sir Anthony Barrowclough, refused to investigate a dispute as to whether a claim form had been received by a department, a typical ombudsman matter, disingenuously advising that recourse to a civil action would be 'a relatively simple and inexpensive matter'.[34] Closer co-operation between courts and the statutory ombudsmen has been suggested;[35] perhaps, however, it is this restriction rather than the MP filter that needs to be lifted.

(c) Fire-watching: Inspection and audit

Ten years after the office had been established, Harlow argued that the PCA had yet to identify a distinctive role. A PCA investigation cost a government department about eighty hours of staff time and the expensive machinery was wasted if treated merely as a small claims court. The Swedish Ombudsman could act without complaints, either by initiating his own investigations, for example after adverse press reports, or by inspecting institutions within his jurisdiction; Harlow argued that the PCA needed similar powers:

> His *primary* role should be that of an independent and unattached investigator, with a mandate to identify maladministration, recommend improved procedures and negotiate their implementation. Changes in his jurisdiction and procedures should be made only if they facilitate the execution of this task. If this is right, the individual complaint is primarily a mechanism which draws attention to more general administrative deficiencies . . . [And]

[33] HC 148 (1980/1), p. 1.

[34] Complaint 45/88, *Annual Review 1988*, HC 480 (1988/9), p. 17.

[35] Law Commission, *Administrative Redress: Public bodies and the citizen, a consultation paper*, CP No. 187 (2008), pp. 99–116.

> the essential question with regard to access is whether the PCA should be given power to intervene of his own initiative. It is submitted that he should.[36]

Acknowledging the function of MPs in filtering simple and trivial complaints, Harlow argued for a strategic role for the PCA. The PCA should concentrate on quality rather than quantity, developing his fire-watching characteristics.

In its ten-year review of the PCA's office,[37] the SC took faltering steps towards a fire-watching function. It recommended that the PCA should, subject to the Committee's approval, be able to mount a systemic investigation where he believed on the basis of previous complaints that a particular department was working inefficiently, with a view to making recommendations for putting things right. Although Sir Idwal Pugh, then PCA, thought this the most important of the recommendations, the Government rejected the idea of an inspectorial power as 'unnecessary and undesirable':

> It would place a heavy burden on the Commissioner if he were required in effect to 'audit' the administrative competence of government departments and would distract him and his staff from *their central purpose of investigating complaints* . . . Where the Commissioner investigates a series of complaints relating to a particular area of administration he is . . . able to form a clear view of the procedures in force there and to make recommendations . . . Any lessons to be drawn from investigations by the Commissioner are already studied by departments and acted upon . . . It should be for Ministers and their departments to decide what action is necessary to prevent further maladministration by a particular branch or establishment, and to be answerable to Parliament for the adequacy of the action . . . taken.[38]

Arguably, a crucial opportunity was lost to put the PCA on a level with the Auditor and Comptroller-General, and his select committee on a level with the far more influential Public Accounts Committee.

In 1993, in a review of competence and functions, the SC again recommended change to allow the PCA both to conduct audits of bodies within his jurisdiction and also to carry out own initiative inquiries at the SC's request but although the Government broadly favoured the recommendations, no steps were taken to implement them.[39] Successive PCAs have, however, found ingenious ways to circumvent the restriction. William Reid, for example, used his power under s. 10(3) of the 1967 Act to group together cases that seemed to suggest endemic maladministration in a particular area, as he did with complaints concerning poor performance in the Child Support Agency (below). He then made general recommendations that were presented to Parliament as special reports. This went some way to fill a glaring jurisdictional gap.

36 C. Harlow, 'Ombudsmen in search of a role' (1978) 41 *MLR* 446, 450–3.

37 *Review of Access and Jurisdiction*, HC 615 (1977/8) [31]. See also First Report of the SC, HC 129 (1990/1) [19–22].

38 *Observations by the Government on Review of Access and Jurisdiction*, Cmnd 7449 (1997/78), pp. 5–6.

39 See HC 33 (1993/4), and for the Government Response, HC 619 (1993/4).

Equally, the SC may adopt a fire-watching stance, taking up cases that suggest endemic failures. After Mr Buckley reported two cases of lengthy delay by the Immigration and Nationality Directorate, for example, resulting in leave to remain being granted 'largely because of the delays rather than because it was judged there had been any original merit in [the] case', the SC sent for and questioned the Director. When he and his staff admitted to 'poor performance, poor working processes and heavy backlogs', the Committee reviewed the department's IT provision, concluding:

> The resultant crisis, with attendant publicity, has led to action being taken. Budgetary constraints have recently been relaxed, and the IND has recruited substantial numbers of additional staff. However, it is important to recognise both that it will inevitably take some months for the benefits of these welcome additional resources to filter through, and, perhaps more fundamentally, that the recent crisis only revealed the extent of the difficulties in which IND has been struggling for some considerable time previously; it did not cause them. An end to the short-term crisis in asylum seekers will not mean an end to the day-to-day problems attendant on the rest of the IND's workload. **A proper assessment must be made of long-term requirements and adequate resources provided to ensure that such backlogs are not permitted to build up again.**[40]

Expressing the hope that it would not 'be necessary to recall the IND for our next inquiry', the SC accepted that 'a corner had now been turned'. This belief, as we know from previous chapters, has not been the case!

In her Special Report on the child and working tax credits system, aimed at tackling child poverty and encouraging more people into work, Ann Abraham also took a broad-brush approach. The system affected around 6 million families, using a wholly IT-based processing system. Given the scale of this undertaking, the PCA concluded, introduction of the scheme had been broadly successful yet the complaints in one single year had amounted to 22 per cent of her total workload. Her Special Report:

> charts the experience for that particular group of tax credit customers. It seeks to understand what has gone wrong in those cases, the impact on customers, the effectiveness of the Revenue's response and the lessons to be learned. However it also raises wider and more fundamental issues, which are not for me, but for Government and Parliament to address, such as whether a financial support system which includes a degree of inbuilt financial uncertainty can meet the needs of this particular group of families. It also suggests that, if such a system is to meet those needs, then a much improved level of customer service is required in the form of better and clearer communications, easier and quicker customer access to Revenue staff who can address problems and queries, and prompt and efficient complaint handling. Without these a sizeable group of families will continue to suffer not just considerable inconvenience, but also significant worry, distress and hardship . . .

[40] 4th Report for 1998-9, HC 106 (1999–2000) [17–20].

> In addition, I believe that this review suggests that there are important lessons to be learned, not just for HM Revenue and Customs, but for all public bodies when implementing new policies and systems. In particular, it highlights the importance, when designing new systems, of starting from the customer perspective and maintaining customer focus throughout the development of the programme. It also highlights the dangers of introducing a 'one size fits all' system. Such systems, whilst superficially providing a fair and consistent and efficient service for all customers can, by failing to pay sufficient regard to the different circumstances and needs of specific client groups, have entirely unintended harsh and unfair consequences for more vulnerable groups.[41]

Twelve very specific recommendations followed. Implementation was monitored and the report followed up two years later, when the office realised that complaints were not, as they had assumed, falling. This report contained six new recommendations, and the PCA said:

> The distress and hardship unnecessarily caused to some low income families faced with the recovery of tax credits overpayments require prompt action. The revisions that HMRC are proposing to make to COP 26 should go some way towards ensuring that decisions on recovery will be far less harsh and more appropriate to this particular customer group. However, those revisions will not be sufficient in themselves to deal with all of the problems identified in this report, nor prevent potential future misunderstandings arising about the proper application of the revised Code.[42]

Seneviratne sees the future of the PCA primarily in firefighting, suggesting that successive PCAs have seen their role 'to be more one of providing an internal administrative audit than of acting as a ready channel for uncovering and investigating citizens' grievances'.[43] The title of the Annual Report for 2007–8 certainly lends support to this view and in her Introduction, Ann Abraham says:

> The work of my Office during the course of 2007–08 reflects its place in the constitution and its twin functions of delivering individual benefit to complainants and serving the wider public benefit. It achieves this larger ambition by drawing on its experience, expertise and independence to right individual wrongs and drive improvements in public services. It is this fruitful mix of individual benefit and public benefit that gives the Office its distinctive character.[44]

[41] PCA, *Tax Credits: Putting things right*, HC 577 (2005/6), pp. 3–4. There had been 404 complaints with 204 in hand; in April 2006, 120 more came in with 314 in hand; by April 2007, 25 were in hand; an average of 74% of complaints were upheld: *Annual Review for 2006/7, Putting principles into practice*, HC 838 (2006/7).

[42] PCA, *Tax Credits: Getting it wrong?* HC 1010 (2007/8) [3]. For comparison with the Revenue Adjudicator, see p. 460. above.

[43] M. Seneviratne, *Ombudsmen in the Public Sector* (Open University Press, 1994), pp. 52, 57–8.

[44] PCA, *Bringing wider public benefit from individual complaints*, HC 1040 (2007/8).

5. Inquisitorial procedure

Ombudsman procedure is investigatory and inquisitorial and hence provides an alternative to the adversarial paradigm. Perhaps the sharpest contrast is that the procedure is free for the complainant! Legal representation is unnecessary and still exceptional (though increasing reference in reports to solicitors suggests a higher visibility for the office amongst lawyers). Once the complaint is laid before the PCA, the investigation is wholly out of the complainant's hands and, although he may be interviewed, this is not a statutory requirement, a point picked up below.

At an early stage, the office evolved a three-stage, investigatory procedure, described by Sir Idwal Pugh as follows.

(a) Screening

The complaint is screened to determine whether it has been properly referred and whether it is within jurisdiction.

Complaints outside jurisdiction still run at about 4 per cent, although this procedure, which drew attention to the disproportionately high number of complaints screened out for lack of jurisdiction, has now, as we shall see, been modified. These figures are, in light of the MP filter, hard to explain away. They are usually attributed to the complexity of the jurisdictional criteria, including the question of overlap with courts and tribunals (s. 5) and the fact that only bodies listed in Sch. 2 to the Act can be investigated. Reversal has been recommended: only bodies *not* subject to investigation should be listed, obviating the need to amend the legislation to reflect the creation of new government bodies.[45] Because it would require amending legislation, however, this sensible change has not been made. The office has always tried to be helpful to disappointed complainants, advising them where else to take their complaints.

(b) Investigation

A statement of complaint setting out the material facts of the case is prepared and sent to the principal officer of the department concerned with a letter requesting his comments. If a complaint names a particular member or members of the department, they receive copies. There are no pleadings and seldom any hearings, though the PCA has power to conduct oral hearings and lawyer-ombudsman Sir Cecil Clothier occasionally did so; oral statements to officers are, however, frequently made. There are no rules of proof or evidence and all information, including comments, may be quoted and relied on in the report. The burden of proof is also unspecified.

[45] Select Committee on the PCA, *Powers, Work and Jurisdiction of the Ombudsman*, HC 33 (1993/4).

Sir Michael Buckley spoke in his 2000–1 Report of lightening the 'evidential burden' placed on the complainant, a change that allowed the office to 'take positive action in a significantly higher proportion of cases'.[46] Section 8 of the Act requires anyone who can furnish information to do so and provides that no claim of public interest immunity, legal privilege or official secrecy shall prevail against the PCA except in the case of the proceedings of Cabinet and its committees. Although it is very rare for such a claim to be made, there have (as we saw in Chapter 10) been several instances.[47]

(c) Report

Sir Idwal Pugh tell us that, when the investigation is complete:

> a draft 'results report' on the case is prepared and is submitted to me and is often the subject of a case conference. This sets out all the facts of the case, the course of the investigation and the conclusion and findings on the complaint. If the complaint is upheld, it will also specify the remedy which is called for. I then send the draft report to the permanent secretary of the department concerned. I do this for the following reasons. First, so that he can check, as far as the department's records are concerned, that I have correctly reported facts. Secondly, so that he can confirm that the department will or will not agree to a remedy where one is included in the report. Thirdly, so that he may also decide whether or not in the very rare case to ask the minister in charge of the department to use the right which he has under the statute to prevent disclosure of information [when it] 'would be prejudicial to If you want a note here it would be in 48 above the safety of the State or otherwise contrary to the public interest'[48]

There is no mention in this passage of the complainant. Yet inquisitorial procedure should also be 'contradictory', a continental term meaning that parties must be given an opportunity to comment on statements and refute any allegations made against them. Current practice is to outline the steps to be taken in a letter to the complainant, who may also be contacted, according to the PCA's website:

> to discuss the details of your complaint and what you would like us to do to make things right . . . We will let you and the MP know what is planned and provide regular updates on our progress with your complaint. At the end of our investigation we will send you and the MP a letter or report explaining our final decision.

This procedure underlines that, technically, the complainant is the MP. Whether the draft report should, in accordance with the rules of natural justice, be sent to the complainant was once considered by the SC, which rejected the

[46] *Annual Report for 2000/1*, HC 5 (2000/1).

[47] An early example is the *Court Line* investigation, where a certificate was issued under s. 11(3) of the Act and the government subsequently refused to accept the PCA's recommendations: see HC 498 (1974/5) and HC Deb vol. 896 cc1812–23. And see p. 472.

[48] I. Pugh, 'The Ombudsman: Jurisdiction, powers and practice' (1978) 56 *Pub. Admin.* 127, 134–6. The statutory requirement referred to is in s. 7(1) of the 1967 Act.

idea on the ground that it would add to delays.[49] There is a contrast to be drawn with the procedure used by the EO's office, where procedure is fully contradictory and involves exchange of documents.

The draft report as sent to the principal officer (PO) normally contains a recommendation as to remedy. The PO should correct any errors, draw attention to omissions and discuss with the PCA proposed action in respect of the recommended remedy. Where compensation is involved, the department may also have to contact the Treasury. Both the SC and the office have expressed concern at the delays occurring at this stage of the investigation. In 2001, Sir Michael Buckley, then engaged in trying to lower the average length of investigations to meet his business plan target of ten to eleven months, expressed concern both at 'the length of time that it takes departments to respond to enquiries and to the statement of complaint which is the preliminary to an investigation, and also to resolve issues, especially issues of redress, after we have sent them a draft report on our investigation'. A special culprit was the Child Support Agency, which frequently overshot the limit of thirty days for a department to respond to the PCA's office, sent 'no more than a holding reply', or sent a reply that did not fully and properly address the issues.[50] Once the reply is received, the report is ready to be sent to the referring MP, to the SC and the complainant.

The thoroughness of this 'Rolls Royce procedure' undoubtedly contributed to the respect in which the office was held, as Sir Idwal Pugh emphasised.[51] The procedure is, however, slow and lengthy – a serious source of public discontent. During the 1990s, delays in the PCA's office grew to the point that they were thought to discourage MPs from submitting complaints. The Select Committee demanded improvements. NPM had hit the Ombudsman's office:

> One of the greatest sources of dissatisfaction with the work of the Ombudsman has been the time it sometimes takes to complete a case. Often this has been for very good reasons. There is a tradition of thorough and complete investigation of complaints which is admirable. As the Ombudsman has said, the Office has 'tended to emphasise thoroughness rather than speed'. But as our predecessors have regularly commented, it is also important to resolve complaints speedily, and they have from time to time voiced their concern about the length of time investigations have taken . . . For cases completed in 1997–98, the average time taken to complete was almost two years (although this figure is somewhat distorted by the clearance of some old cases).
>
> In recent years, both the present Ombudsman and his predecessor have made considerable efforts to reduce the time taken to deal with cases. The main initiatives have been a greater use of more informal techniques to resolve cases; greater delegation; more sophisticated efforts to manage the caseload; and an expansion in staff numbers. The Office began in 1994 to implement a 'fast-track' system, or 'pre-investigation resolution'. Screening is the first

49 Minutes of Evidence, HC 62-i (2000/1), Q 5 to Sir Michael Buckley.

50 See *Annual Report for 2000/1*, HC 5 (2000/1).

51 I. Pugh, 'The Ombudsman: Jurisdiction, powers and practice'.

> stage of the examination of a complaint by the Ombudsman's Office, in which a decision is taken either to reject the complaint or to refer it on for investigation. If it appears at this stage from a complaint that something has gone wrong, the Office may contact the body concerned to ask them informally whether they agree that they have made a mistake. If they do, it asks them to provide a suitable remedy to the complainant . . . In 1997–98 the Office obtained 'due redress' through these means in 110 cases, ranging from an apology to 'the payment of quite large sums of money'. The Ombudsman began to delegate authority to issue reports in 1995. Managers have also been given greater delegated power and freedom to use their staff more effectively depending on the type of cases that they have to deal with. Finally, there is greater stress on concentrating on those aspects of a case which will lead to obtaining redress for the individual complainant 'and less on identifying ancillary systemic weaknesses which it is departments' own responsibility to address'. Such matters 'will be taken up separately with departments, so as not to hold up the processing of individual cases' . . .
>
> We welcome the efforts that have been made to reduce the amount of time taken to deal with cases . . . Like our predecessors, we appreciate the need for thorough investigations in some cases; but we doubt the effectiveness of any system of redress which takes so long to achieve a resolution. **We recommend that the Ombudsman should set as his ultimate aim that all cases should be resolved within six months of their arrival in the Office; and that the Government and he should work together to eliminate the obstacles to achieving this aim. These may include the resources available to him, staff especially, and the powers at his disposal. In particular, it should be made clear to departments that they need to respond fully and urgently to the Ombudsman's requests for information.**[52]

Sir Michael Buckley also decided to change procedure by amalgamating the two stages of screening and investigation:

> After an initial scrutiny to check that a complaint is within my jurisdiction, it is passed to a caseworker who sees it through to a conclusion [which] may range from resolution by making enquiries of the department or agency to a detailed investigation culminating in a statutory report. Investigations are being taken as far, but only as far, as is necessary to reach a fair and soundly based conclusion.[53]

Complaints that fall outside jurisdiction are now classified as 'enquiries' and wherever possible dealt with informally.

The Annual Report for 2003–4 shows the office working more as a modern complaints-handling system:

[52] PASC, *Report of the Parliamentary Ombudsman for 1997-8*, HC 136 (1998/9) [7–9] (fnn. omitted). The SC noted that the number of uncompleted investigations more than one year old had already fallen from 346 in 1997 to 58 a year later. By 2005/6, 38% of PCA complaints were completed in 3 months (target, 80%) 65% in 6 months (target, 85%) 99% within 12 months of being received (target 90%): *Annual Review for 2005/6*, HC 1363 (2005/6). The comparable figures for 2007/8 were: 29% completed within 6 months (target 55%), 75% within 12 months (target 85%) (*Annual Report for 2007/8*, HC 1040 (2007/8)).

[53] *Annual Report for 2000/1*, HC 5 (2001/2) (Sir Michael Buckley). The constant changes in methods of recording not only make comparisons of performance problematic but suggest they may be designed to enhance performance.

The way we work

Once we have received a complaint that has been properly referred by a Member, a named investigator – working under the guidance of an investigation manager and a director of investigations – generally takes responsibility for progressing a complaint from receipt to resolution. Investigation managers and senior investigation officers report the results of all but the most complex or sensitive statutory investigations. Investigators normally issue letters reporting the outcomes of all other consideration of complaints referred by Members, and keep complainants informed of the progress of investigations.

When we receive a complaint from the referring Member we ask four questions:

- Is the complaint about a body and a matter within the Ombudsman's jurisdiction?

If either the subject matter of a complaint or the body complained against is outside the Ombudsman's jurisdiction the matter cannot be considered further. Subject to that:

- Is there evidence of administrative failure?
- Did that failure cause personal injustice which has not been put right?
- Is it likely that the Ombudsman's intervention will secure a worthwhile remedy?

The range of possible outcomes of a complaint to the Ombudsman is as follows:

Outcome 1: If the body complained against or the subject matter of a complaint is clearly outside the Ombudsman's jurisdiction the matter cannot be considered further.

The Ombudsman continues to receive complaints (around 4% of the total received) about areas which are clearly outside her jurisdiction, such as personnel or contractual matters, or decisions which carry a right of appeal. She also receives a number of complaints about planning matters, where the complainants are unhappy with a planning decision, and essentially want her to criticise a planning inspector's professional judgment. In such cases, the most the Ombudsman can do is satisfy herself that the correct procedures have been followed.

Outcome 2: After further consideration of the papers submitted the complaint is not taken further, for example because there is no evidence of maladministration resulting in an unremedied personal injustice, or no added value is likely to be achieved for the complainant.

Outcome 3A: As an alternative to starting an investigation, enquiries are made of the body complained against, and result in an appropriate outcome seen as positive for the complainant. Many complaints can be settled quickly and efficiently in this way without a statutory investigation. It is evident that both complainants and the bodies complained against appreciate the benefits of this approach.

Outcome 3B: Enquiries of the body complained against result in the complaint being seen as one that cannot usefully be taken further, for example because no injustice has been suffered or no added value is likely for the complainant.

When a statutory investigation is initiated, we issue a statement of the complaint to the body concerned; this is copied to the referring Member. One of two possible outcomes will then result:

Outcome 4: The investigation process is taken no further when an appropriate outcome has been achieved or no worthwhile remedy can be achieved.

Outcome 5: A statutory investigation report is sent to the referring Member. It is also copied to the body complained against (which has previously had the opportunity to comment on the facts to be reported and their presentation).[54]

The Annual Report for 2006–7 records further changes in the interests of efficiency:

First, we have introduced a more robust process for deciding whether we could and, if so, whether we should accept a case for investigation. Our aim has been to ensure that our decisions to accept cases for investigation are correct in law, consistent, speedy and strategic in line with the Ombudsman's role as a complaint handler of last resort. Secondly, promoting better local complaints handling and resolution is one of our key objectives. Our assessment process therefore ensures that the body complained about has had an opportunity to resolve the complaint. Also, where appropriate, we ensure that the complainant has made use of any appropriate second tier complaint handler, such as the Adjudicator or the Healthcare Commission. Before we accept a case for investigation we want to be satisfied that:

- the complaint is properly within the Ombudsman's remit and the body complained about has not been able to resolve it;
- there is evidence of maladministration leading to un-remedied injustice;
- there is a reasonable prospect of a worthwhile outcome to our investigation.

We have also established a much clearer distinction between cases where we intervene to secure a positive outcome for a complainant without the need to launch an investigation, and cases where we investigate and report. Therefore, in future we will be able to report more accurately and comprehensively on those cases where our intervention short of an investigation has secured the resolution of a complaint, which is an important aspect of our work. Such cases are now recorded as concluded enquiries. The figures in this Report show a substantial number of cases that were initially accepted for investigation but subsequently closed as an enquiry. This is because we reassessed all cases in hand when we adopted the assessment process described above. Subsequently, 373 cases were closed as enquiries rather than as investigations. Overall, while the number of investigations has reduced, our overall workload remains substantially unchanged as more work is being done at the enquiry stage. The changes are more of presentation than of substance.[55]

Statistics for the years 2006–7 and 2007–8 give a fair indication of how complaints are going.

[54] *Annual Review for 2003/3*, HC 847 (2002/3), pp. 9, 10.

[55] *Annual Review 2006/7, Putting Principles into Practice*, HC 838 (2007/8).

Table 12.1 Complaints to PCA and HSC in 2006–7 and 2007–8

	In hand		Received		Closed		Carried over	
telephone	0	3	5790	5077	5787	4751	3	329
email	7	20	2145	2996	2132	2287	20	129
written	333	644	6575	5048	6264	4651	644	1047
TOTAL	**340**	**667**	**14510**	**13121**	**14183**	**11689**	**667**	**1505**

Source: adapted from HC 838

Table 12.2 Outcomes: The way inquiries ended in 2006–7

	Information requested	Not properly made	Out of remit	Premature – parliamentary	Discretion not to investigate	With-drawn	Accepted	Total
Telephone	4112	620	634	1	1	10	5	5787
e-mail	148	993	579	1	5	15	15	2132
Written	113	1131	593	479	1035	240	1662	6264
TOTAL	**4373**	**2744**	**1806**	**481**	**1041**	**262**	**1682**	**14183**

Source: adapted from HC 838. (N.B. The Table includes complaints to HSC, except in respect of premature complaints. Comparable figures for 2007–8 were not available.)

6. The 'Big Inquiry'

(a) Grouping complaints: The Child Support Agency

Group complaints have been mentioned as a way of surmounting the embargo on 'own-initiative' investigations. In this type of case, the practice is to select around four sample cases from the group, 'parking' the rest and absorbing them into a Special Report under s. 10(3).[56] Before making a Special Report on the CSA, the PCA had received ninety-five complaints of administrative failings in carrying out the agency's statutory functions of tracing 'absent parents' and collecting maintenance payments from them.[57] Complaints were largely associated with failures of the computer system or with delay. Seventy complaints were accepted for investigation and a representative selection compiled, using the wide discretion to filter others off to alternative complaints systems. In a passage that prioritises the inspectorial function, Mr. Reid explained why this was done:

> It was not the best use of my resources to investigate additional individual complaints unless they involved aspects of CSA work which had not previously been brought to my

[56] Sir Michael Buckley, *Oral Evidence*, HC 62-i (2001/2), questions 23, 24.

[57] For fuller accounts of the CSA affair, see C. Harlow, 'Accountability, new public management, and the problem of the Child Support Agency' (1999) 26 *JLS* 150; G. Davis, N. Wikeley and R. Young, *Child Support in Action* (Hart Publishing, 1998). In 2008, the CSA was wound up and replaced by the Child Maintenance and Enforcement Agency: see Child Maintenance and Other Payments Act 2008.

> attention, or unless the complainant had been caused actual financial loss. I took the view that investigation of a number of representative cases should identify any administrative shortcomings needing to be remedied and that any resulting improvements to the system should bring general benefits in which others should share. Many complaints sent to me were about the policy underlying the legislation. That is outside my jurisdiction. Many complaints were about the financial assessment of support for children and single parents. The assessments are open to appeal to Child Support Appeal Tribunals. I have confirmed with the President of the Independent Tribunal Service that it stands ready to handle such appeals.[58]

In common with the various parliamentary committees that have over time investigated this major administrative failure, the PCA identified systemic failures, notably in the IT systems:

> The computer failings have meant that the CSA have had to deal with an increasing number of cases manually. We recognise the need to do so in order to ensure that individual claims are processed as quickly as possible. However, operating both electronic and manual systems alongside one another have given rise to concerns about the impact on standards of data recording. We are concerned that processing claims manually may generate problems of its own. Another area of significant concern centres on the slow progress made by the CSA in processing new claims and the delays in making assessments. The method of calculating child support was changed in 2003. Although the new calculation rules are simpler and more straightforward than before, management of the transition has presented significant challenges. We have received a large number of complaints about delays and mishandling of cases under the old rules. It is disturbing that there have been systemic failures to keep people informed about what is happening in their individual cases – a basic tenet of good customer service.[59]

But the PCA also criticised the hurried way in which the scheme had been implemented:

> Maladministration leading to injustice is likely to arise when a new administrative task is not tested first by a pilot project; when new staff, perhaps inadequately trained, form a substantial fraction of the workforce; where procedures and technology supporting them are untried; and where quality of service is subordinated to sheer throughput.[60]

The SC's response was to register unease at the absence of any in-house complaints machinery. An Independent Case Examiner (ICE) was put in place in 1997 to handle procedural cases. The first ICE (Anne Parker) hit harder than the PCA, accusing the CSA of grossly inconveniencing many of its clients,

58 PCA, *Investigation of Complaints against the Child Support Agency*, HC 135 (1995/6), p. i.

59 PCA, *Annual Review for 2004/5*.

60 HC 135, p. iii.

slating its 'grudging' reports and failure to learn from past mistakes.[61] Despite the new complaints-handling machinery, however, complaints to the PCA continued to multiply, to the point that the office had to enter into a memorandum of understanding with the CSA as to how they were to be handled. Complaints about the CSA rose steadily but by 2007–8, when the ICE was handling complaints for the DWP generally, John Hanlon, now ICE, felt that his widened remit had been broadly speaking successful:

> DWP customers who previously would either have complained through their Member of Parliament to the Parliamentary and Health Service Ombudsman (PHSO) or who would have given up even though they remained dissatisfied, have had their concerns addressed and had the reassurance that the impartial ICE service can bring. DWP businesses have produced good results by their willingness to attempt to promote resolution of complaints at the earliest opportunity, and to take on board feedback and proposals from this office, with a view to improving their approach to resolving complaints.[62]

In respect of the CSA, however, the story was rather different. The intake of CSA cases had been 'higher than expected'. Complaints went randomly to the CSA, to the ICE, to the PCA – and to MPs, who had experienced a big rise. Complaints might or might not be redirected to another part of the system and might also be re-referred or duplicated. This put pressure on those handling complaints and confused complainants. The volume of complaints was so great that the CSA had had to redeploy staff to work on ICE cases. Moreover, it had become necessary:

> to introduce an 'Exit' arrangement, which allowed ICE to disengage from an unacceptably high number of cases where the CSA had not implemented post-investigation ICE resolutions or recommendations within agreed timescales. Between October 2007 and February 2008, it was necessary to 'Exit' 51 cases. In 47 of these, recommendations have subsequently been satisfactorily implemented, but disappointingly 4 remain outstanding. After discussions with senior CSA management, immediate action was taken to ensure that no further 'Exits' would be required from March 2008.

Perhaps complaints are not so much a 'gift' as a distraction.

(b) Political cases

Group investigations may also be used for publicity purposes, to draw attention to 'hard cases' and pressurise government into a change of political position. This overtly political use of the PCA started very early with the *Sachsenhausen*

[61] First Report of the ICE (1998). There were 28,000 complaints of which 1,078 were investigated. The statistics in the ICE's *Annual Report for 2006/7* do not permit comparison.

[62] ICE, *Annual Report for 2007/8*, available online. CSA complaints are not separately recorded.

case in 1967, where the intervention of Sir Edmund Compton persuaded the government to reconsider the case for compensating those who were not strictly prisoners of war but had been incarcerated in this notorious institution.[63] Shortly after, in the notorious *Court Line* affair,[64] the PCA strayed into high politics by criticising ministerial statements that implied that a troubled holiday firm would not collapse. The Labour Government promptly rejected the finding – it was called by one MP 'a political judgement' – but in the end compensation was paid.

Ten years separated *Sachsenhausen* from *Barlow Clowes*, which established the use of the 'Big Inquiry' for campaigning purposes. Barlow Clowes (BC) dealt in 'bond washing' (which enables highly taxed income to be converted into tax-free or low tax capital gains). It had to be wound up in 1988 after its funds were found to have been fraudulently diverted to high-risk ventures and the directors' private use. The issue was the extent to which the DTI had known or ought to have known of this malpractice and taken steps to warn off potential investors; as in *Court Line*, the objective was government compensation. The affair shows a variety of complaint-handling techniques in action. The first step was to complain to MPs, producing a ministerial inquiry, which reported that 'the department's general handling of the licensing of Barlow Clowes . . . was careful and considered and its actions reasonable'; consequently, the findings provided 'no justification for using taxpayers' money to fund compensation'.[65] Immediately, a large number of dissatisfied MPs turned to the PCA, who responded positively but reminded them of s. 12(3) of the 1967 Act, which put *discretionary* decisions to grant, refuse or revoke licences outside his jurisdiction; only if he found maladministration could he examine the minister's decision. The Government agreed nonetheless to co-operate.

With the PCA treading the same ground as the inquiry, duplication was a danger. However, his largely discretionary documentary procedures permitted him to use witness statements from the inquiry. Unusually, we find intervention from lawyers on behalf of investors and detailed submissions from Barlow Clowes's solicitors; unusually too, Sir Anthony Barrowclough – perhaps influenced by his legal background – and his officials took oral evidence from a large number of witnesses, departmental and otherwise. Unlike Mr Le Quesne, who had conducted the inquiry and had confined his remit narrowly to 'fact-finding', leaving evaluation to the minister, the PCA found maladministration on five counts. His 120,000 word report represented a *de luxe* investigation: 'Rarely, if ever, can any record of administration have been so closely scrutinised, and reconstructed in such detail, as in the Commissioner's report on the Barlow Clowes affair; some of the officials subjected to interrogation certainly

[63] *Special Report of the PCA*, HC 54 (1967/8); HC Deb., vol. 758, cols. 112–16. And see A. Bradley, 'Sachsenhausen, Barlow Clowes – and then?' [1992] *PL* 353.

[64] HC 498 (1974/5). And see R. Gregory, 'Court Line, Mr Benn and the Ombudsman' (1977) 30 *Parl. Affairs* 3.

[65] HL Deb., vol. 500, cols. 1255–69.

felt not a little bruised by the experience.'[66] Construing causation in a way familiar to lawyers, the PCA concluded that 'injustice' had been caused and that compensation was due.

What followed raises questions over the effectiveness of any grievance-handling machinery when it comes up against the highest echelons of government. The minister (Mr Ridley) rejected the PCA's findings, criticising him for a trait that also characterises public inquiries and judicial proceedings: measuring departmental action with the benefit of hindsight against 'a way of proceeding which, after the event, can be shown to be more satisfactory than what was actually done'.[67] Taking legal liability as his benchmark, Mr Ridley asserted that the investigation should never have been undertaken: the complainants were not 'directly affected' (the legal test of standing to sue); the findings trespassed on both the discretionary and policy areas of decision-making, proscribed territory for the PCA by s. 12(3); the decision to recommend compensation departed from established principles of civil liability on the part of regulators; and causation had not been shown. Despite the sound and fury, the Government agreed (as governments almost always do) to substantial *ex gratia* compensation 'in the exceptional circumstances of this case and out of respect for the Office of Parliamentary Commissioner'.

Barlow Clowes proved to be the first in a line of high-profile cases in which victim-support groups utilise the PCA as one of several complaints-handling mechanisms to obtain a political outcome in their favour, notable examples being the *Occupational Pensions* case (see p. 554 below), the *Debt of Honour* affair described in Chapter 17, and the *Equitable Life* investigation into the conduct of the Financial Services Authority (FSA) as regulator of an assurance company. After the first PCA investigation into Equitable Life, EMAG, the action group, threatened judicial review, leading to a negotiated compromise after the PCA agreed to a further and fuller investigation. [68] In the meantime, EMAG had taken the matter to the Petitions Committee of the European Parliament, which recommended that the UK government set up a compensation scheme for victims and criticised the light-touch approach of the UK regulatory system.[69] In an unusually complex investigation leading to a five-volume report,[70] the PCA concluded that maladministration in the shape of 'serial regulatory failure' by the FSA had caused injustice, repeating the

66 R. Gregory and G. Drewry, 'Barlow Clowes and the Ombudsman' [1991] *PL* 192 and 408, 439.

67 See HC Deb., vol. 164, cols. 201–12; *Observations on the Report of the PCA,* HC 99 (1989/90). Gregory and Drewy, 'Barlow Clowes and the Ombudsman', p. 429, thought the PCA exceeded his jurisdiction in relation to discretionary decisions and interpreted maladministration very generously.

68 *The Prudential Regulation of Equitable Life*, HC 809 (2002/3); EMAG press release 'EMAG drops judicial review against the PO' (6 Dec. 2004). And see PCA, *Equitable Life: A decade of regulatory failure*, HC 815 (2007/8).

69 European Parliament, *Report on the crisis of Equitable Life Assurance Society* (the Wallis Report) 2006/2199 (INI)) P6-A(2007)0203 Final (4 June 2007). Individual petitions were also presented to the Petitions Committee.

70 PCA, *Equitable Life: A decade of regulatory failure*, HC 815 (2007/8).

recommendation that the Government should 'establish and fund a compensation scheme, with a view to assessing the individual cases of those who have been affected by the events covered in this report and providing appropriate compensation, with the aim of putting those people who have suffered a relative loss back into the position that they would have been in had maladministration not occurred'. The initial response of the Government was sympathetic but it was not until January 2009 that the Government, stating that it accepted only some of the PCA's findings, apologised 'on behalf of public bodies and successive Governments stretching back to 1990 for the maladministration that it believes took place'. An adviser was appointed to advise on an *ex gratia* payment scheme to help victims.[71] With a reminder that it had anticipated this scenario, the PCA referred the matter back to PASC:

> Once again, the government has thought fit to reject findings made by the Ombudsman after a lengthy, detailed, complex, and rigorous investigation. This scenario was one considered by the Committee in its report *Justice Delayed: The Ombudsman's report on Equitable Life*, published in December 2008: We urge the government to act without further delay and to accept the Ombudsman's findings of maladministration. She is Parliament's Ombudsman and it is imperative that the government respects her conclusions. There are valid arguments to be had about the scale of compensation and the way that such cases should be handled in the future, but we would be deeply concerned if the government chose to act as judge on its own behalf by refusing to accept that maladministration took place. This would undermine the ability to learn lessons from the Equitable Life affair.[72]

7. Occupational pensions: Challenging the ombudsman

The prolonged debate over occupational pensions provided – or in practice not provided – by private-sector commercial firms had its roots in the fraudulent activities of Robert Maxwell, whose inroads into the pension funds of his enterprises prompted the establishment of a committee to review pension law. Its report led to the Pensions Act 1995, which established the Occupational Pensions Regulatory Agency (OPRA) and introduced a Pensions Compensation Board. To protect those in occupational pension schemes, it laid down a minimum funding requirement (MFR) to ensure that those in charge of occupational pension schemes could meet their liabilities to existing pensioners and obligations to those not yet on pension. It would seem that the limitations of the MFR were not widely realised or understood even by professional advisers. The Pensions Act 2004 replaced MFR with scheme-specific requirements and a Pensions Protection Fund (PPF) funded by a levy on the pensions industry

[71] See *The Prudential Regulation of the Equitable Life Assurance Society: the Government's response to the Report of the Parliamentary Ombudsman's Investigation*, Cm. 7538 (2009). The claim was for £4.5 million.

[72] PCA, Memorandum to PASC (26 Jan 2009), available on the EMAG website. The reference is to HC 815 (2007/8).

to help those whose schemes had already been wound up. It was widely felt, however, that these measures were still insufficient, as they left around 100,000 people either entirely uncovered or insufficiently funded. At this point, the Government balked at acting as guarantor to private industry, claiming that £15 billion would be necessary to make reparation. This sum was hotly disputed by the Pensions Action Group (PAG), set up to fight for compensation and its adviser, Ros Altmann, who estimated the true figure at £3.7 billion, spread over sixty years. This disagreement lay at the heart of the compensation struggle.

In time, 500 direct complaints from aggrieved pensioners, augmented by over 200 referrals from MPs of all parties, reached the desk of the PCA. The office selected four appropriate test cases for investigation and launched a 'Big Inquiry'.[73] The main allegations were that:

(i) The legislative framework from commencement of the Pensions Act 1995 to commencement of the Pensions Act 2004 had afforded inadequate protection of the pension rights of members of final salary occupational pension schemes.

(ii) On a number of occasions, ministers and officials had ignored relevant evidence when taking policy and other decisions related to the protection of pension rights accrued in such schemes.

(iii) The information and advice provided by a number of government departments and other public bodies about the degree of protection that the law provided to accrued pension rights had been inaccurate, to the extent that it had amounted to the misdirection of the members and trustees of such schemes. Particularly criticised were a 1996 DSS leaflet entitled 'The 1995 Pensions Act' and a 2002 leaflet, 'Occupational Pensions: Your Guide'.

(iv) Public bodies were responsible for unreasonable delays in the process of winding-up schemes.

These complaints posed several jurisdictional problems. First, category (i) was entirely ruled out on the ground that the PCA had no jurisdiction to question the *content* of statute law (see the earlier discussion of the 'bad rule' problem). Secondly, although both the Treasury and Department of Work and Pensions fall squarely within the PCA's remit, the FSA had not been added to the Schedule to the 1967 Act, while other bodies involved, such as the Institute of Actuaries, were private bodies not amenable to the jurisdiction of any public ombudsman. Thirdly, category (ii) complaints involved ministerial discretion and were hence subject to the restrictions of s. 12(3) (see *Barlow Clowes*, p. 552 above). Finally, some allegations, notably those in category (iii) could – and in the event did – give rise to a judicial remedy, requiring the PCA to exercise her discretion under s. 5(2). Undeterred by these obstacles, the PCA told MPs:

[73] PCA, letter to all MPs, 6 Nov. 2004. Full details of the selected cases are given in Ch. 2 of the final Report.

> I had been shown indications that maladministration might have caused injustice to those who had complained to me – and to those in a similar position as those complainants. I also believed that my ability to access evidence which was not available to complainants meant that an investigation by me would achieve a worthwhile outcome, whatever its result. I therefore decided to conduct an investigation.[74]

An unkind critic might call this a 'fishing expedition'.

On 15 March 2006, the PCA laid her mammoth review – in the course of which the office had crawled through departmental files and considered a range of reviews and reports on pension policy – before PASC as a Special Report under s. 10(3),[75] a step necessitated by the Government's unfavourable response to the draft report. There were three findings of maladministration:[76]

- Official information – about the security that members of final salary occupational pension schemes could expect from the MFR provided by the bodies under investigation – was sometimes inaccurate, often incomplete, largely inconsistent and therefore potentially misleading. This constituted maladministration.
- The response by DWP to the actuarial profession's recommendation that disclosure should be made to pension scheme members of the risks of wind-up – in the light of the fact that scheme members and member-nominated trustees did not know the risks to their accrued pension rights – constituted maladministration.
- The decision in 2002 by DWP to approve a change to the MFR basis was taken with maladministration.

The PCA also found injustice in the shape of financial loss, a sense of outrage, and considerable distress, anxiety and uncertainty, coupled with inability to make informed choices or to take remedial action. None of this had been remedied.

In the most controversial section of a controversial Report, Ms Abraham, choosing her words very carefully, made five recommendations as to redress:

> - I recommend that the Government *should consider whether* it should make arrangements for the restoration of the core pension and non-core benefits promised to all those whom I have identified above are fully covered by my recommendations – by whichever means is most appropriate, including if necessary by payment from public funds, to replace the full amount lost by those individuals.
> - I recommend that the Government *should consider whether* it should provide for the payment of consolatory payments to those scheme members fully covered by my

[74] PCA, letter to all MPs, 6 Nov. 2004.

[75] PCA, *Trusting in the Pensions Promise: Government bodies and the security of final salary occupational pensions*, HC 984 (2005/6). Unusually, the Government Response is annexed to the Report.

[76] HC 984 [5.164].

> recommendations – as a tangible recognition of the outrage, distress, inconvenience and uncertainty that they have endured.
> - I also recommend that the Government *should consider whether* it should apologise to scheme trustees for the effects on them of the maladministration I have identified, particularly for the distress that they have suffered due to the events relevant to this investigation.
> - I recommend that the Government *should consider whether* those who have lost a significant proportion of their expected pensions – but whose scheme began wind-up in the year prior to the new regime becoming operational – should be treated in the same manner as those fully covered by my recommendations.
> - I recommend that the Government *should conduct a review* – with the pensions industry and other key stakeholders – to establish what can be done to improve the time taken to windup final salary schemes.[77]

The curt response was that, with the exception of the final suggestion for a review, the Government was 'not minded to accept the Ombudsman's findings of maladministration nor to implement her recommendations'.[78] A statement on the departmental website justified the apparently negative decision:

> Although the Government does not accept liability for these losses, it agrees that there should be a significant package of support, which is why we have committed an additional £2bn to the FAS [Financial Assistance Scheme], which will help about 40,000 people . . . We have real sympathy for those who have lost their occupational pensions and this is why we have put the FAS in place. However, we do not believe that the taxpayer should be expected to underwrite what were private company pension schemes.[79]

Neither the PCA nor PASC was minded to leave matters there. Ms Abraham retorted that nothing in the Response had persuaded her that her findings and recommendations were unreasonable, while Dr Wright, chair of PASC, told the House:

> It is the first time – the only time; the unique time – that a case has arisen in which not only has the finding of maladministration been rejected by the government of the day, but the injustice has remained unremedied. Both components of the ombudsman's work have been set aside: the finding of maladministration and the description of how it might be put right. It is an important moment for the House when Parliament's ombudsman is in such a position over an issue of this kind . . .
>
> I was surprised and disappointed, as no doubt was the ombudsman, by the way in which her report was immediately set aside. I think she was particularly troubled by the fact that,

[77] Selected recommendations from HC 984 [6.15] [6.24] [6.25] [6.28] [6.34], italics and bullet points ours.

[78] HC 984, Annex D.

[79] Mr Purnell (Minister for Pensions Reform), 'Government responds to Public Administration Select Committee' DWP website (2 Nov. 2006).

> in her view, the report had been misrepresented. She had not said to the Government, 'You must sign a blank cheque straight away: that will take care of it.' However, I think she was even more upset by the rejection of her finding of maladministration.[80]

The minister was not minded to back down. The Government respected the role played by the Ombudsman, and would continue to do so but:

> the case we have been discussing is exceptional. The Committee asked us to explain whether it was a new policy or a new approach. The case is exceptional. We shall continue our approach, which is to respect the ombudsman. In fact, in 39 years, this is the first time that my Department has not responded positively to an ombudsman's findings . . .
>
> [The information given] was the right level of information to give, given the context. We are talking about introductory, very general leaflets. . . If we had given the amount of detail that is suggested, with hindsight, we should have done, they would have been not leaflets but handbooks, and they would not have served the purpose for which they were intended.[81]

The next shots in a rapidly escalating war came from PASC, which issued a new report[82] brushing aside as 'simply untenable' the contention that the Government's leaflets were designed 'as part of a wider set of communications to encourage those who had not made provision for their retirement to consider doing so and gave people a starting point for this, as is made clear'. PASC strongly supported the PCA's conclusions and recommendations; the Government was being unreasonable and ungenerous; it should reconsider its parsimonious attitude to redress. Insisting that the disagreement between it and PASC was 'not about *whether* there should be some support, but about *how much* support there should be', the Government held its line. It made a minor concession to look again in the light of the PASC report at what extra support could be made available within the existing framework.[83]

A new attack was about to open on a new battlefield. A test case was brought by four pensioners, arguing that ombudsman findings are binding on the public authority against which they are made, either (a) absolutely, or (b) unless they can be shown objectively to be flawed or unreasonable. Pointing to s. 10(3) of the 1967 Act, the Government replied that the proper recourse was a special report to Parliament; the PCA was 'not there to make binding findings of fact. The function for a s. 10(3) special report is no more and no less than to provide a stimulus to political debate'. Bean J disagreed:

80 HC Deb., col. 512 (7 Dec. 2006). Dr Wright was speaking in a debate on an adjournment motion asking that funds be allocated to the DWP and set aside for full payment of losses.

81 *Ibid.*, cols. 542–5.

82 PASC, *The Ombudsman in Question: The Ombudsman's report on pensions and its constitutional implications*, HC 1081 (2006/7).

83 *Government Response to The Ombudsman in Question: The Ombudsman's report on pensions and its constitutional implications*, Cm. 6961 (2006).

> As it happens, the present case is about a decision of a Secretary of State announced in an oral statement to the House of Commons, affecting many thousands of people, and concerning a significant issue of public policy. But much of the Ombudsman's work concerns decisions of non-departmental public bodies or 'quangos' affecting a single individual or family. If [this] submission is correct, the non-binding nature of the findings of fact would apply equally in such a case.[84]

The judge made three findings: (i) in agreement with the PCA, he found the departmental advice to be 'inaccurate and misleading'; but ruled (ii) that her reasoning on causation was 'logically flawed and in that sense unreasonable'; and (iii) that the department was entitled to accept the 'clear recommendation' from the leading professional body and its own specialist adviser. 'The Ombudsman was in effect expecting the Secretary of State, who is not an actuary, to keep a watchdog . . . and then bark himself.' This reasoning was criticised by the Court of Appeal, which thought the true question was:

> not whether the defendant himself considers that there was maladministration, but whether in the circumstances his rejection of the ombudsman's findings to this effect is based on cogent reasons.[85]

Applying a test of rationality to each of the DWP decisions, the Court of Appeal ruled that it had been irrational to reject one of the PCA's findings of maladministration causing injustice. The DWP had failed properly to consider those findings that dealt with outrage and loss of opportunity to take remedial action. The DWP should therefore reconsider its response.

While PASC maintained its support for the PCA, requiring the Government to respect her recommendations, it also expressed concern over the propensity of dissatisfied complainants to turn for relief to the courts:

> The Parliamentary Commissioner Act was established to deal with maladministration; i.e., actions or failures which cannot be remedied in the courts for either legal or practical reasons, but which nevertheless cause injustice. To ask a court to review the Ombudsman's findings would effectively make matters which are currently not justiciable subject to judicial decision. In these circumstances Parliament's role would be diminished to that of an interested bystander. We believe that when there are disputes between Government and the Ombudsman, Parliament is the proper place for them to be debated.
>
> However, this system will only work if the Parliamentary Ombudsman, the Government and Parliament share a broad common understanding of what maladministration might be and who should properly identify it. If it became clear that the Government routinely considered rejection of a finding of maladministration, then that common understanding would no longer exist. The first step towards resolving such difficulties would be for the House

[84] *R (Bradley) v Work and Pensions Secretary* [2007] EWHC 242.

[85] *R (Bradley) v Work and Pensions Secretary* [2008] EWCA 36 [72].

to debate these matters. However, if that failed, new legislation might be needed, or the Government could attempt to use judicial review to establish where current boundaries lie. We hope it will not come to that . . .

It would be extremely damaging if Government became accustomed simply to reject findings of maladministration, especially if an investigation by this Committee proved there was indeed a case to answer. It would raise fundamental constitutional issues about the position of the Ombudsman and the relationship between Parliament and the Executive.[86]

Next in time came a double-edged reply from the ECJ to a preliminary reference made[87] under TEC Art. 234 by the High Court in an action for damages. Asked to construe an EU directive on the protection of employees in the event of insolvency of their employer, the ECJ issued a cautious ruling: the provision made by the UK government was insufficient to comply with the directive, because it was limited to 20 per cent or 49 per cent of the benefits to which an employee was entitled. On the other hand, the ECJ thought that pension rights 'need not necessarily be funded by the Member States themselves or be funded in full' and, even if the directive had not been properly transposed, state liability was 'contingent on a finding of manifest and grave disregard by that State for the limits set on its discretion'. This would have to be proved to the satisfaction of the High Court. Again the Pensions Action Group claimed victory.

In parallel, changes were taking place as part of a wider review of pension provision.[88] A bill introduced into the House of Commons made improvements to the FAS scheme, guaranteeing 80 per cent of pension for affected employees up to a cap of £26,000 and extending relief to members of some solvent schemes, enough to satisfy the ECJ ruling. Welcoming the improvements, PASC claimed the credit:

Although the Government continues to deny that any maladministration occurred, the Parliamentary Ombudsman's intervention has already resulted in significant improvements to the position of those whose pension funds wound up underfunded.

- Even though the Government rejected the Ombudsman's report, it brought forward its review of the FAS in consequence, and substantially improved the scheme. This initial improvement was itself significant; it meant that some help was available for those within 15 years of scheme pension age, rather than being restricted only to those within three years of retirement.

[86] HC 1081 [75–8].

[87] Case C-278/05 *Robins and Others v Work and Pensions Secretary* [2007] ELR I-1053. See also Art. 8 of Council Directive 80/987/EEC of 20 October 1980 on the approximation of the laws of the Member States relating to the protection of employees in the event of the insolvency of their employer. The state liability principle of EC law, on which the action was based, is explained below at p. 763.

[88] DWP, *Simplicity, Security and Choice: Working and saving for retirement: Action on occupational pensions*, Cm. 5835 (2003); *Security in Retirement: Towards a new pensions system*, Cm. 6481 (2005/6).

> - After our report and the subsequent judgment of the High Court, the Government announced that the FAS would be extended still further, so that all members of affected pension schemes would receive 80% of their core pension entitlements. That promise has resulted in the amendments to the Pensions Bill already described.
> - The Government's review of the FAS will explore whether there are resources, other than the public purse, which can be used to increase the funds available to scheme members.
>
> **We recognize that the Parliamentary Ombudsman's report has already resulted in significant concessions from the Government, and significant improvements in the assistance available to those who have lost their pensions. The Ombudsman system has proved to be effective even in the face of Government resistance.**[89]

But the concessions were not enough to satisfy PASC. It fought on to see the PCA's recommendations fully implemented:

> It might be argued that redress should be offered to those covered by the Ombudsman's finding of maladministration, rather than all those affected by the loss of their pensions during the period in question. We consider on this that the Government approach has been correct. The most effective response to the Ombudsman's report is to amend the Financial Assistance Scheme, particularly since some of the losses were due to policy deficiencies, which fall outside the Parliamentary Ombudsman's remit, but which Parliament can and should remedy. Our remarks apply to all those in schemes which began to wind up before the regime established by the Pensions Act 2004 came into force.[90]

By now the bill was in the House of Lords, where an amendment was inserted, requiring an increase to FAS payments to bring them up to the level of the PPF. Again PASC reported, accusing the Government of 'using the position of scheme members to exert pressure on employers . . . the Government should not use the indigence and distress of those who have suffered considerable losses to try to blackmail them to do so'.[91] The Government did not concede. The Commons rejected the Lords amendment on the ground that it involved the expenditure of public funds. The Lords did not insist and the legislation duly passed into law as the Pensions Act 2007.

What should we make of these two epic inquiries? Like *Barlow Clowes*, both concern the vexed question of compensation for the *supervisory* and *regulatory* functions of government and public bodies. In this way, each is similar, and needs to be related, to the rules of legal liability in cases such as *Three Rivers* case discussed in Chapter 17 (see p. 767 below). In none of these cases is

[89] PASC, *The Pensions Bill: Government Undertakings relating to the Financial Assistance Scheme*, HC 523 (2006/7).

[90] *Ibid.* [12].

[91] PASC, *The Pensions Bill and the FAS: An update including the Government Response to the 5th Report of Session 2005-6*, HC 992 (2006/7).

government the primary wrongdoer; as the most solvent party, it is being asked to stand in as guarantor for risks created by and losses caused by other actors;[92] to put this differently, the end of the security line has been reached. In this respect, the position is broadly comparable to the line taken later in the larger financial disasters caused by the failure of Northern Rock and other banks, the difference being that government was there left free to choose on what terms to intervene. This is what it was arguing for in the *Occupational Pensions* and *Equitable Life* affairs.

Note too how the use of the PCA as a weapon in these political struggles is escalating. Complaints and appeals multiply: to MPs, ombudsmen, Parliament and every court that might have competence, as all available machinery is tested. Note too how the nature of investigations has changed. These are much more like the 'big public inquiry' discussed in the next chapter than standard ombudsman investigations; indeed, as in *Barlow Clowes*, they sometimes run alongside an inquiry. Unlike inquiry panels, however, the PCA is not specially selected for her expertise and this must, over time, bring into question the competence of the office to handle such matters. Finally, the ruling that findings of fact – surely never intended to be binding – now bind the Government invites recourse to the courts. In short, with the 'Big Inquiry', the PCA is moving in a new direction that is not without its dangers and which may end by imperilling the success of the ombudsman scheme.

8. Control by courts?

It is highly improbable that anyone in 1967 foresaw that ombudsman decisions might one day be judicially reviewed. Statute dealt specifically with boundary disputes between courts and tribunals (s. 5(2)) and left the PCA such wide discretion whether or not to investigate that it would have seemed unlikely to be challenged. In fact the first (unsuccessful) application for review of the PCA was not long in coming[93] but it was not until the *Balchin* affair (see p. 481 above) that a PCA decision was quashed and twice sent back for reconsideration on the ground that the PCA had irrationally failed to take account of the supervisory powers of central government departments over *ex gratia* payments by local authorities.[94] In the meantime, as we saw in Chapter 10, courts were happy to review the decisions of other public and statutory ombudsmen. From the standpoint of the judiciary this step is entirely logical: either the ombudsmen, as investigators, are carrying out an administrative function, in which case their decisions are reviewable; or

[92] See for further explanation, J. Stapleton, 'Duty of care: Peripheral parties and alternative opportunities for deterrence' (1995) 111 *LQR* 301.

[93] *Re Fletcher's Application* [1970] 2 All ER 527 was a challenge to the PCA's refusal to investigate.

[94] *R (Balchin and Others) v Parliamentary Commissioner for Administration* [1996] EWHC Admin 152; [1999] EWHC Admin 484.

if the ombudsmen are adjudicators, they can be classified with subordinate jurisdictions.

Not surprisingly, given what has been said about the preference in our legal culture for the adversarial model of justice, challenges were largely on due-process grounds. In the case of the PCA, the natural preference was probably intensified by the reality: the administrative stage of complaints-handling takes place within departments, the process is not transparent and the nominal complainant is the MP. There have been moves towards continental 'contradictory' procedure if not to a full-blown adversarial model; as we have seen, draft recommendations must be presented to the department, giving it an opportunity to respond. Named individuals are also provided with a copy of complaints against them and current guidance warns public servants that any named individual must (i) be notified of the nature of a complaint about them and (ii) be given an opportunity to explain their position with the help of a trade union representative. Where the complainant is legally represented (which remains unusual), anyone complained about has a right to be legally represented.[95] This means that an opportunity must be afforded to contradict and correct findings of fact or inferences drawn by the investigator. Nonetheless, to lawyers trained in adversarial procedure, the procedure of the PCA is criticisable. There is no statutory right for a complainant to see the draft report, while the final report is made to the referring MP, although in practice the complainant receives a copy. This procedure has been condemned by complainants, who feel that they are being pushed to the sidelines. In *Dyer*,[96] however, the Divisional Court rejected an application for judicial review based on breach of the rules of natural justice. The court upheld the standard procedure on three different grounds: (i) the department but not the anonymous complainant is subject to public criticism; (ii) it is essential that the department suggests and discusses redress with the PCA; and (iii) it is necessary, in order for notice under s. 11(3) to be given if documents or information are to be withheld from further disclosure.

In *Cavanagh*,[97] the HSC was approached by a parent who complained that an NHS Healthcare Trust had improperly intervened in the treatment of his epileptic child by setting aside the existing arrangements without providing a satisfactory alternative. The HSC rejected the complaint and, acting on the evidence of two expert reports she had personally commissioned, blamed the consultants in charge of the case. Distressed at the unexpected turn taken by the investigation, the father joined with the impugned doctors to seek judicial review. The Court of Appeal ruled that the investigative and inquisitorial nature of the proceedings

[95] Cabinet Office, 'Handling of Parliamentary Ombudsman Cases', DEO(PM)(96)4 (1996), available online. See also Cabinet Office, 'The Ombudsman in your files' (1995).

[96] *R v Parliamentary Commissioner for Administration, ex p. Dyer* [1994] 1 All ER 375.

[97] *Cavanagh and Others v Health Services Commissioner* [2005] EWCA Civ 1578. In extending the inquiry to the doctors' conduct, the HSC relied on the provisions of the Health Service Commissioners (Amendment) Act 1996, extending the HSC's jurisdiction in matters of clinical judgement, which had just come into force.

did not entitle the HSC simply to investigate and make findings on matters not the subject of the complaint. There were legal limits to her powers:

> *Sedley LJ:* Certain clear propositions emerge from the legislation. First, the Commissioner's functions are limited to the investigation of complaints: she has no power of investigation at large. Secondly, the statutory discretions which she possesses, while generous, go to (a) whether she should embark upon or continue an investigation into a complaint (s. 3(2)) and (b) how an investigation is to be conducted (s. 11(3)). They do not enable her to expand the ambit of a complaint beyond what it contains, nor to expand her investigation of it beyond what the complaint warrants. This legislative policy is emphasised by the distinction contained in s. 11 between persons 'by reference to whose action the complaint is made' and who are automatically entitled to respond, and others who may become implicated but who enjoy no such automatic right. In the present case, one consequence of this scheme was that, although they were interviewed in the course of the investigation, the first the two doctors knew of the full criticism they were facing was when they were sent the draft Report for the purpose only of proposing factual adjustments to it.
>
> This does not mean that the ambit of every complaint or the scope of every inquiry is a question of law: it is for the Commissioner not only to decide what constitutes a discrete complaint but to decide what questions it raises and to investigate them to the extent she judges right. But there are legal limits. One may well be . . . that if she does not elect to discontinue an investigation she cannot truncate it. Another is that how she investigates a complaint is subject not only to the express requirement of notice to those directly implicated (s. 11(1)) but to the common law's requirements of fairness in so far as the statute itself does not restrict them. A third, central to these appeals, is that a point may come at which the pursuit of an investigation goes beyond any admissible view either of the complaint or of what the statutory purpose of investigation will accommodate.

The *Bradley* decision, however, changed the ballgame. In previous cases, complainants were questioning the PCA's discretionary choices. Here they were effectively asking for her findings to be enforced. Yet, as we saw earlier, ombudsman recommendations are not enforceable; this is indeed a characteristic of most ombudsman schemes and one generally regarded by ombudsmen as desirable. Although this is largely a convention, it is highly unusual for the PCA's recommendations to be rejected and, as we have seen, parliamentary pressure usually prevails at the end of the day. There is much force too in the argument advanced by PASC in the *Occupational Pensions* case (see p. 554 above) that enforcement is a matter for Parliament rather than for the courts. Local ombudsmen, who over the years have had more trouble in enforcing their decisions, tend to agree that 'providing a power of compulsion would frankly be overkill and might jeopardise what is a . . . generally very cooperative relationship'.[98] Thus the most curious feature of the *Bradley* ruling is, to quote

[98] Local Government and Health Service Commissioner to Wales, cited by R. Kirkham, B. Thompson and T. Buck, 'Enforcing the Recommendations of the Ombudsman' [2009] *PL* 510, 522.

a recent commentary, 'that it appears to have confirmed in law a position that no one asked for and few people were aware of';[99] and, it might have added, that almost no one seems to have wanted. Let us hope that the more activist line the courts are clearly taking will not do damage to ombudsman schemes.

9. Conclusion: An ombudsman unfettered?

Over its 40 years of existence, the office of PCA has evolved a distinctive role, atypical of most ombudsmen. Successive PCAs have utilised their special position to adopt a firefighting stance, though much has depended on the predilections of the current incumbent. At one end of a spectrum, Cecil Clothier envisaged the office as a substitute for a 'small claims court', handling group complaints only where each complainant could show 'injustice' and often turning away representative actions as political. William Reid, like Idwal Pugh before him, treated multiple complaints as indicative of poor performance, using his discretion to make a selection of symptomatic cases. Ten years on, at the other end of the spectrum, Ann Abraham takes her fire-watching role for granted and 'Big Inquiries' in her stride.

Parliamentary support has been important. When the journey started, the PCA was responsible to the Select Committee on the Parliamentary Commissioner for Administration. PASC, to which the PCA now reports, takes its work seriously under the steady chairmanship of Tony Wright and is, as we have seen in other chapters, ambitious. PASC's interest in good governance has enhanced the fire-watching function and provided support for its officer in hard times. PASC has added legitimacy and authority, enabling the PCA to direct officials and give guidance on good administrative practice, complaints-handling and appropriate redress and remedies. Kirkham, in his fortieth-anniversary review, also focuses on fire-watching, noting a growing tendency to target 'major systemic concerns about the operation of an investigated department'. He warns, however, against settling complaints at an early stage 'before establishing whether there are broader lessons to be learned'.[100]

The PCA now possesses and has used to good effect many of the qualities listed by the EO as characteristic of the office:

- a personal dimension to the office, with an office-holder who is more widely recognised
- independence
- free and easy access for the citizen
- primary focus on the handling of complaints, whilst having the power to recommend not only redress for individuals but also broader changes to laws and administrative practices

99 *Ibid.*, p. 512.

100 R. Kirkham, *The Parliamentary Ombudsman: Withstanding the test of time*, HC 421 (2006/7), p. 11. See also R. Kirkham, 'Auditing by Stealth? Special reports and the Ombudsman' [2005] *PL* 740.

- use of proactive means – successive PCAs have shown creative skill in providing themselves with weapons the legislature deliberately chose not to provide: the power to challenge bad rules, for example, or the 'class investigation' into endemic maladministration.
- effectiveness, based on well-reasoned reports and reliance on persuasion plus the power of the Select Committee rather than on the power to issue binding decisions, as discussed in the previous section – there has been regular publication of guidance on complaints-handling, notably the *Principles of Good Administration* and *Redress*.[101]

These are the qualities that matter from the top-down perspective we have adopted. High visibility and free and easy access for the citizen, qualities rated highly by Gregory and Giddings, are not especially important from this perspective. The PCA gains from the MP filter. It is a cheap and easy way of filtering out 'small claims' with the inestimable advantage of a widely accessible and well-known outreach service: the MP and his or her surgery.[102] We should not necessarily be worried if it has the effect of prioritising the concerns of MPs; MPs are concerned to get re-elected and their complaints reflect the contents of their mailbags, as we can tell from the way they pushed *Barlow Clowes*, the *Child Support Agency*, *Tax Credits* and *Occupational Pensions* investigations. The MP filter might also be credited for acting as a partial substitute for the power to open 'own initiative inquiries' and playing a part in the development of the 'Big Inquiry'.

It might at first seem that the PCA excels in 'big inquiries', where the exhaustive investigative procedure, too costly, cumbersome and slow for trivial complaints, comes into its own. Over the years, the office has honed its techniques until, with *Barlow Clowes*, *Debt of Honour* and *Occupational Pensions*, its 'Rolls Royce' investigatory procedures have evolved into a formidable investigative weapon of inquiry and the relationship with the Select Committee is highly effective, as we saw in the *Occupational Pensions* affair. It is fair to see it as a sort of standing public inquiry, able to handle complex investigations as fast and effectively as a public inquiry but at less expense. Kirkham applauds the tendency for investigations to become 'more high profile', calling the development 'one of the most important contributions that the Office can bring to the constitution'.[103] It could, however, denote politicisation and an element of capture by pressure groups and political institutions. It might too, as we have suggested, have the unintended effect of bringing the ombudsmen into too close a relationship with the courts.

But the PCA has a 'small claims' function and stands at the apex of a complaints-handling pyramid. Evaluating the office from the PDR angle means

[101] PCA, *Principles of Good Administration* (2007) *Principles for Remedy* (2007) and *Principles of Good Complaint Handling* (2008) all available on the website..

[102] R. Gregory and J. Pearson, 'The Parliamentary Ombudsman after twenty-five years' (1992) 70 *Pub. Admin.* 469, 496.

[103] Kirkham, *The Parliamentary Ombudsman.*

prioritising different ombudsman qualities, such as those listed by the BOIA: clarity of purpose, accessibility, flexibility, openness and transparency, proportionality, efficiency and quality outcomes. Lady Wilcox, late of the Citizen's Charter Unit, once argued that all ombudsmen should actively promote their services, seeking the help of the media to advertise their wares; they should appear on 'phone-in' programmes and participate in other high profile events. So far as possible their procedures should be informal; they should accept telephone complaints, travel through the country, and establish local offices. In this way their outreach could be extended to 'people who are not well informed about their rights and entitlements' and 'reach the more vulnerable groups in society, the socially disadvantaged and the underprivileged, whose need for help may be greater'.[104]

Here the PCA scores less highly. There is too much truth in Michael Buckley's first impression of his office as like 'an excellent research department in the Arts faculty of one of our older universities':

> Its staff were careful and conscientious. It had a high regard for truth, intellectual honesty in its investigations, and scholarly accuracy. It had a good deal less regard for urgency, for any practical use to which a particular investigation might be put, or for user-friendliness . . . The Office's Annual Reports were an illustration of these attitudes: around 100 pages of densely packed letterpress accompanied by erudite quotations and scholarly footnotes, and largely unrelieved by such concessions to weakness as side-headings, let alone the expensive frivolity of pictures.[105]

The style of the inquisitorial PCA investigations, anonymous, with restricted rights of participation for the complainant and ending in a report to an MP and Select Committee, all act as barriers to accessibility. Again, no complaints system can honestly be described as accessible if access depends on the unstructured discretion of MP intermediaries. And a good understanding of an ombudsman's powers is only possible if the jurisdictional criteria are simple, which is, unfortunately, not the case. A major obstacle to clarity lies in the fact that only bodies *specifically listed* in Sch. 2 of the 1967 Act can be investigated; legislative action is badly needed to reverse this position. The fuzzy boundaries of the term 'maladministration' are, on the other hand, probably advantageous; they allow the PCA considerable discretion, which has usually been used to good effect.

The appointment of the present incumbent, with her background in citizens' advice bureaux, was a signal for change. Ann Abraham takes visibility and accessibility very seriously. Applauding 'the way in which this now venerable institution has begun to embrace the modernising agenda that has swept through public life in the last decade and more', she has promised a regime 'fit

[104] J. Wilcox, 'A consumer organisation view' in R. Gregory *et al.*, *Practice and Prospects*, pp. 61–6.

[105] M. Buckley, 'Through the retroscope', *The Ombudsman* (December 2003), p. 17.

for purpose well into the twenty-first century'.[106] In line with this promise, the PCA is usually now styled the 'Parliamentary Ombudsman' and the office is less elite and more visible. An up-to-date website enhances visibility, reports are no longer desiccated and impermeable but garnished with pictures and case studies, and some at least of the informal methods recommended by Lady Wilcox are being tried. This is beginning to look like the sort of complaints system that typical NHS patients, pensioners, asylum seekers and those in receipt of income support, might feel comfortable in using. And reforms introduced by Sir Michael Buckley (such as the screening and fast track procedures described above) have had the effect of tilting the balance 'in favour of speed rather than thoroughness'.[107] Turn-around times are now fairly respectable and, even if the office is still below its targets, they compare relatively favourably with other complaints-handling systems.[108]

At the end of the day, however, the public judges effectiveness by final outcome, something that is hard to evaluate. Ombudsman recommendations, we have said, are almost invariably carried out. And if initially apology from a senior officer was seen as sufficient redress, those days are long gone; the CSA was, for example, strongly criticised in a Special Report for failing to provide appropriate remedies other than apologies.[109] Monetary compensation and how it should be calculated was effectively the point of disagreement in the *Channel Tunnel* case, where delays in building the high-speed rail link through Kent had put the project in limbo, causing hard cases of planning blight. There were sharp exchanges between the PCA and Permanent Secretary when the PCA ruled that this was maladministration causing injustice meriting a measure of compensation. The outcome was a new compromise, when the Government conceded new 'Indicative Guidelines' for cases of exceptional hardship, agreed by the SC.[110]

The PCA also requires a general rectification of error, often involving large numbers of cases, and recent Guidance places much emphasis on 'putting things right' and seeking continuous improvement.[111] An earlier statement from William Reid captures the modern priorities:

> Apologies, and acknowledgements of fault and the provision of financial recompense are undoubtedly important – but there is more to redress than that. Complainants need

[106] A. Abraham, 'Introduction' in Kirkham, *The Parliamentary Ombudsman: Withstanding the test of time.*

[107] P. Leyland and G. Anthony, *Textbook on Administrative* Law (Oxford University Press, 2008), p. 136.

[108] The *Annual Report for 2006/7*, HC 838 (2006/7), pp. 58–60, gives clear-up rates of 15% within 3 months; 43% within 6 months; and 79% within one year.

[109] *Investigation of Complaints against the Child Support Agency*, HC 135 (1995/6); *The Child Support Agency*, HC 199 (1994/5), pp. xii–xiv.

[110] PCA, *The Channel Tunnel Rail Link and Blight: Investigation of complaints against the Department of Transport*, HC 193 (1994/5). The Government agreed to look again at a limited scheme 'for those affected to an extreme and exceptional degree'.

[111] PCA, *Principles for Remedy* (2007), available online.

> an assurance that, so far as is humanly possible, identified failings will not be repeated. Appropriate corrective action helps others to avoid sustaining comparable injustices and it improves the quality of service generally available. That is why I attach particular importance to getting rid of systemic defects, those which are liable to affect adversely hundreds or perhaps thousands of individual[s] . . . That is why in their inquiries into a case my staff make a point of ensuring that any wider implications to an individual complaint have been identified and dealt with. That takes time, which I regret. There is still much truth in the old saying that 'Prevention is better than cure'.[112]

This is a firefighting function that courts cannot undertake. Even JUSTICE has admitted that, in respect of redress and enforcement, there is really 'no problem to be tackled'.[113]

[112] HC 20 (1995/6), p. vii.
[113] From JUSTICE–All Souls Review, *Administrative Justice* [5.36–9].

13

Inquiries: A costly placebo?

Contents

Chapter 10 of this book was devoted to complaints. Adopting a 'bottom-up' perspective, we considered the machinery for complaints-handling, its place in the administrative-justice landscape and various possible components of 'proportionate dispute resolution'. In Chapter 11 we turned our attention to tribunals, firmly established by the Franks Committee as 'machinery for adjudication'. We looked at their emergence as a two-tier system of administrative adjudication in terms of the Tribunals, Courts and Enforcement Act 2007. As the JUSTICE–All Souls Committee perceived, inquiries 'though often referred to in the same breath as tribunals . . . have quite a different origin, purpose and status and their development has been somewhat different'.[1] Wade too had noted their ambiguous character: they were, he thought, a hybrid legal-and-administrative process, and 'for the very reason that they have been made to look as much as possible like a judicial proceeding, people grumble at the way in which they fall short of it'.[2] This ambiguity is a central theme of this chapter.

The chapter looks at the genesis of inquiries as 'machinery for investigation', using procedures usually classified as 'inquisitorial'. These, however, both resemble and differ from the investigatory procedures of the Parliamentary Ombudsman studied in Chapter 12. We ask how far this inquisitorial procedure differs from the common law adversarial procedures that we have come to accept as the adjudicative norm. Have inquiries followed tribunals too far down the path of judicialisation, drifting back to the adversarial procedure that common lawyers instinctively prefer? If this is so, we ask in the final section, is the development in some cases necessary to meet the due process requirements of the ECHR? Or is it more generally a necessary step in the evolution of inquiries to yet another mechanism for independent review of government?

Wade seized on the conflictual character of inquiries, which he saw as 'one of the principal battlegrounds between legal and official opinion in the past fifty years'.[3] Since Wade wrote, there has been an exponential growth of inquiries in public life, which have come to be regarded as the cure for every manner of public ill. Somewhat cynically, Louis Blom-Cooper QC, an advocate with much experience of public inquiries, sees them as providing 'the symbolic purpose of holding up to obloquy the particular event that induced the crisis of public confidence':

> The instinct to reach for the solution of a public inquiry stems from a desire to distract the critics or deflect criticism, or to expose some fraud, fault or act of maladministration. It also arises out of the need expeditiously to restore public confidence in government or in public administration, or to scotch ill-founded rumours of scandal, by an independent investigation of the events under scrutiny. The urge also is to establish the facts other than by established methods, such as coroners' inquests, litigation (including judicial review) or criminal proceedings.[4]

1 JUSTICE–All Souls Review, *Administrative Justice: Some necessary reforms* (Clarendon Press, 1988) (hereafter JUSTICE–All Souls).

2 H. W. R. Wade, *Administrative Law* (Clarendon Press, 1961), p. 166.

3 *Ibid.*

4 L. Blom-Cooper, 'Public inquiries' (1993) 46 *Current Legal Problems* 204, 205.

As we shall see, this inclination is not always successful. Several of these 'grand inquests' into the health of the nation have been highly controversial. They have inflamed public opinion and have caused at great expense more problems than they have resolved. What are the reasons for public dissatisfaction and in what respects do public inquiries 'fall short' of public expectations?

Philip Sales, then an experienced Treasury Counsel, takes a high-minded approach. While an inquiry may in practice sometimes 'be a step taken for reasons of political expediency, to meet public pressure on some topic, or as a way of shunting off some difficult matter into a siding so that it can be forgotten about for a while', inquiries do at the same time occupy a vital place in the modern constitution:

> There is an increased recognition that in a modern state the legitimacy of governmental action may be bound up, in part, with the willingness of government to accept public scrutiny of what it has done – to operate with "transparency", to use the short-hand expression . . . Public inquiries can serve an important function in supplementing other processes for scrutiny of government action in the interests of transparency. But it is important to remember that their function is a supplementary one. It must be borne in mind that there are other well-established mechanisms for the scrutiny of government action, particularly in Parliament. The institution of the public inquiry ought not to replace those mechanisms, which are more explicitly linked to the direct democratic political control of what governments do.[5]

Lord Howe, a long-serving minister in Margaret Thatcher's Cabinets with a wide experience of public affairs, depicts inquiries as serving six rather disparate ends. The objective of an inquiry might be:

1. to establish the facts
2. to learn from events
3. to provide catharsis for 'stakeholders'
4. to reassure the public
5. to make people and organisations accountable
6. to serve the political interests of government.[6]

These objectives should be weighed and the balance between them should dictate the procedures selected. We shall find in this chapter that all too many options are available. Recently, however, the Government has moved to rationalise, introducing a model that they hope will be all-purpose in the Inquiries Act 2006.

[5] P. Sales, 'Accountability of government via public inquiries' [2004] *Judicial Review* 173.

[6] G. Howe, 'The management of public inquiries' (1999) 70 *Pol. Quarterly* 294. These objectives will be cited hereafter as (Howe, 1–6).

1. They just grew

Like so much in English administrative law, inquiries did not leap fully fledged onto the public-administration scene; they evolved slowly and without any particular thought being given to functions or shape. Before we can arrive at conclusions as to the place of inquiries in the contemporary system of government, we need to look backwards to see where they came from and how they have assumed their particular shape and characteristics.

(a) Committees and commissions

It has been suggested that planning inquiries have their origin in parliamentary private-bill procedure, which allowed objectors to the bill's procedures to appear before the parliamentary committees. As private-bill procedure fell into disfavour, the cumbersome committee procedure was replaced by inquiries that reported to the minister.[7] Parliamentary committees had other uses; committees of inquiry were commonly appointed during the nineteenth century to investigate issues of public importance and social reform, as was done, for example, to inquire into child-labour exploitation before Peel's Reform Bill in 1816. An alternative might be a royal commission of inquiry, the first of which was established in 1832 to look into reform of the poor laws. Procedurally, these committees collected evidence, listened to witnesses and asked questions, in the same way as modern select committees do. Committees investigated, advised and made recommendations but were not of course able to initiate action. This type of inquiry is either purely advisory or a stage in an administrative process; it is certainly not 'machinery for adjudication', as tribunals are now considered to be.

The pre-war Donoughmore Committee saw inquiries as 'an instrument of government'.[8] Its concern with the terms 'judicial or quasi-judicial decisions' sprang from its terms of reference and would today seem outdated, although it does serve to highlight the hybrid 'legal-and-administrative' position of public inquiries. The committee chose to focus on planning inquiries, which had for some time raised concern over procedures, especially the non-disclosure of inspectors' reports,[9] where openness was recommended: the inspector's report, together with the minister's decision should be communicated to 'the parties concerned'. Otherwise, the committee thought, two types of inquiry should be distinguished. On one side of the line stood 'public inquiries of a judicial character' prescribed by statute, as with the Town and Country Planning Acts, or set up under the Tribunals and Inquiries Act 1921; on the other were inquiries arranged by government 'in

[7] JUSTICE–All Souls [10.1–3].

[8] Terminology borrowed from R. Wraith and G. Lamb, *Public Inquiries as an Instrument of Government* (Allen and Unwin, 1971).

[9] See, e.g., *Local Government Board v Arlidge* [1915] AC 120.

the ordinary course of administration'. In the latter case, the committee 'did not wish to be misunderstood as recommending the adoption of any general rule that reports submitted by inspectors to their ministers should be made available to the public':

> Our recommendation is to be considered as limited to those cases where a public inquiry of a judicial character has been prescribed by Parliament as a step in the process of arriving at a judicial or quasi-judicial decision. It matters not for our purposes whether the holding of such an inquiry is enjoined by the relevant statute or only where certain specified conditions are satisfied or whether it is merely indicated as a step which may be taken if the Minister in his discretion thinks fit so to direct . . . This conclusion follows, as indicated above, from what in our view must be presumed to be the object of Parliament in providing for a public hearing of the parties . . . Our recommendation has no application to those cases where the Minister in the ordinary course of administration may arrange for some local inquiry or investigation, the better to inform his mind before he takes some decision which is in its competence as the head of an executive Department. In such cases the Minister, having full discretion to arrive at his decision in his own way, should be entirely free to deal as he thinks fit with such reports as may be made to him. The ordinary processes of administration might indeed be gravely impeded were the Minister to be tied down to any particular procedure and the fact that the Minister may be armed by statute with a general power to proceed by way of local inquiry in suitable cases makes no difference so long as the matter is essentially administrative.[10]

Donoughmore's uncertainty sprang from the way planning inquiries were beginning to develop and their use when the compulsory purchase of private property for public purposes was involved. While making a distinction that it clearly saw as significant between inquiries 'of a judicial nature' and advisory inquiries, the committee was unable to provide any conclusive criteria for the distinction. Drawing on the intention of Parliament, it insisted at the same time that the test was not whether an inquiry was or was not statutory in origin.

The post-war Franks Committee followed Donoughmore in focusing on planning and land inquiries, numerically the commonest form of inquiry. Once again the hybrid character of inquiries was emphasised:

> The intention of the legislature in providing for an inquiry or hearing in certain circumstances appears to have been twofold: to ensure that the interests of the citizens most closely affected should be protected by the grant of a statutory right to be heard in support of the objections, and to ensure that thereby the Minister should be better informed about the facts of the case.[11]

[10] *Report of the Committee on Ministers' Powers*, Cmnd 4060 (1932), pp. 106–7.
[11] *Report of the Committee on Tribunals and Enquiries*, Cmnd 218 (1957) [269].

Inquiries were not to be classified as 'purely administrative because of the provision of a special procedure preliminary to the decision', which involved the testing of an issue, 'often partly in public'. They were not on the other hand purely judicial, 'because the final decision cannot be reached by the application of rules and must allow the exercise of a wide discretion in the balancing of public and private interest':

> If the administrative view is dominant the public inquiry cannot play its full part in the total process, and there is a danger that the rights and interest of the individual citizens affected will not be sufficiently protected. In these cases it is idle to argue that Parliament can be relied upon to protect the citizen, save exceptionally . . . if the judicial view is dominant there is the danger that people will regard the person before whom they state their case as a kind of judge provisionally deciding the matter, subject to an appeal to the Minister. This view overlooks the true nature of the proceeding, the form of which is necessitated by the fact that the Minister himself, who is responsible to Parliament for the ultimate decision, cannot conduct the inquiry in person.[12]

Tribunals and inquiries differed in their origins and had always served different purposes. There was now general agreement that this was so. 'A reasonable balance' between judicial and administrative functions was necessary. Yet the effect of bracketing inquiries with tribunals was to undercut the emphasis on their administrative functions and the policy element which was always present. An assumption that 'what is right for a tribunal is also right for an inquiry' took hold and grew. The effects as conveniently summarised by Purdue and Popham would be to improve the legitimacy of the standard inquiry by the enactment of procedural rules, which governed not only the conduct of the inquiry but also pre- and post-inquiry procedures. This enactment of procedural rules would, at the same time, accentuate the quasi-judicial aspects of what was originally primarily an administrative function.[13] As Schwartz and Wade put it, after the Franks report the debate crystallised around 'how much "judicialisation" the inquiry procedure can stand'.[14]

(b) The coroner's inquest

A second progenitor of the inquiry is the coroner's inquest, its antiquity attested by the fact that the first edition of the standard textbook dates to 1829.[15] The office was created by Richard I in 1199 to represent the Crown in the administration of justice. Coroners are (and always have been) independent officials

[12] *Ibid.* [272–4].

[13] M. Purdue and J. Popham, 'The future of the major inquiry' (2002) *Journal of Planning & Environment Law (JPEL)* 137.

[14] B. Schwartz and H. Wade, *Legal Control of Government: Administrative law in Britain and the United States* (OUP, 1972), p. 163.

[15] *Jervis on Coroners*, 12th edn (Sweet & Maxwell, 2002).

holding office during good behaviour. They are commonly seen to exercise judicial or quasi-judicial functions, though they do not precisely 'adjudicate'. They are largely independent of central government, being chosen by local authorities, though the Home Secretary's approval is needed.

Under the Coroners Act 1988, which governed the inquests described in this chapter, the coroner has jurisdiction to inquire into the death of any person within his jurisdiction who has suffered a violent or unnatural death, a sudden death from an unknown cause, or who died in prison. The inquest is a limited fact-finding inquiry to establish the answers to who has died, when and where the death occurred, and how the cause of death arose. It is intended to be non-adversarial and in modern times the coroner has been expressly forbidden to consider the potential criminal or civil liability of any named individual, the possible verdicts being: death by natural causes, accident, suicide, unlawful or lawful killing and an 'open' verdict where there is insufficient evidence for any other verdict. (As we shall see, the 'riders' or recommendations added in some inquests can come very close to breaking this prohibition). There is a close parallel here with s. 2 of the Inquiries Act 2005, which provides that an inquiry 'is not to rule on, and has no power to determine, any person's civil or criminal liability'. Inquiries then do not adjudicate; they find facts, investigate, search for and try to discover 'the truth'.[16]

Deficiencies in coronial procedure were highlighted by inquests which took place into the deaths of over 200 elderly people, subsequently shown by a criminal trial and public inquiry to have been murdered by their general practitioner, Dr Shipman. The exhaustive public inquiry conducted by Dame Janet Smith concluded that the 1988 system 'was failing to protect the public and to meet the reasonable expectations of society'. She made important recommendations concerning the need for modernisation, added resources and standardisation of coroners' inquest procedure; these recommendations lie behind the changes contained in the Coroners and Criminal Justice Bill introduced into Parliament in late 2008.[17]

Many of the features of the modern public inquiry are visible in the coroner's inquest, which carries out most of the functions mentioned by Lord Howe (see p. 572 above). The coroner's primary duty is to establish the facts and reassure the public that some notice and action is being taken. Lessons can be learned from the inquest's findings; such recommendations are, however,

[16] *Ibid.*

[17] See *Death Certification and the Investigation of Deaths by Coroners*, the 3rd Report of the Shipman Inquiry, Cm. 5854 (2003); *Death Certification in England, Wales and Northern Ireland: Report of a fundamental review*, Cm. 5831 (2003). And see Home Office, *Reforming the Coroner and Death Certification Service: A position paper*, Cm. 6159 (2004); House of Commons Constitution Committee, *Reform of the Coroners' System and Death Certification*, HC 902 (2005/6); Ministry of Justice, *Coroner Reform: The Government's draft bill*, Cmnd 6849 (2006). Under the Coroners and Criminal Justice Bill, currently before Parliament, there will be a degree of centralisation with a Chief Coroner to lead the service. There will be also be a senior coroner for each coroner area.

not enforceable and no legal consequences flow if they are disregarded. All that the coroner can do is draw attention publicly to some deficiency or write to 'someone in authority', such as a council or a government department about the matter. Recommendations made by the coroner can however be very forthright. A set of inquests, for example, held by coroners into the death of soldiers in Iraq and Afghanistan, attributed the deaths to lack of care for army personnel and to defective equipment. The verdicts, which occasioned much unfavourable publicity, were highly embarrassing to government. They culminated in an unsuccessful application by the Defence Secretary to have one such verdict quashed on the ground that its language appeared to 'determine a question of civil liability'.[18] Shortly afterwards, the Government inserted into a Counter-Terrorism Bill a provision allowing inquests deemed 'a risk to the national security' to be held in secret and without a jury. This proposal occasioned such a public outcry that it was withdrawn by the Home Secretary. However, the Coroners and Criminal Justice Bill would give commensurate powers to the Home Secretary to withdraw an investigation from a coroner in cases involving national security and transfer it to a High Court judge or order that an inquest be held without a jury and in camera.

The inquest can also provide a powerful forum for catharsis, sometimes after other types of inquiry have failed. The inquest into the death of Diana, Princess of Wales in a car accident, for example, followed a French judicial inquiry and an independent inquiry by the Metropolitan Police, which took three years, established the salient facts and was published.[19] It was not, however, until the matter had been investigated in the spotlight of publicity by an inquest where the jury returned a verdict of unlawful killing, laying responsibility at the door of the driver and reporters following the car, that all those involved (the stakeholders) accepted that it must finally be laid to rest. The 'Diana inquest' introduces three recurrent themes of the modern public inquiry: cost, duplication and delay. The final verdict came ten years after her death in 1997. Eight million pounds was spent on the earlier Stevens investigation and £4.5 million on the elaborate trial-type inquest presided over by a High Court judge with a panoply of leading counsel. The proceedings provoked multiple applications for judicial review, starting with a successful application for the inquest to be conducted with a jury.[20]

[18] *R (Smith) v Assistant Deputy Coroner for Oxfordshire & Anor* [2008] EWHC 694 (Admin).

[19] Sir John Stevens, *The Operation Paget Inquiry Report into the Allegation of Conspiracy to Murder Diana, Princess of Wales and Emad El-Din Mohamed Abdel Moneim Fayed* (2006), available online.

[20] *Paul and Ors v Deputy Coroner of the Queen's Household and Anor* [2007] EWHC 408 (Admin). Following the successful review, the Coroner, Lady Butler-Sloss, resigned and was replaced by Lord Justice Scott Baker. See also *R (Mohamed Al Fayed) v Assistant Deputy Coroner of Inner West London* [2008] EWHC 713 Admin. Applications for review of a Coroner's decision my also be made under s. 13 of the Coroner's Act 1988. See also *Assistant Deputy Coroner for Inner West London v Channel 4 Television Corporation* [2007] EWHC 2513 an application by the coroner to order production of documents.

Similar issues arose in respect of the inquest into the death of Jean Charles de Menezes, an innocent man wrongly identified as a terrorist and shot by Special Branch officers following a terrorist attack in London. Death or serious injury caused by the police is routinely investigated by the Independent Police Complaints Commission (IPCC), set in place by the Police Reform Act 2002 in response to complaints that the previous system was insufficiently independent. In the Menezes case, the IPCC did hold an inquiry, initially resisted by the Metropolitan Police. But neither this report nor a subsequent prosecution brought against the police under the Health and Safety at Work Act 1974 for failure to provide for 'the health, safety and welfare of Jean Charles de Menezes' did much to assuage public concern. The inquest, delayed against the wishes of the family to allow the health and safety charges to go forward, opened three years after the shooting and was effectively the first opportunity for evidence to be adequately tested and for the public to learn what had occurred. This raises difficult issues of the relationships between the inquest and other inquiries and of the rights of relatives. The Menezes family withdrew its co-operation after the jury was banned by the coroner, Sir Michael Wright, from returning a verdict of unlawful killing; subsequently an open verdict was returned. This is just the type of inquest that could be deemed 'a risk to the national security' in terms of the new bill.

(c) Inquest procedure

As with inquiries and all inquisitorial procedure, the coroner is in charge. As guidance published by the service puts it:

> The coroner decides who to ask and the order in which they give evidence. Anyone who wants to give evidence can come forward at an inquest without being summonsed by the coroner, but the evidence must be relevant to the inquest . . . A person who wants to give evidence should contact the coroner as soon as possible after the death.
>
> Anyone who has 'a proper interest' may question a witness at the inquest. They may be represented by lawyers or, if they prefer, ask questions themselves. The questions must be sensible and relevant. This is something the coroner will decide. There are no speeches.[21]

This is paradigm inquisitorial procedure.

Over the years, however, the inquest has turned into something of an awkward hybrid. There are juries; 'interested persons' can be legally represented; there are powers to summon witnesses, who can be punished if they do not attend; all evidence is given under oath; witnesses have to answer questions (subject to the important proviso that a 'person or people suspected of causing a death if required to give evidence at the inquest will be protected against

[21] Website of the Surrey Coroner.

answering any question which may tend to incriminate him'). These features of the coroner's inquest give it something of the appearance of a criminal trial and naturally create pressure to make it more so.

2. Inquiries: A mixed bag

(a) Rolls-Royce procedure: The 1921 Act

Until 2005, the only statute of general application to inquiries was the Tribunals of Inquiry (Evidence) Act 1921. Perhaps because it required a motion in both Houses of Parliament, which takes the matter out of the absolute control of ministers, it was very little used, the two most notable examples being the inquiry into the disaster at Aberfan, after a colliery waste tip engulfed the local school, killing 144 people, mainly schoolchildren.[22] Here the choice was undoubtedly cathartic; it expressed deep grief at a national tragedy. In the 'Bloody Sunday' inquiry chaired by Lord Saville (see p. 604 below), the Act was probably invoked to underscore the legitimacy of an inquiry set up many years after the incident by a New Labour Government that wished to demonstrate its 'clean hands'. The Conservative government deliberately chose, against the express wishes of the Opposition, *not* to use the 1921 Act for the Scott inquiry into arms for Iraq (below), the motive almost certainly being desire for ministerial control. The Government left it open for Lord Justice Scott, who conducted the inquiry, to come back to the Government for a tribunal of inquiry to be appointed; in practice, however, it seems that Lord Justice Scott experienced no particular problems. Although they could not technically be subpoenaed, senior civil servants and ministers, including two prime ministers, did give evidence, though occasionally under protest. The Report notes, however, that some departments were not as co-operative as they might have been and used delaying tactics skilfully.

It is sometimes suggested that the 1921 Act was a factor in the judicialisation of inquiry procedure, partly due perhaps to the power to take evidence on oath. Much more influential was the report of another inquiry: the Royal Commission chaired by Lord Salmon, a distinguished Law Lord, into the fairness of tribunals of inquiry.[23] Lord Salmon's professional experience, like that of the High Court judges who habitually chair tribunals of inquiry, was with adversarial trial procedures, for which he may have had a natural preference. There is some support for this in the fact that the Salmon Commission was prompted by Lord Denning's report on the 'Profumo affair'. Revealing his unfamiliarity with inquisitorial procedure, Lord Denning remarked that

[22] Lord Edmund Davies, *Report of the Tribunal Appointed to Inquire into the Disaster at Aberfan on October 21st 1966*, HC 553 (1967).

[23] *Report of the Royal Commission on the Tribunals of Inquiry (Evidence) Act 1921*, Cmnd 3121 (1966); *Government response*, Cmnd 5313 (1973).

he had had to combine the functions of detective, inquisitor, advocate and judge. The procedure, which was often informal to the point of laxness, lay entirely in Lord Denning's hands and raised concerns over the position of witnesses, who had little or no opportunity to challenge evidence that in the event had a very unfavourable effect.[24] Marshall observed dryly that, as no one gave evidence on oath or was cross-examined, 'a large number of conclusions of fact rested on unpublished and unverifiable testimony and it might well have been asked why anyone should be expected to believe a word of it'.[25]

The Royal Commission's formidable list of recommendations was based on trial-type procedures. They covered rights to appear at an inquiry; legal representation; examination and cross-examination of witnesses and notice to witnesses of allegations against them, adding that witnesses should be given an opportunity to prepare a case and be assisted by legal advisers whose expenses were met out of public funds. The Government accepted and promptly implemented as an informal guide to procedure the 'six cardinal Salmon principles', which have formed the bedrock of procedure at public inquiries ever since. It did not, however, legislate. Two committees of inquiry and the unofficial JUSTICE–All Souls Review have since called for a more formal code of inquiry procedure, finally empowered by the Inquiries Act 2005 (see p. 607 below).[26]

(b) Statutory inquiries

It is more common for public inquiries to be set up under subject-specific legislation, most obviously the Town and Country Planning Acts, which are dealt with below. In Scotland, inquiries are devolved by the Scotland Act 1998 but in Wales dealt with on a piecemeal basis by transfer of functions orders made in terms of the devolution legislation. Section 250 of the Local Government Act 1972 contains similar powers. Many other statutes contain similar provisions, such as the National Health Service Act 1977, the Children Act 1989 and Police Act 1996. In a different field altogether, inquiries are authorised by the Companies Acts. This ad hoc way of proceeding can be very confusing, as the inquiry secretary complained in the inquiry into Heathrow's fifth terminal (see p. 586 below). The inquiry had to consider nearly forty linked applications and orders under seven separate pieces of legislation, 'some of which could have been the subject of a major inquiry in their own right'

[24] Lord Denning, *The Circumstances Leading to the Resignation of the Former Secretary of State for War, Mr J. D. Profumo* (HMSO, 1963).

[25] G. Marshall, *Constitutional Conventions: The rules and forms of accountability* (Clarendon Press, 1984), pp. 105–6.

[26] *Report of the Committee on Hospital Complaints Procedure* (HMSO, 1973); *Ad Hoc Inquiries in Local Government* (SOLACE, 1978); JUSTICE–All Souls [10.97].

and 'the sheer scale and complexity of the issues under consideration' had prolonged the length of the hearing considerably.[27]

Accident inquiries are dealt with by the Health and Safety at Work Act 1974 and by a miscellany of different statutes and sets of regulations, such as those made under the Civil Aviation Act 1982, the Railways Act 1974 and Merchant Shipping Act 1995. Usually conducted by inspectors, they are used routinely to investigate the cause of specific accidents, a majority of which are very small and attract only local attention. Occasionally, however, as with the inquiries into train collisions at Ladbroke Grove (Paddington) and Southall in 1999, they are very high-profile indeed, when they may be chaired (as these were) by a judge or distinguished professional expert. The two inquiries, which had occasioned much public disquiet, were followed up by a further joint inquiry commissioned by the Health and Safety Executive into the general safety of train protection systems, with the rather different function of drawing wider conclusions from the facts established by the earlier inquiries.[28] The outcome was a new investigatory body, the Rail Accident Investigation Branch, reporting directly to the Secretary of State, to handle investigations into all railway accidents.[29] Another possibility is a special, non-statutory inquiry, such as the inquiry into the sinking of the *Marchioness* pleasure boat on the Thames[30] or the football-stadium disaster at Hillsborough.[31] Such disasters have occasionally attracted a full-scale tribunal of inquiry under the 1921 Act, as with the shootings at Dunblane primary school[32] and the scandalous case of child abuse in Welsh children's homes, which lasted three years and cost £13 million but resulted in a much needed total overhaul of the child-care system in Wales.[33] All three were chaired by a (retired) judge.

Finally, there is nothing to prevent a government department or public body simply deciding to hold an inquiry without any express authority, as the Mayor of London did recently to investigate allegations of racism in the Metropolitan Police. Inquiries and royal commissions can be set up under the royal prerogative. A statutory power to set up an inquiry can be implied. Again, not every inquiry is a public inquiry; it may simply be part of the normal administrative

27 DoT, 'The Heathrow Terminal 5 Inquiry: An inquiry secretary's perspective' *Planning Inspectorate Journal*, Jan. 2005 (available online).

28 HSE, *The Southall and Ladbroke Grove Joint Inquiries into Train Protection Systems* (HMSO, 2001.) See also Lord Cullen, *The Ladbroke Grove Rail Inquiry* (HMSO, 2000); Professor John Uff, *The Southall Rail Inquiry* (HMSO, 2000).

29 See the Railways and Transport Safety Act 2003.

30 DOE, *The Marchioness/Bowbelle Formal Investigation under the Merchant Shipping Act 1995* (2001). And see *Public Inquiry into the Identification of Victims following Major Transport Accidents*, Cm. 5012 (2001) (Chair: Clarke LJ).

31 *Final Report of the Hillsborough Stadium Disaster*, Cmnd 962 (1990) (Chair: Popplewell J).

32 *Public Inquiry into the Shootings at Dunblane Primary School*, Cm. 3386 (1996) (Chair: Lord Cullen).

33 Department of Health, *Lost in Care: Report of the tribunal of inquiry into the abuse of children in care in the former county council areas of Gwynedd and Clwyd since 1974* (2001) (Chair: Sir Ronald Waterhouse).

procedures of a public authority, like the internal review or inquiry ordered by the Home Secretary in response to the Mayor of London's inquiry into racism. The wish to keep proceedings private in this way is indeed one of the most important reasons for appointing a non-statutory inquiry.

3. Inquiries and the planning process

Although planning inquiries are by no means the only form of inquiry held to advise ministers in making policy decisions, the system is by far the largest, statistically comparable to the large tribunal systems studied in Chapter 11. The final Annual Report of the Council on Tribunals records, for example, that 29,000-odd planning inquiries were held in 2006–7, a rise of 8 per cent. The majority of planning inquiries, whether into local development plans, compulsory purchase orders or planning applications, are small routine affairs which attract little publicity.

To understand the function of these inquiries, it is necessary to understand a little about the planning system, the basis of which is a series of statutes passed after World War II, from which inquiries derive their powers. The most significant was the Town and Country Planning Act 1947 (TCPA), which set in place the general machinery of land-use planning. Planning functions were generally a function of the two-tier district and county local government system, though subject always to departmental co-ordinating functions and ministerial call-in powers. The TCPA laid a positive duty on a planning authority to create development plans. This positive aspect of land use planning was enforced through development control, which required development and changes of use to be submitted to the planning authority for approval. Before a local development plan was made or changed, a local inquiry would be held by an inspector at which objections could be expressed. The inspector, who was in charge of inquiry procedures, reports to the minister or authority that appointed him, subject to cases where the decision-making power is delegated to him. These structures remain largely in place.

The development of a planning inquiry at which objections could be made has been central to acceptance of an increasingly intrusive system of land use planning. As one early study put it, the inquiry is 'part of the institutional apparatus of the state. One of its functions is to secure legitimacy for planning decisions taken by the state.'[34] This is the main reason why, as we saw in Chapter 4, there was so much concern during the 1980s to boost public participation in planning inquiries. This was an aspect of the inquiry that Franks did not consider. There was, however, a negative side to increased participation: cost and delay mounted as inquiries were prolonged. The Local Government, Planning and Land Act 1980, passed by a Conservative government in response to demands to cut the costs and delays associated with planning inquiries, was

[34] N. Hutton, *Lay Participation in Planning Inquiries* (Gower, 1986), p. 1.

a decisive step in the direction of streamlined procedures, restricting the requirement for local inquiries.

Today, most planning applications are dealt with by written representations, though they may occasionally trigger an inquiry or 'hearing'.[35] The 1980 Act was also the start of a steady process of delegation, so that inspectors today not only make recommendations but also take decisions, making the process more adjudicative. Only where the parties to a planning appeal do not agree to a written procedure is an inquiry necessary and even then the planning inspectorate has discretion whether to opt for a hearing, which takes the form of an 'open discussion led by the inspector'. On the face of things, the procedure is fully inquisitorial: the inspector is master of procedure and 'shall identify what are, in his opinion the main issues to be considered at the hearing and any matter on which he requires further explanation from any person entitled or permitted to appear'.[36] Hearings are usually quicker and cheaper than an inquiry and the shortened procedures are popular because they are cheap and speedy and legal representation is unnecessary. Here again we are seeing the search for 'appropriate' and 'proportionate' forms of dispute resolution, discussed in Chapter 10.

On the debit side, hearings are less participatory and offer none of the formal protections afforded by a planning inquiry; third parties are virtually excluded and the wider public interest may also be prejudiced. The Planning Inspectorate (PI), which handles inquiries, promises that its decisions and reports will take into account not only published planning policies and other relevant planning issues but also the views of all the parties; it is, however, far from clear how written representation or hearing procedure can accomplish this promise. Without publicity, how can 'stakeholders', other than those to whom notice must be given, be identified? The Guidance points to some of the difficulties:

> If the appeal is to be decided by a hearing, when the arrangements have been made the [Local Planning Authority] should let you know when and where it will take place. They may also publish details of the hearing in a local newspaper if they think it's necessary. There is usually more publicity about an appeal if there is going to be an inquiry. As with the other appeal procedures, if you have already written to the LPA, they should write to you. The LPA should send you details of the inquiry arrangements once the date is agreed. The appellant must display details of the inquiry, like the time and place, on the site of the proposed development two weeks before the inquiry. These are the minimum publicity requirements . . . Your LPA may give appeals more publicity.[37]

[35] See the Town and Country Planning (Appeals) (Written Representations Procedure) (England) Regulations 2000, SI 2000/1628.

[36] Town and Country Planning (Hearings Procedure) (England) Rules 2000, SI 2000/1626; Circular 05/00 [26].

[37] PI, *Taking Part in Planning Appeals, If you want to comment on someone else's appeals*, available online.

With the aim of making planning applications progress more quickly and efficiently, the Planning and Compulsory Purchase Act 2004 ended the right to a hearing.

(a) Inspectors and independence

Central to the evolution of the modern PI is public perception of its autonomy. Today the PI is an agency, carefully hived-off from central government. It stresses its 'impartial expertise' and has adopted in its mission statement the Franks principles of 'fairness, openness and impartiality' so emphasising the *judicial* nature of its functions. The independence of an inspector handling a planning inquiry is of primary importance because of the wide procedural discretion: the code that covers most routine planning inquiries provides that, 'except as otherwise provided in these Rules, the inspector shall determine the procedure at an inquiry'. In practice, the apparently unfettered discretion is heavily structured by regulations,[38] supported by a departmental code of practice. These cover in some detail the stages from notification of the inquiry: production of documents including a right to copies, appearances at the inquiry, rights to call evidence and cross-examine and, after the hearing, notification of the inspector's reasoned decision in writing and admission of new evidence. Although the rules apply only to planning, Purdue tells us that they tend to act as a benchmark for standardisation and 'although numerous different sets of rules exist for different public inquiries, they tend to follow a standard pattern and indeed, where there are no rules, it is the practice to follow this pattern'.[39]

The introduction of statutory codes opened inquiry procedures to a process of 'judicialisation from within and from without'. With a few exceptions, the regulatory provisions are immediately recognisable by anyone trained in a common law system as following the practice of our adversarial civil procedure (discovery of documents, cross-examination, etc.). Where they do not, they tend to be contested, as with the inspector's right to inspect the site without both parties being present (now statutory) or the obligation to re-open an inquiry, both areas regularly tested by judicial review. A substantial case law has developed, with which we deal in Chapter 14. The case law is equivocal. Sometimes it reflects the general progression towards 'rational decision-making' described in Chapter 3, insisting, for example, that the inspector's report must be intelligible and logical;[40] that ministerial 'policy' decisions must be based on the inspector's findings of fact and supported by sufficient evidence; that a decision to differ from the inspector's

[38] The initial text was the Town and Country Planning (Inquiries Procedure) Rules 1974, SI 1974/419. The rules are now regularly updated.

[39] M. Purdue 'Public inquiries as a part of public administration' in Feldman (ed.), *English Public Law* (Oxford University Press, 2004) [22.14].

[40] See *Save Britain's Heritage v No. 1 Poultry* [1991] 1 WLR 153.

recommendations should be justified in an adequately reasoned letter of decision; and so on. Other rulings, such as a finding that an inspector has no duty to undertake an investigatory function,[41] cast doubt on the very meaning of the term 'inquiry' and it must sometimes seem to the planners that the natural advantages of inquisitorial procedure are being watered down and undercut.

In *Bushell's* case,[42] which situates the inquiry as a step in a holistic planning process designed to 'inform the minister', the House of Lords tried to draw a line under judicialisation. By viewing it in this way rather than hiving off the inquiry as 'machinery for adjudication', judicialisation could be confined to the inquiry procedures. Even here the House of Lords was not especially generous, disallowing cross-examination. Lord Diplock justified his reasoning on the ground that:

> a decision to construct a nationwide network of motorways is clearly one of government policy in the widest sense of the term. Any proposal to alter it is appropriate to be the subject of debate in Parliament, not of separate investigations in each of the scores of local inquiries before individual inspectors up and down the country upon whatever material happens to be presented to them at the particular inquiry over which they preside.

Bushell's case was a serious setback for objectors who, before freedom of information legislation, sought to find a footing in the inquiry to contest government policy. The details of this landmark case are further discussed in Chapter 14.

(b) The 'Big Inquiry'

Purdue and Popham maintain that 'the inquiry process works reasonably well when it is confined to site-specific issues and only a small number of people are involved. It is in the case of the so-called "big inquiry" that problems arise.'[43] They identify four major inquiries involving 'projects of national significance', which have proved particularly troublesome: the site of Stansted airport (1981–3), after which the Government tried to grant permission for a larger airport than had been considered at the inquiry; extension of nuclear power stations at Sizewell B (1983–5) and Hinckley Point (1988–9); and Heathrow airport terminal 5 (1995–9).

[41] *Federated Estates Ltd v Environment Secretary* [1983] JPL 812; *Francis v First Secretary of State and Greenwich LBC* [2007] EWHC 2749 Admin. And see Current Topic, 'The scope of the inquisitorial duty of planning hearings' [2008] *JPEL* 429, 432.

[42] *Bushell v Environment Secretary* [1980] 3 WLR 22. And see p. 647.

[43] Purdue and Popham, 'The future of the major inquiry', p. 138.

Sizewell B[44] was used by protestors to fight government policy on nuclear energy and Purdue saw it as a major shift in the form of the inquiry from:

> its origin in individual rights, resting on property rights, to become an instrument of policy formulation and political decision-making in an open forum. While such a painstaking and public analysis of important national policies can turn the major inquiry into a powerful instrument of accountability and legitimization, from the government point of view it makes the processing of major projects through the planning system increasingly difficult. It also places a strain on the traditional procedures of the public inquiry and increases the costs and delay caused by the inquiry procedure. [45]

This was precisely what *Bushell's* case had tried to prevent.

The inquiry into a fifth terminal at Heathrow cost £80 million and took four years (1995–9); the report was finally published two years later. Handling an inquiry on this scale is a huge responsibility, which lay on the inspector, Roy Vandermeer QC, with a single deputy. Fifty major parties participated, including thirteen local authorities and the local planning authority, local residents and environmental groups, over 95 per cent opposing the application by British Airways. There were 700 witnesses, in excess of 27,500 written representations, mostly opposing the applications, and over 5,500 documents to be considered; in addition, the Inspectors made more than ninety site visits. The length of the inquiry is explained partly by the number of participating bodies and partly because, under the inquiry rules, all objectors, most of whom were legally represented, had a statutory right to be heard and to challenge the views of others, so that 'time had to be set aside to let them have their say'. Much time was also spent in clarifying government policy on a number of important issues, which had neither been updated nor published prior to the inquiry. Did the inquiry legitimate the decision? Not in the eyes of those who opposed the new terminal. Indeed, none of the many airport inquiries have ended protest.

Lord Hart, previously a planning solicitor, has described major inquiries as 'massive debating fora with armies of expensive experts and counsel ranged against each other, many parties with unequal firepower' and as 'a costly and time-consuming process only really suited to a two-party dispute with equal representation'. They place 'a huge and unacceptable strain on the inquiry system'.[46] The Planning Act 2008 is just the latest of many government responses to the defects and irksome delays of major planning inquiries, which include the Planning Inquiry Commission, Special Development Orders and parliamentary committees.[47] The Act facilitates

[44] Sir Frank Layfield, *Report of the Inquiry into Sizewell B* (HMSO, 1987).

[45] Purdue, 'Public inquiries as a part of public administration' [22.09]. And see T. O' Riordan, R. Kemp and M. Purdue, *Sizewell B: An anatomy of the inquiry* (Macmillan, 1988).

[46] HC Deb., col. 1172 (15 July 2008) (Lord Hart).

[47] For discussion, see Purdue and Popham, 'The future of the major inquiry'.

planning applications for 'nationally significant infrastructure projects' – a term very widely defined to extend to generating stations, nuclear reactors, highways, dams and reservoirs, waste treatment plants and much more – by taking them out of the normal planning process. They will be handled by a new Infrastructure Planning Commission appointed by a minister to handle these applications. Applications can be handled by a single Commissioner or three-person panel, though a minister may still call in an application for decision. The Act aims to settle policy and cut short debate by providing that the framework for Commission decisions will be set by 'national policy statements' published by the minister. Inquiries will be replaced by 'examination' of an application, to be conducted primarily through written representations. The Bill does, however, allow for the possibility of an 'open floor hearing' or, at the discretion of the Commissioner/panel, other oral hearings at which interested parties can make representations – subject always to the overriding discretionary powers of the panel or Commissioner as to procedure.

Introducing the bill in the House of Lords, the minister (Baroness Andrews) referred to the 'overdependence on cross-examination as the only way to test evidence':

> Inquiry processes are sometimes slow, intimidating and inefficient not just because of different regimes, different systems and different rules . . . These delays do not, perhaps, prevent those with the most resources having their say, but they make it incredibly hard for those poor in time and expertise to participate . . . The system puts the difficult decisions off until the last stage; it forces inquiries to spend enormous amounts of time debating what government policy is, and whether there is a need for infrastructure. The result is costly and there is uncertainty for communities as well as for developers. [48]

Not everyone was reassured. The government had to fight off a two-sided backbench rebellion. There were complaints of the *autonomy* of the Commission; it would be an agency composed of experts, taking decisions best left to politicians who were accountable to Parliament; and the view of inquiries as an informative and consultative stage in the administrative process would be undercut. From the other side came the familiar plea for justice for the parties: 'removing the right for interested parties to test the evidence through cross-examination' would be a retrograde step. A government concession that the IPC would have to hold a public hearing into a development order whenever 'someone affected wants it, and they will have the right to be heard at that hearing' did not satisfy the rebels, who still felt that the new hearings would prove 'grossly inferior to the current system'.

McAuslan once analysed planning law in terms of three inconsistent and competing ideologies:

[48] HL Deb., col. 1160 (15 July 2008) (Baroness Andrews).

> [First] the law exists and should be used to protect private property and its institutions: this may be called the traditional common law approach to the role of law. Secondly, the law exists and should be used to advance the public interest, if necessary against the interests of private property; this may be called the orthodox public administration and planning approach to role of law. Thirdly, the law exists and should be used to advance the cause of public participation against both the orthodox public administration approach to the public interest and the common law approach of the overriding importance of private property; this may be called the radical or populist approach to the role of law.[49]

These competing ideologies have transformed the planning inquiry into a battleground. Applying this analysis to the development of the planning inquiry, we could see it as a seesaw progression towards judicialisation interrupted at regular intervals by government attempts to 'de-judicialise'. A series of Planning Acts seeks to reintegrate planning inquiries as a stage in policy-making and to strengthen the grip of government over the process. From the standpoint of developers, the move to open up inquiries to community participation is often a threat to private property rights. From the government standpoint, however, the judicialisation of inquiry procedure is more than a take-over bid by the private property lobby and its advisers. They have found new allies in the pressure groups which are using the Big Inquiry as a tin-opener to government policy and to contest the sole right of government to represent the public interest. For both, the new legislation is nothing more than a take-off point to write in new procedural protections.

4. A Spanish Inquisition?

For Blom-Cooper, an experienced inquiry chairman, it is the *investigatory* or fact-finding function of the inquiry that justifies 'inquisitorial' procedure. He feels that:

> The adversarial procedure adopted in the legal system, admirable as it may be for the resolution of defined issues in dispute between identifiable parties, is wholly inappropriate [for an inquiry]. There are, in a public inquiry, no immediately discernible issues to be tried according to well-established rules of evidence . . . Since the parties to litigation formulate their respective cases, call their own witnesses to support one party's case or refute the other party's case, and seek adjudication on the basis exclusively of such evidence, each party may seek to establish its own perceived version of the events. The result may be a satisfactory method for determining who should win or lose the forensic contest. It does

49 P. McAuslan, *The Ideologies of Planning Law* (Pergamon Press, 1981), p. 2. And see B. Hough, 'A material change of use: The rise of the communitarian model' (2001) *JPL* 632, who argues for planning decisions to be taken by 'trained administrators who can identify the common good'.

> not aim to establish an objective truth, still less to identify the relationship between that truth and a wider conception of the public interest. The public inquiry, on the other hand, is constructed – even instructed – precisely to elicit the truth. It will ask itself: what happened; how did it happen; and who, if anybody, was responsible, culpably or otherwise, for it having happened.[50]

This does tend to suggest that there are no conflicts of interest at an inquiry, which our study of planning inquiries shows not to be the case. Purdue, writing more generally about inquiries into appeals or objections, points out that 'there has always been an ambivalence as to whether the primary purpose is to give rights to individuals who will be affected by the outcome or to provide the minister with all the facts and arguments necessary to a sensible and rational decision'.[51] This passage, we would argue, has a wider application. Parties at an inquest may – like Mohamed Fayed at the Diana inquiry – adopt an adversarial and even prosecutorial stance; witnesses may, on the other hand, require the protections typical of adversarial procedure against trial by inquest and the media.

Lord Howe's concern is with inquiries, 'triggered not by some broad policy question but by a specific event or activity which would be inappropriate for consideration by either House of Parliament'.[52] He instances inquiries to investigate allegations of improper conduct in the public service, to establish the cause of some major disaster and learn lessons from it, or to consider some other major issue of public concern. These seemingly disparate types of inquiry have in common that they are '*inquisitorial* in substance and form'. Although he does not specifically say so, inquisitorial procedure is something with which Howe is clearly not comfortable.

We saw that at planning inquiries the inspector was responsible for assembling the evidence, shaping the case, directing the proceedings and asking the questions. In the Heathrow Inquiry, for example, the Inspector held a series of five pre-inquiry meetings to identify the main issues, discover the parties who would to play an active part in the proceedings and agree the ground rules for the day-to-day conduct of the inquiry and formal exchange of evidence. Significantly, it was decided at these meetings to adopt a topic-based and not a party-based approach to the presentation of evidence at the inquiry. Draft lists of topics were circulated for written comments, ending with an Inspector's advice note setting out the agreed list. The Inspector also announced his intention at the first pre-inquiry meeting to have daily verbatim transcripts of the inquiry proceedings.[53] In other types of public inquiry, the Chairman is

[50] L. Blom-Cooper, 'Public Inquiries' (1993) 46 *Current Legal Problems* 204, 205–6.

[51] Purdue, 'Public inquiries as a part of public administration' [22.06].

[52] Howe, 'The management of public inquiries'.

[53] DoT, 'The Heathrow Terminal 5 Inquiry: An inquiry secretary's perspective'. It should be noted that, since the reforms of civil procedure brought in after the Woolf Report on *Access to Justice* (Lord Chancellor's Department, 1996), the role of the judge in civil proceedings is somewhat similar.

responsible for procedure. As inquiry procedure has developed, however, an official counsel to the inquiry is usually appointed to do the questioning. This in itself may stimulate demands for a right to cross-examine.

To lawyers trained in an adversarial system inquisitorial procedure may seem unfair partly because they do not properly understand it, partly because it does not conform to principles of procedural justice derived from proceedings of our common law courts (see Chapter 14). Inquisitorial procedures, in other words, may seem unfair simply because they are *not* adversarial. By inquisitorial procedure, the Council on Tribunals understands that:

> It is the inquiry itself that is responsible for gathering evidence, questioning witnesses, and determining the progress and direction of the proceedings. This differs from the adversarial nature of ordinary litigation in the civil and criminal courts, where each side presents a case which is then tested by the other side. However it is not possible to draw an absolutely hard and fast distinction between the inquisitorial and adversarial modes. For example, accident inquiries can assume something of an adversarial character, with different groups of individuals having different sets of interests. The presence of Counsel to the inquiry may also introduce an adversarial element into the proceedings. Features characteristic of adversarial litigation may properly be introduced into the inquisitorial process, if that assists in the fair and efficient conduct of the inquiry.[54]

'How far this may be appropriate', the paper adds helpfully, 'will vary greatly according to circumstances.'

(a) Scott: a waste of time?

In pursuing these procedural issues, it is helpful to think about the Scott Inquiry, set up to investigate the alleged connivance of ministers and public servants in the illegal export of arms to Iraq between 1984 and 1990. Its terms of reference as agreed between the Government and Lord Justice Scott were to 'examine the facts', 'to report' on whether those involved operated in accordance with government policy, 'to examine and report' on decisions taken by the prosecuting authority and 'to make recommendations'.[55] This remit is clearly investigative and falls within (Howe, 1) and (Howe, 2) (see p. 572 above). The Opposition parties, on the other hand, hoped to use the inquiry to make people and organisations accountable (Howe, 5). As the inquiry unfolded, its

[54] Council on Tribunals, *Procedural issues arising in the conduct of public inquiries set up by ministers* (1996) [7.3] available online

[55] *Inquiry into the Export of Defence Equipment and Dual-Use Goods to Iraq and Related Prosecutions,* HC 115 (1995/6). The Report is the subject of a Special Issue of Public Law: [1996] *PL* 357–527; see also D. Woodhouse, 'Matrix Churchill: A case study in judicial inquiries' (1995) 48 *Parl. Affairs* 24. In our account we omit any reference to the question of claims made by ministers to public interest immunity in court proceedings, a secondary, though important, aspect of the Inquiry: see R. Scott, 'The acceptable and unacceptable use of public interest immunity' [1996] *PL* 427.

outcome and probably its real purpose were shown to be to serve the political interests of government (Howe, 6). The Government had resorted to an inquiry as a means of removing a probably improper set of ministerial actions from the dangerous political forum of the House of Commons and transferring them to a safer, quasi-judicial terrain. Legitimated by the appointment of a disinterested member of the senior judiciary as chairman, a lengthy inquiry would have the effect of sheltering those involved from political attack. Using the vocabulary of ministerial responsibility and accountability (Howe, 5), the Opposition demanded powers to summon witnesses and call for evidence generally reserved for superior courts. Their purposes were no less political; they hoped to use the findings of the 'impartial' inquiry to pull down a weak government. This is the background against which to consider the chosen procedure.

Lord Justice Scott's position with regard to procedure is outlined in the final report at considerable length. As summarised by the Council on Tribunals,[56] the report stated that inquiry procedures need to serve three objectives:

- fairness to witnesses and others whose interests may be affected by the work of the inquiry
- the need for the inquiry's work to be conducted with efficiency and as much expedition as is practicable
- the need for the cost of the proceedings to be kept within reasonable bounds.

Lord Justice Scott refused to allow legal representation of witnesses at the inquiry on the ground of length and prolixity, though he did agree to give some idea of the questions he would be asking and promised to notify in advance anyone who would be criticised in the report. But he thought that the primarily adversarial Salmon principles had little application to inquisitorial proceedings, where those who give evidence are not presenting a 'case':

> The conception that a witness needs to prepare 'a case' introduces an element inherent in adversarial proceedings but alien to an inquisitorial inquiry, at least at the investigation stage. The need to prepare 'a case' may, of course, come at later stage . . . but this stage will not arise until conclusions have been reached by the inquiry.[57]

This implies that an inquiry is purely an investigation, a view we have already contested, and merely confirms well-established principles concerning the rules of natural justice, which kick in only after a certain stage in the investigation.[58]

[56] Council on Tribunals, *Procedural Issues Arising in the Conduct of Public Inquiries Set Up by Ministers* (1996) [4.4].

[57] Sir Richard Scott, 'Procedures at inquiries: The duty to be fair' cited Howe, 'The management of public inquiries'. See also L. Blom-Cooper, 'Witnesses and the Scott Inquiry' [1994] *PL* 1.

[58] *In re Pergamon Press* [1971] Ch 388; *Maxwell v Department of Trade and Industry* [1974] Ch 523.

Lord Howe, a disgruntled witness at the Scott Inquiry, takes a very different view of the procedure:

> Throughout the three working years of the inquiry, all the evidence was adduced in response to questions from Sir Richard Scott himself or from counsel to the Inquiry, Presiley Baxendale, Q.C. No distinction was drawn by either between examination-in-chief or cross-examination of witnesses. There was no cross-examination of any witness save by the Inquiry itself, no closing speeches, no face-to-face dialogue between the Inquiry and any representative of the outside world. When I first complained that this was to be an inquiry at which – as never before in modern times – 'defence lawyers may be seen but not heard', I had scarcely believed myself. But Sir Richard Scott had indeed explicitly discarded almost every one of the established principles.[59]

Although Howe presents the dispute as an argument over adversarial versus inquisitorial procedure, it was, as he himself seemed to realise, partly an argument over the multiple functions of inquiries. Scott saw the inquiry as an investigation designed to establish the 'truth' ending with recommendations, at which stage the 'rights of the defence' may kick in; Howe saw it as a very public forum in which allegations highly detrimental to the individual could be made without any opportunity for self-defence. The victim was, in other words, stripped of the due-process protections inherent in the common law. Against this one might argue that inquisitorial procedure is always 'contradictory' in the sense that parties have an opportunity to make comments and representations; this Lord Justice Scott had given them a chance to do. It might also be argued that *witnesses* at a criminal trial are not entitled to the procedural protections for which Howe is asking; they are not represented by counsel, though there is a right against self-incrimination.

The Scott Inquiry led the Lord Chancellor to ask the Council on Tribunals for advice. Perhaps unfortunately, the Council felt that model rules or even guidance were out of the question, saying:

> It is clear that the infinite variety of circumstances that may give rise to the need for a major public inquiry make it wholly impracticable to devise a single set of model rules or guidelines that will provide for the constitution, procedure and powers of every such inquiry. All that can be done is to set out a number of objectives that should be borne in mind when an inquiry is being established, and to offer guidance in support of those objectives according to the circumstances of the particular inquiry.
>
> The extent to which these four objectives are met for a particular inquiry will be determined by decisions taken early on as to the setting-up, procedure and powers of the inquiry. Suffice it to say that the objectives of effectiveness and fairness should not, as a matter of principle, be sacrificed to the interests of speed and economy.[60]

[59] Lord Howe,' Procedure at the Scott Inquiry' [1996] *PL* 445, 446–7.

[60] Council on Tribunals, *Procedural Issues Arising in the Conduct of Public Inquiries Set Up by Ministers* [2.3] [2.9].

It is what happened when the Scott Report was finally presented to the Government that casts doubt on the absence of general procedural requirements. A public inquiry should surely be *public*. Yet the Government kept the report under wraps for eight days while preparing its own defence. Only at the insistence of the Speaker of the House of Commons was the five-volume report shown to selected Opposition MPs on condition that no photocopies were taken and mobile phones were left outside the room where they were 'carted off and locked up in a farcical test of their abilities to speed-read nearly 2,000 pages in three hours . . . a quite appalling abuse of power on the government's part [which] should never have been agreed to either by Parliament or the Scott inquiry'.[61] The manoeuvre served the Government's purpose. Interest rapidly evaporated after Opposition calls for the resignation of two ministers impugned by Scott were defeated by a slender majority in an adjournment debate on the Report.

Of the many features of inquiry procedure that contributed to this result, delay was probably most important. Set up in 1992, the Inquiry was completed three years later. By the date of publication, the kettle had gone off the boil. It did almost nothing to reassure the public, which had probably lost interest in the affair and nothing at all to secure 'catharsis', whatever that term may mean in the circumstances. Just as the Government had hoped, the inquiry had worked to defeat accountability; indeed from the accountability angle, the inquiry was largely a waste of time. In search of accountability, Lord Justice Scott had produced five very expensive volumes that almost no one would ever read.[62] It is fair to say of Scott that the sole upshot was to serve the political interests of the Government (Howe, 6).

5. Inquiries and accountability

Though primarily directed at Scott, Lord Howe's critique of inquiry procedure extends more widely. Inquiries may fulfil more than one objective: establishing facts and learning from events are not incompatible with public reassurance and catharsis. Potential conflicts are, however, built in. Findings of pervasive managerial incompetence or administrative failure do not serve to reassure the public, which tends to prefer the populist solution of 'name, blame and shame'. This is why Lord Justice Phillips, who chaired the non-statutory inquiry set up 'to establish and review the history of the emergence and identification of BSE and variant CJD in the United Kingdom, and of the action taken in response to it up to 20 March 1996',[63] warned that 'any who have come to our

[61] A. Tomkins, *The Constitution After Scott* (Clarendon Press, 1998), p. 13.

[62] See I. Leigh and L. Lustgarten, 'Five volumes in search of accountability: The Scott Report' (1996) 59 *MLR* 695.

[63] Lord Phillips, *The BSE Inquiry* (HMSO, 2000). BSE (popularly 'mad cow disease') is a neurodegenerative disease in cattle which can be transmitted to humans, when it is known as known as new variant Creutzfeldt-Jakob disease and is fatal. The means of transmission is not definitively established.

report hoping to find villains and scapegoats should go away disappointed'. The Report did not name names. Its overall conclusion was that 'in general, our system of public administration has emerged with credit from the part of the BSE story that we have examined'. It also found that bureaucratic processes had resulted at times in 'unacceptable delay in giving effect to policy' and pointed to a lack of rigour shown at times by officials in considering how policy should be turned into practice, 'to the detriment of the efficacy of the measures taken'. Entirely compatible with establishing the facts (Howe, 1) and learning lessons (Howe, 2) this measured approach deliberately downplayed the accountability function (Howe, 5), thereby attracting criticism that it was a 'whitewash'. It had failed to blame individual civil servants or censure the food industry for its unsavoury practices of recycling animal protein in animal feed (not clearly within its terms of reference).

Mulgan, in his survey of machinery for public accountability, puts considerable emphasis on accountability through the legal system (see p. 47 above). Judicial hearings 'increasingly require the Government to disclose what it has done and why; they allow members of the public the right to contest such government actions, and they can force the Government into remedial action'. This is the main reason, we suggest, why the public reaction to scandals and disasters is so often to demand a public inquiry. But this is a 'thin' definition of accountability, which (i) requires public actors to give an account of what has occurred; (ii) requires them to submit to questioning, and (iii) allows the issues to be probed and publicly debated.[64] A public inquiry is an independent forum well placed to achieve these objects. It is widely felt, however, that a fourth element of sanction is needed to 'thicken' accountability. For a public inquiry to provide reassurance (Howe, 4), it may be that (in common parlance) 'heads must roll'. After the Southall and Paddington Inquiries into serious rail crashes at Ladbroke Grove (see p. 581 above), for example, there were no immediate prosecutions. Even though the cause of the accidents was established and some remedial action taken by the rail operators, it was not until Network Rail was found guilty of an offence under s. 3 of the Health and Safety at Work Act 1974, was fined £4 million and had made financial reparation that the victims spoke of closure.[65] Significantly, this involved litigation and took ten years.

So sanction is not an essential component of the public inquiry; it specifically falls outside the remit of coroner's inquests and (since 2005) inquiries. Howe suggests, however, that it remains a very general expectation that a public inquiry will fulfil this function by pinpointing scapegoats. To offset this very general expectation, modifications of inquisitorial procedures are necessary:

[64] M. Bovens, 'Analysing and assessing accountability: A conceptual framework' (2007) 13 *European Law Journal* 447.

[65] See CPS, Press Release, 'Paddington train crash' (30 March 2007).

> It is for the sake of securing the right balance between these factors (the search for truth, the assignment of responsibility, the reassurance of the public) that certain features have over the years emerged as desirable in the inquiry process, as to the composition of the tribunal, the form of the report, the right to representation, and the nature and extent of appropriate publicity (before, during and after the inquiry itself). These questions have more than once been considered by experts, so that until recently there had been established a widespread consensus about almost all the essentials.[66]

Lord Justice Scott, complained Howe, broke this consensus.

(a) Child-abuse inquiries

Nowhere are problems of balance more evident than in child-abuse inquiries. When a child dies or is injured while in the care of the state, or at the hand of family members in circumstances involving state care services, many bodies and individuals with divergent and conflicting interests may be involved. An inquiry may be set up in one of several ways. A local authority or other body may set up an internal review, whose findings and recommendations may or may not be published. The Minister for Health or Education may set up a statutory inquiry in terms of s. 81 of the Children Act 1989. Criminal prosecutions, actions in negligence, disciplinary proceedings and coroners' inquests are additional possibilities. At least when held in public, such inquiries are inevitably concerned with accountability and even sanction; it is hard to see them as purely investigatory when many of the people involved risk prosecution, disciplinary proceedings, loss of their children or professional reputation.[67] This makes them particularly hard to handle; consequently, those most likely to prove controversial are normally chaired by judges or experienced advocates.

Not only may participants in this type of inquiry have very different interests but they approach the inquiry from different standpoints. Mashaw's models of administrative justice (see p. 447 above) help to explain why. The model of *professional treatment*, interpersonal and based on service, differs greatly from the model of *moral judgement*, Mashaw's term for the legal model we call *due process*. Just such a difference in viewpoint led the three-person panel, chaired by a Crown Court judge, to split and publish opposing reports in the inquiry into the death of Maria Colwell.[68] Professor Olive

[66] Howe, 'The Management of Public Inquiries', p. 296.

[67] A notable example was the Butler-Sloss inquiry: *Report of the Inquiry into Child Abuse in Cleveland*, Cm. 412 (1988). Parents accused of satanic practices were cleared by the inquiry and subsequently compensated, while the medical practitioners were found responsible and suffered very severely: see generally, P. Case, *Compensating Child Abuse in England and Wales* (Cambridge University Press, 2007).

[68] DHSS, *Report of the Committee of Inquiry into the Care and Supervision Provided in Relation to Maria Colwell* (1974). The Report was followed by a second, local inquiry: East Sussex District Council, *Children at Risk: A study by the East Sussex County Council into the problems revealed by the Report of the Inquiry into the case of Maria Colwell* (1975).

Stevenson, from a social-work background, refused to go down the path of the majority, who saw the inquiry as an occasion for accountability and sanction, apportioning the mistakes to individuals as well as 'inefficient systems'. Professor Stevenson called the social workers' decisions 'unfortunate'. She saw them not as breaches of accepted professional standards but as the inevitable consequence of public ambivalence over the rights of parents and the state's right to intervene in protection of children – a clash of values that should be borne in mind.

Add to these diverse viewpoints Mashaw's model of *bureaucratic rationality* and we have scope for further misunderstanding. In this managerial model the primary goal is effective programme implementation and the legitimating values accuracy and efficiency. The managers aim to establish the facts, to learn from events and reassure the public. DHSS guidance that expressed this managerial preference troubled JUSTICE–All Souls.[69] The guidance recommended: (i) that hearings should generally be held in private, as informal hearings or interviews were more effective than formal sessions; (ii) that a 'flexible and inquisitorial procedure' should be used. Conscious of the interests of social workers, the guidance advised (iii) that witnesses should not be 'treated as defendants' but fairly. They should be informed of their rights 'with an opportunity to comment on criticism of their performance made at the inquiry and access to comments on them in the inquiry report . . . Inquiries should not be used for disciplinary purposes and reports of inquiries should not be used in evidence in disciplinary proceedings.' To the JUSTICE–All Souls Committee, a committee largely composed of lawyers, this guidance 'tend[ed] to minimize and obscure somewhat the critical difficulty that confronts any inquiry where reputations are at stake'. This is true if one assumes the purpose of the inquiry is to make people and organisations accountable, more especially if it is held in public, as in the modern age of transparency is likely to be the case. If, however, the primary purpose is to learn from events and the inquiry is internal, the guidance was probably appropriate.

Two particular inquiries stand out in the long and dreary catalogue of investigations into child abuse:[70] the Jasmine Beckford Inquiry, chaired by Louis Blom-Cooper QC, and the Victoria Climbié Inquiry chaired by Lord Laming, a former chief inspector of social services. Blom-Cooper took the view that the function of the inquiry was investigatory but its objective accusatorial: 'to find out what, if anything, people have done wrong or omitted'.[71] The inquiry found systemic failure but allocated responsibility to a named social worker and

[69] JUSTICE–All Souls [10.109–12] citing DHSS Circular, *Non Accidental Injury to Children* (April 1974). See now Dept of Health, *Working Together to Safeguard Children* (1999); Dept of Health Circ, *What to do if you're worried a child is being abused* (May 2000), published in response to the Climbié inquiry, below.

[70] These are recorded in *Child Abuse: A study of inquiry reports* 1980–89 (London: HMSO) 1991.

[71] Brent LBC, *A Child in Trust: Report of the inquiry into the circumstances surrounding the death of Jasmine Beckford* (1985).

health visitor. Dingwall sees both the shape and the outcome of the proceedings as dictated by the appointment of a lawyer-chairman:

> [I]t is clear that the panel, by whatever means, came to accept that Blom-Cooper's appointment should lead to a quasi-judicial model being adopted. Their role was essentially that of spectators to an adversarial drama played by 18 counsel. The Report begins with three chapters which are almost exclusively devoted to procedural questions. Underlying these was the assumption that, just as in a criminal trial, the cause of the untoward event could be located in the behaviour of particular individuals.[72]

The effect was to shift the emphasis of the inquiry from the function of improving social services by objectively establishing facts and drawing lessons from them (Howe, 1 and 2) to the identification of symbolic wrongdoers. But Dingwall rightly goes on to underline that court (and especially criminal) procedures are shaped for the protection of the individual while inquiry procedures are not, while Blom-Cooper, an advocate of inquisitorial procedure, on this occasion combined this with 'accusatorial' goals.

Victoria Climbié was a seven-year-old girl from West Africa whose parents had sent her to Europe for a better life. After she arrived in England, Victoria was battered to death by the two adults in whose charge she was living. They were convicted of murder. There was great media interest and public concern was expressed at the lack of co-ordination between the different public bodies (notably police, education and social services) involved in the episode. It was therefore the Health Secretary who moved to set up a ministerial inquiry. The chairman, Lord Laming, sat with four assessors: a paediatrician, health visitor, detective and social services manager.[73] Lord Laming described what had happened as 'a gross failure of the system':

> Not one of the agencies empowered by Parliament to protect children . . . – funded from the public purse – emerge from this Inquiry with much credit. The suffering and death of Victoria was a gross failure of the system and was inexcusable. It is clear to me that the agencies with responsibility for Victoria gave a low priority to the task of protecting children. They were under-funded, inadequately staffed and poorly led. Even so, there was plenty of evidence to show that scarce resources were not being put to good use . . . Even after listening to all the evidence, I remain amazed that nobody in any of the key agencies had the presence of mind to follow what are relatively straightforward procedures on how to respond to a child about whom there is concern of deliberate harm.[74]

Lord Laming stressed the fact that this inquiry was 'more than just a forensic exercise. It has been charged with looking forward and making

[72] R. Dingwall, 'The Jasmine Beckford affair' (1986) 49 *MLR* 489.

[73] *The Victoria Climbié Inquiry: Report of an Inquiry*, Cm. 5730 (2003).

[74] *Report Summary*, p. 4.

recommendations for "how such an event may, as far as possible, be avoided in the future"' (Howe, 1 and 2).[75] He went on to make more than one hundred detailed recommendations for reform of the child-care services. The inquiry was followed by substantial reforms, including passage of the Children Act 2004, a new government database holding information on all children in England and Wales and the creation of the Office of the Children's Commissioner, empowered to open his own inquiries.[76]

Lord Laming had decided that, in phase one of the inquiry devoted to establishing the facts, procedure would be inquisitorial and not adversarial. Counsel to the Inquiry decided which witnesses to call and examined them. 'Interested Parties' were recognised and a number of witnesses were legally represented. With one exception, there was no cross-examination but representatives were allowed time-limited opportunities to 're-examine' witnesses and make closing submissions.[77] In his Report, he carefully reminded himself that 'those who sit in judgment often do so with the great benefit of hindsight', acknowledging that 'staff who undertake the work of protecting children and supporting families on behalf of us all deserve both our understanding and our support'. He stressed the importance of understanding how *individuals* had acted and how 'deficiencies in their organisations' had contributed to the tragedy as an essential step in moving forward. But he did name names. Several individuals were harshly criticised and suffered from the inquiry; whether their interests were adequately protected is an open question.

Five years after Lord Laming had reported, a baby was battered to death within the same social services area after months of abuse. Baby P, who had more than fifty injuries, was on the children-at-risk register and had been seen sixty times by social workers, doctors and police. Following a letter from a whistleblower, Haringey Council's child protection services were examined by the Commission for Social Care Inspection, an independent agency set up by government 'to promote improvements in social care and stamp out bad practice', which found nothing wrong. After Baby P's mother and boyfriend had been convicted of involvement in the death, the minister asked Ofsted to examine the role of all the agencies involved in this case. He also invited Lord Laming to 'prepare an independent report of progress being made, identifying any barriers to effective, consistent implementation, and recommending whether additional action is needed to overcome them'.[78]

This lends some support to Masson's sceptical view of public inquiries, which she sees as a 'central part of the "scandal politics" which has shaped the child protection system both in terms of public perception and policies and

[75] *Ibid.*, p. 6.
[76] S. 3 of the Children Act 2004.
[77] *Inquiry Report* [2.14–19].
[78] HC Deb., col. 57WS, 12 Nov 2008 (Mr Balls).

practices'.[79] She questions the willingness to commit great sums of money to inquiries as disproportionate. 'Understanding what went wrong is a limited activity to which only modest resources should be committed. Developing the foundations for improving practices requires a more through evidence-based understanding which can only be obtained through research.'

(b) Alternative models

In considering these high-profile public inquiries and the procedures adopted by them, it is helpful to think about two rather similar inquiries. We have mentioned the conciliatory approach adopted by the BSE Inquiry and its efforts to avoid recriminations (see p. 593 above). Lord Justice Phillips, advised by a medical geneticist and an expert in public administration, had to deal with large quantities of technical and scientific evidence. The inquiry sat for two years and published its 4,000 pages of findings in sixteen weighty volumes. Whether the sum of £27 million spent on the inquiry was justified is questionable. If the purpose of the inquiry was *not* to allocate responsibility, less costly alternatives, such as funded research in a high-profile academic institution backed up by a Select Committee inquiry might have been more appropriate. A looser format, that allowed BSE to be considered outside a formal procedural framework and 'outside of technological, scientific and industrial process' – more like that of the Power Commission or Kennedy Inquiry (see below) – might have been more suitable.[80]

The Bristol Royal Infirmary Inquiry into heart surgery had to look back at events that took place over a number of years. It was chaired by Ian Kennedy, a professor of medical law, with a legal sociologist, nursing expert and professor of clinical medicine as panel members.[81] In its first phase, the panel worked its way through 900,000 pages of written evidence from 577 witnesses, including 238 parents. In its second phase, which focused on the future, seminars were held, which took account of the latest research and thinking. At the preliminary hearing, the chairman, introducing the panel, struck the informal note that marked this inquiry:

> I intend to conduct the Inquiry as sensitively and informally as I possibly can . . . There is a [counsel] to the Inquiry . . . His role is strictly impartial. It is to assist the Panel in its

[79] J. Masson, 'The Climbié Inquiry: Context and critique' (2006) 33 *JLS* 221–2, 244. See also B. Corby, A. Doig and V. Roberts, 'Inquiries into child abuse' (1998) 20 *Journal of Social Welfare and Family Law* 377; N. Parton and N. Martin, 'Public inquiries, legalism and child care in England and Wales' (1989) 3 *International J. of Law and the Family* 21.

[80] See K. Jones, 'BSE, risk and the communication of uncertainty: A review of Lord Phillips' report from the BSE Inquiry' (2001) 26 *Canadian J. of Sociology* 655. The Power Inquiry, *Power to the People: An independent inquiry into Britain's democratic system* (Rowntree Trust, 2006) is explained at p. 48 .

[81] *Learning from Bristol: The report of the public inquiry into children's heart surgery at the Bristol Royal Infirmary 1984–1995*, Cm. 5207 (2001). The inquiry sat for 3 years and cost £14.5 million.

> investigation of the facts and its search for the truth. It is not his role to prosecute nor to prove a particular case. Instead, he is there to present all the evidence thoroughly and rigorously, and to advise me and the Inquiry members on matters of law and evidence . . . [T]he objective of the Inquiry is to understand what happened in Bristol, why it happened and what lessons can be learned for the benefit of the National Health Service as a whole. No-one is on trial in this Inquiry; it is not a trial nor a court, nor a disciplinary hearing. It is not a law suit in which one party wins and another loses. There will be no parties. It is not the same as the legal process in a criminal or civil court. We are a team of independent persons working within our terms of reference which involve . . . trying to discover first what happened, secondly why it happened, and thirdly, what lessons can be learned and recommendations made. One of our functions, inevitably, will be to offer constructive criticism. If criticisms are levelled at organisations or individuals which are relevant to these issues, we shall of course consider them and make any necessary finding. It is not our purpose, not the purpose of the Inquiry to sit in judgment. I hope, therefore, that everyone concerned both at the Inquiry and outside it will play their parts responsibly and without rancour. We want to find the facts and learn from them and, as the Secretary of State told Parliament, to do so with all reasonable speed.[82]

Like Phillips, the Bristol inquiry avoided pinning responsibility on individuals, though some 'flawed behaviour' was mentioned. It was, the panel concluded:

> an account of healthcare professionals working in Bristol who were victims of a combination of circumstances which owed as much to general failings in the NHS at the time as to any individual failing. Despite their manifest good intentions and long hours of dedicated work, there were failures on occasion in the care provided to very sick children.[83]

This is to approach the matter, as the Bristol Inquiry did, from the standpoint of professionals imbued with a culture of *professional treatment*. But where the death of a child is in issue, it is likely that both the professional and managerial models will be pushed by public opinion into moral judgements and demands for sanction.

6. The judiciary: 'Symbolic reassurance'

The appointment of an eminent judge to chair a public inquiry is, as we have seen, a common practice. The practice has been supported on various occasions by the Salmon Commission, the Council on Tribunals and more recently, in the context of new legislation, by both the Government and Lord Woolf, then Lord Chief Justice, in evidence to PASC (see p. 603 below). Judges offer obvious advantages. They have the skills needed to chair a complex inquiry,

[82] *Learning from Bristol*, Transcript of Preliminary Hearing, (27 Oct.1998) available on inquiry website.

[83] *Learning from Bristol* (Summary) [5].

deal with witnesses and handle large volumes of evidence. They have authority. Above all, they tend to be perceived by the general public as unquestionably neutral and independent, a helpful attribute in depoliticising political issues. A judicial inquiry provides what has been called 'symbolic reassurance – disinterested authority and dispassionate investigation'. The practice may, however, misfire.

(a) The Hutton Inquiry

The Hutton Inquiry was one of a number of attempts to piece together the truth behind the so called 'dodgy dossier' or, more correctly, the use or misuse by Tony Blair and his staff of intelligence concerning Iraq's possession of weapons of mass destruction in the period leading up to the second Iraq war. The intelligence services held a secret inquiry which reported directly to the Prime Minister. Lord Butler, for many years the Cabinet Secretary, chaired a five-member committee of privy councillors, which reviewed the intelligence coverage of information on 'WMD' programmes. The Butler committee had access to intelligence reports and other government papers and could call witnesses to give oral evidence but, although its report was published, worked in secret and the main Opposition parties refused to participate.[84] When the Foreign Affairs Select Committee examined the decision to go to war it had access to government papers and heard evidence from a wide range of witnesses yet complained of the Prime Minister's failure to co-operate with it; most unusually, the committee split on party lines in seven out of fourteen divisions.[85] The Hutton Inquiry's terms of reference were 'urgently to conduct an inquiry into the circumstances surrounding the death of Dr Kelly' (an official witness before the Select Committee, who had afterwards been found dead in suspicious circumstances).[86]

Twining, an expert in the law of evidence, noted the cross between inquisitorial and adversarial procedure at the Hutton Inquiry: on the one hand the Chairman rather than interested parties controlled who was called as a witness, what documents were produced and to a large extent what questions were asked; on the other hand, oral testimony, examination and cross examination of witnesses in public were allowed. Twining thought the most striking innovation was:

> the creation of a website on which almost all of the evidence was posted immediately, so that although the proceedings were not televised, the media and the public at large had access to almost all of the information presented to the inquiry. This meant that in theory

[84] *Review of Intelligence on Weapons of Mass Destruction*, HC 898 (2003/4).

[85] Foreign Affairs Committee, *The Decision to Go to War in Iraq*, HC 813 (2002/3) and *Government Response*, Cm. 6062 (2003).

[86] *Report of the Inquiry into the Circumstances Surrounding the Death of Dr David Kelly CMG*, HC 247 (2003/4).

> at least everyone could make up their own minds on the basis of almost the same evidence as Lord Hutton.[87]

This was open justice indeed; but it may be one reason why the inquiry failed either to reassure (Howe, 4) or offer any catharsis (Howe, 3). The findings, which cleared the Government of all responsibility, blamed a BBC reporter, prompting the resignation of the Director-General of the BBC. They were, however, largely discounted by the public. For Beloff too, this was an inevitable consequence of the procedure; the wealth of evidence made available on the inquiry's website meant that the public was as entitled, if not actually as qualified, as Lord Hutton to come to its own conclusion: 'judgments were generally formed before [the] inquiry and consequently unchanged by it'.[88] This public inquiry, to put this differently, was all too public.

Lord Hutton himself laid the blame on the media, which had failed to read and accurately report the evidence, concentrating deliberately 'on those parts of the evidence which, viewed in isolation and apart from the surrounding circumstances, could be regarded as harmful to the government':

> If I had delivered a report highly critical of the government in terms which conformed to the hopes of some commentators I have no doubt that it would have received much praise. However, in reality, if I had written such a report I would have been failing in one of the cardinal duties of a judge conducting an inquiry into a highly controversial matter which gives rise to intense public interest and debate. That duty is to decide fairly the relevant issues arising under the terms of reference having regard to all the evidence and not to be swayed by pressure from newspapers and commentators or any other quarter.[89]

It is hardly surprising that in the fraught circumstances after the death of David Kelly the Government should have turned to a judge. However, to ask judges to chair such inquiries places them in a dilemma. If, as Lord Hutton obviously did, they pursue the strictly legalistic line dictated by their adjudicative experience, they 'can produce extraordinary detail and openness, but at the almost inevitable cost of narrowing the issues'.[90] This is, after all, what advocates are trained to do. But, as Beloff pointed out,[91] the issues assigned to Lord Hutton were 'more political than legal. Consequently, although the exercise was in form an inquiry, it rapidly took on – at least in the perception of those that reported it – the appearance of an adversarial contest with the government on one side and the BBC on the other.'

[87] W. Twining, 'The Hutton Inquiry: Some wider legal aspects' in S. Runciman (ed.), *Hutton and Butler: Lifting the lid on the workings of power* (Oxford University Press, 2004), pp. 42, 38.

[88] M. Beloff, discussing Twining, 'The Hutton Inquiry' in *Hutton and Butler*, pp. 52–3.

[89] Lord Hutton, 'The media reaction to the Hutton Report' [2006] *PL* 807, 837.

[90] Twining, 'The Hutton Inquiry: Some wider legal aspects' .

[91] Beloff, in *Hutton and Butler*, p. 53.

The report sparked requests for a fuller inquiry into the legality of the war, firmly refused. Lord MacNally introduced an abortive Iraq War Inquiry Bill in the House of Lords. Coroners' inquests into the deaths of soldiers serving in Iraq led to a judicial application for an inquiry designed indirectly to attack the legality of the invasion by querying the quality of government legal advice. This was fought passionately but unsuccessfully up to the House of Lords.[92] In parallel, as we saw in Chapter 10, there was recourse to all available freedom of information machinery to gain access to the Attorney-General's opinion. For all the £1.7 million spent on it, the Hutton Inquiry had settled nothing. Its findings, one commentator concluded,[93] had probably 'demolished in the public mind any idea that a judicial inquiry can come to a dispassionate, impartial and, most importantly, fair report'.[94] A new inquiry ultimately had to be conceded.

But if not judges, then who? As Twining pertinently asks, 'Who beside a senior judge or lawyer could have designed and presided over an inquisitorial proceeding that involved public examination and cross-examination of witnesses in such an open and revealing manner'?[95] True, but this may be an expedient answer, as PASC has observed:

> Inquiries into issues at the centre of government are . . . by their nature, politically contentious, as well as requiring an understanding of how government works. Criticism of their reports in such cases may undermine the impact of the inquiry and the judiciary as an institution, as well as being detrimental to the reputation of the individual judge.[96]

Conceding that judicial appointments were probably appropriate where an inquiry was designed to establish facts, PASC thought judges less well qualified to deal with 'issues of social or economic policy with political implications'. They lacked appropriate experience. Few judges 'have managed a big workforce, managed a public agency, managed big budgets in competing priorities, dealt with the party-political machine, both locally and nationally, dealt with trade unions going about their perfectly legitimate business and dealt with the media day by day'.[97] As Sir Michael Bichard explained:

> In order to hold public servants to account, I think you need to understand a little of the context within which they are working, though you can get some of that from an assessor and an adviser, but it is second-hand. I do not think a judge is necessarily the best person for that. If you are talking about healing, whether you are talking about healing between some of the parties or actually healing the public confidence, which often this is about, I

[92] *R(Gentle) v The Prime Minister and Others* [2008] UKHL 20.

[93] R. Kaye, '"OfGov": A commissioner for government conduct?' (2005) 58 *Parl. Affairs* 171, 173.

[94] *Ibid.*, p. 176.

[95] Twining, 'The Hutton Inquiry: Some wider legal aspects', p. 38.

[96] PASC, *Government by Inquiry*, HC 51 (2004/5) [48]. And see J. Beatson, 'Should judges conduct public inquiries?' (2005) 121 *LQR* 221.

[97] PASC, *ibid.* [44] and Question 278.

> am not sure a judge has particular qualities to enable him to do that. If you are talking about learning and improving for the future, I am not sure a judge is the best person to do that.[98]

Carefully weighing constitutional arguments based on separation of powers and the dangers to judicial impartiality, PASC concluded:

> With developments in public law, Human Rights Act considerations about impartiality, and the proposed establishment of a Supreme Court, which involves the institutional separation of the judges from the House of Lords, care needs to be exercised in the future use of judges for such work, particularly those from the highest court, and especially in relation to politically sensitive inquiries.[99]

All that it recommended was, however, that decisions about the appointment of judges to undertake inquiries should be taken co-equally by the Government and appropriate senior member of the judiciary. Perhaps more important was the recommendation that, where judges were chosen as the most appropriate Chair, 'they should usually be appointed as part of a panel or be assisted by expert assessors or wing members'. This would lend 'expertise, reassurance, support and protection to inquiry chairs' and also enhance 'the perception of fairness and impartiality in the inquiry process'.[100]

7. Towards reform

Reform of inquiry procedure was overdue. Rationalisation had several times been recommended. Accident inquiries were thought to be too slow. The big political inquiries such as Scott and Hutton had satisfied no one and raised serious questions over the fitness of inquiry procedure. 'Grand planning inquiries', such as Heathrow, had cost a great deal of money without noticeably clearing the way for consensus or appeasing so-called 'stakeholders'. And another mammoth 1921 Act tribunal of inquiry was causing concern.

(a) Bloody Sunday

The Saville Inquiry was set up by Tony Blair in 1998, around the time when a settlement in Northern Ireland seemed on the cards, to establish the truth about 'Bloody Sunday' (30 January 1972) when the British army opened fire on civil-rights protesters in Londonderry, killing fourteen people. This was not the first investigation into Bloody Sunday. A coroner's inquest, which had delivered an open verdict, was followed by a swift and immediate inquiry by Lord

[98] *Ibid.* [45] and Question 679. Sir Michael had chaired *The Bichard Inquiry*, HC 653 (2003/4) into child protection measures after the highly publicised 'Soham murders' of two young girls.

[99] PASC, *ibid.*

[100] *Ibid.* [73].

Widgery, then Lord Chief Justice, which exonerated the army but was widely rejected as a whitewash.[101] What was the object of a new inquiry so long after events that had already been twice investigated? Measured against the Howe objectives, the aim was predominantly catharsis (Howe, 3). The event had been described in *The Irish Times* as reaching 'to the core of the nationalist psyche' and an inquiry would serve both to reassure the public (Howe, 4) and at the same time to serve the political interests of the Blair government by demonstrating a clear break with the actions of previous governments (Howe, 6).

The importance attached to the Inquiry was underlined both by the use of the 1921 Act, endowing it with the powers of the High Court, and by the status of the tribunal members. The president, Lord Saville, was a Law Lord. He was flanked by two distinguished judges from the Commonwealth: the Hon. William Hoyt, Chief Justice of New Brunswick and a member of the Canadian Judicial Council; and the Hon. John Toohey, a retired justice of the High Court of Australia. From the start, however, the tribunal ran into difficulties, arising from the participants' lack of mutual trust and confidence in the proceedings. In four years, £180 million was spent on the Inquiry;[102] its procedures were twice judicially reviewed on the application of soldier witnesses asking for anonymity in reliance on assurances from the Widgery Inquiry and asking to give evidence in London.[103] Approximately 2,500 witness statements were received and there were some 160 volumes of evidence, 13 volumes of photographs, 121 audiotapes and 110 videotapes, all of which had to be sent to representatives of the 'interested parties'. The Inquiry has shown no sign of reporting and is not due to report until late 2009. Even if the Report proves to be the ultimate account of the events of Bloody Sunday, it has been an exercise in 'truth and reconciliation' that failed in this objective. By lasting into the period of reconstruction, it might even come to imperil it.

(b) Rationalisation?

A consultation paper from the DCA in 2004, to consider the need for a new statutory framework for ministerial inquiries, explored some of these problems:

> It can seem wasteful and inefficient for several different sets of proceedings to rake over the same set of events. However, these processes are all designed to perform different

101 *Report of the Tribunal Appointed to Inquire into the Events on Sunday, 30 January 1972, which Led to Loss of Life in Connection with the Procession in Londonderry on that Day*, HC 220 (1972/3).

102 HC Deb., col. 720 WA (11 June 2007).

103 *R v Lord Saville of Newdigate, ex p. A* [2000] 1 WLR 1855; *R v Lord Saville of Newdigate, ex p. B (No. 2)* [2000] 1 WLR 1855; *Lord Saville of Newdigate and Others v Widgery Soldiers and Others* [2002] 1 WLR 1249. And see B. Hadfield, '*R v Lord Saville of Newdigate, ex p. Anonymous Soldiers*: What is the purpose of a tribunal of inquiry?' [1999] *PL* 663. The cases were considered and the issue settled by the House of Lords in a similar case involving the appearance of RUC officers before the Hammill inquiry: see *In re Officer L* [2007] UKHL 36.

functions. Legal proceedings, particularly criminal trials, have important safeguards built into them to protect the rights of all the individuals involved. An inquiry, which does not seek to apportion guilt, has far more flexibility to take the form that will best enable it to establish the facts of the case.

A criminal trial may, through establishing guilt and imposing punishment, be successful in preventing recurrence and may also help to restore public confidence. However, it approaches the case with the primary objective of bringing the guilty to account, whereas the primary purpose of an inquiry is to prevent recurrence. An inquiry identifies ways of preventing recurrence through a thorough exploration of the circumstances of the cases, which it can often do more efficiently and quickly than a criminal trial because it has far greater freedom – it can take an inquisitorial, non-adversarial form; lengthy cross-examinations can be avoided, because the evidence is being tested thoroughly by the chairman; it has discretion to admit a wide range of evidence. This freedom is justified precisely because an inquiry does not seek to determine guilt, and must never attempt to do so. An inquiry is not a court. Its findings have no legal effect.

The presence or absence of any other proceedings should not make any difference to the *aim* of the inquiry. However, if other proceedings have taken place, their outcome may affect the *remit* of the inquiry. If no other proceedings are planned, it is important that there is no attempt to expand the role of the inquiry to fill their place. There may be considerable pressure for this, since those affected by what has happened may well perceive the inquiry as having a wider purpose: to apportion guilt or to provide a basis for claims for compensation. The outcome of an inquiry can help those affected, by satisfying them that an effective investigation has been carried out and that the truth has been established. However, there is also a danger that they may expect more than is within the remit of the inquiry in terms of punishment or retribution, which can lead to a feeling that they have been cheated or disregarded. For the sakes of those involved, it is important to be clear from the outset about the role and remit of the inquiry, including its limitations.

In summary, the government believes that a single inquiry should be sufficient to fulfil the aims of establishing the facts and preventing recurrence. However, an inquiry should not attempt to establish civil liability, or to deal with allegations of professional misconduct or criminal activity. If needed, other mechanisms must be used to deal with these issues.[104]

A later paragraph hints at the Government's true concern with cost:

In recent inquiries there have been demands from numerous potential participants to be granted legal representation, generally at public expense . . . An automatic right to such representation for all participants could potentially lead to enormous expense, and could lengthen the procedure considerably. The inquiry needs to be able to exercise its discretion in controlling the grant of representation, whilst ensuring that all participants are treated

[104] DCA, *Effective Inquiries*, CP 12/04 (6 May 2004) [38] [39] [43] [44]. The paper was based on the *Beldam Review of Inquiries and Overlapping Proceedings*, conducted for the DCA in 2002 and published as Annex C. Annex B consists of a useful table of notable inquiries set up since 1990.

fairly. **The Government believes it is important that inquiries should be able to ensure the most efficient use of representation**, so that, for example:

- Participants with similar interests should have joint representation unless there are strong reasons why they should not do so; and
- Representation should generally be limited to those persons who need it in order to assist the inquiry, or whose conduct is likely to be the subject of criticism by the inquiry. [105]

Government policy had been to pay out of public funds the 'reasonable costs' of 'any necessary party to the inquiry who would be prejudiced in seeking representation were he in any doubt about funds being available.' This policy, which kept the issue of representation firmly within the hands of government, would continue.

Like PASC, the consultation paper tackled the key question of appointments and asked whether inquiries needed procedural rules.[106] It also addressed in cursory fashion two questions that deserved more prominence: (i) whether inquiries had made 'any discernible difference to the conduct of public life' and (ii) whether there should be a formal follow-up system – an idea promptly dismissed as inappropriate.[107]

The Inquiries Act 2005 was, according to the Government, a consolidation measure, which replaced the 1921 Act. Parliament must be informed if a minister sets up a public inquiry (s. 6) but loses its powers of approval under the 1921 Act. The circumstances where an inquiry can be set up are wide: where 'particular events have caused, or are capable of causing, public concern, or there is public concern that particular events may have occurred' (s. 1). Inquiries are to be conducted by a chairman appointed by the minister with or without a panel. The panel is appointed by the minister after consultation with the chairman but the minister may make further appointments or changes (ss. 3, 4 and 7). The terms of reference are settled after consultation with the chairman by the minister, who may change them after consultation with the chairman 'if he considers that the public interest so desires' (s. 5). The only restrictions on ministerial choice are: that no one with a direct interest in the inquiry or close associations with an interested party should be appointed to an inquiry; that the need for balance should be taken into consideration (see ss. 8 and 9); and, where a judge is chosen, there must be consultation with the appropriate head of the of the judiciary. Ministerial control is firmly re-established.

More controversial are ss. 13 and 14, which put into the minister's hands the power to suspend or wind up an inquiry, subject only to notification or consultation of the chairman and appropriate Parliament or Assembly. Although evidence and procedure remain in the chairman's hands (s. 17), the minister

[105] *Ibid.* [93].

[106] *Ibid.* [110].

[107] *Ibid.*, Questions 21–2 and [144].

gains the power to make procedural rules.[108] Access to, and publication of, the report may be the responsibility of the chairman (s. 17) but subject to important provisos: a minister can retain these powers in his own hands. And simply by serving a restriction order on the chairman, (s. 19) a minister can impose restrictions on

- attendance at an inquiry, or at any particular part of an inquiry
- disclosure or publication of any evidence or documents given.

For these purposes, the minister or chairman must take into account 'the public interest' and more specifically (s. 19(4)):

> (a) the extent to which any restriction on attendance, disclosure or publication might inhibit the allaying of public concern;
> (b) any risk of harm or damage that could be avoided or reduced by any such restriction;
> (c) any conditions as to confidentiality subject to which a person acquired information that he is to give, or has given, to the inquiry;
> (d) the extent to which not imposing any particular restriction would be likely—
>
> (i) to cause delay or to impair the efficiency or effectiveness of the inquiry, or
> (ii) otherwise to result in additional cost (whether to public funds or to witnesses or others).

Lord Saville himself wrote to the DCA expressing concern over this draconian power.

In other quarters too the Act was not well received, especially in Northern Ireland. Its provisions could be read as directed at the Saville Inquiry and fears were heightened by the decision to convert several existing inquiries into inquiries under the Act using new powers granted by s. 15.[109] Irish Rights Watch maintained that the Act had 'brought about a fundamental shift'; the powers of independent chairs to control inquiries had been 'usurped' and 'placed in the hands of government ministers'.[110] Amnesty International called on judges to refuse appointment to inquiries established under the Act and demanded its repeal; it dealt 'a fatal blow to any possibility of public scrutiny of and a remedy for state abuses', destroying the chance of 'an effective, independent, impartial or thorough inquiry in serious allegations of human rights violations'.[111]

In an attempt to allay mounting criticism, the DCA issued a press notice arguing that the Act merely filled gaps and codified best practice from past inquiries:

[108] The Inquiry Rules 2006, SI 2006/1838.

[109] See K. Parry, 'Investigatory inquiries and the Inquiries Act 2005' (House of Commons Library SN/PC/2599 (2007), pp. 7–8. The decision was challenged with partial success in *Re Wright's Application* [2006] NIQB 90.

[110] British Irish Rights Watch, 'Summary and critique of the Inquiries Act 2005' available online.

[111] AI press release, 20 April 2005, available online.

> For the first time in statute the Act lays down all key stages of the inquiry process – from setting up the inquiry, through appointment of the panel to publication of reports.
>
> The Act does not, as has been suggested, radically shift emphasis towards control of inquiries by Ministers. Instead, it makes it clear what the respective roles of the Minister and chairman are, thereby increasing transparency and accountability.
>
> It also stipulates that proceedings will be in public unless restrictions on access are imposed by either the Minister or the chairman. Unlike previous legislation, it specifies the ground on which access can be restricted . . . The Act says that inquiry final reports must be published in full unless there are clear reasons for withholding material and lays down what those reasons can be. Once an inquiry ends, any restrictions on public access to any material or evidence will be subject to the Freedom of Information Act.[112]

Read together with the Inquiry Rules, the Act can just be presented as adding to transparency. The Rules do mainly codify practice, though they also restrict third-party rights. Critics of the legislation were, however, right in saying that the main effect of the Bill is seriously to diminish the independence of inquiries by pulling back into ministerial hands many of the powers previously within the remit of the inquiry chairman. A comment in the *British Medical Journal* summarised fears. The 2005 Act, the authors concluded, gave government ministers 'unprecedented' new powers:

> Overall, these changes seem designed to reduce the independence of future public inquiries, and to provide the government with a host of mechanisms for controlling inquiries at every step. This is a considerable departure from past practice, in which the government took the decision to establish an inquiry and set its remit but then played absolutely no part in its subsequent development and progress, which were wholly in the hands of the inquiry chair.[113]

8. Inquiries and human rights

There is one particular situation when the ECHR bites on an inquiry: where it is the main forum for investigation of a death in state custody or at the hands of agents of the state. The state then comes under a positive obligation to set up an inquiry that must comply with criteria of independence, transparency and effectiveness. For this reason, the Joint Committee on Human Rights (JCHR) advised the Government that its draft Bill would be likely to violate ECHR Art. 2. The JCHR took particular exception to the powers now in ss. 13 and 14 for the minister to suspend or terminate an inquiry by notice to the chairman and to the ministerial powers to issue restriction notices and arrange for the publication of reports.[114]

112 See Parry, 'Investigatory inquiries and the Inquiries Act 2005', p. 5.
113 K. Walshe, 'Are public inquiries losing their independence?' (2005) 331 *BMJ* 117.
114 See JCHR, *Scrutiny: First progress report*, HC 224 (2004/5) [2.5-2.28].

In *Jordan v United Kingdom*, considering a coroner's inquest into a police shooting in Northern Ireland, the ECtHR laid out the essentials of an Art. 2 inquiry in some detail:

> The obligation to protect the right to life under Article 2 of the Convention, read in conjunction with the State's general duty under Article 1 of the Convention to 'secure to everyone within [its] jurisdiction the rights and freedoms defined in [the] Convention', also requires by implication that there should be some form of effective official investigation when individuals have been killed as a result of the use of force . . . The essential purpose of such investigation is to secure the effective implementation of the domestic laws which protect the right to life and, in those cases involving State agents or bodies, to ensure their accountability for deaths occurring under their responsibility. What form of investigation will achieve those purposes may vary in different circumstances. However, whatever mode is employed, the authorities must act of their own motion, once the matter has come to their attention. They cannot leave it to the initiative of the next of kin either to lodge a formal complaint or to take responsibility for the conduct of any investigative procedures . . .
>
> For an investigation into alleged unlawful killing by State agents to be effective, it may generally be regarded as necessary for the persons responsible for and carrying out the investigation to be independent from those implicated in the events . . . This means not only a lack of hierarchical or institutional connection but also a practical independence . . .
>
> The investigation must also be effective in the sense that it is capable of leading to a determination of whether the force used in such cases was or was not justified in the circumstances . . . This is not an obligation of result, but of means. The authorities must have taken the reasonable steps available to them to secure the evidence concerning the incident, including *inter alia* eye witness testimony, forensic evidence and, where appropriate, an autopsy which provides a complete and accurate record of injury and an objective analysis of clinical findings, including the cause of death . . . Any deficiency in the investigation which undermines its ability to establish the cause of death or the person or persons responsible will risk falling foul of this standard.
>
> A requirement of promptness and reasonable expedition is implicit in this context . . . It must be accepted that there may be obstacles or difficulties which prevent progress in an investigation in a particular situation. However, a prompt response by the authorities in investigating a use of lethal force may generally be regarded as essential in maintaining public confidence in their adherence to the rule of law and in preventing any appearance of collusion in or tolerance of unlawful acts. For the same reasons, there must be a sufficient element of public scrutiny of the investigation or its results to secure accountability in practice as well as in theory. The degree of public scrutiny required may well vary from case to case. In all cases, however, the next-of-kin of the victim must be involved in the procedure to the extent necessary to safeguard his or her legitimate interests . . . [115]

[115] *Jordan v UK* (2001) 37 EHHR 52 [105–9] omitting all references. See also *McCann v UK* (1995) 21 EHRR 97. In *R (AM) v SSHP* [2009] EWCA Civ 219, the Court of Appeal applied this case law to Art. 3.

These Art. 2 requirements form the basis of a consistent domestic case law consolidated in the case of Zahid Mubarek, a young man on remand at Feltham young offenders' institution. ZM was placed in a cell with a fellow offender who had 'an alarming and violent criminal record, both in and out of custody'. He was killed in the course of a racist attack by his cell mate.

It is to the credit of Martin Narey, Director-General of the prisons service, that he immediately apologised to the family and announced an internal inquiry (the Butt Inquiry) to investigate the circumstances surrounding the murder. The family did not participate. They had written immediately asking for an independent public inquiry into the circumstances of Zahid's death. The minister stalled on the ground that investigations were incomplete. A coroner's inquest was opened but, as is customary, adjourned pending a trial at which the murderer pleaded guilty and was convicted. Unusually, the coroner declined to reopen the inquest. She reasoned that inquests were 'an unsuitable vehicle for investigating publicly the issues raised by this case', that coroners had no investigatory staff at their disposal, that it would be inappropriate and inadequate to rely on an internal investigation by the prison service and, finally, that an inquest was not an appropriate forum in which to make recommendations as to good administrative practice. Clearly, the coroner shared the family's view that a public inquiry was necessary. It was not forthcoming, however. The Commission for Racial Equality (CRE) stepped in, using its powers under the Race Relations Acts to launch a formal investigation, which concluded with a published report.[116] Once again the family did not participate. Instead, they applied for an inquiry in terms of ECHR Art. 2.

At common law, a ministerial refusal to hold an inquiry would be hard to challenge; the applicant would have to show that the decision was '*Wednesbury* unreasonable', a hard standard to meet. Under Art. 2, the position was different. There was, as Hooper J asserted, a *positive* obligation to hold an effective and thorough investigation. On the facts of the case, this obligation could:

> only be met by holding a public and independent investigation with the family legally represented, provided with the relevant material and able to cross-examine the principal witnesses. Against the background of the material which I have set out at some length, the family and the public are entitled to such an investigation.[117]

But no inquiry followed. Instead, the judgment was reversed by the Court of Appeal, reaching the House of Lords only two years later, where the first instance judgment was reinstated. Mirroring the ECtHR jurisprudence, Lord Bingham's speech set out the requirements of an Art. 2 inquiry and summarised its objectives:

116 CRE, *A Formal Investigation by the Commission for Racial Equality into HM Prison Service of England and Wales: Part 1: The murder of Zahid Mubarek* (July 2003).

117 *R (Amin (Imtiaz)) v Home Secretary* [2001] EWHC Admin 719 [91].

- The investigation must be independent
- The investigation must be effective
- The investigation must be reasonably prompt
- There must be a sufficient element of public scrutiny
- The next of kin must be involved to an appropriate extent.

The state's duty to investigate is secondary to the duties not to take life unlawfully and to protect life, in the sense that it only arises where a death has occurred or life-threatening injuries have occurred . . . It can fairly be described as procedural. But in any case where a death has occurred in custody it is not a minor or unimportant duty. In this country . . . effect has been given to that duty for centuries by requiring such deaths to be publicly investigated before an independent judicial tribunal with an opportunity for relatives of the deceased to participate. The purposes of such an investigation are clear: to ensure so far as possible that the full facts are brought to light; that culpable and discreditable conduct is exposed and brought to public notice; that suspicion of deliberate wrongdoing (if unjustified) is allayed; that dangerous practices and procedures are rectified; and that those who have lost their relative may at least have the satisfaction of knowing that lessons learned from his death may save the lives of others.[118]

Firmly rejecting the government argument that any further inquiry would be unlikely to unearth new and significant facts, the House ruled that a full public inquiry was necessary. The Home Secretary obliged, laying down somewhat grudging terms of reference:

In the light of the House of Lords judgment in the case of . . . *ex parte Amin*, to investigate and report to the Home Secretary on the death of Zahid Mubarek, and the events leading up to the attack on him, and make recommendations about the prevention of such attacks in the future, taking into account the investigations that have already taken place – in particular, those by the Prison Service and the Commission for Racial Equality.

The Inquiry Report was to underline that 'this was no ordinary inquiry. It was initially resisted by the Home Office.'[119]

Appropriately, given the circumstances, the inquiry was chaired by a judge (Keith J). The panel of advisers was imaginatively chosen: Lutfur Ali was National Head of Equalities and Diversity for the Department of Health; Bobby Cummines was an ex-prisoner and Chief Executive of the charity *Unlock*; Alastair Papps had been governor of Durham and Frankland Prisons. The inquiry was non-statutory and worked largely from documentary evidence, although it also held oral hearings. The cost was £5.2 million. Calling the tragic death preventable, the inquiry ranged widely. It issued a five-volume report published as a House of Commons paper with eighty-eight detailed rec-

[118] *R v Home Secretary, ex p. Amin* [2003] UKHL 51 [31] [39] (omitting references) reversing *R (Amin (Imtiaz)) v Home Secretary* [2002] EWCA Civ 390.

[119] *The Zahid Mubarek Inquiry*, HC 1082 (2005/6) [1.1]; HC Deb., col. 1186 (24 July 2006).

ommendations for risk assessment and violence reduction in prisons. Many of the Howe objectives were fulfilled: the facts were authoritatively established, as was the willingness of the prison service to learn from events; all of this helped to reassure the public and to provide closure for ZM's family, which had fought so long and hard for justice.

What should we say about accountability, which in many ways had already been established? The murderer had been convicted, the Prisons Service had admitted responsibility, there had already been two inquiries and reforms were in hand. As the Final Report stated, 'many of the recommendations an inquiry of this kind would have made if it had been looking a few months after Zahid's death at what had happened to him have now been overtaken by events. Much of what would have been recommended is now in place – or at any rate plans are well advanced for them to be in place.' Nonetheless, this high-level public inquiry was of great symbolic importance. It was an opportunity for public apology and catharsis. It was a public recognition of commitment to the Franks values of 'openness, fairness and impartiality' and the Nolan standards of integrity in public life.[120] Finally, and perhaps most important, it was a public demonstration of the state's commitment to the rule of law.

This raises very pertinent questions. Why do government and public bodies so often resile from their frequently expressed commitment to the good governance principles of transparency? Why do they so often try to evade their Convention obligations, sheltering behind the ramshackle machinery of coroner's inquests, police investigations, possible prosecutions and a proliferation of inquiries, usually internal and often unpublished? Setting up an inquiry into the death of an innocent Iraqi civilian, Baha Mousa, while in the custody of British soldiers in Iraq, the Defence Secretary asserted that:

> A Public Inquiry into the death of Baha Mousa is the right thing to do. It will reassure the public that we are leaving no stone unturned in investigating his tragic death. The Army has nothing to hide in this respect and is keen to learn all the lessons it can from this terrible incident.[121]

Yet the Baha Mousa inquiry was forced on the Ministry of Defence by a fight lasting nearly five years, ending with a successful appeal to the House of Lords.[122] In ZM's case, it took three-and-a-half years, three fruitless inquiries, an expensive lawsuit and considerable persistence to achieve justice and closure. Similarly, disturbing deaths of young army cadets at Deepcut barracks were considered by four inquests, some seventeen inquiries, an investigative report from the Surrey Police and a wide-ranging report on army training from the

[120] See Lord Nolan, *First Report of the Committee on Standards in Public Life*, Cm. 2850 (1995).

[121] *Times Online*, 13 June 2007.

[122] *Al-Skeini and Others v Defence Secretary* [2007] UKHL 26. Following the judgment, the MoD agreed to pay up to £3m in compensation to those injured.

House of Commons Defence Committee before a 'review' by Nicholas Blake QC – noticeably *not* a public inquiry – was conceded.[123] Both the Defence Committee and the Blake Review criticised the lack of transparency in the army investigative process, commenting that its outcome had 'fuelled the disquiet surrounding incidents'. Blake, concerned at the lack of independence in the investigation and complaints procedures, recommended the appointment of an official with an 'independent ombudsman role'. An independent Service Complaints Commissioner was set in place by the Armed Forces Act 2006 with the aim of making the complaints system 'more independent and more transparent' but, as the Defence Committee had commented earlier, 'the role proposed for the Commissioner falls a long way short of the investigatory body proposed by our predecessor Committee'.[124] The Deepcut deaths clearly raise issues that are, at the very least, closely related to Art. 2, yet no public inquiry has been conceded.

9. Conclusion

This brief survey of public inquiries ends our study of 'alternative' administrative justice before we move on to courts. Whether inquiries really form part of the landscape of administrative justice remains an open question. Precise classification of inquiries defeated both the Donoughmore and Franks committees, set up so many years ago to consider their functions. Both had to classify them as hybrids, exercising both administrative and adjudicative functions. Some inquiries, such as minor accident inquiries or inquiries into regional and local development plans, still retain their original advisory functions. Some major inquiries, such as the Phillips Inquiry into BSE or the Bristol Royal Infirmary Inquiry have also managed, by avoiding the allocation of blame, successfully to hold this line.

Increasingly, however, the public inquiry is coming to be seen as part of the standard machinery for accountability, like freedom of information legislation. In this new context, the expectations of the general public are that inquiries will be fully independent, held in public and that their reports will be published and (as the court ruled in the case of the PCA) binding. In other words, inquiries are increasingly acquiring adjudicative characteristics. Such a classification is in fact fully consistent with Lord Howe's list of inquiry objectives. Civil and criminal courts, tribunals and other adjudicative machinery establish the facts, provide catharsis for 'stakeholders', reassure the public, and, as Mulgan emphasises, hold people and organisations accountable (see p. 47 above). Less directly than inquiries, they provide an opportunity to learn from events. This remains,

[123] Respectively, Surrey Police, *The Deepcut Investigation Final Report* (2004); Defence Committee, *Duty of Care*, HC 63 (2004/5); *The Deepcut Review: A review of the circumstances surrounding the deaths of four soldiers at Princess Royal Barracks, Deepcut between 1995 and 2002*, HC 795 (2005/6).

[124] *Armed Forces Bill: Proposal for a Service Complaints Commissioner*, HC 1711 (2005/6) [4].

however, perhaps the most important independent characteristic of the public inquiry, which it shares with the work of the Parliamentary Commissioner, to whom inquiries have recently been losing ground. The added expertise of the public inquiry, with an appropriate expert panel, must be weighed against the investigatory techniques, largely conducted in private, of the ombudsmen.

Recent years have seen hotly contested and adversarial inquiries, which raise serious questions about appropriate procedure. Inquiries bring individuals into the public eye and, especially when chaired by lawyers, may see it as their function to apportion blame. In a society with a strong tradition of adversarial procedure, the inquisitorial procedure of the public inquiry then becomes problematic. This may be one justification (or excuse) for holding inquiries in private – effectively prioritising the learning function (Howe, 2) over the accountability function (Howe, 5).

At the start of this chapter, we cited Sales's view that inquiries possess an important constitutional function of legitimation in contemporary society. In a governmental system not remarkable for its openness, the willingness of government by setting up an inquiry to 'accept public scrutiny of what it has done – to operate with "transparency"' has undoubtedly been important. The most fundamental and important characteristic of public inquiries in the UK has, however, been their independence. By owing no allegiance to any group of stakeholders – especially not to the Government that sets them up – by having the freedom to investigate openly and impartially and to report without government censorship, inquiries have been able to build consensus and command widespread support for their findings and recommendations. Where – as occurred for different reasons with the Scott and Widgery reports or the internal prisons investigation into the death of Zahid Mubarek – an inquiry has fallen short in this respect it has failed to command public confidence and failed also in its function of providing public reassurance (Howe, 4). It remains to be seen whether the new legislation, by taking so many new powers to control and direct public inquiries, will have stripped them of the independence and impartiality central to their purpose. If so, inquiries will be increasingly discounted. They may then come to be seen as performing Lord Howe's sixth objective of 'serving the political interests of government'.

14

Continuity and change: Procedural review

Contents

As every student of government should know, the administrative process is shaped not only by executive and legislature but also by courts. This chapter focuses on the judicial contribution in the form of procedural review, classically epitomised in the two Latin tags: *audi alteram partem* (hear the other side) and *nemo iudex in causa sua* (no man a judge in his own cause). Suitably hallowed, even hackneyed, the precept that 'justice must not only be done but be seen to be done' is the essence of the rule of law.

A first theme of this chapter is judicialisation and we shall find a general tendency to model the administrative process in the courts' own adjudicative image. We may conceive of a sliding scale: the closer to the 'ideal type' of formal court procedure, the more 'judicialised' the process will be. As emphasised by Lord Diplock's use of the term 'procedural impropriety' (see p. 107 above), this trait is inevitably bound up with the role and form of statutory procedural requirements. Our second major theme is the meeting of a quintessential common law tradition with 'Europe': both the ECHR and Community law are involved. This important constitutional dimension has a two-way aspect. In Art. 6 especially, the Convention wears the genetic imprint of a deep-rooted Anglo-American concern with natural justice and due process.[1] Again, the ECJ in developing general principles of law has drawn directly on common law requirements of a fair hearing.[2] Conversely, we will see how the Human Rights Act (HRA) has ushered in a new round of judicialisation based on the ECHR. Directed to judicial procedures, but casting a wider shadow, the Art. 6 prescription of an 'independent and impartial tribunal' in the determination of 'civil rights and obligations' is today a defining aspect of the administrative law landscape.

We shall also take up a theme discussed in earlier chapters of the use of adjudication to devise and install procedural requirements for other forms of deciding. As noted previously in the context of formal rule-making, this offers a doorway for collective-interest representation, allowing groups to appeal to process values as a way of emboldening the courts: look back, for example, at the *Greenpeace* and *Bapio* cases (see p. 176 above). The scale of the general development of procedural fair play raises the question of judicial discretion. Deepened and widened over the years, procedural review exhibits a determinedly flexible quality. Judges must not only marshal facts and 'weigh' competing considerations but also navigate multiple policy domains and myriad decision-making processes in the cause of variable protection. 'Soft-centred' is an apt description of much in the case law.

The interplay of the twin elements of continuity and change provides a convenient angle of approach to the subject. Much in the general principles has enduring appeal. The courts themselves under the banner of 'procedural fairness' have pursued a course essentially set half-a-century ago in the watershed case of *Ridge v Baldwin*.[3] Looking more closely we identify a whole

[1] A. Lester, 'Fundamental rights: The UK isolated?' [1984] *PL* 46. And see Lord Woolf, 'Magna Carta: A precedent for recent constitutional change' in C. Campbell-Holt (ed.), *The Pursuit of Justice* (Oxford University Press, 2008).

[2] Case 17/74 *Transocean Marine Paint v Commission* [1974] ECR 1063; also Case 222/86 *Heylens* [1987] ECR 4097. And see F. Bignami, *Three Generations of Participation Rights in European Administrative Proceedings* (Jean Monnet WP No. 11, 2003).

[3] [1964] AC 40.

series of developments integral to the 'transforming' of judicial review (see Chapter 3):

- *paradigm shift*: determinedly conceptual/deferential approach ('natural justice') replaced by a more vigorous/open-ended one ('procedural fairness')
- *elaboration of procedural fairness*: adjudicative-type features extended and tailored in contextual fashion, increasingly in the shadow of EU and especially ECHR requirements
- *procedural legitimate expectation*: additional entitlement to judicial protection, ranging across individuated and consultative process (see p. 223 above)
- *cautious experiments with regulating more plural, non-adjudicative types of process*
- *checking for structural as well as personalised forms of bias*: associated with (but not confined to) the Art. 6 Convention right.

There are major stresses and strains. The fact that procedural review is shot through with discretion raises questions about institutional competence, especially when courts venture outside the adjudicative habitat of individuated decision-making and/or begin to second-guess procedural choices expressed in legislation. Again, common law forms of procedural review are designed in a very real sense to enrich the administrative process. But given the many practical demands on government, and especially the need to guard against the limiting effects of judicialisation, how far can the development reasonably go? ECHR Art. 6 has given matters an additional twist. The House of Lords will be seen defending national practices of political and administrative decision-making against demands for a judicialised – 'independent and impartial' – body.

1. Scene-setting

(a) Rationale

In a classic account, the American jurist Lon Fuller identified the distinguishing characteristic of adjudication as being to confer 'on the affected person a peculiar kind of participation in the decision, that of presenting proofs and reasoned arguments for a decision in his favor'.[4] Fuller's general point was that the hallmark of this, and of the other forms of social ordering like contract, negotiation or legislation, was procedural. Each of the forms generates a set of procedural requirements, which protect the integrity of the form; conversely, the integrity of the process becomes eroded if the reality strays too far from the ideal. In the case of adjudication and tribunals, this was the significance of

[4] L. Fuller, 'The forms and limits of adjudication' (1978) 92 *Harv. LR* 353. And see J. Allison, 'Fuller's analysis of polycentric disputes and the limits of adjudication' (1994) 53 *CLJ* 367.

the invocation by Franks and Leggatt of the values of openness, fairness and impartiality, and independence (see Chapter 11). Again, because historically the twin strands in natural justice of the hearing rules and no bias reflected procedure as it developed in English courts of law, the judges in imposing the two principles on the administration have asked for adjudication to be incorporated into the administrative process.

Fuller's ideas have been influential in English administrative law, not least in the quest for 'rational' decision-making. 'Judicialisation', like 'legalisation' or the resort to rules, was to help underpin the integrity of the administration – bringing official conduct under legal control.[5] Yet we find in the literature different justifications for the imposition by the legal system of procedural restraints on administrative decision-making. This has a very practical dimension. Case law stands to be shaped, in Tribe's words, by 'alternative conceptions of the primary purpose of procedural due process and by competing visions of how that purpose may best be achieved'.[6]

One set of justifications is utilitarian and positivist in character, stressing the link between the grant of procedural protection and the quality of substantive outcomes.[7] Participation is required in the service of accuracy and efficiency – a variant of instrumentalist arguments for law as a tool of effective administration. According to theorists of law and economics, the value of due process is quantifiable: the cost of withholding due process can be measured in terms of the probability of error if it is withheld; alternatively, the cost of error can be calculated and weighed against the cost of procedural protection and participation.[8] This form of calculation demonstrates some obvious problems however. What, for example, is the 'error cost' of wrongfully refusing entry to a refugee? And – a question asked in other contexts – is there necessarily a 'correct' outcome? Enough has been said to show that many administrative decisions are not straightforward rule-applications but rather involve questions of judgement or interpretation.

A second set of justifications for fairness or procedural justice is rights-based. In other words, as Dworkin has argued,[9] procedural protections are dependent on, or secondary to, substantive rights. More likely than utilitarian theories to shift the balance in favour of the individual, this model is boosted in Britain by the HRA. Discussed previously in Chapter 13, the 'positive obligation' grounded in ECHR Art. 2 to make inquiries is the most striking example. The duality of Art. 6 – (a) the threshold requirement of a

5 J. Jowell, 'The legal control of administrative discretion' [1973] *PL* 178. And see J. Rawls, *A Theory of Justice* (Oxford University Press, 1973).

6 L. Tribe, *American Constitutional Law*, 2nd edn (Foundation Press, 1988), p. 666.

7 See e.g. J. Resnick 'Due process and procedural justice' in Pennock and Chapman (eds.), *Due Process* (Nomos, 1977).

8 R. Posner, 'An economic approach to legal procedure and judicial administration' (1973) 2 *J. of Legal Studies* 399; L. Kaplow, 'The value of accuracy in adjudication: An economic analysis' (1994) 23 *J. of Legal Studies* 307.

9 See e.g. R. Dworkin, *A Matter of Principle* (Clarendon, 1985), Ch. 4.

determination of civil rights and obligations and (b) a bundle of protections including not only independent and impartial tribunal 'established by law', but also 'fair and public hearing' 'within a reasonable time' and 'judgment . . . pronounced publicly' – also fits. Yet as with rights-based theories of administrative law in general, the model may be seen as not going far enough. Where for example an individual has only a bare 'interest' by reason of the existence of administrative discretion, the case for procedural protection is seen as considerably weakened.[10]

Due process can be said to have intrinsic value – that is to say, as the very essence of justice. An opportunity for affected individuals or groups to participate in the administrative decision-making process 'expresses their dignity as persons';[11] they are otherwise deprived of conditions requisite for continued moral agency. Common in the American literature, 'dignitary theory' has also become prominent in Britain in recent years,[12] again in part through European influences.[13] Mashaw, its leading advocate, does not deny the instrumental value of procedural protection, but rather rejects this as its primary basis. A stress on dignitary values suggests a high standard of protection, for example in those cases where the substantive merits of the individual's case are dubious. Like Dworkin however, Mashaw accepts the case for judicial 'balancing', on the basis that a weighing of competing factors recognises and confronts 'the fundamentally compromised nature of social life'.[14] Indeed, some form of 'balancing' appears inevitable. To classify certain interests as rights for the purpose of procedural protection, and to take no account of other factors in determining its content, has been said by Craig to be 'implausible given that the costs of such protection have to be borne by society'.[15] We see too that dignitary theory and mathematical calculation do not mix. There is an important role here for judicial discretion.

The case for courts rendering non-adjudicative procedures more open to interest representation is naturally informed by ideas of pluralism, diversity, inclusiveness and of direct democracy (see also Chapter 4). Typically a product of American borrowings,[16] this expansionist challenge to the traditional – individuated – approach to 'fairness' was already apparent in

10 D. Galligan, *Due Process and Fair Procedures: A study of administrative procedures* (Clarendon, 1996).

11 Tribe, *American Constitutional Law*, p. 666. A variety of philosophical underpinnings may be used, including natural rights, fundamental liberal values and social contract theory.

12 T. Allan, *Constitutional Justice: A liberal theory of the rule of law* (Oxford University Press, 2001).

13 D. Feldman, 'Human dignity as a human value' [1999] *PL* 682 and [2000] *PL* 61. And see Lord Millett, 'The Right to Good Administration in European Law' [2002] *PL* 309.

14 J. Mashaw, *Due Process in the Administrative State* (Yale University Press, 1985), p. 155

15 P. Craig, *Administrative Law*, 6th edn (Sweet & Maxwell, 2008), p. 393.

16 R. Stewart, 'The reformation of American administrative law' 88 *Harv. LR* (1975) 1776; F. Michelman, 'Formal and associational aims in procedural due process' in Pennock and Chapman (eds), *Due Process*.

Britain in the early 1990s.[17] In jurisprudential terms, there is an evident connection with the permeability of the courts' own procedures to collective or group action (seen in the next chapter as greatly increased in recent times). Splendidly envisioned, procedural fairness is seen here promoting 'independent values of participation, deliberation and consensus' in the governmental decision-making process.[18] More soberly expressed, the courts have a part to play in creating space for different views of 'the public interest' (while at the same time facilitating better flows of information, etc., in instrumentalist fashion). Enthusiasm is tempered by the difficulty (observed in the context of rule-making) of devising procedures which take into account a broad range of views without impairing the efficiency and effectiveness of administration. Nor do the courts exist in a constitutional and historical vacuum. Reflected over many years in patterns of judicial restraint, concern about possible judicial 'interference' with the policy-making process cannot simply be brushed aside.

The legitimating effects of 'fair procedure' are impossible to quantify but perilous to ignore. Signposting contemporary developments in the case law, Bayles, for example, prioritises the value of impartiality by reasons other than 'possible demoralisation effects' or even non-compliance. 'The possibility of partiality should be accepted [only] when the risks of it are small, the costs to parties of an alternative decision maker are great and a failure to decide on the merits might also involve significant injustice.'[19] In similar vein, Solum speaks of 'the hard question' in procedural justice: 'how can we regard ourselves as obligated . . . to comply with a [decision] that we believe (or even know) to be in error?' While procedural perfection is unattainable, and seeking to achieve it intolerably costly, 'procedures that purport to bind without affording meaningful rights of participation are fundamentally illegitimate.'[20] Nor do the advantages in terms of legitimate authority and smooth administration go unremarked in government. *Judge Over Your Shoulder* (JOYS), the Treasury Solicitor's guide to judicial review for civil servants, makes the point explicitly. 'Nobody should be able to allege that the decision is a fix because the decision-maker was biased, whether or not there was any truth in that allegation. The rule must be observed strictly to maintain public confidence in the decision-making process.'[21] The sting in the tail is the evident potential for 'symbolic reassurance', or in Arnstein's terms for therapy and manipulation (see p. 173 above). To ensure they are 'meaningful' requires a close consideration by the courts of the nature of hearings and consultations.

17 G. Richardson, 'The legal regulation of process' in Richardson and Genn (eds.), *Administrative Law and Government Action* (Clarendon, 1994). And see I. Harden and N. Lewis, *The Noble Lie: The British constitution and the rule of law* (Hutchinson, 1986).

18 L. Guinier, 'No two seats: The elusive quest for political equality' (1991) 77 *Virginia LR* 1413, 1489.

19 M. Bayles, *Procedural Justice* (Kluwer, 1990), p. 130.

20 L. Solum, 'Procedural justice' (2004) 78 *Southern California Law Review* 181, 274.

21 TSol, *Judge Over Your Shoulder*, 4th edn (2006) [2.7].

(b) From concepts to contexts

Prior to *Ridge v Baldwin*, natural justice had taken on the character of a highly formalist jurisprudence. Judges attempted to distinguish the 'judicial', 'quasi-judicial' and 'administrative' functions of government in order to determine whether the principles applied.[22] Reflecting and reinforcing a restrictive, deferential response by the courts in the post-World War I period of consolidation of the administrative state, this analytical theory was not wholly devoid of merit, at least for green light theorists. By insulating 'administrative' functions from the common law doctrine, it implied a recognition that adjudicative (adversarial) procedures are of limited usefulness and thus left space for experimentation and innovation with alternative forms of social ordering.

Analytical theory came to be criticised in three main ways. First, it was difficult, if not impossible, to separate different types of function. Terminological contortions and hair-splitting distinctions proliferated.[23] Secondly, with the growth of the state, increasing numbers of decisions were rendered devoid of procedural protections because they were classified as administrative. In *Nakkuda Ali v Jayaratne*,[24] for example, a trader alleged to have acted fraudulently was deprived of his licence. The Privy Council held that this exercise of statutory discretion did not require any kind of hearing; the regulator was acting neither 'judicially' nor 'quasi-judicially', but merely withdrawing a 'privilege'. Thirdly, analytical theory was seen as a break with tradition. Critics like Wade[25] harked back to a 'golden age' of natural justice in the nineteenth century in which, confronted by a nascent administrative state, the courts had demonstrated a robust approach to matters of procedural protection.[26]

Described by a contemporary as 'the Magna Carta of natural justice',[27] *Ridge v Baldwin* fatally undermined the analytical theory. In a brilliant exposition of the common law method, Lord Reid by looking back led the judges forward. Acting under statutory powers, a local police committee had dismissed its chief constable. Seeking financial compensation, not reinstatement, he applied for a declaration that the decision was void for breach of natural justice. The Court of Appeal held that the committee was exercising an administrative function and that the principles of natural justice were not applicable. The House of Lords disagreed:

[22] To trace the development, see *Local Government Board v Arlidge* [1915] AC 120, *Errington v Minister of Health* [1935] 1 KB 249, and *Franklin v Minister of Town and Country Planning* [1948] AC 87.

[23] A feature underlined in the reasoning of the (Donoughmore) *Committee on Ministers' Powers*, Cmnd 4050 (1932).

[24] [1951] AC 66.

[25] H. Wade, *Administrative Law*, 1st edn (Clarendon, 1961).

[26] The classic authority being *Cooper v Wandsworth Board of Works* (1863) 14 CBNS 180.

[27] C. K. Allen, *Law and Orders*, 3rd edn (Stevens, 1965), p. 242.

Lord Reid: The appellant's case is that . . . before attempting to reach any decision [the committee] were bound to inform him of the grounds on which they proposed to act and give him a fair opportunity of being heard in his own defence . . . If the present case had arisen thirty or forty years ago the courts would have had no difficulty in deciding this issue in favour of the appellant . . . Yet the Court of Appeal have decided this issue against the appellant on more recent authorities which apparently justify that result. How has this come about? There have been many cases where it has been sought to apply the principles of natural justice to the wider duties imposed on ministers and other organs of government by modern legislation . . . It has been held that those principles have a limited application in such cases and those limitations have tended to be reflected in other decisions on matters to which in principle they do not appear to me to apply. Secondly . . . those principles have been held to have a limited application in cases arising out of wartime legislation; and again such limitations have tended to be reflected in other cases.

In [the earlier] cases . . . the Board of Works or the Governor or the club committee was dealing with a single isolated case. It was not deciding, like a judge in a lawsuit, what were the rights of the person before it. But it was deciding how he should be treated – something analogous to a judge's duty in imposing a penalty. No doubt policy would play some part in the decision – but so it might when a judge is imposing a sentence. So it was easy to say that such a body is performing a quasi-judicial task in considering and deciding such a matter, and to require it to observe the essentials of all proceedings of a judicial character – the principles of natural justice . . . Sometimes the functions of a minister or department may also be of that character, and then the rules of natural justice can apply in much the same way. But more often their functions are of a very different character. If a minister is considering whether to make a scheme for, say, an important new road, his primary concern will not be with the damage which its construction will do to the rights of individual owners of land. He will have to consider all manner of questions of public interest and, it may be, a number of alternative schemes . . . No individual can complain if the ordinary accepted methods of carrying on public business do not give him as good protection as would be given by the principles of natural justice in a different kind of case.

Although not abandoning terminology associated with analytical theory, Lord Reid's speech worked to liberate the courts from self-imposed conceptual restraints. While at this stage still largely confined to individuated forms of decision-making, today's common law model – *a generalised doctrine of procedural fairness characterised by variable intensity of review* – thus began to emerge in subsequent cases. In *Re H K (An Infant)*,[28] for example, Lord Parker CJ doubted whether an immigration officer in refusing entry had acted in a 'judicial' or 'quasi-judicial' capacity, but thought that in any event the applicant had to be given a chance to explain his position. 'Good administration and an honest or bona fide decision must . . . require not merely

[28] [1967] 2 QB 617. See also *Schmidt v Home Secretary* [1969] 2 WLR 337.

impartiality, not merely bringing one's mind to bear on the problem, but acting fairly.'

Ridge v Baldwin, in other words, had presented the judges with a challenge and an opportunity. Focused on issues of amenability to jurisdiction, the analytical model implied highly judicialised procedure inside a restricted zone.[29] In contrast, prioritising the question of content, 'the duty to act fairly' was indicative of more varied and variable requirements as it ranged increasingly across the piece. Flexibility became the keyword: judicial discretion. Afforded almost Biblical status in recent times, two later House of Lords speeches demanded that judges hold their nerve:

> *Lord Bridge* (1987): The so-called rules of natural justice are not engraved on tablets of stone. To use the phrase which better expresses the underlying concept, what the requirements of fairness demand when anybody, domestic, administrative or judicial, has to make a decision which will affect the rights of individuals depends on the character of the decision-making body, the kind of decision it has to make and the statutory or other framework in which it operates.[30]
>
> *Lord Mustill* (1993): The standards of fairness are not immutable. They may change with the passage of time, both in the general and in their application to decisions of a particular type . . . The principles of fairness are not to be applied by rote identically in every situation. What fairness demands is dependent on the context of the decision, and this is to be taken into account in all its aspects . . . An essential feature of the context is the statute which creates the discretion, as regards both its language and the shape of the legal and administrative system within which the decision is taken.[31]

2. Flexibility: The sliding scale

Such is the realm of the sliding scale of procedural protection. The mass of common law cases on fair procedure incorporates a pool of specific procedural norms, which can be summoned up, and asserted more or less vigorously, by reference to the decision-making context. While the range of possible requirements is (increasingly) broad, the strong genetic imprint of the model of adjudication as 'presenting proofs and reasoned arguments' is clearly visible:[32]

- Give proper notice (*Bradbury* – see p. 176 above)
- Make available relevant information (classically, 'the case against') (*Roberts* – see p. 642 below)

[29] Although the content was never entirely fixed or determinate: *Board of Education v Rice* [1911] AC 179; *Russell v Duke of Norfolk* [1949] 1 All ER 109.

[30] *Lloyd v McMahon* [1987] 2 WLR 821, 878.

[31] *R v Home Secretary, ex p. Doody* [1993] 3 WLR 154, 168.

[32] The list is not intended to be exhaustive. For a detailed survey, see Lord Woolf, J. Jowell and A. Le Sueur, *de Smith's Judicial Review of Administrative Action*, 6th edn (Sweet & Maxwell, 2007), Chs. 6–7.

- Consult and/or receive written representations (*GCHQ* – see p. 107 above)
- Provide oral hearings (*Smith and West* – see p. 641 below)
- Allow legal representation or other assistance (*Tarrant* – see p. 627 below)
- Permit cross examination (*Bushell* – see p. 585 below)
- Give reasons for the decision (*Doody* – see p. 628 below)

(a) Tailoring

The courts have used a variety of techniques for tailoring procedures to the subject matter in hand. Representing a transitional phase in the move from 'concepts' to 'contexts', a modified form of classification was prevalent in the early years of the generalised 'duty to act fairly'. *McInnes v Onslow Fane*[33] concerned a refusal by the British Boxing Board of Control to grant a manager's licence. The court rejected the applicant's argument that he was entitled to an oral hearing and for prior information of any concerns:

> *Megarry V-C*: It must be considered what type of decision is in question . . . At least three categories may be discerned. First, there are . . . the forfeiture cases . . . In these there is a decision which takes away some existing right or position, as where a member of an organisation is expelled or a licence is revoked. Second, at the other extreme there are . . . application cases . . . where the decision merely refuses to grant the applicant the right or position that he seeks, such as . . . a licence to do certain acts. Third, there is an intermediate category . . . the expectation cases . . . which differ from the application cases only in that the applicant has some legitimate expectation from what has already happened that his application will be granted. This head includes cases where an existing licence-holder applies for a renewal of his licence . . .
>
> There is a substantial distinction between the forfeiture cases and the application cases. In the forfeiture cases, there is a threat to take something away for some reason: and in such cases, the right to an unbiased tribunal, the right to notice of the charges and the right to be heard in answer to the charges . . . are plainly apt. In the application cases, on the other hand, nothing is being taken away, and in all normal circumstances there are no charges, and so no requirement of an opportunity of being heard in answer to the charges. Instead, there is the far wider and less defined question of the general suitability of the applicant for a licence . . . The intermediate category . . . may . . . be regarded as being more akin to the forfeiture cases for . . . the legitimate expectation . . . is one which raises the question of what it is that has happened to make the applicant unsuitable.

The obvious danger with this type of reasoning is that the distinctions again become over-rigid. Since a person's livelihood for example can be at stake

[33] [1978] 3 All ER 211. See also from this period, *R v Gaming Board for Great Britain, ex p. Benaim and Khaida* [1970] 2 All ER 528 and *Cinnamond v British Airports Authority* [1980] 1 WLR 582.

in each class of case, the classification may also be criticised for protecting vested interests and/or providing insufficient protection. In other words, a more individuated approach is called for, closely attuned to the effects on the applicant of denial of the application. The judges have taken this on board. Laws LJ has said that *McInnes* 'cannot now be treated as a *vade mecum* to the content of a public body's duty of fairness; it may point the way to an answer, but what is always required is a careful focus on the facts of the given case'.[34]

The tailoring of procedural fairness has seen much transaction typing of different areas of administration. Going in tandem with the explicit recognition of multiple standards of substantive review (see Chapter 3), this is part and parcel of a re-balancing exercise in light of the progressive extinction of judicial 'no-go' areas – more pressure to articulate notions of restraint or constitutional and institutional limitations of review.

Cases touching on national security feature prominently here. A familiar example of procedural protection being 'sacrificed on the altar of substantive advantage'[35] is the decision in *GCHQ* (see p. 107 above) to override a legitimate expectation of prior consultation. Alternatively, take *Cheblak*,[36] where Lord Donaldson spoke of natural justice having 'to take account of realities'. A journalist faced deportation on grounds of national security; the court refused to act on his complaint that the administrative procedure failed to secure to the individual adequate knowledge of the allegations. We note too the 'read-across' in terms of ECHR Art. 6 and the so-called 'war against terror' (see Chapter 3). Take the recent control order case of *AF, AM and AN*.[37] 'It is common ground that the ordinary rule that a party is entitled to know both the case against him and the evidence against him must be modified because of the importance of national security. The question is how and to what extent the ordinary rule should be modified.' While lining up to refute the heresy that an (apparently) unanswerable case cures an otherwise unfair hearing, the judges divided on whether – as basic principle would suggest – there was an irreducible minimum of disclosure. In the light of *MB* (see p. 133 above), the majority thought not.

Raising the standard procedural question of whether a breach of fair procedure can be cured by a subsequent (fair) rehearing or appeal, *Calvin v Carr*[38] is a classic illustration of transaction typing in other contexts. The Privy Council rejected the challenge to a disciplinary decision of the Australian Jockey Club:

[34] *Abbey Mine Ltd v Coal Authority* [2008] EWCA Civ 353 [31]. And see *R (Quark Fishing) v Foreign Secretary* [2001] EWHC Admin 1174.

[35] Solum, 'Procedural justice', p. 182.

[36] *R v Home Secretary, ex p. Cheblak* [1991] 1 WLR 890. Another infamous example is *R v Home Secretary, ex p. Hosenball* [1977] 1 WLR 766.

[37] *SSHD v AF, AM and AN* [2008] EWCA Civ 1148.

[38] [1979] 2 WLR 755.

> *Lord Wilberforce:* No clear and absolute rule can be laid down on the question . . . The situations in which this issue arises are too diverse, and the rules by which they are governed so various, that this must be so . . . While flagrant cases of injustice, including corruption or bias, must always be firmly dealt with by the courts, the tendency . . . in matters of domestic disputes should be to leave these to be settled by the agreed methods without requiring the formalities of judicial processes to be introduced . . .
>
> Races are run at intervals; bets must be disposed of according to the result. Stewards are there in order to take rapid decisions as to such matters as the running of horses, being entitled to use the evidence of their eyes and their experience. As well as acting inquisitorially at the stage of deciding the result of a race, they may have to consider disciplinary action: at this point rules of natural justice become relevant. These require, at the least, that persons should be formally charged, heard in their own defence, and know the evidence against them . . . But it is inevitable, and must be taken to be accepted, that there may not be time for procedural refinements. It is in order to enable decisions reached in this way to be reviewed at leisure that the appeal procedure exists.

Here the relevant area might be defined as 'self-regulation', or alternatively as 'sporting disputes', a light-touch standard of review being justified on grounds of agency expertise and practical exigency. Such definitions, however, may themselves be controversial. We must also keep in mind Lord Mustill's warning that fashions change. As shown earlier with regulatory judicial review cases such as *Interbrew* (see p. 313 above) and *Eisai* (see p. 314 above), the results of transaction typing in one era may be different in another.

The potential of transaction typing as a guide to procedural fairness is necessarily limited. Since precise procedural protections remain to be determined in individual cases within particular areas, further tailoring is required at the micro level. We find decisions explicitly premised on the idea of judicial 'balancing', a process naturally apt to encompass (a) the individual interest in issue; (b) the benefits to be derived from added procedural protections; and (c) the costs, both direct and indirect, of compliance.[39] Framed by the competing justifications for imposing procedural restraints, the scope for differences of opinion within the judiciary is apparent at every stage.

Ex p. Tarrant and Anderson[40] shows the workings of the sliding scale in stylised form. Were prisoners charged with serious disciplinary offences entitled to legal representation? The judge preferred to say that the Boards of Visitors responsible for determining the charges had discretion to allow representation or assistance, the exercise of which the courts would police:

> *Webster J:* The following are considerations which every Board should take into account when exercising its discretion . . . (The list is not, of course, intended to be comprehensive: particular cases may throw up other particular matters.)

[39] Craig, *Administrative Law*, p. 388.

[40] *R v Home Secretary, ex p. Tarrant and Anderson* [1985] QB 251.

> 1. The seriousness of the charge and of the potential penalty.
> 2. Whether any points of law are likely to arise . . .
> 3. The capacity of a particular prisoner to present his own case . . .
> 4. The difficulty which some prisoners might have in cross-examining a witness, particularly a witness giving evidence of an expert nature, at short notice without previously having seen that witness's evidence.
> 5. The need for reasonable speed in making their adjudication, which is clearly an important consideration.
> 6. The need for fairness as between prisoners and as between prisoners and prison officers . . .
>
> In most, if not all, charges of mutiny . . . questions are bound to arise as to whether collective action was intended to be collective . . . Where such questions arise or are likely to arise, no Board of Visitors, properly directing itself, could reasonably decide not to allow the prisoner legal representation.

The House of Lords approved this decision in *ex p. Hone*.[41] Lord Goff took the opportunity to warn against the common law being too generous. (Note however that the rights-based formula of ECHR Art. 6 today compels a somewhat different view (see p. 639 below).

> It is easy to envisage circumstances in which the rules of natural justice do not call for representation . . . as may well happen in the case of a simple assault where no question of law arises, and where the prisoner charged is capable of presenting his own case. To hold otherwise would result in wholly unnecessary delays in many cases, to the detriment of all concerned including the prisoner charged, and to a wholly unnecessary waste of time and money, contrary to the public interest.

A leading case on the duty to give reasons (see below), *ex p. Doody* benchmarks the common law development on the eve of the HRA. *Ridge v Baldwin* and its progeny had, Lord Mustill explained, generated *a presumption* that an administrative power conferred by statute will be exercised in a manner which is fair in all the circumstances.[42] In turn – cutting to the core of the obligation – fairness 'will very often require' that the affected person is provided with the gist of the case against and an opportunity to make representations. Reflecting and reinforcing the trend to rights-based review in the shadow of the Convention (see Chapter 3), Lord Mustill's speech further demonstrates acceptance of a dignitarian as well as instrumental view of procedural protection. Why might the prisoner serving a life sentence wish to know the reasons for the particular tariff or term of imprisonment? 'Partly from an obvious human desire to be told the reasons for a decision so gravely affecting his future, and partly because he hopes that once the information is obtained he

[41] *R v Board of Visitors of HM Prison, The Maze, ex p. Hone* [1988] AC 379.
[42] *R v Home Secretary, ex p. Doody*, p. 168.

may be able to point out errors of fact or reasoning [and/or] challenge the decision in the courts'.[43]

(b) Variation on a theme

It would be strange indeed if the parallel universe of statutory procedural requirements did not exhibit similar features. In 2005, Lord Steyn in *Soneji*[44] effectively crowned an increasing display of flexibility in the case law:

> In the course of the last 130 years a distinction evolved between mandatory and directory requirements [see p. 176 above]. The view was taken that where the requirement is mandatory, a failure to comply with it invalidates the act in question. Where it is merely directory, a failure to comply does not invalidate what follows. There were refinements. For example, a distinction was made between two types of directory requirements, namely (1) requirements of a purely regulatory character where a failure to comply would never invalidate the act, and (2) requirements where a failure to comply would not invalidate an act provided that there was substantial compliance . . .
>
> In *London & Clydeside Estates* [[45]] Lord Hailsham put forward a different legal analysis . . . 'It may be that what the courts are faced with is not so much a stark choice of alternatives but a spectrum of possibilities in which one compartment or description fades gradually into another.' . . . This was an important and influential dictum. It led to the adoption of a more flexible approach of focusing intensely on the consequences of non-compliance, and posing the question, taking into account those consequences, whether Parliament intended the outcome to be total invalidity. In framing the question in this way it is necessary to have regard to the fact that Parliament ex hypothesi did not consider the point of the ultimate outcome. Inevitably one must be considering objectively what intention should be imputed to Parliament . . . The rigid mandatory and directory distinction, and its many artificial refinements, have outlived their usefulness.[46]

The slightly earlier case of *Jeyeanthan*[47] provides some guidance. The minister had fallen foul of the statutory rules on leave to appeal against asylum decisions made by the independent adjudicator by not providing a declaration of truth. Lord Woolf was all for judicial discretion. Faced with a breach of legislative procedural requirement, the court would determine the consequences 'in the context of all the facts and the circumstances of the case in which the issue arises . . . It must be remembered that procedural requirements are designed to further the interests of justice and any consequence which would achieve a result contrary to those interests should be treated with considerable

[43] *Ibid.*, p. 160.

[44] *R v Soneji* [2005] UKHL 49. The Law Lords upheld confiscation orders.

[45] *London & Clydeside Estates Ltd v Aberdeen District Council* [1980] 1 WLR 182.

[46] *Ibid.* [14–15] [23].

[47] *R v Home Secretary, ex p. Jeyeanthan* [2000] 1 WLR 354. And see *Wang v Commissioner of Inland Revenue* [1994] 1 WLR and *Charles v Judicial Legal Service Commission* [2003] 1 LRC 422.

reservation.' Lord Woolf went on to prescribe a little decision-making chain. The question of mandatory or directory was only at most a first step; there are other, more important, questions to answer:

- *The substantial compliance question*: is the statutory requirement fulfilled if there has been substantial compliance with the requirement and, if so, has there been substantial compliance in the case in issue even though there has not been strict compliance?
- *The discretionary question*: is the non-compliance capable of being waived, and if so, has it, or can it and should it be waived in this particular case?
- *The consequences question*: if it is not capable of being waived or is not waived then what is the consequence of the non-compliance?

The procedural complaint failed. While (i) there was a major failure of compliance, (ii) the irregularity had effectively been waived; in any case (iii) it had not affected the applicants.

(c) Standard-bearer: Reasons

Intimately bound up with the quest for administrative rationality and legal control (see Chapter 3), and latterly with more rights-based approaches, the rise of reason-giving requirements is emblematic of the broader development. As regards statutory provision, the Franks Report on Tribunals and Inquiries was an important milestone, with reasoned decisions being seen as an essential part of the package of judicialisation (see Chapter 11). Typical however of the role of 'modest underworker', the courts' own contribution had been muted: there was no general duty to provide reasons for administrative decisions.[48] In 1971, JUSTICE went so far as to say that no single factor had inhibited the development of English administrative law as seriously as this.[49] In 1988, the same organisation expressed a need for statutory reform, on the basis that it was 'not . . . at all probable that the judges here will change their basic attitudes' and develop the obligation at common law.[50] Yet six years later, one commentator was able to identify 'a subtle but real shift in this area', while others spoke of 'a triumph of judicial expansionism'.[51] In fact, reason-giving requirements had begun to epitomise the concept of a 'multi-streamed jurisdiction' (see p. 98 above), with notably strong EU and ECHR prescriptions interacting with and partly overreaching the common law development,[52]

48 See e.g. *Minister of National Revenue v Wrights' Canadian Ropes* [1947] AC 109.

49 JUSTICE, *Administration under Law* (1971), p. 23.

50 JUSTICE–All Souls, *Administrative Justice: Some necessary reforms* (Clarendon, 1988), p. 72.

51 P. Craig, 'The common law, reasons and administrative justice' (1994) 53 *CLJ* 282, 301; R. Gordon and C. Barlow, 'Reasons for life: Solving the sphinx's riddle' (1993) 143 *NLJ* 1005, 1006.

52 P. Neill, 'The duty to give reasons: The openness of decision-making' in Forsyth and Hare (eds), *The Golden Metwand and the Crooked Cord* (Oxford University Press, 1998).

and the HRA then providing a further boost. Today, the situation increasingly resembles 'death by ink-spot', whereby growing 'exceptions' eventually overwhelm – reverse – the general 'rule'.[53] Attention is again directed to the standard of review: what does the judge think are sufficient reasons in the particular context?

Reasons for reasons are not difficult to identify:

- *administrative discipline*: encouraging careful deliberation and consistency
- *citizen interest*: satisfying a basic need for fair play
- *appeal/review*: facilitating checks for e.g. rationality and proportionality
- *public confidence or legitimacy*: promoting the sense of transparency.

Imposing a duty to give reasons can thus serve a mix of instrumentalist and non-instrumentalist rationales; as a principle of good administration, reason-giving is about both fire-watching (quality of initial decision-taking) and fire-fighting (administration under law) and also gives tangible expression to the idea of dignitary values.[54] In seeking so to promote a culture of justification however, the judges cannot ignore a battery of counter-arguments or caveats. 'The giving of reasons . . . may place an undue burden on decision-makers; demand an appearance of unanimity where there is diversity; call for the articulation of sometimes inexpressible value judgements; and offer an invitation to the captious to comb the reasons for previously unsuspected grounds of challenge.'[55] In terms of procedural fairness, this again suggests an important element of 'tailoring'. Alternatively, will judges resist the temptation of utilising the 'procedural veneer' of reason-giving requirements as 'an ideal cover' for substantive merits review?[56]

The absence of a common law duty to give reasons reflected and reinforced the culture of official secrecy which long characterised British government. Giving no explanation was for administrative decision-makers the safe option; a famous dictum referred to 'the inscrutable face of the sphinx'.[57] Conversely, the move to elaborate reason-giving as part of a more comprehensive doctrine of procedural fairness fits the wider constitutional development in favour of transparency signalled by the Official Secrets Act 1989 and – with the broad commitment to give reasons (see p. 471 above) – the 1993 Code on Access to Official Information. Today, this aspect is underpinned

[53] *Stefan v General Medical Council* [1999] 1 WLR 1293, 1301. Though see *R (Hassan) v Trade and Industry Secretary* [2008] EWCA Civ 1311.

[54] J. Mashaw, 'Small things like reasons are put in a jar: Reason and legitimacy in the administrative state' (2001) 70 *Fordham LR* 17; D. Dyzenhaus and M. Taggart, 'Reasoned decisions and legal theory' in Edlin (ed.), *Common Law Theory* (Cambridge University Press, 2007).

[55] *R v Higher Education Funding Council, ex p. Institute of Dental Surgery* [1994] 1 WLR 242 (Sedley J).

[56] The concern famously elaborated in the American administrative law context by M. Shapiro, 'The giving reasons requirement' [1992] *University of Chicago Legal Forum* 179.

[57] *R v Nat Bell Liquors* [1922] 2 AC 128 (Lord Sumner).

by s. 19 of the Freedom of Information Act (FOIA); in fulfillment of the duty to make a publication scheme, the public authority 'shall have regard to the public interest . . . in the publication of reasons for decisions made by the authority'. We would also stress the symbiotic quality of the jurisprudential development in the light of the HRA; proportionality-testing not only informed by, but also generating pressures for, reason-giving (see *Miss Behavin'*, p. 122 above).[58]

The place of reasons as a foundational treaty obligation in the Community legal system[59] constituted a standing rebuke to the common law. With the ECJ soon articulating its role as a vehicle of legal accountability and judicial protection,[60] and with the general principle subsequently applied to Member States in respect of fundamental Community rights,[61] nowhere was the scope for cross-fertilisation or jurisprudential 'spill-over' more obvious. Today, the EU Charter of Fundamental Rights rams home the message, with 'the obligation of the administration to give reasons for its decisions' incorporated in the Art. 41 right to good administration. The national judges, in other words, have had to run hard to keep abreast.

The step-change can be demonstrated by juxtaposing two cases a quarter of a century apart. In *Padfield* (see p. 101 above), the basis of the duty to give reasons was treated as 'little more than a symptom of irrationality',[62] the court being more likely to infer *Wednesbury* unreasonableness in the absence of explanation. This was only to happen if the circumstances pointed 'overwhelmingly' towards one exercise of discretion and no reasons for taking the contrary course were given.[63] *Padfield*, in other words, generated an incentive to give reasons but no free-standing or positive obligation. *R v Civil Service Appeal Board, ex p. Cunningham*[64] authoritatively established that, as part of the decision-making process, the giving of reasons was encompassed by procedural fairness. Castigating the refusal of reasons for an abnormally low compensation award for unfair dismissal, Lord Donaldson looked to the place of openness in buttressing a legal theory of 'control'. 'The Board should have given outline reasons sufficient to show to what they were directing their mind and thereby indirectly showing not whether their decision was right or wrong, which is a matter solely for them, but whether their decision was lawful. Any other conclusion would reduce the Board to the status of a free wheeling palm tree.' No right of appeal from the Board's determination was also viewed as an important factor grounding a reason-giving duty.

[58] See further Ch. 15 as regards disclosure of documents.
[59] TEU Art. 253.
[60] Case 24/62 *Germany v Commission* [1963] ECR 69.
[61] Case 222/86 *Heylens* [1987] ECR 4097.
[62] D. Toube, 'Requiring reasons at common law' (1997) 2 *Judicial Review* 68.
[63] *R v Trade Secretary, ex p. Lonrho plc* [1989] 1 WLR 525.
[64] [1991] 4 All ER 310.

The way was now open for the House in *Doody* to push the boundaries. Though not 'at present' amounting to a general duty, there was, in Lord Mustill's words, 'a perceptible trend towards an insistence on greater openness'. And in this instance the liberty interest was compelling:

> The giving of reasons may be inconvenient, but I can see no ground at all why it should be against the public interest: indeed, rather the reverse. This being so, I would ask simply: is refusal to give reasons fair? I would answer without hesitation that it is not . . . As soon as the jury returns its verdict the offender knows that he will be locked up for a very long time. For just how long immediately becomes the most important thing in the prisoner's life . . .
>
> It is not . . . questioned that the decision of the Home Secretary . . . is susceptible to judicial review. To mount an effective attack on the decision, given no more material than the facts of the offence and the length of the penal element, the prisoner has virtually no means of ascertaining whether this is an instance where the decision-making process has gone astray. I think it important that there should be an effective means of detecting the kind of error which would entitle the court to intervene, and in practice I regard it as necessary for this purpose that the reasoning of the Home Secretary should be disclosed.[65]

It was left to judges in later cases to tease out relevant factors. Deference was on show in the *HEFC* case.[66] A challenge to university research assessment grading for unfairness due to lack of reasons thus proved unsuccessful. Sedley J identified two classes of case founding the duty: (a) the 'Transaction type', where (as in *Doody*) 'the nature and impact of the decision itself call for reasons as a routine aspect of procedural fairness'; and (b) the 'Trigger factor', where 'the decision appears aberrant', namely – building on *Padfield* and *Cunningham* – there 'is something peculiar to the decision which in fairness calls for reasons to be given'. The element of academic judgement was viewed as negating (a), notwithstanding a loss of funding and reputational damage for the institution concerned; as also (b): 'we lack precisely the expertise which would permit us to judge whether it is extraordinary or not'. In contrast, in *ex p. Murray*[67] the Divisional Court rehearsed a classically protective or 'red light' view of judicial review: where the public body has power to affect individuals, the court would 'readily imply' a procedural safeguard such as reasons. An element of old-style analytical theory was also distilled from the cases, with the fact that a tribunal performs 'a judicial function' identified as another positive factor. The ruling opened up the system of court-martial to greater scrutiny; reasons should have been given for punishing a soldier with a term of imprisonment.

65 *R v Home Secretary, ex p. Doody* [18–19]

66 *R v Higher Education Funding Council, ex p. Institute of Dental Surgery* [1994] 1 WLR 242.

67 *R v Ministry of Defence, ex p. Murray* [1998] COD 134. See also *R v City of London Corporation, ex p. Matson* [1997] 1 WLR 765.

The difficult case of *Fayed*[68] dealt with the interplay of common law and statute. Given no prior notice of the minister's concerns, and no reasons for the decision, the Fayed brothers challenged the refusal to grant them citizenship. Government lawyers stood on s. 44(2) of the British Nationality Act 1981: 'the Secretary of State . . . shall not be required to assign any reason' for the relevant – discretionary – decision. Not surprisingly, the Court of Appeal considered that in the absence of this provision there would have been a clear case of procedural unfairness, more especially because of the damage to reputation. Equally, however, an express statutory prohibition on the requirement of reasons could not be overlooked. The majority ruling, that the duty to give notice could be differentiated, is further evidence of the momentum in favour of greater transparency in administrative decision taking (s. 44(2) was subsequently repealed):

> *Lord Woolf MR:* The suggestion that notice need not be given although this would be unfair involves attributing to Parliament an intention that it has not expressly stated. . . English law has long attached the greatest importance to the need for fairness to be observed prior to the exercise of a statutory discretion. However, English law, at least until recently, has not been so sensitive to the need for reasons to be given for a decision after it has been reached. So to exclude the need for fairness before a decision is reached because it might give an indication of what the reasons for the decision could be is to reverse the actual position. It involves frustrating the achievement of the more important objective of fairness in reaching a decision in an attempt to protect a lesser objective of possibly disclosing what will be the reasons for the decision.

But what exactly is entailed in the obligation to give reasons? Classic authority establishes that the reasons given must be proper, intelligible and adequate, dealing with the substantive points which have been made.[69] We learned, however, that a standard such as adequacy is flexible and susceptible to change over time. The dual dynamic of procedural fairness also is in play, with the pressures for variable intensity of review increasing as the coverage of the duty widens. Old arguments against reason-giving are apt to reappear as the rationale for tempering the obligation in the particular circumstances, not least when courts operate outside the familiar paradigm of individualised decision-making. The editors of *de Smith's Judicial Review* find it 'difficult to state precisely the standard of reasoning the court will demand.'[70]

The scope for judicial disagreement is well illustrated by *Save Britain's Heritage v Environment Secretary*.[71] A conservation group complained that the minister, in approving a major development in agreement with the inspector, had failed to indicate with due clarity and precision the extent to which

[68] *R v Home Secretary, ex p. Fayed* [1997] 1 All ER 228.

[69] *Re Poyser and Mills's Arbitration* [1963] 1 All ER 612.

[70] Woolf, Jowell and Le Seuer, *de Smith's Judicial Review of Administrative Action* [7-104].

[71] [1991] 2 All ER 10.

he adopted the inspector's reasoning. In the Court of Appeal, Woolf LJ took a strong contextual approach, tailoring the statutory duty according to 'the nature of the decision . . . the terms of the relevant legislation . . . the importance of the issue' and the need for expedition. His conclusion that the reasons were insufficient was overturned on appeal. Lord Bridge stressed the need to avoid a situation where the minister had 'to dot every i and cross every t', and called for 'a measure of benevolence' in the reading of decision letters.

Where the duty to give reasons is breached, the court can opt to make a mandatory order and/or take the further step of quashing the substantive decision.[72] But what is to happen when (fresh) reasons are adduced after the decision is challenged? This very practical issue cuts to the purpose of the duty, and hence to the basic role of the courts. An instrumentalist view might suggest a relaxed approach: the decision-maker has had the opportunity to reconsider, the decision is now explained, and all should be spared the time and trouble of rehashing the matter. A firm stress on legal control, and especially on promoting good quality decision-making in general, points in the opposite direction. The judges have predictably favoured a middle way, with 'retro-reasons' effectively being made the subject of anxious scrutiny. 'It is well established that the court should exercise caution' before accepting them; reasons put forward after the commencement of proceedings 'must be treated especially carefully'.[73] Is there, in short, 'a real risk' that the 'reasons' are a later invention? The pragmatic bent is manifest.

The case of *Wooder*[74] in 2002 confirms the sense of a continuing dynamic. In an important ruling for the treatment of mental healthcare patients, the Court of Appeal held that a decision forcibly to administer drugs to a competent non-consenting adult called for written explanation (unless this itself was likely to cause serious harm). Brooke LJ based his decision on a common law operating in the context of Convention rights. 'With the coming into force of the Human Rights Act 1998 the time has come . . . to declare that fairness requires that [such] a decision . . . should also be accompanied by reasons.' Sedley LJ went further, basing his decision both on the common law and on ECHR Art. 8. Such was the impact of the medical intervention that it came within the transaction type class of case previously identified in *HEFC*; indeed, *HEFC* was itself ripe for review as overly deferential. And this was an appropriate case in which to trumpet the affirmative concept of personal autonomy elaborated in the Strasbourg jurisprudence.[75] 'The patient is entitled, not as a matter of grace or of practice but as a matter of right, to know in useful form and at a relevant time what the . . . reasons are.'

72 See M. Fordham, *Judicial Review Handbook*, 5th edn (Hart, 2008), pp. 621–2.

73 *R (D) v Home Secretary* [2003] EWHC 155; *R (Nash) v Chelsea College of Art and Design* [2001] EWHC Admin 538. And see *R v Westminster City Council, ex p. Ermakov* [1996] 2 All ER 302.

74 *R (Wooder) v Feggetter* [2002] EWCA Civ 554.

75 See e.g. *Pretty v United Kingdom* (2002) 35 EHRR 1.

3. Pragmatism, rights and the Strasbourg effect

(a) A pragmatic view

Lord Mustill confirms that what fairness requires is 'essentially an intuitive judgement'.[76] A 'broad common sense approach' is one way of characterising much of the jurisprudence.[77] Alternatively, we might describe the rise of procedural fairness in general, and the *Soneji*-type development in particular, as a manifestation of pragmatism in the public law field. As a way of judicial review contributing more liberally to good governance, there is obvious merit in this.

But things may be taken to excess. Even with procedural review we cannot assume the existence of a simple command theory of law: that judges dictate and administrators and politicians obey. Their relationship is far more complex (a theme developed in Chapter 16). The potential of flexible forms of tailoring to obscure the teaching or hortatory function of law[78] should not be glossed over. As Clark has said, 'Natural justice is more than a means to an end (a right decision in individual cases) . . . The essential mission of the law in this field is to win acceptance by administrators of the principle.'[79] The open-ended nature of the reasoning is apt to give ministers and officials ample scope for 'interpretation', a phenomenon illustrated by *Smith and West* (see p. 641 below).

Greater flexibility in procedural review does not always favour the individual. *Jeyeanthan* (see p. 629 above) shows how judicial discretion may operate to whittle down legislative protection. In fact, as red light theories would suggest, a dose of rigidity may be no bad thing. In Lord Woolf's own words, the key argument in *Jeyeanthan* for declaring a nullity was 'to discipline the Secretary of State', so sending a clear message about administrative procedures and the element of judicial control. It would also be foolish to ignore the evident scope for judicial prejudices or favouring of particular social groups. There is a history of striking differences in, for example, the treatment of disciplinary cases involving students (light-touch or pro-authority) and trade union members ('hard look' or sturdy individualism).[80] As the cases involving national security further serve to illustrate, transaction typing need not only be about achieving the 'optimum' in administrative justice.

The rise of procedural fairness also invites consideration of the judicial function – as well as of the courts' own procedures. Are judges properly equipped to identify, assess and 'weigh' competing considerations? Are there not problems of legitimacy in terms of the courts' own adjudicative role and sense of separate identity? Writing in the 1970s on the consequences of adopting a

[76] *R v Home Secretary, ex p. Doody*, p. 168.

[77] P. Leyland and G. Anthony, *Administrative Law*, 6th edn (Oxford University Press, 2008), p. 340.

[78] P. S. Atiyah, *From Principles to Pragmatism* (Clarendon, 1978).

[79] D. Clark, 'Natural justice: Substance and shadow' [1975] *PL* 27, 58, 60.

[80] J. Griffith, *The Politics of the Judiciary*, 1st edn (Fontana, 1977).

highly flexible form of procedural review, Loughlin[81] foresaw a need to admit a wider range of evidence, for example through intervention procedures (see Chapter 16). Judges would have to mould the judicial process in the image of administration. This gives the later judicial embrace of dignitary theory in *Doody* added significance.

(b) Interplay

The interplay of common law procedural fairness with the right to a 'fair and public hearing . . . within a reasonable time' in ECHR Art. 6 naturally assumes greater prominence with the HRA. In terms of *audi alteram partem*[82] however, the civil limb of the Convention right has had only a modest effect.[83] Such is the logic of a powerful indigenous tradition coupled with 'a floor of rights'; of the national courts moving earlier as in *Doody* to minimise differences; and of a threshold unknown to the common law ('the determination of civil rights and obligations'). Efforts to stretch the jurisdiction have again engendered greater variability in the standard of review.

'The lawyers' human rights clause' self-evidently reflects and reinforces an adjudicative model. While ascribed an autonomous Convention meaning, the terminology of 'civil rights and obligations' is itself bound up with the concept of private law as used in civilian systems.[84] On the one hand, faced with growing demands for procedural protection especially in terms of 'the regulatory state', the ECtHR has gradually expanded the application of Art. 6 in cases of administrative decision-making. Is the outcome 'decisive' for private rights and obligations?[85] Licensing decisions furnish many examples.[86] On the other hand, the Court has continued to follow the French model in working a distinction between civil law and public law, with the result of key administrative law areas such as taxes and immigration and citizenship not being amenable to the jurisdiction.[87] Meanwhile, as shown in *Runa Begum* (see p. 663 below), where the Law Lords preferred to sidestep the issue of whether a refusal of

[81] M. Loughlin, 'Procedural fairness: A study of the crisis in administrative law theory' (1978) 28 *Univ. of Toronto LJ* 215.

[82] The structural impact in terms of 'independence and impartiality' is discussed in a later section. And see further, S. Juss, 'Constitutionalising rights without a constitution: The British experience under Article 6 of the Human Rights Act 1998' (2006) 27 *Stat. Law Rev.* 29.

[83] M. Westlake, 'Article 6 and common law fairness' (2006) 11 *Judicial Review* 57.

[84] See J. Herberg, A. Le Sueur and J. Mulcahy, 'Determining civil rights and obligations' in Jowell and Cooper (eds), *Understanding Human Rights Principles* (Hart, 2001). And see now, J. Beatson *et al.*, *Human Rights: Judicial protection in the United Kingdom* (Sweet & Maxwell, 2008), Ch. 6.

[85] *Ferrazzini v Italy* (2002) 34 EHRR 45. The development is traceable to *Ringeisen v Austria* (1979–80) 1 EHRR 455 and *König v Germany* (1979–80) 2 EHRR 170.

[86] See e.g. *TreTraktorer Aktiebolag v Sweden* (1989) 13 EHRR 308. For illustration in the domestic context, see *R (Chief Constable of Lancashire) v Preston Crown Court* [2001] EWHC Admin 928.

[87] See respectively, *Ferrazzini v Italy* (2002) 34 EHRR 45, and *Maaouia v France* (2001) 33 EHRR 1037.

temporary accommodation amounted to determination of a civil right, the position as regards many state benefits has remained obscure.[88]

Viewed from the perspective of the national administrative law system, there clearly is something of a parallel with the expansion of procedural fairness post-*Ridge v Baldwin*. But we note too how the innately flexible common law reaches parts that the codification in Art. 6 cannot reach, both in the case of adjudicative and (see below) non-adjudicative procedures. There would also have been an easier 'fit' with the national system had the relevant 'civil right' been identified as the right to have administrative decisions made lawfully, so vindicating the classic role of judicial review.[89] As we see in a later section, Strasbourg's approach has placed the supervisory jurisdiction itself under pressure.

As regards the substance of judicial protection, the domestic case law shows the relationship of the Convention right with common law requirements taking various forms. The extra potential of legislative review – ss. 3–4 HRA – must obviously be factored in. The control-order case *MB*, where the Law Lords used the civil limb of Art. 6 to enhance 'knowing the case against' in the face of the statute, illustrates the resulting 'added value' (see p. 133 above). Conversely, lesser-known cases demonstrating a rough equivalence are all around. *Adlard*[90] is a good example. The Court of Appeal could find 'no warrant, whether in domestic or in Strasbourg jurisprudence,' for concluding that a local planning authority had to afford objectors an oral hearing. Either way, the practicalities pointed firmly in the opposite direction. On other occasions, we see the Convention right boosting or at least underpinning the common law development. Take reason-giving.[91] With the HRA on the statute book, the Privy Council was soon emphasising that Art. 6(1) would require closer attention to be paid to the duty to give reasons.[92] Today, reversing *Cunningham* etc. is unthinkable.

Determination 'within a reasonable time' is an issue for separate consideration by the reviewing judge.[93] Strasbourg jurisprudence confirms the variable content of the duty, with reference to such factors as complexity of the matter and nature of the applicant's interest;[94] the threshold of proving a breach is generally high.[95] The recent case of *R(FH)*[96] shows the connection with rationality testing. Against the backdrop of huge pressures on the asylum system (see p. 28 above), a group of claimants complained of several years' delay in

[88] *Salesi v Italy* (1998) 26 EHRR 187; *Mennitto v Italy* (2000) 34 EHRR 1122. And see P. Craig, 'The Human Rights Act, Article 6 and procedural rights' [2003] *PL* 753.

[89] See to this effect, Lord Hoffman's speech in *R (Alconbury Developments Ltd) v Environment Secretary*.

[90] *R(Adlard) v Environment Secretary* [2002] 1 WLR 1515.

[91] For the importance which the ECtHR ascribes to reasons, see *Helle v Finland* (1998) 26 EHRR 159.

[92] In *Stefan v General Medical Council* [1999] 1 WLR 1293.

[93] See *Porter v Magill* [2002] AC 357.

[94] *Davies v United Kingdom* (2002) 35 EHRR 720.

[95] See e.g. *Procurator Fiscal, Linlithgow v Watson* [2004] 1 AC 379.

[96] *R(FH) v Home Secretary* [2007] EWHC 1571.

deciding their status as refugees. Accepting that it was implicit in the legislation that asylum claims would be dealt with within a reasonable time, Collins J in applying *Wednesbury* read across the restrictive Art. 6 jurisprudence. The challenge duly failed:

> If unacceptable delays have resulted, they cannot be excused by a claim that sufficient resources were not available. But in deciding whether the delays are unacceptable, the court must recognise that resources are not infinite and that it is for the defendant and not for the court to determine how those resources should be applied to fund the various matters for which he is responsible . . . It follows . . . that claims such as these based on delay are unlikely, save in very exceptional circumstances, to succeed and are likely to be regarded as unarguable. It is only if the delay is so excessive as to be regarded as manifestly unreasonable and to fall outside any proper application of the policy or if the claimant is suffering some particular detriment which the Home Office has failed to alleviate [97] that a claim might be entertained.

Article 6(1) is said by Strasbourg to incorporate the principle of 'equality of arms'; each party must have a reasonable opportunity to present a case in conditions that do not place him at a substantial disadvantage.[98] The acid test is legal representation. From the standpoint of administrative law, the 'added value' has been most apparent at the punitive end. The *Ezeh* litigation,[99] which now requires a more generous approach to that on offer at common law in *ex p. Hone* (see p. 628 above), is the best example. The ECtHR held that where, as in cases of assault, the prison disciplinary offence corresponds to a crime, and the possible sanction extends to further deprivation of liberty, this chief element of judicialisation must be permitted. The Prison Rules have been amended accordingly.[100] At the other end of the spectrum, demands for legal aid under the civil limb of Art. 6, the development has – for the obvious reasons – been thin indeed.[101] The planning cases again show the important role of transaction typing. Faced with vast arrays of lawyers and other specialists, it would have been strange if objectors at major public inquiries had not complained of inequality of arms on grounds of inadequate public funding for legal representation. But as the national courts have been keen to stress, we are back here with the element of inquisitorial procedure (see Chapter 13). *Pascoe*[102] is one in a series of cases rejecting such complaints:

97 See *SSHD v R(S)*, see p. 231 above.

98 *Dombo Beheer NV v Netherlands* (1994) 18 EHRR 213 is the leading case. See C. Harlow, 'Access to justice as a human right' in P. Alston (ed), *The EU and Human Rights* (Oxford University Press, 1999).

99 *Ezeh v UK* (2002) 35 EHRR 691; (2004) 39 EHRR 1. See also *Black v United Kingdom* (2007) 45 EHRR 25.

100 Prison (Amendment) Rules 2002, SI No. 2116.

101 The famous exception being *Steel and Morris v United Kingdom* (2005) 41 EHRR 403 ('the Mclibel trial'). See also *Airey v Ireland* (1979) 2 EHRR 305.

102 *Pascoe v First Secretary of State* [2007] 1 WLR 885. See also *R v Environment Secretary, ex p. Challenger* [2001] Env. LR 12 and *R (Hadfield) v SSTLGR* [2002] 26 EGCS 137.

> *Forbes J*: I accept that inquiry procedures are designed to be more user friendly and less complex than those found in the courtroom. Individuals are enabled to present their own cases, and inspectors will normally adjust the inquiry timetable to facilitate matters for those seeking to put their case . . . In fact, the claimant was much better placed than many litigants in person . . . because she benefited from a considerable amount of legal assistance and other support from witnesses and experts in an inquisitorial rather than an adversarial procedure.

(c) Test bed: Parole

In former times quintessential 'no-go' territory for the courts,[103] nowhere is the widening and deepening of procedural review made more evident than with prison administration in general,[104] and parole in particular. A notorious Court of Appeal decision in 1981 (later overruled in *Doody*), that the Parole Board need not give reasons for refusing to recommend early release, is a suitable benchmark for testing a sea-change in judicial attitudes to intervention. No advocate of transparency, Lord Denning reasoned curiously: 'I should think in the interests of the man himself – as a human being facing indefinite detention – it would be better for him to be told the reasons. But, in the interests of society as a whole at large – including the due administration of the parole system – it would be best not to give them.'[105]

The ECHR was a major driver – well ahead of the HRA. The key to this was the additional protection offered by Art. 5 and especially Art. 5(4). In *Weeks v United Kingdom*,[106] the ECtHR repudiated existing domestic procedures on the ground that the Board, whose sole power at the time was to make recommendations to the minister, was no court substitute. Nor was the fact of judicial review sufficient to remedy the inadequacy. A process of judicialisation was under way, featuring repeated court challenges. On the basis that it might then as 'a court' be Art. 5(4) compliant, the Board would progressively take on the responsibility for decisions on release – at the expense of the minister. The ECtHR rammed home the message in *Stafford*.[107] 'With the wider recognition of the need to develop and apply, in relation to mandatory life prisoners, judicial procedures reflecting standards of independence, fairness and openness, the continuing role of the Secretary of State . . . has become increasingly

[103] With legal accountability being considered fatal to discipline: *Arbon v Anderson* [1943] KB 252.

[104] For the rise of the common law in this context, see successively *R v Board of Visitors of Hull Prison, ex p. St Germain* [1979] QB 425, *Raymond v Honey* [1982] 2 WLR 465, and *Leech v Deputy Governor of Parkhurst Prison* [1988] AC 533. *Daly* signals the immediate impact of the HRA (see p. 118 above).

[105] *Payne v Lord Harris of Greenwich* [1981] 1 WLR 754.

[106] (1987) 10 EHRR 293. See also *Thynne, Wilson and Gunnell v* United Kingdom (1990) 13 EHRR 666, a broader ruling.

[107] *Stafford v United Kingdom* (2002) 35 EHRR 1121, so blurring the distinction previously made between discretionary and mandatory life sentences (see *Wynne v United Kingdom* (1994) 19 EHRR 333).

difficult to reconcile with the notion of separation of powers.' The scene was set for *Anderson*,[108] where the House of Lords declared the relevant statutory provision[109] empowering the minister incompatible with Art. 6.

Turning to the Board's own procedures, a pair of House of Lords cases in 2005 gives a convenient test of temperatures. *Smith and West*[110] raised the question of an oral hearing for prisoners released on licence but then recalled because of concerns about their behaviour. By now making thousands of recall decisions each year, the Board vigorously defended a policy of written representations in the vast majority of cases. The Court of Appeal held that fairness only required oral hearings in respect of disputed primary facts; the Board's assessment of risk to the public was something else. Focusing more on the deprivation of liberty, namely on the nature and impact of the decision for the individual, the House of Lords reversed. The leading speech of Lord Bingham demonstrates the particular strength of procedural fairness in the adjudicative-type situation; and, further, the particular attachment in the Anglo-American tradition to oral hearings:

> The common law duty of procedural fairness does not, in my opinion, require the Board to hold an oral hearing in every case where a determinate sentence prisoner resists recall, if he does not decline the offer of such a hearing. But I do not think the duty is as constricted as has hitherto been held and assumed. Even if important facts are not in dispute, they may be open to explanation or mitigation, or may lose some of their significance in the light of other new facts. While the Board's task certainly is to assess risk, it may well be greatly assisted in discharging it (one way or the other) by exposure to the prisoner or the questioning of those who have dealt with him. It may often be very difficult to address effective representations without knowing the points which are troubling the decision-maker. The prisoner should have the benefit of a procedure which fairly reflects, on the facts of his particular case, the importance of what is at stake for him, as for society.[111]

Showing the possibilities for both overlapping and differential forms of judicial protection, the case powerfully illustrates the complex interplay of common law with Convention rights. The claim for an oral hearing under Art. 5(4) also succeeded, on the basis that the revocation of the licence was a new deprivation of liberty. Procedural fairness, Lord Hope explained, 'is built into the Convention requirement because Article 5(4) requires that the continuing detention must be judicially supervised and because our own domestic law requires that bodies acting judicially . . . must conduct their proceedings in a way that is procedurally fair'. On the other hand, a challenge under the criminal limb of Art. 6 failed; though the prisoner might beg to differ, there was

108 *R (Anderson) v Home Secretary* [2002] UKHL 46; though see, as regards determinate sentence prisoners, *R (Black) v Secretary of State for Justice* [2009] UKHL 1.

109 S. 29 of the Crime (Sentences) Act 1997, repealed by the Criminal Justice Act 2003.

110 *R (Smith and West) v Parole Board* [2005] UKHL 1.

111 *Ibid.* [35]. Lord Bingham referred specifically to *Goldberg v Kelly* (1970) 397 US 254.

found to be no sufficient element of punishment and so no 'criminal charge'. The question whether, alternatively, there was a determination of 'civil rights and obligations' elicited no clear conclusion; even if founded, the majority did not think the prisoners would gain any greater protection. Noting that some determinations do not fall within either limb of Art. 6, Lord Bingham effectively underlined the continuing importance of the flexible common law approach.

Lord Hope's speech in *Smith and West* demonstrates another aspect of judicial assertiveness, the use of procedural review to specify administrative procedures:

> The common law test of procedural fairness requires that the Board re-examine its approach. A screening system needs to be put in place which identifies those cases where the prisoner seeks to challenge the truth or accuracy of the allegations that led to his recall, or seeks to provide an explanation for them which was not taken into account or was disputed when his recall was recommended by his supervising probation officer. Consideration then needs to be given to the question whether it is necessary to resolve these issues before a final decision is made as to whether or not the prisoner is suitable for release. If it is, an oral hearing should be the norm rather than the exception.[112]

The aftermath is instructive. The Board initially adopted the practice of granting an oral hearing to any recalled prisoner who requested one following an initial decision on the papers. However, an internal review two years later led to a substantial tightening of policy. The Law Lords' ruling was effectively 'read down' and procedural discretion reasserted:

> It appears that in many cases the hearing has not been used in order to challenge the recall decision at all and has turned out not to add anything to the information that had been before us on paper. In our view that was not what the House of Lords intended to happen . . . We have taken legal advice and the Board is now in a position to implement the judgment more strictly . . . With immediate effect, therefore, the Board will require reasons from the prisoner when applying for an oral hearing. These will be considered on a case by case basis and an oral hearing will not be granted simply because the prisoner asks for one. Applications will be granted only where it appears to the Board that a hearing is necessary and falls within the ambit of the House of Lords' ruling.[113]

The second case – *Roberts*[114] – concerned the adoption of special-advocate procedure (see p. 129 above) in a new situation. For the purpose of deciding whether to grant a life-sentence prisoner release on licence, the Board had taken the view that if relevant materials were disclosed to the claimant or his

[112] *Ibid.* [68].

[113] Parole Board, *Change of policy on granting oral hearings in Smith and West cases* (February 2007).

[114] *Roberts v Parole Board* [2005] 2 AC 738.

legal representatives the informant(s) would be put at risk. R duly complained that this prejudiced his right to be heard. Whereas in the control order cases the antiterrorism legislation expressly contemplated special advocate procedure, the relevant statute referred in the usual way to the Board taking steps 'incidental to or conducive to the discharge of its functions'.[115] The House held, 3–2, that the Board was acting within its powers and in principle fairly.[116]

The minority (Lords Bingham and Steyn) fastened on the constitutional dimension. In judging the matter in hand, the court had to consider the broader interests at stake; it should stand firm and perform the twin judicial roles of protecting basic rights and buttressing the democratic process. Familiar from *Simms* (see p. 119 above), the common law principle of legality lay conveniently to hand:

> *Lord Steyn:* It is not to the point to say that the special advocate procedure is 'better than nothing'. Taken as a whole, the procedure completely lacks the essential characteristics of a fair hearing. It is important not to pussyfoot about such a fundamental matter: the special advocate procedure undermines the very essence of elementary justice. It involves a phantom hearing only . . .
>
> If the words of the statute do not authorise the power which the Board exercised, the decision is ultra vires. In examining this question the starting point is that the persuasive burden rests on the Parole Board to demonstrate that its departure from ordinary fair procedures is authorised by the statute . . . Parliament has never been given the opportunity to consider the matter . . . If the decision of the Parole Board is upheld in the present case, it may well augur an open-ended process of piling exception upon exception by judicial decision outflanking Parliamentary scrutiny . . . If such departures are to be introduced it must be done by Parliament. It would be quite wrong to make an assumption that, if Parliament had been faced with the question whether it should authorise, in this particular field, the special advocate procedure, it would have sanctioned it. After all, in our system the working assumption is that Parliament legislates for a European liberal democracy which respects fundamental rights . . . The outcome of this case is deeply austere. It encroaches on the prerogatives of the legislature in our system of Parliamentary democracy. It is contrary to the rule of law.[117]

The majority (Lords Woolf, Rodger and Carswell) stressed the legislative expectation that the Board would make, in Lord Woolf's words, 'a practical judgement'. 'In determining the point of principle we are asked to decide, we cannot ignore the reality of certain criminal activity today.' Giving the case a utilitarian twist, the talk was of balancing 'a triangulation of interests' involving the prisoner, the public and the informant, and giving preponderant weight to protection of the public. Whatever Lord Steyn might say, special-advocates

[115] Criminal Justice Act 1991, Sch. 5 [1(2)(b)].

[116] A further challenge based on Art. 5(4) failed on the basis that until the Board's review was complete it was premature. For the sequel, see *R (Roberts) v Parole Board* [2008] EWHC 2714.

[117] *Roberts v Parole Board* [2005] 2AC 738 [88–9] [92–3] [97].

procedure was indeed a glass half-full: the Board had sought an acceptable compromise in exceptional circumstances. Lord Rodger raised the inevitable question: 'what is the alternative?'[118]

> One solution would be to disclose the information to the prisoner's representative and, if possible, to require the informant to give evidence, even though this would risk putting his life or health in jeopardy. That solution would be, to say the least, unattractive and might well give rise to significant issues under Articles 2 and 3 of the European Convention. The other solution would be for the Board to exclude from their consideration any evidence which could not be safely disclosed to the prisoner or his representative. In other words, the Board should close their eyes to evidence, even though it would be relevant to the decision which Parliament has charged them to take for the protection of the public. That solution too would be – again, to say the least – unattractive and, moreover, hard to reconcile with the Board's statutory duty not to direct a prisoner's release on licence unless they are satisfied that it is no longer in the interests of the public that he should be confined.

The *Roberts* case serves to expose underlying tensions in the contemporary model of procedural review. As represented by the majority and minority speeches respectively, the strong pragmatic strand in the common law development is not always reconcilable with a rights-centred view. The unusually strident tone of the judicial disagreement is telling.

4. Broader horizons

Viewed in terms of the transaction-type, *Ridge v Baldwin* was an easy case. What could be more natural than a dollop of adjudicative-style procedural justice in individual disciplinary proceedings? As the student of law and administration well knows however, there are many other forms of decision-making which present differently. The courts must grapple with the question of how far it is appropriate to read across elements of the adjudicatory model in which they are steeped. Predicated on the idea of the flexible rubric of 'procedural fairness' importing a qualitatively as well as a quantitatively different potential for the shaping of the administrative process, there is however the further question of a judicial role in elucidating other species of procedural requirement.

The change from analytical theory to procedural fairness could, after all, be read in different ways. On a narrower interpretation, the expansion of procedural protection did not mark a fundamental change in the nature of natural justice. So, as in the previous section, the working assumption would be that procedural fairness denotes the rendition of adjudicative-style restraint. A more radical interpretation was that abandonment of the 'judicial', 'quasi-judicial', 'administrative' classification ultimately freed the courts not only to discard discredited limitations on the area of review, but also to develop a new agenda of procedural choices no longer confined within a single framework of

[118] *Ibid.* [111].

social ordering. This view echoed classic green light theory in inviting administrative lawyers to question the ideal type of adjudication and to seek out alternative methods of administration (see Chapter 1), but contrariwise assigned the judges a pivotal position in moulding the decision-making process: in effect, 'hands on', not 'hands off'. As envisioned by MacDonald, the banner of 'fairness' stood for 'participation in decision-making'. Rather than ask what aspects of adjudicative procedures can be grafted onto this decisional process, the reviewing court should ask an alternative series of questions. 'What is the nature of the process here undertaken?' 'What mode of participation by affected parties is envisaged by such a decisional process?' 'What specific procedural guidelines are necessary to ensure the efficacy of that participation and the integrity of the process under review?'[119]

The model that English courts seem currently to be elaborating (though 'groping towards' would be a fairer description) is a cautious compromise position. An active 'informalist' mode of judicial supervision – namely, close evaluation of procedures other than against the 'formal' ideal-type of adjudication – is rightly seen as heady stuff, immediately bringing into question the courts' own competency and legitimacy. Conversely, the idea that courts not only mould the administration in their own image but also otherwise desist from fashioning process looks increasingly out of place amid stronger demands for legal accountability and transparency. Then again, the fact of a more difficult terrain impels a more circumspect – deferential – approach in the standard of review to the extent that the notion of procedural fairness can appear largely symbolic. Let us consider two sets of examples.

(a) Competitions

The need to compare applications in competitive situations inevitably causes difficulties in terms of procedural fairness. As illustrated previously with government contract (see Chapter 8), the courts will in the name of even-handedness give some protection to the individual *qua* individual, for example a proper opportunity to put a case.[120] We also know from *Camelot* (see p. 398 above) that the common law notion of a level playing field stretches to a franchisor not moving the goal posts. But what is the scope for procedural review directed to the process of comparison itself? EU law gives us one set of answers in the case of public procurement (see p. 383 above); formal competitions for scarce public resources or government largesse come however in all shapes and sizes.

A clue to the significance of *R (Asha Foundation) v Millennium Commission*[121] is its inclusion as one of the few cases summarised for civil servants in *Judge*

[119] R. MacDonald, 'Judicial review and procedural fairness in administrative Law' (1981) 26 *McGill LJ* 1, 19.

[120] A. Denny, 'Procedural fairness in competitions' (2003) 8 *Judicial Review* 228.

[121] [2003] EWCA Civ 88.

Over Your Shoulder.[122] A charitable organisation had applied unsuccessfully for a grant of £10 million from a lottery fund budget of £19 million. The reason given was truly boilerplate in character: 'Your application was less attractive than others.' It was later confirmed that Asha had been considered eligible for a grant but that the competition was substantially oversubscribed with eligible applicants. The Commission 'had formed its view as to the comparative merits of each eligible project', applying such criteria as degree of public benefit and long-term financial viability, as well as 'the geographical and culture equity' of grant distribution. Unimpressed, Asha sought 'meaningful reasons'; seeking to conjure a legitimate expectation to this effect, counsel duly reminded the court that it was otherwise impossible to tell whether or not the Commission had misdirected itself. Refusing the demand, Lord Woolf fastened on the complex, judgemental nature of the agency's role. Whereas a decision based on threshold criteria or a particular issue of fact would require specifics, the Commission's general explanation was suitably tailored to the context:

> When the Commission is engaged in assessing the qualities of the different applications . . . in competition with each other, the difficulties which would be involved in giving detailed reasons become clear. First, the preference for a particular application may not be the same in the case of each commissioner. Secondly, in order to evaluate any reasons that are given for preferring one application to another, the full nature and detail of both applications has to be known . . . The Commission would have had to set out in detail each commissioner's views in relation to each of the applications and to provide the background material to Asha so that they could assess whether those conclusions were appropriate. This would be an undue burden upon any commission. It would make their task almost impossible. It certainly would be in my judgment impracticable as a matter of good administration.

Even this is an oversimplification. As a distributing body, the Commission had effectively been tasked to make a whole series of mini-decisions about the contrasting merits of multiple applications and to produce a final package of decisions to budget. As against the classic template of bipolar, adversarial adjudication, this decisional process was inherently dynamic and polycentric in character (see p. 125 above): an aspect underscored by the sizeable knock-on effects on other applications of a grant to Asha. Viewed in this perspective, the idea of reconstructing the reasoning process for the particular application appears artificial. In determining the standard of reasons required, the judges must also look to the interests of third parties. The demand for 'meaningful reasons' in competitions sounds well, but what of requirements of commercial confidentiality or, as in the case of university admissions for example, of privacy?

Matters were recently taken a stage further in *Abbey Mine*.[123] The Coal Authority, a statutory agency, had preferred another company's application

[122] TSol, *Judge Over Your Shoulder* [2.65]

[123] *Abbey Mine Ltd v Coal Authority* [2008] EWCA Civ 353.

for a local mining concession, a decision confirmed following a review hearing held at Abbey Mine's request. Counsel argued that Abbey Mine should have been given details of the rival bid – edited if necessary to exclude commercially sensitive information – ahead of the review hearing. The Court of Appeal would have none of it. Reiterating the strong contextual character of procedural fairness, Laws LJ carefully defined the transaction type: 'rival applications for a licence to undertake a commercial venture'. Echoing *Asha*, it was appropriate in such cases to distinguish between a right to know of perceived difficulties with one's own case and a right to know about the competition:

> All the competitors are in the same boat. It would be obviously unfair if one applicant saw his opponent's bid, but the opponent did not see his. But if every applicant (there may sometimes, no doubt, be more than two) saw every other's bid, and was entitled to comment and challenge and criticise, the resulting prolongation and complexity of the decision-making process can scarcely be exaggerated . . . There is no question of sacrificing fairness to administrative convenience. The duty of fairness always takes its place in a practical setting.

In truth, the 'weighing' exercise pointed inexorably in this direction. Why would the notion of 'a level playing field' extend to being told the opposition's game plan?

(b) Consultations

The issue of public consultation, and in particular the judicial role in installing and elaborating relevant procedures, is a familiar battleground in administrative law. As well as formal rule-making process, local and community concerns feature prominently in the cases – charges for day-care perhaps, or the closure of a specialist hospital unit, or even the siting of a pedestrian crossing. At the other end of the scale, think on a huge reservoir for procedural challenge: the 70,000 consultation responses recently generated by plans for a third runway at Heathrow airport. As noted in Chapter 4, the courts' demands remain comparatively muted when set against those made in individual, adjudicative contexts. Together with the use of legitimate expectation to found a duty of consultation (*GCHQ* – see p. 107 above), enhanced statutory requirements, especially as with environmental law under EU tutelage, have given a modest if tangible development some additional impetus.

Bushell's case in 1980 is a key reference point (see p. 585 above). It illustrates how the dominant adjudicative framework of procedural review can operate in a subtle way to close off other procedural choices. Cross-examination of the department's witnesses on its traffic predictions being deemed inappropriate, no other procedural protection was imposed. A broader interpretation of 'fairness' would have meant a duty of consultation to provide objectors with an opportunity of involvement without depriving the minister of the decision-making power. In fact, the House rejected a further procedural challenge, that by following revised methods of traffic calculation after the inquiry the minister took into account new evidence not disclosed to the objectors. As against a requirement to re-consult, Lord Diplock held that procedural fairness stopped at the door of the ministry:

> What is fair procedure is to be judged . . . in the light of the practical realities as to the way in which administrative decisions involving forming judgments based on technical considerations are reached . . . Discretion in making administrative decisions is conferred upon a minister not as an individual but as the holder of an office . . . The collective knowledge, technical as well as factual, of the civil servants in the department and their collective expertise is to be treated as the minister's own knowledge, his own expertise . . . This is an integral part of the decision-making process itself; it is not to be equiparated with the minister receiving evidence, expert opinion or advice from sources outside the department after the local inquiry has been closed . . . Once he has reached his decision he must be prepared to disclose his reasons . . . but he is . . . under no obligation to disclose to objectors and give them an opportunity of commenting on advice, expert or otherwise, which he receives from his department in the course of making up his mind.[124]

In the years following *GCHQ*, the courts began to make increasing forays into the area of consultations. The *Association of Metropolitan Authorities* case[125] illustrates the potential for intra-state litigation founded on the poor treatment of official stakeholders. A bland and tardy consultation letter addressed to the Association of Metropolitan Authorities (AMA) failed to satisfy mandatory procedural requirements for the making of new regulations. A well-known example of intervention on behalf of affected interests is the *British Coal* case,[126] where mass closures of collieries were suspended pending proper consultation under an established review procedure. Reflecting more pluralist ideas, the Court of Appeal reasoned that this alone could allow a discussion of policy issues (not that the Thatcher government was about to be deflected!). More recently, the judges have demanded better consultation in an ever-more diverse range of topics: from funding for the voluntary sector to tax on business, and on through public services and contracting out[127] to – in the *Eisai* case (see p. 314 above) – product regulation. Showing the potential of procedural fairness in mass consultations, the *Greenpeace* case (see p. 177 above) represents the high-water mark in this development.

So far, it may be said, but not so far. The *Bapio* case (see p. 176 above) can be seen now standing four-square against the model of active 'informalist' review.

[124] *Bushell v Environment Secretary* [1981] AC 75, 95–6, 102.. See also *R (Alconbury Developments Ltd) v Environment Secretary* [2003] 2 AC 295.

[125] *R v Social Services Secretary, ex p. Association of Metropolitan Authorities* [1986] 1 WLR 1.

[126] *R v British Coal Corp, ex p. Vardy* [1993] ICR 720.

[127] See respectively, *R (Capenhurst) v Leicester City Council* [2004] EWHC 2124, *R v British Waterways Board v First Secretary of State* [2006] EWHC 1019, and *R (Smith) v North Eastern Derbyshire Primary Care Trust* [2006] EWCA Civ 1019.

In warming to the constitutional argument against a freewheeling judicial role of shaping participative arrangements 'function by function', Sedley LJ looked to some practical reasons 'for being cautious' (to which must be added administrative efficiency and governmental effectiveness):

> It is not unthinkable that the common law could recognise a general duty of consultation in relation to proposed measures which are going to adversely affect an identifiable interest group or sector of society. But what are its implications? The appellants have not been able to propose any limit to the generality of the duty. Their case must hold good for all such measures, of which the state at national and local level introduces certainly hundreds, possibly thousands, every year. If made good, such a duty would bring a host of litigable issues in its train: is the measure one which is actually going to injure particular interests sufficiently for fairness to require consultation? If so, who is entitled to be consulted? Are there interests which ought *not* to be consulted? How is the exercise to be publicised and conducted? Are the questions fairly framed? Have the responses been conscientiously taken into account? The consequent industry of legal challenges would generate in its turn defensive forms of public administration.

Suppose that a duty of consultation is grounded; officials need to know what it entails. JOYS faithfully summarises a set of criteria approved by Lord Woolf in *ex p. Coughlan* (see p. 224 above):

> Where consultation is undertaken, whether or not it is strictly required, it has to be conducted properly, if it is to satisfy the requirement for procedural fairness. Four conditions have to be satisfied:
>
> - Consultation must be undertaken when proposals are still at a *formative stage*
> - Sufficient *explanation* for each proposal must be given, so that those consulted can consider them intelligently and respond
> - Adequate *time* needs to be given for the consultation process
> - Consultees' responses must be conscientiously *taken into account* when the ultimate decision is taken.
>
> Again, when you have consulted before making a decision and have given proper weight to the representations received, you will need to make it clear in your decision that you have done so. This does not mean that you have to recite all representations word for word, but you will have to show that you have grasped the points being made and taken them into account.[128]

Especially if read in tandem with the Cabinet Office code of practice (see p. 172 above), this suggests a more generous spirit, indicating a brighter future for the exercise of individual and collective 'voice'. Words like 'sufficient' and

[128] TSol, *Judge Over Your Shoulder* [2.45]. The criteria were originally set out in *R v Brent LBC, ex p. Gunning* (1985) 84 LGR 168.

'conscientiously' also serve, however, to point up the considerable challenges involved in teasing out and policing the appropriate standard. Even the editors of *de Smith's Judicial Review* have their doubts. 'Where consultations are invited upon detailed proposals which have already been arrived at, the duty of the court to ensure that genuine consideration has been given to critical representations is taxed to the utmost.'[129]

Decided cases show a strong dose of pragmatism, so emphasising the variable nature of the obligation. In determining how extensive the public involvement should be, the court may look for example to how far in the 'formative stage' planning and policy development has reached, and/or the wide implications or otherwise of the project.[130] *Coughlan* serves to underscore the importance of the particular judge's 'feel' for the case. Did the conduct of the local consultation found an alternative basis for resisting closure of the home? Hidden J was in unforgiving mood. Adopting the 'hard-look' approach, the judge replayed the process, seizing on specific items such as late notice of professional advice. Viewing matters more in the round, Lord Woolf thought differently:

> It has to be remembered that consultation is not litigation: the consulting authority is not required to publicise every submission it receives or (absent some statutory obligation) to disclose all its advice. Its obligation is to let those who have a potential interest in the subject matter know in clear terms what the proposal is and exactly why it is under positive consideration, telling them enough (which may be a good deal) to enable them to make an intelligent response. The obligation, although it may be quite onerous, goes no further than this . . . Although there are criticisms to be levelled at the consultation process [it] was not unlawful.

The courts' discretionary control over remedies in judicial review (see Chapter 16) must also be factored in. The very nature of the procedural demand renders it a prime candidate for denial of a remedy even where there is breach of a mandatory requirement. *Ex p Walters*,[131] which concerned the disposal of local authority housing stock, bears testimony to the role of competing considerations. The Court of Appeal rejected the suggestion that unfairness in the consultation led inevitably to the consequence that the procedure should be restarted and the scheme reconsidered:

> *Judge LJ*: It is not irrelevant for the Court to consider what the consultation process required in the particular case and its purpose, what those entitled to be consulted actually understood, and whether compliance . . . would in fact have had any significant impact on them and the decision . . . Where . . . there is overwhelming evidence that . . . judicial review

[129] Woolf, Jowell and Le Sueur, *de Smith's Judicial Review of Administrative Action*, p. 388.

[130] See e.g. *R (Fudge) v South West Strategic Health Authority* [2007] EWCA Civ 803, and *R (Wainwright) v Richmond LBC* [2001] EWCA Civ 2062, respectively.

[131] *R v Brent LBC, ex p. Walters* [1998] 30 HLR 328. The *AMA* case (see n 125 above) provides another example.

> . . . will certainly damage the interests of a large number of other individuals who have welcomed the proposals, and acted on the basis that they will be implemented, it would be absurd for the Court to ignore . . . the relevant 'disbenefits'.

The major environmental protection case of *Edwards*[132] gives a litmus test of current judicial attitudes. Notwithstanding the fears of local campaigners about increased levels of pollution, the Environment Agency had granted a permit for new processes at a cement plant. Predictably in this field,[133] the subsequent judicial review litigation raised points both of EU and domestic law. The broad thrust of the argument was that the Agency did not disclose enough information about the environmental impact of the plant to satisfy its statutory and common law duties of public consultation. Particular objection was taken to the fact that the agency had commissioned, but not released until after the public consultation, a report on likely effects on air quality from an in-house group of scientific experts. The House rejected complaints of breach of the relevant EU directive; the information supplied met the basic requirements of environmental impact assessment.[134] 'Gold-plated' implementing regulations,[135] which extended environmental protection measures to existing plants, proved trickier. A statutory duty to maintain a public register of relevant particulars was held not to preclude the informal garnering of information. 'In a complicated application, one would expect the Agency officials to have discussions with the applicant about matters of concern. It would be extremely inhibiting if the Agency ran the risk that its decision would be vitiated.'[136] From the standpoint of citizen participation however, is this not the slippery slope of 'therapy' and 'manipulation' (see p. 173 above)? Dissenting, Lord Mance spoke tartly of 'a remarkable lacuna'.

Evincing a greater spirit of openness, the lower courts sought in applying the common law to sidestep *Bushell.* Auld LJ explained that if, following public consultation, a decision-maker became aware of 'some internal material or a factor of potential significance to the decision to be made, fairness may demand that the . . . parties concerned should be given an opportunity to deal with it'. This was such a case: breaking new ground, the scientific predictions raised matters 'of which interested members of the public were unaware and might well fail to examine for themselves'.[137] In contrast, Lord Hoffman preached judicial restraint. This was not a case where the un-codified common law principles were needed - in the famous phrase – to 'supply the omission

[132] *R (Edwards) v Environment Agency* [2008] UKHL 22.

[133] R. Macrory, 'Environmental public law and judicial review' (2008) 13 *Judicial Review* 115.

[134] Arising under Council Directive 85/337/EEC on the assessment of the effects of certain public and private projects on the environment.

[135] Pollution Prevention and Control (England and Wales) Regulations 2000, SI No. 1973.

[136] R *(Edwards) v Environment Agency* [2008] UKHL 22 [42] (Lord Hoffman). We touch here on a whole history of planning cases centred on informal methods of communication, most famously *Errington v Minister of Health* [1935] 1 KB 249. And see above, Ch. 13.

[137] *R (Edwards) v Environment Agency* [2006] EWCA Civ 877 [103] [105].

of the legislature'.[138] Quite the reverse: 'when the whole question of public involvement has been considered and dealt with in detail by the legislature, I do not think it is for the courts to impose a broader duty'.[139] 'If the agency has to disclose its internal working documents for further public consultation, there is no reason why the process should ever come to an end.'

The judges all agreed however on another way of skinning the cat. Even if there was a procedural deficiency, a dose of pragmatism should be administered at the remedial stage. By the time the case was heard, monitoring of the pollution levels had confirmed the agency's predictions. Lord Hoffman thought it 'pointless to quash the permit simply to enable the public to be consulted on out-of-date data'. The court had also to factor in 'the waste of time and resources, both for the company and the agency, of going through another process of application, consultation and decision'. The Rule of Law, in other words, had been overtaken by events.

5. Insider dealings

The rule against *bias*, JOYS explains patiently, 'helps to ensure that the decision-making process is not a sham because the decision-maker's mind was always closed to the opposing case'.[140] Raising the functional issue of *impartiality*, there may be concerns about the approach of a particular body or individual – personal prejudice perhaps, or a conflict of interest. Consistent with the rationale for procedural fairness of maintaining public confidence, the courts will typically be testing here for the appearance of bias (and not actual bias – hard to prove). As noted in Chapter 11, the *independence* of the decision-maker from external pressure or influence is a different but closely related question, which concerns the structural or institutional framework.[141] Bound up with the theory of separation of powers,[142] this is classically conceived of in terms of the courts themselves,[143] and thence, in accordance with the adjudicative model of reasoned proofs and arguments, the tribunal system. JOYS happily informs its readers of the polar opposite: 'civil servants appointed to carry out Government policy . . . can scarcely be "independent" in this sense'.[144]

It was the impartiality aspect that featured prominently at common law (*nemo iudex in sua causa*). Establishing a rule that the person who adjudicates

138 Byles J, in *Cooper v Wandsworth Board of Works* (1863) 14 CBNS 180.
139 *Furnell v Whangarei Schools Board* [1973] 2 WLR 92 is the classic authority.
140 TSol, *Judge Over Your Shoulder* [2.47].
141 For the Strasbourg perspective, see *Findlay v United Kingdom* (1997) 24 EHRR 221.
142 R. Masterman, 'Determinative in the abstract? Article 6(1) and the separation of powers' (2005) *EHRLR* 629.
143 *McGonnell v United Kingdom* [2000] 30 EHRR 289. And see Sir D. Williams, 'Bias, the judges and the separation of powers' [2000] *PL* 45.
144 TSol, *Judge Over Your Shoulder* [2.50]. There are also general exceptions to the no bias rule on grounds of waiver and of necessity (no other decision-maker available) (but see *Kingsley v United Kingdom* (2001) 33 EHRR 288).

must have no pecuniary interest in the matter, such that a decision by the Lord Chancellor was set aside, the mid-Victorian case of *Dimes v Grand Junction Canal Proprietors*[145] is suitably hallowed authority. In contrast, reflecting a more pragmatic attitude to the design of institutional settings, the notion of independent adjudication as proclaimed in the Art. 6 Convention right had hitherto received little attention.[146] The HRA duly produced a flurry of activity, not only statutory, as in the case of certain tribunal structures,[147] but also in the domestic jurisprudence. Lord Steyn would soon be claiming 'no difference between the common law test of bias and the requirement under Art. 6 of the Convention of an independent and impartial tribunal'.[148]

The development is again shot through with judicial discretion in the form of transaction typing and variable intensity of review. Questions of institutional competence move centre-stage as the national courts are invited to engage in novel forms of what may be labelled 'structural procedural review'. A pragmatic or cautious accommodation of the Strasbourg jurisprudence, especially as regards judicialisation, is a fair description of much in the case law. Let us look more closely.

(a) Testing times

As a way of promoting the good governance value of integrity, cracking down on apparent bias by invalidating the decision sounds well. But over the years much ink has been spilt on the precise nature of the common law test. Giving 'justice must be seen to be done' paramountcy, the low threshold of 'reasonable suspicion' competed with 'real likelihood' (more respectful of local knowledge and legal certainty).[149] And through whose eyes was the matter to be judged? The ubiquitous 'reasonable man' perhaps?[150] The House eventually moved in the early 1990s to standardise in the criminal law case of *R v Gough*.[151] The court, conveniently considered by Lord Goff to personify the 'reasonable man', should think in terms of 'real danger' – a real possibility (though not the probability) of bias.

Testimony to the broad currents of judicial 'dialogue' in a shrinking world, the Law Lords immediately found themselves pincered. Courts elsewhere in the common law globe held resolutely to a test of reasonable apprehension or suspicion of bias;[152] viewing matters through judicial spectacles jarred with the

145 (1852) 3 HL Cas 759.

146 Though *R (Bewry) v Norwich City Council* [2001] EWHC Admin 657 suggests the existence of the right at common law.

147 The general policy of the Constitutional Reform Act 2005 also fits: see p. 136 above.

148 *Lawal v Northern Spirit Ltd* [2004] 1 All ER 187 [14].

149 See respectively, *R v Sussex Justices, ex p. McCarthy* [1924] 1 KB 256 and *R v Barnsley Licensing Justices, ex p. Barnsley and District Licensed Victuallers' Association* [1960] 2 QB 167.

150 As ventured by Lord Denning in *Metropolitan Properties Co v Lannon* [1969] 1 QB 577.

151 [1993] AC 646.

152 *Webb v The Queen* (1994) 181 CLR 41 (Australia). Likewise in Scotland: see *Bradford v McLeod* [1986] SLT 244.

Strasbourg approach of asking whether there is a risk of bias 'objectively' in the light of the circumstances which the court has identified.[153] The authority of *Gough* soon began to wither inside the domestic system; if maintaining public confidence is the rationale, then, in Lord Steyn's words, 'public perception of the possibility of unconscious bias is the key'.[154] *Pinochet*,[155] the famous case concerning efforts to extradite the former Chilean dictator, further complicated matters. The House had set aside its own decision on the ground that, by reason of his charitable connections with the third-party intervenor Amnesty International, Lord Hoffman was automatically disqualified. A welter of litigation followed on possible attributions of judicial bias with this effect: the courts sensibly held the line that *Pinochet* should be treated as exceptional. A judge 'would be as wrong to yield to a tenuous or frivolous objection as he would be to ignore an objection of substance'.[156] Yet had the House not so pinned its colours to the mast in *Gough*, this expensive and time-consuming detour could have been avoided by considering matters in terms of public perception and the appearance of bias.[157]

The Law Lords apparently recognised their error in *Porter v Magill*.[158] The case had its origins in the 'homes for votes' scandal which engulfed Westminster City Council in the 1990s, where the Conservative-led administration stood accused of corruptly pursuing a policy of council-house sales in marginal wards with a view to garnering political support. M was the local (district) auditor, tasked with policing the lawfulness of the council's expenditure and, *in extremis*, with enforcing financial penalties against named councillors or officials. After a lengthy investigation, he imposed massive surcharges – a very personal form of accountability. But had M overstepped the mark with some excitable comments at a press conference to announce his provisional findings? Proceeding on the basis that the auditor was required to act not only as investigator but also as prosecutor and as judge,[159] the House revisited the case law on appearance of bias. Lord Hope was pleased to confirm a 'modest adjustment':

> The question is whether the fair-minded and informed observer, having considered the facts, would conclude that there was a real possibility that the tribunal was biased.[160]

[153] See e.g. *Pullar v United Kingdom* (1996) 22 EHRR 391.

[154] *Lawal v Northern Spirit Ltd* [2004] 1 All ER 187 [14]. And see especially *Re Medicaments* [2001] 1 WLR 700.

[155] *R v Bow Street Metropolitan Stipendiary Magistrate, ex p. Pinochet Ugarte (No. 2)* [2000] 1 AC 119. See K. Mallinson, 'Judicial bias and disqualification after *Pinochet (No. 2)*' (2000) 63 *MLR* 119.

[156] *Locabail (UK) Ltd v Bayfield Properties Ltd* [2000] QBV 451 [21]. And see A. Olowofoyeku, 'The *Nemo Iudex* rule: The case against automatic disqualification' [2000] *PL* 456.

[157] See to this effect, Lord Hope's speech in *Meerabux v Attorney General of Belize* [2005] UKPC 12; also, *AWG Group v Morrison* [2006] 1 WLR 1163.

[158] [2002] 2AC 357.

[159] The ECHR Art. 6 requirement of an independent and impartial tribunal (see below) being dealt with through a complete rehearing by the Divisional Court.

[160] *Porter v Magill* [2002] AC 357 [103].

Expressly designed as a test 'in clear and simple language' which is in 'harmony' with Strasbourg and with other major jurisdictions, this formulation now rules the roost.[161] In the case itself, the very striking demonstration of audit technique was vindicated. The press conference was 'an exercise in self-promotion in which he should not have indulged. But it is quite another matter to conclude from this that there was a real possibility that he was biased'.

(b) Superwoman

So who is 'the fair-minded and informed observer'? As visualised by Lord Hope, this creation of fiction is really rather remarkable:

> The sort of person who always reserves judgment on every point until she has seen and fully understood both sides of the argument. She is not unduly sensitive or suspicious . . . but she is not complacent either. She knows that fairness requires that a judge must be, and must be seen to be, unbiased. She knows that judges, like anybody else, have their weaknesses . . . She is the sort of person who takes the trouble to read the text of an article as well as the headlines. She is able to put whatever she has read or seen into its overall social, political or geographical context. She . . . will appreciate that the context forms an important part of the material which she must consider before passing judgment.[162]

Two recent House of Lords cases show 'superwoman' in action in the administrative law field. *Al-Hasan*[163] arose from a dispute about the lawfulness of an order for a prison squat search. The deputy governor of the prison presided over disciplinary proceedings, where the applicants were found guilty of disobeying the order and punished. A common law challenge[164] for the appearance of bias succeeded on the narrow ground that the deputy governor had been present when the prison governor approved the search and had not dissented. 'When thereafter . . . he had to rule upon [the order], a fair-minded observer could all too easily think him predisposed to find it lawful.' However, the further argument that the deputy governor could not bring the requisite independence and impartiality to the task because of his knowledge of the prison, and of the security concerns which occasioned the search, signally failed. The evident potential for institutional pressures notwithstanding, 'superwoman' would know her sociology:

> *Lord Rodger*: Nor should it be supposed that only professional judges are capable of the necessary independence of approach. That would be to disregard the realities of life in many organisations today. For example, on a daily basis, head teachers have to apply school rules

[161] For a case showing the positive application of the test, see *Davidson v Scottish Ministers* [2004] UKHL 34.

[162] *Helow v Home Secretary* [2008] UKHL 62 [2–3]

[163] *R v Home Secretary, ex p. Al-Hasan* [2005] 1 WLR 688.

[164] The facts of the case predated implementation of the HRA.

> which they have helped to frame. By virtue of their knowledge of the way the school works and of its problems, they will often be best placed to apply the rules sensitively and appropriately in any given situation. Again, it is not to be assumed that the head teachers' mere involvement in shaping the rules means that a fair-minded observer who knew how schools worked would conclude that there was a real possibility that they would not be able to apply the rules fairly. The same goes for managers in businesses and for officers in the Armed Forces who are committed to upholding the edifice of lawful orders on which the services rest. Equally, I have no doubt that an informed and fair-minded observer would regard prison governors, or their deputies, as being quite capable of interpreting and applying the prison rules fairly and independently, even though they are obviously committed to upholding them.

The place of the professional was directly in issue in *Gillies*.[165] A medical member of a disability appeal tribunal was sitting part-time, while also being contracted to supply expert reports on claimants for the Benefits Agency. Challenge was effectively being made to the workings of a local network; there was said to be a reasonable apprehension that 'doctors who prepared these reports would tend to lean in favour of accepting reports by other doctors in that class'. The Social Security Commissioners accepted the argument; the judges, however, would have none of it. A fair-minded observer would not perceive 'a Benefits Agency doctor'; instead she would appreciate the doctor's 'professional detachment'. Baroness Hale, a former member of the Council of Tribunals, sought to turn the argument on its head. Courts should trust gladly in the neutrality of the profession:

> The relevant facts of tribunal life include the great advantage, both to its users and to its decision-making, of being able to call upon the people with the greatest expertise in the subject matter of the claim. Given the wide variety of disabilities which come before the Disability Appeal Tribunals, it would not be practicable to have a specialist in the particular disability involved in the particular case. The greatest expertise in assessing the claimant's condition and applying the statutory criteria to it is likely to be held by those doctors who are experienced in making these assessments at the point of claim. To have such expertise available on the tribunal can only be an advantage to it.[166]

The trend discernible in these cases[167] of imputing a substantial degree of knowledge to the fair-minded observer clearly has much to commend it; as Baroness Hale suggests, the courts should beware disabling those who by reason of their background knowledge are best able to act. But is there not a danger of drifting too far back towards the elitist view of judicial spectacles promulgated in *Gough*?[168] Superwoman's cape, it seems, is ermine!

[165] *Gillies v Secretary of State for Work and Pensions* [2006] UKHL 2.

[166] *Ibid.* [40].

[167] See also *Taylor v Lawrence* [2003] QB 528 (the fair-minded and informed observer aware of English legal traditions and culture).

[168] S. Atrill, 'Who is a "fair-minded and informed observer"? Bias after Magill' (2003) 62 *CLJ* 279.

(c) Pressure points

As the Supreme Court of Canada has observed, 'the standards for reasonable apprehension of bias may vary, like other aspects of procedural fairness, depending on the context and the type of function performed by the administrative decision-maker involved'.[169] In other words, just as with *audi alteram partem*, matters become more complicated as the parameters of the doctrine expand.

The planning process is fertile territory for this type of litigation. Tackling corruption in property development is one thing, but what is to happen when an elected representative airs views about a particular project? Is this indicative of bias, so cutting against involvement in the legal process of decision by the planning authority? The demands especially of local democracy – positive engagement in producing and applying policy frameworks – point firmly in the opposite direction.

Going back in time, *Franklin's* case (see p. 622 above) gave a clear answer. The minister declared at a public meeting that the new town would go ahead with or without the co-operation of local people; he later confirmed the order. This act was, in Lord Thankerton's words, 'purely administrative' in character. 'The use of the word "bias" should be confined to its proper sphere. Its proper significance is to denote a departure from the standard of even-handed justice which the law requires from those who occupy judicial office, or those who are commonly regarded as holding a quasi-judicial office, such as an arbitrator.'

Almost half a century later, with this form of analytical theory safely entombed by *Ridge v Baldwin*, Sedley J would be found revisiting the matter in a case, *Kirkstall Valley*,[170] concerning alleged bias by members of an urban development corporation. His was a dual approach. First, a complaint that the decision-maker had some personal interest would be determined by the normal test for bias, that is to say irrespective of the nature of the decision-making function. 'What will differ from case to case is the significance of the interest and its degree of proximity or remoteness to the issue to be decided.'[171] Secondly, Sedley J elaborated the distinction between (lawful) predisposition – representatives publicly airing a view – and (actionable) predetermination – a closed mind in fact. Predetermination was an issue separate from bias, such that the court would (only) intervene on grounds of 'no-fettering' (see p. 217 above). 'The decision of a body, albeit composed of disinterested individuals, will be struck down if its outcome has been predetermined whether by the adoption of an inflexible policy or by the effective surrender of the body's independent judgement.'

The merit of this dual approach is the protection afforded not only to affected interests but also to policy and politics – members of the planning

[169] *Baker v Canada (Minister of Citizenship and Immigration)* [1999] 2 SCR 817 [47].

[170] *R v Environment Secretary, ex p. Kirkstall Valley Campaign Ltd* [1996] 3 All ER 304. This was the era of the *Gough* test.

[171] See also *R v Amber Valley DC, ex p. Jackson* [1984] 3 All ER 501.

authority will be shielded from review provided there is no conflict of interest and they exercise judgement.[172] The distinction drawn between bias and predetermination jars, however, with the broad dynamic in procedural fairness of focusing on issues of content and not amenability. *Porter v Magill* opens up another possibility: testing for the appearance of predetermination subject to a high threshold.

This approach, which (given the evident potential for intervention) implies more judicial discretion, was assumed in *Condron*.[173] The chairman of a planning-decision committee in the Welsh Assembly had allegedly remarked that he was 'going to go with the inspector's report' in favour of a scheme for opencast mining. The subsequent decision to grant consent having been challenged, Richards LJ analysed the matter by reference to the normal test for bias. It was necessary to look beyond pecuniary or personal interests and to consider in addition whether, from the viewpoint of the fair-minded and informed observer, 'there was a real possibility that . . . members were biased in the sense of approaching the decision with a closed mind'. This was 'a question to be approached with appropriate caution, since it is important not to apply the test in a way that will render [the] decision-making impossible or unduly difficult'. The challenge failed; in light of the somewhat informal atmosphere of devolved government, superwoman would not apprehend a real risk.

In the 2008 case of *Persimmon Homes*,[174] the complaint went to the heart of the local democratic process. The fair-minded and informed observer, it was argued, would have perceived a real possibility of predetermination when councillors took a critical planning decision with elections pending; counsel conceded however that there were in fact no closed minds. Presented with 'little evidence . . . that members of the Committee were any more politically motivated than would normally be expected from elected policy makers',[175] the Court of Appeal was not disposed to intervene. The exact status of the more flexible *Condron*-type approach was left unresolved. Pill LJ referred to the test in *Porter* not being 'altogether excluded in this context', while Rix LJ spoke of 'a single test', and Longmore LJ of 'the test of apparent bias relating to predetermination'. Happily, all were agreed that the test was an extremely difficult one to satisfy in a situation of democratic accountability. The danger is that over time the high threshold will be whittled down.

The domestic courts have also been subject to increased demands to check for structural elements of bias. While the development is commonly associated with ECHR Art. 6 (below), two very recent cases serve to point up the wider

[172] For practical illustration, see *R v Chesterfield BC, ex p. Darker Enterprises Ltd* [1992] COD 466.

[173] *Condron v National Assembly for Wales* [2007] LGR 87, building in turn on *Georgiou v Enfield LBC* [2004] BGLR 497. See for criticism, J. Maurici, 'The modern approach to bias' (2007) 12 *JR* 56.

[174] *Persimmon Homes v R (Lewis)* [2008] EWCA Civ 746.

[175] In contrast to the situation in *ex p. Beddowes*, see p. 372 above.

possibilities, as also the potential problems. *In re Duffy*[176] concerned a challenge by Nationalists to the minister's appointment of two prominent Unionist activists to the seven-strong Parades Commission for Northern Ireland, a body tasked with facilitating local compromise and if necessary with issuing determinations on the routing of marches. This then was a pre-emptive strike; there were as yet no actual Commission decisions to attack for bias (as also no 'determination of civil rights and obligations'). *Wednesbury* was accordingly centre-stage. From a political standpoint, the minister's decision could be explained as bringing a warring faction 'inside the tent', so neutralising one source of conflict. But was this legally viable? Under the statute, the minister was so to 'exercise his powers of appointment . . . as to secure that as far as practicable the membership of the Commission is representative of the community in Northern Ireland'.[177]

Opening up a new vista of judicial regulation, the judges in Northern Ireland tackled the issue of trawling or targeting in public appointments head on. Disagreement was rife. The trial judge thought the appointment process unlawful because no account was taken of the possibility of encouraging applications from nationalist groups as well as from the strongly loyalist organisations which were targeted. The majority in the Court of Appeal opined that this was not a material factor requiring consideration but merely a matter which some might have considered; the trial judge had gone too far. The dissenting judge discerned an obligation on the minister to encourage applications also from amongst the nationalist residents affected by contentious parades; the trial judge had not gone far enough. Perhaps understandably, the Law Lords chose the safer option of focusing on the two appointments. The minister's own political model was trumped: 'those appointments', proclaimed Lord Carswell, 'failed to achieve the important goal of maintaining the public perception of the impartiality of all of the members of the Commission necessary for its general acceptance'. In accordance with the *doppelganger* test (see p. 43 above), the Secretary of State for Northern Ireland had acted as no reasonable Secretary of State for Northern Ireland could have acted.

The Court of Appeal decision in *R (Brooke) v Parole Board*[178] is the most striking example to date of structural procedural review. The case leads on from the successful struggles to have the Parole Board replace the minister as primary decision-maker on early release (*Stafford* etc.). The challenge could thus proceed on the basis that, both at common law and under ECHR Art. 5(4), the agency was required as a court to show objective independence of the executive. The judges are found examining wide-ranging complaints of ministerial influence – funding arrangements, appointments, etc. – over the adjudicative activities of the Board. The minister's argument that the court should

[176] [2008] UKHL 4.

[177] Public Processions (Northern Ireland) Act 1998, Sch. 1 [2(3)].

[178] [2008] 1 WLR 1950. The companion case of *R (Walker) v Justice Secretary* [2008] 1 WLR 1977 deals with problems of resources.

in orthodox fashion confine itself to correcting specific instances of injustice had been brushed aside. Nor, as the Divisional Court judgment shows, was the scrutiny light-touch:

> There is no question about the independence of mind and impartiality of the individual members of the Board. The issue is whether the relationship with the sponsoring Department of State, formerly the Home Office and now the Ministry of Justice, makes the Board too close to both the Executive and the principal party to all its decisions. We have found no sign of any attempt by the Department to influence individual cases, as distinct from the general approach to release decisions; that is so whether the individual cases are those of the claimants before us or any others. In some respects we have found that the structure of the Board is consistent with the necessary objective independence. But we are satisfied that the relationship of sponsorship is such as to create what objectively appears to be a lack of independence, and to cause the sponsoring Department sometimes to treat the Board as part of its establishment. That has led to inadequate protection for the security of tenure of members. It has also led to documented examples of the use of the powers of the Department which have not been consistent with the need to maintain the Board's objective independence; those have been powers of funding, of appointment and to give directions.

Judicial review on this scale puts in issue the courts' own institutional competence. Attention is immediately directed to the question of remedy. A declaration was granted, which solemnly recorded failure to demonstrate objective independence. However, while recognising that 'it was not appropriate . . . to tell the Secretary of State what action he ought to take', the Court of Appeal willingly provided multiple paragraphs of guidance 'on the areas where action is required'. As discussed further in Chapter 16, the judges will find themselves in a pickle if they go too far down this route.

6. 'Is judicial review good enough?'

ECHR Art. 6 further puts in issue the curative role of judicial review. On the one hand, the Strasbourg jurisprudence confirms that, for the purpose of deciding whether a body is 'independent', the court should – as in *Brooke* – look to the manner of appointment and term of office, the presence of procedural guarantees against external influence, and the general appearance of autonomy.[179] On the other hand, ranging beyond the classic realm of courts as primary decision-makers, by virtue of the increasingly generous interpretation of 'civil rights and obligations', conjures the unenviable prospect of administrative structures at large being vulnerable to challenge: judicialisation gone mad. 'The full judicial model' of Art. 6 falls to be tempered on grounds of constitutional principle – responsible government and democratic accountability – and practical convenience – managerial values of economy, efficiency and effectiveness.

[179] See e.g. on the Gaming Board, *Kingsley v UK* (2002) 35 EHRR 177.

The ECtHR has recognised the problem. The greater amenability to jurisdiction, whereby Strasbourg can effectively demand judicial supervision at the national level, comes with a more holistic approach to decisional processes. First, it need not be the case that each link in the administrative decision-making chain is 'independent'; a lack of independence in the administrative process may be cured by access to an independent judicial body with 'full jurisdiction'.[180] Secondly, 'full jurisdiction' is not to be equated with full decision-making power. Rather, in the words of Lord Clyde, 'full jurisdiction means a full jurisdiction in the context of the case'.[181] To this effect, the ECtHR spoke in *Zumbotel*[182] of the 'respect' that should be afforded decisions taken by 'administrative authorities on grounds of expediency'. The ECtHR judgment in *Bryan*[183] is more explicit. 'In assessing the sufficiency of the review . . . it is necessary to have regard to matters such as the subject matter of the decision appealed against, the manner in which that decision was arrived at, and the content of the dispute, including the desired and actual grounds of appeal.'[184] But this in turn generates uncertainty inside the national administrative law system. There is no single answer to the question of whether judicial review, in its classic guise of a supervisory jurisdiction directed to errors of law and not of fact, has the necessary medicinal quality.

The hybrid nature of the planning process – judicial and administrative elements – saw British lawyers testing the matter in Strasbourg prior to the HRA.[185] The case of *Bryan* concerned an inspector's decision to uphold an enforcement notice. Since the minister could revoke the inspector's power of determination, the inspector could not constitute an independent tribunal. In view however of the specialised nature of the subject matter, and of the 'safeguards' entailed in the inspectorial procedure such as oral or written evidence, legal representation and reasons, the ECtHR held that the common law power to regulate findings of fact via 'irrationality' afforded the requisite measure of protection. *Bryan* thus epitomises the role of transaction typing in determining the question of independence and, further, the idea of 'composite procedure': whether, read together, the administrative and judicial parts of a decisional process effect compliance.

(a) Defensive posture

The House of Lords has now grappled with the issue in two big cases. Involving very different transaction types, they nonetheless share a common thread: defence of national administrative law traditions, the HRA notwithstanding.

180 *Albert and Le Compte v Belgium* (1983) 5 EHRR 533 [29].
181 *R (Alconbury Developments Ltd) v Environment Secretary* [154].
182 *Zumbotel v Austria* (1993) 17 EHRR 116 [32].
183 (1996) 21 EHRR 342.
184 Ibid. [45].
185 See also *ISKCON v United Kingdom* (1994) 18 EHRR CD 133.

The ECtHR having worked to temper 'the full judicial model', the Law Lords are seen moderating it to an extent which may well prove unsustainable in light of the evolving Strasbourg jurisprudence. These cases have a sharp constitutional edge. While both the national and supranational systems display strong elements of pragmatism, there also is an underlying friction between them.

Alconbury[186] was the post-HRA planning case waiting to happen. In issue was the statutory choice of 'call-in' procedure for major – controversial – developments: could there be compliance with Art. 6 when the minister was directly involved? Driving a proverbial 'coach and horses' through a carefully structured system replete with professional inputs, the Divisional Court answered 'no'. Article 6, it was said, meant a separation of powers; the Secretary of State could not be both a policy-maker and decision-taker. The Law Lords would have none of this. In line with classic common law authority,[187] the minister should not be treated as if he were a judge. Precisely because, in Lord Nolan's words, 'the decisions made by the Secretary of State will often have acute social, economic and environmental implications', the political element should be treasured. 'Parliament has entrusted the requisite degree of control to the Secretary of State, and it is to Parliament he must account for his exercise of it. To substitute for the Secretary of State an independent and impartial body with no central electoral accountability would not only be a recipe for chaos: it would be profoundly undemocratic.'[188] Lord Hoffman fastened on the threat of excessive judicialisation. 'The Human Rights Act 1998 was no doubt intended to strengthen the rule of law but not to inaugurate the rule of lawyers.'[189]

The House proceeded to hold judicial review good enough. Echoing *Bryan*, one approach was that of emphasising the procedural 'safeguards': in this case, inquiry by an inspector and subsequent notice and comment procedure. For Lord Slynn, it was these elements, combined with the availability of judicial review, which rendered the decision-making chain as a whole compliant with Art. 6.[190] Reference could also be made to the expansionary tendencies of judicial review – that is to say, an increasingly powerful 'prescription drug' (to ward off Strasbourg). Signalling future possibilities, wherein Art. 6 leads to further intensification of factual scrutiny in judicial review, Lord Clyde emphasised 'the extent to which . . . a decision may be penetrated by a review of the account taken . . . of facts which are irrelevant or even mistaken'.[191] (*E v Home Secretary* (see p. 513 above) would later cast fresh light on this).

[186] *R (Alconbury Developments Ltd) v Environment Secretary* ; and see M. Poustie, 'The rule of law or the rule of lawyers? *Alconbury*, Article 6(1) and the role of courts in administrative decision-making' (2001) *EHRLR* 657.

[187] *Johnson (B) & Co. (Builders) Ltd v Minister of Health* [1947] 2 All ER 395.

[188] *R (Alconbury Developments Ltd) v Environment Secretary* [60]. Note however the move to establish an Infrastructure Planning Commission for large-scale projects (see p. 587 above).

[189] *Ibid.* [91].

[190] *Ibid.* [45–54].

[191] *Ibid.* [169]. The speeches also made reference to proportionality.

Lord Hoffman went further, in a much-cited passage:

> If . . . the question is one of policy or expediency, the 'safeguards' are irrelevant. No one expects the inspector to be independent or impartial in applying the Secretary of State's policy and this was the reason why the court said that he was not for all purposes an independent or impartial tribunal. In this respect his position is no different from that of the Secretary of State himself. The reason why judicial review is sufficient in both cases to satisfy article 6 has nothing to do with the 'safeguards' but depends upon the *Zumbotel* principle of respect for the decision of an administrative authority on questions of expediency. It is only when one comes to findings of fact, or the evaluation of facts, such as arise on the question of whether there has been a breach of planning control, that the safeguards are essential for the acceptance of a limited review of fact by the appellate tribunal.[192]

A judicial policy with much to commend it, Lord Hoffman's aim is clear: insulate key administrative processes from the vagaries of a more context-specific structural procedural form of review (so distinguishing the reasoning (but not the result) in *Bryan*). Transaction typing grounded in considerations of institutional competence thus is the preferred option (*Zumbotel*). The conceptual difficulty is immediately apparent however. What does 'expediency' connote (and why should this not partly depend on the nature of the applicant's interest)? As cases such as *Bushell* remind us, there is much ink wasted on the so-called fact/policy distinction, more especially in terms of 'evaluation of facts'.[193] Paradoxically, in seeking so to distinguish factual matters, Lord Hoffman was incautious.[194] In closing down one avenue of challenge, his speech clearly signposted another – lack of 'essential' safeguards across seemingly vast swathes of routine decision-making. 'Proportionate dispute resolution' at the ground-floor level (see Chapter 10) was now in issue.

The second House of Lords case, *Runa Begum*,[195] promptly highlighted this aspect. RB was offered council accommodation as a homeless person. Complaining of racism and drug problems on the estate, that she had been mugged there, and that her estranged husband frequently visited the building, she refused the offer. As envisaged under the general scheme of Part VII of the Housing Act 1996, a senior housing manager conducted an internal review and decided that the offer was suitable. RB duly appealed to the county court, here exercising judicial-review-type powers. The judge accepted the argument that, since there were disputed facts, the council had breached Art. 6 by not referring the matter to an independent tribunal. The Law Lords again refused to play constitutional architect. On the contrary, explained Lord Hoffman, defences

192 *Ibid.* [117].

193 For further illustration in terms of Art. 6, see *Friends Provident Life & Pensions Ltd v Transport Secretary* [2002] 1 WLR 1450.

194 His own word: *Begum (Runa) v Tower Hamlets LBC* [2003] 2 WLR 388 [40].

195 *Begum (Runa) v Tower Hamlets LBC.*

against Strasbourg-inspired incursions in the general field of administrative law needed tightening:

> The rule of law rightly requires that certain decisions, of which the paradigm examples are findings of breaches of the criminal law and adjudications as to private rights, should be entrusted to the judicial branch of government. This basic principle does not yield to utilitarian arguments that it would be cheaper or more efficient to have these matters decided by administrators. Nor is the possibility of an appeal sufficient to compensate for lack of independence and impartiality on the part of the primary decision maker [[196]] . . . But utilitarian considerations have their place when it comes to setting up, for example, schemes of regulation or social welfare . . . Efficient administration and the sovereignty of Parliament are very relevant. Parliament is entitled to take the view that it is not in the public interest that an excessive proportion of the funds available for a welfare scheme should be consumed in administration and legal disputes . . .
>
> Although I do not think that the exercise of administrative functions requires a mechanism for independent findings of fact or a full appeal, it does need to be lawful and fair . . . In any case, the gap between judicial review and a full right of appeal is seldom in practice very wide. Even with a full right of appeal it is not easy for an appellate tribunal which has not itself seen the witnesses to differ from the decision-maker on questions of primary fact and, more especially relevant to this case, on questions of credibility . . .
>
> In the case of the normal Part VII decision, engaging no human rights other than Article 6, conventional judicial review . . . is sufficient . . . The question is whether, consistently with the rule of law and constitutional propriety, the relevant decision-making powers may be entrusted to administrators. If so, it does not matter that there are many or few occasions on which they need to make findings of fact . . . I entirely endorse . . . courts being slow to conclude that Parliament has produced an administrative scheme which does not comply with constitutional principles. [197]

The concern not to over-judicialise dispute procedures shines through. The distinction made by Lord Hoffman between cases involving property rights – Art. 6 strongly enforced – and those involving social/regulatory schemes – the basic standard of 'lawful and fair' – is nonetheless questionable.[198] The boundary line may well be obscure, for example in planning. Issues of 'error cost' (to a vulnerable group), and of how 'correct' outcomes are constructed, are typically glossed over in the appeal to utilitarianism.

(b) Fresh challenge

In *Tsfayo*,[199] the ECtHR considered the Law Lords' efforts in a judgment difficult to decipher. The case arose from a refusal of a backdated claim for welfare

[196] See *De Cubber v Belgium* (1984) 7 EHRR 236.
[197] *Ibid.* [42–4] [47] [59].
[198] See further, P. Craig, 'The HRA, Article 6 and procedural rights' [2003] *PL* 753.
[199] *Tsfayo v United Kingdom* [2007] HLR 19.

entitlements. Rejecting T's evidence that she had not received the relevant correspondence, the local authority's housing benefit review board upheld the decision; there was no 'good cause' for her delay. A judicial review challenge for irrationality also failed. The ECtHR gave two main reasons for finding a violation of Art. 6.[200] First, the decision-making process was 'significantly different' from that in *Bryan* or in *Runa Begum*. In those cases, the issues to be determined 'required a measure of professional knowledge or experience and the exercise of discretion pursuant to wider policy aims', whereas in this case the Housing Benefit and Council Tax Benefit Review Board (HBRB) was deciding 'a simple question of fact', namely whether there was good cause. Nor were the factual findings 'merely incidental' to the reaching of broader judgements of policy or expediency. The ECtHR, in other words, saw no particular need to temper 'the full judicial model'. Secondly, the HBRB was not only lacking in independence from the executive, but was 'directly connected to one of the parties to the dispute'.[201] An adjudicative body composed of five members of the authority responsible for paying the benefit was tainted at source; there was a 'fundamental lack of objective impartiality'. The fact of HBRBs having already been replaced by a separate system of statutory tribunals[202] was naturally grist to the Strasbourg mill.

Whether or not *Tsfayo* is read expansively[203] will clearly be of considerable importance for the national administrative law system. Dealing with 'double-hatted' tribunal members is one thing, the idea that every minor case of 'pure' fact-finding needs a fully judicialised body quite another! What is also clear post-*Tsfayo* is the scope for expensive and time-consuming litigation on fine points of institutional design – wholly disproportionate.

Two later cases demonstrate the range of possibilities. *Wright*[204] concerned the provisional listing of care workers considered unsuitable to work with vulnerable adults: was the opportunity to petition the minister for removal from the list, coupled with judicial review of the exercise of his statutory power, Art. 6-compliant? The majority in the Court of Appeal thought not.[205] In light of (the second limb of) *Tsfayo*, it was necessary 'to have regard to the nature of the first stage breach . . . The more serious the failure to accord a hearing by an independent and impartial tribunal, the more likely it is that a breach of the process cannot be cured' by judicial review – in this case, 'a denial of one of the fundamental elements of the right to a fair determination', namely the right to be heard, locked up together 'with the (often irreversible) detrimental effect of the inclusion in the list'. On appeal, the House of Lords endorsed this approach and went on to make a declaration of incompatibility.

[200] *Ibid.* [45–7].

[201] A point previously made domestically in *R (Bewry) v Norwich City Council* [2001] EWHC Admin 657.

[202] Child Support, Pensions and Social Security Act 2000.

[203] See e.g. J. Howell, '*Alconbury* Crumbles' (2007) 12 *Judicial Review* 9.

[204] *R (Wright) v Health Secretary* [2008] 2 WLR 536 (CA); [2009] UKHL 3.

[205] For another such example, see *R (Q and Others)*, see p. 741 below.

Ali v Birmingham City Council[206] exposes the faultline between *Runa Begum* and *Tsfayo*. Part VII of the Housing Act 1996 was again in play; had homeless persons declined suitable accommodation? The authority's reviewing officer upheld several decisions to this effect, on the basis that in each case the applicant had received a letter from the council giving the appropriate statutory notice. They all denied this. The first limb in *Tsfayo* was duly invoked; as against a situation calling for specialist knowledge or regard to policy considerations (*Runa Begum*), was it not 'a simple issue of primary fact', namely a matter necessarily open for consideration on the merits by an independent and impartial tribunal? Thomas LJ was naturally horrified by the prospect. There would be 'significant implications for not only the statutory scheme but for the court and tribunal system, if this court were to hold that a full right of appeal was required on findings of primary fact . . . particularly if the appeal encompassed the re-hearing of evidence'. The court clung to *Runa Begum* as binding authority on Part VII and distinguished *Tsfayo* for the nature of the taint.

7. Conclusion

Procedural fairness is an important element in the invigoration of judicial review, at least since the landmark decision of *Ridge v Baldwin*. With significant shifts in the style and substance of judicial protection, and sudden bursts of activity, nowhere is the organic quality of the common law better illustrated. The traditional autochthonous elements of the *audi alteram partem* principle have increasingly been enriched by both ECHR and Community law requirements, most obviously in terms of legislative review but also at the level of principle, for example with reasons. At the same time we note a more circumspect approach to the standard of review in non-adjudicative contexts. Demands for more extensive development, as indicated by the fashionable value of transparency, are matched by genuine concerns about the competency and legitimacy of judicial decision-making based on a broad interpretation of 'fairness'.

Procedural fairness has become a soft-centred legal principle. The scope of judicial discretion manifests itself in a wide range of methodological choices, from the categorisation of functions to interest classification and balancing, and on through macro- and micro-forms of transaction typing. The consequence is a case law which often appears inchoate, due to great variability in the intensity of review, associated with an expanded coverage of *audi alteram partem* situations and, latterly, of the no-bias rule. Equally criticisable is the recourse to 'intuitive judgement' at the expense of theories of process. We find heart-warming 'motherhood statements' (see p. 514 above), utilised to screen the personal choices that judges stubbornly refuse to admit to.

From a broadly instrumentalist approach in earlier years, there has been a shift to dignitary values, attesting the Strasbourg role of 'judge over the judge's

[206] [2008] EWCA Civ 1228. See also *R (Gilboy) v Liverpool CC* [2008] EWCA Civ 751.

shoulder'. A chief 'hot-spot' is structural procedural review directed to the institutional position of the decision-maker. This involves the metamorphosis of a Convention guarantee of 'access to the court' in decisions involving civil rights and obligations into an inherently elusive framework governing both judicial and administrative procedures. As highlighted by *Tsfayo*, there are major problems of 'fit' inside the national polity.

Natural justice lies at the heart of the Anglo-American legal tradition and our courts are naturally proud of their record in establishing the principle and applying it. Looked at through the spectacles of the ECtHR, however, there is room for 'improvement'. But is the ECtHR raising the bar? Or is it inaugurating a world of judicial bureaucracy, where a rule-bound administration is further fettered by complex, costly and time-consuming administrative procedures dictated by judges unfamiliar with the world of administration? For the Law Lords, the challenge has been to limit the disruption to established national traditions and administrative structures, which they deem appropriate. The irony will not be lost on the reader!

15

Elite dimension: Court structures and process

Contents

Although this book does not adopt the court-centred approach of many administrative lawyers, we have learned a good deal about judicial review in its pages. Consideration of the relationship between law and administration, and the contribution law can make to administration, bears directly on the question of the proper constitutional role of the courts. Intended to produce a more rounded picture of the part played by judicial review, the next chapters look to the dynamics, routings and effects of this form of litigation. This chapter focuses on major institutional developments over the last thirty years and on the procedural devices for rationing access to the system. Chapter 16 considers the make-up of the caseload, the workings of the judicial 'tool-kit' of remedies, and the cloudy issues of impact and compliance. What is the value of judicial review read – as the judges are naturally disposed to do[1] – as the 'apex' of a pyramid of dispute resolution (see Chapters 10–11)? Is it, as de Smith thought,[2] sporadic and peripheral? We shall discover that, conveniently obscured by the roll-call of leading cases, judicial review in England and Wales has a secret dimension; the expansion of parameters runs alongside a large-scale exclusion of people.

1. Models of judicial review

'Judicial review' is a slippery concept. Different constitutional systems show a wide range of possible arrangements – for example, constitutional review (United States), a dual jurisdiction (France) and systematised administrative appeals (Australia). As evidenced in the UK with equality and human rights, models of judicial review also change in line with societal values.[3] Wade's classic description[4] of a supervisory – inherent – jurisdiction directed on grounds of legality to the decisions and other public functions of public bodies is no longer sufficient.

Judicial review may have a number of overlapping functions (which different models emphasise to a greater or lesser extent under the broad rubric of legal accountability):

- *upholding the rule of law (control of government)*: constitutional symbolism and legal authority, imposition of law on state actors – the imagery of 'lions behind the throne'
- *protection of the individual*: redress of grievance and defence of private interest – a strong historical theme in the common law
- *determining institutional relationships*: constitutional allocation of powers, intra-state litigation
- *establishing general principles*: as with proper exercise of discretion (rationality, proportionality, no-fettering) – 'hortatory function'
- *vehicle for interest representation*: alternative forum for public discussion – competing conceptions of 'public interest'
- *structuring deliberative and administrative processes*: for example, reason-giving requirements, duty to consult, structural procedural review ('judicialisation')

[1] Not least the influential figure of Lord Woolf, *Protection of the Public: A new challenge,* (Stevens, 1990).

[2] S. de Smith, *Judicial Review of Administrative Action* (Stevens, 1959), p. 3. Even if the hundreds of cases scattered through the footnotes did not give precisely that impression.

[3] For a valuable discussion, see R. Cotterell, 'The symbolism of constitutions: Some Anglo-American comparisons' in Loveland, *A Special Relationship? American influences on public law in the UK* (Clarendon Press, 1995).

[4] H. W. R Wade, *Administrative Law*, 1st edn (Clarendon Press, 1961).

- *insistence on core values of good governance*: normative and expository role associated, for example, with legitimate expectation, *audi alteram partem* and no bias – 'the state must act fairly and honestly'
- *elaboration and vindication of fundamental rights*: increasingly informed by transnational judicial dialogue.

(a) Substance and procedure; a multi-streamed jurisdiction

It is of the essence of the common law tradition that substance and procedure march hand-in-hand.[5] A defining feature of judicial review in this jurisdiction is its strong holistic quality, such that particular procedural and/or substantive changes frequently have significant knock-on effects elsewhere in the system. Viewed from this perspective, the judicial review process is very much a living system, and one that, as history demonstrates, may well take unexpected turns.

For the English lawyer, the classic touchstone is remedy. Suitably lauded in Dicey's formulation of the rule of law, a cardinal feature of common law models of judicial review is the possession of mandatory and stop orders.[6] Together with the famous writ of *habeas corpus*, which allows the court to test the legality of a detention in custody,[7] three 'prerogative orders' traditionally provided the backbone of the supervisory jurisdiction:

- *certiorari* – to quash a decision (now 'quashing order')
- *mandamus* – to order performance of a public duty (now 'mandatory order')
- *prohibition* – to forbid the hearing of a case or taking of a decision (now 'prohibiting order').

In more recent times *injunctions* and *interim injunctions* have also become available generally against public authorities. We noted the symbolism of *M v Home Office* (see p. 10 above), expressed by Lord Woolf in terms of movement towards a model of judicial review premised on coercion, in contrast to one based on trust and co-operation. Yet this is only part of an expanded and expanding judicial toolkit. Centre-stage today is the *declaration*, appropriately termed the judges' 'flexible friend' because of the precise control courts enjoy over the form or writing of declaratory relief,[8] a feature especially prized by reason of the myriad complexities of competing interests familiarly associated with judicial review.[9]

The modern procedural development in England and Wales is also a history

[5] W. H. Maitland, *The Forms of Action at Common Law* (Cambridge University Press, 1968).

[6] Flanked by the contractual (Ch. 8) and tortious liability (Ch. 17) of statutory authorities.

[7] Though with decreasing regularity in the light of judicial and legislative restriction: see Lord Woolf, J. Jowell and A. Le Sueur, *de Smith's Judicial Review of Administrative Action*, 6th edn (Sweet & Maxwell, 2007), pp. 865–71.

[8] As illustrated by *Bibi*, see p. 225 above (drawing the fangs of substantive legitimate expectation).

[9] Lord Woolf and J. Woolf, *Zamir and Woolf: The declaratory judgment*, 3rd edn (Sweet and Maxwell, 2001). The classic authority is *Dyson v Attorney General (No. 1)* [1911] 1 KB 410, *(No. 2)* [1912] 1 Ch 158.

of the distinctive 'permission' (formerly 'leave') stage, whereby, ahead of the full hearing on grounds of review and remedies, cases are subjected to a whole series of filtering mechanisms (or 'safeguards').[10] The reasons for refusing permission to proceed include:

- insufficiently arguable case
- delay (three months time-limit as the 'default' position)
- no sufficient interest in the matter (lack of *locus standi* or standing to sue)
- no issue of 'public law'
- availability of alternative remedies
- challenge is premature.

In so regulating access to their elite system, the judges exercise strong discretion. As well as control for volume, there is much scope for individual fine-tuning in 'the public interest'. We shall see how claimants commonly have their interest in redress of grievance overridden at this point.

Looking more closely at the dynamics of the litigation, we identify several sets of tensions that generate friction and produce pressure points. Prominent among these is the tension between a judicial desire to open up access to the machinery more widely, so facilitating the vital normative and expository function, and a managerial instinct to protect the efficient functioning of that process by keeping litigants out. Particular pressures are generated by the efforts of elite repeat-players to incorporate the idea of judicial review as a surrogate political process, most obviously in the field of human rights law. While the judges have proved increasingly receptive to an open, pluralist form of proceeding, there must be limits in order to maintain, in Fuller's terms (see p. 618 above), the integrity of the adjudicative system. The various interests in litigation also need to be balanced against a wider public interest in the effectiveness of the administrative process, as also in protection of the public purse. The relationship of judicial review with 'ordinary' civil procedure constitutes another source of tension: a tailoring of process to the 'special demands' of the jurisdiction, an approach historically weighted in favour of government ('Crown proceedings'), versus the pull of generalised forms and nostrums of legal practice.

Today, as we have seen in earlier chapters, 'a multi-streamed jurisdiction' has emerged, in which judicial review encompasses not only common law principles as the vibrant senior partner but also applications of EU law and of Convention rights where these are relevant.[11] Increasingly, a public international law dimension is emerging, as unhappily illustrated in the Iraq cases.[12]

[10] A. Le Sueur and M. Sunkin, 'Applications for judicial review: The requirement of leave' [1992] *PL* 102.

[11] R. Rawlings, 'Modelling judicial review' (2008) 61 *Current Legal Problems* 95. And see, R. Gordon, *EC Law in Judicial Review* (Oxford University Press, 2007); and J. Beatson *et al.*, *Human Rights: Judicial protection in the United Kingdom* (Sweet & Maxwell, 2008).

[12] See *R (Al-Jedda) v Defence Secretary* [2008] 2 WLR 31 (see p. 15 above); Sir Stephen Richards, 'The international dimension of judicial review' 2006 *Gray's Inn Reading*, available on the website of the Gresham Society.

AJR procedure is a shared vehicle for all these types of cases. Competing pressures from diversity and commonality are an inevitable consequence (see further below).

(b) Ideal types

How then, both in terms of substance and procedure, might the process of 'transforming judicial review' (see Chapter 3) be visualised? Writing in the early 1990s in the context of a unified common law system still highly insular in character, the authors postulated three sharply differentiated models of judicial review.[13] Today, two further ideal types may help to illuminate basic contours and so the path of historical development and possible futures.

Predominant for much of the twentieth century, the story begins with the 'drainpipe': see Fig 15.1. Narrow, inflexible, and with rigid collars, this is the determinedly formalist model encountered by Davis (see p. 95 above), with the judge as Cotterell's 'modest underworker'. The touchstone is *Wednesbury* in its original guise as a doctrine of judicial restraint and Lord Greene's classic statement of the authority being protected from assault, castle-like, 'within the four corners of . . . jurisdiction' (see p. 43 above). Firmly anchored in the ultra vires justification for judicial review, the model also demonstrates little interest in factual exploration (see below) or reasons-giving requirements.

The 'drainpipe model' was in its own terms both coherent and viable. Infused with Dicey's peculiarly English conception of the rule of law, it was highly individualistic in orientation and essentially geared to the protection of private interests.[14] A strict insistence on the traditional canon of adversarial, bipolar procedure, coupled with strict interpretation of the doctrine of precedent and a remedy-oriented approach as part of the common law inheritance, further underpinned this classic 'private law model' of judicial review.

But the drainpipe model was obviously criticisable as presenting a wholly unreal picture of the adjudicative process. Artificial limitation of the ambit of adjudication associated with the establishment of significant judicial 'no-go areas' put in issue the real accountability of political actors. The break-up of this model through the 'rebuilding' of judicial review in the 1960s, rapid expansion in the 1970s and 1980s targeted on executive discretion and the 'rationality' principle, were assumed in our second ideal type. A snapshot of how things looked at the start of the 1990s, this

[13] C. Harlow and R. Rawlings, *Pressure Through Law* (Routledge, 1992), Ch. 7.

[14] See further, C. Harlow, 'A special relationship? American influences on judicial review in England', in Loveland (ed.), *A Special Relationship? American influences on public law in the UK* (Clarendon Press, 1995); also, M. Taggart, '"The peculiarities of the English": Resisting the public/private law distinction' in Craig and Rawlings (eds.), *Law and Administration in Europe* (Oxford University Press, 2003).

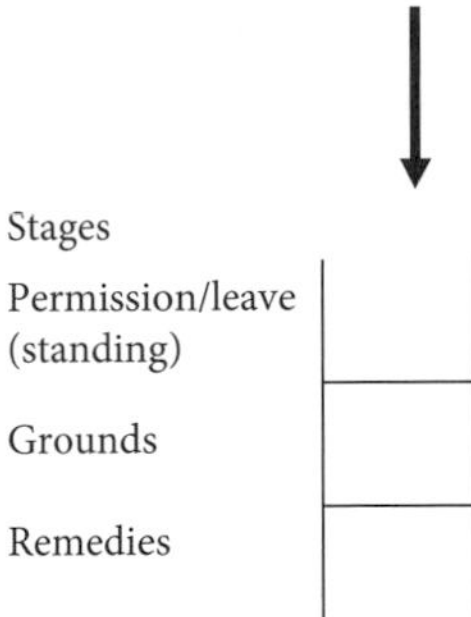

Fig 15.1 The drainpipe

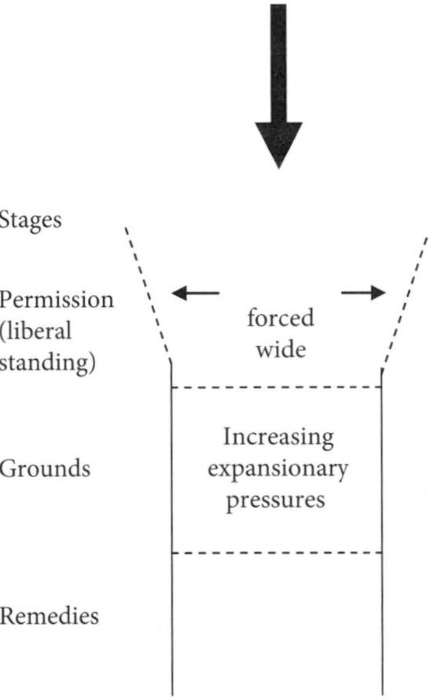

Fig 15.2 The funnel

'funnel model' also reflects the courts' ten years of experience with AJR procedure.

The judicial review process now appeared increasingly permeable at the initial stage, but restrictive later on, especially in terms of information gathering. While the grounds of review continued to expand, orthodox legal remedies remained the order of the day. The funnel model did not represent a state of equilibrium – quite the reverse! It was an obvious compromise whereby the courts had abandoned some of the strict procedural certainties associated with judicial restraint but had not squarely embraced a pluralist logic; a situation in which the close mix of expansive and restrictive elements created much difficulty and pressure for further change.

The hallmark of the 'funnel' was a more relaxed approach to standing to sue *(locus standi)*, whereby the judges determine what types of interest they are willing to protect in judicial review proceedings (see p. 694 below). This represented a departure from the prevailing private-interest rationale ('protection of the individual') and gave explicit recognition to the role of pressure groups as 'public interest advocates'.[15] Based on a concept of public interest in administrative legality, the funnel model thus satisfied a range of normative and expository functions.

Notably however, the funnel model was predicated on a sharp increase in judicial discretion as, for example, by allowing standing to be considered in conjunction with the merits (the *Federation* case, see p. 696 below). And behind the greater liberality on standing lay a tightening of the procedural screw in other respects, an exhibition in judicial mastery of the system. The key criterion at the permission stage is a 'sufficiently arguable' claim. In the light of increasing numbers of judicial review challenges, especially from immigrants and homeless people, a process had already begun of ratcheting-up the interpretation of this most slippery of concepts (see p. 689 below).

Reflecting and reinforcing the rise of a rights-based approach to judicial review (see Chapter 3), later years have seen movement in the direction of our third ideal type, the '(American) freeway'.
Participative and pluralist in orientation, this 'interest-representation' model ultimately stands for judicial review as a surrogate political process. A defining feature is permeability at each stage of the litigation. As well as a generous approach to standing to sue, interventions in the proceedings by third parties (see p. 701 below) are a standard feature, the rules of evidence gathering are enhanced (greater openness), and the approach to remedies becomes that of the interventionist or 'managerial judge'. This in turn links with expansive grounds of review, with heavy emphasis on the constitutional properties of judicial review. Especially favourable to groups, the freeway model is well suited to 'test-case strategy'.

The largely hypothetical or sporadic freeway model[16] was inspired by some famous writings in the heady days of judicial activism in the United States,[17] where judicial review could occasionally provide the hard-biting collective remedy of the 'structural injunction'. The very strength of the model is however its Achilles heel. Concerns about the courts' institutional competence are magnified, threatening the old icon of 'disinterested justice'. The judges'

[15] See further, R. Rawlings, 'Courts and interests' in Loveland (ed.), *A Special Relationship? American influences on public law in the UK.*

[16] Not least, these days, in the US; see M. Feeley and E. Rubin, *Judicial Policy-Making and the Modern State* (Cambridge University Press, 1999); M. Tushnet, *The New Constitutional Order* (Princeton University Press, 2003); J. Beermann, 'Common law and statute law in US Federal administrative law' in Pearson, Harlow and Taggart (eds.), *Administrative Law in a Changing State* (Hart Publishing, 2008).

[17] R. Stewart, 'The reformation of American administrative law' (1975) 88 *Harv. LR* 1776; and A. Chayes, 'The Role of the Judge in Public Law Litigation' (1976) 89 *Harv. LR* 1281.

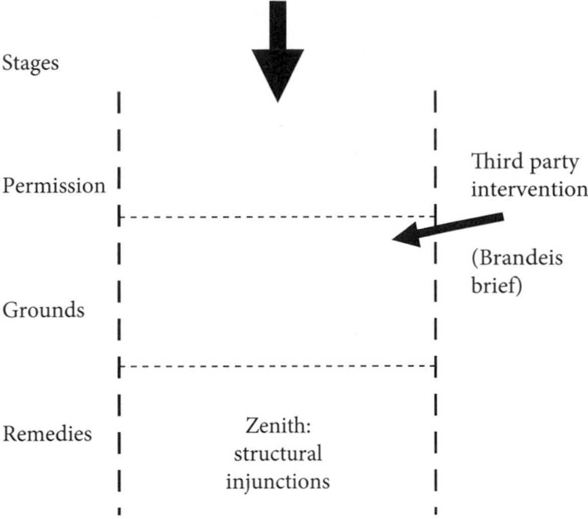

Fig 15.3 The (American) freeway

own representativeness is necessarily called into question. And the freeway's unstructured character means that it can all too easily degenerate into a 'free-for-all' with no clear rules.[18]

The more modest development in this jurisdiction is typically piecemeal in character, a mix of institution-building (see below) and specific procedural amendment.[19] The judges are seen advancing the broad capacities of the system, for example in terms of fact-finding, so further buttressing the normative dimension of legal supervision. The judicial toolkit of remedies is considerably expanded, not least by reason of European requirements and spill-over effects (see further below). Continued development of the declaratory order is an important feature.

This is not a one-way progression however. At the same time, we have noted the prevalence of light-touch approaches under both the *Wednesbury* and proportionality principles; the use of the dubious 'mirror principle' as a limiting device (ECHR 'floor' of rights a domestic 'ceiling' – see p. 136 above); and the scant enthusiasm for structural procedural review under ECHR Art. 6 (see p. 653 above). The machinery has in fact been stretched through formal requirements for early party interaction (see p. 692 below) – a 'front-loading' of the process designed to produce space for settlement and, through better information for the judges at the permission stage, a counterweight for the more intensive judicial scrutiny available on the substantive application. In this way, the judges have constructed the 'British motorway' (see Fig. 15.4).

18 J. Resnik, 'Managerial judges' (1982) 96 *Harv. LR* 374.
19 C. Harlow, 'Public law and popular justice' (2002) 65 *MLR* 1.

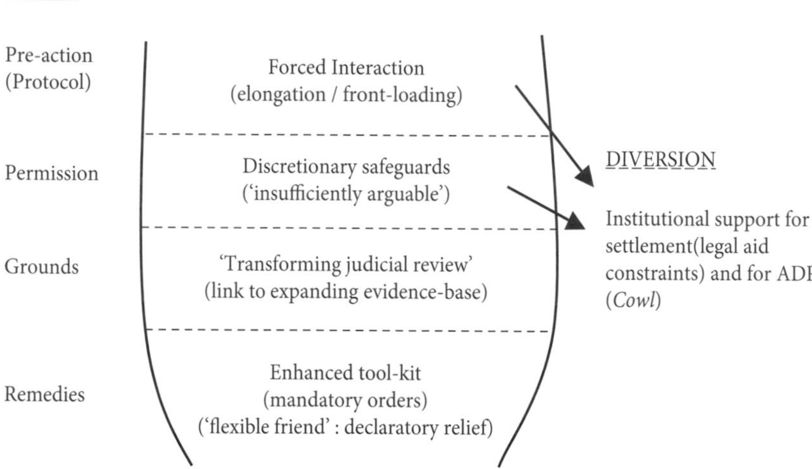

Fig 15.4 The British motorway

(c) Multiple streams

The cluster of legal issues associated with a multi-streamed jurisdiction is scarcely a phenomenon confined to the UK or England and Wales. But in a country in more ways than one the crossroads of the world, the mix is peculiarly potent. There is the historical legacy of Empire, as represented in 'the common law globe'. There is the regional development associated with the 'two legal Europes'. The UK is a big player on the international stage. It would be absurd to ignore the high standing and influence of British courts in many other jurisdictions in an Internet age of transnational judicial dialogue and precedent swaps.

Bamforth has highlighted the scale of the challenge that confronts the national judges in this situation. He describes 'a multi-layered constitution' containing European, state and sub-state systems in which, in determination of the appropriate judicial role, 'red light' and 'green light' perspectives are crosscut by 'minimalist' and 'maximalist' views of the reception of EC law and the ECHR.[20] This is indicative of a changing mindset: a move beyond the (transitional) style of a common law framework subject to 'European influences'[21] to explicit recognition of a sometimes well-suited, sometimes ill-fitting, range of jurisprudential architecture.

So how might the contemporary multi-streamed system of judicial review be visualised? One approach obviously would be to specify three somewhat different ideal types, one for each of the clearly established jurisdictional sources:

[20] N. Bamforth, 'Courts in a multi-layered constitution' in Bamforth and Leyland (eds), *Public Law in a Multi-Layered Constitution* (Hart Publishing, 2003).

[21] Woolf, Jowell and Le Sueur, *Judicial Review*, p. 3.

common law, EC law and Convention rights. But this would obscure the considerable continuity in practice and procedure under the shared umbrella of the AJR, as also the increased influence of comparative materials and the growing public international law dimension. It would too be highly artificial in light of the common experience of different claims mixed in a single case, for example:

- common law/EC law — *Edwards* (see p. 651 above)
- common law/Convention rights — *Daly* (see p. 118 above)
- EC law/Convention rights — *Countryside Alliance* (see p. 113 above)
- common law/Convention rights/ — *A (No. 2)* (see p. 131 above)
- public international law.

Let us instead try a single layout:

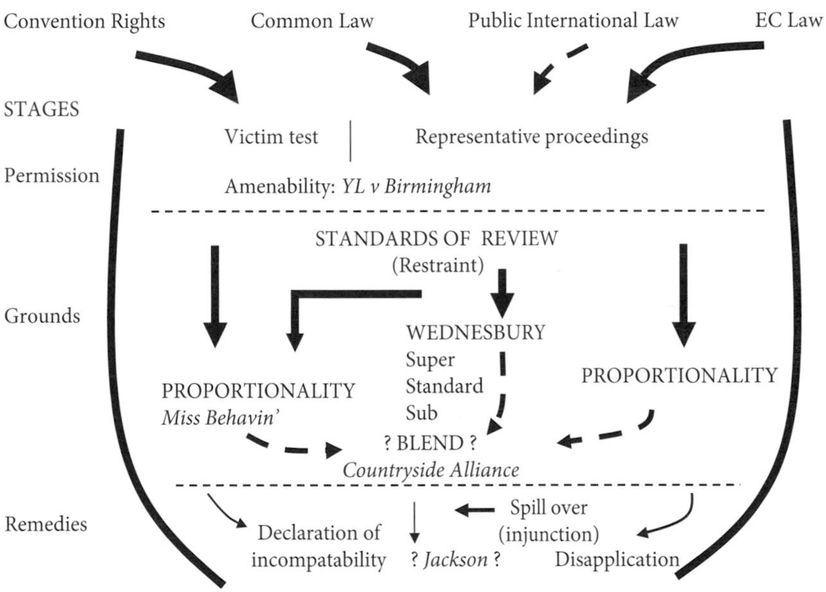

Fig 15.5 Spaghetti junction

As the metaphor implies, our contemporary judicial review framework is apt to appear somewhat bewildering, even a little scary, to the uninitiated.[22] But increased complexity – more problems of navigation[23] – is part and parcel of a system in which major, overlapping jurisdictional sources are more or less closely linked together. This model serves as a reminder, first, of the scope for

[22] Yet the model is highly simplified, the aim again being to focus attention on certain key elements. See further, R. Rawlings. 'Modelling judicial review'.

[23] Particular twists and turns, e.g. as regards standing to sue, are discussed in later sections. See also, in relation to amenability to jurisdiction, p. 380 above.

overlap as regards the pegs on which to hang a case; secondly, that each of the jurisdictional sources reaches parts the others cannot reach; thirdly, of the need not to think in terms of hermetically sealed compartments. The model further highlights the expansionary tendencies of judicial intervention and discretionary control. Since, in Sir Konrad Schiemann's words, 'the light in which a lawyer views a set of facts and the way in which he formulates the legal problem is very much conditioned by the legal system he is applying',[24] some mental gymnastics are also called for.

The 'spaghetti junction' model is exemplified in the debate surrounding the proportionality principle (see p. 106 above). In the domestic law stream of cases, the *Wednesbury* doctrine of unreasonableness is normally applicable; in the two European streams, proportionality is the governing principle. As counsel argued in the *Countryside Alliance* case (see p. 113 above), however, the concept of proportionality does not carry identical meanings in EC and Convention law.[25] British judges therefore have to manoeuvre with three streams of doctrinal traffic at spaghetti junction. With the advent of the Human Rights Act (HRA) and greater familiarity with the proportionality principle, however, pressure for replacement of *Wednesbury* at common law was bound to intensify, pointing up the possibility of a fork in the road whereby *Wednesbury* and proportionality coexist within the domestic law stream. This is already occurring, as statute imposes a proportionality test in particular policy domains, as with the Race Relations (Amendment) Act 2000,[26] or when a particular doctrinal development seems to call for proportionality, as we saw with substantive legitimate expectation in the case of *Naharajah and Abdi* (see p. 229 above).

Similarly, variable demands may be placed on the machinery at the stage of remedies. The pressure for conformity and resultant 'spill-over effect' is strongest in the EU stream, where the doctrines of supremacy and direct effect in EC law and the duty of loyal co-operation operate to push domestic courts towards harmonisation in the interests of the 'effectiveness' of EC law, a principle of primary importance to the ECJ.[27] The most notable example is *Factortame*, where we saw the prohibition against injunctions against the Crown modified (see p. 180 above). The 'spill-over effect' came in *M v Home Office* where the consequent disparity between EC and English law appeared to leave litigants in the domestic stream disadvantaged, an argument that featured in the House of Lords proceedings (see p. 10 above). Something very similar

[24] Sir K. Schiemann, foreword to R. Gordon, *EC Law in Judicial Review*.

[25] Compare G. de Burca, 'The principle of proportionality and its applications in EC Law' [1993] 12 *Yearbook of European Law* 105 and J. McBride, 'Proportionality and the European Convention on Human Rights' in Ellis (ed.), *The Principle of Proportionality in the Laws of Europe* (Hart Publishing, 1999).

[26] See *Defence Secretary v Elias* [2006] EWCA Civ 1293.

[27] See generally, G. Anthony, *UK Public Law and European Law* (Hart Publishing, 2002) and M. Claes, *The National Courts' Mandate in the European Constitution* (Hart Publishing, 2005)

<?> See generally,

has happened in the field of restitution.[28] And just as *Factortame* brought a new remedy in the shape of a power to 'disapply' statutes incompatible with EC law so the HRA brought the lesser 'declaration of incompatibility' with Convention rights.

Looking forwards, the shaping of the streams, with more or less intermingling at spaghetti junction, is likely to emerge as a permanent feature of the new 'multi-layered jurisdiction'. The traffic may of course change. Some streams may gradually merge: proportionality could, as Lord Steyn wished, replace *Wednesbury* unreasonableness altogether (see p. 120 above).[29] New streams might be added. International law might, for example, be pulled more strongly into the system; other streams might be modified, as could be the case if a British Bill of Rights were to be adopted. At least for the foreseeable future, however, a single-track road seems unlikely.

2. Organisational arrangements

Institutional reform is a recurring theme in the recent history of judicial review in England and Wales – in the face of recurring problems of delay and inefficiency, of mismatch between caseload and court resources, and of an inward-looking administrative culture. The period 1977–81 witnessed a major rationalisation of the machinery. Following the introduction of AJR procedure through revision to Order 53, then the governing instrument in the Supreme Court Rules, this phase culminated with s. 31 of the Supreme Court Act 1981, which incorporated some important provisions on access and party delay that remain in place. The years 2000–2 saw a recasting of the process with active case management and regulation and settlement of claims. Grounded in Part 54 of the new Civil Procedural Rules (CPR), this set the seal on the establishment of the Administrative Court, a bastion of judicial power in the constitution. The current phase sees the Administrative Court facing incipient competition from the revamped tribunals structure (see Chapter 11), but opening up the exciting prospect of a regional structure: 'the Administrative Court for users'.

(a) AJR and Crown Office List

Prior to 1977 a mind-numbing complexity surrounded the remedies available in different courts and with different rules on amenability to jurisdiction, standing to sue and time limits. Remedial reform had been a long time coming to this product of the centuries. Whereas Lord Denning had urged replacement of the 'pick and shovel' with 'new and up to date machinery'

[28] See p. 764 above. And see Case 199/82 *Amministrazione delle Finanze dello Stato v San Giorgio* [1983] ECR 3595.

[29] See further, M. Hunt, 'Against bifurcation' in Dyzenhaus, Hunt and Huscroft (eds.), *A Simple Common Lawyer* (Hart Publishing, 2009).

in 1949,[30] it was only in the post-*Ridge v Baldwin* era that successive Law Commission reports helped to generate a sufficient head of steam.[31] With the aim of simplification, the AJR was explicitly designed as an umbrella procedure covering the prerogative orders and the two 'ordinary' remedies of declaration and injunction in cases designated as 'public law'. In addition, the court was empowered to award damages provided there was a recognised cause of action. Such would be the vehicle for judicial review for the next twenty years.

Reform of procedure paved the way for court reform. The impetus came from problems in the Divisional Court, with responsibility for the prerogative orders and traditionally composed of three High Court judges, which in the late 1970s was sinking under an increasing caseload.[32] With AJR procedure it would commonly be single judges who presided at full hearings and the practice was adopted of nominating a small cadre of judges considered specialists in some aspect of administrative law to take Ord. 53 cases. Provision was made for transferring into this 'Crown Office List' other High Court matters seen to involve administrative law issues, as with appeals on points of law from tribunals. The idea of judicial review as a significant and distinctive area of jurisdiction was thus given a powerful boost.

We touch here on Dicey's *bête noire*, a separate system of courts predicated on a jurisdictional distinction between public and private law, alien to the common law tradition (see Chapter 1). Although there had been seeds of this in the shape of the prerogative orders, the Divisional Court was emphatically not an administrative court in the sense to which Dicey had objected; composed of 'ordinary' judges, it possessed no monopoly in remedies against the administration. Declarations and injunctions were available from the Chancery Division, while actions for damages lay in the ordinary civil courts (see Chapter 17). The Law Commission, in proposing AJR procedure, had been looking for more, not less, procedural flexibility, the assumption being that applicants would have the option between AJR and a civil action in cases where both were available on the facts of the case.[33] However, in *O'Reilly v Mackman*,[34] Lord Diplock took it upon himself to invent 'procedural exclusivity', the doctrine that AJR procedure should generally be considered obligatory in public law cases. The case concerned challenges by several prisoners to decisions of the Board of Visitors punish-

[30] A. Denning, *Freedom under the Law* (Stevens, 1949).

[31] Law Commission, *Remedies in Administrative Law* (WP No. 40, 1971); *Report on Remedies in Administrative Law* (Law Com. No. 73), Cmnd 6407 (1976).

[32] See L. Blom-Cooper, 'The new face of judicial review: Administrative changes in Order 53' [1982] *PL* 250.

[33] *Report on Remedies in Administrative Law* [34]. S. 31(2) of the Supreme Court Act 1981 provided that, whereas certiorari, mandamus and prohibition 'shall' be awarded under AJR procedure, declarations and injunctions 'may' be. Ord. 53, r. 1(2) and CPR 54(2)(3) are successively to the same effect.

[34] [1983] 2 AC 237.

ing them with loss of remission; complaint was made of breach of natural justice. Either because they were out of time for judicial review, or because they wanted to be sure of an opportunity to cross-examine on disputed facts (see p. 705 below), the prisoners went by ordinary civil procedure, asking for declarations. They were stopped in their tracks. Lord Diplock stressed the importance of the special 'safeguards' in AJR procedure in guarding against 'groundless, unmeritorious or tardy attacks on the validity of decisions made by public authorities'. It would generally be 'contrary to public policy, and as such an abuse of process' to permit a person 'seeking to establish that a public authority infringed rights to which he was entitled to protection under public law' to proceed by ordinary action and so 'evade' Ord. 53 filtering processes. 'The development of procedural public law' could see exceptions 'decided on a case to case basis'.

The one substantial argument in favour of procedural exclusivity was that for concentration of expertise in a judicial power base: channelling cases in this way helped to cement the position of the 'nominated judges'.[35] *O'Reilly* otherwise represented a variation on a theme: not filtering cases out of the judicial review process, but rather sucking cases in so as to repress them. In this regard, *O'Reilly* was both about rationing – time limits and the choice of a 'wrong' procedure ended it without reference to the merits – and judicial management – with judicial review procedure being seen as more streamlined (especially as regards the evidential techniques: see p. 703 below). The further twist was express provision in Ord. 53 for transfer out of, but not into, AJR procedure.

Lord Diplock had set sail against the tide: an emphasis on internal jurisdictional boundaries at the very time that new modalities of regulatory and contractual governance saw policy and administration moving in the opposite direction. Nor was the Crown Office List about to spread wings; reflecting entrenched interests in an elite system centred at the Royal Courts of Justice, procedural exclusivity worked to cement a London monopoly in public law cases. Little attention was paid to the competing value of access to justice. For example, community lawyers, accustomed to suing local councils in local county courts on behalf of homeless people, now faced an arduous trek.[36]

Entirely predictably,[37] *O'Reilly* resulted in a mass of so-called 'satellite litigation', sterile in the sense of being solely concerned with procedural form, whether one could sue and where one had to sue, and not with the merits.

35 M. Sunkin, 'What is happening to applications for judicial review?' (1987) 50 *MLR* 432.

36 On the basis that the decision whether or not to provide accommodation was a public law matter challengeable solely through AJR procedure: *Cocks v Thanet DC* [1983] 2 AC 286.

37 C. Harlow, '"Public" and "private" law: Definition without distinction' (1980) 43 *MLR* 241. See also, S. Fredman and G. Morris, 'The costs of exclusivity: Public and private re-examined' [1994] *PL* 69.

Gradually a more generous judicial attitude prevailed, with Lord Diplock's concession of possible 'exceptions' being increasingly exploited.[38]Arguments that individuals should be able to invoke the law as a shield against public authorities without bringing separate proceedings prevailed.[39] Prior to the introduction of the CPR, however, the law concerning 'exclusivity' remained exceedingly complex: an object lesson for a whole generation of administrative lawyers in the pitfalls of 'procedural public law'.

(b) CPR and the Administrative Court

Another Law Commission report in 1994 drew attention to major inefficiencies in the handling of Crown Office business, while advocating increased accessibility in the manner of 'the funnel' model as well as enhanced procedural flexibility.[40] Nor could it be expected that Ord. 53 procedure would escape the new orthodoxy of the civil justice reforms promoted in the 1990s by Lord Woolf, not least the twin techniques of forced interaction between the parties at an early stage and active management of individual cases by the judiciary.[41] However, given the recent emergence of judicial review as a specialist jurisdiction, and also the evident constitutional sensitivities, changes had to await detailed consideration of the workings of the Crown Office List.

Eventually published in 2000, the study by accountant Sir Jeffrey Bowman painted a grim picture.[42] After a brief period of respite, delay, which in the early 1990s often involved judicial review cases taking over two years to be heard, was increasing. The work of the review was hindered by a basic lack of management information about the handling of business. Continuing the Dickensian theme, Bowman drew attention to the mishmash of jurisdictions making up the Crown Office List. He stressed the importance of changing the organisational culture; 'reducing delays as far as possible' and 'strengthening the capacity of the list . . . to deal with its expanding jurisdiction'. The HRA was casting a shadow; a further increase in the judicial review workload could reasonably be anticipated once it came fully into force.[43] Bowman demanded careful planning and resource allocation and proper lines of responsibility and firm office management, necessitating 'a

[38] See e.g. *Davy v Spelthorne BC* [1984] AC 264 and *Roy v Kensington and Chelsea and Westminster Family Practitioner Committee* [1992] 1 AC 624.

[39] See *Wandsworth LBC v Winder* [1985] AC 461 and (sharply distinguishing the earlier case of *R v Wicks* [1997] 2 All ER 801) *Boddington v British Transport Police* [1999] AC 143.

[40] Law Commission, *Administrative Law: Judicial review and statutory appeals* (Report No. 226, 1994).

[41] Lord Woolf, *Access to Justice: The final report to the Lord Chancellor on the civil justice system in England and Wales* (HMSO, 1997).

[42] Sir J. Bowman, *Review of the Crown Office List* (Lord Chancellor's Department, 2000).

[43] Previously, not only judicial review and statutory appeals and applications but also matters ranging from extradition to contempt of court were handled by the Crown Office. Bowman actually erred in budgeting for a deluge of human rights claims.

continuing need for a specialised court as part of the High Court to deal with public and administrative law cases'. 'Speed, certainty, efficiency, consistency and quality of decisions in public law cases can only be realised by having a dedicated office to administer cases and dedicated judicial resources to hear them.' The Crown Office List duly metamorphosed into the fully-fledged Administrative Court,[44] better to emphasise the principal nature of the jurisdiction. Dicey's concept of the Rule of Law by 'ordinary courts' had again been stretched but not violated.

Most of Bowman's procedural recommendations were incorporated in the current scheme of Part 54 of the CPR, which – replacing RSC Ord. 53 as machinery for judicial review litigation – was inaugurated in October 2000 to coincide with general implementation of the HRA. Reflecting the ideology of the Woolf reforms to civil justice, and building in turn on the prior trends in judicial review, a strong dose of discretionary judicial control is of the essence of this.[45] Practitioners thus note the creeping tentacles of active case management.[46]

The tailored provisions in CPR 54 are subject to the 'overriding objective' set out in CPR Part 1 'of enabling the court to deal with cases justly'. This includes, 'so far as is practicable', ensuring that the parties 'are on an equal footing'; 'saving expense'; and dealing with the case 'in ways which are proportionate' to its importance, the amount of money involved and the complexity of the issues. So, Administrative Court judges must follow the practice in ordinary civil actions of regulating the conduct of litigation, for example by encouraging co-operation between the parties, fixing timetables or otherwise controlling the progress of the case, helping the parties to settle in whole or in part and encouraging recourse to alternative dispute resolution (ADR). While this may seem unremarkable, we will see how judicial review litigation raises particular problems in this regard, especially at the distinctive permission stage.

Much of the sting of procedural exclusivity was drawn. First, the new formula in CPR 54(1) for identifying cases appropriate for AJR procedure was phrased to reflect the more expansive approach in *Datafin* (see p. 317 above) – 'a decision . . . in relation to the exercise of a public function'. Secondly, as part of the Woolf reforms to civil justice, the stress in judicial review on discretionary 'safeguards' was read across under the CPR to 'ordinary' civil claims via techniques of case management.[47] With procedural differences thus flattened, through greater judicial control across the piece, why not greater

44 *Practice Direction: Administrative Court* [2000] 1 WLR 1654.

45 T. Cornford and M. Sunkin, 'The Bowman Report, access and the recent reforms of the judicial review procedure' [2001] *PL* 11.

46 M. Fordham, *Judicial Review Handbook*, 5th edn (Hart Publishing, 2008), pp. 215–19.

47 E.g. delay could now be taken into account on an application to strike out or for summary judgment. See further, D. Oliver, 'Public law procedures and remedies: Do we need them?' [2002] *PL* 91.

procedural flexibility as between 'public' and 'private' law? Thirdly, underwriting this, there was now provision for transfer of cases into, as well as out of, AJR procedure (CPR 30.5 and 54.20).

Lord Woolf, who had earlier been an advocate of the 'procedural divide' because of the judicial review 'safeguards',[48] duly shifted position. In the key case of *Clark v University of Lincolnshire & Humberside*,[49] C was awarded an inferior degree amid allegations of plagiarism; without a university 'visitor' to complain to, and following dispute about its appeal procedures, she sued the university in contract. Several years later, the point was taken that she should have sought (and so been subject to the strict time limit in) judicial review. The Court of Appeal allowed the private law claim to proceed, saying that, although C could have applied for judicial review, it was not right to deny her access to the courts for abuse of process:

> *Lord Woolf:* The court's approach has to be considered in the light of the changes brought about by the CPR. Those changes include a requirement that a party to proceedings should behave reasonably both before and after they have commenced proceedings. Parties are now under an obligation to help the court further the over-riding objectives which include ensuring that cases are dealt with expeditiously and fairly . . . The intention of the CPR is to . . . avoid barren procedural disputes which generate satellite litigation . . . The emphasis can therefore be said to have changed since *O'Reilly v Mackman.* What is likely to be important . . . will not be whether the right procedure has been adopted but whether the protection provided by [judicial review process] has been flouted in circumstances which are inconsistent with the proceedings being . . . conducted justly in accordance with the general principles contained in [CPR] Part 1.

Attesting to the broad influence of *Clark*, cases on procedural exclusivity are today notable by their absence and as regards 'public' and 'private' functions, it is the issue of amenability to jurisdiction under HRA s. 6 that commands attention! A further development is shown in the *Mullins* case(s).[50] Judicial review proceedings had again been launched against a decision of the Jockey Club; eventually the applicant only sought the ordinary remedy of a declaration. Having held that the *Aga Khan* case (see p. 319 above) still held sway under the CPR, such that judicial review was not available in light of the parties' contractual relationship, the judge transferred the case to himself sitting in the Queen's Bench Division. Echoes of the bridging of the public/private 'divide' in the *Bradley case* (see p. 320 above), the judge then determined it on the basis of

[48] Lord Woolf, 'Droit public, English style' [1995] *PL* 57. See also C. Harlow, 'Why public law is private law: An invitation to Lord Woolf' in Zuckerman and Cranston (eds.), *Reform of Civil Procedure* (Clarendon Press, 1995).

[49] [2001] WLR 1988. See further, Lord Woolf, 'The Human Rights Act 1998 and remedies' in Andenas and Fairgrieve (eds.), *Judicial Review in International Perspective* (Kluwer, 2000).

[50] *R (Mullins) v Jockey Club* [2005] EWHC 2197; *Mullins v McFarlane* [2006] EWHC 986.

a supervisory jurisdiction. Artificial yes, but the prevailing sense of procedural flexibility is palpable.

(c) The Administrative Court in transition

For a little while, Bowman appeared to have done the trick. Armed with a new budgetary allocation, with six courtrooms regularly in use and a lead judge given overall responsibility for speed, efficiency and economy, the Administrative Court exuded a more professional air. As against a mere handful in the early days of AJR, there were by 2003 some thirty 'nominated judges' contributing their services.[51] But with a virtual doubling of the Administrative Court caseload[52] driven by applications to require the Asylum and Immigration Tribunal (AIT) to reconsider (see p. 519 above), things turned sour. By 2007 there were grave delays: on average sixteen weeks for applications for permission to be considered on the papers and eighteen months from initial claim to a substantive hearing. In an embarrassing manoeuvre, the Public Law Project threatened the Ministry of Justice with judicial review proceedings for breach of the common law right of access to justice (*Witham*: see p. 114 above), of the ECHR Art. 6 right (determination of civil rights and obligations 'within a reasonable time') and of the duty to ensure an efficient and effective court system (s.1 of the Courts Act 2003). A significant increase in the numbers of sitting judges was eventually conceded.[53]

We are back too with questions about the relationship between courts and tribunals. In light of the problems afflicting the Administrative Court, pressure from the judges to have the AIT properly nested inside the new two-tier tribunal system (see p. 520 above) was eminently predictable. Asserting the idea of courts as an elite forum of dispute resolution, a judicial working group observed of the reconsideration process: 'each case is intrinsically important, but the applications are numerous and repetitive. We do not consider that this is an appropriate use of High Court judge time.'[54]

Here the use or otherwise of powers in the Tribunals, Courts and Enforcement Act 2007 (TCEA) to order transfer of judicial review cases from the Administrative Court to the Upper Tribunal will be significant. There is provision not only for case-by-case transfer, a sensible element of flexibility, but also for automatic transfer of designated classes of case.[55] The risk is that the inner institutional strength of the Administrative Court, so painstakingly built up, will be diluted by the loss of major categories of case.

[51] Administrative Court, *Annual Report 2003*.

[52] The case load rose from 6,202 new cases to 11,302 between 2002 and 2006; see p. 713 below for further details.

[53] Initially from 7 to between 9 and 12 per week, with more (especially Deputy High Court judges) to follow: see C. Haley, 'Action on Administrative Court delays' (2008) *Judicial Review* 69.

[54] The May Committee, *Justice Outside London* (2007) [46].

[55] TCEA, s. 19, currently with the exception of asylum and immigration matters. But see the Borders, Citizenship and Immigration Bill currently before Parliament.

A study in 2007 of judicial review claims against local authorities threw the issue of 'legal geography' – accessibility and outreach – into sharp relief. All the councils on a twenty-strong list of those most frequently challenged were in London.[56] What about protection of the individual elsewhere? Invocation of the so-called 'radiating effects' of court cases (see Chapter 16) is scarcely an answer. Perhaps hopefully, Lord Justice Sedley spoke of the judges themselves 'starting to appreciate that there are large geographical and social gaps in the legal profession's ability to provide advice and representation' in relation to Convention rights.[57] And if inculcating core values of good governance was important, was there not a case for making the elite machinery more visible and immediate?

In the long view, the facilitative model of 'the Administrative Court in Wales', whereby, post-devolution, judicial review claims against Welsh public bodies could be initiated and determined inside that country,[58] should be seen as heralding a more general break-up of a London monopoly. The May Committee has championed the 'very strong economic, business, professional and social case' for regionalisation of the Administrative Court:

> Proper access to justice is not achieved if those in the regions can only bring judicial review and other claims in the Administrative Court in London. There would be substantial saving in public and private expense. The present system discriminates against those who are not in the South East of England.[59]

Nor was the May Committee much impressed by objections from well-placed functionaries of 'interesting claims' being lost to the provinces, of local hearings leading to 'unacceptable isolation' among senior judiciary, and of something awful called 'a deployment nightmare'.[60] IT could assist in linking different Administrative Court centres, ensuring cohesiveness while allowing judicial review to be brought closer to the people.

Not before time, there are current plans for regional centres of the Administrative Court to open in Birmingham, Cardiff, Leeds and Manchester in 2009, with a further centre planned for Bristol in 2010.[61] Meanwhile, the potential synergies are already evident in the profession. Following the

[56] M. Sunkin, K. Calvo, L. Platt and T. Landman, 'Mapping the use of judicial review to challenge local authorities in England and Wales' [2007] *PL* 545.

[57] Sir S. Sedley, 'The rocks or the open sea: Where is the Human Rights Act heading?' (2005) 32 *JLS* 3, 4.

[58] Even if it has tended to be little more than a 'post-box'. See further, Sir J. Thomas, 'Legal Wales: Its modern origins and its role after devolution' in Watkin (ed.), *Legal Wales: Its past, its future* (Welsh Legal History Society, 2001); M. Williams and N. Cooke, 'The Administrative Court in Wales' (2005) 4 *Wales J. of Law and Policy* 102.

[59] May Committee, *Justice Outside London* [51].

[60] *Ibid.*, annex L.

[61] See further, R. Clayton, 'New arrangements for the Administrative Court' (2008) 13 *Judicial Review* 164.

example of the London-based Constitutional and Administrative Law Bar Association (1986), and the Wales Public Law and Human Rights Association (1999), barristers, solicitors and academics have now joined forces in a Northern Administrative Law Association designed to raise profile and foster specialist expertise.

3. Regulating access

(a) Permission

One justification for permission concerns the prompt and efficient despatch of public business, the need to protect public administration from unmeritorious and/or costly litigation and from the uncertainty engendered by delay. A second justification concerns the efficient use of court time; the preliminary filter may deter unmeritorious applications and facilitate their disposal with the minimum use of resources. According to Lord Woolf,[62] the judges have also been 'encouraged . . . to develop their power to intervene to control abuse of power in a way which they would not have done otherwise'. This may appear a powerful argument – discretionary 'safeguards' as the *sine qua non* of judicial activism – but it is obviously not susceptible of proof.

Prior to the CPR, the applicant had the right to choose an oral hearing at this stage.[63] After Bowman however, early party interaction today grounds the norm of permission decisions 'on the papers'. Other than in truly urgent cases (where application may be made by telephone to a designated out-of-hours judge),[64] oral procedure is typically confined to those initially unsuccessful applications that are renewed.[65] Fortunately, as regards a case challenging precedent for example, permission to appeal against refusal of permission can still be sought from the Court of Appeal.

The statistics testify to the scale of the filtering.[66] In the two years 2006–7 for example, of some 7,500 applications considered, less than a quarter (1,600) were granted permission. Figure 15.6 also reveals that, while the numbers attracted into 'the funnel' have continued to rise, the proportion going forwards has fallen significantly with the CPR framework.[67]

[62] Woolf, *Protection of the Public*, Ch. 1.

[63] As counterbalanced by a right to apply to set aside a permission.

[64] *Practice Statement (Administrative Court: Listing and Urgent Cases)* [2002] 1 WLR 810. E.g. for an interim injunction to protect a vulnerable person: see p. 743 below.

[65] See further, Fordham, *Judicial Review Handbook* , pp. 209–11.

[66] They actually understate it, a further component of the judicial discretion being 'partial filtering' (power to make the permission conditional or restricted to certain grounds). Originally emerging under Ord. 53 procedure, the practice has blossomed as part of CPR-style active case management. See for illustration, *R (Smith) v Parole Board* [2003] 1 WLR 2548.

[67] We noted this trend in the second edition of *Law and Administration*, Ch. 16. The numbers of leave applications increased sevenfold in the period 1981–96, while those successful roughly trebled: from some 550 to 3,900 cases, and 375 to 1,250 cases, respectively.

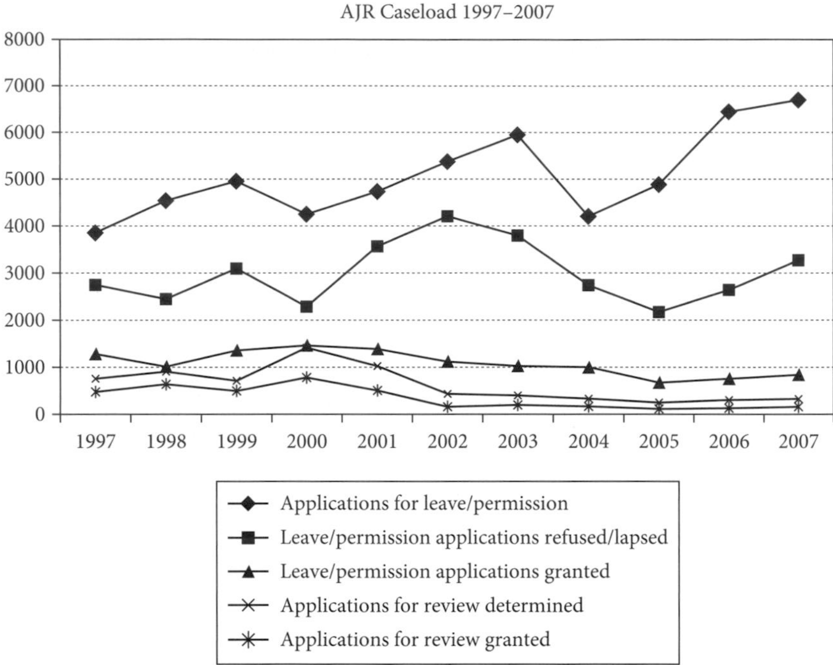

Fig 15.6 AJR caseload 1997–2007

One explanation for the discrepancy is tougher system management of the process by the judiciary – hardened attitudes under mounting pressures of work. This form of judicial gatekeeping is starkly illustrated in two decisions from the 1980s. Bound up in a powerful assertion of public interest, the first one is the homelessness case of *Puhlhofer*,[68] where Lord Brightman decreed 'a very hard look' before allowing legal claims from this vulnerable section of society to proceed. There should be 'a lessening in the number of challenges mounted against local authorities who are endeavouring in extremely difficult circumstances to perform their duty under the Homeless Persons Act, with due regard for all their other problems'. The homelessness caseload promptly fell. In issue in *Swati*[69] was the rule, also operated at the permission stage, against permitting judicial review where an alternative remedy was available. This rule is of long standing in relation to statutory procedures, but exceptionally may be disapplied if the court considers the alternative remedy inappropriate.[70] Refused admission at the port of entry, a foreign visitor only had a statutory right of appeal to a tribunal from abroad, which hardly constituted effective redress of grievance. In turn, a practice had developed in such cases of seeking

[68] *Puhlhofer v Hillingdon London Borough Council* [1986] AC 484.

[69] *R v Home Secretary, ex p. Swati* [1986] 1 WLR 477. The case is a forerunner of the many problems over immigration tribunals, judicial review and ouster previously discussed.

[70] *R v Chief Constable of the Merseyside Police, ex p. Calveley* [1986] QB 424 is a notable illustration.

judicial review; so much so that, by 1985, visitor cases accounted for some 20 per cent of leave applications.[71] The Court of Appeal took action in *Swati* to halt this practice, even though the alternative procedure was unrealistic. 'Where Parliament provides an appeal procedure, judicial review will have no place, unless the application can distinguish his case from the type of case for which the appeal procedure was provided.'

As the commonest reason for refusal of permission, the phrase 'insufficiently arguable' underwrites the innate flexibility of the system. Early *dicta* from Lord Diplock had suggested a relatively open approach under the AJR. 'If, on a quick perusal of the material then available, the court thinks that it discloses what might on further consideration turn out to be an arguable case in favour of granting the relief claimed, it ought to give leave to apply for that relief.'[72] This fitted with the idea of a new procedure sweeping away old limitations and technicalities – a generous 'funnel'. In the wake of *Puhlhofer* and *Swati*, however, Lord Donaldson, then Master of the Rolls, reiterated demands for a harder look, so targeting not only hopeless cases but also those in the 'potentially arguable' category. 'The judicial review jurisdiction . . . should be exercised very speedily and, given the constraints imposed by limited judicial resources, this necessarily involves limiting the number of cases in which leave to apply should be given.'[73] Leave ought only to be given if prima facie there was already clearly an arguable case for granting the relief claimed. In the absence of detailed information, this meant a large dollop of judicial intuition.[74] A contemporary observer duly remarked on the risk of over-regulation. Good applications might be summarily refused access to the courts, so undermining the several judicial review functions of redress of grievance, control of government, and elaboration of legal principle.[75]

Today, with the CPR, testing for the actual arguability of claims is a familiar feature of permission.[76] Recent *dicta* from the Privy Council in *Sharma v Brown-Antoine*[77] show no enthusiasm at the highest levels for a more open approach; it is rather a case of 'pick and choose'. As a vehicle of judicial discretion, the preferred formulation could scarcely be bettered:

> The court will refuse leave to judicial review unless satisfied that there is an arguable ground for judicial review having a realistic prospect of success . . . But arguability cannot be judged without reference to the nature and gravity of the issue to be argued. It is

[71] Sunkin, 'What is happening to applications for judicial review?'.
[72] In *IRC v National Federation of Self-Employed and Small Businesses* [1982] AC 617.
[73] *R v Panel of Take-overs and Mergers, ex p. Guinness Plc* [1990] 1 QB 146. And see *R v Legal Aid Board, ex p. Hughes, The Times*, 29 October 1992
[74] As Lord Donaldson effectively conceded in *R v Home Secretary, ex p. Doorga* [1990] COD 109. (The information-gathering requirements of early interaction were not yet in place.)
[75] R. Gordon, 'The Law Commission and judicial review: Managing the tensions between case management and public interest challenges' [1995] *PL* 11.
[76] V. Bondy and M. Sunkin, 'Accessing judicial review' [2008] *PL* 647.
[77] [2006] UKPC 57.

> a test which is flexible in its application . . . It is not enough that a case is potentially arguable.[78]

The criterion of delay involves an absurdly complicated set of rules. Statute provides that where the court considers there has been 'undue delay' in making an application, it may refuse to grant permission or, at the end of the case, any relief sought; that is, if granting such relief 'would be likely to cause substantial hardship to, or substantially prejudice the rights of any person, or would be detrimental to good administration'. Meanwhile, under the CPR, a claim must be made 'promptly' and in any event within three months of the date on which the decision or action being challenged was taken.[79] The court retains power to extend the time,[80] but there is also discretion to refuse permission even if the claim is made within the period, in a fast-moving commercial/regulatory environment for example.[81]

Taking transaction typing to new heights, the 2008 case of *Finn-Kelcey*[82] graphically illustrates the role of promptness as a rationing device. A local landowner, who was denied permission to challenge the grant of planning permission for a wind farm, filed his claim form a few days before expiry of the three months time limit:

> *Keene LJ:* The importance of acting promptly applies with particular force in cases where it is sought to challenge the grant of planning permission . . . Once a planning permission has been granted, a developer is entitled to proceed to carry out the development and since there are time limits on the validity of a permission will normally wish to proceed to implement it without delay . . . It may often be of some relevance, when a court is applying the separate test of promptness, that Parliament has prescribed a six weeks time limit in cases where the permission is granted by the Secretary of State [[83]] rather than by a local planning authority, if only because it indicates a recognition by Parliament of the necessity of bringing challenges to planning permissions quickly.
>
> What satisfies the requirement of promptness will vary from case to case . . . Knowledge of a resolution to grant permission will often be relevant to whether a person has acted promptly, even though time does not formally run until the grant of permission.[[84]]

[78] *Ibid.* [14].

[79] Supreme Court Act 1981, s. 31, CPR 54.5 – as against the general limitation period of six years, or three for personal injuries.

[80] E.g. because of delay in the grant of legal aid: *R v Stratford-on-Avon DC, ex p. Jackson* [1985] 1 WLR 1319.

[81] See e.g. *R v Independent Television Commission, ex p. TSW Broadcasting Ltd* [1996] *EMLR* 291. For discussion of the 'flipside' doctrine, see J. Beatson, 'Prematurity and ripeness for review' in Forsyth and Hare (eds.), *The Golden Metwand and the Crooked Cord* (Clarendon Press, 1998).

[82] *Finn-Kelcey v Milton Keynes BC* [2008] EWCA Civ 1067; drawing in turn on *R v Hammersmith and Fulham LBC, ex p. Burkett* [2002] 1 WLR 1593.

[83] Town and Country Planning Act1990, s. 288.

[84] *R (Burkett) v Environment Secretary* [2002] UKHL 23. Note also *Hardy v Pembrokeshire CC* [2006] EWCA Civ 2140 (the obligation to act promptly does not offend ECHR requirements of legal certainty).

> In the present case there is a particular consideration because of the nature of the proposed development. The Secretary of State's . . . Planning Policy Statement] stresses the importance of renewable energy projects, referring to the UK target of generating 10 per cent of electricity from renewable energy sources by 2010, so as to comply with its international obligations entered into by the Government. As Sullivan J [has] said, 'the need for promptness in challenging planning decisions within this policy framework is particularly acute. Delay in challenging decisions in respect of renewable energy projects is more than usually prejudicial to good administration.' [[85]]

Discretionary control writ large, the case further illustrates the mixing of threshold requirements with the issue of merits:

> There may be considerations which mean that it is in the public interest that the claim should be allowed to proceed, despite the delay and the absence of any explanation for that delay. If there is a strong case for saying that the permission was ultra vires, then this court might in the circumstances be willing to grant permission to proceed. But, given the delay, it requires a much clearer-cut case than would otherwise have been necessary.

ADR is a classic means of diversion. A step beyond the old-style alternative remedies rule, CPR 1(4) speaks explicitly of 'encouraging' and 'facilitating' the use of techniques like mediation if 'the court considers that appropriate'.[86] In the much-cited case of *Cowl*,[87] which concerned an exhausting *Coughlan*-style controversy about the closure of a residential care home, Lord Woolf emphasised the need for judicial review practitioners to think creatively about ADR, especially where the individual was publicly funded. Judicial review really should be treated as a remedy of last resort:

> The importance of this appeal is that it illustrates that, even in disputes between public authorities and the members of public for whom they are responsible, insufficient attention is paid to the paramount importance of avoiding litigation wherever this is possible. The appeal also demonstrates that courts should scrutinize extremely carefully applications for judicial review in the case of applications of the class with which this appeal is concerned. The courts should then make appropriate use of their ample powers . . . to ensure that the parties try to resolve the dispute with the minimum involvement of the courts. The legal aid authorities should co-operate in support of this approach.

This analysis sits comfortably with the call for 'proportionate dispute resolution' in the White Paper *Transforming Public Services: Complaints, redress and tribunals* discussed in Chapter 11. Here the potential advantages of ADR are said to be greater flexibility, avoidance of confrontation, forward-looking

[85] *R (Redcar and Cleveland BC) v. Business Secretary* [2008] EWHC 1847.

[86] Note however *Halsey v Milton Keynes General NHS Trust* [2004] 1 WLR 3002 (lack of court power to direct parties to enter into ADR).

[87] *R (Cowl) v Plymouth City Council* [2002] 1 WLR 803.

focus and reduced cost. But Lord Woolf glosses over the problems stemming from the rigidity of such a pyramidal framework in the judicial review context. What happens when the alternative remedy proves to be inadequate or partial? Persons eventually driven to litigation are unlikely to see the system as providing speedy and effective redress of grievance.[88] Again, there is an underlying tension between the private function of ADR in meeting the needs of the parties and the normative and expository role of judicial review.

The courts have notably failed post-*Cowl* to generate clear and principled guidelines on the matter. One might hope for a more carefully targeted approach:

> Disputes concerning education and social services provision, in particular, may be among those most amenable to resolution by way of mediation, rather than litigation. These kinds of disputes very often centre on finance, rather than points of principle, and easily lend themselves to mediation as they concern a situation where there is likely to be a long-term relationship between the parties. They also concern a subject matter in respect of which litigation may seem the least appropriate forum for dispute resolution.[89]

(b) Front-loading

Bowman had been particularly concerned with the inefficiencies, for court time and resources, of a high rate of settlement *after* leave was granted.[90] Both parties ought to be encouraged to re-examine the strength of their case at the earliest possible stage. Building on 'best practice' in the profession, a solution lay ready to hand: regulated forms of 'private filtering', that is to say forced preliminaries of party interaction or elongation of the AJR process ahead of any judicial involvement.

Duly incorporated in the CPR framework, this front-loading consists of two main elements. First, a 'pre-action protocol for judicial review' provides that the potential claimant should send a letter before action to identify the issues in dispute and establish whether litigation can be avoided. In Bowman's words, the public body should 'consider such a letter with great care to see whether any settlement or resolution is possible', and then respond conceding all or part of the claim or otherwise explaining its position. Strictly speaking, the protocol as a code of good practice is not mandatory. Non-compliance is effectively sanctioned, however, since the court can take it into account when giving case-management directions or making costs orders.[91]

Secondly, CPR 54 effectively establishes the permission stage as an *inter partes* procedure by requiring service of the claim form and accompanying

[88] S. Boyron, 'The rise of mediation in administrative law disputes: Experiences from England, France and Germany' [2006] *PL* 320.

[89] M. Supperstone, D. Stilitz and C. Sheldon, 'ADR and public law' [2006] *PL* 299, 317.

[90] See further, Ch. 16.

[91] For the practical workings, see C. Banner, 'The Judicial Review Pre-Action Protocol' (2008) 13 *Judicial Review* 59.

documents on, and acknowledgement by, the defendant and any other 'interested parties', and lodging of the papers with the Administrative Court. More particularly, the applicant having communicated a detailed statement of the case, an acknowledgement of service should include a summary of intended grounds of opposition to the claim. Let us hope that not too many individual applicants are lost in this aggrandised paper chase![92]

Bowman had seen other possibilities: not only should the more straightforward cases be weeded out ahead of permission, but also the courts would be better placed at that stage to judge arguability (more information, less intuitive judgement). All of which may help to explain the further decline in permission rates under the CPR. According to the authors of a recent empirical study:

> The greater use of the written process and the greater involvement of defendants at the permission stage have made it more difficult for claimants to persuade judges that their claims are sufficiently arguable, and have enabled the judges to be more discriminating in their assessment of the quality of claims. While there has been no formal change in the permission criteria, the consequence has been to heighten the de facto barrier facing claimants. This, however, is only one aspect of the picture. Following the reforms, greater numbers of claims are being resolved prior to the permission stage. Our interview data indicate that a very high proportion of these are being resolved in favour of claimants . . . Despite the diminishing grant rate, the overall picture may be one in which access to substantive justice in terms of satisfactory outcomes has improved.[93]

(c) Lottery?

The same survey reports 'widespread disquiet' among practitioners about judicial inconsistency at the permission stage. 'The actual test applied depends on which judge you get.' 'You often know that if you get a certain judge you are going to win or lose.' 'There are very similar cases which result in different outcomes.' Statistical analysis confirmed a wide variation in grant rates between individual judges (from 11 to 46 per cent).[94] This is a running sore. One 1990s study had revealed an even greater discrepancy (from 21 to 82 per cent) with no obvious factors to do with the nature or type of cases to explain this;[95] a second showed that in practice a full spectrum of interpretations was in operation, with markedly different emphases being placed on the (apparent) merits of applications.[96] Today, practitioners still find it 'difficult to know precisely

[92] See further on the implications for costs, *Mount Cook Land Ltd v Westminster City Council* [2003] EWCA Civ 1346 and *Davey v Aylesbury Vale DC* [2007] EWCA Civ 1166.

[93] Bondy and Sunkin, 'Accessing judicial review', p. 666.

[94] *Ibid.*, pp. 662–3, 665.

[95] L. Bridges, G. Meszaros and M. Sunkin, *Judicial Review in Perspective*, 2nd edn (Cavendish, 1995), Ch. 8.

[96] A. Le Sueur and M. Sunkin, 'Applications for judicial review: The requirement of leave' [1992] *PL* 102.

what the criteria entail from a claimant's perspective'.[97] The vagueness of the 'sufficiently arguable' test feeds the problem.

Against this backdrop, the question is sharply posed: why retain the permission requirement? Many other jurisdictions, including Scotland, manage without; why not England and Wales? Although Bowman urged retention, procedural developments in the wake of the Woolf report underscore the case for abolition. General provisions ground powers to strike out a case if it discloses no cause of action or is an abuse of process, and to give summary judgment if the claimant has no real prospect of success (CPR 3 and 24). Why not substitute these 'safeguards' for the special procedural protections currently afforded public authorities through the permission requirement?[98]

The judicial fear of opening a floodgate makes such a solution unlikely. If, however, permission is to be used as part of a coherent strategy for managing the case-flow, then, as in other areas of public administration, discretion should be properly structured and confined. It is significant that the major exception to incorporation of Bowman's procedural recommendations in the CPR is the absence in Part 54 of a presumption in favour of permission and explicit statement of relevant criteria. Evidently, behind the scenes, the judiciary was successful in maintaining strong discretion.

4. Matters of interest

(a) Standing. . .

Standing to sue functions as a rationing device by requiring potential litigants to demonstrate some recognised 'interest' in the matter in question. As such, the doctrine has significant constitutional connotations, bearing directly on the nature and purpose of judicial review. How should the balance be struck between (a) an individualist and – prioritising the collective good in vindicating the rule of law – a communitarian analysis of rights and public law, and (b) dispute resolution as the primary role for judicial review and a freer-flowing normative or expository function?[99]

Emblematic of the 'drainpipe' model, standing was long seen as a separate issue or threshold requirement, premised on an interest over and above that of the general public and raising directly the right to apply for a remedy. We noted how, with the 'funnel' model, it subsequently came to be linked more closely to the merits of the case and the grant of remedies. The development, we shall see, has culminated in some remarkably liberal requirements (and legislative reaction in the case of the HRA).

97 Bondy and Sunkin, 'Accessing judicial review', p. 660.

98 The argument is pursued by Oliver, 'Public law procedure and remedies - Do we need them?'.

99 A theoretical framework elaborated by J. Miles, 'Standing in a multi-layered constitution' in Bamforth and Leyland (eds.), *Public Law in a Multi-Layered Constitution*.

The notion of 'interest' is obviously complex. A wide variety of individuals and organisations may subjectively feel themselves 'affected' by an administrative decision. Suppose that a local authority decides to increase its subsidy to the city's public transport system. As a result, fares fall but local taxes increase (the *Bromley* case: see p. 103 above). Who might be said to have an interest in this decision? One answer might be 'local taxpayers and users of public transport', but they are not necessarily the only groups affected. Again, one person may be able to assert a variety of interests. An employer may be a taxpayer or member of an environmental group; a taxpayer may oppose the decision because she lives in the inner city or is offended by urban deprivation.

One approach would be to distinguish 'material interests' (which concern an individual's economic or physical well-being) from 'ideological interests' (which include the affirmation of moral principles).[100] If the classification is applied to our example, however, the open-ended nature of 'material interest' becomes apparent. A restrictive interpretation might confine decisions concerning an individual's well-being to those causing direct financial loss. If, however, the notion encompasses non-pecuniary detriment, where is the line to be drawn? How, for example, should the diffuse interest of city-dwellers in low levels of pollution be treated?

For much of the twentieth century, the approach to standing was essentially two-pronged.[101] First, reflecting and reinforcing the 'protection of the individual' view of the courts' role, applicants were required to show a private interest which had been directly adversely affected. For example, when in *Gregory v Camden LBC*[102] the plaintiff sought to challenge a decision to build a school close by his property, the court accepted that the decision was unlawful but denied standing on the ground that his legal rights as landowner had not been infringed. Secondly it was the Attorney-General who represented the 'public interest' before the courts and possessed public advocacy functions, having automatic standing to initiate or intervene in litigation. The 'relator action' allowed the Attorney-General to authorise a private party to litigate, acting in his name. The Attorney-General's powers then served as a reason why individuals could vindicate only personal, material interests. The public interest, it was said, had been entrusted by the electorate to the Government and was therefore appropriately represented in the courts by the chief Law Officer of the Crown who was directly accountable to Parliament.[103]

Following the reinvigoration of judicial review in the 1960s, criticism of this procedural model became intense. Restrictive standing rules contradicted the idea of a general judicial responsibility to control abuse of power. The

[100] Stewart, 'The reformation of American administrative law'.

[101] From time to time, there were glimpses of an alternative, more liberal, approach: Lord Woolf, Jowell and Le Sueur, *Judicial Review*, Ch. 15.

[102] [1966] 1 WLR 899. The dominant test for the prerogative orders was a 'person aggrieved'.

[103] J. Edwards, *The Attorney-General, Politics and the Public Interest* (Sweet & Maxwell, 1984). And see *Gouriet v Union of Post Office Workers* [1978] AC 435.

twin-pronged approach also contradicted the (then) emergent idea in administrative law of interest representation (see Chapter 4). Today such trust in the doings of the Attorney-General appears somewhat quaint!

A liberalising trend developed in the 1970s, largely under the influence of Lord Denning.[104] Environmental campaigners began to win access, as in *Turner*,[105] where an amenity group seeking to challenge the inspector's decision was held to have standing because it had been allowed to appear at the inquiry. Inspiration for change also came from across the Atlantic, where – experimenting in the direction of 'the freeway' model – the US Supreme Court appeared increasingly willing to open up the judicial system to a broad spectrum of interests.[106] When AJR procedure was introduced in 1978, an American-style test of 'sufficient interest' was included on the advice of the Law Commission.[107] Set out in s. 31(3) of the Supreme Court Act 1981, the test is mandatory: the court 'shall not grant leave . . . unless it considers that the applicant has a sufficient interest in the matter to which the application relates'. But what is a 'sufficient interest'? Narrowly construed it could mean financial or proprietary interest; generously, it could comprise at least some forms of intangible or ideological interest. Absent any statutory guidance about relevant criteria and purpose, the judiciary was effectively free to stage a small but significant procedural revolution.

In the famous case of *IRC v National Federation of Self-Employed and Small Businesses*,[108] the Federation sought to challenge a tax amnesty negotiated between the Revenue and interested trade unions and granted to certain part-time workers in the newspaper industry. While in the event the legality of the amnesty was upheld, the House of Lords recommended a relaxed approach to standing at the leave stage. Lord Diplock's speech would prove particularly influential:

> At the threshold stage, for the federation to make out a prima facie case of reasonable suspicion that the Board in showing a discriminatory leniency to a substantial class of taxpayers had done so for ulterior reasons extraneous to good management, and thereby deprived the national exchequer of considerable sums of money, constituted . . . reason enough for the Divisional Court to consider that the federation, or for that matter, any taxpayer, had a sufficient interest to apply to have the question whether the Board were acting ultra vires reviewed by the court. The whole purpose of requiring that leave should first be obtained to make the application for judicial review would be defeated if the court were to go into the matter in any depth at that stage . . .

[104] *A-G (ex rel. McWhirter) v Independent Broadcasting Authority* [1973] QB 629; *R v Greater London Council, ex p. Blackburn* [1976] 1 WLR 550.

[105] *Turner v Environment Secretary* (1973) 28 P and CR 123.

[106] *Sierra Club v Morton* 405 US 727 (1972). *Lujan v Defenders of Wildlife* 504 US 555 (1992) illustrates the subsequent retrenchment. And see C. Sunstein, 'What's standing after *Lujan*? Of citizen suits, "injuries", and Article III' (1992) 91 *Michigan L. Rev.* 163.

[107] *Report on Remedies in Administrative Law* [48].

[108] [1982] AC 617.

> It would . . . be a grave lacuna in our system of public law if a pressure group, like the federation, or even a single public spirited taxpayer, were prevented by outdated technical rules of [standing] from bringing the matter to the attention of the court to vindicate the rule of law and get the unlawful conduct stopped.

The *Federation* case was an important milestone in the elaboration of a model of judicial review encompassing the public interest in administrative legality. From 'drainpipe' to 'funnel', it thus denoted the shift away from an individualist system, grounded in private interest, towards a collection of 'private Attorneys-General', where anyone could challenge anything claimed to be unlawful.[109] The latter is the pure 'citizen action', the ideal type of a pluralist system of law enforcement. The *Federation* case itself stood for a weakened version of this, representing a judicial willingness to consider some, but not all, instances of administrative illegality.

Further however, the *Federation* case can today be seen inaugurating the current era of rampant judicial discretion. As against the traditional focus on standing as a preliminary issue or 'cap' on entry to the process, the notion of 'sufficient interest' permeating and being permeated by questions of substance and remedy thus sent out a powerful message of less precedent, more freedom of manoeuvre.[110] Transaction-type considerations of the legal and factual context of powers and duties, and of the nature of the alleged breach, were grounded by the formula 'in the matter to which the application relates'. In what would be advertised as 'the proper practical test to apply',[111] Lord Donaldson subsequently recast the place of 'interest' across the procedure as a whole:

> The first stage test which is applied on the application for leave will lead to a refusal if the applicant has no interest whatsoever and is, in truth, no more than a meddlesome busybody. If, however, the application appears to be otherwise arguable and there is no other discretionary bar, the applicant may expect to get leave to apply, leaving the test of interest or standing to be reapplied as a matter of discretion on the hearing of the substantive application. At this stage, the strength of the applicant's interest is one of the factors to be weighed in the balance.[112]

Case law in the 1980s and 1990s generally maintained the liberal trend.[113] In *Leigh*, a journalist was given standing as 'public-spirited citizen' and 'guardian of the public interest in . . . open justice' to challenge a decision of local

[109] Sir K. Schiemann, 'Locus standi' [1990] *PL* 342. One consequence was that relator actions in judicial review withered on the vine.

[110] P. Cane, 'Standing, legality and the limits of public law' [1981] *PL* 303.

[111] *R v Somerset CC, ex p. Dixon* [1998] Env. LR 111. And see Sir S. Sedley, 'The last 10 years' development of English public law' (2004) 12 *Aust. J. of Administrative Law* 9.

[112] In *R v Monopolies and Mergers Commission, ex p. Argyll Group plc* [1986] 1 WLR 763.

[113] Endorsed in turn by the Law Commission, *Administrative Law: Judicial review and statutory appeals*, and by Bowman.

justices that they should have anonymity.[114] Lord Rees-Mogg, a dissident journalist peer, was allowed to challenge the Government's decision to ratify the Maastricht Treaty on European Union 'because of his sincere concern for constitutional issues'.[115] Significantly, he did not win! In a parallel development, public-advocacy functions extending to judicial review proceedings were increasingly granted to statutory agencies along the lines of those given to local authorities to take legal action in the interests of their inhabitants.[116]

As other pressure groups claiming to represent 'the public interest' seized on the *Federation* case, the concept of 'representative proceedings' took over. Collective forms of participation in the legal process were no longer so dependent on finding a 'front-man' with the requisite personal interest. Elite forms of 'test-case litigation' by repeat players thus became a familiar feature of judicial review proceedings, with pressure increasingly being exerted to extend 'the freeway' model. The talk now was not only of 'associational plaintiffs' (organisations suing on behalf of their own members), but also of 'surrogate plaintiffs' (groups claiming to represent the interests of others), and of 'public-interest standing' (groups claiming to stand up for the wider public interest). Notably, the courts showed little interest in testing for the adequacy of representation (what happens, for example, when the view of the public interest presented is hotly contested?).[117]

Presenting representative proceedings in a most favourable light, one case[118] saw the Child Poverty Action Group (CPAG) seek a declaration that the department was under a continuing duty to identify a number of welfare claimants from whom (unbeknown to themselves) benefits had been wrongfully deducted. As a leading provider of public-advocacy services to poor and disadvantaged people, and so in the words of the judge 'very much a body designed . . . to serve their interests in matters of this sort', the group was held to have sufficient interest. The challenge in a second CPAG case[119] was even more wide-ranging, exception being taken to the delays experienced by many people in the handling of benefit claims. Standing was again afforded this surrogate plaintiff. The issues raised were 'not ones which individual claimants for . . . benefit could be expected to raise'.

Environmental litigation was an obvious beneficiary. *R v Inspectorate of Pollution, ex p Greenpeace (No. 2)*[120] saw the group challenge the decision

[114] *R v Felixstowe Justices, ex p. Leigh* [1987] QB 582.

[115] *R v Foreign Secretary, ex p. Rees-Mogg* [1994] 1 All ER 457.

[116] For a striking illustration, see *R v Employment Secretary, ex p. EOC and Day* [1994] 2 WLR 409.

[117] P. Cane, 'Standing up for the public' [1995] *PL* 376, and 'Standing, representation, and the environment' in Loveland (ed.), *A Special Relationship? American influences on public law in the UK.*

[118] *R v Social Services Secretary, ex p. Child Poverty Action Group and GLC,* The Times, 16 August 1984.

[119] *R v Social Services Secretary, ex p. Child Poverty Action Group* [1990] 2 QB 540. The challenge failed on the merits.

[120] [1994] 4 All ER 329.

to allow British Nuclear Fuels (BNFL) to test its new reprocessing plant at Sellafield. Greenpeace claimed to represent both the interests of its local members and the wider public interest in preventing radioactive pollution. Notably however, the decision to grant standing was, in part, premised on the idea of interest representation being more efficient and effective for the court than individual proceedings. 'Greenpeace with its particular experience in environmental matters, its access to experts in the relevant realms of science and technology (not to mention the law) is able to mount a carefully selected, focused, relevant and well-argued challenge.' Values of pluralism, in other words, were now to be harnessed in the judicial service.

The 'Pergau dam' case[121] in 1995 saw the funnel forced wide open. The Foreign Secretary had authorised aid to the Malaysian government to help finance construction of the dam, a major infrastructure project opposed by environmentalists as destructive of natural resources. The World Development Movement (WDM) successfully challenged the decision on the ground that the disbursement was not within the statutory purpose. WDM was described by the court as 'a non-partisan pressure group' and in receipt of funds 'from all the main UK development charities, the churches, the EC and a range of other trusts'. Nobody suggested however that WDM members were affected by the decision or that the WDM was 'representative' of persons affected; like any group or individual in a democracy, it was merely voicing a complaint or opinion. In dealing with standing, Rose LJ established a liberal orthodoxy:

> There [are] a number of factors of significance in the present case: the importance of the issue raised . . . the likely absence of any other responsible challenger . . . the nature of the breach of duty against which the relief is sought . . . and the prominent role of these applicants in giving advice, guidance and assistance with regard to aid. All, in my judgment, point in the present case to the conclusion that the applicants here do have a sufficient interest in the matter to which the application relates.

But is this too liberal? Is it wholly old-fashioned to see in the distinctiveness of courts a set of values which frequent bouts of litigation carried on as a political tactic threaten to undermine? If we allow the campaigning style of politics to invade the legal process, might we end by undermining the very qualities of certainty, finality and especially independence for which the legal process is esteemed, and thereby undercut its legitimacy?[122]

Today, there is in fact a major procedural dichotomy in terms of standing requirements. On the one hand, standing as a rationing device scarcely features in reported cases involving domestic law principles. The House of Lords case of *R (Quintavelle) v Human Fertilisation and Embryology Authority*[123] is

[121] *R v Foreign Secretary, ex p. World Development Movement* [1995] 1 All ER 611. A single decision, *R v Environment Secretary, ex p. Rose Theatre Trust Co* [1990] 1 QB 504, exhibited a different judicial attitude.

[122] C. Harlow, 'public law and popular justice' (2002) 65 *MLR* 1. And see further below.

[123] [2005] 1 WLR 1061.

a suitably striking example.[124] Self-styled as a public-interest group for which 'absolute respect for the human embryo is a principal tenet', an organisation called Comment on Reproductive Ethics (Core) challenged the HFEA's decision to expand the range of licensed IVF treatment on grounds of ultra vires. The agency had been prompted to act by the sad plight of a child desperately needing a bone-marrow transplant whose parents had tried unsuccessfully for a matching sibling. 'Sufficient interest' never seriously featured even though, from the viewpoint of the family, Core surely was 'a meddlesome busybody'. The practical effect of the (ultimately unsuccessful) judicial review proceedings was to leave them in limbo.

EC law in judicial review is treated in the same way. The 'spaghetti junction' model thus illustrates how sufficient interest operates across these first two sources of the multi-streamed jurisdiction. As regards the domestic courts functioning as European Community courts, the liberal approach to standing at national level has a further connotation. The preliminary reference procedure (Art. 234) can be more easily triggered in public law cases, so mediating the effect of the strict standing requirements imposed on direct actions before the ECJ.[125]

On the other hand, as 'spaghetti junction' also points up, s. 7(1) of the HRA imposes a special cap on the added potentials of Convention rights challenge. Mirroring the standing rule in ECHR Art. 34, the public law ground of illegality established by s. 6 of the HRA – acting incompatibly with Convention Rights – can thus be relied upon only by a 'victim'.[126] Ministers were firm that judicial review's traditional role of protection of the individual should not be impeded or obscured by abstract and experimental claims of human rights violations.[127] The ECHR's own jurisprudence, traditionally cast in terms of a person directly affected and so hostile to claims to represent the general public interest,[128] was here seen as a valuable reference point.[129]

This particular rationing device has been much criticised,[130] partly for an excessive individualisation of rights, and partly by reason of the procedural dichotomy itself ('inconsistencies'). In light of the continuing public controversy over the HRA, s. 7 may however be accounted a wise precaution. Another illustration of the many complex dynamics associated with the multi-streamed jurisdiction, it is in fact an incentive for a reworking of Convention rights in

124 Alternatively, see *R (Hasan) v Trade and Industry Secretary* [2007] EWHC 2630.

125 See J. Miles, 'Standing in a multi-layered constitution'.

126 S. 7(3), where 'sufficient interest' is said to incorporate the victim test in relevant proceedings, rams home the message.

127 J. Miles, 'Standing under the Human Rights Act 1998: Theories of rights enforcement and the nature of public law adjudication' (2000) *CLJ* 133.

128 See e.g. *Klass v Germany* (1978) 2 EHRR 214.

129 There is as yet little domestic case law, though see *R (City of Westminster and Others) v Mayor of London* [2002] EWHC 244.

130 See e.g. J. Marriott and D. Nicol, 'The Human Rights Act, representative standing and the victim culture' (1998) *EHRLR* 730.

the image of the common law. The advent of the Equality and Human Rights Commission slightly alters the procedural design giving a limited form of privileged access to the EHRC to 'act only if there is or would be one or more victims of the unlawful act' (Equality Act 2006, s. 30(3)).

(b) . . . and intervention

As an instrument of interest representation, the third party '*amicus* brief' can serve different purposes. Involving seductive ideas of 'enriching the process of deliberation'[131] is the informational or educative function, the court being presented by specialist bodies with materials otherwise unlikely to be gleaned in the adversarial, bipolar process. One variant, developed in America, is the so-called 'Brandeis brief', replete with socio-economic materials. Particularly fitting for this meeting place of a jurisdiction, another one is intervention as a vehicle for comparative legal information delivered via international networks.[132] A pluralist circumvention of the problem of testing for an interest group's 'representivity' is also on offer.[133]

Intervention then, like standing to sue, is not simply a technical matter. Viewed in a positive light, it may be said to enhance the legitimacy of judicial decision-making, precisely because of the wider participation and deeper analytical and evidential base. This may be thought particularly valuable in judicial review, not least when significant constitutional or human rights points arise.[134] Put another way, the informational function may encourage judicial assertiveness and creativity (thus illustrating the mutually reinforcing effect of expansionary dynamics in substance and procedure). Sedley LJ for example has hailed intervention as a way to 'escape the pincers closing in on us': 'The pressures, which cannot be wholly resisted, towards omnicompetent adjudication, and the want of any corresponding expansion in the data and culture with and within which we carry it out.'[135]

As a litigation tactic, intervention has considerable potential as a cost-effective method for targeting likely precedent-setting cases in the higher courts, perhaps as part of a broader litigation strategy.[136] Emblematic of 'the freeway' model, such briefs may serve a discrete lobbying function, the aim being to suggest that the views expressed reflect the attitudes of a wide segment

[131] S. Fredman, 'Judging democracy: The role of the judiciary under the Human Rights Act 1998' (2000) 53 *Current Legal Problems* 99. See also M. Arshi and C. O'Cinneide, 'Third-party interventions: The public interest reaffirmed' [2004] *PL* 69.

[132] So building on long-standing practice at supranational level: Harlow and Rawlings, *Pressure Through Law*, Ch. 6.

[133] R. Rawlings, 'Courts and interests'.

[134] Compare however in the private law field the celebrated 'Siamese twins' case: *In re A (Children) (Conjoined Twins: Surgical Separation)* [2001] 2 WLR 480.

[135] S. Sedley, 'Human rights: A twenty-first century agenda' [1995] *PL* 386.

[136] As long experience across the Atlantic teaches: S. Krislov, 'The *Amicus Curiae Brief: From friendship to advocacy*' (1963) 72 *Yale LJ* 694; P. Bryden, 'Public interest intervention in the courts' (1987) 66 *Canadian Bar Rev.* 490.

of public opinion. The technique can also be used to mitigate the problem of adequacy of representation by allowing for the protection of interests that might otherwise be unrepresented in the litigation ('surrogate intervenor').

The classical design of adversarial, bipolar procedure was by definition antithetical to such interventions, whether in oral or written form. Participation was restricted to an official *amicus curiae*, typically a legal representative of the Crown appointed at the request of the court to assist it with legal argument. Order 53 made provision for intervention only where a party was 'directly affected' (a formula narrowly defined)[137] or where the court considered that a person desiring to be heard in *opposition* to an application was a 'proper person to be heard'. Yet once the drainpipe model had been successfully challenged in terms of standing to sue, pressure to allow interventions was bound to intensify. In facilitating collective or public-interest representation at one stage of the lawsuit and not at others, the pattern of legal procedure in the then funnel model was unbalanced. How could it be that, when a particular individual was allowed to venture the illegality of contraception for young girls, the Children's Legal Centre was denied permission to intervene on behalf of the directly affected class of persons?[138]

The first bodies to make headway had official status and statutory powers: the Equal Opportunities Commission and the Commission for Racial Equality respectively,[139] in the difficult area of discrimination law. Then, in the 1988 case of *Sivakumaran*,[140] the UN Commissioner was permitted to comment through counsel on interpretation of the 1951 Refugee Convention. Pressure groups were not far behind. In *Phoenix Aviation* in 1995,[141] the organisation Compassion in World Farming was allowed to file evidence relating to the treatment of live animals exported for slaughter, and to make legal submissions. A whole new area of legal practice in this country was beginning to materialise in the form of 'public-interest intervention'.

Today, CPR 54 sends out a strong positive signal. As well as providing for service on persons directly affected by the claim, the court is afforded powers to hear 'any person' in support or in opposition.[142] The HRA provides a major catalyst, with the restrictive 'victim' test undercutting a more explicit and broader dimension to rights adjudication and pushing public interest groups towards intervention. Over time we have seen the bipolar format of much important public law litigation reordered.

[137] *R v Rent Officer Service, ex p. Muldoon* [1996] 1 WLR 1103.

[138] *Gillick v West Norfolk and Wisbech AHA* [1985] 1 All ER 533.

[139] *Shields v E Coomes (Holdings) Ltd* [1978] 1 WLR 1408; *Science Research Council v Nassé, Leyland Cars v Vyas* [1980] AC 1028.

[140] *R v Home Secretary, ex p. Sivakumaran* [1988] AC 958.

[141] *R v Coventry Airport, ex p. Phoenix Aviation* [1995] 3All ER 37. See also in the House of Lords, *R v Home Secretary, ex p. Venables* [1997] 3 All ER 97 (intervention by JUSTICE).

[142] 'Any person may apply for permission to file evidence or make representations at the hearing of the judicial review'; such an application 'should be made promptly' (CPR 54.17). See further, Public Law Project, *Third-party Intervention: A practical guide* (2008).

Since 2000, there has been a significant increase in the use of intervention, most obviously in the House of Lords, where groups such as Liberty and JUSTICE have effectively acquired elite repeat-player status.[143] We see clearly here how moving closer to 'the freeway' model multiplies both the opportunities for, and potential scale of the argument in, test cases. The case of *A (No. 2)*, concerning the admissibility of evidence possibly obtained by foreign torturers (see p. 131 above), featured two interventions, the first from a wide array of domestic groups and organisations including Amnesty and the Law Society, the second from transnational legal organisations such as the International Bar Association.

The development is again the product of unfettered judicial discretion. Promptness aside, CPR 54 is silent about the relevant criteria. Judicial failure to explain when, why, by whom and in what form intervention will be permitted, is however a major point of criticism.[144] The courts have effectively adopted a policy of drift.[145]

How far can the use of intervention in judicial review reasonably go? What, one might ask, of the practical considerations of cost and delay, and of the effective impingement on party autonomy? The idea that even with multiple interventions judicial procedure can properly match methodical and transparent processes of consultation, and indeed the flexibility and permeability of the political process at large, is simply an illusion. Intervention as a lobbying tactic also raises concerns for the integrity of the adjudicative process and separate identity of courts.[146] A single case, *R (Burke) v General Medical Council*,[147] shows senior judiciary attentive to the dangers. A terminally ill man with a degenerative condition having won a judgment requiring doctors to honour his wish for life-prolonging treatment, the subsequent Court of Appeal hearing attracted an array of interventions relating to the social, moral and religious dimensions of the matter. Adhering firmly to specific issues, the judges overturned the ruling. The litigation had 'expanded inappropriately to deal with issues which, whilst important, were not appropriately justiciable on the facts of the case'.

5. Fact-base

(a) More rationing

A general limitation of access to government information for the purpose of judicial review reflected and reinforced the traditional notion of a residual,

[143] S. Hannett, 'Third party intervention: In the public interest? [2003] *PL* 128.

[144] For an earlier, unsuccessful, attempt at structuring, see JUSTICE–Public Law Project, *A Matter of Public Interest* (1996).

[145] See Sir H. Brooke, 'Interventions in the Court of Appeal' [2007] *PL* 401; also, M. Fordham, '"Public interest" intervention: A practitioner's perspective' (2007) *PL* 410.

[146] As highlighted by the *Pinochet* case (see p. 654 above).

[147] [2005] EWCA Civ 1003.

supervisory jurisdiction: one concerned with review of, and not appeal from, administrative decision-making. Establishing it as a central component of the 'drainpipe' model, the restriction of proof likewise fitted the formula of judicial restraint – providing, at one level, a strong practical check on invasion of matters of public policy and, at another level, scarce encouragement to expansion of the grounds of review.

Standard information-gathering techniques in the adversarial common law system were then the more notable by their absence with the old prerogative orders. Discovery of documents was not available in applications for certiorari, mandamus and prohibition (one reason why applicants might seek a declaration or injunction). Disclosure of legal error was restricted to what would appear on the face of the record or could be deposed to by way of affidavit. Prerogative remedy procedure thus made no provision for interrogatories, while permission for cross-examination on the affidavits was almost never granted.[148]

Wednesbury itself shows the fit between procedure and substance (see p. 42 above). A chief feature of the case is the lack of evidence demanded by or provided to the court to explain and support the ban: as Taggart put this, 'the high threshold for judicial intervention, coupled with the lack of transparency and difficulties of proof, almost guaranteed' the result. Far from the need to justify, the corporation could proceed in the litigation much like the Sphinx:

> In 1947 the Wednesbury Corporation could have put forward a formidable case. A so-called 'Brandeis brief', containing sociological and economic evidence, could have included studies on the impact of the cinema on children . . . information about the church-going habits of the population . . . and the varying conditions imposed by other local authorities where Sunday cinema opening was allowed. The Corporation never had to do this. Indeed, it never had to give any reasons or provide any evidence at all as to why it did what it did. It was for the challenging cinema to discover and show legal error . . . The collectivity could sit tight-lipped.[149]

Also contributing to the distinctive British climate of official secrecy was 'Crown privilege', whereby ministers could refuse to produce documents by asserting either that disclosure of the contents would injure the public interest or that, for the proper workings of government, the relevant class of document merited protection. Effectively handed 'a blank cheque' by the judiciary,[150] it was in Wade's words 'not surprising that the Crown yielded to the temptation to overdraw'.[151] It would not be until *Conway v Rimmer*[152] in 1968 that,

148 See *George v Environment Secretary* (1979) LGR 689.

149 M. Taggart, 'Reinventing administrative law' in Bamforth and Leyland (eds.), *Public Law in a Multi-Layered Constitution*, p. 329. The *Padfield* criterion of 'no evidence' would later offer some relief: see p. 101 above.

150 In *Duncan v Cammell Laird & Co Ltd* [1942] AC 624.

151 H. Wade and C. Forsyth, *Administrative Law* (Clarendon Press, 2004), p. 844. See *Ellis v Home Office* [1953] 2 QB 153.

152 [1968] AC 910.

recasting the doctrine in the form of 'public interest immunity', the Law Lords would counter-assert the judicial power to determine disclosure by balancing the competing public interests (due administration of justice).[153]

At first sight the establishment of AJR procedure, with facilities for discovery of documents, interrogatories and cross-examination (RSC Ord. 53(8)), promised much. Yet these were quintessentially matters of judicial discretion: namely, part of the special 'safeguards' in public law litigation. Practical arguments now featured prominently. It was of course necessary to discourage lengthy 'fishing expeditions' but in vindicating managerial concerns of streamlined court process, and prompt and efficient despatch of public business, the judges went much further, insisting on a frugal diet of oral evidence, etc.

Lord Diplock's speech in *O'Reilly v Mackman* (see p. 680 above) was at the heart of this. Whereas the new-found power to allow standard evidential techniques was invoked to justify forcing cases down the route of AJR procedure:

> It will be only on rare occasions that the interests of justice will require that leave be given for cross-examination [[154]] in applications for judicial review. This is because of the nature of the issues that normally arise on judicial review. The facts, except where the claim [is] that a . . . public authority . . . failed to comply with the [statutory] procedure . . . or failed to observe . . . natural justice . . . can seldom be a matter of relevant dispute . . . since . . . the authority's findings of fact are [generally] not open to review.

This approach however carried the seeds of its own destruction. 'Catch 22': without the evidence leave could not be obtained ('insufficiently arguable'); without leave the evidence could not be secured (so that it could be well-nigh impossible to sustain allegations such as irrelevant considerations or improper purpose). Attempts to circumnavigate a rigid public/private dichotomy were inevitable.

(b) Degrees of frugality

Although the very restrictive attitude to proof held sway into the 1990s,[155] the stresses and strains associated with the unstable 'funnel' model became increasingly evident. In asylum for example, both *Bugdaycay* (see p. 116 above) and *M v Home Office* (see p. 10 above) demonstrated that the characterisation of disputes of law not fact did not always hold. Meanwhile, the rise of the duty

[153] Including by means of inspection. For later twists and turns, see *D v NSPCC* [1978] AC 171, *Burmah Oil v Bank of England* [1980] AC 1090, *R v Chief Constable of West Midlands Police, ex p. Wiley* [1995] 1 AC 27, and, in terms of ECHR Art. 6, *R v H and R v C* [2004] UKHL 3. Public-interest immunity was also central to the Scott Inquiry (see p. 590 above). And see *R (Binyam Mohamed) v Foreign Secretary* [2009] EWHC 152.

[154] Lord Scarman had earlier stated in the *Federation* case (see p. 696 above) that 'discovery should not be ordered unless and until the court is satisfied that the evidence reveals reasonable grounds for believing that there has been a breach of public duty'.

[155] See e.g. *R v Inland Revenue Commissioners, ex p. Taylor* [1989] 1 All ER 906.

to give reasons (see p. 630 above) both operated to circumvent, and cut across the rationale of, a highly constricted evidential base. Even Griffith, the leading advocate of judicial restraint, thought matters 'the worst of both worlds': 'We have an interventionist judiciary but a judiciary which is limited by procedures and practices designed to exclude certain sources of information and factual investigation without which the policy choices made by the courts – that is, their decisions – are inevitably less good than they could be.'[156]

How then might substance and procedure be brought into kilter, while maintaining a streamlined process? Lord Donaldson in *Huddleston*[157] proffered a doubled-edged sword: a limiting device or justification for the sparing use of formal disclosure orders, an alternative solution to the problem of fact-finding. This was the so-called 'duty of candour':

> [Judicial review is] a process which falls to be conducted with all the cards face upwards on the table and the vast majority of the cards will start in the authority's hands . . . When challenged [the defendant] should set out fully what they did and why, so far as it is necessary, fully and fairly to meet the challenge.

The duty was glossed up in some fine words about 'partnership' between the executive and the judiciary: 'a common aim [of] maintenance of the highest standards of public administration'. Later cases would claim it as a very high duty, one that ranges beyond making candid disclosure of the relevant facts to encompass, so far as this is not otherwise apparent, the reasoning behind the decision challenged.[158] As a matter of good professional practice, the discipline should build at every step of the way (beginning these days with the pre-action protocol). Note however the lack of enforcement method and sanction, other than adverse inferences by the court.[159] At best a partial solution, the duty of candour means trusting the authorities not to be economical with the truth.

There is here a pervasive sense of 'hit and miss'. Take the *Pergau Dam* case (see p. 699 above). How, prior to the Freedom of Information Act, did this most striking of legal challenges to ministers, one that effectively required the court to read the word 'sound' into the statutory purpose of 'promoting . . . development', get off the ground? Although the respondent's affidavit evidence was criticised as being 'economical to the point of being parsimonious',[160] the court declined to order disclosure. Instead, the answer lies in the prior working of the political process, in the form of

156 J. Griffith, 'Judicial decision-making in public law' [1985] *PL* 564, 580. And see JUSTICE–All Souls, *Administrative Justice: Some necessary reforms* (1988), pp. 166–7.

157 *R v Lancashire CC, ex p. Huddleston* [1986] 2 All ER 941.

158 *Foreign Secretary v Quark Fishing Ltd* [2002] EWCA Civ 1409 (Laws LJ); *Belize Alliance of Conservation NGOs v Department of the Environment* [2004] Env LR 761 (Lord Walker). The duty extends to all parties.

159 See e.g. *R (Wandsworth LBC) v Transport Secretary* [2005] EWHC 20.

160 S. Grosz, 'Pergau be damned' (1994) 144 *New Law Journal* 708, 710.

inquiry reports from select committees.[161] The Permanent Secretary, it was revealed, had criticised the proposal to allocate funds in the light of appraisals describing the economic viability of the project as 'marginal' and 'a very bad buy', and had ultimately demanded written authorisation from the minister before making payments. The 'public-interest advocate' had struck lucky.

Today, the CPR affords the judges ample powers of fact-finding in judicial review cases.[162] The standard disclosure order obliges the party to make a reasonable search for, and list, those documents relevant and helpful to both sides; the court can also order specific disclosure and specific inspection of materials (CPR 31).[163] But of course this is all a matter of judicial discretion: to probe or not to probe and the degree of probing. Under Part 54, 'disclosure is not required unless the court orders otherwise',[164] reflecting the original approach of overt access to documentation enforced only in cases of apparent lack of candour in the affidavit evidence.[165]

We note how, underwriting the move beyond the funnel model, the pressures and opportunities for expansion of the judicial review fact-base have continued to multiply. These liberalising factors range from freedom of information legislation (both general and specific)[166] to the proportionality-style review associated with a multi-streamed jurisdiction, Strasbourg's testing of judicial review capacities under ECHR Art. 6 (see Chapter 14) – and indeed mistake of fact as error of law (see p. 513 above). Perhaps then it is no surprise to learn of more cases in which carefully targeted applications for disclosure succeed.[167] Fuelled by 'a greater general awareness . . . of the types of material Government holds', the former Treasury Solicitor sees claimants' lawyers as 'becoming bolder in seeking disclosure',[168] and in the *Health Stores* case

[161] PAC, *Pergau Hydro-electric Project*, HC 155 (1994/5); and, suggesting an improper link between development aid and arms sales, Foreign Affairs Committee, *Public Expenditure: The Pergau Hydro-Electric Project, Malaysia, the aid and trade provision and related matters*, HC 271-1 (1994/5).

[162] Following the Scott Inquiry, ministers declared a more restrictive policy on claims to public interest immunity (a test of real damage or harm): see HC Deb., cols. 949–50, 18 December 1996.

[163] Orthodox informational techniques like cross-examination and expert evidence are part of the package: see e.g. *R (PG) v Ealing LBC* [2002] EWHC250 and *R(Lynch) v General Dental Council* [2004] 1 All ER 1159.

[164] CPR 54 Practice Direction [12.1]. Once permission is granted, the public body should provide the 'detailed grounds' particularising its case together with any written evidence and supporting documents (CPR 54.14).

[165] Reading across pre-CPR practice (*R v Environment Secretary, ex p. Islington LBC* [1992] COD 67): see O. Sanders, 'Disclosure of documents in claims for judicial review' (2006) 11 *Judicial Review* 194.

[166] For the linkage in terms of the Aarhus Convention (see p. 473 above), see R. Macrory, 'Environmental public law and judicial review' (2008) 13 *Judicial Review* 115.

[167] E.g. *JJ Gallagher Ltd v Transport Secretary* [2002] EWHC1195 and *R (Ministry of Defence) v HM Coroner for Wiltshire and Swindon* [2005] EWHC 889.

[168] Dame J. Wheldon, 'Judicial review from the government perspective' (Sweet & Maxwell lecture, 2005).

in 2005,[169] Sedley LJ expressed discomfiture with the 'Catch-22' dilemma. Ordering disclosure only exceptionally 'is unnecessarily protective of government, and of government alone, in public law proceedings brought not as of right but with permission'.

The touchstone is *Tweed*.[170] Invoking the Convention rights of assembly and free speech, T challenged restrictions placed on a parade in Northern Ireland as disproportionate. He sought disclosure of documents, including police reports, summarised in an affidavit sworn by the chairman of the Parades Commission (see p. 659 above). While emphasising that, given the predominance of legal issues, disclosure would generally be more limited in judicial review cases than in ordinary actions, the House found room, in Lord Carswell's words, for 'a more flexible and less prescriptive principle'. The House of Lords substituted for the test of a prima facie inaccurate or misleading affidavit, judicial discretion as to whether, in light of the facts and circumstances of the individual case, disclosure was required to resolve the matter 'fairly and justly'. Proportionality testing in particular required a leg-up. Disclosure orders in such cases should not be automatic, but equally the duty of candour might not be sufficient:

> *Lord Carswell:* The proportionality issue forms part of the context in which the court has to consider whether it is necessary for fairly disposing of the case to order disclosure of such documents . . . Whether disclosure should be ordered will depend on a balancing of the several factors, of which proportionality is only one, albeit one of some significance . . . When one takes into account the proportionality factor, the need for disclosure is greater than in judicial review applications where it does not apply. The duty of candour has been fulfilled by adduction of summaries. Counsel submitted, however, that it is not always possible to obtain the full flavour of the content of such documents from a summary, however carefully and faithfully compiled, and that there may be nuances of meaning or nuggets of information or expressions of opinion which do not fully emerge. I consider that there is force in this view and that in order to assess the difficult issues of proportionality in this case the court should have access as far as possible to the original documents from which the Commission received information and advice.[171]

Demonstrating the significance here of the variable intensity of review, Lord Carswell further stated that 'the degree of deference due is one of the issues which the court must take into account when considering the question of disclosure'. Alternatively, in Lord Brown's words, 'the courts may be expected to show a somewhat greater readiness than hitherto to order disclosure of the main documents underlying proportionality decisions, particularly in cases

[169] *R (National Association of Health Stores) v Department of Health* [2005] EWCA Civ 154. See however, on the dangers of overburdening the process, *R (Prokopp) v London Underground Ltd* [2004] Env LR 170.

[170] *Tweed v Parades Commission for Northern Ireland* [2006] UKHL 53.

[171] *Ibid.* [38–9]. Disclosure to the judge was ordered for the purpose of determining the 'value-added' of the documents and (if raised) the question of public interest immunity.

where only a comparatively narrow margin of discretion falls to be accorded to the decision-maker.' [172]

Tweed is an uneasy balancing act between managerial concern about the courts being flooded 'with needless paper'[173] and the judicial function of redress of a grievance rendered potentially 'non-justiciable' for lack of evidence. A powerful message is sent about the need generally in judicial review to retain rationing yet, in the spirit of *M v Home Office*, the analysis edges towards a mandatory model of judicial review less trustful of the public body. As elsewhere in the multi-streamed jurisdiction, divergent requirements have to be balanced.

6. Conclusion

Over the course of the last thirty years, the judicial review process has been substantially reshaped. Visualised in this chapter through a series of models, attention naturally focuses on the more generous contours of the system. These are represented in procedural terms by liberalised standing and intervention, greater fact-finding powers, and more elaborate legal remedies. We can see how the normative capacities of the elite machinery of the Administrative Court, further fuelled by a mutually supportive relationship with repeat players in public interest cases, have been substantially enhanced. As such, the substantive process of 'transforming' judicial review discussed in Chapter 3 is not only the chief driver but also a product of the new procedures; creative tension is in-built. The emergence of the multi-streamed jurisdiction, while in part operating to curb their autonomy, has also afforded to the national courts fresh opportunities of command and influence.

But it is also a story of double standards. The judiciary shows scant enthusiasm for the application to AJR machinery of the disciplines of structuring and confining discretion so avidly imposed on government since *Padfield*. A 'seedless grape'[174] – little substance at the core – is an apt description of much in AJR practice and procedure, especially at the permission stage. The whiff of judicial lottery is confirmed by empirical studies. Under the mantra of active case management, the CPR framework has facilitated the piling of discretion on the discretion of the individual judge. A series of rationing devices or 'safeguards' applied more or less rigorously at different times and in different situations has ensued, culminating in a basic reorientation of the judicial regulation of access to the system. No longer are there visibly strict standing rules or

[172] 'A fortiori the main documents underlying decisions challenged on the ground that they violate an *unqualified* Convention right': *Tweed v Parades Commission for Northern Ireland* [2006] UKHL 53 [57]. See further, in relation to cross-examination, *R (N) v M* [2003] 1 WLR 562.

[173] *Ibid.* [56].

[174] A metaphor borrowed from E. Gellhorn and G. Robinson, 'Perspectives on Administrative Law' (1975) 75 *Col. Law Rev.* 771.

the threshold requirements of the drainpipe model; there is instead a sharper emphasis on the merits or quality of claim, as in the test of 'arguability' applied when granting or refusing permission. The loose terminology opens the door to enhanced judicial discretion.

In Chapter 3, we tried to show how demands for administrative rationality had stimulated demands for a more rational and principled judicial review. This is emphatically not the picture presented in this chapter. We would not wish to see Lord Hewart's picture[175] of a capricious executive 'unfettered and supreme' displaced by an elite and discretionary system of judicial review unregulated by any strong sense of a need for judicial restraint or accountability.

[175] Lord Hewart, *The New Despotism* (Benn, 1929), p. 17.

16

Judicial review and administration: A tangled web

Contents

Writing in the early 1990s, a future High Court judge was blunt:

> To their shame public lawyers have taken little interest in the impact of judicial review. Yet surely it is the different aspects of this issue which are central to the whole enterprise. Has an applicant actually obtained substantial benefit as a result of successful judicial review? What of others in the same position or a similar position? Are standards of public administration in the relevant public authority better for having been exposed to judicial gaze? Has

there been any improvement in the standards of government in general following this and other instances of judicial review?[1]

In concentrating heavily on doctrinal analysis, public lawyers had tended to assume two key elements of a classical 'control' model of judicial review: that government decision-makers and officials (a) take their lead from courts and not vice versa, and (b) that if proffered the bridle they dutifully put it on. Yet in showing that the administrative process was not, and could not be, a succession of justiciable controversies, de Smith's famous characterisation of judicial review as sporadic and peripheral had also yielded an important clue. The courts as machinery for redress of grievance might need to temper their approach in certain situations; administrative responses to judicial intervention would be many and various.

Stress is rightly laid on the expressive functions of judicial review, whereby – not least these days with Convention rights – certain key values about how public bodies should behave are embodied and proclaimed. From the standpoint of effectiveness and compliance, however, the judicial contribution also falls to be read in terms of the many competing pressures and influences in public administration. Today, research points up a broad range of variables: from subject matter and frequency of court challenge and sculpting of legal remedies to changing organisational priorities and different institutional value systems, and on through hierarchical, cultural and personal factors to issues of legal awareness and expertise.

1. Litigation patterns

Compared with other administrative law machinery (tribunals and ombudsmen, let alone internal complaints procedures) the judicial review caseload is small (see Fig 15.6, p. 688 above). A fifteenfold increase in leave/permission applications since the early 1980s is certainly dramatic,[2] but it should not obscure the fact that 6,000+ cases a year is infinitesimal when measured against the scale of government decision-making. Human rights litigation explosion – what human rights litigation explosion? The graph shows a gentler upward curve since 2000.[3]

Of course the numbers only tell part of the story.[4] Fundamental to 'transforming judicial review' (see Chapter 3) is the sense of courts, with their high

1 R. Cranston, 'Reviewing judicial review' in Richardson and Genn (eds.), *Administrative Law and Government Action* (Clarendon Press, 1994), p. 69.

2 See NAO, *Citizen Redress: What citizens can do if things go wrong with public services*, HC 21 (2004/5).

3 See further, V. Bondy, *The Impact of the Human Rights Act 1998 on Judicial Review* (Public Law Project, 2003).

4 Statistics may also mislead because they are incomplete. Together with statutory appeals and reviews (see further below), we need to bear in mind here actions in contract and tort and also the crosscutting nature of Convention rights. Looking forwards, 'judicial review' in the Upper-tier Tribunal will need to be factored in.

prestige and profile, possessing an influence disproportionate to their caseload. The statistics cannot measure the 'ripple' effect of one decision on, perhaps, thousands of similar cases. The mere existence of judicial review may influence future administrative behaviour (see further below). Litigation has radiating effects, underpinning negotiation, etc., 'in the shadow of the law' in multiple venues outside the courts.[5] The fact remains however that large swathes of public administration have little or no direct contact with judicial review.

(a) Asylum and immigration plus

The judicial review caseload also is highly skewed. Immigration and asylum are the main drivers, with proportions of leave/permission applications of 40, 50, even 60 per cent.[6] As such, the much-advertised growth of judicial review in recent times is in large measure a function of strict immigration policies, the standard of decision-making in a department of state officially characterised as 'unfit for purpose', and the evident incentive for would-be migrants to litigate.[7] In the words of a former Treasury Solicitor, 'the vast majority' of the cases will be 'routine', 'simply . . . part of the process by which public decisions are properly tested and challenged'.[8]

The trend is the more striking because of repeated attempts at diversion out of AJR procedure, epitomised by *Swati* (see p. 689 above).[9] Indeed, the Administrative Court currently gives the impression of a specialist asylum and immigration court with add-ons. One alternative routing, applications to require that the Asylum and Immigration Tribunal reconsider, has also been seen swelling the court's business, with proportions of the secondary caseload of statutory reviews, appeals and applications touching 80 per cent.[10]

Experience teaches that, outside this core area, judicial review can be extremely diverse. We recall the judicial role in determining institutional relationships (as famously with central and local government in the 1980s),[11]

[5] For discussion of such 'bottom-up' or 'decentred' perspectives in this field, see R. Rawlings, 'Courts and interests' in Loveland (ed.), *A Special Relationship? American influences on public law* (Oxford University Press, 1995). And see further below.

[6] In the two years 2006–7 for example, immigration and asylum cases constituted 8,428 of 13,148 permission applications: *Judicial and Court Statistics*, Cm. 7273 (2007), and Cm. 7467 (2008), Table 1.12.

[7] R. Rawlings, 'Review, revenge and retreat' (2005) 68 *MLR* 378. C. Beaton-Wells, 'Australian administrative law: The asylum-seeker legacy' [2005] *PL* 267, gives a valuable comparative perspective.

[8] Dame Juliet Wheldon, 'Judicial review from the government perspective' (Sweet & Maxwell lecture, December 2005), p. 6. And see R. Thomas, 'The impact of judicial review on asylum' [2003] *PL* 479.

[9] See also Practice Direction to CPR Part 54, *Applications for permission to apply for judicial review in immigration and asylum cases – challenging removal* (2007).

[10] 7,036 of 8,601 cases in the two years 2006–7: *Judicial and Court Statistics*, Cm. 7273 (2007), and Cm. 7467 (2008), Table 1.14.

[11] M. Loughlin, *Legality and Locality: The role of law in central-local government relations* (Clarendon Press, 1996).

the push into commercial judicial review (litigation commonly outside the model of 'strong state' versus 'weak individual'), and of course all those 'public-interest advocates' (repeat players as well as 'one-shotters').[12] Empirical analysis of the non-immigration/asylum caseload confirms that 'the absolute numbers of cases involving most other decision areas have been small', and that, 'while challenges are brought against a broad spectrum of bodies, a high proportion . . . involves only a small number of public authorities'.[13]

A study of judicial review challenges to local authorities in England and Wales casts fresh light on this.[14] There were some 5,000 such applications for permission[15] in the period 2000–5, which constituted almost half the non-immigration/asylum caseload. Housing cases (broadly defined) were in the majority, with other significant areas being community care, planning, and education (together some 30% of the sample). Cue 'the London effect' (see p. 686 above): 60% of all local authority challenges were to decisions of London boroughs (which represented 14% of the population of England and Wales). Conversely, 80% of councils together attracted less than 20% of the challenges; 85% had on average fewer than two challenges annually.[16]

The sense of 'different worlds of judicial review litigation' is amply conveyed here. Peripheral in the sense of being unimportant to all save those directly concerned, the bulk of the cases involving inner-city authorities scarcely fitted the comfortable imagery of judicial review as top-tier dispute resolution. Part of the never-ending 'toil of resource management', the litigation typically involved 'a daily response to challenges by claimants seeking to protect their basic housing needs, often in emergency situations'.[17]

(b) Accessibility and outreach

Bottom-up studies of complaints-handling are, as we saw in Chapter 10, preoccupied with questions of accessibility and outreach. Judicial review has received much less attention in these terms. Yet as 'Rolls-Royce' machinery for the redress of grievance, the High Court does not come cheap![18] Costs

[12] For this celebrated distinction, see M. Galanter, 'Why the "haves" come out ahead: Speculations on the limits of legal change', 9 *Law and Society Review* (1974) 95.

[13] M. Sunkin, K. Calvo, L. Platt and T. Landman, 'Mapping the use of judicial review to challenge local authorities in England and Wales' [2007] *PL* 545, 546. And see, L. Bridges, G. Meszaros and M. Sunkin, *Judicial Review in Perspective*, 2nd edn (Cavendish, 1995).

[14] Sunkin *et al.*, 'Mapping the use of judicial review to challenge local authorities in England and Wales'.

[15] Of which 31% (1,582) were successful.

[16] Birmingham and Liverpool led the way among the few 'hot spots' of judicial review activity outside London.

[17] Sunkin *et al.*, 'Mapping the use of judicial review to challenge local authorities in England and Wales', pp. 556, 567. The 's. 55 litigation' discussed later in the chapter raises similar points.

[18] Control of litigation costs is today considered a major failing of the Woolf reforms: Sir A. Clarke, 'The Woolf Reforms: A singular event or an ongoing process?' (British Academy lecture, 2008). Another major inquiry is currently under way, chaired by Lord Justice Jackson.

traditionally fall on the loser, making them hard to predict at the start of the case, an obvious disincentive. 'Front-loading' the judicial review process has given matters a further twist, with the private claimant refused permission made liable for the opponent's costs of working up a defence.[19] Another major obstacle familiar from environmental litigation is the practice of requiring a cross-undertaking in damages in cases where interim relief halting development pending a final determination is requested.[20]

Practitioners complain of 'a large and growing gulf between those eligible for public funding and those who are able to afford to litigate a judicial review'.[21] Eligibility for legal aid, which provides both funding from the Community Legal Service[22] and costs protection, is today severely restricted. The scheme today takes account of the wider public interest[23] but cases still remain subject to a rigorous costs–benefit test. The impecunious litigant may also find a conditional-fee agreement (whereby the lawyer gets his fee on winning) let alone pro bono advice and representation, difficult to secure.[24]

The criteria for legal aid lock up together with the exercise of judicial discretion at the permission stage. For example, where permission is granted, there is a presumption that public funding should be granted or should continue. Conversely, with refusal of permission on the papers apt to see public funding withdrawn, the lack of costs protection may effectively undermine the right to renew an application at an oral hearing. Increased emphasis in funding decisions on alternative dispute resolution (ADR), as by refusing legal representation where an ombudsman system has not been tried, also underwrites the scope for diversion out of the judicial process.[25]

Operating here in defence of the public purse, the courts are understandably cautious about disapplying the general costs rules in judicial review litigation.[26] Occasionally a losing litigant will benefit from after-the-event protection ('no order as to costs') on the ground that he has acted in the public interest by

[19] As now demanded by the acknowledgement of service: *Mount Cook Land Ltd v Westminster City Council* [2003] EWCA Civ 1346. See also *Davey v Aylesbury Vale DC* [2007] EWCA Civ 1166.

[20] So protecting economic interests: see, e.g., *Belize Alliance of Conservation NGOs v Department of the Environment* [2003] UKPC 63. For critical analysis in terms of the Aarhus Convention, see Report of the Working Group on Access to Environmental Justice, *Ensuring Access to Environmental Justice in England and Wales* (2008).

[21] R. Stein and J. Beagent, 'Protective costs orders' [2006] *Judicial Review* 206.

[22] For which the Legal Services Commission has responsibility under the Access to Justice Act 1999. For a convenient overview, see Report of the Working Group on Facilitating Public Interest Litigation, *Litigating the Public Interest* (Liberty, 2006).

[23] LSC Funding Code Criteria, s. 2.4. Third parties standing to benefit may also be asked to contribute. See further the reports by the LSC's Public Interest Advisory Panel.

[24] For the travails of 'the litigant in person', see Bridges, Meszaros and Sunkin, *Judicial Review in Perspective*, Ch. 3.

[25] LSC Funding Code, criterion 5.4. And see J. Findlay, 'Defending judicial review proceedings: Tactical issues' (2005) 10 *Judicial Review* 27. See also, for a broad comparative perspective, J. Resnik, 'Whither and whether adjudication?' (2006) 86 *Boston University Law Rev.* 1101.

[26] Resting easily with active case management, CPR 44 grounds overarching judicial discretion.

raising the matter.[27] Much has also been heard in the last few years of 'protective costs orders', whereby the court takes action to re-balance the financial equation and cap the element of uncertainty by declaring the claimant's maximum (or nil) liability in advance. Reflecting and reinforcing the rise of 'public-interest advocacy', the technique is specifically geared to those cases raising issues of 'general public importance' that 'the public interest requires . . . should be resolved' and where otherwise the applicant would probably have to discontinue the proceedings.[28] As such, the technique is both valuable and inherently limited. It is also an expensive method for arranging 'insurance', one that is prone to engender 'satellite litigation'.[29]

Rules on costs and legal aid are not the only major source of difficulty in terms of access to justice. The uneven distribution of legal expertise to cope with the specialist demands of the judicial review process has scarcely been ameliorated by the current system of legal aid franchising (which includes public law and human rights as a specified subject area of expertise). While clearly welcome, regionalisation of the Administrative Court (see p. 686 above) offers only modest relief. Yet research underscores the importance of professional assistance in the pursuit of formal legal claims.[30] The recent study of judicial review litigation against local government showed an evident correlation between high levels of challenge and concentrations of publicly funded lawyers.[31]

A classic ground-floor study of general legal practice in socially deprived communities in South Wales brings home some grim realities. Human rights litigation was not so much 'sporadic and peripheral' as 'unheard of':

> Under half of the [twenty-one] solicitors had used the HRA . . . It had not been used as a cause of action . . . Only one solicitor had used it as a primary argument . . . A key explanation . . . was uncertainty about how to access the rights . . . A related explanation . . . was a lack of recent, targeted, and practical training . . . A common theme . . . was reluctance to use the HRA for fear that it would give the impression of a weak case.
>
> These sole and small-practice practitioners are operating on tight financial margins . . . They describe themselves as being 'on a production line' with legal aid cases . . . Within such an economic and working environment it is unsurprising that solicitors have little time to consider and work within the new and challenging parameters of the HRA.[32]

[27] *New Zealand Maori Council v Attorney General of New Zealand* [1004] 1 AC466. Likewise, the public body may choose to waive its entitlement.

[28] *R (Corner House Research) v Trade and Industry Secretary* [2005] 1 WLR 2600; also *R (Compton) v Wiltshire Primary Care Trust* [2008] EWCA Civ 749.

[29] *R (Buglife –The Invertebrate Conservation Trust) v Thurrock Thames Gateway Development Corpn* [2008] EWCA Civ 1209.

[30] See generally H. Genn, *Paths to Justice* (Hart Publishing, 1999).

[31] Sunkin *et al.*, 'Mapping the use of judicial review to challenge local authorities in England and Wales'.

[32] R. Costigan and P. Thomas, 'The Human Rights Act: A view from below' 32 *JLS* (2005) 51, 66–7. And see L. Clements, 'Winners and losers' (2005) 32 *JLS* 34.

(c) Iron hand?

At later stages (grounds of review and remedies) the judicial review caseload is diminished.[33] Having peaked at 1,414 in 2000, the numbers reduced rapidly with the CPR framework, totalling just 250–350 AJR cases annually over the last few years (see Fig. 15.6, p. 688 above). The incidence of cases in which public bodies actually experience 'the iron hand' of the court is of course lower still. In the two years 2006–7, 293 applications for review were both determined and allowed[34] – sporadic indeed!

And if the numbers of claims filed have mushroomed, the incidence of final hearings is back to the levels of the early 1980s,[35] with the ratio falling under the CPR from over 20 per cent to some 5 per cent. This recalls the sharpened disciplines – rationing – at the permission stage (see Chapter 15). The dominance of the judicial review caseload by immigration and asylum litigation accentuates the trend; the basic rule of thumb being that the higher the proportion of such cases, the higher the general rate of refusal of permission.[36]

The encouragement of negotiation and settlement via Bowman-type 'front-loading' and Woolf-style active case management must also be factored in. There is much to be said for this in terms of redress of grievance (subject to concerns about inequality of bargaining power),[37] responsive and efficient public administration, and regulating the judicial review caseload. It does however leave fewer opportunities for Administrative Court judges publicly to perform the educative or hortatory function.

2. Tempering: Rights and resources

It is common for courts to temper review by reference to the perceived needs of the administration. This may be done at several stages. In Chapter 15, we saw how this infused the courts' approach to their own procedures (all those 'safeguards' for access and proof). In the next section, we look at a similar tempering process at the stage of legal remedy.

In terms of the variable intensity of review that marks contemporary judicial review, tempering is probably necessary. There are, as we saw in earlier chapters, fewer 'no-go' areas. The courts no longer draw back, for example, in

33 Judicial review cases do however comprise a significant proportion of higher appellate work: A. Le Sueur, 'Panning for gold: Choosing cases for top-level courts' in Le Sueur (ed.), *Building the UK's New Supreme Court: National and comparative perspectives* (Oxford University Press, 2004).

34 *Judicial and Court Statistics*, Cm. 7273 (2007), and Cm. 7467 (2008), Table 1.12.

35 M. Sunkin, 'What is happening to applications for judicial review?' (1987) 50 *MLR* 432.

36 In 2006–7, claimant success rates in permission decisions in immigration/asylum cases and in other civil cases were 13% and 35% respectively.

37 See the findings in V. Bondy and M. Sunkin, 'Accessing judicial review' (2008) *PL* 647, and, for a comparative view, R. Creyke and J. McMillan, 'Judicial review outcomes: An empirical study' (2004) 11 *Aust. J. of Administrative Law* 82. *Practice Direction (Administrative Court: Uncontested Proceedings)* [2008] 1 WLR 1377 facilitates agreed final orders.

the face of prerogative power but there is nonetheless an array of 'light-touch' approaches in matters touching on the paradigm case of national security, defence and foreign affairs, where 'deference', according to Laws LJ (see p. 138 above) should be nearly absolute.[38] Great respect is shown again for the operational discretion of the police, as we saw in *Gillan* (see p. 215 above).[39] In Chapter 7 we saw the courts affording space to regulatory expertise, a second type of deference. Other cases show eminent judges expressing concern about convoluted decision-making pathways *(Denbigh High School*, see p. 121 above; *Miss Behavin'*, see p. 122 above); the troublesome effects of non-discrimination law (*Prague Airport*, see p. 213 above); and onerous adjudicative arrangements (*Runa Begum*, see p. 663 above). All have on occasion been described as unduly burdensome for the administration. Behind the scenes, we find the Attorney-General urging on government lawyers the need to 'educate' judges about the potential administrative consequences of their decisions, not least with respect to resource allocation: it 'is essential to bring home to the court the complexity of the policy background, and the ramifications of unsettling policy decisions in what may, superficially at least, appear to be a discrete area capable of being ring-fenced'.[40] Thus in *Marcic* (see p. 315 above), Thames Water presented a substantial brief to the House of Lords to demonstrate the impact of an adverse liability decision on the countrywide programme for renewal of sewage facilities.

(a) At the sharp end

Let us now turn more specifically to some case law concerning vulnerable sections of society. What, if anything, has judicial review done for them? Legal challenges designed to secure additional resources, or at least maintain existing provision, for a potentially large class of persons are a familiar form of 'test-case activity' or 'public-interest litigation' (see further below). The Diceyan conception of judicial 'control' is largely negative, focusing on protection of the individual in the face of arbitrariness, overweening government authority and excess of power; Dicey indeed expressed his inherent mistrust of what he called 'collectivism'.[41] Here we find judicial review prayed in aid as an encouragement to government intervention on behalf of the under-privileged or,[42] in the terminology of human rights, in support of economic and social rights.

[38] See for a striking example *R v Home Secretary, ex p. Rehman* [2001] UKHL 47.

[39] See also *R v Chief Constable of Sussex, ex p. International Trader's Ferry Ltd* [1998] 3 WLR 1260.

[40] Lord Goldsmith, quoted in M. Sunkin, 'Judicial review and bureaucratic impact: Conceptual issues in researching the impact of judicial review on government bureaucracies' in Hertogh and Halliday (eds.), *Judicial Review and Bureaucratic Impact* (Cambridge University Press, 2004), p. 74. But see J. King, 'The pervasiveness of polycentricity' [2008] *PL* 101.

[41] A.V. Dicey, *Lectures on the Relation between Law and Public Opinion in England during the Nineteenth Century*, 2nd edn (Macmillan, 1914).

[42] See generally S. Fredman, 'Social, economic and cultural rights' in Feldman (ed.), *English Public Law* (Oxford University Press, 2004).

Given the many competing calls on public authorities, not least when economic climes are harsh, this kind of litigation casts a fierce light on the interplay of courts with public administration.[43] How far should the judges go in entertaining pleas of local autonomy and democratic responsibility, of respect for the managerial disciplines of 'new public management' and of polycentricity? Alternatively, with individual claims attractively packaged in terms of welfare 'entitlements' or 'rights', to what extent can the courts grant remedies that seriously impinge on the budgetary allocations of individual public authorities? 'Government by judges' is a charge best avoided!

In this book, the *Coughlan* and *Herceptin* cases (see pp. 224 and 123 above) are striking examples of resource-oriented litigation hitting home. Two further pairs of cases, pre- and post-Human Rights Act (HRA) respectively, are, however, worth a closer look. All involve claims for resources against local authorities on behalf of highly vulnerable people. They point up a natural judicial propensity to 'play safe' with resource allocation,[44] decisions being grounded in precise statutory interpretation and reference to *vires*.

In *Barry*,[45] the council had assessed the elderly and severely disabled applicant as needing home-care assistance, including cleaning and laundry services. After central government reduced its funding, the council informed him, along with many others, that it was forced to prioritise and could no longer offer the services. The case was taken up by the Public Law Project, with an eye on similar developments across local government. It turned on the words 'necessary in order to meet the needs of that person' in s. 2 of the Chronically Sick and Disabled Persons Act 1970. Was the duty such as to provide an individual right to services so that the council was not entitled to take into consideration the resources available to it? The House of Lords (3–2) dismissed the claim:

> *Lord Nicholls*: A person's need for a particular type or level of service cannot be decided in a vacuum from which all considerations of cost have been expelled . . . Once it is accepted . . . that cost is a relevant factor in assessing a person's needs for the services listed in s. 2(1), then, in deciding how much weight is to be attached to cost, some evaluation or assumption has to be made about the impact which the cost will have upon the authority. Cost is of more or less significance depending upon whether the authority currently has more or less money . . .
>
> [It was argued that] if a local authority may properly take its resources into account . . . the s. 2(1) duty would in effect be limited to making arrangements to the extent only that the authority should decide to allocate money for this purpose. The duty, it was said, would collapse into a power. I do not agree. A local authority must carry out its functions under

[43] J. King, 'The justiciability of resource allocation' (2007) 70 *MLR* 197.

[44] E. Palmer, 'Resource allocation, welfare rights: Mapping the boundaries of judicial control in public administrative law' (2000) 20 *OJLS* 63. See also *Holmes-Moorhouse v Richmond upon Thames LBC* [2009] UKHL 7 and *R (Ahmad) v Newham LBC* [2009] UKHL 14.

[45] *R v Gloucestershire County Council, ex p. Barry* [1997] 2 All ER 1.

> s. 2(1) in a responsible fashion. In the event of a local authority acting with *Wednesbury* unreasonableness . . . a disabled person would have a remedy.
>
> *Lord Lloyd* (dissenting): In every case, simple or complex, the need of the individual will be assessed against the standards of civilised society as we know them in the United Kingdom . . . Resources can, of course, operate to impose a cash limit on what is provided. But how can resources help to measure the need? This . . . is the fallacy which lies at the heart of the council's argument . . . It cannot . . . have been Parliament's intention that [a] local authority . . . should be able to say 'because we do not have enough resources, we are going to reduce your needs.' His needs remain exactly the same. They cannot be affected by the local authority's inability to meet those needs . . . The solution lies with the Government. The passing of the 1970 Act was a noble aspiration. Having willed the end, Parliament must be asked to provide the means.

The case of *Tandy*,[46] decided by a unanimous but differently constituted House of Lords, went the other way. T, unable to attend school because of protracted illness, had previously been provided with five hours of home tuition a week. Faced with cuts in central-government funding, the LEA decided to reduce this to three hours a week. The House held, however, that availability of resources was irrelevant to the authority's duty under s. 298 of the Education Act 1993 to provide 'suitable education' to children of school age. The case of *Barry* was sharply distinguished as involving a 'strange' statutory provision that lacked definition, and less faith was put in *Wednesbury*, with local discretionary consideration of resources being effectively corralled as a matter of delivery:

> *Lord Browne-Wilkinson:* The argument is not one of insufficient resources to discharge the duty but of a preference for using the money for other purposes. To permit a local authority to avoid performing a statutory duty on the grounds that it prefers to spend the money in other ways is to downgrade a statutory duty to a discretionary power. A similar argument was put forward in the *Barry* case but dismissed by Lord Nicholls . . . apparently on the ground that the complainant could control the failure of a local authority to carry out its statutory duty by showing that it was acting in a way which was *Wednesbury* unreasonable . . . But with respect this is a very doubtful form of protection. Once the reasonableness of the actions of a local authority depends upon its decision how to apply scarce financial resources, the local authority's decision becomes extremely difficult to review. The court cannot second-guess the local authority in the way in which it spends its limited resources . . .
>
> Parliament has chosen to impose a statutory duty, as opposed to a power, requiring the local authority to do certain things. In my judgment, the courts should be slow to downgrade such duties into what are, in effect, mere discretions over which the court would have very little control. If Parliament wishes to reduce public expenditure on meeting the needs of sick children then it is up to Parliament so to provide. It is not for the courts to adjust the order of priorities as between statutory duties and statutory discretions.

[46] *R v East Sussex County Council, ex p. Tandy* [1998] AC 714.

These two authorities are emblematic of a difficult case law reaching back to the 1960s and 1970s in areas such as health, education and social work, where notions of entitlement are inextricably bound up with deployment of financial resources.[47] Matters have been compounded by a mishmash of intersecting and frequently amended legislative provisions so that (as Lord Nicholls has ruefully observed) identifying parliamentary intention 'is not always easy'. The rule of thumb applied by the courts is that the more specific and precise the duty, 'the more readily the statute may be interpreted as imposing an obligation of an absolute character'; or conversely – low intensity review – that the more general the terms of the duty, 'the more readily the statute may be construed as affording scope for a local authority to take into account matters such as cost when deciding how best to perform the duty'.

The case of *R (G)*, from which this quotation comes,[48] concerned the 'general duty . . . to safeguard and promote' welfare, imposed by s. 17(1) of the Children Act 1989 and, consistent with this, the duty to promote a family upbringing 'by providing a range and level of services appropriate to these children's needs'. The applicant argued that once the needs of the individual child had been established the authority was obliged to provide accommodation. The House of Lords (3–2) dismissed the challenge on the ground that such broad duties were not intended to be enforceable by individuals; it was sufficient that the authority maintained services for which his particular needs made him eligible. It was *Tandy's* turn to be distinguished with Lord Hope expressly linking the generic nature of the obligations to the practical realities confronting the respondents – two hard-pressed London boroughs:

> It is an inescapable fact of life that the funds and other resources available for the performance of the functions of a local social services authority are not unlimited. It is impossible therefore for the authority to meet every conceivable need. A judgement is to be exercised as to how needs may best be met, given the available resources. Parliament must be taken to have been aware of this fact when the legislation was enacted.

Happening post-HRA, this major piece of welfare law litigation also recalls the basic limitations of the ECHR in terms of socio-economic rights.[49] An attempt to invoke Art. 8 (respect for family life) was compromised by the wide margin of appreciation afforded in the Strasbourg jurisprudence.[50]

In *Spink*, s. 2 of the Chronically Sick and Disabled Persons Act 1970 was

[47] As documented in M. Partington and J. Jowell (eds.), *Welfare Law and Policy* (Pinter, 1979). There remains the possibility of the so-called 'default powers 'of ministers being prioritised at the expense of legal action by individuals: for classic authority, see *Watt v Kesteven* CC [1955] 1 QB 408 and *Wood v Ealing LBC* [1967] Ch. 487.

[48] *R (G) v Barnet LBC* [2003] 3 WLR 1194 [1199].

[49] As previously highlighted by *N v Home Secretary*, see p. 127 above. Positive potentials are on show in a case study of Article 3 and asylum seekers later in the chapter.

[50] See especially, *KA v Finland*, [2003] 1 FLR 201.

again before the courts.[51] The claimants argued that the council had to provide and pay for an expensive range of alterations to their home, such that their two severely disabled teenagers could properly enjoy the fruits of family life. The council contended that this depended on whether the parents could reasonably be expected to pay for the improvements. Following *Barry*, the Court of Appeal held that an authority, in determining whether it was 'necessary in order to meet the needs' to make arrangements, was entitled to consider this possibility:

> *Lord Phillips*: As a general proposition a local authority can reasonably expect that parents, who can afford the expense, will make any alterations to their home that are necessary for the care of their disabled children, if there is no alternative source of providing these. It is also reasonable to anticipate that some parents with means will not do so if they believe that this will result in the local authority making the alterations for them . . . A local authority can, in circumstances such as [these], properly decline to be satisfied that it is necessary to provide services to meet the needs of disabled children until it has been demonstrated that, having regard to their means, it is not reasonable to expect their parents to provide [them].

Convention rights again barely featured. There was no break in the line from *Barry* and the fact that 'loving parents' had 'demonstrated their devotion' allowed the court to side-step questions of disability and neglect raised potentially by Arts. 3 and 8.

3. Remedies: A precision instrument?

One of the most important aspects of grievance machinery is that it should provide effective redress. Here the conventional English machinery of judicial review has been seen to posses some notable capacities (powerful mandatory orders and injunctions). Chapter 15 also laid stress on the special attributes of the declaration (the judges' 'flexible friend') and on the expansion of the remedial tool-kit in part under European influence.

The image of 'the British motorway' (see p. 676 above) recalls some important constraints familiarly associated with the adjudicative procedure, however. Continuing pressures for more expansive uses of remedies, as also some judicial disagreement premised on different views of the courts' proper constitutional role, reflect this. For example, English judges have customarily not been enthusiastic to decide hypothetical issues or to lay down rules merely because some individual or group thinks it appropriate.[52] There are though an increasing number of 'exceptions',[53] bound up with the concept of the 'advi-

[51] *R (Spink) v Wandsworth LBC* [2005] EWCA Civ 302.

[52] *Gouriet v Union of Post Office Workers* [1978] AC 435 (Lord Diplock)

[53] To trace the development, see *Royal College of Nursing v DHSS* [1981] AC 800, *Gillick v West Norfolk and Wisbech AHA* [1986] AC 112, *R v Home Secretary, ex p. Salem* [1999] 1 450, and *Kay v Commissioner of Police for the Metropolis* [2006] EWHC 1536.

sory declaration'.[54] Again, the domestic courts have routinely declined to intervene in active administration, although power now exists to make a substitute decision rather than referring the matter back to the original decision-maker[55], and experiments are beginning to be made with structural procedural review (see Chapter 14).

A major limitation on judicial process is the absence of procedures for monitoring impact and implementation. Unlike Parliament, courts cannot call for impact assessments or engage in 'post-litigation scrutiny'; unlike ombudsmen, they lack the ability to monitor treatment of similar cases. Take the case brought by Child Poverty Action Group (CPAG) on behalf of an unidentified class of welfare claimants (see p. 698 above) to establish endemic errors in the payment of benefits. Had the case been won by someone directly affected, an order to make back-payments would be possible, though a declaration of entitlement to back-payment is more likely. But a win by CPAG, which was not directly involved, would create problems of judicial remedy. The court might, in principle, order the department to take out and examine all the relevant files but, as noted earlier, English courts do not deal in 'structural injunctions'. This leaves a declaration that the decision was unlawful as the most likely remedy. The outcome then rests in departmental hands. The department may try to trace the class, as ombudsmen usually advise should be done. Legislation may be required to regularise the position and provide resources for compensation (see Chapter 17). Alternatively, a minister may opt for retrospective legislation depriving everyone of the fruits of the legal victory (see below). The utility of a successful challenge is thus questionable.

In judicial review an otherwise successful claimant has no automatic right to a remedy: even if the agency is held to have acted unlawfully, it is the court's prerogative to deny or fashion any relief. We caught sight of this element in a number of important cases:

- *Datafin* (prospective declaration only so as to avoid market disruption, see p. 317 above)
- *Bibi* (declaration on council house allocation re-written to draw the fangs of substantive legitimate expectation, see p. 225 above)
- *Edwards* (no quashing for failure of consultation in view of actual pollution levels, see p. 651 above)

Judge Over Your Shoulder (JOYS)[56] expands on the possibilities, explaining that relevant matters include:

- any prejudicial delay by the claimant in bringing the case
- whether the claimant has suffered substantial hardship
- any impact the remedy may have on third parties

[54] Sir J. Laws, 'Judicial remedies and the constitution' (1994) 57 *MLR* 213.

[55] See both CPR 54.19 and the Tribunals, Courts and Enforcement Act 2007 (TCEA), s. 141.

[56] TSol, *Judge over Your Shoulder*, 4th edn (Cabinet Office, 2006) [3.37].

- whether a remedy would have any practical effect or the matter has become academic
- the merits of the case
- whether the remedy would promote good administration.

Lord Bingham once sought to justify an element of judicial discretion on the ground that judicial review would enjoy greater legitimacy if it were seen 'as a precision instrument and not a juggernaut'. But given the evident threat to the rule of law and unfairness in sending the individual away empty-handed – not to say the elements of wasted time and expense at the end of a case – the technique should be 'strictly limited and the rules for its exercise clearly understood'.[57]

Yet as the parameters of judicial review expanded under the auspices of AJR procedure, so the extra so-called 'safeguard'[58] of the power to control remedy would take on greater prominence. This was the logic of the transaction typing on offer in *Datafin*, where judicial review was hardly a juggernaut![59] In certain situations, the courts may be surprisingly firm and, in the case of EU requirements, acutely aware of the need to rein in remedial discretion in order to ensure fulfilment of the Member State's obligations.[60] The typically open-ended criteria are nonetheless a recipe for uncertainty in individual cases, with much again riding on the attitude of the particular judge. The fact of considerable overlap with the permission criteria (see p. 671 above) underscores this point.

(a) Case examples

Involving some very different transaction types, a trio of cases will serve to illuminate the range of possibilities. Pointing up the particular difficulties presented by polycentric forms of decision-making, the first one is *Caswell*.[61] A pre-CPR case, it remains the leading authority on refusal of remedy by reason of 'undue delay' (see p. 690 above). Dairy farmers were permitted to produce only the amount of milk allocated to them under an EC quota system. The tribunal had fixed the applicants' quota on the basis of existing production, indicating – erroneously - that they could reapply for additional quota once the size of the herd increased. The applicants only became aware of the possibility of judicial review several years later through an article in the farming

57 Sir T. Bingham, 'Should public law remedies be discretionary?' [1991] *PL* 64, 75. History did not always bear this out, as in a notorious line of cases excusing breach of natural justice: *Ex p. Fry* [1954] 1 WLR 730; *R v Aston University Senate, ex p. Roffey* [1969] 2 QB 538; *Glynn v Keele University* [1971] 2 All ER 89.

58 Lord Woolf, 'Droit public, English style' [1995] *PL* 57.

59 See also *R v Monopolies and Mergers Commission, ex p. Argyll Group plc* [1986] 1 WLR 763. The slightly earlier case of *Chief Constable of the North Wales Police v Evans* [1982] 1 WLR 115 had sent out similar messages in the context of an employment dispute.

60 See to this effect, *Berkeley v Environment Secretary* [2003] 3 WLR 420.

61 *Caswell v Dairy Produce Quota Tribunal for England and Wales* [1990] 2 AC 738.

press. Invoking the statutory discretion, the House of Lords refused to quash the decision and to compel a new allocation; only a declaration was available to mark the invalidity:

> *Lord Goff:* 'S. 31(6) of the Supreme Court Act 1981 recognises that there is an interest in good administration independently of hardship, or prejudice to the rights of third parties . . . In the present context that interest lies essentially in a regular flow of consistent decisions, made and published with reasonable despatch; in citizens knowing where they stand, and how they can order their affairs in the light of the relevant decision. Matters of particular importance, apart from the length of time itself, will be the extent of the effect of the relevant decision, and the impact which would be felt if it were to be reopened. The present case [concerns] a decision to allocate part of a finite amount of quota, and circumstances in which a reopening of the decision would lead to other applications to reopen similar decisions which, if successful, would lead to reopening the allocation of quota over a number of years. To me it is plain . . . that to grant the appellants the relief they sought in the present case after such a lapse of time had occurred, would be detrimental to good administration.

The case of *Caswell* sharply illustrates the clash of values in the judicial review process between on the one hand the rule of law function and effective redress[62] and on the other the efficiency of public administration and court process.[63] There was a strong case for individual protection in the form of financial interest, a claim buttressed by practical problems of access to justice; but, there were important practicalities of administration, with the impugned decision part of a system of rationing. Factoring in the interests of third parties not before the court, judicial review fell to be tempered.

The case of *Burke*,[64] our second selection, involves the difficult area of medical law and ethics. Highlighting the dangers of extravagant use of the judges' 'flexible friend', it bears directly on the constitutional role of the judiciary in this era of Convention rights. B suffered from a progressively degenerative condition similar to multiple sclerosis, which confined him to a wheelchair. He sought to challenge guidance from the General Medical Council to doctors dealing with the termination of life-prolonging treatment. In making a series of declarations under the auspices of ECHR Arts. 2, 3 and 8, only some of which specifically related to the case of the terminally-ill applicant, Munby J had taken it upon himself to rewrite large portions of the guidance. This involved substituting a 'quality of life' test for withdrawal of artificial nutrition and hydration for the tougher 'intolerability' test. On appeal, Lord Phillips took a more balanced view of the court's normative and expository role:

[62] As described in Ch. 17, compensation in such a case might have to be left to *ex gratia* procedures.

[63] The clash would typically be concealed in delay cases by the workings of 'permission'.

[64] *R (Burke) v General Medical Council* [2005] EWCA Civ 1003.

> *Lord Phillips*: It was not the task of a judge when sitting judicially – even in the Administrative Court – to set out to write a text book or practice manual. Yet the judge appears to have done just that . . . Indeed [the judgment] has been understood as bearing on the right to treatment generally, and not merely life prolonging treatment. It has led to the intervention in the proceedings before us [see p. 703 above]. The court should not be used as a general advice centre. The danger is that the court will enunciate propositions of principle without full appreciation of the implications that these will have in practice, throwing into confusion those who feel obliged to attempt to apply those principles in practice. This danger is particularly acute where the issues raised involve ethical questions that any court should be reluctant to address, unless driven to do so by the need to resolve a practical problem that requires the court's intervention . . .
>
> The first three declarations were extraordinary in nature in that they did not purport to resolve any issues between the parties, but appeared to be intended to lay down propositions of law binding on the world . . . The declarations as a whole go far beyond the current concerns of Mr Burke . . . It is our view that Mr. Burke's fears are addressed by the law as it currently stands and that declaratory relief, particularly in so far as it declares parts of the Guidance unlawful, is both unnecessary for Mr. Burke's protection and inappropriate as far as the Guidance itself is concerned.

Quashing the declarations the Court of Appeal nonetheless added as an expository footnote its view that it 'is of the utmost importance that the Guidance should be understood and implemented at every level throughout the National Health Service and throughout the medical profession . . . Having produced the Guidance, the task of the GMC . . . is to ensure that it is vigorously promulgated, taught, understood and implemented at every level and in every hospital.'

Burke sharply poses the question: will other judges prove strong enough to resist the temptation afforded by the 'flexible friend'?[65]

The third case, *R (C) v Justice Secretary*,[66] demonstrates more judicial disagreement over remedial discretion, this time in the parliamentary context of formal rule-making (see Chapter 4). The case concerned the permissible physical constraints imposed on young persons detained in secure training centres. The minister had laid amending regulations extending their use for the purposes of good order and discipline but had unlawfully failed to consult and to carry out a race equality impact assessment (as required by the amended s. 71 of the Race Relations Act 1971).[67] The Divisional Court declined to quash the statutory instrument, giving as reasons (i) that the Upper House had debated it under negative resolution procedure knowing of the failure to consult; and (ii) that the techniques were under active reconsideration. The Court of Appeal granted the remedy:

65 See further, for divergent opinion in the House of Lords, *Oxfordshire County Council v Oxford City Council* [2006] UKHL 25.

66 [2008] EWCA Civ 882.

67 See further as regards s. 71, *R (Kaur and Shah) v Ealing LBC* [2008] EWHC 2062.

> *Keene LJ:* When delegated legislation is found to be ultra vires [this] should normally lead to the delegated legislation being quashed, and only in unusual circumstances would one expect to find a court exercising its discretion in such a way as to allow such legislation to remain in force. [[68]] Such legislation normally changes the law for the public generally or for a class of persons. It should not generally be allowed to stand if it has not come into being in accordance with the law, and certainly not merely because certain checks which should have been carried out beforehand are to be made subsequently. Such a course may well prejudge the outcome of those checks, and yet the public is expected to conduct its life in accordance with such delegated legislation in the meantime. That cannot normally be appropriate.

The judgment of Buxton LJ harks back to Dicey's theory of the 'balanced constitution' (see p. 4 above). (And compare the reasoning in *Huang*, see p. 147 above).

> *Buxton LJ:* There are two objections to reliance on the House of Lords debate, one practical and one of principle. The practical objection is that it is very hazardous to draw any conclusions from the observations of various speakers in a debate, and particularly a debate that is not pressed to a vote, as to what the majority of members understood, let alone decided or were prepared to overlook. To say or suggest that 'Parliament' had approved the failure to consult . . . is therefore an assumption too far. The objection of principle is that the Divisional Court's approach confuses two different constitutional functions. The legal obligation to take certain steps before laying legislation before Parliament is that of the executive. It is not Parliament's role to control that obligation: that is the function of the courts. Rather, the function of Parliament is simply to approve or disapprove the Amendment Rules as laid. Its failure to disapprove the Amendment Rules cannot supply the executive's failure to perform the legal obligations that it bears before laying the Amendment Rules in the first place.

4. In search of 'impact'

(a) Typology

Writing in the 1980s on the theme of legal 'control', Feldman[69] specified three different techniques of judicial intervention or effects on government:

- *directing*: the traditional judicial function of compelling government to adhere to stated legal powers and duties
- *limiting*: establishing the scope of, or setting the limits to the exercise of, discretion (for example, the common law rules against delegation and fettering of powers)
- *structuring*: making explicit values or goals that are to guide decision-making (for example, *Wednesbury* unreasonableness and the duty to act fairly).

[68] The Divisional Court had relied on remarks by Webster J in *R v Social Services Secretary, ex p. AMA* [1986] 1 WLR 1 to the opposite effect.

[69] D. Feldman, 'Judicial review: A way of controlling government?' (1988) 66 *Pub. Admin.* 21.

With 'directing', control is retrospective and specific. The agency is required to take steps to achieve legality, but there might be limited general impact or radiating effects. 'Limiting' potentially has a wider influence on the forms and structures of government (although liable today to be mediated by new modalities of 'governance' (the *Ealing* case, see p. 218 above)). In Feldman's view, 'structuring' affects administrators' day-to-day activities far more significantly than the other techniques, by reason of the greater exercise of prior control or provision of guidance.

This basic typology signals the way in which the various fire-watching functions of judicial review have assumed greater prominence in recent times. From this perspective, the general development in the grounds of review involves a shift of emphasis in favour of 'structuring' (as against the narrow *vires*-based explanation of judicial review exemplified by 'directing' and 'limiting').

The typology also casts light on some of the twists and turns in the cases. We can describe the House of Lords in *Barry* as refusing a request to perform the 'directing' function. Thus, Lord Nicholls was content with only 'structuring' in the form of *Wednesbury* unreasonableness. Conversely, we saw Lord Browne-Wilkinson in the *Tandy* case refuse to 'downgrade' the judicial contribution in this way. Another argument concerns the role of 'structuring'. As noted in Chapter 14, the hortatory or educative function of law, ultimately the internalising by administrators of legal values, may be threatened by flexible application of such an imprecise principle as 'fairness'. As the cases we have been discussing demonstrate only too clearly, the 'intuitive judgment' of courts can be difficult to fathom, let alone predict! Perhaps then it is not surprising to learn that ministers and officials 'complain that the principles of judicial review developed and applied by the courts are too uncertain'.[70]

Excessive structuring – too much juridification of the administrative process – also needs to be avoided. Notably in the *Denbigh High School* case (see p. 121 above), the Court of Appeal was seen moving beyond the expression of values or goals to prescribe in extraordinary detail the steps that headteachers should follow. Conversely, the results-oriented approach of the House of Lords serves both to underscore the importance of Convention rights in discussion of judicial review 'impact' and to limit it.

In view of today's multi-streamed jurisdiction, Feldman's classification can usefully be supplemented:

- *vindicating*: encompasses the transformative potential for judicial review of Convention rights (extending to positive obligations), while also reflecting the rise of merits-based scrutiny of public decision-making more generally.

[70] A. Le Sueur, 'The judicial review debate: From partnership to friction' (1996) *31 Government and Opposition* 8, 22; confirmed by S. James, 'The political and administrative consequences of judicial review' (1996) 74 *Pub. Admin.* 613.

(b) Formal reactions

'Formal' reactions to judicial review, typically a change to, or confirmation of, official agency policy, are usefully distinguished from 'informal' or behavioural or attitudinal ones, which are naturally more elusive. Whereas by definition the very many 'routine' cases can be expected to leave little individual mark, the sequels to particular, sometimes famous, pieces of litigation illustrate the very different ways in which government may respond to judicial decisions.[71] This aspect is further highlighted today by the rise of 'public-interest advocacy', the classic example being as in *Barry* the test case designed to achieve a marked 'ripple' effect, altering or sustaining administrative practice in large numbers of cases.

Negative responses include a strong type of formal reaction – valedictory legislation or nullification. This is classically illustrated in the aftermath of *Anisminic* (see p. 28 above). Another technique is to reaffirm or take the same decision twice as was done in *Padfield* (see p. 101 above). This highlights the limitations of procedural review that has the effect of returning the decision to the original decision-maker. Alternatively, there may be attempts at secrecy, such as by 'boiler-plate reasons'. Other stratagems familiar from the core litigation area of asylum claims bear directly on the court process: if not total ouster then attenuated forms of legal aid and statutory review (see p. 519 above).

As a long-standing public-interest advocate, the endeavours of CPAG are replete with examples of parliamentary sovereignty being used to 'trump' the judicial power. Ministers proved particularly adept at drawing the sting of those challenges designed to benefit a large class of persons that were successful.[72] Statutory provisions might be inserted to the effect that the ruling would not apply to other, similar, claims in the pipeline; alternatively, Parliament might be asked to restrict the back-dating of welfare payments to other, similarly placed individuals. Even on this traditional constitutional scenario however, valedictory legislation does not deprive judicial review of all its 'impact'. As a vehicle of interest representation, one of the functions of court process is to open up a particular policy to public debate. Following the celebrated *Fire Brigades* case (see p. 145 above), for example, the Government had to make substantial concessions when drafting a statutory scheme.[73]

With the multi-streamed jurisdiction, matters are typically more complex. Within the domestic arena, ministers' freedom of manoeuvre may be more circumscribed, partly with the aid of the expanded toolbox of legal remedies. No longer is the judicial power so easily 'trumped' by legislative power, if indeed

[71] Early studies are C. Harlow, 'Administrative reaction to judicial review' [1976] *PL* 116 and T. Prosser, 'Politics and judicial review: The Atkinson case and its aftermath' [1979] *PL* 59.

[72] T. Prosser, *Test Cases for the Poor* (CPAG, 1993). See especially *R v Social Fund Inspector, ex p. Stitt* [1990] COD 288 and *Bate v Chief Adjudication Officer* [1996] 1 WLR 814.

[73] G. Ganz, 'Criminal injuries compensation: The constitutional issue' (1996) 59 *MLR* 95.

it can be. From this perspective, 'transforming judicial review' (see Chapter 3) has a dual effect: not only biting more deeply on the policy-making sinews of government, but also limiting its capacity for a muscular response. The evident difficulties which ministers now face in securing ouster clauses, not least if EC law is in play (*Johnston*, see p. 30 above), and the requirement, through the 'representation-reinforcing' principle of legality (*Sims*, see p. 119 above), to use primary legislation when interfering with fundamental rights, illustrate this further element of judicial 'counter-reaction'.

Having strictly no effect on the validity, continuing operation or enforcement of legislation, the HRA, s. 4 declaration of incompatibility provides a different scenario. In the shadow of the (unincorporated) ECHR Art. 13 right to an effective remedy,[74] implementation is naturally the subject of anxious scrutiny by the Joint Committee on Human Rights.[75] Thus far, legislative action has consistently been taken to remove the defect,[76] underscoring and vindicating the 'dialogue model' of human rights protection (see Chapter 3). As shown in the aftermath of *A (No. 1)* however, there is also the possibility with successful claims of inconsistency or discrimination of 'levelling-down' (see p. 132 above).

(c) Influence: Interpretation and reinterpretation

As against 'red light' views of the chief role of courts, impact studies commonly emphasise 'the limited ability of judicial review to influence administrative decision-making'.[77] Lawyers themselves all too often conflate court orders with enforceability and compliance, so glossing over the kaleidoscopic quality of the relationship between judicial and administrative decision-taking – complex and dynamic, if not always beautiful, in all its varieties.[78]

A pioneering study into the effects on prison administration found 'a legalising of prison culture', with a marked emphasis on process – clear criteria, consistency, and reformed disciplinary procedures – as 'judicial review's most enduring impact'. A theme familiar from procedural fairness (see Chapter 14), the courts had 'been happiest' when imposing adjudicative style constraints. In contrast, in substantive terms:

[74] See now *Burden v United Kingdom*, App. 13358/05 (29 April 2008).

[75] JCHR, *Monitoring the Government's Response to Human Rights Judgments: Annual Report 2008*, HC 1078 (2007/8). By mid-2008, 15 declarations of incompatibility had become final in their entirety. A further 7 had been overturned on appeal.

[76] See for details, J. Beatson *et al.*, *Human Rights: Judicial protection in the United Kingdom* (Sweet & Maxwell, 2008), pp. 522–33.

[77] G. Richardson, 'Impact studies in the United Kingdom' in Hertogh and Halliday (eds.), *Judicial Review and Bureaucratic Impact*, p. 112. For a case study of what happens when judicial review is emphatically not 'sporadic and peripheral', see p. 738 below.

[78] That impact studies are plagued with methodological difficulty itself points up the deceptive simplicity of 'judicial control'. For a valuable comparative perspective, see B. Canon, 'Studying bureaucratic implementation of judicial policies in the United States', in Hertogh and Halliday (eds.), *Judicial Review and Bureaucratic Impact*.

> Judicial review has had less impact on either the framework of policy-making in relation to prisons or on the exercise of low level discretionary powers deemed essential to prison management . . . Judicial review operates primarily to correct aberrations in bureaucratic decision-making but ultimately tends to find itself powerless before the arbitrariness which is often the normality of prison life. This is perhaps why it has had so little impact on prisoners' living and working conditions, a field that probably is best left to the more detailed investigative work of bodies like the . . . Chief Inspector of Prisons.[79]

A study of 'judge-made regulation' in hard-pressed housing authorities points up the difficulty for this 'external control' in penetrating at the ground-floor level. Effectively framed by the availability of empty properties for allocation, the administrative routines were closely governed by such factors as agency relations and expediency:

> Legalistic perceptions of the 'law' will rarely be of more than minor significance. This is not to say that statute or case law has no hortatory role to play in structuring administrative behaviour . . . It is clear that the threat of judicial review can have a marked short term effect on senior officers' perception of the way the administrative process should be controlled. But legalism is an intruder into the administrative arena. It does not prescribe administrative behaviour, but challenges it. It does not facilitate the decision-making process, rather it gets in the way. It is not respected, but ignored. And if it cannot be ignored it is grudgingly accepted as an unrealistic impediment to rational decision-making.[80]

Some studies also suggest that where judicial review does have an influence it tends to be negative. Though a natural accompaniment[81] to 'transforming judicial review', concerns about 'defensive administration' – unduly cautious and inhibited decision-making in the context of threats of litigation (real or perceived) – are hardly new. Take the aftermath of the famous *Bromley* case (see p. 103 above). Confronted by the House of Lords with 'fiduciary duty', some authorities bowed to the spirit of the decision and altered direction, while others resorted to creative lawyering to secure established policy.[82] Further (a standard example of juridification):

> The need to demonstrate the reasonableness of the policy process by routinely consulting political and legal interests has led to greater formality in the organisational arrangements

[79] S. Livingstone, 'The impact of judicial review on prisons' in Hadfield (ed.), *Judicial Review: A thematic approach* (Gill & MacMillan, 1995), pp. 180–2. See also, M. Loughlin and P. Quinn, 'Prisons, rules and courts: A study of administrative law' (1993) 56 *MLR* 497.

[80] I. Loveland, 'Administrative law, administrative processes, and the housing of homeless persons: A view from the sharp end' (1991) 10 *J. of Social Welfare and Family Law* 4, 21–2. See further, I. Loveland, *Housing Homeless Persons: Administrative law and the administrative process* (Clarendon Press, 1995).

[81] See e.g. BRTF, *Better Routes to Redress* (2004).

[82] See *R v Merseyside County Council, ex p. Great Universal Stores Ltd* (1982) 80 LGR 639; *R v London Transport Executive, ex p. Greater London Council* [1983] 1 QB 484.

> of decision-making – in short, to greater bureaucracy. Accompanying the increasing rules and procedures [is] an extension in the amount of time spent in formal meetings and a growth in paperwork . . . The taking of legal advice, of visiting counsel, has now become an established feature of the local authority's policy-making process. . . The intrusion of the legal soothsayers erodes the authority of elected members in quite a fundamental way.[83]

Other research points up the limiting effects for generalist judicial review of highly specialised administrative contexts that are replete with their own institutional frameworks and cultures. For example, the influence on decision-making by the Mental Health Review Tribunal has been characterised as 'patchy at best':

> Admittedly, compliance with certain judicial requirements was high, but wherever there was a conflict between medical and juridical norms the former tended to prevail, even where the juridical norm related to process . . . The MHRT [may be] exceptional in the degree of reliance it has to place on disciplines other than the law. But it is not unique in having to relate to other systems, and reviewing courts must regularly issue rulings which could be expected to apply across competing systems. On the basis of the data from the MHRT, the influence of such rulings on subsequent bureaucratic decision-making is likely to be minimal unless some attempt is made to accommodate alternative value systems.[84]

Nor should it be surprising to learn of changing 'impact' over time. Take the review function performed by the Social Fund Inspectorate (now IRS), itself modelled on judicial review (see p. 503 above). At first, the small stream of court challenges to the agency:

> provided operational clarity to the new organisation. It also served a broader legitimating role. By linking the [inspectors'] approach to judicial review norms such as natural justice, the Commissioner was able to emphasise the legal nature of their task. That the IRS could be challenged in the courts and be held legally accountable was also of importance to the portrayal of IRS as an organisation bedded within the law . . . The ability to withstand judicial review scrutiny was adopted as a key internal measure of the quality of [inspectors'] decision taking . . . Judicial review decisions were also studied in detail and 'milked' for the guidance they offered and for identifying training needs.[85]

Later, however, with new-public-management-style concerns with efficient service delivery increasingly dominating, 'ensuring compliance with the pos-

[83] L. Bridges, C. Game, O. Lomas, J. McBride and S. Ranson, *Legality and Local Politics* (Avebury, 1987), pp. 110–11.

[84] Richardson, 'Impact studies in the United Kingdom', p. 126, drawing on G. Richardson and I. Machin, 'Judicial Review and Tribunal Decision-Making' [2000] *PL* 494.

[85] M. Sunkin and K. Pick, 'The changing impact of judicial review: The independent review of the social fund' (2001) *PL* 736, 746 –7. See also, T. Buck, 'Judicial review and the discretionary social fund: The impact on a respondent organisation' in Buck (ed.), *Judicial Review and Social Welfare* (Pinter, 1998).

sible expectations of judges' took a back seat. 'Juridical norms are expected to serve organisational goals rather than drive them.'[86]

As against simple 'cause and effect', that 'impact' involves interaction with other informing influences is an important sociological theme elaborated in another, more recent, study of judicial review and homelessness decision-making:

> In different ways, professional intuition, systemic suspicion, bureaucratic expediency, judgements about the moral desert of applicants, inter-officer relations, financial constraint and other values and pressures all played a part in how judicial review impacted upon decision-making in the three local authorities . . . The 'impact' of judicial review, of course, is not an 'either/or' matter, but is a question of degree. However, these research findings demonstrate that, despite extensive and prolonged exposure to judicial scrutiny, unlawful decision-making was rife in each authority. In different (and sometimes subtle) ways the local authorities' administrative processes displayed considerable evidence of values and priorities which were in conflict with the norms of administrative law.[87]

Attention is drawn to the contingent meaning of law in the bureaucracy; the way in which messages emanating from judicial review are subject to distortion through processes of interpretation and reinterpretation. 'What the court proclaims is not always what the agency understands . . . there is also an important need for adequate communication within the agency itself.' [88] In helping to point up conditions liable to promote impact – clarity and consistency in the case law, high levels of legal cognisance and competence inside the agency, legal conscientiousness or public service ethos of fidelity to law among officials – this usefully suggests some practical actions. The problem of course is execution across the length and breadth of government.

5. Mainstreaming?

One measure of the increased seriousness with which government regards judicial review is the steps taken to train staff to avoid taking attackable decisions. Already in 1983 the then Treasury Solicitor was complaining publicly about the number of cases the Crown was losing. Perhaps predictably, Sir Michael Kerry[89] identified limited legal awareness among officials as the root cause of government vulnerability. Challenge was here being made to tradi-

[86] *Ibid.*, p. 759.

[87] S. Halliday, 'The influence of judicial review on bureaucratic decision making' (2000) *PL* 110, 116–7, 122. And see S. Halliday, *Judicial Review and Compliance with Administrative Law* (Hart Publishing, 2004).

[88] M. Hertogh and S. Halliday, 'Judicial Review and Bureaucratic Impact in Future Research', in Hertogh and Halliday (eds.), *Judicial Review and Bureaucratic Impact*, p. 280.

[89] M. Kerry, 'Administrative law and the administration' (1983) 3 *Management in Government* 170 and 'Administrative law and judicial review: The practical effects of developments over the last twenty five years on administration in central government' (1986) 64 *Pub. Admin.* 163.

tional civil service views of law and lawyers as peripheral to the administrative process, encapsulated in the confining of departmental lawyers to legal as opposed to policy matters.[90]

Reflecting and reinforcing the trend towards juridification of the administrative process, a more systematic approach designed to anticipate legal challenge became a priority for senior Whitehall officials.[91] As well as in-house legal training, emphasis was laid on such steps as more proactive use of lawyers at the planning stages of policy-making, more thorough review of case work by managers and greater use of counsel especially in the drafting of legislation. The first edition of the Treasury Solicitor's basic guide to judicial review for non-lawyer civil servants also appeared. *The Judge Over Your Shoulder* (JOYS) published in 1987 set out to 'highlight the danger areas' and 'enable warning bells to ring'. By 1994 the then Cabinet Secretary was claiming publicly that 'awareness of administrative law has greatly increased amongst civil servants'.[92]

Notwithstanding the hostile public comment in which ministers have sometimes chosen to indulge (see Chapter 3), later versions of JOYS evince, in the words of a former Treasury Solicitor, a more 'constructive spirit'.[93] Substantially rewritten in light of the HRA, the current edition aims 'to emphasise what is best practice in administrative decision-making, rather than what you can get away with'.[94] Perhaps hopefully, another former Treasury Solicitor believes that 'the principles of good administration . . . developed so assiduously by the courts now form part of every decision maker's frame of reference'.[95] Dame Juliet Wheldon also draws attention here to the 'particular responsibility' of the Government Legal Service; not least, one is tempted to add, in authoritarian times:

> Members of the GLS, as qualified lawyers bound by the same standards of professional ethics as those in practice, must provide objective advice on the legality of Government actions every day. That happens in the development of policy, and in litigation. It does not matter whether the matter is one of high policy or is mundane. My point is that the professional integrity of members of the GLS has a real role to play in embedding the rule of law within Government, and confirming it as a principle of institutional morality. Putting it another way, Government lawyers are the first line of defence when this principle is threatened.[96]

[90] B. Abel-Smith and R. Stevens, *Lawyers and the Courts* (Heinemann, 1967). See further, T. Daintith and A. Page, *The Executive in the Constitution* (Oxford University Press, 1999).

[91] Tracked by M. Sunkin and A. Le Sueur, 'Can government control judicial review?' (1991) 44 *Current Legal Problems* 161.

[92] R. Butler, Foreword to TSol, *The Judge Over Your Shoulder*, 2nd edn (Cabinet Office, 1994).

[93] A. Hammond. 'Judicial review: Continuing interplay between law and policy' [1998] *PL* 34, 39.

[94] TSol, *Judge over Your Shoulder* (2006 version) [1].

[95] Dame J. Wheldon, 'Judicial review from the government perspective', p. 7.

[96] *Ibid.*, p. 8.

(a) Enter Convention rights

Efforts to promote legal learning inside government naturally intensified with the looming prospect of courts adjudicating under the HRA. Lord Chancellor Irvine spoke, no less, of creating a society 'in which our public institutions are habitually, automatically responsive to human rights considerations in relation to every procedure they follow, in relation to every practice they follow, in relation to every decision they take'.[97] A Human Rights Task Force was established by the Home Office, consisting of ministers, civil servants and representatives of public agencies and 'public interest' groups, and given special responsibility for producing and disseminating 'core guidance' for public authorities. 'Respect for Convention rights should be at the very heart of everything you do.' 'You should be able to justify your decisions in the context of the Convention rights, and show that you have considered the Convention rights and dealt with any issues arising out of such a consideration'.[98] Read in light of the subsequent House of Lords ruling in *Denbigh High School* (see p. 121 above), this might even be considered excessively 'positive'!

The scale of the task should not be underestimated. Human rights advocates had to contend here with the workings of multi-layered governance. Central government departments,[99] the new devolved administrations,[100] local authorities,[101] agencies etc.[102] engaged in frontline service provision would all need (continuous) guidance specifically geared to different policy domains. Nor should mere guidance or provision of information be confused with the altogether more demanding activity of 'mainstreaming' human rights principles and values in the administrative process.[103] There would soon be an increasing mound of evidence of problems of compliance.

A report in 2003 from the Audit Commission set the tone:

> The impact of the Act is in danger of stalling and the initial flurry of activity surrounding its introduction has waned . . . 58% of public bodies surveyed [in England] still have not adopted a strategy for human rights. In many local authorities the Act has not left the desks of the lawyers. In health, 73% of trusts are not taking action . . .

[97] Lord Irvine, *Evidence to JCHR*, HC 332-ii (2001/2) [38]. The place of human rights considerations in the legislative process was discussed in Ch. 4.

[98] Human Rights Task Force, *A New Era of Rights and Responsibilities: Core guidance for public authorities* 2000, pp. 3, 17.

[99] See Cabinet Office, *The Human Rights Act 1998: Guidance for departments*, 2nd edn (London, 2000).

[100] See e.g. National Assembly for Wales, *Human Rights Act Implementation: Action plan* (2000); R. Rawlings, 'Taking Wales seriously' in Campbell, Ewing and Tomkins (eds.), *Sceptical Essays on Human Rights* (Oxford University Press, 2001).

[101] L. Clements and R. Morris, 'The millennium blip: The Human Rights Act 1998 and local government' in Halliday and Schmidt (eds.), *Human Rights Brought Home: Socio-legal perspectives on human rights in the national context* (Hart Publishing, 2004).

[102] The NHS Litigation Authority would pioneer an online human rights information service, available on its website.

[103] S. Cooke, 'Securing human rights through promotion and training' 57 *NILQ* (2006) 205.

> The challenge for public bodies is to learn from legal cases in order to avoid similar litigation in the future; and to apply a human rights framework to the decision making across public services in order to achieve better service provision . . . Our assessment showed that 56% of public bodies were not monitoring case law developments on a regular basis . . . The problem is exacerbated in health because it is difficult to identify an appropriate officer who has responsibility for overseeing and monitoring developments.[104]

In urging agencies to adopt creative strategies and techniques of compliance, 'positively promoting human rights', the Audit Commission typically stressed the bottom line. Court cases had 'resulted in legal costs and penalties' and 'damage to an organisation's reputation'. 'Human rights' could do with a dose of 'meta-regulation' (see p. 244 above). As well as the ubiquitous demand for 'risk assessment', the Commission thus stipulated self-assessment tools and checklists, and standardised, periodic reviews of management arrangements. Also pointing up the important role which 'bureaucratic regulators' may play in determining the 'impact' of judicial rulings through follow-up, the Commission looked to include human rights activities as 'scoring elements' in its major inspectorial tool of comprehensive performance assessment.

According to a 2005 report from the Institute of Public Policy Research, the HRA had 'not yet been of demonstrable value in improving standards in public services'. The report referred specifically to:

> the fields of social services, health, social care and housing where a low understanding of the relevance of the Act to service provision combines with a consequent risk that vulnerable and marginalised people will experience breaches of their human rights . . . Most public authorities are struggling to implement a proactive human rights strategy and to achieve changes in practice and consequently the Act is not widely viewed as a tool to achieve better public services.[105]

The report also pointed up the inefficiencies involved in judicial 'firefighting'; even apparently 'successful' test cases had their downside. 'The public authorities concerned could have (and indeed should have) found ways of introducing human rights thinking at the stage when the policies were formulated. There could also have been more effective participation by those affected by the policies before they were implemented, which would probably have avoided the deleterious consequences that followed.'[106] Taking rights seriously was again said to require a strong dose of 'audit technique' involving both quantitative and qualitative indicators.[107]

[104] Audit Commission, *Human Rights : Improving public service delivery* (2003), pp. 3, 7, 15.

[105] F. Butler, *Improving Public Services: Using the human rights approach* (IPPR, 2005), pp. 4, 7. See also, F. Butler, *Human Rights: Who needs them? Using human rights in the voluntary sector* (IPPR, 2004).

[106] The case under discussion is *R v East Sussex CC, ex p. A* [2003] EWHC 167.

[107] As also human rights specifications in contracts with private providers of public services: see above, p. 365.

Concerns about mistaken compliance are common currency with the HRA. A central component of the legal framework is in issue here, the need to strike a fair balance with the wider public interest or rights of other individuals. If judges, according to other judges, sometimes get this wrong, why should one expect front-line staff, especially those working in difficult areas of risk assessment, and possibly subject to threats of judicial review, never to go overboard in respect for a person's rights?

As noted in Chapter 3, the perception of 'public protection versus human rights considerations'[108] has fuelled the debate over a British Bill of Rights (and Responsibilities). Predictably, the resulting government reviews present a more nuanced picture. The Home Office found some evidence of staff in the criminal justice system either being overcautious in applying the jurisprudence when making decisions or using human rights principles as a justification for an overcautious approach; this hardly amounted however to 'a culture of risk aversion'.[109] The Department for Constitutional Affairs' review was more concerned to stress the positive aspects developing over time:

> The evidence provided by Departments shows how the Act has led to a shift away from inflexible or blanket policies towards those which are capable of adjustment to recognise the circumstances and characteristics of individuals . . . As the principles have become more embedded – and in some cases in response to the fear of litigation – policies and practices have been adjusted to ensure compliance with Convention rights and they are a more explicitly recognised part of the decision-making process. In some cases, the attaching of this greater weight to human rights considerations has been a positive move, as shown by . . . decision making in prisons in England and Wales. At this end of the spectrum, it is fair to conclude that this greater weight was necessary and correct. However, at the other end of the spectrum lie examples where this is not the case, and where misinterpretation of the effect of the Convention rights has led to an undue focus upon rights and entitlement of individuals.[110]

A flurry of communications ensued – websites, a Home Office 'hot-line' for frontline staff, and yet more written guidance.[111] 'Myth-busting advice' on how rights should be balanced now took priority.[112]

We are back too with the case for an independent regulatory agency, with limited institutional support[113] for human rights being seen as contributing to

[108] As stated by e.g. the 'Bridges report': HM Inspectorate of Probation, *Serious Further Offence review – Anthony Rice* (2006).

[109] See JCHR, *The Human Rights Act: The DCA and Home Office Reviews*, HC 1716 (2005/6).

[110] DCA, *Review of the Implementation of the Human Rights Act* (2006), pp. 4, 25.

[111] DCA, *Guide to the Human Rights Act*, 3rd edn (2006) and *Human Rights, Human Lives: A handbook for public authorities* (2006).

[112] MoJ, *Guidance on the Human Rights Act for Criminal Justice System Practitioners* (2007).

[113] Otherwise than with the Northern Ireland Human Rights Commission; see C. Harvey, 'Human rights and equality in Northern Ireland' (2006) 57 NILQ 215. And see A. O'Neill, '"Stands Scotland where it did?" Devolution, human rights and the Scottish constitution seven years on' (2006) 57 *NILQ* 102.

a lack of impact in many sectors.[114] The judiciary, in other words, needs help. Pressing the case, the Joint Committee noted that 'litigation is an essential last resort in protecting the rights of the individual or groups, but is not the most effective means of developing a culture of human rights.' 'A human rights commission probing, questioning and encouraging public bodies could have a real impact . . . and complement the courts by preventing breaches of rights occurring through the spread of best practice and greater awareness.'[115]

In the event, one of the very first actions of the new Equality and Human Rights Commission has been the requisite 'benchmarking' exercise of an inquiry into 'how human rights works' in England and Wales.[116] With barriers on the use of human-rights principles in public-service provision as chief focus, the inquiry should further highlight the importance for 'impact' of interlocking roles of judicial review, regulation and inspection, and complaints handling. What Francesca Klug, the lead commissioner on the inquiry, calls the 'long road to human rights compliance'[117] is in truth never-ending.

6. Litigation saga

The scope for reaction and counter-reaction between government and judiciary is particularly well illustrated by the so-called 's. 55 litigation', a main preoccupation for the Administrative Court in the period 2003–5. Characterised by multitudinous individual claims and successive test-case challenges involving a key plank of government policy, this in fact is the most extensive 'litigation saga' to date with AJR machinery. Involving a full set of repeat players (Home Office, campaign groups, specialist lawyers), and eventually culminating in a major House of Lords precedent (*Limbuela*),[118] the affair casts further light on judicial review's function in redress of grievance and on the role and interplay with the common law of Convention rights.[119] Far from the happy idea of 'partnership', there is sharp conflict between the executive and the judiciary in the context of draconian legislation directed at a vulnerable group; exceptional caseload pressures also see tensions rising inside the judicial branch.

114 F. Klug and K. Starmer, 'Standing back from the Human Rights Act: How effective is it five years on?' [2005] *PL* 716.

115 As well as working to raise public awareness: JCHR, *The Case for a Human Rights Commission*, HC 489 (2002/3), p. 6. For the subsequent policy development, see A. Lester and K. Beattie, 'The new Commission for Equality and Human Rights' [2006] *PL* 197.

116 Using its general power of investigation in s. 16 of the Equality Act 2006. The report is expected in mid-2009.

117 F. Klug, 'The long road to human rights compliance' (2006) 57 *NILQ*186. And see D. Galligan and D. Sandler, 'Implementing human rights' in Halliday and Schmidt (eds.), *Human Rights Brought Home: Socio-legal perspectives on human rights in a national context* (Hart Publishing, 2004).

118 *R (Limbuela) v Home Secretary* [2004] 3 WLR 561 (CA); [2005] 3 WLR 1014 (HL).

119 See also E. Palmer, *Judicial Review, Socio-Economic Rights and the Human Rights Act* (Hart Publishing, 2007), p. 254–74.

(a) Scene-setting

Section 95 of the Immigration and Asylum Act 1999 empowered the minister to provide support to asylum-seekers who were destitute, as defined in terms of (no appropriate) accommodation and essential living needs. This would be the day-to-day responsibility of the National Asylum Support Service, a department established by the Home Office.[120] However, s. 55 of the Nationality, Immigration and Asylum Act 2002 provided for refusal of access to NAAS to those making 'late' asylum claims. Support was thus denied to large numbers of asylum seekers who applied for refugee status not at a port of entry but 'in-country'. Section 55 built in turn on another key aspect of government policy – restriction on would-be refugees taking paid employment.[121]

Set in the immediate context of a major bulge of asylum applications, s. 55 served several related policy objectives. By demanding prompt asylum claims, ministers could hit at those who were not genuine asylum seekers, as also those who had demonstrated ability to live without state support. The provision doubled as a way of reducing the (heavy) cost to the Treasury of asylum support and of limiting the attractiveness of the UK for asylum seekers. 'Encouraging' asylum seekers to make application at the ports was helpful to the authorities in determining matters like personal identity or country of origin, as also in making things more difficult for the (criminal) 'facilitators' or agents often accompanying these people.

On the EU front, ministers had successfully prepared the way in negotiations on a directive, securing a special exception to permit this type of statutory restriction.[122] That left ECHR Art. 3 (inhuman or degrading treatment) to contend with. Since the policy amounted to destitution by design, a declaration of incompatibility was in prospect if the legislation said nothing more. Showing the importance of statements of compatibility under s. 19 of the HRA (see p. 148 above), ministers were effectively pressured to demonstrate compliance on the face of the Bill.[123]

The upshot is an unusual statutory equation. First, the minister is forbidden from exercising a statutory function in certain circumstances. The Secretary of State 'may not provide or arrange for the provision of support' to an asylum seeker if he 'is not satisfied that the claim was made as soon as reasonably practicable after the person's arrival in the United Kingdom' (s. 55(1)). Secondly, constituting an exception to the exception to the power to provide for destitute people, 'this section shall not prevent . . . the exercise of a power by the Secretary of State to the extent necessary for the purpose of avoiding a breach of a person's Convention rights' (s. 55(5)(a)).[124] Thirdly, access to the

[120] See JCHR, *The Treatment of Asylum Seekers*, HC 60-1 (2006/7).

[121] See latterly on this aspect, *Tekle v Home Secretary* [2008] EWHC 3064.

[122] Council Directive 2003/9/EC of 27 January 2003, Art. 16(2). This was part of CEAS, the burgeoning Common European Asylum System.

[123] JCHR, *Twenty-third Report*, HC 1255 (2001/2).

[124] Exceptions were also made for children and for those with 'special needs'.

standard appeals machinery of an asylum support adjudicator is blocked (s. 55(10)).

Section 55(5)(a) locks up with the rule of administrative illegality in s. 6 of the HRA – acting in a way that is incompatible with a Convention right. The minister was thus permitted *and* obliged to arrange for the provision of support to avoid this happening. Lord Bingham in *Limbuela* would later elaborate on the somewhat fiendish complications (would the hard-pressed junior officer on the front line understand?):

> The Secretary of State . . . may only exercise his power to provide or arrange support where it is necessary to do so to avoid a breach and to the extent necessary for that purpose. He may not exercise his power where it is not necessary to do so to avoid a breach or to an extent greater than necessary for that purpose. Where (and to the extent) that exercise of the power is necessary, the Secretary of State is subject to a duty, and has no choice, since it is unlawful for him under s. 6 of the 1998 Act to act incompatibly with a Convention right. Where (and to the extent) that exercise of the power is not necessary, the Secretary of State is subject to a statutory prohibition, and again has no choice. Thus the Secretary of State (in practice, of course, officials acting on his behalf) must make a judgement on the situation of the individual applicant matched against what the Convention requires or proscribes, but he has, in the strict sense, no discretion.[125]

Section 55 was not the first such attempt at parsimony. By the time the Court of Appeal first considered the provision in *R (Q)*,[126] there was a whole history of judicial 'guerrilla warfare', the courts repeatedly attacking harsh measures and central government responding with various heavy armaments ranging from primary legislation to propaganda (use of the media). An alternative characterisation is that of a protracted 'litigation game' played for high stakes:

- *Ping* – secondary legislation is introduced in 1996 purporting to restrict entitlement to income support to those asylum seekers who claim asylum on arrival.[127]
- *Pong* – invoking the principle of legality, the regulations are said in the *JCWI* case (see p. 114 above) to be *ultra vires* as contemplating for some 'a life so destitute that . . . no civilised nation can tolerate it'.
- *Ping* – ministers immediately move a new clause to what becomes the Asylum and Immigration Act 1996, so reinstating the 1996 Regulations from the date of the statute; the Act also removes the right to housing benefit and assistance in respect of homelessness.
- *Pong* – asylum seekers thus deprived of the right to benefits are said, in the case of *M*,[128] still to be entitled to care and attention from local authorities, including accommodation, under the National Assistance Act 1948.

125 Lord Bingham in *R (Limbuela) v Home Secretary* [2005] 3 WLR 1014 (HL) [5].

126 *R (Q) v Home Secretary* [2003] 3 WLR 365.

127 Social Security (Persons from Abroad) Miscellaneous Amendments Regulations 1996, SI No. 30.

128 *R v Westminster City Council, ex p. M* (1997) 1 CCLR 85.

- *Ping* – (a) in establishing the central government scheme administered by the National Asylum Support Service (NASS), the Immigration and Asylum Act 1999 counters *M*,[129] excluding the operation of the 1948 Act in cases solely of destitution; (b) the Nationality, Immigration and Asylum Act 2002 amends the scheme, targeting late claims.
- *Pong* – administration of the s. 55 prohibition is successfully challenged in the High Court in *R (Q)*, both for breach of procedural fairness and for contravention of Convention Rights. Home Secretary David Blunkett is reported as being 'fed up' with the wishes of Parliament being overturned by judges: 'Parliament did debate this, we were aware of the circumstances, we did mean what we said and, on behalf of the British people, we are going to implement it.'[130]

(b) Twists and turns

Brought on behalf of six asylum seekers from Africa and the Middle East, some of whom were deeply traumatised, the proceedings in *R (Q)* had been launched within days of s. 55 being implemented; several hundred more claims were soon in the pipeline. Settling on the test for a late claim of whether the asylum seeker could reasonably have been expected to apply earlier, the Court of Appeal took a hard look at the practical workings. A product of poor management and organisation, the lack of procedural fairness was evident; for example, the purpose of the relevant interview was not properly explained and no clear opportunity was provided to rebut the suggestion that the applicant was lying. 'Fairness called for interviewing skills and a more flexible approach than simply completing a standard form questionnaire.' Further, *R (Q)* is the rare example of the national court deciding, for the purpose of the ECHR Art. 6 test of 'full jurisdiction' (see p. 661 above), that judicial review is insufficient: the inadequacies of the procedure 'rendered it impossible for the officials . . . to make an informed determination of matters central to the asylum seekers' civil rights'; 'the court conducting the judicial review was equally unable to do so'.

With Art. 3, the issue of resources cast a shadow; how could the Convention right be used to provide individual protection in such cases without being opened up so as to undermine the rationing of welfare services more generally?[131] In holding that Art. 3 might be engaged, the judges recognised the fact of more than passivity on the part of the state; denying individuals both the opportunity to work and any public assistance effectively differentiated these cases. As to the point at which a lack of support became inhuman or degrading, however, it was 'quite impossible by a simple definition to embrace all human conditions that will engage Article 3'.

[129] Though see *Kola v Secretary of State for Work and Pensions* [2007] UKHL 54.

[130] *The Times* 20 February 2003.

[131] See further, C. O'Cinneide, 'A modest proposal: Restitution, state responsibility and the European Convention on Human Rights' [2008] *EHRLR* 583.

The judges naturally referred to the test in Strasbourg jurisprudence of 'ill-treatment that attains a minimum level of severity and involves actual bodily injury or intense physical or mental suffering'. Degrading treatment occurred where it 'humiliates or debases an individual showing lack of respect for, or diminishing, his or her human dignity or arouses feelings of fear, anguish or inferiority capable of breaking an individual's moral and physical resistance'.[132] But the Court of Appeal went on to impose a high threshold on claims. Whereas the High Court judge had clearly prioritised protection of the individual, saying that 'a real risk' was sufficient, Lord Phillips spoke of a lesser form of public obligation:

> It is not unlawful for the Secretary of State to decline to provide support unless and until it is clear that charitable support has not been provided and the individual is incapable of fending for himself . . . He must, however, be prepared to entertain further applications from those to whom he has refused support who have not been able to find any charitable support or other lawful means of fending for themselves.

What then was the 'impact'? Showing the 'structuring' role of judicial review, the ruling impelled a clean-up of procedures. Sundry improvements were made to the interviewing process, with a view, the minister explained, to ensuring that individual cases received full and fair consideration.[133] Precisely illustrating the contingent meaning of law in the bureaucracy, the court's interpretation of the statutory formula was soon being reinterpreted within the administrative system. Guidance to officials thus placed the burden of demonstrating promptness firmly on the 'in-country' applicant,[134] standard (unpublished) practice being to allow twenty-four hours.[135] Meanwhile, the court's reasoning conjured up the prospect of a further wave of litigation, grounded in multiple or serial applications for asylum support invoking Art. 3. With the charities being all too easily overwhelmed, the Court of Appeal was soon handed a second bite at the cherry.

The case of *R (T)*[136] originally involved several asylum seekers, including S, who had been forced to beg for some considerable time, suffering psychological problems and malnutrition. The judge recognised the degrading treatment: the refusal of public support had 'debased' S and 'diminished his human dignity'. T had been living rough at Heathrow airport, becoming 'increasingly demoralised and humiliated' and finding it 'difficult to rest or sleep'. The Court of Appeal ruled against him however. 'It is impossible to find that T's condition . . . had reached or was verging on the inhuman or the degrading. He had

[132] *Pretty v United Kingdom* (2002) 35 EHRR 1 [52].

[133] HC Deb., col. 522w (1 May 2003).

[134] Home Office Immigration and Nationality Department, *Section 55 (Late Claims) 2002 Act Guidance* (2004 version).

[135] HC Deb., col. 1594 (17 Dec. 2003).

[136] *R (T) v Home Secretary* [2003] EWCA 1285.

shelter, sanitary facilities and some money for food. He was not entirely well physically, but not so unwell as to need immediate treatment.'

R (T) dramatically illustrates the strong factual element in the s. 55 litigation, hence the size of the task facing Administrative Court judges in adjudicating on complicated and fast-changing personal circumstances. So much, it may be said, for the austere view of judicial review proceedings promulgated by Lord Diplock in *O'Reilly v Mackman* (see p. 680 above). Would the Court of Appeal assist?

> What we were being asked to do by both sides in this case was precisely that which was said in *Q* to be impossible, namely to provide a simple way of deciding when Article 3 will be engaged . . . The reality is that each case has to be judged in relation to all the circumstances which are relevant to it . . . But we do consider that a comparison of the facts of S and T may be of assistance to those who have to decide where the line is to be drawn if the obligations imposed by the Convention are to be met . . . It is relevant to have in mind that the boundary – which is not a fixed or a bright line – lies somewhere between the two.

R (T) in fact illustrates how judges may undercut their own contribution, the techniques of 'directing', 'limiting', 'structuring' and 'vindicating' being largely absent. 'No bright line' might sound well in the rarefied atmosphere of the Court of Appeal, but it was apt to ring hollow down on the front line of decision-making. This case too was a recipe for litigation.

Confirmation was not long in coming from Maurice Kay J, the lead judge in the Administrative Court.[137] 'Asylum support cases account for approximately 800 cases in our current workload. Clearly they are having a significant impact on the ability of the Court to process cases in this and other areas. It is [our] experience that, factually, the great majority of cases fall somewhere between *S* and *T*.' The additional twist was the chief place in the litigation of interim relief. In such circumstances of utter destitution, it would typically be a matter of seeking an injunction aimed either at preventing eviction from emergency accommodation or at forcing the hand of NASS to provide some. Far from the idealised form of adversarial court process, studied or even leisurely, happenings at the 'preliminary' stage were never more vital:

> In such circumstances the judges usually grant interim relief on the papers. If, instead, they adjourn the applications into court, the Secretary of State is usually not represented. In some cases a judge refuses to grant the application for interim relief or for permission because he considers it to be premature. In many such circumstances he suspects that a further application before very long would succeed.

Maurice Kay J rightly emphasised the financial wastefulness of all these proceedings; why not use the asylum support adjudicators? Far from judicial

137 *R (Q) v Home Secretary* [2003] EWHC 2507.

review as the 'apex' of a pyramid, 'the Administrative Court is being put in the position of having to act as a first-call dispute resolution forum in an area where there are established alternatives which are better equipped for the task'.[138] In the event, this became the forcing ground for the elaboration of urgency procedures in judicial review (see p. 687 above).

In an unusual move following consultation with colleagues, the lead judge offered the minister some further thoughts. What was said about the impact – or otherwise – of judicial review exposes the fallacy of simple assumptions about court 'control' of the administration:

> There has been some improvement in the Secretary of State's procedures and decision-making since *Q*, but there are still a significant number of cases in which the claimant has at least an arguable case to the effect that the guidance in *Q* has not been followed . . . The answer is simple. It resides in the proper instruction of officials so that they do not resort to generic stereotyping regardless of the accepted evidence to the contrary. The point of test cases is to provide clarification and guidance for those who operate the system at the grassroots. It is a waste of time and ultimately very expensive if the clarification and guidance are ignored. It is the responsibility of the Secretary of State to ensure that it is not.
>
> The main reason why the vast majority of applications are being made and are succeeding is that quite simply there is not in place an adequate and efficient decision-making procedure for the processing of representations and particularly further representations which are made by reference to Article 3. I do not doubt that the Secretary of State wants there to be such a procedure. However, what is in place falls miles short of achieving the targets that were set by the Secretary of State himself.

The following 'guidance' issued by the court recalls the role of remedies as a determinant of 'impact'. Without the American tool of structural injunctions (see p. 674 above), how could it be enforced?

> In an area in which such a large number of claimants are being granted interim relief because they have at least an arguable case, it is incumbent on the Secretary of State to establish an adequate and efficient decision-making procedure which applies the law as set out by the Court of Appeal, which does so within a timescale appropriate to self-evidently urgent issues and which does not give rise to the need for so many applications to this Court.

A report from the Mayor of London[139] provided further insights (and ammunition for the public-interest advocates). Despite a recent policy concession extending the normal claim period from twenty-four to seventy-two hours,[140]

[138] Matters might alternatively be characterised in terms of 'bureaucratic judicial review': P. Cane, 'Understanding judicial review and its impact' in Hertogh and Halliday (eds.), *Judicial Review and Bureaucratic Impact.*

[139] Mayor of London, *Destitution by Design* (2004): see also, Refugee Council and Oxfam, *Hungry and Homeless* (2004).

[140] HC Deb., col. 1594 (17 Dec. 2003).

it was reckoned that some 14,000 people annually might be caught by s. 55, and that 'a large majority of them will find no way out of destitution'. Much charitable relief was being offered, but so many asylum seekers were now living on the streets, especially in London, that there were local concerns about community safety and race relations.

(c) Culmination

The case of *Limbuela* provided the Court of Appeal with a third opportunity. Once again, the case involved several challenges with hundreds more waiting in the wings. There was an additional legal complication. Following the Delphic judgment in *R (T)*, Administrative Court judges had divided, with some giving injunctive relief on grounds of 'imminent breach' of Art. 3, others demanding clear evidence of physical or mental suffering ('wait and see'). The medical evidence in *Limbuela* included muscular pains, heartburn, gastritis, haemorrhoids and deafness.

The Court of Appeal also divided. Laws LJ preferred his form of 'spectrum analysis'[141] whereby the lawfulness of decisions exposing individuals 'to a marked degree of suffering, not caused by violence' depended on the degree of severity. Voicing respect 'for the political domain of State policy evolved in the general interest', he could see no 'exceptional features' in these cases requiring the minister to act. Yet as the majority recognised, it was precisely the generality of the problem that marked the cases out:

> *Jacob LJ:* Although one may not be able to say that there is more than a very real risk that denial of food and shelter will take [a] person across the threshold, one can say that collectively the current policy will have that effect [for] a substantial number of people. It must follow that the current policy . . . is unlawful as violating Article 3. And it follows that the treatment of the particular individuals the subject of these appeals in pursuit of that policy is also unlawful.

This did produce some impact through amendments to the administrative guidance. The caseworker now had to be 'positively satisfied' of some alternative form of support; specific mention was made of such items as 'adequate food', 'washing facilities' and 'night shelter'.[142]

Given the history of the matter, the House of Lords was understandably concerned, in Lord Hope's words, to provide as 'much guidance as we can to the Secretary of State as to the legal framework'. The heresy propounded by Laws LJ was firmly refuted. In Lord Hope's words: 'where the inhuman or degrading treatment or punishment results from acts or omissions for which the state is

[141] See further, *R (Gezer) v Home Secretary* [2003] 3 WLR 365.

[142] Home Office Immigration and Nationality Department, *Section 55 (Late Claims) 2002 Act Guidance* (2004 version), Annex H.

directly responsible there is no escape from the negative obligation on states to refrain from such conduct, which is absolute'.[143] Reasserting the approach taken by the Court of Appeal in *R (Q)*, the next step, explained by Lady Hale, was to differentiate these cases in terms of 'treatment' (and thus resources). 'The State has taken the Poor Law policy of "less eligibility" to an extreme which the Poor Law itself did not contemplate, in denying not only all forms of state relief but all forms of self sufficiency, save family and philanthropic aid, to a particular class of people lawfully here.' Furthermore, as the s. 55(5) language of 'avoiding' a breach itself showed, the policy of 'wait and see' was simply not good enough:

> *Lord Bingham:* When does the Secretary of State's duty under section 55(5)(a) arise? The answer must in my opinion be: when it appears on a fair and objective assessment of all relevant facts and circumstances that an individual applicant faces an imminent prospect of serious suffering caused or materially aggravated by denial of shelter, food or the most basic necessities of life. Many factors may affect that judgment, including age, gender, mental and physical health and condition, any facilities or sources of support available to the applicant, the weather and time of year and the period for which the applicant has already suffered or is likely to continue to suffer privation . . . But if there were persuasive evidence that a late applicant was obliged to sleep in the street, save perhaps for a short and foreseeably finite period, or was seriously hungry, or unable to satisfy the most basic requirements of hygiene, the threshold would, in the ordinary way, be crossed.

Given the evident political sensitivities, perhaps it is not surprising to find the Law Lords at pains to downplay and so justify their role in promulgating this much guidance. As against some naked form of 'common law constitutional rights', the HRA provided useful cover (see Chapter 3). In Lord Hope's words, 'the function which your Lordships are being asked to perform is confined to that which has been given to the judges by Parliament' or as Lady Hale put it, the court was 'respecting, rather than challenging, the will of Parliament'.

Who won what? On the one hand, a major Home Office policy was undoubtedly blunted by the judges' use of Art. 3 to provide 'a last-resort safety net'.[144] Further amendment of the internal guidance would include Lord Bingham's 'imminent prospect' threshold for relief. 'It is vital that caseworkers assess each case individually, including via interview where necessary, and decide in accordance with this test whether it is necessary to grant support to avoid a breach of a person's Convention rights.'[145] In so requiring some extra resource allocation, the decision also brought much-needed relief to the Administrative Court. On the other hand, s. 55 remained on the statute book (and would continue to be used to refuse subsistence-only claims from applicants with

[143] See further, *R (Munjaz) v Mersey Care NHS Trust* [2005] UKHL 58.

[144] O'Cinneide, 'A modest proposal: Restitution, state responsibility and the European Convention on Human Rights', p. 601.

[145] Home Office Immigration and Nationality Department, *Section 55 (Late Claims) 2002 Act Guidance* (2007 version) [7.6].

accommodation).[146] Nor should we be particularly proud of judicial protection at a level just beneath 'destitution'.[147] The Home Office was, of course, free to explore other policy options. Responding to *Limbuela*, the minister announced new processes for 'handling late and opportunistic claims' for refugee status. Those 'who seek to play the system will receive a very quick asylum decision and so will, in reality, have very little access to benefit'.[148]

7. Conclusion

Evaluated as machinery for redress of grievance (see Chapter 10), the courts obviously score heavily in terms of independence, fairness (adjudication), public recognition and visibility. Judicial review also demonstrates important strengths as regards the criterion of effective redress, most obviously the mandatory orders. The very fact of a multi-streamed jurisdiction offers opportunities for judicial protection barely imagineable in the highly formalist and deferential era of the 'drainpipe' model. Once again, however, the expanded capacities of this elite form of administrative law technique ought not to obscure some inconvenient truths. Courts in general, and the judicial review process in particular, are difficult to access. Problems of cost, technical jargon and remoteness, and (dramatically illustrated by 'the London effect') with obtaining specialist legal advice, lock up together here with the various rationing devices elaborated by the courts and operated in typically discretionary style at each stage of the process (see Chapters 15–16). Meanwhile, the missing dimension of follow-up procedures recalls the basic limitations of institutional competence associated with the adjudicative form (see Chapter 14).

Today, we would not wish to describe judicial review litigation in asylum and immigration as sporadic and peripheral. The very fact of draconian countermeasures points up the bureaucratic impact of a large flow of individual challenges (that further constitute a chief reservoir for leading cases). However, at least from the quantitative angle, de Smith's aphorism otherwise retains much of its original force. Indeed, in terms of final hearings, and hence of court-imposed remedies, it is underscored today. Another striking feature is the low-level role in dispute resolution demanded of the courts in judicial review 'hot-spots' such as homelessness and temporary accommodation. Why, it may be asked, do the standard administrative law/judicial review textbooks not focus on this aspect?

All this bears on the contemporary judicial role of spreading the gospel of good governance and human rights (see Chapter 3), or, more modestly,

[146] JCHR, *The Treatment of Asylum Seekers* [91–2].

[147] S. Palmer, 'A wrong turning: Article 3 and proportionality' (2006) 65 *CLJ* 438 discusses the broader connotations of *Limbuela*.

[148] HC Deb., col. 2302W (24 November 2005). There would also be similar struggles about support and accommodation elsewhere in the system: J. Sweeney, 'The human rights of failed asylum seekers in the United Kingdom' [2008] *PL* 277.

of 'fire-watching'. In underwriting values of individualised justice, and of accountability or justification and transparency, judicial review has much to offer public administration. But with such inputs commonly experienced, if at all, at some remove – a feature only underscored by governance trends of agencification and fragmentation – it should not be surprising to learn of patchy effects on the quality or texture of administrative decision-making. While today the multi-streamed jurisdiction buttresses the judicial capacity to structure and confine official decision-making, it is not so easy to secure broad compliance! Perhaps this needs emphasising because of a strong 'top-down' focus in legal writings on the HRA, one that naturally tends to prioritise the role of elite players in enforcement. A 'bottom-up' account of access to justice among the socially excluded gives a very different picture.

Far from the classical model of legal 'control', the short history of Convention rights conveniently illustrates the need for a more holistic view of administrative law tools and techniques. While the courts' role of 'vindicating' is pivotal, their contribution to good governance is largely dependent on the exertions of others (including now the Commission for Equality and Human Rights) in fostering 'radiating effects'. Students of law and administration should take the message to heart.

17

'Golden handshakes': Liability and compensation

Contents

1. Liability or compensation?

In the last three chapters we have looked in some detail at judicial review, today the principal machinery through which courts exercise their function of controlling the executive and for many – especially red light theorists – the centrepiece of administrative law. Judicial review is not the only mechanism for the challenge of executive and administrative action; as we have seen, human rights claims may be raised in every form of judicial process, including criminal proceedings. Judicial review procedure is also subject to the substantial limitation that compensation, in practice sometimes the only suitable remedy, is not usually available. The reformed modern judicial review procedure (see Chapter 15) allows the Administrative Court to award damages on an application for judicial review but *only* when 'the court is satisfied that, if the claim had been made in an action begun by the applicant at the time of making his application, he would have been awarded damages' (s. 31(4)(b) of the Supreme Court 1981). This has the effect of linking damages to the existing law of tort. It has to be said that the writ procedures of the High Court, with detailed pleadings and oral evidence, are in practice better suited for fact-finding in damages actions; these are therefore routinely transferred out of the Administrative Court after the court has determined the public law issues.[1] Cases where a claim for damages is joined to a judicial review application are, however, rare[2] and cases where compensation is actually ordered even rarer.

Judicial review has not always occupied its present paramount position in administrative law. Since time immemorial, wrongful and illegal action by public officials could be challenged by means of an action in tort, as in the famous 'General Warrant cases'.[3] Here warrants issued by the Home Secretary to search premises, seize property and arrest those engaged in the publication of *The North Briton*, a paper published by John Wilkes, a well-known radical deemed dangerous by the authorities, were successfully challenged on the ground that they did not, as they should have done, specifically name the premises to be searched, the owners, or the property to be seized. Wilkes and his printers and publishers sued successfully for trespass to goods, trespass to land and false imprisonment, and the judgments in which the officials were held liable still stand as landmarks in the vindication of civil liberties.[4] Other landmark tort actions should be mentioned. In *Cooper v Wandsworth Board of Works*,[5] C had built houses for which a licence from the Board of Works was necessary but had omitted to apply for the licence. As it was on the face of its statutory power entitled to do, the Board of Works demolished the building. However, in an action for trespass to land, the court found the Board liable in damages, ruling that a hearing ought to have been granted before the extreme course of demolition was taken. In the earlier case of *Ashby v White*,[6] decided at a time when suffrage was very limited, returning officers in a parliamentary election deliberately refused to allow two of the registered electors to vote. The judges were consulted by Parliament as to whether the common law could

[1] Lord Woolf, J. Jowell, A Le Sueur, *de Smith's Judicial Review*, 7th edn (2008) [19-006–009].

[2] But see *R v Deputy Governor of Parkhurst, ex p. Hague* [1991] 3 WLR 340.

[3] *Entick v Carrington* (1765) 2 Wils. KB 275; *Leach v Money* (1765) 19 St. Tr. 1001; *Wilkes v Wood* (1763) 2 Wils. KB 203. Dicey also lists *Mostyn v Fabrigas* (1774) 1 *Cowp*. 161; *Musgrave v Pulido* (1879) 5 App Cas 102; *Governor Wall's Case* (1802) 28 St Tr 51; and the notorious case of *Philips v Eyre* (1867) LR 4 QB 225. These cases are, however, somewhat exceptional in character.

[4] See J. Jowell, 'The rule of law today' in Jowell and Oliver (eds.), *The Changing Constitution*, 6th edn (Oxford University Press, 2007).

[5] *Cooper v Wandsworth Board of Works* (1863) 14 CBNS 180.

[6] *Ashby v White* (1703) 2 *Ld. Raym*. 938. A majority of the judges consulted were of the view that there was no remedy at common law but the dissenting opinion of Holt CJ was later reinstated.

provide a remedy for this 'excessive and insolent use of power'. As Holt CJ put it in his dissenting opinion, which came to be regarded as the law, 'where there is a right there must be a remedy'. The importance of the case is that it concerned intangible rights - though defined in the case as rights of property - which are not normally strongly protected by the common law. It also gave birth to the idea that some rights are constitutional in character or of such importance as to warrant protection by an action in damages. We shall later see *Ashby v White* unsuccessfully invoked in recent cases involving human rights, an outcome that reflects the current unwillingness of the superior courts to allow the ambit of tortious liability to be extended.

From civil actions like these, Dicey extracted the principle of personal responsibility of all public officials to the 'ordinary' courts of the land, on which his doctrine of equality before the law rests. In Dicey's own words:

> In England the idea of legal equality, or the universal subjection of all classes to one law administered by the ordinary courts, has been pushed to its utmost limit. With us every official, from the Prime Minister down to a constable, is under the same responsibility for every act done without legal justification as any other citizen.[7]

This bold assertion actually concealed a position of serious inequality. By virtue of the prerogative powers the Crown had acquired substantial immunity from liability in tort. This exception was to assume greater importance as tort law moved from a system of 'corrective justice' in which individuals sued individuals to a system where the objective was to fix vicarious liability on corporate entities able either to meet or insure against the substantial awards of damages made in personal injury actions. After a long and arduous struggle,[8] the position was righted by the Crown Proceedings Act 1947, which renders the Crown vicariously liable for the wrongful acts of its servants to the same extent as a 'person of full age and capacity'. Despite the ambiguity of this formula, the Act has been largely successful in bringing to an end Crown immunity in tort, subject to a few exclusions covering liability for the armed forces and judicial acts, which have come increasingly under attack in recent years.[9]

Symbolically, the Crown Proceedings Act represented the conclusion of a slow process of bringing the state in all its manifestations – central, local and regional government, agencies and other public bodies – under the

[7] A.V. Dicey, *Introduction to the Study of the Law of the Constitution* (MacMillan, 1959, 10th edn by E. C. S. Wade), p. 187.

[8] See J. Jacob, *The Republican Crown: Lawyers and the making of the state in twentieth century Britain* (Dartmouth, 1996). In other common law jurisdictions, notably Australia, the end to Crown immunity came much earlier; see M. Aronson and H. Whitmore, *Public Torts and Contracts* (Lawbook Co., 1978) and, e.g., the Queensland Claims against the Government Act 1866.

[9] The Crown Proceedings (Armed Forces) Act 1987 repeals s. 10 of the 1947 Act other than for cases which occurred prior to 1987 (see *Matthews v Ministry of Defence* (2003) UKHL 4) but allows it to be revived by ministerial certificate where necessary or expedient because of imminent national danger, etc.

jurisdiction of the 'ordinary courts of the land'.[10] This principle remains the constitutional underpinning for systems of government liability throughout the common law world. It is stoutly defended by Peter Hogg, a leading expert on Crown proceedings, who argues both that 'Dicey captured a fundamental attitude towards government' and that 'the application of the ordinary law by the ordinary courts to the activities of government conforms to a widely-held political ideal' and preserves us from many practical problems.' Hogg believes also that 'Dicey's idea of equality provides the basis for a rational, workable and acceptable theory of governmental liability' and finds least satisfactory 'those parts of the law where the courts have refused to apply the ordinary law to the Crown'.[11] In practice, however, the equality principle was always less clear cut than Dicey suggested. As Dicey's many critics are never tired of reiterating, public officials and public authorities are no longer – if they ever were – in a position of equality with ordinary citizens.[12] They come equipped with a battery of statutory powers to authorise their many incursions, which makes it hard to equate them with private actors who do not possess such powers. A law of torts developed largely to deal with the relationships of private individuals with one another must nowadays be applied to the conduct of public authorities exercising statutory powers and duties for which there is often no obvious private parallel.

The alignment of private and public liability typical of common law systems has advantages: it creates a culture of equality and feeling that public authorities are not above the law. Submitting public authorities to tort law brings its own problems, however. Tort law is a branch of the common law badly in need of reform. It has never been codified nor has the Law Commission ever conducted a consistent overall review of the subject. Left to the judges, progression has been slow and largely achieved through the incremental evolution of negligence into a general principle of liability. But tort law has never fully evolved from the collection of medieval writs or 'nominate torts', each with its own specific requirements, from which it is fabricated. Submitting public authorities to tort law means that problems within the private law of torts are replicated and sometimes magnified in the liability principles applicable to public authorities.[13] Modifications thought necessary by the courts often involve inconsistencies and sometimes result in manifest unfairness. Within this private framework of public liability, attempts to find a general, overall solution to the many problems have largely failed. Currently they are under consideration by the Law Commission, which is suggesting a package of major reforms.[14]

[10] The liability of public bodies other than the Crown had been long ago established by *Mersey Docks and Harbour Board Trustees v Gibbs* (1866) LR 1HL 93.

[11] P. Hogg, *Liability of the Crown*, 2nd edn (Carswell, 1989), p. 2.

[12] See W. I. Jennings, *The Law and the Constitution* (Athlone Press, 1959), p. 312 and the discussion at pp. 16–18 above.

[13] Law Commission, *Administrative Redress: Public bodies and the citizen – a consultation paper*, CP No. 18 (2008) hereafter 'Law Com 187'.

[14] Ibid. And See T. Cornford, *Towards a Public Law of Tort* (Ashgate, 2008).

Perhaps fortunately, the courts are not and never have been the only source of compensation for citizens injured by state action. Before the Crown Proceedings Act the Crown routinely turned to *ex gratia* payments to fill the gap left by Crown immunity, making *ex gratia* settlements whenever Crown lawyers advised that legal liability would have accrued but for the immunity of the Crown. Regulated by the Treasury, this power is still in regular use (see p. 778 below). Recommendations for compensation made by the ombudsmen also rely on the power to make *ex gratia* payments. The *Barlow Clowes* and *Occupational Pensions* affairs described in Chapter 12 showed how in recent years ombudsmen have begun to afford a parallel route to courts for those seeking compensation. Section 5 of this chapter contains a further case study of this road to redress.

The principle that private property cannot be expropriated by the state without compensation is also very ancient, as Lord Moulton remarked in a case concerning wartime requisition of property:

> The feeling that it was equitable that burdens borne for the good of the nation should be distributed over the whole nation and should not be allowed to fall on particular individuals has grown to be a national sentiment. The effect of these changes is seen in the long series of statutes . . . [which] indicated unmistakeably that it is the intention of the nation that . . . the burden shall not fall on the individual but shall be borne by the community.[15]

The 'no taking' principle, strongly represented in American law, ultimately found its way into ECHR Art. 1 of Protocol 1, which provides that 'No one shall be deprived of his possessions except in the general interest and subject to the conditions provided for by law [or international law].'[16] Similar principles operated when, during the nineteenth century, roads and railways were constructed and when, at the end of the century, land was needed for slum clearance schemes or new towns. Statutory compensation was provided by Parliament for the 'taking' of property for such purposes.[17] Compensation for compulsory purchase today has general statutory authority from the Land Compensation Act 1973, probably the largest but by no means the only example of a statutory compensation scheme. The criminal injuries compensation scheme is today statutory, though it originated in the power to make *ex gratia* payments (see below, Section 6).

If the principle of compensation is often overlooked in studies of state liability, this is probably because lawyers are unwilling to recognise systems that

[15] *A-G v De Keyser's Royal Hotel Ltd* [1920] AC 508. And see *Burmah Oil Co Ltd v Lord Advocate* [1920] AC 50.

[16] See now *Marcic v Thames Water Utilities Ltd* [2003] 3 WLR 1603, see p. 315 above.

[17] See e.g., Lands Clauses Consolidation Act 1845 and Railways Clauses Consolidation Act 1845. And see *Hammersmith and City Railway v Brand* 1869 LR 4 HL 171. See also M. Taggart, 'Expropriation, public purpose and the constitution' in Forsyth and Hare (eds.), *The Golden Metwand and the Crooked Cord* (Clarendon Press, 1998).

largely exclude the courts. To put this differently, courts see the civil law system as the general or standard machinery for the allocation of compensation. We, however, see the search for a system of state liability capable of anticipating claims for redress and delivering appropriate compensation in all situations as illusory. Just as we argued in Chapter 10 for systems of proportionate dispute resolution capable of handling the many minor grievances thrown up by the modern administrative state, so here we stress the need for equitable principles of compensation.

The need is all the greater because, in parallel to the 'complaints culture' discussed in earlier chapters, recent years have allegedly seen the development of a 'compensation culture' or society in which there is an increased propensity to seek legal redress when things go wrong.[18] Whether willingness to sue is unreasonable or simply the result of a better-educated public with greater access to information remains an open question. In a variant of the arguments about the 'risk society' that we met in Chapter 2, Atiyah argues, however, that recent extensions of the liability system are partly responsible for 'helping to create a "blame culture" in which people have a strong financial incentive to blame others for loss or death or wrongful injury'. This renders Government:

> particularly vulnerable to litigation when the blame culture gets out of hand. If the public thinks – as some people seem to think – that ultimately the government is responsible for everything that happens in society, then the government (and other public bodies) are liable to get sued, whatever they do or fail to do.[19]

Another reason why the trend has a disproportionate impact on public authorities is that they are assumed to be insured (as local authorities actually are) or otherwise capable (like central government) of recouping their losses through the tax fund. Atiyah, who views the damages system as 'fundamentally an insurance system', sees state liability as 'in effect, an argument that the government should provide free insurance to protect the public against losses and injuries'.[20] This is leading to 'novel' liability actions against public authorities that 'have at least the potential to destabilise some public-sector budgets, such as education and social services, which cannot easily pass on these costs, except to taxpayers of one sort or another'.[21] There are, however, some signs in the case law cited later in this chapter that the response of at least the highest court has been to tighten the liability rules.

[18] See for discussion K. Williams, 'State of fear: Britain's "compensation culture" reviewed' (2005) 25 *Legal Studies* 499. For evidence of government concern, see Better Regulation Task Force, *Better Routes to Redress* (May 2004) and *Tackling the 'Compensation Culture': Government response to the Better Regulation Task Force Report: 'Better Routes to Redress'* (November 2004); Constitutional Committee, *Compensation Culture*, HC 754 (2005/6); Government response, Cm. 6784 (2005/6). And see Law Com. 187, p. 19.

[19] P. Atiyah, *The Damages Lottery* (Hart Publishing, 1997), pp. 138–9.

[20] *Ibid.*, p. 87.

[21] Williams, 'State of fear: Britain's "compensation culture" reviewed', p. 507.

A more logical deduction from Atiyah's argument is that government, if it is effectively to act as insurer, should have some say in the risks that it should underwrite. The courts did not, for example, impose liability on government to make reparation to the victims of criminal violence; they have on the contrary been remarkably protective of the police service in this respect (see p. 775 below). Government chose, as we shall see, to take on this responsibility by setting up a compensation scheme. Similarly, it was unlikely that liability would fall on public authorities if a child who was vaccinated against a serious infectious disease suffered damage from the vaccine administered. Government chose, in the interests of protecting the public, to accept responsibility to compensate the unfortunate few with adverse reactions.[22] These examples might suggest a rather different meaning for the term 'compensation culture'. Rather than designating a society in the grip of litigation mania, perhaps the term should refer to a society moving to a position where a right to compensation is becoming a principle of good administration or good governance principle.[23] Hogg has, for example, argued that it 'ought to be a routine part of the planning for a new government programme to undertake an analysis of the private losses that might be caused by the program . . . the predictable, undesired side effects of a program could and should be analyzed with a view to making legislative provision for private compensation'.[24] For this reason, the final sections of this chapter deal with administrative compensation, which we see as, potentially, a valid alternative to an expanded liability system in respect of the state.

2. Tort law, deterrence and accountability

The story of modern tort law is largely a history of the tort of negligence, the main vehicle for accident compensation. With the rise of negligence has come the view of tort law as compensatory. Lord Bingham quite recently asserted, for example, that 'the overall object of tort law is to define cases in which the law may justly hold one party liable to compensate another'.[25] Dicey, however, saw tort law as a vehicle for accountability, a view that reflects its ancient lineage as a remedy for abuse of power. Punitive and deterrent functions are inherent

[22] See the Vaccine Damages Payment Act 1979 and for criticism of the early operation of the scheme, G. Dworkin, 'Compensation and payments for vaccine damage', (1979) *Journal of Social Welfare Law* 330. In 2007, the original sum of £10,000 was uprated by the Statutory Sum Order, SI 2007/193, to £120,000. Since 1997, £3.5 million has been paid to parents under the scheme.

[23] See for discussion P. Cane, 'Damages in public law' (1999) 9 *University of Otago Law Rev.* 489; D Cohen and J. Smith, 'Entitlement and the body politic: Rethinking negligence in public law' (1986) 64 *Can. Bar Rev.* 1; D Cohen, 'Tort law and the crown: Administrative compensation and the modern state' in Cooper-Stephenson and Gibson (eds.), *Tort Theory* (Captus University Publications, 1993).

[24] P. Hogg, 'Compensation for damage caused by government' (1995) 6 *National Journal of Constitutional Law* 7, 12.

[25] *Fairchild v Newhaven Funeral Services Ltd* [2002] UKHL 22 [9].

in the trespass cases on which Dicey relied and have never entirely been discarded. They are apparent again in the practice of awarding exemplary and punitive damages, endorsed by the House of Lords as an appropriate way to 'vindicate the strength of the law' in cases of oppressive, arbitrary or unconstitutional action by public servants.[26] The constitutional significance of this practice was underlined in *Kuddus v Chief Constable of Leicestershire*,[27] where Lord Nicholls said:

> The availability of exemplary damages has played a significant role in buttressing civil liberties, in claims for false imprisonment and wrongful arrest. From time to time cases do arise where awards of compensatory damages are perceived as inadequate to achieve a just result between the parties. The nature of the defendant's conduct calls for a further response from the courts. On occasion conscious wrongdoing by a defendant is so outrageous, his disregard of the plaintiff's rights so contumelious, that something more is needed to show that the law will not tolerate such behaviour. Without an award of exemplary damages, justice will not have been done. Exemplary damages, as a remedy of last resort, fill what otherwise would be a regrettable lacuna.

The Law Commission, though it hoped to do so, has not felt able entirely to dispose of this practice, recommending in a full-scale survey of the subject a change in terminology to mark the true function of exemplary damages as 'punitive'. According to its final recommendation, a judge should be able to award punitive damages in addition to any other appropriate remedy where the defendant's conduct shows 'a deliberate and outrageous disregard of the plaintiff's rights' and the judge considers other remedies inadequate to punish the defendant's outrageous conduct.[28]

Because they are actionable without proof of damage, the intentional torts convey a powerful deterrent message: officials act at their peril if they misconstrue their powers. In the same way as the ultra vires principle forces a public body to point to the source of its powers, so the trespass action places the onus on the executive to show 'lawful excuse or justification' for its actions. In *R v Governor of Brockhill Prison, ex p. Evans*,[29] the House of Lords construed the defence of 'lawful excuse' very narrowly. A prison governor had miscalculated the length of a prisoner's sentence in reliance on a judicial interpretation of the relevant statutory provisions later held to have been incorrect. It was argued that the governor had had no choice in the matter; he was bound to obey the

26 *Rookes v Barnard* [1964] AC 1129 (Lord Devlin).

27 *Kuddus v Chief Constable of Leicestershire Constabulary* [2001] 2 WLR 1789 [63]. And see *Bottrill v A* [2003] 1 AC 449.

28 Law Commission, *Aggravated, Exemplary and Restitutionary Damages*, Law Com. No. 247 (1997). And see M Tilbury, 'Reconstructing damages' (2003) *Melbourne University Law Review* 27. The report has not yet been implemented.

29 *R v Governor of Brockhill Prison, ex p. Evans (No 2)* [2001] 2 AC 19. The illegality of the detention had already been established in an application for habeas corpus granted by the Divisional Court in *Evans No. 1* [1997] QB 443.

law 'as expounded by the court not just once but several times'. The House of Lords accepted Lord Hope's stern view that it was no answer that the governor took reasonable care or acted in good faith when he made the calculation:

> [F]or the governor to escape liability for any extended period of detention on the basis that he was acting honestly or on reasonable grounds analogous to those which apply to arresting police officers would reduce the protection currently provided by the tort of false imprisonment. I can see no justification for limiting the application of the tort in this way. The authorities are at one in treating it as a tort of strict liability. That strikes the right balance between the liberty of the subject and the public interest in the detection and punishment of crime. The defence of justification must be based upon a rigorous application of the principle that the liberty of the subject can be interfered with only upon grounds which a court will uphold as lawful. The Solicitor-General was unable to demonstrate that the respondent's detention was authorised or permitted by law after the date which was held by the Divisional Court to be her release date. I would hold that she is entitled to damages.

In *ID v Home Office*[30] the claimants were Roma asylum seekers who had spent periods of several months' detention in immigration detention centres. They challenged their detention as 'unlawful, unreasonable and disproportionate'. The Court of Appeal refused to strike out the claims and Brooke LJ cited Dicey to support the view that there was 'on the face of it nothing in the slightest bit peculiar about an individual bringing a private law claim for damages against an executive official who has unlawfully infringed his private rights'. He defended the use of the ancient tort of trespass in circumstances governed largely by statute (here the Immigration Act 1971), regulation and rules, asserting that 'the policy arguments for denying a right to damages for unlawful detention pale by comparison with the policy arguments for admitting such a right, because of the enormous damage that is caused, on occasion, by unlawful detention in terms of suffering and damage to physical and mental health':

> I know that the Home Office is concerned with the practical implications of a decision of this kind. The evidence of the interveners showed, however, that when the Home Office determined to embark on the policy of using powers of administrative detention on a far larger scale than hitherto, the practical implementation of that policy threw up very understandable concerns in individual cases. The transition from a world where decisions affecting personal liberty are made by officials of the executive who operate according to unpublished criteria, and where there is no way of compensating those who lose their liberty through administrative muddles and misfiling, to a world where the relevant criteria have to be published and where those officials are obliged to ensure that their decisions are proportionate and to justify them accordingly, is bound to be an uneasy one in the early years, and mistakes are bound to be made. But so long as detention, which may cause significant suffering, can be directed by executive decision and an order of a court (or

[30] *ID v Home Office* [2005] EWCA Civ 38.

> court-like body) is not required, the language and the philosophy of human rights law, and the common law's emphatic reassertion in recent years of the importance of constitutional rights, drive inexorably, in my judgment, to the conclusion I have reached.[31]

On other occasions, judges have been less stalwart. In *Holgate-Mohammed v Duke*,[32] a ruling that seriously undermines the strict liability of false imprisonment, a police officer detained the claimant at a police station without charging her in the hope of inducing a confession. Considering whether the detention was unlawful, the House of Lords held that the test must be the public law *Wednesbury* standard. This allowed the burden to be discharged by showing that the behaviour was 'common police practice'. It is hard to explain why a prison governor observing the law as the court has ruled it to be is guilty of unlawful detention when a police officer can get away with detaining someone because it is common police practice. Much common police practice is dubiously lawful and it is the duty of our courts to say when this is so.

There is however reluctance to extend the boundaries of strict liability torts. In *Wainwright v Home Office*,[33] a mother and son visiting a relative detained in prison under suspicion of being a drug dealer were subjected to a strip-search. They argued that this was assault and battery even if the prison officers honestly believed the rules authorised a strip search and had neither intended to cause distress nor realised they were acting unlawfully in terms of Rule 86(1) of the Prison Rules 1964. In the case of the son the House of Lords ruled that there could be liability; the search had involved touching his genitals, an improper physical contact of a kind not 'generally acceptable in the ordinary conduct of daily life'. In the mother's case, however, there had been no touching, hence technically no trespass. Unconvinced that strip-searching exceeded what was 'necessary and proportionate' to deal with the serious drug smuggling problem in prisons, the Law Lords, sweeping aside earlier precedents, refused to extend the boundaries of tort law to encompass strip-searching.

The case of *Watkins v Home Office*[34] was remarkable for Lord Bingham's attack on the historic case of *Ashby v White*. In *Watkins*, where prison officers in the course of a cell search had deliberately opened a prisoner's correspondence in violation of Rule 39 of the Prison Rules 1999, which protects the confidentiality of a prisoner's legal correspondence, no physical damage or financial loss had been suffered. The House of Lords refused to extend the scope of the specialised public law tort of misfeasance in public office to cover violations of constitutional or human rights on the ground that the claimant had suffered

[31] *Ibid.* [129].

[32] *Holgate-Mohammed v Duke* [1984] AC 437. See also *Paul v Chief Constable of Humberside* [2004] EWCA Civ 308.

[33] *Wainwright v Home Office* [2003] 3 WLR 1137.

[34] *Watkins v Home Office* [2006] UKHL 16 [24–6]. Cases cited by Lord Bingham include *R v Home Secretary, ex p. Leech* [1994] QB 198; *R v Home Secretary, ex p. Simms* [2000] 2 AC 115; *R(Daly) v Home Secretary* [2001] 2 AC 532. The human rights dimension of these cases is discussed at p. 118–19 above.

no damage, an element of the tort as recently defined by the House of Lords in *Three Rivers*,[35] where it was said:

- the defendant must be a public official
- the act complained of must be an exercise of public power
- the claimant must have suffered damage
- the official must have acted intentionally, maliciously *or recklessly*.

According to Lord Bingham in *Watkins*, the authorities were clear and remarkably consistent:

> The proving of special damage has either been expressly recognised as an essential ingredient, or it has been assumed. None of these cases (and no authority, judicial or academic, cited to the House) lends support to the proposition that the tort of misfeasance in public office is actionable per se. *Ashby v White,* as I have suggested, is not reliable authority for that proposition. I would be very reluctant to disturb a rule which has been understood to represent the law for over 300 years, and which has been adopted elsewhere, unless there were compelling grounds for doing so.
>
> The feature on which the Court of Appeal fastened was the breach in this case of the respondent's constitutional right to protection of the confidentiality of his legal correspondence. That was seen as providing an analogy with the breach of the plaintiff's constitutional right to vote in *Ashby v White.* The respondent relied on the authority of the Court of Appeal (per Steyn LJ) that the right of access to a court, closely linked with the right to obtain confidential legal advice, is a constitutional right. In a number of cases rights of this kind have been described as 'constitutional', 'basic' or 'fundamental' . . . In all these cases the importance of the right was directly relevant to the lawfulness of what had been done to interfere with its enjoyment.
>
> In the present context the unlawfulness of what was done to interfere with the respondent's enjoyment of his right to confidential legal correspondence is clear. I see scant warrant for importing this jurisprudence into the definition of the tort of misfeasance in public office. We would now, of course, regard the right to vote as basic, fundamental or constitutional. None of these expressions was used by Holt CJ in *Ashby v White,* and scarcely could have been given the very small number of adult citizens by whom the right was enjoyed at the time. There is thus an element of anachronism in relying on *Ashby v White* (itself a highly politicised decision) to support a proposition it would scarcely (despite the right to vote being 'a thing of the highest importance, and so great a privilege') have been thought to support at the time. It is, I think, entirely novel to treat the character of the right invaded as determinative, in the present context, of whether material damage need be proved.

Linden once famously described tort law as an 'ombudsman', capable of unlocking the filing cabinets of bureaucrats, bringing their wrongdoing into the open, and making them pay for their misdoings.[36] The civil law is often

[35] *Three Rivers District Council v Bank of England* [2000] 2 WLR 1220.

[36] A. Linden, 'Tort law as ombudsman' (1973) 51 *Can. Bar Rev.* 155 and 'Reconsidering tort law as ombudsman' in F. M. Steel and S. Rodgers-Magnet (eds.), *Issues in Tort Law* (Carswell, 1983).

the last resort of citizens wishing to bring to the attention of the public a serious grievance or wrongdoing, its great advantage being that the levers of the civil action are operated by the individual and not, as with inquests or criminal prosecutions, by public officials. In failing to recognise tort law's deterrent function, the courts may be overlooking its 'ombudsman function'.[37]

3. Duties, powers and omissions

Negligence is, however, the general principle of civil liability and the main vehicle for legal compensation. For central government in particular one case stands as a landmark in the law of liability. In the *Dorset Yacht* case,[38] the House of Lords held that the Home Office could owe a duty of care in respect of damage done when young prisoners camping in open-prison conditions on an island in Poole harbour 'borrowed' a yacht in an attempt to escape. A warning light flashed for public authorities when all but one of the Law Lords (Viscount Dilhorne) rejected the argument that, in the absence of any precedents for liability, no liability could exist. Shortly afterwards, the 'novelty' argument was disposed of in *Anns v Merton LBC*.[39] Here the House of Lords introduced a policy test whereby a court, in assessing whether to impose a duty of care, should ask itself whether any substantial policy reason existed against so doing. This cleared the way to 'novel actions' against public authorities.

The *Dorset Yacht* ruling had a further impact, making it possible to push liability back from the actual wrongdoer (the escaping prisoners) or employees for whom a public authority is vicariously liable (the prison officers) to the public authority as itself in breach of duty. The public authority is a 'peripheral party', by which is meant that a chain of causation may be constructed, allowing liability to be traced back to the actor at the end of a potential liability chain.[40] Take the case of someone who becomes seriously ill with hepatitis after consuming oysters, given to him by a relative (uninsured), bought from a small commercial supplier (limited insurance). He chooses instead to sue peripheral parties: the local authority that owns the lake where the oysters grew, the food-safety authority with powers to regulate the industry and the environmental agency with responsibility for pollution.[41] Unsuccessful treatment in a hospital would add further possibilities! The trend to extend the chain of causation is undoubtedly accentuated by the rule that defendants in a tort action are 'jointly

[37] See C. Harlow, 'A punitive role for tort law?' in Pearson, Harlow and Taggart (eds.), *Law in a Changing State* (Hart Publishing, 2008).

[38] *Home Office v Dorset Yacht Co. Ltd.* [1970] 2 WLR 1140.

[39] *Anns v Merton LBC* [1978] AC 728. This so-called 'two-stage test' was subsequently modified in *Caparo Industries plc v Dickman* [1990] 1 All ER 568, the so-called 'three stage test'.

[40] See J. Stapleton, 'Duty of care: Peripheral parties and alternative opportunities for deterrence' (1995) 111 *LQR* 301.

[41] The facts of *Graham Barclay Oysters Pty ltd v Ryan; Ryan v Great Lakes Council; State of New South Wales v Ryan* [2002] HCA 54.

and severally' liable so that courts do not normally apportion the amount of damage that any defendant should incur.[42]

The rise of negligence as the standard vehicle for compensating victims of accidents had, through the 1970s and '80s, stimulated a 'victim oriented' tort law, by which is meant that courts, especially lower courts, had shown a greater willingness to open up tort law by imposing liability on defendants such as public authorities with 'deep pockets', or which the court assumed to be insured.[43] And as the state came to participate in more activities (education, public housing or social services) and undertook more regulatory functions, public authorities seemed more often to fit the role of guarantor. Just as the Parliamentary Ombudsman was invoked to push the government to make up for lost occupational pensions (see Chapter 12), so damages were sought from bodies exercising regulatory functions. In the *Three Rivers* case, litigants tried an action for misfeasance in public office against the Bank of England for its failure to oversee and prevent the collapse of the BCCI.[44] Again, in *Watson*,[45] liability was imposed on the British Boxing Board of Control (a non-statutory regulator) in respect of inadequate guidance issued to promoters. In *Trent Strategic Health Authority v Jain*,[46] however, the respondents were proprietors of care homes licensed under the Registered Homes Act 1984, whose licenses were withdrawn when the authority suddenly laid a complaint about them. Four months later, the respondents were wholly vindicated in proceedings before the magistrates, who had no compensation powers. As their business had suffered irremediably, the proprietors sought damages for negligence in the exercise of statutory powers and for procedural defects in the conduct of the legal proceedings. Unanimously the House of Lords ruled against them, confirming both that action taken by a public authority under statutory powers designed for the benefit or protection of a particular class of persons (residents) cannot give rise to a tortious duty of care to third parties (the proprietors) and that damage caused through preparation or conduct of court or tribunal proceedings cannot be redressed by means of an action in damages.

Statutory duties are, in principle, mandatory; in other words, they leave the public authority without any power of choice. It might therefore be supposed that omissions to carry out a statutory duty would automatically give rise to a

[42] See J. Stapleton, 'Lords a'leaping evidentiary gaps' (2002) 10 *Torts Law Journal* 376 discussing asbestosis litigation in *Glenhaven Funeral Services* [2002] UKHL 22. Law Com. 187 contains the first serious proposals to tackle this problem: see [4.64–71].

[43] See G. Schwartz, 'The Beginning and the Possible End of the Rise of Modern American Tort Law' 26 *Georgia Law Rev.* 601 (1992); Hon. JJ Spigelman 'Negligence: the Last Outpost of the Welfare State' (2005) available online.

[44] *Three Rivers District Council v Bank of England* [2001] UKHL 6. The choice of misfeasance was dictated by the need to circumvent a 'bad faith only' immunity conferred by section 1(4) of the Banking Act 1987, which restricted liability to cases of bad faith.

[45] *Watson v British Boxing Board of Control* [2001] 2 WLR 1256.

[46] [2009] UKHL 4 [28] [35] (Lord Scott).

right to damages for loss suffered. In practice, however, the courts have shown themselves unwilling to adopt such a stringent approach and the action for breach of statutory duty is a weak one. As the Law Commission complains, the courts have failed to enunciate clear principles and apply them consistently. Their method is to 'look to the construction of the statute, relying upon a number of "presumptions" for guidance, but in practice there are so many conflicting presumptions, with variable weightings, that it can be extremely difficult to predict how the courts will respond to a particular statute'.[47] A statutory power, on the other hand, contains discretion, defined in Chapter 5 as a power of choice; the authority can choose whether to act or not to act; it can also choose how to act. The apparent dichotomy between powers and duties has given rise in tort law to the fallacious argument that bolting a common law duty of care onto a statutory power deprives the public body of its power of choice and transmutes the power into a duty.[48]

If a public body decides not to take action or otherwise fails to act, the presumption against liability is strengthened by the entrenched common law distinction between acts and omissions, where courts are traditionally wary of imposing liability. When, in the seminal case of *Donoghue v Stevenson*,[49] Lord Atkin enunciated his famous neighbour principle that was to form the basis of liability for negligence, he did not confine the circumstances in which a duty of care could exist to positive actions; in fact he said: 'you must take reasonable care to avoid acts or omissions which you can reasonably foresee would be likely to injure your neighbour'. Despite this robust affirmation of liability for omissions, the unwillingness of the common law to impose liability for omissions to act remained. The prejudice was reinforced by an old common law exemption from liability for highway authorities (now repealed) for failure to maintain the highway (nonfeasance). In *East Suffolk Catchment Board v Kent*,[50] where the Board had undertaken to drain the claimant's flooded land but failed to do so, Lord Atkin carefully distinguished the two different categories of duty: statutory duties and the common law duty of care. Despite his vigorous protests, however, the House of Lords declined to find the Board liable, arguing that imposing a duty of care would effectively transform a statutory power into a statutory duty.

Similar confusion is visible in *Stovin v Wise*,[51] where S had been injured in a collision with a driver who negligently turned out of a blind junction. The highway authority had failed to remove a bank that obscured visibility at the junction, previously identified as an accident black spot. It had earlier contacted British Rail, the landowner, for permission to carry out modifications

[47] Law Com. 18 [4.73–4] citing *Clerk and Lindsell on Torts*, 19th edn (2006) [9.02].
[48] On the line between omission and affirmative right see s. 5(a).
[49] *Donoghue v Stevenson* [1932] AC 562. Lord Atkin's position was affirmed in *Anns v Merton LBC* [1978] AC 728.
[50] *East Suffolk Catchment Board v Kent* [1941] AC 74.
[51] *Stovin v Wise* [1996] AC 923, 951 (Lord Hoffman for the majority).

but failed to notice that no reply had been received and to follow the matter up. Essentially, Lord Hoffmann based his refusal to impose liability on the distinction between the two forms of duty:

> One must have regard to the purpose of the distinction as it is used in the law of negligence, which is to distinguish between regulating the way in which an activity may be conducted and imposing a duty to act upon a person who is not carrying on any relevant activity.

He deduced that 'arguments peculiar to public bodies' could and should *negative* the existence of a duty of care, discarding as 'simply unworkable' a more modern distinction made between the 'policy' area of decision-making, to be protected from liability, and the 'operational' acts by which policies and decisions are executed for which liability can accrue.[52] Lord Nicholls on the other hand concluded that the public law elements and 'typical statutory framework' of the decision helped to *create* a duty of care and a 'proximity which would not otherwise exist'.[53] The highway authority had 'failed to fulfil its public law obligations just as much as if it were in breach of a statutory duty'.

In *Gorringe v Calderdale MBC*,[54] the House returned to the problem. A mother had driven over the crest of a hill into an oncoming bus, killing her daughter and two young friends. An action was brought against the highway authority for failing to erect a sign warning of the deep dip in the road. Lord Hoffmann simply said that he found 'it difficult to imagine a case in which a common law duty can be founded simply upon the failure (however irrational) to provide some benefit which a public authority has power (or a public law duty) to provide'. Lord Scott on the other hand returned to the conceptual landmine of statutory duty, reasoning opaquely that:

> if a statutory duty does not give rise to a private right to sue for breach, the duty cannot create a duty of care that would not have been owed at common law if the statute were not there. If the policy of the statute is not consistent with the creation of a statutory liability to pay compensation for damage caused by a breach of the statutory duty, the same policy would, in my opinion, exclude the use of the statutory duty in order to create a common law duty of care that would be broken by a failure to perform the statutory duty.[55]

Public finance does not figure largely in the speeches in these two cases, which focus on the distinction between acts and omissions, statutory and common law duties and the difference between public and private law. Yet the idea of transferring liability from the field of compulsory road-traffic insurance to

[52] See *Anns v Merton London Borough Council* [1978] AC 728.

[53] [1996] AC 938, Lord Nicholls dissenting.

[54] *Gorringe v Calderdale MBC* [2004] UKHL 15; [2004] 1 WLR 1057. There was no possibility of recovery from the bus driver, who was in no way negligent, though an action by the passengers against the negligent driver could succeed. The issues are re-examined in *Mitchell v Glasgow City Council* [2009] UKHL 11.

[55] [2004] UKHL [71].

public funds clearly troubled the House of Lords. In *O'Rourke v Camden LBC*, Lord Hoffmann raised the funding issue more clearly. The claimant had been placed in temporary accommodation pending a final decision on his entitlement to public housing. He was later evicted and claimed compensation for 'sleeping rough'. Lord Hoffmann explained that:

> Public money is spent on housing the homeless not merely for the private benefit of people who find themselves homeless but on grounds of general public interest: because, for example, proper housing means that people will be less likely to suffer illness, turn to crime or require the attention of other social services. The expenditure interacts with expenditure on other public services such as education, the National Health Service and even the police. It is not simply a private matter between the claimant and the housing authority. Accordingly, the fact that Parliament has provided for the expenditure of public money on benefits in kind such as housing the homeless does not necessarily mean that it intended cash payments to be made by way of damages to persons who, in breach of the housing authority's statutory duty, have unfortunately not received the benefits which they should have done.[56]

In an attempt to resolve some of these hard cases, the Law Commission in its 2008 consultation paper suggests radical reform. It asks for special protection for all 'truly public' activities, defining this term to cover any act or omission where:

- The body exercised or failed to exercise, a special statutory power or
- The body breached a special statutory duty; or
- the body exercised or failed to exercise, a prerogative power.

A 'special statutory power' was defined as a power that allows the public body to act in a way not open to private individuals and 'special statutory duty' as a statutory duty placed on the public body that is specific to it and is not placed on private individuals.[57]

4. Defensive administration, 'decision traps' and immunity

Resource allocation is undoubtedly an important dimension of state liability. The decision requiring a retirement home to be kept open (*ex p. Coughlan*, see p. 227 above) may require a wider change of policy, the input of substantial new resources and may even result in worsening the conditions of elderly people in other homes. Tort actions may have similar consequences. Since tortious liability is a blunt instrument, it may, as the House of Lords indicated in the *Marcic* case (see p. 315 above) have the effect of distorting a more appropriate statutory scheme or administrative procedures. Liability may have unforeseen

[56] *O'Rourke v Camden LBC* [1997] 3 WLR 86, 94.
[57] Law Com. 187 [4.131]. And see [4.110–32] and the list of questions at pp. 132–3.

consequences: liability for a playground accident may result, for example, in local authority playgrounds being closed. The impact of imposing a duty of care on a hard-pressed public service may be very similar to that of a judicial review decision that certain drugs are to be made generally available on the NHS, which as we saw with Herceptin in Chapter 3 could cost the NHS millions of pounds annually and result in less treatment for other, less seriously ill, patients. In addition, many tort actions conceal potential claims from groups of people in similar situations. Treasury guidance advises departments in such circumstances:

> to consider whether they should offer compensation . . . in discovered cases of official failure where there has been no complaint. Where, following a particular complaint or the discovery of a particular case, departments discover that other individuals or bodies have suffered in the same way, they should consider whether, in the interests of equity, they should offer compensation to others.[58]

All this leads Cohen to argue for a 'no liability' rule on the ground that government and private employers alike undercut any deterrent effects of liability by failing to enforce liability against employees;[59] indeed, given the trend of modern tort law to vicarious and institutional liability,[60] it would be virtually impossible to do so. Even Schuck, who favours the deterrent use of tort law, has to admit that its deterrent function may be marginal since 'most tort law standards are radically indeterminate; they define legal duties in terms of reasonableness, foreseeability and other similarly ambiguous concepts. Few brightline rules exist; even when they are available, the courts often reject them.' Schuck has also to concede that little is known about impact; 'which remedies deter particular behaviour . . . is ultimately an empirical question, but one that is so elusive that the inquiry must be informed largely by theoretical speculation'.[61] And the deterrence argument should not inhibit us from asking whether some decisions are of such a delicate nature that they should be protected from tortious liability altogether. A common argument against extensions of the liability of public authorities concerns the possible distortion of the decision-making process by introducing into already complex decisions the threat of tortious liability. Arguably, this leads to defensive administration creating 'decision traps' that, by submitting decision-makers to competing pressures, produce a serious freezing effect on administrative action.[62]

[58] Treasury, 'Dear Accounting Officer' (DAO (GEN) 15/92), available online.

[59] D. Cohen, 'Regulating Regulators: The Legal Environment of the State' (1990) 40 *University of Toronto Law Journal* 213, 258.

[60] See *Lister and others v Hesley Hall Ltd* [2001] UKHL 22 (vicarious liability of employers for warden's abuse of pupils in a children's home); *Kuddus v CC of Leicestershire Constabulary* [2001] UKHL 29 (vicarious liability of police authority for misfeasance in public office).

[61] P. Schuck, *Suing Government: Citizen Remedies for Official Wrongs* (Yale University Press, 1983), pp. 16 and 484.

[62] Further discussed in C. Harlow, *State Liability: Tort Law and Beyond* (Oxford University Press, 2004), pp. 24–30.

(a) Social work and liability

The case of *X (Minors) v Bedfordshire*[63] was a test case designed to dispose once and for all of the confusion obscuring negligence actions founded on statutory powers and duties. In two sets of joined cases, the liability in negligence of local education authorities for systemic failures to diagnose and deal with the special educational needs of children and of social workers deciding care cases under the Children Acts was tested. The unanimous opinion of the House was voiced by Lord Browne-Wilkinson, who concluded that liability was possible in the educational cases since the duty of care was well established and did not derive from statute. There was no overriding reason why someone employed by a local education authority to carry out professional services should not in principle owe a duty of care to particular pupils; medical personnel are, after all, liable for their negligence and this liability should therefore extend to psychiatrists whether they work in the private sector or for a public education authority. In the social-work cases, where no private law analogy existed, the House found against the possibility of liability:

> *Lord Browne-Wilkinson:* First, in my judgment a common law duty of care would cut across the whole statutory system set up for the protection of children at risk. As a result of the ministerial directions contained in 'Working Together' the protection of such children is not the exclusive territory of the local authority's social services. The system is inter-disciplinary, involving the participation of the police, educational bodies, doctors and others. At all stages the system involves joint discussions, joint recommendations and joint decisions. The key organisation is the Child Protection Conference, a multi-disciplinary body which decides whether to place the child on the Child Protection Register. This procedure by way of joint action takes place, not merely because it is good practice, but because it is required by guidance having statutory force binding on the local authority. The guidance is extremely detailed and extensive: the current edition of 'Working Together' runs to 126 pages. To introduce into such a system a common law duty of care enforceable against only one of the participant bodies would be manifestly unfair. To impose such liability on all the participant bodies would lead to almost impossible problems of disentangling as between the respective bodies the liability, both primary and by way of contribution, of each for reaching a decision found to be negligent.
>
> Secondly, the task of the local authority and its servants in dealing with children at risk is extraordinarily delicate. Legislation requires the local authority to have regard not only to the physical wellbeing of the child but also to the advantages of not disrupting the child's family environment: see, for example, section 17 of the Act of 1989. In one of the child abuse cases, the local authority is blamed for removing the child precipitately; in the other, for failing to remove the children from their mother. As the Report of the Inquiry into Child Abuse in Cleveland 1987 (Cm. 412) said, at p. 244:

[63] *X (Minors) v Bedfordshire County Council; M v Newham London Borough Council* [1995] 2 AC 633. The cases proceeded on a preliminary point and never came to trial.

> 'It is a delicate and difficult line to tread between taking action too soon and not taking it soon enough. Social services whilst putting the needs of the child first must respect the rights of the parents; they also must work if possible with the parents for the benefit of the children. These parents themselves are often in need of help. Inevitably a degree of conflict develops between those objectives.'
>
> Next, if a liability in damages were to be imposed, it might well be that local authorities would adopt a more cautious and defensive approach to their duties. For example, as the Cleveland Report makes clear, on occasions the speedy decision to remove the child is sometimes vital. If the authority is to be made liable in damages for a negligent decision to remove a child (such negligence lying in the failure properly first to investigate the allegations) there would be a substantial temptation to postpone making such a decision until further inquiries have been made in the hope of getting more concrete facts. Not only would the child in fact being abused be prejudiced by such delay; the increased workload inherent in making such investigations would reduce the time available to deal with other cases and other children.

There is much good sense here. But the floodgates once prised open, further cases naturally followed in which the courts began to look more sceptically at the 'defensive-administration' or 'decision-trap' argument. A cluster of child abuse actions reached the courts, some brought by children taken into care, some by parents wrongly accused of child abuse, whose interests could conceivably conflict.[64] In parallel, the ECtHR had intervened, ruling that the decision in *X v Bedfordshire* violated ECHR Art. 13 since no effective remedy had been available for a grave violation of ECHR Art. 3.[65] The ECtHR did not go so far as to say that *only* a judicial remedy was adequate to furnish effective redress but it certainly hinted as much; the judgment points to the advantages of *judicial* proceedings in affording 'strong guarantees of independence, access for the victim and family and enforceability of awards'.[66] Moreover, the Court laid great emphasis on the importance of monetary compensation as a remedy for violation of individual rights, at least where the right violated was as fundamental as the right to life or the prohibition against torture, inhuman and degrading treatment here in issue. And the damages it awarded in 'just satisfaction' under ECHR Art. 41 were far from negligible: in respect of what was described as 'very serious abuse and neglect over a period of more than four years', the three applicants gained a total of £112,000 for pecuniary damage, with £32,000 per child for non-pecuniary damage, much more than they had been awarded under the criminal injuries compensation scheme (see p. XXX below). It should also be noted, in view of what has been said earlier, that in this case the primary

[64] Notably *Phelps v Hillingdon BC* [2000] 3 WLR 766 and *Barrett v Enfield London Borough Council* [2001] 2 AC 550, where Lords Slynn, Nolan and Steyn dismissed the argument. And see S. Bailey and M. Bowman, 'Public authority negligence revisited' (2000) 59 *CLJ* 85.

[65] *Z v United Kingdom* (2001) 34 EHRR 97, noted by Gearty, 'Oman unravels' (2002) 65 *MLR* 87.

[66] *Z v United Kingdom* [109].

wrongdoers were the parents neither the state nor its officials were actively guilty of abuse, though they were hardly peripheral parties. The state was, in short, being held responsible for a regulatory function and for failure by a public service to react to an allegedly grave and distressing situation – a major extension of liability from misfeasance to nonfeasance.

By the time that the *East Berkshire* case[67] reached the House of Lords, the context had changed again through the introduction of the HRA, making the jurisprudence of the ECtHR a matter to be taken directly into consideration (see below). The question it posed was whether the *parent* of a minor child falsely accused of child abuse could recover common law damages for psychiatric injury in negligence. By a four to one majority, the House of Lords upheld the Court of Appeal's decision that the duty of care was restricted to the children, whose welfare was paramount; for parents, a finding of bad faith might be necessary for liability. The speeches in the House of Lords contain considerable analysis of the process of decision-making in child-care cases, the difficulties of which we explored in the context of child abuse inquiries (see Chapter 13 above). The dangers of skewing the decision-making process were once more emphasised, this time by Lord Nicholls:

> the seriousness of child abuse as a social problem demands that health professionals, acting in good faith in what they believe are the best interests of the child, should not be subject to potentially conflicting duties when deciding whether a child may have been abused, or when deciding whether their doubts should be communicated to others, or when deciding what further investigatory or protective steps should be taken. The duty they owe to the child in making these decisions should not be clouded by imposing a conflicting duty in favour of parents or others suspected of having abused the child.[68]

Lord Bingham, however, was dismissive of this line of reasoning.[69] 'To describe awareness of a legal duty as having an "insidious effect" on the mind of a potential defendant is to undermine the foundation of the law of professional negligence.' Equally, it was out of line with the relevant ministerial guidance, which stressed the need to co-operate closely with parents. He was equally dismissive of the dangers of creating conflicts of interest: 'it was hard to see how imposition of a duty of care towards parents could encourage healthcare professionals either to overlook signs of abuse which they should recognise or to draw inferences of abuse which the evidence did not justify'. On the contrary, tort law 'could help to instil a due sense of professional responsibility, and I see no reason for distinguishing between the child and the parent'. He preferred (on this occasion) to see tort law as evolutionary; it should 'evolve, analogically

[67] *JD and Others v East Berkshire Community Health Trust and Others* [2003] EWCA Civ 1151 (CA); [2005] UKHL 23 (HL). See also *W v Essex County Council* [2001] 2 AC 592.

[68] [2005] UKHL [86].

[69] [2005] UKHL [42] [50]. And see Department for Children, Schools and Families, *Working Together to Safeguard Children* (1999) now (2006), available online.

and incrementally, so as to fashion appropriate remedies to contemporary problems'. He would therefore have preferred to allow the appeals, sending the cases back for trial.

In an age of accountability and human rights this is unlikely to mark the end of the story.[70] Consider the case of Angela Cannings, convicted of murdering her child on flawed medical evidence and sentenced to life. Had Mrs Cannings served her sentence, compensation for wrongful conviction under s. 133 of the Criminal Justice Act 1988 would have been available but the fact that her appeal against conviction succeeded excluded her from the statutory compensation scheme.[71] Can it really be 'fair, just and reasonable' to insist that no duty of care is owed in such circumstances? Would the ECtHR accept that compensation under Art. 5 was not due or that a mother injured in this way was not entitled to 'just satisfaction'?

(b) Policing and the duty of care

There is no immunity from liability for the police force, which is strictly answerable, as we have seen, for the legality of its actions. The imposition of a duty of care in the course of a criminal investigation is, however, another matter. In *Hill v Chief Constable of West Yorkshire*,[72] it was argued that the claimant's daughter would not have been murdered by the 'Yorkshire Ripper' had it not been for the negligence of the police. The House of Lords held that there was insufficient proximity for a duty of care to be owed to the mother, commenting on the inappropriate nature of the tort action for the investigation of such decisions. Lord Keith referred to the waste of police time and trouble and the expense of such proceedings. 'The result would be a significant diversion of police manpower and attention from their most important function, that of the suppression of crime. Closed investigations would require to be reopened . . . not with the object of bringing any criminal to justice but to ascertain whether or not they had been competently conducted.' With a hint of exaggeration, Lord Templeman thought that the way would be opened for every citizen:

> to require the court to investigate the performance of every policeman. If the policeman concentrates on one crime, he may be accused of neglecting others. If the policeman does not arrest on suspicion a suspect with previous convictions, the police force may be held liable for subsequent crimes. The threat of litigation against a police force would not make a policeman more efficient. The necessity for defending proceedings, successfully or unsuccessfully, would distract the policeman from his duties.

[70] See *Lawrence v Pembrokeshire County Council* [2007] EWCA Civ 446 (liability for placing persons on risk register).

[71] The *Independent*, 12 Jan. 2005 and 20 Apr. 2006; *R v Cannings* [2004] EWCA Crim 1. A cluster of these cases led to an inquiry by the Attorney-General and subsequently to proceedings against the doctor by the General Medical Council.

[72] *Hill v Chief Constable of West Yorkshire* [1989] AC 42.

The decision was to rebound on the House of Lords in the unfortunate *Osman* case, where failure by the police to protect a pupil from the attentions of a psychiatrically disturbed teacher led to a death by shooting. This action was struck out by the domestic courts on the ground that the police owed no duty of care, causing the victims to turn to Strasbourg for redress.[73] The ECtHR treated the case as a violation of the Art. 6(1) right of access to the court ruling that, by treating the public-policy immunity as absolute, the domestic courts had ruled out adequate consideration of other public-interest considerations. It then applied Art. 41 to award 'on an equitable basis' a sum of £10,000 to each of the applicants, essentially for loss of a chance fully to present their case.[74]

Undeterred by this warning, the House of Lords went on to apply the *Hill* principle in *Brooks v Metropolitan Police Commissioner*.[75] The claimant, Duwayne Brooks, was a friend of Stephen Lawrence, and a participant in the subsequent inquiry, conducted by Sir William Macpherson,[76] which described the police as 'institutionally racist'. It also found that the investigation had been badly conducted and that the respondent had not been treated appropriately. Yet in a subsequent action for damages for psychiatric injury, the House of Lords nonetheless found that the police force owed no duty of care to accord the claimant reasonably appropriate protection, support, assistance and treatment.

The issue of possible duties of care owed by the police in the course of investigating crime was reopened in *van Colle and Smith*,[77] providing an opportunity for the House of Lords to reconcile two apparently conflicting lines of cases. On the one hand, it confirmed the jurisprudence of the ECtHR in *Osman* to the effect that failure to take measures within the scope of its powers to protect an individual from 'a real and immediate risk to life' would amount to a violation of ECHR Art. 2 (right to life) by a public body. On the other, it affirmed the *Hill* principle that no duty of care was owed; any such duty would cause 'defensive policing' and divert police resources away from combating crime in order to deal with civil litigation. Applying these principles to the fact situations of (i) a vulnerable witness in a criminal case who had been murdered by the suspect and (ii) a young man injured in a series of attacks by his partner after threats of violence had been reported to the police, only Lord Bingham was prepared to consider liability in (ii) on the basis of the Strasbourg principle of 'imminent risk'.

[73] See L. Hoyano, 'Policing flawed police investigations: Unravelling the blanket' (1999) 62 *MLR* 912. And see *Osman v Ferguson* [1993] 4 All ER 344.

[74] *Osman v United Kingdom* (1998) 29 EHRR 245 noted by Gearty 'Unravelling Osman' (2001) 64 *MLR* 159 in a note on *Z v UK* (above), which can be read as a retraction by the ECtHR of *Osman*.

[75] *Brooks v Commissioner of Police for the Metropolis* [2005] UKHL 24.

[76] *The Stephen Lawrence Inquiry: Report of an Inquiry by Sir William Macpherson of Cluny*, Cm. 4262-I (1999).

[77] *van Colle v Chief Constable of Hertfordshire; Smith v Chief Constable of Sussex* [2007] EWCA Civ 325 (CA); [2008] UKHL 50 (HL). And see And see *Mitchell v Glasgow City Council* [2009] UKHL 11 [28–9] (Lord Hope).

What are we to make of this tangled and confusing case law, which imposes a duty of care on the education services and, on a more limited basis, on social workers but not on the police? Are we to conclude that the investigation of crime is more difficult or a matter of greater public interest than decisions to take or not to take a child into care? And what of the tangled jurisprudence of the ECtHR, which in case of apparent violations of ECHR Art. 2 requires both a public inquiry and compensation, and is extending this principle to other cases of human rights violation? There is a danger here of producing a set of parallel, overlapping remedies – some, such as criminal injuries compensation, capable of providing 'just satisfaction, others, such as public inquiries, not.

5. The shadow of Europe

(a) Human rights and 'just satisfaction'

One possible explanation for the negative approach of the Law Lords in these perplexing cases, many of which raise the use of tort law for purposes other than recovery of compensation, is the advent of the Human Rights Act (HRA). The HRA does not preclude the award of damages for violation of a human right but it does make recovery difficult. Section 8(2) restricts the courts able to award damages to those competent 'to award damages, or to order the payment of compensation, in civil proceedings'. Section 8(3) provides that no award of damages is to be made unless, taking account of all the circumstances of the case including alternative remedies, 'the court is satisfied that the award is necessary to afford just satisfaction to the person in whose favour it is made'. Section 8(4) obliges the court to 'take into account the principles applied by the [ECtHR] in relation to the award of compensation under Article 41 of the Convention'.

Strasbourg principles are hard to interpret and Strasbourg awards are relatively ungenerous.[78] This is an open invitation to practitioners to try to bring human rights claims within the compass of domestic tort law. In *Wainwright*, W suffered shame, outrage and a loss of dignity, values discounted by Lord Hoffmann as comparable to the 'lack of consideration and appalling manners' used in institutions and workplaces all over the country, where 'people constantly do and say things with the intention of causing distress and humiliation to others'. Yet the ECtHR subsequently found that the manner in which these searches were carried out was disproportionate to the legitimate objective of fighting the drugs problem in the prison and amounted to a violation of ECHR Art. 8. It also found that the absence of any cause of action in tort, more especially for invasion of privacy, amounted to a breach of Art. 13. Compensation of €6,000 for non-pecuniary damage plus costs was awarded

[78] R. Clayton, 'Damage limitation: The courts and Human Rights Act damages' [2005] *PL* 429, 431.

in 'just satisfaction'.[79] In *Watkins*, the Art. 6(1) right of access to the court and perhaps a right of privacy (ECHR Art. 8) had been violated, so by refusing to extend the tort of misfeasance beyond material damage to cover rights violations, the courts laid themselves open to a finding, under ECHR Art. 13, that no remedy had been provided. In *Z v UK* (see p. 766 above) and *Osman*, this finding materialised.

If the scheme of the HRA is ambiguous, then so is the ECtHR's jurisprudence on 'just satisfaction'. Occasionally, as in Art. 5(5), compensation is prescribed. Sometimes, as with the Art. 2 cases discussed below, jurisprudence makes it virtually axiomatic. Exceptionally, as in *Z v UK* sums awarded in just satisfaction may be very considerable even in cases where the state is not the immediate wrongdoer. The sum awarded in *Watkins* is, however, more typical of the generally insubstantial awards.

Our courts have made three main attempts to deal with the problem of damages in human rights cases. In the first, the claimant, severely disabled and with a large family, had asked the council for housing appropriate to her condition. The council properly took responsibility but through 'operational negligence' left the claimant and her family to suffer conditions of squalor while nearly two years of litigation, delay, failure to carry out statutory duties, and distressing administrative incompetence elapsed.[80] Finally, the claimant's solicitors lost patience and asked for damages under the HRA, claiming in addition to the obvious breach of the right to private and family life (ECHR Art. 8) that the conditions suffered had been degrading (Art. 3).[81] In view of the long period spent by the family in 'deplorable conditions, wholly inimical to any normal family life' and taking into consideration also the absence of explanation or apology, merely to rehouse the family seemed unsatisfactory; Sullivan J insisted on an award of damages. Imaginatively, he fed back into the case law the guidance and practice of the Local Government Ombudsman (below), awarding £10,000 – aptly in the circumstances termed a 'botheration payment'.

In *Anufrijeva*,[82] the second attempt, three claims for damages under ECHR Art. 8 (right to private and family life) were blocked up, respectively based on delay and general maladministration in the handling of asylum applications and on failure to supply accommodation adequate for the infirm and elderly relative of an asylum seeker. In a single judgment delivered for the court by

[79] *Wainwright v United Kingdom*, App. No. 12350/04 (Judgment of 26 Sep. 2006). And see above p. 758. For privacy see J. Morgan, 'Privacy torts: Out with the old, out with the new' (2004) 120 *LQR* 395; *Mosley v News Group Newspapers Ltd* [2008] EWHC 687.

[80] *R (Bernard) v Enfield LBC* [2002] EWHC 2282. The case had been preceded by an unsuccessful application for judicial review of the Council's decision that the applicants had rendered themselves 'intentionally homeless': see *Bernard v Enfield LBC* [2001] EWCA Civ 2717.

[81] The Art. 3 claim was dismissed, as the judge ruled that the 'minimum threshold of severity' had not been crossed: see [26–31]. The case therefore proceeded as a violation of Art. 8.

[82] *Anufrijeva v Southwark LBC* [2003] EWCA Civ 406 (Lord Woolf LCJ, Lord Phillips MR and Auld LJ).

Lord Woolf CJ, a strong Court of Appeal disallowed the claims, ruling that save in exceptional circumstances, ECHR Art. 8 creates no general obligation to provide financial assistance. Its positive obligations stop short at requiring (i) that an appropriate statutory or administrative scheme is in place to ensure that private and family life is protected and (ii) that the scheme is operated with sufficient competence for it to achieve its aim. Thus while error of judgement, inefficiency, or maladministration occurring in the purported performance of a statutory duty could amount in principle to a breach of Art. 8, it would be rare in practice for maladministration to be regarded as a violation. There must, in Lord Woolf's view, be 'an element of culpability. At the very least, there must be knowledge that the claimant's private and family life were at risk.'[83]

The Court of Appeal also chose to highlight 'the different role played by damages in human rights litigation to the award of damages in a private law contract or tort action'. A tentative bright line was drawn between 'liability', resulting in an automatic entitlement to damages, and 'compensation' under the HRA, which was *discretionary*. In considering whether it was just and appropriate to award compensation, courts were therefore entitled to consider not only the circumstances of the individual victim but also what would serve the interests of the 'wider public who have an interest in the continued funding of a public service'. In a human rights application, according to Lord Woolf, the applicant seeks primarily:

> to bring the infringement to an end and any question of compensation will be of secondary, if any, importance. This is reflected in the fact that, when it is necessary to resort to the courts to uphold and protect human rights, the remedies that are most frequently sought are the orders which are the descendants of the historic prerogative orders or declaratory judgments. The orders enable the court to order a public body to refrain from or to take action, or to quash an offending administrative decision of a public body. Declaratory judgments usually resolve disputes as to what is the correct answer in law to a dispute. This means that it is often procedurally convenient for actions concerning human rights to be heard on an application for judicial review in the Administrative Court. That court does not normally concern itself with issues of disputed fact or with issues as to damages. However, it is well placed to take action expeditiously when this is appropriate.[84]

Judges considering human rights claims were reminded to look first to alternative remedies, in particular to investigation by an ombudsman or mediator. In this way, the traditional common law 'pecking order' of public law remedies had been confirmed.

The case of *Greenfield*[85] gave the House of Lords an opportunity to consider the matter. The claimant was a prisoner who had served a disciplinary sentence

[83] [2003] EWCA Civ [45].

[84] [2003] EWCA Civ [52–3].

[85] *R v Home Secretary, ex p. Greenfield* [2005] UKHL 14 [19].

imposed in breach of his procedural rights under ECHR Art. 6(1) and later demanded compensation. Disallowing the claim, Lord Bingham firmly disapproved the idea that compensation under the HRA should approximate to tort law damages:

> First, the 1998 Act is not a tort statute. Its objects are different and broader. Even in a case where a finding of violation is not judged to afford the applicant just satisfaction, such a finding will be an important part of his remedy and an important vindication of the right he has asserted. Damages need not ordinarily be awarded to encourage high standards of compliance by member states, since they are already bound in international law to perform their duties under the Convention in good faith, although it may be different if there is felt to be a need to encourage compliance by individual officials or classes of official. Secondly, the purpose of incorporating the Convention in domestic law through the 1998 Act was not to give victims better remedies at home than they could recover in Strasbourg but to give them the same remedies without the delay and expense of resort to Strasbourg. This intention was clearly expressed in the White Paper 'Rights Brought Home: The Human Rights Bill' (Cm 3782, 1 October 1997), para 2.6:
>
> > 'The Bill provides that, in considering an award of damages on Convention grounds, the courts are to take into account the principles applied by the European Court of Human Rights in awarding compensation, so that people will be able to receive compensation from a domestic court equivalent to what they would have received in Strasbourg.'
>
> Thirdly, section 8(4) requires a domestic court to take into account the principles applied by the European Court under article 41 not only in determining whether to award damages but also in determining the amount of an award. There could be no clearer indication that courts in this country should look to Strasbourg and not to domestic precedents . . . Judges . . . are not inflexibly bound by Strasbourg awards in what may be different cases. But they should not aim to be significantly more or less generous than the Court might be expected to be, in a case where it was willing to make an award at all.

Unless and until Strasbourg again takes a hand in the matter, the law seems to be settled.

(b) The European Union and state liability

In the seminal case of *Francovich*,[86] the ECJ imposed liability on Italy for failure to transpose a European directive. Liability would accrue where:

- a directive was intended to confer rights on individuals
- the content of the rights was clearly spelt out in the directive
- there was a causal link between the failure to implement the directive and the loss suffered, the national court to decide whether a causal link existed.

[86] Joined Cases 6, 9/90 *Francovich and Bonafaci v Italy* [1991] ECR I-5357.

English law collided directly with this European jurisprudence in the *Factortame* case (see p. 180 above), when the 'Spanish fishermen' who had been unlawfully deprived of their right to fish in UK waters sued for damages.[87] On a preliminary reference, the ECJ refined the liability conditions: for liability to accrue, the breach must be 'sufficiently serious'. Today the question normally asked is whether the Member State 'manifestly and gravely' disregarded the limits on its discretion. In *British Telecom*,[88] where BT claimed damages for loss consequential on imperfect transposition of a directive, the ECJ took the opportunity to demarcate the boundaries. Council Directive 90/531 on the co-ordination of national public procurement procedures was notably loosely worded and difficult to transpose; the UK had acted in good faith though making an error in transposition; it had not committed a 'manifestly serious' breach of EC law. In *Factortame (No. 5)*, on the other hand, the English courts ruled that the violation of EC law was 'sufficiently serious' to merit compensation and the action was subsequently settled, allegedly for a sum in the region of £55 million.[89]

No principle of administrative compensation comparable to the *Francovich* principle exists in the English system, where public authorities are subject to the ordinary principles of civil liability, as it does in some continental systems. How to slot the principle of state liability under EC law into the common law was therefore a matter of debate. To treat violations of EU law as a breach of statutory duty is the obvious solution.[90] Misfeasance can also be useful where breaches of EC law are alleged,[91] as the corporate officer of the House of Commons discovered when he turned a blind eye to EC public-procurement law when allotting a contract for the new Parliament building.[92]

The case of *Factortame* is not the only occasion on which the impact of EC law has been felt; in other areas too the 'spill-over' from EC law has been considerable. In *Marshall (No. 2)*, for example,[93] the ECJ considered the statutory tort of race and gender discrimination and ruled the existing statutory cap on damages unlawful under EC law.

[87] Joined Cases C-46/93 and C-48/93 *Brasserie du Pecheur SA v Germany, R v Transport Secretary, ex p. Factortame (No. 4)* [1996] ECR I-1029.

[88] C-392/93 *R v HM Treasury, ex p. British Telecommunications plc* [1996] 3 WLR 203.

[89] *R v Transport Secretary, ex p. Factortame (No. 5)* [1997] EuLR 475 (Div Court) confirmed by the House of Lords at [1999] 3 WLR 1062.

[90] *Garden Cottage Foods v Milk Marketing Board* [1984] 1 AC 130 (Lord Diplock). And see P. Craig, 'The domestic liability of public authorities in damages: Lessons from the European Community' and M. Hoskins, 'Rebirth of the innominate tort?', in J. Beatson and T. Tridimas (eds.), *New Directions in European Public Law* (Oxford: Hart Publishing) 1998. In *Factortame*, the House of Lords did not address the question.

[91] The ruling in *Three Rivers* that there was no liability under EC law is regarded as controversial by M. Andenas and D.Fairgrieve, 'Misfeasance in public office, governmental liability, and European Influences' (2002) 51 ICLQ 757.

[92] *Harmon Facades v Corporate Officer of the House of Commons* (1999) EWHC Technology 199; *Harman No. 2* (2000) EWHC Technology 84.

[93] Case C-271/91 *Marshall v Southampton and South-West Hampshire Health Authority* (*Marshall (No. 2)* [1993] ECR I-4367.

(c) Unjust enrichment and restitution

The *Woolwich* case[94] involved a significant change in the law of restitution, a deeply unsatisfactory area of English law, at the time of the decision under review by the Law Commission.[95] Before the Commission reported, however, the House of Lords was faced with an action for recovery of sums paid by Woolwich to meet tax demands from the IRC that subsequently turned out to have been unlawful. Could the money be reclaimed? Under existing law, money paid to a public authority under a mistake of law in the form of taxes or other levies was not recoverable – 'a shabby rule'![96] In the *Woolwich* case, the House of Lords, in Lord Goff's discreet phrase, 'reformulated the law' to provide a right to restitution in such cases. The House of Lords set out a new principle: that 'money paid by a citizen to a public authority in the form of taxes or other levies paid pursuant to an ultra vires demand by the authority is prima facie recoverable by the citizen as of right'.[97] This conspicuous piece of judicial lawmaking, acceptable to leading commentators and the Law Commission, provoked strong dissents from Lords Keith and Jauncey, concerned that a wide restitution principle could cause 'very serious practical difficulties of administration and specifying appropriate limitations presents equal difficulties'. On the other hand, a factor pointing strongly to the change made in *Woolwich* was that it was required by the jurisprudence of the ECJ, which had already recognised an entitlement to repayment of charges levied contrary to EC law.[98]

The impact of the ECJ was felt again in a later set of claims concerning compensation and restitution for taxes unlawfully demanded. Under the Income and Corporation Taxes Act 1988, corporation tax was payable quarterly in advance on certain distributions made within the UK. In 2001, this provision was ruled by the ECJ to be incompatible with EC law; a right of restitution or compensation must be available.[99] Faced with claims counted in billions, the IR

94 *Woolwich Equitable Building Society v Commissioners of Inland Revenue* [1993] AC 70.

95 Law Com. No. 227, *Restitution: Mistakes of law and ultra vires public authority receipts and payments*, Cm. 2731 (1994). At the time the question was out to consultation with Law Com. No. 120 (1991).

96 S. Arrowsmith, 'An assessment of the legal techniques for implementing the procurement directives' in P. Craig and C. Harlow (eds.), *Lawmaking in the European Union* (Sweet & Maxwell) 1997.

97 [1992] 2 All ER pp. 756, 764 (Lord Goff), approved by Lords Slynn and Browne-Wilkinson. The principle was applied to the situation of an ultra vires contract in *Kleinwert Benson v Lincoln City Council* [1999] 2 AC 349.

98 See Case 199/82 *Amministrazione delle Finanze dello Stato v San Giorgio* [1983] ECR 3595, cited by Lord Goff in *Woolwich* [1993] AC 70, 177. And see Case C-192/95 *Comatch v Directeur Général des Douanes et Droits Indirects* [1997] ECR I-165; M. Dougan, 'Cutting your losses in the enforcement deficit: A Community right to recovery of unlawfully levied charges' (1998) 1 *Cambridge Yearbook of European Legal Studies* 233.

99 Joined cases C-397 and C-410/98 *Metallgesellschaft and Hoechst v Inland Revenue Commissioners* [2001] ECR I-1727. The British government legislated to limit the effect of these judgments in s. 320 of the Finance Act 2003, which takes effect retrospectively to September 2003.

countered with the argument that claims to compensation were time-barred by s. 32(1)(c) of the Limitation Act 1980. The claimants responded that, in respect of claims to restitution, time ran from the date the mistake of law was discovered, namely the date of the ECJ judgment. The House of Lords dismissed this argument, ruling that taxes paid under a mistake of law were reclaimable in restitution, with time running from the point when the mistake was discovered.[100] Whether this is (or should be) purely a public law principle or one generally applicable in private law situations remains undecided, leaving the law of unjust enrichment in an uncertain state.[101]

6. Alternatives to tort law

If, as we are suggesting, the legal system can provide only sporadic and uncertain awards of pecuniary compensation, are more proportionate alternatives available? NHS managers certainly think so. Faced with a fifteen-fold rise in claims for medical negligence between the years 1995–6 and 2002–3, they moved to reform the arrangements for complaints-handling and settlement. The NHS Redress Act 2006 authorises the minister to 'establish a scheme for the purpose of enabling redress to be provided without recourse to civil proceedings'. Such a scheme must provide remedies ranging from an offer of compensation in satisfaction of any right to bring civil proceedings in respect of the liability concerned to the giving of an explanation, an apology or a report on the action which has been, or will be, taken to prevent similar cases arising.[102]

This scheme is not without its problems, as the House of Commons Constitutional Affairs Committee observed when examining the draft Bill. In particular, it does not apply to those with claims over £20,000, which will actually be rejected if they turn out on inquiry to exceed that sum. Questioned by a Select Committee about this negative aspect of the scheme, which the Committee felt would deprive it of much of its usefulness, the minister cheerfully (if ungrammatically) admitted:

> doing regulation by secondary level legislation which we do in Parliament – which when you are in government you love, when you are not in government, you get very frustrated by – is that you can quickly and relatively easily make amendments of that kind to legislation of this nature, so we think that we will be able to do that because of the way we set up the legislation.[103]

[100] *Deutsche Morgan Grenfell Group plc v IRC* [2006] 3 WLR 781.

[101] J. Alder, 'Restitution in public law: Bearing the cost of unlawful state action' (2002) 22 *Legal Studies* 165, argues for a public law principle; G. Virgo, 'Restitution from public authorities: Past, present and future' [2006] *Judicial Review* 370 prefers a general principle. And see generally P. Birks, *Unjust Enrichment*, 2nd edn (Oxford University Press, 2005).

[102] See DoH, *Making Amends. A consultation paper setting out proposals for reforming the approach to clinical negligence in the NHS* (2003) [31] [35]. And see now the NHS Redress Act 2006.

[103] See Constitutional Affairs Committee, *Compensation Culture*, HC 754 (2005/6) [96].

Somewhat sourly, the Committee responded that this 'flexibility' was unlikely to promote confidence in the scheme. The cap is certainly open to the criticism that it leaves the most vulnerable claimants to the forensic lottery of litigation.

It is too early to evaluate this new form of proportionate dispute resolution, which has only just come into operation. In the next sections, however, we shall look more closely at two established models of administrative compensation, asking whether they can provide a viable alternative to courts.

(a) *Ex gratia* payments

Reference has already been made to the Crown prerogative power to make *ex gratia* payments. These powers are routinely used to settle cases of legal liability. The precise nature of the prerogative powers is debatable. The House of Lords has ruled, however, that the powers are discretionary and that, although the discretion is not unlimited, the practice of making *ex gratia* payments does not require parliamentary authorisation.[104] They do, however, need Treasury approval, subject to general authority to make payments up to £250,000, and the conditions for payment are set out and published in the manual of government accounting:

> *Ex gratia* payments other than to contractors are payments which go beyond administrative rules or for which there is no statutory cover or legal liability. Reasons for the payments vary widely; they include, for example, payments made to meet hardship caused by official failure or delay, or special payments to avoid legal proceedings against the government on grounds of official inadequacy.
>
> Extra-statutory and extra-regulatory payments are payments considered to be within the broad intention of the statute or statutory regulation, respectively, but which go beyond a strict interpretation of its terms. Where a payment is of a continuing nature but does not form part of a general concession of sufficient importance to justify separate provision in Estimates, the payment should be noted in the accounts for all years in which it falls. The need for amending legislation should be considered in all cases that arise.[105]

A reorganisation to centralise the disparate practices of *ex gratia* compensation in different departments would have some advantages. It would be less flexible but it would provide greater consistency and transparency, important good-governance values. Just such a scheme is the Australian Compensation for Detriment caused by Defective Administration (CDDA) scheme set up to deal with claims in respect of maladministration.[106] The CDDA scheme

[104] *R v Secretary of State for Work and Pensions, ex p. Hooper* [2005] UKHL 29; *R v IRC, ex p. Wilkinson* [2005] UKHL 30. Both involved the legality of extra-statutory payments to implement ECtHR judgments concerning the compatibility of the British system for widows' pensions with the ECHR.

[105] *Government Accounting* 2000, available online [18.6.5] [18.6.8].

[106] Commonwealth of Australia, *Compensation for Detriment Caused by Defective Administration* (CDDA); *Guidelines for Agencies* (Finance Circular 2001/01/01 Attachment B).

is discretionary but, like the British criminal injuries compensation scheme, is governed by published administrative guidelines. An important difference between it and traditional *ex gratia* payments is the emphasis on consistency and fairness: decisions made under the CDDA scheme must be 'publicly defensible, having regard to all the circumstances of the case'. Only in special circumstances can payments that fall outside the scheme be made and only with the approval of the finance minister.[107]

(b) Criminal injuries compensation

The Criminal Injuries Compensation Scheme (CICS) was first set up and administered under the prerogative powers, though it has since been put on a statutory basis. Use of the prerogative was perhaps justifiable so long as numbers remained small: in its first year of operation, only 554 applications were received and £33,430 paid out in compensation. Thereafter claims increased rapidly: by 1988–9, when legislation was introduced to put the scheme on a statutory basis, there were 43,385 claims and awards of £431,532,702; in 1992–3, when the Government moved to amend the scheme on the ground of cost, claims had risen to 65,977 and compensation totalled £909,446,123. These are considerable amounts of public money to be spent without parliamentary authorisation, especially as questions arise concerning the basis for criminal injuries compensation. Unlike most *ex gratia* payments, criminal injuries compensation is not made in settlement of legal liability nor is it a claim in respect of maladministration. The only explanation afforded by the Home Office working party that advised on the setting up of the plan was that 'although the welfare state helps the victims of many kinds of misfortune, it does nothing for the victims of crimes of violence, as such'.[108] This notably sidestepped the question why anything should be done 'as such' and the equally important question why it should be done without the formal approval of Parliament.

Discussing rules and discretion in Chapter 6, we saw flexibility as an important reason both for discretion and for the choice of soft law. The case put for discretion here was that the CICS was the first scheme of its kind in the world. The Government wished to see how it worked out and retain the ability to make adjustments; moreover, the cost was uncertain. That the organisation and ambit of the scheme was governed by published rules suggested something rather different however. Atiyah[109] was quick to notice the contradiction, calling the denial of a 'right' to compensation 'quite meaningless, because the board administering the scheme has no discretion to refuse claims except within the terms of the scheme itself; and the payment of compensation – though not legally enforceable – follows automatically once

[107] S. 33 of the Financial Management and Accountability Act 1997 (Aus).

[108] *Compensation for Victims of Crimes of Violence*, Cmnd 1406 (1961) [18]. And see A. Ashworth, 'Punishment and compensation: Victims, offenders and the state' (1986) 6 *OJLS* 86.

[109] *Accidents, Compensation and the Law* XXX edn p. 296

the board has determined that it should be awarded'. The Board (now the CICA) set up to administer the scheme also accepted that its discretion was not unfettered:

> The use of the words *ex gratia* means that an applicant has no right to sue either the Crown or the Board for non-payment of compensation. But, in practice, the position is exactly the same as it would be if the Scheme was embodied in a statute with the words *ex gratia* omitted. The Board's view of its legal obligation and duty under the Scheme is that, if an applicant's entitlement to compensation is established there is no power to withhold compensation.[110]

Here the CICA seems to be suggesting that, although the scheme is not justiciable, it is somehow enforceable: the rules of the scheme are sufficiently strict to 'structure' the discretion. Yet a cursory look at the text[111] confirms the rules as 'soft law'. The scheme has two parts: the rules of operation and a 'Guide' or 'Statement' designed to inform applicants and their advisers how applications are likely to be determined. In comparison to statute or the complex regulations on which courts and tribunals typically have to adjudicate, the text is simple to construe and self-explanatory: guidelines or a code of practice aimed at the public and not designed to provide work for lawyers. Indeed, one judge has said that the scheme is unsuited to judicial interpretation:

> The scheme, as the document is entitled which enshrines the rules for the board's conduct, is not recognisable as any kind of legislative document with which the court is familiar. It is not expressed in the kind of language one expects from a parliamentary draftsman, whether of statutes or statutory instruments. It bears all the hallmarks of a document which lays down the broad guidelines of policy.[112]

The Government, while favouring formal adjudicatory methods, originally intended to avoid the courts. The Board would be autonomous, its decisions not being subject to ministerial review or appeal. Claims were submitted and processed on the papers by a single member of the Board; appeal lay to a panel of lawyers, with the possibility of an oral hearing. The only external accountability would be through annual reports submitted to the Home Secretary and laid before Parliament. There were therefore tremors when, in *R v Criminal Injuries Compensation Board, ex p. Lain*,[113] the Divisional Court held that the Board, as 'a servant of the Crown charged by the Crown, by executive instruction, with the duty of distributing the bounty of the Crown . . . came fairly and squarely within the jurisdiction of this Court'. Inroads had been made not

[110] Cmnd 7752 (1979) [15].

[111] Available online at the CICA website.

[112] *R v Criminal Injuries Compensation Board, ex p. Schofield* [1971] 1 WLR 926 (Bridge LJ dissenting).

[113] *R v Criminal Injuries Compensation Board, ex p. Lain* [1967] 2 QB 864.

only on the ambit of prerogative power but also on the scheme's discretionary nature. Discretionary decisions structured by informal rules were now subject to review and interpretation by the courts. Following *Schofield*,[114] where the Board had interpreted the rules to exclude compensation for a bystander knocked down accidentally during a struggle to arrest a shoplifter but the Court of Appeal ruled that the case fell within the rules, the scheme gave rise to legally enforceable entitlements.

But the argument for formalisation through statute would not go away. In 1980, introducing a Private Member's Bill which he later withdrew, Lord Longford argued that 'the establishment of a statutory system would command much more confidence among victims, and certainly could be used to promote much more effective publicity'.[115] He was making the important point that statute is more legitimate, more transparent and more certain than informal rules, which can be – and in the event were – amended from time to time without too much publicity. With the help of the Lords but against the wishes of the Government the scheme finally reached the statute book.[116] It was stated to come into force 'on such day as the Secretary of State may appoint'.

The Act was never activated. An accumulated backlog, long delays and high operating costs of £14.25 million (9 per cent of total expenditure) led the Government to conclude that a scheme based on common law damages was 'inherently incapable of delivering the standard of service claimants should now reasonably expect'. A White Paper proposing drastic change was published.[117] The Government wanted a 'banded tariff' scheme, calculated by averaging past awards. The lawyer-dominated Board would be wound up and replaced by a simple administrative process coupled with two-stage internal review: first, review by a more senior administrator, secondly, an external appeals panel appointed by the minister using documentary procedure. The Home Secretary introduced legislation to replace the 1988 Act but it failed to pass the House of Lords. Hoping to delay implementation indefinitely, he replaced the existing prerogative scheme with a new, less generous, 'tariff' scheme, effectively bypassing the 1988 Act. The legality of this substitution was immediately challenged by a group of unions whose members were likely to be affected.[118] As we saw in Chapter 4, the case, which raised points of great constitutional significance, was decided by a majority of the House of Lords against the Government.

114 *R v Criminal Injuries Compensation Board, ex p. Schofield* [1971] 1 WLR 926.

115 HL Deb., vol. 401, cols. 233–5

116 Ss. 108–77 and Schs. 6 and 7 of the Criminal Justice Act 1988. See P. Duff, 'Criminal injuries compensation: The scope of the new scheme' (1989) 52 *MLR* 518. The Act followed a Report from the Home Affairs Select Committee, *Compensation and Support for Victims of Crime*, HC 43 (1984/5).

117 *Compensating Victims of Violent Crime: Changes to the criminal injuries compensation scheme*, Cm. 2434 (1993). See P. Duff, 'The measure of criminal injuries compensation: Political pragmatism or dog's dinner?' (1998) *OJLS* 105.

118 *R v Home Secretary, ex p. Fire Brigades Union* [1995] 2 WLR 464 (see p. 145 above).

Table 17.1 Awards by tariff level 2004–5 (adapted from Annual Report 2004–5 Table 1)

Level	Tariff in £	Total no. of awards on assessment	Gross value in £
1	1,000	6,735	6,735,000
5	2,000	3,724	7,448,000
10	5,000	198	990,000
15	15,000	45	675,000
20	40,000	34	1,360,000
25	250,000	6	1,500,000

Table 17.2 CIC awards disposed of by level

Year	Disallowed	First level	Review	Appeal	Total awards	Gross value in £
1999–2000	38,157	31,861	5,692	2,147	39,700	108,580,500
2004–5	33,847	27,994	5,352	2,100	35,446	120,845,650

Immediately, a Bill that became the Criminal Injuries Compensation Act 1995 was introduced into the Commons to validate the tariff scheme. It standardised the amounts of compensation. There are today twenty-five bands covering payments between £1,000 and £250,000 in respect of 400 listed injuries. The Act gave the minister wide discretionary powers to 'make arrangements for the payment of compensation' and to appoint an adjudicator; otherwise the scheme had apparently lost both its informal *ex gratia* character and its formal legalistic procedures. Since 2008 appeal lies to the First-tier Tribunal (Criminal Injuries Compensation) under the Tribunals, Courts and Enforcement Act 2006.

As Table 17.1 indicates, the changes have to a certain extent served their purpose. There has been a substantial fall in sums expended in compensation: from a peak of £210 million in 1996–7 and £214 million in 1997–8 (as the changeover was taking place) to average sums of just over £1 million. Note that by far the greatest number of awards comes at the bottom levels of the tariff.

Under the influence of new public management methodology, target-setting is very gradually making an impression on the accumulated backlog, which has moved from a peak of 97,236 cases in 1999 down to 84,581 in 2004–5 (in the last three reported years the backlog has fallen from 91,447 to 84,990 to 84,581). The number of awards contested is dropping slightly, though appeal figures remain fairly constant. The average time to process claims has, however, hardly changed: from around six to eight months, with more than 26 per cent taking more than one year to resolve.

We should not read too much into this brief and selective account of a single statutory scheme but a few general observations are in order. First, time is saved; throughput time compares well with appeals to tribunals or judicial review (see pp. 502 and 685 above). But statutory compensation does not come cheap. The resources required escalate with the number of claims, which in the case of criminal injuries compensation have increased exponentially since inauguration of the scheme. This fact alone may be thought sufficient justification for government insistence on keeping control of resources and ultimately for the fixed-tariff scheme. Compensation cannot be demand-led but it is questionable whether a scheme capped at £250,000, as the criminal injuries compensation scheme currently is, really provides adequately for victims of serious violence. One day the cap may be challenged.

7. Ombudsmen and redress

Over the years, the ombudsmen have handled a good many complaints over compensation, some concerning *ex gratia* payments, others involving the ambit and operation of statutory compensation schemes. *Sachsenhausen* (1967) involved just such an inquiry, as did the *Court Line* affair (1975), the *Channel Tunnel* affair (1995), *Barlow Clowes* (1989), the *Occupational Pensions* affair (2006) considered in Chapter 13 and the *Debt of Honour* affair discussed in this chapter .

Shortly after publication of the Citizen's Charter (see p. 450 above) with its promise of 'better redress for the citizen when things go wrong', the Select Committee on the Parliamentary Commissioner for Administration (PCA), dissatisfied with the haphazard way in which compensation was administered, invited the then PCA (William Reid) to undertake a 'thematic inquiry' into redress.[119] Substantial departmental discrepancies in the practice of *ex gratia* payment were revealed: some departments, like the Home Office, possessed unlimited authority; others needed Treasury authority for all but the most trivial payments. The review also revealed a hotchpotch of compensation schemes, varying in size and scale – some statutory, others *ex gratia*; some, like the CICS, relatively well-known, others entirely unpublicised. There were many anomalies, often creating a strong sense of injustice amongst those left just outside the boundaries, and substantial differences of practice. The Treasury warned departments that 'an unduly liberal regime of compensation would impose an administrative burden on departments . . . Departments needing to distribute codified internal guidance on *ex gratia* payments, in order to permit a measure of delegated authority to local staff, should design it to be exclusive to closely defined cases.' [120]

Rejecting Treasury Guidelines as 'frequently inappropriate' and its advice as 'outdated, restrictive and doctrinaire', the Committee expressed its displeasure at 'the inadequacy of much of the redress offered by departments and agencies, [their] unwillingness to admit fault, refusal to identify and gracefully

[119] PCA, *Maladministration and Redress*, HC 112 (1994/5).
[120] See 'Dear Accounting Officer', DAO (Gen) 15/92.

compensate those affected by acts of maladministration'.[121] William Reid took the view that compensation should be made in all cases of 'abnormal hardship' caused by maladministration. The Committee wished to see established a principle of full restitution: that 'a person who has suffered injury as a result of maladministration should be put back in the same position as he or she would have been in had things gone right in the first place'.[122] A somewhat similar line was taken by the present PCA, Ann Abraham, in a document advising on principles for redress that focuses on 'putting things right':

> Where maladministration or poor service has led to injustice or hardship, public bodies should try to offer a remedy that returns the complainant to the position they would have been in otherwise. If that is not possible, the remedy should compensate them appropriately. Remedies should also be offered, where appropriate, to others who have suffered injustice or hardship as a result of the same maladministration or poor service.
>
> There are no automatic or routine remedies for injustice or hardship resulting from maladministration or poor service. Remedies may be financial or non-financial.[123]

Local authorities have power under s. 92 of the Local Government Act 2000 to make payments to any person who has or may have been affected by maladministration. Guidance covering the way s. 92 powers should be used is published by the Commission for Local Administration.[124] Financial compensation may be appropriate if:

- the authority has taken the appropriate action but has delayed in doing so and the delay has caused injustice
- there is no practical action which would provide a full and appropriate remedy or
- the complainant has sustained financial loss or has suffered stress and anxiety.

The Guidance, which covers quantifiable loss, loss of non-monetary benefits (such as quiet enjoyment of local authority housing), loss of a chance and distress, states that the underlying aim of all such payments must be to put the complainant as far as possible back into the position he or she would have been in but for the fault. Costs and professional fees can be claimed in exceptional circumstances. In general awards are moderate: for example, payments for lost opportunity (such as the right to appeal a council decision) are restricted to around £100, while time-and-trouble payments will normally amount to no more than £50. In respect of distress, the Guidance warns that:

[121] Third Report of the Select Committee on the PCA, HC 345 (1993/4).

[122] *Ibid.*

[123] PCA, *Principles for Remedy* (2007) principle 5, available online.

[124] CLA, *Remedies: Good practice*, available online. These principles were applied in *R (Bernard) v Enfield LBC* [2002] EWHC 2282.

> The level of compensation for distress needs to be carefully assessed in the light of all the circumstances of the individual case. Because these do vary significantly, the guideline has to be broad, but generally it is likely that the appropriate sum would be in the range of £500 to £2,000 for a year, with broadly *pro rata* sums for shorter or longer periods. But a careful assessment of the facts may, on some occasions, point to sums above or below that range.

This fleshes out the PCA's advice to the Select Committee that 'botheration payments' be routinely awarded to cover cases of grave maladministration, where excessive rudeness and malice are involved or exceptional worry and distress caused.

The group dimension of compensation claims means that compensation flowing from a decided case or ombudsman inquiry may be very considerable. In the *Slaughtered Poultry* affair,[125] where the PCA discovered that claims for statutory compensation had been handled by the Ministry deliberately and with the knowledge of the minister so as to minimise the amount of compensation payable, his very negative report resulted in recalculation of sums due to other farmers involving more than £600,000. This did not include the costs in time and labour of identifying those likely to be affected by a ruling. The sheer size of the sums paid out by government in compensation and settlement of legal liability should be – and is no doubt to the Treasury and National Audit Office (NAO) responsible for monitoring payments on behalf of the Public Accounts Committee – a matter of concern. The NAO recently published its 'best estimate' of total compensatory payments across a handful of central government bodies, excluding the very costly NHS, as in the region of £12,448,000, made up of 46,002 individual payments.[126] The Department for Work and Pensions heads the table and makes more than one-third of the total payments. In the single year 2002–3, it made 31,051 payments amounting to £9,047,000 in compensation, of which 10,955 payments (£2,575,000) were in respect of delay.[127] These figures which, it should be noted, cover only central-government departments, may be read in two ways: on the one hand, they can be seen as justifying the courts' cautious approach to extensions of government liability; on the other hand, it could be argued that compensation on such a scale demonstrates society's acceptance of a compensation principle and consequently of a generous and victim-oriented attitude by courts in liability cases.

(a) A debt of honour

An objection often made about ombudsman recommendations is that they are unenforceable (for which reason the ECtHR deems them not to satisfy the

[125] *Compensation to Farmers for Slaughtered Poultry* HC 519 (1992/3), *Annual Report 1993*, HC 290 (1994/5), p. 27.

[126] NAO, *Citizen Redress: What citizens can do if things go wrong with public services*, HC 21 (2004/5), p. 42 and Table 18.

[127] HC Deb., col. 12W (7 Jun 2004) (Mr Willetts).

requirements of an 'effective remedy' under ECHR Art. 13).[128] There is some justification for this attitude in the Government response to the findings of the PCA in the *Occupational Pensions* case (see p. 554 above). The following case study suggests, however, that this reasoning may be fallacious; ombudsmen may sometimes reach the parts that the judicial process cannot reach.

On 7 November 2000, the Parliamentary Under-Secretary for Defence stood up in the House of Commons to make a gratifying announcement:

> I am very pleased to inform the House that . . . the Government have decided to make a single *ex gratia* payment of £10,000 to each of the surviving members of the British groups who were held prisoner by the Japanese during the Second World War, in recognition of the unique circumstances of their captivity . . .
>
> The unique nature of Japanese captivity in the far east was recognised in the 1950s, when those who had been held became eligible for modest payments from Japanese assets[129] . . . In the intervening years, the former far east prisoners pursued the issue of additional compensation with Japan. More recently, they have also campaigned for the British Government to make a payment. However . . . it has been the policy of successive Governments over many years not to make payments in such cases.
>
> We are now making an exception of the British groups that were held prisoner by the Japanese during the Second World War in recognition of the unique circumstances of their collective captivity . . . We estimate that up to 16,700 people may be eligible for the *ex gratia* payments, which will accordingly cost up to £167 million to make.[130]

The House was told that the beneficiaries would be 'former members of the armed forces and Merchant Navy and British civilians who were interned'. No further details were given because, as the public would learn later, they had not yet been agreed. Notes for Guidance published on the same day indicated that 'surviving British civilians who were interned by the Japanese in the Far East during the Second World War' would be eligible.

In July 2001, the minister stated in reply to a parliamentary question that the eligibility criterion for civilian claimants had been clarified: British subjects whom the Japanese interned and who were born in the United Kingdom or had a parent or grandparent born here would be eligible. Intended to be inclusive, these 'birth-link' and 'blood-link' definitions had the unintended effect of excluding some British subjects living overseas who would otherwise have been eligible. ABCIFER, an action group representing British civilians in the Far East, applied for judicial review.[131] It challenged the criteria for the scheme as unlawful, disproportionate and irrational, also arguing that the first announce-

[128] *TP and KM v UK*, App. 2894/95 (10 May 2000).

[129] In practice, around £76.00 for servicemen and £48.00 for civilians.

[130] HC Deb., col. 159 (7 November 2000) (Dr Lewis Moonie). There had been adjournment debates in the House on 10 May 1995, 4 December 1996, 29 April 1998, 9 March 2000 and 6 June 2000.

[131] *Abcifer v Defence Secretary* [2003] EWCA Civ 473 [87].

ment had created a legitimate expectation. But stating that 'anyone who seeks to challenge as unlawful the content of a non-statutory *ex-gratia* compensation scheme faces an uphill struggle', the Court of Appeal dismissed every argument: the statement did not contain a sufficiently clear and unequivocal representation to found a legitimate expectation nor, provided that the criteria were rationally connected with the scheme's objective, was it irrational to exclude certain categories from the class of beneficiaries. 'We do not think that the introduction of this scheme was well handled by the Government. But for the reasons that we have given, the appellant has failed to satisfy us that the scheme was unlawful.'

A second legal challenge to the birth-link criteria was under way, made by a British subject born and resident in Hong Kong. Building on a successful challenge on behalf of the Gurkhas to a recently introduced war-pensions scheme,[132] Mrs Elias pleaded discrimination in terms of the Race Relations Acts 1976 and 2000. Elias J upheld the application, ruling that the scheme adopted was unlawful and indirectly discriminated against those of non-British national origin. The Court of Appeal also thought the chosen criteria discriminatory, despite a wide margin of ministerial discretion in setting the terms of the scheme:

> *Mummery LJ:* Even though UK national origins are not formally specified in the birth link criteria, Mrs Elias' exclusion from the Compensation Scheme is in substance very closely related to her non-UK national origins. It is that exclusion that has to be objectively justified. A stringent standard of scrutiny of the claimed justification is appropriate because the discrimination, though indirect in form, is so closely related in substance to the direct form of discrimination on grounds of national origins, which can never be justified.[133]

After prolonged consideration of the compensation question, the Court of Appeal awarded £10,000 (the statutory sum) in compensation together with £3,000 for hurt feelings in respect of the indirect discrimination.

Alongside, the birth-link criteria had been referred to the PCA by Austin Mitchell MP on behalf of Professor Hayward, a British subject born in Shanghai to British subjects both born outside the United Kingdom. Professor Hayward's education and whole career had been in England where he now lived.[134] Two preliminary points of jurisdiction were raised. First, was the PCA inquiry barred by the possibility of a legal remedy? Secondly, could it be said that maladministration was in issue? Exercising her discretion under s. 5(2) of the Parliamentary Commissioner Act 1967, the PCA ruled that she could investigate; Professor Hayward had not participated in the ABCIFER case nor was it in the circumstances reasonable to ask him to take legal action.

On the second, maladministration, point, the PCA felt that the haste with

[132] *R (Phalam Gurung) v Ministry of Defence* [2002] EWHC 2463 (Admin). But see now *R (Gurung and Others) v Defence Secretary* [2008] EWHC 1496 (Admin).

[133] *R (Elias) v Defence Secretary* [2005] EWHC 1435 Admin; [2006] EWCA Civ 1293 [161].

[134] PCA, *A Debt of Honour*, HC 324 (2005/6).

which the scheme was drawn up was unnecessary. Compensation had been on the agenda for at least five years yet officials were only asked to draw up options two weeks prior to the eventual announcement of the scheme. 'It should have been apparent that drawing up an *ex gratia* scheme in such a short space of time gave no opportunity for the details to be worked out properly and that this inevitably would lead to a lack of clarity.' There had also been misleading press releases, raising expectations that proved illusory. 'Good administration of extra-statutory schemes requires clearly articulated entitlement criteria to ensure that those potentially covered by the scheme are not put to unnecessary distress or inconvenience by uncertainty or conflicting information. Such a need is all the more essential when the relevant issues are sensitive, as is clearly the case here.' This was maladministration, compounded by interdepartmental disagreement and debate over the meaning of the term 'British' for purposes of war-pensions legislation. The PCA also felt concern over equality of treatment. The Government had not been able to reassure her that applications from people in the same situation for the purposes of the scheme's eligibility criteria were not decided differently nor was she satisfied that Professor Hayward and those whose applications were determined after the introduction of the new criterion were afforded treatment equal to those whose applications were determined prior to the introduction of the blood-link criterion.

The PCA made four findings of maladministration, adding two riders:

(i) that the way in which the scheme was devised constituted maladministration in that it was done overly quickly and in such a manner as to lead to a lack of clarity about eligibility for payments under the scheme;
(ii) that the way in which the scheme was announced constituted maladministration in that the Ministerial statement was so unclear and imprecise as to give rise to confusion and misunderstanding;
(iii) that, at the time when the blood link criterion was introduced, the failure to review the impact of that introduction to ensure that it did not lead to unequal treatment constituted maladministration; and
(iv) that the failure to inform applicants that the criteria had been clarified when they were sent a questionnaire to establish their eligibility constituted maladministration.

In addition, I am also concerned about the following two aspects of the operation of the scheme:

(v) that the Government has been unable to provide evidence of the basis on which the early payments under the scheme were made and that thus I have been unable to determine whether the scheme was operated properly; and
vi) that no review of the scheme was undertaken in the light of criticisms of it by the courts, in Parliament, and elsewhere.

Finding that the maladministration had caused injustice, the PCA recommended first that the MOD should review the operation of the *ex gratia* scheme and, secondly, that it should 'fully reconsider' the position of Professor Hayward and those in a similar position. She would expect to monitor the review closely. As to redress, an immediate apology was in order but this was clearly not enough: the MOD should also consider whether they should 'express that regret tangibly'.

In its response, the Government picked up on the variance between the two court decisions and the far more informative PCA inquiry. It refused to accept that a thorough review of the scheme was warranted.

> The Government accepts in full your findings of maladministration in relation to the origination and announcement of the scheme and will apologise for the distress which this maladministration caused to Professor Hayward and others in a similar position.
>
> The Government will also consider expressing its regret tangibly. But we do not consider that these findings warrant a thorough review of the scheme.
>
> The bloodlink criterion does, as both you and the courts have pointed out, create some apparent anomalies.
>
> But, as the courts have recognised, such anomalies are inevitable when devising eligibility criteria for a scheme such as this. They do not make the scheme as a whole irrational or unfair.
>
> Nor is the fact that some payments were made in error to people who are not eligible under the scheme a reason why others in whose cases the same error was not made should now be paid.

The PCA expressed her disappointment; the minister apologised and offered *ex gratia* payments of £500 to Professor Hayward and others affected. But the affair rumbled on. Expressing complete confidence in its officer's decision to investigate and regret that her recommendations had not been fully implemented, the Public Administration Select Committee (PASC) emphasised the difference between judicial review and an ombudsman inquiry:

> In our view, the Ombudsman acted appropriately in investigating this case. The entire basis of the 1967 Parliamentary Commissioner for Administration Act is that it is possible for a measure to be legal, and yet to be maladministered. The fact that legality has been established through Judicial Review may be irrelevant to maladministration. There may even be circumstances where the Ombudsman feels it is appropriate to conduct an investigation while Judicial Review proceedings are taking place, so that she can subsequently report without delay. We would, in principle, support this.[135]

PASC initiated a further inquiry, calling the minister (Don Touhig MP) to give evidence. It now emerged that the criteria might not have been applied consistently. Mr Touhig announced an internal inquiry, requiring a check of nearly 30,000 claim and policy files. The PCA's suspicions were shown to be justified;

[135] PASC, *A Debt of Honour*, HC 375 (2005/6).

for the first time, serious inconsistencies were revealed. After meeting MPs and ABCIFER, the minister decided to modify the scheme once more: anyone who had lived in the United Kingdom for at least twenty years since World War II would now be covered.[136]

The 'Debt of Honour' affair permits us to evaluate the strengths and weaknesses of judicial review and an ombudsman investigation. The first unsuccessful review of legality turned essentially on a distinction between policy and operation; wide discretion was conceded to the Government in setting the parameters of the scheme. It was the Race Relations Acts rather than the HRA that allowed the courts to go further in the second review. The court was then able (albeit unwillingly) to make reparation over and above the lump sum provided by the scheme. The PCA was theoretically hampered by being restricted to maladministration but the flexible, non-legalistic definition allowed her to overcome this obstacle. Under the rubric of operational failure, she was able to attack the scheme's inherent inequalities. The documentary and inquisitorial ombudsman methodology produced a much greater depth of information, used to good effect by PASC, which stood strongly behind its officer when her recommendations were partly rejected. Despite this setback, the inquiry was in the end more successful. On the one hand PASC forced the minister into an internal investigation; on the other, the political solution allowed the Government to climb down gracefully. The unwillingness of the Government to accept her recommendations was reminiscent of its attitude in the *Occupational Pensions* affair but was on this occasion overcome.

The affair also tells us something about the dangers of compensation schemes. Designed to be selective, they create dissatisfaction amongst those who fall just outside the boundaries. This fuels the 'compensation culture', typically stimulating a political battle for inclusion. Also typically the scheme ended up costing much more than had been estimated: costs rose dramatically from the original estimate in 2000 of £167 million; by 2006, around 25,000 claimants had received over £250 million.

(b) Cod wars

The PCA had occasion to return to the *Debt of Honour* affair in considering an *ex gratia* compensation scheme devised by the Department of Trade and Industry (DTI) for Icelandic-water trawlermen made redundant through the 'Cod war' which ran between October 2000 and October 2002.[137]Once again she had to report that maladministration had caused injustice. Reflecting on the experience, Ann Abraham had this to say:

[136] HC Deb., vol. 444, col. 681 (28 Mar. 2006).

[137] PCA, *Put Together in Haste: 'Cod Wars' trawlermen's compensation scheme*, HC 313 (2006/7).

The reader of this report will see that many of the issues I identified in relation to the scheme covered by *A Debt of Honour* arose similarly in relation to the scheme covered by this report. An effective *ex gratia* compensation scheme that accords with principles of good administration would have:

- scheme rules that are clearly articulated and which directly reflect the policy intention behind the scheme;
- systems and procedures in place to deliver the scheme which have been properly planned and tested;
- sufficient flexibility built in to the rules and procedures to recognise the level of complexity in the subject matter covered by the scheme; and
- mechanisms which enable the success of the scheme in delivering its objectives to be kept under review.

That did not happen in either case.

In addition to making recommendations to remedy the injustice I have determined was caused to the representative complainant in this investigation and to others in a similar position to her, I have therefore also recommended that central guidance for public bodies should be developed that specifically relates to the development and operation of *ex gratia* compensation schemes.

The Government have accepted the need for such guidance. The Permanent Secretary at HM Treasury has told me that HM Treasury is planning to take forward my recommendation for specific guidance on the development and operation of *ex gratia* compensation schemes and that this work will be incorporated into the revision of 'Government Accounting', which I understand is due for publication later this year.[138] I welcome this commitment and hope that, through this guidance which should be of considerable assistance to those tasked with the administration of *ex gratia* compensation schemes, this report will make a lasting contribution to the improvement of the delivery of public services.[139]

8. Towards a compensation culture?

Statistical evidence for a compensation culture in the sense of the idea that society is in the grip of litigation fever is thin, ambiguous and easily explained away,[140] but this short survey does suggest increasing willingness to resort to courts. The state's deep pockets make public bodies a magnet for litigants so that 'novel' tort claims are reaching the courts. In parallel, the PCA has been asked to handle a number of highly political compensation claims. The trend has been accentuated by the growing importance of 'affirmative rights' in human rights jurisprudence, which cast obligations of protection on the state,

[138] See HM Treasury, *Managing Public Money* (2008) Annex 4, p. 124.

[139] *Put Together in Haste*.

[140] Williams, 'State of fear: Britain's "compensation culture" reviewed'; Report of a Working Party of the Institute of Actuaries, *The Cost of Compensation Culture* (December 2002); A. Morris, 'Spiralling or stabilising? The compensation culture and our propensity to claim damages for personal injury' (2007) 70 *MLR* 349.

as in *Z v United Kingdom*, where the state signally failed to provide the children with the security underwritten by the Convention on the Rights of the Child. Significantly, the ECtHR saw compensation as axiomatic. The fact that the HRA provides no remedy other than a declaration of incompatibility when statute violates the Convention is a source of grievance mentioned specifically in a Law Commission Scoping Paper as a reason for reconsideration of the law concerning government liability.[141] The courts have so far declined, however, to initiate any serious expansion of legal liability, treating the ECtHR as a ceiling rather than a floor.

Reviewing the evidence, the Commons Constitutional Affairs Committee deduced that the UK was not experiencing a significant increase in litigation. There was, however, 'ample evidence that risk aversion is becoming an insidious problem which the Government and the Health and Safety Executive (HSE) must attempt to address.' This was attributable to a 'grapevine' effect, which spread the popularly held notion that it is easy to obtain compensation and led people to believe that all risk must be avoided. But the Committee did not believe that statutory restatement of the common law would have any useful effect: 'The phenomenon of risk aversion which we have described does not arise primary from the wording of the law or from litigation and will need to be addressed by changing practices and perceptions in the fields of health and safety and risk management.'[142] Thus statutory restrictions on negligence claims, including increased protection for public authorities, have not so far been thought necessary by government. It is the Law Commission that is considering proposals for further protection of 'truly public' activity together with a new test of 'serious fault' for government liability in many cases.

We are perhaps not yet ready to exchange sporadic instances of liability for a general principle of compensation but, in line with the argument in the first section of this chapter, we would interpret the phrase 'compensation culture' positively, to embrace recognition of circumstances where it is morally right that the state should compensate members of the public for loss. This is more a welfare than a liability principle. In this context, a scheme for administrative compensation could be initiated and endorsed by Parliament, giving the present arrangements for *ex gratia* payments greater legitimacy. Such a step is not, however, without its dangers. Greater public awareness of the availability of compensation promoted by the information and guidance increasingly made publicly available by government departments is clearly an element in promoting a compensation culture in the negative sense. The substantial number of statutory schemes already in place must surely also stimulate claims; as we saw in the *Debt of Honour* case

[141] Law Commission, *Monetary Remedies in Public Law: A discussion paper* (11 October 2004); Law Commission, *Remedies against Public Bodies: A scoping report* (10 October 2006).

[142] Constitutional Committee, *Compensation Culture*, HC 754 (2005/6) [112].

study, those on the margins of compensation schemes tend to complain of unfair treatment.

We do not ourselves see a 'compensation culture' as synonymous with a 'blame culture' but rather equate it with a desire for accountability. As Ripstein has observed, 'when injured people clamour for recourse against their injurers, their concern is not just with compensation, but with justice'. Perhaps then it is the courts that need liability most! The ability to award damages against government is a crucial tool in the judicial toolkit and a symbol of subjection of the state to the rule of law. Instances do exist, as this chapter reminds us, where the state or its officials have behaved badly enough to merit public sanction, if appropriate through an award of punitive damages. Before we entirely jettison Dicey's theory of liability, we need to reflect on this.

Index